Twentieth-Century Literary Criticism

Topics Volume

Guide to Gale Literary Criticism Series

When you need to review criticism of literary works, these are the Gale series to use:

If the author's death date is:

You should turn to:

After Dec. 31, 1959
(or author is still living)

CONTEMPORARY LITERARY CRITICISM

for example: Jorge Luis Borges, Anthony Burgess,
Ernest Hemingway, Iris Murdoch

1900 through 1959

TWENTIETH-CENTURY LITERARY CRITICISM

for example: Willa Cather, F. Scott Fitzgerald,
Henry James, Mark Twain, Virginia Woolf

1800 through 1899

NINETEENTH-CENTURY LITERATURE CRITICISM

for example: Fyodor Dostoevsky, Nathaniel Hawthorne,
George Sand, William Wordsworth

1400 through 1799

*LITERATURE CRITICISM FROM 1400 TO 1800
(excluding Shakespeare)*

for example: Anne Bradstreet, Alexander Pope,
François Rabelais, Phillis Wheatley

SHAKESPEAREAN CRITICISM

Shakespeare's plays and poetry

Antiquity through 1399

CLASSICAL AND MEDIEVAL LITERATURE CRITICISM

for example: Dante, Homer, Plato, Sophocles, Vergil

Gale also publishes related criticism series:

CHILDREN'S LITERATURE REVIEW

This series covers authors of all eras who have written for the preschool through high school audience.

SHORT STORY CRITICISM

This series covers the major short fiction writers of all nationalities and periods of literary history.

POETRY CRITICISM

This series covers poets of all nationalities, movements, and periods of literary history.

DRAMA CRITICISM

This series covers playwrights of all nationalities and periods of literary history.

BLACK LITERATURE CRITICISM

This three-volume set presents criticism of works by major black writers of the past two hundred years.

WORLD LITERATURE CRITICISM, 1500 TO THE PRESENT

This six-volume set provides excerpts from criticism on 225 authors from the Renaissance to the present.

ISSN 0276-8178

Volume 46

Twentieth-Century Literary Criticism

Topics Volume

Excerpts from Criticism of Various Topics in Twentieth-Century Literature, including Literary and Critical Movements, Prominent Themes and Genres, Anniversary Celebrations, and Surveys of National Literatures

Laurie DiMauro
Editor

Marie Lazzari
Thomas Ligotti
Roger Matuz
Janet M. Witalec
Robyn V. Young
Associate Editors

 Gale Research Inc. • DETROIT • WASHINGTON, D.C. • LONDON

Contents

Preface

Since its inception more than ten years ago, *Twentieth-Century Literary Criticism* has been purchased and used by nearly 10,000 school, public, and college or university libraries. *TCLC* has covered more than 500 authors, representing 58 nationalities, and over 25,000 titles. No other reference source has surveyed the critical response to twentieth-century authors and literature as thoroughly as *TCLC*. In the words of one reviewer, "there is nothing comparable available." *TCLC* "is a gold mine of information—dates, pseudonyms, biographical information, and criticism from books and periodicals—which many libraries would have difficulty assembling on their own."

Scope of the Series

TCLC is designed to serve as an introduction to authors who died between 1900 and 1960 and to the most significant interpretations of these authors' works. The great poets, novelists, short story writers, playwrights, and philosophers of this period are frequently studied in high school and college literature courses. In organizing and excerpting the vast amount of critical material written on these authors, *TCLC* helps students develop valuable insight into literary history, promotes a better understanding of the texts, and sparks ideas for papers and assignments. Each entry in *TCLC* presents a comprehensive survey of an author's career or an individual work of literature and provides the user with a multiplicity of interpretations and assessments. Such variety allows students to pursue their own interests; furthermore, it fosters an awareness that literature is dynamic and responsive to many different opinions.

Every fourth volume of *TCLC* is devoted to literary topics that cannot be covered under the author approach used in the rest of the series. Such topics include literary movements, prominent themes in twentieth-century literature, literary reaction to political and historical events, significant eras in literary history, prominent literary anniversaries, and the literatures of cultures that are often overlooked by English-speaking readers.

TCLC is designed as a companion series to Gale's *Contemporary Literary Criticism,* which reprints commentary on authors now living or who have died since 1960. Because of the different periods under consideration, there is no duplication of material between *CLC* and *TCLC.* For additional information about *CLC* and Gale's other criticism titles, users should consult the Guide to Gale Literary Criticism Series preceding the title page in this volume.

Coverage

Each volume of *TCLC* is carefully compiled to present:

- criticism of authors, or literary topics, representing a variety of genres and nationalities

- both major and lesser-known writers and literary works of the period

- 10-15 authors or 4-6 topics per volume

- individual entries that survey critical response to each author's work or each topic in literary history, including early criticism to reflect initial reactions; later criticism to represent any rise or decline in reputation; and current retrospective analyses.

Organization of This Book

An author entry consists of the following elements: author heading, biographical and critical introduction, list of principal works, excerpts of criticism (each preceded by an annotation and followed by a bibliographic citation), and a bibliography of further reading.

- The **author heading** consists of the name under which the author most commonly wrote, followed by birth and death dates. If an author wrote consistently under a pseudonym, the pseudonym will be listed in the author heading and the real name given in parentheses on the first line of the biographical and critical introduction. Also located at the beginning of the introduction to the author entry are any name variations under which an author wrote, including transliterated forms for authors whose languages use nonroman alphabets.

• The **biographical and critical introduction** outlines the author's life and career, as well as the critical issues surrounding his or her work. References to past volumes of *TCLC* are provided at the beginning of the introduction. Additional sources of information in other biographical and critical reference series published by Gale, including *Short Story Criticism, Children's Literature Review, Contemporary Authors, Dictionary of Literary Biography,* and *Something about the Author,* are listed in a box at the end of the entry.

• Most *TCLC* entries include **portraits** of the author. Many entries also contain reproductions of materials pertinent to an author's career, including manuscript pages, title pages, dust jackets, letters, and drawings, as well as photographs of important people, places, and events in an author's life.

• The **list of principal works** is chronological by date of first book publication and identifies the genre of each work. In the case of foreign authors with both foreign-language publications and English translations, the title and date of the first English-language edition are given in brackets. Unless otherwise indicated, dramas are dated by first performance, not first publication.

• **Criticism** is arranged chronologically in each author entry to provide a perspective on changes in critical evaluation over the years. All titles of works by the author featured in the entry are printed in boldface type to enable the user to easily locate discussion of particular works. Also for purposes of easier identification, the critic's name and the publication date of the essay are given at the beginning of each piece of criticism. Unsigned criticism is preceded by the title of the journal in which it appeared. Some of the excerpts in *TCLC* also contain translated material. Unless otherwise noted, translations in brackets are by the editors; translations in parentheses or continuous with the text are by the critic. Publication information (such as publisher names and book prices) and parenthetical numerical references (such as footnotes or page and line references to specific editions of works) have been deleted at the editors' discretion to provide smoother reading of the text.

• Critical excerpts are prefaced by **annotations** providing the reader with information about both the critic and the criticism that follows. Included are the critic's reputation, individual approach to literary criticism, and particular expertise in an author's works. Also noted are the relative importance of a work of criticism, the scope of the excerpt, and the growth of critical controversy or changes in critical trends regarding an author. In some cases, these annotations cross-reference excerpts by critics who discuss each other's commentary.

• A complete **bibliographic citation** designed to facilitate location of the original essay or book follows each piece of criticism.

• An annotated list of **further reading** appearing at the end of each author entry suggests secondary sources on the author. In some cases it includes essays for which the editors could not obtain reprint rights.

Cumulative Indexes

• Each volume of *TCLC* contains a cumulative **author index** listing all authors who have appeared in Gale's Literary Criticism Series, along with cross-references to such biographical series as *Contemporary Authors* and *Dictionary of Literary Biography.* For readers' convenience, a complete list of Gale titles included appears on the first page of the author index. Useful for locating authors within the various series, this index is particularly valuable for those authors who are identified by a certain period but who, because of their death dates, are placed in another, or for those authors whose careers span two periods. For example, F. Scott Fitzgerald is found in *TCLC,* yet a writer often associated with him, Ernest Hemingway, is found in *CLC.*

• Each *TCLC* volume includes a cumulative **nationality index** which lists all authors who have appeared in *TCLC* volumes, arranged alphabetically under their respective nationalities, as well as Topics volume entries devoted to particular national literatures.

• Each new volume in Gale's Literary Criticism Series includes a cumulative **topic index,** which lists all literary topics treated in *NCLC, TCLC, LC 1400-1800,* and the *CLC* Yearbook.

• Each new volume of *TCLC,* with the exception of the Topics volumes, contains a **title index** listing the titles of all literary works discussed in the volume. In response to numerous suggestions from librarians, Gale has also produced a **special paperbound edition** of the *TCLC* title index. This annual cumulation lists all titles discussed in the series since its inception and is issued with the first volume of *TCLC* published each year. Additional copies of the index are available on request. Librarians and patrons will welcome this separate index: it saves shelf space, is easy to use, and is recyclable upon receipt of the following year's cumulation. Titles discussed in the Topics volume entries are not included in the *TCLC* cumulative index.

A Note to the Reader

When writing papers, students who quote directly from any volume in Gale's Literary Criticism Series may use the following general forms to footnote reprinted criticism. The first example pertains to material drawn from periodicals, the second to material reprinted from books.

[1] T. S. Eliot, "John Donne," *The Nation and the Athenaeum,* 33 (9 June 1923), 321-32; excerpted and reprinted in *Literature Criticism from 1400 to 1800,* Vol. 10, ed. James E. Person, Jr. (Detroit: Gale Research, 1989), pp. 28-9.

[2] Clara G. Stillman, *Samuel Butler: A Mid-Victorian Modern* (Viking Press, 1932); excerpted and reprinted in *Twentieth-Century Literary Criticism,* Vol. 33, ed. Paula Kepos (Detroit: Gale Research, 1989), pp. 43-5.

Suggestions Are Welcome

In response to suggestions, several features have been added to *TCLC* since the series began, including annotations to excerpted criticism, a cumulative index to authors in all Gale literary criticism series, entries devoted to criticism on a single work by a major author, more extensive illustrations, and a title index listing all literary works discussed in the series since its inception.

Readers who wish to suggest authors or topics to appear in future volumes, or who have other suggestions, are cordially invited to write the editors.

Acknowledgments

The editors wish to thank the copyright holders of the excerpted criticism included in this volume, the permissions managers of many book and magazine publishing companies for assisting us in securing reprint rights, and Anthony Bogucki for assistance with copyright research. We are also grateful to the staffs of the Detroit Public Library, Wayne State University Purdy/Kresge Library Complex, and the University of Michigan Libraries for making their resources available to us. Following is a list of the copyright holders who have granted us permission to reprint material in this volume of *TCLC.* Every effort has been made to trace copyright, but if omissions have been made, please let us know.

COPYRIGHTED EXCERPTS IN *TCLC,* VOLUME 46, WERE REPRINTED FROM THE FOLLOWING PERIODICALS:

Arizona Quarterly, v. 42, Autumn, 1986 for "Yoshie Hotta's 'Judgment': An Approach to the Atomic-Bomb Literature of Japan" by Nobuko Tsukui. Copyright © 1986 by Arizona Board of Regents. Reprinted by permission of the publisher and the author.—*Critical Inquiry,* v. 13, Autumn, 1986. Copyright © 1986 by The University of Chicago. Reprinted by permission of the publisher.—*Cultural Critique,* n. 5, Winter, 1986-87. © 1987 *Cultural Critique.* Reprinted by permission of the publisher.—*Dada/Surrealism,* n. 15, 1986 for "Dada/Cinema?" by Thomas Elsaesser. 1986 © Association for the Study of Dada and Surrealism. Reprinted by permission of the publisher and the author.—*The Dalhousie Review,* v. 67, Summer-Fall, 1987 for "The Literary Crisis: The Nuclear Crisis" by Thomas M. F. Gerry. Reprinted by permission of the publisher and the author.—*Diacritics,* v. 14, Summer, 1984. Copyright © Diacritics, Inc., 1984. Reprinted by permission of the publisher.—*Éire-Ireland,* v. XVII, Summer, 1982 for "Yeats and the Folklore of the Irish Revival" by John Wilson Foster. Copyright © 1982 Irish American Cultural Institute, 2115 Summit Ave., No. 5026, St. Paul, MN 55105. Reprinted by permission of the publisher and the author.—*Extrapolation,* v. 29, Fall, 1988; v. 30, Fall, 1989. Copyright 1988, 1989 by The Kent State University Press. Both reprinted by permission of the publisher.—*Folklore Forum,* v. X, Fall, 1977. Reprinted by permission of the publisher.—*The Georgia Review,* v. XXXIII, Fall, 1979 for "Romance without Women: The Sterile Fiction of the American West" by Madelon E. Heatherington. Copyright, 1979, by The University of Georgia. Reprinted by permission of the publisher and the author.—*German Life & Letters,* v. XXXVIII, July, 1985. Reprinted by permission of the publisher.—*L'Esprit Créateur,* v. XX, Summer, 1980. Copyright © 1980 by *L'Esprit Créateur.* Reprinted by permission of the publisher.—*The New York Times Book Review,* March 13, 1988. Copyright © 1988 by The New York Times Company. Reprinted by permission of the publisher.—*Papers on Language and Literature,* v. 26, Winter, 1990. Copyright © 1990 by the Board of Trustees, Southern Illinois University of Edwardsville. Reprinted by permission of the publisher.—*Science-Fiction Studies,* v. 13, July, 1986; v. 16, March, 1989; v. 16, July, 1989. Copyright © 1986, 1989 by SFS Publications. All reprinted by permission of the publisher.—*The South Dakota Review,* v. 4, Summer, 1966. © 1966, University of South Dakota. Reprinted by permission of the publisher.—*Southwest Review,* v. LI, Winter, 1966 for "The Beginnings of Cowboy Fiction" by Mody C. Boatright. © 1966 Southern Methodist University. Reprinted by permission of the Literary Estate of Mody C. Boatright.—*Soviet Studies,* v. XXXVIII, April, 1986. © 1986 The University of Glasgow. All rights reserved. Reprinted by permission of the publisher.—*West Coast Review,* v. 18, June, 1983. Copyright © June, 1983 West Coast Review Publishing Society. Reprinted by permission of the publisher.—*Western American Literature,* v. XIII, November, 1978; v. XLV, February, 1980. Copyright, 1978, 1980, by the Western Literature Association. Both reprinted by permission of the publisher.—*WORKS,* v. 1, Spring, 1968. Reprinted by permission of the publisher.

COPYRIGHTED EXCERPTS IN *TCLC,* VOLUME 46, WERE REPRINTED FROM THE FOLLOWING BOOKS:

Armitage, Shelley. From "Rawhide Heroines: The Evolution of the Cowgirl and the Myth of America," in *The American Self: Myth, Ideology, and Popular Culture.* Edited by Sam B. Girgus. University of New Mexico Press, 1981. © 1981 by the University of New Mexico Press. All rights reserved. Reprinted by permission of the author.— Barry, Jan. From *Peace Is Our Profession.* East River Anthology, 1990. Copyright © 1990 Jan Barry. Reprinted by permission of the author.—Bigsby, C. W. E. From *Dada & Surrealism.* Methuen & Co. Ltd., 1972. © 1972 C. W. E. Bigsby. Reprinted by permission of the publisher.—Boyer, Paul. From *By the Bomb's Early Light: American Thought and Culture at the Dawn of the Atomic Age.* Pantheon Books, 1985. Copyright © 1985 by Paul Boyer. All rights reserved. Reprinted by permission of Pantheon Books, a Division of Random House, Inc.—Breton, André.

American Western Literature

INTRODUCTION

Uniquely American in its origin and setting, the western is one of the most widely read forms of popular literature, and such writers as Ernest Haycox, Zane Grey, Max Brand, and Louis L'Amour have attracted a worldwide audience. The western novel is a synthesis of many literary forms and traditions, including epic, romance, pastoral, and biography. Many critics consider James Fenimore Cooper's "Leatherstocking Tales," comprising five novels published from 1823 to 1841, as the first works of fiction to exploit the frontier setting and pioneer characters typical of the western genre. Later in the nineteenth century the adventures of various heroes and villains were chronicled in "dime novels," which were often sensationalized accounts of historical figures such as Jesse James, Wild Bill Hickok, and Billy the Kid. In 1902 Owen Wister published *The Virginian,* a novel that formulated the major themes and plots of the western, specifically those deriving from the conflict between the values of civilization and frontier lawlessness. Subsequently, western fiction has featured predictable story lines and a cast of one-dimensional characters, usually with the cowboy as the central figure. Both admired as a rugged individualist and vilified as a violent racist and sexist, the cowboy has been the subject of much critical attention. For many years westerns were neglected by critics who regarded them as formula fiction destined for a low-brow audience. Feminist critics have especially derided westerns for their simplistic and negative portrayal of women. Other commentators, however, have produced thoughtful studies of the western as a literary form, and a large body of criticism now exists analyzing westerns from a variety of cultural and artistic perspectives. The works of such contemporary writers as Larry McMurtry and Thomas Berger have further enhanced the critical reputation of the genre. More complex in structure and characterization than their predecessors, such novels as Berger's *Little Big Man* and McMurtry's *Horseman, Pass By* (also published as *Hud*) and *Lonesome Dove* have attracted readers normally uninterested in westerns. Many critics maintain that no popular genre has influenced American culture more than the western, and due to film and television adaptations the characters and conventions of the western have become familiar to an international audience.

REPRESENTATIVE WORKS

Abbey, Edward
 The Brave Cowboy (novel) 1956
Adams, Andy

 The Log of a Cowboy (novel) 1903
Berger, Thomas
 Little Big Man (novel) 1964
Bradford, Richard
 Red Sky at Morning (novel) 1968
Brand, Max [pseudonym of Frederick Faust]
 The Untamed (novel) 1919
 The Night Horseman (novel) 1920
 The Seventh Man (novel) 1921
 Destry Rides Again (novel) 1930
 Valley Vultures (novel) 1932
 Hunted Riders (novel) 1935
 Dead or Alive (novel) 1938
 The Dude (novel) 1940
Clark, Walter Van Tilburg
 The Ox-Bow Incident (novel) 1940
Cooper, James Fenimore
 The Pioneers (novel) 1823
 The Last of the Mohicans (novel) 1826
 The Prairie (novel) 1827
 The Pathfinder (novel) 1840
 The Deerslayer (novel) 1841
Evans, Max
 The Rounders (novel) 1960
Fisher, Vardis
 The Mothers (novel) 1943
 Mountain Man (novel) 1965
Flynn, Robert
 North to Yesterday (novel) 1967
Grey, Zane
 The Spirit of the Border (novel) 1906
 Riders of the Purple Sage (novel) 1912
 Twin Sombreros (novel) 1941
 Majesty's Rancho (novel) 1942
 Shadow on the Trail (novel) 1946
 The Fugitive Trail (novel) 1957
 Zane Grey's Greatest Western Stories (short stories) 1975
Gruber, Frank
 Outlaw (novel) 1941
 Fighting Man (novel) 1948
 Fort Starvation (novel) 1953
 Johnny Vengeance (novel) 1954
 Tales of Wells Fargo (short stories) 1958
 The Bushwackers (novel) 1959
Guthrie, A. B.
 The Big Sky (novel) 1947
 The Way West (novel) 1949
 These Thousand Hills (novel) 1956
Harte, Bret
 The Luck of Roaring Camp (short stories) 1870
 The Writings of Bret Harte. 20 vols. (novels, poetry, and short stories) 1896-1914
Haycox, Ernest
 Chaffee of Roaring Horse (novel) 1930

Riders West (novel) 1934
Rough Air (novel) 1934
Trouble Shooter (novel) 1937
Sundown Jim (novel) 1938
By Rope and Lead (novels) 1951
Murder on the Frontier (novels) 1953
Vengeance Trail (novels and short stories) 1960
Henry, Will [pseudonym of Henry W. Allen]
No Survivors (novel) 1950
The Last Warpath (short stories) 1966
Hough, Emerson
The Story of the Cowboy (novel) 1897
The Mississippi Bubble (novel) 1902
Heart's Desire (novel) 1905
The Magnificent Adventure (novel) 1916
The Sagebrusher (novel) 1919
The Covered Wagon (novel) 1922
Mother of Gold (novel) 1924
Ingraham, Prentiss
Crimson Kate, the Girl Trailer (novel) 1881
L'Amour, Louis
Hondo (novel) 1953
The Daybreakers (novel) 1960
Sackett (novel) 1961
Ride the Dark Trail (novel) 1972
Comstock Lode (novel) 1981
LeMay, Alan
The Searchers (novel) 1954
Lewis, Alfred Henry
Wolfville: Episodes of Cowboy Life (short stories) 1897
Lott, Milton
Dance Back the Buffalo (novel) 1959
Manfred, Frederick
The Golden Bowl (novel) 1944
King of Spades (novel) 1966
McMurtry, Larry
Horseman, Pass By (novel) 1961; also published as *Hud,* 1963
Leaving Cheyenne (novel) 1963
Lonesome Dove (novel) 1985
Medoff, Mark
The Majestic Kid (drama) 1984
Mulford, Clarence
Hopalong Cassidy (novel) 1910
Portis, Charles
True Grit (novel) 1968
Rhodes, Eugene Manlove
Good Men and True (novel) 1910
West Is West (novel) 1917
The Proud Sheriff (novel) 1935
Richter, Conrad
The Sea of Grass (novel) 1937
The Light in the Forest (novel) 1953
Schaefer, Jack
Shane (novel) 1949
Monte Walsh (novel) 1963
Short, Luke [pseudonym of Frederick Glidden]
Marauders' Moon (novel) 1937
Ride the Man Down (novel) 1942
Vengeance Valley (novel) 1950
Play a Lone Hand (novel) 1951

Silver Rock (novel) 1953
Trouble Country (novel) 1976
A Man Could Get Killed (novel) 1980
South, Frank
Rattlesnake in a Cooler (drama) 1981
Wheeler, Edward L.
Deadwood Dick, the Prince of the Road; or, The Black Rider of the Black Hills (novel) 1877
Wister, Owen
The Virginian (novel) 1902

DEFINITION AND DEVELOPMENT OF AMERICAN WESTERN LITERATURE

Richard W. Etulain

[*Etulain is an American critic and the author of numerous books on American western fiction. His specific interests, as he states, are in the "sociocultural life of the American West and presentation of that region in American popular culture." In the following essay, Etulain traces the historical development of American western literature.*]

A perplexing problem facing the student of western literature is the lack of satisfactory definitions in his field of study. Foremost among these is the need for more precise distinctions between the kinds of fiction written about the American West. In his [*The American Western Novel*], James K. Folsom suggests that all fiction written about the trans-Mississippi West are Westerns. Yet this inclusive definition makes no major distinctions between the writings of Zane Grey and Hamlin Garland, Ernest Haycox and Paul Horgan, Luke Short and John Steinbeck. A more exact categorization (although not an entirely satisfactory one) would be to term the former—Grey, Haycox, and Short—as writers of *Westerns* and the latter as authors of *western novels.* The first group and their writings are the subject of this essay.

It is not difficult to understand the paucity of usable definitions of popular literature. Attempting definitions of the Western is like trying to shovel fleas through a barn door—more escape than are captured. Although I have no hope here of structuring a definitive definition, I do wish to suggest a descriptive one that is usable for subsequent discussions of the Western.

One approach for defining the Western is to scatter along a spectrum the varying kinds of form utilized in western fiction. One might place at the far right the work of Grey, Max Brand, Haycox, and many members of the Western Writers of America. These writers nearly always formulate their fiction from the same ingredients: action, romance, and conflict of good and bad characters. Their plots are predictive; in their narratives the good man always wins. In doing so, he defeats his weak or evil opponents, and he is rewarded for his diligence—most often by winning the thanks of the community he saves, the hand of the heroine, or by gaining wealth. At the opposite end of the spectrum one would place the works of such western writers as Ken Kesey, N. Scott Momaday, Wright Morris, Richard Brautigan, and Larry McMurtry, whose plots are not predictable and who rarely utilize all the ingredients of the Western. Obviously, these extremes on the spectrum leave a good deal of unclaimed middle ground. It is not my purpose here to argue endlessly whether Emerson Hough's *North of 36* or *The Covered Wagon,* Jack Schaefer's *Shane,* or Walter Van Tilburg Clark's *The Ox-Bow Incident* should be branded as Westerns or as western novels. Instead, I am interested in discussing those writers whose works clearly belong in the category at the right end of the spectrum. Too often interpreters have dismissed these men and their writings as not worthy of study; I wish to avoid that mistaken judgment.

To be more specific, the Western is an adventure story, set in the West with major emphasis on action and romance. Its characters are nearly always strictly controlled; that is, they frequently fit into "good" and "bad" categories and are rarely complex or ambiguous. Most fit the type that E. M. Forester labeled "flat" characters. Few writers of Westerns are interested in analyzing or in questioning accepted standards of morality. In fact, they most often want to confirm middle class standards; this being the case, they write within a closed society of rigid restrictions. In Marshall McLuhan's terminology the Western is a *hot* medium, offering the maximum entertainment with the minimum involvement and complexity. As John Cawelti has pointed out recently, the narrative structure of most Westerns is like a game: the good man pitted against the bad man on a field of competition that is definable and predictable. The game operates under a set of rules that are clear to all those involved in the game—and to the reader.

Having suggested the kind of fictional work to be discussed here, let me propose one method of study that illuminates further the meaning of this popular genre. This approach is tracing in broad outline the chronological development of the Western from its birth at the turn of the century until the present time. To imply, however, that the form and content of the Western have remained constant during this period is misleading, for they have changed considerably since the first appearance of the Western. Three periods of development are noticeable as one scrutinizes the rise of the Western.

The Western was born in the first twenty-five years of the present century. Some students trace its origins to the epics, to the historical romances of Sir Walter Scott and Robert Louis Stevenson, and to American adventure fiction of the nineteenth century; but the Western, more than anything else, was the product of several cultural strains in American history surrounding 1900. Though these currents were separate, their cumulative influence helped give rise to the Western.

One of these currents was the long-held interest in the West as a literary topic. Drawing upon the writings of Washington Irving, James Fenimore Cooper, and Walt Whitman and the actions of westward-moving pioneers, and encouraged even further by the successes of such later authors as Bret Harte and Mark Twain, several writers

---

MAJOR MEDIA ADAPTATIONS: Motion Pictures

The Covered Wagon, 1923. Paramount. [Adaptation of the novel by Emerson Hough] Director: James Cruze. Cast: Ernest Torrence, Tully Marshall, J. Warren Kerrigan.

Tumbleweeds, 1925. UA. [Adaptation of the story by Hal. G. Evarts] Director: King Baggott. Cast: William S. Hart, Barbara Bedford, Lucien Littlefield.

The Vanishing American, 1925. Paramount. [Adaptation of the novel by Zane Grey] Director: George B. Seitz. Cast: Richard Dix, Lois Wilson, Noah Beery.

The Virginian, 1929. Paramount. [Adaptation of the novel by Owen Wister] Director: Victor Fleming. Cast: Gary Cooper, Walter Huston, Richard Arlen.

Cimarron, 1931. RKO. [Adaptation of the novel by Edna Ferber] Director: Wesley Ruggles. Cast: Richard Dix, Irene Dunne, Estelle Taylor.

The Squaw Man, 1931. MGM. [Adaptation of the play by Edwin Milton Royle] Director: Cecil B. deMille. Cast: Warner Baxter, Lupe Velez, Charles Bickford.

Law and Order, 1932. Universal. [Adaptation of *Saint Johnson* by W. R. Burnett] Director: Edward L. Cahn. Cast: Walter Huston, Harry Carey, Haymond Hatton.

*Hopalong Cassidy, 1934. Paramount and Universal. [Adaptation of the novels by Clarence E. Mulford] Director: Howard Bretherton. Cast: William Boyd, George "Gabby" Hayes, Andy Clyde.

The Last of the Mohicans, 1936. Edward Small. [Adaptation of the novel by James Fenimore Cooper] Director: George B. Seitz. Cast: Randolph Scott, Binnie Barnes, Bruce Cabot.

The Outcasts of Poker Flat, 1937. RKO. [Adaptation of the story by Bret Harte] Director: Christy Cabanne. Cast: Preston Foster, Jean Muir, Van Heflin.

Wells Fargo, 1937. Paramount. [Adaptation of the story by Stuart N. Lake] Director: Frank Lloyd. Cast: Joel McCrea, Bob Burns, Frances Dee.

Destry Rides Again, 1939. Universal. [Adaptation of the novel by Max Brand] Director: George Marshall. Cast: James Stewart, Marlene Dietrich, Brian Donlevy, Charles Winninger, Una Merkel.

Drums along the Mohawk, 1939. Twentieth-Century Fox. [Adaptation of the novel by Walter Edmonds] Director: John Ford. Cast: Claudette Colbert, Henry Fonda, Edna May Oliver.

Stagecoach, 1939. UA. [Adaptation of "Stage to Lordsburg" by Ernest Haycox] Director: John Ford. Cast: Claire Trevor, John Wayne, Thomas Mitchell, George Bancroft, John Carradine.

The Westerner, 1940. Samuel Goldwyn. [Adaptation of the story by Stuart N. Lake] Director: William Wyler. Cast: Gary Cooper, Walter Brennan, Doris Davenport.

The Great Man's Lady, 1942. Paramount. [Adaptation of the story by Vina Delmar] Director: William L. Wellman. Cast: Barbara Stanwyck, Joel McCrea, Brian Donlevy.

The Ox-Bow Incident, 1943. Twentieth-Century Fox. [Adaptation of the novel by Walter Van Tilburg Clark] Director: William Wellman. Cast: Henry Fonda, Henry Morgan, Jane Darwell, Anthony Quinn.

Duel in the Sun, 1946. David O. Selznick. [Adaptation of the novel by Niven Busch] Director: King Vidor. Cast: Jennifer Jones, Joseph Cotten, Gregory Peck, Lionel Barrymore, Lillian Gish.

My Darling Clementine, 1946. Twentieth-Century Fox. [Adaptation of *Wyatt Earp, Frontier Marshal* by Stuart N. Lake] Director: John Ford. Cast: Henry Fonda, Victor Mature, Walter Brennan, Alan Mowbray.

Fort Apache, 1948. RKO. [Adaptation of "Massacre" by James Warner Bellah] Director: John Ford. Cast: Henry Fonda, John Wayne, Shirley Temple.

The Treasure of the Sierra Madre, 1948. Warner. [Adaptation of the novel by B. Traven] Director: John Huston. Cast: Humphrey Bogart, Walter Huston, Tim Holt.

She Wore a Yellow Ribbon, 1949. RKO. [Adaptation of the story by James Warner Bellah] Director: John Ford. Cast: John Wayne, Joanne Dru, John Agar.

Broken Arrow, 1950. Twentieth-Century Fox. [Adaptation of *Blood Brother* by Elliott Arnold] Director: Delmer Daves. Cast: James Stewart, Jeff Chandler, Debra Paget.

Rio Grande, 1950. Republic. [Adaptation of the story by James Warner Bellah] Director: John Ford. Cast: John Wayne, Maureen O'Hara, Ben Johnson.

Winchester 73, 1950. Universal-International. [Adaptation of the story by Stuart N. Lake] Director: Anthony Mann. Cast: James Stewart, Shelley Winters, Dan Duryea.

The Big Sky, 1952. RKO. [Adaptation of the novel by A. B. Guthrie] Director: Howard Hawks. Cast: Kirk Douglas, Arthur Hunnicutt, Elizabeth Threatt.

High Noon, 1952. Stanley Kramer. [Adaptation of "The Tin Star" by John W. Cunningham] Director: Fred Zinnemann. Cast: Gary Cooper, Grace Kelly, Thomas Mitchell, Lloyd Bridges.

Johnny Guitar, 1953. Republic. [Adaptation of the novel by Roy Chanslor] Director: Nicholas Ray. Cast: Joan Crawford, Mercedes McCambridge, Ernest Borgnine.

Shane, 1953. Paramount. [Adaptation of the novel by Jack Schaefer] Director: George Stevens. Cast: Alan Ladd, Jean Arthur, Jack Palance, Ben Johnson, Van Heflin.

Apache, 1954. UA. [Adaptation of *Bronco Apache* by Paul I. Wellman] Director: Robert Aldrich. Cast: Burt Lancaster, Jean Peters, Charles Bronson.

Hondo, 1954. Wayne-Fellows. [Adaptation of the novel by Louis L'Amour] Director: John Farrow. Cast: John Wayne, Geraldine Page, Ward Bond.

The Searchers, 1956. Warner. [Adaptation of the novel by Alan LeMay] Director: John Ford. Cast: John Wayne, Jeffrey Hunter, Natalie Wood, Vera Miles.

Heller in Pink Tights, 1960. Paramount. [Adaptation of the novel by Louis L'Amour] Director: George Cukor. Cast: Sophia Loren, Anthony Quinn, Steve Forrest.

One Eyed Jacks, 1961. Paramount. [Adaptation of *The Authentic Death of Henry Jones* by Charles Neider] Director: Marlon Brando. Cast: Marlon Brando, Karl Malden, Pina Pellicier.

Two Rode Together, 1961. Columbia. [Adaptation of the novel by Will Cook] Director: John Ford. Cast: James Stewart, Richard Widmark, Shirley Jones

How the West Was Won, 1962. MGM. [Adaptation of the novel by Louis L'Amour] Director: Henry Hathaway, John Ford, and George Marshall. Cast: Debbie Reynolds, Carroll Baker, Lee J. Cobb, Henry Fonda, Karl Malden, Gregory Peck, George Peppard, James Stewart, John Wayne.

Lonely Are the Brave, 1962. Universal-International. [Adaptation of *The Brave Cowboy* by Edward Abbey] Director: David Miller. Cast: Kirk Douglas, Walter Matthau, Gena Rowlands.

Hud, 1963. Paramount. [Adaptation of *Horseman, Pass By* by Larry McMurtry] Director: Martin Ritt. Cast: Paul Newman, Patricia Neal, Melvyn Douglas.

Cheyenne Autumn, 1964. Warner. [Adaptation of the novel by Mari Sandoz] Director: John Ford. Cast: Richard Widmark, Carroll Baker, Karl Malden, Dolores del Rio, Sal Mineo, James Stewart.

El Dorado, 1966. Paramount. [Adaptation of *The Stars in Their Courses* by Harry Joe Brown] Director: Howard Hawks. Cast: John Wayne, Robert Mitchum, James Cann, Ed Asner.

The Way West, 1967. UA. [Adaptation of the novel by A. B. Guthrie] Director: Andrew V. McLaglen. Cast: Kirk Douglas, Robert Mitchum, Richard Widmark, Sally Field.

True Grit, 1969. Paramount. [Adaptation of the novel by Charles Portis] Director: Henry Hathaway. Cast: John Wayne, Kim Darby, Glen Campbell, Dennis Hopper.

The Outlaw Josey Wales, 1976. Warner. [Adaptation of *Gone to Texas* by Forrest Carter] Director: Clint Eastwood. Cast: Clint Eastwood, Chief Dan George, Sondra Locke.

Lonesome Dove, 1991. Motown Production. [Adaptation of the novel by Larry McMurtry] Director: Simon Wincer. Cast: Robert Duvall, Tommy Lee Jones, Anjelica Huston, Diane Lane, Danny Glover, Robert Urich, Rick Schroder, D. B. Sweeney, Frederic Forrest.

*There were 66 films made about Hopalong Cassidy, first as feature length films and then as television shows.

around the turn of century turned to the West for their materials. The chilling conviction that a West, a land linked with freedom, space, and opportunity was rapidly vanishing, nourished further the interest that earlier writers and thinkers had engendered. This interest in and attachment to the past is demonstrated when historical fiction topped the polls of best sellers around 1900.

Concurrently, some Americans of the Progressive Era feared that an industrial society was creeping upon them and devouring their lives. To recapture a past that was less coercive and less dominated by the city, the immigrant, and worker, they turned to the West as a palliative. The West as frontier symbolized a simpler and more primitive and pristine past that many Progressives wished to retain. Confronted with a present and future that conjured a diminished individualism, they embraced, instead, a region in popular literature that was the last opportunity for democracy, individualism, and decency. The West, to these Americans, was more than a satisfactory symbol; it was an attractive emotional experience. The Western was, in large part, the literary by-product of this haunting and fractured emotional experience.

Perhaps Americans in our time can comprehend this tendency of the Progressive Era to evade the most pressing issues of the time and to revert to a nostalgic and sentimental view of the West, for some contemporary Americans avoid the nagging problems of poverty, racism, and pollution by allowing themselves to escape to the mountains or countryside and lose their worries in a symbolic wilderness. In several ways, the popularity of Charles Reich's *The Greening of America* and the writings of Theodore Roszak illustrate this tendency of avoiding harsh realities and of dreaming of what might be. Instead of realizing that the best answer is some kind of difficult but necessary compromise between extremes, many Americans choose to think that back-to-the-land movements or the championing of what they consider the mystical and land-oriented philosophies of Native Americans will solve our complex and traumatic social problems. This desire to avoid a depressing present and the increasing tendency to escape into the past is much with us today; if we comprehend this impulse, it is less difficult to understand the climate of opinion that helped spawn the Western.

Owen Wister illustrates well the desire of some Progressives to recapture the past. A close friend of Theodore Roosevelt, Wister saw the West as the setting for displaying the greatness of the Anglo Saxon past. His West was one that encouraged individualism, democracy, and freedom, and one that weeded out the less desirables—Mexicans, Indians, and immigrants of southern European origin. Wister was an amalgamator; he helped bring together the cultural currents mentioned above and blended them into a paradigm for a new type of popular literature. That is, he played upon the interest in things western, he wrote what he termed an historical novel, he used the new and popular cowboy as a democratic hero, and his work is shot through with the nostalgia that characterized the "strenuous age." Further, he structured these moods in a form that was to pave the way for hundreds of Westerns that were modeled after the form of *The Virginian* (1902).

If Owen Wister was the formulator of the Western, Zane Grey and Max Brand were the systemizers. While Wister chose not to repeat the successful pattern of *The Virginian,* Grey used the formula again and again in his numerous Westerns. There are few major differences between the earlier and later versions of the Zane Grey pattern. Grey saw no need to make revisions in his works, and neither

did his loyal readers, for without his making any large changes his name appeared on the best seller lists for more than a decade. *Riders of the Purple Sage* (1912) is typical of many of his Westerns; it demonstrates both his strengths and weaknesses—an ability at writing description and action-packed adventure but an inability to handle character motivation and human emotion.

Beginning about a decade later than Grey, Max Brand was an even more prolific writer. On one occasion Brand produced an entire issue of a pulp Western magazine—the stories appeared under several names, of course. Brand was superior to Grey in style, characterization, and plot; but Brand could never allow his characters to remain human beings. Frequently, they were not merely heroes but gigantic and mythic super-humans. Brand, once he had discovered an acceptable pattern for his Westerns by the early 1920s, manufactured dozens of the same type before his death during World War II.

Brand published most of his serial Westerns in *Western Story,* a pulp Western magazine that did much to stylize the new popular genre. This Street and Smith publication captured readers who had earlier devoured dozens of Western dime novels and Beadle Story papers. The editors of *Western Story* demanded stories with predictable plots and stereotyped characters. Aspiring writers of Westerns soon learned that stories of sex, ambiguous heroes or villains, or unhappy endings did not win the approval of F. E. Blackwell, the chief editor of the magazine. If one wishes to understand the Western in its formative years, extensive reading in the pages of *Western Story* will reveal the main dimensions of this popular type.

By the end of the 1920s, then, one may use the term *Western* to describe a kind of popular literature that is easily traceable during the first quarter of this century. Some literary students of the period were aware of this new genre, for by 1925 reviewers were using the term *Western* to identify the literary mode discussed above. These novels had dropped many of the specifics of western regional or local color fiction and had instead accepted a design that emphasized, most of all, romance, adventure, and action. This process, which Albert Van Nostrand terms "denaturalization," demands the repression of an author's individual style in favor of the recognizable desires of editors and readers. Strict adherence to or skillful manipulation of the formula is more important than a writer's singular achievements.

A second stage in the development of the Western commences in the later twenties and continues until the Second World War or shortly thereafter. The career of Ernest Haycox during this period illustrates the changes that were taking place in the Western. Haycox, who first appeared in *Western Story* and other Street and Smith publications, grew tired of the restrictions of the pulp Western and tried to make innovations in the formula. He was unable to do so as long as he remained with *Western Story,* so he began sending his work to Doubleday, Doran's *Short Stories* and *Frontier,* both of which encouraged his efforts with more prestige and pay.

First of all, Haycox experimented by using two heroines.

With this technique he could add more tension to his plots and allow for the hero to be perplexed with internal conflicts. (Plots of Westerns written in the early twentieth century were, by in large, limited to external conflicts.) Thus, the rigid dichotomy of good and bad was avoided, for both of the heroines had good qualities. It was only after time and experience that the hero ascertained which gal was "real goodness."

Next, Haycox tinkered with the dimensions of his hero. The pulp Western hero was a doer, an actor, with little emphasis given to his reflections. Haycox sought to give his protagonists broader meaning, to allow them to ponder their circumstances. At first, the results were not persuasive: the "thought" passages had been obviously grafted upon the adventure framework and were out of place. Haycox was attempting what Bernard De Voto and W. H. Hutchinson have called the "Hamlet hero." Actually, the problem that faced Haycox was an old one; it was one that puzzled James Fenimore Cooper, for example, in his Leather-stocking Tales. How could an author give enlarged meaning to the hero of an adventure novel? (James K. Folsom has discussed in detail in his *The American Western Novel* how Cooper successfully solved the dilemma.) But Haycox had further problems. He was writing for an audience that wanted action most of all, and he must give it to them if he was to make his living writing Westerns. His solution was for the hero to "learn" gradually—to act precipitously at first and then to realize that his actions had to be more ordered. Sometimes his "learning" came from his entanglements with the two heroines but more often from the mistakes he made in analyzing himself. His lessons were always tied in with subsequent actions; answers were acted out so that the galloping narrative could keep arm-chair experts happy.

Haycox's most popular innovation came after he began selling his fiction to *Collier's* in 1931, which occurred at the end of a ten-year apprenticeship in the pulps. He began to write *historical* Westerns. Haycox was convinced that if he were to base his Westerns on a solid, historical background he could add to the realism of his final product. Beginning in 1937 with *Trouble Shooter,* a Western based on the building of the Union Pacific Railroad, and terminating with *Bugles in the Afternoon* (1945), an account of Custer's last stand and Haycox's most popular work, he constructed several readable historical Westerns that were a blend of history and adventure. While Haycox's contribution of the historical vista to the Western may not have been his most important one, it has been his most popular and influential one. Such recent writers of Westerns as Dwight B. Newton, Bill Gulick, and Frank Gruber testify to this point. And the agent of Jack Schaefer would bemoan the fact in the 1950s that Schaefer's quality western fiction was not selling because the market was glutted with the inferior Westerns of men all trying to be Haycox.

Haycox's contribution to the development of the Western is difficult to describe and evaluate. Some writers of Westerns have termed his major influence the "feel" he had for his characters and his settings. Others point to his "style" as his difference from other writers of Westerns. Nelson Nye, an old pro at turning out Westerns, says Haycox lifted the Western from the pulps to the slicks, meaning that he elevated the Western from Street and Smith publications into the pages of *Collier's* and *Saturday Evening Post.* Haycox tinkered with the basic structure of the Western, but his changes were gradual enough not to alienate his readers. He avoided the mawkishness of Grey and the superheroes of Brand and added a more realistic treatment of formula characters and a sure grasp of historical detail.

Even more important—and a point not sufficiently noted—Haycox was an immensely successful author financially. While other writers of Westerns were struggling through the Depression, Haycox was selling short stories and serials year after year to *Collier's.* An examination of *Collier's* during the 1930-1945 period shows that Haycox placed more Westerns with this magazine than any other writer, and after 1945 he began to sell his work regularly to *Saturday Evening Post.* No wonder so many other writers tried to imitate his Westerns, for he was the symbol of success and if one were to sell his work, copying Haycox seemed a sure way of gaining an acceptance slip.

World War II killed most of the pulp magazines and seriously wounded the pulp Western, although *Ranch Romances* is still alive and well somewhere in the mythic West. With the termination of these outlets and the lessening number of Westerns appearing in the slicks, writers of Westerns found it difficult to survive. For them the period from the end of the Second World War until the middle fifties was one of great uncertainty.

The most important occurrence within the third stage of the development of the Western was the beginning of the Western Writers of America. Organized in the early 1950s, the WWA has given writers of Westerns the marketplace and meetinghouse they have needed. The organization in its more than two decades of existence has consistently encouraged the writing of better Westerns. In its earliest years, it gave "Ernies" (in honor of Haycox who died in 1950) for the best Western written each year. Recently the number of awards, now called Spurs, has been enlarged to include recognition for such categories as the best western novel, best non-fiction on the West, best Western short and the best western children's book. In the pages of the WWA's house organ, *The Roundup,* tips are given on markets, sales, and improved techniques. On occasion, a maverick like Brian Garfield stirs up a bit of controversy by criticizing recent trends in the Western. But the magazine and the organization are primarily for encouraging writers of Westerns, not criticizing them; perhaps the WWA and *The Roundup* have achieved their major purpose, for the membership list of the group includes nearly all the leading writers of Westerns.

It is impossible to say, however, whether the WWA or its projects has actually aided in the writing of better Westerns. The writers of Westerns think so, and, if one takes time to read Westerns marketed in the last two decades, he will find great improvement over those written twenty years earlier. Large strides have been made in creating more believable characters. Also the best Westerns avoid excessive melodrama and extreme sentimentality. Many recent writers are also utilizing some brand of the historical Western.

If Brand and Grey epitomize the first stage and Haycox and perhaps Alan LeMay the second, it is Luke Short who illustrates the third era in the development of the Western. Short (Frederick Glidden) began writing in the early 1930s. He admits that his first efforts in the pulps were imitations (and bad ones) of Haycox. He read and studied the latter's yearly Westerns in *Collier's* and tried to repeat their successes. But with the gradual demise of the pulps and the death of *Collier's* in 1956, Short had to find new outlets. Like others, he found that several major publishers were willing to flirt with having one or two top-notch writers of Westerns in their stable. For several years Short followed this pattern. But with the increased popularity of the paperback, new opportunities presented themselves. Paperback publishers, at first, were satisfied to reprint Westerns that had appeared previously in hardbound form. But, gradually, those publishers of paperbacks who wished to offer a consistent group of superior Westerns under their trademarks began to give substantial prices for Westerns that appeared as paperback originals. For Short—and for several other superior writers of Westerns—this was the best financial opportunity they could ask for. In recent years nearly all of Short's works have been published as Bantam originals. A recent listing, in fact, includes more than forty of Short's Westerns under the Bantam trademark. The list contains those works that are reprints as well as those that are paperback originals. In the late 1940s Short received nearly $20,000 for his serial Westerns. Although Bantam could not match the lordly prices of the *Post,* it was willing in the early sixties to guarantee Short a minimum of $15,000 a year for at least one new Western per year and the reprint rights on some of his previous work. Probably Short's guaranteed minimum is considerably more now, for this agreement was made more than a decade ago. For Luke Short this type of agreement was stability, and for his publisher it was some order in a chaotic enterprise.

What about the quality of Short's works? Most of his Westerns are skillful blends of the expected tripex: romance, action, and conflict of character. In his Westerns published in the 1960s Short has used more violence than in his earlier works. His heroes engage in vicious fights and argue for the need of brute force to keep law and order. Though their speech sometimes suggests sexual activity, Short's protagonists rarely break (or even bruise) any moral codes. Short is especially adept at mixing the elements of the Western and the detective story. His plots often knit together the standard materials of the Western and the solving of a crime. This fruitful combination of plots freights his Westerns with an extraordinary amount of suspense and tension.

Short obviously knows the details of western life, but most of his works are not historical Westerns. Instead of basing his writings on specific occurrences he stresses general information about such western topics as mining, ranching, railroading, and farming. His Westerns are short—seldom more than 150 pages in paperback form—and rarely emphasize the inner conflicts of his characters. Unlike Haycox, then, he does not consistently utilize the historical Western, the Hamlet hero, and dual heroines. Yet in his convincing portrayal of character conflict, in his "feel" for

western settings, and in his skillful employment of believable plots, Short reminds one a good deal of Haycox. In several ways the ingredients of the fiction of Haycox and Short have become standard fare for contemporary writers of Westerns.

For other authors, different aspects of the Western field have beckoned. Writers like John and Ward Hawkins, the late Frank Gruber, and Tommy Thompson have largely abandoned fiction-writing for the lucrative field of script-writing for movies and television. Still other writers have avoided patterned fiction in some of their novels and have struck out for new ground—for example, Bill Gulick, Giles Lutz, and Will Henry (Henry W. Allen), who continues to write standard Westerns under the name of Clay Fisher. While full-length Westerns sell well, there is almost no market now for the short story Western. This development is unfortunate because frequently the shorter piece demands better characterization and aids writers in not overemphasizing action. At the same time, serial markets in slick magazines have closed up shop. But this change may be one for the better because writers no longer have to tailor their Westerns to fit the demands of the serial marts.

Other signs indicate that the Haycox-Short Western has competition. If one reads Westerns produced by Doubleday in its Double D Western line, for example, he finds a tendency to experiment with topics still taboo in the older format. Sex, dope, and racism—a startling triumvirate for treatment in the Western—are being used with more frequency. Some paperback publishers are also experimenting with these topics. If these signs indicate change, another development may help the Western to calm the heroics of some of its superheroes. Western novelists (but not writers of Westerns) have been making good use of the now-popular anti-hero. The anti-hero diminishes the dimensions of the old adventure hero. If carried far enough and if the elements of the Western are utilized, this type of western fiction becomes an "anti-Western." Max Evans' *The Rounders,* Thomas Berger's *Little Big Man,* Robert Flynn's *North to Yesterday,* Charles Portis' *True Grit,* and Richard Bradford's *Red Sky at Morning* and several western films (for example, *Cat Ballou* and *Butch Cassidy and the Sun Dance Kid*) illustrate this tendency.

Perhaps these alterations will bring new life to the Western. One hopes so. The genre needs once again to undergo the changes that Haycox brought to the Grey-Brand tradition. Now the Haycox-Short type has become too stylized or "denatured"; it too needs an infusion. The hints of change are good signs for the Western, for they will make it even more valuable as an index of the changing dimensions of the American popular mind. (pp. 75-82)

Richard W. Etulain, "The Historical Development of the Western," in The Popular Western: Essays toward a Definition, *edited by Richard W. Etulain and Michael T. Marsden, Bowling Green University Popular Press, 1974, pp. 75-84.*

CHARACTERISTICS OF THE WESTERN NOVEL

John G. Cawelti

[*Cawelti is an American critic. His* Six-Gun Mystique *is a seminal work in the field of western study. In the following excerpt from this work, Cawelti identifies the main features of the western novel.*]

The Western was created in the early nineteenth century by James Fenimore Cooper. Cooper's initial invention of the Leatherstocking (*The Pioneers,* 1823) paved the way for many fictional treatments of the West which strongly resembled his patterns of plot, character, and theme (e.g. R. M. Bird's *Nick of the Woods* and W. G. Simms, *The Yemassee*). By 1860 these patterns had become sufficiently stereotyped that they could serve Edward Ellis as the basis of his *Seth Jones; or The Captives of the Frontier,* one of the most successful early dime novels. In the later nineteenth century, the Western formula continued to flourish in the dime novel and in popular drama. Even the autobiographical narratives of Western experiences and popular biographies of Western heroes like Kit Carson, Buffalo Bill and General Custer, increasingly reflected the main elements of the formula, which was finally enshrined in the great spectacle of the Wild West Show. Gradually the cowboy replaced the frontier scout as the archetypal Western hero. Finally, in a number of works published around the turn of the century, the most important of which was Owen Wister's best-seller *The Virginian,* the western formula arrived at most of the characteristics it has held through innumerable novels, stories, films and TV shows in the twentieth century.

In one sense the Western formula is far easier to define than that of the detective story, for when we see a couple of characters dressed in ten-gallon hats and riding horses, we know we are in a Western. On the other hand, the Western formula contains a greater variety of plot patterns than the detective story with its single line of criminal investigation. Frank Gruber, a veteran writer of pulp Westerns, suggests that there are seven basic Western plots which he lists as: 1) The Union Pacific Story centering around the construction of a railroad, telegraph or stagecoach line or around the adventures of a wagon train; 2) The Ranch Story with its focus on conflicts between ranchers and rustlers or cattlemen and sheepmen; 3) The Empire Story, which is an epic version of the Ranch Story; 4) The Revenge Story; 5) Custer's Last Stand, or the Cavalry and Indian Story; 6) the Outlaw Story; and 7) The Marshal Story. One could doubtless construct other lists of plots that have been used in Westerns, though Gruber's seems quite adequate. . . . [There] is a kind of action pattern that the Western tends to follow whether it be about ranchers, cavalrymen, outlaws or marshals, but the possibility of such diversity of plot patterns suggests that we know a Western primarily by the presence of ten-gallon hats and horses. In other words, the Western formula is initially defined by its setting. Therefore in analyzing the components of the Western formula I will deal initially with the setting.

Tentatively, we might say that the western setting is a mat-

ter of geography and costume; that is, a Western is a story that takes place somewhere in the western United States in which the characters wear certain distinctive styles of clothing. However, this formulation is clearly inadequate since there are many stories set in the American West which we would not call Westerns under any circumstances, for example the novels and stories of Hamlin Garland, or Ole Rolvaag. Moreover, there are novels set in the eastern United States which are really Westerns, for example, the Leatherstocking Tales of James Fenimore Cooper. Our geographical definition must immediately be qualified by a social and historical definition of setting: the Western is a story which takes place on or near a frontier, and consequently, the Western is generally set at a particular moment in the past. (pp. 34-5)

[The] social and historical aspects of setting are perhaps even more important in defining the Western formula than geography. The Western story is set at a certain moment in the development of American civilization, namely at that point when savagery and lawlessness are in decline before the advancing wave of law and order, but are still strong enough to pose a local and momentarily significant challenge. In the actual history of the West, this moment was probably a relatively brief one in any particular area. In any case, the complex clashes of different interest groups over the use of Western resources and the pattern of settlement surely involved more people in a more fundamental way than the stuggle with Indians or outlaws. Nonetheless, it is the latter which has become central to the Western formula. The relatively brief stage in the social evolution of the West when outlaws or Indians posed a threat to the community's stability has been erected into a timeless epic past in which heroic individual defenders of law and order without the vast social resources of police and courts stand poised against the threat of lawlessness or savagery. But it is also the nature of this epic moment that the larger forces of civilized society are just waiting in the wings for their cue. However threatening he may appear at the moment, the Indian is vanishing and the outlaw about to be superseded. It is because they too represent this epic moment that we are likely to think of such novels as Cooper's *Last of the Mohicans,* Bird's *Nick of the Woods,* or more recent historical novels like Walter Edmonds' *Drums Along the Mohawk* as Westerns, though they are not set in what we have come to know as the West.

Why then has this epic moment been primarily associated in fiction with a particular West, that of the Great Plains and the mountains and deserts of the "Far West" and with a particular historical moment, that of the heyday of the open range cattle industry of the later nineteenth century? Westerns can be set at a later time—some of Zane Grey's stories take place in the twenties and some, like those of Gene Autry, Roy Rogers or "Sky King" in the present— but even at these later dates the costumes and the way of life represented tend to be that of the later nineteenth century. Several factors probably contributed to this particular fixation of the epic moment. Included among these would be the ideological tendency of Americans to see the Far West as the last stronghold of certain traditional values, as well as the peculiar attractiveness of the cowboy hero. But more important than these factors, the Western requires a means of isolating and intensifying the drama of the frontier encounter between social order and lawlessness. For this purpose, the geographic setting of the Great Plains and adjacent areas has proved particularly appropriate, especially since the advent of film and television have placed a primary emphasis on visual articulation. Four characteristics of the Great Plains topography have been especially important: its openness, its aridity and general inhospitability to human life, its great extremes of light and climate, and, paradoxically, its grandeur and beauty. These topographic features create an effective backdrop for the action of the Western because they exemplify in visual images the thematic conflict between civilization and savagery and its resolution. In particular, the Western has come to center about the image of the isolated town or ranch or fort surrounded by the vast open grandeur of prairie or desert and connected to the rest of the civilized world by a railroad, a stagecoach, or simply a trail. This tenuous link can still be broken by the forces of lawlessness, but never permanently. We can conceive it as a possibility that the town will be swept back into the desert—the rickety wooden buildings with their tottering false fronts help express the tenuousness of the town's position against the surrounding prairie—nonetheless we do not see the town solely as an isolated fort in hostile country—like an outpost of the French foreign legion in *Beau Geste*—but as the advance guard of an oncoming civilization. Moreover, while the prairie or desert may be inhospitable, it is not hostile. Its openness, freshness and grandeur also play an important role in the Western. Thus, the open prairie around the town serves not only as a haven of lawlessness and savagery, but as a backdrop of epic magnitude and even, at times, as a source of regenerating power.

This characteristic setting reflects and helps dramatize the tripartite division of characters that dominates the Western pattern of action. The townspeople hover defensively in their settlement, threatened by the outlaws or Indians who are associated with the inhospitable and uncontrollable elements of the surrounding landscape. The townspeople are static and largely incapable of movement beyond their little settlement. The outlaws or savages can move freely across the landscape. The hero, though a friend of the townspeople, has the lawless power of movement in that he, like the savages, is a horseman and possesses skills of wilderness existence. The moral character of the hero also appears symbolically in the Western setting. In its rocky aridity and climatic extremes the Great Plains landscape embodies the hostile savagery of Indians and outlaws, while its vast openness, its vistas of snow-covered peaks in the distance, and its great sunrises and sunsets (in the purple prose of Zane Grey, for example) suggest the epic courage and regenerative power of the hero. Thus, in every respect, Western topography helps dramatize more intensely the clash of characters and the thematic conflicts of the story. These dramatic resources of setting can of course be used more or less skillfully by the Western writer or film director, but even at their flattest they have a tendency to elevate rather commonplace plots into epic spectacles. When employed with conscious and skillful intent, as in the Western films of John Ford, the lyrical and epic power of landscape can sometimes transcend even the in-

herent limitations of popular culture and raise escapist adventure to a level of high artistry.

The special qualities of the Western setting emerge still more clearly from a comparison with the treatment of setting in the colonial adventure novels of English writers like H. Rider Haggard. Since it too involved adventures on the periphery of what its readers defined as civilization, the colonial adventure is the closest European analogue to the American Western. Like the Western setting, the tropical jungles of the colonial adventure have both hostile and attractive qualities. Haggard's African veldts, like the Western plains, contain savagery and raw nature which threaten the representatives of civilization. They are also full of exotic animals, beautiful natural spectacles, glamorous and mysterious cults, hidden treasures and other exciting secrets. But, in contrast to the fresh and open grandeur of the Western landscape, these double qualities of the colonial jungle are superficially attractive, but essentially subversive and dangerous. They are associated not with a redeeming hero who saves civilization from the threat of lawlessness and savagery, but with temptations which undermine the hero's commitment to civilization. The Western landscape can become the setting for a regenerated social order once the threat of lawlessness has been overcome, but the colonial landscape remains alien. Its doubleness simply reflects the difference between the overt threat of savage hostility and the more insidious danger of the attractiveness of alien cults and exotic ways of life. Perhaps because it contains an unresolved antithesis between man and the jungle, the colonial adventure has inspired truly profound works of literature, as instanced by such examples as Joseph Conrad's *Heart of Darkness,* while the Western formula has at best produced good novels like Wister's *The Virginian* or Clark's *The Ox-Bow Incident.*

The first major writer who brought together the tripartite division of townsmen, savages, and intermediate hero with a vision of the landscape was James Fenimore Cooper, who thereby became the creator of the Western. Even though Cooper's novels are set in the Eastern forests and many of his thematic emphases are quite different from the later Western, his landscapes show the same basic pattern. The new settlement (*The Pioneers*) or fort (*The Last of the Mohicans, The Pathfinder*) or "ranch" (Hutter's "castle" in *The Deerslayer*) is surrounded by miles of forested wilderness. It is clear, however, that civilization has irreversibly begun its advance. Like many later Western writers, Cooper liked frequently to call his reader's attention to the difference between the peaceful settlements of "today" and the dark mysterious forests of the earlier period of the story, thus insuring that the reader knew he was dealing with a stage of historical development which was definitely in the past. It is implicit in such a setting that the conflict between settlement and wilderness will soon be resolved. Cooper's wilderness also exemplifies the doubleness of the Western formula landscape. The forest is dark and frightening, but also the place where one gets the strongest feeling of the divine presence; it is the locus of the bloodthirsty and savage "Mingos" but also of the noble and heroic Delawares. (pp. 38-42)

A still from Roll Wagons Roll *(1939) depicting one of the most common scenes in western fiction: a wagon train heading West.*

As already indicated, there are three central roles in the Western: the townspeople or agents of civilization, the savages or outlaws who threaten this first group, and the heroes who are above all "men in the middle," that is, they possess many qualities and skills of the savages, but are fundamentally committed to the townspeople. It is out of the multiple variations possible on the relationships between these groups that the various Western plots are concocted. For example, the simplest version of all has the hero protecting the townspeople from the savages, using his own savage skills against the denizens of the wilderness. A second more complex variation shows the hero initially indifferent to the plight of the townspeople and more inclined to identify himself with the savages. However, in the course of the story his position changes and he becomes the ally of the townspeople. This variation can generate a number of different plots. There is the revenge Western: a hero seeks revenge against an outlaw or Indian who has wronged him. In order to accomplish his vengeance, he rejects the pacifistic ideals of the townspeople, but in the end he discovers that he is really committed to their way of life (John Ford's *The Searchers*). Another plot based on this variation of the character relations is that of the hero who initially seeks his own selfish material gain,

using his savage skills as a means to this end; but as the story progresses, he discovers his moral involvement with the townspeople and becomes their champion (cf. Anthony Mann's film *The Far Country*). It is also possible, while maintaining the system of relationships, to reverse the conclusion of the plot as in those stories where the townspeople come to accept the hero's savage mode of action (cf. John Ford's *Stagecoach* or, to a certain extent, Wister's *The Virginian*). A third variation of the basic scheme of relationships has the hero caught in the middle between the townspeople's need for his savage skills and their rejection of his way of life. This third variation, common in recent Westerns, often ends in the destruction of the hero (cf. the films *The Gunfighter* or *Invitation to a Gunfighter*) or in his voluntary exile (*Shane, High Noon, Two Rode Together*). The existence of these and many other variations suggest that the exploration of a certain pattern of relationships is more important to the Western than a particular outcome, though it is also probable that they reflect different components of the mass audience, the simpler variation being more popular with adolescents and the more complex variations successful with adults. In addition, changing cultural attitudes have something to do with the emergence of different variations, since variation two is clearly more characteristic of early twentieth century Westerns, while variation three dominates the recent "adult" Western.

The most important single fact about the group of townspeople is that there are women in it. Character groupings in the Western often show a dual as well as tripartite opposition: the hero and the savages are men while the town is strongly dominated by women. This sexual division frequently embodies the antithesis of civilization and savagery. Women are primary symbols of civilization in the Western. It is the schoolmarm even more than the entrepreneur who signals the end of the old wilderness life. Women are also women, however, and implicit in their presence is the sexual fascination and fear associated with the rape of white women by savages. Though few Westerns explicitly develop this theme and many writers even try to deny its place in their narratives, there seems little doubt that the possible savage capture of women plays a crucial role in many Westerns and an implicit role in most. Leslie Fiedler has done the most interesting work in analyzing the psychological undercurrents of the curious Western triangle between hero, savage, and female. His interpretation stresses the strong emotional, cultural, and even sexual ties between hero and savage which are threatened and finally disrupted by the female. He concludes that the violence endemic to this triangle reflects the terrible incompatibility between the free spontaneity and sexuality associated with savagery and the genteel restrictiveness of civilized monogamous domesticity. Thus, Fiedler interprets the Western as a popular myth embodying the psychological tensions which Freud describes in *Civilization and its Discontents*. Civilization represses spontaneous sexuality and creates a growing neurotic obsession with death and destruction. The hero's destruction of the savage in order to protect the chastity of the schoolmarm symbolizes the repression of his own spontaneous sexual urges and his acceptance of the monogamous sexual pattern of modern middle-class life.

Further evidence for the significance of this Western triangle lies in the frequent presence of two different kinds of women in the Western. This dichotomy resembles the common nineteenth century novelistic dualism of blonde and brunette. The blonde, like Cooper's Alice in *The Last of the Mohicans,* represents genteel, pure femininity, while the brunette, like Cora in the same novel, symbolizes a more full-blooded, passionate and spontaneous nature, often slightly tainted by a mixture of blood or a dubious past. In the contemporary Western, this feminine duality shows up in the contrast between the schoolmarm and the dance-hall girl, or between the hero's Mexican or Indian mistress and the WASP girl he may ultimately marry. The dark girl is a feminine embodiment of the hero's savage, spontaneous side. She understands his deep passions, his savage code of honor and his need to use personal violence. The schoolmarm's civilized code of behavior rejects the passionate urges and the freedom of aggression which mark this side of the hero's character. When the hero becomes involved with the schoolmarm, the dark lady must be destroyed or abandoned, just as Cooper's Cora must die because her feelings are too passionate and spontaneous to be viable in the genteel world of Alice and Duncan Hey-

ward. Even when the relationship between the hero and the dance-hall girl seems to be permanent and almost domestic, like the long-standing friendship between Kitty and Marshall Dillon on the TV series "Gunsmoke," it typically remains in suspension and never leads to marriage.

With women as central agents, the town reflects a somewhat ambiguous view of the values of civilization, an ambiguity which is invariably resolved in favor of social progress, but not without some reluctance and sense of loss. The town offers love, domesticity, and order as well as the opportunity for personal achievement and the creation of a family, but it requires the repression of spontaneous passion and the curtailment of the masculine honor and camaraderie of the older wilderness life. These ambiguities are reflected in the hero's relationship with women. They are also embodied in the three main kinds of townspeople who recurrently appear in Westerns: the pioneers or decent folk, the escapees from civilization, and the banker-villains. The pioneers resemble the hero in being virtuous and honorable people, but they lack his ability to cope with savagery. In addition, their aims are fundamentally different. The hero's primary moral concern is to preserve himself with individual dignity and honor in a savage and violent environment. The pioneers represent a collective force which seeks to transform the wilderness into a new social order. Their values center around the establishment of stable families and the building of homes, farms and businesses. Instead of individual honor, they value hard work, mutual loyalty, and political and economic achievement; in short, the conventional American canons of success. Typically, much of the action of the Western centers around the initial mixture of conflict and sympathy between hero and pioneers, which eventually resolves itself into the hero's commitment to the cause of the pioneers. Sometimes this commitment is happy in its outcome as in Wister's *The Virginian* where the hero is able to synthesize his personal code with the morality of the pioneers and become a successful rancher and political leader. In other cases, the conflict cannot be overcome and the hero's commitment becomes sacrificial. Such was the result of the relation between Judge Temple and Natty Bumpo in Cooper's *The Pioneers,* though in that novel a synthesis between hero and pioneers was attempted in the figure of Oliver Effingham. The sacrificial outcome also characterizes most of the significant recent Westerns. In Jack Schaefer's *Shane,* the hero becomes involved with pioneer Joe Starrett. Throughout the first part of the book we are shown the mixture of mutual sympathy and conflict which characterizes the relationship of two men of equal virtue but different aims and codes. Finally, Shane's commitment to the pioneer cause forces him to reenact his role as a gunman. But, as a killer, he can no longer remain a part of the pioneer community. Wounded in his battle for the pioneers he must ride off into the wilderness again. A similar pattern dominates John Ford's film *The Man Who Shot Liberty Valance.* The hero, Tom Doniphon, must sacrifice himself and his way of life to save the pioneer leader who will be instrumental in destroying the older anarchical society which is the only real background for the hero.

A second group of townspeople, who have become particularly prominent in more recent Westerns, combines in single individuals some of the ambiguities of civilization which appear in the conflict between hero and pioneers. This group consists of people who have fled the East. For them the West is not a place to build up a new civilization, but a haven from failure or personal tragedy in the East. The masculine form of this figure is commonly the drunken professional, particularly a doctor or a lawyer who, we are given to understand, had a promising eastern career which went sour. The female type is the dance-hall girl who, like the drunken professional, has had some shattering experience in the East and has come West to lick her wounds. These figures are commonly alienated from the rest of the townspeople and consequently are better able to understand the hero's moral imperatives. Yet, they cannot function on the hero's ground either since they lack his skills in violence or his strong sense of honor. They often play one or more of three important plot roles: first, they provide sympathy and even assistance to the hero at a crucial time; second, they are better able to initiate the reluctant hero into the virtues represented by the pioneers since they share some of the hero's ambiguity and yet remain basically committed to the town; finally, a savage attack on one of these figures often provides the final push behind the hero's commitment to the cause of the pioneers. In *The Man Who Shot Liberty Valance* it is the savage outlaw's vicious attack on the drunken professional that finally convinces Tom Doniphon of the necessity of playing a role on the side of the pioneers.

Thematically, the escapee from civilization seems to be a means of expressing both some sense of the limitations of civilization and yet of reaffirming what the town stands for. The escapee gains our sympathy and that of the hero by his alienation and failure. Yet from this very position of alienation and failure, he represents the limitations of individualism and the ultimate necessity of commitment to the town, for he, like the hero, discovers that he cannot maintain his prideful isolation when the chips are down and the savage attack has begun. In addition, the escapee serves as an important foil to the hero. His garrulous weakness sets off the hero's silent strength, his enforced alienation and failure contrast with the hero's voluntary isolation and pride. Moreover, his very presence is a testimony to the failure of society to provide an honorable and meaningful role for some of its choice spirits, thus enhancing our sympathy for the hero's own initial alienation from society.

The escapee mediates between the hero and the town and in doing so represents some of the ambiguous feelings toward society which the Western embodies. A third type of town figure symbolizes the negative side of civilization. This is the unscrupulous banker, rancher, or railroad agent who sometimes plays the role of central villain by becoming the employer or manipulator of the Indians or outlaws who actually perform the acts of savagery. This figure represents the decent ideals of the pioneers gone sour. In him, the pioneer goal of building a good society in the wilderness has become avarice and greed for individual wealth and power. Instead of the pioneer's mutual respect and loyalty, the banker-villain possesses skill at manipulating and exploiting the townspeople to his own advantage. This figure appears as the tyrannical rancher Luke Fletcher in Schaefer's *Shane,* as the grasping banker in Richard Wilson's *Invitation to a Gunfighter,* as both the evil gambler Durade and the avaracious capitalist Lee in Zane Grey's *The U.P. Trail.* Sometimes he is the unscrupulous Indian agent who makes corrupt bargains with Indians on the warpath, or the mortgage forecloser who drives the romanticized outlaw into a life of crime. It is tempting to say that in the twentieth century this townsman villain has increasingly usurped the traditional role of the savage as villain, but this would be an overstatement, for the banker-villain was implicit in the Western from the beginning. In *The Pioneers* Cooper clearly adumbrated him in the scheming lawyer Hiram Doolittle and the greedy miner Jotham Riddle. In the dime novel, this character was a favorite villain. Characters like Hon. Cecil Grosvenor of *Deadwood Dick on Deck* resemble one of the recurrent adversaries in the Horatio Alger stories, the greedy squire or avaricious relative who seeks to exploit the Alger hero by keeping him in a servile position, but whose plot is foiled when the hero makes contact with the benevolent merchant (the analogue to the pioneers in the Alger stories.) However, this character does play a more prominent role in the twentieth century and his greater importance reflects the changing thematic content of the Western.

The second major character role in the Western is that of the savage. In his simplest form the savage is the bloodthirsty Indian or lawless outlaw who is the irreconcilable adversary of hero and townspeople. While some Westerns do not get much beyond the simple opposition of good hero and evil savages, the relationship is rather more complex in most examples of the formula. The savages are not invariably villains, for, beginning with Cooper the idea of the noble savage played an important role in the tradition of the Western manifesting itself variously in virtuous Indians and "good" outlaws who exist in complex counterpoint with the evil savages. This double view of the savage mirrors the double meaning of wilderness on which I have already commented. The presence of both noble and diabolical manifestations of savagery reflects the same kind of ambiguity about the progress of civilization which I noted in discussing the townspeople. The savage symbolizes the violence, brutality, and ignorance which civilized society seeks to control and eliminate, but he also commonly stands for certain positive values which are restricted or destroyed by advancing civilization: the freedom and spontaneity of wilderness life, the sense of personal honor and individual mastery, and the deep camaraderie of men untrammelled by domestic ties. In both his roles it turns out that the savage must be destroyed, but in one case we rejoice and in the other feel nostalgically sorry. Two major modes of the Western derive from this distinction. There is the comic-heroic in novels like Wister's *The Virginian,* where the hero destroys the bad savages and achieves a synthesis between noble savagery and civilization in his own person. The second major mode is that of the elegaic which dominates the novels of Cooper and many recent Westerns. Here the imperatives of civilization and the good values of savagery prove irreconcilable and we are invited to lament the passing of these values as the price which must be paid for civilization.

It is possible to have Westerns without Indians or outlaws, but not without somebody playing the role of savage, for the antithesis between townspeople and savagery is the source of plots. Frequently we have a character who changes from savage to hero in the course of the story. For example, in John Ford's *Three Godfathers,* the three central characters are wild outlaws in flight from the law at the beginning of the film. Fleeing across the desert they come upon a lost woman who gives birth to a child and then dies after having made the three outlaws promise to care for the baby. Accepting this responsibility changes the outlaws from savages into heroes by placing them in that typical posture of the Western hero: a situation of divided commitment. As outlaws they are committed to battling with the law, as godfathers to the peaceful domesticity of civilization. In resolving this conflict the film makes use of the comic-heroic mode of the Western. Two of the outlaws are killed while heroically struggling to bring the child safely across the desert. The third arrives in "New Jerusalem" where he refuses to give the child to anyone else for adoption, even though the judge tempts him with a suspended sentence. This proof of a basic commitment to domesticity enables the judge to mete out a minimal sentence and the movie ends happily with the whole town turned out to see the outlaw-hero off to prison.

As I have already noted, the role of savage can be played interchangeably by Indians or outlaws because both groups symbolize the same basic qualities: negatively, lawlessness, a love of violence, rejection of the town and its way of life, and, more positively, the capacity to live and move freely in the wilderness, mastery of the tools of violence, and strong masculinity. Insofar as the Western writer chooses to emphasize the villainous qualities of the savage it is primarily through his ruthless violence. When the writer wishes to present the nobility of savagery, he usually stresses the savage's code of personal honor and his complete physical courage in defending this honor, those qualities which relate him to the hero. In the twentieth century Western, the outlaw has increasingly taken over the role of the "bad" savage, while the Indian seems more and more to embody the positive virtues of savagery. This reverses a relation common in the nineteenth century dime novel in which the outlaw was often romanticized as a noble outcast and the Indian treated as a diabolical villain. (pp. 46-54)

Between the eternally victorious Lone Ranger and the more ambiguous and tragic gunfighter, there exists a whole range of Western heroes more complex than the masked rider but less tragic than the gunfighter. Two types dominate this comic-heroic area of our scale of Western heroes and they are mirror images of each other. The first is the wild cowboy who becomes a pioneer leader, frequently by marrying the schoolmarm. The classic embodiment of this hero is Wister's *The Virginian.* The second type is a dude come West who duplicates the metamorphosis of the cowboy into a pioneer in reverse. This hero starts out as an easterner, usually a very aristocratic one. He has come West because he feels that his way of life has become corrupt and decadent; he seeks regeneration in the great, open spaces. Gradually, he becomes an initiate of the Code of the West, and by the end of the story he has become a cowboy of cowboys. This version of the hero can be found in such novels as Harold Bell Wright's *When a Man's a Man,* and in many of the stories of Zane Grey. He is of particular cultural interest because he was partly inspired by the actual western odysseys of a number of prominent eastern aristocrats like Theodore Roosevelt and Frederic Remington at the end of the nineteenth century.

The hero is a man with a horse and the horse is his direct tie to the freedom of the wilderness, for it embodies his ability to move freely across it and to dominate and control its spirit. Through the intensity of his relationship to his horse, the cowboy excites that human fantasy of unity with natural creatures—the same fantasy seen in such figures as the centaurs of Greek mythology, in Siegfried's ability to understand the language of birds, and in a hero whose popularity was contemporaneous with the flourishing of the Western: Tarzan of the Apes.

The Western hero is also a man with a gun. The interaction of American attitudes toward violence and the image of the Western hero as gunfighter is so complex that it seems impossible to determine which causes the other. Critics of violence in the mass media believe that the heroic romanticized violence of the Western hero is a dangerous model for young people and stimulates then to imitation of the man with the gun. Defenders of the mass media argue that Westerns and other violent adventure dramas simply reflect the culture's fascination with guns. There have been many investigations of violence in the mass media and a large-scale government inquiry has recently been undertaken. Insofar as it seeks to determine the causal role of the Western hero in fostering violence among those who follow his adventures, this inquiry will probably be as inconclusive as the rest, for in my opinion both the tendency to admire gunfighter heroes and the actual social incidence of violence with guns are both symptoms of a more complex cultural force: the sense of decaying masculine potency which has long afflicted American culture. The American obsession with masculinity so often observed by Europeans and so evident in every aspect of our culture from serious artists like Ernest Hemingway to the immense range of gutsy men's magazines, *Playboy* images, and mass sports reflect a number of major social trends which undercut the sense of male security. Among the most important of these developments is the tendency of industrial work to depend increasingly on the superior potency of machines, the increasing importance of women in the industrial economy, the nationalizing trend of American life which has eroded local communities and the individual's sense of control over his life and finally, the decline of parental authority in the family which has undercut the basic source of masculine supremacy. Yet, at the same time, the American tradition has always emphasized individual masculine force; Americans love to think of themselves as pioneers, men who have conquered a continent and sired on it a new society. This radical discrepancy between the sense of eroding masculinity and the view of America as a great history of men against the wilderness has created the need for a means of symbolic expression of masculine potency in an unmistakable way. This means is the gun, particularly the six-gun.

Walter Prescott Webb suggests that the development of Colt's revolver was the critical invention that made possible the American assault on the Great Plains. As Webb sees it, the Plains Indians with their horses and their extraordinary skill with the bow and arrow had a mobility and firepower unequalled until the adoption of the six-gun by the Texas Rangers. From that point on the Americans had a military advantage over the Plains Indians and the rapid development of the "Cattle Kingdom" followed. The historical and cultural significance of the gun as the means by which the cowboy drove out the Indian inhabitants of the plains and shaped a new culture happened to coincide with a long-standing tradition of heroism and masculine honor, that of the medieval knight, and its later offshoot, the code of the duel. For the westerner's six-gun and his way of using it in individual combat was the closest thing in the armory of modern violence to the knight's sword and the duellist's pistol. Thus in a period when violence in war was becoming increasingly anonymous and incomprehensible with massed attacks and artillery duels accounting for most of the casualties, the cowboy hero in his isolated combat with Indian or outlaw seemed to reaffirm the traditional image of masculine strength, honor, and moral violence. The cowboy hero with his six-gun standing between the uncontrolled violence of the savages and the evolving collective forces of the legal process played out in new terms the older image of chivalrous adventure. Not surprisingly an age which so enjoyed the historical romances of Sir Walter Scott would color the cowboy with tints freely borrowed from *Ivanhoe* and *Rob Roy*.

Many critics of the Western have commented upon the gun as a phallic symbol, suggesting that the firing of the gun symbolizes the moment of ejaculation in a sexual act. Insofar as this is the case it bears out the emphasis on masculine potency already noted. However, this kind of phallic symbolism is an almost universal property of adventure heroes. The knight has his sword, the hard-boiled detective his automatic pistol, Buck Rogers his ray gun. The distinctive characteristic of the cowboy hero is not his possession of a symbolic weapon, but the way in which he uses it.

Where the knight encountered his adversary in bloody hand-to-hand combat, the cowboy invariably meets his at a substantial distance and goes through the complex and rigid ritual of the "draw" before finally consummating the fatal deed. The most important implication of this killing procedure seems to be the qualities of reluctance, control and elegance which it associates with the hero. Unlike the knight, the cowboy hero does not seek out combat for its own sake and he typically shows an aversion to the wanton shedding of blood. Killing is an act forced upon him and he carries it out with the precision and skill of a surgeon and the careful proportions of an artist. We might say that the six-gun is that weapon which enables the hero to show the largest measure of objectivity and detachment while yet engaging in individual combat. This controlled and aesthetic mode of killing is particularly important as the supreme mark of differentiation between the hero and the savage. The Indian or outlaw as savage delights in slaughter, entering into combat with a kind of manic glee to fulfill an uncontrolled lust for blood. The hero never engages in violence until the last moment and he never kills until the savage's gun has already cleared his holster. Suddenly it is there and the villain crumbles.

This peculiar emphasis on the hero's skilled and detached killing from a distance has been a part of the Western since its inception. One thinks, for example, of that climactic scene in *The Last of the Mohicans* where Leatherstocking picks the villainous Magua off the cliff top with a single shot from his unerring long rifle. The cowboy hero fights in a little closer within the smaller range of the six-gun, but the same basic pattern of individual combat at a distance with the hero's last minute precision and control defeating the villain's undisciplined and savage aggression is the same. Careful staging of the final duel with all its elaborate protocol became a high point of the film Western, another example of an element of the literary Western which turned out to have even greater potential for the film.

The hero often fights with his fists, but he never kills in this kind of direct hand-to-hand combat. Moreover, he rarely uses any weapon other than his fists, since knives and clubs suggest a more aggressive uncontrolled kind of violence which seems instinctively wrong for the character of the cowboy hero. Thus, the hero's special skill at gunfighting not only symbolizes his masculine potency, but indicates that his violence is disciplined and pure. Something like the old ideal of knightly purity and chastity survives in the cowboy hero's basic aversion to the grosser and dirtier forms of violence. In addition, the hero's reluctant but aesthetic approach to killing seems to reflect the ambiguity about violence which pervades modern society. Twentieth century America is perhaps the most ideologically pacifistic nation in history. Its political and social values are anti-militaristic, its legal ideals reject personal violence and it sees itself as a nation dedicated to world peace and demestic harmony through law and order. Yet this same nation supports one of the largest military establishments in history, its rate of violent crimes is enormously high and it possesses the technological capacity to destroy the world. Perhaps one source of the cowboy hero's appeal is the way in which he resolves this ambiguity by giving a sense of moral significance and order to violence. His reluctance and detachment, the way in which he kills only when he is forced to do so, the aesthetic order he imposes upon his acts of violence through the abstract ritual of the shootdown, and finally, his mode of killing cleanly and purely at a distance through the magic of his six-gun cover the nakedness of violence and aggression beneath a skin of aesthetic grace and moral propriety.

Certain other characteristics are connected with the hero's role as middleman between the pacifistic townspeople and the violent savages. There is his oft-noted laconic style, for example. Not all Western heroes are tight-lipped strong, silent types. Some, like Leatherstocking, are downright garrulous. But the laconic style is commonly associated with the Western hero, particularly in the twentieth century when movie stars like Gary Cooper, John Wayne, James Stewart and Henry Fonda have vied for the prize as the Western hero who can say the fewest words with the least expression. Actually, tight lips are far more appropriate to the formula hero than the torrent of didacticism which flows from the lips of Natty Bumppo, and which most readers of Cooper resolutely ignore. Like his gun, language is a weapon the hero rarely uses, but when he does it is with precise and powerful effectiveness. In addition, the hero's reluctance with language reflects his social isolation and his reluctance to commit himself to the action which he knows will invariably lead to another violent confrontation.

Reluctance with words often matches the hero's reluctance toward women. Cooper's Leatherstocking marked out one basic course that the Western hero would take with respect to the fair sex. The one girl Natty falls in love with, Mabel Dunham in *The Pathfinder,* is too young and civilized to return his love and he gives her up to the younger, less wilderness-loving Jasper Western. On the other hand, the girl who falls in love with Natty, Judith Hutter in *The Deerslayer,* is too wild and too passionate to capture the affection of the chaste and pure Leatherstocking. This romantic situation reflects Natty's position as a man who mediates between civilization and wildness. Cooper found it increasingly difficult to resolve this antithesis and Natty remained caught in the middle between his beloved forest and the oncoming civilization which he had served. At other periods, writers have tried to make a romantic hero out of the cowboy, as in Wister's *The Virginian* and the many novels of Zane Grey. However, even when the hero does get the girl, the clash between the hero's adherence to the "code of the West" and the heroine's commitment to domesticity, social success, or other genteel values usually plays a role in the story. Heroes such as the Lone Ranger tend to avoid romance altogether. They are occasionally pursued by women, but generally manage to evade their clutches.

The hero's true social milieu, until he is transformed by the commitment to civilization forced on him in the course of the story, is the group of masculine comrades, the boys at the ranch, the other horse soldiers, or the Indian sidekicks. However much he may be alienated from the town, the Western hero almost never appears without some kind of membership in a group of males. Often the group of comrades represents a marginal or alienated social class with an ethnic or national background different from that of the hero: the WASP cavalry officer has his Irish sergeant, the cowboy has his Indian, Mexican, and in some recent Westerns his Negro companions. Leslie Fiedler has pointed out how the theme of good companionship between outcast white and men of darker skin plays a complex role in American literature, pointing to such examples as Cooper's Natty Bumppo and his Indian friend Chingachgook, Melville's Ishmael and the South Sea Islander Queequeg, Twain's Huck Finn and Jim, Faulkner's Ike McCaslin and Sam Fathers. Fiedler argues [in his *Love and Death in the American Novel*] that this relationship "symbolically joins the white man to nature and his own unconscious . . . and binds him in life-long loyalty to a help-meet, without the sacrifice of his freedom. This is the pure marriage of males—sexless and holy, a kind of counter-matrimony, in which the white refugee from society and the dark-skinned primitive are joined till death do them part." According to Fiedler, this theme is

an implicit attack on middle-class ideals of gentility, success, and domesticity which repress natural instincts and consequently threaten masculine identity. As we have seen, the concern for masculine potency and the representation of a conflict between civilized order and savage freedom also play a vital role in the Western. However, the formula Western usually attempts to resolve this conflict and to evade some of its deeper implications. While there are Westerns in which the hero remains an outcast, it is more usual for him to move from the milieu of the masculine comrades into a commitment to the town and even into a romance. Moreover, while certain important Western heroes like the Lone Ranger retain the original companion theme, in the majority of Westerns the dark-skinned comrade is replaced by the boys at the ranch, muting the racial significance of the symbolism.

However, though the formula Western may evade the racial or radical undertones which Fiedler sees as typical of the treatment of masculine comradeship in American literature, association with the boys remains one of the most important aspects of the hero's life and style. Not only do the hero's ties of friendship motivate much of his behavior, but in most cases the great sense of honor and adherence to a highly disciplined code of behavior which sharply differentiates hero from savages and outlaws springs from his association with the masculine group. The "code of the West" is in every respect a male ethic and its values and prescriptions relate primarily to the relationships of men. In theory the code prescribes a role for women as an adjunct to masculine honor. Nonetheless the presence of women invariably threatens the primacy of the masculine group. In many Westerns an interesting resolution of this conflict is worked out. The woman in effect takes over the role of the masculine comrades and becomes the hero's true companion. A good example of this is the case of the heroine Georgianna Stockwell of Zane Grey's *The Code of the West.* When she comes West, Georgianna is a flapper and her promiscuity in word, though not in deed, sets her in complete opposition to the "code." After nearly destroying young Cal Thurman, who falls in love with her, Georgianna realizes that her moral outlook has been wrong and that she has herself fallen in love with the simple but dedicated Cal. Once this transformation has taken place, the false eastern sophistication which placed Georgianna in opposition to the "code" gives way and the strength of her new character enables her to confront the villain who threatens to kill her wounded husband. In effect, Georgianna Stockwell becomes one of the boys herself and her final confrontation with Bid Hatfield takes the place of the usual shootdown. While this is an extreme form of the transformation of the female heroine from a threat to masculine identity into a true comrade, the theme is a common one in those Westerns where the hero plays a romantic role as well as his basic one of ambiguous defender of the town.

The hero's membership in the masculine gang and his initial rejection of domesticity relates to another trait he commonly possesses: his desire to keep moving. Just as Natty Bumppo felt he had to move on when the settler's cabins began to impinge on his wilderness, so the modern cowboy hero is represented as a bit of a drifter. As one of his pals tells the hero of Ernest Haycox's *The Man in the Saddle:*

> That's your trouble. Always goin' off to take another look at a piece of country. Fiddle-footed. Always smellin' the wind for scent. And so you lose out.

This quotation neatly sums up the cowboy hero's instinctive rejection of the ethic of success at least in the early stages of the story. The cowboy hero is far from a hero of work and enterprise. Indeed, he is rarely represented as working at all. Nonetheless, the formula requires that the hero somehow possess the necessary funds to maintain himself in horses, food, ammunition and elegant costumes, though it is rarely clear just where or how he gets this money. When one reads a more or less realistic narrative of cowboy life such as Andy Adams' *Log of a Cowboy* or looks at actual photographs of cowboys in action such as those of Erwin Smith, the thing that stands out most strikingly in comparison to the formula Western is the amount of hard, dirty physical labor involved. As Robert Warshow puts it [in his *The Immediate Experience*], "the Westerner is *par excellence* a man of leisure. Even when he wears the badge of a marshal or, more rarely, owns a ranch, he appears to be unemployed." Thus, in many respects the cowboy hero represents an image of man directly opposed to the official American pioneer virtues of progress, success and domesticity. In place of "getting ahead" he pursues the ideal of honor which he shares with his masculine comrades. Warshow neatly summarizes this aspect of the hero's character:

> he fights not for advantage and not for the right, but to state what he is, and he must live in a world which permits that statement. The Westerner is the last gentleman and the movies which over and over tell his story are probably the last art form in which the concept of honor retains its strength.

Even in this case, however, the tendency of popular formulas is to seek for a resolution of thematic conflicts or to evade them altogether. Few Westerns carry out the antithesis between success and honor to its inevitable conclusion: the destruction or exile of the hero from the developing town which can no longer permit the explosions of individual will and aggression necessary to the defense of heroic honor. More typically a way is found in the course of the action to reconcile hero and town and to assimilate the cowboy hero into the world of the pioneers. There are innumerable plot devices which perform this function. The hero falls in love and thus becomes ultimately committed to the pioneer cause. The woman falls in love with the hero and her dedication to him enables her to take over the role of the true male companions. Or the hero simply becomes old and tired and decides that it is finally time to settle down. Different periods in the history of the Western have preferred different kinds of resolutions. For example, the early twentieth century clearly preferred to solve the clash of values through romance, while more recent Westerns have made a great deal of the tired hero who reluctantly gives up the heroic way of life either because he accepts the necessity of civilization or because he is tired of insecurity. The tired hero often shades over into the sacrificial

hero who accepts death or exile because he cannot work out the conflict between the town and his heroic past. It is in treating this version of the Western hero that the formula Western commonly reaches its most moving and significant level as art, a quality which Warshow brilliantly defines in his essay on the Western hero:

> The Westerner is a . . . classical figure, self-contained and limited to begin with, seeking not to extend his dominion but only to assert his personal value, and his tragedy lies in the fact that even this circumscribed demand cannot be fully realized. Since the Westerner is not a murderer but (most of the time) a man of virtue, and since he is always prepared for defeat, he retains his inner invulnerability and his story need not end with his death (and usually does not); but what we finally respond to is not his victory but his defeat.

As these remarks on the variety of hero-types indicate there is a great variety of situations and plots that can be made into Westerns so long as the basic conventions of setting and character relations are maintained. Thus our treatment of situation and pattern of action can be very general and brief here. There is a kind of basic situation which various Western plots tend to embody which I have already defined in my discussion of setting and characters. Basically, this situation develops out of what I have called the epic moment when the values and disciplines of American society stand balanced against the savage wilderness. The situation must involve a hero who possesses some of the urges toward violence as well as the skills, heroism and personal honor ascribed to the wilderness way of life, and it must place this hero in a position where he becomes involved with or committed to the agents and values of civilization. The nature of this situation, and of the conflict between town and wilderness which lies behind it imply that the formulaic pattern of action is that of chase and pursuit because it is in this pattern that the clash of savages and townspeople manifests itself. The savages attack the town and are pursued by the pioneers. Some of the pioneers leave the town and are pursued by the savages. The savages capture one or more of the townspeople and are pursued by the hero. An infinite number of variations are possible within the pattern of capture, flight, and pursuit and the great majority of Westerns are structured around one or more of these types of action. Perhaps the most typical of all such patterns is that of the alternating flight and pursuit. The outlaws or Indians attack the town and are pursued by the hero and the pioneers; something happens to reverse the situation, an ambush, or a mistaken splitting of forces, and the pursuers become the pursued. Finally, the hero succeeds in isolating the true villain from the group of savages and the situation reverses a third time, the hero's pursuit leading to the final confrontation which resolves the story. This built-in structural emphasis on the chase is of course one major reason why the Western has proved so adaptable to film and television presentation. Within these broad outlines the Western has been capable of absorbing many different plots from many different kinds of literature while retaining the flavor of a Western. Or to put it another way, so long as a story can be adapted to Western settings and characters and somehow reduced to the terms of flight, capture and pursuit almost anything can be turned into a Western. Television Westerns in particular have adapted plots from every conceivable source; I recall one episode of "Bonanza" where the plot was clearly derived from a combination of Mary Shalley's *Frankenstein* and John Steinbeck's *Of Mice and Men* manipulated in such a way as to manifest a large proportion of pursuit. Such far-fetched adaptations are generally inferior to Westerns which develop plots which more directly articulate the implicit conflicts of the setting and character roles, but the possible range of Western plots in nonetheless quite wide.

These, then, are the chief characteristics of the Western formula: a particular kind of setting, type of situation, and cast of characters with a strong emphasis on a certain kind of hero. I have indicated several ways in which this combination of elements possesses great dramatic power and unity. In the hands of skillful writers and directors who understand these relationships and know how to exploit them, Westerns can become highly effective works of art. Their actions are capable of arousing strong feelings, their quality of spectacle gives an epic sense to these actions, and their structures are simple and clear enough to be widely understood and appreciated, even by children. This artistic power of unity of character, setting and action is surely the major source of the Western's long-term popularity as a formula. (pp. 56-68)

John G. Cawelti, in his Six-Gun Mystique, *Bowling Green University Popular Press, 1971, 138 p.*

John R. Milton

[*Milton is an American poet and a respected critic of American western literature. As editor of* South Dakota Review, *he was one of the first to give serious attention to the study of westerns as a literary form. In the following excerpt, he discusses the formulaic themes and narrative devices of the western novel, using Owen Wister's* Virginian *as a model of this genre.*]

Whatever the cowboy may have been in real life, he became a hero of popular fiction with the publication of Owen Wister's novel *The Virginian,* joining the ranks of the hunters, scouts, soldiers, Indians, railroad builders, town builders, miners, U.S. marshals, sheriffs, and assorted outlaws who continue to populate the Old West in the type of novel we have long since become accustomed to calling, simply, the western.

The Virginian has probably been talked about more than any other western, and it is often tempting to say that Wister was something more than a writer of westerns. He was a friend of President Theodore Roosevelt (who said that he would like to write a review of *The Virginian* if he were not president) and Henry James (who wrote him a generous letter in praise of the novel, perhaps because of their friendship). His chief literary influence seems to have been Mark Twain. The narrator of *The Virginian* is a tenderfoot reminiscent of Twain's narrator in *Roughing It,* even though in each case the reader is aware of the close relationship between narrator and writer. A Philadelphian,

Owen Wister made fifteen trips to Wyoming between 1885 and 1900, for his health. By the time *The Virginian* was published in 1902 its author was a well man, in body and in mind. And, just as important, he knew the Medicine Bow area of Wyoming as well as Twain had known Carson City, Nevada. Wister is more sentimental than Twain—although *Roughing It* does not lack sentiment—and less humorous, although he occasionally plays upon the tall tale with considerable success. The question of tone—at least in certain passages—also leads to intriguing comparisons. When a tenderfoot in the West says that the foothills are "indefinite and mystic," or "I wanted no speech with any one, nor to be near human beings at all," or "I was steeped in a revery as of the primal earth," it is difficult to determine whether he speaks honestly for himself, sentimentally for himself, sentimentally for the author, or in half jest. Very serious writers were to say almost the same things later on (Mary Austin only a year later), but the most serious statements of this kind prior to Wister had been made by the naturalist John Muir, who was obviously a religious mystic as well. The quotations are, of course, from *The Virginian,* but they would not be out of place in *Roughing It.* In spite of his celebrated cynicism and satire, Twain was not devoid of sentimentality. However, there is no need to associate the words *mystic* and *primal* with sentimentality. It all depends on how easily the words come to mind, on the degree of seriousness of the context and of the writer himself.

Wister moves back and forth between the kind of artistic seriousness that James probably wished for him and the easy response to the western landscape which has characterized most subliterary westerns. In this respect he poses a problem to the critic who is interested in categories and in levels of achievement within the world of literature rather than within the more noticeable world of commerce. For *The Virginian* is in the tradition of western best sellers, and something made it a popular book. When [James Fenimore] Cooper was writing the Leatherstocking Tales, five Walter Scott adventure novels were on—or had just been on—the best-seller list in this country (using the formula of sales amounting to at least 1 percent of the nation's population), and eventually all five of the Leatherstocking novels also became best sellers, as did Bird's *Nick of the Woods.* In the second half of the nineteenth century the only western best seller was Bret Harte's *Luck of Roaring Camp* (1870). Then, in a period of ten years, *The Virginian* and two Zane Grey novels, *The Spirit of the Border* (1906) and *The Riders of the Purple Sage,* made the list. Popularity contests do not always establish relationships among books and authors, but it would appear that the western tradition which appealed to the public began with the Scott romances and established itself in a sequence of Cooper, Harte, Wister, and Grey. Since Wister went west for his health, we cannot insist that his emphasis on the purity of western air is attributable to Harte. Nor can his style be considered a refinement of the styles of Cooper and Harte. He is closer to Twain in this respect. But, in spite of some literary intentions and achievements, Wister established an image of the cowboy and an example of violence which contributed heavily to the stereotypes of character and action in half a century of westerns.

He might have expanded upon one of his more vivid images and given new life to the philosophical discussion—seen in Cooper and Rousseau—concerning the values of the primitive life, the way of the wilderness, as opposed to the values of civilization. Perhaps Wister did not feel strongly enough about this question even though he commuted between Philadelphia and Wyoming for fifteen years. He hits the surface of it when, in *The Virginian,* he mildly laments the tin cans—trophies of civilization—which he finds strewn about on the virgin soil of Wyoming. But only once does he locate an image capable of making a significant statement about the question: "a black pig on a white pile of buffalo bones, catching drops of water in the air as they fell from the railroad tank." The buffalo, on whose bones the pig stands, got water from a stream; the pig, domesticated, representing civilization however ironically, must stand on the bones of a former time in order to get water from a man-made tank which is there primarily to serve the railroad as it carries more and more people into a land that may have been better off without them. If the blackness of the pig represents evil and the whiteness of the bones similarly represents goodness, or purity, then Wister is not only taking a position in the wilderness-civilization controversy but he is also bordering on a mystical condition which, with its own set of ironies, appears again in Holger Cahill's *The Shadow of My Hand* (1956) when the bones of the needlessly slaughtered buffalo come back to the new people of the West, after having been used in the process of refining sugar in the East, to be stirred into their coffee. The various symbolic uses of this image are obvious and may seem farfetched to many readers, but they at least represent a serious attempt to find a thematic link between the past and the present which can illuminate a part of our experience.

Unfortunately, the legacy left by *The Virginian* is much less complicated than that and has been embraced by the writers of formula westerns to the extent that Wister has been called the father of the western. A haphazard listing of some of the ingredients of *The Virginian* will suggest, if not define, the western novel:

1. The cowboy, a drifter, unattached to normal society.
2. The cowboy as hero.
3. The cowboy as gallant in his relationships with women.
4. Emphasis on the purity of the land, the West.
5. Violence caused by evil.
6. A villain, often a shadowy figure, who is defeated by the hero.
7. A moral system based on extremes, on good and evil, on black and white, with few if any complexities in between.
8. Good always wins.
9. More talk than action (although this changed almost immediately in the writers following Wister).
10. People are intruders in the wilderness (although the cowboy is soon seen as a native, much like the Indian, and sees *other* people as the intruders).
11. An attempt at dialect supposedly unique with the cowboy.
12. Little attention given to cattle. (There are none in *The Virginian,* but exceptions can be found in the trail drive novel.)
13. Love, usually between the cowboy and a refined eastern woman.
14. The gun fight, as evil erupts and the hero must destroy it. The confrontation of two gunfighters on a dusty street became important to the western and points up that it is usually not working cowboys who people the western novel but miscellaneous gunfighters, whether they be ranchers by trade, or town marshals, or soldiers, or vague "professional" heroes like Shane.

Essentially, the four ingredients which survive as the so-called formula are the hero, violence, love, and the western landscape, and of these four it is violence that has been refined, not into an art but into a pattern of action and a condition of effect which the standard western cannot do without.

Wister arrives at violence very slowly. It is not until chapter 26 that the Virginian, incensed at Balaam, unleashes his latent power:

> The Virginian hurled him to the ground, lifted and hurled him again, lifted him and beat his face and struck his jaw. . . . [Balaam] felt blindly for his pistol. That arm was caught and wrenched backward, and crushed and doubled. He seemed to hear his own bones. . . . Then the pistol at last came out, and together with the hand that grasped it was instantly stamped into the dust.

Even though some readers objected to this measure of violence, the stamping of the gunman's hand soon became a part of the action—a staple, one of the tricks of the trade—in many westerns that followed *The Virginian.* Who is to say, however, that Wister had betrayed either logic or the principles of justice, since his puritanic sense of right and wrong dictated some kind of punishment for Balaam and the smashing of a gun hand is effective in preventing further use of the gun. When the Virginian changes from a soft-talking, gentle man into a brutal avenger, it is only because justice demands it. Eventually, of course, it becomes difficult to distinguish between justice and an outright appeal to the sensations of the public. As the western evolved over a period of thirty years or so, practiced successfully by Charles Alden Seltzer, B. M. Bower (Bertha Sinclair), Clarence E. Mulford, W. C. Tuttle, Herbert Knibbs, Zane Grey, Max Brand (Frederick Faust), Eugene Cunningham, William McLeod Raine, and Luke Short (Frederick Glidden), violence increased in the stereotyped West, often justified by the need for survival in an untamed land, sometimes found necessary in order to mete out justice in an environment which lacked a legal system such as that found in the civilized lands to the East, but frequently included only because it had become a useful part of the formula. The major image of gunplay comes from *The Virginian* when the hero confronts Trampas on the street, is fired at, almost negligently returns the fire, and kills the villain with two shots. The ingredients for a thousand gunfights are there. Whether the gunfight means anything at all must depend upon the circumstances, the motives, the psychological attitudes of the participants, and the general seriousness of the presentation. With lesser writers, those who look for rather easy or cheap effects, the result is nothing more than melodrama. One illustration will suffice. In Zane Grey's *Heritage of the Desert* (1910), Holderness and his foreman, Snap Naab (the name is interesting), argue over "possession" of a girl. Holderness says abruptly, "Bah!" and shoots his foreman through the heart.

> Snap plunged upon his face. His hands beat the ground like the shuffling wings of a wounded partridge. His fingers gripped the dust, spread convulsively, straightened, and sank limp.

The popularity of the motion picture based on Max Brand's 1930 novel, *Destry Rides Again,* seemed to give public support to the violence, brutality, and exaggeration of the novel. As the western rode into the late 1930s and the 1940s, it was accompanied by increasing doses of bullets and blood. And when it turned from the cowboy or gunman to the wholesale slaughters of range wars, Indian massacres, and the Custer-like confrontations between the Indians and the cavalry, violence had already been accepted (indeed, cherished) by the millions of readers of westerns, most of whom led dull and peaceful lives but perhaps needed a medium through which they could, vicariously, give vent to their inner primitive emotions.

It seems almost contradictory that in the midst of the shooting and the shouting of the western there lies a quiet and chivalric politeness to women. One suggestion is that from the western it is possible for boys (perhaps of all ages) to learn manhood through the exposure to violence and death—the gun fight representing the essence of life's experiences—and that perhaps they could also learn something about women. The latter allegation seems quite far-fetched in the light of the one-dimensional woman who appears in most westerns. (To say two-dimensional might increase the sexual interest slightly but would not affect the shallowness of character.) Whatever truth there may be in Freudian explanations of the western, it is a well-known fact that as the cowboy novel has become deeply imbedded in our myths the analysts have taken increasing interest in it. One such viewpoint may be summarized here to serve as an example. I refer to an article by Warren J. Barker, M.D., "The Stereotyped Western Story, Its Latent Meaning and Psychoeconomic Function," appearing in the *Psychoanalytic Quarterly* in 1955. Dr. Barker recognizes the formula and points out the anonymity of authorship (derived partly, I am sure, from the frequent use of pseudonyms) which is itself characteristic of ancient myths. The cowboy hero is the "eternal son" forever acting out his fantasies. He is both proud and modest, bold and shy. Courageous in righting that which is wrong, he is nevertheless awkward with women. The villain contrasts with the hero, although like the devil he may appear to be a law-abiding citizen and is recognized for what he really is only by the hero. The sheriff is often weak (as most humans are?), so that the hero must usurp his duties for a while. The hero is filled with guilt of one kind or another, although that guilt is attributed to the villain. As the villain thwarts (at least temporarily) the hero in his attempts to win the heart of the heroine, he is really the

hated father of the eternal son, keeping the son-hero from his beloved mother. From this point, Dr. Barker develops the themes of oedipal crimes, incest, and insurance against castration, all seen in the conflict between hero and villain and its resolution. In a sense, one formula yields to another, because a major part of this thesis depends on the villain never being killed. Since the villain is an "isomer" of the hero, his death would mean the castration of the hero, and this would spoil the western formula. The use of the term *isomer* does bring to mind, however, Philip Durham's observation that the western does not have good men and bad men but, instead, good badmen and bad badmen. That is, the distinctions are often blurred.

Because the hero arrives from an unknown point of origin at the beginning of the novel, we are asked to consider the confusion and mystery felt by the average child as it wonders about its own origins. (Do we think of Shane when we recall the nursery rhyme? "Where did you come from, baby dear?" "Out of the everywhere into here.") The western code demands that no one inquire into the origins of the hero. His loneliness at the beginning of his adventure, and again at the end (like that of Shane), runs parallel to the child's recurring wish (never fulfilled) to return to a "blissful symbiosis with mother." Like Adam, the child has been exiled from the Garden of Eden by his new knowledge of sex and hostility. The western is also like *Hamlet;* it is an elaborate account of a boy's love for his mother and the subsequent jealousy and hatred for his father. However, the healthy child will eventually outgrow the "psycho-sexual immaturity" of the western hero until his death wish (symbolized in the hero's act of shooting the villain in order to remove his competition for the woman) turns into activity which is more constructive. At this point, says Dr. Barker, the child will stop reading the stereotyped western novel. If he does not, he has serious emotional problems.

An argument such as this one is, of course, only one of the reasons for the continued popularity of the western. The historian seeks facts of the Old West, even though they may be distorted, or argues with the "mistaken facts" or with the way the writer uses them. The specialized cultural historian looks for low-level, grass-roots evidence of attitudes and characteristics of the common man on the frontier, including his legends and myths. He may also look for evidence of values that originated on the frontier and may have remained in the American character (in support of, or in opposition to, those characteristics named by Frederick Jackson Turner, for example). And the general reading public, for whatever reason, can still turn to the western to escape into a world of adventure that may or may not mean something more than the adventure itself.

What the literary critic looks for is another matter, although his concerns may include all of the others. The western represents one stage in the evolution of the serious or literary novel which emerges in the West in the 1920s. And so we can turn to it to identify some of the problems which even the more sophisticated writers have had as they attempt to wring art out of the western landscape and character, to overcome the established stereotypes, and to

John Wayne as a rugged cowboy in a still from Ride Him Cowboy *(1932).*

give the western experience a depth rarely sensed by the commercial writers who were too busy turning out carbon copies of the formula to stop and think about the philosophical and psychological implications of landscape, of primitive (Indian) religions in relation to modern science, or full character development in a sparsely settled environment. For the literary critic, perhaps, the western is ultimately important for what it is not, rather than for what it is.

Keeping in mind that we are generalizing when we characterize the western, and that it is possible to find exceptions to various elements within the formula, the best that can be said about the conventional western is that it simply portrays the violence of a new and wild land, sometimes describing that land in sensitive terms—however rarely this happens—and occasionally hinting at a significant relationship between man and the land. As John Cawelti has pointed out in *The Six-Gun Mystique* (1970), the conflicts in the western are not often the vehicles for a profound statement about life. The conflict in a conventional western is resolved very simply in terms of plot or "justice," nothing more. The best one sees is a kind of archetypal hero-villain, or the idea of good-evil, with a remote land as a backdrop for the action, partially resembling a medieval morality play but with so little variation that a dozen such novels would be quite enough. There is no need for hundreds, or thousands.

The formula is so limited that Frank Gruber, one of its practitioners who first published in the pulp magazines, could say with apparent confidence that the western exists on an extremely limited number of plots.

> 1. The Rustler Story. Often, the rustled cattle belong to the heroine, and it is the hero who wanders onto the ranch, discovers that the rustlers are in league with a neighbor or friend of the heroine, and after painstakingly convincing her of this fact he resolves the problem.
>
> 2. The Range War or Empire Story. A cattle baron defends his right to graze cattle on the millions of acres of land he wrested from the Indians, ready to kill anyone who puts up a fence. The hero wanders in from nowhere, is shot at, resents it, and takes up with the homesteaders or the small ranchers, winning the war for them.
>
> 3. The "Good But Not Worthy" Story. A variation of No. 2, the hero of this story is a gunfighter or an ex-gunfighter who is trying to quit, who, in the course of his involvement with a range war or a similar conflict, falls in love with the daughter of the homesteader and, after he has defeated the opposing gunslingers, realizes that he is a killer and not worthy of a good woman. He rides away, usually into the sunset.
>
> 4. The Marshal or Dedicated Lawman Story. The honest peace officer stands alone against the evil elements of his town and either wins or dies. If he wins he is often shunned by the community as a killer. If he dies, the good people of the town, formerly afraid to take action, rise up in indignation and clean up the town, so that the death of the hero is not in vain.
>
> 5. The Revenge Story. Something has been done to the hero, or his father or mother or wife or best friend, many years ago. He spends the years looking for the person responsible for his misfortune and eventually catches up with him. This story can also be a variation of the search or the quest and can conclude with a twist of plot, or identity, which is reminiscent of the detective story.
>
> 6. The Outlaw Story. The hero is presented sympathetically, even though he has run afoul of the law. The story may be based upon a historical person such as Billy the Kid or Jesse James, showing that unfortunate circumstances turned a good boy into a bad man. Or a completely fictional hero may be wronged in some way and retaliate by becoming an outlaw. Unable, because of his reputation and the danger which surrounds him, to settle down with a good woman, he frequently seems to commit suicide by inviting death in a gun fight—death being preferable to the alternatives.
>
> 7. The Cavalry and Indians Story. This one is usually a variation of Custer's last stand, often told from the point of view of a cavalryman but occasionally seen from the other side, perhaps through a renegade whose sympathies lie honestly with the Indians.
>
> 8. The Ranch Story. Involving the ordinary working cowboy, perhaps rustlers, perhaps two ranch owners disputing property or water rights, this story has the potential to become a portrait of the authentic cowboy, but a hero usually emerges from the ranch hands to become larger than life.
>
> 9. The Union Pacific Story. Any number of variations are possible within the framework of the building of a railroad. This story might also center on a stagecoach line or the building of a telegraph line. Obstacles arise in various forms.

Plots 7 and 9, in particular, may be subsumed under a wider category called the historical western. Here we run into the point at which the conventional western may most easily merge with a novel which is based upon one or more historical incidents in the nineteenth-century West but which is more artistic or demanding in its intentions, its complexities, its style, and its use of history. Definitions fade when A. B. Guthrie's *The Big Sky* (1947) is included in a Western Writers' list of "best westerns" and is at the same time treated as serious literature by readers and scholars who may shun the western. The question hinges at least partly on the extent to which a historical novel is original in its conception or insights or theme, or whether it follows the formula and the stereotypes of the commercial western novel. It is obvious that in the area of historical fiction of the West we will discover every shade of literary worth, from none to a great deal. The same is true to a certain extent with the more specific plot notations provided by Mr. Gruber. In the degree to which the familiar, or conventional, plot outlines are followed, and the characters within those plots behave like puppets, a novel of the West will be a part of the formula, or an attempt to get away from it, or a successful work of fiction in its own right whose label of *western* is for esthetic purposes a geographical accident or coincidence.

It is the simplified action plot that Gruber identifies, not the complex psychologically motivated or land-determined plot which avoids deliberate manipulation. For his popular audience, Gruber is willing to attach to his plot labels comments whose tone reveals a recognition or admission of the exploitive qualities of the western. For the Revenge Story: "I know he's down in that arroyo, Martha. I swore I'd git him and I will if you'll just hand me my cane and point me in the right direction." For the Empire Story: "Ah got two arrow wounds to take this land and no cotton-pickin' farmer is a-going to fence me in." For the Cavalry and Indians Story: "Did you ever see so many dadblamed Indians, general?" And so it goes. A similar tone seems to permeate the style of many of the pre-1940 writers of westerns, although we can be certain that most of these writers wanted to be taken seriously. It is a characteristic of the formula novel that its romantic ease in describing the landscape, in dealing with love, and in luring the reader into the novel and sharing a little sentiment with him at the end always sounds contrived. The western—even after 1940—frequently opens with a brief look at the landscape, intended to be exotic (though sometimes barren), or with a stilted description of the hero, or with a hint of mystery. The following first sentences may be taken as representative:

> The moon had not yet come to full when Pierce and his two companions rode down from the Sierra Diablos westward across the plain.

> The icy wind came first to the mountains.

> "Silvertip" was what men called him, since the other names he chose to wear were as shifting as the sands of the desert; but he was more like a great stag than a grizzly.

> A fitful breeze played among the mesquite bushes.

> The boy had spent the night at a water-hole in a little draw at the foot of the mesa.

> As his goaded horse plunged into the road, Nevada looked back over his shoulder.

> Goodnight crossed the river at a ford whose bottom sands were scarcely covered by water and made noon camp under the shade of a lonely willow.

> Curt Thompson rode up Gurney's sandy main street through the April dusk.

> Cole Sanborn sat in a tiptilted chair on the porch of the Jonesboro House, the worn heel of one boot hooked in a rung. His long, lean body was slack, apparently relaxed, but its ease was like that of a coiled spring which might be released at the touch of a trigger.

> A sharp clip-clop of iron-shod hoofs deadened and died away, and clouds of yellow dust drifted from under the cottonwoods out over the sage.

These are sentences designed to catch the attention of the reader. The four which say something about the hero are

entirely undistinguished and emphasize either the exaggerated physical characteristics (grizzly, stag, long and lean body, coiled spring) or the mysterious appearance (looked back, arriving at dusk). Landscape ingredients are precisely the ones we expect to find: mountain, plain, wind, mesquite, water hole, mesa, sand, a lonely tree, dust, cottonwoods, and sage. The use of "Diablos" as part of a fictional name for a mountain range is calculated to impress upon the mind of the reader the presence, or potential presence, of evil. Stylistic problems are evident in such phrases as "deadened and died." Altogether, there is nothing in these sentences to distinguish them from thousands of other formula sentences.

Although landscape also plays a part at the end of many westerns, the formula generally called for the happy ending based upon the shallow love story which is an essential ingredient of the commercial western and which leaves the reader in a romantic glow. (This often follows a series of episodes in which violence is the major element, so that the effect is of achievement in the face of adversity—a popular desire and an important basis of fantasy.) Again, the following sentences—in this case last sentences—may be taken as representative:

> With Moira beside him he knew he would never again try to turn his back on the land.

> He walked down the street without looking back.

> He set his teeth firmly and aimed his course toward the blue and crystal-white of distant mountains.

> He took her hand in his, and they rode on silently, a song in the heart of each of them.

> Afterward, Challons forever on the grass of New Mexico as well as under it—Challons with the sun-dark skins of the clean blood of the land.

> Disregarding the group at the far end of the room, she leaned forward and kissed his lips.

> "I'll have a marrying dress on in about two minutes. *If* you'll stop kissing me," she added, in a muffled voice.

> And the two cowboys wandered away in the darkness together.

> The pressure of her hands drew his head down and he met her lips again.

> Mary lifted a rapt young face to his kiss.

Here we have in succession the hero who has found his woman and can cease wandering, the hero who remains relatively anonymous and mysterious, and the hero who seems to have found determination and purpose from the events in which he has just participated. All are consistent with the stereotype. An easy and sentimentalized relationship between a people and their land is the destiny of the Challons. The rest of the story-concluding sentences are conventionally romantic, and almost silly, with the two cowboys wandering away together providing an unintentional chuckle for the modern reader and a small urge to refer to the theories of the psychoanalyst.

The apologetic scholar would like to explain away the sentimentalists of the western by viewing their novels chronologically and discovering that styles and attitudes changed between 1900 and 1960 just as they did in non-western fiction. To a certain degree, the western has indeed undergone a subtle modernization: dialogue is more natural, implied symbolism lends at least the suggestion of multileveled meanings, women are drawn more realistically, the landscape and weather are often a force rather than a decorative backdrop, and more writers of westerns actually live in the West and have some feeling for the place and for the people who roamed over it or settled on it during the nineteenth century. But this argument holds up largely for that rare western which rises above the formula just enough to demand attention but not enough to abandon the genre and become something else. The popular western has remained much the same for sixty years (and more, since it continues to thrive in its own way). If anyone thinks, for example, that the western improved noticeably during the forty or fifty years following publication of *The Virginian,* he need only read tables of contents, chapter titles, to see that he is wrong. From B. M. Bower's *Her Prairie Knight* (1904), "A Handsome Cowboy to the Rescue," "Beatrice's Wild Ride," and "Keith's Masterful Wooing"; from Bower's *Rowdy of the "Cross L"* (1906), "A Shot from the Dark," "Rowdy in a Tough Place," "Pink in a Threatening Mood," and "Rowdy Finds Happiness"; from Clarence Mulford's *Hopalong Cassidy* (1910), "Antonio's Scheme," "Mary Meeker Rides North," "Hopalong Asserts Himself," "Hopalong Grows Suspicious," and "Hopalong's Reward"; from Zane Grey's *Riders of the Purple Sage* (1912), "The Masked Rider," "Love," "Faith and Unfaith," "Solitude and Storm"; from Max Brand's *The Untamed* (1919), "Pan of the Desert," "The Phantom Rider," "The Lone Riders Entertain," "Hell Starts," "Fear," and "Death"; from *Partners of Chance,* by Henry Herbert Knibbs (1921), "High Heels and Moccasins," "Pony Tracks," "More Pony Tracks," and "Two Trails Home"; from Eugene Cunningham's *Texas Sheriff* (1934), "We Need a Shooting Sheriff," "That's Going to Get You Killed," "Dead Man's Hand" (a common title in early westerns), "There Was Bushwhacking Done," and "Inside With You" (a title which becomes meaningful in Guthrie's *These Thousand Hills* [1956] two decades later); from William MacLeod Raine's *Square-Shooter* (1934), "Mary Marries a Dangerous Man," "Hotter than Hell with the Lid On," and "Self-Defense"; from L. L. Foreman's *The Renegade* (1942), "The Deserter," "The Hostiles," "Army Scout," and "The Last Campaign"; from Nelson C. Nye's *The Desert Desperadoes* (1942), "A Man Drifts West," "Two Women," "Forbidden Fruit," "A Man Decides," and "A Man Plays Tag with Hell"; and from *The Wild Bunch,* by Ernest Haycox (1943), "Voice of Hate," "Turn of the Screw" (which appears in more than one western), "Women Meet," "The Taste of a Woman's Lips," and "The Last Decision." Chapter titles went out of fashion in the western in the 1940s, but book titles continued to tip off the reader as to what kind of book he was buying: *Lawman's Feud* (Steve Frazee), *The Bravados, Desperate Rider,* and *Warbonnet Law* (Frank O'Rourke), *The Violent Land* (Wayne Overholser), *Bold Passage* and *Blood on the Land* (Frank Bonham), *No Survivors* and *The Last Warpath* (Will Henry), *Town Tamer, Fighting Man,* and *Fort Starvation* (Frank Gruber), and an almost endless list of one-word titles appearing under the name of the best-selling contemporary writer of westerns, Louis L'Amour. (In each case the title is the name of the chief character who is given a single name which removes some of his humanness and allows him to take on the stature of mythical superman: *Radigan, Taggart, Shalako, Hondo, Flint, Sackett,* and so on.)

If nothing else, chapter and book titles reveal the stasis (stability?) of the western. It may have become slightly more polished in recent years, but in view of its reluctance to make essential changes from the century-old formula it may also have become more tarnished. (pp. 17-34)

> *John R. Milton, "The Popular or Formula Western," in his* The Novel of the American West, *University of Nebraska Press, 1980, pp. 1-40.*

WESTERNS AS HISTORY AND FICTION

Richard W. Etulain

[In the following essay, Etulain discusses historical elements in the western novels of Vardis Fisher, A. B. Guthrie, and Wallace Stegner.]

In this [essay] I shall discuss three ways in which western writers have used history. Vardis Fisher illustrates those who have thoroughly researched their historical subjects in order to write stirring narratives. A. B. Guthrie, Jr., who is also interested in the use of history in fiction, moves beyond Fisher in his desire to interpret as well as narrate his historical materials. Finally, Wallace Stegner takes the giant step. I treat his *Angle of Repose* at length because he has produced a western novel that is more than *about* history; he has written a first-rate fictional interpretation *of* the historical development of the West. I am convinced that an examination of the significant relationship between western history and the western novel will open new vistas of research for historians and literary scholars.

Some students of the life and works of Vardis Fisher are convinced that he was born with a cocklebur in his diaper. They describe his life as one spent either trying to rid himself of the irritant or attempting to understand why he was not chosen one of the elect. It is true that few western writers have been as emotionally involved as he in searching out his own past and that of other persons. From his first novels, published in the late 1920s and early 1930s, until his last novel, *Mountain Man* (1965), Fisher was on a lifelong quest to narrate man's movement through history. During his productive career Fisher dedicated himself to the fruitful union of history and literature in an attempt to recount the past.

For Fisher, first of all, the story was a personal one. His

first seven novels (including the Vridar Hunter tetralogy), published between 1928 and 1937, were regional novels dealing with frontier life in the Antelope Hills area of Idaho. They were autobiographical works that dealt with Fisher's tortured feelings about his early life in the region. The son of pioneer Mormon parents, Fisher battled throughout his early years with his ambiguous responses to his backgrounds. He was not sympathetic to the teachings of the Mormons, and he thought them often bigoted and self-righteous. Yet he praised the leadership of Brigham Young and the loyalty and perseverance he inspired among his followers. Similar tensions are evident in Fisher's feelings about his father. He frequently pictured his father as epitomizing the worst kind of religious fundamentalism. On some occasions his father figures are unfeeling men, introverted and blindly idealistic. But Fisher also admired his father's individualism and his hard work; these were qualities that Fisher tried to emulate in his own life.

In his tension-filled, love-hate reactions to his formative years Fisher displayed his inordinate interest in reporting his past. Some have suggested that his earliest novels were primarily excursions toward self-understanding. What is apparent is that he found some satisfactory answers for comprehending his life, and thus he was able to move back to Idaho—"to come home again"—and to carve out his ranch and build a home in Hagerman Valley. Other questions, however, still vexed him: What about the nature of man? Had people changed through the centuries? What were the forces that had the largest impact on history?

To deal with these questions, Fisher set out on one of the most ambitious projects in American literary history. His ten-volume Testament of Man series (1943-1960) is a monument to Fisher's tenacity, to his unwillingness to let go of the past until it had yielded up at least partial answers to some of its mysteries. The series, which chronicled man from his prehistoric origins to the modern era, was, in one sense, a continuation of his earliest work, although now the issues raised were less personal and more universal. Anyone who has plowed through the series—or even part of it—must admire the prodigious amount of research involved in the project. Fisher the historian-novelist shines through in every volume.

Most of Fisher's western historical fiction also illustrates his thirst for narrating the past. In his most controversial book, *Children of God* (1939), Fisher sought to record how by 1900 the Mormons had evolved into a powerful institution. He had little sympathy for the doctrines and religious practices of the Church, but he exhibited a great deal of interest in the humanity of several of the early Mormon leaders. His own unsatisfying experience with the Latter-day Saints colored his interpretations, but it is noteworthy that, while devout Mormons at first harshly criticized the novel, some have recently recommended it with reservations.

Fisher's search for the historical West led him to the Donner party (*The Mothers*, 1943), the beaver wars of the Northwest (*Pemmican*, 1956), Lewis and Clark (*Tale of Valor*, 1958), and finally the western fur trappers (*Mountain Man*, 1965). His final novel illustrates several of the techniques that he used repeatedly in historical fiction. *Mountain Man* is based on wide research in original sources dealing with the trappers. Fisher seldom wrote about a subject that he had not researched as if he were writing a doctoral dissertation (he received a doctorate in English literature with high honors from the University of Chicago in 1925). At the same time the novel betrays the strong feelings Fisher had about contemporary issues rooted in the freedom, the spontaneity, and the perseverance that the lives of the mountain men illustrated. He also celebrated, through his hero Sam Minard, the strong feelings for nature that he shared with mountain men. In short, Fisher's final novel was a combination of his desire for historical veracity and his goal of demonstrating how the past is related to the present.

A. B. Guthrie, Jr., the Montana novelist, shares Fisher's strong interest in the historical novel. In accounting for his late arrival as a writer of historical fiction (Guthrie was forty-six when *The Big Sky* was published), he says that early in life he fell in love with the West and wanted to explain in fiction the artifacts he found and the men he encountered in diaries and journals. But he kept putting off rounding up his ideas. Then in 1944, on the strength of a Nieman Fellowship to Harvard, he was able to spend a vigorous year reading, researching, and reflecting upon the era of the mountain man. Three years later *The Big Sky* illustrated Guthrie's extensive work in historical documents.

Guthrie's subsequent novels seem less and less based on factual research. As one moves from *The Big Sky* to *The Way West* (1949), to *These Thousand Hills* (1955), to *Arfive* (1970), and on to *The Last Valley* (1975), the last of his five-volume fictional history of the West, one moves gradually across the frontier of fact into the region of Guthrie's remembrances of the West. Each of the first four novels deals with a crucial era in the historical development of the West: the years of the mountain men, the coming of the overlanders, the rise of the cattle ranchers, and the beginnings of town building. The final book in the series treats several themes of the era 1920 to 1945.

In writing *The Big Sky*, Guthrie used many of the standard historical sources dealing with the 1830s and 1840s. He ransacked the works of travelers like Nathaniel J. Wyeth and Washington Irving, as well as the writings of later historians, such as Hubert Howe Bancroft and Hiram H. Chittenden. The writer he seems to have followed most was George Frederick Ruxton, an Englishman who traveled extensively throughout the frontier West. Guthrie may have borrowed much of his trapper talk and perhaps some of his characters from Ruxton's semifact, semifictional work, *Life in the Far West*.

But *The Big Sky* is much more than the scissors-and-paste product of Guthrie's reading and research in western history. He shapes incidents, scenery, and characterizations to fit his thematic concerns. Guthrie once remarked, after finishing his first two novels, that his major thesis was that man kills or destroys the things he loves most. *The Big Sky* illustrates this theme in several ways. Boone Caudill, the major character in the novel, kills his best friend and destroys his marriage to an Indian girl because he mistakenly thinks they have been sleeping together. Besides specific incidents that epitomize Guthrie's thesis, the entire novel deals with the seeds of destruction the trappers bring to the mountains. They love the out-of-doors and sense a new freedom and exhilaration in their occupation. At the same time they strip the Rocky Mountains of its beaver, kill more meat than they are able to use, and exhibit wanton wastefulness in their yearly rendezvous. Boone realizes the destructiveness of his life, as well as that of his companions, when near the end of the novel he tells a friend that they have "spiled" the mountains and that he does not want to return.

In *Arfive*, the penultimate novel of Guthrie's series, he deals with what historian C. Vann Woodward has called the twilight zone of man's experience—that shadowy era in which history and memory overlap. The novel describes a Montana town in the period of Guthrie's boyhood, the years around the opening of World War I. The emphasis is on a small community and its citizens' efforts to adjust their frontier backgrounds to changes thrust upon them. The two major characters have to realize that the past is gone, that new ideas and problems have arisen, and that they too must change if they are to adapt to a fluctuating environment. *Arfive* is a persuasive picture of an important era in our past—when the West ceased to be a frontier and gradually began to take on the appearance of a settled region.

The Last Valley, which Guthrie claims is the last of his fictive treatments of the West, illustrates his absorbing interest in history, his preoccupation with the ideas of change and progress, and some of the similarities in method of historians and novelists. Guthrie uses the central figures of *Arfive*—Benton Collingswood and Mort Ewing—in *The Last Valley.* They are employed as Dick Summers, the mountain man and overland guide, was in *The Big Sky* and *The Way West;* they function as bridges from the past to the present and as commentators on the dangers and benefits of change and progress. And they serve another important purpose. Novelists and historians face analogous tasks of selection and omission when they try to produce a book that portrays a twenty-five-year period without drowning the reader in a deluge of facts. Guthrie attempts to solve this problem by selecting specific events in the 1920s, 1930s, and 1940s and allowing his major characters to react to these occurrences. Their diverse reactions—which Guthrie deals with repeatedly—are similar to what historians call historiography, that is, varying interpretations of a single happening. The technique of probing several reactions to one event or idea allows historians and novelists to broaden the perspectives of their works and to demonstrate the complexity of the past.

Guthrie's most recent novel is also a first-rate treatment of the fluidity of time, of the shadowy boundaries between past, present, and future. Collingswood, Ewing, and Ben Tate, a journalist and Collingswood's son-in-law, are reflective persons, and on several occasions, as they ponder their present circumstances, remembrances of past experiences flood in and condition their thoughts and actions. By uniting past and present—sometimes jamming them together—Guthrie shows how much human history is a

flow, an ongoing current rather than a series of separate, isolated eras. The painting on the dust jacket of *The Last Valley* further illustrates Guthrie's method and message. In the background verdant mountains loom above the rest of the setting, but a town, with its streets, buildings, and smoking chimneys, occupies the center of the painting. In the immediate foreground a single horseman rides away from the town. He is not in headlong flight, but he is leaving. The mountains, the town, and the horseman are not distinctly separated; they are merged. Like the novel, the painting hints at some of the tensions between nature and civilization, between past and present. Alongside the evidences of tension and conflict are emphases on juxtaposition and continuity. In fact, the major themes portrayed in the painting and treated in *The Last Valley* are the key ideas dealt with in all of Guthrie's western historical novels. In a speech he summed up his ambiguous response to the inevitable movement of history and to change: "I accept the fact that progress leaves us no retreat. We can only insist *no undue haste.* We can only try to guide it. We can't stay it. Neither should we."

The interest in history, so evident in the work of Fisher and Guthrie, is even more prominent in the recent work of Wallace Stegner, whom many commentators have come to consider our best contemporary western writer. Norman Cousins, in a review in *Saturday Review/World* of Stegner's superb biography of Bernard DeVoto, has even higher praise for Stegner, calling him the leading man of American letters. Throughout his distinguished career as historian, biographer, and novelist, Stegner has been profoundly interested in western history. Nowhere is this concern better demonstrated than in his novel *Angle of Repose* (1971), which won the Pulitzer Prize for fiction in 1972.

On one level the novel is the story of an eastern woman, Susan Burling, who marries another easterner, Oliver Ward, goes west, and tries to acclimate herself to western ways. On another level the book is about Susan's grandson, Lyman Ward, a retired history professor, who is an amputee and alienated from his world of 1970. By shifting back and forth between the late nineteenth century and events and ideas of the 1960s, Stegner deals with a full century of western history. It is a huge task and one that Stegner accomplishes through two major themes of western history: (1) What is the relationship between East and West? Should the emphases be placed on continuities or on differences? and (2) What comparisons and contrasts can be made between the frontier West and the New West of the 1960s? Because it deals with the major questions involved in a discussion of the nature of western history, Stegner's work is a paradigm for the western novel as history.

The first theme of eastern influence upon the West is developed primarily through the character of Susan Burling Ward. She lives most of her life in the West as she follows her husband to the mining camps of California and Colorado, to the new community of Boise, and finally to Grass Valley, California. Unlike her husband, she never becomes a westerner. Throughout her life she holds on to her eastern, genteel symbols. Her clothing, her maid, and governess (probably the one household in Boise in the 1880s to have both), her eastern literary friends, and her allusions to the East and the classics—all these illustrate her connections with the East.

Through adroit use of symbolic action Stegner represents how much Susan is a stranger to western ways. On one occasion, while standing on an elevated porch and speaking to a Mexican worker, she drops her handkerchief. The laborer quickly retrieves it and hands it up to her. She reaches down for the handkerchief but quickly withdraws her hand when she realizes what she is doing. She cannot—in fact will not—take the handkerchief from his hand; finally she calls her maid to get it back. Another night, while she and Oliver are returning to Leadville—Colorado's rip-roaring mining town—they are forced to bed down in a flophouse. Oliver hesitates, for he realizes that his wife is horrified by the prospect of sleeping in a curtained-off section of a room no more than snoring and belching distance from rough miners and dirty vagabonds. Susan is queasy about the situation, and she lies awake most of the night—first in fear and then, true to her character, in dreaming about how she will picture this "rough" West for eastern magazines. Obviously much of the truth will be brushed away and large doses of romanticism applied before the "dreamed up" West will be publishable in *Century* and *Scribner's*.

A third scene—from which Stegner wrings multiple meanings—is the most revealing incident about Susan's attachment to a nonwestern perspective. Before this scene Oliver and Susan have argued about the suitability of an eastern man who has come west. Susan, overcome by her respect for his reading and his obvious exposure to eastern culture, declares him a cultivated gentleman. She is amazed and upset when Oliver says that the man is worthless in the West—in fact a hazard because he knows so little about mining and engineering. Susan does not see that his lack of experience in these professions should be held against him. One night soon after this discussion Susan and Oliver sit down to dinner, and she mentally criticizes Oliver for not washing before eating—there appears to be smudge on his thumb. Later a third person tells of the day's happenings (the account does not come from Oliver, for, as Susan says, he does not like talkee, talkee). Oliver, the eastern engineer, and others were in the mines when someone shouted a warning. The easterner froze in his tracks, and had it not been for Oliver's quick thinking and fast reactions the gentleman might have lost his life. The smudge on Oliver's thumb is an ugly bruise suffered by aiding a man whom he does not respect. At the end of the scene the reader realizes—and so does Susan—how much her perspective prevents her from understanding the West and what it demands from its residents.

Susan's life in Boise—her longest stay in one place in the West before the family moves to Grass Valley—epitomizes the tensions that eat at her even after she has lived in the West for more than a decade. Stegner catches her dilemmas in one ironic sentence of description: "There sat Susan Burling Ward, tired-eyed after a day's drawing, dragged-out after a day's heat, and tightening her drowning-woman's grip on culture, literature, civilization, by

trying to read *War and Peace*." Like the local colorist she is, Susan loves the scenery, the wild and picturesque part of the Boise Valley; but once she faces the problems of living "in" the Boise area, she finds its remoteness and crassness repugnant and is stifled by the boosterism of its residents. Life in Boise seems acceptable only when she withdraws from it—when she and Oliver move up a river canyon and when she tries to establish a western miniature of Brook Farm.

Yet she becomes attached to the West, despite her reluctance to do so. Near the end of the Wards' stay in Boise, disappointments, failures, and tragedies seem to engulf them. Oliver's irrigation schemes will not hold water, their youngest child drowns (ironically, in an irrigation ditch), Oliver takes to the bottle, and a young engineering friend complicates Susan's problems by declaring his love for her. Susan almost gives up on the West; she leaves Oliver, ships her oldest son to an eastern boarding school, and thinks of remaining in the East. But she cannot remain in the East; something draws her west again—back to Oliver, back to disappointments, back to the dreadful West. She realizes, in spite of herself, that she has become attached to things in the West—even if she is not yet a westerner.

It would be a mistake to picture Oliver as the archetypal westerner—as the exact opposite of Susan. But he does take on characteristics ascribed to many westerners. His dreams are expansive—and expensive—but he is a diligent worker. Because he realizes the need for help in achieving his dreams, he is less class-conscious than Susan and evaluates a person more by his abilities than by his cultural achievements. Though he is overly protective of his wife, he does not allow an excessive gentility to blind him to the realities of a region that demands a ruggedness unknown to Susan's eastern friends.

He is not a local colorist caught up in the picturesque, picnic West. For him the region is a place where his dreams can be put to work; it is a place to be conquered. He finds Susan's classical allusions to miners and their arduous work "about used up," and he bluntly tells her that the cultured gentleman who claims to be an engineer is worthless in the West. At times Susan realizes that Oliver is different: "It was his physical readiness, his unflustered way of doing what was needed in a crisis, that she most respected in him; it made him different from the men she had known."

Oliver's dreams are pregnant with promise, although most of them eventually miscarry. He invents devices to save time and money. He discovers the necessary ingredients to make cement. He lays out a usable scheme to irrigate an entire western valley. But he cannot bring his dreams to fruition, and a major reason for his lack of success is a problem that plagued many western dreamers: he is dependent upon eastern capital, and too often sources of eastern capital are as untrustworthy as Lady Fortuna. All of Oliver's dreams prove workable—but only after he has left the scene. Like many westerners, his schemes and partial successes are destroyed by his inability to control sources of financing.

Stegner, sometimes through his narrator and sometimes

as omniscient author, also comments on the relationship between East and West. Early in the novel Lyman Ward says: "I am impressed with how much of my grandparents' life depended on continuities, contacts, connections, friendships, and blood relationships. Contrary to the myth, the West was not made entirely by pioneers who had thrown everything away but an ax and a gun." On other occasions Stegner contrasts Susan's romantic perceptions with what the West was really like. By depicting these two kinds of Wests, Stegner makes clear how much eastern visions defined what the West was to Americans. Most of these foreign interpreters overstressed the uniqueness of western life and underplayed the continuities between East and West. The point Stegner argues is the central thesis of Henry Nash Smith's brilliant book *Virgin Land* and among the major contentions in the writings of the western historian Earl Pomeroy.

The second theme in Stegner's novel is his depiction of the West as it moves from frontier to settled community and finally on to the Bay Area counterculture of the 1960s. By keeping two eras of western life before the reader and by commenting on the transitions between the two periods, Stegner continually narrates and interprets the historical development of the West. Susan's life, as it moves from raw Leadville to semisettled Boise and finally to the security of Grass Valley, illustrates the flow of western history that Stegner is narrating. Throughout the novel the life and mores of the Wards are placed alongside the Berkeley fever of Lyman's young neighbor, Shelley Rasmussen, and his son, Rodman. And Lyman is the link. As he says, "I really would like to talk to somebody about my grandparents, their past, their part in the West's becoming, their struggle toward ambiguous ends." He likes the idea of seeing how "a fourth-generation Trevithick should help me organize the lives of the first-generation Wards." What Lyman notes is the irony of Shelley, who is a descendant of a Cornish miner, helping him interpret the meaning of the lives of a family who "ruled" her ancestors. And more to the point: It is a Trevithick (Shelley's mother) who, more than any of his kin, keeps Lyman moving physically. Stegner implies that the social and cultural history of the West has leveled some mountains, elevated some valleys, and bridged several chasms.

Stegner also suggests that if contemporary westerners paid more attention to their past they could learn from their history. Shelley is excited about the commune that her husband is planning, and she is disappointed that Lyman does not share her enthusiasm. Her problem, Lyman says, is that she could learn from Susan's experiences in trying to set up a psuedo Brook Farm in the Boise Canyon and from other historical precedents. What Lyman preaches (and one hears Stegner in the background at this point) is that if one knows the past one can better manage the present and plot the future.

It is from Lyman Ward, who acts as narrator, as commentator, as synthesizer, that one receives the most explicit comments about history, especially on the frontier becoming the New West. From the opening pages of the novel Stegner establishes a fluidity of time for his narrator. This fluidity is important, for Lyman switches from present to

past and to present again as he searches for an understanding of his life. As he tries to seize hold of his present circumstances, he perceives the paradoxical truth that as soon as he defines the present it has become the past. And he realizes, too, that his life is cumulative: he is *in* and *of* the past just as he is tied to a complicated present. Both periods impinge upon him; he can escape neither. In his attempt to comprehend fully the relationship between the Old and the New Wests, Lyman utilizes two geological terms. The first is "angle of repose," the incline at which rocks cease to roll. He wishes to study his grandparents to discover how they achieved an angle of repose in their lives. The second term, the Doppler Effect, defines the way in which he wishes to undertake his study. It is not enough, he thinks, to stand in 1970, look back to the late nineteenth century, and write about his ancestors. Instead, he must place himself alongside his grandparents and, in a sense, live their lives with them. Like the good historian, he wishes to be past-minded, to climb into their shoes, and to relive their lives with understanding and objectivity.

But several pressures keep Lyman from producing the kind of history he wishes to write. In the first place, so few of his contemporaries think his subject or his method is correct. Lyman wants his son and the Berkeley generation to understand how much they are tied to the past. The problem is, he says, that they are "without a sense of history. . . . [To them] it is only an aborted social science." His son, Rodman, sums up the view that his father fears: "The past isn't going to teach us anything about what we've got ahead of us. Maybe it did once, or seemed to. It doesn't any more." But Lyman wants to study the past. It is, he argues, "the only direction we can learn from." He continues: "I believe in Time, as they did, and in the life chronological rather than in the life existential. We live in time and through it, we build out huts in its rivers, or used to, and we cannot afford all these abandonings." The Berkeley generation has not yet learned this lesson; the youth of the 1960s, he says, are "by Paul Goodman out of Margaret Mead."

Nor does Lyman want a distorted meaning of the past once it is scrutinized. Too many readers are like Rodman, who wants the drama and the color of something like the life of Lola Montez. But to Lyman this kind of writing is worthless: "Every fourth-rate antiquarian in the West has panned Lola's poor little gravel. My grandparents are in a deep vein that has never been dug. They were *people*."

Most of the time Lyman the historian practices what he preaches. He establishes what the region was like when Susan went west. The reader sees her trip in the context of early transcontinental rail travel and within the tense atmosphere that Americans experienced a few weeks after Custer's defeat in the summer of 1876. Here Lyman utilizes the Doppler Effect when he draws close to his subject, near enough for the reader to discern the sounds of her inner struggles. In addition, he wants to make sure that his readers see the continuities in the time periods he describes. When he summarizes the authoritarianism of mine owners and the ill-treatment of miners in the 1870s, he reminds his listeners that much will change in the next century. The Western Federation of Miners, the Industrial

Workers of the World, and the United Mine Workers are yet to come. One cannot hurry history; one must study it and write about it as it was, not as he wishes it had been. Nor must he remold it entirely by the outlook of his contemporaries. Lyman implies that presentist historians make these mistakes and thus distort history.

Lyman also realizes that the historian (or even an entire society) can easily fall in love with the past and use it as a refuge from an oppressive present. In fact, in spite of his vows not to fall victim to an alluring past, Lyman does so. On one occasion when the counterculture seems to be knocking at his door, he muses: "I am not going to get sucked into this. I'll call the cops in a minute if I have to. And this is all, absolutely all, I am going to think about it. I am going back to Grandmother's nineteenth century, where the problems and the people are less messy." Or, in another situation, he catches an epiphany-like glimpse of himself: "This is not a story of frontier hardships, though my grandparents went through a few; nor of pioneer hardihood, though they both had it. It is only Lyman Ward, Coe Professor of History, Emeritus, living a day in his grandparents' life to avoid paying too much attention to his own."

It would be a mistake to consider Lyman merely the mouthpiece of Wallace Stegner. Students of literature avoid the error of always identifying the ideas of a character with those of its author, but historians need additional warning about the pitfalls of such comparisons. Yet much of what Lyman talks about, Stegner has spoken for on other occasions. Stegner shares some of Lyman's distaste for the student radicalism of the 1960s. Stegner remarked in 1972 that the student movement "started at Berkeley and we inherited it at Stanford. The kids didn't come to learn, they came angry and with answers—not questions." He added, "I don't know why when you get mad at Mr. Smith, you break Mr. Jones's windows."

Much of this misplaced anger, Stegner argued, would have been avoided if we were better students of our past:

> In times of crisis people turn to history. Certainly, as some of the protesters . . . argue, we may be prisoners of the past, but we also are imprisoned in the human species. We have to keep our ties with the past to learn and grow. Cut loose from the past and we become nothing. It doesn't make any difference if there are flaws in the marble or not; that's the marble history must be carved from.

In an interview with John R. Milton, Stegner was even more explicit about some of the ideas contained in his novel: "This is what I would really like to see some western writer manage to do, to put together his past and his present." This statement led to *Angle of Repose,* which Stegner described as

> a novel which involves some pretty refined *eastern* characters who are going to have some of the refinement ground out of them. . . . It's a Willa Catherish kind of theme. She keeps pointing out that the frontier breaks the really refined. . . . The frontier was a brutalizing experience, but it also could be, for people who weren't actually

broken by it, an experience which changed them in other ways. It could be a coarsening experience but also a strengthening one. So I've got some genteel-tradition folks who are going to have to develop a few callouses.

Not only does Stegner ask the most important questions about the making of the modern West; he seems to give the best answers. A full discussion of his answers would be the subject of another chapter, but allow me to summarize briefly what I think he says about the nature of western experiences. Scratch a westerner deeply enough, and one will find an easterner who has carried along much of his cultural baggage and has had to readjust his thinking and living to fit a new environment. In other words, the westerner is not something entirely new; he is a product of his past as well as his present.

Second, if one wishes to understand the modern West, he ought, Stegner hints, to study and comprehend the meaning of such nineteenth-century activities as the gold rush, labor disputes in the mines, and political malcontents like the Populists. In short, what Lyman seems to learn is that the American West is the product of two angles of repose: it is East *and* West; and it is the frontier *and* the Berkeley generation. The answers that Stegner provides are the products of a probing mind trying to decipher the nature of the American West. He shows that the open marriage of history and literature will lead us to the best fictional treatments of the West. And thus, if I were asked to name the most significant western novel of the last decade, I would nominate *Angle of Repose.* I know of no other novel of the last ten years that says as many meaningful things about the American West as Stegner's book. It is a model for subsequent novels written about the West.

At this point one must ask, If such novelists as Fisher, Guthrie, and especially Stegner have made notable use of history in their western novels, why is it that this tendency has not received much notice? I am convinced that the answer to this worthwhile question is rooted in the current trends of scholarship in history and literature and in the inclinations of western historians.

In the past few years historians have been urged to employ more of the research techniques of the social sciences. They are told that the use of statistics, demography, and social psychology, for example, will enhance the specificity of their studies. Many students of history have needed this urging, and historical monographs and essays in historical journals evidence an increasing use of social-science methods. This trend has not been detrimental to historians, for these new techniques have broadened their perspectives. At the same time there is a decreasing interest among historians in utilizing literature in their studies; the scrutiny of novels, poems, and plays as a source for historical knowledge seems less and less acceptable to a generation of historians taught to search for exactness in history.

In the field of American literary studies current research continues to move in the direction of myth criticism and the study of linguistics and popular culture. Here too contemporary emphases have widened our viewpoints and added to our understanding of American literature. On the other hand, few critics emphasize literary history or the historical consciousness of novelists. Thus neither historians nor literary critics have recently shown much interest in trying to focus on subjects that cross the disciplines of history and literature.

There are other reasons why the relationship between western history and western literature has not been studied. By and large, western historians have paid scant attention to the literature of the West. The major western-history textbooks contain no extensive discussions of western writing, and there is no published history of western American literature. Western historians, unlike historians of the South, seem unaware either of the historical value of their literature or the historical consciousness evident in the region's fiction. Part of this oversight is due, no doubt, to the widespread but mistaken notion among historians that any novel written about the West is "just another western." It is true that some western writers have chosen to follow the patterned westerns of Zane Grey and his descendants, but to pigeonhold most western authors as writers of westerns—as some historians have done—is to make no distinctions between Zane Grey and A. B. Guthrie, Luke Short and Wallace Stegner, or Frederick Faust (Max Brand) and Vardis Fisher. As we have seen, Guthrie, Fisher, and Stegner have not written Zane Grey westerns.

Other commentators are equally contemptuous of western historical fiction. As one writer has pointed out, the historical novel is treated as if it were " 'a kind of mule-like animal begotten by the ass of fiction on the brood-mare of fact, and hence a sterile monster.' " Here again there is some basis for this negative attitude. For example, James Michener's bestselling novel *Centennial* (1974) illustrates some of the pitfalls of too much popularization in western historical fiction. Michener gives some sense of the vertical (old to new) and horizontal (East and South to West) history of the West, he deals with some ethnic patterns that helped form the mosaic of western society, and he knows how to write appealing narrative history. But the weaknesses of his popular approach limit the historical value of his widely read novel. He conveniently kills off too many of his characters, and he invokes too many chance circumstances to keep his thousand-page novel on the move. He sensationalizes too much of his material. He places too much emphasis on faddish topics: Indians, cowboys, and mountain men. And, on the other hand, he does little with populism, radical farmer groups, or local, state, and federal governmental squabbles, and he generally scants the twentieth century. Michener has "used" (perhaps "abused") western history; he majors on lively and flashy narrative and minors on useful interpretation of the historical materials he utilizes. But to point to Michener or to writers of westerns as the only source of western historical fiction is to distort the evidence, and some historians have been guilty of this distortion.

Now, allow me to snub down my maverick points. The works of several important novelists, as we have seen, evidence a strong interest in history. But current trends in historical and literary scholarship and contemporary predilections among many western historians have kept stu-

dents from noting this historical consciousness in western fiction. One hopes that western novelists continue to mine the rich lode of western history as well as they have in the past. If they do, literary critics and historians will soon realize that many authors make use of regional history in their western fiction and that this theme merits more attention. (pp. 155-71)

Richard W. Etulain, "Western Fiction and History: A Reconsideration," in The American West: New Perspectives, New Dimensions, *edited by Jerome O. Steffen, University of Oklahoma Press, 1979, pp. 152-74.*

Max Westbrook

[An American educator and critic, Westbrook is an important figure in the development of criticism on American western literature. In the following essay, he addresses the problem of historical authenticity in American western fiction.]

Most readers cheerfully pardon John Keats for mixing his explorers. A change from "stout Cortez" to "stout Balboa" would be awkward, but "On First Looking into Chapman's Homer" is considered, by all evidence, a fine sonnet. No one, thus far, has taken seriously the critic who faulted Stephen Crane for errors of seamanship in "The Open Boat." And we can admire the skill of William Shakespeare, who has Othello's sailing vessels rushing in to park, as if they were automobiles, and who gets away with it.

Distinctions could be made. Shakespeare's double time scheme is an essential part of his genius. Keats just made an error, and Crane, I am willing to believe, must have made several. But the three instances cited concern the authentic, in one form or another; and authenticity, by the mandate of writers and critics, is not a standard for literature.

Verisimilitude is different. The belief, perhaps, is that authenticity restricts the artist's imagination, whereas verisimilitude promotes the reader's "willing suspension of disbelief" and serves, for the writer, as the enabling act of creativity. *Gulliver's Travels* and *Metamorphosis* are not authentic, but both have verisimilitude. Good writers have knowledge relevant to their art, and they use this knowledge with an integrity relevant to their purpose: Jane Austen's finely-tuned sense of upper middle-class speech and manners, Ernest Hemingway's knowledge of bullfighting, Saul Bellow's education in anthropology. But the excellence of *Emma, The Sun Also Rises,* and *Henderson the Rain King* does not consist of territorial accuracy. A work may be authentic and fail as literary art (Upton Sinclair's *The Jungle*), or ignore authenticity and yet be judged an accurate picture of what *is* (Edward Albee's *The American Dream*). The consensus is clear: fidelity to the relevant world is required of literary art, but authenticity is a narrow yardstick and should not be used as a standard of judgment.

This is not true for the literature of the American West. In spite of arguments from theory, in spite of the evidence provided by practical critics, the belief persists that a good Western must be authentic. The belief is not confined to the past or to county loyalists. Those who advocate authenticity in American Westerns are alive and writing, and their numbers include important novelists, critics, and historians. The fallacy of authenticity, furthermore, has been exposed, most recently and ably by Don Walker in *Western American Literature* (February, 1977).

Why does the belief persist? Why do so many good people defend a critical standard that seems so obviously wrong? Who among the believers can refute Don Walker's lucid analysis?

The purpose of this essay is, first, to agree with Don Walker and others who have argued that no literature should be judged on the rack of authenticity and, second, to suggest that part of our difficulty is caused by the fact that we are using a single term, *the authentic,* to describe two fundamentally different directions in Western literature. If by *authenticity* we mean *facsimile,* then we have a restrictive concept, a simplistic formula that is antithetical to the complex and ambiguous world the artist writes about. If, however, the word is used to mean *denotation,* then we have a concept which calls for accuracy and discipline without implying a restriction on the artist's imagination.

Of course, for either direction, we may be using the wrong word, and perhaps my distinction of two types could be expanded to twenty and still not include all of the fundamentally different types of authenticity. Pronouncements about the terminology of literary criticism, however, like the detailed elaboration of sub-categories, are usually ineffective. We are probably stuck with the word, *authenticity.* So I'll accept it and try for progress on the basis of a distinction between two fundamentally different kinds of conceptualization. The Protestant Ethic, for example, is a concept which denies variety: behave by this code of virtue or else you are not virtuous. The Categorical Imperative of Immanuel Kant, by contrast, is a concept which *insists* on variety: your duty is to will toward the good, as best you can see it in local terms, as best you can practice it according to your own abilities and opportunities. Facsimile authenticity is the first type of concept; denotative authenticity is the second type.

The critic who believes in facsimile authenticity believes also that the artist is permitted to create stories and characters, but the permission is granted on condition. The specifics, all details which have a counterpart in the actual world, must qualify by meeting factualist standards. Is the hero wearing bat chaps in a novel set before the time that bat chaps were actually in use? Are the pioneer's wagons drawn by horses *contra* the fact that oxen or mules were used? Did the flowers named grow in this locale and bloom at that time of year?

Advocacy of facsimile authenticity has persisted, at least in part, because the second and quite different type of authenticity wears similar clothing—and thus the two have been confused. My thesis is that the best of Western writers, for all their essential differences as original artists, are devoted to authenticity as denotation, not as a guarantee of aesthetic success, not for the purpose of factual accura-

cy, but as a creative choice among the bounty of Western history, their selected subject. The general intent is not to provide for local readers a nostalgic analogue of regional experience, and thus the standard of facsimile authenticity is not an adequate standard for judgment.

But then comes the rub, the unmistakable fact that so many of the best of Western writers *are* devoted to the authentic. And what a writer chooses (humor, for example) *does* become at least a partial standard of judgment (is it funny?). Consider Harvey Fergusson's *Grant of Kingdom* and *The Conquest of Don Pedro.* Divide either novel into sections, list the subjects, and you have a good enough outline for the scholar planning to research and write a history of the same time and place. Or read Frederick Manfred's *Riders of Judgment* and Helena Huntington Smith's *The War on Powder River,* a novel and a history with the same subject, the Johnson County War. Manfred's fidelity to fact is amazing, even to the detail of a wagon wheel striking a rock and making a loud metallic sound just as the army of cattle barons is trying to sneak up on the cabin of Cain Hammett-Nate Champion. True, Manfred invents freely, especially with his major characters, but a reasonable conclusion from the comparison is that Manfred, whose novel was published before the history, must have gone into archives and done the research of the historian, which, Manfred has told me, is exactly what he did.

Or consider Thomas Berger's *Little Big Man.* The mask of the novel is a hoax, the most famous hoax in the American West, the sole white survivor of Custer's Last Stand; but Berger's research was exhaustive and accurate. As with Manfred, the accuracy includes minute details. Leo E. Oliva has demonstrated, in a major essay (*Western American Literature,* Spring-Summer, 1973), that the cry of an Indian baby, a barking dog, and the appearance of an unusually bright star are incidents which are recorded, for the same time and place, in *Little Big Man* and in Custer's diary. In his selected but thorough study, Oliva reports finding only one instance in which Berger's "history" is different from the actual history.

By a fortunate accident, I once had lunch with Thomas Berger and seized the opportunity to ask the obvious question: "How, in a novel which is so alive, could you be so accurate to history? Did you paper your study wall with notes? Wouldn't such imposed detail dry up your creative juices?"

Writers, I know, enjoy making sport of eager critics asking questions, and I don't blame them; but Berger seemed unoffended and serious and relaxed when he answered No, he did not have historical notes in front of him when he wrote *Little Big Man.* He had read so much for so long, I was told, that he had absorbed the history, and thus he was free to invent within the history.

Examples, I trust, need not be multiplied. Similar stories could be told about A. B. Guthrie, Jr., Vardis Fisher, Frank Waters, Michael Straight, Jack Schaefer, Paul Horgan, Wallace Stegner, John Steinbeck, and so on. Those who write most successfully of the American West live in the country they write about, or lived there long enough to see and feel the land and to know the people. They know the history. And they are devoted to the authentic in a way which *does* suggest that Western literary art is a "make-believe" facsimile written in obeisance to the facts of the relevant time and place. The literary excellence which results from this devotion, however, suggests that authenticity, for the Western artist, is a means and not an end.

Since the theory of denotative authenticity may seem far-fetched, let me try an analogy with familiar territory. Compare—as trial only, for the sake of explanation only—the authenticity of the best Western novels with the denotative level of good poetry. When T. S. Eliot names an object out of Prufrock's life, the denotative meaning of that object is, in a sense, authentic. Prufrock has "measured out" his "life with coffee spoons," and the physical details (a coffee spoon is small, expensive) contain as objective correlative the desired connotations (small, smallness, petty, expensive, effete, purposeless, waste). Change "coffee spoons" to "table spoons" and the necessity for denotative accuracy is clear; for the table spoon is large, it is used in the kitchen, it is a common household object, and the associations are with flour, lard, hearth and home. Or contrast the denotative accuracy of T. S. Eliot with the denotative carelessness of Elizabeth Barrett Browning, who writes (in sonnet 38, *Sonnets From the Portuguese*) of a kiss that "was folded down" (sheets and towels are folded).

Denotative accuracy, clearly, is a characteristic of good poetry. Now I don't want to push the comparison too far, but it is helpful to reflect on this characteristic in order to see the possibility, by analogy, of the suggested thesis. If poets must be accurate to the denotative level of metaphor, without that accuracy being the final intent of the poem or a guarantee of the success of the poem, is it not also possible for authenticity to be a characteristic of Western art but not the final intent, not a guarantee?

If the possibility is granted, the next question is Why would denotative authenticity have a special relevance to Western American literature?

The answer, I think, cannot be found in terms of facsimile authenticity, the use of historical accuracy as a standard of aesthetic judgment. Authentic detail, in fact, can be found even in the popular Western; but detail apart from a vision is not likely to be structured. It becomes an idle shibboleth, a password to gain admittance to the club. Meanwhile, the novel itself may be sentimental, pornographic, romantic, adventure for the sake of adventure . . . whatever. Louis L'Amour, for example, prides himself on living in and writing about the real West. "L'Amour's fans," says Peter Gorner (*Philadelphia Inquirer*, February 17, 1976), "depend on him for . . . authenticity. If he has a cowhand drinking from a spring, the reader can be sure it's there and that the water is good." Again, distinctions could be made. Andy Adams' *The Log of a Cowboy*, for example, is probably better than 99% of the popular Westerns and certainly less successful than the novels of Manfred, Waters, Fisher, Willa Cather, and a dozen others, the writers usually taught in college courses in Western literature. Adams does invent a group of lakes just north of San Antonio, but his motive in writing was to create something more honest than the popular Western of his day. *The Log of a Cowboy* reads like a good documentary account of a cattle drive, and the novel as a novel is honest and rewarding.

But the best of Western American novelists go beyond fidelity to history and find in the Westering experience a vision, a world view. What excites them most about the American West, perhaps, is experience in a nature that is not under human control.

Note, first, the characteristic story lines. Bringing nature under human control—Edwin Corle's *Fig Tree John* or Frank Waters' *The People of the Valley*—is usually associated with the sacreligious. Preference for a place under human control usually signals a failure of the soul. Fear of unaccommodated nature is almost always a disguised fear of the impoverished self within, the "Fort Indian," for example, who deserts his people and hangs around soldiers to beg whiskey. For the Anglo, for the modernist in general, witnessing to the belief that nature is original often takes the compromised form of a devotional journey into the mountains, as in Walter Clark's *The City of Trembling Leaves*. Clearly, story lines in this direction have a universality which may be prompted by the Western experience without being confined to a facsimile version of the Western experience. Clearly, belief in this approach to universal meanings makes it possible for something that seems to be a narrow authenticity to be, in reality, a challenging and open-ended type of authenticity which functions in a way that is comparable to the denotative level of poetry.

Within stories about original nature and the sacrilege of civilization, the representative world is shown to be impersonal (suggesting naturalism), and yet it is a world made by God (suggesting religion). Most of us find this a puzzling combination. We are more accustomed to the alignment found in, for example, Stephen Crane's "The Open Boat." Crane's correspondent learns that nature is indifferent and unanswerable. When a ship sinks, "willy-nilly," when nature seems cruelly unfair to the individual and protest is in order, there are "no temples" and no "bricks to throw" if there were temples, that is, no place of worship, no method of protest. Nature is unresponsive to human beings; it does not speak, and it is deaf. Nevertheless, the men in the boat discover a sense of brotherhood, a humanistic value that is said to be a "reality—stern, mournful, and fine." Thus it is necessary that the men in the boat become "interpreters." They must learn a symbolic level of language ("the great sea's voice") to discover the coherence of a world in which nature is indifferent (literally, practically, nature is voiceless) and yet brotherhood is a reality.

The characteristic world view of the American West is so different from Crane's more familiar dualism that a difference in the art of the West is also indicated. Simply, there *are*, in Crane's sense, "temples." For the Westerner, the forces of nature are *not* symbols. Desert and mountain, unaccommodated nature, are God's desert, God's mountain, an enormous, powerful, and impersonal reality more profound than human inventions, the invented language, for example, which the men in Crane's boat must use in order to make "interpretations."

Thus denotative authenticity in Western literature carries metaphysical implications. To get the physical detail right is a step toward creating the right metaphor. To write accurately of the history of human life on God's land is to discover the proper linguistic base for dramatic studies designed to explore the meanings of human experience.

And this is why the Western hero or heroine has learned to listen, not to make up a language but to learn the *provided* language of reality itself; for the staggering variety of God's physical world exists also, in deep miniature, within the individual. To align one's self with the real, it is necessary to begin with the immense specificity of desert and mountain, of the original, the most profound appearance we human beings can see or imagine.

The pitfalls are obvious. For minor talents with much devotion, the authentic can become a literal report, which is a bore. For writers whose allegiance to the original West is a matter of taste rather than philosophy, the authentic can be used as a cover-up of unauthentic adventures. Or the writer may slide into nostalgia, a maudlin protest that the good old days of the frontier are now gone and never shall return. Even the best of Western writers (and critics) do not always avoid these dangers. In addition, my generalization about denotative authenticity must stand to the rear, with proper modesty. Each artist is individual, keeping the critic's thesis always in jeopardy.

I would like to indicate, however, the presence of denotative authenticity in different types of stories, the purpose being to argue, briefly, that fidelity to the world, in the best of Westerns, represents a vision, a way of seeing, and not merely a devotion to the history of a region.

Walter Van Tilburg Clark's classic Western short story, "Hook," is of special interest here because the subject is, in a sense, nature itself, perhaps the ultimate in authenticity. The story has been widely praised, but why, on what grounds? The main character, almost the only character, is a hawk. The brief appearance of human beings is too little and too late. Readers, apparently, are supposed to admire the young hawk and pity his cruel demise. But if this is valid, then "Hook" is an exercise in the animal story, treading on the edges of sentimentality, and the advertised power of the story is counterfeit. The concept of denotative authenticity, however, suggests a different reading.

If we hypothesize that desert and mountain were made by the personal hand of God, that the energies of the natural world are also the energies within the human being, and that the forces driving Hook are the same forces that drive men and women, then "Hook" is not an animal story merely but a story of the world in which all creatures live. The pure and impersonal story of the consciousness of a hawk is the story of experience which is philosophically alive.

The normal procedure is to look for morals, since our critical training is grounded in symbolism rather than in archetypalism. Is the hawk brave, loyal, cruel? Is this an allegorical tale of human beings? What is the moral lesson that we can learn from the experience of the hawk and apply to the human world? And, if no answers can be found, what can we salvage from the cruelty of the farmer, near the end of the story, or the sensitivity of the farmer's wife?

Such questions, I am arguing, are wrong-headed. Clark is not writing about a world in which the denotative level of experience is symbolical, analogical, or allegorical. Clark is writing from a world view in which nature is seen as animal, desert, mountain, and as intrinsic to human experience, a world view in which the authentic contains metaphysical import in its own tongue. The base—for Hook and for you and me—is the same.

When Hook's parents strike him from the nest, he moves about, not yet able to fly, and discovers that even "in his thickets and near the water, the white sun was the dominant presence." In another Clark story, "The Indian Well," Jim Suttler has long known that in "this dead land, like a vast relief model, the only allegiance was to sun." In other Clark stories—"The Buck in the Hills" and "The Portable Phonograph," for example—the characters and the setting change, but the world view remains the same: the awesome and anonymous powers of the universe are alive, on their own terms, within the creatures of this planet, the two-leggeds as well as the four-leggeds and those that fly, swim, dig, or crawl.

When Hook feels "impelled by the blood appetite," he is feeling something akin to the appetite that stirs the lynch mob in *The Ox-Bow Incident,* something which even Hal in *The Track of the Cat* has to admit is a part of his nature. When Hook is wounded and unable to fly, when he experiences disgrace, shame, and evil, he is being driven by forces which operate inhuman beings. "Once," Clark writes, "he disgraced himself by shrieking challenge at the business-like heron. . . ." Hook's purposeless shrieking is like the hollow and sanctimonious shrieking of the Reverend Osgood in *The Ox-Bow Incident;* his "sensation of evil delight" in attacking the inferior gulls is like the cruelty of the wounded father in *The Track of the Cat,* who strikes out at Grace or Gwyn or Joe Sam, and enjoys doing so, when it is Curt who would make a proper antagonist for him.

Now let's consider, briefly, something quite different from Clark's nature or "animal" story. "Chuangtse and the Prince of the Golden Age," one of Clark's fictive jokes, is set in ancient China, a time and a land quite different from what we find in stories of the American West.

The plot goes like this. A Prince has "labored half of his manhood to secure perfect order in his state." "In the pursuit of this ideal," the Prince gathers a cabinet of Sages, improves agriculture, stocks the fisheries, institutes a forestry program, erects magnificent public buildings, and works out elaborate procedures and ceremonies for handling all human relationships, actions, dress, and behaviour, with a considerable emphasis on rank and station.

Meanwhile, Chuangtse, a combination rascal and wise man, spends a good deal of time stretched out on his back, with his hands folded "across his ample stomach," gazing "fixedly upon his thumbs" or sleeping . . . one can never tell which.

Eventually, the Prince's magnificent engineering of human life turns hollow, and the crops will not grow. The committee-intellect fails to find a solution, as the cabinet of Sages analyzes in vain. But then a gardener does a strange thing: he urinates on the vegetables he has planted. The gardener's personal irrigation plan succeeds, while the Prince's elaborate plans for a perfect agriculture—and society—fail. So Clark is having fun, a very serious, Oriental type of fun.

The joke on the idealist is that the energies of the world, at bottom, are the same for the Prince as for the gardener, for Hook the hawk or Chuangtse, or any of the creatures of the world. Human responsibility, as the Prince finally learns from Chuangtse, is to recognize that autonomous energy cannot be shaped in terms of the invented strategies of human beings. The shaping can be achieved, but it must be developed in nature's terms (a version of the denotatively authentic) and not in the merely personal language of the human intellect.

Herein lies the relevance of Clark's Oriental joke to stories of half-alligator mountain men and pioneers and gun-toting cowboys: the *authentic* energies of the world are obscured by the more personal language of civilization. Here, also, is one reason for Clark's fascination with the Nevada desert. Clark believed that "the moribund city" (see his "Prelude" to *The City of Trembling Leaves*) represents a commitment to the not-real, to death. In the desert, by contrast, "the only allegiance was to sun." Affectations cannot be served in the desert. The thing itself is unmistakably present, the denotative desert, authentic reality. To ignore the sun in the "moribund city" is just as futile as to ignore it in the desert, but the price of negligence is clear in desert or mountain, while city life comforts the ego, protects the unbeliever, and obscures the cause and time of death.

In "The Indian Well," Clark writes that beneath the sounds of swallows, insects, aspens, and the wind, there

> lay still more delicate tones, erasing, in the most silent seconds, the difference between eye and ear, a white cloud shadow passing under the water of the well, a dark cloud shadow on the cliff, the aspen patterns on the stones. Deepest was the permanent background of the rocks, the lost on the canyon floor, and those yet strong, the thinking cliffs. When the swallows began again it was impossible to understand the cliffs, who could afford to wait.

The seconds that are "silent," rather than long or short or numbered, and the "delicate tones" which erase "the difference between eye and ear" are indications of a level of reality beyond the personal language of the individual. Clark is describing the denotative authenticity of nature. It is a permanent power, and it comes into the world in its own right, as "thinking cliffs" which can "afford to wait," for they are the permanent stage of man's little moment in time. This is the impersonal energy which drives Hook the hawk, which makes Chuangtse gaze at his thumbs or sleep in peaceful testimony to his own comic

humility, and which Jim Suttler is able to shape into action. When Suttler finally gets his revenge on the cougar that killed his "Jenny," he fires the rifle by drawing "slowly upon his soul in the trigger." Jim Suttler is at one with the objective world. He is in alignment with the real.

Denotative authenticity, I have suggested, can be illustrated in "Hook" (a nature or "animal" story), "Chuangtse and the Prince of the Golden Age" (a non-Western story by a Western writer), and in "The Indian Well" (representing the quality Western). But what about a more typical cowboy story?

Benjamin Capps' *The Trail to Ogallala* is a trail-drive novel closely modeled on *The Log of a Cowboy*. The reader's attention is focused on the essential task of getting the cattle to market in time to meet a deadline. There are the usual problems with water, stampedes, Indians, swollen rivers; there are the usual stories of information: how the remuda works, what campfire tales were like, how to keep the cattle from losing too much weight, chuck-wagon lore, and so on. But Capps goes beyond the documentary level of the trail drive narrative, beyond the thematic hints of *The Log of a Cowboy* (the allusion to Biblical "pioneering," an occasional concern with the drover's work ethic), and undertakes, also, an important study of leadership.

Billy Scott, the hero, is given an impossible task: he is asked to undertake the responsibility of getting the cattle to market, but he is given no authority. The trail boss is Colonel Kittredge, an honest, brave, and able man whose cold personality incapacitates him for leadership. The Colonel is killed in a stampede, and Billy Scott's untenable assignment becomes even more difficult, for the Colonel's replacement as trail boss is the segundo, Blackie, an incompetent bully with a strong back and a weak but demanding ego.

The Colonel had been too narrowly intellectual. Blackie is pure energy, mindless courage, power, devotion to the work of the drover; but Blackie cannot gaze at his thumbs, cannot wait or listen. He energizes from within himself. In a blind fury, unable to decide which way to go, realizing finally that he had forgotten to retrieve the Colonel's compass before burial, Blackie decides to take a crew and go back down the trail to dig at the Colonel's grave. It's a powerful scene, an excellent example of denotative authenticity. Capps makes no references to sacred time or sacred space. He concentrates on the facts of a cattle drive, as if he were a contemporary version of Andy Adams, but the stuff of the trail drive is shown to have meaning, on its own terms. Blackie unearths the Colonel's body, finds the compass, and discovers what a lover of the documentary could have predicted: the compass was smashed in the stampede. Blackie is centered in his own ego, and he is therefore lost, both geographically and spiritually. He is not in touch with the denotative world. He is a flawed human being and a poor leader.

Billy Scott, a realistic version of the hero, is also flawed. Scott is ambitious. He wants desperately to be trail boss, and he can never bring himself, deep within, to refuse the impossible assignment he says he has refused. Once, in supreme frustration at Blackie's bullying incompetence,

Scott lashes out at the giant and gets himself thoroughly beaten. But fundamentally, most of the time, Scott is in tune with the land and, therefore, in harmony with himself. And this is why Scott can find his way to Ogallala without a compass. The energies within the inner self are in alignment with the energies of nature: his "allegiance is to the sun."

The denotative authenticity of Clark, Capps, and others, of course, is not fixed. There is a large margin for debate even on the level of facsimile authenticity. Contemporaneous experts did not always agree about what had happened or about the way it was done by actual—as opposed to dime novel—cowboys. Most of the important stages of Western history were short-lived, the time of the mountain men, the cattle drive, and the major Indian wars lasting only about twenty-five years or so. Thus the experts were, in a sense, amateurs, beginners, or, at least, people engaged in new activities in a new land. The variety of the "real" West should also serve to humble anyone inclined to think in terms of *the* authentic. Opposites happened. There were drovers who hated all horses (thus authentic) and drovers who loved their favorite horses (thus authentic). There were fools and wise people, the cowardly and the brave, an enormous variety of cultures, the conditions were always changing, and all first-hand reporters (even the honest ones) are subject to the potential trap of the "real" experience: what happened to the reporter is *assumed* to be representative of what happened to others.

From the viewpoint of the writer (Hamlin Garland comes to mind), the search for authenticity amidst such variety led to a belief in the necessity of writing from first-hand experience. The artist must have been there, must have lived the life being reported, and cannot rely on books, second-hand information, or the imagination.

This credo has been advanced by Western as well as non-Western writers, and it nags the literary critic in much the same way as the problem of authenticity. The residence requirement seems too literal, and we think of exceptions, Stephen Crane and *The Red Badge of Courage* being the most obvious. At the same time, in too many instances to ignore, the artist does seem to benefit, as artist, from first-hand experience.

Analogous to the possibility of a denotative authenticity is an old but excellent idea which applies to literature generally. The story teller's "voice," however personal or impersonal, must earn the confidence of the reader. The one who tells the story must be qualified for the job. Simply, if you want to know what is on the other side of the mountain, you can go and see or you can ask the person who has been there. From ancient times to the present, one role of the hero is that of the person who fought the battle or made the journey or performed the task and who is therefore competent to tell the story.

When applied to the American Western, and keeping in mind the distinction between denotative and facsimile authenticity, this means that the artist cannot rely on or ignore the standard of accuracy to the selected subject. I don't know how to define a "quality Western," but one characteristic seems to be that the artist creates the *sense* of having been there. There is an achievement that lies somewhere between fact and magic, in its own special place, and that's why we search for a special and recalcitrant relevance. (pp. 213-25)

Max Westbrook, "The Authentic Western," in Western American Literature, *Vol. XIII, No. 5, November, 1978, pp. 213-25.*

CRITICAL RECEPTION OF AMERICAN WESTERN LITERATURE

James K. Folsom

[*In the following excerpt from his* American Western Novel, *Folsom provides reasons for the critical neglect of American western literature and upholds the value of westerns as a literary genre.*]

One of the most virulent—or perhaps virile—genres of popular modern American art is the Western. On the nation's television screens stories of doctors, psychiatrists, steamboat captains, circuses, and traveling magicians come and go, but always there is a cowboy to be found somewhere. The Western movie is still very much alive, both on the Late Show and in first-run movie houses, and complete with elaborate gadgetry to give the illusion of three dimensions. On the newsstands Westerns of all types and catering to all tastes are readily available in paperback.

Yet when the Western is compared with the other two types of modern American popular fiction—the detective story and science fiction—one peculiarity becomes evident, not so much within the Western story itself as in cultural attitudes toward it; for while the detective story and science fiction have received their share of commentary, the Western is enjoyed in silence. The detective story, perhaps because of certain distinguished practitioners such as Poe and Conan Doyle, is tacitly accepted as a genre with at least the possibility of literary merit. Tired scholars as well as tired businessmen will own up, albeit somewhat shamefacedly, to relaxing with Ian Fleming of an evening after a hard day spent wrestling with Henry James; few, if any, will admit a similar predilection for Zane Grey or, better, for Owen Wister or Eugene Manlove Rhodes. And science fiction, despite an almost complete absence of any work of significant esthetic merit in the genre, has attracted the accolade of book-length studies bursting with high seriousness.

The reason for modern interest in science fiction and the detective story, superficially at least, is not hard to find; for both are genres which are apparently "relevant" to contemporary American culture. This is obviously true of the first, and much pulp science fiction appeals with simple directness to the American fascination with technology—or even gadgetry. Better science fiction, as numerous commentators have pointed out, uses the framework of impossible adventure to discuss the nature of society. Inherent in the theme of confrontation of one culture with another is the moral valuation of the relative merits of each; and serious science fiction quite often concerns itself with a sour evaluation of present society reminiscent in many ways of the radical novels of the thirties. Whatever one may think of the esthetic merits of Ray Bradbury's *Martian Chronicles,* to take a well-known example, its moral purpose is clear, and metaphorical structure typical; for the various chronicles present a history of the loss of Eden in terms of the Earthlings' destruction of the simple, almost golden-age Martian culture. Bradbury's work is certainly among the best modern science fiction, particularly if judged on the basis of moral earnestness; but in a way his concerns are typical, for the genre is almost obsessed with an evaluation of twentieth-century American culture. One could point out that *The Martian Chronicles* particularly—and much science fiction in general—deals with a theme dear to the hearts of writers about the West—the theme of the Last Frontier—and that Bradbury's treatment of the colonization of Mars does not greatly differ from the many novels about the colonization of the West. One *could* point this out, but the fact is that most Americans do not; they tacitly assume that science fiction is relevant while Westerns are escapist. Most science fiction devotees will cheerfully admit that the genre has not lived up to its possibilities; but they will stoutly defend those possibilities as a vehicle for serious literature. The same benefit of the doubt is not given the Western.

Even the detective story has felt the demands of a more sophisticated modern age. The best-known practitioner of contemporary detective fiction, Ian Fleming, has come a long way from his ratiocinative ancestors. It is significant that Fleming's hero—James Bond—is concerned primarily with world affairs. He is a sophisticated connoisseur of exotic drinks and alluring women, and this none too subtle symbolism fixes a great gulf between him and the meek young men in embassies. The same superhuman awareness which enables him to perceive immediately the unwelcome presence of an onion in his very dry martini enables him as well to conquer the knaves who would frustrate the well-meaning but inept statesmanship of others on Her Majesty's service. He is one of a few men to whom a grateful nation allows the privilege of shooting on sight and no questions asked—a dispensation he shares with many a lawman who rides the range of the television Western. In both instances, of course, this is the sheerest fantasy, in Bond's case perhaps tempered with a bit of nostalgia for the grand old days of gunboat diplomacy. But the point is that Ian Fleming is taken at least quasi-seriously while the television marshal is not; and certainly part of the reason for this is that he is involved with world affairs, presented under the aspect of international intrigue—things which are, we trust, of immense importance to us all. We may well weep for the innocent days of that amiable psychopath, Professor Moriarty, who, as nearly as we can tell, loved a good crime in the same way which gentler folk love a good game of chess; or, better still, of Poe's famous ape, vicious it is true, but neither misunderstood, troubled by guilt, nor vexed with the problem of a social conscience. The modern practitioner of the detective story cannot be so naive; he must always take into account the larger picture. His hero's life is not only fraught with peril but freighted with philosophy; as he carefully places his bullets to have maximum effect, he thinks regretfully of the sociological causes which have driven his victim to a life of crime.

All this is not to say that the detective story and science fiction are completely without merit; nor is it to suggest that of all the genres of popular American fiction only the Western can have any claim upon our serious attention. Rather it is to point out an interesting double-think about Western story. Most other genres of popular fiction are assumed to be more profound, at least in implication, than their writers are in performance. The whole is greater than its parts, and though various authors are taken *cum grano salis,* the respective genres are viewed with sophisticated tolerance. Somewhere, it is felt, sometime, a great novel will emerge from the often inferior run-of-the-mill productions, and this faith keeps serious readers as well as escapists interested. Yet the Western is apparently not to be included in this charitable view; it is absolved absolutely from even the possibility of merit.

This tacit denial of the Western's existence is all the more remarkable in light of American interest in so many other things Western. Seminars in "the West" flourish in American universities; commercial and scholarly presses print a constant stream of new historical interpretations of the meaning of the Western experience to American life; and there seems to be no end to the market for reprinted first-hand accounts, from Charlie Siringo to George Armstrong Custer. Yet when the imaginative literary record of the Western experience is approached at all, it is usually peripherally and with condescension. And this even though the reputation of the first great American novelist, James Fenimore Cooper, depends today, and has always depended, on his studies of the West; and though the Western novel today leads a vigorous life which is by no means confined to the sub-literature of the newsstand.

There are many reasons for critical neglect of the Western novel, which though superficially inconsistent, depend upon certain common, inchoate, often only half-formulated assumptions. First, as mentioned above, it is alleged that the Western is an anachronism. Among the perils of the atomic age, stories of Indian raids and cavalry patrols seem to be completely out of touch with the problems facing modern man; and if literature should be a parable of experience, the experience depicted in the Western is too unreal to have meaning today, even granted that it once did. In short, this objection comes down to the allegation that the Western is escape literature, pure and simple. The most that can be said for it is that it gives a harmless retreat from the tensions of modern life to a world of bland adventure where evil and good are easily recognizable, and where the good guy always wins. In support of this assertion it is pointed out that the Western is only very rarely true to the facts of that Western life which it supposedly depicts; and that the landscape of the Western has only a nodding acquaintance with the landscape of the West. As a result, the characters of the typical Western tend toward stereotypes, and the facts of the Western movement are debased into clichés and stock situations.

A more profound statement of this literary objection to the Western novel is that it ignores too many of the facets of human experience with which any art form that claims our serious attention must come to terms. Though—this argument runs—it need not be accepted as axiomatically true that a novel which deals with cowboys and Indians can have no relevance to modern life, yet certainly the very nature of the world of the Western novel is such that it cannot deal with some situations at least which art must interpret. The sexual experience, for instance, is often mentioned as an aspect of life which the Western almost completely ignores.

Many other common critical objections to the Western could be mentioned here, though little purpose would be served by a complete enumeration. What they all ultimately depend upon, however, is a feeling that the picture of western life given by the Western is by and large a false one; considered factually the picture can be shown to be in error, and considered on literary grounds these errors in fact are emblematic of a more profound lack of relevance in the Western novel itself. This criticism is, of course, a particular affront to Americans who—long before Frederick Jackson Turner was to elucidate formally the thesis that the presence of the frontier was the most important single factor distinguishing the American from other peoples—had arrived on their own at the notion that the West was somehow the most expressive part of a culture which likes to think of itself as in all ways peculiarly self-eloquent.

For the distinctively American nature of the American experience has been one of the great themes with which Americans of all times have concerned themselves. From Crèvecoeur's 1782 letter "What is an American?" to Mark Schorer's 1961 biography of Sinclair Lewis subtitled "An American Life," the American-ness of America and Americans has attracted the concern of literary men. And though it is true that there has been singularly little agreement as to just what in fact *is* American about America, it has been just as true that the necessity for defining this American nature has been almost universally understood to be one of the great problems—perhaps *the* great problem—with which the American commentator must concern himself. As a result, a certain coolness in attitude toward the Western is understandable, on the basis that the American life depicted in it can be proved demonstrably false when compared with the "facts" of Western experience.

To add insult to injury, the literary treatment of the West has always been something in which Americans have had extremely high—and generally unrealized—hopes. If the settlement of the West is in fact the American epic, it is an epic not without a hero, but without a poet. Timothy Flint, writing in 1826 of Daniel Boone, reflects sadly that "this Achilles of the West wants a Homer, worthily to celebrate his exploits," a feeling which is more or less endemic among American literary critics. Though Flint himself was later to attempt to remedy this situation, the offhand remark in his *Recollections* reveals a very real bitterness; it is galling to reflect that the epic of America finds, as it were, not Homer but Zane Grey as its chronicler. And

however strongly the writer of a prize essay in the *Western Monthly Magazine* for 1833 may "firmly believe, that within the borders of our country, in the past and in the present, is an abundance of fine materials, endowed with capabilities of being wrought by the hand of genius into an original, a rich, and various literature," he is distressingly silent about how in fact these fine materials have been used. Both these comments reflect an interesting and ubiquitous attitude in literary criticism toward the West. For both these critics tacitly assume the same point of view mentioned earlier—that the literature of the West must somehow deal with the historical facts of western colonization. In fact, the latter critic goes so far as to mention specifically the peculiar desirability of the West as a literary mine because there "society is in ceaseless motion" and "hence is it singularly free from tameness and dull monotony, those fatal foes to the descriptive novelist." The implied canon for literary criticism here is one which by now should be familiar; that the events of western history—*The Romance of Western History,* as James Hall significantly titles an 1857 collection of anecdotes—are somehow inherently so significant in their own right that they require only straight reporting. If such is the case, it becomes easy to understand on a more profound level the critic's instinctive dislike of the "untrue" quality of actual Western literature.

Indeed, if there is one great theme which runs through criticism of the literature of the West, it is precisely this: because they do not understand the "facts" of Western life, Western writers have been unable to present its meaning. The greatest of Fenimore Cooper's literary offenses, Mark Twain thinks, is the fact that five out of six Indians miss an easy jump into a scow in *The Deerslayer.* Somehow to Twain this proves Cooper's complete incompetence as a novelist; yet, if Cooper had pointed out to Twain that it is even more unlikely that any event whatever could transport a nineteenth-century American to King Arthur's court, Twain would probably have thought the criticism rather monumentally beside the point.

If one asks the writers of Western literature themselves what the nature of the genre is, however, the answer he receives will be somewhat different. For the writer of Westerns is not likely to be so dogmatic about the necessity for realistic use of the materials of Western history as his critic would wish. James Fenimore Cooper, in his Preface to the Leatherstocking Tales, refers to the tales as "romances," as does William Gilmore Simms, who subtitles *The Yemassee* "A Romance of Carolina." Owen Wister, too, uses the term in his Preface to what is probably the most popular Western ever written, *The Virginian.*

The term "romance" when applied to the Western is not without interest, as it had a more definite meaning to nineteenth-century literary criticism than it does to us. One remembers Hawthorne's famous Preface to *The House of the Seven Gables,* in which he discusses the differences between the Romance and the Novel. The Romance, Hawthorne says, presupposes "a certain latitude, both as to its fashion and material," which the Novel does not. The distinction he elaborates is more significant than perhaps at first appears. The Novel, he continues, "is presumed to aim at a very minute fidelity, not merely to the possible, but to the probable and ordinary course of man's experience." The Romance, on the other hand, "while, as a work of art, . . . must rigidly subject itself to laws, and while it sins unpardonably so far as it may swerve aside from the truth of the human heart—has fairly a right to present that truth under circumstances, to a great extent, of the writer's own choosing or creation." The distinction between the two, broadly speaking, is that the Romance is presumed to be relatively free from the necessity of presenting historical "truth" in any particular factual sense, though it may well deal with—and Hawthorne's own practice here is instructive—history as myth, or as metaphor.

Hawthorne's distinction between the Novel and the Romance is not by any means confined to his own beliefs. The idea is something of a critical commonplace in the nineteenth century; William Gilmore Simms had noted earlier another implication of the idea in his discussion of the particular genius of the Romance in his Preface to *The Yemassee* (1835). *The Yemassee,* Simms insists, is a Romance and not a Novel, and the two forms of literature are very distinct. To the question he raises, "What is the modern Romance itself?" he notes, "the reply is immediate. The modern Romance is the substitute which the people of the present day offer for the ancient epic. The form is changed; the matter is very much the same; at all events, it differs much more seriously from the English novel than it does from the epic and the drama, because the difference is one of material, even more than of fabrication." The material of the Novel, he continues, is "confined to the felicitous narration of common and daily occurring events, and the grouping and delineation of characters in ordinary conditions of society," while the Romance "does not confine itself to what is known, or even what is probable. It grasps at the possible."

To the interesting comparison between the Romance and the epic we will return in a moment; but first let us note the similarity in Simm's and Hawthorne's distinction between the Romance and the Novel. In both men's phrase, the Novel is confined to the "probable"—that is, the everyday world—while the Romance is by no means so limited. The notion is particularly compelling when the fictional practice of the two writers is recalled; for the Romances of both men are very particularly based in history.

The difference between the Romance and the Novel, then, is ultimately one of what questions may be asked from history. Although the truth which the Novel and the Romance reveal is the same, for the "truth of the human heart" is the truth which fills all history, the Novel must present this truth by means of very particular questions of historical cause and effect, while the Romance need not be so narrowly confined.

Behind Hawthorne's and Simms's discussion of the distinction between the Romance and the Novel stands a very definite, though not explicitly stated, idea of the nature of truth. Truth, for an imaginative writer at least, finally is "the truth of the human heart," meaning that the human heart is the basis of history, not the other way around. Hence the Romance in one sense is just as histori-

cal as the Novel; indeed, from the Romancer's point of view it may well be more so, for the Novel, he thinks, constantly runs the risk of becoming so involved with meaningless detail as to obscure the truth which all art must in some way reveal. The "facts" of history, in other words, may be so inchoate that they only succeed in confusing the reader by concealing its meaning; as a result, the Novel may well be in a profound sense less "historical" than the Romance, though paradoxically the Romance has less to do with the facts of history. It all depends, as Owen Wister points out in his Preface to *The Virginian,* what questions one asks of history. *The Scarlet Letter, Hugh Wynne,* and *Uncle Tom's Cabin* are all "historical," as is "any narrative which presents faithfully a day and a generation." *The Virginian,* then, is just as historical as any of these, even though it is a "colonial romance."

Wister's coupling of these four novels is deliberately paradoxical. Each one, he says, is a "historical novel"; it makes no difference that *Hugh Wynne* contains the historic George Washington while in *Silas Lapham* and *The Scarlet Letter* we find only "imaginary figures." Nor, he goes on to say, does the subject of a "historical novel" necessarily have to be contemporary so long as it presents faithfully its day and generation. And also implicit in Wister's list of four carefully chosen books is the critical position that faithful presentation does not of necessity consist of merely relating the sober historical facts of whatever particular generation is under scrutiny. By faithful presentation Wister means something very close to Hawthorne's "truth of the human heart" which all literary endeavor attempts to discover.

The Novel and the Romance, then, are distinguishable only insofar as they represent different methods of elucidating the "truth of the human heart." The truth which they reveal is finally the same. In any particular case, therefore, the Romance may be more or less novelistic in detail, according to the purpose of its author. It can be completely unnovelistic as (to use an example of Simms's) are the novels of Maturin; or, it may be so close to novelistic historical fact as *Ivanhoe.* Hawthorne, whose knowledge of New England history was profound, implies himself that the separation of the novelistic from the romantic elements in *The Scarlet Letter* is not wholly fortunate; and a recent scholar has shown that this Romance is also concretely enough visualized as a Novel for the reader to create from it a street-plan of seventeenth-century Boston. Yet one has to dig to do it, and this is ultimately the point; the Romancer feels that the Novelist runs the risk of being too much bound to the superficies of things to penetrate to their significance. Still, when properly used, novelistic detail can be a useful tool for the Romancer in his own presentation of the "truth of the human heart."

As a result the Romance often, though not invariably, has about it a certain spurious realism which critics are too often prone to see as its heart rather than as an incidental attribute. Is *Moby-Dick,* to take a well-known example, primarily a Romance or a Novel in the sense in which Hawthorne and Simms would use the terms? Obviously it is a Romance, at least insofar as its core is not basically realistic; yet it contains much concrete detail, which critics on occasion have taken for the center of the work, rather than as a device to give a certain believability to a story which is basically not realistic. The difference between the Romance and the Novel is the difference, as it were, between *Moby-Dick* and *Two Years Before the Mast*. *Moby-Dick* is not about the whale fishery in the same sense in which *Two Years Before the Mast* is about the California clipper trade. The "cetology" and the other factual detail of *Moby-Dick*, though Melville visualizes a whaler as clearly as Dana does a clipper ship, are subsumed as parts of a world which is finally not a "probable" one.

Moby-Dick may have taken us rather far afield from the Western; but a similar confusion in terms to that about the Romance and the Novel may also be seen in the common misunderstanding of the "epic," a term universally applied to the novel of the West.

The "epic of the West" has become so hackneyed a phrase as to have lost almost all meaning whatever. Whether this is due to Hollywood or to the inevitable encroachment of time is not ultimately important; but certainly Hollywood's definition of "epic"—that it have a certain vague historical content and horses—is the unthinking definition which comes to most persons' minds when the term is mentioned. Yet the Hollywood epic is not an epic at all, and the difference between it and the traditional epic is not, as is often assumed, one of execution, but rather one of conception. For the Hollywood epic, however badly executed, is ultimately conceived as historical in a very *particular* way. Press releases for any epic film invariably mention the care with which it has been researched, and on occasion this is even true; yet even when it is, there could be nothing further from the traditional epic than the Hollywood version of it. And the difference between the two is precisely what William Gilmore Simms saw in his Preface to *The Yemassee*. The Hollywood epic is, Simms would say, novelistic. It deals with the world of the "probable," a world which is in the last analysis the world of everyday, though presented, it is true, under the guise of grandiose vulgarity. The appeal of the Hollywood epic is ultimately one of fact; it attempts to convince by the repetitive weight of documentary evidence. Who could disbelieve in Cleopatra after seeing a forty-foot-high Sphinx? And especially a forty-foot-high movable Sphinx pulled by hundreds of slaves?

For Simms, however, and for most later writers about the West, the epic is a very different thing. It is, he says, a Romance. It is a story told about history, but it is not necessarily a story constructed of historical details. A fact which perturbs a modern critic of *The Virginian*— that "there is not one scene set on the range among the cattle"—would not have worried Simms; he might even have thought it to be a point in the book's favor. After all, the Trojan Horse never actually appears in the *Iliad*.

Nevertheless, to assume that all the novels about the West form a self-consistent literary method for the interpretation of experience which has always been totally misunderstood by critics would also be unfair. For writers about the West themselves have not been uniformly of one mind about the possibilities and implications of Western story. Though most of them have felt that the Western is a ro-

mantic parable, some have taken the contrary view that it is basically a novelistic account of the facts of Western colonization. In the last analysis, this latter group of writers about the West forms one category of the "local color" writers who have played a constant, if minor, role in American literature from its beginnings. The purpose of this type of local-color writing has always been more or less openly conceived as a method of publicizing the facts of American life. Whether writing about the settlement of the West, anecdotes of Southern character, or comic tales of Yankee shrewdness, these writers have assumed that their fiction should memorialize bizarre characters, unusual customs, and strange incidents of American life. Where the romantic western novel has always been fabular, tending toward the parable, this novelistic local-color western novel has always been anecdotal; and where the romantic western novel has tended toward synthesis, the local-color western has tended toward fragmentation and individual statement. The difference between the two, to use an analogy suggested before, is the difference between *Moby-Dick* and *Two Years Before the Mast*.

Yet it must not be forgotten that the romantic western has from its beginnings borrowed freely from the anecdotal material of the local colorists. Cooper's characters come immediately to mind; though his romantic young lovers are often sketchily drawn, such figures as Hurry Harry, Uncas, Chingachgook, and even Leatherstocking himself are as particularly conceived as are the characters of Bret Harte. The real difference between Cooper and Bret Harte—or to take two more nearly contemporary examples, Owen Wister and Bret Harte—in their handling of characters is ultimately to be found not in the way the characters are drawn, but in the way they are used.

Bret Harte's characters, like Bret Harte's world, have no significance beyond the statement of a tricky, anecdotal situation. Harte's real interest, and the real concern of Western local colorists from James Hall onward, is finally to be found in the story he is telling. Untoward revelations, trick endings—in a word, "surprise"—are Harte's real aims; by means of manipulation of the machinery of his tales, he attempts to render his anecdotes memorable. The same trick, somewhat less cleverly used, is familiar to all moviegoers at that point in a Hollywood Western where all seems lost, the wagon train is surrounded, the ammunition running low, the Indians massing for a final charge, when suddenly, far away but distinct, the stirring notes of the bugle inform the beleaguered party that the calvary has come to the rescue.

What strikes us funny in such a situation is not the fact itself of the cavalry's fortunate arrival—an event by no means unknown in Western history—but that there is no point to the rescue. The same thing depresses us about the often very cleverly handled tales of Bret Harte, or O. Henry, or Will James. It is that the story has no relevance beyond the realm of anecdote. Romantic western fiction, in contrast, though often as anecdotal as the local-color tale, subordinates the events of the latter to some larger purpose. The point may be made clearer by comparing three often-praised works of Western local-color writing: Andy Adams' *The Log of a Cowboy* (1903), Elliot Paul's

A Ghost Town on the Yellowstone (1948), and John Houghton Allen's *Southwest* (1952). All three of these books are written within a completely anecdotal framework; all purport to be autobiographical; each is told in the first person by a narrator not clearly distinguishable from the author. Yet though the books are strikingly similar in format and in material, the differences between them are unmistakable.

Adams' *Log of a Cowboy* is without doubt the most complete and factual account of trail-driving in our literature. It reports a long drive from the Mexican border north through Texas and the Great Plains to a final destination at the Blackfoot Indian reservation in Montana. Almost every incident of trail-driving is faithfully reported in the *Log;* stampedes, river crossings, debauches in the trail towns, methods of handling cattle, as well as all the other colorful minutiae of cowboy life are painstakingly set down by a man who knew them at first hand. The hero of the book, and ostensible narrator of the log, one "Thomas Moore Quirk," almost exactly resembles Andy Adams himself, and the log of his adventures forms a chronicle of Adams' own colorful experiences on the cattle trail. The book, however, is not really an autobiography; except for a few conventional sentiments the character of the author can scarcely be said to enter the book at all. Adams' focus is consistently outward to the world of events, and his book is truly, as the title says, a *log*— that is, a diary of events told in the order in which they occurred. Even when Adams is reporting campfire gatherings where the cowboys swap stories, his focus is completely external. We get only an occasional glimpse of any emotional effect these stories might possibly have had upon Adams or his hero Tom Quirk, and indeed most of the stories are further anecdotes about cowboy life. Though it is true that once the stories revolve around girls left behind, more often the cowboys reminisce about horses they have known, or dogs, or the hazards of the trail. Adams' relation to these stories is also interesting, for he envisions himself as one who reports them for others, not as one who interprets the stories to himself. Almost invariably he listens to the other cowboys tell of their experiences, and copies their stories down for posterity. He is reluctant to tell stories on his own, nor does he report any effect the others' stories had upon him. Never in his record of cowboy anecdote or of cowboy life does he suggest any frame of reference or interest larger than the often fascinating—and often, it must be added, tedious—world of a particular trail drive. Were one to ask Adams his purpose in recounting this trail drive, his answer would be a historical one; *The Log of a Cowboy,* he would say, attempts a report of the facts of a way of life which has vanished.

Elliot Paul's *A Ghost Town on the Yellowstone* is in many ways reminiscent of *The Log of a Cowboy.* Like Adams, Paul was either involved in, or a first-hand observer of, the events he chronicles: the history of the short-lived town of Trembles, Montana, which was founded accidentally in a stagecoach accident in 1907 and became a ghost town fifteen years later. Like Adams' as well, Paul's account is basically anecdotal, though the subject of his story of necessity focuses his anecdotes around the inhabitants of a

place rather than the events of a journey. But unlike Adams, Paul is personally involved in the fortunes of Trembles, and the ghost town on the Yellowstone becomes a metaphor for his own coming of age. This can be seen in the quality of the anecdotes Paul tells, all of which reflect personally upon himself. Instead of the various good and bad horses which fill Adams' pages, *A Ghost Town on the Yellowstone* contains only one horse, a miserable little pinto named Crocus because, as Paul tells us, "that early spring flower had been used by the Sioux to poison their enemies." Paul inherits Crocus and finally even manages to train her, as he manages to come to terms with the facts of life in Trembles. Indeed, Paul's trials with Crocus are a metaphor for the basic concern of the book, for Crocus is a particular image of the trials of life in general on the Yellowstone, and ultimately the book becomes a story of how one succeeds or fails in a new environment. In juxtaposition to Paul's adaptability—symbolized by his eventual success with Crocus—stands the stubbornness of a surveyor from Bangor, who knows all about cold weather and will not take advice about sensible footwear, and who loses his toes as a result of his obstinacy; and as a final sardonic metaphor we have the pamphlet put out by the Northern Pacific Railroad describing Montana's beautiful climate, which the inhabitants of Trembles take pleasure in reading whenever the temperature hits sixty below. The point of all this is of course clear; one must learn to adapt to the facts of life, rather than attempt to impose an arbitrary scheme upon them.

John Houghton Allen's *Southwest* is, like the two books already discussed, anecdotal in format. Allen tells a number of stories about the area along the Mexican border, an area he significantly calls the "lost world." Unlike Adams' and Paul's, however, Allen's anecdotes are not necessarily of his personal experience. Though some of the stories he tells are stories from his own life, many more have been told him by older men, and of these stories in turn many have not been part of the personal experience of the tellers. On a literal level, the book has really no organization at all. It is a collection of stories arranged according to what appears at first to be a completely random principle of association of ideas. Even the geographical location of Allen's "southwest" is loosely defined, and the definition is broad enough to allow for the inclusion of relevant anecdotes from Old Mexico and even of the American Civil War. Yet though the book does not confine itself to a particular event or place, it cannot really be criticized as random or diffuse except when it is held up to literal-minded canons of organization. Much more than either of the other two books, *Southwest* is a book with a thesis; and the attitude which Allen adopts toward his material is much more personal than Adams' and more overtly reflective than Paul's.

Allen begins his book by calling attention to the present dreariness of the southwest; the first few pages are filled with descriptions of the land, descriptions which conclude with statements of the southwest's ominous and hostile quality. It is, says Allen, a "lonely land," a "sullen land," a "hollow dismal land," a "stagnant land," an "evil land," and so on. From these descriptions he turns to the new American inhabitants of this "evil land," whom he does not like either; "and I am bitter against the land and these people," he concludes, "because I remember when it was a fine place to live." He then goes on to tell of this older, finer land, the Spanish southwest of his youth, concluding with the significant statement that the stories he will narrate "are a poet's tales, a young man's tales; they were my first loves."

It should be emphasized that the stories which he goes on to tell are not in fact much different from the tales of Andy Adams or of Elliot Paul. Moreover, it develops that the tales themselves are relatively unimportant to Allen, whose final concern is with the ironic contrast between the glorious old times of the Spanish southwest and the degenerate new era of the present American southwest. This explains his choice of anecdotes which, while superficially impressionistic, is actually very carefully selected to develop the ironic contrast between the two periods of history.

So short a summary as the above inevitably does a great deal of harm to the books discussed; for our purposes, however, the differences between them should now be sufficiently clear. What one finds in these three books, really, is a kind of progression on the part of their respective authors in the use of anecdotal material. *The Log of a Cowboy* has no relevance at all beyond the particular world it so accurately describes. Like *Two Years Before the Mast,* with which it has been compared, it attempts an honest, thorough, and unbiased report of the particular facts of a way of life, and the reader who finds it interesting must of necessity be one whose interest is primarily historical. *Southwest,* on the other hand, is finally not a historical book at all in any particular sense. Where *The Log of a Cowboy* is specific, impersonal, and detached, *Southwest* is passionately personal and strives always toward a general interpretation of the meaning of the southwest. For such an interpretation, it matters little whether the anecdotes related are, objectively speaking, "true" or not, and many of the stories Allen tells are admitted fables. In a larger sense, however, these anecdotes are true, for they reveal something about "southwestness" which Allen feels could not be shown through purely factual material. Somewhere between these two books stands *A Ghost Town on the Yellowstone.* In many ways almost as particular as Adams, Paul nevertheless feels uncomfortable in the realm of pure anecdote. Though not so personal as Allen, he feels that his book must have some larger concern than the faithful and accurate reporting of events. The stories Paul tells are objectively true—at least ostensibly, though some of them are a little hard to swallow—but they are arranged in such a way as to afford a more than particular insight into the way in which a man must react in order to face life successfully. The unlikely ghost town of Trembles becomes, in Paul's hands, a little world emblematic of the great world from which it apparently stands so far removed.

If one reads these three books in the order in which I have summarized their respective plots, starting with *The Log of a Cowboy* and ending with *Southwest,* one becomes conscious that the basic difference between them lies in their attitudes toward the historical material with which all three deal. Each book asks the question of how the meaning of the Western experience may best be discovered.

Whether the West is best understood in terms of factual anecdotal history or as a metaphorical parable of that history is the real point at issue. In terms of our previous definition, Adams' work is novelistic; Paul and Allen write Romance.

Once this distinction is understood, much of the polemic which surrounds commentary on Western story can be seen in a truer perspective. It is pointless to ask whether *The Log of a Cowboy* is a "better" book than *A Ghost Town on the Yellowstone* or *Southwest.* Adams does not write according to the same standards as the other two authors, and, as the nineteenth century clearly saw, novelistic canons of taste cannot be applied to romantic works of art. No purpose can be served by sneering at romantic western story because it is not true to western life in any specific sense; little is to be gained by wishing Owen Wister were Andy Adams.

And in fact much may be lost; for, if we are to pontificate about the limited success or failure of Western story, we must be very clear about what it has been trying to do. My own position in regard to the novel of the West should by now be obvious. It is, very simply, that the Western has been ignored, condescended to, and maligned largely because the essential nature of Western story has been misunderstood. It has not been sufficiently recognized that this nature is finally unrealistic; that the Western is usually a "myth," or a "fable." The material of this fable is based, at least at one remove, upon American history, but the purpose of the fable is not the realistic explication of a colorful chapter of the American past. It is rather a metaphorical parable of the inconsistencies and contradictions which inhere in the American's paradoxical views about himself, his country, and his destiny. At bottom the Western depicts—often shallowly, sometimes profoundly, but always clearly—the argument which has been with America from the Puritans to the present about what the American experience should be. The question of "What is an American?" is the question the Western novel attempts to answer, though the question is often phrased differently as "What should an American be?" There is of course no answer to this question; art does not give answers to such questions, at least not in any simple way. Yet the Western does attempt to discover what the American is by metaphorical statement of some of the various things he is presumed—or presumes himself—to be. The Western deals in paradox, for the American's view of himself is paradoxical; its material—the Great West—is the material which Americans, rightly or wrongly, have always felt distinguished them from other peoples; and the settlement of the Great West is what tells the American most about himself. The most distinctive fact of American history—the settlement of the Great West—becomes in the Western novel a vehicle which holds in solution the most distinctive fact of the American mind—its obsessive concern with the nature of its own destiny.

A personal anecdote from my own experience may serve to make the point at once more particular and more clear. Some time after the second world war, while a student in Austria, I was invited to have dinner with an Austrian family. The patriarch of this family was an amiable gentleman, a retired industrialist who had spent many years in America and was filled with praise for American ways. He was perfectly clear in his own mind why the Americans had won the war. "We would have won," he said, "had we had such discipline." His notion that, beside the American genius for organization the supermen of the Third Reich were nothing but inefficient bureaucrats, was striking to me at the time. I had not yet discovered Tocqueville's trenchant analysis of the self-deception inherent in American individualism; nor had it occurred to me that there was something profoundly paradoxical in the propaganda war movies I had seen as a youth in which, after the first smashing American victory, a distinguished general would say, "Our men will win because they have been taught to think for themselves," and after the second, "Our men will win because they know the value of teamwork." To both these notions I, and I suppose most Americans, gave unthinking approval; and yet, when one stops to think of it, the two are at least superficially contradictory.

It is beside the point here to attempt a reasoned assessment of which of these ideas best expresses the truth about the American character, or even if indeed they are as contradictory as they appear. Yet it is worthy of notice that this debate is at the heart of a great mass of literature about the West, most apparently in the innumerable works dealing with the conflict between the cattle baron and the "nesters." Superficially this theme is only blood-and-thunder, an excuse for violence in which the sides are easy to distinguish. One can identify the players without a program, if only because the nesters don't have horses. Yet the theme is inherently much more profound than this, as Conrad Richter's *The Sea of Grass* and Jack Schaefer's *Shane,* among others, go to prove. In these works, the antagonists in a blood-and-thunder story are given significance as exemplifying two possible ways of life, both representative of conflicting American values, and the range war which ensues as an inevitable result of their conflict is seen as emblematic of inevitable ideological conflict in a people who simultaneously affirm both sets of values at once.

The conflict in the Western novel, in its broadest terms, is an externalized debate which reflects the common American argument about the nature of, in modern parlance, "the good life." It is no accident that the growth, if not the source, of the Western novel is contemporaneous with the Populist-Progressive attack on the excesses of the Gilded Age, nor that the Western accurately reflects this often acrimonious discussion. The American mental hesitation between the values of urban and rural life is mirrored in the Western novel; whether the coming of civilization is good or ill is the burden of Western fiction. Even the world of Western fiction strangely mirrors the Populist attack in party conventions and the halls of Congress. A cynic might point out that there is precious little fact to be gleaned from the highly emotional discussions of the future of democracy which from time to time erupt violently from the otherwise generally placid American moral landscape; a more compassionate observer might say only that, for all this childish joy in facts, the Ameri-

can does not always confuse the good life with the gross national product.

Perry Miller, in his brilliant essay "Errand into the Wilderness," has mentioned the inherent contradiction in the word "errand." Its denotative meaning, he points out, is "mission"; but combined with this is a contradictory meaning, inherent in the etymology of the word, "to wander," or "to lose one's way." Miller shows that quite early in the American experience both of these meanings come to inhere in the term. Whether in his errand into the wilderness the American has lost his way becomes the burden of Puritan sermons. It is the burden of much later American writing as well, not the least of which is the fictional writing about the West. For the West is unequivocally the wilderness; and it is there that the nature of the errand may best be seen.

When the novel of the West is viewed as a parable, many of the objections raised to it become relatively unimportant. As a fable the Western is not necessarily an anachronism, for it makes little difference whether the Last Frontier is the Great Plains or the moon. If the Western deals in stereotyped situations, if the characters it draws are unreal, if it ignores or misrepresents particular historic facts, so do all fables. For a fable is not ultimately true to the world of everyday; it is rather a projection upon a stage of personal though universalized virtues and vices, hopes, desires, and fears. The Last Frontier is finally something more than an aspect of the American West; its topography comes to resemble the landscape of the human soul. (pp. 13-32)

> *James K. Folsom, in an introduction to his* American Western Novel, *College & University Press, 1966, pp. 13-35.*

THE WESTERN HERO

David B. Davis

[*Davis is an American historian and critic. In the following excerpt, he examines the physical and psychological traits of the cowboy in order to understand the widespread appeal of this mythic figure.*]

In 1900 it seemed that the significance of the cowboy era would decline along with other brief but romantic episodes in American history. The Long Drive lingered only in the memories and imaginations of old cowhands. The "hoe-men" occupied former range land while Mennonites and professional dry farmers had sown their Turkey Red winter wheat on the Kansas prairies. To be sure, a cattle industry still flourished, but the cowboy was more like an employee of a corporation than the freelance cowboy of old. The myth of the cowboy lived on in the Beadle and Adams paper-back novels, with the followers of Ned Buntline and the prolific Colonel Prentiss Ingraham. But this seemed merely a substitution of the more up-to-date cowboy in a tradition which began with Leatherstocking and Daniel Boone. If the mountain man had replaced Boone and the forest scouts, if the cowboy had succeeded the mountain man, and if the legends of Mike Fink and Crockett were slipping into the past, it would seem probable that the cowboy would follow, to become a quaint character of antiquity, overshadowed by newer heroes.

Yet more than a half-century after the passing of the actual wild and woolly cowboy, we find a unique phenomenon in American mythology. Gaudy-covered Western or cowboy magazines decorate stands, windows, and shelves in "drug" stores, bookstores, grocery stores and supermarkets from Miami to Seattle. Hundreds of cowboy movies and television shows are watched and lived through by millions of Americans. Nearly every little boy demands a cowboy suit and a Western six-shooter cap pistol. Cowboys gaze out at you with steely eye and cocked revolver from cereal packages and television screens. Jukeboxes in Bennington, Vermont, as well as Globe, Arizona, moan and warble the latest cowboy songs. Middle-age folk who had once thought of William S. Hart, Harry Carey, and Tom Mix as a passing phase, have lived to see several Hopalong Cassidy revivals, the Lone Ranger, Tim McCoy, Gene Autry, and Roy Rogers. Adolescents and even grown men in Maine and Florida can be seen affecting cowboy, or at least modified cowboy garb, while in the new airplane plants in Kansas, workers don their cowboy boots and wide-brimmed hats, go to work whistling a cowboy song, and are defiantly proud that they live in the land of lassos and sixguns.

When recognized at all, this remarkable cowboy complex is usually defined as the distortion of once-colorful legends by a commercial society. The obvious divergence between the real West and the idealized version, the standardization of plot and characters, and the ridiculous incongruities of cowboys with automobiles and airplanes, all go to substantiate this conclusion.

However, there is more than the cowboy costume and stage setting in even the wildest of these adventures. Despite the incongruities, the cowboy myth exists in fact, and as such is probably a more influential social force than the actual cowboy ever was. It provides the framework for an expression of common ideals of morality and behavior. And while a commercial success, the hero cowboy must satisfy some basic want in American culture, or there could never be such a tremendous market. It is true that the market has been exploited by magazine, song, and scenario writers, but it is important to ask why similar myths have not been equally profitable, such as the lumbermen of the early northwest, the whale fishermen of New Bedford, the early railroad builders, or the fur traders. There have been romances written and movies produced idealizing these phases of American history, but little boys do not dress up like Paul Bunyan and you do not see harpooners on cereal packages. Yet America has had many episodes fully as colorful and of longer duration than the actual cowboy era.

The cowboy hero and his setting are a unique synthesis of two American traditions, and echoes of this past can be discerned in even the wildest of the modern horse operas.

On the one hand, the line of descent is a direct evolution from the Western scout of Cooper and the Dime Novel, on the other, there has been a recasting of the golden myth of the antebellum South. The two were fused sometime in the 1890's. Perhaps there was actually some basis for such a union. While the West was economically tied to the North as soon as the early canals and railroads broke the river-centered traffic, social ties endured longer. Many Southerners emigrated West and went into the cattle business, and of course, the Long Drive originated in Texas. The literary synthesis of two traditions only followed the two social movements. It was on the Great Plains that the descendants of Daniel Boone met the drawling Texas cowboy.

Henry Nash Smith has described two paradoxical aspects of the legendary Western scout, typified in Boone himself. This woodsman, this buckskin-clad wilderness hunter is a pioneer, breaking trails for his countrymen to follow, reducing the savage wilderness for civilization. Nevertheless, he is also represented as escaping civilization, turning his back on the petty materialism of the world, on the hypocritical and self-conscious manners of community life, and seeking the unsullied, true values of nature.

These seemingly conflicting points of view have counterparts in the woodsman's descendant, the cowboy. The ideal cowboy fights for justice, risks his life to make the dismal little cowtown safe for law-abiding, respectable citizens, but in so doing he destroys the very environment which made him a heroic figure. This paradox is common with all ideals, and the cowboy legend is certainly the embodiment of a social ideal. Thus the minister or social reformer who rises to heroism in his fight against a sin-infested community, would logically become a mere figurehead once the community is reformed. There can be no true ideal or hero in a utopia. And the civilization for which the cowboy or trailblazer struggles is utopian in character.

But there is a further consideration in the case of the cowboy. In our mythology, the cowboy era is timeless. The ranch may own a modern station wagon, but the distinguishing attributes of cowboy and environment remain. There is, it is true, a nostalgic sense that this is the last great drama, a sad knowledge that the cowboy is passing and that civilization is approaching. But it never comes. This strange, wistful sense of the coming end of an epoch is not something outside our experience. It is a faithful reflection of the sense of approaching adulthood. The appeal of the cowboy, in this sense, is similar to the appeal of Boone, Leatherstocking, and the later Mountain Man. We know that adulthood, civilization, is inevitable, but we are living toward the end of childhood, and at that point "childness" seems eternal; it is a whole lifetime. But suddenly we find it is not eternal, the forests disappear, the mountains are settled, and we have new responsibilities. When we shut our eyes and try to remember, the last image of a carefree life appears. For the nation, this last image is the cowboy.

The reborn myth of the ante-bellum South also involves nostalgia; not so much nostalgia for something that actually existed as for dreams and ideals. When the Southern myth reappeared on the rolling prairies, it was purified and regenerated by the casting off of apologies for slavery. It could focus all energies on its former rôle of opposing the peculiar social and economic philosophy of the Northeast. This took the form of something more fundamental than mere agrarianism or primitivism. Asserting the importance of values beyond the utilitarian and material, this transplanted Southern philosophy challenged the doctrine of enlightened self-interest and the belief that leisure time is sin.

Like the barons and knights of Southern feudalism, the large ranch owners and itinerant cowboys knew how to have a good time. If there was a time for work, there was a time for play, and the early rodeos, horse races, and wild nights at a cowtown were not occasions for reserve. In this respect, the cowboy West was more in the tradition of fun-loving New Orleans than of the Northeast. Furthermore, the ranch was a remarkable duplication of the plantation, minus slaves. It was a hospitable social unit, where travelers were welcome even when the owner was absent. As opposed to the hard-working, thrifty, and sober ideal of the East, the actual cowboy was overly cheerful at times, generous to the point of waste, and inclined to value friendly comradeship above prestige.

The mythical New England Yankee developed a code of action which always triumphed over the more sophisticated city slicker, because the Yankee's down-to-earth shrewdness, common sense, and reserved humor embodied values which Americans considered as pragmatically effective. The ideal cowboy also had a code of action, but it involved neither material nor social success. The cowboy avoided actions which "just weren't done" because he placed a value on doing things "right," on managing difficult problems and situations with ease, skill, and modesty. The cowboy's code was a Western and democratic version of the Southern gentleman's "honor."

In the early years of the twentieth century, a Philadelphia lawyer who affected a careless, loose-tied bow instead of the traditional black ribbon and who liked to appear in his shirt sleeves, wrote: "The nomadic bachelor west is over, the housed, married west is established" [Edward Douglas Branch, *The Cowboy and His Interpreters*]. In a book published in 1902 he had, more than any other man, established an idealized version of the former, unifying the Southern and Western hero myths in a formula which was not to be forgotten. Owen Wister had, in fact, liberated the cowboy hero from the Dime novels and provided a synthetic tradition suitable for a new century. *The Virginian* became a key document in popular American culture, a romance which defined the cowboy character and thus the ideal American character in terms of courage, sex, religion, and humor. The novel served as a model for hundreds of Western books and movies for half a century. In the recent popular movie, "High Noon," a Hollywood star who won his fame dramatizing Wister's novel, reënacted the same basic plot of hero rejecting heroine's pleas and threats, to uphold his honor against the villain Trampas. While this theme is probably at least a thousand years old, it was Owen Wister who gave it a specifically American content and thus explicated and popularized the modern cowboy ideal, with its traditions, informality, and all-important code.

Of course, Wister's West is not the realistic, boisterous, sometimes monotonous West of Charlie Siringo and Andy Adams. The cowboy, after all, drove cattle. He worked. There was much loneliness and monotony on the range, which has faded like mist under a desert sun in the reminiscences of old cow hands and the fiction of idealizers. The Virginian runs some errands now and then, but there are no cattle-driving scenes, no monotony, no hard work. Fictional cowboys are never bored. Real cowboys were often so bored that they memorized the labels on tin cans and then played games to see how well they could recite them. The cowboys in books and movies are far too busy making love and chasing bandits to work at such a dreary task as driving cattle. But then the Southern plantation owner did no work. The befringed hero of the forests did not work. And if any ideal is to be accepted by adolescent America, monotonous work must be subordinated to more exciting pastimes. The fact that the cowboy hero has more important things to do is only in keeping with his tradition and audience. He is only a natural reaction against a civilization which demands increasingly monotonous work, against the approaching adulthood when playtime ends.

And if the cowboy romance banishes work and monotony, their very opposites are found in the immensity of the Western environment. To be sure, the deserts and prairies can be bleak, but they are never dull when used as setting for the cowboy myth. There is always an element of the unexpected, of surprise, of variety. The tremendous distances either seclude or elevate the particular and significant. There are mirages, hidden springs, dust storms, hidden identities, and secret ranches. In one of his early Western novels William MacLeod Raine used both devices of a secret ranch and hidden identity, while Hoffman Birney combined a hidden ranch, a secret trail, and two hidden identities. In such an environment of uncertainty and change men of true genius stand out from the rest. The evil or good in an individual is quickly revealed in cowboy land. A man familiar with the actual cowboy wrote that "brains, moral and physical courage, strength of character, native gentlemanliness, proficiency in riding or shooting—every quality of leadership tended to raise its owner from the common level" [Philip Ashton Rollins, *The Cowboy*].

The hazing which cowboys gave the tenderfoot was only preliminary. It was a symbol of the true test which anyone must undergo in the West. After the final winnowing of men, there emerge the heroes, the villains, and the clowns. The latter live in a purgatory and usually attach themselves to the hero group. Often, after the stress of an extreme emergency, they burst out of their caste and are accepted in the élite.

While the Western environment, according to the myth, sorts men into their true places, it does not determine men. It brings out the best in heroes and the worst in villains, but it does not add qualities to the man who has none. The cowboy is a superman and is adorable for his own sake. It is here that he is the descendant of supernatural folk heroes. Harry Hawkeye, the creator of an early cowboy hero, Calvin Yancey, described him as:

> . . . straight as an arrow, fair and ruddy as a Viking, with long, flowing golden hair, which rippled over his massive shoulders, falling nearly to his waist; a high, broad forehead beneath which sparkled a pair of violet blue eyes, tender and soulful in repose, but firm and determined under excitement. His entire face was a study for a sculptor with its delicate aquiline nose, straight in outline as though chiselled from Parian marble, and its generous manly mouth, with full crimson and arched lips, surmounted by a long, silken blonde mustache, through which a beautiful set of even white teeth gleamed like rows of lustrous pearls.

While the Virginian is not quite the blond, Nordic hero, he is just as beautiful to behold. His black, curly locks, his lean, athletic figure, his quiet, unassuming manner, all go to make him the most physically attractive man Owen Wister could describe. Later cowboy heroes have shaved their mustaches, but the great majority have beautiful curly hair, usually blond or red, square jaws, cleft chins, broad shoulders, deep chests, and wasp-like waists. Like the Virginian, they are perfect men, absolutely incapable of doing the wrong thing unless deceived.

Many writers familiar with the real cowboy have criticized Wister for his concentration on the Virginian's love interest and, of course, they deplore the present degeneration of the cowboy plot, where love is supreme. There were few women in the West in the Chisholm Trail days and those few in Dodge City, Abilene, and Wichita were of dubious morality. The cowboy's sex life was intermittent, to say the least. He had to carry his thirst long distances, like a camel, and in the oases the orgies were hardly on a spiritual plane. Since earlier heroes, like the woodsman, led celibate lives, it is important to ask why the cowboy depends on love interest.

At first glance, there would seem to be an inconsistency here. The cowboy is happiest with a group of buddies, playing poker, chasing horse thieves, riding in masculine company. He is contemptuous of farmers, has no interest in children, and considers men who have lived among women as effete. Usually he left his own family at a tender age and rebelled against the restrictions of mothers and older sisters. Neither the Virginian nor the actual cowboys were family men, nor did they have much interest in the homes they left behind. Thus it would seem that courting a young schoolteacher from Vermont would be self-destruction. At no place is the idealized cowboy further from reality than in his love for the tender woman from the East. Like the law and order he fights for, she will destroy his way of life.

But this paradox is solved when one considers the hero cowboy, not the plot, as the center of all attention. Molly Wood in *The Virginian,* like all her successors, is a literary device, a *dea ex machina* with a special purpose. Along with the Western environment, she serves to throw a stronger light on the hero, to make him stand out in relief, to complete the picture of an ideal. In the first place, she brings out qualities in him which we could not see other-

wise. Without her, he would be too much the brute for a real folk hero, at least in a modern age. If Molly Wood were not in *The Virginian,* the hero might seem too raucous, too wild. Of course, his affair with a blonde in town is handled genteelly; his boyish pranks such as mixing up the babies at a party are treated as good, clean fun. But still, there is nothing to bring out his qualities of masculine tenderness, there is nothing to show his conscience until Molly Wood arrives. A cowboy's tenderness is usually revealed through his kindness to horses, and in this sense, the Eastern belle's rôle is that of a glorified horse. A woman in the Western drama is somebody to rescue, somebody to protect. In her presence, the cowboy shows that, in his own way, he is a cultural ideal. The nomadic, bachelor cowboys described by Andy Adams and Charles Siringo are a little too masculine, a little too isolated from civilization to become the ideal for a settled community.

While the Western heroine brings out a new aspect of the cowboy's character, she also serves the external purpose of registering our attitudes toward him. The cowboy ideal is an adorable figure and the heroine is the vehicle of adoration. Female characters enable the author to make observations about cowboys which would be impossible with an all-male cast. This rôle would lose its value if the heroine surrendered to the cowboy immediately. So the more she struggles with herself, the more she conquers her Eastern reservations and surmounts difficulties before capitulating, the more it enhances the hero.

Again, *The Virginian* is the perfect example. We do not meet Molly Wood in the first part of the book. Instead, the author, the I, who is an Easterner, goes to Wyoming and meets the Virginian. It is love at first sight, not in the sexual sense, of course (this was 1902), but there is no mistaking it for anything other than love. This young man's love for the Virginian is not important in itself; it heightens our worship of the hero. The sex of the worshiper is irrelevant. At first the young man is disconsolate, because he cannot win the Virginian's friendship. He must go through the ordeal of not knowing the Virginian's opinion of him. But as he learns the ways of the West, the Virginian's sublime goodness is unveiled. Though increasing knowledge of the hero's character only serves to widen the impossible gulf between the finite Easterner and the infinite, pure virtue of the cowboy, the latter, out of his own free grace and goodness recognizes the lowly visitor, who adores him all the more for it. But this little episode is only a preface, a symbol of the drama to come. As soon as the Virginian bestows his grace on the male adorer, Molly Wood arrives. The same passion is reënacted, though on a much larger frame. In this rôle, the sex of Molly *is* important, and the traditional romance plot is only superficial form. Molly's coyness, her reserve, her involved heritage of Vermont tradition, all go to build an insurmountable barrier. Yet she loves the Virginian. And Owen Wister and his audience love the Virginian through Molly Wood's love. With the male adorer, they had gone about as far as they could go. But Molly offers a new height from which to love the Virginian. There are many exciting possibilities. Molly can save his life and nurse him back to health. She can threaten to break off their wedding if he goes out to fight his rival, and then forgive him when he disobeys her plea. The

Virginian marries Molly in the end and most of his descendants either marry or are about to marry their lovely ladies. But this does not mean a physical marriage, children, and a home. That would be building up a hero only to destroy him. The love climax at the end of the cowboy drama raises the hero to a supreme height, the audience achieves an emotional union with its ideal. In the next book or movie the cowboy will be the carefree bachelor again.

The classic hero, Hopalong Cassidy, has saved hundreds of heroines, protected them, and has been adored by them. But in 1910 Hopalong, "remembering a former experience of his own, smiled in knowing cynicism when told that he again would fall under the feminine spell." In 1950 he expressed the same resistance to actual marriage:

> "But you can't always move on, Hoppy!" Lenny protested. "Someday you must settle down! Don't you ever think of marriage?" "Uh-huh, and whenever I think of it I saddle Topper and ride. I'm not a marrying man, Lenny. Sometimes I get to thinkin' about that poem a feller wrote, about how a woman is only a woman but—" "The open road is my Fate!" she finished. "That's it. But can you imagine any woman raised outside a tepee livin' in the same house with a restless man?"

The cowboy hero is the hero of the pre-adolescent, either chronologically or mentally. It is the stage of revolt against femininity and feminine standards. It is also the age of hero worship. If the cowboy romance were sexual, if it implied settling down with a real *girl,* there would be little interest. One recent cowboy hero [in Davis Dresser's *The Hangmen of Sleepy Valley*] summarized this attitude in terms which should appeal strongly to any ten-year-old: "I'd as soon fight a she-lion barehanded as have any truck with a gal." The usual cowboy movie idol has about as much social presence in front of the leading lady as a very bashful boy. He is most certainly not the lover-type. That makes him lovable to both male and female Americans. There can be no doubt that Owen Wister identified himself, not with the Virginian, but with Molly Wood.

While some glorifiers of the actual cowboy have maintained that his closeness to nature made him a deeply religious being, thus echoing the devoutness of the earlier woodsman hero who found God in nature, this tradition has never carried over to the heroic cowboy. Undoubtedly some of the real cowboys were religious, though the consensus of most of the writers on the subject seems to indicate that indifference was more common. Intellectualized religion obviously had no appeal and though the cowboy was often deeply sentimental, he did not seem prone to the emotional and frenzied religion of backwoods farmers and squatters. Perhaps his freedom from family conflicts, from smoldering hatreds and entangled jealousies and loves, had something to do with this. Despite the hard work, the violent physical conflicts, and the occasional debaucheries, the cowboy's life must have had a certain innocent, Homeric quality. Even when witnessing a lynching or murder, the cowboy must have felt further removed from total depravity or original sin than the farmer in a squalid frontier town, with his nagging wife and thirteen children.

At any rate, the cowboy hero of our mythology is too much of a god himself to feel humility. His very creation is a denial of any kind of sin. The cowboy is an enunciation of the goodness of man and the glory which he can achieve by himself. The Western environment strips off the artifice, the social veneer, and instead of a cringing sinner, we behold a dazzling superman. He is a figure of friendly justice, full of self-reliance, a very tower of strength. What need has he of a god?

Of course, the cowboy is not positively anti-religious. He is a respecter of traditions as long as they do not threaten his freedom. The Virginian is polite enough to the orthodox minister who visits his employer's ranch. He listens respectfully to the long sermon, but the ranting and raving about his evil nature are more than he can stand. He knows that his cowboy friends are good men. He loves the beauty of the natural world and feels that the Creator of such a world must be a good and just God. Beyond that, the most ignorant cowboy knows as much as this sinister-voiced preacher. So like a young Greek god leaving Mount Olympus for a practical joke in the interest of justice, the Virginian leaves his rôle of calm and straightforward dignity, and engages in some humorous guile and deceit. The minister is sleeping in the next room and the Virginian calls him and complains that the devil is clutching him. After numerous sessions of wrestling with his conscience, the sleepy minister acting as referee, morning comes before the divine finds he has been tricked. He leaves the ranch in a rage, much to the delight of all the cowboys. The moral, observes Wister, is that men who are obsessed with evil and morbid ideas of human nature, had better stay away from the cowboy West. As Alfred Henry Lewis put it [in *Wolfville Days*], describing a Western town the year *The Virginian* was published, "Wolfville's a hard practical outfit, what you might call a heap obdurate, an' it's goin' to take more than them fitful an' o'casional sermons I aloodes to,—to reach the roots of its soul." The cowboy is too good and has too much horse sense to be deluded by such brooding theology. Tex Burns could have been describing the Virginian when he wrote that his characters "had the cow hand's rough sense of humor and a zest for practical jokes no cow hand ever outgrows."

Coming as it did at the end of the nineteenth century, the cowboy ideal registered both a protest against orthodox creeds and a faith that man needs no formal religion, once he finds a pure and natural environment. It is the extreme end of a long evolution of individualism. Even the individualistic forest scout was dependent on his surroundings, and he exhibited a sort of pantheistic piety when he beheld the wilderness. The mighty captain of industry, while not accountable to anyone in this world, gave lip-service to the generous God who had made him a steward of wealth. But the cowboy hero stood out on the lonely prairie, dependent on neither man nor God. He was willing to take whatever risks lay along his road and would gladly make fun of any man who took life too seriously. Speaking of his mother's death, a real cowboy is supposed to have said:

> With almost her last breath, she begged me to make my peace with God, while the making was good. I have been too busy to heed her last advice. Being a just God, I feel that He will over-

look my neglect. If not, I will have to take my medicine, with Satan holding the spoon.

While the cowboy hero has a respect for property, he does not seek personal wealth and is generous to the point of carelessness. He gives money to his friends, to people in distress, and blows the rest when he hits town on Saturday night. He owns no land and, in fact, has only contempt for farmers, with their ploughed fields and weather-beaten buildings. He hates the slick professional gambler, the grasping Eastern speculator, and railroad man. How are these traits to be reconciled with his regard for property rights? The answer lies in a single possession—his horse. The cowboy's horse is what separates him from vagabond-age and migratory labor. It is his link with the cavalier and plumed knight. More and more, in our increasingly prop-erty-conscious society, the cowboy's horse has gained in importance. A horse thief becomes a symbol of concen-trated evil, a projection of all crime against property and concomitantly, against social status. Zane Grey was ad-hering to this tradition when he wrote [in *Wildfire*], "in those days, a horse meant all the world to a man. A lucky strike of grassy upland and good water . . . made him rich in all that he cared to own." On the other hand, "a horse thief was meaner than a poisoned coyote."

When a cowboy is willing to sell his horse, as one actually does in *The Virginian,* he has sold his dignity and self-identity. It is the tragic mistake which will inevitably bring its nemesis. His love for and close relationship with his horse not only make a cowboy seem more human, they also show his respect for propriety and order. He may drift from ranch to ranch, but his horse ties him down to re-spectability. Yet the cowboy hero is not an ambitious man. He lacks the concern for hard work and practical results which typifies the Horatio Alger ideal. Despite his fine horse and expensive saddle and boots, he values his code of honor and his friends more than possessions. Because the cowboy era is timeless, the hero has little drive or push toward a new and better life. He fights for law and order and this implies civilization, but the cowboy has no visions of empires, industrial or agrarian.

One of the American traits which foreign visitors most fre-quently described was the inability to have a good time. Americans constantly appear in European journals as ill-at-ease socially, as feeling they must work every spare mo-ment. Certainly it was part of the American Protestant capitalistic ethic, the Poor Richard, Horatio Alger ideal, that spare time, frivolous play, and relaxation were sins which would bring only poverty, disease, and other mis-fortunes. If a youth would study the wise sayings of great men, if he worked hard and made valuable friends but no really confidential ones, if he never let his hair down or be-came too intimate with any person, wife included, if he stolidly kept his emotions to himself and watched for his chance in the world, then he would be sure to succeed. But the cowboy hero is mainly concerned with doing things skillfully and conforming to his moral code for its own sake. When he plays poker, treats the town to a drink, or raises a thousand dollars to buy off the evil mortgage, he is not aiming at personal success. Most cowboy heroes have at least one friend who knows them intimately, and

they are seldom reserved, except in the presence of a vil-lain or nosey stranger.

Both the hero and real cowboy appear to be easy-going and informal. In dress, speech, and social manner, the cowboy sets a new ideal. Every cowboy knows how to relax. If the villains are sometimes tense and nervous, the hero sits placidly at a card game, never ruffled, never dis-turbed, even when his arch rival is behind him at the bar, hot with rage and whisky. The ideal cowboy is the kind of man who turns around slowly when a pistol goes off and drawls, "Ah'd put thet up, if Ah were yew." William Mac-Leod Raine's Sheriff Collins [in *Bucky O'Conner*] chats humorously with some train robbers and maintains a calm, unconcerned air which amuses the passengers, though he is actually pumping the bandits for useful infor-mation. Previously, he had displayed typical cowboy indi-vidualism by flagging the train down and climbing aboard, despite the protests of the conductor. Instead of the eager, aspiring youth, the cowboy hero is like a young tomcat, calm and relaxed, but always ready to spring into action. An early description of one of the most persistent of the cowboy heroes summarizes the ideal characteristics which appeal to a wide audience:

> Hopalong Cassidy had the most striking person-ality of all the men in his outfit; humorous, cou-rageous to the point of foolishness, eager for fight or frolic, nonchalant when one would ex-pect him to be quite otherwise, curious, loyal to a fault, and the best man with a Colt in the Southwest, he was a paradox, and a puzzle even to his most intimate friends. With him life was a humorous recurrence of sensations, a hugh pleasant joke instinctively tolerated, but not worth the price cowards pay to keep it. He had come onto the range when a boy and since that time he had laughingly carried his life in his open hand, and . . . still carried it there, and just as recklessly. [Clarence Mulford, *Hopalong Cassidy*]

Of course, most cowboy books and movies bristle with vio-lence. Wild fist fights, brawls with chairs and bottles, gun play and mass battles with crashing windows, fires, and the final racing skirmish on horseback, are all as much a part of the cowboy drama as the boots and spurs. These bloody escapades are necessary and are simply explained. They provide the stage for the hero to show his heroism, and since the cowboy is the hero of the pre-adolescent, he must prove himself by their standards. Physical prowess is the most important thing for the ten- or twelve-year-old mind. They are constantly plagued by fear, doubt, and in-security, in short, by evil, and they lack the power to crush it. The cowboy provides the instrument for their aggres-sive impulses, while the villain symbolizes all evil. The eth-ics of the cowboy band are the ethics of the boy's gang, where each member has a rôle determined by his physical skills and his past performance. As with any group of boys, an individual cowboy who had been "taken down a peg," was forever ridiculed and teased about his loss in status.

The volume of cowboy magazines, radio programs and motion pictures, would indicate a national hero for at least a certain age group, a national hero who could hardly help but reflect specific attitudes. The cowboy myth has been chosen by this audience because it combines a complex of traits, a way of life, which they consider the proper ideal for America. The actual drama and setting are subordinate to the grand figure of the cowboy hero, and the love affairs, the exciting plots, and the climactic physical struggles, present opportunities for the definition of the cowboy code and character. Through the superficial action, the heroism of the cowboy is revealed, and each repetition of the drama, like the repetition of a sacrament, reaffirms the cowboy public's faith in their ideal.

Perhaps the outstanding cowboy trait, above even honor, courage, and generosity, is the relaxed, calm attitude toward life. Though he lives intensely, he has a calm, self-assurance, a knowledge that he can handle anything. He is good-humored and jovial. He never takes women too seriously. He can take a joke or laugh at himself. Yet the cowboy is usually anti-intellectual and anti-school, another attitude which appeals to a younger audience.

Above all, the cowboy is a "good joe." He personifies a code of personal dignity, personal liberty, and personal honesty. Most writers on the actual cowboy represented him as having these traits. While many of these men obviously glorify him as much as any fiction writers, there must have been some basis for their judgment. As far as his light-hearted, calm attitude is concerned, it is amazing how similar cowboys appear, both in romances and non-fiction. Millions of American youth subscribed to the new ideal and yearned for the clear, Western atmosphere of "unswerving loyalty, the true, deep affection, and good-natured banter that left no sting" [Clarence E. Mulford, *Hopalong Cassidy*]. For a few thrilling hours they could roughly toss conventions aside and share the fellowship of ranch life and adore the kind of hero who was never bored and never afraid.

Whether these traits of self-confidence, a relaxed attitude toward life, and good humor, have actually increased in the United States during the past fifty years, is like asking whether men love their wives more now than in 1900. Certainly the effective influence of the cowboy myth can never be determined. It is significant, however, that the cowboy ideal has emerged above all others. And while the standardization of plot and character seems to follow other commercial conventions, the very popularity of this standard cowboy is important and is an overlooked aspect of the American character. It is true that this hero is infantile, that he is silly, overdone, and unreal. But when we think of many past ideals and heroes, myths and ethics; when we compare our placid cowboy with, say, the eager, cold, serious hero of Nazi Germany (the high-cheekboned, blond lad who appeared on the Reichsmarks); or if we compare the cowboy with the gangster heroes of the thirties, or with the serious, self-righteous and brutal series of Supermen, Batmen, and Human Torches; when, in an age of violence and questioned public and private morality, if we think of the many possible heroes we might have had—then we can be thankful for our silly cowboy. We could have chosen worse. (pp. 111-25)

David B. Davis, "Ten-Gallon Hero," in Amer-

ican Quarterly, *Vol. VI, No. 2, Summer, 1954, pp. 111-25.*

Bruce Serafin

[*In the following excerpt, Serafin provides a profile of the fictional cowboy, describing him as both innocent and violent.*]

Probably most people have read cowboy stories or seen cowboy movies at one time or another, and while their appeal is usually associated with childhood, it can extend well into adult life, as anybody knows who has spent time in the libraries of small towns in British Columbia and Alberta. Go into any of these libraries—which are usually located in one storey buildings and have a couple of teenagers wandering around in them and an old man wearing a white tee shirt who sits sleeping at a table—and what you will find besides the usual assortment of books is a revolving rack containing nothing but paperback Westerns. The titles all have the same lowbrow swagger to them— *Hondo, The Tall Stranger, Ride the River, Showdown at Yellow Butte*—and the books have been read and re-read to the point where many of them are falling apart. The librarian will tell you that the people who read these books are adult men. They take them out four or five at a time if they can, and while they sometimes take out a reference or technical book as well, they read almost nothing else in the way of fiction. They may have their favourite authors, but in general any book of the right type will do. What they are looking for, it seems clear, is a kind of story and a way of telling that story that feeds a myth that they wish to hold on to. It is a myth that many men in North America share, I believe, and if they don't nourish it through cowboy stories as such, they very likely read the variants that the genre has produced, the most important of which is science fiction, though war stories and certain kinds of detective stories also fall into this category and are widely read. Here I am not concerned to give an analysis of this myth. What I would like to do instead is describe some of the themes that appear in cowboy stories and suggest why these themes have such an intense appeal.

When I was a boy, part of the fascination of cowboy stories lay in the idea of "sign". You knew that the hero was a hero not only because he looked like a hero and carried a gun, but also by the fact that he could get down on one knee and *read the earth*. Of all his abilities, this was the one that most excited me, since it gave him that aura of power that children envelop anybody with who has a technical competence beyond their own. The drama was always pretty much the same. If he was on a horse, the cowboy would let out a low whistle, stop, and get off; then, with the sharp attentiveness of Sherlock Holmes or Captain Cyrus Smith in *The Mysterious Island,* he would gently finger the broken branch he had spotted or else would roll a cigarette as he studied the barely legible trace of a week-old hoof-print. You could almost hear the wheels going around in his head as he pondered this scrap of information. At such moments he would be as quiet and abstracted as a mechanic, but whenever these moments appeared in cowboy stories I would tense up with delight. For here was the clue; decipher the clue and the whole story would snap into focus. This was marvelous to me, and what I have read suggests that it was marvelous as well to the first audience for Western stories, since it provided a new image of nature, one in which an intense interest attached to its tiniest details, to "a tree stump, a beaver's den, a rock, a buffalo skin, an immobile canoe, or a floating leaf," as Balzac put it in a passage in which the expressed the enthusiasm of Parisian readers for the books of Fenimore Cooper that were then coming out.

In fact, of course, the fascination of "sign" is related to that fascination with detection and technology that North American boys get their first whiff of in the Tom Swift and Hardy Boys books, for example, and later encounter in a horde of writers. That is to say, it is a *modern* fascination, and the cowboy hero is a modern type, not so much a knight dressed up in leather and jeans as a kind of combination detective-engineer. In the cowboy story you get an image of a man *at work,* and while this work is of a special kind, it remains work nonetheless. The cowboy can shoot, read "sign," hunt; he can rope steers, mend fences, and deal with Indians. His competence at what he does is total, and for the readers of cowboy stories this competence is probably the most important aspect of his character. Hence the fact that the classic cowboy story presents the hero's world as a kind of working environment, as grittily actual as the writer can make it. The wierdly shaped rocks, the harsh sun, the buzzards, the cacti, the limping horse, and saddlebags, the stale buckskin shirt and sweaty jeans of the rider—all this is presented with a deliberate matter-of-factness, as if to say that no matter how wild and grand the landscape, the cowboy is utterly at home there and notices the grandeur only out of the corner of his eye, so to speak, if he notices it at all. Naturally there is landscape description here and there—the occasional bit about a sunset, or a valley opening up before a man on a horse, say. But the real interest lies elsewhere. It lies in showing how the dirt crumbles around a bootprint after a day of rain, what snowclouds look like, where a particular mountain pass is located, etc. There is a psychological jargon which is useful here. Psychologists speak of "object-oriented" persons, and it seems certain that the people who read cowboy stories fall into the "object-oriented" camp, which in fact is the camp that all real storytellers write for. (I am thinking of writers like Kipling, Poe, H. G. Wells, Arthur C. Clarke, etc.) They are the sort of people who take motors apart and clip out interesting bits from the newspapers, who hate arguing with their wives and would rather talk about fishing tackle or how a computer works. When they read cowboy stories, they want a hero who can not only shoot, but also rub down a horse and tell the difference between wolf and coyote scat, and in the best cowboy stories—the stories of Louis L'Amour, for example—they get what they are looking for.

But to stress the detective-engineer side of the cowboy hero only gets you part of the way. There is also the warrior side, the freebooter, roving mercenary side which connects the cowboy hero to a long string of heroes that begins with Odysseus and includes in modern times such different figures as Conan the Barbarian and Philip Marlowe. Here you have to be careful. Like the others, the cowboy is definitely a freelance, and the shabby, down-at-heels quality of the freelance is often brought out in cowboy stories; however, the cynicism that tends to characterize this string of heroes is more or less absent from the cowboy. He is made of harder stuff than most of his kind, and while there is a lot of Odysseus in him (cf. John Wayne's cowboys), there is a lot of Achilles as well. The tremendous *pride* of the cowboy hero has rarely been given straightforward attention, first of all, because most commentary concentrates on the movies, which by their very nature reduce the hero's stature, and second of all, because the people who write about cowboy stories would be embarassed to admit that they had ever wanted to wear breastplates and plumed helmets. But if you read the stories of L'Amour and Max Brand, for example, you will immediately notice that the hero projects a pride as elemental as that of Homer's warriors. There is no use denying this, as some writers have done, no use pretending, for instance, that his attractiveness lies in his air of leisure, as if he were a Peter O'Toole in boots, a sort of aristocrat who goes around shooting people and repairing widows' fences. What leisurely air the cowboy might have would be nothing if it weren't for the fact that it masks the tension of a man whose pride in himself as a fighter is the central fact of his existence. This tension colours the drama from beginning to end. Think of those scenes in which the hero rides into town prepared for a shoot-out, for example. The empty doorways and dusty streets, the blank windows, hitching posts and bare false fronts all shout *danger,* but the point of these scenes, the thing that gives them their almost ballad-like quality, is that they define the cowboy: it is just this that he was meant to do—to live at just this pitch of tension and with just this much at stake. And think of the bar-room scenes, with their groups of men, their gloved hands holding cards, etc. The cowboy's quietness and leisurely air in these scenes establish his *control,* not his sense of ease, and when he finally explodes into action he is as singlemindedly murderous as Achilles on the plains of Troy.

Apart from his competence, therefore, his *tension* is the cowboy hero's single most important characteristic, and in this he joins a whole range of figures whose brooding air and animal alertness are the main things that distinguish them. Like Tarzan, for example, he may well appear calm, but he is never slack or unguarded. At the slightest movement he goes from sleep to full wakefulness, for instance, and he often seems to have eyes in the back of his head, so alert is he to the merest crunch of a twig or the taking of a breath. This doesn't just show him to be a hero; it also establishes the fact that the world in which he lives is a hard one, and can't be taken for granted even for a moment. There are two sides to this harshness. First of all, there is the primitive discomfort of the cowboy's world, which is the source of some of the most effective passages the cowboy story has to offer. The simple bedroll; the saddle which is a pillow; the heat; the bare wooden town; the utterly plain corral, hitching post, tin cup; the poor food and clothes—all this comprises an image which is especially appealing to North Americans, who probably live more comfortably than any other people in the world. The great power of this image lies in the fact that it mixes nostalgia with actuality: North Americans love comfort and have built a padded universe for themselves, but you can still get out of your car at night and feel the wind on your face and see the wilderness in front of you, and imagine what it must have been like before the roads were there and the gas stations had gone up. You can step into the wild, in fact, and as long as the wild is there, the image of the cowboy will no doubt continue to exert its power.

But along with the discomfort of the cowboy's world there is the fact that it is a violent, even cruel world. Not only does the cowboy have bandits and Indians on his back, he has the land itself to contend with. It can break his leg, drown him, or make him die of thirst. As the writers often put it, it is a pitiless land, one that cuts and kills, and this is brought out in any number of the images that you find in cowboy stories. For example: a bandit is picked off a cliff and falls onto sharp rocks; a rider is shot off a horse and with a foot still in the stirrup is dragged along the ground; another rider is reduced by thirst to slumping over his horse in the sun like a sack of potatoes; and in *Hondo*—which I believe was Louis L'Amour's first book, and to which I will return again—the hero is almost caught in a flash flood. The point to note, however, is that while the land is harsh, it is never evil. There isn't a trace of that malevolence which is associated with the urban world in detective stories, or with the jungle in stories such as *Heart of Darkness,* for instance. In fact, for all of its harshness, the world of the cowboy story is genuinely exalting, and the reason for this is that it is invariably presented as an *innocent* world. You can get lost, die of frostbite, or be shot off your horse, but in the best cowboy stories such episodes have a note in them that at least for me brings to mind the stories of Kipling, a note that comes not from blurring the harshness, but from quietly stating that this is the way things are, and there is nothing mean or evil about it.

Here you arrive at that element in cowboy stories which bothers a great many people, liberals in particular—the fact that the cowboy story seems to glorify violence and cruelty. It can't be denied that this is sometimes clearly the case. In *Hondo,* for instance, you find the following passage:

> Turning swiftly, Hondo kicked the gun from Lowe's hand, then he grabbed him by the shirt front and jerked him to his feet. Hondo smashed a right into Lowe's stomach, then shoved him away and hit him in the face with both hands. Lowe lunged, swinging, but Hondo knocked down Lowe's right and crossed over his left. Lowe staggered and Hondo walked in. . . . Hondo slapped him. It was a powerful, brutal slap that jarred Lowe to his heels and turned him half around.

Now, this is disgusting, and it is difficult to apologize for it, in the same way that it is difficult to apologize for similar passages in Kipling. The only thing that a reader could possibly get from such a passage is a cheap bit of power. Yet it has to be said that episodes of this kind are rare in cowboy stories, and I feel certain that they would have stood out for me as a boy as much as they do now. Considering the genre as a whole, in fact, I would say that what irritates some readers isn't so much the violence of the hero as it is his innocence—or rather, that combination of

violence and innocence which has been the mark of the cowboy hero right from the start. Let me explain what I mean.

The cowboy is utterly bound up with his world: he can't be separated from it. He is as much a part of it as are the Indians and horses who share it with him. Only in the stories specifically aimed at children do you get characters who wear bright-coloured handkerchiefs and silver spurs, characters who belong to the world of picture books and cap pistols rather than the actual world of the West. In the stories I am examining here, on the other hand, everything emphasizes how much a *part* of the natural world the hero is. His clothes, for example, aren't shiny and bright: they are dusty and stale, and faded to a neutral colour that loses itself against the desert. When he drinks from a spring, he falls to his hands and knees and laps the water like an animal, and as I have shown, he has an animal's alertness as well: that ability to go from utter immobility to explosive action in the space of a second. There is also the fact that he "resembles" the land: his face and body are hard, hint at violence, and with their combination of tension and calmness demand study and reveal "sign" to those who know how to read what is there. (In *Hondo,* for example, there is a shiny spot on Hondo's jeans that tells the woman observing him that Hondo must have worn *two* guns at one time.) And then there is the taciturnity of the cowboy hero. This has been the subject of many jokes (the cowboy with a lantern jaw who says "Yup" and "Nope" when he isn't squirting tobacco juice), but they are urban jokes, with an urban sneer in them, since anybody who has spent time in the bush knows how still it is, and how out of place a talkative person becomes after a few days. However, these facts by themselves are not all that important. What really matters is that in the cowboy story nature is at once innocent and violent, and this extends to the man who inhabits it. It is this that liberals jump on, and for good reason.

The most important feature of the cowboy landscape is the miles upon miles of *distance* through which the hero moves. He has his being in a world of virtually limitless space, and this has an effect on who he is and what his actions amount to which is easy to sense but difficult to pin down in words. One way of expressing it is to say that all of his actions—from rolling a cigarette to fighting an Indian—have an elegaic or poetic significance. They occur in a world of silence and emptiness, a world in which very little happens from one hour to the next, and the result is that they take on that almost ritualistic quality which marks anybody's behaviour—the behaviour of an Eskimo out hunting, for instance—when it appears drastically simplified in comparison to our own. Everything is stripped down and given a sort of heroic, matter-of-fact resonance. Whatever the cowboy hero does, therefore, it seems elemental: whether it is making a fire or killing a man, it has no ethical or moral implications, as if all that distance and silence somehow swallowed up such implications, made them beside the point. If you wanted to reduce it to a formula, you could say: *where there is distance there cannot be evil.*

Now, a great deal of the poetry of cowboy stories relies on

this formula. Take, for example, what is called in *Hondo* the cowboy's "buried core of tenderness." This core of tenderness—which might be thought of as the "truth" about the cowboy—only properly manifests itself in a setting of sky and distance. Seen in a crowded room, the cowboy appears hard and dangerous, but once he is on his horse and dwindling to a dot on the horizon, a sort of poetry attaches to his image, as if the sky itself were memorializing him. Similarly, if the hero's sidekick dies in the cowboy story, he is buried in the open and the long grass of the plains become his monument. Gentleness, tenderness and innocence, in short, are all communicated in the cowboy story in terms of space and distance, whereas evil and malevolence are a matter of bar-rooms and back offices, i.e., places where intimacy is unavoidable and where the elemental quality of the cowboy is forced to contract into an "alert hardness," a "dangerous quiet," etc. Now this is fine in the world of the cowboy story—but *only* in that world; when a figure like the cowboy hero is forced to deal intimately with people you have problems, and it is here that the political argument comes in.

Take the cowboy hero out of his appropriate surroundings and he becomes an eccentric: a hardbitten, laconic egotist, with an unbounded sense of his own worth and a complete inability to communicate with anybody who doesn't appreciate that worth. Certainly he is innocent, but what this innocence amounts to in company is a sort of *bon enfant* brutality that everybody else is supposed to take into account and treat with respect. He is responsible only to himself, and if he steps in and helps somebody out, it is because he perceives that person as weaker than himself and likely to brim with gratitude at what he does. When there are complications, he moves on. Everything that means collective effort is beyond him, whether it is raising a family or becoming a member of a political community. He has a "buried core of tenderness," but the whole point about this buried core of tenderness is that it *is* buried. The cowboy demands to be deciphered, studied: he hates talking about himself and in fact is incapable of doing so—all he can do is *display* himself. In intimate surroundings he falls back on a bundle of mannerisms—a way of moving his mouth, a way of looking out the window—and it is the other person (the widow, the boy) who has to make the effort of communication. Ultimately, in fact, he is vivacious and sociable only when he is among people like himself, sidekicks who will respect his eccentricity and ask nothing of him that might impinge on his essential selfishness.

This is a disillusioned picture of the cowboy hero, but it is an important one; it suggests something of what happens when the image of the cowboy hero is held up as a model for real life. It doesn't work. In real life you cannot be innocent and violent at the same time without appearing like a kid, with all of the kid's willfulness and self-righteousness, not to mention his baffled impulse toward tenderness and stony refusal to explain himself. If you remain adolescent into middle age you become a *character,* and it is a fact that American culture at least is jam-packed with characters, men who refuse to grow up, who hang onto their innocence with their fingernails and confuse brooding with seriousness, a "tough guy" pose with a

sense of responsibility. Yet at the same time there is a political side to all this, and when you examine that political side carefully, the image of the cowboy hero begins to look a bit better. The ideology of the left is an urban ideology. By and large, leftists don't ride horses, they don't own guns, and they aren't especially taciturn. In fact, becoming "politicized" tends to mean becoming aware of the fact that you live with other people and that you have to learn how to communicate with them, i.e., that there is no such thing as being responsible only to yourself. Anybody who says, "I'm doing alright, so don't ask me to get involved," is by definition not a leftist. He is a bit of an innocent, and dangerous for that very reason. Committees, newsletters, rallies, protests—all these activities are collective activities that demand a kind of loss of innocence in the participants, and they are precisely the sort of activities that it is next to impossible to imagine the cowboy hero participating in. The image of the cowboy hero provides a sort of mooring that I think ought not to be underestimated. Certainly it is an inadequate image in many ways, and who would deny that? But at least it is an image which stands for a radical freedom and equality, for *individual* courage, and if only for that reason it is an image that one can respect.

However that may be, I don't want to end this essay on that note. When I was a boy, I read cowboy stories because they presented me with a world that I very much wished to enter. It was a world of guns and violence (and the guns and violence were necessary if I was to get any enjoyment out of the story), but even more it was a world of wolves and deserts, of men in ponchoes riding shaggy horses through snow, of campfires made in the rain and nights spent sleeping on the ground. I grew up close to the bush, and while I read many other things beside cowboy stories, it was in cowboy stories that I first saw reflected something of the world that I actually knew. In Old Hinton there were Indians who rode bareback, with their long legs dangling from either side of the horse, and I myself would carry a B.B. gun when I went into the woods and explored a creek up into the hills. The silence of the winter woods and the intense, aromatic heat of summer, these were available between the lines, as it were, when I read cowboy stories. In short, like everybody else, I responded to the poetry of the stories as much as to the drama, and in fact the poetry and drama were intertwined, since only a free man on a horse could live in such a way as to make the poetry available to me. This doesn't excuse the simplifications of the cowboy story, but it does make the genre valid and worth holding on to, I think. For, crude though it is, the cowboy story has the power to make people dream of a world which is wild to the point of harshness and yet innocent and entirely accessible, and for this reason there is a sense in which all arguments against it are somehow beside the point, including the arguments I have advanced here. Once we have "grown up," we cannot go back to that world, however much we may wish to, but it is something to have known that world at least, and to carry it with you for those nights when only the image of a river and a stand of trees can bring you sleep. (pp. 3-9)

Bruce Serafin, "Cowboy Stories," in West Coast Review, *Vol. 18, June, 1983, pp. 3-9.*

Mody C. Boatright

[*Boatright was an American educator and critic. In the following excerpt, he discusses the portrayal of cowboys in the late nineteenth-century novels of Joseph E. Badger, Prentiss Ingraham, and William G. Patten.*]

If the writer seeking a mass audience is to be successful, he must present his characters in relation to the beliefs and values that this audience holds. This does not mean that he must relate them to a consistent social philosophy. For the intellectual constructs of philosophers, historians, and other learned men become fragmented, broken into myths, symbols, and slogans, and reach the masses as a series of tenets and attitudes often inconsistent with each other. It is by appealing to these attitudes, which he may in fact subscribe to, that the writer makes his characters emotionally satisfying to his audience.

The nineteenth-century writer who wished to present the cowboy in a favorable light to a mass audience had to find some way to relate him to popular values. The first attempt to solve the problem relied on a series of beliefs derived, in part through the Romantic Movement, from a primitivistic social theory popular in Europe in parts of the seventeenth and eighteenth centuries. This philosophy held, in brief, that the earlier forms of social organization were superior to later forms. Thus, an agricultural society was better than an industrial society; a pastoral society was better than an agricultural society; and a savage society was best of all. Hence the noble savage.

The good life was a simple life, lived close to nature, in which all man's natural desires were satisfied. Nature itself, whether thought of as natural law or as natural inclination, was a sufficient guide to the good life. Hence there was no need for elaborate instruction in morals. Indeed, man-made moral systems, being largely sophistry and pedantic learning, more often obscured than enlightened. The simple life lived close to nature was conducive not only to virtue, honor, and happiness, but to physical health as well. Man was naturally endowed, too, with a feeling for beauty and deformity and needed no refinement to respond to the sublime—particularly to the sublimity of nature, which was superior to the sublimity of art.

Civilized man had fallen from his former primitive excellence, and his only hope for redemption was in a return to his early simplicity. For civilization in creating an economic surplus had brought about luxury, with its long train of attendant evils. Luxury had created expensive and artificial tastes and promoted greed manifested in land monopoly, rapine, and fraud. The increasing complexity of society had reduced the freedom of the individual, for freedom was conceived of as consisting in the absence of external restraint, not in the number of alternatives present. Luxury had also created an effete society, governed not by natural human relationships, but by convention, which tended to deprive men of their masculinity and women of their natural social role. The people of the western states should, therefore, be superior to the people of the eastern states.

Many of these ideas are to be found in the writings about the American cowboy. The student of popular culture will not be surprised to find them advocated and contradicted in the same work.

The earliest novel in English I have been able to find with a cattle country setting is William Bushnell's *The Hermit of the Colorado Hills,* published in 1864. This book owes something to Lord Byron and something to Mrs. Radcliffe. The central character, suffering from disappointment in love and remorse for his crimes (his attempt to abduct the woman who had rejected him resulted in her death), becomes the hermit. "Years ago, girl," he says, "I turned my back on my home and swore never to befriend one of my people, even if dying at my door." He nevertheless befriends the girl (he knows by a ring on her finger that she is the daughter of the woman he loved), and thus restores his humanity.

The agents of evil that threaten the rancher are Indians (noble savages occur, but they are rare among the Comanche and Apache), who fear the Hermit, believing that he is a great medicine man in command of supernatural power. The cowboys, consistently called *herders,* play a subsidiary role in the plot, but they are warmly praised for their innocent nobility. They have responded to the ennobling influence of nature.

This chord is struck near the beginning of the story: "What a glorious dream of freedom on the Pampas! Where can the mind, heart, lungs—ay, and the very soul, so drink in a realizing sense of freedom—so full of the perfect expansion that is typical of what we call the infinite."

After a lyric description of the landscape covered with wild flowers, the author proceeds:

> There is no more certain proof to a thinking mind that our good mother Nature intended that the wilderness should be made a home for man—that it should yield bountiful stores of golden grain, and made to blossom like a rose, than the fact that she has created a race of hardy and dauntless men, who throwing aside the trammels of civilized life, and scorning luxuries, boldly compete for the honor of primitive pioneership.

He singles out for special praise Daniel Boone, "nearly forgotten, who planted for the wealth-seekers who followed him to reap."

> Among these hardy and dauntless men are the herdsmen. They are the very picture of health, muscular beasts, daring and graceful as they dash headlong among their unbroken herds. Untrained in schools of fashionable etiquette and effiminacy, uncursed with luxury, conditioned and educated to animal hardships, they get, being with their beasts, truer hearts and a more perfect sense of honor, than many who quibble all a while. . . . There is no half way with the herdsman. Blood alone can pay for blood. Generous to a fault, daring even to rashness, tender hearted even to tears, but stern as death itself, he has made his mark upon the histronic [*sic*] pages of the south-western border, and written his name on the battle fields of Texas and Mexico.

In the use of primitivistic motifs in the interpretation of

Western American life, Bushnell was following a long established tradition. His orginality consisted in the application of these motifs to the cowboy. In making this application he established a lasting precedent, for in the decades that followed, the conventional *persona* of nature's nobleman would become a man in boots and chaps, armed with a six-shooter and mounted on a western pony.

Bushnell, however, had in this respect no immediate successors. Joseph E. Badger, Jr., a prolific writer for Beadle and Adams, turned to the cattle country in 1879, and in 1884 published his best work on this theme. *The Prairie Ranch; or, the Young Cattle Herders* is essentially a ranch country idyl. As a means of conveying to young eastern readers some idea of how ranching was carried on, Badger has two brothers, Ross and Arthur Duncan, spend the fall and winter on a ranch with their cousin, Walter Harvey, whose mother has died, leaving no white woman in the house.

It is a pleasant visit during which the boys are introduced to the ranch buildings and equipment; witness horsebreaking by an expert Mexican rider named Pedillo; take part in a roundup; witness marking and branding; see the mavericks peacefully prorated among the ranchmen (except one five-year-old bull, whose ownership is determined by a roping contest); go on an antelope hunt; camp out on a fishing trip and are serenaded by coyotes, which, Walter assures the tenderfeet, are about as dangerous as so many rats; go with a herd up the trail, witnessing a stampede on the way; and arrive safely at River Bend, Kansas, where one of the cowboys drinks too much, where Pedillo loses his money at monte, and where the herd is sold for eight thousand dollars in cash.

At one place Badger introduces an incident to satirize wild-west fiction, and since he was one of the most active producers of this fiction, had a predilection for highly complicated, melodramatic plots, and was soon to perpetrate such titles as *Solomn Saul, the Sad Man from San Saba; Big Bandy, the Brigader of Brimstone Butte;* and *Daddy Dead-Eye, the Despot of Dew Drop,* he exhibits a capacity for self-ridicule I have not found among his peers. When Walter comes into camp at night to find his cousins waiting with drawn six-shooters, he says: "I expected to find you hid under your blankets, bewailing the unlucky stars that led you out here to fall untimely victims of the Horrible Howler of the Pathless Plains. I'm glad to see you're better grit."

In *The Prairie Ranch* Badger makes one concession to the tradition of violence. In River Bend the cowboy who drank too much talks indiscreetly about the money Walter is carrying home. This is reported to Walter, and when he and his men are overtaken on the road by a stranger who says he wishes to travel back to Texas with them, they disarm him and hold him under arrest, all of which he takes in perfect good humor. Later they are attacked by four men. They release the stranger, who joins in fighting the attackers, three of whom are killed and the other wounded. They are real bandits. The stranger is eventually revealed as the brother of Walter's father. He had got wind of the planned robbery and had overtaken the cowboys to

forestall it. Then, too, he wanted to visit his brother, whom he had not seen in a long time.

These Kansas bandits are the only malefactors in the story. The cowboys are amiable and faithful to their employers. The peaceful division of the mavericks has been mentioned. There is no conflict over grass or water. No Indians disturb the tranquillity of the region. No Mexican bandits attempt to raid the livestock or carry off the women. No rustlers infest the range. The total impression is that of a peaceful community such as the primitivists imagined to exist in pristine times when there was plenty of land and men dwelt in peaceful and harmonious simplicity, uncorrupted by luxury. But in spite of this idyllic quality, we have in *The Prairie Ranch* the most realistic fictional depiction of life in the cattle country before *The Log of a Cowboy.*

Physical health was not the least of the virtues attributed to primitive living. Cowboys of the subliterature of the nineteenth century are never sick, and they recover from their wounds with surprising rapidity. Primitivist thought on this subject received sanction from the medical profession when hundreds of patients, especially those suffering from respiratory diseases, were advised to go West. Examples include Sidney Lanier, Frederick Remington, Owen Wister, and Sidney Porter. The health-seeker became a stock character in Western fiction. His illness might be merely a device to account for his presence in the West, but more often than not he recovered his health and thus testified to the therapeutic qualities of the western climate and way of life.

This is the theme of Edward S. Ellis in *Across Texas* (1894). Herbert Watrous, son of a wealthy New Yorker, suffering from symptoms of "consumption," is advised by his physician to forego entrance to Yale for a year and travel for his health. After considering southern Europe or an ocean voyage, the doctor advises a trip through the American Southwest. Young Watrous is to be accompanied by his friend Nick Ribsam (who in a previous work had hunted moose with him in Maine).

They come to San Antonio by train, where they present their letter of credit to a banker, Mr. Lord, who, coincidentally, is considering the purchase of some ranch property in New Mexico and is preparing to send two of his trusted cowboys to inspect it.

The narrative is mainly concerned with the journey, including adventures with horse thieves and Apaches. Certain chapters, particularly those on Austin and San Antonio, read much like a travelogue. Along the way the men explain their work, and the author intersperses comments in praise of the cowboys. "Men trained in the profession of cowboy think and act quickly." They "were governed by that devotion which belongs to chivalry. There was not one who would not have protected the youth with his life."

But the reader is not permitted to forget the purpose of the journey. The boys had barely reached San Antonio when they were told by Mr. Lord that the city was "a resort for invalids threatened with or suffering from pulmonary weakness, who find the mild equitable climate very helpful. He had known cases in which it had wrought a complete cure." Herbert "showed an improvement within twenty-four hours after arrival in the city of the Alamo."

Climate, however, was only one factor in Herbert's recovery.

> You [the reader] will remember the real cause of Herbert Watrous' journey across Texas, which was to regain his health that was seriously threatened by his bad habits and rapid growth. While he received vast benefit from breathing the pure air of the South-west, it was his forced march, as it may be called, to New Mexico that did the splendid work for him.
>
> The continuous exercise, the crystalline atmosphere, the deep refreshing sleep, the abstention from tobacco [this is the first mention of tobacco, and the only bad habit apparent in the book is studiousness], nourishing food (which, though only partially cooked and eaten at long intervals, was the best diet he could have obtained), in short the "roughing it," in the truest sense, was the "elixir of life," and wrought a change in the young man which, could his parents have witnessed, they would have pronounced marvelous.

The Prairie Ranch and *Across Texas* were intended for juvenile readers. In both, events are reported as witnessed by boys of about eighteen years. In neither is there a hero in the popular sense of the word. Before the cowboy could be made the kind of hero the readers of dime novels and popular weeklies had come to expect, he must be given the major role and allowed to engage in activities other than his routine duties as cowhand. It did not require unusual originality to substitute the fighting cowboy for the fighting scout—the most popular Wild West hero of the seventies and eighties. But even this required caution. The writer was confronted by the same problem that had puzzled Cooper and his immediate successors in the treatment of the frontiersman. Assuming that a love interest involving a genteel heroine was essential to the novel, the problem was to provide her with a suitable lover. In the Leatherstocking tales Cooper had introduced a genteel hero and had left the frontiersman, whose role was what Scott called "the principal personage," as distinguished from the technical hero, in celibacy. In *The Pioneers* Cooper had introduced in Oliver Effinghan a gentleman wearing the garb of a hunter, and Edward S. Ellis in *Seth Jones* had made elaborate use of the same device. After many adventures and much mystification, the disguise, including dialect, is thrown off, and a gentleman worthy of the heroine stands revealed.

Prentiss Ingraham in *Crimson Kate, the Girl Trailer; or, The Cowboy's Triumph,* 1881, apparently his first cowboy novel, had employed a modification of this strategy. The hero, Lester Langdon, is a college-educated gentleman from the East who has come to Texas to be a cowboy. He becomes expert in the skills required, but his language, manner, and bearing distinguished him from the native Texans. There is no secret about his background. Early in the story he rescues the General's daughter by killing one of her abductors and roping the horse upon which she is bound. This done, he introduces himself:

> "My name is Lester Langdon, and I am but a poor cowboy."
>
> "You are a brave one and a gentleman, be your calling what it may."

Later in the story Lester meets the Hermit, who is really Mabry Monkton, a cousin of the General. "Who are you?" asks Monkton.

> "A cowboy."
>
> "You are not one of the rough kind; Texas is not your home."
>
> "No, my home is in the East, but I live in Texas now."

The complicated plot centers around the efforts of Lester's cousin, Loyd Langdon, to do away with him and inherit the estate. He brings false charges of murder against Lester, whose commission in the army (granted as a reward for rescuing Lillian) is revoked, and he is sentenced to die. A remark by Monkton further reveals Ingraham's caution. "Don't call him cowboy, for he was regularly commissioned as an army officer and will be again as soon as the truth is known." After many incidents in which Lester proves adept in wearing disguises and speaking the language of those he impersonates, the truth is known and he inherits the estate.

He is not to marry Lillian, however, but Crimson Kate, introduced relatively late in the story. She is a white girl, ultimately revealed as the daughter of Loyd Langdon, long held in captivity by the Indians. She comes to the army camp to warn of an impending attack, led by a white renegade, who turns out to be Loyd. She is an expert trailer and readily leads the troops to the Indian encampment. After the Indians are defeated and Loyd is killed, Lester puts Kate under the tutelage of a governess, and, we are told in the conclusion, eventually marries her.

For the hero of his next cowboy novel Ingraham used a living person, as he had done frequently, particularly in his numerous fictional stories about Buffalo Bill. At the time *Crimson Kate* was published, William Levi Taylor was a cowboy on Cody's Nebraska ranch. He had been born at Fredericksburg, Texas, in 1857, the son of a Confederate cavalryman, who was killed in the war. "I was dependent upon myself," he said, "when ordinary children are still in the nursery." He went to work as a cowhand, and by the time he was fourteen years old was "able to ride and rope with some of the best of them." Like many Texas cowboys of his generation, he followed the cattle industry north and was a cowboy on Cody's ranch when the Old Glory celebration took place in 1882. He was a member of Cody's Wild West from the beginning. His performances gained wide acclaim. He was billed as "Buck Taylor, King of the Cowboys," a cognomen which by 1887 would be an asset on the title page of a Beadle novel.

In *Buck Taylor, King of the Cowboys; or, The Raiders and the Rangers. A Story of the Wild and Thrilling Life of William L. Taylor,* a story parading as biography, there was no reason to conceal Taylor's background. He is presented as a native Texas cowboy with little formal schooling, whose language, however, is as grammatically correct as

Ingraham's own. But as a working cowhand he could hardly have had the wild and thrilling adventures Ingraham's readers craved. He must leave the ranch, and for laudable reasons. "His uncle had hoped to keep him upon his large ranch, for Buck soon became noted as the best one of the cowboy herders; but the youth was anxious to get beyond the circle of a ranch's herd of cattle." Therefore at the age of eighteen he takes his "old fashioned rifle," calls his dog named Vermifuge, and mounting his scrawny horse named Snakeroot rides off toward the Rio Grande to enlist in McNally's [*sic*] Texas Rangers.

He is not long in demonstrating his prowess. The ridicule of a veteran Ranger, Sal Bradford, leads to a fistfight in which Buck is victorious, and they become fast friends. Buck wins a shooting match, rides an outlaw horse, and, to secure a better mount than Snakeroot, goes in search of a fine roan mustang that had eluded all efforts to capture him. Buck finds three Indians also looking for the roan. He waits until they have trapped him, then kills two Indians and wounds a third, whom he takes care of until he is able to travel and then sends him away. This is Mad Wolf, a noble savage, who later helps Buck escape from captivity. When Buck returns riding the stallion and bearing two scalps, he is welcomed by the Rangers as a peer.

In the course of the story Buck fights against Indians and Rafael's Raiders, a band of Mexican bandits, who have a spy in McNally's company. This man, really one Rodriguez, going under the name of Roddy Armstrong, thinking he has killed Buck (Buck had removed the bullets from Roddy's six-shooter) has him buried. Buck escapes from the shallow grave, and without food walks nearly two hundred miles to camp. This requires three days. Buck later fools a band of Indians by donning in succession five costumes and riding five different horses. Another example of his cleverness brings on the denouement. Rafael is known to watch the Rangers through field glasses from his stronghold. Upon Buck's proposal, he and McNally stage a quarrel in pantomime; Buck draws and fires and McNally falls. Buck mounts and flees. Rafael attacks. He is met and many of his men are killed.

When Ingraham turned to Buck Taylor again in 1891 to produce five novels in rapid succession, he abandoned all condescension and made the series in effect a eulogy to the cowboy. Buck enters as an established hero. In *Buck Taylor, the Saddle King; or, The Lasso Rangers' League* (1891), he is described in these words:

> He was in person over six feet in height by several inches, with a slender form, but athletic, broad shoulders, and the very *beau ideal* of a Texas cowboy.

> He was dressed in somewhat gaudy attire, with a watch and chain, diamond pin in his scarf, representing a miniature spur, and upon the small finger of his hand was a ring, the design being a horseshoe of rubies.

> About his broad-brimmed dove-colored sombrero was circled a miniature lariat so that spur, horseshoe, and lasso designated his calling.

> In the belt were a handsome pair of revolvers

> and a bowie knife, while upon a hook on one side hung a lariat of the very finest manufacture.

> His face was one to remember when once seen, beardless, youthful, yet full of character and fearlessness, amounting to reckless daring.

In *The Cowboy Clan; or, The Tigress of Texas* (1891), Taylor and his men

> were proud to be called "Texas cowboys" and knew the country perfectly.

> They could follow a trail as well as an Indian, ride even better, throw a lasso unerringly and shoot straight to dead center every time.

> A reckless lot of men they were, light-hearted, entirely fearless, generous, noble in the treatment of a friend or fallen foe, and though feared by evil-doers and red-skins, they were admired and respected by the soldiers and the people of the settlements.

In *Buck Taylor, the Saddle King,* Buck admits

> that a great many wicked men have crept into the ranks of our cowboy bands; but there are plenty of them who are true as steel and honest as they can be. . . . We lead a wild life, get hard knocks, rough usage and our lives are in constant peril, and the settling of a difficulty is an appeal to revolver or knife; but after all we are not as black as we are painted.

Taylor and his men are attached to an army post near the Mexican border as "government herders." "I am," he explains, "chief of the cowboys for the Government herd of cattle, only I consented to do a little extra work, you see." This extra work, which is the sole concern of the novels, is pursuing and fighting bands of outlaws who steal and rob and abduct women. There is nothing to impugn the integrity or the efficiency of the army, but the implication is unmistakable that for the job to be done the cowboys are superior to the troopers. This superiority stems partly from their superior knowledge of the country, partly from their superior skill in the use of weapons, including their peculiar weapon, the lasso (it is the means by which Buck kills Tiger Tom), and partly from their greater resourcefulness. Taylor's cleverness matches his prowess. For instance, he is captured by two of the outlaw band. He convinces them that he has gone over to their side and offers them whiskey from a bottle he carried in his saddle bag. The whiskey is drugged and they are soon in his power.

He carried the liquor for just such emergencies, for he never drank, not even a mint julep. His relations with women are scrupulously honorable. He cannot fall in love, first, because even Prentiss Ingraham cannot take wide liberties with the marital facts of a well-known personality, and, second, because he must not marry, but must remain free for further adventures in the sequel.

Ingraham's women, although frequently requiring rescue from the villains who capture them, more often for ransom than for lust, combine the accomplishments of the East with the athleticism of the West. Valerie Tracy, or Trescott as her husband's name turns out to be, was an accomplished musician from a cultured New Orleans family. Indeed, her love of music was her undoing, for it was the fine singing voice of the villain that first attracted her. In *The Cowboy Clan* she plays the guitar and sings, one of her songs being "The Texan Cowboy's" song, probably Ingraham's own composition, only the refrain of which is given:

> Lie down now cattle, don't heed any rattle,
> But quietly rest until morn.
> For if you skeedaddle, we'll jump in the saddle
> And head you off, sure as you are born.

The locally nurtured ranch girl is exemplified by Belle Hassan, described in *Buck Taylor, the Saddle King* as

> fearless as an Indian, and riding like one, a deadly shot with rifle, revolver, bow and arrow, and throwing a lasso unerringly. Belle Hassan was the admiration of all the bold spirits who knew her, and yet under her accomplished mother's tuition, she had become a good student, a devoted reader, a fair artist, and a musician of no mean pretensions, her voice being strangely pathetic and soft in tone.

But in spite of Belle's ability to ride and shoot, she, like many a girl in the Beadle novels, gets herself captured on different occasions by Indians and outlaws, thus providing the hero with opportunities to display his prowess.

Ingraham made no further use of Buck Taylor after 1893, when Taylor left Buffalo Bill's Wild West. He wrote other cowboy novels, including *The Cowboy Clan in Cuba* (1897), in which the cowboys under the leadership of Charlie Chase rescue Lucita and Harry Agramonte from a firing squad. But the works here considered epitomize Ingraham's treatment of the cowboy as a hero. In *Crimson Kate*, 1883, the hero is an educated eastern gentleman who has gone West "a cowboy for to be." In *Buck Taylor, King of the Cowboys*, purporting to be a biography, Taylor is described as a heroic character, who has attained on the cattle range the skills that make him McNally's leading Ranger, but he is commended for wanting to be more than a cowboy. It is more honorific to be a Texas Ranger. In the novels of 1891 Buck and his band are proud to be known as cowboys. Their status is above that of soldiers.

The cowboy warrior band appears in the novels of other writers, including Sam Hall (Buckskin Sam), who in *The Brazos Tigers; or, The Minute Men of Fort Belknap* (1882) inserts a defense of Texas cowboys:

> Many of them are now engaged in driving the immense herds of cattle and horses from Texas north, through the Indian Nation, to the great stock markets, and let me say that these so-called cowboys have been greatly traduced by the American press; for as a class, they are noble, brave, and fearless men, liberal to a fault, tender-hearted, and devoted to each other. In fact, few men can be found, who lead a roaming life in nature's garden, who will not divide their little all with anyone who is in need. Fewer still would desert a friend, or take advantage of an enemy.
>
> If, when they reach town, they are poisoned with "prussic acid and bug juice" until they become

insane and use the weapons they are obliged to carry, too freely—more in sport than otherwise—it is the fault of the town that permits the sale of the vile poison, more than of the poor fellows, whose protracted privation of continuous watchfulness by day and night, naturally causes them to take advantage of a day's rest to have a free and easy jamboree.

But Hall's concern in the story is not with cowboys having a free and easy jamboree in town, but with them as a band of men fighting Indians and outlaws on the range.

The cowboy warrior band, while maintaining its identity, has, like Ingraham's cowboy herders and Hall's Minute Men of Fort Belknap, a quasi-military status and functions under a leader, who overshadows yet represents the group. The lone rider was to emerge in the works of William G. Patten, best known as the creator of Dick Merriwell. The cowboy knight errant is mobile in that he is not committed to a fixed residence and avoids personal involvement with the other characters in the story. As he rides about, he is always ready to take a hand in behalf of the abused and oppressed weak, male or female.

Patten did not create this character overnight, but foreshadowed him in Hustler Harry of *Hustler Harry, the Cowboy Sport; or, Daring Dan Shark's General Delivery*, apparently his first cowboy hero (1889). Harry Hanson, to give him his real name seldom used in the story, "drapped" down from High Notch into Cimarron "on the lookout for sport." He is not long in finding it. He enters a saloon (although he does not drink) and finds the local bully and badman, Hickory Bill, abusing a Negro. He promptly knocks him down and throws him out. The reader is not surprised, for Harry is described as

> a man at least six feet tall and "built from the ground up." Not a thickset, ox-like figure, but one which combined great strength with manly grace. . . . Every limb was rounded and muscular, yet was not overburdened or cumbersome . . . the square, full lower jaw denoted a determined, unswerving nature. His eyes were blue and filled with a half-mirthful yet wholly unfathomable light.

Hustler Harry glories in being a cowboy, declaring,

> "Fact is, if I war rollin' in yeller wealth, I never cu'd give up the range. Just one whiff of the trail, one beller from the hurd, one rattle of long horns set my blood to bilin' and seethin' like I was set fair onto er red-hot furnace an er nigger fireman shovin' in pitchpine an' rosin fer all he was worth."

His ebullience is manifest in frequent boasting reminiscent of the humor of the Old Southwest.

> "I'm er high old maverick fer fun, an' if ye'eve got anything of ther kind in this hyer burgh, u's just trot it out."
>
> "I'm Hustler Harry, ther Hard Nut to Crack from High Notch, an' I'm just a wild maverick on ther stampede w'en I gits ter goin'. If ary of you critters thinks he can put his brand onto me,

just let him tackle ther job. I'm hyer ter 'muse the congregation."

"I'm Hustler Harry ther Hard Nut to Crack. Yer don't want to try any little tack-hammer on my hide. Bring out yer big sledges, an' git yer lives insured w'en yer tackle ther job."

With the help of Detective Daring Dan Shark, Harry rescues a kidnapped girl and brings the outlaws to justice, but he falls short of being the character at first represented. In the first place, he is not entirely disinterested, for he is accused of being a murderer and the leader of a band of outlaws and must clear his name. (The real villain is his double and half brother.) In the second place, he is not a real cowboy but another Seth Jones, and eventually drops his dialect and tells the girl he loves, "In fact, I tell you the truth when I say that I am a gentleman. In becoming my wife you will not have a common brainless husband. I have wealth to a limited extent. Most men would consider themselves fortunate if they possessed a fourth as much."

Whether the girl would have accepted him without this revelation is not clear, but she does accept him and thus makes him ineligible for further heroic roles.

Patten more nearly approached the cowboy knight in *Wild Vulcan the Lone Rider; or, the Rustlers of the Bad Lands. A Romance of Nebraska* (1890). The technical hero is a genuine cowboy, Paul Rickway, "one of those grand creations of the mountains and the plains, a young nobleman of nature." His rival in love goes under the name of Colonel Delos Dangler, but is in reality Lyman Mesurado, a cattle rustler. The principal personage, to use Scott's term again, is Wild Vulcan,

> . . . a strange, gloomy appearing man of mystery, the friend of every honest person, the deadly foe of outlaws and hostile Indians. Involuntarily, with a feeling of awe, the cowboys shrank away from the man sitting so silently in their midst. They had heard strange tales of the prowess of the wild man whom the redskins called the Great Thunder. It was said that single-handed he had attacked and destroyed a dozen hostile redskins, by whom he was greatly feared.

The girl, Nida, has to be rescued more than once; first by Paul, who loses her when he is attacked by an Indian, with whom he grapples and rolls into the river and is presumed to have drowned; but frequently by Wild Vulcan, who can be depended upon to make his appearance at critical times. But since it is eventually revealed that the bogus colonel has murdered Vulcan's wife and stolen his daughter, the Lone Rider, like Hustler Harry, is less disinterested than at first appears.

In this respect he differs from Cowboy Chris, the hero of a half-dozen or more Half Dime novels Patten published under the pseudonym of William West Wilder from 1889 to 1899.

In *Cowboy Chris, the Desert Centaur; or, Hawking the Human Hawk. A Story of the Arid Plains* (1897), two men are riding across the plains. One is Reuben Randall, a man possibly in his fifties, dressed as a cowboy and wearing a "Stinson" hat. The other, Christopher Comstock, in his twenties, is a "square-shouldered, finely built man" who has "the appearance of being a perfect *man*, being one of those persons women regard with frank admiration." At a distance they see a man being chased by Apaches. The younger man says, "We must take a hand someway, old man! It is our duty to aid the weaker party . . . ," to which the veteran replies, "I reckon it is our duty to send as many 'Paches as we kin to ther happy huntin' ground. We'll be doin' the kentry er mighty big favor. 'Paches an' rattlesnakes is just one and the same."

They take a hand and dispatch "several" Apaches, but they are chiefly occupied in rescuing Bessie Pike.

> "Hear me!" cried out Chris Comstock [when her abduction was discovered], placing his left hand over his heart and lifting his right hand toward heaven, "I solemnly swear never to know rest until I have solved the mystery of Little Bessie's fate and punished those who have harmed her, if she has been harmed."

He rescues her not once but twice and punishes those who have kidnapped her. He finds her father "rough and uncouth," but she seemed "refined as if she was the possessor of some education." He admits to himself that "she is a dear little creature for whose sake I would make any sacrifice, but that is no reason why I should desire to make her my wife. My wife! Ha! ha! ha! I will not marry for years, if ever. I am beginning to taste the sweets of a roving life, and I shall not settle down for years to come." Besides, Bessie has a worthy lover in Conrad Vincent, whose failure to rescue her was not attributable to any fault of his own.

But Conrad and Bessie are not to marry until the end of the sequel, *Cowboy Chris, the Vengeance Volunteer; or, the Death Hunt Pards. A Romance of Arizona* (1898). Here she is kidnapped again, this time by a villain named Boone, who murders her father and hopes, by forcing Bessie to marry him, to acquire the estate. Boone disposed of, Chris attends the wedding as best man. He is left free to ride forth like a knight of the Round Table, rescuing other Bessies, but with this difference: women will play little part in his roving life except as they provide wrongs to be redressed. Cowboy Chris will have successors.

By the end of the nineteenth century the cowboy had been admitted to the hierarchy of the heroes of the popular fiction of the American West. First introduced sympathetically as a supporting character to the technical hero and as a symbol of primal innocence, he advanced to the leadership of a warrior band (incidentally adding the lasso to the six-shooter and bowie knife as the conventional weapons of such bands), and in the nineties emerged as the knight of the mountains and plains, "whose glory was, redressing human wrong." In none of these roles, however, had he entirely superseded other western heroes. Numerically he was still overshadowed by the scout and the detective.

Nor was the cowboy a hero to all writers who made use of him as a fictional character. David Druid's Sam Strong, who appears in *Sam Strong, the Cowboy Detective; or, The Ranch Mystery* (1891), is not a cowboy at all, but a detective who brings Sikes Bowles and his cowboy band to justice. Of this band it is said, "For with one exception, all twelve men were cowboys, that lawless class of western plainsmen, to whom are chargeable so many deeds of crime and recklessness [that] are perpetrated daily." And Frederick Whittaker's cowboys are wild barbarians from wild and barbaric Texas. In *Parson Jim, King of the Cowboys; or, the Gentle Shepherd's Big Clean Out* (1882), when they reach town "crazy with excitement and drink . . . and firing all round them into the windows of the houses," the townspeople rush into hiding; that is, all except one, a young consumptive from Boston, who is beaten into insensibility for his presumption. The victim eventually recovers to become first a shepherd and then ranch foreman, in which capacity he shows the westerners how a cattle ranch ought to be run.

As Henry Nash Smith has suggested in *Virgin Land*, the cowboy hero was a son of Leatherstocking's, though considerably less garrulous than his forebear. The fiction in which he appeared followed well-established patterns, imitating that of earlier Wild West fiction, among other ways, by references to recent or contemporaneous events, such as border raids on the Rio Grande, trail driving from Texas, fence-cutting, and the Johnson County War in Montana. The action abounds in disguises; doubles, usually brothers or half brothers, are frequent; lost children and missing heirs are found and identified; secret hideouts—usually caves, but sometimes cabins in secluded canyons—are readily available. The plot is a culmination of a long train of events set in motion years before at another place. Except in the juveniles you may expect a woman to be kidnapped, sometimes by Indians but more often by a white man and his minions. His object may be marriage, prompted either by lust or by a desire to secure her property. It may be revenge. It may be to collect a ransom. The abductor is always guilty of other crimes, but he never beats or in any way physically abuses the woman. In my sampling I have found no instance of a rape and only one of seduction. (This is in Wilder's *Nobby Nat, the Tenderfoot Detective; or, the Girl Rancher's Rough Hustle* (1892), where the father of the victim is dead and she has no brother. Her Amazon sister forces a pistol-point marriage, but the girl, always delicate, pines away and dies, but not before the hero has made her a widow.) The final solution always involves violence, usually the death of the villain, though he may be permitted to escape to reappear in a sequel.

Certain taboos are almost universally observed. Good cowboys may enter saloons and take a hand in a poker game, but they never drink, even in a home where mint juleps are served. If they smoke they smoke a pipe or a cigar, never a cigarette. Even with all the kidnapping of women, there is extreme reticence about sex. Lovemaking is restrained. The hero may resort to the deceptions common in the detective story of the period. He may put on a wig and false beard and spy on the enemy; he can disable him with narcotics, and if he is in captivity he may disable or even kill his guard by any means possible; but under other circumstances he must not stab in the back or shoot from ambush. His nobility of character is also reflected in his attitude toward his horse, a noble animal of great

speed, strength, and endurance worthy of love. As Joseph E. Badger put it in *Laughing Leo; or, Spread Eagle Sam's Dandy Pard* (1887),

> Only one whose life has been passed for the greater part in the saddle can even begin to appreciate the intense love which one comes to feel for a good horse. To such a man, provided he is a *man,* not simply a brute with half the complement of legs, his horse becomes like a wife and children, so far as love and affection are concerned.
>
> (pp. 11-28)

Mody C. Boatright, "The Beginnings of Cowboy Fiction," in Southwest Review, *Vol. LI, No. 1, Winter, 1966, pp. 11-28.*

C. L. Sonnichsen

[*Sonnichsen is an American educator and critic of western fiction. In the following excerpt from his* From Hopalong to Hud, *he studies the unheroic side of the fictional cowboy.*]

"The cowboy," said Owen Wister in his introduction to *The Virginian*, "is the last romantic figure upon our soil." Wister was at least partly right. In American storytelling the cowboy has been a major attraction for almost a century, a focus for public interest on all reading levels. Contrary to the general impression, however, he was never received with unqualified admiration. Writers and readers were ambivalent about him from the start, and a strong undercurrent of disapproval or condescension balanced the fascination felt by the average reader.

In the movies, where leading men demanded and got heroic roles, he did emerge as "the instrument of a just retribution," a "swaggering, self-confident cowboy standing for law and order," a "knight-errant of the plains." But even on the screen he was ambivalent. The first cowboy character to emerge on film (*The Bandit Makes Good,* 1908) was a " 'good-bad' man," as Jon Tuska points out [in *The Filming of the West*], "a Western variation on the Raffles theme." Film historian Jack Nachbar talks about "the rebel-hero's dialectic personality" [*Focus on the Western*], and John G. Cawelti (a leading philosopher in the field) notes the "morally ambiguous character" of the horseman-hero. The Western "fable," says James K. Folsom, summing it all up, is "a metaphorical parable of the inconsistencies and contradictions which inhere in the American's paradoxical views about himself, his country, and his destiny." In short, the cowboy hero was part angel and part devil.

In discussing movie westerns it is possible to talk about myth and symbolism, the working out of Oedipal complexes, and the six-shooter as a phallic symbol. Since 1960 dozens of articles and twenty-odd books have been written about the movie western, many of them dealing with such abstruse matters. About the cowboy in novels and short stories, however, much less has been said. In this field, which provides a good deal of the raw material for movie and television westerns, the reader finds himself on lower ground. The fictional cowboy hero is not so much a mythical figure as a stereotype. True enough, a solemn Lassiter or a mysterious Shane sometimes springs full grown from the head of a Zane Grey or a Jack Schaefer, but Hopalong Cassidy is closer to the norm.

With Hopalong as a model, the specifications for hero status turn out to be quite simple. It can be demonstrated that the one and only trait which every fictional hero had to have was just plain guts. He did not have to have them at the beginning of the story or all the time or any particular time—just at the right time. He suited us because we don't seem to like perfect heroes. They bore us. We can identify best with someone who has a bad side, or some parts missing, like us. Even so, this flawed human being is still a romantic figure, as Wister said, for romantic heroes are often caught between good and evil, starting low like Lazy Hans and finishing high, changing from frog to prince, achieving wisdom or success only after supreme struggles. The point here, however, is that the negative or unheroic side of the fictional cowboy needs to be examined more closely if the truth about him is to be known.

The negative side is and always has been there. All sorts of surprises may be lurking in the enormous and only partially explored jungle of early Western fiction, but if and when all the cowboy characters of the pretelevision years are counted and classified, there will undoubtedly be more immature, uncurried, drunken, ignorant, timid, ugly, funny, and even repulsive types than true heroes in any reasonable sense of the word.

It can be argued, furthermore, that the misfits and rogues of the sixties and seventies, the focal characters of much of the fiction of recent years, are the direct descendants of these early-day caricatures. The doubts and suspicions which from the first attached themselves to the cowboy hero have not diminished. His course has, indeed, been downward, and now in the third quarter of our century he has found his place among the ineffectual, the defeated, the deluded, and even the debased.

The first question to be answered after this introduction is, "How did this descent begin?" The best explanation seems to be a desire on the part of the authors of the early westerns to tell the truth as they saw it. The nonheroic puncher was indeed the son and heir of the real old-time cowhand, the hired man on horseback who chaperoned his employer's longhorns up the Chisholm Trail and roistered in the saloons and brothels of Abilene. He was not well thought of. Most Easterners and some Westerners assumed that he was like Lord Byron: "mad, bad and dangerous to know," reckless when sober and lethal when drunk. Happy Jack Bates in B. M. Bower's *Chip of the Flying U* (1904) complains:

> I know them Eastern folks down t' the ground.
> They think cowpunchers wear horns. Yes they
> do. They think we're holy terrors and eat with
> our six-guns beside our plates—and the like of
> that. They make me plum tired.

There was much firsthand testimony to corroborate this view. Joseph G. McCoy, the founder of Abilene, Kansas, tells how these "drovers" habitually imbibed "too much poison whiskey" and indulged in all kinds of "crazy freaks and freaks more villainous than crazy." The real-life cowboy was reputed to be immature, semi-civilized, and ignorant of everything but cows, horses, and guns. His fictional counterparts down through the years never managed to free themselves from this stigma of original Western sin. When they began to figure in stories just before the year 1900, they retained some or all of their vices and eccentricities. Andy Adams (*Log of a Cowboy*, 1903) was about the only one who avoided the wild and woolly aspects of the cowboy's life-style. The urge to pull the puncher off his pedestal was almost as strong as the impulse to put him up there, and this conflict went on until the nonhero, the antihero, and the SOB took over in the 1960's.

It began to happen as early as 1897 with *Wolfville*, Alfred Henry Lewis' fantasy based on life in Tombstone, Arizona. Wolfville is a mining town, but it is set in the middle of a vast expanse of rangeland, and the narrator is "the old cattleman." Presumably he speaks the language of the cowboys of his region and embodies their attitudes. Hence, although cowboys are conspicuously absent from the scene, they are just around the corner, and they set the tone for later works of fiction which do feature the life and manners of the cowpuncher.

The first notable peculiarity of the old cattleman is his language. Ever since Henry Nash Smith pointed it out in *Virgin Land* (1950), we have realized that the use of dialect puts a man in an inferior social position. Leatherstocking's speech in Cooper's novels is "a constant reminder of his lowly origin." Even Owen Wister's Virginian, since he is an uneducated man, has to prove to Molly Wood, the schoolteacher, that he is worth her attention and respect. Lewis' old cattleman outdoes both Leatherstocking and the Virginian in his colloquial speech, using a dialect that would have astonished Cooper. It involves the use of rather high-flown language disguised by misspelling, dialect pronunciation, adjectives used in place of adverbs, and far-out metaphors:

> Woman's nacher's that emotional, says Enright to the rest of us, she's oncapable of doin' right. While she's the loveliest of created things, still sech is the infermities of her intellects that gov'ment would bog down in its most important functions if left to women.

At the same time, the old man accepts as normal and natural a standard of behavior which turns civilized notions upside down. "Jack Moore . . . does the rope work for the stranglers," he says, referring with complete casualness to the activities of the local vigilantes. The Code of the West is not mentioned, but one thinks of the Virginian hanging his best friend because the code demands it.

Under these circumstances Lewis is an outsider looking in, and although he enjoys and cultivates the old cattleman, he actually treats him with subtle condescension, listening to him as he would to a friendly Hottentot. The old man knows it, too, and sometimes make slighting remarks about "you-alls back East."

The dialect, the macabre morality, and the quirks of personality exploited in the Wolfville series became part of the equipment of later writers, and some of them equaled

In many western novels and films, outlaws rivaled the cowboy in popularity. Here, Walter Miller and his gang rob a train.

Lewis in painting their characters as frontier oddballs. *The Virginian* (1902), for example, is in the tradition, though Wister's book was far more influential than Lewis' work. Jeff, the focal character, is a better man than his fellow cowboys, but he is unlettered and says "haid" for head. When Wister examines Jeff's reactions to the plays of Shakespeare, he is patronizing an inferior, though the point is easy to miss. In *Lin McLean* (1907), the educated Easterner shows his true feelings. Lin, his best friend in Wyoming next to the Virginian, is a young man who never grew up. He has "a boy's soul in a man's body," and Wister remarks, "I looked at him and took an intimate, superior pride in feeling how much more mature I was than he, after all." He probably had a sneaking feeling of superiority to the Virginian, too, but that gentleman, ignorant as he was of Wister's world, did not have a "boy's soul" and demanded courtesy and respect.

The dialect, the eccentric characters, and the image of the cowboy as a perennial adolescent—ignorant but amusing—were standard in the early Western novels. Emerson Hough's Curly in *Heart's Desire* (1905) is Lin's blood brother. Hough, once an extremely popular writer, lived at White Oaks (Heart's Desire), New Mexico, from 1893 to 1898; he knew Pat Garrett well and missed knowing Billy the Kid by just a few years. He loved the newness of the country, enjoyed its good humor in the face of difficulties, and respected its seriousness about serious things (like horse stealing). Curly is his key figure, a delightful, red-headed cowboy who tells Hough about his comical experiences just as the old cattleman recounted his to A. H. Lewis, employing a dialect only a little less outrageous than the language of Wolfville and a philosophy only a little less upside-down. He appeared first in a series of stories written for the *Saturday Evening Post* between 1902 and 1905 (put together as a novel in 1905), and Hough loved him so much that he kept him going, transporting him to Wyoming and giving him a place in the "New West," where he encounters businessmen no better than con artists by whom he is continually "suckered again."

Curly is no hero. He is a "character"—a charming and funny character, it is true, but Hough patronizes him and exhibits his peculiarities of speech and attitude with happy condescension:

> "There's a heap of things different already from what they used to be when I first hit the cow range," says Curly. . . . "Look at the lawyers and doctors there is in the Territory now—and this country used to be respectable."

Curly is really a "picaro," says Carol McCool Johnson, Hough's latest biographer, or even "a barbarian and a Yahoo" by the standards of the East, but he had great staying power, and he has lived on down through the years—the engaging adolescent in chaps. As the western grew into its golden age in the teens, twenties and thirties, Zane Grey's unsmiling heroes threatened to submerge that adolescent, but Lin and Curly were always in there defending their claims. They were often drunk and disorderly, but they managed to be amusing, and when a "sagebrush savior" came along and crowded them to the back of the stage, they played Yorick to his Hamlet and sometimes stole the show.

Clarence E. Mulford, in *Bar-20* (1906), was one who opened the doors of the saloons and kept the tradition of the wild cowboy going. When the Bar-20 cowboys (Hopalong Cassidy's outfit) come to town, "nine happy-go-lucky, dare-devil riders" crowd into Cowan's bar. "Laughter issued from the open door and the clink of glasses could be heard. They stood in picturesque groups, strong, self-reliant, humorous, virile." In about five minutes they are involved in a gun battle, but they kill their enemies more in jest than in anger. And when Hopalong does a concealed enemy in, he takes time out to "lower the level of the liquor in his flask."

When the Bar-20 boys are not shooting up the opposition, they find other diversions:

> "From the bottom of my heart I pity you," called the marshal, watching them depart, a broad smile illuminating his face. "I ain't never seen none of that breed what ever left a town without empty pockets an' aching heads. . . . An' I wish I was one of 'em again," he muttered, sauntering on.

Some of Mulford's cowboys are not just wild—they are also ridiculous, and he likes to group them in pairs. Take Skinny and Lanky in *The Coming of Cassidy* (1908): "Both lean as beanpoles, Skinny stood six feet four, while Lanky was fortunate if he topped five feet by many inches." They resemble Wister's Lin and Hough's Curly in their awkwardness and immaturity, though they seem fully grown when the shooting starts.

This "passel of kids" is composed, of course, of run-of-the-mill cowhands—never intended to be heroes. But Mulford does not want even his top men to come out too near the ideal. An example is Nueces (real name Wilcox), the range detective in *On the Trail of the Tumbling T* (1935). He thinks fast and shoots fast, but he is oversized and incredibly homely. With a horse face and "a big ugly mouth," he is, in fact, so hard to look at that a hotel clerk is "almost fascinated by such an example of human homeliness." Nueces brings the crooks to justice, but his looks would disqualify him in a heroes' sweepstakes.

About the time Mulford was creating Nueces, William Sidney Porter (O. Henry) was writing stories about Texans, including cowboys, which were collected in 1907 under the title *Heart of the West*. His characters are likely to start with two strikes against them. Curly the tramp in "The Higher Abdication" is one of them. He arrives at the

Cibolo Ranch fast asleep in the ranch wagon, having chosen it in San Antonio as a good place to sleep off a drunk. Awakened at last, "up popped Curly, like some vile worm from its burrow. . . . His face was a bluish red and puffed and seamed as the cheapest round steak of the butcher. His eyes were swollen slits; his nose a pickled beet." Snarling and defiant, this human mistake goes off to sleep in a shed. After three weeks with the cowboys on the roundup, however, a "clear-faced, bronzed, smiling cowpuncher" returns, bearing almost no resemblance to Curly. He turns out to be the long-lost son of the owner.

Curly starts lower than anybody in the field of Western fiction, and at the end he is no hero—just a respectable hired man on horseback.

An author in the early days of the western who invented a real hero was likely to balance him with a comic or eccentric foil. Ernest Haycox did that in his early novels. W. C. Tuttle did it, especially in the "Henry" series with Sheriff Henry Harrison Conroy at the center (see *Wildhorse Valley*, 1938, in which the comic characters are knee-deep). The amusing sidekick became a fixture in the movies in the era of the singing cowboy. In stories he often had a partner with a different set of peculiarities. For example, look at Slats Kennedy and Rimfire Boggs in *The Bandit of the Paloduro* (1934), by Charles Ballew writing under his pseudonym of Charles H. Snow.

Slats is "six feet four inches tall, and from either front or side he was a trifle thicker than the edge of a soda cracker." His hair is "the color of a jaundiced carrot." Boggs, on the other hand, is "only five feet six, but he had breadth enough to compensate for what he lacked in height. . . . Rimfire's deeply tanned and wrinkled face invariably reflected august dignity, the proportion depending on the amount of whiskey under his belt." Boggs can quote Shakespeare and the English poets, and he makes such illuminating remarks as, "a bar of justice should not be confused with a slab of mahogany across which stimulants are passed." Although they are "the comedians of the outfit," these two do have thoughtful moments. One such instant comes when they call in a bandit named Red O'Malley to deal with the crooked sheriff. O'Malley shows up and takes care of the situation, but he turns out to be Gion Trask, Jr., a city boy with a flair for guns and gallantry. He is a hero but no cowboy. The others are cowboys but not heroes. They play Yorick to his Hamlet.

Looking forward a little, a curious reader will find a similar situation—cowboy hero, comic foil—in W. C. Tuttle's *Tumbling River Range* (1935), in which Tuttle's peripatetic rangeland sleuth Hashknife Hartley comes to the aid of Sheriff Joe Rick, who fails to appear for his own wedding, apparently because of too much whiskey. Actually he has been doped and kidnapped. Hashknife has a comrade nicknamed Sleepy who provides comic relief, but a better one is already on the ground—"Honey" Bee, the sheriff's best friend and confidant. He is a "medium-sized youth of twenty-five, with tow-colored hair, shading to a roan at the ends, blue eyes, tilted nose and a large mouth." Honey is "a top-hand cowboy, even if he was somewhat of a dreamer." Tuttle never does say so, but he might have noted that this puncher was a great big overgrown engaging boy who could just as well have come out of the pages of Wister or Hough.

Sometimes this character is not even engaging. He can be just plain ridiculous (providing he has guts somewhere in reserve). Henry Herbert Knibbs' Sundown Slim from the novel of the same name (1915) is a good sample. Sundown is a six-foot four-inch hobo. He does a little free-lance cooking when he gets the chance (which is not often), and he writes an occasional bit of doggerel verse when he gets a chance (which is too often). Knibbs, his creator, wrote verse himself. This "poor ramblin' lightnin' rod," looking, as one barroom observer puts it, "like crane in a frog-waller," is not just unprepossessing, he is also "childishly egotistical" and a "self-confessed coward." The man who ought to be the hero is John Corliss, who eventually marries the old sheepman's daughter and puts an end to the range war, but Sundown is the viewpoint character and the real "hero" of the novel. He does make a place for himself, earning the respect of the cowboys, learning to be a cowboy himself, and even winning the affections of Anita, a little Mexican girl who notices none of his handicaps and thinks he is wonderful. Sundown, however, does not change in any essential way. At the end he is still a ridiculous figure with a heart of gold whose loyalty, sincerity, and honest ignorance make everybody like him—even dogs.

Eugene Manlove Rhodes is another writer of the early period who preferred offbeat types. Known as the most knowledgeable portrayer of the real cowboy of his time, Rhodes saw him as habitually outside the law. Legal matters were in the hands of town dwellers—"God's frozen people," he called them—who didn't understand the conditions of a ranchman's life or the principles by which he lived. So Rhodes's heroes often feel the need to circumvent the law in the interests of justice. Says Pres Lewis in *The Trusty Knaves* (1933):

> Really good men, they never do much of anything—not when it's risky. Always fussing about the rules, stopping for Sunday and advice of counsel. Then, they foster a brutal prejudice against guessing, good men do. Worst of all, they wonder does it pay. That's fatal—that last. What you want is a few trusty knaves.

Rhodes's best-known trusty knave is Ross McEwen of *Pasó por Aqui* (1927), a bank robber who gives up all chance of making a get-away to take care of a Mexican family down with diptheria. His most appealing knave is Aforesaid Andrew Jackson Bates—middle-aged, balding, fiddle-footed, generous, and indomitable, who first appeared in a 1917 short story, "The Bird in the Bush." Bates explains his acquired honorific to J. E. Briscoe, who wants Aforesaid's claim in Bottle Basin.

> I've got a positive genius for bad luck—witness them opprobrious syllables, Aforesaid, wished onto me by acclamation of five States and Territories. . . . I've had all the kinds of trouble a mere single man can have, and most generally got the worst of it; but let me tell you, beloved, none of my victorious and laurel-wreathed antagonists has ever bragged about it any, and that includes the sovereign State of California, the Republic of Mexico, the Espee Railroad, the Diamond-A Cattle Company, Yavapai County, Prescott, Buckey O'Neill and the Arizona House of Reprobates, besides Montana and some few other commonwealths whose memory is now fadin' in the mists that rise down the river of Time.

Bates is a man much wanted by the authorities, deficient in personal charm, too old to be really interesting to the heroine, and afflicted with a powerful sense of humor which would always keep him from being a really heroic hero. A man who does not take himself with complete seriousness can hardly qualify. All of Rhodes's leading men are something like Bates: nonchalant, wryly funny, fond of misquoting the monuments of English literature, infinitely resourceful, willing to throw life and limb into the balance—"beyond the pale," as W. H. Hutchinson analyzes them, but fulfilling "the frontier's criterion of a man."

The ugly cowboy, the ignorant cowboy, the stupid cowboy, the lawless cowboy—they are familiar figures in Western fiction. Jeni Calder, in her 1974 discussion of Western movies *There Must Be a Lone Ranger,* calls the interest in these shaded characters "a profoundly romantic preoccupation" and quotes actor and director Robert Redford, who says he wants to make movies about "a guy who is outside society, who is flawed and a loner . . . the kind of guy who appears to be a hero but isn't." Mr. Redford should have a field day looking for plots in these early novels.

Destry of *Destry Rides Again,* perhaps the most famous of all Western heroes, could serve as a model. He is a social liability before he becomes a social asset. "You began as an industrious boy," says the judge who sends him to prison; "you end as a man who scorned any tool other than a Bowie knife or a Colt's six-shooter. You gambled for a living and fought for amusement."

Destry makes no defense: "What you said is plumb true. I been a waster, a lazy loafer, a fighter, a no-good citizen, but what I'm getting the whip for now is a lie! I never robbed the Express!"

Destry does have a useful set of guts, however, and he proves it in a most unusual way: he poses as a spineless weakling, accepting all insults and allowing himself to be branded as a coward, in order to expose the man who framed him, almost losing the girl as well as his character and reputation in bringing the guilty man to justice.

A special kind of negative hero is the rogue—the picaro—a staple item in the Western bill of fare. He could have come out of the Spanish Renaissance if the writers had ever heard of Gil Blas. Nelson Nye introduced a good example in a 1934 novel called *Wild Horse Shorty.* The scene is just south of Tucson in the Santa Cruz Valley. Shorty, a lover of horses who owns sixteen "bangtails," shows up at a country store, intent on finagling sustenance for himself and his herd on credit. Everybody knows he is a deadbeat, and it looks as if he and his equine relics are at the end of their string. He is not without friends, however. One of them says, "He's a good lad at heart—he don't mean nothin' by it; all this borryin' an' chargin's on account of his horses—he's a natural born horse lover. He jest can't help it."

Besides being a horse lover and a deadbeat, he is a con man whose "line of blarney would move a dead Indian" and something of an actor. Nye mentions "the Bill Hart look which he had taken such pains to cultivate," and he loves to appear in costume:

> He was clean and close shaved, and his five-foot-seven was clothed in rare splendor. . . . His big San Fran hat, white and red-striped shirt and cowhide boots with that dilly of a cactus painted on each were brand new.

And there were "gaudy-gay flowers" on his vest.

Shorty is not easy for his neighbors to love, but he starts a horse ranch by claiming title to land being used by a local horse-and-cattle baron, takes on two eccentric but knowledgeable partners, finds that one of his deceptively ugly horses is a champion racer, and wins all the money, plus the girl, at the end. It is almost as if Mr. Nye had announced at the beginning, "I'll show you that a cowboy doesn't have to be a hero to be interesting and successful."

The con man, of course, cannot exist independently. He has to have somebody to con, and the authors of westerns show considerable ingenuity in digging up victims. Frank X. Tolbert reached a sort of plateau in this respect in 1954 with Bigamy Jones, "tall and red haired and ornery looking" but so irresistible to women that he was married more than thirty times—"He never kept a good tally." In his defense it should be said that he never let marrying interfere with his business, "which was making a real hand."

The rangeland Romeo is sometimes a Hero in Spite of Himself. Lee Hoffman conceived such a character in 1966 in *The Legend of Blackjack Sam*. Bo Johnson enters the picture in his underwear, having jumped out of a bedroom window just ahead of a charge of buckshot. He tore the buttons off the rear flap as he departed and is plodding down the road in this unheroic condition when he encounters first a riderless horse and then a man with good clothes, a money belt, and a hole in his head. He puts all the material wealth to good use and is consequently mistaken for Blackjack Sam, a gunman hired by the citizens of the town of Bottleneck to do away with a local menace named Diamond Dick Durston. With good luck and the help of a perceptive and resourceful young woman, Bo carries out the assignment. He is not very bright, and he is anything but brave. He is a hero by accident—a type which reappears again and again in western fiction. Other examples include John Reese's *Sure Shot Shapiro,* about a Jewish drummer who acquires a reputation as a gunman purely by chance, and the same author's *Singalee,* which deals with the adventures of a charming jack-of-all-trades who works magic as an auctioneer in the daytime and performs other miracles at night. A ruthless and determined woman almost gets him shot. He emerges unscathed, however, and about to be married. No hero! Just a lucky man.

It can go the other way. The man can be an anti-Romeo or an un-Romeo, in flight from romance. Take the title character of John and David Shelley's *Hell-for-Leather Jones,* a little fat man who "tops his skinny animal like some bulbous tumor." He has incautiously praised the cooking of the Widow Beeson and is in danger of spending the rest of his life working on her farm. Hence his flight. Booger Jones doesn't look like a hero, and he has shaky knees in ticklish situations, but he doesn't back off from difficulties. He subdues two sets of bad men, brings peace to a feuding village, collects five thousand dollars for finding a missing person, and emerges intact. He is a man with guts, but never—no, never—a hero!

Half a dozen more types of unheroic hero could be cut from the herd of early-day novels and stories. One would be the funny cowboy who describes his predicaments and escapades solely for entertainment, as cowboys really did in the bunkhouse and around the campfire. S. Omar Barker sold some thirty stories about a character named Boosty Peckleberry to *All Western* and *Short Story Magazine* back in the thirties, and there were a good many more.

Another category includes the youngsters, all the way from little fellows up to apprentice cowboys, who have filled the role in the years between the publication of Andy Adams' *Wells Brothers* in 1911 and Ben Capps's *True Memoirs of Charley Blankenship* (1972) or Stephen Overholser's *A Hanging at Sweetwater* (1974). Most of them just want to get a job done or be accepted and are not in line for hero status, but they will probably always be with us because readers, remembering their own painful approaches to maturity, identify readily with them. Like their elders, they can even be repulsive, just so they have the requisite quota of guts. Examples are plentiful, but let one suffice: Earl Hardin in Carolyn Lockhart's 1929 story, "No Redeeming Trait." Earl is a chore boy at the Bar B Ranch owned by a female skinflint named Mrs. Rhoda Rice, who is in financial straits. She detests her boy-of-all-work. Earl is "mouthy," a braggart, and a snoop, "lying as easily as he breathes and unabashed when caught." Along with these qualities he has "a rhinoceroslike hide which no amount of sarcasm could penetrate." He steals oats at night for an old cowhorse named Shorty, which he loves, and is suspected of pilfering Bull Durham and socks from the ranch hands. He laughs when accused and replies, "I come by it honestly. . . . Pa done two jolts for rustlin' and I had an uncle made his livin' by selling damp horses till a posse got him."

The showdown comes when Mrs. Rice tries to solve her financial problems by selling her horse herd, including Shorty, to a buyer for a dog-food factory, and Earl lets all the horses out of the corral. When he is caught and brought to trial for horse theft, with the penitentiary just around the corner, he speaks up in his own defense:

> It wasn't right to do Shorty thataway, after all the work he'd done on that ranch. It would 'a' been pure murder and I'd 'a' been yallerer than she says I am if I hadn't took a chance to save his life. . . . She says I haven't got a redeemin' trait, and maybe I ain't, but . . . I'll set in the Big House till the walls turn green 'fore I'll say I'm sorry fer what I done.

The judge, with an oversize lump in his throat, turns the boy loose. Earl has guts and loyalty, but if he is a hero, the definition will have to be broadened.

Naturally, as the years went by, the world changed, and the western changed with it. The 1950's were pivotal. Television was born, giving the Western myth tremendous acceleration and attempting (unsuccessfully, it turned out) to make epic heroes out of such unlikely specimens as Wyatt Earp. Faith in the American Dream began to fade. The pioneer, once credited with bringing "civilization" to a savage land, was downgraded in the sixties, and his Indian foe was transformed into a noble being outraged by brutal whites. Conventional standards of decency went overboard, and permissiveness about sex and violence neutralized the old taboos. Cowboys talked with less restraint. Finger bones cracked, and eyeballs popped, and Apache tortures were described in great detail. The writing of westerns began to be a new ball game, and the cowboy hero was naturally affected.

The change did not come at once, and it did not go all the way. The continual reprinting of thirty-year-old westerns—for example, the stories about Ranger Jim Hatfield—kept the old traditions alive, and reader interest on the paperback level remained more or less constant. But more and more nonformula, unconventional Western stories were published, and at the same time, academic critics and historians of culture began to take a passionate interest in fictional accounts of the early West. Psychologists, sociologists, and popular culturists followed suit, and for the first time in its history the western was taken seriously. In fact, the shoot-em-up or horse opera was in danger of being analyzed to death. Most of the commentators were talking about movie westerns, but the stories on which the movies were based could not be left out. What was true for the Western moving picture was at least partly true for the Western novel.

A good sample of the kind of discussion that has become familiar is found in a well-known essay by the Swedish movie historian Harry Schein. The Western hero, he observes, has become "an omnipotent father symbol," always "alone in the little community" and often "one of those exceptional human beings who seem never to have had a mother" [Philip Durham and Everett L. Jones, *The Western Story: Fact, Fiction, and Myth*]. An American political scientist adds, "The Western hero is rarely a Sir Galahad in chaps; he is instead what might be termed a Madisonian hero. . . . reaffirming our deep political skepticism" [Walter S. Karp, *Horizon* 17 (Summer 1975)]. Today's directors, says another motion picture specialist [Philip French, *Westerns*], are reacting to "a deadening mass society and a dehumanized technology," pitting their central characters against the establishment.

It would be difficult to think seriously of Hopalong Cassidy or Sundown Slim as "omnipotent father symbols" or "Madisonian heroes." As examples of "the predominant figure in American mythology" [Eugene Manlove Rhodes, in *Best Novels and Short Stories*], Shane and a few others might qualify, but only a few. These generalizations do show, however, how seriously the cowboy is being taken, especially as he appears in the movies. What they do not show is how low the fictional cowboy has fallen, still paying his debt to his flesh-and-blood cowboy ancestor and still less than a hero in public opinion.

Skeptics there have always been who insisted that he was only a hired man on horseback. Eugene Manlove Rhodes resented these doubters and in a famous poem pictured him at the end of his earthly career riding into heaven with head held high to the welcoming shouts of the "gentlemen adventurers" of all the ages. Today's skeptics will not allow him even this much dignity. William Savage, Jr., their latest spokesman, warns that a distinction must be made between an intelligent, aggressive, and successful cattleman and the cowboy, a rangeland dropout who worked for wages and died poor because he lacked the ability to own and operate a ranch of his own. His life, says Mr. Savage, was "dull," and he himself was "an individual of little or no significance"—definitely "not the stuff of which legends are made."

How, then, did he become a legend? Easily answered, says Savage [in *Cowboy Life*]. In order to make him interesting, the fiction writers gave him a six-shooter and transformed him "from ranch hand to gun hand." The gun made the difference, and very soon the cowboy became a symbol of "courage, honor, and individualism." So he did, if Lassiter and Shane are the models. But what about Curly and Lin McLean and Sundown Slim and Wild Horse Shorty and the rest who are, at best, hired men on horseback with guts? Mr. Savage is ignoring the unheroic cowboy of the early novels, a man who had courage and sometimes nothing else. His descendants are still here, still not quite making it with other people.

These bedeviled characters are particularly prevalent in the hardback novels with some pretensions to literary merit—books which have only a nodding acquaintance with the Hopalong Cassidy tradition, still represented by soft-cover westerns on the newsstand racks. It is on this upper or hardback level that most of the changes are taking place. In such books the nominal heroes fall into fairly obvious categories. The main ones would be misfits, failures, and SOB's.

It is an ironic coincidence that one of the best of the cowboy-as-misfit novels was published in 1956, the very year in which television began to apply hothouse treatment to the Western myth. This book was Edward Abbey's much-admired *The Brave Cowboy*. Critics hailed it as "highly original," meaning that Mr. Abbey had thrown the cowboy-hero formula, as generally understood, into reverse.

Jack Burns, the cowboy, is an anachronism when he rides his mare Whisky into contemporary Albuquerque. He is still young, crowding thirty, but he belongs back in the eighties. There is no place for his kind of rugged independence anymore.

He has come on an impossible mission. His friend Paul Bondi is in the Albuquerque jail, on his way to prison, for refusing to cooperate with the provisions of the Selective Service Act. Jack gets himself into the jail in order to get Paul out. They are both rebels against the rule of "law," but in different ways. Jack wants to take Paul back to the wilds where civilization has not arrived—the West of frontier times. He knows it can be done, because he has been doing it, though he has had to descend to herding sheep in order to put distance between himself and the things he despises. The proof of his success is the absence among his scanty possessions of a social security number and a draft card. "Come with me," he pleads:

> We'll go high up in the Rockies—maybe the Shoshone forest in Wyoming. I know where there's a cabin, a good tight windproof cabin, at the foot of a glacier. . . . We'll lay in a good supply of venison and elk and pine logs and just sit tight while the snow falls. I'll write songs and you can work on your treatise or whatever you're working on now.

Paul won't go. He wants to make his protest where he is, and Jack has to escape without him. Once outside, Jack heads for the mountains and touches off one of the great pursuits in Western fiction as the forces of the law, reinforced by the United States Army, follow him and Whisky up the cliffs of the Sandia Mountains east of Albuquerque, where only eagles and the cable car should go, all the way to the top and down on the other side with the Manzanos just ahead and Mexico beyond. Whisky hates pavement, however, and the end comes on Highway 66 when the horse and rider go down before a truck loaded with plumbing fixtures intended for the comfort of civilized Americans with draft registrations and social security cards.

Jack is no hero. He overcomes nothing and rights no wrongs. His appearance is enough to keep him outside the boundaries of heroism. He has a "long scrawny neck" and a nose "like the broken beak of a falcon," and his skin, "bristling with a week's growth of black whiskers," has "the texture of a cholla and the hue of an old gunstock." He does have guts and a horse, but they are not enough to save him from futility. It is not fate which opposes him. He has no real tragic flaw. He is just born at the wrong time. In his Quixotism and recklessness he reminds us of something we learned from Sigmund Freud: there is no such thing as a hero, anyway. The man who appears to be one is just compensating for something. We can admire Jack Burns. We can pity him. But we can't identify with him. He is not one of us. And we can't let him win, because nobody does.

He does throw some of our assumptions into reverse. We are often told that the quest for law and order is the backbone of the Western story—a "republican law and order" which will not tolerate "usurpation" of the functions of society by the rich rancher or the sheriff or anybody else [Karp]. In novels like *The Brave Cowboy,* society is the usurper. "The old heroes used to protect society from its enemies," Paul Newman says. "Now it's society that is the enemy."

It is easier to find such crypto-revolutionary commentaries in the movies than in novels, but Abbey is by no means the only one to paint the cowboy hero as a victim. In Jack Schaefer's *Monte Walsh* (1963) the aging punchers are exploited by the faceless money merchants of Wall Street. In J. P. S. Brown's *The Outfit* (1971) the working cowboys are pawns in the plans of a Hollywood character who uses the ranch as a hobby. Most of the time the man in the foreground, as Savage argued, does not have sense enough or luck enough to get ahead. He is ineffectual,

frustrated, or unlucky. No matter how hard he climbs, he winds up back in the ditch.

We may miss the point because he is funny, as in Max Evans' *The Rounders* (1960). The book was made into an "engaging" movie in 1965, and readers may miss the underlying pessimism because Dusty Jones and Wrangler Lewis, the men under the gun, are funny in speech and hilarious in action. What we laugh at, however, are broken bones, irrational behavior, and exploitation of the weak by the strong.

The boys work for a predatory cattleman named Jim Ed Love and are breaking wild horses for him when the story opens. It is brutal work, and they show it:

> [Wrangler] looked just like a ground hog coming up for air when he crawled out of his bedroll in the morning, and he didn't look a hell of a lot better now except that I stood so far above him I couldn't see much but the brim of his hat and his potbelly hanging out over his droopy britches. What his britches was hanging on I don't know.

> They looked like they would droop right down around his knees any minute, but that was as far as they would have gone. His legs was bowed so bad that if you was to straighten them up, he would have been twice as tall.

Dusty doesn't describe himself, but the pair resemble the funny cowboy combinations of forty years before. The difference is, these two can't win.

Deceived by Jim Ed's persuasive tongue, they settle down for the winter at a camp out in the wilds where they are to gather wild cattle at five dollars per head for themselves. They are accompanied by an equine demon known as Old Fooler because of his deceptively meek demeanor just before he starts bucking. They are about one hundred miles from anywhere, have not been to town for a year, and are in for everything unpleasant, unforeseen, or crippling that could possibly happen. A branding scene is typical:

> Those were big calves—wild and mean. We were shorthanded and had only a bunch of raw broncs and an outlawed roan son of a bitch to rope off of. Wrangler said the irons were ready. He went out and fit a loop on a big white-face calf. Then he fought his bronc around and started dragging him to the fire. I went down that rope and reached over his back with one hand in his flank and the other on the rope. The calf jumped straight up and kicked me in the belly with both feet. While he was up I heaved and down he went.

> Wrangler bailed off his horse and came to help. In the meantime the calf had got one foot in my boot top and tore the bark off my shin. Then he kicked me in the mouth with the other foot. I had only one tooth in front that hadn't been broke, and now I didn't have that.

This is one of the milder episodes in the epic of Dusty and Wrangler. In the spring when three of Jim Ed Love's hands ride in to help get the reclaimed livestock out,

Dusty says, "It's a good thing you boys showed up when you did because me and old Wrangler had just one catch rope left between us, and we would have had one hell of a fight to see which one got to use it to hang himself with."

Again the cowboy hero has nothing going for him but guts. We know because they are frequently showing. The point of view could be called realistic if his luck were not so consistently bad. His trail goes back to Andy Adams' *Log of a Cowboy* (1903), Ross Santee's *Cowboy* (1928), and on down to Ben Capp's *The Trail to Ogallala* (1964). It reaches a sort of plateau with William Decker's highly praised *To Be a Man* (1967), the life story of Roscoe Banks, who doesn't lose as much blood as Dusty and Wrangler but has all he can do to survive.

Roscoe is left an orphan when his father is killed by a party of resentful Wyoming ranchers who suspect him of cattle theft. The father's partner gives the boy a good start before sending him off at sixteen to become a wandering puncher and rodeo performer. In his old age he settles down at Coconino, Arizona, and is mourned by the entire population of perhaps four hundred people when he is killed by a young punk who is robbing the post office.

Roscoe learns to be master of his job and master of himself, but his life is commonplace if not, in Mr. Savage's term, "dull." Skeptical as we are about our fellow men, we can admit that something may be said for people in former times, and that fact gives the book a nostalgic appeal. Roscoe makes the point when a dissatisfied puncher is trying to promote a strike:

> We've got a lot of holes in us. Me and the men on that crew, we'll never amount to a damn and likely we'll all die broke. We're easy to fault. But I'll tell you this: there isn't one I can't count on. They may look like dumb dirty hillbillies to the likes of you, but they'll go out alone and get the job done knowing that they won't get thanked or paid extra for it. Maybe nobody would ever know he did the job or if it was tough or if he hurt doing it. We could all soldier on the job. Easy. . . . But we don't and, like I said, if you have to ask why, you'll never know.

When Roscoe is in his coffin, the preacher says, "Here was a man whose like few of us will ever see again." He is a nonhero, an ordinary man whose virtues are "integrity, responsibility, and an abiding code of personal honor"—not enough to make him a hero, but too much to make him anything else.

J. P. S. Brown's *Jim Kane* (1970) is one of the many more which expose the somber side of the cowboy hero's life and portray him as a man with more guts than luck. Jim is a cattle buyer operating in Sonora, Mexico, who survives incredible difficulties getting his cattle to Chihuahua only to find at the end of the trail that his employer won't give him a square deal. Like the cowboys in *The Rounders,* he heads for the wilds to start over.

Then there is C. W. Smith's prize-winning novel of West Texas called with some preciosity *Thin Men of Haddam* (1973), with a Chicano in the leading role. Rafael Mendez is foreman of a ranch owned by a rich man who is city bred and unmindful of others. Mendez dreams of acquiring the spread and making a cooperative Chicano Utopia out of it where all his stagnating, outraged, hopeless compatriots, personified by his cousin Manuelo, can be useful and happy. The Mexicans can't realize, of course, that he has this vision, and they call him "Tio Taco" because he won't find jobs for them on the ranch. He can't tell them that he is only a "glorified flunkey." The plight of these people who can't get work and must endure the insults of the egregious gringos is harrowing, and the climax, a manhunt, leaves Mendez crucified and defeated.

Perhaps the best of these novels about men who can't make it is Elmer Kelton's Spur Award winner, *The Time It Never Rained* (1973). It tells the story of Charley Flagg of Rio Seco in West Texas—too old to be a cowboy and more sheepman than cattleman anyway—who won't accept government help or subsidies for anything, but manages, with the help of the local banker, to survive a seven-year drouth that sweeps men of less principle away. Ironically, the rain, when it finally comes, brings Charley's ultimate defeat, but he goes down fighting, his head bloody but unbowed. The book is not a western, but it is a fine novel of the West which reveals much about the life and the people of its region.

Among the defeated are a small group who feed on their illusions and refuse to live in the present. Jack Nachbar calls their stories "anti-Westerns" and says that "the central tension is invariably between a cynical contemporary knowledge of the horrors of the westward movement and past idealism about the glories of the great Western migration." The theme is central in Richard Gardner's *Scandalous John* (1963), which is about a demented old ranchman named John McCanless, a sagebrush Don Quixote with a long, skinny body, a leathery face, a scraggly mustache, and a complete set of illusions about who, when, and where he is. With the help of a Mexican Sancho Panza named Francisco Jimenez Xumen, he drives a single cow (his "herd") north to market. After incredible adventures, including some time spent at a Western Days celebration at Warbag, Colorado, he dies in a battle with police on the streets of Chicago.

In the estimation of almost everybody who knows him, he is a "nut," and even his daughter Amanda, who loves him, wails that she is tired of being his "keeper." Only one man sees the truth. Billy, his future son-in-law, says, "He's a hero, and we haven't got many of those left . . . part of the great American myth, an as yet unheroed Nibelung."

Scandalous John is more than a satire on the mythical West. It is a lament for an age which exploits the violence of the frontier without understanding the solid qualities on which the Western myth is built. It raises the question: Does a man in our time have to be crazy to be a hero?

Robert Flynn's *North to Yesterday* (1967) tells a similar tale without the thunder and lightning. Lampassas, "a little man, wrinkled, dried up and soured . . . old and frail," has dreamed all his life of being part of a trail drive, and he finally does gather a herd of wild cattle and harries them all the way to Trail Town. He arrives ten years too late, however. The trail is closed and nobody wants his cows. A number of similar stories have appeared on the screen and in nonfiction.

The disillusion which produced these chronicles of wasted time gathered momentum in the fifties and produced the antihero or SOB. He appeared as an isolated example as early as 1944 in the person of Lewt McCanles in Niven Busch's *Duel in the Sun*. Lewt has no conscience and no scruples about anything, and eventually he has to be shot for his own good by the girl who loves him. He is not a real cowboy since his father is rich and powerful and a U.S. senator, but as an SOB he could not be more authentic.

He reappears in 1960 in Larry McMurtry's *Horseman, Pass By,* which was made into the movie *Hud* (the name of the central character, a complete SOB). The time is the 1930's. Children ride to school in yellow buses, and Grandma has a radio. Granddad, once known as Wild Horse Homer Bannon, is old and out of place. Hud, in his red suede boots, pursues blondes and booze in the nearby town of Thalia and personifies the New Day on the Texas range. He gets anything he wants, and he wants Granddad's ranch. When the hoof-and-mouth disease is detected in the Bannon herd, Hud tells his stepfather, "Some day I'm gonna have your land, Mr. Bannon, and right here may be where I get it. You're an old senile bastard who bought them Mexican cows, and you're the one who better get us out of this jam, if you don't want to end up workin' from the shoulders down yourself."

Just to show his true colors, Hud rapes the negro cook Halmea before the eyes of Lonnie, the fifteen-year-old narrator, and when Granddad, half crazy over his losses, falls off the porch and breaks his hip, Hud puts a bullet in him. "He was just an old worn-out bastard," he explains. "He couldn't a made it no way in the world. He couldn't a made it another hour."

Nobody calls him to account.

There is some question about what Mr. McMurtry means by such a display of heartlessness. Philip French, analyzing the movie version, thinks this "unattractive Texan" represents a "perversion of Western ideals, the decadent fag end of a tradition." The publishers believe that the book "paints a picture of ranching Texas as it exists today." Either way, Hud brings seventy years of doubt about the cowboy hero to final disillusion.

In 1975 the novelists continued to deny that there was anything heroic about the cowboy. George L. Voss did it with a minimum of subtlety in *The Man Who Believed in the Code of the West,* which follows the fortunes of Thaddeus Baldwin of Chicago, educated at Harvard, who establishes a ranch at Flat Butte, Montana, under the illusion that in the West there is honor even among thieves. In the first chapter he encounters Steve Hurd's collection of hard cases on the porch of Hochler's store. "In the course of reading many books on the frontier," he says,

> I have often encountered allusion to the Code of the West, one apparently as rigid in its way as the code of chivalry was in an earlier time. Therefore I was in no real danger from five over-armed men when it could be plainly seen that I

carried no weapon of any kind, neither pistol, rifle nor knife. The code would obviously protect me.

His perception of the truth is delayed for a while, but when it comes, he develops into a true Westerner and fights lead with lead. Fortunately, he learned to shoot before he left Chicago. Furthermore, he learns to speak in "the local patois" and wins so much money at blackjack that he comes to be known as "Bet a Bundle Baldwin." And he stops talking about the Code of the West. He is a cowboy only by adoption, but he is useful in making the point that the cattle country was not a haunt of heroes.

A funnier and less labored attempt to downgrade the cowboy hero and put the western in its place is Gary Jennings' *The Terrible Teague Bunch*. The man to watch is L. R. Foyt, a broken-down old cowpuncher who organizes a train robbery in 1905, driving a herd of stolen culls from Shreveport to Teague, Texas, where the holdup is to take place. Trail-driving days were never like what Foyt and his assortment of odd characters (an oil-field rigger, a Cajun lumberjack, and a former soldier with half a mind) encounter on their month-long odyssey. The story is a good takeoff on the epics of the trail, and Foyt adds a finishing touch. He wears bib overalls and implies that all sensible cowboys do so too on account of the extra pockets. He carries his six-shooter in the bib and has surprised more than one opponent who was not expecting a fast draw from such a place of concealment. The tone of events is forecast as the conspirators make their plans and the whiskey begins to take effect:

> It was getting to all of them. Karnes's normally brick-red face was now darkened to puce. Boudreaux was slumped so low in his chair that he seemed to be hanging on the edge of the table by his mustache, and Foyt's ordinarily pale gray eyes now looked like the ends of two severed veins. None of them probably, could have stood up and walked very gracefully, but their thinking and speaking functions seemed relatively unimpaired.

Not a hero among them. And the leading man in bib overalls! That really removes the cowboy from his pedestal.

This discussion has penetrated only a little way into the mighty forest of Western fiction, but what has been said should discourage easy generalizations about the cowboy hero. He is not always heroic. A sizable number of examples paint him in shades of gray and sometimes black, and as we approach the present, the shades deepen. (pp. 103-28)

> C. L. Sonnichsen, "From Hopalong to Hud: The Unheroic Cowboy in Western Fiction," in his From Hopalong to Hud: Thoughts on Western Fiction, *Texas A&M University Press, 1978, pp. 103-28.*

Daryl E. Jones

[*Jones is an American critic and author whose work examines the relationship between popular literature and cultural values. In the following excerpt, he discusses the appeal of the outlaw hero by examining the character of Deadwood Dick, a less than noble figure who has rivaled the cowboy in popularity. He also examines revenge and persecution as forms of law in American western writing.*]

Among the select brotherhood of Western heroes who live eternally in the popular imagination, one figure is strangely prominent—a man clad wholly in black, seated astride a black horse. Characteristically, his fist is raised in defiance, his teeth are clenched, and from the shadow obscuring the top half of his face two black, magnetic eyes are smoldering. He is, of course, the noble outlaw, Robin Hood in New World guise, a synthesis of timeless human desires and the unique combination of forces operating upon the development of popular American fiction in the last half of the nineteenth century.

Inasmuch as the dime novel was the age's most widely read form of fiction, it is not surprising that the noble outlaw made his debut in one of these pulp thrillers. He did so on October 15, 1877, when the House of Beadle and Adams released Edward L. Wheeler's *Deadwood Dick, the Prince of the Road; or, The Black Rider of the Black Hills.* Intelligent, handsome, and chivalrous, Deadwood Dick gunned and galloped his way into the hearts of the reading public. So popular did the black-clad road agent become, in fact, that soon no profit-minded publishing firm was without its own dashing lawbreaker. Moreover, these outlaws were not exclusively the products of imagination; in the desperate search for new material, dime novelists often turned to historical accounts of actual Western badmen, a practice which spawned countless novels sensationalizing the notorious careers of such desperadoes as Jesse and Frank James, the Younger brothers, the Daltons, Rube Burrows, Joaquin Murieta, Tiburcio Vasquez, and Butch Cassidy and the Sundance Kid. Nevertheless, whether purely fictional or modeled after a legendary figure, the dime novel outlaw hero exhibited extraordinary appeal; by the 1890s, one series which printed a high percentage of outlaw stories, Street & Smith's Log Cabin Library, boasted a weekly circulation of 25,000 to 30,000 copies, and other outlaw series were equally popular.

This popularity may be explained in part by the manner in which the stereotyped outlaw hero embodied certain cultural values and satisfied, through his conventionalized role in the dime novel Western formula, the sociopsychological needs of the reading public. In one sense, of course, the outlaw was simply a reincarnated archetype, a nineteenth century American manifestation of the devil-may-care European rogue or highwayman traditionally prominent in popular fiction. In another sense, however, he was the unique product of a specific cultural context—a cultural context which, through a complex interplay of several aesthetic and cultural dynamics, fostered the development of those character types most responsive to its own social imperatives and psychological preoccupations.

The nineteenth century, despite its expressed optimism and faith in progress, was an age preoccupied by all of the problems which inevitably accompany rapid social change. It was an age of industrialization, urbanization, class polarization, and control of society by big business and the international agricultural market. It was an age in which new values seemingly threatened established morality. Above all, it was an age in which the average individual found his freedoms severely abridged by gargantuan social and economic forces. Totally subject to these forces, powerless to effect any real change in his life, the common man could still escape into the pages of a pulp thriller and become, if only temporarily, a self-reliant Western hero eminently free in a fantasy realm where every problem had a swift and clear-cut solution. Thus, the astounding popularity of the outlaw hero may be explained in part by his capacity for resolving in fantasy the otherwise insoluble cultural conflicts of the age.

One such conflict in particular played a crucial role in the development and consequent popularity of the outlaw hero: namely, the ambivalent American attitude toward law and the legal system. While most citizens professed belief in the value of law as a positive, organic force which served to build freedom into society, they felt that the legal system was largely unresponsive to the needs of the average individual. Undoubtedly, the intricacies of the judicial process contributed to this notion. More importantly, however, the majority of Americans suspected a nefarious association between law and special privilege. In an age of increasing class polarization, of growing antagonism between labor and capital, it seemed that unscrupulous members of the upper class were exploiting the intricacies of the legal system as a means of furthering their own interests while simultaneously denying the fundamental democratic rights of the majority. By the last half of the nineteenth century such sentiments were sufficiently widespread as to constitute a general antipathy toward law and the legal system. In addition to harboring a natural distaste for artificial restraints, the average individual doubted the ethics of pettifogging lawyers, regarded courtroom procedure as mere chicanery, and looked upon law itself as a tool employed by a vast conspiracy of the rich to subjugate and exploit the poor. In sum, the average American could no longer see a connection between moral and civil law. Too often there seemed to be a wide and unsettling disparity between that ideal justice which *ought* to prevail in the application of law and that lesser justice which, in fact, *did* prevail.

This concern for the meaning and value of law had long been a central theme of the Western. "There are regions," observes Natty Bumppo in *The Prairie* (1827),

> where the law is so busy as to say, In this fashion
> shall you live, in that fashion shall you die, and
> in such another fashion shall you take leave of
> the world, to be sent before the judgement-seat
> of the Lord! A wicked and troublesome meddling is that, with the business of One who has
> not made his creatures to be herded like oxen,
> and driven from field to field as their stupid and
> selfish keepers may judge of their need and
> wants. A miserable land must that be, where
> they fetter the mind as well as the body, and
> where the creatures of God, being born children,
> are kept so by the wicked inventions of men who
> would take upon themselves the office of the
> great Governor of all!

Natty speaks from bitter experience, for he had come into conflict with the law a short time before. In *The Pioneers* (1823), the novel commonly credited with providing the Western's characteristic setting, character, and themes, Cooper brings the anarchic world of the wilderness personified by Natty Bumppo into conflict with the ordered, law-governed society personified by Judge Marmaduke Temple. Natty, schooled in Nature but untutored in the ways of the law, lives an upstanding life regulated solely by his own personal moral code. In contrast, Judge Temple lives by the maxim that "Society cannot exist without wholesome restraints." These opposing philosophies clash when Natty kills a deer out of season; accordingly, he is charged with a violation of the game laws and brought before the bench. But when asked whether or not he is guilty, the old trapper resolutely replies, "I may say not guilty with a clear conscience . . . for there's no guilt in doing what's right. . . . "

These same words might have been spoken by any one of the stereotyped Western heroes who attained popularity more than forty years later in the dime novel. Whether trapper, plainsman, cowboy, or outlaw, each of these popular heroes was, like Natty, characterized by his asocial status and his intuitive recognition of the disparity between that which was merely legal and that which was morally just. But this similarity between the venerable trapper and his pulp successors should not be construed simply as a naive and unimaginative attempt by second-rate writers to follow an old trail blazed by Cooper. Instead, dime novelists recognized in the disparity between morality and legality a sure-fire method for creating popular heroes; specifically, it offered them a magic formula whereby they might synthesize in the person of a single fictional character the two ostensibly irreconcilable traits which the reading public most highly prized and most often demanded of those it would venerate: virtue and rebelliousness. On the one hand, public demand had always existed for a standard hero who, guided by his own unerring sense of right and wrong, would lead the forces of good into battle against evil. On the other hand, in an age in which socioeconomic forces suppressed individual freedoms, public demand also existed for a hero who would reject any and all forms of artificial restraint, especially law. The dime novel Western hero satisfied both of these demands; wholeheartedly engaged in fighting villainy, he sometimes found it necessary to subvert the law in the interests of a higher justice.

The introduction of heroes who occasionally acted without regard to the law touched off an ascending spiral of rebelliousness in the dime novel. Evolving through respective incarnations as trapper, plainsman, cowboy, and outlaw, the Western hero progressively abandoned traditional social and legal codes of behavior in favor of sensationalism and absolute self-reliance. In one sense the outlaw hero was merely the culmination of this trend; in another sense, however, he was a unique figure whose characterization posed a singular problem for dime novelists. While previous Western heroes had either acted in the absence of law or, on occasion, bypassed legal formalities in an attempt to exact a more nearly perfect justice than that which an imperfect legal system could ever hope to real-

ize, never before had a Western hero openly opposed the law; never before had a Western hero reacted against societal restraint so violently as to waylay stages and rob banks. How then might this new and virulent strain of rebelliousness be reconciled with the hero's traditional virtue? And how might the outlaw hero be differentiated from that mob of ordinary badmen who, in league with the forces of evil, also opposed the law?

Dime novelists attacked the problem in two ways. First, they masked the bandit hero's questionable behavior with a thin veneer of respectability, always emphasizing his social polish, courtly manners, and chivalrous conduct toward friend and foe alike, particularly women. Second, and more importantly, they provided him with a justification for his rebelliousness. Though his heart was as true as steel, they explained, he had been unjustly persecuted and driven outside the law. Thereafter, a good but dangerously embittered man, he lived solely for revenge.

Once instituted, the theme of persecution and justifiable revenge rapidly assumed the nature of a formal plot convention in the outlaw story. Indeed, so pervasive did it become, and so familiar to readers, that authors merely needed to refer to "a thin smile" or "eyes glowing like coals" in order to supply all necessary character motivation. Of genuine significance, however, is the manner in which dime novelists tailored the timeworn theme of persecution and revenge to their own cultural context, consciously transforming it into a narrative convention which enabled them to instill in the outlaw hero that quality most responsible for his appeal—the violent but morally justifiable rejection of all forms of restraint, especially the law.

One of the more prolific writers on the staff of Beadle and Adams was a flamboyant Philadelphian who wore a Stetson hat, saluted strangers as "Pard," and billed himself "Edward L. Wheeler. Sensational Novelist." Acquaintances thought Wheeler somewhat odd, but no one could dispute his knowledge of the writing business, for it was his pen that produced one of the most popular fictional heroes of the age: Deadwood Dick, the Black Rider of the Black Hills. Galloping through a series of adventures in more than thirty novels, the dashing Prince of the Road embodies all of the attributes of preceding Western heroes. A deadly shot and skilled equestrian, a master in the art of disguise, he cleverly evades pursuit or tracks down villains—tasks facilitated by a guaranteed income of five thousand dollars a year from his own gold mine. Forever young, handsome, and chivalrous, Deadwood Dick brings a blush to the cheeks of the beautiful and yearning women who abound in the novels; usually he resists their awkward advances, but he does marry three times and father two children. Each time, however, his wife's unfaithfulness or death shatters his domestic bliss, banishing him once again to a rootless life roaming the hills with his two valiant sidekicks, Calamity Jane and Old Avalanche, the Indian fighter.

In the first novel of the series, *Deadwood Dick, the Prince of the Road; or, The Black Rider of the Black Hills,* Wheeler begins to define the outlaw hero in terms of persecution and revenge, a theme he would return to in later novels, consciously developing and refining it as a narrative convention. When first introduced to the reader, Deadwood Dick is already a road agent. Though he spends considerable time eluding those who would claim the price on his head, he is actually in hot pursuit of Alexander and Clarence Filmore, two crafty malefactors who, we are given to understand, figure prominently in the outlaw's mysterious past. As the novel nears its conclusion, Deadwood Dick captures the villains and spirits them off to his mountain stronghold. Preparations are made for a hanging, and Deadwood Dick's loyal followers only await a signal from their captain before hoisting the two Filmores into eternity. But that signal is long in coming, for the outlaw chieftain must first justify the deed to all present, including the reader. Flinging aside his black mask and addressing the crowd, Deadwood Dick reveals that his real name is Edward Harris; an orphan, he had been taken in and raised by the kindly Harris family. But this home was soon denied to him, for the scheming Filmores successfully managed the "accidental" deaths of his foster parents. Then, as executor of the Harris estate, the elder Filmore swindled Edward and his lovely sister out of their share of the family wealth. Moreover, he foully mistreated them. "Finding that this kind of life was unbearable," the outlaw explains, "I appealed to our neighbors and even the courts for protection, but my enemy was a man of great influence, and after many vain attempts, I found that I could not obtain a hearing; that nothing remained for me to do but to fight my own way. And I did fight it." Taking his sister with him, Deadwood Dick continues, he escaped from the Filmores, but not until he had first gone to his father's safe and "purloined a sum of money sufficient to defray our expenses." Though the money was rightfully his, its theft branded him a criminal in the eyes of the law. As a result, the outlaw concludes, "The Hills have been my haunt ever since. . . . Now, I am inclined to be merciful to only those who have been merciful to me. . . . Boys, string 'em up!"

Insofar as it is embodied in the plot of this, the first of the Deadwood Dick stories, the theme of persecution and revenge manifests itself primarily through a relationship between individuals: the Filmores persecute Deadwood Dick and he takes revenge upon them. But the theme also has an obvious social dimension in that Deadwood Dick's justification for taking the law into his own hands rests on society's refusal to take a stand against the social evil which the Filmores represent. Were it not for the unresponsiveness of the legal system and the inaction of the public, Deadwood Dick contends, he would not have been forced to act on his own. And had he not been forced to act on his own he would not have become involved in that chain of events which ultimately deprived him of his rightful place in the community. Through a kind of emotional transference, then, Deadwood Dick comes to resent not merely those villainous individuals who actually precipitated his problems but the whole of society as well.

This anti-social sentiment assumes much wider scope in subsequent Deadwood Dick novels, largely as a result of a significant refinement made by Wheeler in the manner in which he implemented conventional persecution and revenge. Whereas he had instituted the convention in the original Deadwood Dick story primarily to justify Dead-

wood Dick's attack upon specific individuals, he utilized it in later novels to create stock situations which would afford the outlaw an opportunity to justifiably attack society in general. Usually Wheeler employed one or the other of two situations, each of which placed society in the role of oppressor and Deadwood Dick in the role of misunderstood defender of virtue. In the first, Deadwood Dick attempts to aid a party in distress but finds himself repeatedly hampered by an ignorant populace. This, of course, provokes the outlaw's wrath. In the second situation, Deadwood Dick renounces his life on the road and strives to become a law-abiding member of the community; invariably, however, he is persecuted by an unforgiving public and driven back into the hills where he broods over his unjust treatment and swears vengeance.

By depicting Deadwood Dick's encounters with society in terms of conventional persecution and revenge, Wheeler gained two artistic advantages. First, it allowed him to employ the community as a foil against which to define in the noble outlaw an essential trait common to all Western heroes: namely that he is a man possessed of superior powers of moral perception. Inasmuch as the Western hero is able to detect the presence of evil when the general public is not, he takes it upon himself to protect the community by acting swiftly—even if this entails subverting those social and legal codes which the public holds most dear. Unlike other Western heroes, however, the outlaw hero does not merely subvert these codes; he violates them outright, and since the public remains unaware of the need for prompt and decisive action it inevitably misinterprets such violations. Hence, the outlaw hero incurs the animosity of the very community he is striving to protect—a bitter irony which, in turn, transforms his previously latent disdain for the credulous public into overt enmity. By depicting the outlaw's encounters with society in terms of conventional persecution and revenge, then, Wheeler dramatized that tension which exists between the alienated individual and the community, between insight and credulity, and between morality and legality. It is from this tension that the central ambivalence of the outlaw hero arises; he is at the same time a paragon of virtue and a confirmed rebel, a public servant and an expendable martyr.

A second advantage stemmed from Wheeler's use of conventional persecution and revenge. Deadwood Dick's banishment from the community affords him an opportunity to vent his righteous indignation in the form of bitter social criticism. Throughout the Deadwood Dick saga, the outlaw's attacks focus essentially upon the same three interrelated issues which he initially raised in his justification for lynching the Filmores: first, the stolidity of a citizenry that either cannot or will not distinguish between good and evil and which, through its inaction, consequently furthers the spread of evil; second, the iniquity of a social system which sanctions the exploitation of the common man by an unscrupulous ruling class; and, finally, the fundamental injustice of a legal system which, while it permits those of wealth and influence to perpetrate the most heinous crimes, at the same time severely punishes the common man for the least indiscretion.

The artistic advantages which Wheeler gained by defining

the outlaw's relationship to the community in terms of conventional persecution and revenge become apparent in two consecutive stories which relate Deadwood Dick's encounters with the citizens of the bustling boom town of Leadville, Colorado. In each of these tales, Deadwood Dick is portrayed as both a misunderstood protector of the people and an outspoken social critic. In *Deadwood Dick in Leadville; or, A Strange Stroke for Liberty,* the outlaw holds up a stage but takes great pains to assure the passengers that he means them no harm: "These mountain districts are infested with ruffianly bands of road-agents and outlaws, who prey not only upon one another, but upon all who come within their reach, often resorting to the most fiendish torture to extort money. It does me proud to claim that Deadwood Dick and his followers are in no way allied to such gangs." Instead, maintains the outlaw chief, he is "a protective agent for the people." Though he waylays stages and deprives the passengers of their money, he does so only to prevent the unscrupulous Captain Hawk from getting his hands on it when he halts the stage farther down the road. After the passengers have arrived safely in Leadville, Deadwood Dick explains, he will see to it that their money is returned. In spite of this valuable service, Deadwood Dick and his men are nevertheless ostracized by a society which refuses to make a distinction between good and bad outlaws. Still, it is of little consequence, notes the outlaw proudly: "Let the world regard us as it will—we care not. We are a band, to a man, who hate the world and everything worldly. . . ." And as for the citizens themselves, he continues, unable to repress a bitter laugh: "The people—well! . . . they would smite me down, were I to do them each and every one a blessing. They have a grudge against me which only my death can appease."

Though Deadwood Dick is persecuted by a community which fails to recognize that he is acting in its best interest, it is nevertheless apparent that such individual action is necessary. Lamentably, Leadville's legal system is clearly unresponsive to the needs of the people—so much so, in fact, that a number of citizens have, "in defiance of the law, set themselves up as adjusters of their own wrongs. . . . Almost to a spirit of insubordination has this thing amounted to among those who plead for justice without receiving it, and hence came the organization known as the Regulators and Adjusters, making Leadville the possessor of two laws—a law of the State and a law of the people."

In essence, the remainder of the novel contrasts the relative effectiveness of each of these forms of law. On the one hand, the law of the State is plainly inept. When Noel Farnsworth complains to the town sheriff that his sister has been abducted, the genial but incapable lawman throws up his hands in resignation. After a moment's hesitation, he feebly suggests the Farnsworth offer an ample reward in hopes that his sister will be returned unharmed. Then too, Ralph Gardner, the miscreant who has engineered the abduction, repeatedly uses his influence as "one of the richest men in Leadville" to bend the law in his favor, even invoking it in his defense when caught cheating at cards. And on still another occasion, Beautiful Bill, an inaptly named town bully who refers to himself as "a respected and law abidin' citizen," harasses the cowed citizenry. But the officers of the law are afraid to oppose him, so "Justice let him alone." On the other hand, the law of the people is not without its failings either. Too many of Leadville's citizens glory "in taking human life, whether in self-defense, in justice, or cold-handed." Blinded by mob psychology, manipulated by those "ruffianly and villainous characters . . . who literally 'boss' the town," the enraged populace is not only ineffective but potentially dangerous as well. At last, in a revealing scene which follows the capture of the notorious road agent Captain Hawk, the two alternative forms of law come into direct conflict:

> An instant trial was ordered by the people, and though the sheriff should have waited the slow motion of the law, by rights, he could not resist without running the risk of having his own life taken by the mob. . . . Accordingly a jury was selected, and the case was brought up, with a prominent lawyer as prosecutor. . . . A young pettifogger undertook the defense, but after he had spoken a few words, the crowd grew so excited, and revolvers were displayed in such profusion, that he wisely took a seat. A verdict of 'guilty' soon followed—the jury not leaving their seats.

On the following morning, just as the sun edges up over the horizon, Captain Hawk is hanged.

Against this backdrop of confusion, coercion, and iniquity, Deadwood Dick stands out as a cool and incorruptible enforcer of true justice. Guided solely by his own infallible sense of right and wrong, unrestricted by legal impedimenta, he is the defender of unarmed virtue, the champion of the downtrodden. And yet he is not free; he is an exile, a lonely and homeless man untiringly persecuted by the very community for which he fights. Confiding to Calamity Jane his grim conviction that the "justice grabbers . . . will never get over their antipathy toward me, until they see me dangling in mid-air beneath a tree-limb," Deadwood Dick resolves to surrender to the people and pay his debt to society. However, he has an ulterior motive, and therefore extracts from Calamity Jane a promise that she will cut him down immediately after he is hanged and, if possible, resuscitate him. "After that," he explains, "I am not afraid of them, for they cannot hang a man but once, and that satisfies the law for all previous misdemeanors. I have but to hang, and then I can laugh at them all, for I shall be a free man—free to go where, or do whatsoever I choose." Accordingly, Deadwood Dick rides into Leadville and surrenders himself to mob justice. Permitted a few last words before being hanged, the Prince of the Road defends his notorious past in such a way as to implicitly contrast the true justice he has enforced with that lesser justice exacted by the law:

> Some of you may say that my life as a road-agent has been highly criminal. I don't agree with you on that score, for where I have tapped you, I have done so in a gentlemanly manner, and have, as a rule, circulated the spoils among poor and needy families. . . . I have aided a few ruffianly characters in getting a grand send-off, to be sure, but they were the worst of human

brutes, and feared neither God nor man, and whose lives were a curse to the country and a discredit to the name of man. . . . Therefore, in balancing my accounts, I have not much to regret. But the law has seen fit to regard me as a ferocious criminal, and not wishing to offend the law—the great, majestic law—I do deliver myself up to be lynched from the nearest limb of the nearest tree.

Moments later, "in the name of the law," Deadwood Dick makes his exit at the end of a rope.

It proved to be a brief exit, however, and when Deadwood Dick appeared in the next number of Beadle's Half Dime Library he was eminently free. As he explained in a later novel, "while I hung and paid my debt to nature and justice, I came back to life a free man whom no law in the universe could molest for past offenses." Yet his days of freedom were numbered. Resurrecting his hero in *Deadwood Dick's Device; or, The Sign of the Double Cross,* Wheeler again constructed his story in terms of conventional persecution and revenge.

The plot involves Deadwood Dick's efforts to maintain ownership of a mine which he has inherited upon the death of a friendly miner. The Howells, the miner's avaricious family, resent Deadwood Dick's acquisition of the property and use all of their vast wealth and power to wrest it from him. It is clearly a class struggle, for Wheeler intrusively describes the Howells as "a leading family, both financially and socially—for Leadville, mind you, has its social world as well as its Eastern sister cities, formed out of that class whom fortune has smiled upon. And surrounded by a great superfluity of style, pomp and splendor, they set themselves up as the 'superior class,' ye gods!" Using their influence, the Howells prejudice the citizens against Deadwood Dick, and soon the servile sheriff makes a rash attempt to arrest him. Cornered, his vehement protest that he is "lawfully a free man" ignored, Deadwood Dick regretfully guns down the sheriff's men and effects his escape—but not before he utters a fearful proclamation: "To-night I have been forced again into crime, and am an outlaw, by the decree of the people. Let them look out, for I will not stop now, but they shall learn to fear my name as an omen of death."

Characteristically, Deadwood Dick's oath of vengeance is justified on the grounds that he has been unjustly persecuted by a society which, lacking his own "keen sense of perception," too often honors its enemies and maligns its benefactors. As he declares in a rare moment of self-revelation:

> I despise a man who is proud of himself, his name, or any worldly possession. No! I am not proud of the name of Deadwood Dick—I should be a contemptible sinner were I. It is not a name to be proud of, for there are many stains upon it, never to be washed out; yet, outlaw, road-agent, dare-devil though I have been, and am now, I have been driven on, step by step, by a people who have no mercy—who refuse to let me alone, after I had hanged and thus paid the penalty of crime. So that, though my future prospects may not be pleasant to reflect upon, I

have the consolation of knowing that no man was ever paid nature's debt by my agency, who was not at heart a ruffian and villain, and whose death was not a relief to the community, and a favor to every honest man.

And again, when asked if he must always live such a "wild, strange life," the noble outlaw fiercely replies, "Always! . . . I am an outcast, and as such I have only to remain. Society or the public at large refuse [sic] to receive me. They are everlasting enemies. . . . They curse me, and drive me about, and I have no choice except between this life and death." Reflecting upon Deadwood Dick's blighted life, Old Avalanche mutters, "He's bin treated like as ef he war sum dishonorable coyote, an' ef he ain't got cause fer revenge, I don't know myself." Calamity Jane heartily agrees, and together they join Deadwood Dick in a campaign of terror against the citizens of Leadville.

Throughout the remainder of the Deadwood Dick saga, Wheeler again and again utilized conventional persecution and revenge as a means of creating stock situations which afforded the invincible Prince of the Road an opportunity to justifiably defy the law in order to defend the downtrodden and, in the process, bring swift justice to a society in which affluent evil-doers further their own ends by duping the public and manipulating the hopelessly ineffective legal system. In *Deadwood Dick on Deck; or, Calamity Jane, the Heroine of Whoop-Up. A Story of Dakota,* the outlaw hero comes to the aid of an honest miner who feels, "that very few men are so poor but what they can stand firm for their rights"; if there were more men in the country like him, we are told, "there would, undoubtedly, be a change for the better, when every man would, in a greater or lesser degree, have an independence, and not be ground down under the heel of the master of money." In *Deadwood Dick of Deadwood; or, The Picked Party,* the outlaw chief cooperates with a detective to topple the corrupt business empire of a "purse-proud aristocrat" who lives by the maxim that "wealth is omnipotent." For his efforts, however, Deadwood Dick is sentenced to death by a drunken judge, and it is only because of Calamity Jane's quick thinking that he manages to escape. On another occasion, while defending the rights of a peaceful Crow Indian whose lands have been usurped in *Deadwood Dick's Claim; or, The Fairy Face of Faro Flats,* the noble outlaw threatens to kill Philander Pilgrim, the local attorney and editor of the town newspaper. "A man is liable to arrest, sir, for uttering a threat!" exclaims the attorney. "Good Blackstone," the outlaw chuckles, "but it don't answer here. If you have ever heard of me you will know that I am the man who has found it right, necessary, and convenient to defy arrest." Always defiant, the prince of outlaws continues to lead the forces of good into battle against evil until, in *Deadwood Dick's Dust; or, The Chained Hand. A Strange Story of the Mines, Being the 35th and Ending Number of the Great 'Deadwood Dick' Series,* he is killed while successfully destroying a town whose citizens have appropriated his own tract of land and lynched Calamity Jane. Thus, ironically, the valiant hero who has spent his life defending the rights of others in the end loses it in defense of his own.

During the eight years that Wheeler concentrated his efforts primarily on the Deadwood Dick series, he penned a number of other novels which also illustrate his awareness of the fact that the noble outlaw's source of popular appeal lay in his justifiable rebellion against society. In these tales Wheeler consistently implemented the narrative convention of persecution and revenge to explain his hero's death as a social being and rebirth as a free individual immune to law. Fred Brayton, formerly a detective, and hero of *A No. 1, the Dashing Toll-Taker; or, the Schoolmarm o' Sassafras,* takes to the road as a result of a false conviction of murder. In *Solid Sam, The Boy Road-Agent; or, The Branded Brows. A Tale of Wild Wyoming,* Solid Sam turns to a life of crime because a band of ruffians has appropriated his gold mine. Though he plans to waylay them individually and collect the gold which is rightfully his, he finds this impossible and instead demands that the citizens of Placer City restore his gold and pay him protection money. When they refuse, the outlaw and his men "justifiably" reduce the town to a "series of heaps of smoking ashes and charred embers, to tell of the vengeance of Solid Sam." One of the clearest examples of the noble outlaw's vindication occurs in *Apollo Bill, the Trail Tornado; or, Rowdy Kate from Right-Bower. A Story of the Mines.* Approaching the problem laterally, Wheeler explains that "circumstances have been chronicled of a brave and gallant man, with a spice of nobility in his heart, who has taken to the profession of stage robbery, more on account of some secret life trouble, than taste for the business itself." Soon Wheeler reveals the "secret life trouble" that has caused law-abiding citizen Bill Blake to be reborn as the dashing Apollo Bill. His home and family, it seems, were destroyed by a roving gang of border ruffians. Swearing an oath of vengeance, Blake set out to track down the murderers; in the process, however, he accidentally shot and killed an innocent man. Pursued thereafter by the untiring

> minions of the law . . . hunted down to the last resort, he rallied around him a band of fellows and took to the mountains. They were discovered in their first retreat and branded road-agents ere they had earned the right to such a calling. Assailed by despondency and anger at this injustice, Apollo Bill fled to this fastness and organized his men into what is known as Apollo Bill's road-agents.

Like so many other fictional outlaws, Apollo Bill has been falsely accused by a society ignorant of the nature of true justice; he is given no choice but to rebel.

On the basis of these tales and those in the Deadwood Dick saga, it is possible to outline the structure of persecution and revenge as a narrative convention. Essentially, it may be divided into three separate phases. In the first, a good man unjustly persecuted by one or more evil individuals discovers that the legal system can neither protect him nor punish his oppressors—a fact usually attributed to the villain's ability to use wealth and influence either to manipulate the law itself or to corrupt those involved in the slow and complex judicial process. On occasion, though, the hero simply refuses to entrust his fate to a jury composed of citizens who lack his own moral insight. In the second phase, the hero undertakes individual action to avenge his wrongs but, through a fatal misstep, breaks the law and becomes a social outcast. In some instances, the hero does not himself break the law; rather, he is framed by the villain. In the final phase, the outlaw's hatred for the evil individuals who initially persecuted him changes to hatred for society in general. This hatred invariably finds expression in violent action against the community; implicit at all times, however, is the fundamental assumption that such chastisement is merely part of the hero's paternalistic duty as protector of the people and enforcer of true justice.

Although Edward L. Wheeler was the first dime novelist to employ the timeworn theme of persecution and revenge as a means of creating a Western hero capable of responding to the social and psychological imperatives of the nineteenth century, he was by no means the last. Other dime novelists followed his lead, and conventional persecution and revenge soon became a standard device in the outlaw story. Moreover, although originally formulated as a means of fashioning fictional outlaws, conventional persecution and revenge also played a profound role in the development and popularization of legends about actual Western badmen. Seizing upon those few facts which were germane to the convention, and shamelessly altering those that were not, dime novelists portrayed famous outlaws of the West as victims of an oppressive social system—a practice which influenced the legends of men like Jesse and Frank James, Bob Ford, and Joaquin Murieta.

But whether used to create fictional outlaws or implemented as a means of transforming actual Western badmen into misunderstood rebels, the narrative convention of persecution and revenge enabled dime novelists to provide the American public with heroes who possessed a capacity for resolving in fantasy the otherwise insoluble cultural conflicts of the age. In essence, the outlaw hero served two interrelated cultural needs. On the one hand, he was a projection of the widespread American preoccupation with the meaning and value of law. As a good man victimized by the unsettling disparity between that which was morally just and that which was strictly legal, the outlaw hero won a kind of immunity from restraint. Thereafter, guided solely by his own infallible sense of right and wrong, he could resolve that disparity between moral and civil law by taking swift and decisive individual action which insured the execution of true justice. On the other hand, the outlaw hero was a projection of the average American's growing alienation in a modern society characterized by industrialism, materialism, class polarization, and the suppression of individual freedoms by a rigid socioeconomic structure. Eminently free, the invincible outlaw hero was a man who would not, in Edward L. Wheeler's words, "be ground down under the heel of the master of money." Neither would he stand idly by in an age of apparent moral decline; inevitably, he punished the wicked and triumphed over evil. And if, like an angel of wrath from *Revelation,* he sometimes found it necessary to purify an entire society with thunder and pillars of fire, then this too was just. (pp. 10-22)

Daryl E. Jones, "Clenched Teeth and Curses: Revenge and the Dime Novel Outlaw Hero,"

A still from The Wild Bunch, *with Ben Johnson, Warren Oates, William Holden, and Ernest Borgnine as outlaws who plan a robbery.*

in The Popular Western: Essays toward a Definition, *edited by Richard W. Etulain and Michael T. Marsden, Bowling Green University Popular Press, 1974, pp. 10-23.*

WOMEN IN WESTERN FICTION

Jenni Calder

[*Calder is an American educator and the author of* There Must Be a Lone Ranger, *a study of themes in western novels. In the following excerpt from this work, she describes the various types of women in western fiction, including the pioneer woman, dance-hall girl, female outlaw, and prostitute.*]

> She looks like one of the English poor women of our childhood—lean, clean, toothless, and speaks like one of them, in a piping, discontented voice, which seems to convey a personal reproach. All her waking hours are spent in a sunbonnet. She is never idle for one minute, is severe and hard, and despises everything but work.

We cannot recognise this as the Western screen heroine. This is a woman in Colorado described by Isabella Bird, herself a most proper but delightfully unconventional traveller in the West. 'She' is typical, unlovely, hardworking, characterised by her sunbonnet, a strictly utili-

tarian piece of apparel, worn from sunrise to sunset, day in, day out, limp, sweat-soaked, layered with dust, as necessary, and in its way as symbolic, as the cowboy's wide brimmed hat. More than anything else the sunbonnet represented a combination of drudgery and respectability. The heroine of the Western does not wear a sunbonnet. Nor does the dance hall girl. The woman who did was a woman who worked in the sun, washing clothes at the pump, trudging beside a covered wagon.

The sunbonnet suggests also a married woman, or a woman whose vision is encompassed by the idea of marriage, not a girl on the make, coming West with a good nose for a boom town, nor the pretty rancher's daughter whom the hero will probably win. The sunbonnet suggests a mate for the dirt farmer, not for the range rider. The heroine of the Western must, generally, have either more or less than the sunbonnet represents.

Women were not a plentiful commodity in most parts of the frontier. It was often easier to import pianos and champagne than to bring out suitable mates for frontiersmen. The motives that took women West were limited. They might go as wives, daughters or nieces. They might go as adventuresses—the only equivalent of the heroic man who sets forth to open up new territories is a woman of dubious reputation. The only respectable job that could take a woman West was school-teaching, and for that smaller communities would tend to rely on local talent. Or they might go, occasionally, as 'mail order' brides, lonely wives for lonely ranchers brought together through correspondence.

History has institutionalised the frontier woman, and she is trapped in a narrow image. It is an image that interweaves decency and endurance—look at the tight lips and scraped hair of the women in any old photograph of a frontier family—and an aggression that echoes that of the men. The legend has done nothing to free women from this narrowness: the conventional Western can only offer a romanticised alternative. Occasionaly the courage, determination, independence and incredible capacity for endurance is allowed to contribute richly to the Western, but not as a rule.

Some argue that the Western could profitably dispense with women altogether. Frederick Woods wrote in 1959, 'Time after time, one can detach the females without endangering the structure of the main plot. The West is a man's world, and the women are relegated to mere decoration . . . most often they are prizes only, to be gathered in by the handsome hero when the gunsmoke has drifted away.' Yet the woman as a prize only echoes long established narrative conventions. The Western incorporates a treatment that has long existed. To the extent that the Western often imports its characterisation of women from another convention Frederick Woods is right. To argue that the Western cannot legitimately use women characters, and cannot do so without retaining the romantic conventions that much of its audience will look for, is misleading. It consigns to oblivion the women who were there.

The ordinary pioneer woman is elusive on the screen. The glimpses that we do catch are most often of a hatchet-faced caricature. She is sometimes comic. She is sometimes helpless. She is almost always peripheral. She is the lean housekeeper in *The Oxbow Incident* spitting her sour aggression at the range hands. Transformed, her origins unacknowledged, she is Lola Albright in McLaglen's *The Way West* (1967) in unconvincing middle age, charmingly tousled and dirt-smudged, crossing the plains and mountains bare headed. More genuinely, and very rare, she is Eva Maria Saint in *The Stalking Moon,* yet even here, though we see a raw, bewildered woman, the screen star is too attractive to be entirely honest to the original book's portrayal. In the book T. V. Olsen emphasises throughout the physical and mental damage that ten years of Apache life have done to a woman who was once a pretty, over-protected girl. There is an appropriateness in this scarred woman finding a home with a rough-living scout who has in his way been equally damaged by his years of killing and bare survival.

It is a little easier to track down something reminiscent of reality in print. The pioneer heroine appears in her most noble and solid form in Willa Cather's novels of Nebraska life; in them we can see how the demands of the frontier linger on long after the frontier itself has ostensibly passed. It was not only a hard life on the frontier for a woman accustomed to any kind of comfort or even a minimal relief from hardship, it was often bitterly resented. The celebrated woman of courage is difficult to square with the embittered helpmeet who has long ago relinquished the possibilities of choice in her own life. 'Virgin land usually spelt to a woman isolation, disease and hopelessness,' writes An-

drew Sinclair, historian of woman's emancipation in America. Walter Prescott Webb wrote that the Great Plains 'repelled the women as they attracted the men. There was too much of the unknown, too few of the things they loved.' This is perhaps meant to suggest that for women the trivialities of civilisation were more precious than for men, but perhaps a more useful emphasis is on the fact that women had limited opportunities and experience to deal with the unknown. While the men rode out to meet it the women stayed at home trapped in a gruelling round of tasks that were necessary in order to convince themselves that decency could be preserved. In *The Siege at Dancing Bird* Alan Le May provides us with a striking picture.

> Matthilda Zachary would have hated and feared the prairie if no Indian had ever ridden it. The galling month-long winds; the dust that sifted forever from the walls and roof of the hole in the ground where they lived; the spreading stains of mud that leaked through with every rain; the few poor things they had to do with, so the endless toil showed no return; the cruelly harsh home-boiled soap, which made cracked, hurting hands the price of keeping clean—all this Matthilda could have forgiven. But she could not forgive what seemed to her the prairie's vast malignance, as boundless as its emptiness, and as mighty as its storms.

Although there is a young, attractive and less bitter woman in the novel, it is Matthilda Zachary that the novel is about. Le May has shown in an number of his novels that he has strong grasp of the quality of life on the frontier, and much of this is presented through a sympathetic portrayal of women. Matthilda does not survive, but she fights, in spite of the fact that she hates what she is fighting for. There must have been many like her. Even Miss Bird's pioneer, soured and grim as she was, had courage, though it may seem to us now to be perverse and negative.

The tragedy of the frontier woman was that she so rarely did share all that we celebrate in the frontier man. She acquired some extradomestic skills, riding and shooting, but had not the scope to employ them in a positive way. Yet the type of heroine that gives most pleasure in the Western is precisely the hard riding, tough girl who helps herself to a share of the frontier's freedom. (Just as there can scarcely be a single reader of Scott's novels who does not find the adventurous Di Vernon the most attractive of his heroines.) It is a positive claim that can be made for the Western, that its climate of anarchy *can* grant women a greater than conventional licence in their actions. It is all the more pity that so often it does not.

In the Western context one might look for heroines who are in fact heroic. They are rare. Where they do occur they are generally comic or caricatured, like the numerous Calamity Janes. Most of these are glamorous, jolly, gun-toting females without the remotest suggestion of the original. Calamity Jane was in fact a repulsive character, though an interesting example of what could happen to a woman on the frontier. She was crude, frequently drunk, and unparticular about whom she shared her bed with. Most of her heroic exploits were, as far as can be judged, fabrications, and her romantic link with Wild Bill Hickok seems to be a myth.

A more authentic female tough with a greater heroic potential, though scarcely more attractive than Calamity Jane, was Belle Starr. She was leader of an outlaw gang, probably the mother of Cole Younger's child. She was no glamour girl. Photographs show her, in a long velvet dress and riding sidesaddle, looking grim, prim and stone faced. She operated in Indian Territory, and was killed more or less in action in 1889. She has since featured in a number of movies, all of which have emphasised femininity at the expense of what might be seen as heroics.

The nearest we can get to a genuinely glamorous female outlaw is Etta Place, who, in her photographs, is beautiful and, as we know from *Butch Cassidy,* was a close associate of Harry Longbaugh, alias the Sundance Kid. Etta Place is a truly fascinating woman, in many ways both more mysterious and more appealing in history than the solidity Katharine Ross gave her in the film suggests. Although there is some doubt as to whether she was a schoolteacher or the inmate of a Fort Worth brothel it is well established that she could ride and shoot and that she accompanied Butch Cassidy and the Sundance Kid on a number of their exploits. She had both elegance and courage, and Butch Cassidy's verdict—'She was the best housekeeper in the Pampas but she was a whore at heart'—adds a further dimension to our picture of her.

Etta was an outlaw of dubious morality. It is generally true that the women who achieved any kind of success comparable to that of men were not the respectable citizens, the wives and daughters whose presence helped to transform the frontier town to a civilised community on something like an Eastern pattern. The only women who were able to make use of the flexibility of an untamed society were those who risked their reputations—or had no reputations to risk. The woman who made money and owned property and had the kind of power money and property grant was most often a brothel or saloon owner. And there were not many such women. The fate of those who started out in such professions was generally less enviable.

In George Roy Hill's movie Etta Place says she will follow Butch and the Kid because they represent the only excitement that ever came into her life. It was a romantic, heroic dream come true. Etta is genuinely absorbed into the myth, on more or less the same terms as the heroes. It is a distinctive feature of the film. She is wholly untypical of what the Western generally supplies, but contains perhaps a promise for the future. How many young girls, trapped in the isolation of the prairies and the mountains, must have longed for the frontier legend to appear on their door-step? Most women in the West were victims of the consequences of the fight against the wild, victims of drudgery and loneliness, their own and that of the men around them. Those who survived into respectability felt that their endurance gave them a natural superiority over the fallen. It was an echo of the heroic Western male, the character that John Wayne plays repeatedly, who considers that he has won his right to be right. While the heroes killed to confirm their status the women could only confirm theirs by giving no quarter to those who had no pretensions to achieving it.

The cowboy's respect for womankind is a powerful feature of the legend. It was said that a woman could travel the length and breadth of the Western territories in greater safety than she could walk the streets of New York. In the 1870s Isabella Bird calmly travelled alone for hundreds of miles in the Rockies, sometimes with the company of one or two men. Never did she tremble for her safety. She was a good rider and quite handy with a gun, and she even developed what she considered a practical form of dress for her rugged life: she called it 'The American Lady's Mountain Dress' and it consisted of 'a half-fitted jacket, a skirt reaching to the ankles, and full Turkish trousers gathered into frills which fall over the boots—a thoroughly serviceable and feminine costume for mountaineering and other rugged travelling in any part of the world.' She rode astride, unthinkable for a well brought up woman, although she sometimes switched to sidesaddle in populated areas.

For hundreds of miles and many months she was unmolested. We may be sceptical about Western, clearly derived from Southern, courtesy, but there is nothing to suggest that any of the West's heroes, good or bad, behaved reprehensibly to a decent woman. But the Western has nursed a sense of threat, a murky shadow, a hint of a fate worse than death, usually administered—or rather, *nearly* administered—by a whisky breathing desperado in need of a shave. Rape, the dread word, has hovered just behind the print of page after page of Westerns since they began. It is in part carrying on the tradition of the rescue of the maiden in distress by the gallant knight. As in a medieval landscape populated with dragons and sorcerers and wicked barons the Western terrain could contain special hazards for the vulnerable female. In many cases these are deliberately exploited to make the most of that most enduring aspect of femininity, sexual helplessness. Every aggressive phrase, every lowering look, every degree of rough handling, can be made to suggest the possibility of rape.

In the Western less trustful women, or more experienced, carry a lady-like derringer which a gloved hand can produce from the front of a dress if the need arises. According to Hamlin Garland such a precaution would have been unnecessary. He wrote, in *The Moccasin Ranch* (1909):

> Formalities counted for little, and yet with all this freedom of intercourse, this close companionship, no one pointed the finger of gossip towards any woman. The girls in their one-room huts received calls from the bachelor neighbours with the confidence that comes from purity of purpose, both felt and understood.

This is in the halcyon days of the early settlement, and the enterprise is regarded both romantically and from a sternly conventional viewpoint: it is the women who might have been the victims of gossip. This transplantation of a very limited social attitude does not read well in a Western context.

It does not always happen that respectability breeds respect, and it is here that the Western does manipulate the more open society of the frontier. There *are* circumstances under which a decent woman might be molested without reflection on her character. It is tempting to make the most of female frailty in a situation that would seem to demand more toughness than we would expect from an Eastern young lady. And it is tempting to provide an opportunity for the hero to exhibit his gallantry. An impeccable attitude to women, whether or not he becomes romantically involved, has always, with occasional exceptions, been an important facet of the hero's character.

It is, for instance, easier in a Western context to allow a hero to behave with courtesy towards a prostitute. The first Western writer to allow his hero to treat a tart like a lady was Bret Harte in his famous story *The Outcasts of Poker Flats*. John Oakhurst the gambler is the only man to treat the prostitutes evicted by the town's moral citizens with any decency or kindness. The situation reappears with distinction in *Stagecoach* (which is to say Ernest Haycox's story *Stage to Lordsburg*, on which the movie is based) where the Ringo Kid behaves with quiet gallantry towards the sad and nervous prostitute who has been run out of town by upright ladies.

At one time it was felt that the Western hero didn't have much to do with women.

> . . . the Western hero stands apart from all other male 'leads' of the screen. Romance is barred from his life. Always impeccably good-mannered and gallant towards women in an aloof, impersonal way, he never becomes emotionally involved—and certainly, for all the rough stuff to which he treats the villain, would never behave with the famous James Mason brutality.

But this has never been quite true. A strain of romance has run right through the Western, certainly from *The Virginian* on, although the hero who rides off into the sunset to pursue his lonely way is possibly the most significant type of Western hero. In most cases the fact that the hero will be romantically involved is established from the outset. It certainly is in Zane Grey's stories, in which women feature prominently. They are often quite tough heroines, but always beguilingly feminine, and frequently in real danger with the hero suitably arriving at the eleventh hour to perform his rescue.

Grey dwells salaciously on the virgin innocence of hero and heroine, and we find lingering descriptions of narrow escapes from fates worse than death. In *To the Last Man* Grey reaches great heights in this vein. In a heavily breathing scene witnessed by the hero the villain rips off the heroine's blouse. As Grey puts it, 'the unleashed passion of the man required violence'. The hero tries hard to avert his eyes from the girl's nakedness, but as he must also be poised to save her (he is wounded, which gives Grey an opportunity to prolong the scene) this proves difficult. The scene is a stew of lust, blood and nudity with Grey holding the reins of propriety with practised ease. He is a master at this: it is allowable for the girl's breasts to be bared if the ostensible motive is to appall us through the eyes of the hero, and not to titillate. He renders the conclusion of *Riders of the Purple Sage* acceptable, by tak-

ing the edge off its impropriety—unmarried hero and heroine are trapped in a sealed valley, perhaps for ever. He deftly blurs the issue in a haze of romance lit by a glow of purity, purity all the more powerful, not to say astonishing, for the burgeoning sexuality of both throughout the book.

Ellen, the heroine of *To the Last Man,* escapes. In 1921 this was obligatory: it also makes the element of exploitation more apparent. The heroine of *Hang 'Em High* (1969) is the victim of rape, and lives, respected, in a bustling frontier community. She is a competent woman, aloof, certainly not helpless. Her fascination (she is played by Inger Stevens) is due precisely to the fact that she is not a pathetic female ruined by rape, and her unconventionality makes a good partner for Clint Eastwood's Marshal Cooper. It is of interest that the Western context is flexible enough to make both this situation and its opposite equally convincing. In *Duel at Diablo* the young woman who returns to her community after a period of captivity by Apaches is treated like dirt. It is known that she was forced to marry an Apache and the town feels that a woman who has submitted to an Indian might as well submit to the whole town.

The film, encased as it is in a thoroughly conventional plot, becomes interesting through that part of the plot that concerns the heroine's escape from her white husband, who can barely tolerate her, in her attempt to recover her half Apache baby. It shares some of the characteristics of *The Stalking Moon*. Both films make the point that if a woman is forced to choose between death and an Apache husband she is likely to choose the latter, and she is likely also to love her child even if she has little affection for the father. And as in *The Stalking Moon* a loner hero is drawn to a woman who is as unfit for a conventional life as himself.

In a novel by Will Cook, *Two Rode Together,* a white woman rescued from the Comanches has some feeling for her Indian husband and expresses her grief in traditional Indian fashion when he is killed by the white men who rescue her. Significantly when she is safely returned to the fort no one will dance with her at a ball given in honour of her deliverance. She is soiled goods. It is a sad little episode not, in the novel, central to the theme. What is of interest is that we have, though not as heroine this time, a woman forced into an isolated independence in much the same way as is a particular kind of Western hero.

The numb, inarticulate Sara Carver in *The Stalking Moon,* without relations or friends, an embarrassment to the army, unacceptable in normal white society, is like these other women an outcast, and it is by being an outcast that she achieves something close to the status of the loner hero. But neither she, the victim, nor the more active Etta Place, are typical Western heroines of the last ten years. The mode remains, as a rule, traditional. We have slightly less glamorous prostitutes, and rather more glamorous gunslingers, a sprinkling of more realistic victims, but very, very few Western makers who have made convincing use of women's life in the West, either in terms of conveying something like the reality of their existence or of dramatising their mythic potential.

So the frontier woman has neither enjoyed the expansion of the myth nor a genuine attempt to present her difficulties. There is a great deal of potential and so far we have only had hints of the possibilities. Yet it would be misleading to underestimate the significance of the women who do appear. If many Western heroines are superfluous many of the women in secondary roles are of some importance: they are, in their way, essential to the myth. The myth cannot survive with only the support of the characterless, unsmudged heroine.

We are used to seeing the dance hall girl or the town tart as a brash, gay, sometimes witty woman with nerves of steel. She is of course a necessary foil to the young innocent whom the hero may win. She is also an important gesture towards the West's wildness and to a situation which everyone accepts but few care to elaborate. Sometimes she is a pretty little plaything, like the big-eyed lisping blonde in *Rough Night in Jericho;* sometimes a more sombre woman, suggestive of depths of character and passion. She can be anything from a floosie to a woman of power, and there is, not surprisingly, a much greater range of character amongst the fallen than amongst the virtuous.

The inmates of the Fort Grant brothel in *Hang 'Em High* are under the strict control of a regal and matronly woman who looks after her girls with some affection. The establishment has some elegance. But if here the relationship between drifter and brothel is all ease and relaxation it does ignore some problematic issues. The more comfortable, clean and acceptable such an establishment is the more ambiguous is the situation of those who work in it. Are they well-groomed, decent young women or are they victims of exploitation to be pitied and saved, or are they irredeemable sluts regarded with suspicion and bitterness by the community's respectable females? There was always the possibility that their own husbands and sons were customers.

In the Western we get most versions of the woman of ill repute, but least frequently do we get the girl who is really down and out. The life of a prostitute could be as grim, lonely and loveless as that of the most remote settler's daughter. They shared the same lack of choice in what they did with their lives. Girls came West lured by hopes of financial gain, like anybody else, and pushed by a grim understanding of the lack of opportunities in the East. Once West there was little a single girl could do. The dance hall, the saloon and the brothel were usually the only alternative sources of employment. A woman in the West was above all a commodity. If it was not her entertainment value that was bought and sold it was her domestic value. It was of course a situation not confined to the West, but the bareness of Western society emphasised it. It was, for so many women, their last hope.

As we have seen, women were one of the diversions a town had to offer men on the move. A girl's function in the dance hall or saloon was to look decorative and get the men to spend money. They were at the mercy of the proprietor on the one hand, the customers on the other. If they were not exactly prostitutes they were assumed to be of easy virtue. The Western has presented distinct types of the woman of not necessarily irreclaimable but certainly dubious morality. They are often of European origin—'Frenchie' appears in more than one Western. There are many Irish girls. 'Frenchie' is usually tough, resilient, influential, the Irish girl often worn out and bitter. The mainstream Western frequently presents the buxom blonde with a heart of gold, occasionally a fallen angel struggling to abandon a life she hates. Towns in the southwest always seem to be densely populated with sultry flesh at easy rates. In *The Wild Bunch* it is certainly not to Peckinpah's credit that he makes use of that opprobious cliché that all Mexican girls are tarts. Mexican women, like the men, are expendable.

There are a few memorable exceptions. *Ride the High Country's* massive whore is probably the nearest the screen has got to what John Coleman called 'a gen-yew-ine clapped-up tart' and she is superb. The climate of the film is such that we can readily imagine this queen of revelry spreading disease and Billy, a young resident of the mining camp who has clearly made use of its amenities, passing it on to his newly-wed wife. The self-hating, dignified Irish girl in *Killer on a Horse* is memorable for a different reason. She communicates a drastic loneliness, a depth of private suffering. But in recent years the brothel and the prostitute have become vehicles for comedy and light relief with no suggestion of misery or disease or desperation. Comedy that turns on sex always has immense potential, but the jollity and the wholesomeness that forms the dominant image leaves out a great deal.

William Cox's novel *The Duke* indicates a little of what most Westerns ignore. There are two women in this story who are important characters, one a twenty year old girl from New England who has come West for lack of opportunity back home, the other an older, experienced, toughened woman. The younger has a job in a bar; she serves drinks and wanders amongst 'the Saturday night gamblers, smiling at one and all'. The older woman is a waitress, but is obviously not what she seems. She has behind her a mysterious, embittering past, has survived an overdose of laudanum, and before the book finishes contemplates another. The barrenness and cheapness of her life pushes her to desperation, yet she is not weak, but a positive and sympathetic character. The book ends, of course, happily for her, united with a man who understands the kind of life she has led. She is romanticised, she is beautiful, cultivated, educated, but she does suggest quite powerfully the vulnerability of a woman alone on the frontier.

Laudanum provided a not uncommon solution to misery, opium too. Neither were difficult to come by. Both were standard nineteenth century palliatives. There was not much in life for the ageing prostitute unless she was one of the few who rose to the heights of proprietorship, and the young were just as likely to succumb to depression and self-disgust. Andy Adams, writing from experience, describes the Dew-Drop-In Dance Hall in Ogallala.

> Here might be seen the frailty of women in every grade and condition. From girls in their teens, launching out on a life of shame, to the adventuress who had once had youth and beauty in her favour, but it was now discarded and ready for the final dose of opium and the coroner's ver-

dict—all were there in tinsel and paint, practising a careless exposure of their charms.

Occasionally in the Western we do come across a whisky-sodden, worn-out woman, but the effects of liquor are usually represented in girlish giggles. It is curious that the descent of the innocent girl into the depths of prostitution, a much worked plot in fiction, has not found its way into the Western.

In 1893 a Colorado newspaper recorded a suicide attempt by a girl called Rose Vastine. The glib tone of the report does not disguise the underlying tragedy.

> Rose Vastine, known about the camp as 'Timberline', became weary of the trials and tribulations of this wicked world and decided to take a trip over the range, and to this end brought into play a forty-one calibre pistol. With the muzzle at her lily white breast and her index finger on the trigger she waited not to contemplate the sad result. A slight contradiction of the muscles caused the gun to empty its contents into Rose, the ball passing through the upper portion of her left lung.

The wound was not fatal, but Rose's action, if not typical, was symptomatic.

The nature of her usual occupation meant that the drifting female made little impression on the communities that sustained her. Influence came from success, money and staying put. Those who did not reach the top had nothing to contribute—or were prevented from contributing—to the process of development. Her respectable sister could do little more than attempt to impose a well-understood old order.

> There must have been times when she could have cried bitterly as she saw the few obvious pleasures monopolised by the young and the immoral. Understandable is the difficulty of choice when her husband died and her only possible occupations were boardinghouse keeper or prostitute. Every fibre of her being called for a new and better social order where the usual social values were respected and where children could be reared without contamination from a crude and lawless society.

Almost every woman in the West felt threatened. The hold onto a conventional, protected life was so tenuous, the reversals could be so drastic, and any attempt to undertake an unprotected, unconventional life so demanding. In such a society the women, like the men, most often had to make a choice between feeding on the crudity and lawlessness and condemning out of hand anything that did not conform to a limited and unforgiving attitude.

Yet there were women who made a good thing out of their immoral trade, had no doubts about its value, and took a certain pride in handling things properly. There were standards in prostitution just as in any other form of business. Elliot Paul describes in his autobiographical *A Ghost Town on the Yellowstone* two establishments in Glendive at the turn of the century.

> The principal madams in the Glendive stockade

were both smart women and fine troupers, but not at all alike. Jack Little, short, squat and stocky, had a hoarse whisky baritone voice. She wore black silk stockings and a short, stiff ballet skirt that left quite an area of flesh tones uncovered, and was the 'hail-fellow-well-met type'. Mona Mason, on the other hand, had been a Southern society belle before, as she put it, she 'got on to herse'f'. Jack, in a tough land, wanted her cat-house to be the toughest spot, and attended to the bouncing herself, if anybody got unruly enough to warrant being thrown out. Jack's theory was that 'men don't shoot women unless they love 'em'. Mona was a soft-spoken, polite and languorous woman, who seemed to have no bones, and never raised her voice. She thought that, since Montana was doing so well by her, she could bring some Southern grace and hospitality into Montana, and she did. She could not get many Southern sporting girls, that far away from home, and the few she got from Dixie could not stand the Montana climate. So she trained the Middle-Western hookers who drifted West from Chicago, Omaha, Kansas City and St. Paul not to shout or drink beer from bottles, and no matter how many times they had to leave the dance hall or the parlour in the course of a night, they were required to put their corsets back on and hook them properly before they appeared again.

As with the hero, fashions in heroines change. In the early days the helpless maiden was popular, and alongside these—they are regular denizens of W. S. Hart's pictures—are toughies in the shape of blatant bar-room girls. Zane Grey's books introduced some more active heroines, although as we have seen in a crisis they were suitably helpless. Ernest Haycox wrote about interesting women, though they suffered in translation to the screen. It was more than anything fashions in the cinema that forced the Western to be merely decorative. The Gene Autry era produced the heroine it deserved, a rigorously permanent-waved cowgirl in fringes and boots. The successor to this, reflecting a more general trend, was the woman who emphasised the positive good of domesticity, the woman who waited loyally for her man to return, prayed that he would give up his gun. We see women tending and feeding their men.

But almost from the start the most attractive kind of Western female is the girl who wears jeans and rides a horse and, to some extent at least, responds to an adventurous, demanding man's world by doing a man's work. There is something particularly appealing in a woman, with of course her femininity never in question, in masculine garb tackling masculine difficulties. The fact that this is usually manipulated in such a way as to enlarge the hero does not destroy the fact that in a context where a woman is allowed to enter a man's world there is much more scope for female action.

Emerson Hough's Taisey, young ranch owner in his novel *North of 36* (filmed two years later by Irvin Willat) dresses like a man and accompanies the herd she owns on the trail drive. Of course without the help of a dedicated man she would never win through, but although ultimately she is dependent she is able to make something of both her freedom and her responsibility. One of the nicest of tomboy heroines is Mariette Hartley's role in *Ride the High Country*. We respond to her partly because she does seem to be a genuine product of rough isolation. She shares the life of a demanding father and has to act as ranch hand, cook and cleaner. With cropped red hair and freckles and shapeless grubby trousers her transformation to a bride wearing her mother's wedding dress in a raucous mining camp has a wistful quality of reality.

There have been some long haired, wild riding female hellions. The girl in *El Dorado* has been brought up by a father amongst brothers (so often the wives have not survived) and is as instinctive and skillful as an animal who has to fight for existence. She is won by James Caan as the enigmatic knife-thrower and it seems a suitably eccentric match. These tough frontier women have been appearing quite frequently in the television serials, again reflecting trends elsewhere, in *The Virginian* for instance, a much needed contrast to the wholesome Betsy. There was a splendid though sad version of a Calamity Jane in *The High Chaparral* who shoots, holds her whisky and cusses with the best of the men. She runs her own freighting company, drives the wagons herself, completely untramelled by civilised life. Yet even here the emphasis is on the waif-like quality of this young, tough woman fending for herself, and she is not regarded as a suitable mate for the hero: he may be a degree uncouth but he belongs to a well-established, successful ranching family.

The particular appeal of the girl dressed as a boy, of the highlighting of femininity through masculine actions, is a vein the Western is likely to continue exploiting. What is to be hoped is that much more will be made of the immense potential for heroines that lies in the anarchy of the Western situation. For now, the tomboy remains an eccentric. What still dominates the Western is a changing image of the chocolate box heroine, who was so firmly established in the forties and reigned triumphant throughout the fifties. Raquel Welch with a rifle in her hand is really little more than an up-dated version of chocolate box. Her function is inevitably primarily decorative.

The chocolate box heroine has become more versatile, but her versatility has not made her more interesting. Although the stetsoned cowgirl never wholly emerged from the B Western there is now a more sophisticated heroine recognisable as being of a similar species. We find her most frequently in the television series. She does as well as a hostess in an evening gown as she does on a horse, and she can converse with State Governors as easily as with cowpunchers. She has the confidence that arises from a secure status. She is an all-purpose horse-opera heroine and she is generally very, very dull.

This all-purpose heroine is a fusion of what have been traditionally in the Western two general types: the decorative heroine, who is associated with civilisation, domesticity, the schoolhouse and the church, and the spunky heroine, who is not averse to riding the range and encountering man-sized dangers but who is almost always sufficiently tamed to provide a suitable mate for the hero. A lack of conformity to these types provides a clue to the more in-

teresting Western movies and the more readable Western books. The fusion suggests that taste has outgrown the negative heroine, but it does not suggest that Westerns are in general responding to this. Traditional versions are being stretched to provide opportunities for more screen sex, but the new realism only seems able to cope with women in the West on these terms. Of course there are exceptions, some of which have been noted, but it is worth repeating that the Western has not incorporated women significantly and creatively into the myth although the potential is there.

Allied with the traditional division between chocolate box and spunky, and allied more closely with the rigid separation of decent and fallen, is a conventional pattern of dark and fair. Often enough to be of some significance the respectable heroines are blonde and ladies of dubious morals are brunette. The classic oppositions of *High Noon* provide an excellent example of this dark/fair pattern. The Quaker wife is fair, the woman with whom the hero has clearly been involved in the past is dark. The Quaker wife becomes a symbol not so much of love and purity as of lawfulness and civilisation, again a traditional role for the woman in the Western. The woman in Will's past is a reminder of passion and recklessness. With some irony the fact that Will's wife, once more a Quaker armed, takes unto herself a gun helps the balance in favour of the blonde. A touch of spunk is needed to match her with the hero. In terms of this pattern the redhead provides a useful compromise. A significant number of the Western's spunky but respectable heroines have red hair. It suggests spirit without vice, virtue without insipidness.

A majority of Westerns have the idea of marriage present at some point. What in fact is the Western's ideal of a wife? The wife, whether existing or intended, has a role of the greatest importance to play in the Western, for without her the note of romance, of reconciliation, of promise for the future on which so many Westerns end would not be possible. A few end with regret and parting or death and are sometimes equally romantic. But this does not change the predominant emphasis, which remains squarely on the fate of hero and heroine. The powerful, traditional belief that hope lies in a repetition of a conventional, sanctioned cycle, however extraordinary and anarchic the context, communicates itself in the Western as it does elsewhere.

Sometimes the ending is more than just a clinch, but a positive if highly romantic statement about the hero's new life. 'This was what he had to live for. And as he drew her closer, feeling the giving in her, he knew that all the uncertainty and the emptiness of his tomorrows was gone.' This is taken from the last page of a Western by a highly prolific writer. The suggestiveness is pervasive but vague. The hero, a drifter, a fighter, can never, whatever his courage and physical achievements, fulfil himself without a woman. This is what it was all for. No more loneliness, no more emptiness. A life of mutual comfort and companionship. A standard theme of countless songs, novels and poems, and of course, which we all recognise, an undermining of most of what makes the action hero what he is. Because the Western heroine is repeatedly characterised as a civilising influence her effect on the independent hero can only be destructive.

The hero who rides off womanless on the final page retains his integrity. He has not been enticed by visions of domestic bliss, or if he admits their attractions he dismisses them. Every hero who continues on his lonely way protects something vital about himself. Yet the solitary exit does not occur as frequently as might be supposed. The fact that *Shane* embodies so much that is best about the Western almost makes us believe that its ending is typical. Shane is certainly so powerful that he carries the myth onwards and we see in him the preservation of the lonely freedom that countless lesser heroes, brought to a halt by the fair sex, lose. And Shane's attraction is enhanced by the fact that he knows he is leaving behind him a woman who loves him, and he knows he is right to do so.

For those who relinquish that particular brand of independence it is not just any woman who can fill the emptiness of those tomorrows. Time after time the Western hero unites himself with vacancy and thus does graver damage to the Western's total effect. It is a symptom of the failure to recognise that more positive heroines can only enhance the value of the myth. In the Western context, with hardship a part of everyday life, it is particularly crass to present marriage as a passport to ease and happiness, especially when it is so often to a woman who is ignorant, or at least not convincingly knowledgeable, of frontier life.

We look for wives who will not negate the heroes, and sometimes we can find them. At the end of Louis L'Amour's *Heller With a Gun* the hero significantly gets the tough, Denver-bred youngster who is ready to ride after him rather than the more proper and superficially more attractive young woman from the East. This is a favourite contrast of L'Amour's. In *Last Stand at Papago Wells* the sophisticated Jennifer has to learn from the rough and ready Junie before she can qualify as mate for the hero, whose initial remark is 'You look nice but you don't mean anything.' In the course of an Indian attack Jennifer acquires some meaning. Yet there has to be more to the perfect mate than toughness. If a woman has to pass certain frontier tests she will not do to share the life of the Westerner if she cannot also make a home, a home that will be a refuge from the wild, and this has all the traditional connotations. L'Amour ends another of his books like this:

> But he was remembering a long meadow fresh with new-cut hay, a house where smoke would soon again rise from the chimney, and where shadows would gather in the darkness under the trees, quiet shadows. And beside him a woman held in her arms a sleeping child . . . a woman who would be there with him, in the house before that hearth.

A quiet vision consistent with the deep current of sentimentalism that runs through the Western as through all other forms of popular literature. But no soft moment can disguise the real content of such a vision. We are back to the harsh experience of Matthilda Zachary, dimmed and blurred. The Indians have been defeated, but that vision cannot be sustained without heart-breaking toil. No hero

can soften the reality, though there is quite a chance that the idyllic picture will soften the hero. We can find a corrective, unexpectedly, in one of the later books of Eugene Cunningham, *The Trail from the River* (1939). His hero says:

> You have read a book about the big handsome cowboy marrying the lovely school-ma'am. What you and the other fool-cowboys didn't read, though, was the book for grown-ups about the married life they had, people as different as day and night penned up in the same house year after year, one of 'em eating with a knife and the other eating with a fork!

The big handsome cowboy is clearly the Virginian. Wister's Eastern school teacher gave the Western heroine a discordant start. The screen now trails behind the novel in giving us interesting and convincing heroines. Not only for the sake of the Western hero, who now seems more inclined to die than to marry, which is one way of preserving his independence, but even more for the sake of the unfulfilled potential of women in myth since the time of classical Greece, a test of the Western's ability to grant women a positive contribution to the myth would be a welcome experiment. (pp. 157-73)

Images of women and minorities in westerns:

The manliness of our cowboy myth-hero has been maintained at the expense of women. One of the oldest American clichés describes the West as a place where "men are men, and women are glad of it." Another describes the West as being "hell on women and horses." And the Western story is unique in popular literature in making prostitution glamorous. The hero spends his leisure in saloons with whores or "dancing girls," open hearted ladies who understand that "a man's gotta do what a man's gotta do." Even "Gunsmoke"—the most long-lived, carefully edited, and cunningly produced of television series—made the only permanent female member of its cast the owner of a saloon, happily neglecting the historical fact that no respectable woman in the real Dodge City ever entered, let alone owned, such an establishment. The fictional cowboy hero is usually uncomfortable with a "good girl," who would curb his freedom and deplore his violence. Marriage to her may be his reward, but it also is usually the end of his story. And almost never, of course, does he meet an intelligent, adult woman who could both complicate and enrich his life . . .

Until very recently, Western heroes held that the only good Indians were dead Indians and that most blacks and Mexicans were ignorant, cowardly, or treacherous. Only occasional exceptions were made for an Uncle Tom or an Uncle Tonto, a faithful companion who held the hero's horse or bound his wounds. Occasionally a Cisco Kid emerged as a "proud Spanish American of the Southwest"—but only occasionally. And only in the recent self-conscious times have Western heroes stopped praising their comrades by saying, "That's damned white of you."

Philip Durham and Everett L. Jones in their
The Western Story, *Harcourt Brace Jovanovich, 1975.*

Jenni Calder, "Women in the West," in her
There Must Be a Lone Ranger, *Hamish Hamilton, 1974, pp. 157-73.*

Madelon E. Heatherington

[*In the following excerpt, Heatherington contrasts two
types of women in American western fiction: the "princess" and the "poison queen," describing the former as
the embodiment of conventional feminine virtues and
the latter as a destroyer of men.*]

In recent years, virtually every art form dealing with the
American West has become fashionable, profitable, and
therefore to some extent respectable—every art form, that
is, except fiction. Most novels and short stories about the
West are still regarded as merely "pulp" trash, widely read
but rarely taken seriously. Ph.D. candidates have written
dissertations on Western music, films, sculpture, and
painting, but the fiction still limps along on the critical and
academic blacklist, lower than Women's Studies or Science Fiction. I propose that a significant reason for this respectability gap, as it might be styled, is that unlike other
art forms taking the American West as their source or subject, the fiction has for the most part stayed at the simplistic level of its dime-novel origins and its early popularizers
(Owen Wister, Zane Grey, et al.), especially in characterization, and has therefore failed to take into account the
complexities both of human behavior, actual or fictional,
and of the Western's own genre, the romance.

An important manifestation of Western fiction's arrested
development occurs in its treatment of women characters.
Even the best of recent fiction about or based on myths of
the West, like Thomas Berger's *Little Big Man* and Ken
Kesey's *One Flew over the Cuckoo's Nest,* has generally
continued to perpetuate a puerile fantasy—by males,
about males, for males—that has restricted most such
novels to a realm of escapism in which Hawkeye, Shane,
or Hud grows solitarily gray, hunting and fishing, building
forts and "shootin' Injuns," happily removed from all
adult women forever. Not merely the formulaic pulp novelists (such as Louis L'Amour), but often the most respected of Western writers still manufacture the same
dreary female stereotypes as Wister and Grey did (types
who are by no means confined to fiction about cowboys
and Indians, but who appear in some form in virtually all
literature): the basic division of women into the purely
good and the utterly bad; the virgin and the bitch; Northrop Frye's "the lady of duty and the lady of pleasure";
the Princess and the Poison Queen.

But simply to identify such characterization as shallow, or
to disparage it as merely another form of male chauvinism, is to overlook more salient consequences in favor of
an equivalently simplistic revisionist-feminist attack. It is
a commonplace among students of literature, especially of
Westerns, that women have received short shrift in the fiction, that most fictional women are flat and peripheral,
and that even when a woman is a central figure (like Cath-
arine the shrew, tamed in one of the few Westerns written
by a woman: Marilyn Durham's *The Man Who Loved Cat
Dancing*), she is handled in a manner so predictable as to
be formulaic. It would be equally commonplace to observe
that such treatment is unfair, a shame, a gross misrepresentation, etc. More important, I believe, is the examination of two further consequences arising from such limited
characterization of women in Westerns: the basic dynamics of romance are aborted in these novels, and therefore
most fiction of the American West has never allowed itself
to explore and develop its own full potential.

Doubtless one of the reasons that much Western fiction remains at best a problematic genre for critics is that the
West itself is still ordinarily seen, even by many who live
there, as an uneasy mixture of mythic fantasy and social
inertia. The region itself is vague, uncertainly located
somewhere over the Mississippi and south of Philadelphia.
What "the West" means is even less clear. To many Americans, it stands for the last U.S. frontier, final refuge of the
disaffected, inspirational locus of true Marlboro *macho*
where people and things were simpler, cleaner, and wiser
than in the East. To others, the West is a cultural desert
littered with radioactive sheep and half-ton Chevy pickups
bearing bumper stickers which vow, "You can have my
gun when you can pry my cold, dead fingers off the trigger." The same schizoid response appears toward art
about the West, long dismissed by most critics as regional
sentimentalism which only the proletariat favor, presumably moving their lips and stroking their Winchesters the
while. But suddenly Wall Street brokers are wearing Justin boots, and all of the arts except fiction have acquired
a WASP-ethnic cachet.

Western fiction has earned its lack of status, however, for
most of it is still as limited as it was seventy years ago—a
striking contrast with what is happening in the other arts
about the West. These others have so managed to adapt
Western formulas as to have it both ways: they are keeping
pace with a more sophisticated (or perhaps a more realistic) apprehension of history and of human beings, but they
have also continued drawing on the Western's traditional
resource of romance myths. Consider country-western
music as an example-a hybrid of country and western,
granted, but sharing enough of the Western's resources to
participate in its myths. It is clear that at least some of this
music has changed in recent years. David Allen Coe wrote
a song in 1977 with these lines: "I was drunk the day my
ma got out of prison / And I went to pick her up in the
rain"—a deliberate parody of the hillbilly's preoccupation
with Mama and prison and being drunk, as Coe's lyrics
cheerfully declare. Or take Jerry Jeff Walker's "Up against
the wall, redneck mother, / Mother who has raised her
son so well"—a play on the radical sloganeering of the
1960's, as well as an ironic treatment of the conventionally
syrupy portrait of Mother by such singers as Roy Acuff
and the Carter Family. A few other female stereotypes are
changing in the music, too: along with Tammy Wynette's
conventional injunction to "Stand by Your Man" or
Waylon Jennings' eulogy of the "Good-Hearted Woman,"
loyal as a hound, there is also Loretta Lynn snarling
"Don't Come Home a-Drinkin' with Lovin' on Your
Mind" or the Amazing Rhythm Aces' sardonic vignette,
"Third-Rate Romance."

No equivalent transformations are occurring in Western

fiction, which for the most part still gives us shallow demi-types of no complexity whatever. Not even stereotypes, much less archetypes, most Western women are characters so formulaic, so diluted, so single-dimensional that their functions in various novels are usually as interchangeable as assembly-line carburetors. To be sure, there are a few exceptions; Sissy in Tom Robbins' *Even Cowgirls Get the Blues,* Susan in Wallace Stegner's *Angle of Repose,* and Beret in O. E. Rölvaag's *Giants in the Earth*—quite early, as Westerns go—are examples. None of these women could be removed or exchanged with another female character without seriously damaging each novel's effectiveness and impact. All of these women's presences and perspectives are crucial in the development of their novels. Sissy's spacy gallantry as a focus for Robbins' philosophical meanderings make her the nexus of the whole picaresque book; every character in it functions because of some connection, however tenuous, to her. Susan's and Beret's struggles to come to terms with the frontier (Susan more successfully than Beret) form such an essential part of each work that what Stegner and Rölvaag were saying about human life under alien, often hostile circumstances could not have been so fully realized without these women. But Sissy, Susan, and Beret are exceptional creations.

Much more common are the legions of faceless women who service, follow, or prompt the men—motivators, not actors, important only to the plot, which is primarily concerned with the maneuverings of males. Note, for instance, the roster of "good woman" demi-types customary in the fiction, dominated by Molly Wood's Schoolteacher in Wister's *The Virginian:*

> THE TRANSPLANTED LADY (Stewart White's *These Folded Hills,* A. B. Guthrie's *These Thousand Hills,* William Goldman's *Butch Cassidy and the Sundance Kid*)
>
> THE INDIAN VIRGIN (Vardis Fisher's *Mountain Man,* Frederick Manfred's *King of Spades,* A. B. Guthrie's *The Big Sky*)
>
> THE FARM WIFE, often combined with EARTH MOTHER (A. B. Guthrie's *The Way West,* Jack Schaefer's *Shane,* Larry McMurtry's *Leaving Cheyenne*).

Who can name more than a few of the main female characters in these novels? And these are not the pulps; these are the good books, among the best in Western writing. But even here, the ladies of duty blend into a single creature, whose fictive function is to swell a procession, to gather firewood, to keep the children out of the way and the dishes unbroken in the flour barrel, to minister to her man's marital advances, and occasionally to be abducted, raped, or murdered in order that the men might avenge her. On the whole, the good demi-types are no more distinguishable from one another than are Isolde the Elder and Isolde White-Hands in *Tristan.*

Curiously, neither are the bad demi-types, even though naughty women are ordinarily more distinctive in literature since they cause more trouble; their comparatively greater freedom of action makes them more of a threat to the homeostatic well-being of the heroes than are the duti-

ful ladies. In our wider literary typology, for every St. Anne, Griselda, Ophelia, or Marmee March, there are a half dozen memorably wicked women like the Apocryphal Judith, Lady Macbeth, Amber St. Clare, Scarlett O'Hara, Brett Ashley, Carol Kennicott, Jo March, Lady Chatterley, Isadora Wing: rebellious figures, one might almost say "masculine" in their ingenuity, self-sufficiency, and assertiveness. But the appearance in Western novels of even demi-typed Poison Queens is much rarer than in the rest of our fiction; indeed, there is only one type, the Outlaw Girl. Sometimes she is a literal felon like Cat Ballou or Etta Place, sometimes a perverse Earth Mother like Ma Grier in Walter Van Tilburg Clark's *The Ox-Bow Incident,* but most popularly, she is the Soiled Dove (also known as The Dance-Hall Girl), as in Schaefer's *Monte Walsh,* Steinbeck's *East of Eden,* or Guthrie's *These Thousand Hills.*

Now contrast these indistinguishable figures with the full-blooded archetypes, of which most Westerns' women are but featureless copies. The good woman can be identified in Jungian terms as the beneficent *anima,* the soul mother objectified as a goddess adored from afar: Isis, Athena, Mary, Beatrice. Whether as Leslie Fiedler's "Blue-Eyed Protestant Virgin" (i.e., a true Princess) or as the domesticated Princess (the Earth Mother), the good woman stands for transcendence of human baseness, the incarnation of virtue, chastity, mercy, and no bad habits or internal organs. She is the antithesis of the hero, his secular pipeline to the other world of divinity. The bad-woman archetype is more complicated, in part because she does share some wicked ways with the hero, particularly sexuality, and in part because her power over him can interfere with his mythic function as hero, the attempted mediation between savagery and civilization. The Poison Queen is the destroyer of men's souls and the ruination of their bodies, Jung's maleficent *anima,* the seductive castrator feverishly chased but despised once had: Ishtar, Aphrodite, Lilith, Magdalene, Morgan le Fay. her encouragement of the hero's sensuality (i.e., secularity) can doom him unless he establishes his dominance over her—and over those impulses in himself which she represents—for if he does not de-fang her with his magical, symbolic weapon, he cannot go on to save the world in the name of righteousness, the Princess, and Manifest Destiny.

Given these two points of comparison (the small number of exceptional female characters in Westerns, and the romance-myth archetypes on which Westerns draw), the trail of flattened women in most Western fiction is faint indeed. The paradox is that the vehicle of romance by which these demi-types are carried to readers is potentially quite powerful—but not if it is limited by internal constraints. Assuming that Stanley Fish is correct, the best "self-consuming artifacts" are designed to push their readers beyond the text and beyond their own minds. Good books, that is, do not merely affirm what a reader already believes, but induce in him a disequilibrium, a happily anxious quest that carries him out of his own assumptions, in fact, beyond the book itself. But most Westerns are self- and reader-affirmative; they reassure the reader that his attitudes are right and just, that he need not bestir himself to question them. Worse, many readers of Westerns, especially of the pulps, believe that those novels are almost telling the literal truth, as if they were honest-to-God historical case studies about the way the West really was, including the way men and women really were in the West—and possibly should be still. By appealing to this kind of search for affirmable bias, and by fixing characterial "truth" at the level of Barbie and Ken dolls, most Western novels have left unexplored the nonliteral, ambivalent, but nevertheless far more powerful truths of their own origins in romance.

Even the most conventional Westerns rest on a foundation of romance mythology that can sometimes elevate novels above the limits of formula—a mythology both received and created about the nature of America, of the West, of good and evil, of solitude and solidarity, of heroism and salvation, of savagery and civilization . . . and of men and women. In his important study of Western American fiction, *The Six-Gun Mystique,* John G. Cawelti has observed that good Western novels "can be seen as the embodiments of the archetypal pattern of the hero's quest which Frye discusses under the general mythos of romance." As Frye notes, romance is characterized by "its extraordinarily persistent nostalgia, its search for some kind of imaginative golden age in time or space," and by its ritual quest or chase structure, the whole set in an idealized universe removed from the ordinary (real) world. The Western, we know, is ordinarily located in some region of the West, usually takes place in the past (often between 1830 and 1890), and nearly always involves a chase of villains by the hero, with civilization—the Princess, the town—as the prize. Like all romances, too, the Western is usually stripped of mundane concerns like hemorrhoids or excise taxes that might distract the hero from the ritual tests and confrontations required by romance as prelude to deliverance.

Deliverance, the romance/Western hero's principal duty, can be subdivided into two related and sequential tasks. First, the hero must confront evil, usually by undertaking an arduous journey during which he encounters several preliminary sources of conflict before he meets and slays the symbolic dragon which has been ravaging the princesses, ruining the crops, and generally rendering the landscape sterile. So the romance hero's social obligation is to eliminate the savagery that has disrupted the community. His second task is to return the community—however illusorily, however momentarily—to the purified, prelapsarian, neoplatonic paradise from which souls are expelled when they are born into this ordinary world of bills, beans, and boredom. The hero's anagogic function, then, is to give us a glimpse of what we could be if we were better than we are.

The point here is that in order to carry out this two-stage process of deliverance, any hero of romance (and therefore of a Western) must accept and conquer various initiating challenges which prepare him for the task ahead. It is because of the initiatory tests that he progresses first to mastery of himself and his world and thence to the salvation of lesser mortals from sterility and despair. In the romance mythos, women play a crucial part in this preliminary testing and therefore in the preparation for deliverance,

for because of his encounters with various female archetypes, the hero learns to accept various aspects of himself. He must undergo confrontation and acceptance so that he can recognize the synthesis of those archetypes in what Joseph Campbell calls "the goddess of the world" (figures like Gē or Parvati or H. Rider Haggard's "She"), and then he must symbolically marry the goddess, metaphorically becoming or absorbing her and thereby multiply enhancing his own powers. At that point, says Campbell, the hero will have achieved "total mastery of life; for the woman *is* life, the hero its knower and master."

Suppose, however, that the hero cannot or will not attempt that confrontation, assimilation, and mastery: then he has three less acceptable (because more restrictive) choices. As one, he may project his lack of fulfillment, his insecurity, and his concomitant self-loathing directly onto women, seeing them as figures of the sexuality in himself which, being unacknowledged and untested, has therefore destroyed him. This first choice forces him to fixate on woman as Poison Queen, whom he now sees as an enemy. To some extent, McMurphy takes this stance in *Cuckoo's Nest;* many writers have contended that it is Don Juan Tenorio's choice, too. As the second, the hero can take the opposite tack and deny his fear and rage about his own reluctance to encounter the goddess; he projects an overcompensatory reversal of loathing onto woman and now sees her as his antithesis, the Princess, an icon. Most fictional cowboys may seem to have made this choice—Jack Crabb appears to have done so in *Little Big Man*—but I suggest that in most Westerns, the hero's awe around women stems less from throttled rage disguised as reverence than from his having made the third, and worst, choice: the denial that women exist in any significant way at all. This attitude is the worst because if a hero tries to proceed on his task in ignorance of women and what he can learn from them, his capacity for deliverance is severely weakened because *he* is. He becomes vulnerable to unexpected assaults from enemies who take advantage of his ignorance, as Ishtar does in her first encounter with Enkidu or as Brunhild does with Siegfried. Thus undermined, the hero becomes essentially powerless to effect his primary task of salvation, so he wastes his regenerative energies in mere adventure for its own sake.

Sadly, this is what has happened with most fiction about the West, even the best novels. Hugely and deservedly popular (and not just with readers of the pulps), wonderfully ironic in tone and in their manipulation of Western formulas, provocative and perceptive works in nearly all respects, *Cuckoo's Nest* and *Little Big Man*—representative of the best of Western fiction—still avoid confrontation with the goddess, still use female characters as narrowly and as peripherally as Wister did in 1902, and consequently still deny their heroes full romance status.

Kesey's novel is a marvelously complex anticipation of psychiatrist R. D. Laing's proposition, rather like Scaramouch's, that insanity is the only sane reaction to a universe gone mad. Everything in *Cuckoo's Nest* compels us to deal with the clash between individuality and conformity, between self-definition or -discovery and and institutional prescription, even between the East and the West:

East Coast technology *versus* West Coast naturalism—the Promised Land re-created by all writers of Westerns. As Kesey advances these oppositions in order to argue for their synthesis, he invokes and then inverts nearly every tradition of Western fiction: the Promised Land becomes an insane asylum, the Lone Ranger helps the Indians to win, the Lone Ranger himself (Randle Patrick McMurphy) is enormously compelling but still a wheel-spinning con man dodging the work farm. Through such inversions and resultant ambiguities, Kesey shows us that the contest is not a simplistic one between McMurphy and the Combine, libido and super-ego, good and evil, Dionysiac rebellion and Apollonian restraint. Granting McMurphy's powerful appeal, granting his vigor and his necessary potency as an antidote to the entrenched sickness of the asylum, nevertheless, Kesey's central point is that balance rather than extremes produces health, and McMurphy is as unbalanced in one direction as Big Nurse is in the other. Were McMurphy's iconoclasm and self-indulgence left unchecked in the world outside the asylum, he would be as dangerous there as the nurse is inside.

But despite her status as the hero's opponent, and therefore despite the necessity of her individuation as part of Kesey's Hegelian argument, Big Nurse gets nothing like the artfully distinctive treatment which Kesey affords the male characters. True, she is made a formidable antagonist. No single character so clearly stands for regimented oppression as does Nurse Ratched, always surrounded by mechanical imagery as harsh as her name: the tools she supposedly carries in her purse, her switchboard nurse's station, her black "robots," even her incongruously maternal, implausibly sexual breasts, as machined as the rest of her, "skin like flesh-colored enamel." But hers is basically a one-dimensional evil, for her power is largely derivative, not something she has earned or can exercise on her own; she merely symbolizes the impersonality of power. Consequently, when McMurphy attacks her, his act is primarily a political one, a defiant trust-busting assault on the Combine she represents. The Chief implicitly recognizes the political nature of McMurphy's charge when, using Western-formula terms, he describes the scene prompted by McMurphy's responsibilities to his constituents: "We couldn't stop him because we were the ones making him do it. It wasn't the nurse that was forcing him, it was our need. . . . We made him stand and hitch up his shorts like they was horsehide chaps, and push back his cap with one finger like it was a ten-gallon Stetson, slow mechanical gestures," directed against a mechanical woman.

In demonstrating that the Western paradise no longer exists unless people deliberately create it, Kesey shows the danger of imposing any single perspective, even McMurphy's, onto reality. But in not allowing Big Nurse any more complexity of characterization than Trampas got in *The Virginian* or Big Brother in *1984,* Kesey thereby weakens the mythic confrontations. The cardboard characterizations in Berger's *Little Big Man* have the same effect. In this episodic *tour de force* (which, one could argue, turns Kesey's tragi-comic vision into unbridled satire and demythologizing), the force of romance is dissipated, its generative power weakened, and its salvatory function aborted. Like many contemporary novels, *Little Big Man*

focuses on deconstructive processes more than on certification of any product. For example, Berger plays with our preconceptions about heroes and heroines throughout the novel, mixing the generic preconceptions in figures like Caroline, so that none of the women is taken seriously because few of the characters are. Consequently, neither of Berger's Princess-types has even the little substance that Kesey's Poison Queen-type did, for Amelia and Mrs. Pendrake simply invert the Princess model.

The original Western Princess, Molly Wood, is "spunky," Wister says, so her innocence and her virginity—the sine qua non of Princesshood, as experience is of Queenhood—become valuable symbols of virtue and self-control. Her eventual submission to the Virginian may be retroactively predictable, but nevertheless the submission is a gallant, self-determined act of completion: "She knew her cow-boy lover, with all that he lacked, to be more than she ever could be with all that she had." With their chaste union, the robust West is given authentication and value by the refined East—a typical "civilizing" role assigned to women in Westerns/romances, but in Wister's book a profound act. Berger's Amelia and Mrs. Pendrake, however, are as ephemeral in their influence on Crabb as each is shabby in her origins: Mrs. P. impeccably blue-eyed and a minister's wife to boot but a closet Soiled Dove who has taken on nearly the whole town; Amelia the Dance-Hall Girl whom Crabb fancies just long enough to give him time to learn shooting from Wild Bill Hickok. Like Molly and most Princesses, both women are unattainable, but here they are out of reach by Crabb's choice, not their own. He says he was only interested in Amelia because "all my life I had yearned for a bit of class, and I purposed to achieve it in this niece of mine," but once she has attained classiness, Crabb abandons her to the lawyer in the Kansas City Hotel. Similarly, he runs away from Mrs. P., not because of anything so personal as queasiness about her behavior or his, but because he was "just worn out with the whole business" of living among Caucasians.

Thus, what these two represent to Crabb is approximately what Molly represented to the Virginian, but the concept of civilization that the two books examine has degenerated considerably since Wister's time. Where Wister was attempting to redefine American society in terms of the code of the West, Berger's hero first can "see no sense to it [civilization] whenever Mrs. P. wasn't around" and then later, through Amelia, translates "civilization" into all those useless arts for which Amelia had showed no talent in the saloon: piano playing, refinement of accent, lifting the pinkie while drinking tea. The point is not merely that Molly stood for something powerful, thinned out to silliness by Amelia and Mrs. P. Rather, it is that both Wister and Berger portray civilization as approximately equivalent to manners, gentility, fashion, behaviors to be studied rather than ideas or ethics to be learned—in short, trivialities women are as well suited to symbolize as Big Nurse symbolized an equivalently shallow evil. Once understood, the evil is overcome as easily as the useless good (signified by Amelia and Mrs. P.) is forgotten.

In *The Virginian, Cuckoo's Nest,* and *Little Big Man*—the fountainhead of Westerns, and two of the best Westerns in recent years—the women are significant in a catalytic, supportive fashion, but not as characters. They are props in front of whom the men may strut or snarl but from whom little independent action is expected or required. Molly feeds the conflict of the Virginian with Trampas, but as another representative of good, not as a participant in the conflict with views of her own. Big Nurse is not much more than the figuration of the Combine; Amelia and Mrs. P. are toys. Even love, a most natural response between hero and heroine in a romance, plays no significant part in the major conflict of such novels as these, for few fictional Western males ever feel their hats, horses, or sleep—much less their world—well lost for love.

Should the usual Western hero fall in love, and particularly should he marry any woman but an Indian, he is automatically removed from the action. If he does not voluntarily take himself out, as the Virginian does, then his cronies will remove him. To cite only three representative examples, Crane's "The Bride Comes to Yellow Sky," Schaefer's *Monte Walsh,* and Guthrie's *These Thousand Hills* show that in most Westerns, married males figuratively become geldings, appallingly sensible, and unheroically grounded—literally as well as metaphorically, for a woman takes a man off his high horse. Marriage virtually unmans a Western hero, removing him from truly masculine pursuits, which are essentially celibate and therefore perhaps more holy as well as more fun than those accessible to domesticated males. So a "real" Western man, like a horseback Simon Stylites, lives, works, and plays alone or with other males, saving his *virtú* and his *preux* for roping calves, shooting scoundrels or strangers, and swatting flies on the bunkhouse wall.

That is to say, like most protagonists of heroic literature, the Westerner is typically unmarried and earns respect in the eyes of other would-be heroes through his self-sufficiency and his expertise with the weapons of his trade. Unlike the others, however, the usual Western hero *stays* unmarried, uncommitted, arrested at an adolescent level of sexual and psychological development, possibly because the risks in attaining further maturation would be frightening, certainly because that attainment would exclude him from the atmosphere of pubescent play hovering behind even the direst straits of a fictional cowboy's life. When the hero stutters and stumbles like a thirteen-year-old in the presence of a woman, his ineptitude is only partially the result of naïveté, only partially an outsider's unease with the unknown, the seldom seen, the rarely realized. His discomfort is also as symptom of his own (or his creator's, or his reader's) repressed fears about himself, fears too alarming ever to be consciously acknowledged and therefore impossible to overcome, because nobody—character, writer, or readers—admits the fears are real.

But it is not a homosexual panic at all; it is an *a*sexual panic, a terror at the possibility of any kind of full emotional sexuality lurking anywhere. A Western hero might get his ashes hauled in Dodge City, if the book were written after 1950, but a committed and loving attachment—even to a stereotyped Princess or Poison Queen—is usually beyond not only his ken but his impulses as well. Any woman is a threat to the Westerner's monastic play-

ground, so for the most part, he simply ignores women altogether. There are exceptions here, too—the Virginian, for example, spends so much time courting Molly that we are obliged to wonder how he gets his chores done—but the more common case in a Western is that only men have status, respect, and the chance to earn the same, from other men, because only men are familiar threats, externalized versions of the hero himself, predictable, safe, known.

The bulk of fiction about the American West, then, does something virtually unparalleled in romance: it vigorously celebrates the *divorce* of psycho-sexual maturation from growth, heroism, and ultimate salvation. Instead of an encompassing, restorative fertility, the typical Western novel supports an erotic ignorance, a debasement of that pubescent, "chaste," Edenic love labeled by Frye as "erotic innocence" characteristic of romance. The taboo against sexuality in any form is deeply hidden in most Western fiction beneath paeans to the charms of rugged individualism and to the moral enlightenment supposedly inherent in an amorphous "code of the West" derived from nineteenth-century industrial/expansionist dogma and hellfire theology. But as a result of repression, the quest of a typical Western hero almost never takes him deeply into himself by way of significant contact with a woman, since what she might teach him is more dangerous than his willed ignorance. Consequently, almost never does a Western novel free itself from psycho-sexual stagnation.

"Translated into ritual terms," Frye writes, "the quest-romance is the victory of fertility over the wasteland" but the Western romance is designed precisely to keep fertility at bay. The Western version has little or nothing to do with rejuvenation or with civilization, and, like Natty Bumppo, its hero becomes attenuated—even dangerous—once the town has arrived. This literary West, this American version of Avalon, the Hesperides, the Isle of Cockaigne, is a dry land in more ways than one, for in order to keep his own narrow myth of autonomy intact, the Western hero has been forced to refuse the responsibility of furthering the community's needs, and has thereby niggardly withheld fulfillment not only from himself but from all the barren land. Constrained in his quest even before he begins by his inability to accept the most frightening challenge of all, the typical Western protagonist has neglected his best chance of saving his soul and encasing eternity in his mortal lifetime. As a hero, he has been sold short because he has not been allowed to take the one risk that can bring him true salvationary stature: the risk of losing his soul, not to a Princess or a Poison Queen, but to a woman. (pp. 643-56)

Madelon E. Heatherington, "Romance without Women: The Sterile Fiction of the American West," in The Georgia Review, *Vol. XXXIII, No. 3, Fall, 1979, pp. 643-56.*

Shelley Armitage

[*In the following excerpt, Armitage describes and praises the cowgirl in western fiction, claiming that she best represents the historical women of frontier America.*]

Kirk Douglas torn between Eve Miller, an upstanding woman, and Patrice Wymore, a saloon-singer, in The Big Trees *(1952).*

Woman's place in the myth of America may be measured by a simple story. Two Indians are sitting on a fence. One is a big Indian, the other, a little Indian. The little Indian is the big Indian's son, but the big Indian is not the little Indian's father. How can this be? David Potter, who relates the riddle, solves it with this explanation: the big Indian obviously is the little Indian's mother, but we may initially fail to see this since social conditioning often makes us conceive of relationships from a masculine perspective. Potter's story has particular import when we examine the myth of America specifically as the Western or frontier myth in which the qualities of heroism are traditionally masculine ones. Rugged individualism, bravery, nobility, and a love of the wilderness are noted by historians such as Frederick Jackson Turner and writers from Cooper on as traits indigenous to the frontier experience. Turner sees these qualities as part of the national character and evoked by the frontier's challenge to the *civilizing instinct;* yet woman, typically the civilizer, is not typically thought to exhibit them. Our imaginative writers, unlike the historians, view the frontier as *an escape from civilization* and thus seldom treat women heroically. Heroes, like Natty Bumppo, are not the apostles of progress but the an-

tisocial, misanthropic refugees from civilization who bemoan the descration of the wilderness and wish to defend it from settlement. It follows that such heroes, as William Humphrey observes [in *Ah Wilderness: The Frontier in American Literature*], avoid the trappings of civilization by avoiding marriage:

> . . . if we are to judge by our imaginative literature, we are, beneath all the slogans extolling the democratic social organization and the virtues of family life, a nation of secret bachelors, hermits of the woods and the plains. In books about such figures there is no place for any heroine.

If heroines have not emerged from western history and literature, however, a predominant stereotype has—an image perpetuated by writers and historians as appropriate to woman's role in the Western myth. Emerson Hough describes her thus [in *The Passing of the Frontier*]:

> She is the chief figure of the American West, the figure of all the ages. This major figure is not the long-haired, fringed legging man riding a rawboned pony, but the gaunt and sad-faced woman sitting on the front seat of the wagon . . . her face hidden in the same ragged sunbonnet which

had crossed the Appalachians and the Missouri long before. There was America. . . . There was the seed of America's wealth. There was the great romance of all America—the woman in the sunbonnet; and not, after all, the hero with the rifle across his saddle horn.

This image of the sunbonnet woman is popular for a number of reasons. On a psychological level, her implied status as mother satisfies the needs of our writers to reconcile their attitudes about women. Leslie Fiedler says, "Women represent at once the ruined and redeeming virgin-bride dreamed by Sentimentalism, and the forgiving mother, necessary to sustain an imaginary American commonwealth of boy-children. . . . Both marriage and passion impugn the image of woman as mother and mean the abandonment of childhood." The passivity of this creature on the wagon seat further compliments predominant nineteenth-century beliefs about women's natures and their roles. Emerson noted that civilization was the power of "good" women. Such a woman remained in the home and did all that was necessary to maintain that home, even to following her husband overland from friends, family, culture, and precious possessions. Any penchant for the wilderness, therefore, was regarded as evil on a woman's part; certainly in literature "white women who refuse to restrict their behavior to what society intends for them find the wilderness a natural habitat for forbidden sexuality, and for them, separation from the male, and solitary wandering in the wilderness are considered equivalent to the fall." Thus, Hough's description of the pioneer woman as "gaunt" and "sad-faced" is appropriate to her expected sacrificial role. She was the "seed of America's wealth" in part because she perpetuated its seed. Men who had subdued the wilderness for its great riches were interested in establishing a "line." Material exploitation and sexual exploitation were closely aligned. This sunbonnet woman is therefore "the great romance of all America" because "she stoically transcended a situation she never would have freely chosen." Long-suffering, pure, persevering, this pioneer woman reaches mythic proportions in her celebration in statues, histories, and literature across the country because she became the symbolic repository of values revered by men but often personally ignored for their own materialistic ventures on the frontier.

The sunbonnet woman thus seldom reaches the status of a true heroine. Unlike the dynamic heroines of European literature, Jane Eyre or Anna Karenina, for instance her compliance to tedious tasks has none of the heroic cut of her male counterparts in the West—the trappers, miners, cowboys, or soldiers. Characters like Beret Hansa in Rolvaag's *Giants of the Earth* (1926) or Dorothy Scarborough's crazed character in *The Wind* (1925) are not memorable but predictable. Such a woman most often serves as a plot motivator for the more dramatic activities of the hero, making Huck Finn "light out for the territory" or Daniel Boone move West one more time. For the most part, western writers have been content to follow the example of what Judith Fryer notes is a pattern of our major writers:

> Significantly, the women in the novels of Hawthorne, Melville, Oliver Wendell Holmes, Har-

old Frederic, Henry James, and William Dean Howells are not women at all, but images of women. They are reflections of the prevailing images of women in the nineteenth century, and like the predominantly male creators of utopian schemes, their male creators perceive with cultural blinders the women in the New World Gardens of their imaginations [*The Faces of Eve*].

Yet the real frontier offered a unique situation for altering these images. Recent historians such as Gerda Lerner suggest the sunbonnet stereotype is far too limiting, for pioneer women often had to be independent and frontier men and women were interdependent. Current efforts to reconstruct history from diaries, letters, and newspapers indicate that historians such as William Sprague and Francis Parkman had not only a narrow but sometimes an erroneous view of women's attitudes, status, roles, and occupations on the frontier. Moreover, one frontier not only necessitated unique behavior by women, but engaged the popular imagination sufficiently to inspire the emergence of perhaps the only true American heroine. That frontier was the cattle frontier, and the "new woman" was the "cowgirl"—the rustler, wrangler, outlaw, or ranch woman whose occupation depended on her mastery of the horse. In real life, she had to exercise the masculine traits revered by historians such as Turner and by western writers. She attracted no attention from major American writers—perhaps because her character was particularly antithetical to their image of the American woman—but her character as it evolves in popular culture from the dime novel to films comes close to resolving the dilemma of the woman in American fiction as Fiedler and others see it. She was neither mother nor virgin-bride. At times she was a full-fledged partner of the hero; at times she was the hero herself. (pp. 166-68)

During the height of the cattle industry, the dime novel, which had popularized western characters and action since 1860, transformed heroines from crinoline objects to active participants in the plots. First came the use of Indian girls who could ride and shoot. Then writers disguised women in men's clothing and explained their acts of violence and aggression in terms of revenge. But by 1878, in Edward L. Wheeler's *Bob Woolf, the Border Ruffian; or the Girl Dead-Shot,* Hurricane Nell assumed all the skills and functions of a Western hero. There may be several explanations for this transition of the heroine's role, and each indicate that real cowgirls could to some degree capture the popular imagination.

First, there were the requirements of Erastus Beadle, head of the firm of Beadle and Adams, who had been to the frontier twice. Beadle recognized the impact of good storytelling that had dramatized the opening of the Eastern states, the Revolutionary War, and the War of 1812, and he expected his writers to achieve verisimilitude through adequate research or, even better, first hand knowledge of the West. Thus, at least some of his stable of writers—Joseph E. Badger, Prentiss Ingraham, Sam Hall, Mayne Reid, and E. L. Wheeler—were not only familiar with the West but had lived there. Certainly, they would have had opportunities to observe real cowgirls, and several examples illustrate a direct connection between real women and the characters in dime novels. For instance, Rowdy Kate of *Apollo Bill, The Trail Tornado; or Rowdy Kate From Right Bower* (1882) boasts in a typical Southwestern style: "I'm a regular old double distilled typhoon, you bet." There was a Rowdy Kate in the 1870s who was a dance-hall girl, among other things, and possibly could pass as a double-distilled typhoon. In *The Jaguar Queen or, the Outlaws of the Sierra Madre* (1872), Katrina Hartstein goes about with seven pet jaguars on a leash and is the leader of a gang. Anne Sokalski, who accompanied her soldier-husband to his duty post in the mid-1860s, took along her thirteen trained hunting dogs which she kept on a leash. She wore a riding habit made of wolfskin and trimmed with wolf tails, topped with a fur hat. She spent hours at target practice, was a deadly shot, and could out-ride some of the cavalry. The author of *The Jaguar Queen,* Frederick Whittaker, who had served in the army, would have found Anne inspiration for his character. Even Hurricane Nell has authentic roots. Mountain Charley (Mrs. E. J. Guerin) joined miners at Pike's Peak in 1859. She was dressed like, and passed for, a man. In 1861, she published her autobiography—ample time for the dime novel author to have heard of her.

With the availability of real models—women, we must remember, who were at home with horses, guns, and even violence—the addition of the "Amazon" character in the dime novel was an effort to reconcile reality with certain social predilections of an Eastern audience. Erastus Beadle's list of rules for writers ended with "We require unquestioned originality," but it began with "We prohibit all things offensive to good taste in expression and incident." Though critics of the dime novel are quite right to note the disintegration of the novels due to overt sensationalism after about 1880, the development of two types of Amazon characters dramatized the cowgirl folk heroine and indicated a growth in the Western myth since Cooper. Dime novels, of course, were fashioned after Cooper's Leatherstocking adventures with a backwoods hero—comic, dialectal, unsuited for marriage—contrasted to his Eastern sidekick who, by virtue of his aristocratic breeding, always got the girl. As the writers refined the bifurcated plot—one part adventure, and one love interest—into the activities of a single, cultivated protagonist, the two new heroines emerged. One, the "Sport," was usually a beautiful woman dressed in a mannish fashion, who performed manly feats with gun, whip, and knife, drank liquor straight, and swore expertly. She might save the hero from danger, but she almost never got his romantic attention. In this way, she replaced the noble backwoodsman, since she was strong, brave, capable of action. Moreover, since there was no love interest, she in no way threatened the hero with her strength; she was his equal, his friend. A classic example of the "Sport," and probably the most famous, is E. L. Wheeler's Calamity Jane. In *Deadwood Dick on Deck; or Calamity Jane, The Heroine of Whoop-Up,* she has a pretty, but hard face, wears buckskin pants, "met at the knee by fancifully beaded leggins," dainty slippers, a velvet vest, a velvet jacket, and a Spanish broad-brimmed hat "slouched upon one side of a regally beautiful head." Wearing one revolver on her waist and a rifle on her back, she rides a black pony fitted out Mexican

style. When asked why she dresses like a man, she replies: "I don't allow ye ken beat men's togs much for handy locomotion and so forth, an' then, ye see, I'm as big a gun among men as any of 'em." In *Deadwood Dick in Leadville; or A Strange Stroke for Liberty* (1881), she saves a man's life and calls ammunition "condensed death."

The "Pard" character, on the other hand, often won the hero. She was also masculine in her skills, but did not try to pass for a man like the rougher "Sport." Rather she was a partner to the hero, capable of doing what he did, sharing equally in danger and daring with occasional concessions to femininity. Probably she is one of the few egalitarian female creations. Two classic "Pards" ran in dime novel series from 1900 to the 1920s—Arietta Murdock, created by Cornelius Shea for *Wild West Weekly,* and Ned Taylor's Stella, the cowgirl heroine of *Rough Rider Weekly.* Arietta, displayed on about 80 percent of the *Wild West Weekly* covers, regularly rescued the hero by hurling dynamite, leaping chasms, shooting her gun, riding for the posse, and stealing guns or horses from outlaws. Like Arietta, Stella was a blonde, known in her native Texas as "Queen of the Range." She sidekicks with ex-Rough Rider Ted Stong and cuts a dashing figure in her white stetson, bolero jacket, white leggings, and red skirt, with her gun strapped to her hip. Thus, unlike the earlier pale heroines of Cooper's novels, these western women, whether friends or lovers, were strong, independent, brave, athletic, and full partners to the hero. Like their historic sisters, the ranch women, they fill a unique literary role.

An indication of this uniqueness, outside the fact that these heroines are fully "heroic" and share in the Western myth, is that they are called "Amazons." The use of this classical character for reference indicates the lack of any American literary predecessor. Unlike the dime novel hero, who has as his native reference the backwoodsman, the mythical forerunner of the cowgirl character is rooted in a legendary female culture where strength and athletic prowess were aspects of female heroism. The reference also indicates the difficulty of perpetuating a myth that runs so counter to nineteenth-century sensibilities about women. Perhaps only in popular culture, where myth making is intricately involved with entertainment, could such a heroine evolve. Nevertheless, in the pattern described by Richard Slotkin, the character of the cowgirl moves through the primary, romantic, and consummatory stages of myth development. That is, the character is identified in the repetition of formulas (as in the dime novel); the character is adapted to specific social and literary requirements by artists, thus obscuring the original meaning of the myth (as in the Wild West Shows, some literature, and films); and, finally, an attempt is made to recapture the real meaning of the myth by providing new visions (as in some recent novels and films). Moreover, as Slotkin points out, the effective use of myth depends on the development of traditional metaphors in the narrative that indicate change. Crucial to this acculturation is the medium; in the case of the cowgirl character the narrative is told through literature, sport, and film.

Along with the dime novel, the evolution of the "Pard" or "Sport" characters continued in western literature dating from the turn of the century. Unlike the dime novels which emphasized action to the exclusion of character development, the evolution of the cowgirl in this Western popular literature establishes a workable metaphor for this character. As Slotkin notes, "The success of the myth in answering questions of human existence depends upon the creation of a distinct cultural tradition in the selection and use of metaphor. Thus, the dime novel established the formula for the myth—action, dress, character type. Other writers adopted the formula but discarded the Amazon reference for an American metaphor: the natural woman."

In 1908, Lester Shepherd Parkman wrote a story in verse introducing this natural woman. *Nancy MacIntyre,* though strictly inferior poetry suitable perhaps for recitation, is about cowboy Billy, owner of eighty acres in Kansas and his love for Nancy, a cowgirl "Pard" who dresses in long skirt with a gun and cartridge belt. Nancy possesses all the attributes of a hero: she saves Billy from an ambush, stands off a posse in behalf of her father, and shoots Jim Johnson who steals Billy's eighty acres. But Billy admires her lack of artificiality:

> Now, those women that you read of
> In these story picture books,
> They can't ride in roping distance
> Of that girl in style and looks.
> They have waists more like an insect.
> Corset shaped and double cinched,
> Feet just right to make a watch charm,
> Small, of course, because they're pinched.
> This here Nancy's like God made her—
> She don't wear no saddle girth,
> But she's supple as a willow
> And the prettiest thing on earth.

Though Billy speaks in part of natural beauty, the poem connects scenes of the western landscape, and of her ability to deal with the harsh life of the prairie, with her authenticity.

Thus, like the pastoral hero, the natural woman as cowgirl is at one with nature. In the works of Eugene Manlove Rhodes, for instance, love of the land is connected to the heroine's capabilities. Eva Scales in "Maid Most Dear" (1930) says this about the desert country of New Mexico:

> "I've lived here all my life. Except for a few trips
> to Silver City and El Paso. I've never been out
> of these hills." Her head lifted, her eyes lingered
> on the long horizons, lovingly. "If it is any better
> outside, I'm willing to be cheated."

Eva is the brave and daring heroine of the story who shoots it out with a lynch mob in order to save Eddie and Skip, the heroes of the story. Other Rhodes stories reiterate the same idea. In "The Desire of the Moth" (1902), "Beyond the Desert" (1914), and "Bird in the Bush" (1917), the heroines derive their strength from nature.

Thus the "Pard's" ability to take full responsibility for her life depends on her capacity to enjoy harmony with man and nature. In the novels of Bertha "Muzzy" Sinclair, the cowgirl heroines often choose this harmonious relationship at the cost of approval by townspeople. Though Sinclair's novels often are humorous and avoid historical

themes, she often juxtaposes the heroine's character, formed and sustained by the range land, against the expectations of society. In *Rim O' the World* (1919) Belle Lorrigan is a tough, athletic heroine. She races across the prairie in a buckboard pulled by two pinto ponies, Rosa and Subrosa. A sure shot, she teaches her three sons manners by plugging a hole in one boy's hat when he forgets to remove it. When the sheriff arrives to check the brands on some green hides, she threatens to put a bullet "about six inches above the knee," if he doesn't leave. He continues to talk and she determines to shoot his front tooth out. Needless to say, the women in town dislike Belle, but the author clearly illustrates that the "natural" woman maintains integrity by answering to the laws of the land, not the conscience of snooty town women.

The reconciliation of the strong woman with her role in the family further is handled by William Sydney Porter in his story "Hearts and Crosses" (1907). After Santa inherits a ranch from her father, she runs it so expertly that her husband leaves to become foreman of another ranch. When he orders a shipment of cattle from her, she sends a pure white steer with the brand—a cross in the center of a heart— which she and Webb had used before their marriage to denote a secret meeting. Webb returns to find he is father of a son, and he and Santa continue to share equally in the running of the ranch. Santa's acumen as a "Pard" is memorably described in the night scene when she ropes, ties, and brands the white steer single-handed.

The early literature of the cowgirl heroine, therefore, seized on the distinctive "active" behavior of the heroine—the skills necessary to survival and to heroism—and added to the one-dimensional dime novel authentic frontier situations. Character thus was a matter of independence, ingenuity, and physical skill fostered by the demands of the environment. The heroine typically coped with so-called female concerns—love, marriage, family, societal expectations—by exhibiting "masculine" traits. The metaphor of the "natural" women was a statement of her ability to cultivate these traits, yet still be a woman, and to achieve equal status with the hero or even be the center of the work herself. Other writers such as Owen Wister in *The Virginian* (1902) used this metaphor to test the fitness of Eastern values. In the westering of Molly Wingate, Wister indicates that her acquisition of the skills of the cowgirl favorably influence her character. But in the novels of Zane Grey, the cowgirl character changed and the metaphor of the natural woman was diverted to an earthiness that suggested sexuality rather than heroic dimension. In novels such as *Hash Knife Outfit* (1920), Grey, like Wister, tested the Eastern girl against the land or against western values, but, like his heroes, he essentially domesticated the heroines' love of independence and sense of freedom. The later novels of Luke Short, Max Brand, Nelson Nye, and Louis L'Amour continue this trend, returning to the pat stereotype of the woman as either "good" but inert, or active and assertive but sexual. Gone is the girl "Pard" who can coexist with the hero because of her androgynous abilities. The myth, therefore, is diverted from its original sources and content to a reflection of social or literary obligations—the second stage of mythogenesis Slotkin speaks of when the nature of reality is less important than the social requirements of the artist.

Grey, for example, uses the Western myth to work out his own picadillos. John Cawelti notes [in *Adventure, Mystery and Romance*]:

> In a period where . . . traditional American values were under attack, Grey and other contemporary novelists . . . transformed the western formula into a vehicle for reaffirming a traditional view of American life. . . . In contrast to contemporary American society where women were increasingly challenging their traditional roles, the West of Grey . . . was, above all, a land where men were men and women were women. In novel after novel, Grey created strong, proud, and daring women and then made them realize their true role in life as the adoring lovers of still stronger, more virtuous, more heroic men.

Another explanation for the loss of the original thrust of the cowgirl character was the historic or personal distance writers such as Grey had from the West. By contrast, many of the dime novelists and other writers such as Parkman, Sinclair, Rhodes, and O. Henry had either grown up in the West or spent time there. Their interest, though the works often were melodramatic, was in recording real Western characters and experiences. As an example, Joe B. Frantz and Julian Choate write of "Muzzy" Sinclair: "She had what so many cowboy writers lack, a real background of life among the bowlegged brethren. . . . She was reared in Montana where she rode the range and fraternized with men on horseback. She did not try to pontificate about the epic role of the cowboy, and she had no pretense to history as such, but she was faithful to the Western historical milieu which she knew first hand." (pp. 171-76)

The athletic ability of the cowgirl . . . is her unique and sustaining attribute. From the deeds that distinguished her in real life throughout the physical escapades in the dime novel, western literature, the Wild West Show, rodeo, and film, her identity is grounded in physical capability. Studies show that athletically oriented people identify themselves with athletic traits associated with success—aggressiveness, tough-mindedness, dominance, self-confidence, and risk taking. These traits, of course, are antithetical to those usually attributed to women. Hence, the cowgirl who can ride and rope and run her ranch as well as a man is able to carve out a portion of the Western myth for herself by means of her athletic bearing. Such talents not only put her on equal footing with the hero, but they allow her the very traits our writers attribute to the Western hero. Thus, if the behavior and attitudes of the hero are of interest because he exhibits these characteristics as a trapper or cowboy or soldier, the cowgirl also commands this interest. Indeed, one of the complaints of novelists such as Wallace Stegner is that women's lives on the frontier constituted a view "from the inside," that is, only from the home. Such drama of dailiness has proved uninteresting to our novelists. No doubt the cowgirl had special appeal because she exhibited behavior thought to be unusual for women. She was, in fact, the "New Woman" of the frontier, and her popularity parallels new freedoms women were experiencing toward the end of the nineteenth century and during the 1920s. In this sense, however, her athletic inclinations presented as much of a problem as they did a unique status. Because she did contradict the typical female role, writers tended to refine her by centering her in melodrama or even making her exploits so sensational, they bordered on comedy. Audiences, no doubt, found this treatment of her entertaining and therefore acceptable. Later, of course, writers and film makers converted the qualities of the athletic heroine to sexual energy, so that she became the "dark" heroine.

But the athletic "Pard" offered an opportunity for writers to resolve their dilemma over the "masculine wilderness of the American novel," as Carolyn Heilbrun calls it. Rather than pose a sexual threat to the hero by representing the marriage and civilization that inimitably followed association with a woman, the girl "Pard" functioned as a buddy would: she was friend, sidekick, and, if she became a wife, at least she could rescue the hero from a jam. If this cowgirl character was an "Amazon" she nevertheless was described by the dime novelists as a "honey-throated" Amazon; her androgyny made her a companion of the hero. The alternative—more prevalent in our literature—fits this description of Texas by J. B. Priestly in 1956:

> I am convinced that good talk cannot flourish where there is a wide gulf between the sexes, where the men are altogether too masculine, too hearty and bluff and booming, where the women are too feminine, at once both too arch and too anxious. Where men are leavened by a feminine element, where women are not without some tempering by the masculine spirit, there is a chance of good talk. . . . But here was a society entirely dominated by the masculine principle. Why were so many of these women at once so arch and anxious? . . . Even here in these circles, where millionaires apparently indulged and spoilt them, they were haunted by a feeling of inferiority, resented but never properly examined and challenged. They lived in a world so contemptuous and destructive of real feminine values that they had to be heavily bribed to remain in it. All those shops, like the famous Neiman-Marcus store in Dallas, were part of the bribe. They were still girls in a mining camp. And to increase their bewilderment, perhaps their despair, they are told they are living in a matriarchy.

Priestly not only gives good reason for a balance of male and female elements, but he fingers the reason for the dearth of heroines in western literature: heroic stature is conceived in purely masculine terms. Unlike the Greek goddesses and British, French, Russian, or Spanish women who assumed leading roles in mythology, literature, and history, American heroines are a pale lot—except for the cowgirl, whose evolution from the lives of real women on the frontier makes her embodiment of masculine and feminine traits unique. (pp. 179-80)

Shelley Armitage, "Rawhide Heroines: The Evolution of the Cowgirl and the Myth of America," in The American Self: Myth, Ideology, and Popular Culture, *edited by Sam B.*

*Girgus, University of New Mexico Press, 1981,
pp. 166-81.*

LATER WESTERN FICTION

Michael T. Marsden and Jack Nachbar

[*In the following essay, Marsden and Nachbar compare
the westerns of the early 1900s with those of the 1970s
and 1980s.*]

Unlike the Western radio or television series whose popularity waxed and waned according to various media-
specific developments, the popular Western novel has enjoyed a consistent and notable following from the nineteenth century to the present. With its foundation firmly
in the dime novels, the Wild West shows, the pulps, and
the popular Western formula, Western fiction has simply
been more fully developed than its counterparts in the
other mass media. From its earliest manifestations
through the writings of Owen Wister, Zane Grey and Max
Brand, the popular Western novel appealed to eastern sensibilities rather than western. Other Western writers, such
as Ernest Haycox, Luke Short and Louis L'Amour,
weaned the form away from its eastern mindset and planted it more firmly in western soil.

The Western of post—World War II years is marked by
two major tendencies. First, because novels, like radio,
had to compete against the ever more popular television,
like radio they fought back with realistic, tough-minded
content. However, despite changes in content, the tone has
continued to be romantic and idealized. The contemporary Western novel thus strikes a precarious balance between the audience's need for realism and romanticism;
however gritty the plot becomes, the results remain hopeful and optimistic.

The second major distinguishing characteristic of the
postwar Western is its emphasis on reality of setting. What
Western writers and Western readers are interested in is
a good story which not only entertains but also informs
them about the American West. In his fine study *The
Dime Novel Western,* Daryl Jones notes that the late nineteenth-century public grew less and less tolerant of the increasing sexual and violent content of many of the dime
novels, whose sales fell off notably. The Western story, in
fact, seems to have gone through several cycles of birth,
sordid adulthood, and rebirth during its one hundred and
fifty-plus years of existence. Jones quite accurately pinpoints the popular appeal of the "cleansed" Western story:

> That we are still reluctant today to abandon our
> vision of an ideal world, a moment's glance at a
> newsstand, a theater marquee, or a television
> program guide will instantly confirm. The medi-
> um has changed, but the popular Western lives
> on. To be sure, the message is neither so simple
> nor so reassuring as it once was. With the ad-
> vance of the twentieth century have come cul-

tural and world-wide dilemmas which have
brought about significant alterations on the familiar formula. . . . Altered, inverted, even
parodied, the popular Western formula nonetheless survives. And it will continue to survive as
long as it extends to humanity some glimmer of
hope that a golden age still lies ahead.

The modern popular Western, like its early predecessors,
views the American West as a "golden age" which did not
allow spiritual or physical weaknesses among the survivors. The heroes of the modern Western, however, can be
philosophers on the range, men used to wrestling with
ideas as well as cows, like those found in the novels of Ernest Haycox. Haycox, like a number of his contemporaries
in the post-1930 period, added a historical dimension to
some of his Westerns which, while heightening the realism, did not diminish the idealism. The author of twenty-
four novels from the late '30s to early '50s, Haycox penned
several classic Westerns, including *Trouble Shooter, The
Border Trumpet, Alder Gulch, Bugles in the Afternoon,*
and *The Earthbreakers.* Henry Wilson Allen in his "Will
Henry" Westerns followed in the same tradition. In his
Maheo's Children, the Sand Creek massacre plays a prominent role in the plot, and his *From Where the Sun Now
Stands* depicts the annual trek of the Nez Perce Indians
to follow the buffalo. Luke Short also wrestled with the realities of the West in his works of romance. In *Paper Sheriff,* which is considered one of his best Westerns, the focus
is on the importance of "group needs over individualistic
interests," a theme which marks a certain maturity of the
Western formula. The emphasis on the historical West in
each of their works allowed these writers to meet effectively the changing needs of the audience by providing them
with hard information about the West, while at the same
time engaging them in a romance. This compromise is not
without its price, however. Paperback Westerns, which
had been a staple of the publishing industry for more than
three decades, have begun to decline in popularity. In
1975, for example, only sixty-five new paperback Westerns were published out of a total of 177 which were distributed; the other 112 were reissues.

The most dominant type of Western on the newsstands at
present is the adult Western series, which does not exclude
sex and violence. George G. Gilman's "Edge" series, Jake
Logan's "Slocum" series, and Tabor Evans's "Longarm"
series are only three of the many adult Western series now
commanding an impressive part of the popular Western
marketplace, leaving the casual peruser of the paperback
racks with the impression that in the Western market the
only competition adult Westerns have are reissues, or
Louis L'Amour's novels. While adult Westerns do not
seem to be consistent with the mainstream popular Western tradition, at least one critic, Gary Hoppenstand, has
suggested [in an unpublished essay] that rather than a "bizarre outgrowth of the genre," adult Westerns might be
an evolution of the approach of the Western romance towards sex and violence. He argues that the sex and violence of the adult Western series have been there all
along—they have simply been more fully developed in this
stage of the Western romance's evolution.

While other writers like Jack Schaefer, whose *Shane*

helped to elevate the Western paperback to new levels of respectability, deserve serious analysis as well, perhaps the most representative author of the mainstream popular Western tradition is the best-selling and prolific Louis L'Amour, who has been ranked by *Saturday Review* as the third top-selling writer in the world. L'Amour clearly believes in a responsible and responsive West populated by the restrained and civilized. He has a considerable talent for perceiving the needs and interests of his audience and, after three decades of writing Western novels, has been able to establish his own genre against which the works of other popular Western writers are judged. L'Amour has developed a strong, personal relationship with many of his readers. He writes:

> As for myself, whatever else I may be I am a storyteller. I see myself as carrying on the story of my people just as the shanachies in Ireland and the Druids before them, and as Homer did in Greece. . . .
>
> Telling stories is my way of life. . . . My intention has always been to tell stories of the frontier, the sort of stories I heard when growing up.

L'Amour's fiction can be used as a touchstone for the modern popular literary Western because of its universal appeal and continuing success in the marketplace. In addition to providing his audience with enjoyable stories, he also provides them with a popular history of the settlement of America by focusing on family dynasties, vernacular architecture, the cultural history of the American Indian, women's roles on the American frontier, cowboy customs, and myriad other details of nineteenth-century American life.

From the 1950s *Hondo* to his most recent Sackett novel, Louis L'Amour's works remain convincing examples of the viability of the mainstream popular Western story, presenting the historical West in something like an oral tradition. But the successes of the adult Western series also serve as convincing examples of what many perceive to be the evolution of the Western story form into a distinctly different type of story. Still others perceive the two forms, the mainstream popular Western story and the adult Western series, as linked in an evolutionary process where the latter is developing elements already present in the former. Whatever the specific form or forms the popular Western story takes, it seems reasonable to suggest that it will continue to remain a strong force in the popular literary marketplace. One possible explanation for the longevity of the popular Western story in its many forms is that writers like Ernest Haycox, Luke Short, and Louis L'Amour are really telling versions of one, long epic tale unfolded over an extended period of time through the efforts of a number of skilled storytellers.

The death of John Wayne, the movies' greatest Western star, symbolically suggests a place to mark the demise of the modern popular Western. By that date, hoofbeats on the radio had been silent for a generation. Both the film and television media had become incapable of producing a Western hit. Even the long-lived Western novel showed signs of aging. However, though the popularity of the Western theme has declined, its struggle to maintain a place in American life has brought about a thematic maturity and dignity to the popular Western formula. Where early or "classic" Westerns had affirmed the European-American taking and taming of the West, modern Westerns often did not. Radio and television Westerns such as *Gunsmoke* sometimes suggested that pioneering could mean no more than a slow death on a barren prairie. Movies often explored the negative side of the settlement of the West, such as the pathology behind much outlaw violence and the racism at the heart of the Indian wars. Even Western novels, the form that most strongly retained the values of "classic" Westerns, moved in the direction of stronger characterization and a closer fidelity to historical accuracy.

During the 1980s the formula Western refuses to pass completely from the scene. Western novels stubbornly maintain their slots in paperback book racks. Just as significant, perhaps, is the persistence of images from popular Westerns in the media. Popular music stars such as Willie Nelson and Waylon Jennings still sell millions of records featuring songs about cowboys. During the early '80s, Western-style bars and cowboy clothes were a billion-dollar fad. On television, ads for chewing tobacco, gum, beer, aftershave lotion and numerous other products all ride into American homes on the shoulders of popular Western heroes. The continuing presence of these images suggests the remaining, latent attraction of the popular Western. When the national mood changes and is again receptive to frontier stories, it is not unlikely that a third significant period of popular Western storytelling will engage America's national imagination. (pp. 1276-80)

> *Michael T. Marsden and Jack Nachbar, "The Modern Popular Western: Radio, Television, Film and Print," in* A Literary History of the American West, *edited by Max Westbrook, Texas Christian University Press, 1987, pp. 1263-82.*

C. L. Sonnichsen

[*In the following essay, Sonnichsen examines the works of modern western writers Larry McMurtry, Max Evans, and Benjamin Capps.*]

In his introduction to the 1942 Readers Club edition of Walter Van Tilburg Clark's *The Ox-Bow Incident*, Clifton Fadiman, speaking as usual *ex cathedra*, makes the following remark: "I suppose every folk-form bears within itself the possibility of a corresponding art form. One of these folk-forms is the horse-opera or western."

He goes on to point out that *Ox-Bow* follows the stereotype but goes far beyond it. "Now *The Ox-Bow Incident* has all the ingredients: monosyllabic cowpunchers, cattle rustlers, a Mae Western lady, a sinister poker game, barroom brawls, a villainous Mexican, and a lynching. Why doesn't the whole thing add up to another *Destry Rides Again*? Simply because Mr. Clark is an artist and because his materials are merely a pretext for saying something that goes beyond them."

Although he is almost innocent of information about

Western regional writing, Mr. Fadiman in this instance tells the truth. Mistakenly, however, he regards Mr. Clark's book as the first attempt since Bret Harte to raise the Western story to the level of art. Actually, the Western tradition divided over sixty years ago into at least two categories. With Owen Wister's *The Virginian* (1902), or if you prefer, with *Wolfville* (1897) or *The Log of a Cowboy* (1903), a small group of writers took a high road, leaving the formula writers, descendants of the dime-novelists of a generation or two before, on the old sub-literary popular level.

It could be shown that these sons of Zane Grey exhibit a great deal more resourcefulness and literary skill than has generally been conceded by their critics, but to save time let us call them "formula" writers and identify them by the following characteristics: sterotype characters; standard plots; a black-versus-white system of morality (*Time* magazine calls the Western the American Morality Play), and a setting in a semi-mythical region on the cattle-and-mining-frontier. The last two elements, the view of life as a struggle between good and evil and the heightened or the mythical Western setting, seem to be the permanent and stable ingredients in the formula.

The High Road writers differed from their more popular brethren in two ways. First they wrote better. Owen Wister is said to have brought the Western story up to *Atlantic Monthly* standards. Second, they aimed at more or less realism, and struggled to free themselves from the myth of the Old West.

I know more about the Southwest than I do about the West in general, and names from other regions could well be added to my list of High-Road Western writers: Steward Edward White, Eugene Manlove Rhodes, Conrad Richter, Walter Van Tilburg Clark. Between the High and the Low there should probably be a Limbo for Emerson Hough, Ernest Haycox, Jack Schaefer, A. B. Guthrie and some others.

The *Ox-Bow Incident* was not the beginning of something new on the High Road, as Clifton Fadiman supposed. It was really the end of all activity on the upper level. I find very little on a par with Mr. Clark's work during the forties and fifties. Instead, traffic on the Low Road built up as television programs dispensed mythology and symbolism and assured us that the West was won by noble pioneers who battled savages and wicked white men to assure a safe and decent life for a grateful posterity.

One result, as we all know, was the apotheosis of Wyatt Earp and Bat Masterson *et al*, an error which produced a violent and continuing reaction. But that is another story.

Among the readjustments which followed the take-over of the Wild West by television was the death of the pulp Western magazines, a severe weeding out of writers, and an upgrading of the product by those who survived. The soft-cover Westerns on the racks in the corner drug store and the hard-cover Westerns issued by Macmillan and Houghton Mifflin are several notches above the products of twenty years ago.

The High Road has changed too. After remaining comparatively untraveled for twenty years, it has recently been showing signs of renewed activity. Three new Southwestern writers have helped to change the picture: Larry McMurtry, Max Evans and Benjamin Capps.

All three are Texas boys with ranch backgrounds. Each has published several books and has an established following. Each one has found a different answer to the question: "How can we revive the Western novel?"

McMurtry, still under thirty and now an English teacher at Rice University, entered the field in 1961 with *Horseman, Pass By*. You saw it in the movies under the name *Hud*. It applied to the Western background the techniques and attitudes of what we used to call the Hard Boiled School. The viewpoint character is an adolescent named Lonnie Bannon who thinks and talks like Holden Caulfield in *The Catcher in the Rye*, only more so. In fact, the book might have been appropriately titled *The Catcher in the Prickly Pear*. Lonnie lives with his grandfather "Wild Horse" Homer Bannon and his step-grandmother. The grandmother's son Hud lives with them too, and he is a bad one. He wants the old man's ranch and says so. Complications set in when an outbreak of hoof-and-mouth disease makes it necessary to slaughter Homer Bannon's cattle. Homer loses his mind as a result, has delusions, falls off a porch, and breaks his hip. Hud, accompanied by a blonde belonging to somebody else, finds the old man crawling across the road, delirious, with his hip bone protruding through the flesh. Hud shoots him to put him out of his pain—as a short cut to ownership of the ranch. At the end of the story it looks as if he is going to get away with it.

The only really sympathetic character in the book is the negro cook Halmea, whom Hud rapes while Lonnie has to look helplessly on.

As one would expect, Mr. McMurtry's philosophy is Existential. He introduces the Anglo-Saxon monosyllables frequently, whether they are needed or not, and the whole thing adds up to what would be called in Houston (where Mr. McMurtry is much admired) raw, dynamic, and rank with the bitter smell of life.

It will not do to downgrade Mr. McMurtry, however, for he can write vivid and often moving prose, and his West is real, in a gruesome sort of way. "When I knew Grandad was in bed," he writes, "I went back to the windmill and stopped the blades, so I could climb up and sit on the platform beneath the big fin. Around me, across the dark prairie, the lights were clear, the oil derricks were lit with strings of yellow bulbs, like Christmas trees. The lights were still on in the kitchens of the pumpers' cabins, the little green-topped shacks scattered across the plain, each one propped on a few stacks of bricks. Twelve miles away, to the north, the red and green and yellow lights of Thalia shimmered against the dark. I sat above it all, in the cool breezy air that swept under the windmill blades, hearing the rig motors purr and the heavy trucks growl up the hill. Above the chattering of the ignorant Rhode Island Reds I heard two whippoorwills, the ghostly birds I never saw, calling across the flats below the ridge."

John Wayne and Ward Bond in the film adaptation of The Searchers *by Alan LeMay.*

When Lonnie goes back inside, he picks up a well thumbed copy of *From Here to Eternity.* What Mr. Mc-Murtry does in this novel and its successor, *Leaving Cheyenne* (1964), is to add four parts James Jones and four parts J. D. Salinger to about two parts Owen Wister to make a new formula for the novel of ranch life in the West.

Max Evans is headed in an entirely different direction. A ranch manager since he was fourteen, he belongs out of doors as McMurtry belongs in the classroom. His first short story appeared in the *Empire* magazine in 1951 when he was twenty-six years old. His first collection called *Southwest Wind* was published by the Naylor Company in 1958. His two novels are *Hi-Lo Country* (1961) and *The Rounders* (1960), the latter having been made into a movie. A collection of stories called *The One-Eyed Sky* appeared in 1963 and *The Mountain of Gold* was published by a regional press in Georgia in 1965.

He believes that "All lasting literature stems from the land," and he himself is as close to the land and its creatures as anyone now writing, including Walter Van Tilburg Clark. His domain is the cattle country of northeastern New Mexico, which he has recreated and renamed as William Faulkner revised the geography of northern Mississippi. The inhabitants, human and animal, are his friends and neighbors, and he is deeply impressed by the grimness of the lives they lead.

"The One-Eyed Sky," for instance, is about an old cow and her newborn calf, and old coyote and her four pups. The coyote must kill the calf to feed her starving offspring. The cow must destroy the coyote in order to preserve her calf. Into this desperate predicament steps a far-riding cowboy who sees and understands the situation and knows that he must take a hand.

The grimness of life, however, occupies only one half of Evans' mind. The other half is devoted to the absurdity of people and the situations they get into. *The Rounders* is the best example. Two authentic cowboys, Dusty Jones and Wrangler Lewis, spend the winter in a lonely line camp catching wild cattle for a predatory rancher named Jim Ed Love. Their constant and only companion is Old Fooler, a mild-appearing horse who conceals homicidal tendencies. In the spring they take their accumulated cash, plus Old Fooler and a couple of girls, to the big Rodeo at Hi-Lo, the capital city of Max Evans' little kingdom. At the end of the celebration, thanks to Old Fooler, they are broke and ready to go back to Jim Ed Love.

Dusty and Wrangler talk like real cowboys but their talk is not offensive because it is natural. They are naive and ignorant, but they are also brave, generous and humane. Evans looks at them as Steinbeck looks at the inhabitants of cannery row—with humor and affection. He shows, through their activities, how cowboys live and work. Sometimes he even gives brief lectures on the subject. Mostly, however, he comments with wry and earthy humor on the vicissitudes of their lives.

When Dusty asks Wrangler one time how he came to be in his present situation, Wrangler says it was the fault of Toy Smith, a guest at a dude ranch where he happened to be working. She took him to her bosom and her bed.

> "At nights when we got back and I got the horses unsaddled and fed, there would be Toy Smith hangin' over the corral gate waitin' for me to go for a swim in them hot-water tanks. She sure was a swimmer," said Wrangler. "And float! Hell, she looked like a whole mountain range lyin' out there on her back."
>
> "Was she big?" I asked.
>
> Wrangler looked at me and snorted through his flat nose. "Big? Why Dusty, you couldn't get her in a hay barn without widenin' the doors. . . . She got to where she follered me every place I went except the toilet. Ever'time we'd have a dance for the cowboys and dudes, she just grabbed little old me and waltzed all night. I couldn't see past her for all that belly and there weren't no use lookin' up, for there was about forty pound of bosom hangin' over my head. There was just one thing to do and that was hold on tight and pray."

The romance ended when Wrangler began staying out nights with another girl. He came back to Toy's room one evening to find a ball-pein hammer under her pillow, a clear invitation, he figured, for him to move on.

Evans moves about in the timeless West of the cattleman, like his predecessors in Western fiction, but the greasy spoon restaurants and asphalt pavements and neon lights of today's cow towns are only a few miles down the road. Out of the tragedy and hilarity of the ranch life he knows he has constructed his own escape from the formula.

Benjamin Capps is not the least interesting or the least successful of the three. He studied at Texas Tech and the University of Texas, navigated bombers in World War II, taught briefly in an Oklahoma College, and was working as a welder in Grand Prairie, Texas, when a successful novel made it possible for him to write full time. His first extended piece of fiction, *The Hanging at Comanche Wells* (somewhat reminiscent of *The Ox-Bow Incident*) was an original paperback in 1962. *The Trail to Ogallala* followed in 1964. His publishers expected a moderate run and printed less than 3,000 copies. In three months 7,000 copies had been sold and it brought Mr. Capps several literary awards and citations as well as a comforting sum of money.

The Trail to Ogallala is so much like Andy Adams' *Log of a Cowboy* that one can hardly believe Capps did not have that book in mind. It is the story of a cattle drive, but whereas Adams' 1903 volume was a simple and factual account of what happened on the Western Cattle Trail, Capps' book recreates the inner as well as the outer lives of men on a long drive. Like Adams' tale it has no complication of plot, no heroine, no passionate love story. But character is behind every bit of action and Mr. Capps displays extraordinary skill in transporting his reader to another time and place. Take for instance the storm scene which precedes a stampede: "Below the roll of cloud was a spreading expanse of solid color, dark dirty gray tinged with green, ominous in its dead hue, as if it were the silent deadly center of all the threats of the clouds. When the expanse lighted up inside, it revealed light purple highlights. To Scott, the green tint meant hail. He tightened the neck string of his hat snug under his chin and began to sing 'Rock of Ages' to the cattle. The nervous steers and cows were moving about, soemtimes stumbling over the ones that were lying down. A big drop of rain spattered against his hat."

Like his predecessors on the High Road, Capps is trying to write not better Westerns but better fiction about the West. In *Trail* and in *Sam Chance*, his second novel (1965), he has risen above the formula.

In their different ways, McMurtry, Evans and Capps have added something new to regional fiction about the cattle country and have made it clear that the horse opera may indeed be the take-off point for a body of writing of which we need not be ashamed. After all, the West of the cattleman is our number-one fictional resource. For sixty years we have been trying to make literature out of it, and it looks as if we are doing better as time goes on. (pp. 22-8)

> *C. L. Sonnichsen, "The New Style Western," in* The South Dakota Review, *Vol. 4, No. 2, Summer, 1966, pp. 22-8.*

William Bloodworth

[*In the following essay, Bloodworth compares popular and "literary" westerns.*]

This paper proposes to define the relationship between the so-called Formula or Popular Western and a still-emerging tradition of American writing which draws upon the Formula Western for setting and characters but which does not sit easily under the rubric of popular culture.

The non-popular (that is, not popular in the way that Zane Grey, Luke Short, or Louis L'Amour have been popular) tradition may have had its earliest expression in Walter Van Tilburg Clark's *The Ox-Bow Incident* in 1940. However, it did not really begin to flourish until the late fifties and early sixties, during the heyday of popular western entertainment on television and at the movies. Berger's *Little Big Man* (1964) has considerable claim to being the most widely respected novel within the tradition. Other examples would most certainly include E. L. Doctorow's *Welcome to Hard Times* (1960), Robert Flynn's *North to Yesterday* (1967), John Seelye's *The Kid* (1972), and novels by R. G. Vliet and David Wagoner—all of which incorporate aspects of the classic Popular Western in fiction which, in its purposes and results, seems to go considerably beyond its popular origins.

Two other kinds of novels belong in this discussion. One is the western with a contemporary setting like Edward Abbey's *The Brave Cowboy* (1956), Max Evans' *The Rounders* (1960), or Larry McMurtry's *Horseman, Pass By* (1961). The other is the western that at first seems almost identical to the popular story but which turns out to be a horse opera of a slightly different color, as is the case with Frederick manfred's *Riders of Judgment* (1957) and, I think, with Charles Portis' *True Grit* (1968).

Somewhere within the tradition I am trying to describe there may even be a place for such idiosyncratic works as Richard Brautigan's *The Hawkline Monster* (1972)—subtitled "A Gothic Western"—or Tom Robbins' *Even Cowgirls Get the Blues* (1976), provided that they are accompanied by several question marks.

A good term to identify this motley and variform category of American fiction is hard to come by. C. L. Sonnichsen a few years ago proposed the term "New Style Westerns" to describe fiction by McMurtry, Evans and others. Leslie Fiedler's "New Westerns," as used in *The Vanishing American,* is also a possibility. "Anti-Westerns" seems to apply in some cases. "Off-Trail Westerns" is somehow the most appealing term by virtue of its implied reference to a departure from the crowded trail of popular culture. "Literary Westerns" may be the most useful term, however, by drawing attention to the conscious (or self-conscious) literary intentions behind all of the novels that I have mentioned and a good many others that, I am sure, could be brought into this discussion. Perhaps it will be best to talk off-trail qualities in Literary Westerns, reserving the usual upper case letters for the latter term. An obvious off-trail—and, by extension, "literary"—quality of the Literary Western can be seen in the comments of an unnamed "Western Writer" quoted by Russell Nye in *The Unembarrassed Muse.* According to this writer, when a character in a story is shown to have missed in his attempt to solve problems, "the academic pinheads call it art, a complex human document full of ambiguities." But, he goes on to say, "Mine don't miss because I make a living at it." The point here is obvious. Ambiguity is held to a minimum in Popular Westerns. Literary Westerns, on the other hand, involve a liberal infusion of attitudes distilled from modern literature.

This point is so obvious, in fact, that having made it, I don't really care to emphasize it. Instead, I want to draw attention to the *similarities* between Popular and Literary Westerns, to their common ground, and to the ultimate thematic reliance of the latter on the former.

My general argument runs something like this: although many critics and scholars have drawn attention to the Literary Western as a way of criticizing, satirizing, or making other kinds of negative judgments about the formula stories, the literary story actually tends to affirm rather than deny some of the basic themes of its more widely circulated popular cousins. The Literary Western represents an extension of the Popular Western as much as it represents a departure from it. Furthermore, the success (the quality, if we wish) of the Literary Western often seems to depend on its retention of mythic aspects of the Popular Western.

Using the term "mythic aspects" in reference to the Popular Western is like opening Pandora's box, the concept of "myth" being subject to dozens of definitions and the word "mythic" often used so loosely as to have little denotative value. To clarify matters I must admit to using "mythic" somewhat generally myself to refer to something imaginary (a particular kind of narrative, a character type, a specific setting for a story) which serves as a consistent source of meaning and vicarious emotional response for many members of the society in which it circulates.

The terms "formulaic" or "conventional" might be used to describe the same thing since I am not referring to elements that have their origin in some ancient, primitive narrative. However, "mythic" does a better job of drawing attention to the possibility that many elements of the western have a validity and an appeal beyond that of familiarity or repetition. Exactly how far beyond is a question lying outside the scope of this essay; I can only refer to Will Wright's *Sixguns and Society,* which makes the general claim that popular western films work like primitive myths in communicating the basic concerns of their society.

At any rate, the tradition of the Literary Western since the 1950s draws heavily upon several elements of the formula stories which I think we can refer to as "mythic." The arid landscape of the West, the western hero, and the disjunctive sense of time and history incorporated in Popular Westerns are three obvious ones.

Literary versions of the western sometimes treat these elements in ironic ways for the apparent purpose of demonstrating the difference between the way things really were and the way that people have often imagined them to be. When they do this they follow the example of *The Ox-Bow Incident,* which reduces the mythic heroism of the western character to cowardice and moral ambiguity. (Clark's novel—published before the heyday of the Pop Western in the fifties—is perhaps a genuine anti-western in this respect.) In some cases the Literary Westerns work toward a *Blazing Saddles* kind of comic send-up of western stereotypes.

In most cases, however, the mythic elements of the western are treated with a surprising and perhaps even unconscious degree of respect even when irony or humor are the obvious intentions of the narrative. For the sake of argument I would claim that the spirit of the Popular Western is almost impossible to break—even with the bit and spurs of writers whose purpose is to produce "complex human documents."

Landscape is the most obvious example of how undeniable a mythic aspect of the Popular Western can be. As John Cawelti points out in *Adventure, Mystery, and Romance,* the defining element of the western is "the symbolic landscape . . . and the influence this landscape has on the character and action of the hero." The geography of the western—be it the "World of crystal light, a land without end" in *The Virginian,* the romantic color and canyons of *Riders of the Purple Sage,* or the harsh character-testing land of Louis L'Amour—is sacred territory and clearly inseparable from the values and meanings that are expressed through character and plot.

Even in those Literary Westerns which tend towards irony and parody, the land retains an inescapable significance. In Doctorow's *Welcome to Hard Times,* for instance, the landscape is described in such harsh terms as to make the efforts of people to establish a town seem ludicrous. The Dakota Territory of the story is "nothing but miles of flats" where wagon trains leave "a long dust turd lying on the rim of the earth." The only aspect of the land that justifies human habitation is a water well in the town of Hard Times. No crops can be grown on the land, no trees provide lumber, and the nearby mine soon plays out. Blue, the mayor of the town and the narrator of the story, learns that the West is a "fraud," "a poor pinched-out claim."

Yet Doctorow's novel—which, among other things, can be seen as an attack on Turnerian ideas about the benefits to be derived from the frontier experience—only reinforces the mythic significance of the western landscape by overstating the qualities of aridity and inhospitability. The Bad Man from Bodie in the novel, the mysteriously inhuman villain who twice destroys the town and most of its inhabitants (and who, curiously, is named Turner), seems to be an allegorical representative *of* the landscape rather than a person simply on it. And in his malevolent violence he suggests the untamed and untameable West. Doctorow's landscape *is* the West *in exremity,* a literary resurrection of the Great American Desert notion, and—above all—a place where Eastern ideas and habits have little effect. In a sense, the real villain in the novel is the kind of artificial commercialism that Blue and others attempt to establish in Hard Times through the selling of water and women. From Wister on, the West has been an exposer of sham and artificiality, and it retains this function in *Welcome to Hard Times.*

Some Literary Westerns which are set after the years of settling the West seem to be conscious efforts at avoiding the classic landscape of the formula. In McMurtry's *Horseman, Pass By* (renamed *Hud* in order to capitalize on the Paul Newman movie in 1962) and Flynn's *North to Yesterday,* the landscape of the Old West exists primarily in the dreams and fantasies of the main characters. In the mid-1950s setting of McMurtry's novel, the West Texas landscape is a place of tractor-trailer rigs, Cadillacs, government cattle inspectors, and honky-tonk music. In *North to Yesterday* Flynn's story concerns a central Texas storekeeper and would-be cowboy named Lampassas who organizes a cattle drive to Trail's End in Kansas some twenty years after the end of the trail drives.

Although the mythic landscape of the Popular Western is acknowledged as nothing but a myth in both of these novels, the main intention of the stories is not so much to contrast the myth with the reality of history but, almost conversely, to show its retention in *spite* of history. In *Horseman, Pass By* young Lonnie Bannon has a dream in which he rides a Texas landscape "like the opening scene in a big Western movie," and he obviously yearns for the kind of

place that the West was when his grandfather, now passing away, was young. In *North to Yesterday* Lampassas' quixotic faith in trail driving is so strong that he convinces several others to join in his attempt to take a herd of scraggly longhorns to Trail's End. When he finally gets there with a few of his cows he learns that the cattle market no longer exists and cowboys of the old kind are no longer welcome. Undaunted, however, he is still driving cattle when the novel ends, forcing his belief in the trail onto a changed landscape. In both of these novels the landscape of the Popular Western, internalized within characters or frozen in their memories, is a positive element and a means of gaining the reader's sympathy.

Whereas it is difficult to find a Literary Western that successfully explodes popular attitudes towards landscape, it is uncommonly easy to cite examples which seem to revise or eliminate the traditional character traits of the western hero. Much in line with modern literature, the protagonists of the Literary Western tend to be antiheroes, nonheroes, or—at the very least—unsuccessful heroes. At one end of the spectrum are the characters whose bravery exceeds their ability to survive, as is the case with Jack Burns in Abbey's *The Brave Cowboy* or Cain Hammett in Manfred's *Riders of Judgment.* At the opposite extreme is the sexually deceptive Kid of John Seelye's novel by that name, Brautigan's two killers in *The Hawkline Monster,* or the homosexual Bonanza Jellybean of Robbins' *Even Cowgirls Get the Blues* (that is, if the spectrum goes as far as these last two examples). Somewhere in between—as usual—is Jack Crabb of *Little Big Man.* A strange assortment to compare with the likes of the Virginian, Lassiter, Shane, William Tell Sackett, and others of popular vintage.

The protagonist of the Literary Western differs from the hero of the Popular Western mainly by not actually being heroic or by not being successfully heroic. Villains are generally not gunned down. Instead, the hero himself often meets death, sometimes in decidedly unclassical ways, as in *The Brave Cowboy* where Jack Burns is hit by a tractor-trailer rig loaded with toilet fixtures. Often, as in *North to Yesterday* and Evans' *The Rounders,* there are simply no opportunities for "heroic" action of the kind associated with the Popular Western. At times a would-be hero is simply unable to act in a heroic manner even when a situation arises, as Lonnie Bannon is unable to shoot his half-brother Hud when he sees Hud raping their black maid in *Horseman, Pass By*—or as Mayor Blue is unable to stand up against the Bad Man from Bodie in the opening scene of *Welcome to Hard Times.*

Furthermore, the romantic involvement that has been such a great part of the western hero's personality since *The Virginian* is seldom depicted in Literary Westerns. Shane-like shades of it remain in *The Brave Cowboy* and *Riders of Judgment* with the hero attracted to somebody else's wife, but nowhere does the hero win the heart of the heroine in classical fashion. A list of the acute violations of the romantic conventions of the formula would include Jack Crabb's multi-ethnic sexual services, the bitterness of the relationship between Blue and his Molly (as compared to Molly Stark Wood in *The Virginian*) in *Welcome to*

Hard Times, and the miscegenous relationship implied between Seelye's Kid (actually female) and a black sidekick. (I think it would be unnecessarily messy to mention all that goes on in this regard in the novels by Brautigan and Robbins.) Sexual relations are easily the most "off-trail" aspect of the Literary Western.

Yet the differences between literary hero and formula hero may not be as extreme as I have made them out to be. One underlying and rather general similarity remains. Most of the central characters in the Literary Westerns are alienated from conventional social values and many are proponents, intuitively, of justice and right. As is so often the case in the Popular Western, the idea of good that the character represents is not based on the social values of churches, schools, and commerce. In contrast to the behavior of the hero, ordinary society is intolerant, foolish, dull, or just plain unpleasant.

All of which may only mean that both varieties of the western build stories around uncommon personalities, not that one continues a tradition begun by the other. However true this fact may be, it seems important to note that the most essential quality of the formula hero is not seriously challenged. Specific traits are radically different in places, and "the certainty of resolution" that Cawelti says is expected of formulaic characters is almost entirely missing, but the western hero—or antihero—remains larger than life in his attachment to values that transcend those around him.

"It is a vanished world," Owen Wister wrote in 1902 of his setting for *The Virginian.* His words describe the mythic projection of a world removed from that of the present not so much in number of years but by virtue of a felt temporal disjunction resulting in a sense of loss, of nostalgia, even of alienation from ordinary historical time. Wallace Stegner refers to this as "a past which has no present." It is related to what Cawelti calls "the slightly removed imaginary world of formulaic fiction." A standard feature of the Literary Western, the sense of "a past which has no present" is an unmistakable affirmation of the Popular Western tradition.

Those Literary Westerns which stress the mythic sense of time most obviously are the ones which have some or all action occurring *after* the classic years of cowboys, trail drives, and Indians. In *Little Big Man* the effete present (exemplified in the narrator Ralph Snell) is a sorry contrast to the heroic past of Chief Lodge Skins, George A. Custer, and Jack Crabb. A similar contrast appears in *The Brave Cowboy, Horseman, Pass By, The Rounders, North to Yesterday* and *True Grit* (with the narrator looking back on her adventures with Rooster Cogburn).

But the sense of a vanished world in which action, gesture, and character had more significance than it does in the present turns up as well in stories set entirely in the past. One of the best examples of a recent evocation of mythic frontier time is R. G. Vliet's short novel, *Rockspring.* Vliet's story may serve, in fact, as a perfect example of the continuing literary vitality of all three mythic aspects—landscape, character, and time—which represent the heritage of the Popular Western.

First published as the feature item in the twenty-fifth anniversary issue of *Hudson Review* in 1973, *Rockspring* can lay claim to critical recognition of the most respectable kind. The novel tells the story of a fourteen-year-old girl, the daughter of white settlers in Texas during the wild 1830s, who is kidnapped by three Mexican *bandidos.* Written in achingly poetic prose, *Rockspring* develops the theme of maturation in a wild and threatening western landscape—a maturation which culminates in the girl's eventual love for one of the Mexicans who, like the typical formula hero, turns out to be capable of incredibly gentle and sensitive responses in spite of his hardened exterior.

Vliet departs in his novel from the Popular Western in many ways—his heroine is actually and repeatedly raped, and at the end of the story his Mexican hero is killed by the girl's Anglo relatives—but essential elements of the formula are unmistakably present. *Rockspring* also represents a modern version of the Indian captivity narrative, that very first Popular Western, with the woman first seeing her captors as heathen devils but eventually learning a strange and ambivalent respect for them. Combined with Vliet's poetic powers, particularly with his extraordinary ability to depict the heroine's response to the Southwest landscape and to the alien culture and language of her Mexican abductors, the formula elements result in a novel of remarkable power. This work shows how far the western can go in the direction of sheer literary excellence, and can serve as sufficient proof of the western's continued potential not only as popular culture but also as cultural resource.

By stressing the influence of the Popular Western I do not mean to imply that key differences between formula and literary stories should be ignored. For instance, the typical way that violence in Popular Westerns is either justified as a necessary means to an end or is rationalized as the result of unambiguously evil motives differs elementally from the more truly "senseless" violence of the Literary Western. Custer's masacre of Cheyennes at the Battle of Washita in *Little Big Man* would be a case in point.

Yet I am convinced that we let such differences obscure the ways in which the formula story has been translated, so to speak, instead of transformed, into a minor but important contemporary literary tradition. One of the underlying points of this paper—perhaps *the* underlying point—has to do with the typical hands-off attitude of many literary critics, scholars, and practitioners towards the Popular Western. In its most obvious form my point is something like, "We can't really appreciate *Little Big Man* or *True Grit* until we have read the likes of Ernest Haycox and Luke Short." But I also mean to say that we can't really appreciate Haycox and Short, or any other writers of genuine Popular Westerns, until we have read works by Berger, *et al.* That is, not until we recognize the persistence of popular themes—particularly their persistence even in works that often seem to parody the formula, that seem bent on chasing popular conventions into box canyons of ambiguity and complexity—can we really begin to understand the heritage of the Popular Western. (pp. 287-96)

William Bloodworth, "Literary Extensions of

the Formula Western," in Western American Literature, *Vol. XLV, No. 4, February, 1980, pp. 287-96.*

FURTHER READING

Anthologies

Coleman, Rufus A. *Western Prose and Poetry.* New York: Harper & Brothers, 1932, 502 p.
  Western poetry and stories from the nineteenth and early twentieth centuries.

Taylor, J. Golden, ed. *Great Western Short Stories.* Palo Alto: American West Publishing Company, 1967, 572 p.
  Collection of western short stories.

Secondary Sources

Berkhofer, Robert F., Jr. "The Western and the Indian in Popular Culture." In his *White Man's Indian: Images of the American Indian from Columbus to the Present,* pp. 71-111. New York: Random House, 1978.
  Examines the negative portrayal of Native Americans in American western literature.

Branch, E. Douglas. *The Cowboy and His Interpreters.* New York: D. Appleton and Co., 1926, 277 p.
  Collection of essays on the portrayals of the cowboy in fiction.

Dinan, John A. *The Pulp Western.* San Bernardino: The Borgo Press, 1983, 128 p.
  Study of theme, plot, and style in pulp westerns.

Eastlake, William. "The Failure of Western Writing." In *Old Southwest/New Southwest,* edited by Judy Nolte Lensink, pp. 91-9. Tucson: University of Arizona Press, 1987.
  Laments the lack of well-written modern westerns and urges writers to draw from first-hand experience when writing about the West.

Elkin, Frederick. "The Psychological Appeal of the Hollywood Western." *The Journal of Educational Sociology,* No. 24 (October 1950): 72-86.
  Examines the reasons for the widespread popularity of American western literature and films.

Erben, Rudolf. "The Western Holdup Play: The Pilgrimage Continues." *Western American Literature* XX, No. 4 (Winter 1989): 311-22.
  Defines the western holdup play as a drama involving a cast of characters involuntarily confined to an area and forced to interact. The critic evaluates *The Petrified Forest, Bus Stop, When You Comin Back, Red Ryder?, The Holdup,* and *Angels Fall* as typical of the western holdup play.

Erisman, Fred, and Etulain, Richard W. *Fifty Western Writers.* Westport, Conn.: Greenwood Press, 1982, 562 p.
  Biographical and bibliographical sourcebook on fifty well-known western writers, including Max Brand, Zane Grey, Louis L'Amour, and Ernest Haycox.

Etulain, Richard W. "Frontier and Region in Western Literature." *Southwestern American Literature,* No. 1 (1971): 121-28.
  Examines the problem of terminology in the field of western literature and attempts to define such terms as "frontier," "region," and "the West."

———. *Western American Literature: A Bibliography of Interpretive Books and Articles.* Vermillion, S. D.: Dakota Press, 1972, 137 p.
  Bibliography of western literature, with sections on individual authors.

Folsom, James K. "Good Men and True." In his *American Western Novel,* pp. 99-140. New Haven: College & University Press, 1966, 224 p.
  Comments on the favorable portrayal of cowboys in western fiction.

———. *The Western: A Collection of Critical Essays.* Englewood Cliffs, N.J.: Prentice-Hall, 1979, 177 p.
  Collection of essays on American western literature, including commentary by W. H. Hutchinson, Vardis Fisher, Richard Etulain, and Max Westbrook.

Frantz, Joe B., and Choate, Julian Ernest, Jr. *The American Cowboy: The Myth and the Reality.* Norman: University of Oklahoma Press, 1955, 232 p.
  Compares the cowboy of literature to the real cowboy.

Graham, Don. "Old and New Cowboy Classics." *Southwest Review* 65, No. 3 (Summer 1980): 293-303.
  Compares Andy Adam's *The Log of a Cowboy* to Benjamin Capps's *The Trail to Ogallala,* stating that the latter work is more accurate in its description of cowboy life and use of history.

Gurian, Jay. "The Possibility of a Western Poetics." *The Colorado Quarterly* XV, No. 1 (Summer 1966): 69-85.
  Evaluates western poetry, finding that most western verse lacks "wit, irony, paradox, metaphor, or symbol."

Haslam, Gerald W. *Western Writing.* Albuquerque: University of New Mexico Press, 1974, 156 p.
  Ten essays on western literature, writers, and criticism. Includes articles by Bernard DeVoto, Wallace Stegner, A. B. Guthrie, Vardis Fisher, John R. Milton, and W. H. Hutchinson.

Hutchinson, W. H. "Virgins, Villains, and Varmints." *Huntington Library Quarterly* 16 (1953): 381-92.
  Identifies and discusses three character types in western fiction: "good women," "bad guys," and the hero.

Jones, Daryl. *The Dime Novel Western.* Bowling Green: The Popular Press, 1978, 186 p.
  Examines characterization, theme, structure, and plot in the dime novel western.

Lojek, Helen. "Reading the Myth of the West." *South Dakota Review* 28, No. 1 (Spring 1990): 46-61.
  Discusses Frank South's *Rattlesnake in a Cooler* and Mark Medoff's *The Majestic Kid* as two plays that examine the discrepancy between the myth and reality of the American West.

Lyon, Thomas J. "Western Poetry." *Journal of the West* XIX, No. 1 (January 1980): 46-53.
  Examines themes and style in a selection of western poetry.

Meldrum, Barbara. "Images of Women in Western American Literature." *The Midwest Quarterly* XVII, No. 2 (Winter 1976): 252-67.

Assesses the role of women in western fiction.

Milton, John R. "Conversations with Western American Novelists." *South Dakota Review* 9, No. 1 (Spring 1971): 16-57.

Interviews western writers Frank Waters, Walter Van Tilburg Clark, Harvey Fergusson, and Wallace Stegner.

————. "The Evolution of the Western Novel." In his *Novel of the American West,* 65-116. Lincoln: University of Nebraska Press, 1980.

Traces the history and development of the western novel.

Munden, Kenneth. "A Contribution to the Psychological Understanding of the Cowboy and His Myth." *American Imago* 15, No. 2 (Summer 1958): 103-48

Attempts to understand the appeal of the cowboy by examining his personality traits.

Nussbaum, Martin. "Sociological Symbolism of the Adult Western." *Social Forces* 39 (October 1960): 25-8.

Studies adult westerns as reflections of social attitudes and beliefs.

Smith, Henry Nash. "The Dime Novel Heroine." In his *Virgin Land: The American West as Symbol and Myth,* pp. 126-35. New York: Vintage Books, 1950, 305 p.

Discusses the depiction of women as "soft-hearted Amazons" in American western literature.

Tuska, Jon, and Piekarski, Vicki. *Encyclopedia of Frontier and Western Fiction.* New York: McGraw-Hill Book Company, 1983, 365 p.

Provides biographical and critical information on the major writers of western and frontier literature and includes essays on "Historical Personalities," "Native Americans," "Pulp and Slick Western Stories," and "Women on the Frontier."

Walker, Don D. "Can the Western Tell What Happens?" *Rendezvous* 7, No. 2 (1972): 33-47.

Studies the link between literature and history and how western writers have rendered American history in their fiction.

Westbrook, Max. "The Themes of Western Fiction." *Southwest Review* XLIII, No. 3 (Summer 1958): 232-38.

Examines the "revolt-and-search" motif in westerns, defining the term as an act of rebellion against institutional evil and the search for a personal code of ethics.

————. "The Practical Spirit: Sacrality and the American West." *Western Literature Association,* No. 3 (1968): 267-84.

Relates American western writing to the concept of "sacrality," maintaining that modern life has "lost contact with the source, with sex, God, land." He suggests that western writers have recognized this failure and have tried to restore the connection through their fiction.

Dadaism

INTRODUCTION

Dadaism was a highly influential literary and artistic movement of the World War I era. Founded in Zurich in 1916 by European writers and artists who had been displaced by the war, the movement quickly spread to other cities in Europe, with the main groups being located in Paris and Berlin. The Dadaists—or "Dadas," as members of the movement referred to themselves—believed that the carnage of World War I was evidence of the failure of western institutions, and consequently they rejected culturally sanctioned values and conventions in art. The result was uninhibited experimentation with forms of "anti-art": poetry composed in invented languages, plays performed with inaudible dialogue, objects such as snow shovels and urinals exhibited as works of art, and numerous other displays of flamboyant nonsense designed as an affront to traditional aesthetics. Much of the direction for these activities was given by Tristan Tzara, the titular leader and chief polemicist of Dadaism whose manifestos established the outrageously illogical and, to many commentators, indefinable nature of the movement. With such statements as, "the true Dadas are against Dada," the Dadaists set out to undermine conceptualizations of their movement and assault traditional ideas about art.

While criticized for what some have viewed as nihilistic and meaningless antics, Dadaism is more often seen as the source of later movements and innovations in the arts, including Surrealism, the Theater of the Absurd, performance art, and various avant-garde trends in painting, music, and film.

REPRESENTATIVE WORKS

Aragon, Louis
  Feu de joie (poetry) 1920
  Anicet (novel) 1921
  Les aventures de Télémaque (novel) 1922
  Le libertinage (short stories) 1924
  Le mouvement perpétuel (poetry) 1926
Arp, Hans (Jean)
  der vogel selbdritt (poetry) 1920
  die wolkenpumpe (poetry) 1920
  Der Pyramidenrock (poetry) 1924
  Gesammelte Gedichte. 2 vols. (poetry) 1963-73
Ball, Hugo
  Die Nase des Michelangelo (drama) [first publication] 1911
  Der Henker von Brescia (drama) [first publication] 1914

Flametti oder vom Dandysmus der Armen (novel) 1918
Zur Kritik der deutschen Intelligenz (nonfiction) 1919
Tenderenda der Phantast (prose and poetry) [written 1914-20] 1967
Breton, André
  Mont de piété (fiction) 1919
Breton, André, and Soupault, Philippe
  Les champs magnétiques (poetry) 1920
Duchamp, Marcel
  Marchand du sel: Ecrits de Marcel Duchamp (essays) 1958
  [*Salt Seller: The Writings of Marcel Duchamp*, 1973]
  The Bride Stripped Bare by Her Bachelors, Even (notebooks) 1960
  Entretiens avec Marcel Duchamp (interviews) 1967
  [*Dialogues with Marcel Duchamp*, 1967]
  Marcel Duchamp: Notes and Projects for the Large Glass (notebooks) 1969
Éluard, Paul
  Répétitions (poetry) 1922
Hausmann, Raoul
  Material der Malerei Plastik und Architektur (nonfiction) 1918
  Hurra! Hurra! Hurra!: 12 Satiren (satire) 1921
Huelsenbeck, Richard
  Phantastische Gebete (poetry) 1916
  Azteken oder die Knallbude (novel) 1918
  Verwandlungen (novel) 1918
  Doctor Billig am Ende (novel) 1921
Picabia, Francis
  Poèmes et dessins de la fille sans mère (poetry and drawings) 1918
Ribemont-Dessaignes, Georges
  Manifeste à l'huile (manifesto) 1920
  Manifeste selon Saint-Jean Chrysopompe (manifesto) 1920
  L'empereur de Chine (drama) [first publication] 1921
Richter, Hans
  Rhythm 21 (screenplay) 1921
  Rhythm 22 (screenplay) 1922
  Rhythm 23 (screenplay) 1923
  Vormmittagsspuk (screenplay) 1927
  [*Ghosts Before Breakfast*, 1927]
  Dada, Kunst und Antikunst (criticism) 1964
  [*Dada: Art and Anti-Art*, 1965]
Schwitters, Kurt
  Anna Blume (poetry) 1919
  Die Kathedrale (poetry) 1920
  Memoiren Anna Blumes in Bleie (poetry) 1922
  Die Blume Anna (poetry) 1923
Soupault, Philippe
  Aquarium (poetry) 1917

Rose des vents   (poetry)   1920
Tzara, Tristan
   La première aventure céleste de Monsieur Antipyrine
      (drama) [first publication]   1916
   Vingt-cinq poèmes   (poetry)   1918
   Manifestes Dada   (manifestos)   1924
      [*Seven Dada Manifestos*, 1977]
   L'homme approximatif   (poetry)   1930
      [*The Approximate Man* published in *Approximate
      Man, and Other Writings*, 1975]

BACKGROUND AND MAJOR FIGURES

Jerold M. Starr

[*Starr is an American sociologist and educator. The following excerpt provides an introduction to the social, political, and artistic origins of Dadaism and examines the
major figures and principle tenets of the movement.*]

For years a world war seemed both impossible and inevitable. The doctrines of competitive capitalism, utilitarian-
ism, and Spencerian evolutionism held that war was part
of the barbaric feudal past and not possible within the
modern network of economic interdependence. Nevertheless, major European crises had erupted almost every year
after 1895: the Boer War, Fashoda, the Russo-Japanese
War, Agadir, the Balkan wars. Moreover, "Germany's determinism to dominate the continent and challenge England's control of the world's seas and markets" made war
in Europe appear "inevitable."

Middle-class intellectuals, particularly educated youth,
welcomed the war as the one "blow of fate" that could reconcile class conflict, mobilize the spiritual interests of the
nation, and give birth to a "new, more ethical and less
commercial man" to replace the mundane, interest-bound
bourgeoisie and proletariat. Indeed [in his *Generation of
1914* Robert] Wohl reports, "When war did break over
Europe, it was interpreted by intellectuals as an hour of
redemption, a rite of purification, and a chance, perhaps
the last, to escape from a sinking and declining civilization."

The reality of the war made a mockery of such hopes and
dreams. Before long, the organized bloodbath drove many
to disillusionment and despair. In England the "war poets
provided the theme: doomed youth led blindly to the
slaughter by cruel age." Although the carnage was confined to the combatants, the suffering was widespread.
Wohl explains:

   All inhabitants of Europe were exposed to the
   militarization of life and language, the erosion of
   individual freedom and social differences, the
   disruption of economic life, the drain of wealth,
   the hardship caused by food shortages, the
   growth of collectivism and bureaucracies, the
   collapse of the international system and the re-

lease of huge reservoirs of aggressivity and violence.

The artistic world suffered serious disruption from the
war: "During the first weeks of the war there was a rash
of emigrations, voluntary and involuntary." The Germans
had to leave France, the Russians had to leave Germany,
and many pacifists left their own countries "to avoid conscription or escape the hysteria and suspicion at home."
Colonies of émigré artists, writers, and political activists
grew up in the large cities of neutral countries: Amster-
dam, Barcelona, Lisbon, New York, Geneva, and Zurich.

The art market stopped functioning, making it difficult for
even the well-known to make a living. Schools and gal-
leries were closed and publications were censored. Cultural radicalism generally was suppressed by the patriotic
conformity demanded by the state in the name of the war
effort. [In her *Painters and Politics: The European Avant-
Garde and Society, 1900-1925* Theda] Shapiro writes: "As
the war ground on, the painters more and more frequently
complained of their forced artistic inactivity." They kept
in touch with each other by mail and an occasional inter-
mediary, sharing their concerns.

For various reasons Zurich became "the meeting ground
for exiles of all sorts—the safe, though scarcely calm, eye
of the hurricane" (Shapiro). Because of its size, location,
and ethnic diversity, Switzerland had an established policy of military neutrality. This allowed Zurich to serve as
the unofficial capital of world capitalism, its international
banking system preserving the assets of elites and the integrity of capitalist economic relations during periods of
defeated diplomacy and military confrontation. As a consequence Zurich, paradoxically, also served as the center
for radical refugees seeking asylum from the war. The Rumanian artist Marcel Janco, one of the original Dadaists
and himself a Zurich refugee during the war, has written:

   Zurich was a haven of refuge amid the sea of fire,
   of iron and blood. It was not only a refuge but
   the trysting place for revolutionaries, an oasis
   for the thinker, a spy exchange, a nursery of ideologies, and a home for poets and liberty-loving
   vagabonds. . . . It became a meeting place of
   the arts. Painters, students, revolutionaries,
   tourists, international crooks, psychiatrists, the
   demimonde, sculptors, and polite spies on the
   look out for information, all hobnobbed with
   one another.

It was in Zurich in 1916 that all the young century's trends
and movements in art and politics climaxed in what came
to be called Dada. Conceived in a spirit of artistic and political revolt, Dada was born into the horror of world war
and, over the next seven years, grew to encompass three
continents.

The Dadaists accepted the Marxist interpretation of the
war as representing the greedy adventurism of a capitalist
class grown fat with political power. In the words of the
Dadaist Richard Huelsenbeck, "In Zurich the international profiteers sat in the restaurants with well-filled wal-
lets and rosy cheeks, ate with their knives and smacked
their lips in a merry hurrah for the countries that were
bashing each other's skulls in."

The essential spirit of Zurich Dada was protest. Its attitude was outrage at the destruction of beauty, goodness, and truth by the culture of industrial capitalism, which, collapsing under the weight of its own contradictions, had degenerated into wholesale human slaughter. Dada's artistic and political posture was radical negation, the complete destruction of all traces of the past in order to purify humanity and build a new society on the ruins of the old. Despite the positive affirmation implicit in their position, the Dadaists concentrated on negative action, practicing provocation, not contestation. Zurich Dada constituted a great refusal. It eschewed any desire to convince anybody of anything. Its goal was more direct and simple: to shock a bourgeois public out of its apathy. By unblocking communication and returning people to primary awareness, it hoped to overcome passivity and create movement. In short, in the words of Hannover Dadaist Max Ernst, "Dada was like a bomb." Dada declared its own war on the smug bourgeoisie that was carrying on business as usual, safely behind the lines. It sought to blow middle-class cultural assumptions into little pieces, to bring the war home.

[In 1953, *The London Times* commented on "The Dada Movement"]:

> It is true that the original adherents of the movement claimed to be pacifists, but they nevertheless took a paradoxical delight in destruction; they loathed, yet made capital out of, the battles of Verdun and the Somme because the war represented the triumph of chaos over law and order—all that the nineteenth century had most revered. It would have been cowardly and dishonourable, they felt, as well as being opposed to their inverted principles, to refrain from the holocaust. So they proceeded to contribute to it as effectively as possible in their own way. Art, religion, literature, politics, logic, "all social hierarchies" must be abolished they decreed, and Dada (i.e., the cult of negation and anarchy) set up in their stead.

Those who came to launch Dada in Zurich in 1916 had been influenced by the various movements of the period preceding the war, especially Futurism. The founder of the Cabaret Voltaire, where Dada was born, was a 30-year-old German Catholic named Hugo Ball. Experienced in all aspects of stage work, Ball had come from Munich, where he had collaborated with Kandinsky in trying to found an Expressionist theater. Ball also had worked as a radical journalist, contributing to the pro-youth, anti-war, and graphically Expressionist review *Die Aktion,* and collaborating on a periodical entitled *Die Revolution.*

Appalled by his firsthand view of the war in Belgium, Ball had fled to Zurich with forged papers under an assumed name, accompanied by his mistress, Emmy Hennings, a 31-year-old cabaret singer. To make ends meet, Ball and Hennings took jobs as piano player and diseuse for a troupe of circus-style entertainers. They "then decided to open their own Zurich cabaret as a center for any performers who might care to volunteer." For Ball, the aim of the cabaret was to "transcend the War and jingoism and recall the few independents who live for other ideals." In Febru-

ary 1916 the Cabaret Voltaire was opened with Ball as manager and Hennings as star.

Also on hand was Ball's friend from Munich, 22-year-old Richard Huelsenbeck. Huelsenbeck was an Expressionist poet who also had written for *Die Aktion.* Ball and Huelsenbeck shared an interest in the Futurist "Marinetti's phonetic, telegraphic, typographic use of language, and had organized a reading in his honor in Berlin only two weeks before Italy's entry into the war." Once the war broke out, Huelsenbeck found Germany "unbearable." He received permission from the army to study medicine in Switzerland and arrived in Zurich just six days before the opening of the Cabaret Voltaire.

Also in attendance that first evening of the Cabaret Voltaire was a small, monacled, dapperly dressed 20-year-old Rumanian named Sami Rosenstock. He had been studying mathematics at Zurich University and writing symbolist poetry under the name Tristan Tzara. Tzara joined the Dada group instantly, and became its strategist, publicity manager, and, in 1917, editor of the periodical *Dada.* Impudent, witty, and contentious, Tzara feuded with Huelsenbeck, André Breton, and others over the direction of Dada.

Marcel Janco was a 21-year-old countryman of Tzara's who had come to Zurich to study architecture. He created posters, decorations, and masks for the Cabaret Voltaire. Janco was a participant in many of the Dada exhibitions, and his woodcuts illustrated the first book of the *Collection Dada,* edited by Tzara.

The one major artist of the original Zurich group was 30-year-old Hans Arp. Born in Alsace, Arp moved in 1904, at the age of 18, to Paris, where he was greatly impressed by modern painting. Over the next four years he studied at the Weimar School of Applied Art and the Academy Julian. After working alone in Switzerland for three years, Arp emerged in 1911 as cofounder of Der Modern Bund. Arp then collaborated with Kandinsky on the book *Der Blau Reiter* and participated in several exhibitions. Arp's other pre-Dada acquaintances included Guillaume Apollinaire, Max Jacob, the Cubists Pablo Picasso and Georges Braque, and Amedeo Modigliani, who drew his portrait.

At the outbreak of the war, Arp returned to Switzerland, where, in November 1915, he exhibited his first abstract collages, and tapestries at the Tanner Gallery in Zurich. It was at this exhibition that he met another artist, Sophie Taeuber, whom he was to marry in 1922. Between 1916 and 1919 Arp and Taeuber illustrated Dada journals and exhibited at the Dada "manifestations." Arp took little part in the soirées, but Taeuber frequently performed modern dance under a pseudonym at the Galerie Dada. In 1917 Arp made his first wood relief, initiating his distinctive style of unadorned, undulating, abstract forms.

Sophie Taeuber was born in Zurich in 1889 and studied art at the Technical School in St. Gall from 1908 to 1910, and with Wilhelm von Debschitz in Munich from 1911 to 1913. Active in the Dada movement from the beginning, she also taught at the School of Applied Arts from 1916 to 1929. Writing about those early years, Arp said, "The pictures she [Sophie] was doing at the time exercised a decisive influence on my work."

For the six months of its operation, the Cabaret Voltaire presented performances every evening that, in Janco's words, were "pregnant with a spirit of protest." Janco's account of the Dada ethos confirms Hauser's claim that Dada represented "Romantic Rousseauism in the most extreme meaning of the term":

> We had lost confidence in our "culture." Everything had to be demolished. We would begin again after the tabula rasa. At the Cabaret Voltaire we began by shocking the bourgeoisie, demolishing his idea of art, attacking common sense, public opinion, education, institutions, museums, good taste, in short, the whole prevailing order.

The name Dada was taken to signify the new movement. One account attributes the find to Ball and Huelsenbeck; another to Tzara. In both cases the discovery occurred through a chance exploration of the French dictionary. The word, translated as "hobbyhorse," had instant appeal for everyone. Childlike, musical, and international, it seemed suspended between mystery and nonsense, a favorite position of the Dadaists.

The stylistic innovations of all of the modern art movements were assimilated into Dada's eclectic search for a new art. Huelsenbeck recalls:

> All of us were enemies of the old rationalistic art which we regarded as symptomatic of a culture about to crumble with the war. We loathed every form of an art that merely imitated nature and we admired, instead, the Cubists and Picasso. We agreed with the Futurists that most public monuments should be smashed with a hammer, and we delighted in the nonrepresentational experiments of Arp, van Rees, and Marcel Janco.

From their friend Kandinsky and the Expressionists, the Dadaists adopted the free use of color. Janco's woodcuts and his personal view that "the sculptor must become an artisan" bring to mind the Expressionist group that called itself Die Brücke. From the human figures in Cubist paintings, especially those of Picasso, came the inspiration for "the grotesque cardboard costumes, used in Dada stage performances to create an alienation-effect." Dada also borrowed the collage form from the Cubists.

The movement with the largest impact on Dada was Futurism. From the Futurist Umberto Boccioni the Dadaists adopted the use of new materials, such as cardboard, wire, and pieces of wood, in constructing the collage. When the Cabaret Voltaire opened, it was decorated with Futurist posters that were characterized by "the free use of typography, in which the compositor moves over the page vertically, horizontally and diagonally, jumbles his type face and makes liberal use of his stock of pictorial blocks" [Hans Richter, *Dada: Art and Anti-Art*]. Dada borrowed this technique for its own posters, fly sheets, and periodicals, and improved on it by developing the photomontage, the intended effect of which was to give "to the individual letter, word or sentence a freedom it had never possessed" (Richter).

In music and poetry the Futurists had pioneered what they called "bruitism." In 1911 Luigi Russolo built "a noise organ in which he could conjure up all the distracting sounds of everyday existence," modern sounds for modern times. Bruitistic poems alternated noises with words. The logical extension of these became Marinetti's and Kruchenykh's phonetic poems, consisting solely of nonsense syllables, a completely abstract and nonrepresentational poetry divorced from any association with established meaning.

The Dadaists adopted the idea of abstract and phonetic poetry, then developed it much further. Nonsense poems were composed by picking words out of a hat; static poems were made by rearranging chairs upon which posters, each with a word, had been placed; "gymnastic poems" were recited in which Tzara and Huelsenbeck did deep knee bends in between verses; "Ball composed 'sound poems' in which he did his best to avoid anything that sounded like any word in any language; and groups of Dadaists spoke and chanted simultaneous poems, each speaking a different language or saying different words," thus, in the words of Tzara, "showing the struggle of the human voice with a threatening, entangling, and destroying universe whose rhythmical sequence of noise is inescapable."

[Martin Esslin, in his *Theater of the Absurd*] describes Dada plays as "essentially nonsense poems in dialogue form . . . accompanied by equally nonsensical business and decorated with bizarre masks and costumes." [Georges Hugnet, in his essay "Dada"] comments:

> For these performances Janco designed paper costumes of every color, put together with pins and spontaneous in the extreme. Perishable, purposely ugly or absurd, these materials, chosen by the chance action of eye and mind, symbolized in showy rags the perpetual revolt, the despair which refuses to lose itself in despair.

Two longer plays by Georges Ribemont-Dessaignes were greatly admired by the Dadaists. The first, *L'empereur de Chine* (The Emperor of China), written in 1916, deals with the themes of sexuality, slavery, imperialism, war, rape, violence, and cannibalism. Its intention, according to Esslin, was "to shock a bourgeois public" as well as "create a poetic universe with validity on the stage." The second play, *Le bourreau du Pérou* (The Hangman of Peru), is concerned with the seduction of the state by the forces of destruction.

Most important, Dada took from Futurism its whole posture of provocation, including its improvisatory cabaret theater, with its shock effects, its literary and spoken manifestos, and its general emphasis on spontaneous action. When he took Dada with him to Berlin in 1918, Huelsenbeck credited Tzara with enunciating the principle of the literary manifesto in 1916 and explained: "The manifesto as a literary medium answered our need for directness. We had no time to lose; we wanted to incite our opponents to resistance, and, if necessary, to create new opponents for ourselves" (Richter).

Despite its continuities with earlier movements, Dada represented something qualitatively new in the history of modern art. [Werner Haftman, in his *Painting in the 20th Century*] states:

> Dada has its own place in history and its own originality. In Dada these isolated elements formed a unity for the first time. Dada took up all these separate ideas, assembled them and established them as a unified expression of experiences and emotions that were wholly of the present. In this way, Dada finally cut the umbilical cord that bound us to history.

Despite its attacks on the past and present, Futurism worked to promote its program for the future. Dada completed Futurism's project of destruction by rejecting all programs for the future as well. Hans Richter, who joined Dada in its early years, writes:

> Dada not only had *no* programme, it was against all programmes. Dada's only programme was to have no programme . . . and, at that moment in history, it was just this that gave the movement its explosive power to unfold *in all directions,* free of aesthetic or social constraints . . . this freedom might (and did) lead either to a new art—or to nothing. Unhampered by tradition, unburdened by gratitude (a debt seldom paid by one generation to another), Dada expounded its theses, anti-theses and a-theses.

The basic principles of Dada art—the core of its praxis—were chance creation and the particularization of elements. Richter declares, "Chance became our trademark." He explains, "The official belief in the infallibility of reason, logic and causality seemed to us senseless—as senseless as the destruction of the world and the systematic elimination of every particle of feeling." Chance was adopted as "a protest against the rigidity of straight-line thinking." For example, here is Tzara's prescription for making a Dada poem:

> To make a dadaist poem
> Take a newspaper.
> Take a pair of scissors.
> Choose an article as long as you are planning to make your poem. Cut out the article. Then cut out each of the words that make up this article and put them in a bag.
> Shake it gently.
> Then take out the scraps one after another in the order in which
>   they left the bag.
> Copy conscientiously.
> The poem will be like you.
> And here you are a writer, infinitely original and endowed with a
>   sensibility that is charming though beyond the understanding of the vulgar.
>   Tristan Tzara

As is apparent, the practice of chance creation subverted the bourgeois rationalistic value of utilitarian means-ends logic and expressed the bohemian Romantic values of spontaneous creation and presentness. The practice of chance creation, as in Tzara's poem, produced a random juxtaposition of dissimilar elements that dislocated the given frames of reference, exploded the reified categories of bourgeois thought, and aspired to shock the audience

into a new awareness of the primary power of language and art.

Thus, the logic of chance creation also was integrally related to the other salient feature of Dada art, the particularization of elements. Such particularization was expressed visually in the photomontage. Richter describes the process briefly: "They cut up photographs, stuck them together in provocative ways, added drawings, cut these up too, pasted in bits of newspaper, or old letters, or whatever happened to be lying around—to confront a crazy world with its own image." The photomontage did more than simply mirror the disintegration of the bourgeois order. By uprooting elements from their conventional contexts, it subverted their taken-for-granted meaning.

In speech the particularization of elements was expressed through a form of "chatter" dissociated from language. Discourse is constructed according to the rules of language, with the intention of meaningful communication. Chatter, on the other hand, is immediate, unplanned, and uncensored. "It can easily do without meaning: it need only be information, indication, or merely a means of relieving one's feelings, relaxing, or passing the time." As Tzara declared, "Thought is produced in the mouth."

The very idea of explanation was rejected, and contradictions were used as a way of "blowing up" the language of the bourgeoisie and, thus, of "destroying the main bridges between 'them' and 'us,' by incommunicability" [Alfred Willener, *The Action Image of Society: On Cultural Politicization*]. Willener observes, "Having brushed aside all obstacles, all justifications and all obligations—including that of explaining oneself—they reached that vital level where joy, movement, spontaneity, and metamorphosis have their being; language is no longer a poor means, but a game, a celebration."

Through the use of chance and radical particularization the Dadaists sought to transcend the bourgeois image of society and history as mechanistic and determined. Their quest led in two directions. One was Freudian in thrust; chance construction was like the free association that emancipates feelings and unlocks the secrets of the unconscious mind. The other was Jungian in thrust, the search for the ineffable higher consciousness of the universe. Richter reflects that the experience of chance creation

> . . . taught us that we were not so firmly rooted in the knowable world as people would have us believe. We felt that we were coming into contact with something different, something that surrounded and interpenetrated *us* just as we overflowed into *it* . . . beneath it all lay a genuine mental and emotional experience that gave us wings to fly—and to look down upon the absurdities of the "real" and earnest world.

There was more than a little mysticism in the Dada attitude. Richter refers to chance as "a magical procedure" whose "secret" purpose "was to restore to the work of art its primeval magic power. . . . " Ball urged all to "withdraw into the innermost alchemy of the word." This attitude was a current in the Romantic wave that flowed from avant-garde circles throughout the period. Artists and intellectuals aspired to initiate works that seemingly created

The Paris Dada group, circa 1921. Tristan Tzara wears the monocle in the second row; Paul Eluard and Georges Ribemont-Dessaignes are at his right. In the first row, Benjamin Peret wears the monocle, Philippe Soupault is on the left without the mask, and an unidentified workman is on the right.

themselves, developed their own independent life, and provoked onlookers into a qualitative transformation of consciousness. Such an epiphany was not possible within Rationalist thought. It was a celebration of the triumph of the spirit over its materialist adversaries.

The emphasis on presentness served to deny continuity in historical development. In contrast, it implied the power of individual acts to create unique moments or "free spaces" in time, in which the radically new might suddenly emerge. The Russian Suprematist painter Varvara Stepanova wrote in 1919: "Non-objective creation is still only the beginning of an unprecedented Great Creation, which is destined to open the doors to mysteries more profound than science and technology."

Max Ernst and Johannes Baargeld must have felt themselves close to such "Great Creation" when, as Hugnet reports, they began to discover in their automatic drawing another drawing, the contours of which appeared "slowly out of the tangled lines—like an apparition, like a prophecy. . . ." Certainly, the Dadaists' posture of anti-art expressed the mystic attitude that seeks to explode all

forms so as to be absorbed into the "all oneness" that lies beyond the cultural veil.

Since the basis for a technical elite lies in its mastery of the established rules, the rejection of such rules also constituted the rejection of such elites. The Dadaists were contemptuous of the art establishment and wished to elevate practicing artists to the level of aesthetic lawgivers, visionary prophets in an age of decadence. As Arp was to claim later, "At the time the action of opening a zip-fastener for a beautiful woman was called sculpture." Within such a broad definition anything might be considered art.

No more graphic illustration of this idea can be found than Duchamp's submission of ordinary functional objects as works of art to be displayed in museum showings. From 1913 on, he submitted such objects as a bicycle wheel fastened to a kitchen stool (*Bicycle Wheel*), a snow shovel (*Shovel*), and a public urinal (*Fountain*). Only the latter was rejected. In 1915 he coined the term "ready-made" to refer to such works of art by decree.

At one New York showing the artist-photographer Man

Ray exhibited a metronome with an eye on it, entitled *Object to Be Destroyed.* His stated intention was to show the visual in a sound-producing object. When the public responded by destroying his object, Ray filed a claim with the company insuring the exhibit, arguing that because he had signed it, the metronome was a work of art.

Of course, if anything can be considered a work of art, then anyone can be considered an artist. Consequently, there was no great need for "artists." Duchamp promptly retired from painting altogether and spent the rest of his life in various private activities, including playing chess with his friend Man Ray.

In June 1916 the Dadaists published the only issue of the periodical *Cabaret Voltaire,* which included contributions by Apollinaire, Picasso, Modigliani, Kandinsky, Marinetti, and others in addition to the Dada nucleus of Arp, Ball, Huelsenbeck, Janco, and Tzara.

The Cabaret Voltaire closed in July 1916, forcing the Dadaists to find new settings for their evening performances. The "First Dada Evening" was held July 14, 1916, at the Wuag Hall and, according to Tzara's notes, featured numerous "demonstrations" (including Tzara's demand for "the right to piss in different colours"), Cubist dance, "gymnastic poem, concert of vowels, bruitist poem, static poem, chemical arrangement of ideas," and the African rhythmic pounding of Huelsenbeck's "big drum." The evening ended when the performers' cardboard costumes were torn off by the audience, windows were smashed, and the police were called in to restore order.

Ultimately this succès de scandale constituted the essential spirit of all Dada creativity. It made the movement truly public and provided the necessary social context within which their various artistic experiments could be understood. Hugnet recalls the pandemonium of the Dada "manifestations":

> The Dada activities in Zurich from 1916 to 1918 shook off their literary character and directly attacked the conventions and stale responsibilities of a public which in the face of such effrontery wavered between rage and amazement. On the stage of the cabaret keys were jangled until the audience protested and went crazy. . . .

Shapiro adds, "Another favorite technique in those days of hourly war bulletins was the fake news release in which true information about the far-flung members of the avant-garde was mixed with absurd or apocryphal reports." Although few would admit to any intentions, Dada's project was to deflate all pomposity, pull the rug out from under all pretensions, put a tack on the chair of decorum, and enjoy a collective belly laugh forceful enough to shake the rafters of the creaky establishment. The Dadaists worked in a spirit of subversion more akin to Groucho than to Karl Marx. For them, all society was Margaret Dumont.

In January and February 1917 the Dadaists staged their first exhibition at the Galerie Corray on Bahnhofstrasse, and on March 23 they held the "Grand Opening of Galerie Dada." Over the next two months they staged two more exhibitions and four evening events at the gallery,

the most ambitious of which was a performance of the Expressionist play *Sphynx and Straw Man* by the Austrian painter Oscar Kokoschka. Janco directed the production and designed the masks.

Tzara took over the editorship of the periodical *Dada,* and in July the first issue appeared. Over the next few years several more followed (at the rate of about two a year), featuring the works of Braque, de Chirico, Duchamp, Ernst, Feininger, Klee, Laurens, Masson, Matisse, Miró, Picabia, Ray, and Tanguy, among others, in addition to the Dadaists themselves. Despite this prestigious assembly, Dada's proudest creation remained public chaos. Not content with their popular triumph at the Cabaret Voltaire and Galerie Dada, the Dadaists proceeded to spread their campaign of disorder into the streets of Zurich. "The Dada Movement" reports: "Appalling rumors were circulated; fictitious reports were sent to the newspapers; entertainment innocently advertised to attract middle-brow aesthetes, lady water colourists and members of choral societies, would turn out to be obscene and blasphemous displays."

Dada's position that anyone can be an artist was radically democratic. If common people could create a new art, could they not also create a new reality? Did the Dadaists really believe in the creative potential of the common people? Probably not. Despite their anti-militarist, anti-capitalist, and radically democratic stance, the Zurich Dadaists did not make common cause with the political left. Shapiro states: "They ignored Bolsheviks such as Lenin and pacifists such as Romain Rolland, or else ridiculed them; they mocked revolutionaries for assuming that people were capable of reason and worthy of salvation. All they were willing to concede was the absurdity of life."

Hugo Ball, the founder of the Cabaret Voltaire, was unable to reconcile himself to this position and took his leave of Dada around June 1917. He went to Bern, where he helped edit a democratic, anti-kaiser weekly. Within a year he retired to a Swiss village to write a biography of Bakunin and to study anarchism. Perhaps Ball was initially attracted to Dada because of his understanding of Bakunin's position that during the early stages of a revolution, destruction and construction are one and the same. It became apparent to him, however, that Dada represented "a new nihilism which not only questioned the value of art but of the whole human situation." This was too much for Ball, who explained, "I have examined myself carefully, and I could never bid chaos welcome."

The political and economic deterioration associated with the war brought forth a storm of protest throughout Europe and Russia. Everywhere authority was under attack. Shortages and inflation provoked food riots in many cities. Soldiers mutinied and deserted in large numbers. The labor unions and left parties grew rapidly in size and militancy.

The most significant transformation occurred in Russia. In March 1917 the aristocracy was overthrown and replaced by a democratic republic. Eight months later the new government was overthrown by Lenin and the Bolsheviks in the name of socialism.

Europe was in turmoil by the end of the war. Peasants seized estates in Italy and Spain. Defeat brought the collapse of the Austro-Hungarian and Ottoman empires. In Germany, on November 9, 1918, Kaiser Wilhelm II abdicated his rule and Frederick Ebert became president of the new Weimar Republic. The new republic's Liberal/Democratic Socialist ruling coalition continued to be challenged aggressively from both the right and the left. To many, the roaring cannons had sounded the death knell of liberal capitalism. The rise of the new Soviet state appeared like a harbinger of the new age, almost a historical imperative. In 1919 Soviets were set up in Berlin and Munich, as well as Vienna, Budapest, Turin, Fiume, and Glasgow.

The spirit of the revolution burned brightly in the arts as well. In Russia the Futurists had labored to advance the cause of modern art. With the triumph of the Bolsheviks in 1917, modern art suddenly achieved official support in Russia. Under the direction of Anatole Lunacharsky, director of the Commissariat of Enlightenment (Narkompros), the progressives sought to bring the best of art and science to the masses, to complete the political revolution by replacing the peasant culture of the czarist period with a new proletarian culture for industrial socialism.

Lunacharsky appointed David Petrovich Shterenberg, a progressive painter who had lived in Paris the last years before the war, to head the graphic arts division (IZO) of Narkompros. Between 1918 and 1921, IZO set up 36 museums around the country, 13 of which provided art education for the proletariat. Modernism in all the arts, abstract painting in particular, "established a virtual dictatorship over the museums, the art schools and the cultural bureaucracy. For the first time in history, the avant-garde was elevated to the position of power, charged with the task of remaking an entire civilization" [Hilton Kramer, "Beyond the Avant Garde," *New York Times Magazine* (1979)].

Three weeks after the establishment of the Weimar Republic, Shterenberg directed a manifesto at "progressive" German artists. He pointed to the Russian government's support of "the new tendencies" in art and declared that only "the new creations that came into being shortly before the world upheaval can be in step with the rhythm of the new life being created." Shterenberg called for intellectual exchanges leading to an international organization of Russian and German artists.

Greatly impressed with the openness of the Bolsheviks to modern art, "Western intellectuals replied to this manifesto with expressions of solidarity with Russian artists and the Russian people; many spoke out against the Allied anti-Bolshevik intervention in the Civil War in late 1918 and 1919" (Shapiro). Exhibitions of each other's art were organized in both Russia and Germany.

Three German editors/correspondents—Alfons Paquiet, Alfons Goldschmidt, and Arthur Holitscher—traveled often to Russia and reported on cultural-political relations between the two countries. The latter two, along with Ludwig Rubiner, went on to found the Berlin League for Proletarian Culture in 1919 and later the Proletarian The-

ater. By 1919 artists all over Germany, especially the young generation that had come of age during the war, had "embraced the Left, determined to have some say in the rebuilding of German society. In a spate of manifestoes, painters and writers proclaimed their adherence to the proletariat, and then to the Spartacists, as the government brought in the counter-revolutionary Freikorps to crush them" (Shapiro).

Berlin was the center of this movement for a revolutionary art. In 1918 two new organizations were formed, the Arbeitsrat für Kunst (Works Council for Art) and the November-Gruppe. Both groups sought to overthrow the conservative art establishment and to bring modern art to the people through publications, exhibitions, and entertainments. The Arbeitsrat barely survived the brief revolutionary period, but the November-Gruppe lasted until 1932. The principal achievements of these movements were to liberalize museum leadership and to increase government support for teaching the new art and applying it to the design of buildings and tools.

The most famous experiment of this kind was the founding of the Staatliches Bauhaus in 1919 under the direction of the architect Walter Gropius. Organized like a medieval craft guild, instruction in the Bauhaus "sought to combine esthetics with practicality," training students in both manual labor and the "fine arts." "Everything from the theory of abstract art to the revival of crafts to the design of factories, office buildings and entire cities, was joined in a program to reform the look and feel and function of virtually every aspect of modern civilization" (Kramer).

The dominance of Expressionism in German popular art became a subject of debate. Supporters asserted that Expressionism was the broadest-based movement against nineteenth-century representational art and that its exhibition and impact still had a public character. Critics countered that the Expressionists' tendency to keep their art separate from their politics was no longer progressive. Many on the left now demanded an art explicitly committed to the aims of socialist revolution. They scoffed at Expressionist works like Ernst Kirchner's self-portrait of his personal war trauma. According to them, in the current revolutionary political climate, mere expression of the artist's feelings was no longer a sufficiently radical act. The historical possibilities of the moment demanded a more deliberately political art.

Some argued that art must be unionized and subsidized by the state, but remain free of political control in a manner comparable with academic science. They proposed that artists must develop their own revolutionary commitments freely in order to create anything with true artistic value. Allowing this to occur would protect the people from the implicit materialism of the socialist leaders and preserve the spirit of revolutionary freedom in the production of popular culture.

Still others rejected the very concept of proletarian art, on both practical and theoretical grounds. Practically, some pointed to the conservative tastes of the proletariat and proposed that, as a mass, it would never be responsive to the distinctively individualistic expression required of authentic modern art. Theoretically, some objected to art designed exclusively for any stratum in the class structure, arguing that true art must be rooted in the basic species/being of the whole human community.

Dada was perhaps the most incandescent of the revolutionary flames that burned across the continents. From 1918 to its self-willed demise in 1923, Dada spread to Germany, France, Spain, Italy, Holland, Yugoslavia, Czechoslovakia, as far west as the United States, and as far east as Russia. While communication, even collaboration, continued between artists in most of these Dada centers, Dada assumed a distinctive character in each location. In the process, breaches occurred between branches of the movement over its future direction. The critical issue was the relationship of art to politics, and the positions adopted clearly reflected the different sociopolitical contexts of the movement. (pp. 86-103)

> *Jerold M. Starr, "Revolutionary Art Versus Art for the Revolution: Dadaists and Leninists, 1916-23," in* Cultural Politics: Radical Movements in Modern History, *edited by Jerold M. Starr, Praeger Publishers, 1985, pp. 79-130.*

Walter Benjamin on Dadaist Art:

The revolutionary strength of Dadaism consisted in testing art for its authenticity. Still lifes put together from tickets, spools of thread, cigarette butts, were linked with artistic elements. They put the whole thing in a frame. And they thereby show the public: Look, your picture frame ruptures the age; the tiniest authentic fragment of daily life says more than paintings. Just as the bloody finger print of a murderer on a page of a book says more than the text.

> *Walter Benjamin, in his "The Author as Producer," published in* The Essential Frankfurt School Reader, *Andrew Arato, Eike Gebhardt, eds., The Continuum Publishing Company, 1990.*

Robert Motherwell

[*In the following excerpt, Motherwell discusses some of the major and minor figures associated with Dadaism.*]

The origins of dada as a historical movement are variously attributed—to the arrival in neutral Zurich, Switzerland, of young intellectuals from all over warring Europe, to the visit to New York of Cravan, Duchamp, Picabia and others, to the meeting in Nantes of Jacques Vaché and André Breton—all events taking place in 1915 or 1916, bloody years in the first world war.

It might be well to add something about the locale, Zurich, substantial, old, well-to-do, a university town, perhaps not too different in felt tone from Cambridge, Massachusetts or New Haven, Connecticut. . . . (p. xvii)

It was the sons of the Zurich bourgeoisie, the university students, who used to go to the Cabaret Voltaire, a beer parlor. Hugo Ball, the German poet who ran it, improvised entertainment to draw trade, playing the piano himself, while Huelsenbeck, a young German student of medicine, who was against the war, danced pseudo-African dances in black-face. In looking for a stage name for a singer whom they wanted to hire—a young woman who never returned—they are said to have found, in a French-German dictionary, the word "dada," which is French baby-talk for anything to do with horses. The dictionary was at hand because Ball was writing a learned history. One cannot but wonder whether the young Zurich students had any sense of who was entertaining them along with their beers. One might say that the public history of modern art is the story of conventional people not knowing what they are dealing with.

The protest of dada in Zurich against the war is touching; a few sensitive and intelligent men, hardly more than boys, insisting on the sense of shame that all of Europe ought to have admitted. The dada movement was an organized insulting of European civilization by its middle-class young. A healthy feeling that gave a new vitality to European painting by everyone who felt it, dada or not.

Lenin was in exile in Zurich during the dada days. . . . Marcu, a young Roumanian (as were Janco and Tzara), has left us a memoir:

> When we left the restaurant, it was late in the afternoon. I walked home with Lenin.
>
> "You see." he said, "why I take my meals here. You get to know what people are really talking about. Nadezhda Konstantinovna is sure that only the Zurich underworld frequents this place, but I think she is mistaken. To be sure, Maria is a prostitute. But she does not like her trade. She has a large family to support—and that is no easy matter. As to Frau Prellog, she is perfectly right. Did you hear what she said? Shoot all the officers! . . . "
>
> . . . . .
>
> "Do you know the real meaning of this war?"
>
> "What is it?" I asked.
>
> "It is obvious," he replied. "One slaveholder, Germany, who owns one hundred slaves, is fighting another slaveholder, England, who owns two hundred slaves, for a 'fairer' distribution of the slaves."
>
> "How can you expect to foster hatred of this war," I asked at this point, "if you are not, in principle, against all wars? I thought that as a Bolshevik you were really a radical thinker and refused to make any compromise with the idea of war. But by recognizing the validity of some wars, you open the doors for every opportunity. Every group can find some justification of the particular war of which it approves. I see that we young people can only count on ourselves . . . "
>
> Lenin listened attentively, his head bent toward me. He moved his chair closer to mine . . .

Lenin must have wondered whether he should continue to talk with this boy or not. I, somewhat awkwardly, remained silent.

"Your determination to rely upon yourselves," Lenin finally replied, "is very important. Every man must rely upon himself. Yet he should also listen to what informed people have to say. I don't know how radical you are or how radical I am. I am certainly not radical enough. One can never be radical enough; that is, one must always try to be as radical as reality itself . . . "

Zurich was, in those days, as it is now the home of Dr. Jung and of the so-called Zurich school of psychoanalysts. Huelsenbeck himself is now a Jungian psychoanalyst, practicing in New York City, under the name of Charles R. Hulbeck.

The appropriation by dada of these three principles, bruitism, simultaneity, and, in painting, the new medium [collage], is of course the "accident" leading to psychological factors to which the real dadaist movement owed its existence.

This statement by Huelsenbeck, is one of the few attempts that have been made, and it only in passing, to formulate the nature of dada in terms of its own expressive means. (p. xviii)

In 1917, some time after he founded the Cabaret Voltaire [Hugo Ball] went to Berne, Switzerland, where he helped to edit an anti-Kaiser weekly. By the time of Ball's death, in 1927, he had become an ardent Roman Catholic, almost a "holy man," greatly admired by the natives of the Swiss province in which he lived, and had made a pilgrimage to Rome. Yet it was he who had named his cabaret the "Voltaire." (p. xix)

When I started the Cabaret Voltaire, I was sure that there must be other young men in Switzerland who, like myself, wanted not only to enjoy their independence, but also to give proof of it.

I went to Mr. Ephraim, the owner of the Meierei, and said to him: "I beg you, Mr. Ephraim, please let me use your place. I should like to start an artists' cabaret." We came to terms, and Mr. Ephraim gave me the use of his place. I went to some of my acquaintances. "Please give me a picture, a drawing, an etching. I should like to have a little exhibition in connection with my cabaret." To the friendly Zurich press, I said. "Help me, I want to start an international cabaret; we'll do some wonderful things." I was given the pictures, the press releases were published. So we had a cabaret show on February 5th [1915]. Mme. Hennings and Mme. Leconte sang, in French and Danish. Mr. Tristan Tzara read some of his Roumanian poetry. A balalaika orchestra played popular tunes and Russian dances.

I got a great deal of support and sympathy from Mr. Slodki, who made the cabaret poster, and from Mr. Arp, who loaned me some original works of art, Picasso etchings, and some pictures by his friends, O. van Rees and Artur Segal. A lot more support from Mr. Tristan Tzara, Mr. Marcel Janco and Mr. Max Oppenheimer, who all appeared many times on the stage. We organized a Russian evening, then a French one (during which works by Apollinaire, Max Jacob, André Salmon, Jarry, Laforgue and Rimbaud were read). Richard Huelsenbeck arrived from Berlin on February 26th, and on March 30th we played two admirable negro chants (always with one big drum: boom boom boom boom drabatja mo gere, drabatja mo booooooooooooo); Mr. Laban helped and was amazed. And (on the initiative of Mr. Tristan Tzara) Mr. Huelsenbeck, Mr. Janco and Mr. Tzara recited (for the first time in Zurich and in the whole world) the simultaneous verses of Mr. Henri Barzun and Mr. Fernand Divoire, and a simultaneous poem of their own composition. . . . It is necessary to define the activity of this cabaret; its aim is to remind the world that there are independent men—beyond war and Nationalism—who live for other ideals.

The intention of the artists here assembled is to publish an international review. The review will appear in Zurich, and will be called, DADA Dada Dada Dada Dada.

Of equal interest is Ball's account of his "sound poems" read at the Cabaret Voltaire:

I invented a new species of verse, "verse without words," or sound poems, in which the balancing of the vowels is gauged and distributed only to the value of the initial line. The first of these I recited tonight [1915]. I had a special costume designed for it. My legs were covered with a cothurnus of luminous blue cardboard, which reached up to my hips so that I looked like an obelisk. Above that I wore a huge cardboard collar that was scarlet inside and gold outside. This was fastened at the throat in such a manner that I was able to move it like wings by raising and dropping my elbows. In addition I wore a high top hat striped with blue and white. I recited the following:

gadji beri bimba
glandridi lauli lonni cadori
gadjama bim beri glassala
glandridi glassala tuffm i zimbrabim
blassa galassasa tuffm i zimbrabim . . .

The accents became heavier, the expression increased an intensification of the consonants. I soon noticed that my means of expression (if I wanted to remain serious, which I did at any cost), was not adequate to the pomp of my stage-setting. I feared failure and so concentrated intensely. Standing to the right of the music, I recited "Labada's Chant to the Clouds," then to the left, "The Elephant Caravan." Now I turned again to the lectern in the center, beating industriously with my wings. The heavy vowel lines and slouching rhythm of the elephants had just permitted me to attain an ultimate climax. But how to end up? I now noticed that my voice, which seemed to have no other choice, had assumed the age-old cadence of the sacerdotal lamentation, like the chanting of the mass that wails through the Catholic churches of both the Occident and the Orient.

I don't know what inspired me to use this music, but I began to sing my vowel lines recitatively, in the style of the church, and I tried to remain not only serious but also to force myself to be grave. For a moment it seemed as if, in my cubist mask, there emerged a pale, disturbed youth's face, that half-frightened, half-curious face of the ten-year-old lad hanging trembling and avid on the lips of the priest in the funeral masses and high masses of his parish. At that moment the electric light went out, as I had intended, and I was carried, moist with perspiration, like a magical bishop, into the abyss. Before the words, I had read a few programmatic words:

With these sound poems we should renounce the language devastated and made impossible by journalism.

We should withdraw into the innermost alchemy of the word, and even surrender the word, in this way conserving for poetry its most sacred domain. We should stop making poems second-hand; we should no longer take over words (not even to speak of sentences) which we did not invent absolutely anew, for our own use. We should no longer be content to achieve poetic effects with means which, in the final analysis, are but the echoes of inspiration, or simply surrepti-

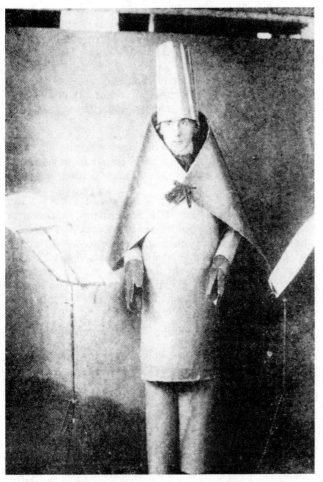

Poet Hugo Ball performing at the Cabaret Voltaire in 1916.

tiously proffered arrangements of an opulence in cerebral and imagistic values.

Hans Richter wrote me of the death of Hugo Ball's wife, Emmy Hennings, as follows:

> I wish to make a correction—a sad one—in my short essay about the dada people. Emmy Hennings died in Magliaso (Tesson) in a small room above a grocery store in August 1949 [sic]. In order to make a living (to survive) she had to work during the day in a factory.—We had not heard from her since years.—Arp told me that he saw her in Lugano 1 ½ years ago.

Since Richter's letter is dated January 26, 1949, the date of Emmy Hennings' death is evidently 1948.

Richard Huelsenbeck kindly supplied (1950) the following note on Marcel Janco, the Roumanian artist who painted the *Cabaret Voltaire:*

> When I had entered the place called Cabaret Voltaire, I saw many people sitting behind round tables, drinking beer, yelling about something that I couldn't understand. Through the cigarette smoke that hung in big clouds above the head of the audience I finally saw Hugo Ball and Emmy Hennings, the owners and founders of the Cabaret. Ball came over to me and introduced me to a little man wearing a monocle and throwing shrewd glances left and right. This was Tzara. Tzara turned around and introduced me to a man much taller than himself. "This is my friend, Marcel Janco," he said.
>
> Janco was a tall, friendly man from Roumania. He had an easy smile, and would talk to you about everything, and discuss with you any question of the universe, from morning to night, or from night to morning. We would sit in the Baserbas, a Spanish restaurant, and rant about the misery of the war. Or we would take a row-boat, sometimes with girls, sometimes without, and discuss abstract art. Janco was a young architect, deeply in love with the revolution in art that had begun with cubism and that was then throwing its lightning from the Futurists' camp in Italy.
>
> Janco was as good in discussion as in rowing, as in love, as in everything. He did all the decorations of the Cabaret; he painted the pictures, made the exotic looking masks, and talked the hesitant proprietor (who had never seen anything like it) into accepting and even hanging modern posters.
>
> Janco danced, recited and showed his art in the Cabaret Voltaire. I see him today as one of the great pioneers of our movement, a man with many talents but without arrogance, always helpful and never interfering with other persons' ambitions. But the best of him was, and still is, his warmth, his affection for his friends, his loyalty to Dadaism, which he understood deeply and profoundly.

Arp has written of Janco as follows in his volume of poems and prose in the Documents of Modern Art, *On My Way* (N.Y., 1948):

Secretly, in his little room, Janco devoted himself to a "naturalism in zigzag." I forgive him this secret vice because in one of his paintings he evoked and commemorated the "Cabaret Voltaire". On a platform in an overcrowded room, splotched with color, are seated several fantastic characters who are supposed to represent Tzara, Janco, Ball, Huelsenbeck, Madame Hennings and your humble servant. We are putting on one of our big Sabbaths. The people around us are shouting, laughing, gesticulating. We reply with sighs of love, salvos of hiccups, poems, and the bow-wows and meows of medieval bruitists. Tzara makes his bottom jump like the belly of an oriental dancer. Janco plays an invisible violin and bows down to the ground. Madame Hennings with a face like a madonna attempts a split. Huelsenbeck keeps pounding on a big drum, while Ball, pale as a plaster dummy, accompanies him on the piano. The honorific title of nihilists was bestowed on us. The directors of public cretinization conferred this name on all those who did not follow in their path.

. . . . .

Are you still singing that diabolical song about the mill at Hirza-Pirza, shaking your gypsy curls with wild laughter, my dear Janco? I haven't forgotten the masks you used to make for our Dada demonstrations. They were terrifying, most of them daubed with bloody red. Out of cardboard, paper, horsehair, wire and cloth, you made your languorous foetuses, your Lesbian sardines, your ecstatic mice. In 1917 Janco did some abstract works that have grown in importance ever since. He was a passionate man with faith in the evolution of art.

From a letter in French by Marcel Janco to Hans Richter, dated 10 March 1950, Tel Aviv (Israel):

You are not any younger, but believe me, I am also "a bit" changed. Having fled Europe, I hoped to find a "Tahiti" like Gauguin for my painting, but I was mistaken, because the climate here is difficult and one works savagely in order to exist. . . . With my peregrinations and migrations during 12 years, I have lost all international contacts. On the other hand, I believe that my painting, for which I have sacrificed everything, as for a true mistress, has kept all its force. It is true that not always have I painted abstractly, because I believe that one must also say something, but, without being deformist or expressionist, my painting is oriented towards a strong expression, like you find in folk art. I believe that at bottom I am still very close to "dada," to the true dada which at bottom always defended the forces of creation, instinctive and fresh, colored by the popular art that one finds in all peoples. I do not like anymore the literary mystifications of the Surrealists, and Arp always pleased me with his purity and the instinctiveness of his abstractions, which are not dry outmoded mathematical complications, but on the contrary always filled with some spiritual associations. . . . A group retrospective exhibition, with Klee, Arp, Richter, Calder, Eggeling, Janco, Hulbeck, Man Ray, Ernst and others,

would still be an event in Paris in 1950 or 1951. What do you think? Could we not throw a little light with such an exhibition on the development of the art to come in order to prevent a fall into the gulf of "social realism"? I think that the problems that we posed in 1917-1919 are still not resolved. . . . Is it true that in America there is also a tendency toward that miserable "realism"?

In terms of ultimate accomplishment, the important dada painters were Arp, Marcel Duchamp, Max Ernst, Francis Picabia and Kurt Schwitters—that is, apart from George Grosz, who now prefers to forget his part in the movement. Schwitters, an eccentric, sincere, humorous man, who gathered from the débris of the streets the materials for his collages, has been commonly underestimated. "In order to achieve insight, you must work" is not a sentiment that the dadas would have found especially sympathetic. Schwitters seems to have called his version of dada "merz" in order to preserve his independence. He was against past art, not because it was art, but because it was *past,* and we see now, so many years later, that his work of the period, like that of the best dada painters, is at home in an exhibition of "abstract" art, that the dada painters' "anti-structure" position in their search for the "new" itself produced a new structure not unrelated to the new structure of the "abstract" painters, that the dada painters were never able to reduce themselves to mere sensation or social activity, as many of the writers were able to do. It is as though the desire to shake off structure and the search for new structure had to arrive at the same place, because in both cases the means had to be the same, rejection of traditional modes of composition. The nature of Schwitters' work changed hardly at all up to the day of his death in 1947; it never lost its freshness, unpretentiousness, nor perfection of scale. (pp. xix-xxi)

[He] once came to Mies van der Rohe's Berlin office and said to the renowned abstract architect, "I know you think I am insane, but let's do a book on architecture together."

In George Grosz's recent autobiography, *A Little Yes and a Big No* (N.Y., 1946) there is an unfriendly account of Schwitters, as well as of Johannes Baader, the latter of whom Grosz regards as mad; Grosz asserts that the meaning of "merz" is garbage, and that consequently Schwitters' "merz" pictures and "merz" poems are "garbage" pictures and "garbage" poems; this is not out of accord with Schwitters' strange but touching habit of collecting everything he found as he walked along the street; but it must be remembered that the word "merz" is a neologism, invented by Schwitters. Sibyl Moholy-Nagy, in her biography of her husband (N.Y., 1950), gives the following account of Schwitters' invention of the word: "The name was accidental and came from the four central letters of the word 'komMERZiell,' which appeared on a scrap of newspaper in one of the MERZ collages."

Mies van der Rohe tells that once Schwitters was on a train, carrying great roots from trees with him. Someone asked him what the roots were, and he replied that they constituted a cathedral. "But that is no cathedral, that is only wood!" the stranger exclaimed. "But don't you know that cathedrals are made out of wood?" Schwitters replied.

Moholy-Nagy writes, in *Vision in Motion* (Chicago, 1947), of Schwitters' extremely popular poem, "Anna Blossom Has Wheels" ["Anna Blume"] (1919), "At first reading the poem seems to be only double-talk. In reality, it is a penetrating satire of obsolete love poems." Here is the poem, which became famous in Germany, translated by Mrs. K. Klein:

Anna Blossom Has Wheels
(Merz poem No. 1)

Oh thou, beloved of my twentyseven senses, I
    love thine!
Thou thee thee thine. I thine, thou mine.
—We?
That belongs (on the side) not here.
Who are thou, uncounted woman? Thou art—
    art
thou?—People say, thou werst,—let them
say, they don't know, how the church tower
    stands.
Thou wearest thy hat on thy feet and wanderest
    on
your hands, on thy hands wanderest thou.
Hallo thy red dress, clashed in white folds. Red
    I
love Anna Blossom, red I love thine! Thou thee
thee thine, I thine, thou mine.—We?—
That belongs (on the side) in the cold glow.
Red Blossom, red Anna Blossom, how say (the)
people?
Prize question:
1. Anna Blossom has wheels.
2. Anna Blossom is red.
3. What color are the wheels?
Blue is the color of thy yellow hair.
Red is the whirl of thy green wheels.
Thou simple maiden in everyday-dress, thou
    dear
green animal, I love thine!—Thou thee thee
    thine,
I thine, thou mine.—We?—
That belongs (on the side) in the glowbox.
Anna Blossom! Anna, A-N-N-A, I trickle thy
name. Thy name drips like soft tallow.
Dost thou know Anna, dost thou already know
    it?
One can also read thee from behind, and thou,
    thou
most glorious of all, thou art from the back, as
from the front: A-N-N-A.
Tallow trickles to strike over my back.
Anna Blossom, thou drippes animal, I love
    thine!

Josef Albers, the abstract painter, tells that Schwitters used to listen to the conversations of women on street-cars and trains, and to the sentimental popular songs liked by servants and working girls, and that many of his writings were based on what he heard on these occasions, filled with parodies and puns. Albers also remembers with a smile a story Schwitters used to tell about a parrot that had a hernia; but he cannot remember the details.

Moholy-Nagy writes that without

trying to define Schwitters' peculiar poetic quality, it can be said that most of his writing is emotional purgation, an outburst of subconscious pandemonium. But they are fused with external reality, with the existing social status. His verbal "collages" are good examples of this. There the current of his thoughts is mixed with seemingly random quotations from newspapers, catalogues and advertising copy. With this technique—like Gertrude Stein—he uncovers symptoms of social decay known to all, but neglected or dodged in a kind of self-defense. The scene is Germany. Inflation after the war; corruption, waste, damage to material and man. An abortive social revolution makes the situation even more hopeless. Schwitters' writings of that time end with a desperate and at the same time challenging cry.

In one of his demonstrations, he showed to the audience a poem containing only one letter on a sheet [a large "W"].

Then he started to "recite" it with slowly rising voice. The consonant varied from a whisper to the sound of a wailing siren till at the end he barked with a shockingly loud tone. This was his answer not alone to the social situation but also to the degrading "cherry-mouthed"—"raven-haired"—"babbling-brook"—poetry.

The only possible solution seemed to be a return to the elements of poetry, to noise and articulated sound, which are fundamental to all languages. Schwitters realized the prophecy of Rimbaud, inventing words "accessible to all five senses." His *Ursonata* (1924) ["Primordial Sonata"] is a poem of thirty-five minutes duration, containing four movements, a prelude, and a cadenza in the fourth movement. The words used do not exist, rather they might exist in any language; they have no logical, only an emotional context; they affect the ear with their phonetic vibrations like music. Surprise and pleasure are derived from the structure and the inventive combination of the parts.

Mies van der Rohe says that Schwitters was extremely disturbed when Mies pointed out that one of his "sounds" was identical in sound with the Roumanian word for "Schnapps"—Schwitters was distressed at any possibility of denotative reference to the world. Hausmann claims to have originated the idea of "sound poems" as we shall see; we have already seen the evidence that neither he nor Schwitters, but Hugo Ball did. In any case, it is a pity that Schwitters's *Ursonata* is not brought into print again; it is beautiful to look at, and shows an extraordinarily exact and complicated structural sense. Schwitters simple sound poem called *priimiitittiii* follows (*Transition*, no. 3):

priimiitittiii	tisch
tesch	
priimiitittiii	tesch
tusch	
priimiitittiii	tischa
tescho	
priimiitittiii	tescho
tuschi	
priimiitittiii	
priimiitittiii	

priimiitittiii	too
priimiitittiii	taa
priimiitittiii	too
priimiitittiii	taa
priimiitittiii	tootaa
priimiitittiii	tootaa
priimiitittiii	tuutaa
priimiitittiii	tuutaa
priimiitittiii	tuutaatoo
priimiitittiii	tuutaatoo
priimiitittiii	tuutaatoo
priimiitittiii	tuutaatoo

The following is from a letter by the artist's only living relative, his son Ernst (Oslo, Norway, 26 August 1948):

[For] Kurt Schwitters political tendencies of any kind in art have always been and remained anathema.—As late as during the latter part of the war, my father resisted the so-called "Deutscher Kulturbund," an association of refugee artists in England [where Kurt Schwitters spent the second world war], because of their definite political tendencies. He rather suffered their hatred, which, as is well enough known, in the case of political agents, may be very injurious, indeed, [rather] than yield to their view. My father remained faithful to his principle, "Merz aims only at art, because no man can serve two masters."

(pp. xxi-xxiii)

Finally I add a long quotation from *Moholy-Nagy* by his wife Sibyl: . . . (p. xxiii)

[The] German Press Association gave a banquet for the Italians, to which we had received a personal invitation from Marinetti [Emilio Filippo Tommaso Marinetti, founder of the Futurist movement]. Moholy was unwilling to go. He had been shadowed by the SS; his refusal to submit his paintings to the censorship of the National Socialist Art Chamber to obtain a "working permit" had been followed by threats of arrest. His cleaning woman had stolen his mail and had delivered it to the Blockwart (political district warden), and some of his associates had disappeared mysteriously. He was done with Germany, and on his last night in Berlin he didn't feel like sitting down with the new rulers. But Kurt Schwitters, who was our house guest at the time, insisted on going, to honor the revolutionary in Marinetti, and he finally persuaded Moholy to join him.

Kurt was profoundly worried about the political tide. His rebellious days were over. At forty-six he wanted to be left unmolested, enjoying a secure income from his real estate and his typographical work, and puttering away on his gigantic MERZ plastic, a sculpture of compound forms which extended from a corner of his studio through two stories of his house, winding in and out of doors and windows, and curling around a chimney on the roof. There was nothing he dreaded more than emigration. He died a broken man in England in 1948. [sic]

The banquet offered a very different picture from the lecture the night before and confirmed all of Moholy's misgivings. Short of Hitler, all the Nazis were present: Goebbels and Goring, August Wilhelm of Hohenzollern, the president of the Berlin University, Gerhart Hauptmann, once the torchbearer of revolution but now a chipped plaster image of Goethe. Hess was there, and with him was fat Röhm, whose days were already numbered. These officials were sitting along a huge horseshoe table, while Nazi underlings and the artists whom Marinetti had insisted upon inviting sat at individual tables. Moholy, Schwitters, and I were sandwiched between the head of the National Socialist Organization for Folk Culture, and the leader of the "Strength Through Joy" movement. The disharmony between the guests was accentuated by the absence of speeches and an unlimited consumption of excellent German Rhine wine. Moholy was silent. His face was shuttered, and when our eyes met I saw that he was full of resentment. The more Schwitters drank, the more fondly he regarded his neighbor.

"I love you, you Cultural Folk and Joy," he said. "Honestly, I love you. You think I'm not worthy of sharing your chamber, your art chamber for strength and folk, ha? I'm an idiot too, and I can prove it."

Moholy put his hand firmly on Schwitters' arm and for a few minutes he was silent, drinking rapidly and searching the blank face of his neighbor with wild blue eyes.

"You think I'm a Dadaist, don't you," he suddenly started again. "That's where you're wrong, brother. I'm MERZ." He thumped his wrinkled dress shirt near his heart. "I'm Aryan—the great Aryan MERZ. I can think Aryan, paint Aryan, spit Aryan."

He held an unsteady fist before the man's nose. "With this Aryan fist I shall destroy the mistakes of my youth"—"If you want me to," he added in a whisper after a long sip.

There was no reaction at all from the "Strength Through Joy" man while the official from the Folk Culture Organization nodded droolingly, his round cheeks puffed up with wine and amazement. Schwitters took a sudden liking to him.

"Oh joyful babyface," he muttered, tears running down his cheeks. "You will not prohibit me from MERZing my MERZ art?"

The word "prohibit" had finally penetrated the foggy brain of the "Strength Through Joy" man.

"Prohibited is prohibited [Verboten ist verboten]," he said with great firmness and a heavy tongue. "And when the Führer says 'Ja' he says 'Ja' and when the Führer says 'Nein' he says 'Nein.' Heil Hitler!"

Schwitters looked wildly at Moholy, at me, at Marinetti, but before he could incite anyone to action, Marinetti had risen from his chair. He swayed considerably and his face was purple.

"My friends," he said in French. "After the

many excellent speeches tonight"—the silent officials winced—"I feel the urge to thank the great, courageous, high-spirited people of Berlin. I shall recite my poem "The Raid on Adrianople.""

There was polite applause. Some nice poetry would break the embarrassing dullness of the dinner.

"Adrianople est cerné de toutes parts SSSSrr-rr zitzitzitzitzi PAAAAAAAAAAgh rrrrr-rrrrrrrrr"

roared Marinetti

"Ouah ouah ouah, départ des trains suicides. ouah ouah ouah."

The audience gasped; a few hushed giggles were audible.

"Tchip   tchip   tchip—féééééééééééééééééééélez!"

He grabbed a wineglass and smashed it to the floor.

"Tchip tchip tchip—des messages télégraphiques, couturières Americaines Piiiiiiiiii-iiiiiing, ssssssssssrrrrrrrr, zitzitzit toum toum Patrouille tapie—"

Marinetti threw himself over the table.

"Vanitéeeee,   viande   congeléeeeeeee—veilleuse de La Madone."

expiring almost as a whisper from his lips.

Slowly he slid to the floor, his clenched fingers pulling the tablecloth downward, wine, food, plates, and silverware pouring into the laps of the notables.

Schwitters had jumped up at the first sound of the poem. Like a horse at a familiar sound the Dadaist in him responded to the signal. His face flushed, his mouth open, he followed each of Marinetti's moves with his own body. In the momentary silence that followed the climax his eyes met Moholy's.

"Oh, Anna Blume," he whispered, and suddenly breaking out into a roar that drowned the din of protesting voices and scraping chair legs, he thundered:

Oh, Anna Blume
Du bist von hinten wie von vorn
A-n-n-a.

(pp. xxiii-xxiv)

It is difficult to convey the force of André Breton's personality, whose domineering is perhaps welcomed by his followers because of his insistence on "moral" and "serious" goals. One might say, knowing it to be an oversimplification, but perhaps not misleading in view of the events of the past thirty years, that surrealism was what Breton did to dada. Not only that, after the collapse of the Congress of Paris ("to establish new directives for the modern mind") in 1922, the majority of the dadas went with him, rather than with Tzara, or that publication of

the *First Manifesto of Surrealism* by Breton in 1924 is often taken to mark not only the birth of that movement, but the official end of dada as a movement; but that, in proposing that surrealism undertake psychic researches, investigate automatism, etc., and, ultimately, embrace the politics of the left (this last in turn brought about dichotomies when later surrealism became hostile to the U.S.S.R., Aragon, Eluard, Naville and others being Russian sympathizers), Breton turned "the gay blasphemy" of Duchamp and other "natural" dadas into a world of serious, organized aims. Yet Breton has always had the deepest respect for Duchamp, the arch-dada, who has been a kind of mediator, because of his detachment and fairness, in some of the conflicts among the surrealists. One of the important surrealist painters says of the various ideological quarrels that are part of the surrealist story that, although Breton does not always seem to have been right (even from a surrealist point of view), somehow he always *was* surrealism, and no one wrested the leadership from him. The painter remarked, in passing, that it was Breton who was the one who would have "died" for surrealism—not merely the idea, for many artists and poets were committed to that—but for the *word*.

In 1932, nearly a decade after the dada movement, Breton wrote a preface, "Surrealism: Yesterday, Today, and Tomorrow" for the surrealist number of *This Quarter* (vol. V, no. 1, September, 1932), edited by Edward W. Titus, and published in English in Paris. Breton in an aside wrote:

> There is no doubt that before the surrealist movement properly so-called, there existed among the promoters of the movement, and others who later rallied around it, very active, not merely dissenting, but unfortunately, antagonistic dispositions which, between 1915 and 1920, were to align themselves under the sign-board of *Dada*. Post-war disorder, a state of mind essentially anarchic that guided that cycle's many manifestations, a deliberate refusal to judge—for lack, it was said, of criteria—the actual qualifications of individuals, and perhaps, in the last analysis, a certain spirit of negation which was making itself conspicuous, had brought about the dissolution of a group as yet inchoate, one might say, by reason of its dispersed and heterogeneous character, a group whose germinating force has nevertheless been decisive and, by general consent of present-day critics, has greatly influenced the course of ideas. It may be proper before passing rapidly—as I must—over this period, to apportion the, by far, handsomest share to Marcel Duchamp (canvasses and glass objects still to be seen in New York), to Francis Picabia (reviews 291 and 391), Jacques Vaché (*Lettres de Guerre:* "War Letters") and Tristan Tzara (*25 Poems, Dada Manifesto 1918*)" [trans. by Mr. Titus].

It is Breton who wrote, "A monstrous aberration makes people believe that language was born to facilitate their mutual relations." (pp. xxvi-xxvii)

> *Robert Motherwell, in an introduction to* The Dada Painters and Poets: An Anthology *by*

Arp and others, edited by Robert Motherwell, George Wittenborn, Inc., 1951, pp. xiv-xxxvii.

DEFINITIONS

C. W. E. Bigsby

[*Bigsby is a Scottish critic and educator who has written extensively on the theater and radical social movements. In the following excerpt, Bigsby presents various "definitions" of Dada offered by principal figures associated with the movement.*]

> Dada was a literary and artistic movement, international in scope and nihilist in character, which lasted from 1915 until 1922.
>
> *(Encyclopedia Britannica)*

The search for origins, the attempt to trace and define this most quixotic of phenomena, has provided futile amusement for academics and artistic speleologists for the last fifty years. There can be few movements, however, which lend themselves less to solemn exegesis. Indeed, the would-be explicator of Dadaism soon encounters well-prepared defences. Fully alive to the fact that criticism has a tendency to fossilize the vital and the evanescent, the Dadaists took pains to discourage future generations of historians and critics. The Rumanian painter, Marcel Janco, refused to conceive of a valid history; Max Ernst, the German painter and poet, pointed out the impossibility of capturing the ephemeral; while Jean Arp ridiculed critical methodology in an ironical account of the founding of Dada which is a particularly effective satire of ponderous academicism:

> No dadaist will ever write his memoirs! Do not trust anything that calls itself 'dada history', however much may be true of Dada, the historian qualified to write about it does not yet exist.
>
> (Marcel Janco)

> . . . a Dada exhibition. Another one! What's the matter with everyone, wanting to make a museum piece out of Dada? Dada was a bomb . . . can you imagine anyone, around half a century after a bomb explodes, wanting to collect the pieces, sticking it together and displaying it?
>
> (Max Ernst)

I hereby declare that Tristan Tzara found the word DADA on February 8th, 1916, at 6 p.m. I was present with my five children when Tzara uttered this word for the first time—filling us with justified enthusiasm. This took place in the Café Terrace in Zurich—I was putting a roll into my left nostril at the time. I am convinced that this word is not of the slightest importance and that only morons and Spanish professors can be interested in dates. What interests us is the Dada spirit and we were all Dada before Dada ever ex-

isted. The first Holy Virgins I painted date from 1886 when I was only a few months old and used to amuse myself by pissing graphic impressions. The morality of idiots and their belief in geniuses gives me the shits.

> (Jean Arp)

Despite their distrust of programmes and their revolt against formalized systems the Dadaists delighted in publishing numerous and frequently contradictory statements of their beliefs. While considering that to define Dada was 'un-Dadaistic' they constantly attempted to do so, in the process revealing a characteristic predilection for paradox and contradiction. Thus Tzara could announce that there should be 'No More Manifestoes' while devoting considerable time and energy to compiling a large number of them. But, as he was later to say in one of his poems, 'If each man says the opposite it is because he is right.' It is scarcely surprising that Max Ernst should have listed Walt Whitman as one of his favourite poets.

The manifesto seemed to answer the public need for direct, polemical statement. Yet, perversely, it served merely to further the Dadaists' aim of taunting the bourgeoisie. For while the public looked for a plain statement of intent, the bare bones of the latest artistic movement, they were caught in a web of words whose primary purpose was to demonstrate the redundancy of language. Nevertheless, though wildly and intentionally contradictory, these statements and manifestoes do serve at least obliquely to convey something of the tone and essence of Dada:

> To be against this manifesto is to be a Dadaist.

> . . . in principle I'm against manifestoes, as I am also against principle . . . I write this manifesto to show that people can perform contrary actions together while taking a fresh gulp of air.
>
> (Tristan Tzara)

> Nothing was holy to us. Our movement was neither mystical, communistic nor anarchistic. All of these movements had some sort of program, but ours was completely nihilistic. We spat upon everything, including ourselves. Our symbol was nothingness, a vacuum, a void. . . .
>
> (George Grosz)

> The honorific title of nihilists was bestowed on us. The directors of public cretinization conferred this name on all those who did not follow in their path.
>
> (Jean Arp)

> . . . the misunderstanding from which Dadaism suffered is the chronic disease that still poisons the world. In its essence it can be defined as the inability of a rationalized epoch and of rationalized men to see the positive side of an irrational movement.

Over and over again, the strumming, shouting and dancing, the striving to épater le bourgeois, have been represented as the chief characteristics of Dadaism. The riots provoked by Dadaism in Berlin and Paris, the revolutionary atmosphere surrounding the movement, its wholesale attacks on everything, led critics to believe that its sole aim was to destroy all art and the blessings of culture. The early Dada manifestoes, in which nonsense was mixed with earnestness, seemed to justify this negative attitude.

In the considered opinion of this Manifesto, Dada had both destructive and constructive sides.

(*Dada Manifesto,* 1949)

Dada was anything but a hoax; it was a turning on the road opening up wide horizons to the modern mind. It lasts and will last as long as the spirit of negation contains the ferment of the future.

(Marcel Janco)

Art demands clarity. . . . We are fighting the lack of system for it destroys forces.

(Arp, Janco, etc.)

I'm against systems, the most acceptable system is on principle to have none.

(Tristan Tzara)

At Zurich in 1915, uninterested as we were in the slaughterhouses of the world war, we gave ourselves to the fine arts. While the cannon rumbled in the distance, we pasted, recited, versified, we sang with all our soul. We sought an elementary art which, we thought, would save men from the curious madness of these times. We aspired to a new order.

(Jean Arp)

Art is a pharmaceutical product for morons.

(Francis Picabia)

Dada has launched an attack on the fine arts, an enema to the Venus de Milo, and finally enabled 'Laocoon and Sons' to ease themselves after a thousand-year struggle with the rattle-snake.

(Jean Arp)

Art is going to sleep for a new world to be born. 'ART'—parrot word—replaced by DADA . . . Art is a PRETENSION warmed by the TIMIDITY of the urinary basin, the hysteria born in THE STUDIO.

(Tristan Tzara)

Dada hurts, Dada does not jest, for the reason that it was experienced by revolutionary men and not by philistines who demand that art is a decoration for the mendacity of their emotions . . . I am firmly convinced that all art will become dadaistic in the course of time, because from Dada proceeds the perpetual urge for its renovation.

(Richard Huelsenbeck)

Cubism was a school of painting, futurism a political movement. Dada is a state of mind. To oppose one to the other reveals ignorance or bad faith.

(Tristan Tzara)

Dada is German Bolshevism.

(Richard Huelsenbeck)

Do not trust Dada. Dada is everything. Dada doubts everything. But the real Dadas are against DADA.

(Tristan Tzara)

A movement which includes the nihilistic Walter Serner, the effervescent Tristan Tzara and the sober intelligence of Hugo Ball is difficult to categorize. Most of the Dadaists were young men united in a temporary alliance against the past but all were working their own way towards a personal response to art and a world in which personal maturity seemed to coincide with universal dissolution. Hugo Ball, who founded the Cabaret Voltaire in Zurich, defined the purpose of his venture as an attempt to 'draw attention across the barriers of war and nationalism, to the few independent spirits who live by other ideals'. Although by degrees the Dadaists did formulate more specific objectives it is worth bearing in mind that their primary emphasis was laid on the need for individual freedom in a time of political, moral and aesthetic crisis. This is the core of Dada—the foundation of all that was to follow. (pp. 3-7)

C. W. E. Bigsby, in his Dada & Surrealism, *Methuen & Co. Ltd., 1972, 91 p.*

John Erickson

[*In the following excerpt, Erickson discusses the importance of irony to defining the nature of the Dada movement.*]

Irony: true freedom, it is you who liberates us from the ambition of power, from the slavery of parties, from the respect of habits, from the pedantry of science, from the admiration of the great personages, from the mystification of the reformers, and from the adoration of one's self.

(Pierre-Joseph Proudhon, *Les Confessions d'un révolutionnaire,* 1848)

No revolutionary groups born out of protest of the threat of ideological power structures to individual self-determination have met with more calumny and misinterpretation than anarchism and Dada. The fact that neither has carried through a successful revolution has, with some truth, relegated them in the minds of critics to the deviant, criminal fringe of society. With less truth, they have been judged as given over to nearly total nihilism.

Without dwelling on the history and pre-history of Dada as an outgrowth of 19th-century collectivist anarchy, I wish to look at the Dada perception of the self and the world which, through the attempts of commentators to define and classify, has been formulated around specious half-truths that continue to cloud our understanding. These formulations concern such notions as the cult of the self and nihilism, but turn on the notion of Dada irony or humor.

Michel Sanouillet discusses with probity in a recent essay the terms of self-designation chosen by the proto-Dadas. Despite the predilection of detractors and sympathizers alike for the terms Dadaism and Dadaist instead of Dada and Dadas, the former terms serve primarily as negative signifiers, whose suffixes presuppose the existence of a movement, school or codified group which Dada never was nor ever could have been. They signify the absence or, perhaps, failure of Dada and serve as linguistic traces of the incapacity of the critical intellect to verbalize an un-verbalizable phenomena.

Many critics of Dada conveniently or carelessly overlook Tzara's marginal note to his *Manifeste Dada 1918* that appeared in *Dada 3:*

> Le DADAISME. Pour introduire l'idée de folie passagère en mal de scandale et de publicité d'un "isme" nouveau—si banal, avec le manque de sérieux inné à ces sortes de manifestations, les journalistes nommèrent Dadaïsme ce que l'intensité d'un art nouveau leur rendit impossible compréhension et puissance de s'élever à L'ABSTRACTION, la magie d'une parole (DADA), les ayant mis, (par sa simplicité de ne rien signifier), veaux devant la porte d'un monde présent: vraiment trop forte éruption pour leur habitude de se tirer facilement d'affaire.

One misconception about Dada centers in its emphasis on individual subjectivity, which is usually interpreted as the unqualified aggrandizement of self. Commentaries on the origins of Dada often remind us of the *fin de siècle* and early century *culte du moi* exemplified in Huysmans' *A Rebours,* Barres' trilogy by that name, Gide's *Les Nourritures terrestres* and *L'Immoraliste,* etc., before entering upon a discussion of how the Dada(ist)s opposed the value of individual expression to the machinery of academic art and all other forms of artistic, social, moral, and political strictures. Commentators can accept Tzara's tirade even against avant-garde movements that were to influence Dada, such as Cubism and Futurism, which Tzara called "laboratoires d'idées formelles." They often seize on Tzara's description of the new literature as "Œuvre de créateurs, sortie d'une vraie nécessité de l'auteur, et pour lui-même. Connaissance d'un suprême égoïsme, où les lois s'étiolent," while only partially reconciling the equations set forth in the *Manifesto* a few lines earlier: *Ordredésordre, moinon-moi, affirmationnégation:* rayonnements suprêmes d'un art absolu." If one were intent on looking for nihilist tendencies in Dada, one could easily assimilate the equation *orderdisorder* and, with little difficulty, *affirmationnegation.* But if one were seeking confirmation of a Dada glorification of the individual self, one might tend to gloss over the cryptic equation *selfnon-self* and move on quickly to Tzara's reference to a supreme egoism.

The fact is, Dada's preoccupation with self bears only the most tenuous resemblances to the earlier *culte du moi.* Negation carried to its logical conclusion by the Dadas excludes nothing in its pre-existing or crystallized form, neither self nor Dada itself.

That paradox has remained one of the *pierres d'achoppement* for critics and has provided them reason to dismiss Dada summarily, as an irrational nihilism that can lead only to the ultimate cancellation of every form of life. Several critics (even Dadaist Richter) have proposed that suicide or self-annihilation is the ultimate form of Dada, and a book has appeared on that very subject with a chapter entitled: "Dada: Suicide as an Art" [Alvarez, A. *The Savage God: A Study in Suicide*], which offers a brilliant but faulty analysis of the Dada regard for self. We should be little surprised, however, for thought and

art founded on "paradoxical dialectics" (Sanouillet), while demanding recognition by their intellectual contentiousness, have down through the ages been interpreted in terms of sickness, madness or self-destruction—a recent example being the numerous references to the schizoidal character of Samuel Beckett's art.

Suicide and self-annihilation? Of course, critics can refer to Jacques Vaché and speculate on the suicide of Arthur Cravan whom they might romantically envisage as sailing away on his boat from Mexico into a sea of oblivion. But Vaché and Cravan, for all their Dada-like characteristics, were decidedly secondary figures in the phenomenon of Dada. When the proto-Dadas—Tzara, Picabia, Duchamp, Hugo Ball, among others—speak of the negation of self, they hardly speak in terms of suicide, for such an act would represent the atrophy or fixation of "le chaos quiconstitue cette infinie informe variation: l'homme" (Tzara). It would be tantamount to existential death—the cessation of becoming.

The Dadas were not death-oriented; they were insistently life-oriented. Their conceptualization of the negation of self ("non-moi") refers rather to the institutionalized self, for which biological death serves only as a metaphor. Their negation of self parallels, I believe, Proudhon's injunction to free ourselves from the adoration of self, and they use essentially the same means: irony. The term irony goes back to the type of the *eiron* Aristotle describes in Book Four of the *Nichomachean Ethics.* The *eiron* or ironical man is a man "who professes that he does not have, or has in less measure than the world supposes, the good qualities which he does in fact profess." He dissembles, depreciates his self, as opposed to the *alazon* or boaster who holds himself up as being more than he is. As Northrop Frye says, the *eiron* "makes himself invulnerable, and, though Aristotle disapproves of him, there is no question that he is a predestined artist, just as the *alazon* is one of his predestined victims."

If we replace the term "artist" used by Frye with "anti-artist" (or "an-artist," as Duchamp would prefer), we acquire a working definition of the Dada ironic attitude. Like Proudhon, their anarchist predecessor, however, they go beyond the root-sense of *eiron* as well as the commentative-sense of Frye. While their object is to make themselves invulnerable to mystification by self or other, they do not seek invulnerability through mere dissimulation. Dada irony, like that of the anarchists, is not passive but aggressively carried out, in order to achieve the effect of distancing or standoffishness, in Kenneth Burke's sense, which alone allows the human individual to achieve proper perspective. The anarchists and Dadas have transposed the biblical injunction, that we must die in order to be reborn spiritually, onto secular plane. To obtain authentic freedom, they sought to liberate the self from materialistic motives, habits, mystification and idolatry in any form—political, moral, scientific, or egoistic. The ultimate preservation of the natural self, lying hidden beneath the layers of sentiment, memory, and self-pride, is at stake for the Dada individual as for *all* individuals (Tzara: "en sachant toutefois respecter les autres individualités"). Thus, when Tzara enounces his belief that "ce qu'il y a de divin en nous est l'éveil de l'action anti-humaine," he alludes not to biological destruction but the destruction of the conscious ego, mediator and construct of empirical reality, which makes us vulnerable to the inroads of social, political, artistic and personal vanity and blinds us to our authentic self. Suicide represents just another form of vanity, morbid preoccupation with ego, antithetical to the proto-Dadas.

The proto-Dadas all express doubt in the efficacity of self (ego). In an interview, Marcel Duchamp has referred to his activity of earlier years as consisting of

> pushing the idea of doubt of Descartes to a much further point than they ever did in the School of Cartesianism: doubt in myself, doubt in everything. In the first place, never believing in truth. In the end it comes to doubt "to be." Not doubt to say "to be or not to be"—that has nothing to do with it. There won't be any difference when I'm dead and now, because I won't know it. You see the famous "to be" is consciousness [i.e., ego], and when you sleep you "are" no more. That's what I mean—a state of sleepingness, because consciousness is a formulation, a very gratuitous formulation of something, but nothing else. And I go further by saying that words such as truth, art, veracity, or anything are stupid in themselves. Of course, it's difficult to formulate, so I insist *every word I am telling you is stupid and wrong.*

If we understand this attitude towards self/ego, we understand why Duchamp spoke so disparagingly of self, why he cultivated his famous attitude of *indifference* (a form of "sleepingness"), why he set about removing art from the personal (egoistic) domination of the artist by distancing himself from art through experimentation with unconventional media and impersonal instruments of artistic creation. He turned, for instance, to painting on glass, as we know, and experimenting with the techniques of draftsmanship, which intrigued him because of the "impersonality of the ruler."

Apollinaire was unusually prophetic when he remarked about Duchamp in 1913 that "il sera peut-être réservé à un artiste aussi dégagé de préoccupations esthétiques, aussi préoccupé d'énergie que Marcel Duchamp, de réconcilier l'Art et le Peuple" (*Les Peintres Cubistes*). For Apollinaire, Duchamp offered the reconciliation of art and the ordinary by bringing art down from its pedestal through his detached attitude. And Breton, nearly ten years later would note the same detachment after the fact in speaking of Duchamp's indifference and "dédain de la thèse."

This same ironic attitude, towards art, towards self, explains another aspect of Dada art which often has been misinterpreted: Dada's interest in machines and mechanical artifacts—the very incarnation of scientific and social order. But this Dada interest went hand in hand with an inseparable corollary, which was the urge for liberation from enslavement to the very objects they chose to elevate. That the Futurists exerted an important influence on Dada in general is incontestable (particularly through the effect of their notion of *parole in libertà* on Dada poetry and typographical layout). That the Futurist interest in ma-

chines and technological objects paralleled that of the Dadas is likewise undeniable, but commentators have often overlooked that radical difference underlying their attitudes towards machines and technology.

So far as Duchamp's relationship with the Futurists, he disclaimed their influence on the kinetic characteristics of his early work, while convincingly maintaining that those characteristics grew out of his interest in Jules Etienne Marey's chronophotographs of the 1890's which depicted, through multiple camera exposures, human figures in movement. To Marey, Duchamp owes in part his *Jeune homme triste dans un train* and the first version of his *Nu descendant un escalier* (both from 1911). As for his versions of the *Broyeuse de chocolat,* which would be incorporated into his *Large Glass,* he brings to mind the Futurist interest in manufactured objects. But the versions of that work show the same impersonality (ironic distance) at work in his readymades, a value distinctly opposed to those found by the Futurists in machines and artifacts of urban technology. The Futurists glorified the machine, virtually transformed it into an object of worship because of its inherent dynamism and energy. They viewed the machine, taken as it was, as the epitome of art. In Marinetti's *Manifesto of Futurism* (February 20, 1909), he stated his feeling that "A racing car whose hood is adorned with great pipes, like serpents of explosive breath—a roaring car that seems to ride on grapeshot—is more beautiful than the *Victory of Samothrace.*"

But Duchamp's readymades, usually constructed from objects "found" in the urban landscape, destroy the very value treasured by the Futurists—*function.* In defending in *The Blind Man* his entry in the 1917 Exhibition of Independents held in New York of the famous urinal entitled "Fountain," which he signed "R. Mutt," Duchamp insisted that "Whether Mr. Mutt with his own hands made the fountain or not has no importance. He CHOSE it. He took an ordinary article of life, placed it so that its useful significance disappeared under the new title and point of view—created a new thought for that object." Whereas, it was the function of the machines, which released the energy latent in them (the roar of a racing car's exhausts), that fascinated the Futurists, the ironic "blocking" of the object's function (an act of distancing it from its technological context) was crucial for Duchamp.

Nowhere do we see expressed more eloquently the radical difference in attitude between the Futurists and the Dadas in regard to machines than in the construction by Man Ray entitled Dancer (*Danger*), from 1920. This work consists of a grouping of cogwheels on a sheet of glass with the word DANCER superimposed on them. The "C" of the word DANCER, however, carries the suggestion of a bar on its lower prong, which upon close scrutiny spells out the word DANGER. Two details of this construction subtly reveal the ironic, anti-Futurist statement of Man Ray. The word DANCER, while calling to mind his interest in dance and its dynamism, in accord with the latent movement of the cogwheels, concurrently, through its decipherment as DANGER underscores the Dada awareness of the potential tyranny of the machine. Man Ray reenforces this idea by interlocking the cogwheels in such a way as to render them unfunctionable. Hence, through ironic manipulation and control the artist simultaneously conveys the dynamic potential of the machine and wards off the threat of it. "It illustrates," as Roland Penrose asserts, "Man Ray's reverence and distrust of the machine god. . . . "

No better example exists of Dada liberation through irony from the mystification and worship of objects. From those same objects, we might add, adulated so much by the Futurists that certain of them were to turn to the grand god of the Fascist war machine. No less than Duchamp and Man Ray, did Picabia, through the humorist distance he placed between himself and his machine drawings, through his conscious manipulation of them that transformed function into pseudo or mythic (as opposed to mystifying) function, preserve his control over and freedom from technological systems.

Dickran Tashjian speaks of how the Dadas in New York, in particular Picabia, brought about a reconciliation between the simplicity of rural-frontier America (American primitivism) which so intrigued them and the complexities of urban technology. In an essay accompanying Picabia's machine drawings in Stieglitz's review *291* in 1915, Marius de Zayas observed that Picabia "had broken away from Europe and accepted America as it was by living in its a-historical present, dominated by the machine and cut off from tradition."

The machine itself might indeed be viewed as a liberation from tradition, but through his double-edged humor Picabia achieved a liberation twice removed by freeing the artist from the machine. The clean, concise lines of his depiction of a sparkplug bearing the title "Portrait d'une jeune fille américaine dans l'état de nudité" shows both a celebration of technological simplicity and a renunciation of the machine through whimsy. His machines are parody-machines by means of which he seeks to attain "the summit of symbolism." The anti-artist, not the machine, dominates.

Irony or ironic humor was one of the most effective devices of the Dadas to denigrate or destroy those instruments of human invention (whether the artificiality of the ego or the machine) that through mystification entrap and enslave the individual. No community of individuals has understood the liberating force of irony better than the anarchists and the Dadas. To limit our view of Dada activities to the nihilism it advocated, and to see in that nihilism nothing more than a dead-end playfulness (at its most innocent) or a corrosive destructiveness (at its worst) is to focus on the headlines without reading the fine print.

We misunderstand Dada as much as Breton if we insist that it step forth and identify itself. Breton, in spite of the fascination he and certain of his Parisian followers had for Dada, and in spite of their eagerness to play the Dada game for the space of a few years, were never Dadas. A Dada could not have proposed a congress that would draw together the avant-garde groups with their diverse aspirations into a unified movement, as did Breton. A Dada would have comprehended why Tzara would wish to turn such a congress into derision, as Breton could not. As

Sanouillet points out, a Dada could not have defined Dada in the way Breton defined Surrealism in his first *Manifesto,* and through such codification turned it into an un-Dada *ism.* A Dada could never have envisaged the creation of a review entitled *Dada au Service de la Révolution,* as did certain of the surrealists (causing even Breton to realize that political involvement had been carried too far). A Dada could not have flirted with Marxist or Communist ideology without ceasing to be a Dada, or with any such system, much less a system given to the idea of historical evolution and set upon the mastery of man and nature.

One may well point out that the Surrealists were not alone in being drawn into political wedlock, that the "artistes radicaux" who founded the Bund Revolutionärer Künstler in 1919 in solidarity with the political uprisings in Germany and the Balkans, and whose manifesto stated their desire "to take part in the ideological evolution of the state," included such Dadas as Arp, Janco, and Richter. Their disagreement with the determined detachment of Tzara manifested itself in their statement that "We are fighting the lack of system, for it destroys forces. It is our highest aim to bring about a spiritual basis of understanding for all mankind." In expressing these thoughts, some of the Dadas, for the moment at least, had become Dadaists. Their statement exposes the first fissures in the walls of that fragile structure called Zurich Dada, which had been held together until then by enthusiasm and conflicting temperaments in precarious balance.

One might also assert that German Dada, in Cologne where Baargeld held forth, and Berlin where Raoul Hausmann, Johannes Baader and Richard Huelsenbeck (who had returned to Germany in January 1917) kicked up their heels, had indeed become politically involved. To be sure, instead of adamantly yielding to the strict party line of Berlin Communism, German Dada parodied rather than parroted it in such documents as the manifesto of the so-called Dada Revolutionary Central Council published in 1919. But, in measure as Zurich, Berlin, and Paris Dada lost their ironic distance and took themselves seriously, they were on their way to becoming un-Dada. Or, as Sanouillet states, "In moving from Zurich to Berlin in 1917, the *Dada* Huelsenbeck had become a *Dadaist,* i.e., a militant concerned with the activity of a movement and the efficiency of an ideological platform." With Huelsenbeck's and Hausmann's argument for the communization of Dadaism in the manifesto of the Dadaist Revolutionary Central Council, we can contrast Hugo Ball's view that Dada was the opposite of Bolshevism, in that it contrasted "the completely quixotic, inexpedient, and incomprehensible side of the world with [Bolshevism's] destruction and consummate calculation."

The infinite shadings of Dada and Surrealism, and the inconsistencies, contradictions, and varying attitudes of the Dadas and Surrealists, complicate any effort to contrast the two. But generally speaking, Dada's relationship with Surrealism was the encounter of a state of mind with a structured system. Surrealism indisputably picked up and refined many of the activities with which Dada toyed in Zurich and New York, in particular automatism and dream activity, but it differed integrally from Dada. Perhaps the most striking difference is that, Dada, through its ironic detachment, playfulness and humor, preserved its life-giving perspective and freedom. While, though enjoying Dada moments, insofar as it lost its detachment Surrealism became historical process and system.

One point to be made concerning the dispersal of the Dadas, the metamorphoses of certain Dadas into Dadaists, and the emergence of Surrealism from its structured chrysalis, is that Dada in New York and Zurich, which in large part preserved its ironic distance from world events during the conflagration of a world at war, found itself beset by two divisive forces in the years 1917-1919. One force was the Bolshevist Revolution which lured some of the Dadas with its illusory and paradoxical (even for a Dada) promise that a new system had arisen which would end systems. The other force was the Armistice itself, which broke down the barriers which had until then protected the small and isolated Dada groups and allowed them to maintain their delicate equilibrium. After the Armistice, with the pilgrimage to Paris and Berlin, the Dadas moved into a much vaster arena filled with such a conflict of opinion and ideas that they could no longer exert control over events as they formerly had. The complexity of the situation they found themselves in called for organization and structure, whereas before "a fluid set of concepts" had been enough (Sanouillet).

Dada never coalesced into anything resembling a school or a movement. Its very existence depended upon its keeping its "distance," that sense of liberating irony of which Proudhon spoke. If it appeared to fall apart in the early twenties, it was only that it could not by nature materialize as movement/ego, as abstract *ism,* as it was under pressure to do. So some of the Dadas went off to play chess, some became Dadaists, and some of the Dadaists Surrealists. Dada, on the other hand, did not end. In character, it simply withdrew. As spirit, instinct with deathlessness, it is still capable of stirring at times, in a Tinguely, a Christo, or a Stoppard. (pp. 41-50)

John Erickson, "Dada Distance," in L'Esprit Créateur, *Vol. XX, No. 2, Summer, 1980, pp. 41-50.*

Dada aimed to destroy the reasonable deceptions of man and recover the natural and unreasonable order. . . . Dada gave the Venus de Milo an enema and permitted Laocoon and his sons to relieve themselves after thousands of years of struggle with the good sausage Python.

—Hans (Jean) Arp, in Dada: Monograph of a Movement, *1957*.

Michel Sanouillet

[*In the following excerpt, Sanouillet examines the diffi-culty of defining the ideology and aesthetics of Dada-ism.*]

[In] recent years an increasingly large number of people, both in university circles and among the public at large, have been attracted to, even fascinated by, and sometimes addicted to the Dada movement, to Dadaists, men and women, to Dada artistic or literary productions, but above all, to what must be called the Dada spirit. . . . [So] many books, articles, television and radio programs have been devoted to Dada in recent years that some degree of saturation has been reached. So many new trails have been blazed by new breeds and generations of critics that it has become hard to see one's way very clearly. In fact, most scholars in the field would contend at this time that what we need most is not another book or some clever exegisis of Dada texts, but simply a good five-cent definition of what Dada is. (p. 16)

I feel deep sympathy for the scores of scholars who, in the last decade or so, have attempted to write historical accounts of the Dada movement, and who eventually have had to be satisfied with a collection of texts, or have given up the task altogether, unable as they have been to come to grips with that unlikely mass of documentary evidence and that bunch of sarcastic people all gathered under one elusive trade mark: Dada. The cause and nature of their ordeal were best described, I think, by the anonymous contributor to *The Times Literary Supplement,* who wrote in 1953, no doubt out of despair, the following complaint:

> How is one to define, let alone confine, a movement which cannot be identified with any one personality or place, viewpoint or subject, which affects all the arts, which has a continually shifting focus, and is moreover intentionally negative, ephemeral, illogical, and inconclusive.

This state of affairs helps explain why, until twenty years ago, no book and only a dozen articles had been written on the subject. Of course one could find passing references in art primers and literary histories. The Dada saga was condensed into a paragraph, or even a footnote, somewhere in between Cubism and Surrealism, generally serving as a cursory introduction to the latter.

Perhaps this would be a good starting point towards a definition of Dada; trying to explain what Dada is *not,* and how it can be distinguished from neighboring avant-garde movements. In the public mind, Dada and Surrealism, for example, have always been mixed in a general feeling of estrangement and repulsion born of our inability to work out simple criteria to define specifically the Dada work or concept. Pataphysician Jean Ferry observed in 1960: "Surrealism today means: something a bit weird, slightly porno around the edges, a hole in a pebble, Dali's moustache in Louella Parsons' column." This is true and applies to Dada as well as to any avant-garde movement as long as it goes against the grain of contemporary public taste. Picasso, even at this late date, is still viewed by 80 per cent of our civilized populations as a successful con man who managed to make a fortune painting three-eyed women endowed with cubic buttocks.

We should not lose track of the fact that the public mind,

consciously or not, needs a definition, any definition, not so much to have a precise idea of what is being talked about, but because public taste, as Duchamp showed it, is based on stereotypes which most of the time bear no relation to truth or reality.

The lack of clarity which surrounds the Dada story proceeds from the aura of legend attached to the word itself. As is well known, none of the protagonists, Tzara, Huelsenbeck, Arp or Richter agreed on the way the word Dada was found and the movement founded, just as nobody is absolutely sure of the origins of the great myths of the past, Homer, Shakespeare or the Holy Grail.

Dada thrives on its mysterious origins. Once I told Tzara that new evidence I had uncovered seemed to contradict his version of the genesis of Dada. He just smiled and said: "Why do you professors always want to destroy legends?" In fact, this avowed scorn for university scholars was only a smokescreen behind which most Dadas hid their fear of seeing the truth unearthed. Arp wrote that "only imbeciles and Spanish professors are interested in dates" and Tzara himself: "The first thought that comes to these people [he is referring to us professors] is bacteriological in character: to find the etymological or at least the historical or psychological origin of a word that means nothing. We see by the papers that the Kru negroes call the tail of a holy cow Dada. The cube and the mother in a certain district of Italy are called: Dada. A hobby horse, a nurse, both in Russian and Roumanian: Dada." You see that very little help is to be expected from the Dadaists, not even the most vocal and literate.

What I would like to do . . . is to examine whether Dada can be confined to a domain of its own, and then whether it is feasible and desirable to work towards a definition which might be acceptable if not to everybody, at least to most specialists.

Let us look first at the definitions of Dada given in dictionaries, encyclopaedias and textbooks; that is, definitions given by people outside the movement itself. The *Petit Larousse Illustré,* that cultural staple of the French school system, out of which legend has it that the word Dada was picked by chance, in 1915, in Zurich, by Hugo Ball, provides a good beginning. In the 1913 edition of the Larousse, of course, only the literal meaning of Dada appears: "Noun, masculine. Linguistics. Funny or childish term, used to describe a horse. Plural: des dadas.— Figurative: obsessive idea, leaning, project one endlessly toys with, and always comes back to."

In the 1924 edition, after the last Dada manifestations in Paris, Dada enters the dictionary for the first time and here is what we read: "Dada. Noun, masculine. A name voluntarily devoid of meaning, adopted by a literary and artistic school which appeared around 1917, and whose platform, entirely negative, tends to make extremely arbitrary, if not to suppress completely, any connection between thought and expression. (One can also say Dadaism.) Adj. The Dada school."

Follows a short list of Dada writers (Breton, Tsara [sic], Picabia, etc.) and this conclusion: "If we make allowance for a—large—portion of humor and hoax, one may consider Dadaism as the extreme limit of the possible divorce between words and their meanings, one of them saying that the meaning of words is not an assured property."

Before poking fun at this first definition of Dada, we should stop for a moment to consider the many interpretations given in the press of the period and which, by comparison, appear not only extravagant, but completely untrue. The Larousse definition, although limited to problems of language, is by no means absurd. In fact, we'll see in a moment that the unknown contributor pinpointed the most important objective of the Dada enterprise, from which all others will follow; that is, to create the conditions of a new language, conditions outlined by Duchamp in his *Green Box:* "Take a Larousse dict. [Once again, you see the important part played by didactic books in spelling out the Dada ideology] and copy the so-called 'abstract' words, i.e. those which have no concrete reference. Compose a schematic sign designating each of these words. [. . .] These signs must be thought of as the letters of the new alphabet. A grouping of several signs will determine what would correspond in this literature to the substantive, verb, adverb, declensions, conjugations, etc."

In fact, if we understand this search for a new dictionary as Duchamp sees it, that is, as a search for a new *concrete* alphabet based on a non-linguistic semiotic system, the Larousse definition pretty well covers most of Dada's written and plastic productions.

In order to be useful a definition must unequivocally enunciate the specific and essential properties of an object. It must include all the definite and nothing but the definite. It must be affirmative, that is, state what Dada *is* and not what it *is not.* It must allow anybody to understand the term itself, the idea expressed by the word, and the various extensions of that idea: extension in time, in space, etc. Finally, it must be as concise as possible.

Starting from these premises, one soon realizes that he can not possibly give a conventional definition of Dada. Of course we could proceed through a series of approximations: "Dada is an avant-garde movement, located in time between Futurism and Surrealism," for instance. But then we find that Futurism lasted for a few years after the birth of Dada, and that the Surrealists claimed that their movement started as early as 1918, long before Dada's demise in 1924. Even that date is controversial: Georges Ribemont-Dessaignes and Marcel Duchamp remained staunch advocates of Dada well into the thirties.

One could approach the problem differently, by referring to another avant-garde school of similar character and stressing what is called the "specific difference:" Dada would be Futurism *plus* or *less* something. But here again we enter a dead-end street, because Dada was never clearly differentiated from companion movements. This is particularly true in connection with Surrealism. Nobody can tell exactly when Breton, or Eluard, or Man Ray, or Arp, or Max Ernst ceased being Dadas to become Surrealists. Nor can we use other visible standards like specific properties of Dada texts or paintings.

When we look closely at Dada productions in the light of art or literary history, we may well wonder whether anything really original was unearthed by the movement: "words in liberty," free typography had been widely used by the Futurists; simultaneous poetry was invented by Unanimists Romains and Barzun; similarly neither the phonetic poem, nor automatic writing, neither collage nor photomontage were *stricto sensu* Dada discoveries, although Dada played a part in their propagation throughout the artistic world of their time. In fact, none of these techniques can be used as a sure-fire criterion of what is, and what is not, a Dada poem or a Dada work of art. The Surrealists were eager to point out that they were instrumental, for example, in the inception and perfection of automatic writing. And Dada's early publications such as *Cabaret Voltaire* or *Dada 1-3* are nothing more than a medley of modern art productions in France, Italy, Germany, Austria, Russia, etc. . . . an eclectic panorama of 1917 avant-garde, by no means a program. Consequently it appears that any quest for a definition of Dada which would rest on technical criteria only would be at best misleading, if not totally wrong.

Perhaps the dialectical relation between Dada and Dadaism would help us leap over the initial paradox which has stopped many a budding scholar and which Lucy Lippard [in *Dadas on Art*] has excellently summed up as follows: Dada, "this agent of immediacy and destruction, has created some of the most enduring objects and attitudes of our times." In other words, was Dada a negative or positive force? We will see in a moment that asking the question in this logical and cartesian fashion will lead us nowhere. The assumption, which we find in all art primers, that Dada was essentially a negative movement, soon to be turned into a positive school called Surrealism, was promoted by the Surrealists themselves who had good strategic reasons for doing so. And we must concur with Huelsenbeck that: "It is ridiculous and a sign of idiocy exceeding the legal limit to say that Dada . . . is only of negative value" [Richard Huelsenbeck, *En Avant Dada: Eine Geschichte des Dadaismus*].

But it would be just as idiotic and exceeding the speed of light to deny the negative side of Dada, which is so closely linked with its philosophy and historical development.

I have dealt at length in my books on what seems to me a basically false problem, and only an apparent paradox. Dadaism created while Dada was destroying, which is what we all do unknowingly. That is why it is absurd to oppose two currents within Dada: one, negative and anti-artistic represented by the writers Tzara and Huelsenbeck, the other positive and creative, by the painters Arp, Janco and Ernst. The best examples of positive/negative dialectics is given by the work of Kurt Schwitters. As Huelseneck put it: "If the Dadaist movement is Nihilism, then Nihilism is a part of life, a truth which would be confirmed by any professor [again!] of zoology."

A much more promising domain of research seems to be that of Dada as Logos. Most scholars, interested as they are primarily by Dada's history and achievements, have lost track of an essential factor; that before being anything else, Dada was a word, a brand new, meaningless and magic word, a "jewel-case word" as Gide defined it. No other literary or artistic movement ever depended so much on the contents of its name for its reception by the public at large.

Tristan Tzara once told me how furious he was when critics began using the expressions Dadaism, Dadaist, dadaistic to refer to himself, his friends and their productions. This, in his mind, was a desecrating gesture which amounted to equating Dada with all other preceding—and for that matter subsequent—*isms*. He always strongly believed that Dada was *essentially* different: other *isms* were meant to structure and base in history some form of ideology, theory or aesthetic system. Romanticism, Realism, Naturalism, Symbolism, Futurism, Expressionism, Surrealism, etc. were all explicit in their formulation, even if they later somewhat overgrew their original semantic connotation. Even today we find romance in Romanticism, reality in Realism, nature in Naturalism and surreality in Surrealism.

Dada, on the contrary, is what Duchamp called a "Prime Word," one which can be divided only by itself and by unity. Tzara insisted on many occasions that it was silly to try to evolve a concept out of an empty shell. Dada means nothing, he said, and nobody can cause it to signify. Of course, from a strictly linguistic point of view, such a statement does not hold water. To say that Dada means nothing has no meaning. As Jean-Claude Chevalier puts it: "As long as a succession of sounds, always identical, is used with a specific function in a given language [. . .], it has a meaning. There is no linguistic structure which is not a signifying structure (Greimas)." Further along Tzara contends that "Dada is arbitrary." Of course, because any isolated word is arbitrary and acquires its meaning only through the position it is given within the linguistic system.

We know that in most Indo-European languages, the "consonant + vowel" system is the basic expressive unit that children learn first: mama, papa, pipi, lolo, which is why Dada means hobby-horse in baby talk and yes in Russian. Thus the Dada repetitive phoneme is, so to speak, at the root of a number of elementary combinations, all loaded with what we call a heavy emotional semantic charge. Consciously or not, whether it was found by accident in a dictionary or coined to suit a ballet dancer, the word Dada was felt as a linguistic toy, which could not be compared with other literary names. Breton: "One can say that the word Dada lends itself easily to puns. That is why we selected it."

That is why we find the word Dada at the centre of numerous linguistic combinations, out of which I'll select a few: Raoul Hausmann calls himself *Dadasophe;* Ernst *Dadamax* or *Dadafex maximus;* Johannes Baader *Oberdada;* George Grosz *Propagandada;* Huelsenbeck *Huelsendada.* Tzara's periodical *Dada* has a special number named *Dadaphone* and a projected anthology called *Dadaglobe;* Baader's "Bible," a huge scrapbook *Dadacon.* There is a weird fascination attached to the word and I would contend that some of the awe we feel toward the person and behaviour of this new impersonation of Ubu called Idi Amin Dada is due to the incongruous sound of his name. On that subject, Jacques Rivière and André Gide, who were both editors of the influential Parisian periodical *La*

Nouvelle Revue Française, wrote in 1920, at the peak of the Paris Dada movement, two articles which appear today in retrospect as quite remarkable in their foresight: "The day the word Dada was found," writes Gide, "there was nothing left to do. All that was written later appeared a bit washed out. Nothing equated *Dada.* Those two syllables had reached the goal of 'sonorous vacuum,' a total lack of meaning. In that single word Dada, they had expressed all they had to say *as a group.* '""

And Jacques Rivière: "Man cannot express something which has no meaning [. . .] The Dadas consider words only as accidents: they let them happen. Language for them is no longer a means, it is a *being.*"

That Dada was felt by its promoters as a being endowed with a special status, rather than as a concept, is obvious in the way the word was used, at least at the beginning of the movement; that is, with a capital and without an article. But what kind of a being remains to be defined. When confronted with the need to explain what they were and what they were trying to do, to people outside their *bund,* newspaper men for example, or the Parisian bourgeois crowd flocking to their public manifestations, they resorted most of the time to jokes, insults, or obviously nonsensical definitions.

In no movement or literary school I know did the exponents go to so much trouble to try to indicate what it was that made their enterprise worthy of interest. I have encountered and classified over a hundred sentences in manifestoes, letters, poems or other writings, beginning with "Dada is" . . . or "Dada wants" . . . , or "Dada does" this or that. This attitude reveals that the Dadaists' major concern was to make sure themselves that they were dealing with a series of aesthetic and philosophical problems never before encountered, and which needed to be dealt with in an unprecedented manner. They felt that Dada was some kind of outside phenomenon over which they had little control and whose scope was much larger than that of a literary theory.

Subconsciously, by the very number of their divergent and sometimes conflictual definitions, they give us a rough idea of what Dada was *for them* and *to them,* which is not necessarily what it is for us. First of all, they saw Dada as a living entity, free to act as it chose, without worrying about problems of logic. To Arp, for example, "Dada is devoid of meaning, like Nature." This implies that each artistic experiment has a spontaneous, playful, irrational and individual character.

Dada, that biological entity, can take on various appearances, that of a vegetable: "Dada is a fruit that grows on man;" "Dada is a tomato;" of an animal: "Dada is a virgin microbe;" "Dada is the chameleon of interested change;" "Dada's tail is warped like an eagle's beak;" of a specific human being: "Dada is Tristan Tzara;" "Dada is Francis Picabia." Dada has human attributes: a nationality: "Dada is American;" "Dada has a French appearance;" it—he—is physically described as "having a China ass" and being able "to kick you in the behind and you like it." "Come to Dada if you like to be embraced and embarrassed;" "Dada will rattle his jawbones as a sign of friend-

ship" (Ribemont-Dessaignes); Dada "invites you to the opening of the Max Ernst exhibition." He even has feelings: "Dada is very happy," Georges Ribemont-Dessaignes keeps repeating.

But we must never forget that Dada was a *group* of people closely knit together, a *bund,* whose purposes were identical, and who had banded together their talents and energies to wage an excruciating war against society as a whole. That is why we find constant references, in the members' own writings, to Dada as a collective being ("Dada, a corporation for the exploitation of vocabulary"), or to Dada as a combination of individuals ("Us, Dada"), without an *s,* which will degenerate, later on, into "Us, the Dadas."

The main difference between the collective being Dada and the Surrealist group is that the former never felt the need to be structured. This is apparent from the start in the early publications and manifestations in Zurich: "Dada was born of a need for independence, of a distrust towards community" (Tzara); "I am against systems, the most acceptable system is on principle to have none" (Tzara); "All Dadas are president." The anarchistic government of Dada is drastically opposed to the ecclesiastical organization of Surrealism, in which the Pope was infallible and all those not deemed to conform to the official truth were excommunicated and henceforth treated as outcasts.

A further inquiry into the many Dada texts where the word is mentioned and reflected upon will show that in fact *Dada* is used as a standard module which can be substituted for any other word or expression. One of the favorite techniques will be to take a stereotyped sentence, a popular saying, and to alter it by inserting the word Dada: "*Dada, Dada* über alles" (*Deutschland,* Grosz); "*Dada* today, *Dada* tomorrow, *Dada* forever" (*Germany,* Herzfelde); "*Dada* in, *Dada* out" (*Day,* Ernst); "*Dada* lifts everything" (*Faith,* Soupault).

The conclusion to all this is that Dada "is nothing, nothing, nothing" and that "everything is Dada." Dada, noun and adjective, subject and object, encompasses practically the whole spectrum of grammatical interplay. Dada is all that exists and cannot exist outside existence. Therefore it cannot be used as a normal semantic unit. There is only one word in our languages which enjoys so many privileges: the word *God.*

Dada, like the Christian Trinity, dons three appearances: the Dada father, the original eternal power, whose shape cannot be seen or even conceived by limited human beings; Dada the son, which is the movement itself, inscribed in history, time and space, endowed with a form which, according to Gustave Thibon, is both a perfection and a limit; and finally, Dada the Holy Ghost, the Dada spirit, present in a number of men and their works, visible to the happy few, but without discernable form or limit.

And, in fact, all the Dadaists, without any exception, kept making references to Dada in terms descriptive of superhuman, God-like creatures: Schwitters: "Jesus Christ was the first Dada." Picabia: "Dada knows everything: the Holy Virgin was already a Dadaist," Breton: "Dada is a new cult. The oldest and most fearful enemy of Dada is God." Schwitters: "Dada comes and the sick are healed, move about and sing." Huelsenbeck: "Dada is the War Bond of Eternal Life. Invest in Dada (Jesus saves)." "Dada floated over the waters before dear God created the world and when he said: Let there be Light!, there was not light, but Dada."

I do not think Arp was really joking when he wrote: "What interests us is the Dada spirit. And we were all Dada before the existence of Dada." Neither did Janco: "Dada was anything but a hoax; it was a turning on the road opening up wide horizons to the modern mind. It lasts, and will last as long as the spirit of negation contains the ferments of the future."

This helps explain the mystic tendencies of a Hugo Ball who saw in the Dada adventure the necessary set of tools to break the old chains, and who later chose to retire into a Catholic retreat. It also explains why there is no contradiction between Ball and the violently radical and political turn taken by the Berlin Dadaists under Baader, Hausmann, and Huelsenbeck. For the latter "Dada is German Bolshevism," and the red god demands, among other things, "compulsory adherence of all clergymen and teachers to the Dadaist articles of faith."

Consequence: to speak of Dada, to analyse the Dada language, one needs a new language, a Dada metalanguage, which only Dada can use and understand. With Dada, we live inside a closed world, within Félicien Marceau's "egg shell" which nobody can penetrate without first breaking it. The critic or the historian can only write or talk about *Dadaism* and the *Dadaists,* not about Dada and the Dadas. As long as we look at Dada from the outside, and only from that vantage point, we are well founded to treat Dadaism as any other concept or school, like Futurism and Surrealism. But the latter offers only one viewpoint, whether it is investigated from the outside or from the inside.

From the *Dada* root, the linguist will normally coin the whole sequel of derivatives: Dadaism, Dadaist, Dadaistic, etc., nouns and adjectives. The "emptiness" of the word Dada helps us understand the disconcerting varieties of its impersonations in so many places and times; why, for instance, Dada in Zurich was mainly concerned with art—or anti-art, while in Germany, it engaged in practical politics. While Tzara was still writing "Dada means nothing," in Germany Dada had lost its art-for-art's sake character with its very first move. *"The Dadaist,"* says Huelsenbeck, *"sees his mission in the smashing of the cultural ideology of the Germans."* In moving from Zurich to Berlin in 1917, the *Dada* Huelsenbeck had become a *Dadaist,* i.e. a militant concerned with the activity of a movement and the efficiency of an ideological platform.

In fact, when we peruse manifestoes and other documents put out by Dada painters and poets, we come to realize that the very abundance of their definitions of what they thought Dada was, conceals their main concern which is to avoid being cornered into giving a final, precise and all-inclusive definition of their private and public objectives, of their aesthetic theories on art and poetry, of their philosophy of life. This was due, not so much to their inability to see clearly into themselves or their friends, as to a fundamental impulse to resist falling into the historical pattern typical of all other avant-garde movements which were doomed from the moment a younger and newer form of protest was found. Thus the scholar and the critic keep playing an endless game of hide and seek with the exponents of a movement which, like Pascal's sphere, has its centre everywhere and its circumference nowhere.

It would therefore be nonsensical to attempt to give a definition of Dada the way Breton did of Surrealism, again in the form of a dictionary entry, and again, you will notice, in verbal and linguistic terms: " 'Surrealism,' noun. Psychic automatism in its pure state, by which one proposes to express—verbally, by means of the written word, or in any other manner—the actual functioning of thought. Dictation by thought, in the absence of any control exercised by reason, exempt from any aesthetic or moral concern."

Such a definition of Surrealism, although it is now considered as fragmentary, still stands because it describes a static ideology. Dada, on the other hand, being essentially movement, can aptly be portrayed only by a fluid set of concepts, and this must be done in terms of what I'd call paradoxical dialectics.

One might say that the best criterion of a Dada piece is that it escapes definition, whereas a surrealist work can always be ascribed to a particular series of identical items. Whenever we feel we have pinned down Dada to what appears to be a specific domain, within safe and recognizable boundaries, we can bet we are no longer on Dada grounds. That is, I grant you, a very unpleasant position for a scholar to find himself in, but any other would entail a misconception of the very nature of the movement. Only a fluid analysis of Dada's ingrown paradoxes, conducted in dialectical terms, can account for its impact on our civilization and concepts. Dada is the essence of contradiction: born out of Expressionism, Cubism and Futurism, it will pretend to die in the marshes of Surrealism, only to pop up again decades later in a dozen unrelated new guises. It claimed to have at last murdered Art, while giving us canvasses by Ernst, Picabia, Schwitters and Duchamp, which, for all practical purposes, vie today with oils by Rubens and Renoir for record prices and prime gallery space. Dada yearned for the end of an era and was dangerously fascinated by the attraction of vacuum and nothingness, but ended up by singing a hymn to light and life.

It is not sheer coincidence if Dada has come to acquire such an important position in the intellectual spectrum of our century. We live in a period which is itself a tissue of contradictions. Having reached an unprecedented level of technological and scientific achievement, we are witnessing a general caving-in of all rational grounds. Never have we seen so many cults, sects, tea-cup readers, gurus, UFO watchers and ESP enthusiasts. These are also the times when the principle of dialectical revolt has infiltrated modern societies, from Red China to Baader's Germany. No sooner have we uttered a considered statement than we are compelled to admit that its opposite may be just as valid.

Moreover, our epoch is beginning to experience the short-comings of what the 19th Century thought was the panacea of all economic ills: gigantic structures, dehumanized plants and factories, state-controlled bureaucracies. The trend now is to a return to private, diversified initiative. Small is beautiful. And Dada, in its spirit and its operating mode, seems to be well adapted to this new way of thinking, much more so for example than Surrealism, based on autocratic government and stringent moral rules.

For Dada has all the attributes of successful living organisms in the process of evolution. It is what we call, at our Centre du XXe Siècle in Nice, a "soft structure." It behaves like those rhizomorphous underground roots, which are strong and determined enough to proceed and expand, however slowly, but flexible enough to constantly adapt to changing environments and to circle around obstacles.

The danger for all living structures is to become lignified, ossified, woody, hard. Only then, of course, can they be clearly identified and classified: such is the case for most literary and artistic movements. But when they do, they die like coral in their petrified shells. Consciously or not, the Dada painters and poets have understood that their best chance to remain alive was to refuse to grow old. And like all adolescents in their prime, Dada will be forever a rebel with many causes. (pp. 16-27)

> *Michel Sanouillet, "Dada: A Definition," in* Dada Spectrum: The Dialectics of Revolt, *edited by Stephen C. Foster and Rudolf E. Kuenzli, The University of Iowa, 1979, pp. 15-27.*

MANIFESTOS AND COMMENTARY BY DADAISTS

Tristan Tzara

[The following is excerpted from Tzara's Seven Dada Manifestoes. The first, "Manifesto of Mr. Antipyrine," was originally a monologue spoken by a character named "Tristan Tzara" in Tzara's play La Première aventure céleste de M'Antipyrine.*]*

1. Manifesto of Mr. Antipyrine

Dada is our intensity: it sets up inconsequential bayonets the sumatran head of the german baby; Dada is life without carpet-slippers or parallels; it is for and against unity and definitely against the future; we are wise enough to know that our brains will become downy pillows that our anti-dogmatism is as exclusivist as a bureaucrat that we are not free yet shout freedom—

A harsh necessity without discipline or morality and we spit on humanity. Dada remains within the European frame of weaknesses it's shit after all but from now on we mean to shit in assorted colors and bedeck the artistic zoo with the flags of every consulate

We are circus directors whistling amid the winds of carnivals convents bawdy houses theatres realities sentiments restaurants HoHiHoHo Bang

We declare that the auto is a sentiment which has coddled us long enough in its slow abstractions in ocean liners and noises and ideas. Nevertheless we externalize facility we seek the central essence and we are happy when we can hide it; we do not want to count the windows of the marvelous élite for Dada exists for no one and we want everybody to understand this because it is the balcony of Dada, I assure you. From which you can hear the military marches and descend slicing the air like a seraph in a public bath to piss and comprehend the parable

Dada is not madness—or wisdom—or irony take a good look at me kind bourgeois Art was a game of trinkets children collected words with a tinkling on the end then they went and shouted stanzas and they put little doll's shoes on the stanza and the stanza turned into a queen to die a little and the queen turned into a wolverine and the children ran till they all turned green

Then came the great Ambassadors of sentiment and exclaimed historically in chorus

psychology psychology heehee

Science Science Science

vive la France

we are not naive

we are successive

we are exclusive

we are not simple

and we are all quite able to discuss the intelligence.

But we Dada are not of their opinion for art is not serious I assure you and if in exhibiting crime we learnedly say ventilator, it is to give you pleasure kind reader I love you so I swear I do adore you

2. Dada Manifesto 1918

The magic of a word—Dada—which has brought journalists to the gates of a world unforeseen, is of no importance to us.

To put out a manifesto you must want: ABC

to fulminate against 1, 2, 3,

to fly into a rage and sharpen your wings to conquer and disseminate little abcs and big abcs, to sign, shout, swear, to organize prose into a form of absolute and irrefutable evidence, to prove your non plus ultra and maintain that novelty resembles life just as the latest appearance of some whore proves the essence of God. His existence was previously proved by the accordion, the landscape, the wheedling word. To impose your ABC is a natural thing—hence deplorable. Everybody does it in the form of crystal-bluffmadonna, monetary system, pharmaceutical product, or a bare leg advertising the ardent sterile spring. The love of novelty is the cross of sympathy, demonstrates a naive je m'enfoutisme, it is a transitory, positive sign without a cause.

But this need itself is obsolete. In documenting art on the basis of the supreme simplicity: novelty, we are human and true for the sake of amusement, impulsive, vibrant to crucify boredom. At the crossroads of the lights, alert, attentively awaiting the years, in the forest. I write a manifesto and I want nothing, yet I say certain things, and in principle I am against manifestoes, as I am also against principles (half-pints to measure the moral value of every phrase too too convenient; approximation was invented by the impressionists). I write this manifesto to show that people can perform contrary actions together while taking one fresh gulp of air; I am against action; for continuous contradiction, for affirmation too, I am neither for nor against and I do not explain because I hate common sense.

Dada—there you have a word that leads ideas to the hunt: every bourgeois is a little dramatist, he invents all sorts of speeches instead of putting the characters suitable to the quality of his intelligence, chrysalises, on chairs, seeks causes or aims (according to the psychoanalytic method he practices) to cement his plot, a story that speaks and defines itself. Every spectator is a plotter if he tries to explain a word: (to know!) Safe in the cottony refuge of serpentine complications he manipulates his instincts. Hence the mishaps of conjugal life.

To explain: the amusement of redbellies in the mills of empty skulls.

DADA MEANS NOTHING

If you find it futile and don't want to waste your time on a word that means nothing. . . . The first thought that comes to these people is bacteriological in character: to find its etymological, or at least its historical or psychological origin. We see by the papers that the Kru Negroes call the tail of a holy cow Dada. The cube and the mother in a certain district of Italy are called: Dada. A hobby horse, a nurse both in Russian and Rumanian: Dada. Some learned journalists regard it as an art for babies, other holy jesusescallingthelittlechildren of our day, as a relapse into a dry and noisy, noisy and monotonous primitivism. Sensibility is not constructed on the basis of a word; all constructions converge on perfection which is boring, the stagnant idea of a gilded swamp, a relative human product. A work of art should not be beauty in itself, for beauty is dead; it should be neither gay nor sad, neither light nor dark to rejoice or torture the individual by serving him the cakes of sacred aureoles or the sweets of a vaulted race through the atmospheres. A work of art is never beautiful by decree, objectively and for all. Hence criticism is useless, it exists only subjectively, for each man separately, without the slightest character of universality. Does anyone think he has found a psychic base common to all mankind? The attempt of Jesus and the Bible covers with their broad benevolent wings: shit, animals, days. How can one expect to put order into the chaos that constitutes that infinite and shapeless variation: man? The principle: "love thy neighbor" is a hypocrisy. "Know thyself" is utopian but more acceptable, for it embraces wickedness. No pity. After the carnage we still retain the hope of a purified mankind. I speak only of myself since I do not wish to convince, I have no right to drag others into my river, I oblige no one to follow me and everybody practices his art in his own way, if he knows the joy that rises like arrows to the astral layers, or that other joy that goes down into the mines of corpse-flowers and fertile spasms. Stalactites: seek them everywhere, in mangers magnified by pain, eyes white as the hares of the angels.

And so Dada was born of a need for independence, of a distrust toward unity. Those who are with us preserve their freedom. We recognize no theory. We have enough cubist and futurist academies: laboratories of formal ideas. Is the aim of art to make money and cajole the nice nice bourgeois? Rhymes ring with the assonance of the currencies and the inflexion slips along the line of the belly in profile. All groups of artists have arrived at this trust company after riding their steeds on various comets. While the door remains open to the possibility of wallowing in cushions and good things to eat.

Here we cast anchor in rich ground. Here we have a right to do some proclaiming, for we have known cold shudders and awakenings. Ghosts drunk on energy, we dig the trident into unsuspecting flesh. We are a downpour of maledictions as tropically abundant as vertiginous vegetation, resin and rain are our sweat, we bleed and burn with thirst, our blood is vigor.

Cubism was born out of the simple way of looking at an object: Cézanne painted a cup 20 centimeters below his eyes, the cubists look at it from above, others complicate appearance by making a perpendicular section and arranging it conscientiously on the side. (I do not forget the creative artists and the profound laws of matter which they established once and for all.) The futurist sees the same cup in movement, a succession of objects one beside the other, and maliciously adds a few force lines. This does not prevent the canvas from being a good or bad painting suitable for the investment of intellectual capital.

The new painter creates a world, the elements of which are also its implements, a sober, definite work without argument. The new artist protests: he no longer paints (symbolic and illusionist reproduction) but creates—directly in stone, wood, iron, tin, boulders—locomotive organisms capable of being turned in all directions by the limpid wind of momentary sensation. All pictorial or plastic work is useless: let it then be a monstrosity that frightens servile minds, and not sweetening to decorate the refectories of animals in human costume, illustrating the sad fable of mankind.—

Painting is the art of making two lines geometrically established as parallel meet on a canvas before our eyes in a reality which transposes other conditions and possibilities into a world. This world is not specified or defined in the work, it belongs in its innumerable variations to the spectator. For its creator it is without cause and without theory. *Orderdisorder; egonon-ego; affirmationnegation:* the supreme radiations of an absolute art. Absolute in the purity of a cosmic, ordered chaos, eternal in the globule of a second without duration, without breath without control. I love an ancient work for its novelty. It is only contrast that connects us with the past. The writers who teach morality and discuss or improve psychological foundations have, aside from a hidden desire to make money, an absurd view of life, which they have classified, cut into sections, channelized: they insist on waving the baton as the categories dance. Their readers snicker and go on: what for?

There is a literature that does not reach the voracious mass. It is the work of creators, issued from a real necessity in the author, produced for himself. It expresses the knowledge of a supreme egoism, in which laws wither away. Every page must explode, either by profound heavy seriousness, the whirlwind, poetic frenzy, the new, the eternal, the crushing joke, enthusiasm for principles, or by the way in which it is printed. On the one hand a tottering world in flight, betrothed to the glockenspiel of hell, on the other hand: new men. Rough, bouncing, riding on hiccups. Behind them a crippled world and literary quacks with a mania for improvement.

I say unto you: there is no beginning and we do not tremble, we are not sentimental. We are a furious wind, tearing the dirty linen of clouds and prayers, preparing the great spectacle of disaster, fire, decomposition. We will put an end to mourning and replace tears by sirens screeching from one continent to another. Pavilions of intense joy and widowers with the sadness of poison. Dada is the signboard of abstraction; advertising and business are also elements of poetry.

I destroy the drawers of the brain and of social organization: spread demoralization wherever I go and cast my hand from heaven to hell, my eyes from hell to heaven, restore the fecund wheel of a universal circus to objective forces and the imagination of every individual.

Philosophy is the question: from which side shall we look at life, God, the idea or other phenomena. Everything one looks at is false. I do not consider the relative result more important than the choice between cake and cherries after dinner. The system of quickly looking at the other side of a thing in order to impose your opinion indirectly is called dialectics, in other words, haggling over the spirit of fried potatoes while dancing method around it.

If I cry out:

> Ideal, ideal, ideal,
> Knowledge, knowledge, knowledge,
> Boomboom, boomboom, boomboom,

I have given a pretty faithful version of progress, law, morality and all other fine qualities that various highly intelligent men have discussed in so many books, only to conclude that after all everyone dances to his own personal boomboom, and that the writer is entitled to his boomboom: the satisfaction of pathological curiosity; a private bell for inexplicable needs; a bath; pecuniary difficulties; a stomach with repercussions in life; the authority of the mystic wand formulated as the bouquet of a phantom orchestra made up of silent fiddle bows greased with philtres made of chicken manure. With the blue eye-glasses of an angel they have excavated the inner life for a dime's worth of unanimous gratitude. If all of them are right and if all pills are Pink Pills, let us try for once not to be right. Some people think they can explain rationally, by thought, what

they think. But that is extremely relative. Psychoanalysis is a dangerous disease, it puts to sleep the anti-objective impulses of man and systematizes the bourgeoisie. There is no ultimate Truth. The dialectic is an amusing mechanism which guides us / in a banal kind of way / to the opinions we had in the first place. Does anyone think that, by a minute refinement of logic, he has demonstrated the truth and established the correctness of these opinions? Logic imprisoned by the senses is an organic disease. To this element philosophers always like to add: the power of observation. But actually this magnificent quality of the mind is the proof of its impotence. We observe, we regard from one or more points of view, we choose them among the millions that exist. Experience is also a product of chance and individual faculties. Science disgusts me as soon as it becomes a speculative system, loses its character of utility—that is so useless but is at least individual. I detest greasy objectivity, and harmony, the science that finds everything in order. Carry on, my children, humanity . . . Science says we are the servants of nature: everything is in order, make love and bash your brains in. Carry on, my children, humanity, kind bourgeois and journalist virgins . . . I am against systems, the most acceptable system is on principle to have none. To complete oneself, to perfect oneself in one's own littleness, to fill the vessel with one's individuality, to have the courage to fight for and against thought, the mystery of bread, the sudden burst of an infernal propeller into economic lilies:

DADAIST SPONTANEITY

I call *je m'enfoutisme* the kind of like in which everyone retains his own conditions, though respecting other individualisms, except when the need arises to defend oneself, in which the two-step becomes national anthem, curiosity shop, a radio transmitting Bach figures, electric signs and posters for whorehouses, an organ broadcasting carnations for God, all this together physically replacing photography and the universal catechism.

ACTIVE SIMPLICITY.

Inability to distinguish between degrees of clarity: to lick the penumbra and float in the big mouth filled with honey and excrement. Measured by the scale of eternity, all activity is vain—(if we allow thought to engage in an adventure the result of which would be infinitely grotesque and add significantly to our knowledge of human impotence). But supposing life to be a poor farce, without aim or initial parturition, and because we think it our duty to extricate ourselves as fresh and clean as washed chrysanthemums, we have proclaimed as the sole basis for agreement: art. It is not as important as we, mercenaries of the spirit, have been proclaiming for centuries. Art afflicts no one and those who manage to take an interest in it will harvest caresses and a fine opportunity to populate the country with their conversation. Art is a private affair, the artist produces it for himself; an intelligible work is the product of a journalist, and because at this moment it strikes my fancy to combine this monstrosity with oil paints: a paper tube simulating the metal that is automatically pressed and poured hatred cowardice villainy. The artist, the poet rejoice at the venom of the masses condensed into a section chief of this industry, he is happy to be insulted: it is a proof of his immutability. When a writer or artist is praised by the newspapers, it is proof of the intelligibility of his work: wretched lining of a coat for public use; tatters covering brutality, piss contributing to the warmth of an animal brooding vile instincts. Flabby, insipid flesh reproducing with the help of typographical microbes.

We have thrown out the cry-baby in us. Any infiltration of this kind is candied diarrhea. To encourage this act is to digest it. What we need is works that are strong straight precise and forever beyond understanding. Logic is a complication. Logic is always wrong. It draws the threads of notions, words, in their formal exterior, toward illusory ends and centers. Its chains kill, it is an enormous centipede stifling independence. Married to logic, art would live in incest, swallowing, engulfing its own tail, still part of its own body, fornicating within itself, and passion would become a nightmare tarred with protestantism, a monument, a heap of ponderous gray entrails. But the suppleness, enthusiasm, even the joy of injustice, this little truth which we practise innocently and which makes us beautiful: we are subtle and our fingers are malleable and slippery as the branches of that sinuous, almost liquid plant; it defines our soul, say the cynics. That too is a point of view; but all flowers are not sacred, fortunately, and the divine thing in us is our call to anti-human action. I am speaking of a paper flower for the buttonholes of the gen-

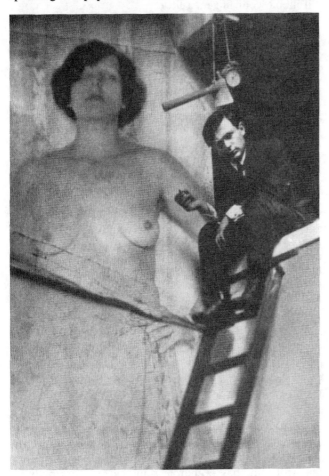

Photograph of Tristan Tzara by Man Ray, 1921.

tlemen who frequent the ball of masked life, the kitchen of grace, white cousins lithe or fat. They traffic with whatever we have selected. The contradiction and unity of poles in a single toss can be the truth. If one absolutely insists on uttering this platitude, the appendix of a libidinous, malodorous morality. Morality creates atrophy like every plague produced by intelligence. The control of morality and logic has inflicted us with impassivity in the presence of policemen—who are the cause of slavery, putrid rats infecting the bowels of the bourgeoisie which have infected the only luminous clean corridors of glass that remained open to artists.

Let each man proclaim: there is a great negative work of destruction to be accomplished. We must sweep and clean. Affirm the cleanliness of the individual after the state of madness, aggressive complete madness of a world abandoned to the hands of bandits, who rend one another and destroy the centuries. Without aim or design, without organization: indomitable madness, decomposition. Those who are strong in words or force will survive, for they are quick in defense, the agility of limbs and sentiments flames on their faceted flanks.

Morality has determined charity and pity, two balls of fat that have grown like elephants, like planets, and are called good. There is nothing good about them. Goodness is lucid, clear and decided, pitiless toward compromise and politics. Morality is an injection of chocolate into the veins of all men. This task is not ordered by a supernatural force but by the trust of idea brokers and grasping academicians. Sentimentality: at the sight of a group of men quarreling and bored, they invented the calendar and the medicament wisdom. With a sticking of labels the battle of the philosophers was set off (mercantilism, scales, meticulous and petty measures) and for the second time it was understood that pity is a sentiment like diarrhea in relation to the disgust that destroys health, a foul attempt by carrion corpses to compromise the sun. I proclaim the opposition of all cosmic faculties to this gonorrhea of a putrid sun issued from the factories of philosophical thought, I proclaim bitter struggle with all the weapons of

DADAIST DISGUST

Every product of disgust capable of becoming a negation of the family is Dada; a protest with the fists of its whole being engaged in destructive action: *Dada; knowledge of all the means rejected up until now by the shamefaced sex of comfortable compromise and good manners: Dada; abolition of logic, which is the dance of those impotent to create: Dada; of every social hierarchy and equation set up for the sake of values by our valets: Dada; every object, all objects, sentiments, obscurities, apparitions and the precise clash of parallel lines are weapons for the fight: Dada; abolition of memory: Dada; abolition of archaeology: Dada: abolition of prophets: Dada; abolition of the future: Dada; absolute and unquestionable faith in every god that is the immediate product of spontaneity:* Dada; elegant and unprejudiced leap from a harmony to the other sphere; trajectory of a word tossed like a screeching phonograph record; to respect all individuals in their folly of the moment: whether it be serious, fearful, timid, ardent, vigorous, determined, enthusiastic; to divest one's church of every useless cumbersome accessory; to spit out disagreeable or amorous ideas like a luminous waterfall, or coddle them—with the extreme satisfaction that it doesn't matter in the least—with the same intensity in the thicket of one's soul—pure of insects for blood well-born, and gilded with bodies of archangels. Freedom: Dada Dada Dada, a roaring of tense colors, and interlacing of opposites and of all contradictions, grotesques, inconsistencies:

LIFE

3. Proclamation without Pretension

Art is going to sleep for a new world to be born
"ART"—parrot word—replaced by DADA,
PLESIOSAURUS, or handkerchief

The talent THAT CAN BE LEARNED makes the poet a druggist TODAY the criticism
of balances no longer challenges with resemblances

Hypertrophic painters hyperaes-
theticized and hypnotized by the hyacinths
of the hypocritical-looking muezzins

CONSOLIDATE THE HARVEST OF EX-
ACT CALCULATIONS

Hypodrome of immortal guarantees: there is
no such thing as importance there is no transparence
or appearance

MUSICIANS SMASH YOUR INSTRUMENTS
BLIND MEN take the stage

THE SYRINGE is only for my understanding. I write because it is
natural exactly the way I piss the way I'm sick

ART NEEDS AN OPERATION

Art is a PRETENSION warmed by the
TIMIDITY of the urinary basin, the *hysteria* born
in *THE STUDIO*

We are in search of
the force that is direct pure sober
UNIQUE we are in search of NOTHING
we affirm the VITALITY of every IN-
STANT

the anti-philosophy of *spontaneous* acrobatics

At this moment I hate the man who whispers
before the intermission—eau de cologne—
sour theatre. THE JOYOUS WIND

If each man says the opposite it is because he is right

Get ready for the action of the geyser of our blood
—submarine formation of transchromatic aeroplanes, cellular metals numbered in
the flight of images

above the rules of the
and its control

BEAUTIFUL

It is not for the sawed-off imps
who still worship their navel

4. Manifesto of mr. aa the anti-philosopher

without searching for I adore you
who is a french boxer
or irregular maritime values like the depression of Dada
in the blood of the
bicephalous
I slip between death and the vague phosphates
which scratch a little the common brain of the dadaist
poets
luckily
for
gold
undermines
prices and the high cost of living have decided me to give
up D's
it is not true that the fake dadas have snatched them away
from me for
repayment will begin on
that is something to cry about the nothing that calls itself
nothing
and i have swept away sickness in the customs house
i tortoise shell and umbrella of the brain rented out from
noon to 2 p.m.
superstitious individual releasing the wheels
of the spermatozoidal ballet that you will encounter in
dress rehearsal in the
hearts of all suspicious characters
I'll nibble your fingers a little
I'll buy you a re-subscription to love made of celluloid that
squeaks like metal doors
and you are idiots
I shall return some day like your urine reviving you to the
joy of living the midwife wind
and i'll set up a boarding school for pimps and poets
and i'll come back again to begin all over
and you are all idiots
and the self-kleptomaniac's key works only with twilight
oil
on every knot of every machine there is the noise of a newborn babe
and we are all idiots
and highly suspicious with a new form of intelligence and
a new logic of our own which is not Dada at all
and you are letting yourself be carried away by Aaism
and you are all idiots
cataplasms
made of the alcohol of purified sleep
bandages
and idiot
virgins
tristan tzara
Take a good look at me!
I am an idiot, I am a clown, I am a faker.
Take a good look at me!
I am ugly, my face has no expression, I am little.
I am like all of you!

But ask yourselves, before looking at me, if the iris by which you send out arrows of liquid sentiment, is not fly shit, if the eyes of your belly are not sections of tumors that will some day peer from some part of your body in the form of a gonorrheal discharge.

You see with your navel—why do you hide from it the absurd spectacle that we present? And farther down, sex organs of women, with teeth, all-swallowing—the poetry of eternity, love, pure love of course—rare steaks and oil painting. All those who look and understand, easily fit in between poetry and love, between the beefsteak and the painting. They will be digested. They will be digested.

I was recently accused of stealing some furs. Probably because I was still thought to be among the poets. Among those poets who satisfy their legitimate need for cold onanism with warm furs: *H o h o,* I know other pleasures, equally platonic. Call your family on the telephone and piss in the hole reserved for musical gastronomic and sacred stupidities.

DADA proposes 2 solutions:
NO MORE LOOKS!
NO MORE WORDS!
Stop looking!
Stop talking!

For I, chameleon transformation infiltration with convenient attitudes—multi-colored opinions for every occasion dimension and price—I do the opposite of what I suggest to others.
I've forgotten something:
where? why? how?
in other words:

ventilator of cold examples will serve as a cavalcade to the fragile snake and i never had the pleasure of seeing you my dear rigid the ear will emerge of its own accord from the envelope like all marine confections and the products of the firm of Aa & Co. chewing gum for instance and dogs have blue eyes, I drink camomile tea, they drink wind, Dada introduces new points of view, nowadays people sit at the corners of tables, in attitudes sliding a little to left and right, that's why I'm angry with Dada, wherever you go insist on the abolition of D's, eat Aa, rub yourself down with Aa toothpaste, buy your clothes from Aa. Aa is a handkerchief and a sex organ wiping its nose, a rapid noiseless—rubber-tired—collapse, needs no manifestoes, or address books, gives a 25% discount buy your clothes from Aa he has blue eyes.

mr. aa the anti-philosopher sends us this manifesto

Hurrah for the undertakers of combination!
Every act is a cerebral revolver shot—the insignificant gesture the decisive movement are attacks—(I open the fan of knock-outs to distill the air that separates us)—and with words set down on paper I enter, solemnly, into myself.
I plant my sixty fingers in the hair of notions and brutally shake the drapery, the teeth, the bolts of the joints.
I close, I open, I spit. Take care! This is the time to tell you that I lied. If there is a system in the lack of system—that of my proportions—I never apply it.
In other words I lie. I lie when I apply it, I lie when I don't apply it, I lie when I write that I'm lying, for I am not lying for I have seen my father's mirror—chosen among the advantages of vaccara—from city to city—for myself has never been myself—for the saxophone wears the murder of the visceral chauffeur like a rose—it is made of sexual

copper and tip sheets. Thus drummed the corn, the fire alarm and the pellagra down where the matches grow.

Extermination. Yes, of course.
But it doesn't exist. Myself: mixture kitchen theatre.
Hurrah for the stretcher bearers armed with ecstatic convocations! The lie is ecstasy—what transcends the duration of a second—there is nothing that transcends it. Idiots brood the century—idiots start some centuries all over again—idiots belong to the same club for ten years—idiots play see-saw on the clockface for the space of a year—I (idiot) leave after five minutes.
The pretension of the blood to pour through my body and my factitiousness the random color of the first woman I touched with my eyes in these tentacular times. The bitterest banditry is to complete a sentence of thought. Gramophone banditry little anti-human mirage that I like in myself because I think it absurd and insulting. But the bankers of language will always get their little percentage on the discussion. The presence of one boxer (at least) is indispensable for the bout—the members of a gang of dadaist assassins have signed a contract covering self-protection for operations of this order. Their number was very small—since the presence of one singer (for the duet), of one signatory (at least) for the receipt, of one eye (at least) for sight—was absolutely indispensable.

Put the photographic plate of the face into the acid bath. The disturbances that sensitized it will become visible and will amaze you.

Give yourself a poke in the nose and drop dead.
dada

5. manifesto on feeble love and bitter love

I
preamble = sardanapalus
one = valise
woman = women
pants = water
if = mustache
2 = three
cane = perhaps
after = decipher
irritating = emerald
vice = vise
october = periscope
nerve =

or all this together in any arrangement at all whether savorous soapy brusque or definitive—picked at random—is alive.

So it is that above the vigilant mind of the clergyman set up at every animal vegetable imaginable or organic street corner, everything is equal to everything is without equal. Even if I didn't believe it, it is the truth just because I have set it down on paper—

because it is a lie that I have PINNED DOWN as you pin a butterfly to your hat. The lie moves about greeting Mr. Opportune and Mr. Convenient: I stop it, it becomes truth.

As a result Dada undertakes police duty with pedals and

muted morality. Everybody (at some time or other) was complete in mind and body. Repeat this 30 times. I consider myself very charming

Tristan TZARA

II
A manifesto is a communication addressed to the whole world, in which there is no other pretension than the discovery of a means of curing instantly political, astronomical, artistic, parliamentary agronomic and literary syphilis. It can be gentle, good-natured, it is always right, it is strong, vigorous and logical.
A propos logic, I consider myself very charming.

Tristan TZARA
(pp. 75-86)

How I became
charming delightful
and delicious

I sleep very late. I commit suicide 65%. My life is very cheap, for me it is only 30% of life. My life contains 30% of life. It lacks arms strings and a few buttons. 5% is consecrated to a state of semi-lucid stupor accompanied by anemic râles. This 5% is called Dada. So you see that life is cheap. Death is a little more expensive. But life is charming and death is charming too.

A few days ago I attended a gathering of imbeciles. There were lots of people. Everybody was charming. Tristan Tzara, a small, idiotic and insignificant individual, delivered a lecture on the art of becoming charming. And incidentally, he was charming. And witty. Isn't that delicious? Incidentally, everybody is delicious. 9 below zero. Isn't that charming? No, it's not charming. God can't make the grade. He isn't even in the phone book. But he's charming just the same. Ambassadors, poets, counts, princes, musicians, journalists, actors, writers, diplomats, directors, dressmakers, socialists, princesses and baronesses—all charming. All of you are charming, utterly subtle, witty, and delicious. Tristan Tzara says to you: he would be quite willing to do something else, but he prefers to remain an idiot, a clown and a faker.

Be sincere for an instant: Is what I have just told you charming or idiotic? There are people (journalists, lawyers, dilettantes, philosophers) who even regard the other forms—business, marriages, visits, wars, various congresses, joint stock companies, politics, accidents, dance halls, economic crises, emotional crises—as variations of dada. Since I am not an imperialist, I do not share in their opinion—I prefer to believe that dada is only a divinity of a secondary order, which must simply be placed beside the other forms of the new mechanism for interregnum religions.
Is simplicity simple or dada?
I consider myself quite charming

Tristan TZARA

Colonial syllogism
No one can escape from destiny
No one can escape from DADA

<hr>

Only DADA can enable you to escape from destiny.

<hr>

You owe me: 943.50 francs.
No more drunkards!
No more aeroplanes!
No more vigor!
No more urinary passages!
No more enigmas!

(pp. 97-8)

Tristan Tzara, "Seven Dada Manifestoes," in The Dada Painters and Poets: An Anthology *by Arp and others, edited by Robert Motherwell, George Wittenborn, Inc., 1951, pp. 74-98.*

Marcel Duchamp on Dada:

[*George Heard Hamilton*]: *You said once to me, some years ago, that the Dada spirit had been operating in New York—with you, for instance, and with Man Ray—before Dada was named as a movement?*

[Marcel Duchamp]: Oh yes. It was in the air, as many of these things are, and we certainly had the same spirit as that in Zurich, and started under the same name. They invented a name and of course the name was a good sort of flag around which all these ideas crystallised and that But even before the war there was a Dada spirit. It has always existed. Rabelais is in essence a Dada.

[*Hamilton*]: *Would you consider that Dada is more than just a criticism of art?*

[Duchamp]: It is—much more. It has many more intentions. It is the nonconformist spirit which has existed in every century, every period since man was man. It is just that this time round they found a name for it.

Marcel Duchamp, in an interview originally broadcast on BBC, November 1959, and later published in The Art Newspaper, *February 1992.*

André Breton

[*The following are Breton's "Two Dada Manifestos."*]

I

The historical anecdote is of secondary importance. It is impossible to know where and when DADA was born. This name which one of us was pleased to give it has the advantage of being perfectly equivocal.

Cubism was a school of painting, futurism a political movement: DADA is a state of mind. To oppose one to the other reveals ignorance or bad faith.

Free-thinking in religion has no resemblance to a church. DADA is artistic free-thinking.

As long as the schools go in for prayers in the form of explanation of texts and walks in museums, we shall cry despotism and try to disrupt the ceremony.

DADA gives itself to nothing, neither to love nor to work.

It is inadmissible that a man should leave any trace of his passage on earth.

DADA, recognizing only instinct, condemns explanation *a priori*. According to DADA, we must retain no control over ourselves. We must cease to consider these dogmas: morality and taste.

II

We read the newspapers like other mortals. Without wishing to make anyone unhappy, we feel entitled to say that the word DADA lends itself readily to puns. To tell the truth, that is in part why we have adopted it. We are incapable of treating seriously any subject whatsoever, let alone this subject: ourselves. Everything we write about DADA is therefore for our pleasure. There is no petty news item for which we would not give the whole of art criticism. Finally, the wartime press did not prevent us from regarding Marshal Foch as a faker and President Wilson as an idiot.

We ask nothing better than to be judged by appearances. It is rumored everywhere that I wear spectacles. If I told you why, you'd never believe me. It is in remembrance of a grammar example: "Noses were made to hold up spectacles; accordingly, I have spectacles." What's that you say? Ah, yes! That doesn't make us any younger.

Pierre is a man. But there is no DADA truth. One need only utter a statement for the opposite statement to become DADA. I have seen Tristan Tzara without words to ask for a box of cigarettes in a tobacco store. I don't know what was the matter with him. I can still hear Philippe Soupault asking insistently for live birds in paint stores. Perhaps I myself am at this instant dreaming.

A red host is after all as good as a white host. DADA doesn't promise to make you go to heaven. It would be absurd, *a priori*, to expect a DADA masterpiece in the fields of literature and painting. Nor, of course, do we believe in the possibility of any social betterment, even though we have conservatism above all things and declare ourselves the partisans of any revolution whatsoever. "Peace at any price" is the slogan of DADA in time of war, while in time of peace the slogan of DADA is: "War at any price."

The contradiction is still only an appearance, and doubtless of the most flattering sort. I speak and I have nothing to say. I find not the slightest ambition in myself: and yet it seems to you that I am animated: how is it possible that the idea that my right flank is the shadow of my left flank does not make me utterly incapable of moving? In the most general sense of the word we pass for poets because we attack language which is the worst of conventions. One may very well know the word Hello and say Goodby to the woman one meets after a year's absence.

In conclusion, I wish only to take into account the objections of a pragmatic order. DADA attacks you with your own idea. If we reduce you to maintaining that it is more advantageous to believe than not to believe what is taught by all religions of beauty, love, truth and justice, it is because you are not afraid to put yourself at the mercy of DADA by accepting an encounter with us on the terrain that we have chosen, which is doubt. (pp. 203-04)

André Breton, "Two Dada Manifestoes," in The Dada Painters and Poets: An Anthology *by Arp and others, edited by Robert Motherwell, George Wittenborn, Inc., 1951, pp. 203-04.*

André Breton

[*In the following essay, Breton attacks Tzara and expresses his dissatisfaction with Dadaism.*]

My friends Philippe Soupault and Paul Eluard will not contradict me if I say that we have never regarded "Dada" as anything but a rough image of a state of mind that it by no means helped to create. If, like me, they come to reject its label and to note the abuse of which they are the victims, perhaps this initial principle will be saved. Meanwhile they will pardon me if, in order to avoid any misunderstanding, I inform the readers of *Commoedia* that M. Tzara had nothing to do with the invention of the word "Dada," as is shown by the letters of Schad and Huelsenbeck, his companions in Zurich during the war, which I am prepared to publish, and that he probably had very little to do with the writing of the *Dada Manifesto 1918* which was the basis of the reception and credit we accorded him.

The paternity of this manifesto is in any case, formally claimed, by Max Serner (sic), doctor of philosophy, who lives in Geneva and whose manifestos written in German before 1918 have not been translated into French. Moreover it is known that the conclusions formulated by Francis Picabia and Marcel Duchamp, even before the war, plus those formulated by Jacques Vaché in 1917, would have been sufficient to guide us without the manifesto. Up to now, it has seemed distasteful to me to denounce the bad faith of M. Tzara and I have allowed him to go on using with impunity the papers of those whom he robbed. But now that he has decided to exploit this last opportunity to be talked about, by wrongfully attacking one of the most disinterested undertakings ever put under way, I am not reluctant to silence him [Breton is referring to the International Congress For the Determination of Directives and the Defense of the Modern Spirit, which led to the demise of Dadaism and the Formation of Surrealism under the leadership of Breton].

Dada, very fortunately, is no longer an issue and its funeral, about May 1921, caused no rioting. The cortège, not very numerous, took the same road as the followers of cubism and futurism, drowned in effigy in the Seine by the students of the Beaux-Arts. Although Dada had, as they say, its hour of fame, it left few regrets: in the long run its omnipotence and its tyranny had made it intolerable.

Nevertheless I noted at that time not without bitterness that several of those who had given to it, of those in general who had given the least, were reduced to misery. The others were not long in rallying to the powerful words of Francis Picabia, inspired, as we know, solely by his love of life and horror of all corruption. I do not mean to say that Picabia was thinking of reconstituting our unity around himself:

> It is hard to imagine
> How stupid and tranquil people are made by
>   success

and he is more inclined than anyone I can think of to dispense with it. But, although there is no question of again substituting a group for individuals (M. Tzara has such lovely ideas!), Louis Aragon, Pierre de Massot, Jacques Rigaut, Roger Vitrac and myself can no longer remain insensitive to this marvelous detachment from all things, of which Picabia has set us an example and which we are glad to attest here.

For my part, I note that this attitude is not new. If I abstained last year from taking part in the demonstrations organized by Dada at the Galerie Montaigne, it is because already this type of activity had ceased to appeal to me, that I saw in it a means of attaining my twenty-sixth, my thirtieth birthday without striking a blow and therefore decided to shun everything that wears the mask of comfort. In an article of that period, which was not published and is known to few persons, I deplored the stereotyped character our gestures were assuming, and wrote as follows: "After all there is more at stake than our carefree existence and our good humor of the moment. For my part, I never aspire to amuse myself. It seems to me that the sanction of a series of utterly futile 'dada' acts is in danger of gravely compromising an attempt at liberation to which I remain strongly attached. Ideas which may be counted among the best, are at the mercy of their too hasty vulgarization."

Even though our epoch has not achieved a high degree of concentration, shall we always consent to pursue mere whims? "The spirit," we have been told, "is not so independent as not to be upset by the slightest hubbub that occurs around it." What future shall we predict for the spirit, if it maintains this hubbub itself?

Far be it from me, even today, to set myself up as a judge. "The essence and the formula" will perhaps always evade me, but, and this cannot be repeated too often, it is the search for them that matters and nothing else. Hence this great void that we are obliged to create within ourselves. Without evincing an extreme taste for the pathetic, I am willing to do without almost everything. I do not wish to slip on the floor of sentimentality. There is, strictly speaking, no such thing as error: at the most one might speak of a bad bet; and those who read me are free to think that the game isn't worth the candle. For my part, I shall try, once again, to join the fight, as far forward as possible, although I do not, like Francis Picabia: "One must be a nomad, pass through ideas as one passes through countries and cities," make a rule of hygiene or a duty out of it. Even should all ideas be of a nature to disappoint us, I propose none the less to devote my life to them. (pp. 204-06)

> *André Breton, "After Dada," in* The Dada
> Painters and Poets: An Anthology *by Arp and
> others, edited by Robert Motherwell, George
> Wittenborn, Inc., 1951, pp. 204-06.*

Richard Huelsenbeck

[The following "Dada Manifesto" was written in 1949 for inclusion in Robert Motherwell's book The Dada Painters and Poets: An Anthology.]

The signers of this manifesto are well aware that the recent venomous attacks on modern art are no accident.

The violence of these attacks stands in direct proportion to the worldwide growth of the totalitarian idea, which makes no secret to its hostility to the spiritual in art or its desire to debase art to the level of slick illustration.

The signers of this manifesto are not political thinkers; but in the matter of art they believe they have something significant to say because of a particular experience that made a lasting impression on them. The experience—Dadaism—occurred many years ago, and it is still too soon to foresee all its possible reverberations.

Dadaism was founded in Zurich in 1916 (see the note at the end of this manifesto). As an active movement it has long since gone the way of all things. Its principles, however, are still alive, and have demonstrated their vitality, although many of the founders, charter members and original supporters are dead.

This strange, surprising vitality has convinced the signers of this manifesto that the experience of Dadaism and its innermost creative principle endowed them (and others) with a special insight into the situation of modern art.

And because the creative principle in Dadaism has survived, we are at last in a position to pass fair judgment on Dadaism itself.

The more we contemplate, the more evident it becomes that the creative principle developed in Dadaism is identical with the principle of modern art. Dadaism and modern art are one in their essential presuppositions; consequently the misunderstandings that arise in connection with modern art are identical with the misunderstandings that have pursued Dadaism since its founding in 1916.

The signers of this manifesto believe, therefore, that if we can dispel the widespread misapprehensions about Dadaism, we shall have rendered an appreciable service to modern art in its struggle against popularization and sentimentalization. It is difficult to sum up the innumerable expressions of hostility to Dadaism in a few words. Nevertheless, at the risk of one more misunderstanding, we shall attempt a brief formulation; the misunderstanding from which Dadaism suffered is a chronic disease that still poisons the world. In its essence it can be defined as the inability of a rationalized epoch and of rationalized men to see the positive side of an irrational movement.

Over and over again, the drumming, shouting and dancing, the striving to *épater le bourgeois,* have been represented as the chief characteristics of Dadaism. The riots provoked by Dadaism in Berlin and Paris, the revolutionary atmosphere surrounding the movement, its wholesale attacks on everything, led critics to believe that its sole aim was to destroy all art and all the blessings of culture. The early Dada manifestoes, in which nonsense was mixed with earnestness, seemed to justify this negative attitude.

In the considered opinion of the signers of this manifesto, Dada had both destructive and constructive sides. The destructive aspect is obvious and requires no further description; the constructive aspect is not so easily discernible. It lies hidden beneath the manifest destructivism and must be elucidated in some detail if it is to be understood.

To forestall any possible misunderstanding, the signers of this manifesto wish to state that this document is not the confession of a superannuated criminal who has espoused the principles of the YMCA. Nor should it be identified with the protestations of a lady of easy virtue who takes up the Victorian way of life at the end of her career. This manifesto is rather a free declaration of men who have recognized the need for a constructive movement and discovered to their joy that they have never been far removed from such a movement. The worst that could be said is that the world has indeed come to a sorry pass if even the Dadaists feel it necessary to stress the positive and constructive aspect of their nature and principles.

The positive element in Dadaism is not a mere accident deriving from the structure of the mind (the positive always turns up when the negative goes out the door); on the contrary, Dadaism was positive and pursued positive aims from the very beginning of its existence. If this positive element has always been disregarded, any innate nastiness in Dadaism is less to blame than the generally negative, critical and cynical attitude of our time, which drives people to project their own vileness into persons, things and opinions around them. In other words, we believe that the neurotic conflict of our time, that manifests itself in a generally negative, unspiritual, and brutal attitude, discovered a whipping boy in Dadaism.

But let us consider the credit side of Dadaism. In this credit column stands first of all the uncontested fact that Dadaism became the father and grandfather of many artistic and philosophical movements; we can go so far as to say that Dadaism provided us with a precept for life, by expressing the principle that you must attain to the Ultima Thule of self-renunciation before you can find the way back to yourself. The Surrealist movement, founded by André Breton (whose writings should be reread from this angle), is a scion of Dadaism. Surrealism undertook to realize the spiritual aspiration of Dadaism through an artistic direction; it strove for the magical reality which we Dadaists first disclosed in our constructions, collages, writings, and in the dances at the Cabaret Voltaire. As the philosophical consequences of Dadaism represented a positive reaction to a long series of negativistic, neurotic and aggressive manifestations, Dada was and is the termination and rejection of everything that had been said by Rimbaud, Strindberg, Ibsen, Nietzsche and others. Unconsciously or semi-consciously, Dadaism anticipated many formulations that are now current—Sartre's Existentialism for example. It is no accident that Sartre calls himself "the Nouveau Dada." But we believe that there is an essential difference between Dadaism and Existentialism. Existentialism is essentially negative, whereas Dada lived its extreme despair, expressed it in art, and in this "participation créatrice" found a therapy for itself.

The work of the Dadaists asks those men who have con-

quered the negative within themselves to band together for constructive deeds. The work of the Dadaists, we firmly believe, makes it clear that the goal of Dadaism was human development, towards spirituality and freedom. This is particularly expressed in the Dadaist rejection of totalitarian solutions to the present conflicts of mankind. The signers of this manifesto wish here to repeat that they dissociate themselves radically and permanently from all those who either seek such solutions or who support a party or society that stands for such solutions. For Dadaists, the State cannot be the ruler of man; it is man who must rule the State.

Adolf Hitler's rage against the Dadaists proves that they were on the right path. He mentions them in *Mein Kampf.* The fact that in Russia art is compelled to dedicate itself to patriotic illustration clearly shows on what side Dadaism stood and where modern art must stand. Consciously or unconsciously, the adversaries of modern art, no less than the enemies of Dadaism, are totalitarian types. On the positive side of Dadaism stands its courage; it is as famed for the baldness of its formulations as for the force of its convictions.

The force and integrity of the Dadaist position make it easy for the signers of this manifesto to say once again that they condemn the use of art as an instrument of propaganda. Art is spiritual and the first characteristic of the spiritual is freedom. Creative expression is an expression of man's most authentic personality, identical with the divine act of creation. It is therefore a blasphemy to make art dependent on the State or to debase it by compelling it to illustrate misunderstood political theories. Art is spirit and as such can accept no master, neither the aristocrat nor the proletarian. It can bow to one master alone, and that master is the great spirit of the universe.

Yet precisely because art is spirit, it has the mission to expose the unspiritual; this it does in its own symbolic language. In this symbolic language, in its close relationship to the archetypes of mankind, in the representation of the creative tension between forms and colors, in the restoration of the original feeling of space and direction in the aesthetic and ethical sense, Dadaists see the essence of all artistic activity.

For Dadaists, art has a lofty, solemn mission, and nothing must be allowed to divert it from its eternal and essential aims. The signers of this manifesto therefore repeat that the value-giving function of art is the purpose and end of all human activity, and that this mission must be subordinated neither to politics, to social considerations, to friendship, nor to death. Returning to the positive in Dadaism, it is perhaps most evident of all in the lives of the individual Dadaists since the closing of the Café Voltaire.

Hugo Ball and Emmy Hennings became mystics soon after their departure from Zurich. Ball wrote his famous book: *Die Flucht aus der Zeit (Flight from Time)* (1927). It was a work far in advance of its time, and even at that early date Ball rejected all totalitarian solutions. In *Das Byzantinische Christentum (Byzantine Christianity)*, Ball demanded a return to a spiritual attitude, and attacked materialism, machine worship, and overestimation of mass organization. Ball came out for spiritual individualism; this alone he believed could lead to new values, restore peace, and create a new world. Emmy Hennings, who first influenced Ball in many ways, wrote magnificent poems and books, demonstrating her great love for the spiritual in man and art.

Hans Arp and Sophie Taeuber agreed from the very beginning of the Dada movement that art had to be freed from illustration and imitation and carried back to its spiritual sources. They worked on constructions, collages and reliefs which today bear witness to a brilliant anticipation of modern directions in art. Eggeling, van Doesburg and Richter—to mention only a few—revealed in their works not only their joy in Dadaism, but also an ability to say positive, constructive, direction-giving things. In his paintings and objects the legendary Marcel Duchamp, who loved and championed Dadaism from the first, showed more than anyone else in our time the influence of Dada's turn from the cynical to the positive.

The development of Max Ernst, who was one of the first Dadaists and who later, along with Breton and Tzara, founded Surrealism, clearly reveals the constructive side of Dadaism.

In his *Phantastische Gebete* (*Fantastic Prayers*), in his writings on Dadaism and in other verse and prose works, Richard Huelsenbeck (now Charles R. Hulbeck) fought for the spiritual concept and the establishment of a new world of values in opposition to the old chaos and disintegration. Like Ball, he found in certain psychoanalytical works an intimate *rapport* with his own ideas and with the requirements resulting from the demise of Dadaism. With Ball, Carl Jung and others, he stood for the restoration of man by the intellect, against the disintegration of friendship, human relations and society.

The signers of this *Dada Manifesto 1949* wish (in the firm belief that it is the last of all Dada manifestoes) to stress once more their belief that the problem of Dadaism is identical not only with the problem of modern art, but with the problem of mankind in our time and perhaps in all times. They further believe that the small group of Dadaists in the Cabaret Voltaire in Zurich in 1916 were, more than any other men of our day, seized with despair at the evil of the times and overcame this despair, theoretically as well as practically, by setting up certain principles relevant both to the situation of art and the situation of the human community. Previous Dada manifestoes have been documents of accusation. This last Dada manifesto is a document of transcendence.

Note

For reasons of historical accuracy, the undersigned consider it necessary to state that Dadaism was not founded by Tristan Tzara at the Cabaret Voltaire in Zurich. It is self-evident that Dadaism could not be invented by one man, and that all assertions to this effect are therefore false. Dadaism was a child of chance. The undersigned hereby state that the "discovery" of Dadaism was truthfully and correctly described by Richard Huelsenbeck in his book *En avant Dada* (published by Steegemann, Hanover, Germany, in 1920) and published in English in volume 8 of "The Documents of Modern Art": The Dada Painters and Poets. (pp. 390-94)

Richard Huelsenbeck, "Dada Manifesto, 1949," in The Dada Painters and Poets: An Anthology *by Arp and others, edited by Robert Motherwell, George Wittenborn, Inc., 1951, pp. 390-94.*

Tristan Tzara

[*The following essay, "An Introduction to Dada," was written in 1948 for inclusion in Robert Motherwell's book* The Dada Painters and Poets: An Anthology.]

From the point of view of poetry, or of art in general, the influence of Dada on the modern sensibility consisted in the formulation of a *human constant* which it distilled and brought to light.

It was in the same way that Romanticism, by defining an existing *state of mind,* was enabled, not only to delimit a permanent aspect of the individual sensibility but to broaden this state of mind so as to constitute a source of intellectual values which in certain epochs was to play an important role in the interpretation of social phenomena. It is too soon to estimate the historic importance of Dada, but even now it can be stated that by supplying the germ of surrealism it created, in the realm of poetry and art, a new intellectual climate which in some measure still survives.

Two traditions, one ideologically (the French Revolution, the Commune, etc.) the other poetically revolutionary (Baudelaire, Nerval, Rimbaud, Lautréamont, etc.), reacted simultaneously on the dadaists and the surrealists. An inner conciliation of these two currents was a constant preoccupation with us, yet even today this endeavor cannot be said to have lost its meaning and urgency.

When I say "we," I have primarily in mind that generation which, during the war of 1914-1918, suffered in the very flesh of its pure adolescence suddenly exposed to life, at seeing the truth ridiculed, clothed in the cast-off garments of vanity or base class interest. This war was not our war; to us it was a war of false emotions and feeble justifications. Such was the state of mind among the youth when Dada was born in Switzerland thirty years ago. Dada was born of a moral need, of an implacable will to achieve a moral absolute, of a profound sentiment that man, at the center of all creations of the spirit, must affirm his primacy over notions emptied of all human substance, over dead objects and ill-gotten gains. Dada was born of a revolt common to youth in all times and places, a revolt demanding complete devolition of the individual to the profound needs of his nature, without concern for history or the prevailing logic or morality. Honor, Country, Morality, Family, Art, Religion, Liberty, Fraternity, etc.—all these notions had once answered to human needs, now nothing remained of them but a skeleton of conventions, they had been divested of their initial content. We took Descartes' phrase: "I don't even want to know that there were men before me," as a motto for one of our publications. This meant that we wished to regard the world with new eyes, to reconsider the very fundamentals and test the truth of the notions handed down to us by our elders. On a completely unsystematic plane, our ideas ran parallel to those of the men of science who, at about the same time, were reconsidering the most widely accepted theories of physics, finding its deficiencies and going on from there to build the monumental edifice that is modern physics. Our own modest attempts at renewal occurred in the moral field of poetic or artistic research in its close association with the social order and the conduct of everyday life. The Russian Revolution was saluted by some among us as a window opened upon the future, a breach in the fortifications of an outmoded civilization.

Our horror of the bourgeois and the forms in which he clothed his ideological security in a world which he wanted to be congealed, immutable and definitive, was not, literally speaking, an invention of Dada. Baudelaire, Lautréamont and Rimbaud had already expressed it; Gerard de Nerval, at the antipodes of the bourgeoisie, had constructed his special world in which he foundered after attaining to the limits of the most universal knowledge; Mallarmé, Verlaine, Jarry, St. Pol Roux and Apollinaire had shown us the way. But our impertinence went perhaps a little farther. We proclaimed our disgust, we made spontaneity our rule of life, we repudiated all distinctions between life and poetry, our poetry was a manner of living. Dada opposed everything that was literature, but in order to demolish its foundations we employed the most insidious weapons, the very elements of the literature and art we were attacking. Why, nurtured as we were on the work of certain poets who were our masters, did we turn against literature? It seemed to us that the world was losing itself in idle babbling, that literature and art had become institutions located on the margin of life, that instead of serving man they had become the instruments of an outmoded society. They served the war and, all the while expressing fine sentiments, they lent their prestige to atrocious inequality, sentimental misery, injustice and degradation of the instincts. Man stood naked in the presence of life. The ideologies, dogmas, systems, created by the intelligence of man, could no longer reach him in the essential nakedness of his consciousness. It was no longer a question of resistance to an obsolete society: Dada took the offensive and attacked the social system in its entirety, for it regarded this system as inextricably bound up with human stupidity, the stupidity which culminated in the destruction of man by man, and in the destruction of his material and spiritual possessions. But these ideas, which today seem natural and obvious, were at the time of which I am speaking the mark of so subversive a spirit that we were bound to scandalize society, to scandalize it so drastically that it could only regard us as criminals or imbeciles. We did not preach our ideas, we lived them, somewhat in the manner of Heraclitus, whose dialectic implied that he himself should participate in his demonstrations at once as subject and object of his conception of the world. This conception was one of continuous movement, perpetual change, a headlong flight of time. This led us to direct our attacks against the very fundaments of society, language as the agent of communication between individuals, logic as the cement. Our conception of spontaneity and the principle according to which "thought is made in the mouth" led

us in full awareness to repudiate the primacy of logic over living phenomena.

Everything connected with language was for Dada a constant problem and preoccupation. In all this tentacular activity that was Dada, poetry was harassed, insulted and despised,—I am referring of course to a certain brand of poetry, "art poetry" or "static beauty." When in 1919 Picabia, at a gathering sponsored by *Littérature,* exhibited a drawing which he executed on a blackboard and erased as he went along; when I myself, on some pretext which I no longer remember, read a newspaper article while an electric bell drowned out my voice; when, a little later, under the title of *Suicide,* Aragon published the alphabet in the form of a poem in *Cannibale;* when in the same magazine Breton published an extract from the telephone book under the title *Psst* (dozens of other examples might be cited)—must we not interpret these activities as a statement that the poetic work is without static value, that the poem is not the aim of poetry, since poetry can very well exist elsewhere? What better explanation can I offer of my instructions for the manufacture of a Dadaist poem (draw words at random out of a hat)? It is certain that this Dada objective of destroying poetry with its own weapons was inspired in part by our hatred of the poetry which had been unable to escape from its role as an "instrument of expression," which, despite everything, was still literature. At this point Dada sought an issue in action and more especially in poetic action, which is often confused with the gratuitous. I shall cite examples: the series of visits to more or less absurd places in Paris and the art exhibition organized by Max Ernst in a Cologne urinal.

Another current came into being with the publication of *La Ière Aventure Celeste de M. Antipyrine (First Celestial Adventure of Mr. Fire-Extinguisher)* (1916) and it was not until after its appearance that we began to write series or words having no apparent consecutive sense. Usually devoid of any grammatical tie (elliptical style), these poems were a part of the general tendency which expressed itself in the form of an organized struggle against logic. This method presupposed that words could be stripped of their meaning yet still be effective in a poem by their simple evocative power—a kind of magic as hard to understand as it is to formulate. The analogy between this use of words and the flight of images was known to us, as was the role of words in *non-directed* thought, although we never gave expression to these ideas. Explaining was repugnant to us, for Dada was a dictatorship of the spirit. Attempts were made to compose new words but only a few poems were written entirely in an invented language. If the experiment was justified from the point of view of consequences to be drawn from the use of words without meaning, it became ineffectual as soon as the poem was reduced to a succession of sounds.

Apollinaire in *Les Soirées de Paris* and Reverdy in *Nord-Sud* had established a parallelism between cubist painting and poetry. Into the domain of poetry they introduced the "commonplace," a language pill based on a minimum of collective understanding, the popular wisdom which passes the findings of *directed thought* through the sieve of its intelligence. Both these men contributed to Dada magazines at the beginning of the movement. This new element of poetry was an important acquisition for Dada. It was the point of departure for Paul Eluard's researches in his magazine *Proverbe*.

Dada was opposed to cubism on the ground that cubism tended, in its finished work, to express an immutable and static beauty, while everything in Dada stresses its *occasional*, circumstantial nature, the real aim of art being integration with the present-day world. With Dada the work serves only as an identification. Poetry is defined as a reality which is not valid aside from its future.

I shall not take space here to describe in detail the scandalous aspect of Dada, which was itself envisaged as a poetic factor. But I remember a snapshot taken on the stage during the demonstration at the Salle Gaveau in 1921; it showed the public standing, shouting, waving their arms. The spectacle was in the hall, gathered on the stage, we observed an audience gone wild. A play by Paul Eluard figured in the program. Two characters meet on the stage. The first says: "The post-office is across the street." The second replies: "What's that to me?" Curtain. The play was ended. In another sketch, by Breton and Soupault, entitled *S'il vous plaît*, only the first act was played. In the second act, according to the text since published, the authors were supposed to come out on the stage and commit suicide. The program also announced that the Dadaists would have their hair cut on the stage. Ribemont-Dessaignes performed a dance in which the upper part of his body was covered by an immense cardboard funnel and—this was a memorable innovation—not only tomatoes were hurled at the stage to be caught in the funnel but, for the first time anywhere in the world, beefsteaks. Numerous were the inventions with the gift of exasperating the public. The public was divided into several clans. One believed that we were masters of mystification, another that we were real imbeciles; not very numerous in any case were those who gave us a little real credit. And among these last must be counted Valéry and Jacques Rivière. There was good cause for dismay, for, while we voluntarily made ourselves into objects of scorn and vilification, while we did not hesitate to offer ourselves up as a holocaust to every mockery and humiliation, while from all this we even drew a kind of glory,—the writings of Aragon, Breton, Eluard and others evinced a clarity and vigor calculated to disconcert the most convinced adversaries.

Was this movement, only the destructive side of which had been seen by most critics, really necessary? It is certain that the *tabula rasa* which we made into the guiding principle of our activity, was of value only in so far as *something else* would succeed it. A state of affairs considered noxious and infamous demanded to be changed. This necessary disorder, of which Rimbaud had spoken, implied nostalgia for an order that had been lost or a new order to come.

Arp, Aragon, Soupault, Eluard, Breton, Picabia, Ribemont-Dessaignes, Crevel, Rigaud, Péret, Max Ernst, Duchamp, Man Ray, myself and a few others were the Dadaists of the first hour in France. The magazine *Littérature* was the organ of Dada in Paris, side by side with *391, Cannibale, Proverbe*, etc. It was Valéry who gave the name *Lit-*

térature to the magazine, as an antithesis in allusion to Verlaine's celebrated phrase. Dada, which had broken not only with the traditional succession of schools, but also with those values which were ostensibly most unassailable, actually prolonged the unbroken line of schools and poets; by this marvelous chain it was connected with Mallarmé, Rimbaud, Lautréamont, and going still farther, with Baudelaire and Victor Hugo, thus marking the continuity of the spirit of revolt in French poetry, that poetry which is based on concrete life and situated at the very center of the preoccupations which become all the more universal in proportion as they are localized.

Dada was a brief explosion in the history of literature, but it was powerful and had far-reaching repercussions. It lay in the very nature of Dada to put a term to its existence. Dada was one of those adventures of the spirit in the course of which everything is put in question. It undertook a serious revision of values and confronted all those who participated in it with their own responsibilities. From the violence and sacrilege of Dada was born, if I may so express myself, a new literary heroism and a sense of moral danger and courage unaccustomed in the field of literature; here, as in the field of physics, danger and courage were the elements making possible the fusion of a categorical principle: Life and poetry were henceforth a single indivisible expression of man in quest of a vital imperative. Dada taught us that the man of action and the poet must commit their whole being to their principles, uncompromisingly and with complete self-abnegation. For Dada, a literary school, was above all a moral movement. It was individualistic, anarchic in certain respects, and it expressed the turbulence of the youth of all times. A product of the disgust aroused by the war, Dada could not maintain itself on the dizzy heights it had chosen to inhabit, and in 1922 it put an end to its existence.

Surrealism rose from the ashes of Dada. With some intermittences, most of the Dadaists took part in it. But that is the beginning of another story. (pp. 394-98)

Tristan Tzara, "An Introduction to Dada," in
The Data Painters and Poets: An Anthology
by Arp and others, edited by Robert Mother-
well, George Wittenborn, Inc., 1951, pp. 394-
98.

Hans Richter

[*In the following essay, Richter equates Dadaism with Abstractionism in art.*]

Art historians and critics have recently discovered dada. They have decided the movement to be something like a glorified practical joke that had some useful destructive function at the time.

This definition has now been sanctioned by repetition and has become a "historical fact". But we, who were all together there when it happened look at it from another angle, not from the big noise we made at the time to "épater le bourgeois" but from the ideas and problems with which we, the artists, were then concerned and which were the bone and flesh, though not necessarily the skin of this movement. The nucleus of the artistic endeavour

Man Ray on the state of Dadaism:

Now, we are trying to revive Dada. Why? Who cares? Who doesn't care? Dada is dead. Or is Dada still alive? We cannot revive something that is alive just as we cannot revive anything that is dead.

Is Dadadead?

Is Dadaalive?

Dada is.

Dadaism.

> *Man Ray, in Robert Motherwell's* The Dada Painters and Poets: An Anthology, *George Wittenborn, 1951.*

of dada as it appeared in Zurich 1916/19 was abstract art. Abstract art was at that time a fighting proposition not a four-lane highway on which everybody travelled who was faced with an empty canvas. Abstract painting that *was* dada. When Arp and van Rees had painted and been paid for two abstract frescoes in the hallway of a school in Zurich, the school board, sustained by public opinion, insisted that these dadaistic (in fact just plain abstract) ventures be immediately painted over with normal human figures. And they were.

Even before I joined dada in 1916 I had lost more and more interest in subjects like apples, nudes, madonnas, guitars, and concentrated upon this realm in which color and form, a line and surface started to become meaningful by themselves: abstract art.

In these years 1913/17 I found myself attracted on one side towards uninhibited freedom and spontaneous expression and on the other side fascinated by the problem of gaining an objective understanding of fundamental principles which might govern and control these heaps of fragments which we had inherited from the cubists. One day at the beginning of 1918, Tristan Tzara knocked at the wall which separated our rooms in the Hotel Limmatquai in Zurich and introduced me to Viking Eggeling. Our complete agreement from the very first moment on aesthetic as well as on philosophical matters, a kind of enthusiastic identity led spontaneously to a collaboration and friendship which lasted until Viking Eggeling's death in 1925.

This collaboration led us over a small bridge from painting to scrolls and finally in 1920 into an adventure none of us had ever dreamed of: film. In these years between 1918 and 1920 our research led us to study the "behaviour" of line and surfaces towards or against each other. We deducted from these exercises a kind of method which allowed us to "orchestrate" a line and a form from the very simplest to the most complicated expression. Eggeling called it "Generalbass der Malerei". We used these drawings on small pieces of paper to study the relationships of

simple and complicated forms, arranged them and rearranged them on the floor till one day we discovered a kind of continuity evolving from these lines of drawings. It was then that we decided to make purposely a continuous development of forms and form groups on long scrolls of paper: our first scrolls. Eggeling's was "Horizontal-Vertical Mass", mine "Preludium".

These scrolls, when we looked at them, imposed upon us the wish to realize the "movement" they implied: real movement: that meant film and that is how we came to make films.

It is therefore no accident that the first abstract films were made by two members of the original dada group, Eggeling and myself. And they certainly did not demonstrate the officially acknowledged spirit of dada: the Mona Lisa with a moustache, the toilet-seat or the nail flatiron . . . but they grew nevertheless straight from the art-, and -nothing-but-art problems which had drawn us into them. I remember very well though, that I had kind of a row with Tzara, the publisher of our dada magazine about this point. He was against reproducing Eggeling's classic abstract drawing in *Dada* (Giorgione, Renaissance and all that), and I had to use all kinds of protest, pressure and arguments to convince him.

Sure, we were all for the law of chance, but if there were a law of chance, then there should by the same logic also be a law of "rule". And to approach, to discover this "Rule" seemed to make the law of chance meaningful: the just balance "between heaven and hell" (Arp). It was the obvious question which this new liberated form of expression (abstract art) had put before us.

After I have stated this fact: Dada = abstract art, I happily wish to insist on the other point: Dada = non-abstract art. And that is also true—if not truer and is documented by a different series of films. *Entr'acte* 1924 after a story by Francis Picabia produced by René Clair: a funeral, a hearse led and drawn by a slow- and fast-moving camel, a dancing girl with a flowing beard, and the whole story ending in the reappearing of the dead and the magic dissolution of the mourners. It bends over backwards to laugh over and with the paradoxical happenings, dada! Nothing abstract there except the tension between the overly fast or overly slow rhythm of the action itself.

Fernand Léger's "ballet mécanique" also 1924: An integration of abstract forms, rhythms and objects (kitchenware) with a bit of a story ("On a volé un collier de perles de 5.000.000"). The zeros become pearls, abstract form and part of the story again. They dance, split and transform, become round and sharp, disappear. Though Léger was never a dadaist, the film is 100%. It is one of the most imaginative of this kind. It is just that Léger had sensed the ambiguity in the ordinary: serious beauty turns into laughter and laughter into abstract beauty, without denuding the one or the other of their inherent meaning and integrity.

More abstract in the proper sense of the word are my *Filmstudy* and Man Ray's *Emak Bakia,* both 1926.

The pre-surrealistic poem *Filmstudy* uses floating heads

and eyes connected with luminous circles like moons rising from the surface of the screen in gentle ripples and exploding waves. Abstract forms, objects on the same rhythmical level relieved of their explainable and useful function, talk their own sensitive but irrational language. *Emak Bakia* is a beautiful poem created by a string of objects, abstract symbols dancing in the nude, shirtcollar slowly turning one way—turning the other, moving, measuring the time of a studio-locked universe.

Though these two films were at that time already called surrealistic (after the fashion) they are more dada. I wonder, if the distinguishing line between the two can be drawn exactly as surrealism jumped out of the left ear of dada fully equipped and alive, making dadaists = surrealists overnight. Anyhow in these two films there is no "moral" issue involved as surrealism demands, nor a Freudian party line drawn. Though interpretations in the Freudian direction are never lacking. The same goes for my film *Vormittagsspuk* (1927). It is really simple: Four bowler hats, some coffeecups and neckties "have enough" (are fed-up) and revolt from 11.50 to 12 a.m. Then they take up their routine again. (Darius Milhaud and Hindemith are actors in the film, the original score was composed by Hindemith, but later destroyed by the Nazis.) The chase of the rebellious "Untertanen" (objects are also people) threads the story. It is interrupted by strange interludes of pursuit which exploit the ability of the camera, to overcame gravity, to use space and time completely freed from natural laws. The impossible becomes reality and reality, as we know, is only one of the possible forms of the universe.

To accept the paradox that the genuine and sincere can walk hand in hand, foot to foot, foot in mouth, and hand to foot with the spoofy, nonsensical, that is what makes the understanding of dada difficult.

But just there new avenues are opening, and the chase after the self-freed independent bowlerhats, flying through the landscape, becomes symbolic: the rebellion of the objects against their daily routine in a too-well regulated world. (The social critics discovered in it a satire against the Nazis.) The psychoanalysts found it a story of the libido on a weekend spree.

The spirit of dada, whatever it is called, is bitterly needed today. Is needed to brace us against the fatal world we presume to understand when we blow it to pieces; is needed against the topheavy symbolists who know the numbers of all the missing pieces in their subconscious attic; against the impotent Eliot-frame-of-mind imitators; against the new mystics and the older nonmystics; against the serious concrete-blockbuilders and against the busy cloud magicians; against the world planners and the plumbers, the cheaters and the humorless in art, in film-art, in everything. (pp. 39-43)

Hans Richter, "Dada and the Film," in Dada: Monograph of a Movement, *edited by Willy Verkauf, Academy Editions, 1975, pp. 39-43.*

THEATER AND FILM

Günter Berghaus

[*In the following excerpt, Berghaus discusses Dada theater.*]

DADA is generally considered to have had its beginning in the founding of the Cabaret Voltaire in Zurich in early 1916, by the German poet, novelist and cabaret performer Hugo Ball. Around the year 1915/16, however, similar phenomena can be traced in artistic circles throughout the Western world, and all of them to some extent deserve to be called Dadaist.

The First World War had triggered off an intellectual revolt against the existing capitalist, militarist and imperialist society and the arts which had traditionally supported this system. All of these disenchanted artists and intellectuals owed a great deal to pre-war Futurism, but contrary to other innovatory art movements, which had come into being since the turn of the century, the 'Protodadaists' were not so much concerned with artistic improvements, but with a complete revaluation of the moral basis of all the arts and cultural phenomena in a bourgeois society.

Futurism was the first movement with an artistic concept based on the rejection of traditional society and the establishment of a 'modern spirit' in the world of arts. The Futurists used performance as a medium of expression, and their *serate* in many ways prefigured the later soirées of the Dadaists. They chose the theatre as an arena to propagate their artistic, philosophical and political ideas, and to stage an assault on tradition, education, religion and bourgeois values, making use of onomatopoeic poetry, noise music, simultaneous declamations, alogical playlets, improvised sketches, gymnastic movements and fantastic costumes.

From 1909 onwards there was a steady surge of influence from the ideas and attitudes of the Futurists into the intellectual and artistic circles of Paris. Here several movements since the end of the nineteenth century had attempted a revitalisation of the arts, but with nothing approaching the measure of success the Futurists achieved in establishing a united front against traditionalism.

In the years 1913-14 many of the artists who later played a major rôle in the Dada movement met for the first time in Paris. José Pierre, in an examination of Dadaist tendencies in pre-war art movements, suggests that DADA was conceived in Paris during these years, to be born a year later in New York, where the *émigrés* Marcel Duchamp and Francis Picabia formed the centre of a cosmopolitan ferment of intellectual agitation, and christened in Zurich, where a group of radical artists around Hugo Ball and Tristan Tzara practised a new concept of Anti-Art, to which they gave the name DADA: 'In Rumanian "dada" means "yes, yes", in French a rocking-horse or hobby horse. To Germans it is an indication of idiot naivety and of preoccupation with procreation and the baby-carriage' [Hugo Ball]. In short, it did not mean anything in particular, but was considered by the Dadaists to be 'wholly appropriate. Nothing could better express our optimism, our sensation of newly-won freedom, than this powerfully reiterated *"da, da"*—"yes, yes" to life' [Hans Richter].

There are innumerable theories about who invented the name DADA. But there can be no doubt that it appeared for the first time in print on 15 June 1916 in *'Cabaret Voltaire. Literary and Artistic Anthology. Edited by Hugo Ball'*.

Hugo Ball, the founder of *Cabaret Voltaire*, was a man with considerable theatrical experience. From September 1910 to May 1911 he had been a student at the Max Reinhardt school in Berlin, where he received instruction in acting, directing, dramaturgy and theatre criticism. In autumn 1911 he became 'Dramaturg' at the Stadttheater Plauen, and in October 1912 he took over the post of 'Dramaturg' at the Kammerspiele in Munich. He played several minor parts and wrote two plays, *Die Nase des Michelangelo* (*Michelangelo's Nose*) and *Der Henker von Brescia* (*The Hangman of Brescia*).

His theatrical ideas at that time were greatly influenced by Nietzsche's Dionysian-Apollonian theatre (which he had studied as a student of philosophy in Munich), by Wassily Kandinsky's theories of abstract theatre, and by the staging practice at the Künstlertheater, which, under the direction of Georg Fuchs, was the centre of a theatre reform similar to that propagated by Adolphe Appia and Edward Gordon Craig.

As Ball wrote in a programmatic article in *Phöbus,* he intended to carry further the ideas of the Künstlertheater and create a 'Gesamtkunstwerk', combining dance, mime, words, music, colour and taking recourse to the 'Geburtsgrund allen dramatischen Lebens' ('the original cause of all dramatic life'). In his diary he wrote about his ideas of this time:

> The idea behind the Expressionist theatre is that of a festival ('Festspiel'); it contains a new concept of the total work of art ('Gesamtkunstwerk'). The artistic form of present-day theatre is impressionistic. Events on stage appeal to the individual and his intellect. The subconscious is not touched at all. The New Theatre will use masks and stilts again. It will recall archetypes and use megaphones. Sun and moon will run across the stage and proclaim their sublime wisdom.

Ball was not only interested in the development of a new theatre, but like Kandinsky aspired to 'a rebirth of society through a union of artistic means and forces'. In another diary entry we read: 'Only theatre is capable of forming a new society.' Ball at that time saw himself as an Expressionist, who wanted to recreate an archaic, mystical form of theatre, which would have a strong impact on the audience's emotions and profound influence on society as a whole (emulating an ideal, which he saw realized in early Greek theatre).

His ideas took a new direction when he met Richard Huelsenbeck in the avantgarde circles of the Café des Westens in Berlin. Together they wrote a manifesto in 1914, in which they defined the function of art as 'to provoke, to

overthrow, to bluff, to vex, to tickle to death, to be chaotic and incoherent, to be a daredevil and a negationist'.

There can be no doubt that in 1914 Hugo Ball had reached a pre-dadaist position, when the outbreak of war prevented him from further developing his ideas on the New Theatre. First hand experience of the mass killings on the western front opened his eyes to the barbarity of the war. Deeply shocked he noted in his diary: 'The whole machinery and the devil himself have broken loose now. Ideals are only labels that have been stuck on. Everything has been shaken to its very foundations.' A few days later he concluded: 'One has to break with the system of reason, for the sake of a higher reason.' He began to study socialism, communism and anarchism, without being able to favour any of these systems. The senseless destruction around him even caused him to consider giving up the theatre altogether:

> I am still concerned about the theatre, and yet it all has no sense any more. Who wants to produce plays nowadays, or who wants to see them? . . . The theatre is like a man who has suddenly been decapitated. He might stand up again and walk a few steps. But then he will fall and lie there dead.

He felt that, as an artist, he could not survive in this destructive climate. In May 1915 he moved to Switzerland, where he continued his artistic activities and his political studies. 'Switzerland is like a bird-cage surrounded by roaring lions', he wrote on 15 October 1915 in his diary. Despite the peaceful environment he had great difficulties finding firm ground in his ideological struggle: 'The collapse is beginning to take on gigantic dimensions. We will no longer be able to refer to the authority of the old idealistic Germany; so we will be completely without any basis. . . . That whole civilisation was ultimately only a sham.'

None of the traditional beliefs, nor any of the alternative social utopian philosophies, could satisfy his quest for a secure framework of ideological reference.

> Know thyself! As if it were so simple! As if only good will and introspection were required. Whenever an eternal ideal is firmly anchored in the solid traditions of education and culture, literature and politics, the individual will be able to compare himself, see himself, correct himself. But what when all norms are shaken and in a state of confusion?

Ball's mental crisis was aggravated by his desperate financial situation, and his spiritual exasperation was soon equalled by his physical decline. Eventually his wife, Emmy Hennings, found employment as a singer in a cabaret. Ball himself was forced to take a job playing the piano with a 'variété' troupe. While touring the country with the 'Maxim Ensemble' he made the acquaintance of a great number of exiled artists, and developed a considerable talent for organising shows, hiring halls and artists, writing songs and rehearsing performances.

> We have to work from 8 a.m. to 10.30 p.m. and get a good wage. I am writing small pieces for the troupe (an Apache number, a harem num-

ber). During the daytime I read and write. We
have a charming room in the variété-restaurant.
It is large with heavy wall-panelling like in a
Gothic castle. We smoke endless cigarettes and
write our diaries. There are contortionists and
tightrope walkers, fire-eaters and soubrettes.

Ball and Hennings were quite taken with their lives as
strolling cabaret artists. They only regretted that they did
not have complete control over the venture. 'To have our
own troupe, to write our own material, to work towards
having a real theatre: this is our ultimate ambition.'

The opportunity to fulfil this dream arose in January 1916,
when a Mr Ephraim offered them the lease of the
'Meierei', a rather run-down bar in the disreputable
'Nierendorfviertel' in Zurich. A press notice on 2 February announced:

> Cabaret Voltaire. Under this name a group of
> young artists and writers has formed with the
> object of becoming a centre for artistic entertain-
> ment. The Cabaret Voltaire will be run on the
> principle of daily meetings where visiting artists
> will perform their music and poetry. The youn-
> ger artists of Zurich are invited to bring along
> their ideas and contributions, regardless of their
> artistic direction.

The cabaret was opened on February 5th. The first shows
were played to a largely foreign and literary audience and
provided rather conventional fare of light entertainment
(cabaret songs, music recitals, literary readings, dances
etc.), in no way reflecting Ball's artistic philosophy, which
on 25 November 1915 he had described as follows:

> The creation of any art (painting, writing, com-
> posing) will do people good, provided that they
> do not pursue any purpose in their subjects, but
> follow the course of their free, unfettered imagi-
> nation. The unrestrained process of fantasizing
> never fails to revoke those things that have
> crossed the threshold of consciousness unana-
> lysed. In an era like ours, when people are as-
> saulted daily by the most monstrous things with-
> out being able to keep account of their impres-
> sions, in such an age aesthetic production be-
> comes the diet we feed on. But all living art will
> be irrational, primitive, and complex. It will
> speak a secret language and leave behind docu-
> ments not of edification but of paradox.

Nothing could be in greater contrast to these ideas than
the note in Ball's diary on 7 March 1916:

> The Sunday was given over to the Swiss. But the
> young Swiss are too cautious for a cabaret. A
> fine gentleman paid tribute to a timid form of
> freedom and sang a song about 'Pretty Virgin
> Lisa' ('Schöne Jungfer Lischen') which made us
> blush and look away in embarrassment. Another
> gentleman recited his 'oaken' poems.

The 'Swiss Evening' seems to have convinced Ball that
drastic changes were necessary if the Cabaret Voltaire was
ever going to be more than a tame entertainment venture.
He convinced his old friend Huelsenbeck that new methods had to be adopted, and he, who 'wanted most to drum
literature into the ground', complied with Ball's wishes.

They put together a performance which for the first time
well and truly deserved the epithet 'Dadaist'. On 29
March Huelsenbeck, with trembling nostrils and raised
eyebrows, a Spanish cane in his hand, 'recited' his poetry
to the accompaniment of his bass drum, and was received
with shouting, whistling and laughter from the audience.

The next step in the direction of DADA performance was
the simultaneous poem 'L'admiral cherche une maison à
louer', presented on 29 March by Huelsenbeck, Janco and
Tzara in three different languages to the accompaniment
of a whistle, rattle and bass drum. The Dada circus, which
according to Ball was 'both a buffoonery and a requiem
mass', had begun. Ball discovered a new aim in life. His
diary for these months is full of new ideas and reflections
about the nature of the new art which they were in the process of developing:

> Our cabaret is a gesture. Every word that is spo-
> ken or sung here proves at least that this humili-
> ating age has not succeeded in winning our re-
> spect. What could be respectable and impressive
> about it? Its cannons? Our big drum is louder.
> Its idealism? That became a laughing stock a
> long time ago, in its popular as well as in its aca-
> demic form. The grandiose butchery and canni-
> balistic exploits? Our deliberate foolishness and
> enthusiasm for illusion will annihilate it.

> One can almost say that when belief in some-
> thing comes to an end, the object or cause of our
> belief returns to chaos and becomes common
> property again. But perhaps this resolutely, forc-
> ibly produced chaos and thus a complete with-
> drawal of faith is necessary before a new and
> solid edifice, based upon a changed basis of be-
> lief, can be erected. Then the elementary, the de-
> monic will break forth. The old names and
> words will fall. For faith is the measure of things
> by means of the word and denomination.

The performance of poetry (one can no longer speak of
'readings'), which had begun at the Cabaret Voltaire, became one of the trademarks of DADA and was repeated in
various forms and configurations at nearly every soirée in
Zurich, Berlin and Paris. Dada poetry was not written in
order to be printed and read in private. It could only be
brought to life in a performance and relied on an actor in
order to fulfil its functions. It required theatrical representation, and the acoustic effect (produced by voice or instruments) was enhanced by visual presentation (through
gesture, mime and movement), so that the audience could
actually *hear* and *see* the poem.

The most famous example of this type of performed poetry
was Ball's 'gadji beri bimba', which he presented on 23
June 1916 in the guise of a 'magical bishop'. His costume
complemented the quasi-religious intensity of his delivery.
He made great efforts to find the right rhythm, inflexion
and accentuation for his verses, modulating his enunciation and projecting his voice in a way that proved him to
be a true Max-Reinhardt-pupil. The poem culminated in
a cadence inspired by liturgical chant, revealing the religious, magical and irrational undertones in Ball's art. He
did not just perform his poetry, but celebrated it with the
dignity and solemnity of a high priest.

Ball himself described his poetry as an attempt to 'protect poetry's last holy precinct', as 'a retreat into the alchemy of words', which 'rejects the language which has become spoiled by journalism and, therefore, made useless. In another passage in his diary he analysed the aims behind Dadaist performed poetry:

> We tried to give the isolated vocables the fullness of a magical invocation, the glow of a star. And curiously enough, the magically inspired vocable conjured up and gave birth to a *new* sentence that was not conditioned or limited by any conventional meaning. Touching upon a hundred ideas without naming them, this sentence made resound the innately playful, but hidden, irrational nature of the listener. Our experiments touched upon areas of philosophy and life that our rational and precocious environment scarcely allows us to dream of.

The performance of simultaneous and sound poems could involve up to twenty people on the stage. None of the text, of course, could then be understood. The only impression the audience got was that of chaos and unbridled vitality, which, according to Huelsenbeck, was exactly the effect the performers had intended:

> Simultaneity is a direct reminder of life . . . , which defies formulation, because it is a direct symbol of action. And so ultimately a simultaneous poem means nothing but 'Long live life!' ('Es lebe das Leben').

The simultaneous poems were not only a symbol of life in an ossified, moribund society; they also reflected the chaos in a war-stricken world and a civilisation which was falling apart. Ball characterised these performances in the following terms:

> The 'simultaneous poem' has to do with the value of the voice. The human organ represents the soul, the individuality in its wanderings between its demonic companions. The noises represent the background—the inarticulate, the fatal, the decisive. The poem tries to elucidate the fact that man is wound up in the mechanistic process. In a typical abridgement it shows the conflict of the *vox humana* with a threatening, ensnaring and destroying world, whose rhythm and noise are inescapable.

A variant to the sound poems were the noise poems or 'poèmes bruitistes', invented by the Futurists and introduced to the Zurich Dada circles by Richard Huelsenbeck, who considered this type of art to be 'a direct objectivisation of the dark, vital forces' and 'a rather violent reminder of the colourfulness of life'. Here the text was only a skeleton, a sort of libretto, which was overlaid with an orchestration of noises, produced on drums, rattles, whistles, pots and pans. The performer would speak, shout, yodel or sing on top of this noise, and the result of this was seen as 'an attempt to capture in a clear melody the totality of this unmentionable age, with all its cracks and fissures, with all its wicked and lunatic cosiness, with all its noise and hollow din. The Gorgon's head of boundless terror smiles out of the fantastic ruins.'

Another form of Dada performance was the gymnastic poem, or 'poème mouvementiste', which was recited to the accompaniment of certain movements. It depended on the performer's physical skill to combine his utterances with kinetic creations, which could be simple movements such as knee bending, or more complicated 'dances'. An explanation of these works is given by Tristan Tzara:

> The gymnastic poem which we have invented is designed to accentuate and to articulate the meaning of words through primitive movements. What we want to represent is intensity. It is for this reason that we go back to primitive elements. . . . The actor ought to add primitive movements and noise to his voice, of a kind where the exterior expression corresponds with the meaning of the poetry. The artist has the freedom to arrange and to compose the movements and noises according to his personal understanding of the poem.

A more refined version of these gymnastic poems were the dances carried out by members of the Laban ballet group. Here a professional dancer interpreted the rhythms and sounds of the poems kinetically and created a synaesthetic 'artwork', which according to some descriptions must have looked very convincing and effective:

> Abstract dances: a gong beat suffices to stimulate the dancer's body to the most fantastic formations. The dance has become an end in itself. The nervous system explores all vibrations of the sound, perhaps all the hidden emotions of the gong beater too, and turns them into an image. Here, in this special case, a poetic sequence of sounds was enough to bring to life each of the individual word particles in a strange and visible way in the hundred-jointed body of the dancer. The *Chant of the Flying Fish and the Sea Horses* (*Gesang der Flugfische und Seepferdchen*) turned into a dance full of spiky bones, full of flickering light and cutting sharpness.

A further type of performed poetry was the static poem, or 'poème statique'. Tzara distinguished it from the simultaneous poems thus:

> We looked for a simultaneity which is relative because its duration is inherent in space. With the static poem we have for the first time created an immobile poem, where the relationship of distances remains stable. This equilibrium allows one to begin reading the poem simultaneously from all sides. The emphasis is given in depth and its representative force determines the purity of abstraction. Uniformly dressed people carry signs on which the words of the poem were written. They arrange and rearrange themselves in groups according to the (classic) law which I impose on them.

A variation on this form of performance were the static poems where the words were written on cardboards and rested on chairs arranged on the stage in a certain order. From time to time the curtain was lowered and the words were rearranged or exchanged.

The Dadaists realized that art and society are always closely related to one another and that one could not reject the one and accept the other: 'The artist never stands above his surroundings and the society of those who admire him. His small brain does not produce the content of his creations but merely processes the ideologies of his market (just as a sausage machine processes meat)' [George Grosz and John Hearztfield]. So if they wanted to subvert bourgeois values they had to subvert art itself. This did not mean the abolition of artistic creativity, but of the aura around art works and the artist's dependence on the bourgeois art market: 'We are not artists in order that we might live comfortably and irresponsibly from the exploiters' craving for luxury [Otto Dix].

The Dadaists felt that the beauty, harmony and rationality of academic art served as a prop of bourgeois society, of 'the hierarchy in the state' [Tristan Tzara]. What was generally considered 'intelligent', for the Dadaists was nothing but 'the triumph of good education and pragmatism. But life, thank goodness, is something else, and its pleasures are limitless' [Tristan Tzara]. Consequently they put their emphasis on the non-rational, non-logic, non-intelligent: 'The unconscious is inexhaustible and uncontrollable. So let us do away with the conscious, with philosophy. What matters is: *we are;* we dispute, we agitate, we discuss. . . . What we want now is spontaneity. Not because it is more beautiful or better than other things. But because everything that comes out of us freely without the intervention of the speculative mind is a representation of ourselves' [Tristan Tzara].

Art had to be taken out of the hands of academic teachers and turned into something personal again. It had to be produced as a creative act, free of any restrictions normally imposed by taste, rules, logic etc. The artist had to give in to his spontaneous impulses and create without premeditation, relying purely on chance and automatism. What mattered was the creative process and not the aesthetic quality of the final product.

But no artist could prevent the fact that the results of his creativity could be turned into collectable art objects. So he had either to destroy the products of his imagination or choose a medium which did not leave any traces behind. For this reason the most transitory art form possible, performance, became the favourite medium of expression for the Dadaists.

Most of the Dada performances were improvised and depended for their success on chance, the inspiration of the moment, and the audience's reaction. 'All of our sketches were of an improvised nature, full of fantasy, freshness, and the unexpected' [Marcel Janco]. Few of the Dada performers had any professional training, there were no rehearsals or directions. Tzara's well known saying 'Thought is produced in the mouth' captures well the spontaneous nature of Dada performances. The actor did not exhibit the results of an artistic process, but rather performed an uncontrolled rendering of his own instantaneous ideas. He did not *represent* another character, but rather *presented* himself.

The performances did not relate to any other place or time but the here and now. 'Here' normally meant a small, bare platform stage, without set and with only few props. Sometimes there was a backdrop, but this never related to the performance itself. Considerable effort, however, was put into the costumes and masks, which in Zurich were produced by Marcel Janco and in Paris by Francis Picabia and Sonja Delaunay. They greatly enhanced the effect of the productions and must be regarded as an important ingredient of Dada performances.

Although the actor's 'self-exhibition' on the stage was a largely improvised event, the whole soirée was nevertheless well organised. Richter, for example, recalls the 'Non Plus Ultra' Ninth Dada Evening in the Saal zur Kaufleuten (19.4.1919): 'Tzara had organised the whole thing with the magnificent precision of a ringmaster'. This in no way contradicted the improvised nature of the stage events themselves. Apart from allowing the performers room for creative self-expression, the soirées had the equally important function of provoking the largely bourgeois audience, and this could only succeed if the whole programme was well organised.

Whatever happened on the stage was directed towards an audience. The Dadaists did not experiment with the architectural structure of the theatre, but basically accepted the spatial differentiation between performers and spectators. However, the forms of communication between stage and auditorium were challenged in every major performance.

After the first production of Kokoschka's *Strohmann und Sphinx* (*Straw Man and Sphinx*), during the *Sturm* soirée on 14 April 1917, Tzara wrote: 'This performance decided the role of our theatre, which will entrust the stage direction to the subtle invention of the explosive wind, and the scenario to the audience'. Here, as in every other of the following major soirées, the Dadaists succeeded in shocking, provoking and enraging their audience to an extent that the direction of communication between performer and spectator was reversed. Looking back on the soirée in the Salle Gaveau (26.5.1920), for Tzara the most important experience was that 'the spectacle took place in the auditorium. We were gathered on the stage watching the audience let loose.' Georges Charensol in *Commoedia* reported on the 'Manifestation Dada' in the Salle Berlioz at the Maison de l' Oeuvre:

> The public lashed out against, booed and jeered at the Dadaists, who received their injuries with grinning faces. One would have thought oneself in a madhouse, and the spirit of madness shrieked from the stage as well as in the hall. The Dadaists have exasperated their spectators and I think this is exactly what they wanted to do.

The situation was slightly different at the Kaufleuten soirée, where a certain section of the audience had become familiar with the Dadaists' provocation and had arrived with what the performers considered the 'wrong' kind of expectation. Tzara decided that they needed 'special treatment' and devised a programme which delivered exactly the opposite of what these spectators had come for:

> Eggeling appeared first . . . and delivered a very serious speech about elementary 'Gestaltung' and abstract art. This only disturbed the audience insofar as they wanted to be disturbed but weren't.

After this prosaic beginning, which provoked simply by being so unprovocative, there followed dances by Suzanne Perrottet and poems by Käthe Wulff. These prepared the ground for Tzara's simultaneous poem for twenty performers, *La fièvre du mâle* (*The Fever of the Male*). This hellish spectacle enraged the other half of the audience and unleashed the 'signal of blood. Revolt of the past and of education' [Tristan Tzara]. All 1500 spectators were now in a state of agitation; but before they could bring the evening to a standstill, an intermission was called.

In the second half the same crescendo effect was used and the audience was brought to new heights of indignation. There was a talk by Richter on Dadaism, which 'cursed the audience with moderation', atonal music by Hans Heusser, a recitation by Arp from his *Wolkenpumpe* (*Cloud Pump*), and more dances by Perrottet. This led [as Hans Richter recalled] to the climax of the evening, the entrance of

> Dr Walter Serner, dressed as if for a wedding, in immaculate black coat and striped trousers, with a grey cravat. This tall, elegant figure first carried a headless tailor's dummy onto the stage, then went back to fetch a bouquet of artificial flowers, gave them to the dummy to smell where its head should have been, and laid them at its feet. Finally he brought a chair, and sat astride it in the middle of the platform with his back to the audience. After these elaborate preparations, he began to read from his anarchistic credo, *Letzte Lockerung* (*Final Dissolution*). At last! This was just what the audience had been waiting for.

> The tension in the hall became unbearable. At first it was so quiet that you could have heard a pin drop. Then the catcalls began, scornful at first, then furious. 'Rat, bastard, you've got a nerve!' until the noise almost entirely drowned Serner's voice, which could be heard, during a momentary lull, saying the words 'Napoleon was a big strong oaf, after all'.

> That really did it. What Napoleon had to do with it, I don't know. He wasn't Swiss. But the young men, most of whom were in the gallery, leaped on to the stage, brandishing pieces of the balustrade (which had survived intact for several hundred years), chased Serner into the wings and out of the building, smashed the tailor's dummy and the chair, and stamped on the bouquet. The whole place was in an uproar.

So finally the provocation had worked. But this was only due to the fact that Tzara had masterminded the show with a clear vision of how the various sections of the programme would affect the audience, who after three years of Dada activities in Zurich were no longer innocent in their expectations, but arrived in order to be shocked and affronted. Once the spectators began to enjoy the spectacle on the stage, and the accepted rôles of performers and onlookers were reinstated, Dada performance had failed in one of its major functions: to provoke its bourgeois audience to the extent that they reversed the direction of theatrical communication and took over 'le scénario dans la salle'. [Tristan Tzara]

In an interview with the BBC, recorded in 1959, Tristan Tzara explained at great length the position of the Dada artists concerning art and anti-art:

> At the time of the congress in Paris exactly, we declared Dada was not modern, because Dada was anarchic and the modernism of the time tended to become a dogma, a sort of institution. . . . For us, 'modernism' had a pejorative meaning; it was almost an insult to call us 'modernes', because modernism was in fashion and we were against this fashion. . . . The fact is that there is confusion about our negativism. It was not an absolute negativism, but a sort of dialectic negativism, in the sense that we wanted to make a clean break with everything that existed before us, to see life and everything with new eyes, with new and fresh feeling.

Though statements made by the Dadaists in later years do not necessarily comply with what they thought in the heyday of their activities, this interpretation—though made with hindsight—in my view sums up the complex nature of the Dadaists' relation to *the arts* better than any of the many studies written in the 1950s and 1960s under the influence of Existentialism and the Theatre of the Absurd. Certainly, there was a very strong destructive, negativistic, anarchic, even nihilistic strain in Dada art, but it would not capture the essential ambition of the Dadaists to stress too strongly this aspect of their production. As Hans Richter rightly emphasized, 'in spite of all our anti-art polemics, we produced works of art'. They did not write any plays which had any lasting artistic value; but they loved the medium of theatre and used it aptly in order to express their ideas and feelings.

Their creations were highly unorthodox and the meanings of these 'artworks' cannot be described in terms of traditional aesthetics. The Dadaists did not want to produce meaning in the traditional sense. To a great extent the meaning of Dada art depended on the exclusion of distinct meanings and the provocative effect this had on the unprepared onlooker. The meaninglessness of Dada art was only a camouflage for a new kind of meaning, hidden behind a surface of pure nonsense.

Dada art, however, should never be taken at its face value. The strong *anti* stance only disguised an equally strong positive impulse. Richter characterized this balance:

> We were all propelled by the same vital impulse. It drove us to the fragmentation or destruction of all artistic forms, and to . . . a raging anti, anti, anti, linked with an equally passionate pro, pro, pro!

Tzara was even more specific on this subject:

> Is not art, with a capital A, inclined to take a privileged or tyrannical position on the scale of values, which in turn causes it to sever all connections with human qualities? In this sense Dada declared itself anti-artistic, anti-literary, and anti-poetic. Its desire to destroy was much more an aspiration towards purity and sincerity than a tendency towards a sort of acoustic or spatial inanity, confining itself to immobility and absence. Dada's presence in the most immediate,

the most precarious and improvisory reality was its counter-blow against that pursuit of eternal beauty which, existing beyond time, aspires to attain to perfection.

Tzara, in his first Dada manifesto, had described this positive aim as the 'pursuit of life's essence' ('nous cherchons l'essence centrale'); Hugo Ball named it 'die Reinheit, die wir erstreben' ('the purity for which we are striving'). Hans Arp described it in similar terms: 'We were looking for a more elementary art to cure mankind of the madness of our times and to establish a new order, a balance between heaven and hell.'

In order to achieve this aim the artist had to undergo a process of curing, which Raoul Hausmann described as 'praktische Selbstentgiftung' ('practical self-detoxication'), that is: 'negation of the traditional meaning of life or culture, which is not tragic, but barren'. The process of destruction was carried out with a positive aim in mind: 'It is certain that the *tabula rasa,* which we made the guiding principle of our activities, only had value in so far as it prepared the way for other things to follow.' Hugo Ball reminded Huelsenbeck in a private conversation:

> What we need is the preservation of the deeper identity of our Western civilisation, and because of this you should oppose everyone who does not understand Dada's ambivalence with regard to the question of tradition. What we wanted was not only the destruction of a tradition, but also the creation of a new one. When Dada turned against humanism and its overestimation in the arts, we were nevertheless afraid of the inhumanity in war and politics, which we were fighting against.

By many of its followers Dada was regarded as a vital link between the old and the new:

> In a state of suspension between two worlds, when we have broken with the old one and have not yet been able to establish the new one, satire, the grotesque, caricature, the clown and the puppet make their appearance. It is the deeper meaning of these forms of expression to reveal, through the mechanisation and marionette-like quality of life, another kind of existence beyond the seeming and actual torpor.

Hans Arp also had this idea of another life in mind when he spoke of 'Dada as a crusade in order to win back the promised land of creativity'. But how was one to achieve this ideal? Arp's metaphor of a 'crusade' was not chosen at random. Ball compared his position in Zurich to that of a fighter in the trenches, and the bellicose language becomes even more obvious when one examines the Dada manifestos published in Berlin.

Eventually the Dadaists realized that confronting the bourgeoisie in the theatres was not enough. They had to move into more political areas. Particularly in Berlin, Dada was taken out of the cafés into the public arena and connected with the revolutionary movements in society:

> We know that we have to be an expression of the revolutionary forces, an instrument of the masses and the necessities of our times. We deny any

similarity with the aesthetic profiteers and academics of tomorrow. [Berghaus explains in a footnote that this is part of an open letter signed by Housmann, Dix, Grosz, Höch, Schlichter and others.'']

In their 'Manifesto Against the Weimar Spirit of Life' they declared Dada 'an international antibourgeois movement', and in their 'Manifesto Against the Petit Bourgeois Spirit (Puffkeismus) of the German Soul' they defined their aim as follows: 'The old state and economic structures change under the approach of the working class. It is our duty to bring the realities of the intellectual life (the so-called "Arts and Sciences") up to date.'

Erwin Piscator, the champion of Epic Theatre and one of the most influential directors of the 1920s, is a good example of an artist who, having experienced the barbarity of war at the Ypres front, was totally disillusioned about the role art could play in modern society. Immediately on his return to Germany he joined the Club Dada in Berlin and underwent a 'self-purification', which completely changed his attitudes towards art and life:

> In Berlin I saw Herzfelde again. He introduced me to his circle . . . Most of them belonged to Dada. There was a great deal of discussion about art, but always in relation to politics. We came to the conclusion that art had to be a weapon in the class struggle, otherwise it had no value at all. Full of memories of the past, deceived in our hopes for life, we saw the salvation of the world in terms of ultimate logic: organized struggle of the proletariat, seizure of power. Dictatorship. World Revolution. Russia was our ideal . . . Under the slogan, 'Art is shit', the Dadaists began with the demolition of art. . . . These iconoclasts made a clean sweep, they reversed gear, abandoned the bourgeois position, and returned to the point of departure from which the proletariat also had to approach art.

For a great number of artists Dada meant an important transitional period in their lives. Their connection with the movement led to a radical reorientation of their outlook on art and society. Many of the Berlin Dadaists later joined the Communist Party (Erwin Piscator, George Grosz, John Heartfield, Wieland Herzfelde, Franz Jung), as did Paul Eluard and Louis Aragon in Paris. Dada became a training ground for radical, politically active artists. Even the arch-bohemian, anarchist and nihilist Tristan Tzara later turned socialist. Hugo Ball converted to Catholicism, but did not give up his belief 'in a holy Christian revolution and a mystical union of a liberated world'.

The effects Dada had on the art world in general are too manifold to be related here. In the theatre Dada had great influence on the development of Surrealist drama, the Theatre of the Absurd, Happenings and Performance Art. But how did Dada work in the field of drama? So far, we have only discussed Dada performances based on poetry, dance and music. But what did a Dada *play* actually look like?

Though performances were the most important form of artistic expression used by the Dadaists, plays as such were only rarely performed. In Zurich, only one 'proper' play was presented (Kokoschka's *Strohmann und Sphinx* at the *Sturm* soirée on 14 April 1917), and in Paris only three soirées included performances of plays (27 March 1920 at the Maison de l'OEuvre: *Le serin muet* by Georges Robemont-Dessaignes, *S'il vous plaît* by André Breton and Philippe Soupault, *La première aventure céleste de M. Antipyrine* by Tristan Tzara; 26 May 1920 at the Salle Gaveau: *La deuxième aventure céleste de M. Antipyrine* by Tristan Tzara, and *Vous m' oublierez* by André Breton and Philippe Soupault; 10 June 1921 at the Galerie Montaigne: *Le coeur à gaz* by Tristan Tzara).

However, it would be wrong to assume that the Zurich soirées, because they did not include the performances of plays, were less theatrical than those in Paris. Analysing the first Dadaist play, Tzara's *La première aventure céleste de M. Antipyrine,* one finds that this 'double quadrologue' is rather static and consists of an odd mixture of sound poems, automatic writings and a Dada manifesto. The static quality of the play was underlined in the first production, where the actors recited the text wearing multi-coloured paper bags which hindered their every movement. The understanding of the text was not exactly improved by the 'diabolic sound machine' which Tzara had specially constructed for the occasion. It consisted of 'a klaxon and three successive invisible echoes, for the purpose of impressing on the minds of the audience certain phrases describing the aims of Dada. The ones which created the most sensation were: "Dada is against the high cost of living" and "Dada is a virgin microbe".' Around their necks the actors carried signs on which the names of the characters (M. Antipyrine, Boumboum, Tristan Tzara etc.) were inscribed. How much of the performers on the stage, bathed in green light, was to be seen from the auditorium is difficult to assess. The decoration, consisting of a bicycle wheel, some ropes strung across the stage, and a few placards with hermetic inscriptions ('Paralysis is the beginning of wisdom', 'Stretch out your hands, your friends will cut them off etc.), was placed not behind, but *in front* of the actors. It is no wonder that the play, which Tzara described as 'a boxing match with words', excited the audience to such an extent that no single word from the stage could be understood.

Whereas Dada poetry can only be analysed properly in performance, the rather untheatrical production of Tzara's first *Celestial Adventure* did not help in any way to understand the meaning of the play. The first impression one has after reading the text (which was written as a typical Dada exercise in automatic writing) is that of total chaos. Sounds, words and phrases are thrown together and no regard is paid to rules of grammar or even logic. The play bears no relation to any dramatic convention. It is an anarchic explosion of the author's imagination, which, because of the spontaneity of its creation, must be seen as an expression of his subconscious feelings and concerns.

Long before the Parisian Surrealists invented the 'écriture automatique', this new technique had been employed by the Dadaists in Zurich. Poetry in action, as being practised in the Dada soirées, was nothing but 'parole automatique'. Since these creations represent the author's dreams, wishes, desires and obsessions, and since they were produced without any aesthetic considerations, it is easier to gain access to their meaning with the analytic tools of psycho-analysis than with those of philology. Tzara stressed the close connection between dreams and what he called 'penser prélogique' or 'non dirigé' (prelogic and non-directed thought). With special reference to the first *Celestial Adventure* he explained: 'This method presupposed that words could be stripped of their meaning yet still be effective in a poem by their simple evocative power—a kind of magic as hard to understand as it is to formulate.' In another article he wrote: 'A world placed by a secret association, not discernible by known methods of investigation, next to another, may, by means of a *shock*—strange process—disclose to certain readers, who are particularly sensitive or experienced, an emotion of a poetic nature.'

Analysing the text of the *Celestial Adventures* one finds that the word-material used evokes different types of association. Passages such as:

Mr. CRICRI	zdranga zdranga zdranga zdranga
Mr. BLEUBLEU PIPI	di di di di di di di di zoumbai zoumbai zoumbai zoumbai
Mr. ANTIPYRINE	dzi dzi dzi dzi dzi dzi dzi dzi

or word-play such as:

> rendre prendre entre rendre rendre prendre prendre endran drandre

conjure up images of childlike innocence or playful Negro mumbo-jumbo. Both, of course, are interrelated. Primitive Negro cultures were regarded as reminders of mankind's infancy and Negro art as 'an expression of purity'. Several programmes of Zurich soirées mention the recitation of 'vers nègres' or the singing of 'Negerlieder'. Huelsenbeck was particularly fond of Negro rhythms, Janco's masques were inspired by those found in Africa and Oceania, and Tzara's cycles of Negro poems were based on actual African songs collected and translated by European missionaries.

In a very similar way the Dadaists 'welcomed the child in art as well as life'. They wanted to use 'childhood as a new world: all the directness of childhood, all its fantastic and symbolic aspects, against the senilities, against the adult's world.' Ball, however, was aware of the fact that children were more than playful innocents:

> A child's innocence, I mean, borders on the infantile, on dementia, on paranoia. It stems from the belief in a primeval memory, in a world that has been repressed and buried beyond recognition, a world that is saved in art by unrestrained enthusiasm, but in a lunatic asylum is freed by a disease. The revolutionaries I mean are sooner to be found there than in the mechanised literature and politics of today. The primeval strata, unreached by logic and the social apparatus, emerge in the inconsiderate infantility and madness, where all inhibitions are removed. This is a world with its own laws and its own form; it

poses new problems and new tasks, just like a newly discovered continent.

Later he remarked on the same subject: 'Certainly, the naïveté of children can be heartless and cruel, and all laughter, because it distorts certain muscles, indicates a strange origin.'

This 'primeval' world is stressed in the *Celestial Adventures* by the presence of a character called 'Npala Garroo' and dialogues such as:

> Mr. CRICRI (. . .) Dschilolo Mgabati Bailunda
> LA FEMME ENCEINTE Toundi-a-voua Soco Bgai Affahou
> Mr. BLEUBLEU Farafamgama Soco Bgai Affahou

There is also a character called 'La femme enceinte' and childish names such as 'Pipi', 'Cricri', 'Bleubleu'. There is a great amount of vocabulary with childlike associations and words linked with the process of pregnancy, birth, motherhood and procreation: 'accoucher', 'nouveau-né', 'parthénogenèse', 'foetus', 'organe sexuel', 'savon testiculaire', 'ballet spermatozoïde' etc. Several of the phrases related to the child's world have a very aggressive quality, such as: 'oiseaux enceints qui font caca sur le bourgeois. le caca est toujours un enfant' ('pregnant birds shit on the bourgeois. shit is always a child').

One should note that the 'oiseau' is the animal that is used most in the play. Most of the other animals are lesser creatures such as 'serpent', 'grenouilles', 'tortue', 'souris', 'scarabée', 'vers', 'coccinelle', 'mollusque', 'microbe', 'protozoaïres' etc. The bird is one of the few animals with a positive connotation. It is also related to the extensive vocabulary of upward movement, such as 's'envoler', 'grimper', 's'élever', 'monter', 'l'aviateur', 'ange', and objects such as 'clocher', 'poteau télégraphique', 'arbre', 'montagne', 'cathédrale', 'Tour Eiffel', and the nine times repeated 'réverbères', which, of course, is related to the 'boucle de lumière', 'lampion', 'soleil', 'lucidité', 'ciel', 'arc-en-ciel' etc.

On the other side of the spectrum are the words with a negative connotation. These may be words such as 'malheur', 'catastrophe', 'douleur', 'peine', 'maladie', 'écoeurement', 'décombres', 'débris', expressions of separation ('évacuer', 'abandonner', 'violer'), secretion ('chier', 'pisser', 'urine', 'merde', 'crachat', 'WC', 'cul', 'aaïsme', 'hémorroïdes', 'maillots mouillés et jaunes') and of hostile landscapes ('désert', 'cimetière', 'glacier putride', 'neiges pourrissantes', 'marécages pétrolifières'). This world of hostility, decomposition and desintegration is linked to and supported by a vocabulary of mechanical order. There is the 'langouste mécanique', the 'bras polygone irrégulier', the 'parallélépipède', 'ellipse pudibonde' and 'magnéto poignard'. That this world of order has no positive meaning is revealed in the sentence: 'A l'arrivée de la police il est dégoûté' ('at the arrival of the police he feels disgusted').

This can in many ways be regarded as the world the Dadaists felt surrounded by and against which they reacted so strongly. They saw themselves as the 'oiseaux enceints',

i.e. the artists who wanted to rise to higher things and transcend the decomposing world around them. Their 'médicin' against the rampant 'fièvre' in Europe was Dada art. They were creative and acted like children, shitting on the bourgeois and thoroughly enjoying doing so. Behind this aggressive attitude there was the desire to give birth to something pure and beautiful. So out of the decomposing, putrefying surroundings the flower of Dada grew, or, as M. Antipyrine expressed it: 'Un lys vient d'éclore dans le trou de son cul' ('a lily begins blooming in his arsehole'). This can be regarded as a central metaphor of the play, which, when related to the 'caca sur le bourgeois' and the phrase 'Car l'art n'est pas sérieux, je vous assure, . . . c'est pour vous faire du plaisir' ('art is not serious, I assure you, it is there to give you pleasure'), leads us to an understanding of the aspirations, dreams and obsessions of a Dada playwright such as Tristan Tzara, and, on a more general level, to an appreciation of the aims and the essence of Dada performance art. (pp. 293-309)

> *Günter Berghaus, "Dada Theatre or: The Genesis of Anti-Bourgeois Performance Art," in* German Life & Letters, *Vol. XXXVIII, No. 4, July, 1985, pp. 293-312.*

J. H. Matthews

[*A Welsh critic, Matthews is considered one of the foremost scholars specializing in Surrealist literature, music, art, and film. In the following excerpt, Matthews discusses the difficulty of distinguishing Dadaist from Surrealist plays and questions the viability of Dada theater given its combative attitude toward the public.*]

Relatively little has been said on the subject [of Dada's attitude toward the theater], so that one may be forgiven for concluding that Dada's approach to the stage, and surrealism's too, is unworthy of attention. By and large, it appears, the whole question has been pushed aside, and for good reasons, it seems at first glance.

The fact of the matter is that it is as unfruitful as it is foolhardy to speak of Dada theatre or of surrealist drama. Even a preliminary consideration of the available evidence recommends that we limit ourselves, instead, to acknowledging the existence of a certain number of texts by writers of Dada or surrealist persuasion which, sometimes for want of a better definition, may be called plays. To begin with, at all events, our inquiry appears not merely unpromising, but denied definite orientation.

When we take up the question of theatre in the perspective of Dada or surrealism, our initial impression is that the best guidelines may well be of the most unsophisticated kind. Thus, it would appear, the plays of Tristan Tzara could be considered an expression of Dada primarily because their author was one of the founders of Dada in Switzerland. As for Georges Ribemont-Dessaignes, his *L'Empereur de Chine* could be termed a Dada text because it was the first piece of writing in dramatic form to be published in France—during 1921—in the "Collection Dada." Results are likely to be less than satisfactory, though, if we go about things in this fashion. Tzara's plays and Ribemont-Dessaignes's plainly have little in common.

What is more, the theatrical works of neither of these authors offer very clear affinities with, shall we say, *S'il vous plaît* by André Breton and Philippe Soupault, performed on March 27, 1920.

But our problems do not end here. *S'il vous plaît* was presented under Dada aegis. The fact is especially worthy of note because Breton and Soupalt had co-authored, a year earlier, a series of texts they called *Les Champs magnétiques*. The historical importance of these texts is that they were produced by the very process of verbal automatism which, in his 1924 surrealist manifesto, Breton was to salute as basic to surrealist expression. In fact, *Les Champs magnétiques* has never ceased to be considered, in surrealist circles, the first attempt to explore the surrealist potential of language, to adapt language to purposes quite different from those that interested Dada. The existence of *Les Champs magnétiques* is proof, then, that chronology offers no safe-conduct through the confusing and sometimes apparently conflicting evidence that has come down from the period when Dada was active and surrealism in gestation. *L'Empereur de Chine* was written at the beginning of 1916, before its author had ever heard the word "Dada." While one critic at least gives precedence to surrealism over Dada in this play, Ribemont-Dessaignes speaks in his memoirs of merely having "flirted" with surrealism. He did not find it to his liking at all to cast off his Dada identity, when Dada yielded to surrealism. Yet we cannot attach too much importance to his hesitations, since there is reason to suspect his actions of being motivated by personal antipathy for André Breton, far more than by deeply held convictions, aesthetic or anti-aesthetic. As for Breton, his respect for *L'Empereur de Chine,* we should notice, was in no way diminished by its author's aversion to surrealism. Breton and Soupault, meanwhile, wrote *S'il vous plaît* before they made Tzara's acquaintance. At that time, Tzara had not yet left Zurich for Paris, where Dada really took root only after his migration from Switzerland to France. Later, after the demise of Dada, Tzara joined the surrealists, freely associating for a while in surrealism's program of revolt, which had replaced Dada's.

Unfortunately, no guaranteed criterion exists that, cutting across misleading chronological boundaries, would permit us to classify this play as unquestionably of Dada inspiration and that play as of purely surrealist derivation. The thesis advanced by Michel Sanouillet, who contends in his *Dada à Paris* that surrealism in France is merely an extension of Dada, is no less tendentious than arguing that Dada is surrealism in disguise or in search of its true identity. Progress is likely to be more sure if the liberty granted all creative writers within Dada is recognized as having direct consequences for the theatre: absence of a consistent and consecutive approach to drama as well as absence of a unified program for the stage.

To begin with, at any rate, avoidance of dogmatism and rigid controls on the part of Dada writers of plays bids us be wary of attempting to determine where Dada in the theatre stops and where surrealism begins. It is advisable to note, rather, how often attitudes taken by writers in the Dada tradition were adopted by the first surrealists also.

Iconoclasm, for instance, is fundamental to theatre as understood and practiced both in Dada and in surrealism. Hence the exuberant aggressiveness of the following notes by Tristan Tzara represents equally the approach of the latter and of the former:

> Première: "Sphynx and Straw Man" by O. Kokoschka. Firdusi, Rubberman, Anima, Death.
>
> This performance decided the role of our theatre, which will entrust the stage direction to the subtle invention of the explosive mind, scenario to the audience, visible direction, grotesque props: the DADAIST theatre. Above all masks and revolver shots, the effigy of the director. Bravo! & Boom boom!

Naturally, it would be difficult to deduce from these few phrases any theory destined to modify or question playwriting constructively, in the name of Dada. At best, one senses that certain ideas on the methods and purposes of dramatic composition were to grow only incidentally out of a distinctive conception of communication and expression, affecting the drama among other literary modes. These ideas reflected no preconceived intent, no concerted effort by Tzara and his associates—either those he knew in Zurich during the First World War or encountered later in Paris—to improve, update, or otherwise revitalize the playwright's art. On the contrary, it is in its negative aspects that Dada treatment of theatre can be said to manifest the greatest measure of unity. At the same time, there is no occasion to speak of a sudden and intentional change of emphasis, subject matter or style, deliberately adopted once Dada gave way to surrealism. Since Breton's outlook upon life was basically incompatible with Tzara's, during the early days of surrealist activity temperamental differences contributed more to indicating where boundaries eventually would be erected than did distinctions on the plane of theory. Hence estimates of the theatre could not be characterized as marking an entirely new departure, during the middle twenties; or so it seems at first. After all, Breton had been motivated to join Dada largely by disgust for literature as nothing more interesting than a succession of aesthetic exercises carried out in accepted literary forms. His eventual disagreement with Dada's philosophy of nihilism, as expressed by Tzara, did not dispose of that disgust altogether. Disgust continued to nourish many of the attitudes we identify as typical of the surrealist posture.

Surrealism agrees with Dada in opposing any compromise with rational, emotional, and moral preoccupations of the kind traditionally underlying the theatre in France, no less than elsewhere. Instead of these, Dada developed a form of spectacle—the word *manifestation* ("demonstration," "celebration," "outburst," "revelation") being used in French to describe performances put on before the public by those militating for Dada—that was essentially a deliberate act of provocation. From the first, an instinct for showmanship in Tzara guided Dada toward exhibitionism. And this, for a time anyway, fascinated those in Paris who were not to declare themselves surrealists until after brief but impassioned association with Dada. We find Breton beginning a lecture at the Ateneo in Barcelona on November 17, 1922, with the following words: "In general,

I consider that a critical study is quite out of place in the present circumstances and that the smallest theatrical effect would serve my purposes better." Significantly, he went on to speak of Alfred Jarry, seated at a table with a bottle of absinthe in front of the curtain at the Salle du Nouveau Théâtre in 1896, on the first night of his *Ubu Roi.* Breton mentioned also Arthur Cravan in wartime New York, having to be dragged in a state of intoxication onto the rostrum from which he was supposedly to lecture about modern humor, and where he started to undress before his audience. Breton's conclusion was unequivocal: "All things considered, the sense of provocation is still what is to be appreciated most in this matter. A truth will always gain from taking an outrageous turn when finding expression."

In his essay entitled "Après Dada," Breton dates the "funeral" of Dada from about May 1921. Yet there is no immediately observable difference between the statement just taken from his 1922 address in Barcelona and an affirmation of Tzara's, the next year: "Dadaism has never rested on any theory and has been only a provocation." Before the days of surrealism, Dada recognized the theatre as a valid expression of the principle of provocation, when it is treated as somewhat self-contradictory, when, for example, the form of drama is adopted to nondramatic ends. In part, this is what Tzara's *1918 Dada Manifesto* implied: "Let every man cry out: a great destructive negative work needs to be accomplished. To sweep away, to clean up." All things considered, one might hope, then, to begin dealing quite practically with the question of drama in Dada by identifying what drama is not, for Dada—categorizing the things Dada writers do not wish to do and noting what they reject. For elements of negativity are paramount, even when they engender innovative features leading in some cases to distinctly positive results, as Dada gives way to surrealism. All the same, consistency is far from the Dada playwright's mind, and concerns the surrealist little if any more. Tzara neglects plot entirely in two plays (1916 and 1920) about the celestial adventures of someone he calls Monsieur Antipyrine. In *S'il vous plaît* Breton and Soupault handle plot with undisguised irony. Ribemont-Dessaignes, though, develops a relatively firm plot line in *L'Empereur de Chine,* as he does also in *Le Bourreau du Pérou* (1926). In addition, he declares that all his plays— even the enigmatic playlet *Le Serin muet* (1919)—have a philosophical import patently lacking in, for example, Louis Aragon's *L'Armoire à Glace un beau Soir* (written between 1922 and 1923) and in Aragon's *Au Pied du Mur* (first performed in 1925), as it is absent, too, from the Breton-Soupault sketch *Vous m'oublierez* (1920).

The only truly common feature of early surrealist playwrighting, one thinks at first, is certainly its most durable link with drama of Dada inspiration: denial of the right of conventional and conservative forces to inhibit free expression in the theatre. As is the case with Dada, it is in the nature of surrealism to cast down sacrosanct forms, repudiate established aesthetic principles, and be wary of all rules in deference to the spirit of revolt and iconoclasm. This is why theatre *per se* is of no more value to Breton and his companions than to Tzara and his. The defenders of Dada and those of surrealism are far from being concerned with making a memorable contribution to the literature of the stage. To borrow a phrase used in 1968 by José Pierre, as a title for a volume of surrealist short stories and plays, they have *D'autres Chats à fouetter:* other fish to fry. In surrealism as much as in Dada, the idea of a play as a conventional form is valid only so long as the drama provides a framework into which writers can conveniently pour their material. It is a matter of indifference to them if this material does not quite fill the mold where it has been cast, or if it overspills the limits we are accustomed to see dramatists respect. Indeed, in the theatre perhaps more than anywhere else, one is made aware of the things that Dada and surrealism have done *to* a given literary form, rather than *for* it.

When we have said this much, we still cannot point, either in Dada or in surrealism, to proof of a well-planned, concerted attack upon the medium of theatre. The most we can do, at this juncture, is indicate certain characteristic trends that appear common to both.

In writers to whom the idea of professionalism in literary or artistic production is abhorrent, it is only to be expected that distaste for ordained approaches and perspectives should provoke striking departures from the norm of playwriting. When bringing people on stage before an audience, neither Dada nor surrealism displays consistent regard for characterization. In fact, the very idea of character is ridiculed quite frequently, as in the dramatis personae of Tzara's *Le Cœur à Gaz.* In surrealism, notably, skepticism about the unity of character in theatrical presentation is plain to see. No doubt this reflects, at least in part, Breton's marked dislike for conventional drama and the roles it offers as exemplary. "Oh eternal theatre," he exclaims in his *Introduction au Discours sur le Peu de Réalité* (1927), "you demand that not only to play the role of another but also to dictate this role, we mask ourselves in his resemblance, that the mirror before which we pass send back a foreign image of ourselves. Imagination has every power except that of identifying ourselves in spite of our appearance with a personage other than ourselves." What could be more logical to Breton than this conclusion, which deeply influences the surrealists' conception of drama: "Literary speculation is illicit as soon as it sets up, facing an author, personages he declares to be in the right or in the wrong, after having created them out of nothing"?

In his *Nadja* (1928), Breton confided, "I who never go to the theatre [. . .]." The revised version of his text (1963) changes the phrasing of this admission without betraying its meaning, or suggesting even a minor modification in attitude: "Braving my distaste for the boards [. . .]." The realistic prejudice of conventional drama held as little appeal for him as for Tzara. Indeed Breton preferred to give attention to the "question of reality, in its relationship to possibility, a question which remains the great source of anguish." The general orientation of his thinking thus dictated his views upon theatre. In Paul Palau's *Les Détraquées,* performed at the Théâtre des Deux Masques, following one of the fundamental principles of surrealism Breton was responsive to the "latent content" that he detected behind the "manifest content" of a lurid drama. In his *Anthologie de l'Humour noir,* reviewing various interpretations of Synge's *Playboy of the Western World,* he asserted that a most satisfying explanation of the play rested, to his mind, on the Oedipus complex. He added, "The important thing is that exploration of the 'latent content' leads here to confronting a rosette of meanings tending to have value on several planes at once and to have value for everyone, as if, with *The Playboy,* we were dealing with a precipitate of the universal dream."

Where Breton consistently distinguishes latent content from manifest content, Tzara separates the spirit from technique in a manner that strengthens, rather than weakens, the parallel between Dada and surrealism in matters pertaining to theatre. "It is not a new technique that interests us, but the spirit," averred the Dada leader in a lecture delivered in 1922. From both Dada and surrealism, respect for theatrical form, convention, and technique draws nothing but suspicion, because it endorses submission to temptations of a literary nature. As a result, if we try to evaluate the plays . . . on their literary merits, we are in danger of losing sight of what is essential, as much to practitioners of Dada as to defenders of surrealism. So long as we confine ourselves to estimating the supposed worth of these texts as works of literature, we must expect to find ourselves not only less than pleased with the quality of the material we are handling, but actually engaged in diverting it from its true purpose. For, in surrealism no less than in Dada, the conflict between form and technique, on the one hand, and expression of latent content and a nonliterary anti-artistic spirit, on the other, is resolved invariably to the detriment of formal and technical requirements, and in disregard of aesthetic standards.

The theatregoer tends to find established dramatic forms reassuring and considers technical competence essential in the playwright. But Dada and surrealism believe it salutary to outrage their public by refusing to meet expectations or to abide by specifications. It is not enough to notice that, coming to plays written in the spirit of Dada or surrealism with the hope of seeing some tangible contribution made to the art of the theatre or the technique of dramatic presentation, spectators and readers are more in danger of being disappointed than they are likely to be rewarded. At the very least, Dada and surrealist writing for the stage demonstrates indifference to the medium of the play. In its most aggressive forms, such writing constitutes a frontal attack upon the very idea of dramatic communication. For this reason, it casts the audience in an unaccustomed and disconcerting role.

It was typical of Dada to challenge its audience in direct confrontation. Mounting a Dada spectacle meant putting on a public show. Success depended, therefore, upon the presence of spectators who would find themselves witnessing a performance for which they were unprepared. Surprise was a key element in Dada provocation and could be replaced effectively by no other ingredient. This largely is why the manner of making contact with audiences favored in Dada was destined to have a limited potential. It was just a matter of time before participants ran out of ideas for taking the public off guard. It was equally predictable that, quick to learn from experience, the public

soon would be alerted to Dada's methods. Discovering that Dada used terrorist tactics to ridicule good taste, culture, reason, and even the spirit of inquiry, people either stayed away from the next spectacle or returned in a state of mind quite different from before and even prepared, in some cases, to enjoy what was intended to aggravate. There seems little doubt, therefore, that the distinctive posture of the surrealists, who for more than forty years took care to keep their distance from the public, resulted from one of the lessons Dada taught Breton and several of the friends who followed him out of the Dada camp into surrealism.

So far as they relied upon the audience's trust in the playwright's responsibility to his craft, those undertaking to express the mood of Dada on the stage paid the drama a compliment, in a roundabout fashion. But when doing so, they indicated how little, really, their interest in plays had to do with dramatic ambition. Within the framework of a Manifestation Dada held at the Théâtre de la Maison de l'Œuvre (Salle Berlioz) on March 27, 1920, Tzara's *La Première Aventure céleste de Monsieur Antipyrine* was termed a "double quatrologue." But *Le Serin muet* was presented as a one-act play and *S'il vous plaît* called a comedy. The program of the Festival Dada at the Salle Gaveau on May 26 listed Tzara's *La Deuxième Aventure céleste de Monsieur Antipyrine* without explanatory subtitle, while *Vous m'oublierez* was classified as a sketch. Viewed by traditional standards, classifications in this manner represented an act of literary piracy. Dada-affiliated writers were providing their public with a yardstick for measuring the distance separating their theatre from familiar dramatic forms. So they invited the audience to ponder the significance and implications of that distance, just as the surrealist Georges Hugnet was to do when giving his play *Le Droit de Varech,* published in 1930, the subtitle of melodrama.

In advance of surrealism, Dada had this as one of its essential qualities: it guaranteed individual writers the greatest possible liberty. "The work of art is never beautiful by degrees, objectively, for everyone," declared Tzara's 1918 Dada manifesto. "Criticism is therefore useless, it exists only subjectively, for each person, [. . .]. Thus DADA was born from a need for independence, for mistrust before community of of ideas. Those who belong with us retain their liberty. We recognize no theory."

Although formulating no positive theory of drama, those who elected to speak for Dada or surrealism from the stage necessarily had to face the consequences of having chosen the theatre as their means of expression. Drama poses a special problem for any writer, that of communication with an audience seated beyond the footlights. Release from the necessity to face this problem cannot be obtained by the simple expedient of denying that the audience is present. However grudging it may be, adoption of theatrical form betrays the assumption that an assembled group of people are listening and reacting to what they hear. The author has agreed to meet his public collectively, to solicit the attention of a number of persons at once. He therefore anticipates certain reactions more or less consciously, and writes accordingly. And so, when one is dealing with a theatrical mode as unconventional and self-consciously anti-conformist as is the case in Dada and surrealism, the question of justification for presentation in dramatic form is of central concern. More especially, one must ask what the author is free to do, what the audience is justified in expecting—and with what results. (pp. 3-12)

Dada and surrealist writers attack the structure of drama because they have no faith in the viability of theatrical structure and hence have no ambitions to bring anything new to it. The surrealist, especially, is more concerned with what Breton terms "*poetic* intuition" than with consecrated literary modes. He recognizes, as does Breton, that the intuition claiming his exclusive attention "wants to be not only assimilative of all known forms but boldly creative of new forms." But none of these new forms could ever be an art form which, as [Martin Esslin has noted in his *The Theatre of the Absurd*], Esslin "necessarily relies on constructive cooperation." Whatever Dada and surrealism give to the theatre, they give incidentally, neither by design nor by intent. The seeds they sow in the theatre produce a harvest that they are quite content to let others gather. (pp. 285-86)

J. H. Matthews, in his Theatre in Dada and Surrealism, *Syracuse University Press, 1974, 286 p.*

Thomas Elsaesser

[*In the following excerpt, Elsaesser examines what qualities constitute a Dadaist film.*]

The cinema, displaying a flagrant (and ironic) discrepancy between the bricolage of its mechanical, optical, chemical processes on the one hand, and the homogeneity, unity, illusory cohesion of its effects on the other, would seem to be a quintessentially Dada artifact—a contention which conversely might suggest that Dada artifacts are quintessentially nineteenth-century technological fantasies.

The combination Dada/cinema is thus interlaced with the more general history of inventions and apparati, and with the crises provoked in the arts when it became impossible to separate technology from technique or scientific from artistic experiment. The explosive development of new means of representation and reproduction towards the end of the nineteenth century, indicating for the first time that aesthetic effects can be attributed to machine-made objects or images, had profoundly ruptured a traditional relation between art and mimesis. It had also cruelly exposed the delicate relationship between crafted object and art object in respect to labor, skill, and value.

Two aspects are worth singling out. One is to look, especially in the context of Germany and Berlin Dada, at the forms of spectatorship and pleasure that might be associated not so much with watching Dada films but watching films as Dada. The second point concerns the kinds of reflection which the cinema as total apparatus—psychic, economic, erotic—occasioned among the avant-garde and Dadaists in particular, as a model or metaphor for representing the relation of body to social environment, or even for conceptualizing the art-work as event, rather than as

object, no longer as products but as circuits of exchange for different energies and intensities, for the different aggregate states matter can be subjected to between substance and sign through an act of transposition, assemblage, division, and intermittence. The cinema, in other words, between photo-montage and meta-mechanics.

Unlike "Surrealism and Cinema," on which one can consult volumes, the subject "Dada and Film" has not entered into the histories of the movement, nor into film history as a distinct entity. Apart from a short, mainly autobiographical essay by Hans Richter in Willy Verkauf's monograph, references to Dada films have until a few years ago only turned up in histories of avant-garde cinema, experimental or abstract film. The focus of these accounts tends to sever the examples from their Dada connections and to annex them as the precursors of a tradition either of graphic or structuralist cinema. Dada films thus appear briefly in the prehistory of the New American Cinema, but the connections seem rather tenuous compared, again, to the profound influence of Surrealism on the American film avant-garde.

The problems of talking about Dada film are twofold. Firstly, the question of attribution and contribution. Should one resist calling *Ballet mécanique* a Dada film, because Léger is usually considered a Cubist? Hans Richter did not think so:

> Though Léger was never a Dadaist, his *Ballet mécanique* is 100% Dada.

Do Francis Picabia's disagreements with the Paris Dadaists disqualify *Entr'acte*? We know that the ballet *Relâche*, for which Picabia and René Clair conceived *Entr'acte*, was in part a protest against Breton's takeover of the Surrealist movement. By a reverse logic, should Hans Richter's *Rhythm 21* and *Rhythm 23* be discussed as Dada films because Richter makes a case for Dada art as abstract art? Candidly, he himself admitted:

> After I have stated this fact "Dada equals abstract art" I happily wish to insist on the other point, "Dada equals non-abstract art." And this is also true if not truer.

Ambiguity of one form or another surrounds most other potential candidates. Duchamp's *Anémic cinéma* is usually called a Dada film, with which Duchamp would presumably not have quarreled, if he had not baulked at calling it a film at all, preferring to see it as part of his "precision optics." In Man Ray's case, we have *Retour à la raison*, first performed at the famous "Soirée du Coeur à barbe" in July 1923, an occasion which signaled the break-up of Paris Dada. Man Ray considered his subsequent two films *Emak Bakia* and *L'Etoile de mer* to be Surrealist films. Hans Richter calls his own *Filmstudie* "rather more surrealist." This only leaves two or three short films by Richter: *Ghosts before Breakfast* and *Two-Penny Magic* as uncontested Dada films.

The second problem is chronology. If one takes a generous view, one can start with 1920, the year Richter and Eggeling applied for facilities and funds to the UFA Film Company in order to carry out work which resulted in *Rhythm 21, Rhythm 23*, and *Diagonal Symphony*. In the same year

Duchamp and Man Ray conducted the first and almost lethal experiments with revolving glass discs and 3-D stereotypes, out of which grew *Rotating Demisphere* and *Anémic cinéma.* It is not until 1923 that *Retour à la raison* appears, and in 1924, *Entr'acte. Ballet mécanique* follows in 1925, and in 1926 comes Hans Richter's *Filmstudie,* Man Ray's *Emak Bakia,* and Duchamp's *Anémic cinéma.* Finally, in 1927 Richter completes *Ghosts before Breakfast* and *Two-Penny Magic,* and in 1928 Man Ray's *L'Etoile de mer* is shown. No chronology of Dada stretches that far.

The reasons for the sparse and late appearance of Dada films are in part financial and in part geographical. There was little commercial interest in either Richter's or Eggeling's work, even though it was sponsored by the powerful UFA Studio, which successfully marketed other types of animation film (Walther Ruttmann's or Lotte Reiniger's). *Entr'acte* was specifically commissioned, and Man Ray's films were made with money from a wealthy expatriate, Arthur Wheeler, who had tried to persuade Man Ray at one stage to become a professional film-maker, with his backing. During the 1920s, France was more receptive to experiments in the cinema, not least because the flourishing ciné-club movement gave film-makers an outlet and a form of distribution, however marginal in relation to the commercial cinema. In Germany, by contrast, the artistic avant-gardes were quite hostile to the cinema during most of the 1910s and early 1920s mainly for political reasons: Germany had a very powerful and successful commercial film industry, and only the arrival of the "Russenfilme" sparked off practical interest in an "alternative cinema." There was, in consequence, less of a viable exhibition system for experimental shorts produced outside the film industry.

One of the few times that one can talk of a Dada film soirée occurred in May, 1925, in Berlin, when Eggeling's *Diagonal Symphony,* Richter's *Film is Rhythm* (the two Rhythm films spliced together) Ruttmann's *Opus I, II* and *IV,* Léger's and Murphy's *Ballet mécanique,* Picabia's and Clair's *Entr'acte,* as well as three films by Moholy-Nagy (made at the Bauhaus) were screened together.

More recent literature has in contrast stressed the ways in which Dada techniques or practices were inherently "cinematic." Anton Kaes, in an article on "Verfremdung als Verfahren: Film und Dada," argues that the cinema suggested to the Dadaists the need to represent "the hectic acceleration of life," and in particular, he compares Hans Richter's work with the "Cinematism" in painting (Balla's famous *Dog on a Leash*), with "Fotodinamismo" and the multiple-exposure studies popular among not only avant-garde photographers in the early teens. But more important for Kaes is the fact that a revolutionary conception of cinema has in common with Dada the principle of montage "because it problematizes the relationship between object of perception and the subject of perception. Montage does not allow for a coherent perspective in which the subject is in control." Kaes quotes Franz Kafka and Thomas Mann to indicate that even the commercial cinema caused an experience of shock to its earliest spectators.

This approach goes beyond the more traditional histories of avant-garde movements, where Dada or Surrealist films are simply searched for examples of techniques already familiar from the literary or visual productions. Kaes can point to a potential area of research, where historical investigations of Dada converge with questions of current film theory, once more interested in the ideas about spectatorship first formulated by Siegfried Kracauer and Walter Benjamin, and recently given a more explicitly psychoanalytical turn.

The general shift from an environment experienced through all the senses to one increasingly dominated by the eye and obeying its control undoubtedly forms part of both the history of the cinema and of Dada. The confusion of active and passive roles under the rule of spectacle is well caught in a poem by George Grosz: "I am like a filmstrip and like a child in a thousand luna parks . . . someone is always cranking the handle."

In this sense, the cinema is indeed that "phenomenon par excellence which has to be traced along the minute cracks and fault-lines that run through late Victorian society in Europe." It is the expression of a sensibility excited by motion, by the means of locomotion, relishing dioramas and panoramas, flocking to world fairs, crowding into the Crystal Palace and climbing the Eiffel Tower. The need for physical mobility, spatial displacement, for the bird's eye view and for being driven or carried along precede the cinema at the same time as these pleasures were significantly transformed, realized, and interpreted by the cinema. Their social dimension leads one inevitably to demographic facts: for the cinema is unthinkable without the big cities. Perhaps the best guide through its prehistory is Benjamin's Baudelaire. In order to understand the changes in perception forced upon people living in the cities as well as for intimating the implications of those changes, Benjamin constructed a Baudelaire who serves him as a poetic "precision instrument" to trace those very fault-lines. The poem about wandering the suburbs at daybreak like a fencer thrusting and parrying imaginary blows suggests to Benjamin that Baudelaire reacted to "ennui," the spectre of specular fascination and voyeuristic control, by a new involvement of the body in the very act of writing, modeled on the experience of fighting one's way through crowded streets and public places:

> The meaning of the hidden configuration (which reveals the beauty of that stanza to its very depth) probably is this: it is the phantom crowd of the words, the fragments, the beginnings of lines from which the poet, in the deserted streets, wrests the poetic booty.

However fanciful this reading may be to a Baudelaire scholar, Benjamin isolates an important aspect of Dada technique: a reaction to, as well as an exploitation of the tyranny of total vision which invaded the early decades of the century. When characterizing the (to him ambiguous) contribution made by Dada to avant-garde art, in his essay on the "Work of Art in the Age of Mechanical Reproduction," Benjamin sees Dada objects replacing one kind of spectatorship (contemplation) with what he calls "a new tactility":

> In the decline of middle-class society, contem-

plation became a school for asocial behavior; it was countered by distraction as a variant of social conduct. . . . From an alluring appearance . . . the work of art of the Dadaists became an instrument of ballistics. It hit the spectator like a bullet, it happened to him, thus acquiring a tactile quality.

One might compare this negation of contemplation to Duchamp's categorical demand to destroy the "retinal" aspect of painting, and thus to counteract the supremacy of the eye. Whereas the Russian post-revolutionary avant-garde abandoned painting and turned to film and photography, Duchamp and other Dadaists on the whole rejected the cinema, not least because, even in its avant-garde forms, it seemed too close to the synesthesia of the Impressionists and the advocates of the Gesamtkunstwerk. That the difference in political situation between East and West played its part is accurately perceived by Benjamin:

> Dadaism . . . sacrificed the market values which are so characteristic of the cinema in favor of higher ambitions. . . . The Dadaists attached much less importance to the sales value of their work than to its uselessness for contemplative immersion. The studied degradation of their material was not the least of their means to achieve this uselessness.

Dadaism in many of its manifestations was reactive, seeking ways of radically short-circuiting the means by which art objects acquire financial, social, and spiritual values. Thus, while from the point of view of the material base, the cinema seemed an art of waste-products, and its conditions of reception were anything but auratic, the very popularity of films meant that the cinema soon represented tremendous financial, and with it, social value. This paradox marked the Dadaists' involvement from the start: the cinema seemed initially anti-contemplative as an entertainment, and at least Benjamin saw in its visual forms an element of tactility; but it soon acquired its own aura: that of glamor and total specular entrancement. It is therefore perhaps not surprising that interest of some Dadaists focused in the first instance on the behavior of the crowds, the character of a happening, and the "degraded" nature of film spectacle, parodying subversively the theater and the concert hall. A certain physicality and body-presence of the first cinema audiences is what might be called the Dada element in film.

While few theorists today would be very satisfied with drawing a dividing line between Meliès and Lumière when it comes to establishing an opposition between "realism" and "fiction" or documentary and fantasy, there has recently been a great deal of interest and controversy around the possibility of distinguishing between so-called "primitive cinema" (up to 1917) and "classical narrative cinema" on the basis of different types of spectatorship. Alongside oppositions such as commercial versus avant-garde cinema, illusionist versus materialist film, historians have speculated on the kind of involvement and participation elicited by early cinema. In one of the most interesting formulations, Noel Burch contrasts two kinds of Imaginary underpinning different practices: the "Edisonian" (a fascination with the apparatus of cinema in view of a total sim-

ulacrum of life, and the "analytical" one, aiming to break down movement into smaller and smaller particles. Both seem relevant to Dada, whose interest in the cinema was in some sense a nostalgic one, attached to the film performance of the 1910s and the figure of the inventor-bricoleur. What remains problematic about both the generic distinction and the definition of a filmic avant-garde in the context of early cinema is that we still know very little about the actual viewing experience during the period in question.

In a typical program, say in Berlin in 1913 (but surviving in the suburbs well into the early 1920s), non-narrative films would be mixed with sketches and fantasies. The Kaiser (or Hindenburg) would be shown on parade right after a filmed variety number. The items would be introduced, a lecturer would stand at the back of the room or hall and comment sarcastically or pathetically on the action, explain, or provide the kind of epic distance that Brecht, copying from the cinema, tried to create in his theater. There was little sense of "illusionism" or any suspension of disbelief.

Skepticism and sarcasm mingled freely with wonder and amazement. The viewing experience seemed, as it were, embedded in drinking and furtive sex, and if it was "structured," it derived this structure from the ambience of the event as much as from the films. "Das Kino" or "Kintopp" was characterized by its communality of reception on the one hand, and its discontinuous flow on the other. Here is an early testimony of a film-show in Berlin:

> The room is darkened. Suddenly the Ganges floats into view, palms, the temple of the Brahmins appears. A silent family drama rages with bon vivants, a masquerade—a gun is pulled. Jealousy inflamed. Mr. Piefke duels headlessly and they show us, step by step, mountaineers climbing the steep, demanding paths. The paths lead down through forests, they twist and climb the threatening cliff. The view into the depths is enlivened by cows and potatoes. And into the darkened room—into my very eye—flutters that, that . . . oh, dreadful! One after the other! Then the arc lamp hissingly announces the end, lights! And we push ourselves into the open . . . horny and yawning.

Van Hoddis's response is to the total environment, of which the film is only one part. The interest in early cinema on the part of today's theorists like Noel Burch resides in the fact that the so-called "codes of representation" have not yet become hierarchized and subjected to certain "laws" whose ideology a later (film-)avant-garde was to deconstruct. This hierarchy is above all one organized around the dominance of the look; it becomes the distinguishing mark of the cinematic watershed between "primitive" and "Griffithian" film-making. To quote from an article by Pascal Bonitzer:

> The look in Griffith was not something that had been there since the beginning of the cinema. There was, first of all, the 20 years during which the cinema was content merely to be the object of viewing, recording phenomena and movements and the sights of the world. When today

we see these early films . . . we are seeing the varied fruits of a cinematic Eden where the coldness and sophistication of the look had not yet penetrated. . . . A cinema where the only currency was that of gesture, where the viewers' eyes are functioning but not looking. According to Edgar Morin . . . it wasn't until 1915-1920 that the gesticulation typical of actors gave way to a degree of immobility. This is the turning point represented by Griffith. . . . What we have here is a cinematic revolution. With the arrival of montage, the close-up, immobile actors, the look (and its corollary—the banishment of histrionics) an entire facade of the cinema seemed to disappear and be lost forever, in a word, all the excrement of vaudeville. . . . The cinema was innocent and dirty, it was to become obsessional and fetishistic. The obscenity did not disappear . . . it passed into the register of desire.

As Bonitzer goes on to show, it is the look circulating within the fiction that, inducing desire, produces narratives, which are in turn based on subjecting to a more or less rigid logic the articulation of cinematic space and sequence. And as Bonitzer also remarks, it is the German Expressionist cinema which for the first time systematically exploited the look as the cinematic signifier par excellence. The introduction of the look into the film diegesis thus constitutes the end point of a development, the final cornerstone of the edifice of control and containment which has governed the development of mainstream cinema. If I claimed that Dada spectatorship is nostalgic, it is perhaps because the presence or absence of the charged look as the agent and motivator of both continuity and discontinuity, of sequence and cut distinguishes Surrealist interest in *film* (consider the importance of the eye and of point of view in *Un Chien andalou*) from Dada interest in *cinema*.

What was Dada in regard to cinema was not a specific film, but the performance, not a specific set of techniques or textual organization, but the spectacle. One might argue that in order for a film to have been Dada it need not be made by a Dadaist, or conversely, that there were no Dada films outside the events in which they figured. "What is a Dada film?" would resolve itself into the question "*When* was a film Dada?" This gives a special place to the screening of *Entr'acte* as part of *Relâche* (as opposed to its cinema première a year later at the Studio des Ursulines), and to the Soirée du Coeur à barbe. At a time when the cinema had become itself a thoroughly respectable (and "institutionalized") form of entertainment, both film text and viewing context had to combine in order to defamiliarize the occasion, in order to recapture the cinema's "excremental" age of scandalously guilty innocence.

Entr'acte works hard at "deconstructing" what had already become set as the conventions of the feature film and the cinema experience. It mocks the solemnity of state-occasions as they might have been presented in contemporary newsreel. By its satirical look at funerals, parades, and photo features from the world of arts, entertainment and leisure, *Entr'acte* explodes the conventions of the newsreel in forms themselves borrowed from the cinema (American slapstick, the Keystone Cops, for instance), and thus could be considered as being in turn part of a filmic genre—that of parody, were it not for the event for which it was conceived.

Picabia and Satie had wanted the audience to whom *Entr'acte* was shown during the intermission of the ballet *Relâche* to provide their own "musical" accompaniment by the mumbling, scraping, protesting, guffawing and general noise to be expected during an intermission. To their disappointment the spectators remained respectfully in their seats, silent, staring at the screen. The projection failed to ignite into a Dada performance.

This incident, I think, is symptomatic of a problem that made film a less than perfect medium at Dada events. For the conditions of a reception in the cinema—the dark room, the stable rectangle of the screen, the fixed voyeuristic position of the spectator—all counteract not only the sense of provocation, but they also compensate for the absence of a coherent diegesis and for the non-narrative organization in the filmed material. Under normal viewing conditions, that is, in a movie theatre and not as part of a performance aspiring to the condition of the happening, Dada films such as *Entr'acte, Ballet mécanique,* or Hans Richter's works are almost inescapably contained, unified and finally recuperated in a way that the classic examples of Surrealist cinema are less vulnerable to, for reasons which have mainly to do with the fact that Surrealist films so closely mimic the figurative operations of narrative cinema, and compensate for the ruptures of their time-space continuum by a massive investment in the on-screen and off-screen look, which lures the spectator into the play of projection, fetish, and identification described by Bonitzer as typical for illusionist cinema.

Film technology confers on even the most banal object the aura of erotic presence. The scandal resides in the cinema bypassing aesthetics while at the same time providing a source of aesthetic appeal. It opened an old wound in German literary culture—the debate about "form" and "material" ("Geist" and "Stoff"). The very achievement of classical literature (no less than of Romantic art) had been the suppression of materiality, its total transfiguration into "form." What for some writers categorically excluded the cinema from being art ("in the cinema, the material substance is preserved in its crude factuality, whereas in drama the material is wholly consumed and transformed by form, of which the main agent is language"), was for others the cinema's chief claim to attention: that it could produce emotion of an aesthetic kind out of pure materiality. Thomas Mann recognized the same dilemma when in 1928, after seeing the first film version of his novel *Die Buddenbrooks,* he wrote:

> A pair of lovers, both young and beautiful, who in a real garden with billowing grass say goodbye "forever" . . . who could resist, who would not enjoy letting it all pour out. This is pure material, not transformed by anything.

Mann concluded from this that it was pointless to try to apply to cinema the criteria developed by classical aesthetics. Sixteen years earlier, Georg Lukacs had already warned against solving the problem in this fashion:

. . . something new and beautiful has developed in recent times, but instead of taking it as it is, people are attempting to classify it. . . . The cinema is regarded either as an instrument of education or as a cheap substitute for the theater; either didactic or economic. Few people if any remember that something beautiful belongs first and foremost to the realm of beauty and its definition and evaluation is properly a task for aesthetics.

Lukacs, in other words, recognized clearly that the cinema posed a challenge to classical aesthetics which had to be answered, and not as Mann was to suggest, by merely relegating it to the side of "life" as opposed to "art." Lukacs goes on:

> The images of the cinema . . . possess a life of a completely different kind [from those on the stage]; in one word, they become—fantastic. But the fantastic is not the opposite to living, it is another aspect of life: life without presence, without fate, without causality, without motivation; a life with which the core of our being will never be identical, nor can it be; and even if it—often—yearns for this kind of life, this yearning is merely after a strange precipice, something a long way off, inwardly distanced. The world of the cinema is a life without background or perspective, without difference of properties or qualities. [The cinema] is a life without measure or order, without being or value, a life without soul, mere surface . . . the individual moments, whose temporal sequence brings about the filmed scenes, are only joined with each other insofar as they follow each other without transition and mediation. There is no causality which could join them, or more precisely, its causality is free from and unimpeded by any notion of content. "Everything is possible": this is the credo of the cinema, and because its technique expresses at every moment the absolute (even if only empirical) reality of this moment, "virtuality" no longer functions as a category opposed to "reality": both categories become equivalent, identical. Everything is true and real, everything is equally true and real; this is what a sequence of images in the cinema teaches us.

What Lukacs here analyzes with a certain lugubrious melancholy is nothing other than what Raoul Hausmann or Kurt Schwitters celebrate: "Everything is true and real, everything is equally true and real." The fundamental Dada paradox, namely that the real is the material, but that this irreducible materiality has no reality other than as a sign or a representation, finds its implicit resolution, if Lukacs is right, in the cinema—except in a cinema equated philosophically if not empirically with life itself. It is in this theoretical impasse that Dadaists remained caught when thinking about the cinema, and it gives some justification to Benjamin's assertion that the Dadaists' attitude to the new technologies of visual reproduction and imaging was retrograde, but necessarily so, given their radical aspirations:

> The history of every art form shows critical epochs in which a certain art form aspires to effects which could be fully obtained only with a

changed technical standard, that is to say, in a new art form. The extravagances and crudities of art which thus appear . . . actually arise from the nucleus of its richest historical energies . . . : Dadaism attempted to create by pictorial—and literary—means the effects which the public today seeks in the cinema.

From Benjamin's perspective and vantage point this estimation of Dada technique as anachronistic in relation to a revolutionizing technology seems at least strategically plausible. But it may also (perhaps deliberately) misread Dada activities and their main thrust. The Berlin Dadaists, for instance, were finally only interested in two kinds of cultural objects: live performance and the newspaper, prototypes of an interventionist use of the mass-media. In both cases, by utilizing already existing forms and formats, maximum effect could be achieved through a minimum of effort—a reversal of bourgeois value-creation which the labor-intensive and time-consuming process of filmmaking does not exemplify particularly well. The principle of the ready-made (the spectacular ratio of effort to effect of an upturned urinal labeled "Fountain" and exhibited in a gallery) was generally of cardinal importance to the Dadaists, not only because it suited the movement's libidinal economy (the excremental against the obsessional): it demonstrated Dada's anti-mimetic concept of realism (preferring material literalism over metaphoric constructions of the materials of art), while at the same time undercutting the traditional equation of skill, effort or inspiration with art, value, status and morality. Wieland Herzfelde wrote:

> The tasks [of painting] have been taken over by photography and film, and they solve them infinitely more perfectly than painting ever could. . . . [Since their invention] all art movements can be characterized as having, despite their differences, a common tendency to emancipate themselves from reality. Dada is the reaction to all these attempts at disavowing the factual, which has been the driving force of impressionists, expressionists, cubists and even futurists (in that they refused to capitulate to film); however, the Dadaist doesn't try to compete with the camera, or to breathe soul into it (as did the impressionists) by giving the worst lens—the human eye—priority, or (like the expressionists) turn the apparatus round and simply depict the world inside their own bosom.

> The Dadaists say: Whereas once inordinate amounts of time, love and exertion were expended on the depiction of a body, a flower, a hat, the shadow cast by a figure, etc., today all we have to do is take a pair of scissors and cut whatever we need out of the paintings, the photographic reproductions of these things; if the objects are small, we don't even need the representations, but take the objects themselves, e.g. pocket knives, ash trays, books, etc.—things which in the museums of old art are wonderfully painted, but only painted.

This passage from Wieland Herzfelde's "Zur Einführung in die Erste Internationale Dada Messe" seems to illustrate Benjamin's point even as it tries to embrace the cinema, only to reject film as not material enough. Herzfelde, despite his bold polemics, does not fully rise to the challenge of the problem already posed by Lukacs: how does the apparently unmediated reality conveyed by the photographic image constitute itself as a sign?

In practice, Dada products were often far from subscribing to Herzfelde's naive literalism of taking the objects themselves and putting them on display. The typical Dada artifact, the photomontage, indicated that the materials were not primary materials, but already formed by mechanical processes, which meant that what in one context constitutes the end-product is treated by Dada as raw material. Likewise, the point about Duchamp's ready-mades is that a semantic transformation has taken place, and not only a transgression of space, status, and use. The shift from end to means in the case of Duchamp especially is always doubled by what might be called a process of semiotization, where an object of little or no value is transformed not into a value but into an (ironic) signifier of value. Raoul Hausmann, in looking back at Berlin Dada, makes a similar point:

> Anti-art withdraws from things and materials their utility, but also their concrete and civil meaning; it reverses classical values and makes them half-abstract. However, this process was only partially understood and only by some of the Dadaists.

Hausmann's notion of "half-abstract" would be worth following up further, if one wanted to situate more precisely the Dadaists' use of images and the critical status of photographic or filmic illusionism in the early practice of photomontage. From the vantage point of an interest in non-linguistic sign systems and visual sign production, the work of Grosz, Hausmann, and Heartfield has yet to be fully explored, because—and here Benjamin is undoubtedly right—Dada "anti-art" contributed less to the overturning of contemporary value systems than it participated in the transformation of a perceptual apparatus which the cinema changed so drastically and rapidly that it seemed to put the intellectual avant-gardes on the defensive.

The pre-history of the cinema comprises two quite distinct strands: that of the spaces and places where the new mass-public gathered for entertainment—fairgrounds, traveling circuses, vaudeville and nickelodeons—, and that of the optical or scientific toys, such as the zoetrope or the phenakistoscope, where images—painted, printed, or photographed—deceived the eye into perceiving movement and continuity where there was merely intermittence. If the Dadaists took an interest in the phenomenon of the masses eroticized by cinematic spectacles, they were equally alert to the fact that here was a machine organized in a peculiarly contradictory way: the cinematic apparatus is devised to function so as to disguise the actual movement *of* the image (passing through the projector gate) in order to create a non-existent movement *in* the image. Energy in the cinema appears not as in productive machines, to transmit, transfer, or transform movement, but in order to nullify, disguise, and revalue movement: mechanics has become the metamechanics of imaginary motion. This

gives the cinema, in terms of its apparatus, the status not of an optical toy, but rather, it makes it available as a philosophical toy, a machine transforming the useful energy of cogs and transmission belts into a useless energy of illusionist simulation. It is this aspect of the cinema—the devaluation of matter through its perfect reproduction, as in the photograph, but coupled with the transformation of mechanical movement from one aggregate state to another—which is explored and elaborated in Duchamp's *Anémic cinéma*. The film grew out of lengthy and dangerous experimentations with glass discs on which geometrical segments and lines were painted in such a way as to produce particular illusionist effects when put in revolving motion.

The rotoreliefs by themselves were illusionist devices, where motorization created a sense of depth and of spatial extension, a movement from inward to outward and vice versa. As such, Duchamp's work is comparable to that of Richter and Eggeling, only that *Anémic cinéma* plays with more overtly anthropomorphic sensations of heaving or breathing, and thus focuses on the eroticizing effect of animating the inanimate by a cunning arrangement of geometrical lines. But what decisively distinguishes Duchamp's film from other work is that the painted discs are intercut with other discs on which a series of ingeniously punning sentences are inscribed, whose semantics and syntactics exploit the mirror effect of syllabic division ("L'aspirant habite Javel, et moi, j'avais l'habite en spirale"). The two types of discs taken together create contrasts between flatness and depth, between negative and positive space, between reading and illusion, between literal and metaphoric. Furthermore, the puns themselves, which are almost all erotic, interact by a sort of metaphoric contagion with the shapes and movements of the discs, to create the impression of seeing male and female protuberances in endless motion, whose consummation is frustrated through the intervention of the machine, a typically Duchamp topos.

Indeed it is not simply the intervention of one machine, but rather the synchronization of two machines: the recording camera and the revolving motor that spins the discs—two circular motions, distinct from each other, synchronized and dephased to produce endlessly closed circuits. Useless energy has been transformed into semiotic energy, via punning and mirroring effects, and the film—referring the spectator to the apparatus that makes its effect possible—reveals itself as peculiarly auto-erotic. The cinema-machine has become a bachelor-machine.

The insertion of art into the sphere of technological, capitalist modes of production becomes, according to Benjamin, the only position from which a critique of that mode of production is possible. In this respect, the idea of cinema, viewed from the perspective of its particular apparatus, could serve as a sort of model for the representation of the relation between body and matter, "Geist" and "Stoff," which goes beyond the disavowal of Thomas Mann as well as the polemical-sadistic materialism of the Berlin Dadaists.

When Hausmann compares the soul of the Berlin bourgeois to a "libretto machine with a reprogrammable morality disc," the metaphor brutally substitutes the spiritual connotations of soul with the image of a gramophone. Hausmann's *Tatlin at Home* or Grosz's *The Engineer Heartfield,* on the other hand, depict precision machines carefully inserted in the place of brains and heart respectively. Clearly there is a difference, both actual and intended, between these two uses, and it highlights the ambiguity of the machine metaphor in much Dada work, poised between futurist machines, which were, invariably, mimetic representations of machines in the conventional media of bourgeois art (oil paint, bronze, etc.), and constructivist machines which were, in a fundamental sense, real machines.

In Picabia's *Portrait of Marie Laurencin,* however, the machine parts neither propose a likeness, nor a polemical statement. The work suggests a coalescence of heterogeneous attributes whose perfection, harmony, or subtle interaction is signaled by machine elements. Similarly, in Man Ray's famous *Dancer/Danger,* the cogs are interlocking so tightly that, as a machine, it cannot function. The picture needs a dancer, a human element with the precision and dexterity of a machine, to make the mechanism turn. But it also remains blocked as long as it is viewed as the representation of a real machine. Only when we notice and thereby activate the energy of the pun (doubled by the fact that it works in two languages) does the cog of the letter G "make the connection": the Dada machine is not so much a metaphoric machine, as it is a metonymic machine which solicits the imaginary participation by an act of displacement, requiring the viewer to look and think in several dimensions at once. Secondly, as the examples from Duchamp, Man Ray, and Picabia make apparent, Dada machines are word machines; they explicitly semiotize the relations that exist between the parts.

Dada practice, like the cinematic apparatus, redefines the relation of part to whole, the relation of part to part. It is the cut, the montage principle that makes the energy in the system visible and active. However, unlike the cinematic apparatus, where heterogeneity at the level of the material components and technologies becomes "retinal" and fantasmatic, Dada machines, whether drawn on paper or printed, enacted in front of a public or built out of glass and wire, use the contradictions and frictions in the system to remain non-mimetic. A Duchamp ready-made invites both tactile and conceptual viewing, but never contemplative attention. The bicycle wheel mounted on a stool is only complete as a "work" when it arouses the desire to make it revolve, and it apparently was installed in a place where, to Duchamp's quiet satisfaction, no-one passed without at least attempting to give it a furtive spin.

Where the Dada machine thus differs from the cinematic apparatus is that at the level of the representations it remains intentionally anti-psychological. The obsessional, projective-introjective functions of the cinema contrast with Duchamp's lifelong exploration of natural processes, of mechanics and optics in search of material supports for the play of ideas which are anti-intentional and non-expressive, but articulate themselves as traces of a presence figured in metonymies. Duchamp's representational systems and constructs—even those which most obviously parody the cinema by figuring it as "nature morte," such as *Etant donnés*—eschew the kinds of closure and homogeneity which typify the developments of film form.

Thus, the complex combination of mechanics, optics, chemistry and timelag which makes cinematic reproduction possible was an invention very much in the Dada spirit, for the Dada object always manipulates the materials of technical reproduction (and not those of expression). The few Dada experiments in film pushed in this direction, as did Dada interest in spectatorship, since it recognized the cinema as a machine not only in view of the recording/screening apparatus of camera, film-strip and projector, but also as a social machine, in which the spectator had a programmed place, physically, physiologically and economically.

Yet that which made cinema so powerful a social institution—its ability to simulate in its *textual* effects the psychic apparatus as a desiring machine (the cinema as the most efficient simulacrum of the psychic apparatus when mapped onto the perceptual system, as has consistently happened since Freud—by and large ran counter to Dada: it was the Surrealists who saw in filmic processes a way of representing the relation of psychoanalysis to matter, mediated through rhetoric and figuration. If, as Benjamin suggested, there is something anachronistic about Dada and cinema, the difference between Dada and Surrealism in this respect parallels and repeats the development of the cinema generally: the first focus of attraction for a paying public was the machinery itself, its novelty, its intricacy, its basic effects. Only subsequently was this fascination displaced to the stories, the stars, the spectacular and the specular. Recent film theory, however, seems to indicate that interest in the apparatus has staged its own return. Perhaps the contradictions and frictions of Dada/cinema may yet become productive. (pp. 13-26)

Thomas Elsaesser, "Dada/Cinema?" in Dada/Surrealism, No. 15, 1986, pp. 13-27.

NATURE AND CHARACTERISTICS OF DADAIST WRITING

Peter Demetz

[*Demetz is an American educator who has written extensively on German literature and literary theory. In the following essay on phonetic poetry, Demetz introduces his terms "logopoeia", "phonopoeia", and "graphopoeia"—the three fundamental aspects of all poems— and analyzes how Dada poetry upsets what is classically a perfect balance between meaning, sound, and appearance.*]

Our renewed consciousness of poesy carried by organized streams of sound has a long history in which times of the finest hearing alternate with epochs of the deaf ear. The Russian Formalists, more than fifty years ago, were certainly right in suggesting that friends of literature should be *ear*- rather than *eye*-people, and even if the Formalists in their time did not convince everybody of the necessity of listening to poetic sounds, our age of renascent semiotics, intent upon making important distinctions between visual and auditory signs, and perhaps the new grassroots, communal, oral poetry, in this country as well as among the restive Soviet writers, have done much to change our encounters with poetic texts. We are aware again that we have to listen more carefully than we have in the past and, encouraged by the late Marshall McLuhan, if not by contemporary linguistics committed to analyzing everyday speech acts, we are less disturbed than previously by a growing suspicion that poetry or even literature at large, as something kept in the written or printed records, is but an island in oceans of oral communications. In my interest in modern phonetic poetry, in which sound more often than not prevails over meaning, I find myself in an ambivalent position. I am respectful of tradition, but am not a traditionalist entirely, and I am far from wanting to suggest that we should regress to the *Urschrei,* the primal scream, or to mere babble as the true source of poetry. Yet I do not want to close my ears to some recent experiments because I suspect that these articulations (in which our usual expectations of what a poem should be are ruthlessly counteracted) offer something we should know about the uneasy relationship of sound, meaning, and writing.

It was Roman Jakobson who (building on Karl Bühler's model) defined the different functions of language potentially present in any utterance and, by distinguishing between poetic and referential functions, as well as among a few others, made it less difficult for us to deal with what traditionalists may term mere "sound." He suggested that a self-concerned poetic utterance was characterized by withdrawal from the referential sphere, and made it more legitimate to bracket questions of imitation, reference, and denotation. In following his example, I do not want to revive issues of *l'art pour l'art,* but to emancipate questions of poetic discourse, at least for the time being, from problems of social, philosophical, or metaphysical relevance, and, by narrowing our field of observation, I hope to sharpen our perception of the smallest parts. Keeping Jakobson's methodological assumptions in mind, we are free to postpone either/or decisions about some disturbing texts which we barely tolerate in our inherited canon of literature; and once we are courageous enough to assume that there may be an *imbalance* of functions in *all* utterances (Dada or not) we may be more willing to look at language experiments which radically *un*balance that which we believe to be proper balance, proportion, and integrity. We have to overcome our belief that verbal experiments are egotistic games played by poetic narcissists, and accept the possibility that in these challenges to our sensibilities poetic discourse wants to *show* and *tell* of what it consists.

The process of unbalancing operates in more than one way and involves the presence or absence of semantic, phonetic, and graphic qualities which are all of importance in constituting a literary text as a device to provoke and, perhaps, to control a reader's or listener's response. If I call the potential of meaning *logopoeia,* using Ezra Pound's

term in a simplified way, that of sound *phonopoeia,* and that of visual shape, in writing or printing, *graphopoeia,* I assume that in a main-stream poem, as *e.g.* in Goethe's "Über allen Gipfeln ist Ruh" or Heine's "Mit deinen blauen Augen," there is an efficient alliance of all three elements that dominates the encounter of text and reader. I also believe that in certain moments of literary history, widely dispersed in time, particular texts are produced which may cease to be texts in the accepted sense of the term: a predominance of *phonopoeia* pushes the text into the realm of a-semantic sound or, as we would say metaphorically, of music; or the hegemony of *graphopoeia* changes the text, beyond the borderline between the arts, into a picture which we may or may not hang on our wall. In the absence of these experiments, our concepts of tradition are blind and incomplete, for it is precisely the disturbed balance and the emancipation of elements in pictorial and phonetic poetry which teaches us to perceive what kind of happy alliances are alive in those poems which do not challenge our assumptions any more. Only in encountering so-called nonsense poems, *e.g.* by Wassilij Kandinsky, Lewis Carroll, Paul Scheerbart (much admired by Walter Benjamin), or Kurt Schwitters, we suddenly realize how much we thirst for meaning; and only after we have observed how intense *phono-* or *graphopoeia* may change a text into a sound composition or a potential picture, we are sharply aware of the virtualities dominant in any utterance of poesy. Babble and doodle do offer potential enlightenment.

In saying that the process of unbalancing occurs in many centuries and in many literatures, I want to imply that I do not wish to see these imbalances as something exclusively modern, but merely prefer to deal with some more recent developments because they strike me as more radical and more revealing than what we may observe in the more distant past. There are, of course, the famous poems in the shape of wings, eggs, axes, and altars in the Greek Anthology (some possibly from the 3rd century B.C.) as well as in the 16th- and 17th-century poetry in England, Germany, Italy, and elsewhere; yet there is little in these past ages to compete with what was done by the Italian Futurists, the Russian *Zaum* poets, the Dadaists of all nations, or, in our own days, by concrete poets here and abroad, engaged as they are in ingeniously testing the materials of poetic language if not of all language inside and outside the sphere of poetry. It is only the unbalancing of elements that teaches us what balances are.

But, instead of discussing ideas of balancing and unbalancing, it might be more useful to demonstrate a few actual unbalancing acts in more or less recent practice, and to observe closely what happens when the phonic and semantic elements turn into a state of fragile disequilibrium.

In Edgar Allan Poe's "The Bells" (which may stand for many other poems of sound imitation) the process of dislocation away from the proportionate contributions of all elements to an integrative effort has long begun, and it is not difficult to hear how *phonopoeia* strains against the traditional structure:

> Hear the sledges with the
> bells—

Silver bells!
. . . Keeping time, time,
time,
In a sort of Runic rhyme,
To the tintinnabulation that so musically wells
From the bells, bells,
bells, bells,
Bells,   bells,
bells . . .

What emerges with particular force, even in a few isolated lines, are repetitions of stressed sound rather than meaning, and even the graphic shape of the text on the page is arranged to impress on the reader—or, better, the listener—that recurrent sounds, as well as individual words in which particular sounds recur, are in undisputed positions of rhythmic privilege. The poem almost shamelessly shows its phonetic materiality, trying to imitate tinkling bells, regardless of a few bits and pieces of rather silly *logopoeia* still residing in syntactic constructions, "keeping time, time, time, in a sort of Runic rhyme." Yet, compared with other experiments in verbal sound, we have to admit that the phonetic impulse has not yet destroyed the inherited phonemes or morphemes of the English language. The language of the text may not be particularly sophisticated, but its individual components are not beyond the accepted lexicon; perhaps with the exception of "tintinnabulation," the native speaker will not have much difficulty, and children especially will be delighted to hear how bells tinkle under the twinkling of the stars. Poe uses the phonetic potentialities of his native tongue, and while his mobilization of recurrent phonemes may guide *graphopoeia,* and reduce the semantic charge of the text, we continue hearing a poem which still accepts a traditional consensus about the collaboration of elements, even if the element of sound, as an icon of tinkling bells, asserts itself with preponderant energy.

My excerpt from a second example would possibly disturb many readers or listeners if I did not add immediately that it is taken from a Dada poem by Hugo Ball, entitled "Katzen und Pfauen":

siwi faffa
sbugi faffa
olofa fafamo
faufo halja finj

sirgi ninga banja sbugi
halja hanja golja biddim . . .

It is not difficult to suggest that in such a text *phonopoeia* has come to exert its undisputed energies. Without the title directing our hermeneutic efforts in a particular direction, any attempt at establishing meaning would be totally futile, and even so we cannot hear more than sounds cleverly organized in two systems in which we are urged to hear what irritated cats and peacocks are telling each other. *Phonopoeia,* as an impulse to imitate animal articulation, has gone far beyond human—or, in Ball's case, German—morphology and lexicon, and yet it has not gone *at all* beyond the continuing habits of a German native speaker who articulates halja / hanja in ways prescribed by German rather than by American or French pronunciation. In spite of all efforts to liberate the pristine essence of language, untouched by ideological disease,

there are barriers inherent in any act of habitual articulation, and a native German speaker cannot but differ in his acoustic projections of peacock or cat idiom from native American or French speakers; we all know that French roosters awake us in the morning by saying "cocorico" (or so the French speakers assure us), and German roosters on the other side of the Rhine, by saying "kikiriki." It is ironic to hear that even the most desperate striving for the purity of absolute poetry cannot quite overcome the basic habits of native *parole.*

I am not certain that Ball knew of his ally inside Germany who was similarly concerned with preserving the purity of poetry in the age of war, chauvinism, and cheapening convention. Hugo Blümner, who lived and worked in Berlin, had been a lawyer before he turned, as so many intellectuals of Schiller's and his own time, to the theater, trained as an actor under the supervision of Max Reinhardt, and established himself, in the later years of World War I and the early 1920's, as a defender of avant-garde art, travelling speaker of expressionist verse, and a phonetic poet in his own right. I am quoting the initial passage of his "absolute" sound poem, entitled "Ango Laina," of 1921:

Oiaí laéa ofa ssísialu
Ensúdio trésa súdio míschnumi
Ia lon stuáz
Brorr schjatt
Oiázo tsuígulu
Ua sésa masúo tülü

Ua sésa maschiató toró
Oi séngu gádse ándola
Oi ándo séngu
Séngu ándola
Oi séngu
Gádse

Ina
Leíola
Kbaó
Sagór
Kadó
Kadó mai tiúsi
Suíjo ángola . . .

Blümner's "Ango Laina" is a poem that wants to communicate feelings, not meanings, in an absolute way: that is, free of all *logopoeic* burdens, references, and potential denotations. We have to admit that Blümner is very careful not to include any sound strings reminiscent of Latin or Greek, as Ball does on occasion, for instance in his "Labadas Gesang an die Wolken," or morphemes suggesting particular inflections. Another example to clarify the point: If Rudolf Carnap, in his *Logical Syntax of Language,* uses a sentence of invented words, "Pirots karulize elatically," we are still tempted, as Jakobson remarked, to think of the "pirots" (whatever they are) as something in the plural, and to believe that a single "pirot," whatever it, she, he is, "karulizes" because we find familiar signs of inflection. Yet I wonder whether it is possible to communicate without shaping sounds in a characteristic way set by the habits of a particular *parole.* We do not know much about Blümner's technique of recitation, but I suspect that he articulated his sounds as a native speaker born in Berlin, and trained in German theater elocution; dreaming of an absolute language, he was, as soon as he articulated aloud, incapable of going beyond the phonetic barrier inherent in his speech habits and, inventing sound strings of unheard-of courage, did not escape the prison of his set ways of, *e.g.,* pronouncing the long *u* in the German way.

But that is not all. I think he was a captive of his native German in a more paradoxical way, and I suspect that his emancipated sound actually responded to the inherited German sound structure in the manner of a dialectical inversion. He wants to go as far as possible beyond all German sound configurations, and yet, because he wants systematically to avoid the usual German distribution of sounds, he creates new patterns which are indirectly defined by the structures he wants to oppose in his ear and in our hearing. A statistical analysis of sound distribution in modern spoken German would clearly indicate that the unstressed *e,* as in the second syllables of *geben, leben, reden,* recurs most often among all German speech sounds (11.95%), and if other variants are added, the index increases to 17.66%. It is revealing that such an unstressed *e,* the most characteristic of all German sounds, does not appear in Blümner's poem once. But there are other indications that Blümner's "skew," or pattern of sound distribution, is designed radically to negate the traditional sound patterns of his native tongue. The sequence "unstressed *e* + *n*" present in nearly 5% of all German sound strings, does not appear either, and the German "skew" of vowels and liquids is nearly reversed in Blümner's idiom. He avoids most *Umlaute,* dramatically increases the recurrence of long stressed *o,* which in his native tongue provides a mere 0.86% of all sound materials, and in a striking way increases the occurrence of *l* which in German figures only in the middle ranks (4.25%) between *n* (9.32) and *p* (1.2). These sound statistics, however unusual in discussions of poetry, are helpful in suggesting that Blümner, in developing his absolute language, really works with a statistical "skew" of sounds *against* German, as something to be opposed, to be argued against. Spoken German is the auditory ground against which Blümner's absolute idiom operates, and, as a sound poet, he reminds me of one of those atheists who cannot explain what they really believe unless they discuss the entire history of theology.

It is perhaps little known that Blümner was among those writers and art critics who convinced Kurt Schwitters to experiment with colors and sound, rather than to cultivate what he had learned at the Dresden Academy. Blümner recited his poetry in Hanover in the fall of 1918, and the young graphic artist and writer Schwitters, who was among his listeners, began to experiment himself and, within a year or two, was as radical as anybody among the *Sturm* people or the Dadaists in Zurich and Berlin. In the United States, Schwitters is known as the ingenious and witty master of collage, but his many and variegated verbal experiments are far less known; the trouble with him is, of course, that he was a totally unorthodox and playful artist who happily let the hundred flowers of his talents bloom. Early and late in his life, he painted old fashioned landscapes and traditional portraits while, at the same time, competing with the Russian and Dutch Constructiv-

ists in brilliance and courage of graphic experiments; and in his literary work he was equally willing to write funny fairy tales, charming nonsense verse, or to engage in the most ruthless and witty experiments with syntax or sound. I should like to concentrate on Schwitters' much disputed text "Wand":

> Fünf Vier Drei Zwei Eins
> Wand
> Wand
> WAND
> WAND WAND WAND
> WAND WAND WAND
> WAND   WAND   WAND   WAND
> wände
> wände
> Wände
> WÄNDE WÄNDE WÄNDE
> WÄNDE   WÄNDE   WÄNDE   WÄNDE
> WAND
> WAND   WAND   WAND
> WAND WAND WAND
> wand wand wand
> wand
> wand
> wand
> wand

Schwitters himself would have said that his poem belongs to his "konse-quente Dichtung" in which he explores what he terms "internal rhythm," the constituent basis of all works of art. The actual text starts, after a countdown or blast-off line, with the rocket-like propulsion of a single word or, rather, its recurrence regulated by three organizational principles. There is, first, the morphological distinction between the singular "Wand" and the plural "Wände"; second, the intervals within the sequence of articulations, and, finally, the force of articulation, indicated by different graphemes suggesting (I think) a *piano, mezzoforte,* and *forte* level of voice. The semantic charge amounts to a minimum, but there is a complex and sophisticated organization of the morphological signals, the presence/absence of the continuous sound stream, and the changing intensity of voice; and if I listen carefully to the sound string, I may discover that the text operates with proportions and symmetries which can be formalized in a numerical way. Morphologically, the text offers, in its central part, 10 plurals of the basic element, surrounded, or preceded and followed, by 13 singulars (the coda echoes the title); and concentrating on the indications of sound level, I would say that the text forms three parts in which the first and second prompt me to read with ascending pitch while in the third part my voice descends. The point is that from the collaboration of sounds, intonations, and intensities an intricate and attractive experience of our aural sensibility results which refuses to yield sense in a traditional way.

Critics have had considerable difficulties with Schwitters' "Wand," and interpretations (if it is possible to speak about hermeneutic efforts) have ranged, in my experience, from the assertion that the text, as a performative act, builds up a wall of sounds, to the helpless suggestion that we are in the presence of one of those Dada jokes which do not merit closer attention whatsoever. I take the joke as seriously as Schwitters who, as a verbal and graphic artist, was very much concerned with fundamental questions of art, and I submit that in "Wand" he wants to test the possibility of creating a verbal structure which would have all the organizational characteristics of a highly structured field of formal interrelationships, except that of making sense. "Wand" may be an experiment crossing the boundaries between the arts, yet it derives its considerable charm from Schwitters' attempt to transfer insights about the composition of a graphic art work to literature, or, to be more precise, from his abstractions in the graphic arts to poetic discourse. In the early 1920's the industrial designer Schwitters came to the conclusion that a work of art, in order to be one, had to fulfill two basic requirements—the requirement of showing an "internal rhythm," that is, a rich and intricate interrelationship of parts with each other, and the requirement of being isolated by a *découpage,* a cut, a line, a threshold, or a white space from surrounding sensory experience which does not show an equally high degree of formal organization. He suggests that any work of art consists of an "internal rhythm" disengaged from the surrounding experience of a lesser structure—the problem is, however, that such an "internal rhythm" (the idea of which Schwitters derived from Herwarth Walden's articles about expressionist painting) functions differently in the different systems of the graphic and the verbal arts; and while shifting his ideas and his terms from speaking about his collages to verbal experimentation, Schwitters creates revealing difficulties for his readers/listeners because he assumes that words which have lexical meanings can be used, within disengaged fields of formal intricacy, as if they did not carry with them a resilient power of semantic direction at all. Schwitters leaves us productively puzzled by the question of whether the internal patterns of "Wand" actually enhance or diminish the semantic load of the basic material; and if it is diminished or perhaps destroyed, we are challenged by the further question of whether there can be verbal art constituted by an intentional lack of sense, and yet of a significance of another kind.

Schwitters' Viennese friend Raoul Hausmann had particular reasons for misunderstanding Schwitters' texts because he had long developed radical "soundings" of his own which sound as if they were to end all sound poetry. Hausmann (who survived the Nazis by hiding in Southern France) went so far in his ruthless negation of any establishment, mainstream *or* avantgarde, as to find himself in fierce opposition against the Expressionists, the *Sturm* people, and the Dadaists, declaring in his many manifestoes that the best Dada was *anti-dadaist*—negation itself had to be negated again and again. Hausmann, as did Ball and Schwitters, recited his texts publicly, to shock his audiences; and while we have the texts of some of his theoretical writings, we do not have many scores of his sound performances. I offer here a notation from one of them:

```
K P' E R I   U M   L P' E R I O U M
N M' P E R I I I    pernoumum
bpretiberrerre-
    bee  onnooooooooh   gplanpouk
komnpout  perikoul
rreeeeeEEErreeeee      A
oapderree  mglepadonou   mtnou
```

tnoumt

We do not have many scores because Hausmann rarely intended to transform his sounds into graphemes; in striking contrast to Schwitters, who works on his sound texts with great care and uses many signs usually found in musical scores, Hausmann never bothered systematically to preserve his recitations in print. Perhaps I should say that while seemingly belonging to the early phonetic poets of our century, he was not really one of them; to him, I suspect, it was not the sound and the sound strings that mattered but only the way in which the sounds were produced by the human apparatus of articulation. Ultimately it was not the phonetic element which was of concern to him, but the exercise of the articulatory motor impulse in a physiological sense.

We have at least some indication in one of his confusing Dada manifestoes about the "Legitimacy of Sound" (1921) which, in pretending to oppose traditional essays by speaking nonsense, nevertheless suggests something of the ideas which he had in mind. He does not speak about sounds at all, but about the relationship or, rather, the analogies that obtain between art and smoking—what art and smoking have in common is the fact that they create a moment of "serenity as such in the infantile behavior of life," offering us, in the middle of hectic experience, the "consoling certainty of the uniqueness of what happens" (when we meditate on art or smoke a cigarette, leisurely inhaling and exhaling the air). Hausmann speaks a good deal about *Navy-cut* tobacco but deals with smoking as a convenient metaphor; to him, smoking is a productive emblem of how breathing is disciplined in a recurrent rhythm, and it is the willed act of breathing which is of central interest. We are immersed in a unique moment in which all virtualities of life are gathered, our social alienation is negated, and we feel in a nearly mystical way that we are liberated from the confinements of time and space. I am speaking of a nearly mystical experience because Hausmann himself pushes us in that direction; in his manifesto, he alludes to the *Prana* ("wisdom") and the *Tattwa* (force field of change), and the presence of these terms, ultimately derived from the old religions of India, reveals the full implications of what he wishes to say. Smoking stands here for the exercise of breathing, and breathing for the exercise of motor energy in producing sound by pushing a stream of air past and against particular obstructions in the upper part of our body—what we achieve when we exercise our physiological powers is that we release energy and approach a moment of unique serenity which takes us out of a world of intolerable pressures. I suspect that what is called Hausmann's "sound poetry" is but a sediment of his articulatory exercises which, as activating energy, are far more important than what they actually produce; and even if Hausmann may have a rather fragmentary knowledge of Yoga, he is well on his way to longing for a spiritual *Mantra* to guide and govern life. What he recites may sound like phonetic poetry, but I think that we are moving towards motor exercises, into a realm of therapy using the healing release of body energy.

Most of my examples of sound poetry have been selected from experiments of the productive years 1916 to 1921, and another essay would be needed to discuss the resuscitation of phonetic poetry after the hiatus of the war years and the transformations of sound poetry by electronic hardware after the mid-1950's. I have been tempted to deal with sound problems from a perspective of synchrony, but I think I know what I had to ignore and to sacrifice. Much of a theory of phonetic poetry, as far as the relationship of sound and meaning is concerned, develops together with semiotics and the philosophy of language in Plato's *Cratylos,* in Stoic logic, in Locke and Leibniz; and a critical analysis of these problems in historical perspective would not neglect to discuss Jacob Böhme's language speculations (recently analyzed by Steve Konopacki) and the sound experiments of the international Baroque. Yet I believe that our modern concerns with what language can do, and what the materials of poetic discourse are, have pushed us to more radical insights and demands; and we have yet to analyze dispassionately how it happened and what it implies that the posthumous publication of de Saussure's *Introduction to General Linguistics* in 1916 coincides with the first Dada manifestoes in Zurich, very much concerned with language, and the question of public and private meaning.

Listening to phonetic poetry, even of a particular period in history, challenges our aesthetic habits, I think, in very important and productive ways. We are less certain, after listening to Schwitters, that a close collaboration of sound, writing, and meaning is an absolute, necessary, and unchangeable condition of poetry, and we begin to suspect that the functional togetherness of *logopoeia, phonopoeia,* and *graphopoeia,* which is characteristic of the central body of our literary tradition, may be close to being another social convention, brittle, unstable, and fragile, rather than something given by nature once and for all. But there are other challenges of a social and aesthetic kind. In the texts of Ball and Blümner, our options concerning ethics and language are at stake because these writers are desperately concerned with rescuing what they believe to be the absolute purity of language, outside their infected and diseased native tongue, or any natural tongue if it cannot be done otherwise, and we have to ask ourselves whether they do not confuse the system of *language* with the particular ways in which individual speakers actually behave (I remember many people of my generation who in exile refused to speak or write German because they believed that, somehow, the language itself was sick). Kurt Schwitters provokes our ontological ideas about how works of art exist; and while he organizes his patterns and rhythms of whatever materials, sound among them, he really asks the question whether meaning is among the essential or peripheral necessities of art. Hausmann pushes his experiments beyond the confines of literature to anthropology or physiotherapy; exploring the physiological circumstances of human articulation, he moves into a space in which questions of meaning and writing are totally irrelevant, and we are asked whether we can achieve a healing moment of serenity by employing our organs of sound articulation.

Yet I would like to place my discussion of sound and meaning in the wider context of the present moment, and I am asking myself whether these questions are not also relevant in view of Susan Sontag's demand that we need

an erotics, not a hermeneutics, of art—that is, that we should be eager to feel the sensual pleasures yielded by art, rather than to exert our energies in the hermeneutic search for meaning. Considering the inclinations and predilections of our contemporary discussions of literature, largely dominated by the friends and adversaries of Hirsch, Gadamer, or Derrida, I suspect that we are committed once again to assuming that poems are philosophical or theological statements of sorts. We grapple with the potential presence or absence of meaning, and totally neglect, underrate, or forget that the idiom of poetry, if it is that of poetry, has a sensual quality that, unlike philosophical assertion (whether or not under deconstructionist "erasure"), directly affects us as human beings who touch and feel. Phonetic poetry undoes balances within the poem but restores balances of a humane kind. We may be hermeneutic animals who cannot live without meaning, but it is the ultimate challenge of sound experiments to remind us that in a particular discourse called poetry there is something that has to strike our senses before making sense. (pp. 23-33)

Peter Demetz, *"Varieties of Phonetic Poetry: An Introduction,"* in From Kafka and Dada to Brecht and Beyond, *Reinhold Grimm, Peter Spycher, Richard A. Zipser, eds., The University of Wisconsin Press, 1982, pp. 23-33.*

Judi Freeman

[*In the following excerpt, Freeman discusses the graphical use of language—what she calls "word-images"—in Dada art, focusing on pre-1920 works by Marcel Duchamp.*]

Dada was as much about the act of making—or orchestrating—art as it was about the work of art itself. Words, present in titles or inscriptions, were integrated into pictures or objects, establishing alternate interpretations of the meaning of the work; witness, for example, Duchamp's *In Advance of the Broken Arm* (1915), the title accompanying his readymade shovel.

The first wave of word-images in Dada occurred in the period that coincided with the end of the war and the early postwar years. Discursive elements played an integral role in Marcel Duchamp's readymades, which relied upon their titles or inscriptions to convey the ironies intended by the artist. Perhaps his most controversial readymade, his *Fountain* (1917), focused attention on the irony of presenting a mundane, even vulgar object as if it were an *objet d'art*. The urinal was labeled, turned on its side, installed like a fountain, and signed, albeit pseudonymously, R. Mutt. Duchamp later explained that

Mr. Richard Mutt sent in a fountain. . . .

Now Mr. Mutt's fountain is not immoral, that is absurd, no more than a bathtub is immoral. It is a fixture that you see every day in plumbers' show windows.

Whether Mr. Mutt with his own hands made the fountain or not has no importance. He *chose* it. He took an ordinary article of life, placed it so that its useful significance disappeared under the new title and point of view—created a new thought for that object.

This was not the first time that Duchamp incorporated an inscription into a work as a way of invoking or undermining a concept. He had placed inscriptions on the front of such canvases as *Chocolate Grinder, No. 1* (1913), effectively transforming relatively cubist canvases or realistically rendered objects into more poetic plays on meaning.

Duchamp was not mobilized during the war due to a heart condition; instead he left France for New York in June 1915. There he was closely associated with Francis Picabia and the poet/artist Marius de Zayas, with whom he engaged in an exploration of language and meaning through the creation of an unconventional rebus. In the rebus the visual image was completely disconnected from the verbal reference. The result was a text that, though it initially seemed to be comprehensible, was fundamentally absurd. The jarring visual-verbal confrontation requires the viewer to come to grips with its content in some fashion. In this text, entitled *"The"* (1915), each time the definite article was to appear, it was replaced by an asterisk. The text is grammatically correct but lacks meaningful content. Years later Duchamp described those experiments with language to Arturo Schwarz, his erstwhile dealer:

> There would be a verb, a subject, a complement, adverbs, and everything perfectly correct, as such, words[;] but meaning in these sentences was a thing I had to avoid. . . . The verb was meant to be an abstract word acting on a subject that is a material object, in this way the verb would make the sentence look abstract. The construction was very painful in a way, because the minute I *did* think of a verb to add to the subject, I would very often see a meaning and immediately [when] I saw a meaning I would cross out a verb and change it, until, working for quite a number of hours, the text finally read without any echo of the physical world.

The sophisticated manipulation of language in Duchamp's readymades grew out of this experimentation. In one, two brass plates sandwich a ball of twine that hides a small object that created a noise whenever the assembled work was moved. The readymade was labeled *A Bruit secret* (*With Hidden Noise;* 1916). If this inscription made the object's function too explicit, additional texts confused the issue. Inscribed on top in white paint are the phrases:

> P.G..ECIDES DEBARRASSE.
> LE D.SERT F.URNIS.ENT
> AS HOW.V.R. COR.ESPONDS
> *Convenablement choisie dans la même colonne*

and underneath:

> .IR CAR.ELONGSEA
> F.NE,HEA., O.SQUE
> TE.U S.ARP BAR AIN
> *Remplacer chaque point par une lettre*

Duchamp described these as "three short sentences in which letters were occasionally missing like in a neon sign when one letter is not lit and makes the word unintelligi-

ble." These were a Dada act of scrambling any legible reference, much as Duchamp had already done in *"The."*

The meaning of these phrases remains obscure, even when the words are completed and finished phrases are read vertically as well as from left to right. When asked about the inscription in the 1960s, Duchamp claimed that the text could be read as a fusion of French and English:

First line lower plate: Continuing on first line upper plate:	*Fire. Carré longsea;* *Peg decides débarrasse;*
Second line lower plate:	*Fine, cheap, lorsque;*
Second line upper plate:	*Les déserts fournissent;*
Third line lower plate: Continues third line upper plate:	*Tenu sharp bargain;* *As however corresponds.*

These snippets, almost impossible to decode without the artist's instructions, are absurd and, what is more, seemingly irrelevant to the work of art. They demonstrate the deliberate cloaking of tangible references in Duchamp's work.

In other readymades created in the teens Duchamp opted for a more direct use of language. His *Traveler's Folding Item* (1916) consisted of an Underwood typewriter cover elevated on a pole. The temptation Duchamp sought to encourage was that of the voyeur: the desire to see what was hidden. As he noted in the 1950s, "The onlookers are the ones that make the picture." *Underwood,* the name of a typewriter manufacturer, functioned as part of the work. Whether *Underwood* referred to being "under wood," or whether it represented a play on notions of being "under," as in looking under the skirtlike typewriter cover, is never made clear by Duchamp.

The ambiguity of language's precise role in the meaning of a work is further evident in *Apolinère Enameled,* a readymade of 1916-17 in which Duchamp paid homage to the avant-garde critic Apollinaire. Starting with an advertisement for Sapolin Enamel paints, Duchamp rearranged the lettering by adding new letters and blacking out others, deliberately misspelling the poet's name. The company's motto, inscribed in the lower right-hand corner, was rendered by Duchamp into words, much like those used in the *A Bruit secret:* "Any act red by her ten or epergne, New York, U.S.A." The advertisement was further altered by Duchamp's rendering of the little girl's hair in reflection in the mirror, further transforming the readymade into an assisted readymade.

Certainly L.H.O.O.Q. (1919) operates on one level as a bowdlerized image of the iconic Mona Lisa, supplemented by a goatee and mustache. A second reading incorporates the inscription but only the cryptic reference it creates. Only a third reading, quickly and out loud, reveals L.H.O.O.Q. stands for *"Elle a chaud au cul"* ("She has a hot ass"). Is the inscription essential to an understanding of the work? The content of the words was certainly secondary in importance, if for Duchamp the significance of L.H.O.O.Q. was the act of designating a postcard reproduction an equally authentic work of art. (pp. 21-5)

With André Breton's organization of a 1922 International Congress for the Direction and Defense of the Modern

Marcel Duchamp - photographed by Man Ray - as his alter-ego Rrose Sélavy. The name is derived from the sentence: "Eros, c'est la vie."

Spirit, the various factions in the Dada movement began to splinter. The differences among the poets hastened Dada's demise; Tzara and Breton are the most obvious examples, but Jean Cocteau's distance from all circles and Paul Eluard's and Robert Desnos's ties to artists and philosophers both inside and outside of the Dada movement may also be cited. The end of Dada coincided with the end of the first wave of a significant body of word-images. The subsequent birth of surrealism did not inspire a similarly ambitious investigation of language for several more years. (p. 36)

> *Judi Freeman, "Layers of Meaning: The Multiple Readings of Dada and Surrealist Word-Images," in* the Dada & Surrealist Word-Image *by Judi Freeman with John C. Welchman, The MIT Press, 1989, pp. 13-56.*

Richard Kostelanetz

[Kostelanetz is an American critic who has written extensively on English and American literature. In the following essay, he shows that although the Dadaists produced no significant amount of prose fiction, the Dada ethos and aesthetic philosophy can clearly be seen in the novels of Alfred Jarry as well as in the work of a number of more recent writers, including John Barth, Tom Veitch, and Thomas Pynchon.]

The literary innovations of Dada stemmed from disrupt-ing or, more literally, decomposing conventionally sensible forms. "We began to write series of words having no apparent consecutive sense," remembers Tristan Tzara. "This method presupposed that words could be stripped of their meaning and yet still be effective in a poem by their simple evocative power—a kind of magic as hard to understand as it is to formulate." Around the same time, just before 1920, Hugo Ball declaimed similarly non-syntactical "poetry" in Zürich, and Kurt Schwitters infused a kind of doubletalk into a satirical love poem entitled *Anna Blume* (1919). The climax to this tendency was Schwitters' *Ursonata* (1924), which Moholy-Nagy describes as "a poem of thirty-five minutes' duration containing four movements, a prelude, and a cadenza in the fourth movement. The words do not exist; rather they might exist in any language. They have no logical, only an emotional context; they affect the ear with their phonetic vibration like music." However, if only because Schwitters uttered these sounds in a situation where poetry was expected, they should be considered not music but literature. "Abstract poetry," he later wrote, "released the word from its associations—this is a great service—and evaluated word against word and, in particular, concept against concept, with some thought paid to sound." Had Schwitters perhaps chosen to announce, in a galvanized gesture, that his words comprised a story, rather than a poem, and since both artists and critics invariably attribute significance to such acts of imposed definition, Schwitters might have made an equally revolutionary contribution to the art of prose fiction, as well as further challenged, as much avant-garde activity does, academic conceptions of the boundaries separating one art from another.

Another extreme literary innovation occurred twelve years later when Marcel Duchamp was asked for his autobiography. "With a typical Dadaist gesture," writes Moholy-Nagy, "he emptied the contents of his desk—notes, drawings and photographs of the last twenty-five years—into a cardboard box. All this was faithfully reproduced and put into a portfolio without chronological or any other order, leaving the 'mess' to be disentangled by the reader." The ultimate theme of Dada esthetics was artistic freedom—that literally anything was possible in any art, including the forms of literature; and even though most practitioners could not overcome the constraints that every artist inherits with his training and self-apprenticeship, those who took the leaps of freedom established radical precedents for future work.

The double paradox is that even anti-art inevitably reveals the influence of previous arts, as well as creates esthetic examples that shape future art. Perhaps because the ideas informing Dada were in essence quite simple, although original and unfamiliar to both art history and most artists, its impact upon functioning creative intelligences was liable to be both quicker and more subliminal than the complex thought of, say, Wittgenstein's philosophy or contemporary physics; thus, I suspect that the Dada spirit has probably infiltrated all contemporary minds whose sensibilities were susceptible, slipping, for instance, into the fiction of writers only dimly aware of the original work. What supports this conjectural measure of Dada's impact is my sense that some of the most inventive and profound fictions of recent times are indebted in perceptible respects to its ideas; for as Tzara judged in 1951, he and his colleagues created "a new intellectual climate which still in some measure survives."

What makes the Dadaists' neglect of prose fiction so surprising is the fact that one of their heroes and acknowledged precursors, Alfred Jarry, had twenty years before Dada's heyday written an innovative fiction that realized in prose many of Dada's esthetic and metaphysical prejudices. *Exploits and Opinions of Doctor Faustroll, Pataphysician,* sub-titled "A Neo-Scientific Novel" (although it runs to only eighty pages in Simon Watson Taylor's Grove Press translation,) was drafted in 1898, when Jarry was twenty-five, nine years before his premature death. Unable to publish his manuscript at the time, he entrusted it to friends, who provided it for the first French edition in 1911, more or less when the spirits that became Dada were fermenting.

The narrative's opening paragraph, which follows after a fictitious document that serves as an introductory framing device, establishes an absurd tone, beneath a veneer of reasonableness, that the novel sustains:

> Doctor Faustroll was sixty-three years old when he was born in Circassia in 1898 (the 20th century was (−2) years old).

> At this age, which he retained all his life, Doctor Faustroll was a man of medium height, or to be absolutely accurate, of $(8 \times 10^{10} + 10^9 + 4 \times 10^8 + 5 \times 10^6)$ atomic diameters: with a golden-yellow skin, his face clean-shaven, apart from a sea-green mustachios [sic], as worn by king Saleh; the hairs of his head alternately platinum blonde and jet black, an auburn ambiguity changing according to the sun's position; his eyes, two capsules of ordinary writing-ink flecked with golden spermatozoa-like Danzig Schnapps.

What plot there is, amidst the numerous digressions, consists of Faustroll's adentures, in the company of the bailiff Panmuphle and an idiotic creature named Bosse-de-Nege (literally "bottom-face"); and this narrative thoroughly violates several kinds of mundane credibility—chronological, geographical, psychological, social and biological.

In the course of the fiction, the absurd surface progressively assumes metaphysical resonance, as at one point Faustroll says in passing, "I am God," and at another point Jarry introduces " 'pataphysics," which he then defines as "the science of that which is superinduced upon metaphysics, whether within or beyond the latter's limitations, extending as far beyond metaphysics as the latter extends beyond physics." A few lines later Faustroll feigns the processes of expository elaboration: " 'Pataphysics is the science of imaginary solutions, which symbolically attributes the properties of objects, described by their virtuality, to their lineaments." The climax to this book, which has a surprisingly linear structure (imposed partly by the adventure-story motif), comes in the forty-first and last chapter, which ends a section wittily entitled "Ethernity." "Concerning the Surface of God," as the chapter is called,

is a fiction in the form of a scientific proof, in which the narrator uses geometrical hypotheses and algebraic equations, the highest rituals of reason, eventually to prove:

> GOD IS THE TANGENTIAL POINT BETWEEN ZERO AND INFINITY. Pataphysics is *the* science . . .

In *Faustroll* alone, Jarry initiated several revolutionary precedents for modern fiction—among them the familiar devices of "Black Humor" and moderately expressive typography and, more importantly, the principles that all kinds of printable material could be incorporated into the text of imaginative prose and that literally anything can occur in a fiction; indeed, he suggested stylistic possibilities that went unheeded by the Dadaists themselves. Perhaps because this masterpiece, probably the first thoroughly absurd novel, has gone surprisingly unread, as has Jarry's later fabulous fiction, *The Supermale* (reprinted in *New Directions No. 18*), even today, seventy years after *Faustroll* was written, it seems ahead of current advanced fictional practice. . . .

In a Faustrollian fantasy that denies all verification, I once imagined that certain prematurely deceased Dadaists were reborn as American writers named John Barth, Joseph Heller, Thomas Pynchon, Harry Mathews, Donald Barthelme, Claes Oldenburg, William Burroughs and Tom Veitch (perhaps midwived by Ionesco's acknowledged three greatest influences—Harpo, Chico and Groucho); for they have realized in extravagant prose fiction certain Dadaist inventions and biases, such as totally exterior representation, the absence of narrative resolution, unmitigated blasphemous comedy, the decomposition of traditional forms, and the rendering of wordly absurdity.

For instance, even though the narrative line of John Barth's *The Sot-Weed Factor* (1960) is as horizontal as *Faustroll,* the book is structurally vertical, systematic mockery, mostly in thoroughly detailed parodies, of several contemporary and ancient philosophical ideas, the eighteenth-century English novel, seventeenth-century English and American history, a cartload of literary conventions, and much else besides, all to convey the Dadaist theme that history itself is as ridiculous as most attempts to definitively understand it. In a more recent story, "Title," Barth creates three simultaneous but overlapping narrators—one the writer contemplating his inability to finish a novel, the second the writer considering the decline of a love affair, the third the writer worried about the decay of the culture; and in reading this story live, with two of the voices pre-recorded on stereophonic tape, Barth adapts the Dadaist invention of *poème simultané* to invigorate the decadent art of a literary recital.

Heller's *Catch-22* (1961), whose subject is the absurdity of modern war, contains qualities reminiscent of Dada, if not Jarry, who wrote in *Supermale,* "In fact, Marcueil embodied so absolutely the average man that his very ordinariness became extraordinary." Conspicuous evidence of Dada infuses Harry Mathews's less comprehensible but marvelously witty novels, *The Conversations* (1962) and *Tlooth* (1966) and the better-known fictions of both Donald Barthelme and Thomas Pynchon. Claes Oldenburg's *Store Days* (1967), ostensibly a book about a neo-Dada environmental work of art entitled *The Store* (1962) that Oldenburg had previously constructed, is not a work of criticism but a critical fiction whose semi-sensible tone, overall structure, conglomerate texture, use of "found" printed materials, discontinuous syntax and cohering themes approximate, by esthetic analogy, in hardbound prose the original work of art. [Parallelly, Kenneth King's "Super-Lecture" (1966), reprinted in my *Young American Writers* (1967), is also an ironic critical fiction cast in the form of a dancer's statement, whose narrator is partially a fictitious creation, expressing partial sense beneath a veneer of fantastic nonsense; John Cage's *Talk I* (1965), reprinted in *A Year from Monday* (1967), recalls Schwitters' *Ursonata* in its intentional incomprehensibility in a situation where sense is expected; and Emmett Williams' *Sweethearts* (1967) makes a narrative out of one resonant word, "Sweethearts," designed across the left-hand pages in various ways.]

Both William Burroughs and Tom Veitch have successfully exploited the Dada painters' technique of randomly incorporating whole chunks of quoted or "found" material into their own narrative texts. The result is an art by accident that even for Burroughs fails more often than not; but when the technique works, the result can be radically original and yet suggestively coherent. Let me quote in their entirety the stunning second and third paragraphs of Veitch's fiction, "The Luis Armed Story" (from *Art and Literature No. 11,* also reprinted in *Young American Writers*).

> In the dimness of the cafe, the manager is arranging the tables and chairs, the ashtrays, the siphons of soda water; it is six in the morning. I awoke early, shaved, dressed, draped myself with cameras and equipment, and went on deck to record our entry into the port of Gothenburg. In the beginning was the Word, and the Word was with God; and the Word was God. The Agon, then. In her tight fitting Persian dress, with turban to match, she looked ravishing.
>
> This is the story of a man, one who was never at a loss. I can feel the heaty . . . heaty closing in, feel them out there making their moves, setting up their devil droll stood pigeons, crooning over my spoon and dropper I throw away at Washington Square Station, vault a turnstile and two flights down the iron stairs, catch an uptown A train. . . . For the reader familiar with analytical psychology there is no need of any introductory remarks to the subject of the following study. An eight-year decline of syphilis ended in 1955. "For a pansy." The purpose of this book is to provide a concise yet comprehensive guide to the history and understanding of philosophy for the general reader.

To achieve this sense of fractured coherence and convey perceptual disorientation, Veitch actually used verbatim the opening sentences—randomly "found" passages—of several books, including one by Burroughs, that were lying near his writing desk. In short, several significant Dada strategies—rendering the fixed unfixed and the comprehensible absurd, appropriating unretouched the materials of the environment, parodying familiar conventions,

creating uncompromisingly thorough blasphemy—continue to inform significant recent fictional work; so that although the original Dadaists themselves did not create any significant prose literature, there was and still is, in the history of narrative art, a distinctly Dadaist fiction.

The relevance of Dada for the future of fiction lies first in its emphasis upon external reality at a time when, since the environment undergoes greater discernible change than the heads of men (although change they likewise do), the commonly perceived world is likely to be a more fertile subject for radical formal invention and, concomitantly, innovative truth, than psychological processes.

> One thing that is new is the prevalence of newness, the changing scale and scope of change itself, so that the world alters as we walk in it, so that the years of a man's life measure not some small growth or rearrangement or moderation of what he learned in childhood, but a great upheaval. [J. Robert Oppenheimer]

Perhaps because the world around us continually evades all neatly encapsulating definitions, Dada esthetic revolutions seem especially persuasive to writers and readers who seek an appropriate form, if not the semblance of illusory wisdom, for their not-knowing-profoundly about contemporary life. Indeed, artfully disordered literature, in posing challenges to comprehension, also serves the beneficial function of honing the reader's mind for the task of making sense of the chaos in his environment.

A second continually relevant thesis of Dada esthetics holds that all forms and materials are available to literary artists—algebraic equations, maps and charts, graphic illustrations, pictures, types of various sizes and styles; unfamiliar or inscrutable languages, etc., etc. The highly decomposed narrative of Michel Butor's *Mobile* (1963), which I consider one of the most spectacular forays beyond the frontier, collects and juxtaposes long lists of words commonly *found* around America, such as billboard slogans or inscriptions on road signs; and this use of raw verbal data, within the compositional structure of comprehensive collage, makes *Mobile,* to my mind, one of the very best microtreatments of the large subject of America today. Furthermore, since anyone who reads a great number of novels eventually learns all the old tricks (and perhaps tries a few of them himself), the problem for creators of imaginative prose is no longer infusing life into familiar conventions but filling up the sheets of paper with persuasive fictions; and to this end, the writer should feel free to employ all the discipline, cleverness, imagination and intellect he can muster. "A page is an area," writes B. S. Johnson's narrator in *Albert Angelo,* "on which I may place any signs I consider to communicate most nearly what I have to convey."

From the esthetic assumptions of Dada inevitably follows the idea that a fiction could viably consist primarily of pictures, perhaps abetted by obliquely relevant texts and perhaps a few attached props like Andy Warhol's imaginatively conceived but trivially executed *Index* (*Book*) (1967); and one of the most exciting fictional narratives I read recently, *Saga* (1968), by the French concretist Jean-

Francois Bory (in *Approaches,* No. 3), consists of twenty-eight pages of illustrations, each of which contains, among other expressive designs, certain resonant words. (These observations persuade me to note in passing that certain children's books at times seem formally more adventurous than adult fare.) In that *Tri-Quarterly* review mentioned before I now find a sophisticated wisdom that I remember asserting out of innocence: "There really exist no limits upon the kinds of fictions that can be put between two covers."

On second thought, however, this particular espousal of unfettered possibility now strikes me as needlessly conservative, if not compromised, in one crucial respect; for if limits exist not to be respected but exceeded, why should fictions, even those created out of words, necessarily be printed on paper of uniform size and bound between covers? And why should a writer piously accept the convention that all his words be printed in type of the same size and style and then laid in evenly measured and modulated grey lines? Why should a work of imagination necessarily have a discernible beginning and an equally definite end? Why could not a narrative be framed on a continuous sheet of paper wound, say, between two rollers, printed not perpendicularly, like the *Torah,* but in lines parallel to the spindles' shafts? Could one not create a room full of words cunningly chosen, expressively designed, resonantly arranged, and artfully draped, that would evoke the coherence of both environmental art and literature? (Maybe such an environmental fiction could be mass-produced or "published" on screens that the purchasing "reader" could then circulate to his taste around his own home.) In fact, why should authors of fiction necessarily deal in linear modes; for just as the French novelist Marc Saporta created a book, offered in a box whose unbound pages can be read in any order, so a fiction appropriate for storage on an advanced computer (which, given time-sharing, can be electronically linked into an individual reader's home) should be similarly non-linear. That is, the random-access, as opposed to serial-access, memory of an advanced machine would enable the reader to appreciate discrete segments in any order over his home console; and ideally, every sequence of the fiction's would provide him with more or less the same interest, coherence and pleasure. Indicatively, such discontinuous fictions as *Finnegans Wake* or *Naked Lunch* (1958) or Marvin Cohen's *The Self-Devoted Friend* (1967) would store more suitably than nineteenth-century novels or, say, Mary McCarthy's *The Group* (1963).

What will, I think, primarily distinguish fiction of the future from the other arts will be an emphasis upon words selected and arranged out of a taste for language, a measure of human significance, a sense of potential linguistic articulations, and an awareness of the viable traditions of literature, all informing works for a public of readers attuned to words; for the ultimate challenge of the new electronic media to printed literature consists not in appropriating its audience but in forcing everyone who writes to eschew purposes that other media can realize more successfully and, instead, consider profoundly the most propitious forms for his own devices and the manifold evocative possibilities of words. (pp. 19-26)

Richard Kostelanetz, "Dada and the Future of Fiction," in Dada/Surrealism, *No. 1, 1971, pp. 19-26.*

Manuel Grossman

[*Grossman is an American critic and educator. In the following excerpt, he discusses the influence of Dada on later literary figures and movements.*]

[In discussing] the Dada poets and antipoets, we must take up the complex question of their influence upon later writers. Despite the differences that existed between Dada and Surrealism . . . the Surrealists, at first, bore the brunt of this influence. This is not surprising if we take into account that there were bound to be essential similarities in two movements like these, which had developed out of the same climate of artistic protest and revolt.

According to Ribemont-Dessaignes, one of the few members of Paris Dada who never became a Surrealist, "everything in Surrealism which belonged to the domain of liberty, revolt, and non-conformism was contained in Dada." Although he tried to minimize its importance, even Breton could not help but admit the debt he and his fellow Surrealists owed to Dada. In an essay in which he explained why he was abandoning the Dada movement, Breton wrote that "it should not be said that dadaism would have served other than to keep us in that perfect state of non-attachment that we are at."

Breton tried to play down the significance of this "perfect state," but there are indications that, if not for him, then for his colleagues Soupault and Aragon, it was a crucial experience. Soupault, in particular, had found it so necessary that it was virtually impossible for him to break with Dada, even though he had no illusions about its future. Breton himself noted this in a lecture he gave in Barcelona in 1922, when, with a mixture of sadness and irony, he informed his audience that "at the present time only Philippe Soupault has not lost hope in Dada, and it is rather moving to think that until his death he will perhaps live as Dada's toy as we have seen Jarry live as Ubu's."

Aragon also experienced a sense of loss over Dada. But he found it easier than Soupault to embrace Surrealism. Even though he became Breton's greatest ally and was an important figure in the Surrealist movement in his own right, however, Aragon continued at times to express himself in what can only be called a Dadaist style. Thus, as late as 1927, he was still writing poems like the following wry account of Dada's impact:

> Old Combatant
> I did the Dada Movement
> said the dadaist
> I did the Dada Movement
>
> and in effect
> it did me

As Aragon's case illustrates, the influence of Dada was so all-pervading in the early days of Surrealism that it is often impossible to distinguish what was Surrealist from what was Dadaist. Gradually, however, as the Surrealists began to move in the direction of politics and became involved in their doctrine of love, the Dada influence vanished.

Although not as directly affected as the Surrealists, other writers, such as the expatriate American novelist Henry Miller, who lived on the fringes of both the Dada and Surrealist movements, also felt the impact of Dada. In "An Open Letter to Surrealists Everywhere," which was part of his *The Cosmological Eye,* Miller testified to the influence of both movements on his work. But he went on to say that he preferred the Dadas because "the Surrealists are too conscious of what they are doing."

Miller made the kinship which existed between himself and the Dadas even clearer in the concluding passage of *The Cosmological Eye.* "I have no interest," he declared, "in the intentions of the existing governments of the world. I hope and believe that the whole civilized world will be wiped out in the next hundred years or so. I believe that man can exist, and in an infinitely better, larger way, without civilization."

While they were not as outspoken in acknowledging its influence as Miller, writers like James Joyce and E. E. Cummings may also have absorbed something of the Dada spirit from the literary climate in Europe. Joyce was living in Zurich when Dada first emerged, and although there was never any question of his joining the movement, he frequented the same cafés as the Zurich Dadas and shared their fascination with the turbulent world of the irrational.

According to A. W. Litz in *The Art of James Joyce,* it was during this period that Joyce began to perfect his "stream of consciousness approach" which, interestingly enough, closely parallels the Dadas' free-association techniques. Since there is no evidence that the Dadas' revolt against language and rationality had a direct influence upon Joyce's approach, this similarity may be coincidental, but this does not preclude the possibility of some form of indirect influence. Certainly Joyce's work was affected by both the literary and psychological climate of Zurich, a city which, in addition to being the place of exile of the Dadas, was also the center of the International Psychoanalytic Movement led by Carl Jung.

The manner in which Joyce's technique developed lends further credence to this idea. In moving from *Ulysses* to *Finnegans Wake,* he followed a path similar to that of the Dadas. As David Grossvogel has pointed out, "the evolution that leads him from *Ulysses* to *Finnegans Wake* indicates a change in the author's concerns, from the inner representation of character through analysis of consciousness to a freer enjoyment of words and their revelatory possibilities." And with this last stage in his evolution, Grossvogel concluded, "Joyce ends close to the unstructured fun of the Dadaists and relatively free of the formal concerns that normally limit the author through an awareness of his audience."

Cummings came in contact with the Dada movement in Paris during the early twenties. Like Joyce, he was too much of an individualist to join the movement, but he did become friends with the Paris Dadas, whose boisterous antics made a lasting impression upon him. Looking back

nostalgically to this period, just after the demise of the Dada movement, Cummings asked:

> What's become of (if you please)
> all the glory that or which was Greece
> all the grandja
> that was dada

Further evidence of the impression which Dada made upon Cummings comes from his poetry in general and his play *Him* in particular. By devising his own system of punctuation and grammar and making use of popular expressions and slang in his poems, Cummings served notice that he, like the Dadas, was intent upon capturing life's essential spontaneity before it could be frozen into rational form.

The Dada influence underlying this preoccupation with the immediate and the spontaneous is also marked in *Him,* Cummings's most ambitious attempt at playwriting. Making use of a nonlinear plot and nondiscursive symbolism to express the ambiguities of the modern artist's life, this play anticipated many of the innovations of the theater of the absurd; its juxtapositions of serious love scenes and raucous circus acts and bawdy burlesque routines looks ahead to the attempts of Beckett and Ionesco to create a new form of experience based upon the spontaneities of popular theater.

The dialogue in *Him,* if that term can be used to categorize speeches which often border on the unintelligible, is characterized by the kind of word play which is most often associated with Dada. Moreover, there is even a scene (one of the scenes in the play-within-a-play, in which the curtain rises, stays up for about a minute, then falls again with no other action taking place) in which Cummings makes use of an empty stage in a manner that one astute critic has termed "pure Dada."

That Cummings' kinship with the Dadas goes even deeper than this, however, is illustrated by his view of the tenuousness of communication. In the second scene of the play, Him, the poet, describes his art as a perilous acrobatic act, balancing three chairs in the sky. When asked by his mistress, Me, what will happen to the chairs (the completed work), the poet answers:

> The chairs will all fall by themselves down from
> the wire and be caught by anybody, by nobody;
> by somebody whom I don't see and who doesn't
> see me; perhaps by everybody.

By the 1930s and 40s, Dada had become so submerged that it is virtually impossible to trace its influence, except as a kind of underground force. But toward the end of World War II, seemingly as the result of two new phenomena on the literary scene, this situation began to change. The first of these was the development of Lettrism, a movement led by Isidore Isou, a young writer who, like Tzara, was a Rumanian exile living in Paris. Taking off from where the poetic experiments of Ball, Schwitters, and Tzara had ended, Isou systematically began to explore the possibility of creating poetry out of letters rather than words. While the originality of Isou's experiments has been questioned, it is difficult to deny that he and his followers helped provide the impetus that was necessary to bring Dada back to the surface.

The second phenomenon which contributed to this postwar Dada renaissance was the emergence of Existentialism. Declaring that "I am the new Dada," Jean-Paul Sartre called attention to the fact that some of the basic ideas of his philosophy had already been expressed, in a rudimentary form, by the Dadas. Richard Huelsenbeck has elaborated on this in his essay "Dada and Existentialism," in which he proposed, among other things, that the atmosphere of Berlin Dada was very close to that of Existentialism. Moreover, Huelsenbeck concluded that "the new man" whom he and his colleagues had envisioned was similar to Sartre's image of Existential man. In exploring this new image of man, the Dadas touched upon the concept of absurdity, which is a basic tenet of the Existential philosophy, and anticipated the Existentialists' tendency to elevate action above systems of thought.

We must be careful not to overextend the analogy between Existentialism and Dada—the one a serious, philosophical movement, and the other an elusive, more or less spontaneous outcry in the arts—but we can perhaps now see why the development of the former helped bring the latter back into prominence. The same postwar atmosphere, which was conducive to a philosophy of despair, like Existentialism, also brought about a reconsideration of Dada. That this atmosphere is still very much with us was made clear by a reviewer for a Düsseldorf newspaper who commented upon a Dada exhibit which was held in West Germany in 1958. "In its origin," this reviewer wrote, "Dada is the radical protest of artists with a prophetic vision against the suicide of Europe in the First World War, something which, in the middle of the twentieth century, one can see to have been only the overture to that senseless suicide of the world which has in the meantime become possible."

The Dada rebirth was first heralded in the plastic arts with its quick succession of Dada-inspired phenomena—Abstract Expressionism, Pop Art, Assemblage, and the various other forms of "Neo-Dada." Paralleling these developments, certain new literary forms, such as the New Novel and Beat poetry, have appeared, raising the possibility that just as viable a Dada tradition exists in literature as in painting and sculpture. Having already discussed the ways in which Aragon's *Anicet* anticipated the experiments of the New Novelists, we might add that, in general, when the Dadas and Surrealists stripped the word of its denotative and connotative function, they were paving the way for the phenomenological approach of writers like Alain Robbe-Grillet and Michel Butor.

For the main thrust of Dada's influence on recent literature, however, we must look beyond the New Novelists, with their spirit of scientific detachment, to another group of writers who have adopted the techniques, if not the spirit, of the Dadas. Numbered among this group are Samuel Beckett, whose manner of expressing metaphysical anguish both in his novels and his plays sometimes calls Dada to mind; William Burroughs, whose novels are often constructed according to those principles of chance which were so dear to the Dadas; and John Barth, whose most

recent work is an attempt to translate certain Dadaist concepts into the novel form.

But, above all, it is the free-wheeling poets of the Beat generation who have not only inherited the Dadas' taste for absolute freedom, but also their radical ways of expressing it. For the Beats, Dada was a multifaceted symbol of modern nihilism: to LeRoi Jones, it was "Black Dada Nihilismus"; to Allen Ginsberg, it was the memory of heaving "potato salad at CCNY lecturers on Dadaism"; and to Lawrence Ferlinghetti, it was an intimation of life's everyday absurdities. (pp. 152-57)

> *Manuel L. Grossman, in his* Dada: Paradox, Mystification, and Ambiguity in European Literature, *Pegasus, 1971, 192 p.*

FURTHER READING

Anthologies

Motherwell, Robert, ed. *The Dada Painters and Poets: An Anthology.* New York: George Wittenborn, 1951, 464 p.
    Important source of Dadaist writings, including manifestos, essays, histories, and reproductions of Dadaist art.

Secondary Sources

Ades, Dawn. *Dada and Surrealism Reviewed.* England: Westerham Press, 1978, 475 p.
    Catalog of an exhibition held in London that includes essays on the history and aesthetics of Dadaism as it was practiced in Europe and the United States.

Barr, Jr., Alfred H., ed. *Fantastic Art, Dada, Surrealism.* New York: The Museum of Modern Art, 1936, 271 p.
    Includes Georges Hugnet's essays "Dada" and "In the Light of Surrealism," as well as many reproductions of Dadaist paintings and graphic art.

Bergius, Hanne. "The Ambiguous Aesthetic of Dada: Towards a Definition of Its Categories." *Journal of European Studies* 9, No. 192 (1979): 26-38.
    Discusses Dadaist aesthetics in a historical context and identifies the print media and advertising as significant influences.

Caws, Mary Ann. "Dada's Temper, Our Text: Knights of the Double Self " and "Outlook and Inscape in Dada and Surrealism." In her *The Eye in the Text: Essays on Perception, Mannerist to Modern,* pp. 133-40, pp. 87-103. Princeton: Princeton University Press, 1981.
    Discusses the Dadaist poet's use of wordplay and visual dissonance—what Caws calls "Dada's choreography"—to distance the reader from the text and promote a self-conscious, critical way of reading. The second essay combines a thematic discussion of Dadaist and Surrealist art with an examination of theories on seeing and perception.

Edenbaum, Robert I. "Dada and Surrealism in the United

States: A Literary Instance." *Arts in Society* 5 (1968): 114-125.

Distinguishes between Dadaism and Surrealism by examining the influence of the latter on the American novelist Nathanael West.

Erickson, John D. *Dada: Performance, Poetry, and Art.* Boston: Twayne Publishers, 1984, 152 p.

Historical and aesthetic analysis of Dadaism with chapters on the characteristics and emphases that distinguished the major Dadaist groups.

Gershman, Herbert S. "From Dada to Surrealism." *Books Abroad* 43, No. 2 (Spring 1969): 75-81.

Examines the differences and similarities between Dadaism and Surrealism through close thematic analyses of some representative poems by Tristan Tzara and André Breton.

Hamilton, George Heard. "Mr. Duchamp, if you'd only known Jeff Koons was coming." *The Art Newspaper* III, No. 15 (February 1992): 13.

Transcription of Hamilton's 1959 BBC radio interview with Marcel Duchamp in which they discuss Duchamp's "readymades," his final masterpiece *The Large Glass* (*The Bride Stripped Bare by Her Bachelors, Even*), and the fact that he feels his art "has no appeal for the public at large."

Hardison, O. B., Jr. "Dada, the Poetry of Nothing, and the Modern World." *The Sewanee Review* XCII, No. 3 (Summer 1984): 372-96.

Assesses Dadaism's significance in the history of modern art.

Joselit, David. "Marcel Duchamp's *Monte Carlo Bond* Machine." *October,* No. 59 (Winter 1992): 8-26.

Close analysis of the philosophical and theoretical implications of Duchamp's performance art piece called the *Monte Carlo Bond* as well as his "Rrose Sélavy" persona.

Lemoine, Serge. *Dada.* Translated by Charles Lynn Clark. New York: Universe Books, 1987, 120 p.

History of the Dadaist movement.

Melzer, Annabelle Henkin. *Latest Rage the Big Drum: Dada and Surrealist Performance.* Ann Arbor: UMI Research Press, 1976, 272 p.

Discusses the performance aspects of Dadaist writing and analyzes Dadaist acting, plays, and performances.

Sheppard, Richard. "Dada and Politics." *Journal of European Studies* 9, No. 192 (1979): 39-74.

Detailed discussion of the various Dada groups and their political views and actions.

———. "What is Dada?" *Orbis Litterarum* 34, No. 3 (1979): 175-207.

Theorizes on the philosophy of Dada and discusses various artists' views on such thinkers as Henri Bergson and Sigmund Freud.

———. "Tricksters, Carnival and the Magical Figures of Dada Poetry." *Forum for Modern Language Studies* XIX, No. 2 (April 1983): 116-25.

Examines Dada poetry from a perspective influenced by the literary theory of Mikhail Bakhtin and by the concept of "archetypes" developed by psychologist Carl Jung.

Irish Literary Renaissance

INTRODUCTION

The Irish Literary Renaissance refers to a period during which Irish writers drew upon Celtic mythology, folklore, and the peasant culture of Ireland to develop a national literature distinct from that of England. Known by various designations, including the Gaelic Revival and the Celtic Twilight, the Irish Literary Renaissance is generally considered to have spanned the years from 1885 to 1940. While this movement encompassed diverse literary traditions, styles, and genres, scholars have identified several unifying elements in the works of such key figures as William Butler Yeats, J. M. Synge, A. E. (George Russell), Lady Gregory, Padraic Colum, George Moore, and Sean O'Casey. These include the belief that the realities of Irish peasant life, including poverty, isolation, and powerlessness, were legitimate subject matter for a national literature and that Ireland's distinct language, culture, and history could be elevated to literary importance. Writing during an extremely turbulent period in Irish history, when the Irish people were struggling for independence from Great Britain after nearly two hundred years of cultural and political domination, the writers of the Irish Literary Renaissance recognized the necessity of reigniting interest in Ireland's ancient literary traditions as well as promoting national unity and cultural pride. Scholars concur that the premier achievement of the Irish Literary Renaissance was the establishment of the Abbey Theatre in 1904. The most celebrated playwrights of the Abbey, including Synge, Yeats, and O'Casey, are best known for plays in which they incorporated Anglo-Irish vernacular, satire, symbolism, and epic lyricism to explore the social and political concerns of the Irish peasantry. While some Irish writers advocated reestablishing Gaelic as Ireland's official language, most recognized that it was necessary to utilize Anglo-Irish dialect to create an authentic national literature. Modern commentators agree that the Irish Literary Renaissance as an active movement came to an end shortly before the advent of World War II. Factors generally believed to have contributed to its dissolution include the trend toward modernism in art and literature, declining artistic standards within the movement itself, and the decreasing intensity of the Irish Nationalist movement following the establishment of the Irish Free State in 1922.

REPRESENTATIVE WORKS

A. E. [pseudonym of George Russell]
Homeward: Songs by the Way (poetry) 1894
Deirdre (drama) 1902
The Candle of Vision (autobiography) 1918
The Interpreters (novel) 1922
The House of the Titans, and Other Poems (poetry) 1934

Boyle, William
The Building Fund (drama) 1905
The Eloquent Dempsey (drama) 1906

Bullock, Shan F.
By Thrasna River (novel) 1895
Ring O' Rushes (short stories) 1896
The Barrys (novel) 1897
Irish Pastorals (short stories) 1901
The Squireen (novel) 1903
Dan the Dollar (novel) 1905

Clarke, Austin
The Vengeance of Fionn (poetry) 1917
The Bright Temptation (novel) 1932

Cockery, Daniel
A Munster Twilight (short stories) 1916
The Threshold of Quiet (novel) 1917

Colum, Padraic
Broken Soil (drama) 1903
The Land (drama) 1905
Wild Earth (poetry) 1907
Thomas Muskerry (drama) 1910
Castle Conquer (novel) 1923

Dunsany, Lord Edward
The Sword of Welleran (short stories) 1908
The Glittering Gate (drama) 1909
A Dreamer's Tale (short stories) 1910
The Book of Wonder (short stories) 1912

Ferguson, Sir Samuel
Lays of the Western Gael (poetry) 1865
Congal (poetry) 1872
Poems (poetry) 1880

Fitzmaurice, George
The Country Dressmaker (drama) 1907
The Pie-Dish (drama) 1908
The Magic Glasses (drama) 1913
The Dandy Dolls (drama) 1914

Gregory, Lady
Cuchulain of Muirthemne [translator] (folklore) 1902
Gods and Fighting Men [translator] (folklore) 1904
Spreading the News (drama) 1904
Kincora (drama) 1905
The White Cockade (drama) 1905
The Canavans (drama) 1906
The Gaol-Gate (drama) 1906
Hyacinth Halvey (drama) 1906
The Rising of the Moon (drama) 1906
The Image (drama) 1910
Our Irish Theatre (autobiography) 1913
The Wrens (drama) 1914
Dave (drama) 1927

Hyde, Douglas
Love Songs of Connacht (poetry and folklore) 1893

Casadh an tSúgáin   (drama)   1901
Joyce, James
  Dubliners   (short stories)   1914
  A Portrait of the Artist as a Young Man   (novel)
    1916
  Exiles   (drama)   1918
  Ulysses   (novel)   1922
  Finnegans Wake   (novel)   1939
MacDonagh, Thomas
  When the Dawn is Come   (drama)   1908
MacManus, Seumas
  The Humours of Donegal   (novel)   1898
  A Lad of the O'Friels   (novel)   1903
MacNamara, Brinsley   (John Weldon)
  The Valley of the Squinting Windows   (novel)   1918
  The Clanking of the Chains   (novel)   1920
Martyn, Edward
  The Heather Field   (drama)   1899
  Maeve   (drama)   1900
Milligan, Alice
  The Last Feast of the Fianna   (drama)   1900
Moore, George
  A Mummer's Wife   (novel)   1885
  A Drama in Muslin   (novel)   1886
  Celibates   (novellas)   1895
  Evelyn Innes   (novel)   1898
  The Bending of the Bough   (drama)   1900
  Diarmuid and Grania   [with William Butler Yeats]
    (drama)   1902
  The Untilled Field   (short stories)   1903
  The Lake   (novel)   1905
  Hail and Farewell. 3 vols.   (autobiography)   1911-
    14
Murray, T. C.
  Birthright   (drama)   1910
  Maurice Harte   (drama)   1912
  Autumn Fire   (drama)   1924
O'Byrne, Dermot
  Children of the Hills   (short stories)   1913
  Wrack, and Other Stories   (short stories)   1918
O'Casey, Sean
  The Shadow of a Gunman   (drama)   1923
  Juno and the Paycock   (drama)   1924
  The Plough and the Stars   (drama)   1926
O'Grady, Standish James
  History of Ireland: The Heroic Period   (history)
    1878
O'Kelly, Seumas
  The Weaver's Grave   (novella)   1917
  Waysiders   (short stories)   1918
Plunkett, Joseph
  The Circle and the Sword   (poetry)   1911
Reid, Forrest
  The Bracknels: A Family Chronicle   (novel)   1911
  Following Darkness   (novel)   1912; also published as
    Peter Waring, 1937
  At the Door of the Gate   (novel)   1915
  The Spring Song   (novel)   1916
Robinson, Lennox
  The Clancy Name   (drama)   1908
  The Whiteheaded Boy   (drama)   1916
  Crabbed Youth and Age   (drama)   1922
  Drama at Inish   (drama)   1933
Stephens, James
  Insurrections   (poetry)   1909

The Charwoman's Daughter   (novel)   1912; also
  published as *Mary, Mary,*   1912
The Crock of Gold   (novel)   1912
The Hill of Vision   (poetry)   1912
The Demi-Gods   (novel)   1914
Deirdre   (novella)   1923
Synge, J. M.
  In the Shadow of the Glen   (drama)   1903
  Riders to the Sea   (drama)   1904
  The Well of the Saints   (drama)   1905
  The Playboy of the Western World   (drama)   1907
  The Tinker's Wedding   (drama)   1909
  Deirdre of the Sorrows   (drama)   1910
Yeats, William Butler
  The Wanderings of Oisin, and Other Poems   (poetry)
    1889
  *The Countess Cathleen, and Various Legends and
    Lyrics*   (poetry)   1892
  The Celtic Twilight   (folklore)   1893
  The Secret Rose   (short stories)   1897
  The Wind among the Reeds   (poetry)   1899
  The Shadowy Waters   (drama)   1900
  Cathleen ni Houlihan   [with Lady Gregory]
    (drama)   1902
  The Hour-Glass   [with Lady Gregory]   (drama)
    1903
  In the Seven Woods   (poetry)   1903
  The King's Threshold   [with Lady Gregory]
    (drama)   1903
  On Baile's Strand   (drama)   1904
  Deirdre   [with Lady Gregory]   (drama)   1906
  The Unicorn from the Stars   [with Lady Gregory]
    (drama)   1907
  The Golden Helmet   (drama)   1908
  The Green Helmet, and Other Poems   (poetry)
    1910
  Responsibilities, and Other Poems   (poetry)   1914
  At the Hawk's Well   (drama)   1916
  The Wild Swans at Coole   (poetry)   1917
  Michael Robartes and the Dancer   (poetry)   1920
  A Vision   (essay)   1925; also published as *A Vision*
    [enlarged edition],   1937
  On the Boiler   (essays and poetry)   1939

OVERVIEW

Phillip L. Marcus

[*Marcus is an American educator, critic, and editor who
specializes in Irish studies. His works include* Standish
O'Grady *(1970) and* Yeats and the Beginning of the
Irish Renaissance *(1970). He is also a contributor to
such journals as* James Joyce Quarterly *and* Irish University Review. *In the following excerpt, he provides a
comprehensive overview of the Irish Literary Renaissance, or what he terms the Celtic Revival.*]

[The Celtic Revival in Ireland] depended for its existence
upon the growth during the 1800s of an awareness of na-

tionhood, encouraging the creation of a 'national' literature and a 'national' art.

Such aspirations Ireland shared with many other European countries seeking to reassert their historic identity. But Ireland faced peculiar difficulties. The number of native Irish speakers was steadily and rapidly declining in most of the country and the new literature would have to be in English. The movement looked back to and derived part of its inspiration and imaginative energy from the Celtic golden age; but in speaking of a 'Revival' we risk obscuring the crucial fact that the bulk of the modern literature was written in a different language, often by men and women whose ancestors had not even come to Ireland until long after the end of that remarkable medieval era.

In the visual arts, the situation was closely parallel. During most of the 19th century Irish artists were forced to make their careers abroad, usually in England. The bulk of the work they produced had nothing to distinguish its nationality. Any that did manifested it in the choice of subject matter, or in the revival of ancient Celtic art, rather than in any distinctly Irish style. The question is complicated by the fact that it is difficult to distinguish between those artists whose choice of Irish subjects, contemporary or ancient, was prompted by a search for the romantic or the picturesque, and those who were looking for a national identity.

The story of the Celtic Revival in literature is essentially the story of how these drawbacks were surmounted, and a vigorous and wholly authentic national culture brought into being. In the visual arts the final verdict must be one of qualified success only. But it is an exciting story, featuring strong, colourful personalities, memorable events, a closer involvement of art in the public world of politics than we can easily imagine today and of course a substantial number of literary and artistic masterpieces.

Poems written in English by Irishmen had begun to appear by the 14th century, but so long as Irish remained the primary language of most of the country no appreciable body of such literature could be expected. By the 1700s there were large numbers of 'new' settlers who considered themselves Irish but whose native language was English; and, while many authors of that era looked to England for their subjects, form and style, others did take an interest in the indigenous culture. From the 1790s on, political ballads in English enjoyed wide circulation. The immensely popular *Irish Melodies* of Thomas Moore (1779-1852), which began appearing in 1808, gave a rather facile lyric expression to national themes, with a prevailing note of post-Union melancholy. It was only with the Young Ireland movement of the 1840s, however, that we find an organized, self-conscious effort to develop a literature that would be primarily English in language but distinctively national, 'racy of the soil', in character.

Nationality as the Young Irelanders defined it embraced all creeds and races and classes in the country. They wanted to bring together Irish-speaking Gaels, direct heirs of the pre-Norman people whose traditions the Penal Laws had driven into refuge in the impoverished world of the cabins and the turf fires; and men who were English in an-

cestry and language but identified themselves nevertheless with Irish political, economic and cultural interests. Literature was to be an important binding force. The leaders of the movement, the most famous of whom were Charles Gavan Duffy (1816-1903) and the revered Thomas Davis (1814-45), founded the weekly paper the *Nation* in 1842 to serve as a focal point for the encouragement of national literary effort and dissemination of the fruits of that effort. Because the leaders were strongly nationalistic in their politics, the most characteristic literature of the *Nation* and the 'Library of Ireland' (a series of inexpensive books for popular consumption) was often little more than anti-Unionist propaganda:

> How thrive we by the Union?
> Look round our native land;
> In ruined trade and wealth decayed
> See slavery's surest brand;
> Our glory as a nation gone,
> Our substance drained away;
> A wretched province trampled on,
> Is all we've left today.
> Then curse with me the Union,
> That juggle foul and base—
> The baneful root that bore such fruit
> Of ruin and disgrace.

Intended to be immediately intelligible to great masses of ill-educated readers, it was superficial and sometimes distorted in content, conventional and mechanical in style. Only a poet of real talent such as James Clarence Mangan (1803-49), author of 'Dark Rosaleen' and 'O'Hussey's Ode to the Maguire', was able to transcend the pressures of expediency. Thus, while the Young Ireland movement certainly did contribute greatly to the strengthening of national sentiment in Ireland, it could not by itself constitute the nucleus of a revival.

At the same time, however, complementary forces were at work. One of these was a vein of acute realistic social observation in novels of Irish life, a vein which perhaps originated in 1800 with Maria Edgeworth's *Castle Rackrent*. The tradition was extended by such writers as Gerald Griffin, John Banim and William Carleton (best known for his *Traits and Stories of the Irish Peasantry*, 1830-33). Like Mangan, Carleton was for a time associated with the *Nation*, but never fully identified himself with its aspirations. *Knocknagow* (1879), probably the most popular Irish novel of the period, was contributed by the Fenian patriot Charles Kickham; it chronicled lovingly the life of a Tipperary village. The work of these novelists was sometimes low in quality or marred by class or religious bias, but it did significantly expand the range of appropriate subject matter for national literature. The youthful W. B. Yeats would praise Banim and Carleton as writers who 'saw the whole of everything they looked at . . . the brutal with the tender, the coarse with the refined . . . [and] tried to make one see life plainly but all written down in a kind of fiery shorthand that it might never be forgotten'. While James Joyce would have had nothing but scorn for these native predecessors, his own fiction continues the tradition they helped begin and embodies the receptivity to a wide spectrum of experience for which Yeats had praised them.

Between them and Joyce the most powerful representative

of that tradition was George Moore (1852-1933), who carried it on under the stimulus of Zola and French naturalism in his fine novel *A Drama in Muslin* (1886). It provides a panoramic view of contemporary Irish life and a merciless indictment of the entire country, urban and rural, Ascendancy and peasantry. His view of Dublin clearly prefigures Joyce's:

> The weary, the woebegone, the threadbare streets—yes, threadbare conveys the moral idea of Dublin in 1882. . . . The Dublin streets stare the vacant and helpless stare of a beggar selling matches on a doorstep, and the feeble cries for amusement are like those of the child beneath the ragged shawl for the red gleam of a passing soldier's coat. On either side of you, there is a bawling ignorance or plaintive decay. Look at the houses! Like crones in borrowed bonnets some are fashionable with flowers in the rotting window frames—others languish in silly cheerfulness like women living on the proceeds of the pawnshop; others—those with brass plates on the doors—are evil smelling as the prescriptions of the threadbare doctor, bald as the bill of costs of the servile attorney. And the souls of the Dubliners blend and harmonize with their connatural surroundings.

This was the tract of Irish life that Joyce was to develop and make his own; and the virtual interpenetration of setting and character which Moore re-creates through metaphor was to receive its ultimate expression in the phantasmagoria of *Finnegans Wake,* the central character of which is both man and city.

A second major force which complemented Young Ireland efforts to create a national literature was a growing scholarly and imaginative interest in the Irish past, especially in the old Gaelic literature and legends. The Young Irelanders themselves encouraged this pursuit; but it had originated long before and many of its greatest enthusiasts were men who could not accept the nationalistic (as opposed to the merely national) elements in the Young Ireland political programme.

English-language accounts of Irish legends and bardic literature began appearing in the 16th and 17th centuries. Scholarly and literary attention increased rapidly during the later part of the next century, receiving a stimulus from the controversy over James Macpherson's alleged Ossianic 'translations'. (There was a corresponding concern with Irish traditional music, manifested in Edward Bunting's *General Collection of Ancient Irish Music*—a book which in turn influenced Moore's *Melodies.*) The Union caused only a temporary check; in the 19th century, massive contributions were made by the two great Gaelic scholars John O'Donovan (1809-61) and Eugene O'Curry (1796-1862), while the publication in 1825 of Thomas Crofton Croker's *Fairy Legends and Traditions of the South of Ireland* opened the rich related vein of Irish folklore. Meanwhile, the famine and its aftermath led to a drastic decline in the use of Irish, which had been under increasing pressure since the 1700s. By 1891, over 80 per cent of the population would speak no Irish at all.

Once these traditional stories were readily available in translation, their suitability as the basis for a new literature in English seemed obvious. They were fresh; had not been mined again and again like the Classical materials; and appeared virtually inexhaustible—'the most plentiful treasure of legends in Europe', Yeats was to assert. Their distinctively Irish features offered Irish authors a way of breaking with the custom of merely echoing at a distance their counterparts in England. On the other hand, they represented a subject that, while intensely national, was uncoloured by modern politics and sectarian religious controversy and thus might appeal to a wider, more heterogeneous audience. Mangan, who contributed to the *Nation,* had worked as a copyist for O'Donovan and O'Curry and derived from them the strong interest in the Irish past which informs some of his best poetry. Aubrey de Vere (1814-1902), in contrast, refused to countenance agitation for independence and was very critical of what he termed Irish 'jacobinism'; but he produced a number of poetic adaptations of the early Gaelic tales. And the two most important predecessors of the Revival, Sir Samuel Ferguson and Standish James O'Grady, were both supporters of the Union.

Ferguson (1810-86) briefly sympathized with some of the less extreme Young Ireland views, but before and after that era identified himself with the forces of the Unionist Ascendancy. He by no means considered himself a 'West Briton', however, and both as antiquarian and as poet he was deeply absorbed in the early literature and culture of the country. Clearly the motives underlying his interest in this material were different from Davis's; but he was a man of real, if limited, poetic ability, and thus was able to reveal as no one before him the potential of such material as a foundation stone for a national literature. His epic poem *Congal* (1872) had many flaws; but it, along with a number of poems based on legendary and folk subjects in *Lays of the Western Gael* (1865) and *Poems* (1880), constituted the most substantial body then available of work in which the fresh national subject matter was combined with a high level of technical proficiency. It was primarily for this reason that Yeats was moved to praise him so extravagantly in 1886:

> The author of these poems is the greatest poet Ireland has produced, because the most central and most Celtic. Whatever the future may bring forth in the way of a truly great and national literature—and now that the race is so large, so widely spread, and so conscious of its unity, the years are ripe—will find its morning in these three volumes of one who was made by the purifying flame of National sentiment the one man of his time who wrote heroic poetry—one who, among the somewhat sybaritic singers of his day, was like some aged sea-king sitting among the inland wheat and poppies—the savour of the sea about him, and its strength.

The praise itself was certainly excessive, but Yeats was right in giving Ferguson so high a rank among his contemporaries; and the prediction that a new literary movement was at hand of course proved prophetic.

Yeats made even greater claims for Ferguson's friend O'Grady (1846-1928), asserting that his *History of Ireland* 'started us all'. His enthusiasm was matched by others, including T. W. Rolleston, who called the *History* 'the first book I ever read which convinced me that there was such a thing as a spiritual Ireland'; and George Russell, who declared that 'whatever is Irish in me he kindled to life'. What was the cause of this remarkable impact? It lay precisely in the vision of early Irish tradition embodied in O'Grady's famous work.

O'Grady's background, like Ferguson's, allied him with the Ascendancy; and only by chance did he discover that his country had a noble and inspiring past. Once he had made this discovery, however, he rapidly gave it memorable expression in his *History of Ireland* (1878-80). This was a strange book, partly prose epic and partly scholarly study, devoted to the deeds of the most famous of all Irish legendary heroes, Cú Chulainn. Some writers had already begun using the new source of subject matter for less than elevated purposes: the Gaelic scholar P. W. Joyce, writing in 1879, spoke of stories which had been 'presented in a very unfavourable and unjust light—distorted to make them look *funny,* and their characters debased to the mere modern conventional stage Irishman'. In contrast, O'Grady regarded 'this age and the great personages moving therein as incomparably higher in intrinsic worth than the corresponding ages of Greece. In Homer, Hesiod, and the Attic poets, there is a polish and artistic form, absent in the existing monuments of Irish heroic thought, but the gold, the ore itself, is here massier and more pure, the sentiment deeper and more tender, the audacity and freedom more exhilarating, the reach of imagination more sublime, the depth and power of the human soul more fully exhibit themselves.' For him Cú Chulainn's combat with his blood-brother Ferdiad was 'the most profoundly tragic scene in all literature', and Cú himself, 'the noblest character'.

This vision, too, involved distortion: in the Gaelic originals, the heroic and noble are mixed inextricably with the comic, the fantastic, the coarse. In his desire to give them the acclaim they deserve O'Grady did them the disservice of presenting only a partial—and thus a false—image. But appearing as it did during a period of burgeoning national consciousness, that was precisely the image which could most powerfully affect the minds of those who were to determine the course of subsequent Irish literature and history. For O'Grady, as for so many other Irishmen, the present moment was haunted by awareness of the past. In his own case the result was an obsession with the painful contrast between the modern landlord class, with whom he continued to sympathize, and what he imagined to be their enlightened and exemplary counterparts in the heroic period. For several other writers there would be material and inspiration for a new literary movement. And for Patrick Pearse, who was to declare that 'what Ireland wants beyond all other modern countries, is a new birth of the heroic spirit' and that 'we must re-create and perpetuate in Ireland the knightly tradition of Cuchulain', O'Grady's image combined with the words of Theobald Wolfe Tone, Robert Emmet, who led a brief rising in 1803, and Thomas Davis and John Mitchel to help form the consciousness behind the Eastern Rising.

The Irish critic Ernest Boyd hailed O'Grady as 'the father of the Literary Revival in Ireland'; and, as we have seen, Ferguson, Davis, and several other 19th-century authors could also take a share of the credit. But there is no doubt that the greatest contribution was made by William Butler Yeats (1865-1939). The poetry he wrote as a youth had imitated English models. In 1885 he met the old Fenian exile John O'Leary, and, under the influence of O'Leary's maxim that 'there is no great literature without nationality, no great nationality without literature', decided to become an *Irish* writer. Almost at once he transformed himself into the guiding force in contemporary Irish writing, giving cohesiveness and direction to the vague impulses that were in the air.

His first task was to define precisely what the distinguishing characteristics of a genuinely national literature might be. As he surveyed the efforts of his predecessors he found much to ponder. The most *popular* literature had come from the patriotic tradition inaugurated by the Young Irelanders, with whose radical political aims he was sympathetic; but he was offended by the weaknesses of that work and preferred on literary grounds the work of men like Ferguson and William Allingham, which lay outside the tradition epitomized by *The Spirit of the Nation* and was consequently little read yet seemed to him distinctively Irish. Resisting the pressures towards immediate political usefulness, he called for writing that would be Irish in subject and spirit and style but not necessarily politically nationalistic. Against the Young Ireland view that 'Patriotism . . . can *make* poetry' he argued that the writer must always put the demands of his art before those of politics. To counter the urge towards provincialism he asserted that 'a writer is not less national because he shows the influence of other countries and of the great writers of the world'. Foreign influences could be particularly valuable in the area of artistic craftsmanship, where so much of the 19th-century literature had been woefully deficient. As particularly important indigenous subject-matter he stressed legend, folklore and 'the spiritual life'—the last a manifestation of his own passionate life-long concern with the occult but which he nevertheless sought to establish as primally and essentially Celtic. And he expressed confidence that his country could 'build up a national tradition, a national literature, which shall be none the less Irish in spirit for being English in language'.

Yeats strove diligently to spread these ideals to others. In a steady stream of articles and reviews he propagandized for them and for writers whose work gave them substance. He defended the nascent movement against such critics as Gavan Duffy, who, returning to Ireland at the end of his life, wanted only patriotic writing in the old Young Ireland mode; and the famous Irish Shakespearean scholar and Trinity don Edward Dowden (a close family friend), who preferred the literature of England and the Continent to anything his own country might produce. As editor of a variety of anthologies, Yeats featured the work of the new authors and of those earlier writers who had prepared the way for them. He was also instrumental in founding Irish literary societies in Dublin and London, organizations which performed the important function of giving a sense of *group* effort, of a real *movement* in progress. Most dramatically of all, he provided a concrete illustration of his literary programme in his own increasingly prominent creative work.

His principal volumes before the turn of the century were *The Wanderings of Oisin and Other Poems* (1889), *The Countess Cathleen and Various Legends and Lyrics* (1892), *Poems* (1895), *The Secret Rose* (1897) and *The Wind Among the Reeds* (1899): narrative and lyric poems, stories, dramas—an impressive body of evidence that there was indeed something to his claims concerning the possibility of a great national literature. 'The Valley of the Black Pig', short enough to be given in its entirety, will serve to epitomize these early efforts:

> The dews drop slowly and dreams gather: unknown spears
> Suddenly hurtle before my dream-awakened eyes,
> And then the clash of fallen horsemen and the cries
> Of unknown perishing armies beat about my ears.
> We who still labour by the cromlec on the shore,
> The grey cairn on the hill, when day sinks drowned in dew,
> Being weary of the world's empires, bow down to you
> Master of the still stars and of the flaming door.

Here Yeats has subjected Young Ireland poetry to a kind of 'spiritual' sublimation process. The militancy of the earlier school is there, and many of the country people from whom Yeats had heard the legend upon which the poem is based saw in the battle a coming struggle between Ireland and England. But he himself makes the political subsidiary to the occult, identifying the poem in its original title as part of a group 'concerning Peasant Visionaries' and (as his notes make clear) associating the legend with other mythological battles about which he knew from books of comparative anthropology such as Rhys's *Celtic Heathendom* and Frazer's *Golden Bough*. The resultant vision of apocalypse also draws upon the poet's Blakean and hermetic studies, and the poem is intensely national (even tied to the Sligo of Yeats's own youth) but not at all parochial. In technique, too, it shows a modification of the *Nation* tradition in the light of Yeats's contact with the literature of other countries. The subject of the poem (first published in the English *avant-garde* magazine *The Savoy*) demanded not the conventional energetic but mechanical ballad rhythms of Davis and his followers but rather 'wavering, meditative, organic rhythms' that would liberate the reader's mind from 'the pressure of the will' and make him receptive to communication by symbol and archetype. The sound patterns, the repetitions, the high percentage of monosyllabic words are designed to push audiences not to the barricades but rather to the quiet, awesome shores of trance.

The disillusionment with practical politics following [Irish nationalist leader Charles] Parnell's death in 1891 caused many sensitive minds to seek other outlets for their national impulses, and this obviously aided Yeats's efforts. Ireland in the 'nineties was becoming a lively place culturally. Most of the early stars in the literary firmament seem to

us today to be distinctly minor talents: John Todhunter, Katharine Tynan, Nora Hopper, Lionel Johnson. But the mere fact of their involvement generated further interest and thus prepared for the advent of greater figures who might otherwise have written differently or not at all; and these years did see the emergence of one Irish writer of considerable ability and significance, George Russell (1867-1935), popularly known as 'AE'.

AE was in fact among the most remarkable and engaging personalities in the history of modern Ireland. He was an unlikely blend of mystic, artist and practical man, equally familiar with newspaper editing, the economics of cooperative farming, the Sacred Books of the East and the composition of poetry. He shared many of Yeats's occult interests and came to share his national ones, though he felt a tension between nationalism and 'the politics of eternity'. In 1898 Yeats observed that 'Dublin is waking up in a number of ways and about a number of things. Russell is doing a good part in the awakening.'

His poetry is generally inferior in quality to Yeats's work, perhaps because the fullness of his commitment to a transcendent reality made him less inclined to consider craftsmanship as an ideal. The folk subject (a fairy luring a mortal out of life), the apocalyptic note and the very language and verbal effects of the following stanza from his 'The Gates of Dreamland' remind us of the Yeats of 'The Valley of the Black Pig':

> 'Come away,' the red lips whisper, 'all the earth is weary now;
> 'Tis the twilight of the ages and it's time to quit the plough.
> Oh, the very sunlight's weary ere it lightens up the dew,
> And its gold is changed and faded ere its falling down to you.'

Not surprisingly, Yeats praised such work as 'more Irish than any of those books of stories or of verses which reflect so many obviously Irish characteristics that every newspaper calls them, in the trying phrase of 1845, "racy of the soil" '. AE himself wrote 'I feel in a frenzy when I see the "Spirit of the Nation" referred to as literature' and praised Yeats in turn for providing an alternative. AE was also a great discoverer and encourager of young writers, including Joyce, Sean O'Faolain and Austin Clarke. Not all his 'finds' were so fortunate as these, and Yeats came to feel that his friend had also nurtured too many mediocre talents with whose contributions the movement could afford to dispense. Nevertheless, AE certainly played a key role in turning Irish literature away from the Davis tradition and keeping the new movement alive.

It seems appropriate at this point to emphasize that there were a number of writers of this era who did not follow the programme Yeats and his associates were championing. Oscar Wilde (1854-1900), for example, had by birth impeccable credentials for becoming involved with the Irish literary scene: his father Sir William Wilde was a noted Irish antiquarian and his mother, known as 'Speranza', had actually contributed verse to the *Nation*. But Wilde himself preferred a larger, cosmopolitan literary world. Similarly George Bernard Shaw (1856-1950), though he wrote frequently about social and political questions involving his homeland, made Ireland the subject of only one of his major plays. It would be possible to argue that his work and Wilde's reveal an 'Irish sensibility'; but clearly neither man wrote out of a conscious desire to contribute to the development of a national literature or identified himself integrally with the Revival. Considering their great creative abilities, the loss to that movement was a considerable one. Edward Plunkett, Lord Dunsany (1878-1957), provides another example. Although he sometimes came into contact with the Revival and was encouraged by Yeats to involve himself more closely, he was basically a 'West Briton' and thus out of sympathy with its aims.

Unlike these men, the fox-hunting cousins Edith (Enone Somerville (1858-1949) and Violet Martin (1862-1915), who as 'Somerville and Ross' collaborated on a number of novels, did make Ireland the primary concern of their work. Nevertheless, their relation to the movement was a tenuous and uneasy one. In 1894 they had published *The Real Charlotte,* which has been called the best Irish novel of the century, and it looked as if they might fit into Yeats's plans. But when their tremendously successful collection of stories *Some Experiences of an Irish R. M.* appeared in 1899 its comic treatment of Irish life reminded many readers of the 'stage-Irish' tradition and the patronizing works of the popular novelists Charles Lever (1806-72) and Samuel Lover (1797-1868). Somerville and Ross were in fact class-conscious members of the Ascendancy, though also shrewd observers of the social scene and often brilliant writers. Thus it was difficult for Yeats and his closest associates to claim them for the national effort, and they themselves were careful to remain detached. Yet their work, in contrast to that of the cosmopolitan writers, can indeed be studied profitably in the context of Irish literature.

At the opposite extreme from authors who did not share the intense national impulses of Yeats were others who felt that the movement he was fostering was not Irish *enough.* The key figure here was undoubtedly Douglas Hyde (1860-1949). As a child he had become fascinated with peasant life and with the Irish language. His collections of folklore soon brought him to Yeats's attention, and the bilingual *Love Songs of Connacht* which he published in 1893 seemed to Yeats a major step towards the development of a distinctively Irish form of English prose to replace the comic brogue that had been the staple of the novelists. But Yeats was mistaken in thinking that Hyde had any serious interest in creating a national literature in English. Hyde felt that the only way the modern nation could preserve its ancient Celtic heritage was through the Irish language, and it was towards saving and reviving the dying tongue that he devoted the greatest share of his energies. In November 1892 he gave these ideas memorable expression in his influential lecture on 'The Necessity for De-Anglicising Ireland', and when the Gaelic League was founded the following year he became its first president. Soon he was at the centre of a growing cultural movement of his own, and one that, at least implicitly, questioned the right of Yeats, AE and the others to call themselves *Irish* writers. Hyde himself, though he confessed in 1900 that

he would rather have written one good poem in Irish than an entire volume of English verses, was indulgent towards their efforts, which he looked upon as a halfway house; but some of his followers, including the fiery journalist D. P. Moran, were not. Their 'Irish Ireland' programme asserted that the national literature *must* be in the native language. This position led to some vigorous clashes with Yeats and those identified with his ideals; it also contributed substantially to the militant nationalism which erupted in 1916.

The single most significant and well-known of Yeats's efforts to stimulate the development of a national literature was the Irish dramatic movement now universally associated with the Abbey Theatre, its home since 1904. Yeats had been drawn to the drama since the beginning of his literary career, and during the 1890s he became increasingly conscious of the suitability of the stage as a means of reaching the large potential audience who could not be interested in *reading* serious literature. A preliminary manifesto shows the way in which the theatre movement was conceived as a medium for the propagation of Yeats's literary ideals:

> We propose to have performed in Dublin in the spring of every year certain Celtic and Irish plays, which whatever be their degree of excellence will be written with a high ambition, and so to build up a Celtic and Irish school of dramatic literature. We hope to find in Ireland an uncorrupted and imaginative audience trained to listen by its passion for oratory, and believe that our desire to bring upon the stage the deeper thoughts and emotions of Ireland will insure for us a tolerant welcome, and that freedom to experiment which is not found in theatres in England, and without which no new movement in art or literature can succeed. We will show that Ireland is not the home of buffoonery and of easy sentiment, as it has been represented, but the home of an ancient idealism. We are confident of the support of all Irish people, who are weary of misrepresentation, in carrying out a work that is outside all the political questions that divide us.

At the time this manifesto was written there was, in addition to the old opposition of nationalist and Unionist, the new bitterness left by the split in the nationalist ranks following the fall of Parnell. Consequently the position that political relevance was not an essential requirement for national literature was particularly useful in providing a sufficiently broad basis of appeal for what was intended to be a national theatre. The claims of art were to come before all others; 'freedom to experiment' was to be essential. But the dramatic movement *would* be intensely national, drawing its strength from the heroic past and giving particular attention to mythological and early historical subjects. The playwrights, Yeats suggested in a contemporary essay, would be primarily authors 'who have never doubted that all things are shadows of spiritual things'.

Yeats himself energetically set about the task of realizing this programme. He plunged into the practical aspects of 'theatre business, management of men', and also wrote a number of plays, including *The King's Threshold, On*

Baile's Strand and *Deirdre,* that showed growing mastery of theatrical techniques. Almost from the start, however, he encountered problems and disappointments. A controversy concerning the theology of his own *Countess Cathleen* (part of the programme in 1899, his Theatre's first year) was the first of many clashes with audiences that proved far less tolerant than the manifesto had predicted. There were also internal conflicts among the dramatists and the actors. Most seriously of all, the traditional romantic and heroic subjects that Yeats favoured as matter for the new drama failed to take hold. Among his associates in the early years of the movement, both Edward Martyn and George Moore preferred modern work in the vein of Ibsen. 'Peasant' plays became increasingly popular, and a strain of harsh realism emerged and began to dominate the stage.

The peasant material was primarily the province of two of the Theatre's greatest figures, Lady (Augusta) Gregory and John M. Synge. Lady Gregory (1852-1932), a woman of the 'Big House' and the Protestant Ascendancy, had immersed herself in the life and literature of her native land and became one of Yeats's closest friends and literary allies. Her Galway estate, Coole Park, served as a focal point and matrix for much of the new literary activity. The rich heritage of the house and the great natural beauty of the surrounding area impressed themselves deeply upon the imagination of Yeats and many others: their visits were memorialized by initials carved in the trunk of a great beech tree in the garden. Lady Gregory was attracted by Hyde's work, learned Irish, and in the cabins surrounding Coole she and Yeats sought to make contact with the living folk-mind. In her *Cuchulain of Muirthemne* (1902) and *Gods and Fighting Men* (1904) she synthesized the great cycles of early Irish legend and retold them in 'Kiltartan', an English prose coloured by Irish idiom and constructions:

> Then Cuchulain stood up and faced all the men of Ulster. 'There is trouble on Cuchulain,' said Conchubar; 'he is after killing his own son, and if I and all my men were to go against him, by the end of the day he would destroy every man of us. Go now,' he said to Cathbad, the Druid, 'and bind him to go down to Baile's Strand, and to give three days fighting against the waves of the sea, rather than to kill us all.'

This prose, though disparaged by some as artificial, was in Yeats's eyes the perfect medium for making the old stories part of the modern Irish consciousness.

Lady Gregory played from the first a major role in planning the theatre movement; she collaborated with Yeats on several plays, and, when it became apparent that appropriate works were in short supply, set about providing them herself. Her specialty was comedy, but she also wrote tragic-comedies, tragedies and 'wonder plays'. An element of fancy generally tinges the world of the country people depicted in her work. These plays appealed to a wide audience and thus helped keep the Theatre going in difficult times. Nevertheless, she shared Yeats's high standards and supported them vigorously: as she put it in *Our Irish Theatre,* her chronicle of the movement, 'we went on giving what we thought good until it became popular'.

John Synge (1871-1909) was yet another writer from an Ascendancy background who developed a deep commitment to Irish folk life; and the quality of the work he produced after foregoing a cosmopolitan career in Paris to write about the culture he had observed on the Aran Islands and elsewhere in his own country gave weight to Yeats's assertions that nationality was an essential element in great literature. But Synge was tenaciously sincere in his vision of that life ('what I write of Irish country life I know to be true and I most emphatically will not change a syllable of it because A. B. or C. may think they know better than I do'), and thus the plays in which he embodied it provoked tempestuous controversy. As a dramatist he believed that 'on the stage one must have reality, and one must have joy . . . '. In most modern literature these qualities had bifurcated into the naturalistic and symbolist schools; but in countries such as Ireland, 'where the imagination of the people, and the language they use, is rich and living, it is possible for a writer to be rich and copious in his words, and at the same time to give the reality which is the root of all poetry, in a comprehensive and natural form'. This theory justified Synge's dramatic prose, which has general characteristics similar to Hyde's and Lady Gregory's but is even more vibrant and poetic:

> Where now will you meet the like of Daneen Sullivan knocked the eye from a peeler, or Marcus Quin, God rest him, got six months for maiming ewes, and he a great warrant to tell stories of holy Ireland till he'd have the old women shedding down tears about their feet. Where will you find the like of them, I'm saying?

The reality underlying this passage from *The Playboy of the Western World* involved elements of violence, social decline and sexual frustration: the 'real men' are all gone and blooming girls have to make do with the runts who remain. Synge, preoccupied by death and actually destined to die in the fullness of his powers, was attracted by all manifestations of life lived to the utmost and did not feel compelled either to obscure or to condemn elements embarrassing to public morality or national self-images: 'the wildness and, if you will, vices of the Irish peasantry are due, like their extraordinary good points of all kinds, to the *richness* of their nature—a thing that is priceless beyond words'.

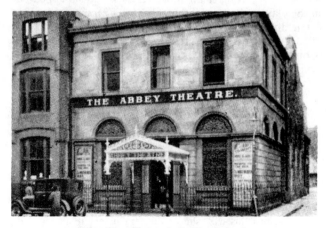

The Abbey Theatre in Dublin, Ireland.

Many of the extreme nationalists could not admit that Synge's picture of Irish life had any truth in it. Their minds, conditioned by Young Ireland stereotypes, needed to see the English-Irish conflict in simple black-and-white terms; any admission that the Irish character had flaws would weaken the development of patriotic feeling and strengthen the oppressors' hand. So Synge, although his own national feeling probably ran deeper than that of most of his antagonists, became the target of virulent attacks. The powerful tragedy *Riders to the Sea* gave relatively little offence, but *The Shadow of the Glen* was considered 'a libel on Irish womanhood' and sparked a controversy in the newspapers. Another play, *The Tinker's Wedding,* was too strong even to be performed in Ireland; and there were riots in the theatre over *The Playboy* in 1907. (Hostile elements in the audience even sang Young Ireland ballads such as Davis's 'A Nation Once Again'.)

Yeats, who had been fighting the super-patriots since the 'nineties, took advantage of the *Playboy* controversy to re-assert the supreme claims of art; but such quarrels made it harder and harder for him to believe in the possibility of a *popular* literary movement and helped produce his own gradual alignment with a very different strand of Irish tradition. Synge and Lady Gregory were themselves both strong-minded individuals who did not always agree with Yeats (or with each other), but the poetic retrospect of 'The Municipal Gallery Revisited'—

> John Synge, I and Augusta Gregory, thought
> All that we did, all that we said or sang
> Must come from contact with the soil, from that
> Contact everything Antaeus-like grew strong.
> We three alone in modern times had brought
> Everything down to that sole test again,
> Dream of the noble and the beggar-man.

—shows that to Yeats their differences seemed insignificant in the face of their common enemy.

There were in fact other talented dramatists connected with the theatre movement, but the work of many of them portrayed with grim faithfulness areas of modern Irish life in which little or no joy could be discerned; and although Yeats recognized this work as satisfying his own requisites for national literature he could not fully sympathize with its vision. A strong element of that dark realism appeared in the plays of Padraic Colum (1881-1972), especially *The Land* and *Thomas Muskerry.* Lennox Robinson (1886-1958), often linked with T. C. Murray and R. J. Ray as 'Cork realists', explained this new mood as a direct reaction against their more romantic predecessors:

> We young men, a generation later than Yeats . . . didn't see [Ireland] as a queen, didn't see her all fair in purple and gold, we loved her as truly as Yeats . . . and the rest—maybe we loved her more deeply, but just because we loved her so deeply her faults were clear to us. Perhaps we realists saw her faults too clearly, perhaps we saw her too often as a grasping, middle-aged hag. She was avaricious, she was mean, for family pride she would force a son into the Church against his will, she would commit arson, she would lie, she would cheat, she would murder

and yet we would write all our terrible words about her out of our love.

To such observers as AE and Ernest Boyd the prominence of the realists was a sign that the theatre movement had entered a period of decadence; contemporary sensibilities conditioned by Joyce are less likely to be disturbed by the plays in this vein and can see that their vision of Irish life, although admittedly narrow, was a powerful and genuine one that needed dramatization.

Yeats's own discouragement with the theatre movement requires qualification. That the Abbey Theatre did not take the course he sought for it is undeniable, but it certainly catalysed concern with the development of a national literature. The activity it generated was abundant. Besides Yeats's own circle at the Abbey there were splinter groups, an Ulster dramatic movement, and plays in Irish. In addition to names already mentioned, Alice Milligan, AE, Hyde, Joyce, the Reverend Patrick S. Dinneen, James Cousins, William Boyle, George Fitzmaurice, Conal O'Riordan, W. F. Casey, Seumas O'Kelly, St John Ervine, Rutherford Mayne, Joseph Campbell, Thomas MacDonagh and Patrick Pearse were among those who tried their hand at writing plays. Prominent actors and actresses included Frank and W. G. Fay, Máire Ní Shiubhlaigh, Sara Allgood, Maire O'Neill, Arthur Sinclair, J. M. Kerrigan and Fred O'Donovan. Whatever the merits of individual plays and performances, their cumulative effect contributed substantially to increasing cultural (and political) awareness.

And it is a misconception to think that Yeats turned away from the Abbey. A study of the Theatre records and of his own correspondence reveals that he never surrendered active involvement in either the artistic or the business ends of play production. However, he was impressed by the failure of his own early plays to find a popular audience, and this led him to search for a dramatic form oriented towards performance but not tied to the public stage. By 1914 he had found what he sought in the aristocratic Noh theatre of Japan, brought to his attention by Ezra Pound. This mode seemed to him ideal for plays concerned with the supernatural, with legend and myth, and expressing their vision by means of symbol and esoteric allusion. It would also free him from popular taste: he boasted that he had 'invented a form of drama, distinguished, indirect and symbolic, and having no need of mob or press to pay its way—an aristocratic form'. A minimum of props and scenery meant that the new plays were performable in a drawing room before a select, highly educated audience. (The appeal of private performance was enhanced when a 1914 crisis in Abbey finances made expensive experimental productions of Yeats's earlier plays temporarily impossible.) And certainly the plays he wrote under this influence, beginning with *At the Hawk's Well,* were too esoteric ever to become crowd-pleasers. Yet even as he turned in this new direction he felt he was 'working for my own country. Perhaps some day a play in the form I am adapting for European purposes shall awake once more, whether in Gaelic or English, under the slope of Slieve-na-mon or Croagh Patrick ancient memories. . . . ' In 1916 he admitted to having the dream that such plays, perhaps translated into Irish, might be taken into the country districts.

And plays of his, including some of the most esoteric ones, appeared on the Abbey stage right up to the time of his death.

When we move from the theatre to examine other aspects of Irish literature from the turn of the century to about 1920, we do so only to meet Yeats once more. Despite the fact that he devoted so much attention during these years to drama, he remained the central figure in Irish poetry. The new century brought a new emphasis to his vision, and thus to his work. He described the change in Nietzschean terms:

> I have always felt that the soul has two movements primarily: one to transcend forms, and the other to create forms. Nietzsche . . . calls these the Dionysiac and the Apollonic, respectively. I think I have to some extent got weary of that wild God Dionysus, and I am hoping that the Far-Darter will come in his place.

This statement was by no means a *renunciation* of the 'spiritual': the soul is still supreme. But whereas his poetry in the 'nineties had increasingly concerned itself with the soul's transcendence of the phenomenal world, now he would give more attention to its incarnation in that world. Writing for the theatre, which demanded language that men could *speak,* reinforced this shift in emphasis: it led him to seek for 'a more manful energy . . . and for clean outline, instead of those outlines of lyric poetry that are blurred with desire and vague regret'.

During this same period, Yeats was defending the primacy of art in controversies with the extremists among his nationalist political allies over such issues as *The Playboy* and the proposed gallery for the great collection of paintings which Lady Gregory's nephew Hugh Lane wished to give Dublin, and trying to keep the literary standards of the writers themselves as high as possible. The bitterness which so often resulted and his own increasing unpopularity brought him to see the value of his more 'masculine' style for *satiric* poetry and helped provoke him to a redefinition of his own national tradition. More and more he turned from the 19th-century nationalism with which he had originally identified back to the heyday of the Ascendancy in the decades preceding the Union. Grattan, Burke, Berkeley and Swift took on a new value in his eyes, became sources of political and philosophic and literary wisdom; and he saw himself and such congenial contemporaries as Synge, Lane and Lady Gregory as their heirs.

Both the satiric note and the sense of alienation from the nationalists are already discernible in poems like 'To a Wealthy Man . . . '

> You gave, but will not give again
> Until enough of Paudeen's pence
> By Biddy's halfpennies have lain
> To be 'some sort of evidence',
> Before you'll put your guineas down,
> That things it were a pride to give
> Are what the blind and ignorant town
> Imagines best to make it thrive.

His assertion in 'September 1913' that the revolutionary movement itself had lost its strength was disproved dramatically by the Easter Rising three years later. He recog-

nized his misjudgment, and made brilliant art of the recognition in 'Easter 1916'; but he continued to pursue his new direction. It was a direction that he considered no less Irish, no less patriotic, than that chosen by the rebels; and it led him towards Thoor Ballylee, the Norman tower near Coole which he bought in 1917 and which became a dominant symbol in the great poetry of his mature years.

One of the disadvantages of a literary movement is that its most original authors almost invariably call forth imitators. By the first decade of the new century, a great many of the young poets were beginning to explore the early manner which Yeats had already moved beyond—an effect Joyce was to characterize in *Finnegans Wake* as the 'cultic twalette'. AE also had his disciples, and the new work often seemed to have drawn inspiration from both sources. Colum, 'Seumas O'Sullivan' (James Starkey), Ella Young and Susan Mitchell—who proved to be an excellent poetic satirist—were among the young writers emerging at this time. Ulster, of course, had its poets, including Alice Milligan and Joseph Campbell.

A literary movement consists of half a dozen writers living in the same city who cordially detest one another.

—*A. E. (George Russell), in an undated statement published in* Irish Literary Portraits, *British Broadcasting Corporation, 1972.*

James Stephens (1880-1950), whose first volume of verse appeared in 1909, eventually developed into a poet of considerable stature; but after *The Crock of Gold* (1912) he was best known as a writer of prose romances. Oliver St John Gogarty (1878-1957), model for the notorious 'Buck' Mulligan of *Ulysses,* was actually a talented poet and another remarkable all-round man, involved in virtually every aspect of contemporary Irish life. He supported the Sinn Fein movement and later served with Yeats in the Senate of the newly established Free State. Much of his poetry, written out of a deep love of Classical literature and culture, seems by Yeatsian standards cosmopolitan; but he also produced witty satires on local themes.

Patrick Pearse, Thomas MacDonagh and Joseph Plunkett, three other poets whose work was becoming known during this era, were to achieve their greatest fame outside the sphere of literature. For them, their country literally meant more than life, but they too had been affected by the climate Yeats had created and did not repeat the Young Irelanders' mistake of confusing patriotism and poetry. Pearse, although like Hyde he really desired a national literature in Irish, praised Yeats as a 'great artist' and 'the poet who has most finely voiced Irish nationalism in our time'. Pearse did not feel that a writer who chose to advance a cause was automatically weakening his work, but neither did he believe that by doing so he would be strengthening it. In his study of Irish literature the scholarly MacDonagh observed that 'propaganda has rarely produced a great poem'. Each of these poets was a conscious craftsman and rigorously pruned his *oeuvre* with posterity in mind.

Nineteen-sixteen took all three men from the scene; in the following year Austin Clarke published his first volume, *The Vengeance of Fionn.* Clarke was to become arguably the best Irish poet after Yeats, but it was not until many years after this era that he developed the distinctive style found in his finest work. In retrospect the poetry of the 1900-20 period seems transitional: more sophisticated and self-conscious, attaining a generally higher level of artistry than the work of the formative years of the Revival; but providing nothing to equal the fullest flowering of the movement in Yeats's major lyrical volumes of the 'twenties and 'thirties.

To Ernest Boyd, writing in 1916, fiction seemed 'the weak point of the Revival'. However, he was among those who did not take Somerville and Ross seriously; he had only recently discovered Joyce; and Seumas O'Kelly had not yet published his great novella *The Weaver's Grave.* When one adds the contributions of these writers to the work of Stephens, Moore and the Ulster novelist Shan F. Bullock, it becomes obvious that the prose of the first two decades of the 20th century is one of the strongest areas in modern Irish literature.

The fiction writers of this era struck every tonal note, from whimsical fantasy to brutal realism; lyricism, comedy and satire flourished; and there were major experiments in form and style. Somerville and Ross, O'Kelly, and Stephens all deserve more attention than they have received. For the purposes of this survey, however, Moore and Joyce must be given the fullest consideration—because their work, in addition to its excellence, embodies an appraisal of the Revival itself. Each of them produced a volume of stories chronicling the deadness of much of modern Irish life as they saw it (Moore focusing upon the countryside, Joyce upon the metropolis) and a novel that dramatized in detail a sensitive mind's efforts to escape this constricting environment; and each followed these works with a *magnum opus,* a Sacred Book, in which the entire Irish literary movement was subjected to a highly personal and generally negative scrutiny.

After writing *A Drama in Muslin* and *Parnell and his Island* in the 1880s, Moore had absented himself from his homeland until the turn of the century when the nascent theatre project aroused his national enthusiasm. In addition to his brief involvement with that project (which included collaboration with Yeats on the play *Diarmuid and Grania*) he took an interest in the language movement; the stories in *The Untilled Field* (1903) appeared also in Gaelic to serve as models for potential writers of fiction in Irish. It was almost certain, however, that the picture of Irish life presented in them would not be well received among the priests and Irish Irelanders who comprised the backbone of the Gaelic League. Moore depicts the country as debilitated by poverty and emigration, with its aristocracy in decay, the Church in control of people's lives, and no room for love, beauty or art. While some of the priests in the stories are treated sympathetically, the volume as a whole puts Catholicism in a very bad light.

Not surprisingly Moore's novel *The Lake* (1905), originally conceived as a story for *The Untilled Field,* charted the course of a priest's abandonment of his religion in order to seek 'life'. The book made an innovative contribution to the development of the psychological and symbolic novel. Father Gogarty's metamorphosis is effected by his plunging into a lake and swimming to freedom; the connection between the external and internal worlds is made explicit in his final reflection that 'There is a lake in every man's heart. . . . And every man must ungird his loins for the crossing.'

Moore had come to feel that no artistic and cultural awakening was possible in Ireland so long as the country remained primarily Catholic. In addition to rather ostentatiously renouncing the faith himself, he made this perception the shaping principle in his fictional-autobiographical trilogy *Hail and Farewell* (1911-14). All his literary associates appeared under their real names, with no major figure spared from some degree of satire.

Moore's description of Yeats giving a speech about the Lane gallery provides a delightful counterpoint to Yeats's own poem on the subject:

> We . . . could hardly believe our ears when, instead of talking to us as he used to do about the old stories come down from generation to generation, he began to thunder like Ben Tillett himself against the middle classes . . . and all because the middle classes did not dip their hands into their pockets and give Lane the money he wanted for his exhibition. . . . And we asked ourselves why Willie Yeats should feel himself called upon to denounce the class to which he himself belonged essentially: on one side excellent mercantile millers and shipowners, and on the other a portrait painter of rare talent. With so admirable a parentage it did not seem to us necessary that a man should look back for an ancestry, and we had laughed at the story . . . that on one occasion when Yeats was crooning over AE's fire he had said that if he had his rights he would be Duke of Ormonde, and that AE had answered, 'In any case, Willie, you are overlooking your father'—a detestable remark to make to a poet in search of an ancestry. . . . AE . . . should have guessed that Yeats's belief in his lineal descent from the great Duke of Ormonde was part of his poetic equipment. . . . AE knew that there were spoons in the Yeats family bearing the Butler crest, . . . and he should have remembered that certain passages in 'The Countess Cathleen' are clearly derivative from the spoons.

There was genuine insight here about the importance of tradition for a writer like Yeats, but Moore scarcely did justice to Yeats's complex motives for attempting to realign himself and failed to see the extent of his achievement in stimulating a genuine Revival. Moore emerges as his own hero, the messianic artist who tried unsuccessfully to bring light to the Gentiles. The book was witty and beautifully written, but left much unhappiness among those who felt that the vision it presented was inaccurate and unfair. With the appearance of the first volume Moore emulated the protagonist of *The Lake,* leaving his house in Ely Place after a decade of residence and crossing the sea to London once again.

This pattern of voluntary 'exile' was echoed by James Joyce (1882-1941) in both his life and his work. When Joyce decided in 1902 to make himself known in Dublin literary circles, Yeats and AE thought that a highly promising young recruit had been found. Though they recognized his ability they did not know their man. Joyce admitted Yeats's greatness as a writer, but he could not accept what he saw as a catering to the 'rabblement' in the theatre movement. Already *au courant* with the latest Continental literary trends, he was suspicious of 'the folk' and feared that the Irish movement was essentially parochial. Thus he resisted the kindnesses and encouragement the older figures offered and in 1904 left the country to write abroad.

In the same year he had already begun the stories eventually collected as *Dubliners.* In them he left no doubt about his attitude towards the country he was fleeing: 'my intention was to write a chapter of the moral history of my country and I chose Dublin for the scene because that city seemed to me the centre of paralysis'. The volume begins with the death of a priest and each succeeding story adds images of sterility and corruption. The great final story, 'The Dead', does contain a positive picture of Irish hospitality and possibly some suggestions (more typical of Yeats than Joyce) of a greater vitality in the primitive west; but it too ends with death. The new movement is reduced to a handful of ludicrous images: a would-be poet who desires to be recognized as 'one of the Celtic school by reason of the melancholy tone of his poems'; a politician's bad patriotic verses about the death of Parnell; and a disastrous concert offered as emblematic of the contemporary musical scene. (The grasping Mrs Kearney of 'A Mother', the story in which the concert occurs, may be an ironic counterpart of Yeats's Cathleen ni Houlihan, who in his famous play has given up everything for Ireland.) Also in 1904 Joyce read *The Untilled Field;* although he called it a 'silly, wretched book', he must surely have recognized in it a response to Irish life very similar to his own, and he may well have absorbed from it certain images and situations.

Joyce was equally derogatory in his comments about *The Lake,* but a reading of his own *A Portrait of the Artist as a Young Man* reveals resonances everywhere with Moore's novel. Stephen Dedalus, the largely autobiographical hero of *A Portrait,* rejects a potential career in the priesthood in order to become an artist, a 'priest of eternal imagination'. Such values make him an outsider, virtually alone in a hostile milieu—a uniqueness Joyce dramatizes in part by showing Stephen's fellow college-students participating in the demonstrations against *The Countess Cathleen.* Stephen does care about Ireland, and desires to forge 'the uncreated conscience' of his race; but before he can do so he must leave, must escape the 'nets' of nationality, language and religion which threaten to hold back his soul from its full development. Thus the book ends with his preparations to depart for Paris.

But Stephen was to find (as had some of Moore's characters) that 'escape' is not so simple. In his next novel, *Ulysses,* Joyce brought him back to Dublin, sadder and possibly wiser but with little creative work to show for his efforts. The central question of whether his contact with Leopold Bloom, citizen of the city he had fled, will make him into the great artist who will go forth to write the novel in which he appears is beyond the scope of this essay. We may notice, however, that at last Joyce has deigned to acknowledge the Revival in progress in the Dublin of 1904—Joyce's own *annus mirabilis*—to which Stephen returns. In doing so, however, Joyce's purpose was certainly not primarily historical verisimilitude. His deeper motives are suggested by a passage in which, during an interlude in Stephen's exposition of his theory about Shakespeare, the other characters discuss the literary movement: "Our national epic has yet to be written, Dr Sigerson says. Moore is the man for it.'

At one level *Ulysses* can be read as Joyce's evidence that *he,* not Moore, was the man who would write 'the Irish epic'. Joyce suggested this not only by recreating Homer's *Odyssey* in modern Dublin but also by embedding in his novel a sort of literary history of Ireland. Working primarily through parody, he destroyed all his chief competitors, leaving the field to himself. There are marvellous burlesques of Hyde, O'Grady, AE and Synge; an obscene parody of one of Yeats's most romantic poems; and satiric hits at Gogarty, at Moore himself and at lesser figures. In addition, medieval Irish literature, the folk tradition, the patriotic strain and the language movement are all found wanting. As Joyce had so ostentatiously dissociated himself from the Revival, the implication was that the efforts of Yeats and the others had been misguided, while the lonelier course elected by Joyce was the true course.

Yet half a century later we can see that in the end Yeats, too, was right. Joyce had left his country, but he never stopped writing about it; and perhaps no one ever gave it fuller expression in literature. Joyce's work was national if not nationalistic, and he avoided parochialism through his increasingly complex practice of telescoping the particular and the mythic or archetypal. Furthermore, he brought to the task of creating a national literature an incredible artistic sophistication which he developed, as Yeats had predicted would be necessary, by putting himself to school to the great European masters. Joyce, in so many ways Yeats's opposite, demonstrated that extremes often meet; and Yeats's tower in Galway and the Martello tower that dominates the opening chapter of *Ulysses* stand as twin symbols of the triumph of the modern Irish literary movement. (pp. 199-225)

Phillip L. Marcus, "The Celtic Revival: Literature and the Theatre," in The Irish World: The Art and Culture of the Irish People *by E. Estyn Evans & others, edited by Brian de Breffny, Harry N. Abrams, Inc., 1977, pp. 199-225.*

DEVELOPMENT AND MAJOR FIGURES

William Irwin Thompson

[*Thompson is an American educator, critic, and editor. His writings include* Passages about Earth: An Exploration of the New Planetary Culture *(1974) and* The Celtic Renaissance *(1982). In the following excerpt, he traces the historical, political, and cultural origins of the Irish Literary Renaissance.*]

Nothing ever begins where one thinks it should. The child learns that his father had a father, and then there's no stopping. Historical movements are not different: for every famous beginning there are a dozen other obscure beginnings that preceded it. Yeats is the prominent figure of the movement known as the Irish Literary Renaissance, but Yeats merely led the national movement into international recognition; he did not begin it. What was reborn in the Irish Renaissance was the Irish past, but if one looks for a beginning of that interest in the past, he will end up in the "dark backward and abysm of time."

Things do change, however. Gradually and almost unnoticeably they emerge into the more conspicuous existence that we call a beginning. The idea of a movement, with a start and finish, is an intellectual convenience we cannot do without, but like all convenient things, it is a great oversimplification. When we say that something began in such a year, we often mean that a greater number of people paid attention to it in that year than in the previous one. Clearly Ireland has always had a past, and there have always been Irishmen interested in it; but there have also been times when men have tried to forget the past, and have left it for their grandchildren to return in peace to what they themselves left in pain.

There was Elizabethan England. The men of that time wished to forget the Wars of the Roses, the crude, vulgar days of baronial strife. The story of Elizabethan England is one of zest for the present, for the new Italian clothes, the new refinement, the new literature, and the New World. The land was coming to consciousness of itself in a city; civilization and elegance were the exciting values of the time. But excitements cannot endure forever, and even civilizations are subject to boredom and changes of interest. A century and a half would make any nation bored with civilization and elegance. By the middle of the eighteenth century a gentleman seated in a rococo drawing room might look out of the window at some wild and rugged prospect and think of the country as a place holding some values the city had overlooked. In a quiet mood, he might dream fondly of the good old days. He would dream, not of civilization, but of a simple community; not of elegance, but of energy; not of the city, but of the moor or glen. In Tudor days the country folk were moving into the city and doing their best to become refined. The country held no romance for them, but painful memories of drudgery. The myth of the pastoral landscape where the shepherd sweetly pipes to his innocent lass is the dream of a busy man of city affairs. To an eighteenth-century London gentleman, the descriptive poetry of primitive places, the meditations among ruins, the Norse and bardic odes of Gray, and most sensationally of all, the lays of Ossian by James Macpherson, offered a new mode of consciousness. We have since named this mode romanticism, and the Irish Literary Renaissance has its beginnings in this larger movement.

The first scholar to reach into the Celtic past was James Macpherson, but by a quirk of Celtic contrariness this scholar's Scottish appropriation of Irish materials was published in Dublin [*Temora, An Ancient Epic Poem*, 1763]. Macpherson had published fragments of Highland poetry in 1760, but in his publications of 1762 and 1763 he tried to convince the guardians of neoclassical taste that epic poems had been written in Scotland in the third century. Dr. Johnson, who made a journey to the western islands of Scotland, was not convinced, but the more romantic Goethe was only too willing to believe in an ancient and heroic Northern literature; and in translating the poems, Goethe created an enthusiasm among students of the time for literature that bore a closer ancestral relation to the Germans than did the famous works of the Romans and Greeks. In the nineteenth century these students, turned philologists, were to take the lead in the study of the Celtic past. The Irish, however, did not wait a century to respond to Macpherson's insulting remarks.

> While some doubt the authenticity of the composition of Ossian, others strenuously endeavour to appropriate them to the Irish nation.

Scottish scholars like the Reverend Hugh Blair or David Hume were apt to dismiss the Irish claim to a history older than Christendom, for the Irish were generally regarded as a savage and rebellious people who knew nothing of civilization until they were conquered by the Normans. Hume's sentence on the case was considered final.

> The Irish, from the beginning of time, had been buried in the most profound barbarism and ignorance; and as they were never conquered or even invaded by the Romans, from whom all the western world derived its civility, they continued still in the most rude state of society, and were distinguished only by those vices, to which human nature, not tamed by education nor restrained by laws, is for ever subject. [*History of Great Britain*, I, 1767]

Readers in Great Britain were, of course, only too eager to believe this, and the Irish were not in a position to argue. And so when the Irish claimed Ossian for themselves, the British saw only further evidence of their thievish instincts. But unkind as Macpherson was, the Irish are in his debt, for his embellished version of the detritus of Irish sagas that he encountered in the Highlands started the gradual landslide of Celtic materials. Soon after the poem's publication, newly founded Ossianic societies rediscovered the imaginary island of Finn, Oisin, and Cuchulain.

That the insult of Macpherson stirred the Irish into looking into their own past is clearly seen in the career of Sylvester O'Halloran. Even while he was working on a history, O'Halloran took time out to issue a shorter pleas for the establishment of a foundation devoted to the preservation of the ancient Irish annals. The tone of his plea reveals the incentive behind his scholarship.

> Even in these modern days of erudition and curiosity, we have seen such monstrous accounts of this country and people, as are truly astounding. . . . Since then we have had further attempts on our History and Annals in Macpherson's famous poems. [*Insula Sacra*, 1770]

O'Halloran was angered by the scholarship of the Scots, but he was himself no mere provincial Irishman incensed by the slurs of rival Celts. Though a physician in Limerick, he had studied medicine on the Continent, and in his medical career published treatises on glaucoma and gangrene, and helped found the Royal College of Surgeons. A gentleman of the Enlightenment, O'Halloran was impressed with the effect learned societies could have in the advancement of knowledge. With this effect in mind, he campaigned for the establishment of an academy devoted to the study and preservation of Irish antiquities, and to this study he contributed by publishing Irish histories of his own in 1772 and 1778. In the earlier history, O'Halloran included an appendix devoted to a refutation of Macpherson's claims [*An Introduction to the Study of the History and Antiquity of Ireland*, 1772]. The doctor's work was successful, for in 1785 the Royal Irish Academy was founded to further the study of science, polite literature, and antiquities, and the doctor now became Sylvester O'Halloran, M.R.I.A.

In the following year one of the charter members of the Academy, Charles Vallancey, published his *Vindication of the Ancient History of Ireland*. General Vallancey, like Dr. O'Halloran, was a gentleman, but unlike the man of science, the general was a man of the world; therefore, his interests were more apt to drift toward the exotic and dilettantish. Vallancey was interested in comparing Irish, Phoenician, and Hindustani words, and, on the basis of early Christian monuments, he elaborated a theory about Ireland in a Buddhist, pre-Christian era. Even in its early days the Academy was showing that learned societies can move in two directions in the advancement of knowledge. The British cult of the amateur had made its appearance in Irish scholarship, and for a hundred years to come it would continue to infuriate the Irish into redoubling their own efforts. Whether minuet or jig, the pace of Irish scholarship continued to quicken, and in 1789 Charlotte Brooke, with somewhat effusive apologies for leaving her pianoforte and needlepoint to take up the pen, published her very important *Reliques of Irish Poetry*. This volume was indeed a milestone, for here was a bilingual edition of the poems concerning the figures that were about to become legend once again: Cuchulain, and Deirdre, and Finn. Significantly, it was O'Halloran who wrote an introduction for the young lady's work.

When General Vallancey attempted to establish some relationship between Irish and Hindustani, he was, of course, groping in the dark toward the Indo-European hypothesis that was to be articulated in the later and more famous work of Jakob Grimm. The General was mistaken not in his hunch, but in his method and in his efforts to hinder more prosaic scholars in pursuing theories that were not sweeping embraces of universal history. Nevertheless much good can often come from crank notions and irresponsible methods; historically, a few proud sciences have had such humble origins. The Scots and the Irish had had their say, and now it was time for the Welsh to come forth. In 1831 a Welshman, James Prichard, published a work devoted to the study of the relationship between the Celts and the Eastern peoples, but this volume was dedicated to the German philologist, Grimm. Prichard's work showed that the Welsh were as eager as the Irish to defend themselves from the attacks of the English. Prichard quotes a Mr. Pinkerton as revealing the general attitude of the time concerning the Celts.

> The real Celtic is as remote from the Greek as the Hottentot from the Lapponic. . . . The mythology of the Celtae resembled, in all probability, that of the Hottentots, or others of the rudest savages, as the Celtae anciently were, and are little better at present, being incapable of any progress in society. [*The Eastern Origin of the Celtic Nations*, 1831]

This new tone of English vexation, so different from the Royal patronage that had founded the Royal Irish Academy, was apparent, no doubt, because in 1798 the Irish had again rebelled against the Crown and, what was far worse in the minds of the terror-stricken British Establishment, had sought the aid of Revolutionary France. For a brief period it had seemed that Irish history and poetry could be a matter of *belles-lettres*, but with a new rising to prove the incorrigibility of the Irish, Irish history and poetry again became a political matter. This did not hurt the Welsh, however, and six years later, in 1837, another woman did for the Welsh what Charlotte Brooke had done for the Irish, for in that year Lady Charlotte Guest published the Welsh legends in the *Mabinogion*. It was to go through many editions and was influential in creating the neo-medievalism of Tennyson and Morris.

Precisely because Irish literature had fallen from scholarship into politics, the next advances in the study came from the Continent. In 1837 Adolphe Pictet published his *De l'affinité des langues celtiques avec le sanscrit*, and in 1838 Franz Bopp published his *Über die celtischen Sprachen vom Gesichtspunkte der vergleichenden Sprachforschung*. This work was part of the great movement of Continental philology, for Bopp had published early studies in 1816, which were followed by the more famous work of Rasmus Rask in 1818 and Jakob Grimm in 1819. Whereas Vallancey had made rather unsystematic comparisons of Irish words with similar words in Phoenician and Hindustani, the Germans argued that systems rather than words should be compared. Irish scholarship received an even more secure footing when Johann Kaspar Zeuss began a study of the Celtic place names in his native Bavaria and ended up writing the definitive *Grammatica Celtica* in 1853. If all this sounds like incredibly heavy Germanic scholarship, one should not be deceived into thinking it was all a dry business. The Germans were passionately interested in discovering the *Urmythologie* of the ancestral *Volk*. The ancient form of a word was not merely a lexical unit; it was a relic of a time when the heart ruled a body that lived outdoors, a relic of that exalted time when the mind knew no French and the body was free of silks. In Goethe's Ossian the Germans had a living incarnation of the world view they were looking for.

The Germans were not alone in their romantic enthusiasms. What had begun in the work of Macpherson and the bardic odes of Gray became a general fashion in literary taste. The Scottish poetry of Burns and Sir Walter Scott flowed upon the crest of a new sensibility. Thomas Moore was becoming rich by singing his *Irish Melodies* in the drawing rooms of ladies of fashion, and Lady Morgan, authoress of the best seller, *The Wild Irish Girl,* was creating a sensation by appearing at parties in the imaginary native dress of her characters. It was a time for effusions of sensitivity in countless meditations among ruins, graveyard poems, and lays of minstrels of forgotten kingdoms. Lady Morgan was quick to sense the possibilities of the graveyard and ruin genre, and taking advantage of the instinctive desire of the wealthy to be accused, she attempted to show the English that if they must weep over ruins, they might weep over the ruins they had created.

> I sat down on the tomb of the royal O'Connor, and plucked the weed or blew away the thistle that waved there its lonely head. The sun was setting in gloomy splendour, and the lofty angles of the Abbey-tower alone caught the reflection of his dying beams, from the summits of the mountains where they still lingered. [Quoted in *The Irish Novelists,* by Thomas Flanagan, 1959.]

When the romantic's eye had tired of viewing the ruins of time, it might wander to take in the eternal hut of the peasant, to see that there in spite of the ravages of wars, the ancient, and therefore sacred, way of life was still preserved. And who could be certain that in a humble peasant the blood of a vanished king did not flow? The romantics were in the habit of climbing mountains and meditating upon the prospect, but the movement up for them always involved a movement down for someone else. As divinity no longer hedged a prince, it began to gather about the peasant, and the romantic might dream in apocalyptic reverie of a time when every valley would be exalted, and every hill made low. It was perhaps in this general spirit of the time that the Third Estate in France discovered its own nobility.

> The French were told by no less a person than Siéyès that all their troubles came from the usurpation of the Franks over a thousand years ago. French noblemen in 1789 were descendants of barbarous Germans, while French commoners were descendants of civilized Gauls and Romans. [Crane Brinton, *The Anatomy of Revolution,* 1956]

The peasant was coming into his own, and in the future the usurpation of the Gall would be righted by the Gael, but in the early half of the nineteenth century the image of the peasant was not so fixed and hard and sharp. He could at one moment be a symbol of tears and grief, and in the next a figure of laughter with his comic face of loutish expression. William Carleton had begun his *Traits and Stories of the Irish Peasantry* (1830) as a commission to ex-

press the evils of popery, but he went far beyond that to describe the primitive mode of life where grotesque humor and sudden violence are part of the day-to-day matters of experience. As true an artist as Carleton was (and Synge credits him [in *The Aran Islands, and Other Writings,* edited by R. Tracy, 1962] with being the father of modern Irish literature), it was only too easy for the Tory Englishman to mock the Liberal's pathetic, long-suffering Irish peasant with the image of the violent, *shillelagh*-wielding Paddy of Carleton's stories, who became, through frequent journalistic use, the simian-featured Irishman of the London illustrated papers.

Writers of the first half of the nineteenth century like Lady Morgan, Thomas Moore, and William Carleton had created a superficial fashion for things Irish, but their success in this was based more upon their ability to exploit an already existing market for the ethnic and exotic than on their ability to create an understanding and appreciation of Irish culture. Their work had its importance in placing a romanticized image of the Irish past before the public eye, but the public mind was freighted with other images so that Ireland's tended to blur out of focus. As late as 1853 the founders of the Ossianic Society could still complain of Ireland's mistreatment.

> Though Ossianic lore has been almost neglected by most writers, nevertheless, it is but fair to record a few honourable and praiseworthy exceptions. The first is C. Wilson, who published a small quarto volume of Ossianic poetry in 1780, and next Miss Brooke, who published in 1786 [sic] a large volume which has been reprinted by the patriotic and enterprising Christie of Dublin, in 1816. The Ossianic poems afterwards remained unnoticed until the late Edward O'Reilley and the Rev. D. Drummond wrote their prize essays on their authenticity, and in refutation of Macpherson's false assertions. . . . [*Transactions of the Ossianic Society,* edited by Nicholas O'Kearney, 1853]

One of the members present at the founding of the Ossianic Society was John O'Donovan, and with O'Donovan, George Petrie, and Eugene O'Curry, Irish scholarship takes on a more professional character. The previous generation of gentlemen-scholars were, at their best, men of the Enlightenment; at their worst, they were dilettantes who wished to do more than ride to hounds. O'Donovan and O'Curry, however, were men without an independent income; they worked, and the work did not pay well at all. In 1833 O'Donovan went to work, for shilling wages, mapping the antiquities of Ireland for the Historical Department of the Ordnance Survey. His superior in this position was George Petrie, an artist and scholar who had visited the Aran Islands in 1820 to collect music and make sketches. Petrie's most famous works were to be his studies of the round towers in particular and ecclesiastical architecture in general, and all this was done to disprove the common notion that Ireland had had no civilization before the Norman Conquest. Together with Petrie and O'Donovan, Eugene O'Curry formed a triumvirate that gained European attention. Petrie's task was to administer the survey, O'Donovan's was to do the field work, and O'Curry's was to do the manuscript research. In over a decade of ascetic conditions in the field, O'Donovan managed to produce one hundred and fifty volumes of descriptive letters on Irish monuments. These letters, however, are not merely archaeological catalogues; they are also romantic meditations among ruins.

> I was moved by various emotions upon viewing the graveyard which encloses the ashes of Prince Eoghan, the first Christian convert in Inishowen, and of fifty generations of his descendants, and these emotions were heightened by viewing the princely figure of MacLaughlin, the eldest branch of his descendants, who is now the actual possessor of the old graveyard and of the field in which the celebrated Uisige Chaoin or Clarifont flows. [Quoted in P. M. MacSweeney, *A Group of Nation Builders: Petrie, O'Donovan, and O'Curry,* 1913.]

The romantic style of O'Donovan's prose indicates that history for this Irish scholar was not merely a matter of facts, but even more than that, the passage illustrates the particular *idea* of Irish history that was beginning to emerge in Irish archaeology. The past is perceived to be a realm of value that gives meaning and directives to the present, and the survivor of this past, the peasant, is seen to be a noble creature whose veins contain the blood of a lost kingdom, of a kingdom older and more noble than Great Britain. Not surprisingly, the English were not oblivious to the nationalistic power of such historical scholarship; as the facts began to gather around the hypothesis that there was a civilization in Ireland long before the English could boast of one, the government stopped its subsidy for the Survey in 1840. But since these men received little in the way of salary, the suspension of the subsidy did not stop their work. They carried on their research in the newly founded Irish Archaeological Society, and from there moved into the Royal Irish Academy. Once in the more prestigious Academy, these professional scholars encountered the gentlemen-dilettantes. Sir William Betham, the president of the Academy at the time, had a polite knowledge of philology that he exercised in free associations of Celtic with Etruscan. When other members of the Academy insisted on recognizing Petrie's considerable achievements by presenting him with a gold medal, Betham resigned. Petrie was also responsible for the discovery of the poet James Clarence Mangan, and it was Petrie who had given the poet a position on the Ordnance Survey, where Mangan could turn into verse the literal translations provided him by O'Donovan and O'Curry.

Mangan was a legendary figure of the Dublin of the 1830's. He published his poems in the *Dublin University Magazine,* where the tales of William Carleton were also appearing. With the labors of the scholars and the imaginations of the writers, Dublin was beginning to have a literary existence. The *Dublin University Magazine* is, admittedly, not as historically important as Scotland's *Edinburgh Review,* and the movement that gathered about the Trinity College journal was tiny in comparison with the later Dublin movement of the early twentieth century. Mangan was not Yeats, and Carleton was not Joyce, yet both Yeats and Joyce paid tribute to these writers of the early movement. Mangan is now chiefly remembered for his poem, "Dark Rosaleen," and it is hard to make sense of the esteem Yeats and Joyce bestowed upon him. But as legend and not artist he makes some sense. The figure in broad-brimmed hat and flowing cloak, the figure lost in meditation upon a high ladder in the long hall of the Trinity College Library, the tortured soul who consumed liquor and opium and died at forty-six: all add up to the Edgar Allan Poe variation on a theme from Byron. As common as such a figure might be in the French artists' war against the complacent piety and greed of the bourgeoisie, it was something new for provincial Dublin. In Ireland the breach between poet and society was not so extreme—if the voice of the poet was raised in the cause of the downtrodden Irish nation. Mangan was on the right side, so his personal mannerisms were overlooked. Mangan did not restrict himself to publishing in the intellectual *Dublin University Magazine,* for he also published in the more popular *The Nation.* This magazine was the journal of the younger generation of mid-nineteenth-century Ireland; its editor, Thomas Davis, was a graduate of Trinity College who had become dissatisfied with the garrison mentality of his fellow Anglo-Irishmen and wanted to catch Ireland up in the romantic nationalism that was rising in Germany and Italy. Davis and his associate Gavan Duffy tried to create a Celtic national identity by fostering a literature of patriotism. Impatient with the parliamentary politics of Daniel O'Connell, these members of Young Ireland celebrated the glory of Ireland's heroic past. Through countless battle poems the new ideology of physical force galloped anapestically until an entire generation knew *The Nation* by heart. Unfortunately for Yeats, who would later have to fight his way free of this mnemonic literature, it was *The Nation,* and not the *Dublin University Magazine,* that was to pass on a standard of taste to the end of the nineteenth century.

But while the broadsides and ballads circulated among the politically awakening masses, Petrie, O'Donovan, and O'Curry continued their slow work of translating the immense number of manuscripts that were untouched in the libraries of Trinity College and the Royal Irish Academy. O'Donovan's works were his *Irish Grammar* and his edition of the *Annals of the Four Masters.* For these works he was, with the help of Jakob Grimm, elected in 1856 to a corresponding membership in the Royal Academy of Berlin. O'Curry's great achievements were his translations and his detailed descriptive catalogue of the Irish manuscripts in the libraries of Ireland and England. Petrie, O'Donovan, and O'Curry all died in the 1860's, but in that decade the work of O'Curry was noticed and praised by Matthew Arnold, and it was this English poet who made the next significant contribution to the Literary Renaissance.

In 1867 Matthew Arnold published his Oxford Lectures *On the Study of Celtic Literature.* These lectures are not the best of Arnold, for they are dated by his facile notions of race and national temperament, but at the time they were a welcome advocacy of the Irish cause. As Professor Kelleher has said [in "Matthew Arnold and the Celtic Revival," *Perspectives of Criticism,* edited by Harry Levin 1950]:

When Matthew Arnold set out to describe the characteristics of Celtic literature and to analyze its effects, he paid the Celtic world the first valuable compliment it had received from an English source in several hundred years.

Arnold was quick to attack the willful misconception that there was not a great quantity of Irish literature by quoting O'Curry's estimate that there were thousands of manuscripts (so many, in fact, that O'Curry could not even complete the task of cataloguing them). Arnold as an Englishman had something other than a patriot's interest in eliminating anti-Celtic prejudice. He saw Celtic literature as a useful antidote for the poisons of philistinism and materialism that corroded the society of industrial England. With this purpose in mind it is not surprising that Arnold saw only sweetness and light, mist and faery magic in the literature of the Celt. Overlooking the hard, sharp, and often fierce qualities, Arnold saw precisely what he was looking for. In spite of all his writings on culture, Arnold was not an anthropologist interested in reconstructing a primitive world view, and his ethnocentric perceptions became the official Victorian view. This Victorian Celt of Arnold proved to be as long-lived as his grandfather, the Georgian Celt of Macpherson, for even Lady Gregory, who knew modern Irish, came to see Cuchulain through Arnold's mist. Yeats, Lady Gregory's collaborator in folklore, never learned more than a few words of Irish, so Arnold's antinomies were perhaps irresistibly attractive. Arnold contrasted the yeomanly sense of form of the Saxon with the magical qualities of the Celt, and thought that English literature was in need of the spirituality of the Celt. The Professor of Poetry at Oxford was, of course, not primarily interested in Celtic literature, for it was scarcely available to him; instead he was interested in the Celtic element in English literature. He believed that it had made a significant contribution to the poetry of the past, and concluded that modern England had an even greater need of it.

> Now, then, is the moment for the greater delicacy and spirituality of the Celtic peoples who are blended with us, if it be but wisely directed, to make itself prized and honoured. [*On the Study of Celtic Literature,* 1867]

Arnold was not parochially interested in the preservation of Welsh and Irish as spoken languages; he wanted to see the Celtic element take part in the immense future he foresaw for English poetry. In this, he was a good prophet. In the work of Tennyson and Morris, the Arthuriad and the *Mabinogion* had shown their possibilities for contemporary poetry; therefore it seemed reasonable to think that the Irish legends as well could be put to such high use.

One Irish poet attempted to do just that. Sir Samuel Ferguson was in the center of the Irish literary activity of his time, for as a member and president of the Royal Irish Academy, he was familiar with O'Donovan and O'Curry, and as an editor of the *Dublin University Magazine,* he was well acquainted with Mangan and Carleton. But Ferguson was also a man whose Irish sensibility was prudently modified by an extensive knowledge of English poetry and a late nineteenth-century taste. That this opposition between England and Ireland caused him divided loyalties

is seen clearly in the preface to his epic poem, for there he says of the Irish sagas:

> They seemed to possess, to a remarkable degree, that largeness of purpose, unity, and continuity of action which are the principal elements of Epic poetry, and solicited me irresistibly to the endeavour to render them into some compatible form of English verse. After some time, however, I found the inherent repugnancies too obstinate for reconcilement, and, with some regret, abandoned that attempt. [*Congal, A Poem,* 1872]

The pagan light of ancient Irish poetry did not pass through Pre-Raphaelite stained glass, and the Christian conventions of the poet laureate completely blacked out the force of a battle poetry that was not chivalric. Ferguson could not hope to re-create either the compression of the Irish line or the cascades of epithets and kennings. Following Tennyson, Ferguson's approach was to seize upon the lyric moment that was framed by the entire tragedy. The approach was naturally more congenial to short poems than "epics," and in his lyrics Ferguson directly influenced Yeats. In his lyric on the abdication of King Fergus, he does not tell the entire story of King Fergus and the boy Conchubor, but concentrates on the moment of abdication. (Cf. Yeats's "Fergus and the Druid.") Ferguson's poetic career extended over five decades, and though he never achieved fame as a poet, he was an important influence. In him the continuity of Irish poetry is maintained, for he connects the literary movement of Dublin in the 'forties with the later revival of the 'nineties. As early as 1834 his "Versions from the Irish" began appearing in the *Dublin University Magazine* and eventually were published in book form as the *Hibernian Nights' Entertainment* in 1857. His production kept up its slow but steady pace and he published books of poetry taken from the Irish in 1864, 1872, and 1880. This poetry seems now exactly what it is: part of the literary history of the mid-nineteenth century in Ireland; but what appealed to Ferguson appealed to others, so he has his place in the line of men and women who created an audience for the Irish past. Yeats, in his first venture in literary criticism, tried to make a case that the only reason Ferguson turned from poetry to antiquities and the presidency of the Royal Irish Academy was because he did not have, in Ireland, an audience sensitive to poetry. There were more obvious reasons for Ferguson's failure as a poet, but Yeats was not entirely overstating the situation. Because of the wretched educational system, the reading public in Ireland was pitifully small. From the beginning the Irish artist was placed in that psychologically painful situation which the American Negro writer now encounters: the audience for his art is not with his own downtrodden people but with the educated classes in power, and success in that art lifts him out of the togetherness of propaganda into the aloneness of poetry. But for the uneducated members of his former world, the movement into art always seems like a betrayal, and that is why only a genius can stand the aloneness, for he has his genius to fill up the space once owned by the crowd. The others return to the shouting. But the young writer can avoid the problem and postpone a decision until the years of mastery. The young Yeats was not yet troubled with such problems; he wished to create an audience for poetry among his countrymen and hoped, with the example of the neglected Ferguson, to shame the Irish into making up their losses with him. He was not yet accusing the Irish of debasing literature into political cant; quite the opposite, he was yoking the ethereal Pegasus of the quiet scholar's poetry to the bandwagon of Irish nationalism.

> Of all the many things the past bequeaths to the future, the greatest are great legends; they are the mother of nations. I hold it the duty of every Irish reader to study those of his own country till they are familiar as his own hands, for in them is the Celtic heart.
>
> If you will do this you will perhaps be saved in their high companionship from that leprosy of the modern—tepid emotions and many aims.
>
> . . . I appeal . . . to those young men clustered here and there throughout our land, whom the emotion of patriotism has lifted into that world of selfless passion in which heroic deeds are possible and heroic poetry credible. ["The Poetry of Sir Samuel Ferguson," 1886]

The essay was printed in Trinity College's successor to the former *Dublin University Magazine,* the new *Dublin University Review,* and the appearance of a sermon on Irish nationalism that took the work of a past president of the Royal Irish Academy as its text did not fail to startle and annoy the very pro-British community of Trinity College. Ferguson never made his poetry a war-cry for independence, but he had helped to find an Irish past that was to dominate the future.

Although the work of Sir Samuel Ferguson is artistically not very interesting, his synchronic structures of history do arouse an intellectual curiosity. In his early *Hibernian Nights' Entertainment,* Ferguson superimposes Irish history on Irish legend. Here the story of the fall of the kingdom of Emain Macha and the death of Deirdre and the sons of Usnach is told through an interesting technique. The book opens with a sentinel keeping his watch, and because, from the Table of Contents, one is expecting to hear the story of Deirdre, the sentinel's speech immediately recalls the opening of the *Oresteia;* but the sentinel is not of the time of Deirdre, but of the sixteenth century, and the story he tells is of Red Hugh's captivity; it is in the dungeon that a companion of the Irish prince tells the story of the fall of Emain Macha to pass away the hours of imprisonment. For the reader, this is a double past: he goes back to the sixteenth century only to find within the frame of this picture another and more ancient past. The fall of the ancient kingdom of Ulster is thus juxtaposed with the fall of Ireland to the English, for "Hugh was to be the last of the old Gaelic kings" [Edmund Curtis, *A History of Ireland,* 1964]. But even beyond this double-time, the literary echo of the sentinel's speech suggests a comparison of Deirdre with Helen of Troy, and another thousand years is added to the horizon. All this is, of course, implicit, but it is arresting to see that the early Irish writers, even in the act of recapturing the past, were reaching for the synchronic structures that were to become so fully realized in the late poetry of Yeats and the last work of Joyce. Yeats acknowledged his debt to Ferguson, made a prophecy, and lived to fulfill the terms of the prophecy himself:

"Whatever the future may bring forth in the way of a truly great and national literature . . . will find its morning in these three volumes."

By 1880 well over a century had been devoted to the study of early Irish literary remains. And that was the chief difficulty: the ancient writings were literary remains and not living legends. Neither the work of literary archaeologists nor the polite literature of academy presidents could affect the public lack of interest. The Irish, from a popular point of view, simply had failed to put forth anything to compete with the Scottish *Ossian* or the Welsh *Mabinogion.* From the beginning the Irish response to Macpherson had been scholarly, and ultimately this response was very important to the general fund of knowledge, but the knowledge remained in the libraries. Even among the educated classes, Irish history was an arcane subject. The historian who changed this, Standish James O'Grady, described the situation as follows.

> At school and in Trinity College I was an industrious lad and worked through curriculums with abundant energy and some success; yet in the curriculums never read one word about Irish history and legend, nor even heard one word about these things from my pastors and masters. When I was twenty-three years of age, had anyone told me—as later on a professor of Dublin University actually did—that Brian Boromh was a mythical character, I would have believed him. I knew absolutely nothing about our past, not through my own fault, for I was willing enough to learn anything set before me, but owing to the stupid educational system of the country. I knew Sir Samuel Ferguson and was often his guest, but knew him only as a kind, courteous and hospitable gentleman; no one ever told me that he was a great Irish poet. [*Standish O'Grady: Selected Essays and Passages,* edited by Ernest Boyd, 1918]

The paradox of Irish studies at the time was that the more educated a man was, the more likely he was to know absolutely nothing about Irish history. It was a simple matter of geography that when a member of the ruling Anglo-Irish Ascendancy directed his gaze toward London, he turned his back on Ireland. The Catholic middle classes kept memories of Catholic Ireland alive, but even they knew little or nothing of pagan Ireland. Other than the scholars, only the Irish-speaking peasants of the very primitive west had any knowledge of the ancient days, for they still told the stories of the Fianna, but even the peasants had forgotten Cuchulain. O'Grady might never have discovered the past if it had not been for an accident. Once when this young landlord and barrister was a house-guest in the country, the rain prevented him from following the usual round of upper-class diversions. Wandering into the library, the young man happened to come upon a copy of O'Halloran's history. What followed must have been something like a conversion experience, for this enthusiast of Carlyle stumbled upon heroes and histories he had never even dreamed of. What Odin was for Carlyle, Cuchulain became for O'Grady. The shock of encounter must have been explosive, for judging by the history he was to write, the Georgian front of Dublin was lifted out of sight like a stage-prop and a cosmic drama began to unfold itself beyond the bounds of little time or local space. The young man hurried off to the Royal Irish Academy to find the books that no one read, but not even knowing where to begin and what sources to trust, he wandered into the blind alley of Vallancey. Fortunately, the librarian came to his aid and set him on the track of O'Donovan and O'Curry. Interested as O'Grady was, he was not fascinated by what he found, and this, he thought, was a serious problem. Dissatisfied, he set out to right the situation himself.

> In history, there must be sympathy, imagination, creation. The sorry remnants discussed by the antiquarian do not themselves supply a picture. . . . Until this mass of information is popularized, and by being popularized, secured and appropriated, it is unlikely that any new surge of antiquarian enthusiasm will again ruffle the tranquil mind of the intellectual classes of Ireland. [*History of Ireland: Heroic Period,* 1878]

O'Grady lacked the intellectual metabolism of the scholar. Modern Irish was difficult; ancient Irish, extremely difficult; consequently he chose not to go over the same ground with the philologists. O'Grady chose instead "the reconstruction by imaginative processes of the life led by our ancestors in this country." This imaginative reconstruction was not intended as merely another book to put away on a shelf in the Academy. "I desire to make this heroic period once again a portion of the imagination of the country, and its chief characters as familiar in the minds of our people as they once were."

O'Grady's approach was to take the Cuchulain legends from the Ulster Cycle and place them in a context of a cosmic drama, for his vision extended even beyond the life of the ancestors. His history practically begins in the brooding anticipation of the silent instant before Creation. What unfolds is not Eden again, but a visionary Darwinism in which huge monsters, the as yet clumsy laborings of some inchoate passion yearning for expression, lumber across the stage of Pleistocene Ireland. Across the frozen island that awaits its destiny pass Gods, Fomorians, Firbolgs, and, finally, the high Milesian race that is brought to consummate expression in its Hero, Cuchulain. The work is fascinating in its imaginative conception and narration, and for such a thoroughly a-Christian and immense vision of history, one would have to go to Wagner's *Ring* for a comparison. And it was precisely a Wagnerian excitement that the work was most likely to generate. The later writer, A. E., said that in reading O'Grady, "It was the memory of race which rose up within me, and I felt exalted as one who learns he is among the children of kings." O'Grady's history is, therefore, not simply a retelling of past events, but a conjuration that overwhelms the present, and, further, gives the present its full meaning. In imaginatively handling such an idea of the past, O'Grady uses an *entrelacement* whereby the reader moves from the past to a more ancient past and back again. In relating the story of the flight of Lara to Slieve Mish, he introduces a chapter that tells the ancient tale of the Milesian invasion of Ireland. It seems that the Tuatha de Danan goddess, Bamba, was awaiting the predestined moment. She appears to the

leader, Heber, and blesses him and his descendants, and tells him that this is the last time that she will be seen by the Gael, for she will live, unseen by men, in the fairy mound of Slieve Mish. The chapter is sufficiently long that the reader is allowed time to forget Lara, but upon turning to the next chapter, he is brought forward in time again.

> This then, Slieve Mish, of the Shiel Heber, was the territory, and this the city to which the exiles of Dinn Rie came flying from the unjust king. [*History of Ireland: Heroic Period*]

A sequence of events, the present, is set off with its own day-to-day consciousness, then suddenly it intersects with another sequence of events, the past, with a consciousness that understands it even though the present had no knowledge of the other's existence. In juxtaposing past and present, O'Grady re-created the structure of his own conversion experience on that rainy day. As an Anglo-Irish gentleman, O'Grady was involved in the life of the definite and circumscribed values of the British Empire; suddenly he encountered a world in which the horizon expanded to infinity, but yet, and most importantly, it was a world that had a place for him. This is the messianism of the elect and it is a motif that was to linger on in Irish affairs, for from such imaginings of the past it was only natural to reason that the future contained a destiny befitting such an exalted heritage.

In ancient days the memory of the past exerted a conservative force on society: the models of the ancestors served to keep the young in harmony with the social order. It is then not as surprising as it would seem to note that O'Grady was a conservative Unionist and not a Liberal Home-Ruler or a radical Nationalist. For O'Grady, Cuchulain was the model of aristocratic virtue; he was appreciated because he was a far cry from the vulgar, commercial, and ignoble man of the modern industrial world. O'Grady did not want to awaken a nationalistic consciousness in the mob, but he did want to awaken the moribund class of Irish landlords to a sense of nobility and duty. For O'Grady the agricultural turmoil of the Land Campaign came about because the landlords were apeing the penurious small-mindedness of shopkeepers. O'Grady tried to fight the coercion and boycotting of Michael Davitt's Land League, but his brand of benevolent despotism whereby the state attempted to guarantee the employment of the working classes did not open up the treasure-chest of the Tory's heart. Michael Davitt scoffed at O'Grady's futile stance, and the landlord class continued on its way to extinction. The man who could not find a publisher for his history of Ireland and had to pay for its publication himself did not succeed in finding a political audience either. It was not until ten years later when the scandal of Parnell and the collapse of his Home-Rule movement had turned people away from politics that O'Grady found an audience in the young men of a generation with new interests. It was as editor of the warm and personally engaging *All-Ireland Review* that Standish O'Grady became respected [according to Ernest Boyd in *Ireland's Literary Renaissance,* 1922] as "the father of the Irish Literary Renaissance." From time to time O'Grady would scold Yeats for his affected manners and his letters to the *Review* that read as if they were intended for the

London *Times,* but when Yeats in his own aristocratic old age looked back, he looked back with respect.

> All round us people talked or wrote for victory's sake, and were hated for their victories—but here was a man whose rage was a swan song over all that he held most dear, and to whom for that reason every imaginative writer owed a portion of his soul. In his unfinished *History of Ireland* he made the old Irish heroes, Fion, and Oisin, and Cuchullan, alive again, taking them, for I think he knew no Gaelic, from the dry pages of O'Curry and his school, and condensing and arranging, as he thought Homer would have arranged and condensed. Lady Gregory has told the same tales, but keeping closer to the Gaelic text, and with greater powers of arrangement and more original style, but O'Grady was the first, and we had read him in our teens. [*Autobiographies*]

If O'Grady started the imaginings of a literary movement, he also shared in the beginnings of other imaginings, for in the Cuchulain of this Irish Unionist, one revolutionary nationalist saw the supreme glorification of violence when sanctified by a noble cause. This revolutionary, Padraic Pearse, as a schoolmaster had a mural painted at the entrance to his school: there the boys could see the boy Cuchulain taking arms from the Druid, and there they could read the Irish motto, "I care not if my life have only the span of a night and day if my deeds be spoken of by the men of Ireland." O'Grady achieved his goal, and certainly and ironically more than was ever his goal. But the Ireland of revolution was not O'Grady's Ireland and "He did not know what his own work meant to Padraic Pearse" [A. E., *The Living Torch,* edited by Monk Gibbon, 1938]. O'Grady wrote many books, newer Cuchulain versions, short stories, historical novels, even a critical history in answer to the objections of scholarship to his romantic history; he tried newspapers, publishing, and political schemes from benevolent despotism to socialistic communities, but his masterpiece remained the *History of Ireland: Heroic Period* that he had published in 1878. By 1916 O'Grady had retired from public life into the absolute silence of advanced old age.

While O'Grady was at work bringing the translations of the scholars to a wider public, the philological movement was itself gaining momentum. Whitley Stokes, a young man who had accompanied Petrie, O'Donovan, O'Curry, and Ferguson on a visit to the Aran Islands in 1857, now collaborated with the German philologist, Ernst Windisch, in publishing the *Irische Texte* (1880) in Leipzig. The production of scholarly translations was, perhaps, accelerated beyond the usual academic rate because there arose an almost militant competition between Windisch in Leipzig and Heinrich Zimmer (the elder), Professor of Sanskrit and Celtic, in Berlin. This competition was not restricted to the Germans, for in 1899 the Irish Text Society began its publications with the hope that it could do for Irish literature what the Early English Text Society had done for the study of medieval English literature. The competitive spirit even touched family relations, for Standish James O'Grady's cousin, Standish Hayes O'Grady, published a large two-volume collection of translations in 1892. Unfortunately the prose style of Hayes's *Silva Gadelica* shows that he provided no literary competition at all for his cousin; his work was purely scholarly.

Scholarship and literature had been combined in the work of Standish James O'Grady, but the combination made his *History of Ireland* a thing apart from either pure scholarship or pure literature. The relationship between scholarship and art was not always so ambiguous. John Synge had a sensibility that was more alive to the ironies and contradictions of human nature than to the historical conflations of Teutonic messianism. In his plays he was to make the most original and authentic portrayals of Irish peasant life. Perhaps Synge's originality was helped by the fact that he came to the Aran Islands by way of a detour through Europe. In 1893 Synge was in Paris living the usual life of starvation in a garret while at work on translations of Rabelais, Ronsard, and Petrarch. But Synge was not an expatriate; he was also in touch with the philological movement, for he was attending de Jubainville's lectures on Celtic mythology at the Sorbonne.

The relationship between literature and scholarship was equally distinct in the work of the philologist, Kuno Meyer. As a schoolboy Meyer had spent two years in Scotland; as a student his interest in Celtic matters was stimulated by the lectures of Ernst Windisch. But Meyer was not merely a man of academic interests. As consulting philologist to the writers of the literary revival, he earned his place in George Moore's gossip-novel *Hail and Farewell.* Meyer was often on hand for the cultural activities in Dublin, for as Professor of Romance Languages in Queens College, Liverpool, it was a simple matter to cross over and maintain a double life, teaching in Liverpool and doing research in Dublin. Meyer was able to keep visionary schemes and Celtic mist out of his philology; he was, however, unable to keep out of politics. In the First World War the Professor remarked on the strong ties that bound Ireland and Germany. Becoming something of a recruiting sergeant, he suggested that captured Irish soldiers should form an Irish Brigade to fight against England. Not surprisingly, the Professor lost his Chair at Liverpool while he was making banquet speeches in America.

If all the German professors did not make their presence felt in such dramatic ways, the high seriousness of mind that was the natural tone of Germanic scholarship helped in convincing the Irish that they possessed a tradition to be proud of. Together the German and the French scholars were winning an international audience for ancient Irish literature, but the Anglo-Irish professors at Trinity College refused to alter their opinions. Professors Dowden and Mahaffy were rather vocal on the aboriginal crudity, if not outright obscenity, of the Irish sagas. Expelled from the university, the Irish movement had to find a home elsewhere; fortunately for the revolution that was to come, the movement found a home in the lower classes.

By the twentieth century, a hundred and fifty years of scholarship had given Irish writers a substantial tradition. O'Grady had popularized the scholars' work for readers at home, and now Yeats, Synge, and Lady Gregory extended the campaign to the entire English-speaking world.

With the appearance in 1902 of Lady Gregory's *Cuchulain of Muirthemne* the legend reached its widest audience: President Theodore Roosevelt kept a copy to pass away the time on his long political train-journeys. Now the people of the great cities of England and America could read the story of Cuchulain told in the charming dialect of the peasants of Kiltartan. Yeats thought it one of the best books to come out of Ireland. Lady Gregory was not Synge's patron, so he felt free to be a little more critical. Synge was grateful enough for Lady Gregory's experiments in dialect, but he preferred to take his Irish straight.

> For readers who take more than literary interest in these stories a word of warning may be needed. Lady Gregory has omitted certain barbarous features, such as the descriptions of the fury of Cuchulain, and, in consequence, some of her versions have a much less archaic aspect than the original texts. Students of mythology will read this book with interest, yet for their severer studies they must still turn to the works of the German scholars and others, who translate without hesitation all that has come down to us in the MSS. [*The Aran Islands, and Other Writings*]

The important point, however, was that the reader now had a choice he never had before, and the range of choice from Lady Gregory to Ernst Windisch was a genuine one indeed.

Now in twentieth-century Dublin began the literary movement that was to prove far more successful than the earlier one that had centered on *The Nation* and the *Dublin University Magazine.* The earlier movement had ended in delusion, frustration, failure, and silence; for the curtain that fell upon its act was really a shroud: the million deaths of the famine, the typhus-infested "coffin ships" of the mass emigration, and the utter failures of the rebellions of 1848 and 1867 had exhausted the energy of the nation. But even of their own accord the earlier efforts would probably have come to a halt. Here the judgment of this movement's best historian is necessary.

> If we were to judge it by its bulk alone, we would be tempted to say that nineteenth century Irish fiction was devoted primarily to the production of historical novels, sumptuously bound in green and lavishly decorated with gilt shamrocks. For the most part they have fallen into a merciful oblivion. It could be argued that their lack of literary worth reflects invidiously upon the shallow and constrictive nationalism to which Davis committed his contemporaries and his successors. It was upon this charge that Davis would be arraigned by a later generation of Irish writers. But in fact Davis's larger error lay in his failure to see that the Irish mind had always been influenced, to the point of obsession, "by the deeds and passions of the past." And when, at his bidding, Irish writers turned directly to national history for material, they brought with them the old, sullen grudges and the old, delusive lies. He had asked for a school of historical fiction which transcended hatred, accusation, and guilt. He had forgotten that these were the very forces which had shaped and determined

the history of Ireland. [Thomas Flanagan, *The Irish Novelists*]

The past that the earlier writers had used for their work hurt too much for art and was still too painfully present. Another past was needed, a past not owned by hatred. Unlike the writers, the scholars were motivated by patriotism, but not possessed by it. It was this deeper past that stood before history that Yeats and Synge inherited. (pp. 3-29)

> *William Irwin Thompson, "The Past Recaptured," in his* The Imagination of an Insurrection, Dublin, Easter, 1916: A Study of an Ideological Movement, *1967. Reprint by The Lindisfarne Press, 1982, pp. 3-29.*

Estella Ruth Taylor

[*In the following excerpt, Taylor describes the Irish Literary Renaissance as a distinct literary school.*]

There was a central coterie among the modern Irish writers [of the Irish Literary Renaissance], who early established the fact that they looked upon themselves as a school, although more than one of their contemporaries among the Irish and the English have explicitly denied to them sufficient cohesion of purpose to entitle them to any such claim. George Moore, who has given us the most celebrated, though probably not the most accurate, of all the treatments of the men and women who were engaged in the reform of Irish literature, records their recognition of themselves as a coterie who were consciously endeavoring to build a new Ireland intellectually and politically worthy of all the sufferings that every class and creed had endured in the past. Padraic Colum also recognized this coterie as rising after the downfall of Parnell. He described the group as one in which a homogeneous and enthusiastic leadership prevailed in spite of the fact that everybody knew everyone else's foibles and oddities.

Who, then, were those who felt the obligation to build a new Ireland? Who may properly be considered members of the Dublin school? Where do we draw the line of exclusion? Who are within the pale, and who stand independently without? And what have they themselves declared to be their purposes?

As a matter of fact, there were circles within circles, concentric, eccentric, and overlapping. As the wheel turned and gained momentum, a few on the outer rim were thrown off and never re-established a personal connection. All those who were participants in the theatre movement, either as writers of or producers of plays, all the members of the Irish Academy of Letters, and all those who with regular frequency met together informally for literary repartee have voice in this interplay of criticism. They may be considered in one of two categories, either as the creative writers, who were also the movers and instigators of artistic fulfillment, or as the journalistic spectators and reporters of the doings and sayings of the creative members.

If one were to set down merely those names which appeared on that unique social register, the great copper beech in Lady Gregory's garden at Coole, he would have

Left to right: William Butler Yeats, J.M. Synge and A.E. (George Russell) fishing on Coole Lake. Drawing by H. Oakley.

the roll of the prime movers, the central coterie. But the larger circles include the membership of the Academy, some of whom were journalists by profession, and, as previously suggested, those connected with the Abbey Theatre at one time or another. Such connections entitle one to be heard wherever Irish comment upon Irish literature leads to a final decree. Beyond the core, comprised of William Butler Yeats, George William Russell (A. E.), John Millington Synge, Lady Augusta Gregory, George Moore, Edward Martyn, and Douglas Hyde, there appear in the second circle Padraic Colum, James Stephens, William Kirkpatrick Magee (John Eglinton), Lord Dunsany, Stephen MacKenna, and Oliver St. John Gogarty. As the circle expands, Lennox Robinson, Stephen Gwynn, Denis Gwynn, L. A. G. Strong, St. John Ervine, E. A. Boyd, Frank O'Connor, Susan Mitchell, Daniel Corkery, Darrell Figgis, and A. E. Malone are drawn within its sphere.

At the dawn of the awakening stands Katharine Tynan, who was well aware of what forces were shaping things to come in the literary world of Dublin, but whose own work is distinctly allied to that of the English Victorians. Stephen Gwynn establishes her relationship to the Irish school. It will be noted that he draws this distinction, that she was never self-consciously Irish: "In so far as the creation of a distinctive Irish literature was organized and worked for, she [Katharine Tynan] never belonged to the movement. Yet appearing when it did, her work strength-

ened the movement. In it Ireland had something to show, not the less Irish because it was never self-consciously Irish; something Irish because it could be no other." Her critical comment, while distinctly feminine in character, and rather more sentimentally reminiscent than logically disinterested, will, nevertheless, be taken into account as adding that detail which offers at times a clue to a fuller comprehension.

James Joyce stands somewhat apart from the other members of the school for the reason that, as an expatriate, he did little or nothing to foster even the most tenuous of personal relationships with his Irish contemporaries. There is less cross/comment between him, whose view was universal, and the Dubliners who remained more provincial, than was circulated constantly in critical exchange among those who were in more continuous contact in Ireland. His work is, however, paramount in the study of the city, the atmosphere, the milieu in which the work of all the others was largely done. It is not necessary here to acknowledge the greater magnitude of his genius nor the more distant extensions of his influence. Stephen Gwynn credits him with recalling the Dublin scene: "Dublin of these years [early years of the Abbey plays] is recalled to us in part by George Moore, but far more intimately by James Joyce, in his *Portrait of the Artist as a Young Man,* which describes the student life. We can learn there that lines from Yeats haunted the young men—not recalled as ringing phrases that prompted action, but simply as melodies filling the mind with high and delicate beauty."

That Joyce himself felt no allegiance to the group no one will deny. Padraic Colum notes the fact in *The Road Round Ireland:* "He talked of Ibsen on the night I first spoke to him. . . . The Irish Revival had no allegiance from him—he distrusted all enthusiasm, he said. The prospect of creating a national theater was already discounted by him." Charles Duff sees in Joyce the personalization of the reaction to the school: "We often see it stated that Joyce is one of the figures thrown up by the Irish literary revival, but this is true only in the sense that he was a reaction *against* it. It is entirely erroneous to associate him in any other way with the general tendencies shown in the work of contemporary Irishmen, most of which was propagandist and therefore contrary to his whole conception of art."

No one who has read *Ulysses* can accuse Joyce of indifference, however, although he may agree that Joyce felt no allegiance to, and is in practice wholly divergent from, the literary aims of that coterie who formed the nucleus of literary life in Dublin.

The recognition of Yeats and A. E. as leaders of a school may be found with monotonous regularity, but perhaps is nowhere more singularly expressed than by Darrell Figgis, who calls them "apostles" while he is distinguishing them as "conductors" of the revival:

> What was called the "Irish Literary Revival" was truly an English literary revival conducted by Irishmen. In this W. B. Yeats had a conscious part; but A. E. was rather caught into it from his own separate world, that was only literary in the sense that to convey spiritual experiences from

soul to soul was to put them into writing, and that to convey them justly was to write them finely, with a commensurate music and imagination. W. B. Yeats' apostleship was designed and deliberate, and the immediate results were excellent though the work became spoiled in time; but A. E. was rather an unsuspecting apostle, a little bewildered in the white light of publicity that had so suddenly fallen about him in his emergence from the household in Ely Place.

Darrell Figgis, after speaking of A. E.'s life of mystical experience and experiment, of his study of the writings of the ancient seers, of his habits of contemplation and meditation, defines his place in the school—"that very rare circle of friendship that became, before its members were scattered through the world, almost a community of mind"—as that of "almost a spiritual dictatorship."

As one explores the criticism of the modern Irish writers by their fellow-Irish, he soon finds conflict of opinion as to who was the actual founder of this or that society, the strongest influence upon a particular genius, or even the founder of the Gaelic League or the Abbey Theatre. Denis Gwynn is as ardent a champion of Edward Martyn as a leader as Figgis is of A. E., disputing the generally accepted view that Yeats and Lady Gregory were the "primum mobile" as far as the Literary Theatre is concerned. Gwynn would even have us feel that

> No other Irishman, in the various movements which together may be generally described as the 'Irish Revival'—between the eighteen-nineties and the establishment of the Irish Free State in 1921—occupies the same prominent place as Edward Martyn as a connecting link between so many intellectual activities. . . . He had already made a reputation among men of letters when Mr. W. B. Yeats was beginning to be known as a poet; and it was he who introduced Mr. Yeats to both Mr. George Moore and to Lady Gregory and obtained their collaboration with him in founding the Irish Literary Theatre. It was Edward Martyn who not only provided the money with which the first group of actors were got together, but who also wrote the first play which attracted favorable attention when it was acted in Dublin, and so made the subsequent development possible.

Gwynn shows some resentment over the brevity of Yeats' acknowledgment before the Swedish Royal Academy of Martyn's part in the founding of the Irish Literary Theatre and adds that Yeats' account in his book is an incomplete version:

> The Irish Literary Theatre, and the Abbey Theatre which arose from its early beginnings would never have come into existence if it had not been for the public spirit and the enthusiasm of Edward Martyn, who is dismissed with this melancholy gesture of condescension. And although quite a number of large books have been written concerning the modern Irish drama, the story remains curiously unconvincing without any full record of Edward Martyn's own part in bringing it to life.

Gwynn denounces Lady Gregory more specifically than by merely alluding to "a number of large books." He complained that in her book on the Irish theatre she leaves the impression that at the time of her meeting with Yeats at Comte de Bosterot's, where they laid the ground plan for the theatre, Edward Martyn was by mere chance paying a call, there being no indication of the fact that the Comte was Edward's cousin and most intimate friend. By this curiously extraneous detail he seeks to establish that Lady Gregory failed to give credit where credit was due.

Martyn's own statement, provided us in a manuscript left by Martyn to his literary executor, Denis Gwynn, and now in print in Gwynn's life of Martyn, shows a little testiness that hints at underlying temperamental differences. Surely Martyn stands alone in his reference to *Cathleen ni Houlihan* as "a silly little play." It is clear that Martyn looks cynically at the Abbey and feels his isolation:

> We all know how useless it is to push a person without talent. . . . These are the sort of persons, however, whom Mr. Yeats and Lady Gregory triumphantly succeeded in pushing. . . . He proclaimed their merits in his most dictatorial vein until they actually got to believe in themselves and even to show signs of some improvement. Meanwhile the mediocrities taking their cue from the dictator went about fussing over the art of those players until they made them notorious enough to attract silly little people with silly little plays like *Cathleen ni Houlihan* and *The Pot of Broth* to the amused surprise of those who were in the habit of thinking for themselves.

Martyn said, frankly, that he himself could not write peasant plays, for the simple reason that they did not interest him, and that because he did not furnish such plays for the Abbey Theatre, he became an isolated figure. He criticized the Abbey players for limiting their acting powers, declaring that they had confined themselves to the acting of peasant and middle class roles until they had become totally unfitted to portray the upper classes.

Whatever the merits of the case may be (and the claims of Lady Gregory and Yeats are too widely supported to need defense here), it is well enough understood that Martyn did belong to the inner circle, and he has the unenviable distinction of having drawn more comment from George Moore than any other writer of the period. It was Moore who said in *Hail and Farewell* that Martyn had telegraphed him, "The sceptre of intelligence has passed from London to Dublin." But Yeats says in *Dramatis Personae* that that sounds more like Moore than like the "economical tongue-tied Martyn."

Colum claims Lord Dunsany for the movement, and by virtue of the pertinent comment that Dunsany has made upon his contemporaries as well as for the fact that four of his plays were produced at the Abbey, his attitudes should be taken into account. Colum has said that although Dunsany never used an Irish name in any of his plays or stories, he was, nevertheless, under the influence of the Irish literary movement. Dunsany himself was proud to be of the company. In his memoirs he refers to the pride he felt in having one of his early stories, "Time and the Gods," included in *The Shenachie,* a magazine which published in the same issue "charming tales" by Bernard Shaw and George Moore.

The connections of Douglas Hyde were almost wholly centered in the Gaelic League, and critical references to him in that relationship abound. Since all members of the school were acutely aware of the problems raised by the Nationalists' language movement, a study of their reflections upon the significance of Gaelic demands a separate treatment. (pp. 7-13)

James Stephens was brought into the coterie by A. E., whose satisfaction in his protégé seems to have annoyed Yeats to such a degree that he was tardy in his extension of welcome. As the years passed, Stephens' place was acknowledged even by Yeats, who could not be blind to the popularity of the Puckish writer whose place in the affections of the English reading public was securely established.

It would be impracticable to set down here every testimony relative to each individual's title to membership in the school. It suffices to have drawn together here representative statements wherein the terms "circle," "coterie," and "school" occur frequently enough to establish the fact that the attributions were actually those of the Irish writers themselves.

The consciousness of themselves as a coterie is further attested by their development of another institution symptomatic of a school of writers, the *salon,* though the term connotes a greater formality than may rightfully be associated with the Irish. From the time of the beginning of the revival certain gathering places were recognized centers of literary life, and there both the poets and the critics assembled, and "for the most part the critics were the poets, and the poets were the critics." In this way Stephen MacKenna made himself felt: "At MacKenna's evenings I would meet A. E., occasionally Arthur Griffith, occasionally John Eglinton, occasionally Arthur Lynch, in the early days John Synge who had been a comrade of Stephen's in Paris, Joseph Hone, Rudmore Brown, Osborn Bergin, Thomas Bodkin. The talk was the best that could be heard anywhere."

George Moore prophesied well, though egotistically, of Coole as a sort of Minstrelburg:

> Coole was beginning to be known to the general public at the time I went there to write *Diarmuid and Grania* with Yeats. Hyde had been to Coole, and had been inspired to write several short plays in Irish. . . . If Yeats had not begun *The Shadowy Waters* at Coole he had at least written several versions of it under Lady Gregory's roof tree. A. E. had painted in the park; now I was going there. "In years to come Coole will be historic; later still it will be legendary, a sort of Minstrelburg, the home of the Bell Branch Singers," I said.

One could continue endlessly with references to A. E.'s Sunday evenings. Dunsany tells of meeting James Stephens in A. E.'s house in Rathgar Avenue, where "on Sunday evenings he always had a reception for such as cared to come, mostly poets." At that time, Dunsany relates,

James Stephens was excited by the approaching appearance of his first book, not yet quite believing that it should actually come to pass that he should see his book in a shop window.

Yeats refers to the "writers or would-be writers, among them James Stephens," who gathered at A. E.'s rooms regularly on Sunday evenings after A. E. had become a magnet because of his publication of *Homeward, Songs by the Way.* Yeats attended, but he confesses that he was "not friendly with that center, considering it made up for the most part of 'barren rascals'—critics as Balzac saw critics."

Consistent with the usual pattern of development in a school there developed out of the associations of these literary men the Irish National Literary Society, the National Theatre Society, which was to develop later into the Abbey Theatre, and the Irish Academy of Letters. Yeats defined the purpose of the Irish National Literary Society, founded in Dublin in 1893, referring at the same time to the Irish Literary Society founded two years earlier in London: "These societies had given, as I intended, opportunity to a new generation of critics and writers to denounce the propagandist verse and prose that had gone by the name of Irish literature, and to substitute for it certain neglected writers."

Yeats recognized that they would have a hard fight before they would get the right of every man to see the world in his own way admitted. He said in a letter to John Quinn:

> Irish national literature, though it has produced many fine ballads and many novels written in the objective spirit of a ballad, has never produced an artistic personality in the modern sense of the word. Tom Moore was simply an incarnate social ambition. And Clarence Mangan differed merely from the impersonal ballad writers in being miserable. . . . We will have a hard fight before we get the right of every man to see the world in his own way admitted. Synge is invaluable to us because he has that kind of intense narrow personality which necessarily raises the whole issue.

Yeats' point of view was subscribed to wholeheartedly by Lady Gregory and A. E. and continues to be upheld by Daniel Corkery, an influential voice from southern Ireland. Corkery has said that the difference between Anglo-Irish literature and Irish literature is the difference between Maria Edgeworth's *Castle Rackrent* and Lennox Robinson's *The Big House,* that exploring one's own land for a foreigner is not expressing one's land for itself, and that much so-called Anglo-Irish literature might better be called Irish-English.

Yeats and his followers were determined, obviously, to make of the new Irish literature a sincere expression of the Irish, an expression that would reflect the native culture and the character of the Irish stripped of all superimposed Anglican veneer. All pseudo-patriotism, all exaggerations such as had been perpetuated in the "stage-Irishman," all false wit, in short, all aspects of the literary lie were to be denied through the conscious agency of the Irish National Literary Society. In the application of the new spirit to the drama Yeats and A. E. were determined to go even further than they had in their treatment of the lyric and the short-story writer. The drama, the reformers felt, should stem from the heroic matter of the Gaelic legends.

Not all members of the group were in complete agreement with Yeats on this point. John Eglinton, better known by his pseudonym than by his real name, William Kirkpatrick Magee, a distinguished essayist, held divergent opinions regarding the Gaelic legends as adaptable subjects. A. E., while asserting his own faith in their continued power as symbols, records Eglinton's attitude:

> I know John Eglinton, one of our most thoughtful writers, our first cosmopolitan, thinks that 'these ancient legends refuse to be taken out of their old environment'. But I believe that the tales which have been preserved for a hundred generations in the heart of the people must have had their power, because they had in them a core of eternal truth. . . . These dreams, antiquities, traditions, once actual, living and historical, have passed from the world of sense into the world of memory and thought. . . . They have now the character of symbol, and as symbol, are more potent than history. . . . Deirdre is, like Helen, a symbol of eternal beauty, and Cuchulain represents as much as Prometheus the heroic spirit, the redeemer in man.

Yeats was informed of Eglinton's view and made note of it as follows:

> Let a man turn his face to us, accepting the commercial disadvantages that would bring upon him, and talk of what is near to our hearts, Irish Kings and Irish legends and Irish Countrymen, and we would find it a joy to interpret him [on the stage]. Our one philosophical critic, Mr. John Eglinton, thinks we were very arbitrary, and yet I would not have us enlarge our practice. England and France almost alone among nations, have great works of literature which have taken their subjects from foreign lands, and even in France and England this is more true in appearance than in reality.

Stephen Gwynn, though not antagonistic, does not completely support the prevailing opinion and remains impenitent:

> The rest of us had not been taught as yet that it was unpatriotic to be amused by the songs which Robert Martin and Percy French were writing. I remain impenitent and think that what is called "Anglo-Irish" humour, when at its broadest, as in Robert Martin's *Ballyhooly* is very good fun indeed, and at its subtlest, as in Maria Edgworth or in much of Lever, or in the work which Robert Martin's sister, Martin Ross, did with Edith Somerville, is as good a humour as the modern world can show. As for its fidelity to life, no one who has lived in the west of Ireland, and, above all, no one who has taken part in Irish politics, is going to be convinced that the "stage Irishman" as Irish authors represented him is not a legitimate caricature. The truth has been that people took it for a complete representation.

But these differences of opinion were but slightly felt and, in the main, one common purpose, the presentation of the real Ireland and the truly Irish, actuated the practice of the members of the Irish National Literary Society, whose dramatic expression led to the founding of the Abbey Theatre.

This is not the place wherein to recount the history of the Abbey Theatre, the facts of which are already too well known to demand notice here, but a few statements pertaining to the development of the theatre and the Academy are necessary at this point, however repetitious, to establish the base from which explorations depart into that morass of interlocking comment upon the persons engaged in these organizations. The comments selected are chosen to show again that common purpose which is requisite to any acknowledgment of the group as a school.

Lady Gregory confesses that the statement which was circulated in the form of a news letter at the time of the founding of the Irish Literary Theatre seems a little pompous. It begins:

> We propose to have performed in Dublin, in the spring of every year certain Celtic and Irish plays, which, whatever be their degree of excellence, will be written with a high ambition, and so to build up a Celtic and Irish school of dramatic literature. We hope to find in Ireland an uncorrupted and imaginative audience trained to listen by its passion for oratory, and believe that our desire to bring upon the stage the deeper thoughts and emotions of Ireland will ensure for us a tolerant welcome, and that freedom to experiment which is not found in theatres of England, and without which no new movement in art or literature can succeed. We will show that Ireland is not the home of buffoonery and of easy sentiment, as it has been represented, but the home of an ancient idealism. We are confident of the support of all Irish people, who are weary of misrepresentation, in carrying out a work that is outside all the political questions that divide us.

Yeats felt the necessity, even the urgency, of utilizing the national heritage for drama and roused in his contemporaries a sense of obligation toward their own people who had suffered from exploitation by writers in the old tradition. "All Irish writers," he wrote, "have to choose whether they will write as the upper classes have done, not to express but to exploit this country; or join the intellectual movement which has raised the cry that was heard in Russia in the seventies, the cry 'To the people'."

Later, in the same work, he accents again the reference to class when he says: "Our opportunity in Ireland is not that our playwrights have more talent—it is possible that they have less than the workers in an old tradition—but that the necessity of putting a life that has not hitherto been dramatized into their plays excludes all these types which have had their origin in a different social order."

But Yeats had no intention of sealing off the Irish dramatist in a provincial world of his own. He knew that a full knowledge of the history of the drama and its modern trends in other countries than his own was essential to the craftsman. With Martyn and the youthful Joyce, he recognized the master Ibsen:

> It is of the first importance that those among us who want to write for the stage should study the dramatic masterpieces of the world. . . . At the present moment [1901], Shakespeare being the only great writer known to Irish writers has made them cast their work too much on the English model. . . . If Irish writers had studied the romantic plays of Ibsen, the one great master the modern stage has produced, they would not have sent the Irish Literary Theatre imitations of Boucicault, who had no relation to literature. . . . We Irish have, I think, far greater need of the severe discipline of French and Scandinavian drama than of Shakespeare's luxuriance.

At the same time he felt that the impulse toward dramatic expression lay in the people themselves: " . . . we have turned a great deal of Irish imagination towards the stage. We could not have done this if our movement had not opened a way of expression for an impulse that was in the people themselves. The truth is that the Irish people are at that precise stage of their history when imagination, shaped by many stirring events, desires dramatic expression."

Stephen Gwynn attributes to George Moore the calling of the Irish Literary Theatre to the attention of the English critics. Moore, he said, could never resist putting his finger into any new literary pie:

> Mr. Yeats understands to perfection the arts of the propagandist. This was quickened about March by the publication of . . . Mr. Edward Martyn's prose-drama, *The Heather Field,* accompanied by a preface from Mr. George Moore, who has throughout acted as sandwich man to the movement. Mr. Moore has the talent of awakening controversy, and though in describing Mr. Martyn's play as a masterpiece unique in modern prose-drama, he did Mr. Martyn a very ill turn, he certainly succeeded in calling the attention of English critics to the Irish literary Theatre and *The Heather Field* in particular.

But Moore was apparently both a benign and an evil influence, in the opinion of Gwynn, who said that "the Irish Literary Theatre died either from inanition or a surfeit of George Moore." Yeats, however, is generous in his acknowledgment of Moore's contribution: "Looking back now upon our work [The Irish Literary Theatre], I doubt if it could have been done at all without his [George Moore's] knowledge of the stage; and certainly if the performances of this present year [1901] bring our adventure to a successful close, a chief part of the credit will be his."

Joseph Hone, Yeats' biographer, modifies this acknowledgment somewhat by calling attention to the fact that Yeats had "admitted that Moore was an embarrassing ally":

> At this time [1897] neither Yeats nor Martyn had any working knowledge of the theatre, and Lady Gregory had never given a thought to the stage—was not even much of a theatre-goer. Yeats at once realized that Moore, who had always been knocking about theatres and had produced a play of his own in London, would be essential to their rehearsals. But several prominent characters of the Irish revival—George Russell among them—resented the introduction of Moore into the movement on the ground of his political as well as his religious shortcomings. Yeats admitted that Moore was an embarrassing ally ("he must always be condemning or worshipping") but found his "moral enthusiasm" inspiring.

The loss of Synge, Colum suggests, rather than "a surfeit of George Moore" initiated the decline in this phase of the Irish literary movement. Colum sums up the accomplishment:

> Synge died in 1909 and though his last play, *Deirdre of the Sorrows,* was still to be produced, and although many other important plays were afterwards put on, the date of Synge's death marks the end of a period of growth. We can now ask what the movement that created the Abbey Theatre has actually accomplished. Briefly stated, it has produced a national drama for Ireland: it has intensified in Irish writers national characteristics, and it has encouraged them to write plays that are charged with Irish temperament, the Irish instincts, the Irish tradition.

A. E. Malone felt that the triumvirate, Yeats, Synge, and Lady Gregory, had no successors among the new dramatists of the Irish Theatre "where farce, melodrama, and cynicism now hold dominant sway." This situation did not disturb Colum, who said, "After all, it is too much to ask of a country that she should look upon the production of literature as the be-all and end-all of the national life."

We have yet to consider the Academy as a tangible evidence of a conscious school of writers. George Moore, who "would have a finger in every pie," ignored the invitation to membership, and there were other refusals, as will be seen later. Perhaps Moore's dislike of Lady Gregory carried over finally to her last great project, for:

> She [Lady Gregory] remained to the last by the side of Irish literature, and it was in her house that Yeats and George Russell discussed the project of an Academy of Letters which should carry on the tradition of their movement, make known the views of Irish authors on such questions as censorship and call attention to the respect due to the intellectual and poetical quality in the national life. Bernard Shaw consented to become President of the Academy, and George Russell drew up the rules and the constitution.

Frank O'Connor, himself a member of the Academy, reflects the attitude of A. E. as an academician, an attitude not characteristic of that modest poet, as will be apparent later:

> It [The Academy of Letters] was Yeats' idea, an institution whose authority might override mob law and fight the absurd censorship of books. A. E. was gloomy. He feared and distrusted those enthusiasms of Yeats and prophesied that the

Academy would be asked to award a prize to some of Yeats' protégés.

. . . Once when I questioned the name of some suggested Academician, he said, "Why worry about literary eminence? You and I will provide that."

Hone indicates the more inclusive nature of the Academy as compared to that of the more limited theatre group:

The formation of the Academy was announced at a meeting in Dublin on September 18, 1932, when Lennox Robinson read out the letter, signed by Bernard Shaw and Yeats, which had been addressed to each of those invited to become members. The list was inclusive enough: The Celtic poets were there alongside the Cork Realists of 1910, Gaelic modernists like F. R. Higgins and Frank O'Connor, St. John Ervine and Peadar O'Donnell, two Northerners, and Edith Somerville the "Big House" novelist. George Moore ignored the invitation and refusals came on various grounds from Douglas Hyde, Stephen MacKenna and James Joyce. Joyce's refusal was the chief disappointment. He . . . recalled that it was thirty years since Yeats had first held out to him a "helping hand" but added that his case being as it was and probably would be, he saw no reason why his name should have arisen at all in connection with such an Academy.

The literary society, the theater, the academy were, indeed, both centers of and culminations of influences. John V. Kelleher in the *Atlantic* (March, 1945) pronounced the extinction of an Irish school of literature. He said that the death of F. R. Higgins, which had followed so closely the death of Yeats, had suddenly revealed the scarcity of poets in a country where poets had been as plentiful as journalists elsewhere. "Those who are left," he said, "do not coalesce into a school." He also noted the cessation of interlocking critical comments.

St. John Ervine had said much earlier that the Irish Literary Renaissance had perished for lack of staying power. . . . A. E. protested a slightly earlier pronouncement: "A writer in the American *Dial* suggested lately [1923] that the Irish literary movement had come to an end, but the funeral oration he pronounced was premature. Since he wrote, Irish literature has been enriched by three notable books, *The Return of the Hero,* by Michael Ireland, the beautiful *Deirdre* by James Stephens, and lastly by the long expected novel of Padraic Colum, *Castle Conquer.*"

Three years later Colum, expanding his *Bookman* article of July, 1926, acknowledged that the coterie had broken up, and he assigned a reason:

In the space between the downfall of Parnell and the rise of the Irish Volunteers the intellectuals had the whole stage in Ireland—I mean intellectuals in the best sense of that abused word. They formed a coterie that was homogeneous, in which everybody knew everybody's oddity. . . . They are still in Dublin, most of them; but the coterie has broken up; ideas have been

de-limited, and have taken on a practical tinge because of the demands of the new state.

James Stephens saw that the school had been absorbed into the world, that the culture of the Irish could no longer be considered as growing from its own root. He said, "We have entered the world. More, the world has entered us, and a double, an internal and external, evolution is our destiny."

That the Irish literary revival was accompanies by the typical manifestations of a school—namely, a central coterie, a salon, a theatre, and an academy—is obvious, and, except for the less evident nature of the salon, was recognized by outsiders from the first. The whole activity was constantly under scrutiny and was being criticized by the participants themselves. The associates in the movement were conscious of themselves as playing a role and have left a record of a self-conscious expectancy of being acknowledged in literary history. (pp. 13-23)

> *Estella Ruth Taylor, "The Typical Manifestations of a School," in her* The Modern Irish Writers: Cross Currents of Criticism, *University of Kansas Press, 1954, pp. 7-23.*

George Moore on W. B. Yeats's role in the Irish Literary Renaissance:

[The] Irish movement rose out of Yeats and returns to Yeats. He wrote beautiful lyrics and narrative poems from twenty till five-and-thirty, and then he began to feel that his mission was to give a literature to Ireland that should be neither Hebrew, nor Greek, nor French, nor German, nor English—a literature that should be like herself, that should wear her own face and speak with her own voice, and this he could only do in a theater. We have all wanted repertory theaters and art theaters and literary theaters, but these words are vain words and mean nothing. Yeats knew exactly what he wanted; he wanted a folk theater, for if Ireland were ever to produce any literature he knew that it would have to begin in folk, and he has his reward. Ireland speaks for the first time in literature in the Abbey Theater.

George Moore, in his Hail and Farewell, *D. Appleton and Co., 1914.*

R. A. Scott-James

[In the excerpt below, Scott-James identifies the major figures of the Irish Literary Renaissance.]

A few years before the end of the [nineteenth] century a breath of wind blew from the west over England and made English readers aware of something new, strange and alluring, as novel in its way as the romanticism of Wordsworth and Coleridge had seemed a century earlier. Borne on this western breeze were voices, as if heard from afar, of minstrels singing songs of old times cherished in the minds of a living people. It was the beginning of the 'Celtic revival' and for Englishmen of new awareness of 'the Celtic Twilight', an expression derived from the title of Yeats's book published in 1893. For some time these words were used, often by people who had not read the book, to indicate something vague, misty, unsubstantial, like the romantical outpourings of the Highland Scottish poet, Fiona Macleod, who on his death was discovered to have been William Sharp. But this Irish literature, which was destined to make so deep an impression on the English as well as the Irish mind between 1900 and 1914, was to take on clear lineaments; it was to be at its best an expression of the Irish character in a unique moment of Irish history, when the more scholarly and more imaginative of the Irish nationalists were rediscovering the ancient history of their race and seeking both to revive its language and literature and write a new literature in the spirit and as far as possible in the language of the old.

Henry W. Nevinson, writing in the *London Mercury* in March 1939, just after Yeats's death, spoke of the effect which the young Irish writers had on Englishmen in the 1890's:

> At that time there was something in the real Irish or Celtic nature that was wanting to our souls. It had been hinted to me a few years earlier by the great Celtic scholar, Kuno Meyer, who went about Ireland searching for old Irish manuscripts, long obscured in the peaty smoke of Irish cabins. And I had known the distinguished Fenian, old John O'Leary, when he was an exile in Paris, where I induced him to talk to me almost every night upon Ireland while we drank the innocent *mazagram* in a little café on the Left Bank. 'AE' and Douglas Hyde, just then becoming a little known, helped our enthusiasm. But, true poets as both were, it was Yeats who fulfilled our vague and undefinable desire for something outside the limits of even the finest English thought and language in those days.

The Irish Literary Movement must not be identified with the political movement for Home Rule, but both came from the same impulse. It should be remembered that the political movement evoked widespread sympathy in Great Britain, and had the open backing of the official Liberal Party which ultimately passed a Home Rule Bill through Parliament and had it put on the Statute Book. But the literary movement, which early won the esteem of British readers, was watched through all its phases with intense interest without any intrusion of political feeling. Englishmen followed the activities of the Irish National Literary Society (founded in 1892), the Gaelic League (founded in 1893, under the presidency of Douglas Hyde, that indefatigable Gaelic scholar who strove hard if in vain to restore the use of the ancient Irish tongue) and the Irish National Theatre Society (1903); and it was an Englishwoman, Miss Horniman, who provided the money for founding the Abbey Theatre in 1904. Under the ægis of Yeats, Lady Gregory, Edward Martyn and a company of actors attuned to their spirit, the Abbey Theatre became the home of a distinguished drama which, if both drama and acting were taken into account, could scarcely be equalled anywhere else in the English-speaking world.

The men and the women who were protagonists in this movement were united by the sense of a mission—a mis-

sion to unearth what was inherent both in Ireland's memory of her past and in the life of the simple, unspoilt peasants of to-day; to reclothe the ancient heroes and make them live again in prose or verse; to penetrate to the beliefs and half-hidden secrets which lie behind the customs and superstitions of the folk; to submit to the romance which romantic stories engender and to reconcile this, if need be, with gritty realism—for perhaps Ireland was the one place in the world where the actual and the ideal were inseparable, or at least always contiguous. The language, too, was to be simple and racy of the folk. Since the old Gaelic was too difficult and too rarely understood, then a vernacular should be found which would be in essentials that of the folk, but slightly conventionalized for the purposes of literature. Lady Gregory (1852-1932) and J. M. Synge (1871-1909) laboured successfully to develop such a language, the one using it with rare humour and charm in her short plays, the other to more tragic purpose in such plays as *Riders to the Sea* (1903), or the tragi-comedy of *The Playboy of the Western World* (1907). George Russell (AE) felt the inspiration and was carried along by it in his lyric poetry, and in his play *Deirdre* which, produced in 1902, marks the beginning of the Irish Theatre movement. For AE the legends of Ireland stirred in every Irish scene, and his feeling for them, combined with his love of the occult and his mystic studies, led him as often to pantheistic imagery as to otherworldliness. Lady Gregory's *Gods and Fighting Men* (1904) and other records of Ireland's legendary past thrilled Yeats and peopled his mind with heroic figures. They moved in his imagination side by side with those of the recently living whom he added to the heroes. We can hardly think of Yeats without Lady Gregory and AE, or any of these without Synge, whom Yeats had first met in 1896 when Synge was a student in Paris. Around them were others—George Moore, first friendly and cooperative, afterwards hostile—many lesser poets and playwrights, and the players of the Abbey Theatre. But these four were the nucleus of what became a sacred company, a priesthood; they were guardians of the gods and fighting men and the mystical communion between a splendid past and the folk of to-day in whom they believed its spirit to be preserved; they had charged themselves with the duty of rendering the life and spirit of a race in a language which, while inspired by Ireland, would also lend itself to universal literature.

Synge was twenty-five years old, studying in Paris, when Yeats first met him. Yeats, thinking too much, perhaps, of Arthur Symons and other friends among the French Symbolists, recommended Synge to make a thorough study of contemporary French literature; but a little later, knowing him better, urged him to give up France and 'seek in the Aran islands a life that had never yet been expressed in literature'. The advice was taken. He went to the Aran Islands, and to the Irish counties of Wicklow and Kerry, and to the Congested Districts. He listened to the folk; he studied their manners and speech; and out of this material, though he had only eleven years of life remaining, wrote two books descriptive of the places and people he had visited, some poems and translations, and six plays by virtue of which he ranks as a major dramatist.

The last of these, *Deirdre of the Sorrows* (1909), is the least satisfactory, because here he left the common folk whom he knew so well and turned to the ready-made tale of the old heroic Saga whose conventional trappings had inspired AE and Yeats, just as the familiar tales of ancient heroes suited the genius of the Greek tragedians; but for Synge they were an embarrassment, restricting his fancy, and affording no scope for the grim humour which was of his essence. It was Synge's forte, not to turn the heroes of tradition into living men, but to make ordinary men into heroes; to show the lives of common peasants with unsparing realism, speaking their common speech racily, evoking the humorous together with the intensely emotional, laughter moving side by side with horror. Modestly, and no doubt rightly, in his Prefaces to *The Tinker's Wedding* (1909) and *The Playboy of the Western World,* he attributes half his success to the people of the time and place in which he lived.

> Anyone who has lived in real intimacy with the Irish peasantry will know that the wildest sayings and ideas in this play are tame indeed, compared with the fancies one may hear in any little hillside cabin in Geesala, or Carraroe, or Dingle Bay. All art is a collaboration; and there is little doubt that in the happy ages of literature, striking and beautiful phrases were as ready to the story-teller's or the play-wright's hand, as the rich cloaks and dresses of his time. It is probable that when the Elizabethan dramatist took his ink-horn and sat down to his work he used many phrases that he had just heard, as he sat at dinner, from his mother or his children. In Ireland, those of us who know the people have the same privilege. . . . In a good play every speech should be as fully flavoured as a nut or apple.

But his success sprang not only from the fact that in Ireland he found 'a popular imagination that is fiery, and magnificent, and tender'. He found that, and used it; but other Irishmen have known it, too, and been led astray by it. Even Yeats, at times, in his youth, was seduced by its sweetness, its strangeness, its fancy. But Synge discovered also something else that lies at the very core of his genius and gives it strength. 'It may almost be said,' he wrote, 'that before verse can be human again it must learn to be brutal.' If I may quote words that I have used before, 'he does not mean the brutality of our English or French realists, or ugliness, sheer fact, miscalled truth, without beauty; what he wants is fidelity to *common* truth, a realization of the root, primitive facts—the most grim primitive facts—that hard basis of fact which must be accepted before the imagination can bear fruit'. In his greatest play, *The Playboy of the Western World,* there is a certain brutality of frankness even in the choice of theme, in which the audience at the Abbey Theatre, violently protesting, were not wrong in detecting a criticism of the Irish character. Who can say that to describe the romanticizing of a supposed murderer who boasts that he has killed his father, and the scorn that follows when it is found that the father was not killed, is not a criticism of a quality of the Irish? ('There's a great gap,' Pegeen alone perceives, 'between a gallous story and a dirty deed.') But who will say, on the other hand, that he is not as lavish with his praise when he shows the Playboy at the end driven on by the fire of imagination to display the very courage he is sup-

posed to lack? The poetic spirit, after all, could be the spur to action. Pegeen perceives it. 'Oh my grief,' she cries, 'I've lost him surely. I've lost the only Playboy of the Western World.'

But it is something more than purely Irish character that Synge displays in the poetry and humour of his dialogue and the tense dramatic situations in which his persons behave. In *Riders to the Sea* (produced 1904), the whole of human nature is in Maurya, the 'old woman with one thing and she saying it over', who, lamenting the death of four sons by drowning, and becoming almost demented from fear that a similar fate will befall her remaining sons, hears of the death of the last of them with fortitude and is reconciled to her fate.

> Michael has a clean burial in the far north, by the grace of the Almighty God. Bartley will have a fine coffin out of the white boards, and a deep grave surely. What more can we want than that? No man at all can be living for ever, and we must be satisfied.

It is an ending in the manner of Greek tragedy, and as universal.

William Butler Yeats (1865-1939) was at the centre of the Irish Literary Movement, and indispensable to its existence; it was fruitful in inspiration for him. But he transcended it, and lived long, at his best, after it had faded. The early influences in his life were not exclusively Irish. For twelve of his first fifteen years his parents' home was in London, though his most cherished memories were of the long holidays spent at the home of the Pollexfens in the Irish County of Sligo. In 1880 his father, John Butler Yeats, took his family back to Ireland, but again settled in England in 1887; and a few years later W. B. took a flat for himself in Woburn Buildings in Bloomsbury, and retained it for twenty-four years. This is not to say that in youth and middle ages Yeats was not constantly in Ireland. He went to and from between London and Dublin, and Dublin and Sligo and the western counties. His earlier literary friends were poets who lived in London, English and Irish—Dowson, Arthur Symons, Lionel Johnson, AE, John Davidson, Selwyn Image and Ernest Rhys—it was the last who, recognizing his sense for Irish lore, set him to compile a book of Irish fairy tales. It was in Ireland of course that he developed his enduring interest in legends, fairy tales and the supernatural, and his Irish friend AE encouraged his instinct towards the mystical. It was in Dublin that he joined the Hermetic Society, which was started to promote oriental religions and theosophy, but equally in London he pursued his inquiries into Buddhism, Spiritualism, and the occult in many forms, including astrology, and other researches that were to earn him a reputation for being a magician. But though an interest in the occult and in spiritualism remained with him throughout his life, and he was wont, like Blake, to talk familiarly about his spirit acquaintances, he kept such things in their place. His official biographer, J. M. Hone, asking whether he really believed in the occult, or was playing with fantastic images, replies that 'his poetic genius halted half-way between faith and simile, so as to preserve the sibylline quality of his own experience'.

But it was at least with enduring passion that he pursued his dream of Ireland, and his intellectual arguments about his dream; it was an element in his romantic relationship with Maud Gonne, the beautiful woman who loved political notoriety and adventure among revolutionaries in all the capitals of Europe; but it was with a devotion practical as well as passionate that he set himself to build up an Irish theatre in Dublin. The seduction of his language and his romantic themes and the sweet distillation of emotional experience moved English no less than Irish readers in the nineties and made them aware of a new lyrical voice that had a fay quality, a wild tenderness, something which, in Nevinson's words, 'was wanting to their souls'. They heard him chaunting (not chanting) 'a tongue men do not know'. They became familiar with the 'Rose' symbolism which first appeared in

> Red Rose, proud Rose, sad rose of all my days!
> Come near me, while I sing the ancient ways.

and the deeper notes of Innisfree, and the sad lyrics of old age:

> When you are old and grey and full of sleep

and the eeriness they felt

> When we bent down among the fading coals
> And talked of the dark folk who live in souls
> Of passionate men, like bats in the dead trees.

and the wild love poems of *The Wind among the Reeds* (1899).

Here in one person seemed to be the bard of ancient times and the accomplished poet who, while he was absorbing old Irish lore, was moved also for a short time by the verse forms of Rossetti, was enchanted by the ritual enjoined by Pater, and was giving much of his mind then, as always, to William Blake. But at that stage it was the Blake of *The Songs of Innocence* rather than of the Prophetic Books who influenced his verse, as we may see in such lyrics as *Never Give all the Heart,* which contains the same idea and many of the words of Blake's:

> Never seek to tell thy love.

The ending

> For he gave all his heart and lost

lacks the poignancy of Blake's

> Ah, she did depart.

It is interesting that Robert Bridges, who wrote his best poems in old age, should have advised the young Yeats to devote himself more exclusively to verse, on the ground that youth is the time for poetry. It is true that the poetic vein which yielded *Innisfree* and the beautiful idealistic play, *The Countess Cathleen,* would never appear in the later years with the same softness and assonance. Yet as it turned out not only was Yeats to go on writing poetry all his life, but the best was to be at the last. It has been pointed out that his poetic career divides into three parts, like a Greek tragedy, with a beginning, a middle and an end. If so, the middle is less clearly definable than the beginning or the end. The practical activities in which he engaged, at the time when Irish drama was being put to the

test at the Abbey Theatre, undoubtedly had much effect on his character. He was compelled to concern himself with the material details of the theatre (not excluding its finance), the training of actors and teaching them how to speak verse, and the political prejudices and frequent obstruction of societies and cliques in Dublin, some of them led by narrow-minded fanatics. Maud Gonne, too, often dragged him into a political atmosphere from which he would have preferred to stand aloof. When he experienced the pettiness of men in whom he might have expected comradeship and the excesses of some of the leaders of Sinn Fein he suffered disillusion, or rather release from illusion, and at the same time acquired a sort of worldly-wisdom, a capacity for judging life realistically, yet without loss to his imagination. He knew where his own strength lay, and was not to be easily diverted from his proper work—though we must remember that for him full living was always the necessary experience for the poetic life. When someone in the war period asked him for a war poem he replied:

> I think it better that in times like these
> A poet's mouth be silent, for in truth
> We have no gift to set a statesman right.

Yet when some men for whom previously he had had no great regard died in the Easter Rebellion of 1916 he could not but be profoundly moved, however little he agreed with their politics. Out of their sacrifice, however misguided, he was constrained to feel that 'a terrible beauty is born'. The spectacle of war in Europe and war in Ireland and quarrels between well-meaning men induced bitter reflection:

> Things fall apart; the centre cannot hold;
> Mere anarchy is loosed upon the world,
> The blood-dimmed tide is loosed, and every-
>   where
> The ceremony of innocence is drowned;
> The best lack all conviction, while the worst
> Are full of passionate intensity.

I cannot here discuss the part that Yeats played as a Senator, as eloquent public speaker, as defender of the lost cause of freedom from censorship in Eire, and an honoured elder in the State. In his later years he withdrew from public life, travelled, saw those friends he cared to see and pursued his vocation. Poetry meant not less to him now, but even more. He wrote with no less passion, no less imagination, but with far greater force. His gentleness gave place to a sort of ironic fierceness and grim frankness. Something hard and earthy was substituted for the softness of the romantic lyricism of his youth. This later thing had a sterner ring of truth, a virility, a grip on experience as a whole, and he found a new idiom and a new imagery with which to express it. He had not given up his dreams, or even his spirits, or his wilder flights of imagination; but it was now the imagination of a man who had trodden the earth, had known men and been undeceived about women (without ceasing to love them). His poetical excitement remains.

> Never had I more
> Excited, passionate, fantastical
> Imagination, nor an ear and eye

That more expected the impossible.

In the last year of his life he was writing:

> When a man grows old his joy
> Grows more deep day after day.

He does not shrink from 'the foul rag and bone shop of the heart'. He compares himself to the Stilt-Jack who walks on high stilts in procession:

> Malachi Stilt-Jack am I, whatever I learned has
>   run wild,
> From collar to collar, from stilt to stilt, from fa-
>   ther to child,
> All metaphor, Malachi, stilts and all. A barnacle
>   goose
> Far up in the stretches of night; splits and the
>   dawn breaks loose;
> I, through the terrible novelty of light, stalk on,
>   stalk on;
> Those great sea-horses bare their teeth and laugh
>   at the dawn.

He read the younger modern poets, and was eager to understand what they were doing and seeking. But he insisted that great subjects were needed for great poetry, and that its true function was to evoke joy and minister to the emotions. 'The arts are all the bridal chambers of joy', he wrote in *On the Boiler,* and he even added that artists should praise or represent 'great or happy people'. 'To me it is a fundamental defect in modern art,' he said in 1938 to the present writer, 'that it too much provokes to thought; classical art engenders feeling.' For this reason it seemed to him that Ibsen was a sign of decadence and Bernard Shaw more so. He delighted in theorizing about art, but he had no patience with art which begins in theory—it will begin, he said, 'with the thing seen, and felt, the dream, it may be, the poetical facts'. Even in his youth

> Players and painted stage took all my love
> And not those things that they were emblems of.

The old man with his 'eagle eye', rejoicing in 'an old man's frenzy' went on to the end living his poetical life, looking askance at 'the cavern of the mind', peopling his world with images

>   those images
> That constitute the wild,
> The lion and the virgin,
> The harlot and the child

writing with irony and measured vehemence, still respecting 'the aristocracy who are above fear, the poor who are beneath it, and the artists whom God has made reckless'. The whole of Yeats's life was the life of poetry, and each part enriched and added splendour to that which followed. (pp. 89-98)

> *R. A. Scott-James, "The Irish Literary Movement," in his* Fifty Years of English Literature, 1900-1950, *second edition, Longmans, Green and Co., 1957, pp. 89-98.*

INFLUENCE OF IRISH FOLKLORE AND MYTHOLOGY

John Wilson Foster

[*In the excerpt below, Foster discusses the impact of folklore on the Irish Literary Renaissance.*]

Assessing the role of folklore in the Irish Literary Revival, a complicated business, involves questions about the Revival concept of folklore; about the status of Revival collections of folklore, as archives and as literature; about the structural and thematic impact of folklore on Revival literature; and about the reaction against folklore by Revival or counter-Revival writers, notably James Joyce. At the center, radius, and circumference of these issues moves the protean, restless figure of Yeats—poet, playwright, fictionist, collector and theorist of folklore, student of matters spiritual. In this brief essay, I can merely glance off these issues and Yeats's involvement with them, and restrict myself to discussing—superficially, even so—two others: the Revival image of the Irish countryman, author of the folklore, and the nature of belief in folklore and literature.

As early as Patrick Kennedy, whose *Legendary Fictions of the Irish Celts* (1866) offers Wexford material, readers associated writer-collectors in Ireland with local areas: when we think of T. Crofton Croker, we think of Cork, Waterford and Limerick; of Hyde, Connacht; of Yeats, Sligo; of Lady Gregory, Galway and the Aran Islands. Later, the motor car and bus, and a superior train service, enabled such folklorists as O'Sullivan and Delargy to roam freely and repeatedly throughout Ireland, giving them a greater sense of the national picture in folklore. Lady Gregory explained in *Visions and Beliefs in the West of Ireland* (1920) how the spur to her own collecting was affronted local patriotism: "*The Celtic Twilight* was the first book of Mr. Yeats's that I read, and even before I met him, a little time later, I had begun looking for news of the invisible world; for his stories were of Sligo and I felt jealous for Galway." From Kennedy onwards, but before a scientific interest in local variants, collectors understood folklore as the expression of the *genius loci,* not as mere variations of international patterns. All localities were not equal in purity or quantity of folklore, of course, and the best-rewarded collectors were those who went West; Douglas Hyde, Jeremiah Curtin, William Larminie, W. B. Yeats, and Lady Gregory.

During the Revival, local folklore collections, like studies of the old sagas, were placed at the service of Irish nationalism. There was a nationalist counterpart of Lady Gregory's local pride; Hyde's industriousness, for example, owed something to his recognition that Ireland was falling behind Scotland in folklore collecting and that no Irish collector rivalled Campbell of Islay. Since cultural nationalism interested itself more in the past than in the present, and since the present was a betrayal and a decline, and yet an opportunity and climacteric, the study of folklore was governed by what we might call "survival" and "nonliteracy" theories. According to the first, current lore is vestigial, a diminishing survival of the past. According to the second, since folklore comprises the beliefs, customs, and expressive products of primitive peoples and of illiterate members of civilized societies, folklore must cease to be a living thing with the eradication of illiteracy. In his preface to *Legendary Fictions of the Irish Celts,* Kennedy bemoaned the fate of folktales at the hands of emigration and halfpenny journals, and he confessed to "the horrid thought that the memory of the tales heard in boyhood would be irrecoverably lost." This sentiment achieved the status of refrain in introductions to later folklore collections, suggesting that it might be a motif in such collections. A quarter of a century after Kennedy, Joseph Jacobs, referring to Irish storytelling, feared that "there are signs that its term of life is already numbered." J. H. Delargy announced, in 1945, that "The days of the folk-tale are numbered even in Ireland," while exactly one hundred years after Kennedy Séan O'Sullivan wrote, in his *Folktales of Ireland,* that "Very soon, memories of Irish storytelling on the grand scale will be found only in recordings and in books such as this."

If the folklorists tended to pessimism, the cultural nationalists proved recklessly optimistic. The discovery of folklore was held to be a *re*discovery on the assumption that all Irishmen had been, and could be again with effort and guidance, participants in the irreplaceable world and wisdom of the folk. The writers, too, had optimistic confidence—though in a more respectful manner than the early 19th-century writers, Lover and others—that Irish folklore could be reborn as literature. It must not be forgotten, of course, that the folklorist, cultural nationalist, and writer often coincided in the same Revival figure.

Creators and custodians of the folklore, embodiments of the past, the Irish "folk" or "peasantry," as Irish countrymen were deemed, became vitally interesting to the Revival, especially if they also inhabited the remote and primitive West. Certain upper-class Irishmen, usually Protestant, believed they shared with the peasant a disdain for worldly possessions—although they unlike the peasant, already enjoyed them—as they believed that worldly possessions inimically influenced the folklore that allegedly defined the peasant. "It is in many ways a mystery," Hyde confessed, when musing on the genesis of the folktale, "part of the flotsam and jetsam of the ages, still beating feebly against the shore of the nineteenth century, swallowed up at last in England by the waves of materialism and civilization combined; but still surviving unengulfed on the western coasts of Ireland." Only a later generation of folklorists in Ireland—and elsewhere, be it said—realized that folklore has no exclusively spiritual or highly artistic cast; that industrialism and materialism can generate their own folklore; and that folklore has its "hardware"—crafts and artifacts—as well as its "software"—songs, tales, customs, and beliefs. Such idealization of Irish country people suggests how deeply the folklore enthusiasm of the Irish cultural Revival had set its roots in the primitivist and occult romanticism of the late 19th-century British and European folklore movement.

The notion among Irish Revivalists that the Irish countryman has no interest in worldly possessions was a shallow and self-deceiving one. The peasant may not have had worldly goods, but he certainly *wanted* them, though generations of poverty may have taught him to tell others, in self-compensation, that the opposite was the case. In large measure a history of voluntary, enthusiastic materialism, the history of independent Ireland merely corroborates the romantic absurdity of the Revival view of the peasant. The peasant may have been more spiritual, in Yeatsian terms, than the rest of his compatriots—he was certainly more superstitious—but this did not cancel out his normal human cupidity. Nor had he any sustained *intention* to be spiritual, in a pagan rather than Christian sense, at the expense of material well-being. And I do not deny that the countryman loses a great deal of his irreplaceable lore when he graduates into the middle class, or into the city, or into the age of technology and print. I would certainly deny, however, that the upper-class personage has any natural affinity with the peasant and his lore, a notion current among certain Revivalists. Some of the Revivalists thought that the peasant and aristocrat alike lacked the anxieties associated with acquisitiveness and, consequently, could cultivate a spiritual existence. According to Yeats, the peasant, aristocrat, and artist all create beautiful things; enjoy long tradition; possess a special kind of knowledge or wisdom; and are above, like the aristocrat; beneath, like the peasant; or beyond, like the artist, merely materialist concerns. As believers in folk systems of expression and belief, however, the Irish gentry lived even farther apart, from the peasantry than did and do the Irish middle classes, which emerged in recent times and which possess, along with the normal anxieties associated with possessiveness, that anxiety attending the vivid remembrance of a poverty associated with the folklore that, even in the city, they remember and try to forget. Middle-class disdain of peasant lore rests as much on close and uncomfortable succession or "similarity" in time as on difference in class, wealth, or attitude. Signs of this discomfiture occur throughout *A Portrait of the Artist as a Young Man* (1916): for example, at the end of the novel when Stephen Dedalus records in his diary his response to John Alphonsus Mulrennan, the old man Stephen met during his sojourn in the West of Ireland.

Moreover, well-off Irish Protestants who discovered and collected peasant lore frequently became black sheep among their families and delinquents among their class—one thinks of Lady Gregory and Douglas Hyde. Such collectors did not entirely represent the gentry some Revivalists endeavored to see as having affinities with the folk. The attitude of upper-class folklorists to their subject resembled that of an adult, free from the troubles of adolescence, such as middle-class anxieties, trying to recover the faintly recalled bliss of childhood, such as the folk existence. That in the Irish context, if not a universal one, folk life was not the childhood of *their* race did not faze the Anglo-Irish. Indeed, their consciousness of dealing with *another* race was what made possible the folkloric side of the Literary Revival. For the early folklorists, the peasantry was exotic, and upper-class collectors had the outsider's curiosity, condescension, and brashness that unearthed a great quantity of data. Roman Catholic collectors of less exalted social station could not—out of shame, fear, and politeness—have mustered the same curiosity or data. They also had the leisure which Lady Gregory, in *Visions and Beliefs,* deemed a vital attribute—alongside patience, reverence and a good memory—of the field collector. Professionalism has since removed the necessity of leisure, just as the Ediphone recording machine and later, the tape-recorder, have removed the necessity of a good memory.

According to some, the affinity between gentry and peasantry rests on a half-historical, half-legendary conviction that the latter, or at least the seers and storytellers among it, held in protective custody the memory and art of a native aristocracy dispersed with the overthrow of the Gaelic order, an idea given most vivid expression in Daniel Corkery's *Hidden Ireland* (1924), but prefigured in Yeats's equation of peasant, artist, and aristocrat. It was a short step from this to seeing the Irish peasantry as itself an honorary or emblematic aristocracy driven West and underground by successive invasions. For the Anglo-Irish Revivalists, culture and class proved faster bonds of sympathy and identity than race. There was another fancied bond. A romantic notion of a fugitive folklore and aristocracy accorded with a more realistic, if largely unconscious, self-image held by the more perceptive landed gentry in Ireland. Standish James O'Grady told the landlord class what it might have hitherto suspected: that, unless its members mended their ways, it was finished in Ireland. In reading the history of folklore studies during the Revival, one cannot avoid sensing members of one endangered species—the Ascendancy—seeking in imagination the fellowship of another endangered species—the Gaelic-speaking peasant. A measure, perhaps, of guilt and uncertainty caused a few well-born Protestant nationalists to wish they *were* peasants; James Stephens later recalled hearing Yeats and AE actually express the desire to be reincarnated as such. The interest in folklore had a spiritualist cast might partly because of a wider reaction in Europe to rationalism, but also because it expressed a turning away of the more sensitive members of the Ascendancy from the material world—the city, capital, industry, the bourgeoisie—in which they were faring ill in reputation and general fortunes. This interest has the character, in other words, of a rearguard action, and this might serve to explain Ascendancy enthusiasm for the past, for the Otherworld, for the West, as well as that desperate rounding upon their own class and forebears, for their frivolousness and insensitivity, in which O'Grady, Lady Gregory, and Yeats from time to time engaged. The spiritual world that the more poetic and mystical Revivalists turned to for solace and escape was not one defined by their inherited Protestantism, but one defined by paganism, occultism, and the more mystical versions of Roman Catholicism. It would hardly be going too far to describe the Irish Literary Revival, whether we think of its Catholic or its Protestant writers and scholars, as an anti-Protestant movement. The Protestant, after all, was too readily identified with the hated merchant, as well as with the scientist and democrat. The indisputable paganism of the Irish peasant, lying as an elder faith beneath his more recent Catholicism, had another useful contribution to make to the Revival. The Revivalist who identified with this paganism felt his Irishness now had a spiritual dimension which the Catholicism of his countrymen, especially the candles of the Irish poor, had

hitherto prevented him from sensing. Here was an ironic reversal of the soup-kitchen conversions of the Famine.

From his introductions and appendices to *Fairy and Folk Tales of the Irish Peasantry* (1888) and *Irish Fairy Tales* (1892), Yeats, like Lady Gregory, seems to have thought the Irish countryman believed in the supernatural the way all of us believe in, say, the law of gravity, and that Yeats considered himself a fellow-believer. Lady Gregory and Yeats assumed that belief rested not just on the received wisdom of tradition but also on actual experienced vision. But peasant belief has to be expressed and in the expression arises a series of complications neither Yeats nor Gregory took sufficiently into account. To begin with, before scientific folklore studies developed, informants conveyed these beliefs to sophisticated collectors who, in Ireland, claimed a different religious persuasion and a vastly different social station. The informant must surely have tailored what he said to such a collector by playing the expected role and telling the collector what he wanted to hear—that the peasant believed intensely in the supernatural—thus taking advantage of the collector's earnestness and credulity, and then embroidering along the way so that he too might enjoy this peculiar occasion. Having written this, I came upon a passage in *We Two Together* (1950), the autobiography of James and Margaret Cousins, in which James recalls an Englishwoman "keen on the Irish fairies" who comes to Donegal and is initiated into fairy lore by her local host, one MacGarvey. "I stopped MacGarvey," Cousins remembers

> and asked him if he knew Mr. Russell (AE) who painted pictures of the countryside, and sometimes painted things that nobody saw but himself. "Now *that's* a rare gentleman," he replied, apparently as irrelevantly as I had asked the question, "and I say so, although he never stud me a drink." "And what about the English lady and the fairies?" "She knows the world and all about fairies." "Yes, but how much does she know herself, and how much have you told her?" "Well, Mister Cousins, it's the way with us we mebbe say more than the God's truth, just to plaze people that want to know more than you know yourself." "And what do you know about the fairies? Have you ever seen one?" "Damn the fairy or ghost or divil ever I've seen, or anything worse than meself, thanks be to God."

The danger of distorted recording data lessened when local and Roman Catholic folklorists took to the field and could not, and would not, be hoodwinked to the same extent.

Secondly, the Irish countryman, whose practical world is literal and devoid of humor, has a strong vein of playfulness, mocking, ironic, sometimes cruel, when it comes to the word. This simply reminds us, however, of the large element of play in traditional as well as sophisticated culture that Huizinga postulates in *Homo Ludens.* Any attempt to apply wholesale what Joseph Jacobs called "the anthropological method"—that is, taking stories and testimony of the folk as literal evidence, against which Jacobs cautions interpreters in his *Celtic Fairy Tales* (1892)—is frustrated by the element of play, which Yeats the dramatist recognized in the fairy cast of the Irish countryside he discusses in his two early folklore collections—pookas, gancanaghs, dullahans, etc.—but which Yeats the folklorist did not recognize in the folk *belief* in these colorful figures. If the peasant's responses to the early collectors were sometimes playful, so too were his imaginative inventions and his belief in them.

Thirdly, even if the belief is sincerely held—and the formerly widespread sincerity of belief in the supernatural in Irish country districts is hardly in question—the countryman might still be thought of as holding contradictory views, by a kind of cognitive dissonance, which become "views" and, hence, contradictory only during the reflection and explanation the collector demands of him. He might be thought of, in other words, as inhabiting two different worlds at once—one normally invisible, one visible. We might think of him as reconciling the two worlds by dividing the day and the calendar, his daily environment, and even his habits and behavior between them. Yeats felt at one with the peasant because vision, he was sure, provided the basis of their respective systems of belief. But did not Yeats, mystic poet and cultural manager, exercise his own kind of cognitive dissonance? In *Fairy and Folk Tales of the Irish Peasantry,* he adds a personal note to an anecdote by Letitia Maclintock:

> There is hardly a village in Ireland where the milk is not . . . believed to have been stolen times upon times. There are many counter-charms. Sometimes the coulter of a plough will be heated red-hot, and the witch will rush in, crying out that she is burning. A new horse-shoe or donkey-shoe, heated and put under the churn, with three straws, if possible stolen at midnight from over the witches' door, is quite infallible.

Does Yeats believe the last counter-charm *is* infallible, or does he merely tell us it is *believed* to be so? Does he fully believe in the original charm? Perhaps he merely reports a belief as a folklorist, but he may also be writing as a sophisticated fellow-believer, a casual epistemologist. Perhaps, again, he writes as a poet, and the whole question of a poet's belief becomes difficult because of the exigent mediation of poetic form, barely discernible in this passage in Yeats's folklore writing, which informs Yeats's poetry as a skeleton informs flesh, or blueprint a building. We know that folklore, and the forms and content of supernatural belief, enhanced the beauty and power of Yeats's poetry, but we do not know to what extent his own belief was a poetic one, sustained in aesthetic illusion for the sake of the poetry. In what sense did Yeats believe in, say, the complex system of *A Vision?* Is it primarily an intellectual artifact, complement to a poetic canon, an ultimate mask among masks?

Yeats himself would probably have refused to partition himself, where the supernatural is concerned, as folklorist, epistemologist, or poet; he would no doubt have seen himself as all three, which itself is a poetic idea. Yet, he preceded his commentators in acknowledging his epistemological ambivalence towards the mystical and supernatural. In his introduction to *The Wind Among the Reeds* in the *Collected Works* (1908), he spoke of moments of vision in sleep and waking and of the images of a mystical language, but, then, in the words of A. Norman Jeffares, "Being troubled by what was thought to be reckless obscurity he tried to explain himself in lengthy notes into which he put 'all the little learning I had, and more wilful phantasy than I now think admirable, though what is most mystical still seems to me the most true'." In his *Yeats: The Man and the Masks* Richard Ellmann describes Yeats as

> Latently sceptical by nature, but craving the irrefutable evidence of the supernatural which would finally lay his doubts at rest. . . . This attitude may be fairly described as a predisposition to believe and a desire to find fair evidence which would convince people lacking the predisposition.

"Yeats," claims Kathleen Raine,

> was not more sceptical than AE; indeed all those from whose writings I have quoted [Douglas Hyde, Y. Evans-Wentz, Andrew Lang, William James, Carl Jung] were too subtle in their thought for scepticism. But he was more analytical, more aware that of "facts of mind" there are many possible explanations. [Foreword to *Fairy and Folk Tales of Ireland*]

In spite of his repudiation of science, Yeats, said Edmund Wilson during the poet's life, "has always managed to leave himself a margin of scientific doubt . . . the romantic amateur of Magic is always accompanied and restrained by the rationalistic modern man." "He believes, but—he does not believe," Wilson epigrammatizes, and his quotation of Yeats from *A Vision* might seem to answer the question I earlier posed:

> Some will ask if I believe all that this book contains, and I will not know how to answer. Does the word belief, used as they will use it, belong to our age, can I think of the world as there and I here judging it? [*Axel's Castle: A Study in the Imaginative Literature of 1870-1930.*]

"And he intimates," Wilson concludes, "that, after all, his system may be only a set of symbols like another—a set of symbols, we recognize, like the Irish myths with which he began."

Something less problematic than the nature of Yeats's belief is the image of the Irish peasant, in Yeats and other Revival writers, as inhabitant of a world primarily spiritual and magical. Justifiably, I think, we demand that this image, purported in folklore and autobiographical writings, which resemble scaffolding around the brilliant incontestable structures of Revival literature, to be verifiable—that it accord with the best evidence, including one's own experience, as far as that extends. I believe Yeats, in fashioning his images of the peasant on which so much of the Revival depends, did not adequately take into account the playful, sceptical, and dramatic qualities of the peasant's testaments of belief that Yeats reserved for his own treatments—folkloristic, epistemological, poetic—of those testaments. Scepticism and distrust constitute a genuine aspect of the countryman's personality—making him such a shrewd and penny-wise marketeer—but Yeats saw it as an uncommon attitude imported from

William Butler Yeats.

the outside. In the introduction to *Fairy and Folk Tales of the Irish Peasantry,* Yeats writes:

> . . . the Sceptic is [not] entirely afar even from these western villages. I found him one morning as he bound his corn in a merest pocket-handkerchief of a field. Very different from Paddy Flynn—Scepticism in every wrinkle of his face, and a travelled man, too!—a foot-long Mohawk Indian tattooed on one of his arms to evidence the matter. "They who travel," says a neighboring priest, shaking his head over him, and quoting Thomas A'Kempis, "seldom come home holy." I had mentioned ghosts to this Sceptic. "Ghosts," said he; "there are no such things at all, at all, but the gentry, they stand to reason; for the devil, when he fell out of heaven, took the weak-minded ones with him, and they were put into the waste places. And that's what the gentry are. But they are getting scarce now, because their time's over, ye see, and they're going back. But ghosts, no! And I'll tell ye something more I don't believe in—the fire of hell;" then, in a low voice, "that's only invented to give the priests and the parsons something to do." Thereupon this man, so full of enlightenment, returned to his corn-binding.

I have a sneaking regard for this curmudgeonly fellow. He is impertinent to his better and unaccommodating enough not to believe in ghosts; he has been presumptuous enough to have left Ireland, and even exhibits foolish pride in binding his corn in so diligent and self-absorbed a manner in his "merest pocket-handkerchief" of a field. It is telling that the poet, foiled in his preconceptions, reverts to a superficially irrelevant snobbery in recollecting the exchange. But many a spalpeen or emigrant to America saved, with his remittances, many an Irish family from going the roads. His energy in having left Ireland, even for a short time, is not to be sneered at by someone who took the packet-steamer any time he felt like a change of air or company. The curmudgeon may not even be a rationalist at all, but merely had a sense, perhaps, of the difference between fact and fiction and between the occasions appropriate to each, and considered the binding of corn in the uncertain weather of the West far more pressing than any chat about ghosts with the idle gentry.

The curmudgeon rather deftly, I think, turns the upper-class chap's curiosity about folklore against itself by insulting the real gentry under cover of insulting the fairy gentry in whom he believes, apparently with some reluctance. Perhaps he rightly suspected that he was not the subject but the object of the curiosity. The fairies were, of course, called "gentry," as Yeats later informs us in his introduction to *Irish Fairy Tales,* and he says it is "for politeness' sake." I wonder. He could be right if, to the country people, the real gentry were proper recipients of their politeness, and if the fairies were regarded as the fled and defeated gods, the Tuatha Dé Danann, who shrank physically in the imagination of the people as they faded in their historical memory. But many of the local legends and ghost stories of Ireland recount the doings of the real gentry, and not always to the credit of the latter. If the fairies were thought of as fallen angels and mischievous creatures, then to call them "gentry" is, it could be argued, for impoliteness' sake. Since the mischievous fairies commanded respect, on the one hand, and fear and dislike, on the other, like the real gentry, the issue is a mixed one.

Lastly, an obstacle to our applying the anthropological method too readily to oral folklore—as the Revivalists, even the writers among them, tended to do—is that the casting of a belief in narrative form would seem to change its order of existence. An experience or event becomes a first-person anecdote; thereafter, it becomes a third-person anecdote, and perhaps eventually a local legend. And a local legend may eventually become a fairy tale or folktale proper. I suspect, too, there might be some devolution: *Märchen* are localized; local legends are passed off to the outsider as personal experience. The transformation from personal experience to story does not mean that the original conviction or belief becomes unfounded, insincere, or duplicitous; but it does mean that validity, or sincerity, or verifiability becomes irrelevant. The events of the story, as story, exist independent of the credence of both storyteller and listener. In expression, an experience or event accrues or assumes motifs and formulas, and passes under the jurisdiction of narrative laws of type and genre. At that point we have to make the distinction drawn by Douglas Hyde:

The *sgeal* or story is something much more intricate, complicated, and thought-out than the belief. One can quite easily distinguish between the two. One (the belief) is short, conversational, chiefly relating to real people, and contains no great sequence of incidents, while the other (the folk tale) is long, complicated, more or less conventional. [Quoted by Raine.]

The transformations are not just from subject, or witness, to informant, or retailer, to anecdotalist or storyteller, but also from personal to impersonal modes of narration, and from local and specific place and historical and specific time to those conventional generalities of time and space we find in *Märchen*. An appreciation of the conventional structures of oral lore, be it personal anecdote or hero tale, became possible only with the rise in Ireland of scientific folklore studies. The second generation of Irish folklorists—mostly local men, Roman Catholics, inhabitants of no Big House or Georgian terrace, tutored by the Scandinavian pioneers—had no personal system of belief to corroborate, no romantic image of a fey and credulous peasantry to project, and only little more desire than their contemporaries, the New Critics, to apply the anthropological method to texts. By the time they emerged, partly *because* they emerged, the Irish Literary Revival was finished. (pp. 6-18)

> *John Wilson Foster, "Yeats and the Folklore of the Irish Revival," in* Éire-Ireland, *Vol. XVII, No. 2, Summer, 1982, pp. 6-18.*

Phillip L. Marcus

[In the following excerpt, Marcus examines how the writers of the Irish Literary Renaissance incorporated Irish folklore and mythology into their work.]

One of the major contributions to the development of modern Irish literature in English was the rediscovery of the old Irish legends. References to them had begun to appear in English-language works in the late 1500's, and during the ensuing centuries they attracted increasing scholarly attention, so that by the second half of the nineteenth century a substantial body of fairly accurate translations was available. By that time there were also many Irish writers who had to use English as their medium but were interested in Irish subject-matter, and they saw the early stories as perfect material for a creative literature. Not only were they fresh and unexplored, but they also seemed virtually inexhaustible—"the most plentiful treasure of legends in Europe." There was much discussion of how many hundreds of octavo volumes it would take to publish all the surviving texts. In fact, there proved to be far more than were necessary, as most of the writers stuck to a few particularly appealing characters and tales.

Furthermore, these legends, although of course in origin connected with those of other countries, had taken on distinctively Irish features, and being national they offered Irish authors a way of breaking with the custom of merely echoing at a distance the writers of other countries. On the other hand, they represented a subject that, while intensely national, was uncolored by modern politics or sectarian religious controversy and thus might appeal to writers of differing persuasions and to a wider, more heterogeneous audience. Stopford Brooke epitomized this virtue in his [1893] address at the inaugural meeting of the Irish Literary Society, London:

> The earliest and noblest part of the [ancient Irish] literature was national, but not nationalist. It was fully Irish; written out of the heart of her own people, it was but little influenced by other literatures; and in it, at least, we can forget our quarrels of party, and quarrels of religion. It is not so easy to forget these quarrels when we read the literature which followed the invasion of Ireland by the English. . . . That literature may be said to be nationalist as well as national. It was forced to conceive Ireland as a whole and as set over against England. [*The Need and Use of Getting Irish Literature into the English Tongue*]

These theoretical advantages had already been abundantly exemplified in practice, for Ferguson and de Vere, both non-Nationalists politically, had been early users of the legendary materials; another example, their contemporary T. Caulfield Irwin, seeking to avoid political themes in his *Irish Poems and Legends* (1869) in order that it might "be acceptable to *all* classes who read Irish or English verses," had included several poems based on Irish myths. Finally, contrasted with an often sordid present, the Ireland depicted in the old texts, full of beauty and epic heroism, appeared extremely attractive; the contrast in fact made that earlier period seem far more noble and idealistic than it really was.

As soon as the Irish writers began turning their attention to the old stories they were faced with determining precisely *how* they were to be used. No one answer seemed obvious, and consequently extremely diverse solutions were adopted.

The most rudimentary literary approach can be seen in Gerald Griffin's "The Swans of Lir" (1842). In this rendering of *Aided Chlainne Lir* (The Fate of the Children of Lir) Griffin stayed so close to his original that the eminent Irish scholar Eugene O'Curry, in a note to his own edition of the Irish text with literal translation, gave special praise to his fidelity. Griffin took what was virtually a piece of scholarship and used it in a collection of stories linked by a frame tale. Obviously he hoped the novelty of the story, not anything unique in his handling of it, would appeal to his readers.

A similar approach was used by Denis Florence MacCarthy in his *Ferdiah* (1882), a retelling of the most famous of Cú Chulainn's battles, except that while Griffin had reproduced the prose with interspersed lyrics of his source, MacCarthy tried to give his work more literary appeal by using a poetic medium throughout. The structure and content of the source were preserved intact: he neither rearranged his material nor omitted any incident. And his fidelity to the language was equally great. . . . (pp. 223-25)

For most of the early myth-users, however, such scrupulous faithfulness to the old texts was impossible. Sometimes the reason was artistic: many of the texts survived in corrupt form, aesthetic virtues they may once have had blurred through centuries of oral transmission and manual copying. Often elements in the stories were judged repugnant on moral grounds or conflicted with idealized visions of the heroic age.

Both artistic and moral or idealistic objections can be seen in the work of P. W. Joyce, whose *Old Celtic Romances* (1879), a pioneer book in the field, was used by many more significant figures. Joyce was a scholar, but, as he indicates in his preface, his renderings were not done "for linguistic purposes":

> A translation may either follow the very words, or reproduce the life and spirit, of the original, but no translation can do both. If you render word for word, you lose the spirit; if you wish to give the spirit and the manner, you must depart from the exact words and frame your own phrases. I have chosen this latter course. My translation follows the original closely enough in narrative and incident; but so far as mere phraseology is concerned I have used the English language freely, not allowing myself to be trammelled by too close an adherence to the very words of the text. The originals are in general simple in style; and I have done my best to render them into simple, plain, homely English.

This suggests that Joyce, like MacCarthy, deviated from his sources only in not always using their very words. And yet, as other passages in the same preface reveal, Joyce did occasionally tidy up the "narrative and incident" of certain tales. For example, in "The Pursuit of the Giolla Dacker and his Horse" he "omitted altogether a long episode towards the end, which travels away from the main story," and in the Diarmaid and Gráinne story he made several changes:

> I cannot help believing that this fine story originally ended with the death of Dermat, though in all the current versions . . . there is an additional part recounting the further proceedings of Grania and her sons, after the death of the hero. But this part is in every respect inferior to the rest—in language, in feeling, and in play of imagination. It seems to me very clear that it was patched on to the original story by some unskilful hand; and I have accordingly omitted it, and ended the story with the death of Dermat. I have also omitted two short episodes—that of the *cnumh* or reptile of Corca Divna, as a mere excresence; and Finn's expedition to Scotland for aid against Dermat. And, for the sake of clearness, I have slightly changed the place of that part of the tale which recounts the origin of the Fairy Quicken Tree of Dooros. There are one or two other trifling but very necessary modifications, which need not be mentioned here.

Some of the changes, such as the elimination of the expedition to Scotland, were certainly aimed at structural improvement; but prudishness may have prompted the omission of the conclusion, in which Gráinne, instead of remaining faithful to Diarmaid, gives herself to Fionn. Recent scholarly opinion supports Joyce's assertion that the episode is not of the same origin as the rest of the tale [See

Tóruigheacht Dhiarmada agus Ghráinne, edited by Nessa Ní Sheaghdha]; nevertheless, it is clear from Joyce's comments that he *wanted* it not to be canonical. And one of those "trifling but very necessary modifications" involved the bowdlerization of a passage which relates that "Diarmuid kept himself from Grainne, and . . . he left a spit of flesh uncooked in Doire dha bhoth as a token to Fionn and to the Fenians that he had not sinned with Grainne." [The omitted passage is quoted from the version of Standish Hayes O'Grady, *The Pursuit of Diarmuid and Grainne.*]

Thus, Joyce did take considerable liberties with his sources in regard to rearrangement and omission, but he did not take the far greater liberty of *adding* to the original texts. Other, less scholarly minded writers of the time, in trying to make the old legends into "good stories," resorted to modifying plot through invention as well as deletion, expanding the characterizations and making them consistent and convincing, and combining elements from different versions.

A good example of a formal justification of this approach is found in de Vere's preface to *The Foray of Queen Maeve* (1882), where he asserted,

> It is not in the form of translation that an ancient Irish tale of any considerable length admits of being rendered in poetry. What is needed is to select from the original such portions as are at once the most essential to the story, and the most characteristic, reproducing them in condensed form, and taking care that the necessary additions bring out the idea and contain nothing that is not in the spirit of the original.

Joyce had been rather apologetic about his structural alterations; but in de Vere's case modification of the plot structure of the original was taken for granted, even elevated into an ideal in its own right. Such alterations were to preserve "the spirit of the original," but that was quite another thing than merely diverging from the letter of the *language,* for it involved a diminished concern with adherence to the *content* of the original texts: additions as well as omissions would be necessary.

De Vere's own modifications of his sources were numerous but fairly restrained. He toned down certain elements and omitted others, such as the passage in the Fight at the Ford in which the combatants' wounds are said to be big enough for birds to have flown through. Elsewhere he expanded the scope or significance of incidents present in the source: the banquet at which Medb bribes Fer Diad to fight Cú Chulainn was developed into a little dramatic scene, and the encounter of Findabair and Reochaid became a romantic tragedy. Sometimes elements were introduced that had *no* basis in the source: he brought in a banshee howling on the night of Deirdre's birth and, to heighten the pathos of Fer Diad's feelings toward Cú Chulainn, fabricated the idea that the former had been in love with Aoife and had lost her to his friend. He frequently added "poetic" descriptive passages such as the following, again from the Fight at the Ford:

> . . . the vernal day
> Panted with summer arduous, while aloft

Noontide, a fire-tressed Fury, waved her torch,
Kindling the lit grove and its youngling green
From the azure-blazing zenith.

Here the spirit of the originals has vanished.

Unlike de Vere, John Todhunter did not in practice always exemplify his theory. His statement, in regard to his versions of the "Three Sorrows," that "in telling again these old stories, I have freely rehandled my materials—not following precisely any one of the many versions of each legend, but appropriating and adopting whatever best suited my purpose in each" [*Three Irish Bardic Tales*], was misleading in its suggestion of radical modification of his sources. In fact he stayed rather close to the original stories in structure and incident, modifying them mainly by adding copious quantities of often trivial detail.

Katharine Tynan, in her *The Pursuit of Diarmaid and Grainne* (1887), was another writer who used the "good story" approach. Like P. W. Joyce, she omitted the serpent, Fionn's expedition to Scotland, and most of the events following the death of Diarmaid. But she went even further than he had: she dropped also the rather dull opening of the tale, in which Fionn sends emissaries to propose to Gráinne, and began her poem with the more dramatic marriage banquet. Furthermore, in the received tradition, the years in which the lovers lived together in peace are only referred to briefly; Miss Tynan picked up the hint and created a highly sentimental domestic scene:

> And lovely was the wedded life,
> For sixteen years unclouded over
> Of noble husband, tender wife,
> Each still the constant lover;
>
> They loved as in the hour's surprise,
> When, with a sudden flush and quiver,
> Each looked to meet the other's eyes
> And knew they loved for ever.
>
> [*Shamrocks*]

This sort of treatment certainly was not faithful to the emotional tenor of the legend; nor could it be harmonized with Gráinne's final apostasy, and thus she found that episode as unacceptable as Joyce had.

The story as she presented it was still not sufficiently modified to suit Rolleston, who felt very strongly that "these old Celtic tales do not bear retelling in the form in which they have reached us" ["Shamrocks," *The Academy*, July 9, 1887]. He was disturbed by her retention of the incidents in which Diarmaid slew a giant, singlehandedly dispatched two thousand warriors, and leaped unseen over an encircling army:

> This turgidity is a blot in the ancient Irish mythic poetry, and it is neither wise nor patriotic to reproduce it. We want the Irish spirit, certainly, in Irish literature; but we want its gold, not its dross; its spirituality, not its superstition; its daring fancy, not its too frequent recourse to mechanical exaggeration.

Joyce had tended to excuse the imperfections he found as not being genuine parts of the legends, though this was only partially true. Rolleston readily admitted the undeniable fact that the early Gael *was* capable of grossness and

other faults, and thus he had to advocate a highly selective form of rehandling.

An exponent of the "good story" method who exploited its possibilities much more fully was Robert Dwyer Joyce. An Irishman by birth, he emigrated to America, where he wrote two long poems on heroic subjects, *Deirdre* (1876) and *Blanid* (1879). These works, immensely successful when they first appeared, soon fell into virtual oblivion; but they were read by a number of other Irish writers who were working with similar materials, and Yeats wrote one of his earliest "Irish" articles about them ["The Poetry of Robert Dwyer Joyce," *Irish Fireside*, December 4, 1886].

The brother of P. W. Joyce, he shared none of the latter's reverence for the original texts; both of his poems contain such extensive elaboration and addition of invented material (sometimes even long episodes) that the sources are often altered almost beyond recognition. For example, in *Deirdre* thirty pages are devoted to a manufactured episode in which Naisi's forces seize a fleet of Fomorian galleys in which to sail to Scotland. *Blanid*, a poem several thousand lines in length, is elaborated from a few pages in Keating: the incidents are greatly expanded, long descriptive passages abound, and there is an attempt at fuller characterization. The alterations were not only extensive but also violated the spirit of the old texts. This is particularly true of *Blanid*, in which the source is transformed into a satiny medieval romance: Cú Chulainn and the other warriors are called "knights," Blanid is the maiden in distress, and there are castles, dungeons, and even some Spenserian dragons.

In Samuel Ferguson's first treatment of a heroic subject, an 1834 prose retelling of the Deirdre story, he anticipated Griffin by using an almost literal translation as one of a series of stories set in a frame tale. Generally, however, he disliked too much in the legends to reproduce them virtually intact. His books are full of references to "vulgarity" and "turgid extravagances and exaggerations" in the old stories. *Congal* was originally to have been a translation, until he found his source's "inherent repugnancies too obstinate for reconcilement." He remedied the problem partly by omitting or changing offensive elements, as in the case of the following vivid battle detail:

> He . . . made a drag and mighty pull to draw back the spear, but he failed; he made a second effort, and failed; but in the third effort he dragged out his viscera and bowels between his skin and his warlike attire. [*The Banquet of Dun Na N-Gedh and the Battle of Magh Rath*, edited and translated by John O'Donovan, 1842]

In *Congal* this passage became

> And with both hands essayed to drag the weapon from its seat
> But failed: a second time he tugged with painful sick essay,
> And failed: but at the third attempt the javelin came away.

Although a scholar and antiquarian, he felt free also to make numerous and extensive additions. Many of these have an obviously artistic motive: in *Congal*, for instance, he developed the defiant old warrior Kellach, one of the most vivid and successful characters in the poem, from a mere sketch in the source, and entirely invented the maiden Lafinda and betrothed her to Congal in order to provide a love interest.

But Ferguson was an earnest Victorian, not an aesthete, and his conception of good literature included edification. Consequently he praised de Vere for giving "the dignity of a high religious philosophy to his subjects" and sought to do the same. Many of his works illustrate a variation upon the "good story" method in which the author chooses from among the old texts subjects conducive to edifying moral or religious interpretation and even fabricates suitable vehicles when he cannot find them to hand. Lady Ferguson thus approvingly quoted T. W. Lyster's observation that in nearly all the poems based on Irish heroic myth her husband had been "attracted by some moral, or religious, or humane idea, either inherent in the myth or read into it in his imaginative scrutiny" [*Lays of the Red Branch*]. One of Ferguson's favorite devices was to conclude poems with one of the characters having a prescient vision of Christianity. *Conary,* "Mesgedra," "The Healing of Conall Carnach," "The Burial of King Cormac," and "The Death of Dermid" all fit this pattern. In *Congal,* Ferguson attributed to the title character (who is definitely pagan throughout the original text) an apparent death-bed religious illumination. His Naisi is given a long invented speech, unlike anything the Naisi of the original texts would say and reminiscent of Ulysses on "degree" in *Troilus and Cressida,* the burden of which is

> Man lives by mutual trust. The commonwealth
> Falls into chaos if man trust not man.
> For then all joint endeavours come to naught,
> And each pursues his separate intent
> Backed by no other labour than his own.
>
> [*Poems,* 1880]

In these and other instances Ferguson, too, clearly deviated from the spirit of his originals.

Like all other fresh sources of subject-matter, the legendary materials had sometimes been appropriated for less elevated purposes, a practice lamented by P. W. Joyce [in *Old Celtic Romances*]:

> Scraps and fragments of some of these tales have been given to the world in popular publications, by writers who, not being able to read the originals, took their information from printed books in the English language. But I am forced to say that many of these specimens have been presented in a very unfavourable and unjust light—distorted to make them look *funny,* and their characters debased to the mere modern conventional stage Irishman.

Surely one of the main reasons for the tremendous impact produced upon reader after reader by Standish O'Grady's work was the greatly idealized image it embodied of the Irish heroic age. In contrast to the debased visions described by Joyce, O'Grady depicted it as a culture of which any nation could be proud:

> I cannot help regarding this age and the great

personages moving therein as incomparably higher in intrinsic worth than the corresponding ages of Greece. In Homer, Hesiod, and the Attic poets, there is a polish and artistic form, absent in the existing monuments of Irish heroic thought, but the gold, the ore itself, is here massier and more pure, the sentiment deeper and more tender, the audacity and freedom more exhilarating, the reach of imagination more sublime, the depth and power of the human soul more fully exhibit themselves. [*History: Critical and Philosophical*]

He stressed the tradition's nobility and excitement:

> Out of the ground start forth the armies of her demigods and champions—an age bright with heroic forms, loud with the trampling of armies and war-steeds, with the roar of chariot-wheels, and the shouting of warriors.

Cú Chulainn's combat with Fer Diad was "the most profoundly tragic scene in all literature," and Cú himself "the noblest character."

AE's description of his own feelings upon first reading O'Grady reveals that it was this heroic grandeur that moved him: he felt like a man "who suddenly feels ancient memories rushing at him, and knows he was born in a royal house, that he had mixed with the mighty of heaven and earth and had the very noblest for his companions" ["A Tribute by AE," *Standish O'Grady: the Man and the Writer*]. Rolleston's reaction was similar:

> The shadowy gods and warriors ceased to be mere names; they took heroic shape and form. They were filled with passions, terrific and superhuman sometimes, but profoundly moving. Anger was there, and vengeance, malice and craft, honour and loyalty, self-sacrifice and devotions, and at times a pathos and tenderness which, in their poignant keenness, matched the gigantic scale on which all the passions of this early legendary age were conceived.
>
> This [the *History*] was the first book I ever read which convinced me that there was such a thing as a spiritual Ireland. [*Portrait of an Irishman*]

O'Grady consciously fostered this idealized image of the period. As he later admitted, he found in the early texts things that he "simply could not write down and print and publish," such as the "very loose morality" of Queen Medb. An even greater problem was presented by the central figure of the Red Branch cycle of legends, Cú Chulainn himself: at times he appeared extremely noble and heroic, but other features of the story tended to undercut this image. O'Grady could not accept Cú's three-colored hair, the seven pupils in each of his eyes, the seven digits on each of his hands and feet, let alone his grotesque "distortions." . . . (pp. 226-35)

Only MacCarthy faithfully reproduced such descriptions: all the other early writers, and Yeats and Lady Gregory after them, followed O'Grady's example and omitted them. Nor did O'Grady find congenial the idea of Cú Chulainn having an invincible weapon; consequently he made the fearful *ga bulga* into a "rude spear," thrown in the ordinary manner [*History of Ireland*]. And if he knew the Stowe version of the *Táin* he must have found elements even harder to reconcile with his own vision of his hero, for in that manuscript there is a passage in which Cú and two invisible fairy helpers gang up on Fer Diad and attack him from all sides simultaneously. O'Grady's general practice was to make Cú Chulainn seem more heroic by depriving him of all his superhuman features and advantages.

Despite the title of his most famous work, he did not really pretend he was dealing with the past in a scholarly manner. His *History* was almost immediately reprinted, with a few introductory chapters omitted, under the title *Cuculain: An Epic,* and in a new preface he declared, "The style which partly as a substitute for metre I have adopted, and partly in imitation of the bards, would seem rather to relegate [the book] to that species of composition which is termed epic, than to any of the other known kinds of literary workmanship." He was quite concerned with the aesthetic values of the legendary tales and sought to enhance them. In his method, as he himself described it, "actual historical fact" was "seen through an imaginative medium" and the whole of the original account reduced to its "artistic elements." This was essentially the "good story" approach, and he used it fully, adding as well as omitting. He introduced not only descriptive passages and details for creating atmosphere, but also elements of characterization and even, on occasion, whole incidents. The degree of freedom he allowed himself is indicated by the episode in which he depicted Cú Chulainn and Láeg visiting Dublin on Christmas and seeing there in a shop window a shiny toy chariot, which they buy for Cú's small son.

This incident was certainly a gross breach of both the fact and the spirit of the heroic period, but O'Grady's motive in fabricating it was probably "literary." In at least one case, however, he altered his sources in a way comparable to Ferguson's interjection of religious pieties. In the chapter of the *History* entitled "A Pioneer," Láeg, rushing to rejoin his master, seeks lodging for the night at the house of a former slave who has attained his freedom and purchased some land of his own, but the niggardly, base-minded owner refuses to offer any hospitality without recompense. In creating this episode O'Grady set up a contrast with the heroic magnanimity of the great warriors and provided a change of tempo from the scenes of combat, but his main purpose was almost certainly the introduction of a commentary upon the Ireland of his own day. His political preoccupation with the Irish aristocracy is well known. Elsewhere in the *History* there is what seems to be a direct reference to them and to what O'Grady considered their fallings-off: "In the days of Maeve, the great knights and champions of Eire concerned themselves more with knightly deeds and thoughts, and relinquished to the base born excessive zeal concerning wealth and its distribution." "A Pioneer" offered that aristocracy he both loved for their virtues and hated for their weakness a picture of what would come if they did not assert themselves: the land passing into the hands of men with no trace of the old heroic qualities, "a hungry, greedy, and anarchic *canaille.*" It was, in other words, a moral parable in which the primitive events had a modern application.

O'Grady himself soon became a source for another myth-user, William C. Upton, whose *Cuchulain: The Story of his Combats at the Ford* appeared in 1887. The Irish myths had already been recast in a wide variety of forms, from short lyrics to prose epic; Upton added yet another, the "dramatic poem." He accepted the image of Cú Chulainn and the *Táin* as O'Grady presented it, but instead of relating it in a leisurely narrative he tried to compress it into a drama: his work was divided into scenes, observed the unities, had a list of *dramatis personae,* and even stage directions. It was, however, neither a satisfactory rendering of the story nor a performable work. The limitations of time and place and of dramatic probability ruled out direct representation of almost all the more exciting parts of the tale, and Upton had to compensate by using the very awkward and inadequate device of having Cú Chulainn simply *tell* Láeg at great length about his exploits. The form, certain elements in his vocabulary, and the presence of spirits singing short lyrics, all suggest that Upton's model was Shelley's *Prometheus Unbound.* The combination of Shelley and O'Grady was a strange one, but no stranger than that in the Noh-patterned Cú Chulainn plays Yeats would later write.

Upton's use of O'Grady was indicative of the fact that literary renderings of the early legends were beginning to attract attention. During the seventies and eighties there were many other examples of one laborer in the field being aware of his fellows. De Vere and Todhunter, for instance, both referred to O'Grady in their own works; de Vere also praised Ferguson and MacCarthy and was in return recommended by them. P. W. Joyce presented a copy of *Old Celtic Romances* to Katharine Tynan, and Ferguson was even familiar with the work of R. D. Joyce. There was by this time a substantial quantity of literature in the new mode, and nearly all of what would become the most frequently used legends were available in at least one version.

It is hardly surprising that Yeats's own attention was soon drawn to the old myths and their modern advocates. He read what scholarly translations he could find, and Ferguson, R. D. Joyce, de Vere, Katharine Tynan, and O'Grady. His earliest published articles were almost all on writers who had used legendary material, and he absorbed what they had to teach him in regard to method. But when, as could be expected, he began to draw upon that material for his own work, he went beyond them and introduced an important new approach.

So rich a body of traditional stories offered the poet abundant potential means for self-expression. They could serve him as allegorical vehicles, sources of symbols, "objective correlatives" for his own feelings and ideas. A story in its received form might prove suitable for such interpretation, might fit perfectly the elements he wished to express; or some modifications of the original myth might be required, either rearrangement of existing features or addition of entirely new elements. The subjectivity of the personal content would be balanced and controlled by the public, traditional nature of the myth. This approach was at least as old as Classical Greek drama: in *The Trojan*

Women, for example, Euripides "used heroic legend for the expression of his feelings about the horrors of aggressive war in his own time." It was of course common in English literature: Keats, turning the Endymion story into an allegory concerning the human imagination; Shelley, imprinting the Prometheus legend with his own idiosyncratic world vision; and Tennyson, embodying aspects of his feelings about the death of Hallam in the myths of Ulysses, Tithonus, and King Arthur, are only a few of the writers who might be mentioned. But as the preceding survey illustrated, it was not found in Irish literary tradition before Yeats. Ferguson and O'Grady approached it in some of their modifications of the early texts, but neither of them was egoistic enough to actually cultivate it; it was one thing for Ferguson to add a conventional love affair or religious sentiment, but quite another to distort the texts for *personal* ends; and O'Grady, in the preface to his *History,* expressed his *regret* that he could not efface from the work all traces of his own personality.

The first two legendary poems Yeats wrote were "The Madness of King Goll" and *The Wanderings of Oisin.* It is probable that Yeats began *Oisin* before writing "King Goll"; Richard Ellmann says the former was begun in 1886, and on June 25, 1887, Yeats indicated [in a letter] that the first two sections of it had been composed, while "King Goll" was first mentioned on July 1, 1887. However, that letter speaks of "King Goll" as ready to be sent out, and it was therefore his earliest complete poem based on Irish myth. In it his new approach to such material seems already to be present. (pp. 236-41)

This legend (which may be a confusion of the story of Goll the boy-king of Ulster in *Cath Finntrága* with that of Suibhne Geilt) was not well known, nor did O'Curry present it as particularly interesting or important. A mere summary of a minor event, with no aesthetic form, it must have attracted Yeats for other reasons.

To suggest that he found in this story a vehicle for personal feelings is not to insinuate that he ever had fears of madness. His father did a picture of him as King Goll to accompany the poem, and Yeats's humorous later recollection of the incident gives a clue to the nature of his empathy with the figure:

> I write for boys and girls of twenty but I am always thinking of myself at that age—the age I was when my father painted me as King Goll, tearing the strings out [of] a harp, being insane with youth, but looking very desirable—alas no woman noticed it at the time—with dreamy eyes and a great mass of black hair. It hangs in our drawing room now—a pathetic memory of a really dreadful time. [*Letters*]

In the pathetic boy-king Yeats found an image of his own youthful unhappiness.

In *The Wanderings of Oisin,* Yeats used his approach with much greater complexity. His principal source for the story of Oisin's adventures was an eighteenth-century Irish poem attributed to Michael Comyn, which he found translated in the fourth volume of the *Transactions of the Ossianic Society.* In reshaping this material he made a very significant structural alteration. In Comyn's poem, Oisin visited only two places, a Land of Virtues and a Land of Youth, stopping at the former on the way to the latter. Yeats brought him to three: the Island of the Living (corresponding to Comyn's Land of Youth), the Island of Victories (the equivalent of Comyn's Land of Virtues), and the Island of Forgetfulness. Furthermore, he altered the order and relationship as found in Comyn, making Oisin go to the Island of Victories after he has lost his desire to stay on the Island of the Living, and to the Island of Forgetfulness when he is no longer content on the Island of Victories. In a contemporary letter Yeats himself confessed that his intention in modifying his sources was the creation of an allegory: in 1889 he wrote to Katharine Tynan, "There are three incompatible things man is always seeking—infinite feeling, infinite battle, infinite repose—hence the three islands." At the end of his life, in "The Circus Animals' Desertion," he still saw the poem this way, as indicated by the reference to "three enchanted islands, allegorical dreams, / Vain gaiety, vain battle, vain repose."

Two other allegorical interpretations have been suggested by Professor Ellmann, who argues that "on a personal level [the three islands] represent Yeats's idyllic boyhood at Sligo, his subsequent fights with the English boys in West Kensington because he was Irish, and his daydreaming adolescence on Howth," as well as paralleling "the periods of childhood, of aggressive maturity, and of senility in the lives of all men." Yet another reading of the pattern was offered by Yeats in a retrospective account:

> When I was a boy everybody talked about progress, and rebellion against my elders took the form of aversion to that myth. I took satisfaction in certain public disasters, felt a sort of ecstasy at the contemplation of ruin, and then I came upon the story of Oisin in Tir nà nOg and reshaped it into my *Wanderings of Oisin.* He rides across the sea with a spirit, he passes phantoms, a boy following a girl, a hound chasing a hare, emblematical of eternal pursuit, he comes to an island of choral dancing, leaves that after many years, passes the phantoms once again, comes to an island of endless battle for an object never achieved, leaves that after many years, passes the phantoms once again, comes to an island of sleep, leaves that and comes to Ireland, to Saint Patrick and old age. I did not pick these images because of any theory, but because I found them impressive, yet all the while abstractions haunted me. [*Explorations*]

In another passage written during the same period he put it more tersely: "The choral song, a life lived in common, a futile battle, then thought for its own sake, the last island, Vico's circle and mine, and then the circle joined" [*Explorations*]. Of course Yeats did not know Vico's theories at the time he wrote the poem, but as Thomas Whitaker has shown, he had already found similar ideas in Theosophy, Balzac, and Blake. From this perspective Oisin's travels represent a cyclical theory of history.

In connection with the introduction of the three-island pattern, Yeats greatly expanded the nostalgia felt by Oisin for his Fenian companions in Comyn's poem: in *The Wanderings,* Oisin's departure from each of the immortal realms is precipitated by contact with some item that calls to mind his former life. In making this modification Yeats made central to the poem a theme that runs throughout all his work: the "choice" dichotomy, a tension between the claims of this world and the one beyond. Oisin, like Yeats himself, was continually drawn back to the former.

This theme was reinforced in the poem by the conflict between Oisin and Saint Patrick. In Comyn's poem this conflict was very muted: Patrick is mainly interested in hearing the tale, and when their differences of opinion at one point threaten to get out of control, he says, "Let us leave off our controversy on each side / And continue thy story, O valiant Oisin!" Yeats strengthened the tension by drawing upon other dialogues between them in the same volume of the *Ossianic Society* series, in which the opposition is virulent and unremitting. In this form the two figures represented perfectly the attractions of the antithetical realms. Yeats was eventually to make the parallel overt, and in the process to relate it to one of his most famous "choice" poems, "Vacillation," and to the development of his entire literary corpus: "The swordsman throughout repudiates the saint, but not without vacillation. Is that perhaps the sole theme—Usheen and Patrick—'so get you gone Von Hügel though with blessings on your head'?" Read from this point of view, *The Wanderings of Oisin* can be seen as a personal *psychomachia*.

The Oisin-Patrick controversy also helped develop the theme of historical cycles. As Whitaker points out, Yeats was already familiar with theories of the alternation of "pagan" and "religious" eras, and his poem focuses upon a man caught in the transition. Patrick seemed victorious, but in one popular Fenian legend the heroes were said to be still alive and only awaiting the proper time to return; Yeats, seeing himself at the end of the Christian period, would suggest a similar hope in his last poem, "The Black Tower."

In 1888, while preparing a corrected fair copy of *The Wanderings,* Yeats made an important comment on his technique in the poem:

> In the second part of "Oisin" under the disguise of symbolism I have said several things to which I only have the key. The romance is for my readers. They must not even know there is a symbol anywhere. They will not find out. If they did it would spoil the art. Yet the whole poem is full of symbols—if it be full of aught but clouds.

There is something here of the mystery and secretiveness with which the French *Symbolistes* approached their art, and also perhaps an element of personal reticence; but Yeats did want at least some of his many meanings discerned, for when the early reviews of the poem proved uncomprehending, he wrote to Katharine Tynan, " 'Oisin' needs an interpreter" and then—possibly hoping that she herself would review it—dropped the hint about the "three incompatible things."

In addition to the larger "structural" symbolism already discussed, the poem is full of specific symbols. In several instances vehicles already present in the sources were merely endowed with the desired significances. This was particularly true in the case of the dear-hound-lady-youth procession. It appears only once in Comyn, and its meaning is never explained. Yeats brought it in three times, always in relation to the love of Oisin and Niamh and always during the crucial periods in which the lure of the mortal world is being evaded by flight to one of the islands: thus he set up a pattern emblematical of eternal desire and pursuit. The lines written long after in "The Circus Animals' Desertion" about Yeats's having been "starved for the bosom of ['Oisin's] faery bride" suggest also a personal level to Niamh, though this may be only an anachronistic reference to Maud Gonne, whom he had not even met by the time he finished the poem. And the burden of old age that descends upon Oisin may have reflected Yeats's feelings about having lost the gift of spontaneous composition or a facet of the sense of *fin de siècle* and premature decrepitude that pervades his early volumes.

In other cases Yeats modified his sources more radically or even introduced new elements with symbolic value. For example, in Comyn's poem Oisin fights a battle with a Fomorian giant. Yeats turned the giant into a demon of vague origins and unspecified nationality and thus paved the way for widely varying interpretations of him as representing England (with the maiden he holds captive corresponding to Ireland), Yeats's own father, and "orgasm incarnate." Furthermore, whereas in the earlier poem Oisin dispatched his opponent permanently after a fight of only three days and nights, Yeats supported some of his main themes by making the combat recur every few days for a hundred years and "end" only when Oisin departs. In greatly elaborating upon Comyn's description of the palace in which the fight took place, Yeats added the detail of two statues, one associated with the heavens and the other with the seas, which have been identified as "spiritual and physical man." He also brought into the poem two of his favorite symbols, the dance and the rose. Dancing constitutes the main activity of the immortal inhabitants of his first island; and in the course of their dancing he had them come to a grove of "damask roses" which, because they never decay, represent the eternality of life there. The poem also contained many other, less precise hints of hidden meaning, such as the reference in one of the Immortals' songs to "Asian trees."

It should be clear by now that Yeats's response to the myth materials was far more involved than those of writers who were concerned merely with improving them aesthetically or morally: it was an act of personal interpretation and personal expression. Yeats's one contemporary account of the process of composition of *The Wanderings* is illuminating in this respect:

> I have corrected the first two parts of "Oisin." The second part is much more coherent than I had hoped. . . . It is the most inspired but the least artistic of the three. The last has most art. Because I was in complete solitude—no one near me but old and reticent people—when I wrote it. It was the greatest effort of all my things. When I had finished it I brought it round to read to my Uncle George Pollexfen and could hardly read, so collapsed I was. My voice quite broken. It really was a kind of vision. It beset me day and night. Not that I ever wrote more than a few

lines in a day. But those few lines took me hours. All the rest of the time I walked about the roads thinking of it. I wait impatiently the proofs of it. With the other parts I am disappointed—they seem only shadows of what I saw. But the third must have got itself expressed—it kept me from my sleep too long. Yet the second part is more deep and poetic. . . . The first parts I felt. I saw the second [the third?]. Yet there too, perhaps, only shadows have got themselves on to paper. [*Letters*]

The shadowiness is certainly present, but Yeats's vision did get expressed; the content seems almost over-rich. He was so deeply engaged with the problem that both the approach of *The Wanderings* and some of its key themes also pervaded the story "Dhoya," which he was writing at about the same time. Yeats himself created the character of Dhoya, the giant abandoned in Sligo by the Fomorians who had held him captive, but the basic situation of the story, the man who marries a fairy bride and then loses her to her fairy husband in a chess game, was borrowed from the Irish legend of King Eochaid, Edain, and Midhir. Yeats used it to express the tension between the immutable realm and the world of change: the woman of the *sidhe* cries,

> "Dhoya, I have left my world far off. My people—on the floor of the lake they are dancing and singing, and on the islands of the lake; always happy, always young, always without change. I have left them for thee, Dhoya, for they cannot love. . . . I left the places where they dance for thee!"

Here was a variant of Niamh's love for Oisin, the chief difference being that in "Dhoya" the lovers do not try to escape the mortal world—and consequently their relationship becomes the victim of the inevitable change. Yeats set the story long before Fenian times, but twice in the story drew parallels with Diarmaid and Gráinne.

At the time he wrote these early works Yeats was deeply caught up in philosophical speculations and occult studies and naturally tended to see the early legends in their light. But even before *The Wanderings of Oisin* was actually published, Yeats had found scholarly "support" for his interpretations. In a letter of October 8, 1888, he spoke of a desire to review John Rhys's "book on ancient Celtic religion," *Lectures on the Origin and Growth of Religion as Illustrated by Celtic Heathendom* [*Letters*]. His interest in this book is easy to explain: Rhys treated all the heroic stories as religious myths, Cú Chulainn, Fionn and the rest as euhemerized deities; and he constantly drew parallels between his Irish examples and Welsh, Continental, Classical, and Eastern legends. At this time or shortly afterwards Yeats was also impressed by the French scholar Henri D'Arbois de Jubainville's *Le Cycle Mythologique Irlandais,* which had been published in 1884. This book was not translated until 1903, and the apparent feebleness of Yeats's French may have made reading it difficult: possibly Hyde, O'Leary, or Maud Gonne (who knew de Jubainville personally) helped him or outlined its main concerns. It interpreted the early texts in a manner similar to that of Rhys, but with much more emphasis upon the Tuatha Dé Danann and the other pre-Milesian groups, and discussed Celtic conceptions of reincarnation and the other world. (pp. 242-50)

During the following decade Yeats found further support in Alfred Nutt's long study of Irish tales dealing with the other world. Yeats reviewed this study, which was written to accompany Kuno Meyer's edition of *The Voyage of Bran,* and asserted, "D'Arbois De Jouvainville's 'Mythologie Irlandaise [*sic*],' Professor Rhys' 'Celtic Heathendom,' and it are the three books without which there is no understanding of Celtic legends." By the end of the century this triumvirate seemed so important to him that he saw it as virtually the main force behind the literary renaissance:

> Most of us who are writing in Ireland now are dreaming of a literature at once romantic and religious, and . . . we search for the religious life of other times among old Irish monuments and legends. The work of Mr. Nutt and Professor Rhys and M. De Joubainville has made known something of the religious life in the Pagan legends, and the greater part of contemporary Irish and Highland literature has come of the discovery. ["High Crosses of Ireland," *Daily Express* (Dublin), January 28, 1899]

This was certainly too great a claim for such studies, but they had indeed been important in the development of his work from the time he read them, increasing his confidence in the approach he had already taken in using the old legends and providing him with further interpretations along the same lines.

In the nineties Yeats continued to use the myth materials as vehicles for expressing himself and his world vision. His two "Fergus" poems provide an interesting example. Fergus Mac Róich, as Yeats knew from O'Grady's *History* and other sources, was a warrior of tremendous prowess who was tricked into giving up his throne. Yeats disregarded this image in favor of the dreamy and most unwarlike monarch of Ferguson's "The Abdication of Fergus Mac Roy." In this form he was a suitable vehicle for expressing Yeats's "flight into fairyland" motif ("Who Goes With Fergus") and the pursuit of occult knowledge in which he himself was engaged ("Fergus and the Druid"). The "dreaming wisdom" Fergus obtained included the doctrine of reincarnation, which Yeats knew to be found in a poem attributed to the Welsh bard Taliesin and paralleled by de Jubainville with the "pantheistic" "Song of Amergin":

> I have been many things:
> A green drop in the surge, a gleam of light
> Upon a sword, a fir tree on a hill,
> An old slave grinding at a heavy quern,
> A king sitting upon a chair of gold.

In the same passage Yeats also drew upon Rhys's and de Jubainville's interpretations of the battle between the Tuatha Dé Danann and the Fomorians at Magh Tuireadh as a mythic version of the opposition of light and darkness, heat and cold, good and evil:

> . . . in my heart the daemons and the gods
> Wage an eternal battle, and I feel
> The pain of wounds, the labour of the spear,

But have no share in loss or victory.

[*The Variorum Edition of the Poems of W. B. Yeats* (In a footnote, the critic adds: "These lines were eliminated in revised versions of the poem.")]

The unfortunate end of Fergus's quest showed Yeats's awareness of the potential limitations of such a life. A related perspective appears in the story "The Wisdom of the King." In writing it he made use of the legend of Fergus Mac Leide, a king with a facial deformity the presence of which his retainers tried, and ultimately failed, to keep secret from him. Yeats would have known Ferguson's version of the story, "Fergus Wry-Mouth," but his immediate source was probably Katharine Tynan's "The Fate of King Feargus," for his plot is much closer to hers. While Ferguson had depicted him as a bluff warrior, she makes the king a sensitive, poetic man, thus opening the way for Yeats to blend him with his other Fergus. His character's philosophy had a familiarly Yeatsian ring: in order to woo his beloved, "he poured his wisdom at her feet, and told her how the heroes, when they die, return to the world and begin their labour anew; . . . and of the great Moods, which are alone immortal, and the creators of mortal things." But he loses her to a virile boxer and horse-trainer (who is not in either Ferguson's version or Miss Tynan's), probably reflecting Yeats's realization that he must be a man of action to win Maud Gonne.

The Countess Cathleen was an attempt to do with Christian Irish legend what he had already done with pagan sources: "to mingle personal thought and feeling with the beliefs and customs of Christian Ireland." (Yeats had included the story of Countess Kathleen O'Shea in *Fairy and Folk Tales,* believing it to be a traditional Irish tale.) But in the play, as in the narrative poem, Yeats brought one era to bear upon the other. In the first version he included, along with the "Who Goes with Fergus" lyric, references to the ride of Oisin and Niamh and to Edain [*The Variorum Edition of the Plays of W. B. Yeats*]. In revising the text for *Poems* (1895), he drew upon the *Magh Tuireadh* legend as a parallel to the struggle of Christian angels and devils for the soul of Cathleen:

Angels and devils clash in the middle air,
And brazen swords clang upon brazen helms.
[*A flash of lightning followed immediately by thunder.*]
Yonder a bright spear, cast out of a sling,
Has torn through Balor's eye, and the dark clans
Fly screaming as they fled Moytura of old.

The "spear" was hurled by Lugh, the sun god, whose killing of Balor precipitated the rout of the Fomorians.

The Shadowy Waters, which Yeats apparently conceived even before his dedication to national concerns, and upon which he continued to work after the emergence of the theater movement, contained at various stages a considerable quantity of mythological material. The work itself was not a retelling of any traditional Irish story, though Forgael's voyage with a woman towards an unchanging realm can be seen as simply another version of the personal concern expressed in *The Wanderings* by the ride of Oisin and Niamh. Because his central plot, being self-fabricated, was highly subjective, Yeats sought to surround and ballast it with as much traditional legend as possible. During the early nineties his main source was again the stories of the Tuatha Dé Danann and Fomorians and their conflict. At the beginning of the work Forgael is in league with the forces of evil, and the index of the psychological change he undergoes is his eventual resolution to love "none but the children of Danu." Yeats also worked in a reference to the youth and lady of *The Wanderings* (another indication of the connection between Forgael and Oisin) and an allusion to the birds of Óengus.

There was one disadvantage to this method, as Yeats revealed in an 1894 letter: "In my struggle to keep it concrete I fear I shall so overload it with legendary detail that it will be unfit for any theatrical purposes." However, he still believed in the truth of the principle, for he recommended it two years later in an article on "Fiona Macleod" [in *The Bookman,* December, 1896]: "Emotions which seem vague or extravagant when expressed under the influence of modern literature, cease to be vague or extravagant when associated with ancient legend and mythology." And when at the end of the century he took up the *Shadowy Waters* manuscript again he indicated—in phrasing that perfectly epitomizes the highly personal nature of his approach to the old stories—that such materials still played a key part in his plans:

I am working at my *Shadowy Waters* and it is getting on far better than when I left it aside a couple of years ago. Since then I have worked at Irish mythology and filled a great many pages of notes with a certain arrangement of it for my own purposes; and now I find I have a rich background for whatever I want to do and endless symbols to my hands. [*Letters,* 21 June 1899]

Yeats was, with considerable reluctance, persuaded to eliminate the Fomorians, but he compensated for the loss by expanding the role of Óengus. He now brought in the story of Óengus' relations with Edain before she become the wife of King Eochaid, interpreting it "in my own way." On the basis of dreams and visions experienced by himself and AE, he endowed Forgael with a harp supposedly sent by Óengus and having strings woven by Edain from Óengus' hair. The procession from *The Wanderings of Oisin* also reappeared; Yeats made it a more integral part of the new version by having the hound and deer function as signs to Forgael and Dectora, as they had before to Oisin and Niamh:

The pale hound and the deer wander for ever
Among the winds and waters; and when they pass
The mountain of the gods, the unappeasable gods
Cover their faces with their hair and weep.
They lure us to the streams where the world ends

Further proof of Yeats's later remark that "for a long time symbols of this kind had for me a very intense, a very personal importance" was the contemporary lyric "The Desire of Man and of Woman," in which the deer and hound were depicted as being in reality human lovers whose shapes had been transformed by Óengus.

After the turn of the century, Yeats occasionally directly revealed the personal element in works based on Irish myth. Thus, in *Baile and Ailinn* the parallel between the title characters and Yeats and Maud Gonne, implicit in such lines as "Being forbid to marry on earth / They blossomed to immortal mirth," is made explicit at the end of the poem:

> Let rush and bird cry out their fill
> Of the harper's daughter if they will,
> Beloved, I am not afraid of her,
> She is not wiser nor lovelier,
> And you are more high of heart than she
> For all her wanderings over-sea;
> But I would have bird and rush forget
> Those other two, for never yet
> Has lover lived, but longed to wive
> Like them that are no more alive.

Similarly in *The Old Age of Queen Maeve* he interrupted his description of the legendary character with the question

> O, unquiet heart,
> Why do you praise another, praising her,
> As if there were no tale but your own tale
> Worth knitting to a measure of sweet sound?

But during the inaugural period of the Renaissance, and generally even thereafter, he avoided such definite internal evidence. Consequently, awareness of his particular concerns in the rehandling of a given legend depends upon a combination of knowledge of the received form of the legend (so that variations will be apparent and their significance pondered) and of Yeats's personal vision and sometimes even his personal affairs. Nor can one always be sure even then. The early poem "The Death of Cuchulain" (later retitled "Cuchulain's Fight with the Sea") is a case in point. In a contemporary note, Yeats himself pointed out his source as Jeremiah Curtin's *Myths and Folk-lore of Ireland*, adding, "The bardic tale of the death of Cuchullin is very different." As Curtin gives it, the folk tale is far less noble and heroic than O'Grady's rendering of the "bardic" version in the *History*. Yeats's choice of the former suggests that it fit a need which the "better" story did not, and Richard Ellmann has suggested that he found in it a vehicle for expressing his own often antagonistic relations with his father. There is, however, nothing specific in Yeats's handling of the story to support this reading: he makes the young man Cú Chulainn's son by Emer rather than by Aoife (Curtin has simply "a son whose mother was called the Virago of Alba") and changes his name from "Conlán" to "Finmole," but neither of these changes point to a personal motivation. Yeats also added a scene in which Emer is told by a swineherd named Aleel of Cú's arrival with another woman. "Aleel" was obviously a name of personal importance to him at this period, for he used it in the first revised version of *The Countess Cathleen* as the name of the bard, and in one early draft of *The Shadowy Waters*, again for a poet, Dectora's lover when she is captured by Forgael. However, while the poet in *The Countess Cathleen* can easily be seen as representing Yeats, and while the same is true of the corresponding figure in *The Shadowy Waters* (Forgael's having him put to death reflecting the rejection of the more purely subjec-

tive, dreamy aspect of Yeats's personality by a more powerful, active side), any attempt to identify Aleel with Yeats in "The Death of Cuchulain" produces only confusion. The best arguments in support of a personal reading of the poem are therefore the choice of the subject, Yeats's contemporary practice in other myth-based works, and his repeated later use of various portions of the Cú Chulainn legend. Beginning with *On Baile's Strand* he drew upon it repeatedly to express himself and his world-view (*The Only Jealousy of Emer* and "Cuchulain Comforted," for example, both being full of *Vision*-type doctrine) and at the end of his life reverted to the "bardic" version of the death of Cú, which now fit his own situation better than the folk tale.

Throughout the early years of the movement Yeats propagandized for study and literary recreation of the legends, and even in the first article he published ["The Poetry of Sir Samuel Ferguson," *Irish Fireside*, 1886] praised their potential for "healing our nation" and helping Irishmen "to live the larger life of the spirit." It was not until 1892, however, that he made any public reference to the approach towards such materials that he personally favored, and even then he did so briefly and obliquely: "If we can but take that history and those legends and turn them into dramas, poems and stories full of the living soul of the present, and make them massive with conviction and profound with reverie, we may deliver that new great utterance for which the world is waiting" ["Hopes and Fears for Irish Literature," *United Ireland*].

He became more explicit as the years passed. In 1895, having predicted the replacement of the current "age of criticism" with an "age of revelation," he went on to suggest, "This revolution may be the opportunity for the Irish Celt, for he has an unexhausted and inexhaustible mythology to give him symbols and personages" ["Irish National Literature. III.—Contemporary Irish Poets," *The Bookman*]. Two years later, in an article on "Fiona Macleod," he referred to contemporary Irish writers taking "a peasant legend" and making it "the symbol of some personal phantasy" ["Miss Fiona Macleod," *The Sketch*] The influential essay "The Celtic Movement in Literature," which dates from the same period, placed the approach in an international perspective:

> A new fountain of legends, . . . a more abundant fountain than any in Europe, is being opened, the fountain of Gaelic legends. . . . "The Celtic Movement," as I understand it, is principally the opening of this fountain. . . . It comes at a time when the imagination of the world is as ready as it was at the coming of the tales of Arthur and of the Grail for a new intoxication. The reaction against the rationalism of the eighteenth century has mingled with a reaction against the materialism of the nineteenth century, and the symbolical movement, which has come to perfection in Germany in Wagner, in England in the Pre-Raphaelites, in France in Villiers de l'Isle-Adam, and Mallarmé, and in Belgium in Maeterlinck, and has stirred the imagination of Ibsen and D'Annunzio, is certainly the only movement that is saying new things. The arts by brooding upon their own in-

tensity have become religious, and are seeking, as I think Verhaeren has said, to create a sacred book. They must, as religious thought has always done, utter themselves through legends. . . . [The] Irish legends . . . have so much of a new beauty that they may well give the opening century its most memorable symbols.

And in one of the introductions he wrote for *A Treasury of Irish Poetry* he referred to the Irish poets seeking "to express indirectly, through myths and symbols, or directly in little lyrics full of prayers and lamentations, the desire of the soul for spiritual beauty and happiness."

Even these passages do not refer to specific instances in Yeats's own work; it was only in private letters that he became so personal. As a result, the readers most likely to have been aware of his approach towards the myth materials were those who knew him well or had a substantial knowledge of the traditional forms of the legends so that they could distinguish the idiosyncrasies in his treatment of them. When these circumstances are understood, it will not seem surprising that Yeats's example did not at once attract numerous emulators. Legendary works employing the "good story" approach continued to appear. Even the debased, stage Irish treatment calumniated years before by P. W. Joyce remained alive: in 1893, *United Ireland* printed (next to an article by Yeats) a story by P. J. M'Call entitled "Cuchullin and Emir," which reduced O'Grady's "noblest character" in all literature to a ludicrous clown. . . .

A few writers, however, did begin to treat the early literature in the Yeatsian manner.

One such writer was Larminie. His first volume, *Glanlua and Other Poems,* appeared in the same year as *The Wanderings of Oisin.* It contained, in addition to "The Return of the Gods," a short poem on Óengus and Edain, and the long titlepoem itself. There is nothing about the lyric to suggest a personal reading, and *Glanlua* seems a most unlikely vehicle. The plot tells the story of one Dohnal, a Firbolg monarch whose mother Morna, one of the Tuatha Dé Danann, has given him invincibility in battle. He is married to Glanlua, whom he loves but who despises him; they are said to be the parents of Cú Chulainn's future friend and adversary Fer Diad. Fergus Mac Róich and a warparty come and attack Dohnal, but all are slain except Fergus, who is taken prisoner. Glanlua develops a passion for him and, obtaining from Dohnal's mother the secret of his strength, reveals it to Fergus. He kills Dohnal and flees with Glanlua, but Morna arouses the elements and the birds against them, and finally forces Fergus to cast Glanlua into the sea, from which she rises incarnate as a crane. On Fergus, Morna places the curse that he shall lose his throne and be unhappy through love. The poem is laced with ghosts, skulls, and other bizarre manifestations of the supernatural and seems to represent an example of the "good story" approach used to create a gothic romance. A personal interpretation here would be almost out of the question.

Moytura, in Larminie's *Fand* volume of 1892, does reveal a treatment comparable to Yeats's approach. He not only equated the Tuatha Dé Danann with good and the Fomorians with evil, but also placed their conflict within a larger scheme of cosmic origins. His account begins with the creation of the world by the Tribes of Danu, brings in the evolution of lower forms of life, including dinosaurs, and culminates with the good gods, having routed evil, willingly turning over the earth to men and endowing them with various gifts. Larminie had read de Jubainville's *Cycle Mythologique,* for he quoted from it in his first book, and consequently could have derived the religious interpretation of the myth independently of Yeats, who had referred to it in articles but not yet used it in his own work. On the other hand, Larminie did know the old legends well, and if he had read *The Wanderings of Oisin* he may have sensed something of what Yeats was doing.

AE was a second writer in this category. In March, 1895, he published an article on "The Legends of Ancient Eire," and in September of the same year Yeats noted, "A.E. has begun to dig for new symbols in the stories of Finn and Oisin, and in the song of Amergin." AE himself formally stated his position a few years later, during the Eglinton controversy:

These dreams, antiquities, traditions, once actual, living, and historical, have passed from the world of sense into the world of memory and thought; and time . . . has not taken away from their power nor made them remote from sympathy, but has rather purified them by removing them from earth unto heaven: from things which the eye can see and the ear can hear; they have become what the heart ponders over, and are so much nearer, more familiar, more suitable for literary use, than the day they were begotten. They have now the character of symbol, and, as symbol, are more potent than history. They have crept through veil after veil of the manifold nature of man, and now each dream, heroism, or beauty, has laid itself nigh the divine power it represents the suggestion of which made it first beloved; and they are ready for the use of the spirit, a speech of which every word has a significance beyond itself. [*Literary Ideals in Ireland*]

The world-vision that AE was to employ those symbols to express was epitomized in his first article on the legendary materials:

Life is one; . . . nature is not dead but living; the surface but a veil tremulous with light—lifting that veil hero and sage of old time went outwards into the vast and looked on the original. All that they beheld they once were, and it was again their heritage, for in essence they were one with it—children of Deity. The One gave birth to the many, imagining within itself the heaven of heavens, and spheres more shadowy and dim, growing distant from the light. Through these the Rays ran outward, falling down through many a starry dynasty to dwell in clay. Yet— once God or Angel—that past remains, and the Ray, returning on itself, may reassume its old vesture, entering as a God into the Ancestral Self. ["The Legends of Ancient Eire," *Irish Theosophist,* 1895]

In that article he showed how this vision could be discerned in the legend of Oisin in Tir-na-nOg, and his interpretation makes an interesting contrast with Yeats's poem:

> We . . . are met on the threshold of diviner spheres by terrible forms embodying the sins of a living past when we misused our spiritual powers in old Atlantean days. These forms must be conquered and so Oisin battles with the Fomor and releases the power—a princess in the story. This fight with the demon must be fought by everyone who would enter the land of the Gods. . . . Tir-na-noge, the land of Niam, is that region the soul lives in when its grosser energies and desires have been subdued, dominated, and brought under the control of light; when the Ray of Beauty kindles and illuminates every form which the imagination conceives, and where every form tends to its archetype.

In the second installment he used in a similar manner Fionn, Diarmaid and Gráinne, and Cú Chulainn.

Soon, however, he began drawing most of his symbols not from the Ulster and Fenian cycles, but rather from the "mythological" cycle, that of the old Irish deities. This was quite natural: his vision, though unorthodox, was essentially religious, and a key element in it was his belief that man is incarnate divinity. The early Celtic mythology offered a ready-made pantheon, including some figures po-

A.E. (George Russell).

tentially equatable with the One and many gods in human form. Furthermore, AE seems to have had at about this time an actual visionary experience in which his world-view was represented by various members of the Tuatha Dé Danann. His efforts to embody that experience in a long poem lasted far into the next century and finally culminated successfully in *The House of the Titans,* of which AE wrote to a friend that it "does not follow legend. It is a symbolic treatment of the tale." Among the earlier poems using figures from the mythological cycle was "Twilight by the Cabin." This lyric began with a description of a peasant girl staring into the twilight from her cabin door. AE then equated her with Edain while the latter was in human form. . . . He also used Óengus in an 1897 story, "A Dream of Angus Oge," the god summoning a boy to come away with him to the realm of the immortals.

Perhaps the most imaginative and successful of all AE's interpretations of Irish myth is "The Children of Lir," a short lyric probably written at about the turn of the century:

> We woke from our sleep in the bosom where cradled together we lay:
> The love of the Dark Hidden Father went with us upon our way.
> And gay was the breath in our being, and never a sorrow or fear
> Was on us, as singing together, we flew from the infinite Lir.
>
> Through nights linked with diamond and sapphire, we raced with the Children of Dawn,
> A chain that was silver and golden linked spirit to spirit, my swan.
> Till day in the heavens passed over, and still grew the beat of our wings,
> And the Breath of the Darkness enfolded to teach us unspeakable things.
> Yet lower we fell and for comfort our pinionless spirits had now
> The leaning of bosom to bosom, the lifting of lip unto brow.
> Though chained to the earth yet we mourned not the loss of our heaven above,
> But passed from the vision of Beauty to the fathomless being of Love.
>
> Still gay is the breath of our being, we wait for the Bell Branch to ring
> To call us away to the Father, and then we will rise on the wing,
> And fly through the twilights of time till the home lights of heaven appear;
> And our spirits through love and through longing made one with the infinite Lir.

In the original legend (*Aided Chlainne Lir*) the Lir is a deity of ordinary, finite proportions and has none of the shadowy, mysterious grandeur of Lir as the "Great Deep" (to borrow a phrase from AE's note to the poem). AE substituted this image for the swan-children's father, so that Lir could represent the One and they the many springing from the One. Their sojourns upon increasingly more harsh waters then become, in AE's system, the stages of the divine soul's descent towards mortal existence. Once on earth the soul loses memory of its former nobility and finds satisfaction in human love, represented by the close bond among the swan-children. And the ultimate baptism and salvation of the children of Lir becomes the return after long ages of the many—conscious once more of their own divinity—to the One.

Certainly AE came as naturally as did Yeats to this way of treating the old legends, and it may well be that he began using it independently. The evidence for Yeatsian influence is primarily indirect: AE's intimate knowledge of his friend's work, and the fact that he showed himself to be conscious of Yeats's approach—and of its essential agreement with his own—in the exchange with Eglinton. Something must also be said of the possibility that Larminie's example affected him. Exactly when AE read the *Fand* volume is not known, but it is perhaps significant that his first full-length literary recreation of an Irish myth, a prose "Enchantment of Cuchulain," was based on the story of Fand. By 1898, in any case, he had not only read Larminie, but also found very sympathetic the vision and approach of *Moytura:*

> The genius of our modern writers has caught the last tales told in the cabins, and the dying fall of the songs: they have given them new meaning. They retell the old stories with a hitherto unknown splendour, and find in them a universal significance and fitting symbols for moods which never die. The battle fought in the tumultuous dawn-light of legend, between gods and demons at Moytura on the shores of the west, has been retold with profound spiritual significance by Larminie, and in his mystical drama it becomes the eternal battle between good and evil. . . . The battle is over in the heavens perchance, but it has yet to be fought out on earth, and the interest we feel in the antique story is that it is the fittest symbol for the conflict today. ["In the Shadow of the Gods," *The Internationalist,* 1898]

This passage was followed immediately by a poem on the subject by AE himself, "The Everlasting Battle":

> When in my shadowy hours I pierce the hidden
>   heart of hopes and fears
> They change into immortal joys or end in imme-
>   morial tears:
> Moytura's battle still endures, and in this human
>   heart of mine
> The Golden sun-powers with the might of
>   demon darkness intertwine.
>
> I think that every teardrop shed still flows from
>   Balor's eye of doom,
> And gazing on his ageless grief my heart is filled
>   with ageless gloom.
> I close my ever weary eyes and in my bitter spirit
>   brood
> And am at one in vast despair with all the demon
>   multitude.
>
> But in the lightning flash of hope I feel the Sun-
>   god's fiery sling
> Has smote the horror in the heart where clouds
>   of demon shades take wing.
> I lay my heavy grief aside and seize the flaming
>   sword of will.

> I am of Dana's race divine and know I am im-
>   mortal still.

The proximity of the poem to the comment on Larminie certainly suggests a direct connection, though in form AE's lyric is much different from the long, semidramatic *Moytura*. The periodical version of Yeats's "Fergus and the Druid" provides a closer parallel in that it uses the myth to express a psychological state and is similar verbally as well, with "the demons and the gods" waging "an eternal battle" in the speaker's "heart." Even if AE's turn to the old stories was spontaneous, his awareness of their literary potential may well have been reinforced by the twin examples of Yeats and Larminie, the two contemporary Irish poets he ranked highest.

Nora Hopper borrowed so much from Yeats that he must surely have influenced her also in her use of and method of treating the Irish legends. It is difficult to credit her with a genuine personal vision, but her myth-based works do have a distinctive characteristic, which might be termed "extreme deconcretization." This is well illustrated in her treatment of the Diarmaid and Gráinne tale, the prose story "Boholaun and I." The story is set at some unspecified but apparently modern period, and the author provides almost no information about the narrator of the story, one Maurice Cahill. Cahill tells how Boholaun, an ordinary ragweed by day, was transformed by the twilight into a fairy steed with "a shining silken coat of elfin grey, and a flowing mane and tail of hair fine as woven glass, and moonshine coloured." In a dream vision Cahill mounted the horse, and

> lough and valley flashed by us, a medley of green and grey, and next, sharp spears of mountain glorious with sunset: after that a blinding mist, and then a flash of pearl and rose that may have been a gate, and then—Ah! *then!* Asleep or awake, I slid from the saddle, and sank at the feet of a great and gracious figure, robed with mist. And as I lay at her feet, other figures came and closed about me, grave and splendid and stately, looking at me with eyes that probed my soul.

Maurice Cahill is really Diarmaid reincarnate, and one of those spirits is Gráinne: "The body of Maurice Cahill holds the soul of Diarmuid, and Grainne is weary till the twain come to her." The story ends with the narrator, who has returned to consciousness, yearning for the same reunion.

It should be clear from this sketch that very little of the original myth remains: Miss Hopper took up the strength of passion between the two lovers and used it to suggest the imperishability of the things of the soul. Her interest lay there, and not with the present, the fleshly, not with Maurice Cahill. Yeats felt that she had gone too far, that by using the legends in this manner she had stripped them of their power to counterbalance the subjective elements added by the author. Her uncertainty about specific settings seemed to him particularly unfortunate: "Our legends are always associated with places, and not merely every mountain and valley, but every strange stone and little coppice has its legend, preserved in written or unwritten tradition. Our Irish romantic movement has arisen out of this tradition, and should always, even when it makes new legends about traditional people and things, be haunted by places" ["The Poems and Stories of Miss Nora Hopper," *Daily Express* (Dublin), 1898]. The two other stories based on mythological materials, "The Sorrow of Manannan" (which stays fairly close to the original legend) and "Cuchullin's Belt" (which does not), are open in varying degrees to the same criticism. Yeats could not fully accept her legendary works, but he did recognize her as following the path that he had been the first to mark out.

By the end of the century, then, at least four writers had made use of the personal approach; and Yeats repeatedly, and AE more sporadically, continued to do so.

Meanwhile, some authors did continue to rely upon the "good story" method. "Ethna Carbery," for example, retold a number of tales in her *In the Celtic Past* (1902), using prose as her medium and modifying minor elements freely but adhering quite closely to the major outlines of her sources. . . . (pp. 250-69)

Rolleston's *The High Deeds of Finn* (1910) began with a theoretical statement of method recalling the comments years before of P. W. Joyce, Todhunter, and de Vere:

> My aim, however I may have fulfilled it, has been artistic, not scientific. I have tried, while carefully preserving the outline of each story, to treat it exactly as the ancient bard treated his own material, or as Tennyson treated the stories of the *Mort d'Arthur*, that is to say, to present it as a fresh work of the imagination. In some cases . . . I have done little more than retell the bardic legend with merely a little compression; but in others a certain amount of reshaping has seemed desirable. The object in all cases has been the same, to bring out as clearly as possible for modern readers the beauty and interest which are either manifest or implicit in the Gaelic original. [*The High Deeds of Finn*]

He knew P. W. Joyce's work and was aware of how he had changed the ending of the Diarmaid and Gráinne story from a "tough" to a "romantic and sentimental" one. In his own book he went even further, omitting the story entirely, "partly because it presents the character of Finn in a light inconsistent with what is said of him elsewhere, and partly because it has in it a certain sinister and depressing element [i.e., sexual passion] which renders it unsuitable for a collection intended largely for the young." A third writer, James Stephens, rehandled his sources freely, telescoping events to increase dramatic effect, filling in gaps in tales that have survived only in fragmentary form, and imbuing them with his own brand of delicate humor and whimsy, but apparently never used them as vehicles for self-expression.

Nevertheless, many of the more important Irish writers who turned their attention to the myth materials did treat them in what was essentially the personal manner. Thus, an already much retold story like that of Diarmaid and Gráinne continued to prove viable in the hands of such diverse figures as Lady Gregory, Austin Clarke, and James Joyce.

In *Gods and Fighting Men* (1902) Lady Gregory had sim-ply given the traditional version of the ending, and it is strongly hinted at in Yeats and Moore's *Diarmuid and Grania,* for the writing of which she prepared a synopsis of the legend (*VPlays,* 1169). But her own play *Grania* (1912) showed her taking a different course, retaining the apostasy but inventing a rationale for it. In the last act Diarmaid is brought in, dying. His last thoughts are all of Fionn—for whom his old affection returns strongly—and the world of men and battle. He has completely forgotten Gráinne, who finds herself ranked as nothing in comparison with the heroic life. After this she is of course very bitter, and her return to Fionn, whom she practically has to force to take her, becomes intelligible, even natural. Why did Lady Gregory make this change? The unusual modification calls attention to itself, and her biographer, Elizabeth Coxhead, has argued cogently that she was sublimating in the feelings of Gráinne her own frustration at the masculine society in which her closest friends moved but "from which a woman, through her talent as much a part of the movement as any of them, would be forever excluded."

Clarke's first treatment of the legend, *The Vengeance of Fionn* (1917), was a long poem full of hazy romanticism. Such modifications as he made do not suggest a strong personal element, but it may be that in the "flight" episode he found a correlative for some of the anxieties that later culminated in his breakdown. Fear and flight are also central in his second work employing the Diarmaid-Gráinne story, the novel *The Bright Temptation* (1932). But here he gave the legend a new interpretation or at least a fresh emphasis. The book is about the initiation into love of a youth and a girl in medieval Christian Ireland, and Clarke treated their innocent delight in each other as something beautiful and good. Throughout the book he repeatedly paralleled their love and flight together with the love of Diarmaid and Gráinne, which he suggests was equally innocent and beautiful. Furthermore, both levels are meant to function together as an oblique comment upon the repressive sexual morality in Ireland of the Free-State period.

The approach Joyce adopted in *Finnegans Wake* clearly falls into the personal category. He selected from among the many available stories those most adaptable to the highly idiosyncratic vision expressed in the book. In the interest of inclusiveness he referred in one place or another to most of the famous incidents in the life of Fionn, but the two most important elements from his point of view were the tradition that Fionn still lived and would return, and the Fionn-Diarmaid-Gráinne triangle. The former naturally appealed to him because it could be harmonized with the cyclical theories of history that dictated the structure of the *Wake*. He interpreted Fionn's fate in the light of Vico, as Yeats did retrospectively in regard to Oisin. Furthermore, Joyce's identification of Fionn as "the dreamer," while it has not been widely accepted, can in any case be seen as an improvisation upon the same tradition. And if he was familiar with Lady Gregory's reference to this part of the legend in *Gods and Fighting Men*, he must have found the version she gave attractive, for it included the suggestion that Fionn had already "been on the earth now and again since the old times, in the shape of one of the heroes of Ireland."

Not, of course, that Joyce felt himself in any way bound by received versions of the figure and his actions. His pleasure at finding a scholarly theory that Fionn was of Scandinavian origin came from having "discovered" the connection himself (in the same way he was delighted by the resurgence of Finland), and not from any scholarly reverence for the integrity of his sources. In Clarke's *Bright Temptation* the images and behavior of the more modern characters are reflected back upon their mythological counterparts, and something similar happens in the *Wake* with Fionn. His modern avatar HCE is a tremendously comic figure, and references like that to "the explots of Fjorgn Camhelsson when he was in the Kvinnes country with Soldru's men," an obvious permutation of HCE's crime in the park, transfer much of that comedy to the "heroic" level in a way that makes Joyce's Fionn contrast strikingly with the idealized heroes which other writers had sought in the early stories. Joyce's closest kinsman in this respect was probably James Stephens.

Fionn's relationship with Diarmaid and Gráinne fit without modification one of the basic patterns of *Finnegans Wake,* the old man loving a young girl and losing her to someone of her own generation. Joyce gave this episode particular emphasis by including a great many references to even small details: thus "Clanruckard for ever!," Clann Riocaird being the first place Diarmaid and Gráinne stopped in their flight, and "Three climbs threequickenthrees in the garb of nine," the nine Garbhs being henchmen of Fionn who lose their lives trying to dislodge Diarmaid from a quicken tree. He also exploited the comic potential of such details, so that the hound Bran's aid of the lovers emerges as "buy bran biscuits and you'll never say dog" and Diarmaid's "feats" become attractions in a circus sideshow—"Kniferope Walker and Rowley the Barrel", but he readily modified the order in which they traditionally occurred. Moreover, free of the prudishness which had characterized many of his predecessors, he quite openly emphasized the element of sexual passion in the incident, Gráinne's physical desire for Diarmaid ("The eitch is in her blood, arrah! For a frecklesome fresh-cheeky sweetworded lupsqueezer") and the calculating nature of her treatment of Fionn ("that . . . hot coney *a la Zingara* which our own little Graunya of the chilired cheeks dished up to the greatsire of Oscar, that son of a Coole.") Both points, of course, coincided with the general "triangle" pattern in the book. Most important of all, he found a new value in Gráinne's final apostasy. Gráinne as a young girl corresponds to Issy, but the older Gráinne who survives the death of Diarmaid becomes an ALP role, and "E'en Tho I Granny a-be He would Fain Me Cuddle" includes a reference to Fionn's continuing desire for her. Thus ALP's "Finn, again!" on the final page proclaims not only his "resurrection" but also her eventual return to him, and ties together the two major Fionn motifs.

In the middle of a section of the "Night Lessons" chapter dealing mainly with Tristan and Isolde, Joyce planted a few references to Diarmaid and Gráinne to indicate his awareness of the parallel nature of the two stories. The following passage adds another level to the parallel:

> Wait till they send you to sleep. . . . Then old Hunphydunphyville'll be blasted to bumboards by the youthful herald who would once you were. He'd be our chosen one in the matter of Brittas more than anarthur.

The primary allusion here is to the drugging of Fionn at the marriage banquet, but the final sentence brings in the adulterous Arthur-Lancelot-Guinevere triangle. It might seem surprising that Joyce did not connect this complex with the even more famous Irish story of Conchobor, Deirdre and Naisi, especially since Naisi and his two brothers provided a perfect embodiment for the "three soldiers" motif. Possibly the idea never occurred to him, though this seems unlikely. The passage quoted above from "Ethna Carbery," with its contrast between the morals of Gráinne and Deirdre, suggests another reason: the long-standing associations of the latter figure with purity and virtue make her much less suitable to his purpose.

In many ways *Finnegans Wake* was a literary dead end, but it did not have this effect on the Diarmaid and Gráinne tale: as recently as 1964, Eugene R. Watters drew upon its structure for a modern poem, *The Week-End of Dermot and Grace.* In that poem the flight of the legendary lovers underlies a romantic interlude in the lives of a post-World War Two Irish couple, with Fionn apparently represented by all the troubles from which they are trying to escape.

Even John Synge, who is more often thought of in connection with folk subjects and who spoke scornfully of the mythological figures and their literary use in "The Passing of the Shee"—

> Adieu, sweet Angus, Maeve and Fand,
> Ye plumed yet skinny Shee,
> That poets played with hand in hand
> To learn their ecstasy.
>
> We'll search in Red Dan Sally's ditch,
> And drink in Tubber fair,
> Or poach with Red Dan Philly's bitch
> The badger and the hare.

—turned to legend in his last play, *Deirdre of the Sorrows.* AE and Yeats had both written plays on Deirdre in the years immediately preceding Synge's decision to do so, yet when he was asked if he would not be accused of copying them he replied "There isn't any danger of that. People are entitled to use those old stories in any way they wish. My treatment of the story of Deirdre wouldn't be like either of theirs." His estimate was correct, for AE had given prominence to the druid Cathbad and Yeats had embodied in his version aspects of his response to Maud Gonne's marriage to John MacBride, while in Synge's hands the legend became a vehicle for personal feelings about imminent death and the ephemerality of mortal happiness.

This survey should illustrate that Yeats's early myth-based works occupy a pivotal position in the development of this literary mode during the modern Irish literary movement: before he began to write, variations upon the "good story" method predominated; in the mature years of the Renaissance the personal approach came to the fore. This change was certainly not due entirely to Yeats, but it must have received a powerful stimulus from his own repeated practice. (pp. 269-75)

> *Phillip L. Marcus, "Old Irish Myth and Modern Irish Literature," in his* Yeats and the Beginning of the Irish Renaissance, *second edition, Syracuse University Press, 1987, pp. 223-75.*

IRISH POETRY

Richard Fallis

[*In the excerpt below, Fallis examines Irish poetry published between 1900 and 1923, focusing on the contributions of A. E., Padraic Colum, J. M. Synge, and William Butler Yeats.*]

The Irish Renaissance began with poets and poetry, and it would not be an exaggeration to say that it produced little significant fiction or drama until at least fifteen years after it began. Nevertheless, once the movement had started in earnest, it gave rise to less poetry of lasting merit than fiction or drama for several decades. There were many poets working in Ireland in the first quarter of this century, but few of them wrote many poems which seem of much significance today. Thomas Kinsella, a distinguished Irish poet of our own time, attributes this to the presence of Yeats as too strong a poetic model: "As to Yeats's contemporaries, my own impression is of a generation of writers entranced, understandably, by the phenomenon of Yeats among them, and themselves going down in a welter of emulation and misunderstanding of his work" ["The Divided Mind," *Irish Poets in English,* edited by Sean Lucy, Mercier, 1973), p. 217.]. Kinsella is probably right, but even if there had been no Yeats, the Irish poets of this period would have faced some formidable problems. There was, at the most basic level, the problem of recognition; would it be possible for any Irish poet to find an audience inside the country and abroad? Beyond that, the Irish poet had to deal with the problem of Irishness in subject matter and style; how would he define his Irishness? Some poets did it largely by using something like the old style of the poets of *The Nation,* writing poems of patriotic sentiment in high, emphatic language. Other poets, looking to the more recent literary past, continued to find a definition of Irishness in the mysticism, reverie, and wavering rhythms of the Celtic Twilight. A few poets, influenced by the techniques of their English contemporaries, the Decadents and the Georgians, used urban impressionism and elaborate technical forms to portray the Irish experience. Yet others, looking to Douglas Hyde's translations from Gaelic and Gaelic poetry itself for models, found ways to create what came close to folk poetry.

Especially in the years before World War I, there were plenty of theories of how to write Irish poetry, and there were plenty of poets. The Dublin literary world of that time, like the one of today, was small and self-inclusive. Young nationalists and writers would gather at Seumas O'Sullivan's on Sunday mornings; AE held open house at his home in Rathgar Avenue on Sunday nights. Maud Gonne was At Home on Monday nights, Padraic Colum on Tuesdays, and when writers were not at someone's house, they were in the pubs and the newspaper offices. Joyce's description of the newspapers as Aeolian halls of the winds should not make us forget that they took an active interest in the literary revival. The daily papers, even the Unionist *Irish Times,* gave generous space to reviews of the work of the Abbey and the Irish writers. In addition, Ireland was beginning to develop a good range of literary and intellectual magazines. The *New Ireland Review, The Shanachie,* Standish O'Grady's *All-Ireland Review,* John Eglinton's *Dana,* the *Irish Review,* and even AE's farmers' magazine, *The Irish Homestead,* all played parts in the development of a significant literary culture. There was sometimes too much self-congratulation, rivalry, and laxness of standards, but Dublin was becoming an exciting place in which to be a writer.

Yeats used to refer to some of the younger poets as AE's canaries, and the bird image is not far wrong, for AE was a sort of mother hen to many of them, regularly clucking over his chicks. He taught them his philosophy, a pantheistic adoration of nature, and he argued that the essential value of Ireland lay in the primitivity of the country and its people. His own poetry was less an influence than his ideas and his personality. A few of his poems from after 1900 carried on the wavering rhythms and pale imagery of the Celtic Twilight successfully, but his poetic voice remained a faint one. One of his best poems, "Carrowmore," is attractive enough as an evocation of fairyland, but its images owe too much to the Yeats of "The Lake Isle of Innisfree" and "The Song of Wandering Aengus" for it to seem more than a good pastiche. AE taught his followers that "the province of a national literature" was "to create the Ireland in the heart," and his prose writings all during this quarter-century were valuable for their intelligent definitions of the relationship between the artist and his nation. The interest in Theosophy which he had shared with Yeats and others in the nineties remained important to him, although his work with Irish farmers taught him that the Ireland of the mystical imagination was a different thing from the Ireland of the bogs and the dairy farms. Nevertheless, his belief in the divinity of nature never wavered nor did his belief in an easy intercourse between the spiritual world and the human. AE's candor about his mystical experiences was sometimes disconcerting, as when he would show friends pictures he had painted of the spirits who visited him, but his spiritual autobiography, *The Candle of Vision* (1918), is a glowing interpretation of the visionary life. His insistence on a relationship between visionary experience and nationalism did much to establish among some of the writers the belief in the "national being" itself as a motive for their lives. It is unkind to charge so good a man as AE with racism, but there is no doubt that his acceptance of the idea of a collective Irish consciousness with emphases on spirituality and immateriality was a dangerous mixture of nationalism and mysticism. AE himself had nothing but good will toward others, but such beliefs could, and did, lead to the violence he deplored.

AE's greatest service to Irish literature, though, came neither in his poetry or his ideas. It came, instead, in his unceasing kindness to younger writers. Some of them may later have disparaged him as "Dublin's glittering guy" and laughed about the "at homes" in which a comment from Mrs. Russell would set him off on an hour's monologue, but he was, as Frank O'Connor said, the father of three generations of Irish poets. Among his "discoveries" were James Joyce, Padraic Colum, James Stephens, Frank O'Connor, Austin Clarke, and Patrick Kavanagh. AE's genius was for dealing with writers at the very beginnings of their careers, and often, as they matured, their allegiances turned from him to Yeats. Yeats was his closest and oldest friend, and yet there was often antagonism between them. Yeats envied his friend's ability to attract the young, and perhaps AE was dismayed by Yeats's toughness and egotism. Yeats's wife described the problem exactly when she told her husband that he was the better poet, but AE was a saint. One friend, when asked what AE was like, replied: "Well, there was the beard and the hair and the glasses and the brown, large clothes. . . . He was very large, he had a sort of wild look, but it wasn't wild with fury, he was wild with warmth and vitality and terrible interest in everything" [Comment of Lady Glenavy in W. R. Rodgers, *Irish Literary Portraits*.]

His interest in the young led him, in 1904, to sponsor the publication of a collection of poems by younger writers, *New Songs*. Some of the poets who appeared in it are thoroughly forgotten today, but it was an important volume because it introduced some good young talent and because it suggested that a new movement was coming in Irish poetry. The best of the poets in that volume turned away from the style of the Celtic Twilight toward new ways of interpreting the Irish experience. Often they replaced the mazy rhythms of the poetry of the nineties with an energy which came from folk song; in general, they avoided the legends which had attracted the earlier generation and wrote instead of the ordinary experiences of peasants, tinkers, and tramps. For the vague and evocative visions of the older poets, they substituted hard, clear pictures. The interest in peasant life which Yeats, Hyde, and AE had stimulated in the nineties led some of the younger poets to a fuller knowledge of traditional Irish music, Gaelic folk poetry, and English ballads. Love songs such as "My Love is Like the Sun," political ballads, and such masterpieces of the ubiquitous Anon. as "The Night Before Larry Was Stretched" and "The Willow Tree" were a far cry from the highly wrought Celticism of the nineties, and the younger generation benefitted from the concision, firmness, and energy of the old songs.

Padraic Colum wrote several poems which have by now become a part of the folk tradition in Ireland, and Colum was in some ways the best of the poets AE sponsored around the turn of the century. Born in 1881, the son of the master of a workhouse in Longford in the dull center of Ireland, Colum's first successes had come in his plays for the Irish National Theatre. He was a good dramatist, and could have been a better one, but the publication of

a little collection of poems, *Wild Earth,* in 1907, was perhaps his most lasting contribution to Irish literature. The influence of Douglas Hyde's translations from the Gaelic is strong in this collection, but the entire volume has a freshness and spontaneity which marked Colum as something more than anyone's imitator. Bryan MacMahon writes [in "Place and People into Poetry," *Irish Poets in English*] that "Colum's view of life is in essence that of the peasant as a noble savage endowed with the secrets of life and death. This valuable but somehow simple viewpoint is projected in poetry where not alone sowers and reapers but honey-sellers, drovers, blacksmiths, ballad-singers, bird-catchers, and tin whistle-players move in delightful but somehow silent mime." Not all of this is in *Wild Earth,* but Colum shows a good mastery of the dramatic lyric and a striking sense of the wonder in elemental things. "An Old Woman of the Roads," "The Plougher," and "Achill Girl's Song" are all sentimental poems, but their sentiment is the true one of folk song rather than the meretricious one of bad poets and cheap entertainers. As one commentator on Colum's work has written, Colum often shows a "childlike power to see straight to the soul of things" and thus "presents us with poetic experience in its most innocent and naked form." And, he adds, "Often there are no allusions, no symbols, only the simplest images, nothing but the singing tone and the thing itself " [L. A. G. Strong, quoted in Zack Bowen, *Padraic Colum*]. From the plainness of such poets as Colum has come one important strand in more recent Irish poetry, a strand of simplicity and openness.

Unlike Colum, Joseph Campbell was not one of AE's proteges, but he shared with Colum the ability to create a simple poem which seems to be the thing itself. He was, in fact, one of a number of writers from Ulster who were involved in a literary revival in their province which drew its inspiration from what was going on in Dublin and other parts of Catholic Ireland. He was involved in the Ulster Literary Theatre, Belfast's counterpart to the Abbey, in its early days. Moreover, Campbell did important work in collecting the folk songs of his province, and these, with their distinctive north of Ireland and even Scottish idiom, colored his creative work. His first collection of poems was unremarkable, but his second, *The Rush Light* (1906), showed an impressive awareness of the techniques and simplicity of folk poetry. The first stanza of one of his early poems aptly expresses his outlook:

> I am the mountainy singer—
> The voice of the peasant's dream,
> The cry of the wind on the wooded hill,
> The leap of the fish in the stream.

There is little of AE's mysticism in his work and less of Yeats's arcane symbolism; his interest in the precise presentation of experience led him to experiment with Imagism, the technique of modernist poetry which values clarity of objective pictorialization above all else. *The Mountainy Singer* (1909) contains much of his best poetry, but *Irishry* (1913), a collection of poetic impressions of peasant types, is perhaps his most characteristic work, a bit sentimental but moving in its honesty of observation.

As much or more than any other Irish poet of his time,

Campbell caught the voice of peasant song, and such poems as "The Ninepenny Fidil" and "My Lagan Love" have, in fact, become now part of Irish folksong. Most of his poetry from after about 1914 is disappointing, but his earlier work gives him a place as an important minor poet. Several religious poems, including the well-known "I am the Gilly of Christ," suggest his fundamental strength, the ability to turn the most complex sort of experience into something simple and precise. His most memorable images are often his simplest: the dancer with music in his feet and death on his face, the days of his life as a black valley in which silence is audible. He lacks some of Colum's energy and too often he confused sentimentality with sympathy, but "The Old Woman" is only one of many poems which seems right as only perfected simplicity can be:

> As a white candle
> In a holy place,
> So is the beauty
> Of an agèd face.
>
> . . . . .
>
> Her brood gone from her,
> And her thoughts as still
> As the waters
> Under a ruined mill.

If Colum is the representative poet of the midlands of Ireland in these years and Campbell of Ulster, then James Stephens is the representative of Dublin and the dream world of the Dublin slum dweller. Stephens did not appear in *New Songs,* but he was an important follower of AE, and his first collection of poems, *Insurrections* (1909), marked him as a major voice in Irish poetry. His subject is primarily the city; there is little interest in ancient legend or folklore. Natural or racial mysticism is largely absent; vague imagery and the desire for evocation are replaced by colloquialism and the sound of an ordinary voice:

> I saw God! Do you doubt it?
> Do you dare to doubt it?
> I saw the Almighty Man! . . .

Stephens owed a good deal to Browning for this colloquialism, and one of his best poems, "Mac Dhoul," is a kind of Irish revision of the end of Browning's "Fra Lippo Lippi." The plain talk and the almost breezy mysticism are welcome, but like Colum and Campbell, Stephens wore out as a poet too early, and his best work was done by 1920, thirty years before his death. Even so, his second collection, *The Hill of Vision* (1912), had such good poems as "Why Tomas Cam was Grumpy" and "What the Devil Said," and in 1918 he published what may have been his most interesting poetry, a volume called *Reincarnations.* The poems here are based on the Gaelic poets of the seventeenth, eighteenth, and early nineteenth centuries. Stephens did not intend to make scholarly translations; instead, his poems are re-creations in English of the Gaelic originals, and they catch much of their spirit and vigor. "A Glass of Beer," perhaps Stephens's best-known poem, comes from this collection; it is not characteristic of all the poems in it by any means, but its invective against the

serving girl in the inn who will not give the poet "the loan of a glass of beer" is unforgettable:

> If I asked her master he'd give me a cask a day;
> But she, with the beer at hand, not a gill would arrange!
> May she marry a ghost and bear him a kitten, and may
> The High King of Glory permit her to get the mange.

For even more potent invective, we could turn to J. M. Synge's "The Curse." One of Synge's ablest critics, T. R. Henn, feels that Synge's achievement as a poet was slight, and sometimes the poems do not seem as finished as they ought to be. But slight and casual as many are, they ring true to their maker's vision of life, his glorification of the roughness and energy of peasant Ireland, and his fear of death. Synge wisely observed that the poetry of his own time needed to learn to be brutal in order to become human again. That was good advice; Yeats took it, wrote some brutal epigrams, and then some intensely human meditations and lyrics. Synge himself never moved far beyond brutality, but his command of imagery is consistently striking, even in the violent tale of how a score of Erris men got "shut" of the Danny who was "playing hell on decent girls" and "beating man and boy." There is no romanticization of peasant life in the ballad of Shaneen and Maurya Prendergast who own just "a cur-dog, a cabbage plot, / A goat, and cock of hay," and very little Celtic Twilight glamor in "Beg Innish."

"The Passing of the Shee," written, the poet tells us, after looking at one of AE's pictures, is a satiric comment on vague and glamorous Irishism. Poets would continue to write in the Celtic Twilight manner long after Synge's death, but Synge was right in asserting that all that was finished for any real creative purpose:

> Adieu, sweet Angus, Maeve, and Fand,
> Ye plumed yet skinny Shee,
> That poets played with hand in hand
> To learn their ecstasy.
>
> We'll stretch in Red Dan Sally's ditch
> And drink in Tubber fair,
> Or poach with Red Dan Philly's bitch
> The badger and the hare.

Synge's abrupt dismissal of the Celtic Twilight, its gods, its style, and its ethos suggested one important direction Irish poetry would eventually take. But, historically, Synge was as ahead of his time in his poetry as he was in his plays and his vision of Ireland. He had no use for what he saw as nationalistic nonsense about his country, but some other poets still found in nationalism a powerful means of expression. The mystic vision of Ireland, the nationalism religious in its intensity, implicit in the early work of Yeats and AE remained an important factor in Irish verse as well as in Irish politics. For one group of poets and nationalists, in fact, the vision of Ireland was so real that they were ready to die for it. Only an extreme nationalist would now claim that Padraic Pearse, Thomas MacDonagh, and Joseph Mary Plunkett were important poets, but each died to give birth to a free Ireland in 1916, and their poetry and their nationalism were intimately connected.

Pearse's place in history is as the creator of the Irish Republic, but he was considerably more than the man who led the troops on Easter Monday of 1916 and read the declaration of Irish freedom. Born in Dublin in 1879, he worked for several years as a journalist and editor for the Gaelic League before founding St. Enda's School in 1908. At ten he had gone down on his knees to vow that he would spend the rest of his life trying to free Ireland, and St. Enda's was one way of carrying out that vow. St. Enda's taught its students in Gaelic and English, and Pearse, interested in educational reform, had even gone to Belgium to study that country's system of bilingual schooling. Nevertheless, St. Enda's real purpose was to teach patriotic idealism. Visitors to the school found in its entrance hall a mural of the arming of Cuchulain because Pearse's aim was to arm a generation of Irish boys with Cuchulain's courage, devotion, and passion for Ireland. A shrewd commentator has noted that Pearse "read the Ulster Cycle as allegory, as an image of the story of Calvary. Emain Macha was a kingdom afflicted with a primal sin that was redeemed by the blood sacrifice of Cuchulain. Pearse's writing, political or literary, is filled with the imagery of apocalypse and one must go to Revelation to encounter the Christ-Cuchulain figure that he envisioned" [William Irwin Thompson, *The Imagination of an Insurrection*]. In his poetry, as in his life, Pearse saw himself as a redeemer, misunderstood and maltreated, who would nevertheless redeem his people from their political bondage to Britain and their spiritual bondage to English materialism.

In Gaelic Ireland he found purity, passion, and purpose, and so he learned the language, bought a cabin in the west of Ireland, and even wrote poetry in Gaelic. Yet much of his poetry is far removed from the usual verse of Gaelic Ireland, for it is really an allegory of his own tortured imagination. There is a strong streak of asceticism, even masochism, in it; it is almost as though the beliefs of the Gaelic League and the most intense antiphysicality of Irish Catholicism had found expression in the language of a Biblical prophet. Such poems as "The Rebel" and "The Fool" have an impressive Biblical cadence in their parallelisms and repetitions, but they are also mawkish and embarrassingly self-pitying. His best play, *The Singer* (not produced during his lifetime), is just as clearly an autobiographical allegory. Pearse himself is surely MacDara, the wandering singer of patriotic songs, "shy in himself and very silent, till he stands up to talk to the people. And then he has the voice of a silver trumpet, and words so beautiful that they make people cry. And there is terrible anger in him, for all that he is shrinking and gentle." At the end of the play, MacDara's obsessions with his mother, patriotism, and sacrificial death (all obsessions Pearse shared) lead him out to die alone for his nation: "One man can free a people as one Man redeemed the world. I will take no pike, I will go into the battle with bare hands. I will stand up before the Gall as Christ hung naked before men on the tree!" MacDara-Pearse's death is to be, really, suicide, a death consciously sought for its symbolic significance. Padraic Pearse chose just this sort of death, a blood sacrifice which would redeem his people, and perhaps he could be dismissed as nothing more than a neurotic rebel if it were not for the incontestable fact that the death he and his colleagues chose was indeed a symbolic act which led to the liberation of their country. Pearse would rank as an insignificant poet if the idea of blood sacrifice for national redemption, so clearly stated in his poems, had not changed the course of Irish history and made him one of the truly prophetic voices in modern Ireland. Pearse's obsession with Mother Ireland lets him speak as archetypal patriot, a nationalist for whom death for a glorious thing is preferable to any sort of life. And perhaps it is not entirely accidental that the one great poem he wrote does not speak of himself or Mother Ireland but speaks as the voice of a human mother grieving and praying for the sons she has lost in the struggle for liberation; it is a sentimental poem, but a true and moving one. It begins:

> I do not grudge them: Lord, I do not grudge
> My two strong sons that I have seen go out
> To break their strength and die, they and a few,
> In bloody protest for a glorious thing,
> They shall be spoken of among their people. . . .

Pearse was not the only poet to die before the firing squads in 1916; Joseph Plunkett and Thomas MacDonagh died with him. Plunkett, who was only twenty-eight, published a single volume of poems, *The Circle and the Sword* (1911), but his work shows a strongly Catholic mysticism and a Pearse-like concern with personal sacrifice. Thomas MacDonagh was a more considerable poet and a playwright whose *When the Dawn is Come* was produced at the Abbey in 1908. Although he helped Pearse found St. Enda's in that same year, he spent much of his career as a lecturer in English literature at University College, Dublin. "The Yellow Bittern" shows that MacDonagh was alert to the voice of Gaelic poetry in a way Pearse was not; that poem and "John-John" could almost be by Colum or Stephens. Much of his poetry which comes out of his own imaginative experience rather than the Gaelic is conventional Romantic melancholy, and William Irwin Thompson may be right in suspecting that MacDonagh was fundamentally an intellectual who found that the intellectual can be little more than sacrificed in Ireland. Certainly, he was a shrewd thinker, and his posthumously published *Literature in Ireland* (1916) is an important study of Gaelic and Anglo-Irish poetry. In it MacDonagh rightly observed that any true Irish poetry must draw a significant part of its inspiration from Gaelic literature and that the "Celtic mode" created out of Standish O'Grady and the poets of the Celtic Twilight was based on a misunderstanding of the Gaelic tradition.

Yeats, in his great elegy for the poets and rebels of 1916 wrote:

> Hearts with one purpose alone
> Through summer and winter seem
> Enchanted to a stone
> To trouble the living stream.

But the Yeats of "Easter 1916" was clearly disturbed by the "excess of love" for Ireland which he saw in the rebels, an excess which had given birth to a "terrible beauty."

The road of excess may lead to the palace of wisdom, as Blake said, but the seeming excesses of Irish nationalism, of which the Easter Rising was only one climax, frightened Yeats. He had come into the twentieth century with a vision of Ireland based on his own idiosyncratic mixture of Theosophy, occultism, folklore, and Celtic saga, and even the disturbances at the premiere of *The Countess Cathleen* in 1899 had not completely shaken his faith in this vision. Those disturbances were, though, the first quarrel in an increasing controversy between the Yeatsian vision of Ireland and the nationalists' vision of political liberation, material improvement, a peasant-centered culture, and Catholic piety. Yeats would eventually announce furiously that "Romantic Ireland's dead and gone, / It's with O'Leary in the grave," but, in fact, O'Leary's kind of literary nationalism still had great truth in it, truth which Yeats was sometimes too egocentric to see. With his shyness, his haughtiness, and his interest in esoteric matters, Yeats was frequently out of sympathy and even out of touch with the Ireland of the first quarter of this century. But his detractors underestimated his immense imaginative power and even his rocky character as they laughed at his mannerisms. It has sometimes been said that the other poets in Ireland during these times had genius but lacked the talent to sustain it; Yeats had both, and through his bitter quarrels with Ireland and himself, he became the greatest poet in English of our century.

He sometimes spoke of his involvement in Irish affairs as a baptism in the gutter; those are strong words, but they are not entirely inappropriate as a description of his experiences in the Irish dramatic movement between 1899 and the death of Synge in 1909. The baptism turned the gentle and dreamy poet of the nineties into a combative man. Through writing plays, Yeats gradually learned to objectify even himself and his own emotions. When AE sent him a copy of *New Songs,* Yeats replied [in a letter]: "Some of the poems I will probably underrate . . . because the dominant mood in many of them is the one I have fought in myself and put down. . . . an exaggeration of sentiment and sentimental beauty which I have come to think unmanly. . . . We possess nothing but the will and we must never let the children of vague desires breathe upon it nor the waters of sentiment rust the terrible mirror of its blade. I fled from some of this new verse you have gathered as from much verse of our day knowing that I fled that water and that breath." The shift from poetry imaged as water and breath to poetry imaged as sword was immensely important to him, and the image of the sword reflected a new-found toughness in his own imagination. During the years of his day-to-day involvement in the Abbey and its affairs, he demonstrated a surprising particality and harshness. Sometimes his sharp tongue enraged the actors, but he proved himself an adroit manager of theatrical business. He told a friend in 1906 that Dublin needed "some man who knows his own mind and has an intolerable tongue and a delight in enemies," and his vigorous defense of Synge during the *Playboy* riots showed he was that man.

Some old friends lamented the loss of the gentle Willie Yeats, but in Synge and Lady Gregory he had found powerful reinforcements for his new self. Synge's relentless clarity and his call even for brutality in poetry stiffened Yeats's resolve to remake himself. Lady Gregory's Coole Park offered a place of seclusion and order in his tumultuous life, and Lady Gregory herself was a firmly supporting presence. In her he saw a living example of an aristocracy which had roots in the past as well as the courage and the stability Yeats sought. His father wisely observed that his son was a conservative at heart, and so he was. The new glorification of Anglo-Ireland was a conservative development of the old theories of the Celtic Twilight days: Anglo-Irish aristocrats and Gaelic peasants had much in common, he decided, and the praise of both, together with the attacks on the supposed materialism and religious narrowness of the urban middle class, became Yeats's way of asserting his primitivism and his belief that simplicity, nobility, and passion were the shared characteristics of aristocrat and tinker. Some of the glorification of aristocratic values was absurd, as when Yeats claimed that he ought to have been the Duke of Ormonde, but it enriched and broadened his imagination even as it made him a snob personally. For his poetry's sake, though, it was not a bad thing; the discovery of a deep-rooted past helped sustain his creativity through some difficult times and it led, eventually, to some of his greatest poetry.

That happened slowly, and admirers of the poet who bought his new collections of poems, *In the Seven Woods* in 1903 and *The Green Helmet* in 1910, were sometimes dismayed by the changes in his work. Much of the intricacy, some of the verbal magic, and almost all of the Celticism of previous volumes were gone. *The Wind Among the Reeds* in 1899 had opened with an evocative description of the Sidhe riding the air and calling, "Away, come away: / Empty your heart of its mortal dream," but the title poem of *In the Seven Woods* was a compact, freely rhymed sonnet in which vision still hangs in the air but our attention is drawn to the earthly woods of Coole Park and the poet's modest contentment in the Quiet that wanders among the bees and pigeons there. Maud Gonne shocked Yeats by marrying a soldier, Major John MacBride, in 1903, and in place of the earlier passionate love poetry, there is an aging and chastened voice. He insists that there is still folly in being comforted for his lost love, but he knows there are threads of gray now in Maud Gonne's hair, and much of the love poetry concerns old memories. Most remarkably, the Yeats of 1903 was willing to say what the Yeats of the nineties could not possibly have said: "Never give all the heart." The finest poem of *In the Seven Woods,* and one of the finest Yeats ever wrote, "Adam's Curse," is also a poem of disappointed love, but it is most impressive in its command of things which would become central to his later poetry: dialogue, meditation on the craft of poetry, closely controlled irony, beautifully plain language, and, at the end, a coalescence of image, thought, and emotion into a magically right stillness.

"Adam's Curse" has the inevitability of great poetry, but its rightness was something Yeats found only intermittently in these years before World War I. *In the Seven Woods* and *The Green Helmet* are both small collections, and Yeats wrote little lyric poetry during this period. The writing of plays and Abbey business kept him from that work, of course, but his personal and emotional turmoil cost him even more creatively. *The Green Helmet* is interesting for its identification of Maud Gonne with Homer's Helen and for its sharp little epigrams which show Yeats had learned much about concision and clarity from Synge and the poets—Catullus, Ronsard, and Villon—Synge loved. Still, it does seem, as Yeats said, that

> The fascination of what's difficult
> Has dried the sap out of my veins, and rent
> Spontaneous joy and natural content
> Out of my heart.

The death of Synge in 1909, a resumption of the unhappy relationship with Maud Gonne after her separation from John MacBride, increasing bitterness about Irish affairs, and a gradual disengagement from the Dublin scene marked the Yeats of this time. An expensive, multivolume *Collected Works,* published in 1908, looked suspiciously like a handsome end to his career; by 1910 he had accepted a pension from the British government, and there were those who expected him to live out his days as a conventional man of letters in London.

They were wrong, thoroughly wrong. Controversies in Ireland and bitterness over developments at the Abbey did cause Yeats to move back to London, but once there, he began again to rediscover and remake himself once again. The interest in the esoteric revived, leading to a new interest in mediums, spiritualism, and attempts to contact the dead; out of this, he gradually began to find answers to his questions about the supernatural and even answers about human personality, history, and creativity. In London, too, he met Ezra Pound, the American expatriate poet, who became his secretary and adviser. Yeats was furious when Pound edited some of his poems before submitting them to an American magazine, *Poetry,* but gradually he realized that his friend's insistence on precise imagery and clarity was exactly what he needed to continue the work of remaking himself as a poet. Pound also introduced him to some manuscripts of translations of Japanese Noh plays, and Yeats found in these a model for the sort of drama he now wished to write, an aristocratic drama of mime and suggestion which came still closer than the symbolist plays of the decade before to the theater of ritual and intimation he had always sought. The publications of George Moore's *Hail and Farewell* and Katharine Tynan's indiscreet autobiography turned his attention, also, towards his own past and his family's. His next volume of poems, *Responsibilities* (1914) reflected several of these new interests. It opens with an apology to his ancestors that there is "nothing but a book . . . to prove your blood and mine." *Responsibilities* has many sorts of poems in it, from the powerful invective of "September 1913" with its attack on an Ireland turned grubby and mean to the fragile lyricism of "To a Child Dancing in the Wind," but the collection as a whole is notable for a regathering of poetic power. None of the poems quite equals Yeats's best work, but they clearly show that the process of remaking was coming towards a successful conclusion:

> I made my song a coat
> Covered with embroideries
> Out of old mythologies
> From heel to throat;
> But the fools caught it,

> Wore it in the world's eyes
> As though they'd wrought it.
> Song, let them take it,
> For there's more enterprise
> In walking naked.

Still, Yeats was hardly ready, then or ever, to walk naked, and around 1917 he began to restitch his coat into a new mythology. In that year, after a final proposal to Maud Gonne and subsequent a proposal to her daughter, Iseult, he married an Englishwoman, George Hyde-Lees. Although he had had an interest in mediums and automatic writing for several years, it seemed to him almost a miracle when his young bride began to write out for him messages from the spirit world. At first, the messages seemed confused, but gradually he pieced them together into a coherent philosophy of life and art, a philosophy which taught that eternal, preordained change was the condition of history, that all kinds of human personality could be understood in terms of common types, that human creativity was an attempt to work out an understanding of one's self and one's inherent opposite or antiself. The theories Yeats eventually developed in his prose testament, *A Vision* (1925) were complex and esoteric, but their importance for his poetry lay in the fact that he believed them to be at least an approximate answer to the questions of human existence which had troubled him all his life. The theories, and perhaps marriage and its stability, liberated his imagination in an astonishing way.

His next two collections of poems, *The Wild Swans at Coole* (1919) and *Michael Robartes and the Dancer* (1921) were the products of that liberation. In poem after poem, he asserts his greatness. "The Wild Swans at Coole" itself is an exquisitely poised lyric in the Romantic nature tradition; the elegy for Lady Gregory's son, Robert, killed fighting in the British air force in Italy in 1918, is the first of a long series of personal elegies, a complex meditation of death, personality, and the creative imagination. Some of the poems, "Solomon to Sheba," for example, reflect the happiness of the married man. In the later volume, the title poem reveals a new sense of humor, and several poems in both volumes turn the anger and point of the earlier epigrams and invectives toward a new breadth. "Easter 1916" is a triumph of the plain style, an honestly doubting poem which carefully examines the poet's response to the rising in Dublin while admitting that in their deaths the leaders of the rising and Ireland itself have been "changed, changed utterly." Change becomes a dominant theme in *Michael Robartes and the Dancer,* and the poet who once had sought apocalypse now becomes a powerful voice for humane conservatism in a world changing violently and not knowing how or why it changes. "On a Political Prisoner" laments change at the personal level, regretting the politics that have turned Constance Gore-Booth, the old friend from Sligo, from "youth's lonely wildness" to a bitter and abstract mind. In "The Second Coming" Yeats finds the true prophetic voice as he gives us in his image of "A shape with lion body and the head of a man, / A gaze blank and pitiless as the sun" the ruling phantasm of our times. "A Prayer for My Daughter" offers one solution to the problems of a changing world and a pitiless future: let the soul recover "radical innocence" by driving out hatred and learning that it is

> self-delighting
> Self-appeasing, self-affrighting,
> And that its own sweet will is Heaven's will.

All through the 1920s Yeats's imagination would run free and wide, giving us some of the great lyrics in our language. He was by no means the only valuable Irish poet of his time, but he was the one whose works last. He never quite found the open-hearted simplicity of a Colum, Stephens, or Campbell; Synge was better at bitter invective; Pearse expressed a mystical nationalism Yeats was too complex to accept. Part of Yeats's superiority to his contemporaries lay in his astonishing command of the English language; is there any other poet who wrote so few bad lines? Part of his superiority lay in the intricacy of his mind and emotions; Yeats simply lived and experienced more fully than his contemporaries. In many ways, he was an outsider to Ireland; it is difficult to imagine him at Mass in the parish church, at the races at Fairyhouse, or gossiping in a pub. Often his themes and images seem far outside the mainstream of Irish verse, and yet he seems the most essentially Irish poet of them all, perhaps only because in his poetry he was most essentially himself. His presence on the Irish scene and his mastery of his art probably harmed the development of Irish poetry. He had too many imitators, in all his styles, and too many poets who were not imitators could only react against his work. Still, bet-

ter one master, with all the problems that implies, than a dozen evanescent talents. (pp. 116-32)

> *Richard Fallis, in his* The Irish Renaissance, *Syracuse University Press, 1977, 319 p.*

Patrick C. Power

[*In the following excerpt, Power provides a stylistic analysis of poetry written prior to and during the Irish Literary Renaissance.*]

Standish James O'Grady [greatly influenced] the poets of the so-called Irish Literary Renascence or Irish Literary Revival. . . . As far as supplying material for the poets is concerned, his was not the only influence, but nevertheless it was not inconsiderable and the style of some of the verse found a model in O'Grady's style of writing.

O'Grady took the old Gaelic tales, mythological and semi-lengendary and moulded an heroic literature out of them in English. His stories are wholly fanciful. The originals were legendary but they had a hard core of realism. O'Grady changed all this and his version of them is a veritable fantasy-land of words; a flight from reality. It is not without interest to note that he published them in his *History of Ireland.* O'Grady's style bears the same relationship to the original Gaelic style as his stories to true history; both are unreal, but the result is magnificent in its own way.

Here is a short excerpt from O'Grady's *History of Ireland* to illustrate the quality of his style. The writer is speaking of Cuchulainn:

> . . . and, as he thought on these things, lo! the dawn trembling through the forest, and the hoar-frost glittering on the grass.
>
> Then started forth Cuchulainn, and drew from the chariot the venison which he had cooked, and ate thereof, and drank his last draught of ale, making a gurgle in his strong bare throat, and his strength revived in him. Nevertheless, his countenance was hollow and wan, dull were his splendid eyes, and there was a wound in his hand and in his leg and in his left side, and his noble breast was mangled and all his body black with dried gore.

This was the style of writing that inspired Todhunter, Larminie and W. B. Yeats. Although it is not the style of the Gaelic sagas, and is often described as merely derivative, it must be emphasised that the literary Finn tales in Gaelic, such as *An Bhruidhean Chaorthainn* and *Eachtra an Ghiolla Dheacair,* are all written in a bombastic rhetorical style resembling O'Grady's. However, this does not apply to the ancient sagas. Years later, Yeats wrote of O'Grady these unconsciously ironical words:

> Standish O'Grady supporting himself between the tables
> Speaking to a drunken audience high nonsensical words.

But to a generation of Anglo-Irish poets, the disenchantment with O'Grady was all in the future. For the poets of the Cheshire Cheese in the Rhymers' Club, O'Grady was

---

Yeats on Irish literature:

[I have said] that all great literature is a battle. Tragic literature, as I see it, is battle in the depth of a man's soul. He feels the lack of something and he creates, as Dante did, the vision of divine justice. Beatrice dies, and he creates a vision of divine love. It would take me too long to give proof that the ecstasy of tragic art differs from happiness, because it can only exist with pain . . . whereas ecstasy is got when the intellect has shown you the whole vision of reality and you have brought your imagination to peace by bringing something from the invisible world, the compensating dream . . . you have completed the picture so that your imagination is at peace. Realism is a battle in the outer world; it is the contest of two realities, and we have come to realise that Ireland is in the midst of that contest. Out of that battle is coming our art, and it is because of the stupidity of our opponents. . . . The battle that began with Synge is going on for generations, and there is growing up among the young a passionate hatred of that row of china figures. They are beginning to break them one by one and as they continue our Press becomes more and more indignant. We have to bring together in Ireland the remnants of that old folk faith, giving us a beautiful romantic literature if we see it rightly. . . . Then we can create a great imaginative poetical literature for the internal and external battle.

> *W. B. Yeats, in a lecture delivered in 1913 and later published in* Theatre and Nationalism in Twentieth-Century Ireland, *London Oxford University Press, 1971.*

---

the one who gave them an *Irish* style to imitate and base their own on.

John Todhunter was one of the Rhymers' Club. He had written some verse before 1888 but after that he turned to Ireland and her past for inspiration. Todhunter was the first poet to write in the misty style of the Celtic school, whose master was Standish James O'Grady. In Todhunter there is posturing and lack of strength but the importance of O'Grady may be gauged from the fact that his influence could cause a mature writer such as Todhunter to change his style and direction in middle age.

Here is an excerpt from 'The Lament of Aideen for Oscur' which appeared in the volume, *The Banshee,* published in 1888:

> The wan woods are quailing
>   In the wind of their sorrow,
>   Their keene they might borrow
> From the voice of my wailing.
>   My bed's the cold stone
> By the dark flowing river
>   Ochone-a-rie! Achone!
> Thou art gone and forever.

Later on the O'Grady influence becomes more apparent and one finds this kind of writing which appears in 'The Death of Conlaoch' published in 1896:

> O Strand of the sorrowful waves! Oh Strand of
>   Bala!
> Once more
> The wind-swept grass of your dunes is my whis-
>   pering bed,
> and I hear
> The songs your sorrowful waves moan always
>   along the
> shore,
> The old stories your winds through the grass
>   come
> whispering in my ear.

Todhunter's inclination to a prosy verse is very marked at times, as in the above quotation. But this has nothing to do with his prose sources, it seems, because his verse before 1888 was inclined to prosiness except when he used a short line.

In Todhunter's Irish poetry one comes on what Dr. Robin Flower called 'the direct passion of the folk-singers' in Gaelic. A good example of this is found in 'Meeting' which begins:

> Oh! come to me in the morning, white Swan of
>   the
> thousand, charms
> Or come to me in the passion of day, the rapture
>   of the
> noon,
> Or come to me in the twilight hour, sweet long-
>   ing of my
> arms,
> In the hush when day kisses night our two hearts
>   beating
> one tune.

The passionate extravagance of this owes more than a little to O'Grady and it appears also in three other poems by Todhunter on love-themes viz. 'Parting,' 'Oh Day of Days' and 'Maureen.'

On another occasion, Todhunter happened to strike an undeniable Gaelic note. This was when he wrote 'Agha-doe.' This written in the style of the Gaelic ballads of the 17th and 18th centuries and surpasses even those Anglo-Irish street-ballads that are most Gaelic in style. 'Agha-doe' begins:

> There's a glade in Aghadoe, Aghadoe, Aghadoe,
> There's a green and silent glade in Aghadoe,
>   Where we met, my love and I,
>   Love's fair planet in the sky,
> In that sweet and silent glade in Aghadoe.

The use of the phrase 'planet of the sky' as a term of endearment is obviously a paraphrase of a Gaelic one, 'spéir-bhean' ('sky-lady'). Incidentally, J. J. Callanan's paraphrase, 'fair one of heaven' is more poetical.

In the second verse of 'Aghadoe,' a note of ferocity appears which is found in the Gaelic verse:

> Oh! my curse on one black heart in
>   Aghadoe, Aghadoe,
> On Shaun Dubh, my mother's son in
>   Aghadoe,
>   When your throat fries in hell's drouth,
>   Salt the flame be in your mouth,
> For the treachery you did in Aghadoe.

Nowadays, John Todhunter's poetry is read only as a literary curiosity, apart from 'Aghadoe.' As to the rest of his poetry on Gaelic themes, he depended almost completely on his literary sources and his work often sounds like a mere literary exercise. It was a case of art for art's sake and not very good art at that. Todhunter was completely cut off from the living Gaelic tradition by his long residence abroad, his ignorance of Gaelic and his lack of contact with even English-speaking Irishmen who were close to the Gaelic tradition. Todhunter depended on O'Grady mainly for his Gaelic inspiration, and he thus helped to create a poetic school whose style was based on a literature he did not know and for a people from whom he was largely cut off. The same remarks apply to William Larminie.

If only for writing one poem, 'The Dead at Clonmacnoise,' T. W. Rolleston deserves some notice in any work on Anglo-Irish poetry. But there is a further very good reason for speaking of him, for he was one of the Rhymers' Club out of which arose the Irish Literary Society in London in 1891 with Yeats, Todhunter and others, and which led directly to that flowering of Anglo-Irish literature which is usually described as an Irish Literary Revival or Renascence.

Like his companions, he came under O'Grady's influence also. W. P. Ryan, one of the founder-members of the Irish Literary Society, said in 1894:

'The reading some ten years ago of Standish O'Grady's *Heroic Ireland,* was a turning point in his intellectual career!'

But Rolleston did not confine himself to Gaelic themes in his literary work and a mere handful of verses is all that he left behind him as a reminder of his interest in a poetry created on Gaelic models. Geoffrey Taylor says:

'His verse is, on the whole, undistinguished, but "The Dead at Clonmacnoise," is, I think, the best Irish poem of the nineteenth century.'

The poem is based on a Gaelic one but is in many ways original. Here is the second stanza:

> There beneath the dewy hillside sleep the noblest
> 　Of the clan of Conn,
> Each below his stone; his name in branching
> 　Ogam
> And the sacred knot thereon:

The delicacy of touch which Rolleston shows here, appears also in another poem on a Gaelic theme, 'The Grave of Rury,' which speaks of Cong Abbey where Ruaidhrí Ó Conchubhair, the last High King of Ireland is buried. Here are the first two verses.

> Clear as air, the western waters
> 　evermore their sweet unchanging song
> Murmur in their stony channels
> 　round O'Conor's sepulchre in Cong.
>
> Crownless, hopeless, here he lingered;
> 　felt the years go by him like a dream,
> Heard the far-off roar of conquest
> 　murmur faintly like the singing stream.

The dream-like quality of this style owes much to O'Grady but there is a sureness of touch here which Todhunter and Larminie lacked. It is to be regretted that Rolleston wrote so little in this fine style.

In the poetry of W. B. Yeats, we find not only the result of mere literary influences but also of the living tradition of Ireland derived ultimately from Gaelic. The ways of the street-ballads were not above his notice, neither did he hesitate to notice the noisy jingles of the political ballad-makers of Young Ireland. In fact, Yeats endeavoured to make himself the literary heir of all the diverse elements that made up the tradition of Anglo-Irish verse before his time. To quote his own words:

> Know that I would accounted be
> True brother of that company
> Who sang to sweeten Ireland's wrong,
> Ballad and story, rann and song . . .

Yeats was in a particular way the heir of the Gaelic tradition in his attitude to the literary heritage of Ireland, his feeling for style, the way in which he devoted his attention to technique and, above all, in his pride in the profession of poetry. It should be remembered that the person of the poet was sacred in ancient Ireland and he alone could cross hostile borders with impunity. Vivian Mercier says:

> Their Irish background gave (or at any rate offered) Joyce and Yeats those four priceless gifts: contact with a living folklore and thus with myth; contact with a living folk-speech; a traditional sense of the supreme importance of technique to a writer, coupled with the realisation that technique must be learned, by imitation, study and practice.

But one cannot advance seriously the opinion that Yeats'

poetry is Gaelic in its style throughout. One thing that inhibited him in this matter was his lack of a working knowledge of Gaelic. His sources were all second-hand—texts in translation, Anglo-Irish folklore derived from Gaelic and the works in English of Lady Gregory and John Synge. He never bothered to learn Gaelic and go to the original sources.

Yeats' early poetry is art pure and simple and a flight from realism. The first poem in this period which is based on Gaelic sources and attracted notice to him as a purely Irish poet is 'The Wanderings of Oisin.' In later times, Yeats himself was far from being satisfied with it. Louis Mac Neice says:

'As for the long narrative poem, "The Wanderings of Oisin" itself, it is very derivative (he later considered it to be full of the Italian colour of Shelley) and no more Irish than Tennyson's "Voyage of Maeldune." '

Despite the truth of this statement, the poem does have some features in its style which are borrowed from Gaelic literature. For example, there are phrases here and there that come directly from Gaelic. In one case Yeats describes Hell in this way:

> Where the flesh of the foot-sole clingeth on the
> 　burning stones . . .

And in yet another place, Hell is described as 'flaming stones'. It happens that in Gaelic verse, Hell is described regularly as 'leaca na bpian', 'the flag-stones of pains'. In another place in his poem, Yeats makes Oisin remark to Padraic when the latter urges him to embrace Christianity, that he would spend his life in that case

> Awaiting in patience the straw-death,
> croziered one, caught in your net.

This term 'straw-death' is similar to the Gaelic 'bás le hadhairt' i.e. 'pillow-death' because in ancient times, pillows were made of straw. The reference here is to the disgrace it was for a warrior to die peacefully in bed.

However, throughout 'The Wanderings of Oisin,' Yeats uses a style that owes little to Gaelic literature. He uses phrases like 'soft her eyes like funeral tapers' and shows that he had not yet learned to avoid the epithet that was pretentious and artificial and was still like Sigerson and those who 'shuddered at all that was not obviously and notoriously refined'.

There is another criticism of 'The Wanderings of Oisin' by the poet himself which is worth a little scrutiny. He says:

'Years afterwards when I had finished "The Wanderings of Oisin," dissatisfied with its yellow and its dull green, with all that overcharged colour inherited from the romantic movement, I deliberately re-shaped my style . . . '

One cannot deny that there is plenty of colour in the poem, but a count of the colours mentioned and the frequency of their occurrence gives interesting results:

Colours are mentioned eighty-two times throughout the poem. Of these, eight are greens and one is yellow. Whites are predominant and there are twenty-nine of them in all. This is very interesting when one counts the colours in all the verse extant written by a typical Bard such as Tadhg Dall Ó hUiginn. Here also the whites predominate, in fact they account for about half of all the colours mentioned. And so, not only is Yeats shown to be incorrect in his remark but also he uses the same predominant colour as one of the last of the Gaelic Bards. Since the choice in both cases must, of necessity, have been subconscious, it is all the more significant for that reason.

Of all the poems of Yeats on Gaelic mythological themes, none illustrates so well the influence of O'Grady on his style as a short poem called 'The Valley of the Black Pig.' One does not always find such a resemblance between Yeats and another writer as in this. Here is an excerpt from it:

> The dews drop slowly and dreams gather: un-
>   known spears
> Suddenly hurtle before my dream-awakened
>   eyes,
> And then the clash of fallen horsemen and the
>   cries
> Of unknown perishing armies beat about my
>   ears.
> We who still labour by the cromlech on the
>   shore,
> The grey cairn on the hill . . . bow down to you,
> Master of the still stars and of the flaming door.

This was published in 1899 but even in 1904 there is the glimpse of a more vigorous and a starker style in a little epigram of four lines commenting on whether or not he should praise some indifferent poets who were imitators of his style:

> You say, as I have often given tongue
> In praise of what another's said or sung,
> 'Twere politic to do the like by these;
> But was there ever dog that praised his fleas?

This is not unlike what that master of salty invective and satire, Dáithí Ó Bruadair, might have written in Gaelic.

One aspects of Yeats' style is his particular use of Gaelic mythology which is quite unlike that of Ferguson, for example, or of any of the other Anglo-Irish poets. Hilary Pyle says on this point:

'Only Yeats had the intuition to see that writers with a background of the Ascendancy could never be completely at home in an adopted tradition. Irish legends provided much symbols for his poetry . . . and the power of his symbols lies in the essence he derived from them rather in the fact that they are Irish.'

One sees the beginning of this in 'The Wanderings of Oisin.' The basic narrative is purely Gaelic, of course, but one feels that the poet was giving expression to something that the Gaelic writer never intended. The latter was telling a wonder-tale; the former was indulging in a kind of Pre-Raphaelite escapism from reality on the wings of an old story.

'The Song of Wandering Aengus' is full of the Gaelic-derived symbolism. The distracted Aengus cut a wand of the hazel tree (a tree sacred to the Druids) and with a berry on it caught a silver trout. (A fish figures in Gaelic saga as the source of omniscience). Then Aengus sees 'a

glimmering girl' who fades away leaving him distracted. All this recalls the ancient 'Aisling Oengusso' of Gaelic literature where a vision of a girl which fades sway leads the visionary to madness. But Yeats changes it somewhat and transposes it into an atmosphere of unGrady-like simplicity. Here is the vision being introduced:

> When I laid it on the floor
> I went to blow the fire a-flame
> But something rustled on the floor
> And someone called me by my name.

The poem 'Red Hanrahan's Song about Ireland' is also full of symbolism. In the first stanza, which was quoted in the chapter, 'Metrics', one reads of 'black wind'. In Gaelic, the winds are described by colours still, but long ago there was an elaborate system of wind-colours as the ancient text *Saltair na Rann* proves. The north wind was black and, furthermore, such a wind was a bad omen. The thorn tree was the sacred tree of the fairies and misfortune came when a thorn tree was broken or destroyed. Finally, the name 'Cathleen, the daughter of Houlihan' was a poetic name for Ireland.

In the 'Withering of the Boughs' Yeats evokes a famous Gaelic story-motif in these two lines:

> I know of the sleepy country, where swans fly
>   round
> Coupled with golden chains, and sing as they
>   fly . . .

It should be recalled that Étaín and her lover, Midir, eloped from the house of Étaín's husband joined together with golden chains. Yeats found the same motif in the story of Baile and Aillinn, a story which he made his own in verse. The chained swans symbolise liberation from the cares of life as well as untramelled love.

Yeats occasionally tried to write in the style which he found in the translations of *Love-Songs of Connacht* by Dr. Douglas Hyde. In these, poetry is made from the ordinary things of daily life and is sometimes full of naivete. Here is part of Yeats' poem 'To An Isle in the Water' which seems to be modelled on Hyde's translations:

> Shy one, shy one,
> Shy one of my heart,
> She moves in the firelight
> Pensively apart.
>
> She carries in the dishes,
> And lays them in a row,
> To an isle in the water
> With her would I go . . .

But there is more than one example of the effect that Hyde's work had on his style. Let us look, for example, at 'My Paistin Finn' which is found in the farce *The Pot of Broth* (1902) Apart from the fact that the poem has the title and first line of a Gaelic poem of the same name, this kind of thing is found:

> I would that I drank with my love on my knee,
> Between two barrels at the inn . . .

Is it too much to say that he found his idea in Hyde's 'An Tuirse 'san Brón' where this line is: 'A sprightly bohaleen / that would coax awhile on his knee,'? Hyde, also, made a translation of the Gaelic *Páistin Fionn.* In another poem of Yeats, 'The Ragged Wood,' there are definite Gaelic-type phrases which he may have got from Hyde. Here are some lines from Yeats:

> . . . (the) Pale silver-proud queen-woman of
> the sky . . .

> . . . O my share of the world, O yellow
> hair . . .

It just happens that Hyde has in his version of 'An Bhrigh-deach' these phrases: '. . . Fine long yellow hair . . . ', '. . . the bright brown sky-lady, Who is after destroying my heart'. It is possible that Yeats picked up these phrases in that source. At all events they are thoroughly Gaelic.

Synge was another writer who influenced Yeats in the early years of this century and the influence might be described as Gaelic, although very much at second hand. It is not at all comparable to Hyde's in this respect. The beggar poems in the 1914 volume of Yeats' verse, *Responsibilities,* seem to have all been a result of the influence of Synge. A good example of what this meant in Yeats' style is found in this extract from 'The Hour before Dawn' which recalls the tramp in the play *The Shadow of the Glen:*

> The beggar in a rage began
> Upon his bunkers in a hole,
> 'It's plain that you are no right man
> To mock at everything I love,
> As if it were not worth the doing.
> I'd have a merry life enough
> If a good Easter wind were blowing,
> And though the winter wind is bad
> I should not be too down in the mouth
> For everything you did or said
> If but this wind were in the south.'

The syntax has definite signs of Gaelic influence here, mixed with forms seldom if ever used by Irish people, such as the 'were' in the fifth and last lines above. 'Was' is the proper Anglo-Irish word in both these places.

To sum-up: Yeats' style shows some signs of Gaelic influence but this is only a part of the general tapestry. Many things came to its formation; Pre-Raphaelitism, O Grady's prose works and Synge's plays with their dialect. The street-ballad did not have any influences such as that of the French Symbolists. He did succeed in forming something distinctively Irish with certain Gaelic elements in it but, as has been said somewhere, 'he was disposed rather to halt and counter than to continue and round-off the work of Mangan and Ferguson'. That about summarises the position. It is of some significance that the greatest poet that Ireland has ever produced should be ignorant of Gaelic. It may have done him good; he was not obsessed by the ghost of the last remnants of Gaelic literature, as others were later.

In Pádraic Colum's poetry, we hear the voice of the folk-singer; the ballad-maker who has written in a manner akin to the Gaelic poets. In Colum's verse, as in the verse of the 18th century Gaelic poets, there is the same narrowness of scope as well as the same simplicity and even naivete. The chief literary influences on Colum's style seem to have

been Yeats and Sigerson, but he does not have the scope of the former nor the Victorian style of the other. But there was also Hyde and he may be said to have been the most influential of those who affected the style of Pádraic Colum. Beside his influence, that of the other two is negligible.

Like the Gaelic poets, Colum has an inability to 'sustain long works'. His long poem *Lowry Maen* is tedious. The same thing cannot be said about the short lyrics he wrote. For example, there is 'The Mountaineer' which concerns the poor hill-man who looks at the pillar-stone over an ancient burial and remembers that he too belongs to the old order that is gone, and dispossessed by the British. His final thought is

> But he remembers
> The pillar-stone
> And knows he is
> Of the race of Conn.

'The Ballad of Downal Bawn' has been referred to already. It shows Gaelic influence in a marked way. For instance there is the use of Gaelic-type syntax such as this:

> The hound in his loop by the fire.

Furthermore, there are the references to the traditional story-lore of the people, such as:

> The hoard of the men who had raised the
> mounds,
> Who had brewed the heather ale.

This is a reference to the two beliefs about the Vikings viz. that they had a secret method of brewing heather-ale which had died with them and that they were the ones who built the prehistoric tumuli in Ireland. Another poem which enshrines a reference to the story-telling of the country-people borrowed from Gaelic are the lines from 'The Drover':

> And my mind on white ships
> And the King of Spain's daughter.

Colum shows the absence of mere mawkishness and sentimentality especially in poems such as 'The Landing.' It is an 'exile-poem', a type very common in both Gaelic folk-song and more sophisticated Gaelic verse. Here are some lines from it:

> . . . And names are called and spoken—
> 'Nancy', 'Mary', 'Owen',
> 'Goodbye, and keep your promise!'
> Farewell to you, my son!

> Green, greener grows the foreland
> Across the slate-green sea,
> And I'll see faces, places,
> That have been dreams to me.

This is the simplicity of the Gaelic folk-singer. The naivete and uncomplicated mind of the Gaelic peasant poet is found in much of Colum's poetry but there is one group of poems which reflects it more than any other; they are his three poems on tramp women in *Wild Earth.* The best-known one of them is 'The Old Woman of the Roads' but more typical of Colum's style is the one entitled 'What the

Suiler said as she lay by the fire in the farmer's house': It is the tramp-woman's day-dream of an easy life:

> I'd lie up in my painted room
> Until my hired girl would come . . .

This, however, she can do only if she 'had the good red gold'. Her concluding remark is the pathetic statement:

> And it's well for them whose bit is sure.

Colum makes judicious use of dialect, much of which is of Gaelic origin. Some of the above quotations illustrate this. The type of dialect is different from Synge's in that it is more restrained and as Yeats says: 'Unlike Synge's and Lady Gregory's, his is the dialect of the non-Irish-speaking district.' Here is a typical verse from 'Interior':

> The sons that come home do be restless,
>   They search for the thing to say;
> Then they take thought like the swallows,
>   And the morrow brings them away.

Colum is not only the folk-singer but, more than that, he is the sophisticated one who brings to his art the ability to sketch in rapidly the salient points well. Unlike Yeats, he was very much inside the life of the Ireland he sang of; an Ireland with a Gaelic heart. Yeats was often a little outside it but he had much wider horizons. This is what Colum lacks.

Francis Ledwidge's verse has been described thus by Padraic Colum: 'Francis Ledwidge's is the poetry of the plain—specifically of the demesne land that is the county of Meath.' This alone makes him an Irish poet but not necessarily indebted to the old Gaelic literary tradition. And this is how it was until the last year of his life when a different note begins to be heard. But he was killed before full maturity.

The early poems are full of biblical and classical allusions in the conventional English poetic tradition, such as

> And drooping Ruth-like in the corn
> The poppies weep the dew.

> And meads begin to rise like Noah's flood.

> When will was all the Delphi I would heed.

And so on. It often sounds like Keats. There are the same sensuous lines overflowing into one another. For instance, there are these lines from 'The Vision on the Brink.'

> Jonah is hoarse in Nineveh—I'll lend
> My voice to save the town—and hurriedly
> Goes Abraham with murdering knife and Ruth
> Is weary in the corn. Yet will I stay,
> For one flower blooms upon the rocks of truth,
> God is in all our hurry and delay.

Then at the beginning of the last year of his life, a change came. The Easter Rising of 1916 had come and gone and Ledwidge's loyalties were divided between the country in whose army he served and his own which was under the heel of his fellow-soldiers. This seems to have caused him to turn to a more Gaelic mode in the last year of his life.

One of these is 'Had I a Golden Pound' which is quite different from anything he had written heretofore. It is the folk-song with the Gaelic echo in it. Here is a verse from it:

> Had I a golden pound to spend,
>   My love would mend and sew no more,
> But I would buy her a little quern,
>   Easy to turn, on the kitchen floor.

This is the new Ledwidge who also wrote a few poems about the Rising. One is on MacDonagh, another on the execution of poets after the Rising which he entitled 'The Blackbirds.' In this poem he represents Ireland as an Old Woman, a Gaelic poetic convention. Here are some lines from this delightful lyric:

> I heard the Poor Old Woman say:
>   'At break of day the fowler came
> And took my blackbirds from their songs
>   Who loved me well through shame and blame.

> 'No more from lovely distances
>   Their songs shall love me mile by mile,
> Nor to sweet Ashbourne call me down
>   To wear my crown another while.'

This new style never came to maturity. Time was running out on the soldier-poet. Shortly before his death in the Flanders' battles of 1917, he wrote a little poem in a palpably Gaelic style which he called 'Fate' and in it he predicted his death. He said:

> These things I know in my dreams,
>   The crying sword of Lugh,
> And Balor's ancient eye
>   Searching me through,
> Withering up my songs
>   And my pipe yet new.

Perhaps, it is the fame earned by his plays that has made John Millington Synge so little known as a poet. There is also the important fact, of course, that he wrote so little verse but of this. L. A. G. Strong makes the astonishing assertion that 'Great as his influence has been upon the theatre, it may well be that as a poet he will best prove to have been the prophet of a new time.'

It is noteworthy that the same Synge who wrote his plays in an English markedly like Gaelic, modelled on it, in fact, should avoid this completely in his verse. For the arty style of AE and some others; Synge would substitute the realities of life as he saw them in the West of Ireland:

> We'll stretch in Red Dan Sally's ditch,
>   And drink in Tubber fair,
> Or poach with Red Dan Philly's bitch
>   The badger and the hare.

This cannot be said to be based on Gaelic literature, yet there is some link between the two here. At all events, it is the life of the Gaeltacht. To anyone remembering the young Yeats' dreams of beans and honey on Inisfree, this vignette of life in the real Gaeltacht from 'Patch-Shaneen' is almost piquant:

> Shaneen and Maurya Prendergast
>   Lived west in Carnareagh,
> And they'd a cur-dog, a cabbage plot,
>   A goat and cock of hay.

It might be said that Synge achieved the wild energy of

some of the street-ballads in much of his poems, especially in 'The Mergency Man and Danny.' The latter speaks of the brutal murder of a seducer of innocent girls in the Erris district in Mayo. It ends up:

> And when you're walking on the way
>   From Bangor to Belmullet,
> You'll see a flat cross on a stone,
>   Where men choked Danny's gullet.

The poetry of Synge, slight though the quantity be, was surely a warning to Irish poets from one who knew the living Gaelic culture of the West to avoid making a kind of poetic formula of it all. This was the danger and Synge's verse does fulfil his requirements that 'it is the timber of poetry that wears most surely, and there is no timber that has not strong roots among the clay and worms.' It might be said that the strongest and finest Gaelic influence of all is apparent in Synge's few poems namely the effect that the people whose culture was Gaelic had on his mind, out of which sprang plays which are often pure poetry. (pp. 152-71)

> Patrick C. Power, "Style—Poets of the Revival," in his Story of Anglo-Irish Poetry (1800-1922), The Mercier Press, 1967, pp. 152-71.

IRISH DRAMA AND THE ABBEY THEATRE

Richard Fallis

[In the excerpt below, Fallis traces the development of the Abbey Theatre.]

On a wet afternoon in the summer of 1897, three people sat talking in the office of a country house in the west of Ireland: W. B. Yeats, Edward Martyn, a well-to-do landowner, and Augusta Gregory. Martyn had written two plays which he had been unable to get produced in London; both he and Yeats lamented the fact that there was no theater in Ireland willing to present serious Irish drama. Lady Gregory knew little about the theater, but she was interested in writers and was already making her house, Coole Park, into a refuge for Yeats and some others. Lady Gregory was also a great organizer, and, as she tells it [in *Our Irish Theatre*], that afternoon's conversation about the theater turned into something more than idle talk: "We went on talking about it, and things seemed to grow possible as we talked, and before the end of the afternoon we had made our plan. We said we would collect money, or rather ask to have a certain sum of money guaranteed. We would then take a Dublin theatre and give a performance of Mr. Martyn's *Heather Field* and one of Mr. Yeats's own plays, *The Countess Cathleen*. I offered the first guarantee of £25."

For Augusta Gregory, nothing she believed in was impossible, and once she came to believe in it, an Irish theater was no impossibility. A public letter was written with which she began the work of asking wealthy and interested

Lady Gregory, 1911.

friends and acquaintances to guarantee the funds. The public letter said that the plan was to perform "Celtic and Irish plays, which whatever be their degree of excellence will be written with high ambition, and so to build up a Celtic and Irish school of dramatic literature." The letter went on to assert that the "passion for oratory" in Ireland ought to provide these plays with an "uncorrupted and imaginative" audience, one which would be tolerant and anxious to support plays which would portray the true Ireland, "the home of an ancient idealism." The letter also insisted that the plays would be apolitical, and the list of subscribers who eventually offered support certainly shows that contributions were solicited from people of every kind of politics. Nationalists like Maud Gonne and John O'Leary were subscribers, but so was Parnell's heir, John Redmond, and Parnell's fiercest opponent, T. M. Healy; AE and Douglas Hyde signed up, and so did members of the Anglo-Irish aristocracy.

The idea of regular performances of serious Irish plays by Irish playwrights was indeed a new and attractive one, but drama had existed in Ireland for centuries before the first performances of the Irish Literary Theatre in 1899. Dublin's first theater had gone up in 1637, and it was there that the first historical play on an Irish subject, James Shirley's *St. Patrick for Ireland,* had been staged in 1640. In the latter part of the seventeenth century and on through the eighteenth, Dublin had a lively theatrical tradition, producing such splendid comic playwrights as George Farquhar and William Congreve, both graduates of Trinity

College, as well as actress Peg Woffington, the Elizabeth Taylor of the mid-eighteenth century. Goldsmith and Sheridan, too, in that century continued the tradition of Irish comic writers of genius, but all these figures made most of their careers in London, as did Dion Boucicault, the enormously popular Irish playwright of the nineteenth century. After the Act of Union in 1800, Ireland had become increasingly a theatrical backwater. Dublin was an important stopping place for traveling companies from England, and most of the major Irish towns had their occasional theatrical presentations, but what Irish drama there was existed primarily for the English stage. Even so, Boucicault had some spectacular successes in Ireland as Irish audiences found in his *Colleen Bawn* and *Arrab-na-Pogue* "colour, romance, high-sounding words, deeds of daring, and the spirit of sacrifice" [Andrew Malone in his *The Irish Drama*]. They found the same in the patriotic melodramas of J. W. Whitbread toward the end of the century, while Dublin audiences loved the farces which regularly filled the Queen's Theatre and the spectacular productions of English touring companies which played at the Gaiety. Still, none of these really made for an authentic national drama, and Lady Gregory, Yeats, and Martyn had their work cut out for them.

But if a national drama were to be created, what sort of drama should it be? Even as people of all sorts of political views agreed to subscribe their money to support the Irish Literary Theatre out of feelings of national pride, an interest in drama, or just friendship for Lady Gregory, the two playwrights themselves were fundamentally at odds over the sorts of plays they thought ought to be the basis for an Irish dramatic movement. Edward Martyn, strongly influenced by Ibsen, believed Ireland needed plays which dealt with social and personal problems as the plays of the Norwegian master and the new school of "problem plays" did. Yeats, just as strongly influenced by French symbolism, found the realism of much of Ibsen repugnant and dull. Yeats believed that Ireland needed myth, symbol, and high poetry so as to appeal to what he understood to be the Celtic imagination. The play Martyn planned to stage, *The Heather Field*, tells the story of an Irish landowner, Carden Tyrrell, who is obsessed by his estate and his desire to turn a tract of unproductive heather into good farmland. His wife and his close friend fear that he will ruin himself financially with his reclamation project, but he goes on with it, even though it turns him into a tight-fisted landlord, hated by his tenants, who eventually sinks to madness and ruin. *The Heather Field* is a strong play, if sometimes stilted and derivative, in which the conflict of idealism and realism together with some effective handling of symbolism and dream make for more than an ordinary "problem play." Nevertheless, its setting, language, and theme are very different from Yeats's play, *The Countess Cathleen*, an elaborate poetic tapestry shaped into a modern version of a medieval morality play. It, too, has a landowner as its central figure, but Cathleen is by no means a realistic figure nor is the world she inhabits. In Yeats's tale, there is famine in medieval Ireland and two demons, disguised as merchants, come to Cathleen's peasants offering to buy their souls in exchange for gold the peasants need to buy food. Cathleen, moved by the peasants' plight, gives the merchants her own soul instead,

but she is redeemed from her Faustian compact with evil by the nobility of her intention, for "the Light of Lights / Looks always on the motive, not the deed." The play was one of a series of symbolic dramas Yeats then planned to write about the history of Ireland, choosing stories which would somehow define and exemplify the soul and experience of the Irish people. Of the two plays, Martyn's is arguably the better, but what was important at the time and for the future of Irish drama was the fundamental difference between them. Martyn saw the theater as a place of intellectual argument and social commentary on the problems of the contemporary world; Yeats saw it as a place of reverie and imagination about the timeless world of eternal truth. There was room enough for both kinds of drama, and more, but the differences between the two show that the intention of portraying a "true" Ireland was going to be a very complicated matter.

The two plays were scheduled for production in Dublin on May 8 and 9 of 1899, with actors mostly brought over from England, at the Antient Concert Rooms, a large hall seating about 800 people. Because Lady Gregory and both playwrights were almost entirely ignorant of stagecraft, Martyn's cousin, George Moore, hired the actors and organized the rehearsals. Moore was already a famous man; although born into a prominent Irish family, he had made his reputation as a novelist in England, and had only recently begun to see himself also as an Irish writer, one who might have a role in the burgeoning literary revival. Moore was an odd and difficult character, a man who prided himself on his knowledge of the world and his sophistication, but a congenital liar and exceedingly erratic in his behavior. His years as a collaborator in the Irish movement were to prove him at least as much a nuisance as a help.

Even so, the problems Moore sometimes helped make and the usual problems with actors, sets, and costumes were as nothing compared to the problems created by Yeats's seemingly harmless play, *The Countess Cathleen*. Martyn, a devout Catholic, became alarmed when he was warned that the play's action of bartering souls was theologically unacceptable. Moore and Yeats eventually convinced him, with the help of letters from prominent clergymen, that the play was not heretical, but then an old enemy of Yeats's from the nationalist movement, F. Hugh O'Donnell, published a pamphlet, *Souls for Gold,* which brought the theological controversy out into the open. A political controversy sprang up when ardent nationalists began to insist that the play was a slander on the Irish peasants, honorable folk who even in time of famine would never be so base as to sell their souls. Cardinal Logue, the Catholic primate of Ireland, entered the controversy (without having read the play) by charging in a public letter that "an Irish Catholic audience which could patiently sit out such a play must have sadly degenerated both in religion and patriotism." Intentionally or not, the Cardinal was almost asking for a riot at the first performance. With one newspaper charging that *The Countess Cathleen* was "a blasphemous perversion" and "a hideous caricature of our people's mental and moral character," Yeats, fearing violence, arranged to have police present at the premiere. There was some hissing and booing from students at the Catholic university (young James Joyce refused to join them), but they did not really interfere with the performance. One viewer wrote in his diary, "I watched enraptured, as if I were in fairy land" as "a spiritual, half-mystic, visionary sensation crept over my senses." *The Countess Cathleen* worked its intended magic on a good section of the audience, but there was no question that Martyn's *Heather Field,* done the next night, was the greater success. Yeats, with his Protestant background and long immersion in Blake, the occult, and Celticism, misjudged his audience. Believing that the Irish were a naturally mystical race whose highest visions could be embodied on the stage through elaborate poetry, complex symbols, and passionate speech, he was out of touch with Dublin and perhaps with the real Ireland. A poet's theater such as he imagined could not succeed, and his plays never exercised the power over a large audience of which he had dreamed. Instead, Martyn's play was the forerunner of the type which would become the basis of much Irish drama, a play dealing with recognizably real people in real situations but in a balance of realism and idealism.

Meanwhile, the first season of the Irish Literary Theatre had generated plenty of publicity, including some favorable reviews in the English newspapers, and a sense of accomplishment. As an Irish movement, it was somewhat tainted by the fact that the police had been called on the first night and that almost no Irish actors had participated. It was very much an Anglo-Irish theater, and the seasons of 1900 and 1901 did not do much to change that. In 1900 the Irish Literary Theatre presented three new plays, *The Bending of the Bough,* a satiric comedy about Irish politics originally written by Martyn but rewritten by Moore, Martyn's *Maeve,* and *The Last Feast of the Fianna* by Alice Milligan. The newspapers still grumbled about the absence of Irish actors, but there was no real controversy, and the productions, considerably more adept than in 1899, took place before a fashionable audience in the huge Gaiety Theatre. October of 1901 brought the final performances of the Literary Theatre, the new plays being a jerry-built collaboration between Yeats and Moore called *Diarmuid and Grania* and a play in Gaelic, *Casabh an tSúgáin,* by Douglas Hyde. Even with a splendid production and incidental music by the greatest living English composer, Edward Elgar, *Diarmuid and Grania* failed to rouse much enthusiasm. Much of the audience seems to have left when it was over, thus missing Hyde's play—the more important of the two—a retelling of a folktale, neatly constructed if amateurishly acted. Its importance, though, was that it was a play in Gaelic, something never before seen in Dublin, and a play acted entirely by Irishmen, something not before seen in the Irish Literary Theatre and a portent for the future. After these performances, the Irish Literary Theatre ceased to exist. It had produced two or three good plays, but it was essentially a toy for some theatrical innocents. A real Irish drama would take more than plays by Yeats, Martyn, and their friends and more than the occasional two- or three-night season.

The next step in the development of Irish drama takes us from the relative splendors of the Gaiety Theatre to a very modest and drafty room, St. Theresa's Hall, in a back street. It was there, on a stage 30' x 21' in a hall seating

only 300 that the National Dramatic Society staged AE's *Deirdre* and Yeats's *Kathleen ni Houlihan* in April of 1902. No longer were the actors English professionals; instead they were enthusiastic Irish amateurs led by Maud Gonne as the heroine in Yeats's one-acter. The moving forces behind these productions were William Fay and his brother, Frank, an electrician and an accountant's secretary. Both had been involved in theatricals in Dublin for years; as early as 1891 their "W. G. Ormonde Combination" had presented a comic "screaming sketch" at a temperance hall. Later on, they organized groups to play in "coffee palaces," places of wholesome entertainment operated by total-abstinence organizations. The brothers were amateurs, and most of what their groups had performed had been very amateurish stuff indeed, but both were already expert theater-men. Frank was interested in acting techniques and in the new movements in the theater in his time; he read and took careful notes on all he could learn about Ibsen's National Theatre in Norway, the Théâtre Libre André Antoine had organized in Paris, and J. T. Grein's Independent Theatre in London, the first serious theater there in a century. He became a commentator on drama for the nationalist newspaper, *United Ireland,* where he preached that the Irish Literary Theatre would never really take root until it used Irish actors and created a truly Irish style. His work for the newspaper brought him into contact with Maud Gonne and the Daughters of Ireland, a nationalist women's group she led. Helping them with some tableaux and plays probably brought him to Yeats's attention. At about the same time, AE had written a one-act play, *Deirde,* which the Fays were interested in producing. With encouragement from them and Yeats, AE slowly turned it into a full-length drama, the last act having to be almost squeezed out of him. The Fays' company of amateurs began rehearsals of *Deirdre* with the enthusiasm that only amateurs can have; one of the actors later recalled: "Everybody learned everybody else's part for sheer love of the thing. The lack of a curtain-raiser worried the management. But their worry disappeared when it was whispered that Yeats had had a dream, and had put it into a one-act play, and that Maud Gonne would have the central part."

Finally, on April 2, 1902, the curtain went up on these productions. The audience had to hear the plays over the noise of popular songs, dancing, and billiard balls from the room next door. St. Theresa's Hall was small and uncomfortable; the stage was too small, and the sets were crude. But AE's play was discovered to be rather effective anyway, and Yeats's a good deal more than that. *Cathleen ni Houlihan,* which was really a collaboration between Yeats and Lady Gregory, was, in fact, the first masterpiece of Irish dramatic nationalism. It tells the story of a family in the west of Ireland in 1798, the year of the French invasion and the rebellion against British rule. As the family prepares for the wedding of a son, Michael, to a wealthy girl, a haggard old woman enters their cottage. Asked why she is poor and vagrant, she replies that strangers have stolen her four green fields, and Michael offers to help her recover them. A shiver of recognition must have gone through the audience as it recognized that the old woman (played by Maud Gonne) was Cathleen ni Houlihan herself, the embodiment of Ireland; the four green fields were the provinces of Ireland; and that the robbing strangers were the British. "It is a hard service they take that help me," the old woman tells Michael. "They that have red cheeks will have pale cheeks for my sake, and for all that, they will think they are well paid." As she leaves the cottage, Michael stands entranced by the door, watching her. His brother enters with the news that the French have landed at Killala to aid the rebellion, and his father asks him, "Did you see an old woman going down the path?" "I did not," Patrick answers, "but I saw a young girl, and she had the walk of a queen." The Irish dramatic movement was conceived on the afternoon Yeats talked with Martyn and Lady Gregory in the great house in County Galway, but it was born at that production of *Cathleen ni Houlihan.*

The success of these performances encouraged the Fays and the others to go on with more plays. They rented a small hall in Camden Street to give them a permanent home for rehearsals and productions and organized themselves into the Irish National Theatre Society with Yeats as president, Maud Gonne, Douglas Hyde, and AE as vice-presidents, and William Fay as stage manager. In spite of the impressive name and the roster of notables, things sputtered for a while. The Camden Street hall was good enough for meetings and rehearsals, but its stage was only six feet deep and a mere fifty spectators could sit on its wooden benches. The company, all amateurs still, worked up a program of four short plays, three in English, one in Gaelic, which it presented for a nationalist organization at the Antient Concert Rooms in October. Thanks to a sympathetic audience, these were well received, but when the company put on three of these plays at its own hall in December, the audiences were small, the theater was bone-chillingly cold, and the reviews unfriendly. The movement could have died right then, but these were determined people and they kept going. In March of 1903, they were back on the stage, but the stage was now the more adequate one of the Molesworth Hall, rented for the occasion. The plays were Yeats's ornate morality, *The Hour-Glass,* and a funny little farce by Lady Gregory, *Twenty-Five.* Between the two plays, Yeats gave a lecture, "The Reform of the Theatre." Joseph Holloway, an incurable theater-goer who was present that night as he was present at virtually every theatrical production in Dublin for more than forty years, found Yeats's lecture a ridiculous bit of posturing, and so it must have seemed to listeners accustomed to traditional theories of drama. Yeats began by observing that the commercial theater of 1903 was in a "deplorable condition" and that it was necessary to reform it so as to make it again "an intellectual institution." To do this, three basic reforms were necessary: a new emphasis on the importance of "beautiful speech," a simplified acting style which would not detract from speech, and the development of scenery which would be "inexacting to the eye, so that the great attention might be paid by the ear." Yeats probably owed some of his ideas to the Fays, but they were also a logical extension of his own belief in the power of language and his father's emphasis on drama as intense reverie. Yeats was thinking, of course, of reforms which would be necessary for the successful staging of his own symbolist plays, but his emphases on language and simplicity became the governing ones

in the best of Irish drama. Even today, good actors trained in the modern Irish tradition are notable for their ability to handle language and their ability to make small gestures count for much. In 1903, with the commercial theaters dominated by ranting actors, extravagant sets, and plays which turned on conventionally "effective" situations, all this was revolutionary talk.

With the development of a theory and practice of performance, the training of some actors, and the development of a sympathetic audience in Dublin, the Irish movement was on the way to success. What it still needed, though, were more first-rate plays and a permanent home. Both came in remarkably short order.

Only two-and-a-half years after the premiere of *Cathleen ni Houlihan,* Irish drama had its home in the Abbey Theatre, the gift of an Englishwoman who insisted she cared nothing about Irish nationalism, Annie E. F. Horniman. Annie Horniman did care about drama though—care enough to give Ireland the Abbey and encourage in England the development of the Manchester Repertory Theatre and the Old Vic. Miss Horniman was a wealthy woman, from a family which had made a fortune in tea, and she shared Yeats's interest in the occult. She had helped him as his secretary and had occasionally come over to Dublin to help also with the Irish National Theatre Society's productions. As the productions continued during 1903 and 1904, she must have become increasingly impressed by the work being done in Dublin. According to one story, she had some stock which she promised the Fays she would use to pay for a theater if its value increased; according to another, in 1903 she heard Yeats make an appeal to the audience at the Molesworth Hall for financial support for the drama group. He had hoped that she might give a small donation; instead, she said, "I will give you a theatre." Both stories may well be true, for both seem characteristic of her impulsiveness and her generosity. Certainly, performances by the Irish players in London in 1903 and 1904 helped her make her decision. For the first time, the company acted in a real theater on those whirlwind tours, and the English critics were much impressed by the plays and the acting. In any event, in April of 1904 she wrote a formal letter to Yeats and the company to say that she had bought a theater in Dublin which she proposed to give to them.

What she gave them was part of the old Mechanics' Institute in Dublin's Abbey Street and another building which had once been a morgue. With the advice of Joseph Holloway, who was an architect as well as a theater buff, she turned these into the Abbey Theatre. For more than forty years it would remain essentially unchanged, the cradle of Irish drama. The renovation of the buildings cost her £1,300, a huge sum in those days, and what she got for her money was a small and adequate theater, but hardly, in view of the Abbey's subsequent fame, a luxurious one. The theater-goer entered through a small vestibule which with its paneling and stained-glass windows looked more like the anteroom to a Presbyterian church than a theater. In the theater itself were, downstairs, rows of plain wooden theater-seats, pit and stalls, and upstairs, a rather narrow, horseshoe-shaped balcony. Altogether, the room would hold about 500 patrons. The stage was forty feet wide and about sixteen feet deep. That meant that it was too small for a cyclorama, but the stage lighting was fairly good for its time. It was all a great improvement on the hired halls the company had used previously. The backstage facilities were limited at first, but, by adding more space, Miss Horniman eventually provided acceptable dressing rooms, a good scenery dock, and a pleasant green room for the actors. To the gift of the building itself, she added an annual subsidy to keep the company going. Her generosity was to prove very great; before her association with the Abbey ended in 1910, she had given it more than £12,000. She was amazingly free with the money, but she was also cantankerous and much given to interference. She subjected the actors and management to a barrage of advice, harassed the Fays continuously, bickered with Lady Gregory, and sometimes drove Yeats to distraction. But though she must sometimes have seemed to be the Wicked Witch of the East, she was also Irish drama's fairy godmother. Without her gift of a theater, the Irish movement could not possibly have prospered and developed as it did.

By the time the company moved into the Abbey in December of 1904, it was already developing its other necessity, more good plays and good playwrights. Martyn and Moore were no longer part of the movement, but with Yeats, Lady Gregory, J. M. Synge, Padraic Colum, and William Boyle writing plays for it, the company in the new theater could look to the future with a good deal of confidence. Yeats's best play so far, *On Baile's Strand,* and Lady Gregory's little masterpiece, *Spreading the News,* had their premieres on the night the Abbey opened, December 27, 1904. Later that season, a strong play by Synge, *The Well of the Saints,* Lady Gregory's first tragedy, *Kincora,* and a funny comedy by William Boyle, *The Building Fund,* were added to the repertory. The move to the Abbey, and the subsequent decision to go from an amateur group to a largely professional company, cost the Irish National Theatre Society some of its actors and actresses, mostly nationalists who wanted to serve the cause through an amateur group rather than become professionals. Nevertheless, a company that included Frank and William Fay, Arthur Sinclair, George Roberts, and Sara Allgood had plenty of talent and dedication.

Yeats remained a dominant figure in the theater. He was gradually learning the playwright's craft to add to his immense talent as a poet. Too often in his earlier plays, the poet got the best of the playwright, but through seeing his plays on the stage and by continuous revision, he was making himself into a fine dramatist. *The Countess Cathleen* benefitted from that process of revision, though even more revision never turned *The Shadowy Waters,* first produced in January of 1904, into a stageworthy piece. Too much symbolism and too much beautiful language suffocated it. But one of Yeats's strengths as a playwright was his willingness to continue to experiment, and in the early days before and after the opening of the Abbey, he contributed a number of strikingly different plays to the Irish repertory. *Cathleen ni Houlihan,* the patriotic tragedy, and *The Pot of Broth,* a farce, were produced in 1902; both owed a good deal to Lady Gregory for their effective dialogue and peasant speech. Yeats's first attempt to tell a

story from heroic legend, *Diarmuid and Grania* (1901) was a fiasco, but free of George Moore's collaboration, he went on to write increasingly effective plays based on this kind of material. *The King's Threshold* (1903) is a striking allegory of the relation of the artist to society cast into the days of the legendary King Guaire of Cort, and *On Baile's Strand* (1904) is a masterpiece. It is Yeats's first dramatization of the Cuchulain legends, telling the story of Cuchulain's battles with his son and the sea, but telling the story through the very effective ironic distancing provided by a fool and a blind man who are commentators on the central plot as well as agents in it. *Deirdre* (1906) treats the greatest of Irish love stories very beautifully and with a good attention to characterization, while *The Golden Helmet* (1908) was an amusing demythologizing of another Cuchulain tale. With the exception of *At the King's Threshold,* Yeats's best plays from this period were the ones in which he did not attempt to work out his own myths about himself as a personality and artist but found his overt subjects elsewhere. Personal plays such as *The Shadowy Waters* and *The Unicorn from the Stars* (1907) were too private and involuted to make effective drama; *The Hour-Glass* (1903), for all the beauty of its language, does not quite hang together.

Yeats was a consummate literary artist who had to learn the craft of the stage by trial and error; Lady Gregory was a natural mistress of dramatic situations who sometimes had difficulty in being more than merely effective. Few of the Irish playwrights had more inherent talent, but it was a talent Lady Gregory discovered only after she was fifty. When she was a very old woman, Sean O'Casey wrote to her: "You can always walk with your head up. And remember you had to fight against your birth into position and comfort, as others had to fight against their birth into hardship and poverty, and it is as difficult to come out of one as it is to come out of the other, so that power may be gained to bring fountains and waters out of the hard rocks." O'Casey, whose childhood in the rough Dublin slums was utterly different from Augusta Gregory's in a well-to-do-house in County Galway was exactly right. Born into the Persse family of the Anglo-Irish Ascendancy at Roxborough in 1852, she grew up a typical member of the Protestant aristocracy. In 1880, she married Sir William Gregory, a retired civil servant who was thirty-five years her elder, and until his death she devoted herself to him and their only son, Robert. Through her connections and his, she knew all sorts of people from Robert Browning and Henry James to William Ewart Gladstone, and she spent much of her time in London or abroad. After her husband died, she settled at their Irish country house, Coole Park, to supervise her property and raise her son. In the early nineties, living at Coole, she came face to face with the Irish world around her, the world of servants, peasants, and the little nearby town of Gort. She had once opposed home rule, but she gradually became a convinced nationalist; she learned Gaelic and became interested in folklore, the stories she heard reminding her of the ones her Irish nurse, Mary Sheridan, had told her during her childhood at Roxborough. Gradually, she made Coole a haven for Irish writers, and after 1897 Yeats, among others, came every summer to write, talk, walk in the woods around the estate, and fish its lake.

When Lady Gregory first asked Yeats what she could do to help the Irish literary movement, he merely told her to buy its books, but soon she began to write them as well. Her interest in folklore and legend led her to think of retelling the stories of Ireland in a style and dialect like the one she had heard in childhood and heard around her at Coole every day. *Cuchulain of Muirthemne* (1902) was her first important effort, a very successful version of the stories of Cuchulain and the Red Branch in a good approximation of west of Ireland dialect. Her retelling lacks the flamboyance of Standish O'Grady's, but it is a more coherent narrative and less diffuse than O'Grady's *History,* moreover, it is invaluable for its dialect—clear, sensible, but with the swing of authentic Irish speech. Lady Gregory was claiming her due when she said, "I have told the whole story in plain and simple words, in the same way my old nurse Mary Sheridan used to be telling stories from the Irish long ago, and I a child at Roxborough," and Yeats only exaggerated a little when he called it the best book to come out of Ireland in his time. It and *Gods and Fighting Men* (1904), a retelling of Irish mythology and the stories of the Fianna, became basic source books of Irish legend for many writers who could not read the tales in their Gaelic originals. Both books, and others which followed, showed that Lady Gregory was very skillful in adapting the work of scholars to the style, point of view, and idiom of native storytelling; she was, in fact, the best popularizer of legend and folklore the Irish Renaissance produced.

These books proved her to be a superb storyteller, and it was not long before she began telling stories for the stage. She was a woman who was always willing to do the work at hand which needed doing, and in the early days, the dramatic movement needed short plays, comedies preferably, which would be effective curtain-raisers for the longer and more serious plays. Lady Gregory took to writing these, and she quickly developed into a fine playwright, one who could tell a good story, create strong characters, and handle dramatic situations. *Spreading the News* (1904) was the first play to show her true merit. It is an excruciatingly funny little farce in which deaf Mrs. Tarpey, an apple-seller from the mythical village of Cloon (the town based on Gort which Lady Gregory frequently used as her setting) creates a crazy disturbance through her talk. Working from Mrs. Tarpey's misinformation and using what Lady Gregory once called the incorrigible genius of the Irish for mythmaking, half a dozen other characters decide a murder has occurred, a belief which is not thoroughly discredited even when the supposed victim casually ambles back on stage. *Spreading the News* develops a farcical situation deftly, and it also presents a series of characters, all stereotypes in one way or another, who have the breath of life in them: Mrs. Tarpey herself, the typical village gossip; the English magistrate, always referring to his valuable experience from service in the Andaman Islands and blind to what is going on around him; guillible Shawn Early; frightened Bartley Fallon who makes a life out of bemoaning his misfortune; Tim Casey, a man most adept at adding two and two to make five. *Spreading the News* is characteristic of her farces, a deft, funny play made out of the experiences of small-town Ireland, a world full of isolated personalities who are resis-tant to alien authority and exuberant in their disregard of mere fact.

In one sense, Lady Gregory's comedies are further exploitations of stage Irishmen and conventional aristocratic attitudes towards "the natives," but there is a truth and rightness in them, too, as well as a consistent comic vision of Ireland as a land of mad sanity in which order can be restored, but not for long. *The Gaol-Gate* (1906) and *The Rising of the Moon* (1907) show that she could also write strong plays of sentiment, plays sensitive to the darker side of the Irish experience. *The Gaol-Gate* is a very moving study of women waiting for a man to be released from prison and a passionate cry against British oppression; *The Rising of the Moon* is a surprisingly effective play of patriotism in which the old revolutionary ballad which gives it its title causes a policeman to let a rebel slip away from him. Both plays turn on what is really stage irony, and an O. Henry-like sense of irony informs much of her work. In *Hyacinth Halvey* (1906), it makes for hilarious comedy as Hyacinth, the new Sub-Sanitary Inspector in Cloon, is trapped in the myth of his own virtue; in *The Wrens* (1914) it makes for a kind of bitter amusement as we watch a quarrel in the street cause a servant to forget to tell his master to return for a vote in the Irish House of Commons, a vote on the Act of Union which brought so much trouble to Ireland. The focus on these ironies restricts Lady Gregory's artistic vision, but it makes her small world theatrically effective and involving. Although she constantly experiemented—"Desire for experiment is like fire in the blood," she wrote—she was at her best in small forms. Her big tragedies tend to sprawl, and some of her historical plays are clever ideas which do not quite come off. But she was an acute satirist, as *The White Cockade* (1905), *The Canavans* (1906), and *The Image* (1909) show. Later in her career, she wrote some attractive childrens' plays, clever parodies, many of them, of the conventions of fairy tales, and her last play, *Dave* (1927), is one of her several sentimental but touching religious plays.

She was a very productive writer during a career which began when she was almost fifty and only ended with her death at eighty, producing several books of legend and folklore, more than twenty original plays plus almost as many collaborations and translations, books on the Irish theater, and autobiographies. All this was the product of constant hard work, hard work which also extended to years of day-to-day management at the Abbey, an enormous correspondence, the upkeep and supervision of Coole, and constant attention to her family and to younger writers. Those who knew her often describe her strength and purposefulness, and she must have been a rather daunting figure at times. Yet there is a controlled twinkle in the eye in her best photographs; control of herself and amusement at the world's foibles were two of the secrets of her career. A third secret was her passionate love for Ireland, the Ireland of Coole with its beautiful house and deep woods, but love also for the Ireland of dull little Gort, the Ireland of urgent nationalism, and the Ireland which the Abbey embodied. She was a persistent and courageous woman, fearless in defending her friends, the theater company she nurtured and sustained, and the ideals she came to believe in. One night during the Anglo-Irish

War, when she was in her late sixties, she was waiting for a tram with the secretary of the Abbey after the night's performance. Shots rattled in the street, and she was begged to lie down on the pavement. "Never!" she answered as she shouted out encouragement to the rebels. That courage carried her through "the troubles" in Ireland, the death of her son in World War I, and the eventual sale of Coole. She was herself a great rebel against her background and her class, a fighter determined to do all she could for Ireland and Irish drama, a rebel who knew that every cause worth fighting for has its funny side. Only a person of great courage and great humanity could write as she did toward the end of her life, "Loneliness made me rich—'ful' as Bacon says."

Lady Gregory's early plays did much to define the direction of modern Irish drama. Many of the good but unremarkable plays which made up the bulk of the Abbey's repertory owed more to her than to Yeats's symbolism or Martyn's earnest Ibsenism. Today it is fashionable to undervalue the plays which can be categorized as peasant and village comedies or tragedies, yet these plays, pictures of a life any Irish person could recognize, were central to the dramatic movement and the process of national self-understanding it fostered. From its early days, these were the Abbey's most successful plays, and two of the Abbey's most successful early playwrights, William Boyle and Padraic Colum, were masters of the genre. Boyle caught the flat facts of life in Louth and Meath in several of his plays. His work was fairly conventional in style, but *The Building Fund* (1905) with its wonderful old miser, Mrs. Grogan, is still amusing as is *The Eloquent Dempsey* (1906), a satire on the double-dealing politicians. His situations were stock ones, but he had a good control of acidulous irony, and his plays had a professional competence some other Irish plays of the period lacked. In the early years of the century, it seemed that Padraic Colum might develop into the best of the younger Irish playwrights. He was only in his early twenties when he had his first success with *Broken Soil* (1903), the first impressive play of that kind of peasant realism which was to help make the Abbey famous. His next play, *The Land* (1905), was a strong study of a recurring problem in Ireland: who will inherit the little patches of land on which a farm family lives? In Colum's play, as too often in reality, the weak and conniving eventually inherit the property the older generation has ruined itself striving to preserve, while the strong and imaginative emigrate to America. Colum's command of a realistic dialect and his ability to deal interestingly with serious social problems ought to have made him a continuing figure in Irish drama, but after *Thomas Muskerry* (1910) he wrote no more for the Abbey. Conn Hourican, the central figure in *The Fiddler's House,* the revised version of *Broken Soil,* is a fiddler with equally strong instincts for wandering and artistic creation; Colum's own instincts were very much like his Conn's. He left Ireland for America when he was only in his thirties, and spent much of the rest of his life wandering and writing. He wrote some fine poems and many books of folklore, but his promise as a dramatist remained unfulfilled. Given his talent, there is something disappointing about his later career.

Colum, Boyle, and Lady Gregory all wrote good plays about the Irish farms and villages and helped establish one kind of modern Irish drama, but nothing better illustrates the difference between the good and the great in drama than comparing their work with that of John Millington Synge. Lady Gregory's Hyacinth Halvey, for example and the Christy Mahon of Synge's *Playboy of the Western World* are rather similar characters in somewhat similar situations, but Hyacinth is an amusing stage-figure while Christy is alive as few people we know in real life are alive. His creator, John Synge, was a complex man and a complex playwright, but Yeats probably came closest to defining him when he wrote: "He was a solitary, undemonstrative man, never asking pity, nor complaining, nor seeking sympathy . . . knowing nothing of new books and newspapers, reading the great masters alone; and he was but the more hated because he gave his country what it needed, an unmoved mind where there is a perpetual Last Day, a trumpeting, and coming up to judgment."

Yeats's emphasis on the hatred Synge's plays aroused reminds us that Synge's entire career at the Abbey was controversial. His masterpiece, *The Playboy,* provoked riots after its premiere in 1907, but even his first play, the one-act *In the Shadow of the Glen* (1903), created its share of trouble. It tells a simple story of a tramp seeking shelter for the night at a lonely cottage in County Wicklow. He is welcomed by a woman whose husband has just died, and the corpse is laid out on the table for the wake. The woman leaves the tramp and the corpse alone in the room while she goes out to find the young farmer she loves. Terrified, the tramp sees the "corpse" rise from the dead; he explains that he has pretended to die so that he can catch his wife and her lover together. The husband again pretends to be dead. When the wife and her farmer return, he "rises from the dead" a second time. He drives his wife from the house, but her cowardly lover stays behind to drink with her husband, and the tramp and the young wife set out into the world together. The story is, of course, a traditional folk tale found in many cultures, but to the good Irish nationalists of 1903 it was a slander on the virtues of the Irish peasantry. No peasant woman would be unfaithful to her husband; there was no such thing in Ireland as a loveless marriage, or so they said. More sensitive viewers than these nationalists might have been delighted by the play's powerful evocation of the dark glens of Wicklow and its subtle symbolism, but Synge's characters seemed too real and his language too idiomatic for much of his audience to believe that *In the Shadow of the Glen* was anything more than a realistic "slice of life" created to offend them.

For Synge, though, the wild and chaotic life of the peasantry was a source of constant wonder. Born in 1871 into an Anglo-Irish family fearfully contemptuous of its Catholic tenants, Synge had originally hoped to be a musician. That career never developed because of his intense shyness, but by the time he finished his education at Trinity College in 1892, he had learned Gaelic and already had a good knowledge of Irish rural life. There seemed to be no career in Ireland for him, so he went abroad, first to Germany and then to Paris, to try to make his way. Yeats encountered him in a cheap hotel in Paris in 1896, supporting himself as a literary journalist. Somewhere in their conversations Yeats told him, "Give up Paris. You will never create anything by reading Racine, and Arthur Symons will always be a better critic of French literature. Go to the Aran Islands. Live there as if you were one of the people themselves; express a life that has never found expression." It was, in fact, two years before Synge went to Aran, but when he did go he began to discover himself as an artist just as so many Irish writers did, by encountering the peasant life of the country. Beginning in 1898, Synge spent parts of five summers on these isolated, primitive islands. Almost untouched by the rest of the world, they then preserved the closest possible approximation of traditional Irish life: Gaelic was the native language, and modern comforts were few indeed. Men still fished from the high cliffs, took cattle to the mainland in small, frail boats and farmed tiny, rock-enclosed fields. Synge learned to love the islanders for their openness and their passion, and from their English dialect he partially made the language which gives his plays their life and poetry. He made good friends on the islands, and during his winters abroad (he continued to try to get along in Paris), letters full of simple eloquence came from them. In February of 1902, for example, Martin McDonagh wrote to him: "Johneen, Friend of My Heart. A million blessings to you. It's a while ago since I thought of a small letter to write, and every day was going until it went too far and the time I was about to write to you. It happened that my brother's wife, Shawneen, died. And she was visiting the last Sunday in December, and now isn't it a sad story to tell? But at the same time we have to be satisfied because a person cannot live always." Out of McDonagh's letter came the climactic lines of the mother's lament in Synge's *Riders to the Sea,* as out of the peasant world of Aran, Wicklow, and West Kerry came Synge's greatness.

Synge was a genius, but he could be a difficult genius. Neither Yeats nor Lady Gregory, with him the directors of the Abbey in its early days, liked him thoroughly. There was something wild about this quiet man, something dangerous, something disturbing. Both had difficulty in persuading him to tone down the language in his plays; neither was quite sure of the common sense of one who would talk of writing a play for an Irish audience in which a Protestant woman would choose to be raped by soldiers rather than stay in the house of a Catholic. One of his plays, *The Tinkers' Wedding,* was too roaringly anticlerical for the Abbey to dare produce; all of his plays were too full of a passionate vision of Ireland to make them please complacent audiences. The critics saw *Riders to the Sea* (1904) as "hideous realism," and failed to understand that it was Synge's moving tribute to the indomitable spirit of the Aran women and a tribute to all the Aran peoples' steadfastness in the hands of fate and its agent, the sea. In a single scene it tells how Maurya, an old woman, loses her remaining sons to the eternal tides. The "action" is simplicity itself, but it has the simplicity and force of the greatest tragedies, and *Riders to the Sea* is surely the great short tragedy in our language. Its protagonists are, in T. R. Henn's words, "enclosed in an inflexible circle of destiny" [*The Plays and Poems of J. M. Synge*]. The play reminds us of tragedy's origins in the lyric; Synge's powerfully plain lyricism and his subtly unified symbolism make the

little play a perfect whole. Maurya's concluding lament for her sons is one of those rare moments when dramatic language transcends itself to become a vision of eternal truth:

> Michael has a clean burial in the far north, by the grace of the Almighty God. Bartley will have a fine coffin out of the white boards, and a deep grave surely. . . . What more can we want than that? . . .
> No man at all can be living for ever, and we must be
> satisfied.

In the Shadow of the Glen and *Riders to the Sea* made it clear that in Synge Irish drama had found a new master; *The Well of the Saints* (1905), his first three-act play to be produced at the Abbey, solidified his reputation. Again there were complaints from the nationalists who claimed, rightly, that the action of the play was based on a foreign source and that, therefore, the play could not possibly be Irish. But its characters and its setting are thoroughly Irish, as is its theme, that illusion is often more satisfactory than reality. That theme, one which runs through all his later plays, finds its great expression, though, in *The Playboy of the Western World* (1907), a play which would

J.M. Synge.

be a comedy if it were not so close to tragedy, a tragedy if it were not a comedy.

It was his masterpiece, but it was simply too much for most of his audience. Irish nationalists were infuriated by the portrayal of brutal peasants who condoned violence and murder and were vulgar, crude, and small-minded. In three acts of realistic fantasy, Synge more or less destroyed a century of myth about the peasantry of the west of Ireland, myth which had held that their sufferings had made them into quintessential Irishmen, a "saving remnant" which had to be honored for its patience, fortitude, and piety. The myth was based on the modern urban belief that country people who live close to the natural world are somehow made holy by it; in Ireland, the myth had been encouraged by Catholic piety and the nationalist theory of the innate superiority of spiritual Ireland to materialistic England. In fact, centuries of ignorance and oppression had left much of the Irish peasantry degraded, superstitious, and violent. Synge himself also idealized peasant Ireland, but the peasants he loved were the traditionally oppressed: tinkers, tramps, and the poor. In these real people, rather than the imaginary mystics of the Celtic twilight or the plaster saints of Irish nationalism, he found his myth of the Irish soul—passionate, hard, unforgiving, and wild. As he wrote to a young admirer who praised *The Playboy*, "In the same way you see—what it seems so impossible to get our Dublin people to see, obvious as it is,—that the wildness and, if you will, vices of the Irish peasantry are due, like their extraordinary good points of all kinds, to the *richness* of their nature—a thing that is priceless beyond words."

The troubles with *The Playboy* began long before the first performance. Yeats, W. G. Fay, and Lady Gregory were all concerned about the strong language in it from the first time they heard it read, and some of the actors objected strenuously to the words they were made to say. Eventually, the company made cuts or emendations in more than fifty speeches. Still, no one expected really serious disturbances, and Yeats, for one, went off to Scotland to lecture. But the opening night's audience erupted during the third act. The next day the newspapers were indignant, the *Freeman's Journal* calling the play a "libel upon Irish peasant men and, worse still, upon Irish peasant girlhood," and the *Evening Mail* saying it implied Irish people were "gorillas." With excitement in Dublin rising, Synge and Lady Gregory thought it might be well to have police in the theater for the next performance, but that only helped incite the audience. The performance turned into a riot. Yeats returned from Scotland, gave a newspaper interview in which he said those who disliked the play were illiterates being led by ignorant patriots, then let into the theater a group of drunken students from Trinity College to shout down the nationalists. For several of the performances, the actors could not be heard over the racket. Ironically, the crowds which came to damn *The Playboy* or praise it made it an enormous box-office success, but at the cost of losing much of the Abbey's position as a national institution. Some nationalists swore never to enter it again; Boyle and Colum withdrew their plays from its repertory in protest against the management's continued defense of Synge. Joseph Holloway, the architect-playgoer,

probably reflected much Dublin opinion when he wrote in his journal that *The Playboy* "is not a truthful or a just picture of the Irish peasants, but simply the outpouring of a morbid, unhealthy mind ever seeking on the dunghill of life for the nastiness that lies concealed there." The worst row in Irish theatrical history did not end in 1907 or in Dublin. The Board of Guardians of the Gort workhouse hurt Lady Gregory deeply by forbidding its orphans picnics at Coole in retaliation for her support of Synge. In 1911, Irish-Americans in Philadelphia had the Abbey company, then touring the United States, arrested for presenting the "immoral and indecent" *Playboy*. Lady Gregory's life was threatened when the company reached Chicago, but the mayor there, asked to stop performances of the play in his city, read three pages of it and reported, "instead of finding anything immoral I found the whole thing was wonderfully stupid."

What sort of play was it, then, that could cause so much trouble? Its plot is simple enough, as Synge's usually are. Christy Mahon appears in a village in the wilds of County Mayo saying that he has murdered his father. The peasants take him in, admiring what they see as his daring, although we in the audience can see that he is nothing more than a shy, frightened boy. Killing his father was not, Christy insists, your "common, week-day kind of murder," and the legend he and the villagers create around it and him makes a man of him while it simultaneously entraps him. He falls in love with the pub-keeper's daughter, Pegeen Mike, in spite of the efforts of the cantankerous Widow Quin and Pegeen's old boyfriend, the snivelling, pious Shawn Keogh. But Christy's fame and his newfound manhood collapse when his "murdered" father reappears, bandaged yet full of life after the blow from his son's spade. Christy tries to kill him again and apparently succeeds. Now faced with the reality of murder and realizing "there's a great gap between gallous story and a dirty deed," the peasants turn on Christy, bind him, and try to cripple him to make it easier to get him to the police. But Old Mahon revives once more; he and his son go off together with the old man saying, "We'll have great times from this out telling stories of the villainy of Mayo and the fools is here." Pegeen, who has loved and betrayed Christy with equal passion, is left with the knowledge of what she has lost: "Oh my grief, I've lost him surely. I've lost the only playboy of the western world."

Around this series of comic reversals with motifs of ironic resurrection, frustrated romance, and Oedipal conflict, Synge creates a wonderfully extravagant verbal construct. No play of the Irish Renaissance has a richer, more various language, language better fit for cursing or lovemaking. Pegeen Mike assaults the Widow Quin and her scheme for stealing Christy from her by saying of the Widow, "Doesn't the world know you reared a black ram at your own breast, so that the Lord Bishop of Connaught felt the elements of a Christian, and he eating it after in a kidney stew?" Christy, pouring himself out to Pegeen, cries, "It's well you know it's a lonesome thing to be passing small towns with the lights shining sideways when the night is down, or going in strange places with a dog nosing before you and a dog nosing behind, or drawn to the cities where you'd hear a voice kissing and talking deep love in every shadow of the ditch, and you passing on with an empty hungry stomach failing from your heart."

Yet for all the glory of its language, *The Playboy* is a strange play. In one sense, it is a Dionysiac comedy in which anything goes, a fulfillment of Synge's desire to create what is "superb and wild" in reality. In another, it is a satire on the traditional lawlessness of Ireland and a satire, too, on its patterns of courtship and marriage. It is more than a little a tragedy in which the hero, Christy, discovers his identity and his "fate," but only by leaving Pegeen, the archetype of the strong woman of so much Irish drama, bereft of all comfort. There is that and more in the play, and critics have found everything in it from an allegory of Irish political history to a retelling of the myth of sacrificial expiation with Christy as Christ-bearer. Cyril Cusack, one of the finest of the recent actors who have played Christy, tells how it took him years of performances to realize fully how the play moves through a series of anticlimaxes towards a resolution in which "reality disappears in a balloon-burst of disillusionment and the person of Christopher Mahon suddenly resolves itself into a dew" ["A Player's Reflections on the Playboy," *Twentieth Century Interpretations of the Playboy of the Western World,* edited by Thomas R. Whitaker].

The Playboy was the last of Synge's plays to be produced during his lifetime. Two years after those riotous nights in 1907 he was dead. He left unfinished his last play, *Deirdre of the Sorrows,* it is his only full-scale tragedy, a play which misses greatness only because its author did not live to give it the final revisions which would have made it an artistic whole. Even with its imperfections, notably a second act that drags, *Deirdre* is a powerfully moving work. Many other playwrights of the Irish Renaissance tried to tell the story from the *Táin* of Deirdre and Naisi, their flight from the wrath of old king Conchubor who had meant to marry Deirdre, and their eventual deaths through his vengeance, but none did it better than Synge. Still employing his dialect, Synge made what was really a dramatic poem on the themes of love, death, and old age which so obsess him in his lyric poetry. He subtly turns the old tale of fated love into a study in heroic pride; Deirdre is the last in his line of proud and determined women. She is as much a relation of Pegeen Mike and Maurya as a figure from ancient legend. Her pride and her determination never to lose Naisi's love drive her to return with him to Conchubor and inevitable death. There is no greater speech in Irish drama than Deirdre's last, as she keens over the grave of Naisi and prepares for her own suicide.

> I have put away sorrow like a shoe that is worn
> out and muddy, for it is I have had a life that
> will be envied by great companies. It was not
> by a low birth I made kings uneasy, and they sitting
> in the halls of Emain. It was not a low thing to
> be
> chosen by Conchubor, who was wise, and Naisi
> had no
> match for bravery. . . . It is not a small
> thing to be rid of grey hairs and the loosening
> of the teeth. . . . It was the choice of lives
> we had in the clear woods, and in the grave
> we're safe surely. . . .

John Synge, too, found safety in the grave after a career which made Irish drama uneasy and himself immortal. As Una Ellis-Fermor observed long ago, much of Synge's greatness came from the fact that he knew Ireland itself rather than what was written about it. His travel books, particularly his superb memoir of the Aran Islands, show an open-eyed delight in the life around him that is reminiscent of the open wonder of early Gaelic nature poetry. His ear for Irish speech was as fresh. He was surely the greatest playwright Ireland has produced and, in a special way, the most Irish. A decade after his friend's death, Yeats remembered him as one who came

> Towards nightfall upon certain set apart
> In a most desolate stony place,
> Towards nightfall upon a race
> Passionate and simple like his heart.

> ["In Memory of Major Robert Gregory," *Variorum Poems*]

By the time John Synge died in 1909, modern Irish drama and the Abbey Theatre had passed through its first years of greatness. A disagreement over the management of the theater had caused the Fays and some others to leave, losing for the company some of its best actors and effective directors. But even if Synge had lived and the Fays had stayed, the excitement and achievement of those first ten years of the movement probably could not have been sustained. It is almost impossible to overestimate the sense of purpose and commitment in those early years of collaboration between some fine playwrights and a devoted group of actors. Lady Gregory would give a party at the end of each week of rehearsals; barmbrack from Gort was always in the green room for snacks between sessions. Miss Horniman would sometimes be there, drinking claret cup and smoking a cigar. In the early days, Frank Fay would come directly from his employer's office to type scripts and teach elocution. Synge would silently sit in the wings during performances, rolling cigarettes to hand to the actors as they came off stage. Yeats would fuss over whether the theater were warm enough for its few patrons; sometimes the box-office take was only a few pounds, and even with Miss Horniman's subsidy there was hardly enough money. The salaries of the company were ridiculously low considering the talent involved; even as late as 1914 Arthur Sinclair, one of the best actors Ireland produced, was earning only four pounds a week. The actors were paid double salaries and the theater took in the amazing sum of £160 during the week of the first performances of *The Playboy,* but, during the week before, a triple bill of *Kathleen ni Houlihan, Spreading the News,* and *Hyacinth Halvey* earned only slightly more than £37. Still, the money was not the important thing, and one actress who played minor roles with the company looked back after forty years to remember fondly Lady Gregory telling the company to be quiet while Mr. Yeats read "his new masterpiece," and, not so fondly, an occasion when Yeats was so rude that one of the actors threatened to push him into the footlights. There were some bitter quarrels and the kinds of personal rivalries that always come in a theater, but there was also a sense of purpose and community.

Both of those continued even after the death of Synge and

the Fays' departure, but the Abbey was becoming increasingly an ordinary professional theater. Miss Horniman withdrew her subsidy in 1910, something she had been threatening to do for several years and finally did when the theater failed to close in mourning on the death of King Edward VII. With the subsidy gone, the Abbey had to pay even closer attention to the box office; the "theatre of beauty" Yeats had envisioned or even the theater of dramatic nationalism others had imagined gradually turned into a commercial playhouse. But it was a playhouse which was still committed to Irish drama and Irish playwrights. The Abbey's acting style remained uniquely its own. The actors who had been trained by the Fays had mastered the art of spare and forceful gesture as well as the technique by which to convey the power of language. Some might cynically observe that the Abbey's small stage and primitive facilities precluded any elaborate sets, but there was still something very effective in the modest and often beautifully simple ones used. The Abbey drew on some of the best experimental stage designers of the day, Gordon Craig being the most important, and many Abbey actors gradually achieved international fame. To the theater buff those old cast lists are still tantalizing: W. G. Fay as Christy Mahon, Maire O'Neill as Pegeen Mike or Deirdre, Sara Allgood as Synge's Lavarcham, or Arthur Sinclair as his Conchubor.

As the Abbey acclimated itself to the loss of Synge, the Fays, and Miss Horniman's subsidy, its new concern with the box office and its continuing interest in finding good Irish playwrights led it to produce more plays that were realistic, more plays that dealt with contemporary problems. Two new playwrights who helped fill the need for those sorts of plays were Lennox Robinson and T. C. Murray, both natives of Cork and sometimes grouped with some other writers as the "Cork realists." Robinson discovered his interest in drama when he saw the Abbey perform in Cork while he was still a young man, and he was only twenty-two when the company did his first play, *The Clancy Name,* in 1908. It was a gritty melodrama of family pride, and all of his early plays were grimly realistic in their recurring theme of the disastrous results to rural life when its values came into conflict with those of urban society. Robinson's career at the Abbey went on for half a century. His most lasting plays were two comedies, *The Whiteheaded Boy* (1916) and *Drama at Inish* (1933), but he could write well in many dramatic forms. His construction was almost always effective and his dialogue alert to the patterns of real speech. He was probably too fluent a writer for his own good, but his plays were very popular with Abbey audiences, and in *Crabbed Youth and Age* (1922) he showed that he could write a clever comedy of manners, something few modern Irish playwrights have been able to do.

Like Lennox Robinson, T. C. Murray tried his hand at several styles, but his best plays were careful expositions of emotional conflicts in provincial life. A Catholic native of Macroom in West Cork, a gray and ugly town stretched out along the road from Cork to Killarney, Murray was the first good playwright of the Irish Renaissance to write of country and village life from the inside, and his portrayals of Catholic farmers and townspeople have a ponderous

truth to type. His themes are the permanent ones of provincial life: frustrated ambition, exile, loveless marriage, the persistent care of motherhood, and the dull bleakness of old age. *Birthright,* produced at the Abbey in 1910, is a story of fraternal conflict, while *Maurice Harte* (1912) deals sensitively with the problems of a mother who wants her son to be a priest and the son who feels no vocation for the priesthood. These two and *Autumn Fire* (1924), a powerful study of inevitability and quiet despair, are among his best work; *Autumn Fire* uses much the same situation as Eugene O'Neill's *Desire Under the Elms* and is probably the better play. Murray was a conscientious playwright, but too often his plots were melodramatic and coincidental, and his characters were sometimes talking cliches. Nevertheless, he, Robinson, and some others wrote strong plays which helped define the norms of modern Irish drama. Rather conventional plays such as these can be important in their time, but they do not necessarily last well. A repertory theater such as the Abbey was then needs this kind of drama, but if they become all the theater has to offer, then something is wrong.

Looking back, it seems that something was wrong with the Abbey around the time of World War I. The new plays kept coming and the acting was often excellent, but the old excitement was gone, and too many of the new plays were earnest, worthy, and similar. The tragedies were melodramatic tales of village frustration; the comedies were laughing presentations of Irish stereotypes. Two playwrights, both fantasists, seem sharply differentiated from all this sameness: Lord Dunsany and George Fitzmaurice. Neither had a very long career at the Abbey; both had that remarkable Irish talent for imagining mad and cosmic worlds of fantasy which, psychologically, are alarmingly real. Lord Dunsany's *The Glittering Gate* (1909) is almost Swiftian in its lunatic irony and wisdom. Bill and Jim, two burglars in this life, wait at what they think is the gate of Heaven for it to open. While they wait, they talk out their lives on earth. Beer bottles, reminders of their chief pleasure when alive, rain down on them, but all the bottles are empty, and when the gate finally opens, there is only mocking laughter and "Stars. Blooming great stars."

Dunsany's forte was prose fantasy rather than drama, and he went on to write some of the best fantasies of the century. George Fitzmaurice's forte, unfortunately for him, was drama, but after successes with his first few plays, the Abbey failed to produce any more of his work. Fitzmaurice died in 1963 with a trunk full of unproduced plays, and it is only since his death that he has been recognized as a major Irish playwright and a startling original. He was born in 1877 near Listowel in the northern part of County Kerry. As the child of a Protestant clergyman in Catholic Kerry, Fitzmaurice seems to have developed early the sense of detachment which eventually led him to spend his life watching but not participating in the world around him. Kerry is a proverbially old-fashioned and idiosyncratic part of Ireland, and it is from the folklore of Kerry that Fitzmaurice drew his sense of rural fantasy as well as interests in the grotesque and the violent. He spent most of his life, though, in Dublin as a not very successful member of the civil service. In 1907 the Abbey produced his first play to be staged, *The Country Dressmaker,* it enjoyed a great success and remained for more than forty years one of the most popular plays in the repertory. Like most of Fitzmaurice's plays, its setting is Kerry, and its plot involves two factions in a village which are scheming to marry off Pats Connor, a villager who has gone to America and returned. The plot is unremarkable, but Fitzmaurice demonstrated in this play that his mastery of Kerry dialect was as good as Synge's mastery of that of Aran and County Wicklow and that there was a vein of fantastic humor in him.

If Fitzmaurice had continued to write comedies like *The Country Dressmaker,* he might have remained a successful dramatist. But the best of his subsequent plays are private fantasies, plays which begin by being firmly fixed in the real world but quickly veer off into nutty imaginings. *The Pie-Dish* (1908) is that unusual thing, a tragic fantasy, or, perhaps more accurately, a pathetic fantasy. In one very short act, it tells how old Leum Donoghue has spent twenty years making an ornamental pie dish; dying, but in a frenzy to complete his masterpiece, he calls on the devil to give him more time. When he does, he falls dead, and the dish drops from his hands, smashing. This is a strange little play; dead accurate in its dialogue and characterization, and a quirky variation on the Romantic theme of the Faustian desire of the artist to create a perfect work. The audiences of 1908 laughed heartily at it, and perhaps it was the laughter where none was intended that encouraged Fitzmaurice to go on to make wilder fantasies in which abnormality overtaken by the supernatural is the norm. In *The Magic Glasses* (1913), laughing madness ends in death for Jaymoney Shanahan, a thirty-eight-year-old man who spends his time in the loft of his father's farmhouse looking through nine glasses he has bought from a fairy. Through the glasses, Jaymoney can enjoy an immensely satisfying fantasy world, strikingly different from the everyday: "'tis better than being in the slush—same old thing every day—this is an ugly spot, and the people ignorant, grumpy, and savage." His parents call in Morgan Quille, a quack medical man, to cure him, but Quille's efforts to exorcise Jaymoney's demon leave the exorcist himself in convulsions; Jaymoney returns to the loft. It collapses with him, and the play ends with Jaymoney dead, his throat slit by his magic glasses. The play is a brilliant parable on the power of the imagination as well as a satire on the escapism of the writers of the Celtic twilight, all this placed in the context of characters and language skillfully drawn from Kerry originals. It was the next to last of Fitzmaurice's to be produced at the Abbey, and its author gradually became as reclusive as Jaymoney himself. Still, he continued to write plays, fantasies as well as realistic ones. *The Dandy Dolls,* which was published in 1914, was probably his masterpiece. Its theme, as in so many of Fitzmaurice's plays, is the intrusion of the supernatural into the ordinary world of County Kerry. Its action and language are a perfect farrago of farce, but just beneath the surface are inexplicable magic, violence, and grotesquerie. Roger Carmody devotes his life to making dandy dolls, what they are Fitzmaurice never really explains; a priest as well as all sorts of supernatural powers would like to get their hands on them, but Roger's most recent creation, like all the others, is eventually stolen by a mysterious figure, the Hag's Son. Roger's earthy wife,

Cauth, explains the process: "For the Hag's Son is against them to the death, and so sure as Roger makes a doll, so sure will the Hag's Son, soon or late, come at it, give it a knuckle in the navel, split it in two fair halves, collar the windpipe, and off with him carrying the squeaky-squeak." This time, though, Roger is stolen along with his doll, and we are left to wonder if normality has returned finally or if it ever will.

Fitzmaurice once said the characters in some of his plays were "wicked old children." His best work depends on the conflict of crazy innocence and uncomprehending experience. He was a great tale-teller, one who could spin a yarn as well as any Kerryman by the fire, and there is something absorbing still in his parables of frustrated vision and artistry. Because of his command of peasant character and dialect, he is often compared to Synge, but Fitzmaurice's imagination was more narrow and less disciplined. A few of his characters have the rich humanity of most of Synge's, but the majority are whirling caricatures. During the last forty years of his life the Abbey produced none of his new plays, but that did not keep him from writing, and apparently he did not care whether the plays were staged or not. Increasingly he became a recluse in his own fantasy world, coming out only to go to work and for his regular pints of stout at Mooney's and other Dublin pubs. When he died in 1963, a pathetic note was found in his effects: "Author is prepared to sell outright all rights in 14 plays dealing intimately with life in the Irish countryside." There had been no buyers in his lifetime, but Fitzmaurice was exactly right in his phrasing: his plays to deal "intimately with life in the Irish countryside," not the day-to-day life of north Kerry farmers, perhaps, but the imaginative life which still exists inside the head of many a village storyteller.

The failure to encourage Fitzmaurice after 1913 is one of the mysteries of the Abbey's history, but by that time the theater was probably too concerned with commercial success to want his work. The years between 1913 and 1923 were a difficult time for it, years in which it took great effort simply to stay in business. The building survived the devastation of the 1916 rising, but one of the actors died in the fighting and a promising writer, Thomas MacDonagh, was among the patriots shot in the aftermath. The new plays continued to come, but the exhaustion of those times is indicated by the fact that most of the 1916-17 season was given over to the plays of George Bernard Shaw, an Irishman, admittedly, but one who was no more than tangentially associated with Irish drama. The "troubles" brought the company to the edge of bankruptcy, and in the spring of 1921, Lennox Robinson, then the manager, had no choice but to tell the actors that the theater was giving up its struggle for survival. But, in spite of all odds, it reopened that fall in the lull between Ireland's war for independence and her civil war, and it kept going. In 1924 the new Free State offered a subsidy, and that seemed to guarantee some financial security for the future. The Abbey had become Ireland's state theater, the first state-supported theater in the English-speaking world.

John Synge would have seen some irony in that. The nationalists who execrated his *Playboy* had become the guarantors of his theater. Yet there was something appropriate in this decision, for the Abbey had done as much and more than any nationalist to prove that Ireland was indeed "the home of an ancient idealism." Yeats's plays spoke to one vision of Ireland in their intricate symbolism and passionate reverie. Lady Gregory's spoke to another, Synge's to yet a third, Colum's, Murray's, Fitzmaurice's to others still. No one vision was complete or perhaps even ultimately true, but each was a kind of truth about the Ireland that was and the Ireland that could be. Those visions, the products of the dramatic genius of Ireland's playwrights, had made drama one of the great and lasting achievements of the Irish Renaissance. (pp. 87-115)

> *Richard Fallis, in his* Irish Renaissance, *Syracuse University Press, 1977, 319 p.*

Lady Gregory recalling the mission statement of the founders of the Abbey Theatre:

Our statement—it seems now a little pompous—began:

"We propose to have performed in Dublin in the spring of every year certain Celtic and Irish plays, which whatever be their degree of excellence will be written with a high ambition, and so to build up a Celtic and Irish school of dramatic literature. We hope to find in Ireland an uncorrupted and imaginative audience trained to listen by its passion for oratory, and believe that our desire to bring upon the stage the deeper thoughts and emotions of Ireland will ensure for us a tolerant welcome, and that freedom to experiement which is not found in theatres of England, and without which no new movement in art or literature can succeed. We will show that Ireland is not the home of buffoonery and of easy sentiment, as it has been represented, but the home of an ancient idealism. We are confident of the support of all Irish people, who are weary of misrepresentation, in carrying out a work that is outside all the political questions that divide us."

> *Lady Gregory, in her* Our Irish Theatre: A Chapter of Autobiography, *Lady Gregory Estate, 1913.*

David Krause

[*In the following excerpt, Krause examines the relationship between Ireland's move toward political independence and the development of an Irish national theatre.*]

The rebirth of a nation's literature . . . is not an immaculate conception. It is a painful process of renewal that grows out of attrition and contention, a civil war of violent words and conflicting aspirations. Therefore, instead of presuming to interpret the Irish literary renaissance as a predestined revelation of the Celtic mystique, whatever that might be, or daring to provide a capsule account of all the volatile forces involved in that complex process, I want to limit myself to what I believe to be the period of crisis—the catalytic stage during the first quarter of the twentieth century when the nation's new literature began

to emerge out of the seemingly irreconcilable struggle between political necessity and the creative imagination.

Paradoxically, though Irish nationalism and literature had an urgent need of each other's vitality and vision, their spokesmen were from the start suspicious of their respective methods and values; they were sharply divided by the common goal of seeking to reassert the national heritage and pride. On the nationalist side, there was the hortatory attempt of the political apologist to glorify individual behaviour in terms of a purification and idealisation of national life; and on the literary side, there was the imaginative attempt of the artist to express his own vision of experience in terms of the reality of national life. Militant nationalism often seems at the point of winning the struggle, especially during a revolutionary period, when in the name of national honour the writers are urged to celebrate the proposition that all the men are courageous patriots, all the women are paragons of virtue, and love of country is the greatest glory. But even when they have been inspired by unimpeachable principles of revolutionary justice, such attempts to canonise the national character ironically threaten to become the occasion of national hypocrisy. They also become the inevitable target of those uncompromising writers who gain the final victory because they owe their Irish allegiance to what might be called the higher nationalism—the search for the truth about man, the quintessential nature of his character and his world.

In Ireland at the turn of the twentieth century, the development of the literary renaissance and the movement for national independence naturally coincided after the death of Parnell, each force guiding and inspiring the other in the early days as they worked towards the common goal of liberating the country from British domination. Nevertheless, it soon became clear that literature and nationalism were destined to collide with each other when they weren't colliding with Britain. The record of that internal collision can be observed in the lives and works of Ireland's major writers, Yeats and Synge, Joyce and O'Casey, four men who stubbornly maintained their loyalty to the higher nationalism. What W. R. Rodgers once wrote about Synge effectively expresses the writer's responsibility to his nation: 'A writer's first duty to his country is disloyalty, and Synge did his duty by Ireland in presenting her as he found her and not as she wished to be found.' Synge is the seminal figure, and this view has its roots in Yeats's comment on the genius of Synge and the way it exposes the gap that exists between the artist and the nation: 'When a country produces a man of genius he is never what it wants or believes it wants; he is always unlike its idea of itself.'

Synge had raised the whole issue with his very first play, *In the Shadow of the Glen* (1903), a mock-heroic portrait of Irish peasant life which was completely at odds with the country's romantic idea of itself. And Yeats was also early in the field. On the controversial occasion of that first performance of Synge's play, presented by Yeats's Irish National Theatre Society at Molesworth Hall on 8 October 1903, the company also performed the première of Yeats's new play, *The King's Threshold,* which could be described as an ironic comment on, perhaps even a recantation of, his glowingly nationalistic play of the previous year, *Cathleen ni Houlihan.* It was no surprise, then, that Synge and Yeats were accused of disloyalty to Ireland by the Dublin newspapers, the self-appointed guardians of the national honour and were vehemently attacked by Arthur Griffith, one of the leading apostles of the new nationalism. Founder of Sinn Fein, the formidable Griffith, in the 17 October 1903 issue of his nationalist weekly, *The United Irishman,* launched the first of his unrelenting assaults against Synge and Yeats and the new theatre movement. About Synge's play he wrote the following comment:

> The Irish National Theatre Society was ill-advised when it decided to give its imprimatur to such a play as 'In a Wicklow Glen' [*In the Shadow of the Glen*]. The play has an Irish name, but it is no more Irish than the Decameron. It is a staging of a corrupt version of that worldwide libel on womankind—the 'Widow of Ephesus,' which was made current in Ireland by the hedge—schoolmaster . . . Mr Synge's play purports to attack 'our Irish institution, the loveless marriage'—a reprehensible institution but not one peculiar to Ireland. We believe the loveless marriage is something of an institution in France and Germany and even in the superior country across the way, and, if we recollect our books, it was something of an institution in that nursery of the arts—ancient Greece . . . Man and woman in rural Ireland, according to Mr Synge, marry lacking love, and, as a consequence, the woman proves unfaithful. Mr Synge never found that in Irish life.

Well, hardly ever. Since Griffith subordinated literature to his quixotic defence of Irish womanhood, he was disinclined to judge Synge's play as a work of art. According to his national ideals, the play was a profane and dangerous foreign influence, a serious libel against Irish women, and therefore false. Nor was he alone in holding this chauvinistic view, for the performance of the play was greeted by some hissing and a minor disturbance when three prominent members of the Theatre Society who were in the audience walked out in protest and resigned from the company. Dr James H. Cousins, who was present at the time, accurately described the motive for the walkout in the memoir he wrote with his wife, *We Two Together* (1950): 'Maud Gonne, Maire Quinn and Dudley Digges left the hall in protest against what they regarded as a decadent intrusion where the inspiration of idealism rather than the down pull of realism was needed.' The Irish artist, therefore, was a decadent intruder, and by these nationalistic standards a fabricated idealism was more palatable than the ironic reality.

If the three protesters had remained for the performance of Yeats's new play, they probably would have been exposed to another shock. They had all acted in his *Cathleen ni Houlihan* in 1902, with Maud Gonne in the title role of the heroic Old Woman who exhorts the men of 1798 to die a martyr's death for Ireland—'They shall be remembered for ever.' But now in *The King's Threshold,* although he continued in the heroic mode, Yeats turned away from the national symbolism of Cathleen ni Houlihan and created a martyred poet as 'the inspiration of idealism,' the higher idealism of art. This Celtic parable is Yeats's manifesto in defence of poetry, an heroic defence of the poet's great gift of lyric power and his ancient right of high honour in the state. When King Guaire, following the advice of his national councillors, the bishops and soldiers and judges, insults the poet Seanchan by dismissing him from the state council—'it is against their dignity / For a mere man of words to sit amongst them'—Seanchan acts to uphold his sacred right by going on a hunger strike on the palace steps. Rejecting all compromise as a defeat of his principles, he sacrifices his life for the belief that the arts must never be controlled or diminished by the state. At one point Seanchan reminds his disciples that poetry is 'One of the fragile, mighty things of God, / That die at an insult'; and later he offers a Dionysian vision of the poet's great gift of tragic joy, a vision that owes more to Nietzsche than to nationalism:

> And I would have all know that when all falls
> In ruin, poetry calls out in joy,
> Being the scattering hand, the bursting pod,
> The victim's joy among the holy flame,
> God's laughter at the shattering of the world.

The later and major Yeats is prefigured in these apocalyptic lines. Only poetry can transform the tragic patterns of life and triumph over them, a mythical process of aesthetic joy which Yeats later embodied in such brilliant poems as 'Sailing to Byzantium' and 'Lapis Lazuli.' Seanchan's fight for the absolute supremacy of poetry led Una Ellis-Fermor to make the following comment on Yeats's aesthetic in her *Irish Dramatic Movement* (1939): 'It is a flaming exaltation of that vision which is the symbol of all spiritual knowledge and the gift of the spirit beside which all other values are disvalued. Poetry is either the root of life or it is nothing . . . Even Brand himself never proclaimed more unflinchingly the doctrine of "all or nothing." ' In the light of such wisdom it is only surprising that Mrs Ellis-Fermor, instead of looking to Ibsen's Brand for a parallel to Yeats's Seanchan, did not more appropriately turn to Ibsen's great Irish disciple, James Joyce; for Seanchan is a blood-brother of Joyce and surely anticipates his martyred high priest of art, Stephen Dedalus. More precisely, perhaps the priority of kinship between Yeats and Joyce on the absolute supremacy of art should be reversed, with Joyce as the initiator of the principle. It was the young Joyce, disdainfully aloof from both the literary and national movements in Ireland at the turn of the century, who in 'The Day of the Rabblement' in 1901 had warned Yeats of the danger of allowing the Irish Theatre to become a part of the new nationalism. In that prophetic essay the nineteen-year-old Joyce had written with characteristic arrogance that 'Mr Yeats's treacherous instinct of adaptability must be blamed for his recent association with a platform from which even self-respect should have urged him to refrain.' By 1903 the disenchanted Yeats had created his 'all or nothing' Seanchan, and it would be fair to say that he had abandoned his not-so-treacherous 'instinct of adaptability'—with the national cause, and with men like Edward Martyn and George Moore who were grinding the wrong axes. Therefore, when Joyce in his 'all or nothing' essay went on to state the crux of the issue he was speaking to all Irish artists, he was invoking the fervour and dedication of a Seanchan and a Dedalus:

> If an artist courts the favour of the multitude he cannot escape the contagion of its fetishism and deliberate self-deception, and if he joins in a popular movement he does so at his own risk. Therefore, the Irish Literary Theatre by its surrender to the trolls has cut itself adrift from the line of advancement. Until he has freed himself from the mean influences about him—sodden enthusiasm and clever insinuation and every flattering influence of vanity and low ambition—no man is an artist at all.

Needless to say, Yeats did not surrender to the Irish 'trolls,' those who distrusted and compromised the artist and were determined to limit literature to a subordinate position in the new Ireland. No less than Joyce, he spent the rest of his life fighting them, and Arthur Griffith was one of his first significant opponents. Predictably, then, Griffith did not like *The King's Threshold,* mainly because his sympathies were all with King Guaire and against what he called the 'selfish' poet who was foolishly and unreasonably fighting the wrong battle against the wrong enemy. Yeats wrote a formal reply, 'An Irish National Theatre and Three Sorts of Ignorance,' which Griffith printed in the 24 October 1903 issue of *The United Irishman.* In this article he defended his theatre and Synge from his version of trollism, the 'obscurantist' attacks of the three main pressure groups in Ireland that made it their mission to protect the national honour from the profane artist: the political, religious and Gaelic language propagandists. There is a direct parallel to this attitude in Joyce's *A Portrait of the Artist as a Young Man* (1916), when Stephen Dedalus, in rejecting the arguments of the nationalistic Davin, also identifies the triple-enemy of the artist: 'When the soul of a man is born in this country there are nets flung at it to hold it back from flight. You talk to me of nationality, language, religion. I shall try to fly by those nets.'

So Griffith had flung up his net. Thereafter he became even more narrowly nationalistic in his views, and he remained a thorn in the side of the Abbey Theatre. Several months after Yeats's article appeared, he wrote in a letter of 2 January 1904 to Lady Gregory: 'Did I tell you of my idea of challenging Griffith to debate with me in public our two policies—his that literature should be subordinate to nationalism, and mine that it must have its own ideal?'

That public debate did not materialise; nevertheless, the substance of the issue, literature *v.* nationalism, can be found not only in the heroic stance of Yeats's Seanchan and Joyce's Dedalus but also in the mock-heroic strutting of Synge's 'playboys' and O'Casey's 'paycocks.' For instead of defending the sanctity of the artist, these two playwrights instinctively adopted this idea as an implicit principle and went on to launch a comic attack upon the sanctity of the national idealism. As a result Synge and O'Casey were more violently controversial figures than Yeats and Joyce, though this was partly due to the fact that the theatre is a more public and more immediately provocative art form than poetry and fiction; and irreverent comedy is a more recognisably subversive weapon

than literary martyrdom. This is in no way meant to belittle the massive influence of Yeats, or the versatile power of Joyce. Far from being limited to the arrogant aesthetics of Stephen Dedalus, for example, Joyce was a master of comic irreverence in most of his works, particularly in his satiric exposure of nationalistic follies in the hilarious Cyclops chapter of *Ulysses,* where Bloom plays the sensitive mock-hero as comic scapegoat at the expense of the roaring Citizen. But few Irishmen had the opportunity to read Joyce during his lifetime when the unofficial censorship kept his books hidden from most of the people, and Yeats's verse plays never achieved popularity in the theatre and were actually written to be performed in drawing-rooms for carefully chosen audiences of no more than fifty sympathetic listeners.

So we must turn to the plays of Synge, and even more to those of O'Casey, performed in the Abbey Theatre to the accompaniment of riots and protest demonstrations, to discover what amounted to a comic desecration of Ireland's household gods. Under the banner of the new nationalism those household gods or lesser deities—pieties might be a more accurate term—were now equated with the sacredness of everything that was true-green Irish, from Cathleen ni Houlihan to Molly Malone. Though it was understandable and even inevitable that the change should take place in a time of incipient revolution, the impossible pieties of British domination had been replaced in the popular mind by the improbable pieties of Irish idealism. Such a situation was ripe for comic desecration by courageous writers like Synge and O'Casey who questioned and mocked the inviolability of that idealism by relating it to the mundane and ironic realities of Irish life. To the militant and moralistic guardians of the household gods, such as Arthur Griffith and Maud Gonne, and their counterparts out in force now across the land, these two playwrights were guilty of a serious libel against Ireland; but in the hindsight of history and the assessment of literary values it should be clear now that Synge and O'Casey, though they are still regarded with suspicion and enmity by some of their die-hard countrymen, were only guilty of presenting Ireland 'as they found her and not as she wished to be found.'

Synge found the Irish peasants in varying states of comic paralysis and contradictory tensions, straining under the complex moods of frustration and wild fantasy, vicarious exuberance and farcical despair, and therefore his dark comedies were a necessary desecration of those sentimental pieties of the idyllic and pure peasant life. One should have little difficulty in sympathising with the dispirited and potentially vibrant young Nora Burke, in *In the Shadow of the Glen,* over her inability to love her cold and cantankerous old husband, always wheezing like a sick old sheep and with nothing but rough words in his toothless mouth. She openly admits that she married him because he had a bit of a farm that might provide her only security against the fears of old age and insanity. She is terribly depressed and especially afraid of the threat of madness since even a mysterious and magnificent figure of a man like Patch Darcy was finally broken, driven to insanity and death in the desolate hills. And if she does not go the way of Patch, she will in all probability end up like Peggy

Cavanagh, as she tells us in one of those dithyrambic sentences of Synge's which achieve a lyrical union of insight and tragicomic anguish: 'And saying to myself another time, to look on Peggy Cavanagh, who had the lightest hand at milking a cow that wouldn't be easy, or turning a cake, and there she is now walking round on the roads, or sitting in a dirty old house, with no teeth in her mouth, and no sense and no more hair than you'd see on a bit of a hill and they after burning the furze from it.'

With such prospects of tragic waste ahead of her, it is no surprise that Nora decides to go off with the poetic Tramp, who in spite of his fine 'blather' and his affinity with Patch Darcy can only give her an uncertain if immediate refuge from her sour and vindictive husband. Thus, the elaborate scheme of the mock-wake, the farcical revenge which Michael Burke concocts to trap Nora finally helps her to escape to her perilous freedom. By what parody of marital bliss and womanly virtue, then, did the nationalistic guardians of the household gods presume to lecture Synge that a woman like Nora should reflect 'the inspiration of idealism'?

But presume they did, and with such cumulative objections that *The Well of the Saints* (1905) was put down by Griffith as another anti-Irish attempt to imitate an alien and unsavoury story, this time from Petronius; *The Tinker's Wedding* (1907) was considered to be so outrageously 'beyond the beyonds' that it was never performed at the Abbey; and *The Playboy of the Western World* (1907) provoked a week of stormy riots in the theatre. Eleven days after the opening of *The Well of the Saints,* Yeats in a letter of 15 February 1905 to John Quinn wrote in part:

> The audiences always seemed friendly, but the general atmosphere has for all that been one of intense hostility. Irish national literature, though it has produced many fine ballads and many novels written in the objective spirit of a ballad, has never produced an artistic personality in the modern sense of the word. Tom Moore was merely an incarnate social ambition. And Clarence Mangan differed merely from the impersonal ballad writers in being miserable . . . We will have a hard fight before we can get the right of every man to see the world in his own way admitted. Synge is invaluable to us because he has that kind of intense narrow personality which necessarily raises the whole issue.

Synge and O'Casey, like Joyce and Yeats, carried on the fight for the artist's right to present his own vision of Ireland, for they were fiercely subjective men who provoked an atmosphere of intense hostility because they went against the grain of the national and patriotic sentiments. Refusing to pander to those sentiments, Synge and O'Casey created anti-heroic characters who had to fulfil their tragicomic aspirations beyond the conventional paths of Irish life. These playwrights desecrated the national character initially by the very fact that they chose to write sympathetically as well as ironically about cowards, hypocrites, liars, drunkards, tinkers, tramps, beggars, braggarts, parasites, and prostitutes, as well as an odd assortment of peasants, publicans, priests, pedlars, charwomen, carpenters, chicken butchers, bricklayers,

poets, gunmen, hungry old men and women, and consumptive children. To such marginal people living for the most part on sheer guile and pride, the world of reality in early twentieth-century Ireland was something of a nightmare that could easily have driven them to madness or death. Their basic problems and needs were of necessity more personal than national, their impulses and desires were more earthy than ideal, and their only weapon for survival was an improvisational instinct for staying alive through comic resilience, a resourceful display of imagination and mendacious rhetoric which kept their tormentors off balance. It was only natural, then, that they could turn a deaf ear on pious principles with the same instinct for self-preservation that inspired Falstaff to cock an irreverent finger at an honourable corpse on the battlefield.

In *The Well of the Saints,* Synge's satiric parable on the vanity of human wishes, the religious miracle that temporarily restores the sight of the blind beggars, Martin and Mary Doul, reveals their follies and fantasies, as well as the cruelties of the villagers who mock and torment them with the merciless mirrors of reality; but it also convinces Martin that he is more likely to survive in the blind world of his unfettered imagination where his heightened senses allow him to 'feel' the joys and surprises of his vagrant adventures on the road—and that poetic choice is a greater miracle for him. Like Nora Burke, the Douls turn their backs on the sanctity of village life, they become itinerant exiles from the household pieties because experience has taught them a universal truth: a dangerous freedom is preferable to a safe incarceration. It was a similar decision which led Mary Byrne in *The Tinker's Wedding* to 'save' her son and his woman from the respectability and security of a proper Christian marriage so that they could all be free to follow the pagan pleasures of wild tinker life. And again it was a parallel choice which drove the miserable Christy Mahon to mock-parricide and mythic liberation in Synge's masterpiece, *The Playboy of the Western World.* After the repressed and adventure-starved villagers in Mayo transform Christy into a triumphant playboy because he 'murdered' his father in a daring act of defiance; after he is forced to 'kill' his father a second time in front of them and they suddenly turn against him, in the name of their outraged household gods; after he breaks free from their cruel torture and resurrects his playboy legend to become his own hero—after all this, it is his impetuous sweetheart, the tragic Pegeen Mike, who loses her nerve at the moment of crisis, Pegeen with her wild lamentations at the end of the play—'Oh my grief, I've lost him surely, I've lost the only Playboy of the Western World.'—Pegeen who has been terribly defeated by her unfortunate loyalty to those enslaving household gods.

The victors in Synge's plays are forced to leave the community as tragicomic scapegoats who must improvise their hazardous freedom outside the norms of Irish society. They have liberated themselves, and the community, after it recovers from its ambivalent mood of outrage and loss, sinks back into its normal state of paralysis. Perhaps Synge's itinerant heroes are the original outsiders or rebels of the twentieth century, the early comic anarchists of modern literature. And behind them, behind O'Casey's tragicomic clowns, too, as an indirect and presiding influence, there is the archetypal desecrator of sacred things in Ireland, Oisin, the mock-heroic old warrior-poet of Celtic myth, the Playboy of the Pagan World as he appears in the medieval and later Oisin-Patrick dialogues, the *Agallamh Oisin agus Padraig* of dramatic ballad poetry. And in the line of descent from Oisin, there is also the mischievous and mock-heroic 'shaughraun' or vagabond of Dion Boucicault's Irish comedies, *The Colleen Bawn* (1860), *Arrahna-Pogue* (1864), and *The Shaughraun* (1874), plays heavy with sentimentality but also so rich in comic invention, farcical irreverence, and sly Irish humour that they were admired and imitated by Synge and O'Casey.

When we come at last to the tragicomedies of O'Casey, plays dealing directly with the bloody events of the War of Independence, from the 1916 Rising to the Free State settlement in 1923, the desecration of Ireland's household gods increased in proportion to the accelerated fanaticism of Sinn Fein. From O'Casey's point of view, if the patriots were now the guardians of the national honour, the playwright had to be the guardian of the national honesty. No matter how noble the cause, death was a dirty business, and the attempt to die for one's country could bring out the worst as well as the best in men, particularly as it was seen through the eyes of the dispossessed poor people of the Dublin tenements. That was O'Casey's initial desecration, his decision to make the grotesque scapegoats of the slums his main concern instead of the patriots at the barricades, his refusal to sing the Sinn Fein slogans and wave the tri-colour flag. The disciples of Griffith and Maud Gonne never forgave him for these offences and he had to fight them throughout his long life, in his six-volume autobiography, a work full of mighty and profound desecrations, and in most of his later plays.

In his first play, *The Shadow of a Gunman* (1923), set in 1920 at the time of the guerrilla fighting between the IRA and the British forces, his chief spokesman is Seumas Shields, the anti-heroic pedlar and wise fool who can assess the ironic realities of Irish life and deflate the new pieties with painful accuracy. In his characteristic method of creating mock-heroes, O'Casey laughs at as well as with Shields, a man of exaggerated devotion who often uses his faith as a cloak for his cowardice, yet a man of insight and candour who is sickened by brutality and fears that the revolution is devouring its children. In discussing the war with his friend, Donal Davoren, the self-deceived sentimental poet pretending to be a gunman, Shields exposes the danger of fanatical patriotism:

> I wish to God it was all over. The country is gone mad. Instead of counting their beads now they're countin' bullets; their Hail Marys and paternosters are burstin' bombs—burstin' bombs, an' the rattle of machine guns; petrol is their holy water; their Mass is a burnin' buildin'; their De Profundis is 'The Soldiers' Song'; an' their creed is, I believe in the gun almighty, maker of heaven an' earth—an' it's all for 'the glory o' God an' the honour o' Ireland.

When Shields is reminded that he himself had once been a militant Republican—'I remember the time when you yourself believed in nothing but the gun,' Davoren tells

him—Shields justifies his past loyalty and present horror with the best of all possible replies:

> Ay, when there wasn't a gun in the country; I've a different opinion now when there's nothin' but guns in the country—An' you daren't open your mouth, for Kathleen ni Houlihan is very different now to the woman who used to play the harp an' sing 'Weep on, weep on, your hour is past,' for she's a ragin' divil now, an' if you only look crooked at her you're sure of a punch in th' eye.

O'Casey was trespassing on sacred ground here by taking a crooked look at the new Cathleen ni Houlihan. The romantic and sentimental woman with the harp had been transformed into an angry and righteous woman with a gun who demanded absolute loyalty and hit out savagely at anyone who doubted her ruthless methods. But the bold Shields, more effective with words than deeds, went on to question the heroism of her chief cohorts, the bloodthirsty gunmen, insisting that the defenceless people who were supposed to be saved by the war were becoming its main victims.

> It's the civilians that suffer; when there's an ambush they don't know where to run. Shot in the back to save the British Empire, an' shot in the breast to save the soul of Ireland. I'm a Nationalist meself, right enough—a Nationalist right enough, but all the same—I'm a Nationalist right enough; I believe in the freedom of Ireland, an' that England has no right to be here, but I draw the line when I hear the gunmen blowin' about dyin' for the people, when it's the people that are dyin' for the gunmen! With all due respect to the gunmen, I don't want them to die for me.

The scepticism of Shields was O'Casey's humanistic attempt to measure the cost of patriotism. Although it is difficult to stem the tide of bloodshed in a time of war, he was outraged over the way the nationalist rhetoric ignored the indiscriminate slaughter. And in his next play, *Juno and the Paycock* (1925), dealing with the Civil War between the die-hard republicans and the free-staters in 1922, O'Casey moved on to another group of forgotten victims, the Irish mothers on both sides who lost their sons in the bitter fighting. In the stoical and proud figure of Juno Boyle he created his own symbol of Cathleen ni Houlihan, a black-shawled woman of the tenements who had a heart instead of a harp or a gun. When her son Johnny, who was crippled in the hip and lost an arm fighting in the Easter Rising, tells her he would gladly sacrifice himself again for Ireland, 'for a principle's a principle,' she also speaks for Ireland when she opposes his gesture of heroics with an ironic appeal to the higher reality: 'Ah, you lost your best principle, me boy, when you lost your arm; them's the only sort o' principles that's any good to a workin' man.' And later, when Johnny is slain by the republicans for the betrayal of his friend, Hughie Tancred, O'Casey again turns away from the stock responses of patriotic grief as Juno utters her classic lament for the higher idealism, the sacredness of life itself:

> Maybe I didn't feel sorry enough for Mrs Tancred when her poor son was found as Johnny's

been found now—because he was a Die-hard! Ah, why didn't I remember that then he wasn't a Die-hard or a Stater but only a poor dead son! It's well I remember all that she said—an' it's my turn to say it now: What was the pain I suffered, Johnny, bringin' you into the world to carry you to your cradle, to the pains I'll suffer carryin' you out o' the world to bring you to your grave! Mother o' God, Mother o' God, have pity on us all! Blessed Virgin, where were you when me darlin' son was riddled with bullets, when me darlin' son was riddled with bullets? Sacred Heart o' Jesus, take away our hearts o' stone, and give us hearts o' flesh! Take away this murdherin' hate, an' give us Thine own eternal love!

With these elegaic words of anguish O'Casey had touched a universal nerve before which all appeals for national sacrifice must be held mute. For the Juno Boyles of Ireland and the world, suffering and slaughter are the immediate enemies of man. This theme was extended in O'Casey's next play, *The Plough and the Stars* (1926), in which he turned an ironic and irreverent eye upon the Easter Rising itself, one of the most significant moments of sacrifice in Irish history. Perhaps it was no surprise, then, that the mixed praise and hostility which had greeted his previous plays now exploded into riots in the theatre and provoked Yeats's famous 'You have disgraced yourselves again' speech to the protesting audience. The disgrace was nationalism's continuing attempt to intimidate and control literature in Ireland.

Again O'Casey had desecrated the household gods by identifying his Cathleen ni Houlihan with the ragged women of the Dublin tenements, with Nora Clitheroe and Ginnie Gogan and Bessie Burgess, instead of with the 1916 martyrs. This did not mean that he was against the revolution and the martyrs, it meant that he was for the forgotten mothers and wives. In the second act when the Figure at the street meeting outside the pub speaks the actual words of Patrick Pearse in exhorting the people to rebellion, three of the patriots in uniform come into the pub for a drink, Clitheroe and Brennan and Langon. They carry the national flags, and this, too, was interpreted by the rioters as a desecration of the national symbols, for we are to believe that the uniforms and flags never saw the inside of a pub; just as the appearance of the prostitute, Rosie Redmond, was a similar insult to Ireland, for we are to believe that no Irish girl ever laboured in that profession. The three men 'have been mesmerised by the fervency of the speeches,' they have heard the words of Pearse: 'Bloodshed is a cleansing and sanctifying thing, and the nation that regards it as the final horror has lost its manhood'—and over their drinks they cry out:

> LIEUT. LANGON. Th' time is rotten ripe for revolution.
>
> CLITHEROE. You have a mother, Langon.
>
> LIEUT. LANGON. Ireland is greater than a mother.
>
> CAPT. BRENNAN. You have a wife, Clitheroe.
>
> CLITHEROE. Ireland is greater than a wife.

But in the ironic context of the play, Ireland is no greater than her mothers and wives for whom bloodshed has indeed become the final horror. Juno Boyle made that point in her heartbreaking prayer to the Blessed Virgin, and Nora Clitheroe underscores it when she returns from an unsuccessful attempt to find her husband at the barricades and cries out wildly: 'An' there's no woman gives a son or a husband to be killed—if they say it, they're lyin', lyin' against God, Nature, an' against themselves!' The fierce honesty of Nora stands in contrast to the vanity and heroism of her husband, who sulked when he thought he had not been promoted to Commandant and later rushed out to die for Ireland in what his General called 'a gleam of glory.' Brennan brings the tragic news at the end of the play, and the irony grows darker with his empty words of hope: 'Mrs Clitheroe's grief will be a joy when she realises that she had a hero for a husband.' It is a meaningless heroism for poor Nora, who in her hysterical grief has lost her baby and her sanity, as well as her husband. Nor is there any joy for Ginnie Gogan, who lost her consumptive daughter, and Bessie Burgess, who lost her life trying to save Nora.

These tragic ironies reflect a major aspect of O'Casey's view of Ireland, yet they are balanced by a series of comic ironies which also desecrate the Cathleen ni Houlihan pieties and provide that comic view of life which allows some of the characters to survive and even achieve a degree of redemption amidst the disorder and death. This brings us to O'Casey's anti-heroes or clowns, men like Seumas Shields, Captain Boyle, Joxer Daly, Fluther Good, The Covey, and Peter Flynn—cowards and braggarts who manage to temper their folly with an instinctive shrewdness and wisdom that is attractive and reprehensible and human. Unlike Yeats's Seanchan and Joyce's Dedalus, they are unable to issue aesthetic manifestos and wage a private war against the Irish establishment; unlike Synge's peasants and tinkers, they cannot leave the community and seek their uncertain freedom on the road. They have been trapped in their Dublin tenements by a lifetime of poverty and hunger, and now by the terror of the revolution. They are only free in their own conception of themselves, in their eloquent lies and fantasies, in their selfish preservation of their lives in a ridiculous and dangerous world. What they do share with Synge's anti-heroes is their guile and bravado, their comic defences which function best in a spirit of anarchy and belligerent imagination. Their own type of guerilla warfare must be fought with words and motherwit, the only weapons of the dispossessed; and, therefore, their lyrical and over-leaping rhetoric provides a vicarious gratification of their impossible dreams. The very language that Synge and O'Casey created for their characters must then be considered as an organic aspect of their tragicomic themes and structures.

Like Seumas Shields, all of O'Casey's clowns cross their eyes at Cathleen ni Houlihan; and in their irreverence they themselves become an essential part of the national symbolism they mock. They, too, are Ireland, with all their magnificent follies and outrageous derelictions of duty. O'Casey never lets them down lightly, constantly exposes them to satire as well as sympathy. Shields, whose conscience is seldom engaged and is only as honest as it suits him to be, unmasks himself as well as his countrymen when he declares: 'They've made Balor of the Evil Eye King of Ireland, an' so signs on it there's neither conscience nor honesty from one end of the country to the other.' Captain Boyle, that master of self-preserving hypocrisies and strutting masquerades, reveals his serious failures in the same breath that he asserts his anarchic freedom when, for example, he rebels against Juno's attempt to find out which pub he's hiding in to avoid the prospect of a job: 'Is a man not to be allowed to leave his house for a minute without havin' a pack o' spies, pimps an' informers cantherin' at his heels? . . . I don't want the motions of me body to be watched the way an asthronomer ud watch a star.' Like his clever parasite, Joxer Daly, he is the cause as well as the victim of the 'chassis' that threatens to destroy him and his family. But for all their transgressions, these men also possess an indestructible spirit of fun and revelry which keeps them alive in a terrible time and reminds us that their frailties and fantasies could easily be ours under similar conditions.

It is central to the tragicomic genius of O'Casey that he is able to maintain his dual view of these grotesque clowns, mocking them for their irresponsible follies, admiring them for their irreverent victories. Therefore, the mock-heroics of the Captain are as much a part of Ireland as the stoical heroism of Juno. This was one of O'Casey's methods of resisting the nationalist pressures to idealise the Irish people. Perhaps he resisted those pressures most successfully in *The Plough and the Stars* by giving his derelict comedians a kind of left-handed heroism, which is richly shared by Ginnie Gogan and Bessie Burgess and Rosie Redmond, as well as by Peter Flynn and The Covey, and most of all by that wise and boozy lord of misrule, Fluther Good. Though they 'twart and torment' each other through most of the play, they are finally forced to unite and help each other when the street fighting and looting break out and they realise they have a common enemy in the war. They risk their lives for each other and some of them even die for each other; and thus they create their own ways of living and dying for Ireland.

Their mock-battles against each other also develop a further pattern of ironies, as in the second act pub scene, for one of many examples, when Pearse's call for the sacrifice of Irish blood is rewarded with a screaming hair-pulling brawl about illegitimacy and a quixotic fight over the honour of a prostitute. And this type of comic-ironic desecration must finally be linked to the mock-heroic deeds of that superb fool, Fluther Good, who could defend the honour of the prostitute and then go to bed with her; who could risk his life to save Nora and then take the same risk to loot a pub and become blind drunk; who could argue on all subjects with the grandiose illogic of a bragging buffoon and then silence the British soldiers with a devastating retort: 'Fight fair! A few hundred scrawls o' chaps with a couple o' guns an' Rosary beads, again' a hundhred thousand thrained men with horse, fut, an' artillery—an' he wants us to fight fair! D'ye want us to come out in our skins an' throw stones?' There must be some redemption for such an Irishman.

Perhaps the rebirth of a nation cannot be celebrated apart from the rebirth of its literature; perhaps a nation needs the comic wisdom of its irreverent fools as well as the martyred blood of its patriots; perhaps Ireland was not ready for her freedom until her conception of herself was broad enough for the national character to encompass a Fluther Good as well as a Patrick Pearse. There are many ways to redeem Cathleen ni Houlihan besides dying for her, and Sean O'Casey dramatised some of them. In his own way he was the artist as total Irishman, and perhaps his was the higher nationalism. (pp. 114-33)

David Krause, "Sean O'Casey and the Higher Nationalism: The Desecration of Ireland's Household Gods," in Theatre and Nationalism in Twentieth-Century Ireland, *edited by Robert O'Driscoll, Oxford University Press, London, 1971, pp. 114-33.*

Mary Colum on Lady Gregory:

With all her faults and snobbery, [Lady Gregory] was a great woman, a real leader, one of those who woke up Ireland from the somnolence and lassitude it was too prone to fall into. It is very doubtful indeed if Yeats could have produced as much work as he did without her help. It is almost certain that, but for Lady Gregory, the Irish national theater would have remained a dream, or ended in being that failure that so many hopeful undertakings in Ireland became.

Mary Colum, in her Life and the Dream, *Doubleday & Company, Inc., 1928.*

W. B. Yeats

[*Below is a letter Yeats wrote to a group of Californian students following a lecture he gave at their school in 1904. It was originally published in* The Voice of Ireland: A Survey of the Race and Nation from All Angles, by the Foremost Leaders at Home and Abroad *in 1924. In the letter, Yeats expresses the impulse behind the formation of the Abbey Theatre and outlines the fundamental literary tenets and techniques that characterized Irish drama at that time.*]

Some twenty-four years ago, Lady Gregory, who was near her fiftieth year, and I, who was in my early thirties, planned the foundation of an Irish Theatre, and we were soon joined by John Synge, who was in his late twenties. Lady Gregory had spent most of her life between two great houses in South Galway, while Synge had wandered over half Europe with his fiddle, and I had gone to and fro between Dublin and London. Yet Synge and I—like Lady Gregory—were people of the country; I because of my childhood and youth in Sligo, and he because of his in Wicklow. We had gone, all three, from cottage to cottage, collecting stories and hearing songs, and we thought that in these we had discovered that portion of the living mind of Ireland that was most beautiful and distinguished, and we wished to bring what we had discovered to Dublin, where, it seemed to us, the popular mind had grown harsh and ugly. We did not think that the Irish country lacked vice; we were even to be denounced because we insisted that they had the brutalities of country people elsewhere; but we were certain of the beauty of the songs and stories.

Lady Gregory had taken down a song in Irish—'The Grief of a Girl's Heart' it is called—and one day she showed it to a Gaelic-speaking man at her door, and asked what were the best verses. He picked just those verses that I would have picked—those that are most wild and strange, most unlike anything that is called 'popular poetry':

> My heart is black as the blackness of the sloe, or as the coal that is left on the smith's forge; or as the sole of a shoe left in white halls; it was you put that darkness over my life.
>
> You have taken the East from me; you have taken the West from me; you have taken what is before me and what is behind me. You have taken the moon, you have taken the sun from me; and my fear is great that you have taken God from me!

Amid your semi-tropical scenery, you think of Ireland as a far-off country of romance, and you will find it hard to understand one very prosaic reality. If a man is creating some new thing he has to question the taste of others, and that makes those others angry, and all the more if that new thing is a part of something they have long looked down upon as ignorant or foolish or old-fashioned. Then, too, even if he does not openly question the taste of others, it will be a long time before they can see the beauty that he has seen. I think it was George Henry Lewes who said that at first he could see no merit in the Elgin Marbles; and I remember an essay by Andrew Lang, in which he apologised for some attack on the poetry of my generation by saying that when he first met with the poetry of that very great poet, Paul Veraine, he thought it no better than the rhymes in some country newspaper. George Henry Lewes and Andrew Lang had much taste and great erudition. We had to convince average men and women, and to do this by an art that must blunder and experiment that it might find some new form.

If any of you become artists or poets, do not ask a welcome from great crowds, but write at first for a few friends, and always for a comparatively few people—not because you scorn the crowd, but because you think so well of it that you will offer it nothing but your best. In a few generations—but a short time in the history of a masterpiece—that crowd will speak of you with respect, if you are a great artist or poet, and a sufficient number will study what you have made with pleasure and profit.

We thought that Irish drama would be historical or legendary, and in verse or romantic prose; neither Synge nor Lady Gregory had written plays, nor had indeed thought of doing so; so it was I—my head full of poetical drama—that gave the theatre its first impulse. After an experiment with English actors, we began our real work in 1902 in a little temperance hall in a back street, and chose our players from boys and girls, whose interests were, with a couple of exceptions, more political than literary. For the next two or three years we moved from hall to hall making some reputation among students of literature, and among young patriots who thought a theatre with Irish plays might strengthen national feeling, but [we were] much derided by the newspapers. One night I came in front of the curtain and asked the audience to support us against our enemies. I quoted from a leading article in one of the morning newspapers, which had said: 'Mr Yeats proposes to perform foreign masterpieces'—that was part of our project at the time—'Foreign masterpieces are very dangerous things.' I was angry; I should, perhaps, have remembered that the Elgin Marbles are 'foreign masterpieces,' and that some of the figures are very unclothed. Among my audience was an English friend, Miss Horniman. I had been hoping—she had made one or two hints—that she would give us a subscription, and as she was rich, I had fixed upon twenty pounds as the amount. She came up to me the moment I had finished, and said: 'I will buy or build you a theatre.' In the next few months she bought and rebuilt a little old theatre that had been part of a Mechanics' Institute, and we opened there in the winter of 1903-4.

Our obscurity made it possible to create a new kind of acting, for it gave us time to prepare and experiment. If our players had been stage-struck young men and women of the usual kind, they would have developed much more quickly; but their art would have been the ordinary stage art of their time. I had once been asked, at the end of a lecture, where we would get our players, for at that time there were neither Irish players nor Irish plays. I answered with the first thing that came into my head: 'I will go into a room where there are a lot of people, and write all the names on slips of paper and drop them into a hat, shake them up, and take out twelve slips. I will ask those twelve people to act our plays.'

Certainly William Fay, an electric light fitter, who was also an actor of genius, had some experience, for he had toured Ireland in a company with a Negro actor-manager; and his brother, Frank Fay, was learned in the history of the stage, and fond of reciting poetry. But our women players were almost chosen at hazard. They all belonged to a political association, 'The Daughters of Erin,' that described itself as educating the children of the poor, but was described by its enemies as teaching a catechism that began with the question: 'What is the origin of evil?' and the answer was—'England!' From this Association we got two actresses of genius—Miss Sara Allgood, and Miss Moira O'Neill. They grew but slowly to skill and power because, acting at first more from patriotism than ambition, they were never tempted to copy some popular favourite. They copied, under the guidance of William Fay, the life they had seen in their own homes, or saw during some country visit; or they searched, under the guidance of Frank Fay or of myself, for some traditional measured speech to express those emotions that we feel, but cannot observe.

I soon saw that their greatest success would be in comedy, or in observed tragedy; not in poetical drama, which needs considerable poetical and general culture. I had found an old Dublin pamphlet about the blind beggar, 'Zozimus,' and noticed that whereas the parts written in ordinary English are badly written, certain long passages in dialect are terse and vivid. I pointed this out to Lady Gregory, and said if we could persuade our writers to use dialect, no longer able to copy the newspapers, or some second-rate English author, they would become original and vigorous. Perhaps no one reason ever drives one to anything. Perhaps I do not remember clearly after so many years; but I believe it was that thought that made me write, with Lady Gregory's help, *The Pot of Broth,* and *Cathleen ni Houlihan.* The dialect in those two plays is neither rich nor supple, for I had not the right ear, and Lady Gregory had not as yet taken down among the cottages two hundred thousand words of folklore. But they began the long series of plays in dialect that have given our theatre the greater portion of its fame.

I once said to John Synge, 'Why is it that an early Renaissance building is so much more beautiful than anything that followed?' And he replied, 'Style is from the shock of new material.' It was the shock of new material that gave our plays and players their admirable style. I insist on the word 'style.' When I saw Miss O'Neill play the old drunken woman in *The Tinker's Wedding,* at the Birmingham Repertory Theatre a few years ago, I thought her performance incredibly distinguished—nothing second-hand, nothing from the common stock of the stage; no *cliché,* no recognition of all that traditional humour about drunken women.

Lady Gregory's little farces are the only farces of modern times that have not only humour but beauty of style; and her tragedy, *The Gaol Gate,* is a classic, and not because of its action, for it has no action, but because of its style. One need not commend the style of John Synge's famous plays—*The Well of the Saints,* or *The Playboy, The Riders to the Sea, Deirdre of the Sorrows.* Should our Abbey Theatre come to an end, should our plays cease to be acted, we shall be remembered, I think, because we were the first to give to the English-speaking Ireland a mastery of style by turning a dialect that had been used hitherto with a comic purpose to a purpose of beauty. If I were your professor of literature (I must remind myself that *you* hear me, while others but overhear) and were compelled to choose examples of fine prose for an Irish reading book, I would take some passages from Swift, some from Burke, one perhaps from Mitchel (unless his mimicry of Carlyle should put me off), and from that on find no comparable passages till *The Gaol Gate* and the last act of *Deirdre of the Sorrows.* I would then set my pupils to show that this strange English, born in the country cottages, is a true speech with as old a history as the English of Shakespeare, and that it takes its vocabulary from Tudor England and its construction from the Gaelic.

The dialect drama in the hands of Mr Fitzmaurice, Mr T. C. Murray, Mr Lennox Robinson, Mr Boyle, Mr Daniel Corkery, and Mr Seumas O'Kelly, and of Mr Padraic Colum in one of his plays, took a new turn. Synge and Lady Gregory were as little interested in social questions as the old men and women whose stories they had heard and copied; but our new dramatists were, in imagination and sympathy, mainly of the city. The countryman is much alone, and if, as happened through all the Middle Ages, when the most beautiful of our stories were invent-

ed, he is of a violent and passionate nature, he seeks relief from himself in stories or in songs full of delicate emotion: he delights, perhaps, in Arthur and his Court. In the cities, however, men who are in continual contact with one another have for their first need not the beauty but, as I think, the truth of human life. They suffer much from irritation, anger, jealousy; and in their hearts they desire to be shown that, though capitalist and labourer, Nationalist and Unionist, Republican and Free Stater, even honest men and bribed, differ in one thing, they are alike in a hundred. They wish to see themselves and the enemy of their working hours explained, derided or bantered, with at least occasional good humour, though they are not philosophic enough to know that art is the chief intellectual form of charity. When some play of this kind is acted, they are startled, sometimes angry, sometimes incredulous; but they are not bored. They cannot be shown too many such plays if we are not to murder or be murdered because we have given or received some partisan name. Such plays, in the hands of the writers I have named, have dealt with the life of the shop and workshop, and of the well-off farmer, more often than of those small farms of Connaught where there is so much folklore; and the scene is laid, as a general rule, in or near some considerable town, and their speech comes close to modern English. Except in the plays of Mr Lennox Robinson, however, where some character is introduced whose speech has no admixture of dialect, characterisation becomes conventional and dialogue stilted. They introduce such characters so often that I wonder at times if the dialect drama has not exhausted itself—if most of those things have not been said that our generation wants to have said in that particular form. Perhaps, having created certain classics, the dramatic genius of Ireland will pass on to something else.

What new form shall we invent? Or shall we but find new material, and so give the old form new interest? Perhaps on the whole it is likely that we shall but find new material. Ireland is full of tragedy and ruin; and though at the moment we have to reject the few new plays that deal with it, because they are full of the distortion of party feeling, that phase will pass. In a year or two there will be personal narratives, separate incidents which detach themselves. Motives will become apparent; we shall be able to see it all separated from our own fears and hopes, as if upon the luminous table of a *camera obscura.* We have to make peace among so many passions that are the most violent Ireland has known in modern days—violent not only because there has been so much suffering, but because great intellectual questions are involved.

When should we distinguish between political and private morality, or is there only one morality? What is the part of the Catholic Church in public life? How far must the State respect humanitarian emotion? As all these things have been fought out in country districts, or, if in towns, by those classes which still use a language that has in some degree what is called 'dialect'—that is to say, elements peculiar to Ireland—I have a little hope that I shall not be compelled, as one of the readers for the Abbey Theatre, to read through a great number of plays in ordinary English, where all is bookish and pedantic, or full of humorous or sentimental *clichés.*

A cartoon by Tom Lalor of William Butler Yeats addressing the audience at the Abbey Theatre about J.M. Synge's The Playboy of the Western World.

Yet perhaps my first thought is correct, and that we are about to create a new form, and that this form will deal more with those classes who have lost almost every distinctive Irish form of speech. The other day a strange Irish novel was published—*Ulysses,* by Mr James Joyce—which is certainly a new form. You are too young to read it—your master would rightly take it from you. It would cost you some pounds to buy a copy, and if you bought it you would be too startled by its incredible coarseness to see its profundity.

Every other successful Irish novel—certainly every other whose name I can recall at the moment—resembles our plays in dealing with some simple story of public or private life by the light of a morality which everyone accepts without hesitation. Great works of art have been written in that way—the comedies of Oliver Goldsmith, and nearly all the comedies of Molière, for instance. But there are other works which are also, as a famous Belgian poet said a masterpiece must be, a portion of the conscience of mankind, and which judge all by the light of some moral discovery. Something which has been there always—more constantly there, indeed, than Tony Lumpkins or the miser—but which has not been noticed, is brought out into the light that we may perceive [that] it is beautiful or

good, or most probably that it is evil or ugly. The plays of Strindberg or Chekov are of this kind, and it is such works, whether novels or plays, that are most characteristic of intellectual Europe today.

We have already two such plays in Mr Lennox Robinson's *Round Table* and his *Crabbed Youth;* and it looks as if the audience that welcomed his *White-headed Boy* and the other plays in his old manner will give them a sufficient welcome. It is wavering; the shorter play it has delighted in, but the longer, which more openly calls in question a traditional point of view, leaves it a little cold. Mr Robinson has taught us to laugh at, and therefore to judge, a certain exaggeration of domesticity, a helpless clinging to the one resolute person that we had all perhaps noticed in some Irish house or other without knowing that we had noticed it.

He has not made his characters speak in dialect, for he is describing a characteristic that, though it may exist among peasants, needs a certain degree of leisure for its full display; one of those tragedies almost that only begin, as Maeterlinck said, when we have closed the door and lighted the lamp—almost a malady of contemplation. Should some other of our dramatists use the same form, he will have spent many years, like Mr Joyce or like Mr Lennox Robinson, in the education of his judgment, and not only that he may keep his dialogue pure without the protection of a particular form of speech, but that he may judge where judgment has hitherto slept. Then he must be ready to wait—his audience may be slow to understand—for a long time, it may be, to do without all that pleasant companionship that belongs to those who are content only to laugh at those things that everybody laughs at.

He will have to help him a company of players who, though they are still masters of dialect alone, love work and experiment, and so constantly surprise us by some unforeseen success, and a theatre that, having no director or shareholder to pay, uses the profits on its more popular plays to experiment with plays that may never make a profit at all. The audience, though it has coarsened under the influence of public events and constant political discussion, is yet proud of its intelligence and of its old hospitality, and may be won over in time. Yet it may be a bitter struggle—one can never tell; as bitter as any Synge had to endure. And you, perhaps, walking among your palm trees under that Californian sunlight, may well ask yourself what it is that compels a man to make his own cup bitter? (pp. 80-8)

W. B. Yeats, "Two Lectures on the Irish Theatre by W. B. Yeats," in Theatre and Nationalism in Twentieth-Century Ireland, *edited by Robert O'Driscoll, Oxford University Press, London, 1971, pp. 80-8.*

IRISH FICTION

Ernest Boyd

[*Boyd was an Irish-born American critic and translator who is best known for his examinations of Irish literature. In the excerpt below, taken from his influential study* Ireland's Literary Renaissance, *he surveys prose works of the period, stating that in comparison to the poetry and drama produced, fiction was the "weak point of the revival."*]

Anglo-Irish literature has been rich in poetry and drama, but the absence of good prose fiction is noticeable, when it is remembered that the romances of O'Grady were the starting point of the Revival. Indeed, were it not for the essays of John Eglinton, the occasional prose pieces of A. E., and Yeats's two volumes of stories, one might say that the art of prose has been comparatively neglected. For many years John Eglinton was the only writer of the Revival who wished to be known solely as a prosaist, but there is nowadays a perceptible tendency amongst the new writers to seek expression outside the limits of poetry and drama. They do not, however, seem interested in the novel as such, and prefer some even more amorphous form. Even those who write short stories, the most popular form of fiction in contemporary Anglo-Irish literature, rarely

conform to the traditions of the *conte* or *nouvelle*. They either connect their narrative by some loose thread, or they reduce their stories to the dimensions of a sketch. Of novelists in the proper sense of the word we have very few, and they do not appear so intimately related to the literary movement in Ireland itself as the poets and dramatists. A vast quantity of purely "circulationist" fiction must be laid to the charge of Irish writers. Much of it is frankly potboiling; some of it is doubtless intended as a contribution to literature. For obvious reasons, only the more significant novelists call for such reference as is possible in dealing with a large field whose prevailing flatness is its most prominent characteristic.

Emily Lawless was the first of the modern writers of fiction to obtain recognition, when *Hurrish* was published in 1886. This story of Land League times was an early manifestation of that interest in peasant conditions which has become the special feature of the Revival. It must, however, be said that at this point the connection ceases, for Emily Lawless wrote her book entirely as an unsympathetic observer. The agrarian movement is seen in the darkness of anti-national prejudice, not in the light of understanding, and the caricatural rendering of Irish dialect stamps the book as intended for foreign consumption. More fortunate was the choice of the Elizabethan wars in *With Essex in Ireland* (1890), followed in 1892 by *Grania*, an interesting picture of life in the Aran Islands, unspoiled by any misconception of Irish politics or Irish speech. *Maelcho* (1894) is a second attempt at historical fiction hardly to be compared with the earlier story of Essex's expedition, to which a certain charm is lent by the convention of a style contemporary with the events related. In her narrative of the Desmond rebellion there is something of that hostility to the "mere Irish" which was felt in *Hurrish,* and which contributed to the failure of Emily Lawless as an historical novelist. Compared with the glowing enthusiasm of O'Grady's Elizabethan stories her work appears colourless. She is most likely to be reread for the sake of *Traits and Confidences* (1898) and *The Book of Gilly* (1906), two delightful volumes of Western sketches and impressions. In these later works there is a modification of that attitude of aloof superiority, which seems to have sensibly weakened as a result of the changed conception of nationality effected by the Revival. In 1886 *Hurrish* expressed the only possible point of view in respectable circles. But, as time went on, Emily Lawless found that she could permeate her work with the spirit and colour of the West, without prejudice to her political and social convictions. Instead of uncouth, almost non-human beings, living in a savage land, she shows us the wild and simple beauty of life on the shores of the Atlantic, whose fascination haunted her verse, and finally found expression in her prose.

More properly to be counted among the prose writers of the Revival is the author whose poems, *Bogland Studies,* have already been mentioned as preliminary to that part of her work which now calls for attention. Jane Barlow had just only begun to write for *The Dublin University Review* when Emily Lawless was known as a novelist of some standing. Her career coincides, therefore, with that of the poets so exclusively identified with the renascence in Ireland. In 1892 *Irish Idylls* was published, the first of the long series of "bogland studies" which includes *Kerrigan's Quality, Maureen's Fairing, Strangers at Lisconnell* and many others. Sometimes, as in *Kerrigan's Quality* and *The Founding of Fortunes,* a slight plot gives an air of cohesion to these stories, but the author is always and essentially a short-story writer. She depends entirely upon the natural charm of the scenes and incidents depicted, and reduces construction to a minimum. She has a fine selective instinct which rarely betrays her into the trivial or absurd, and this, coupled with a remarkable knowledge of the simpler aspects of peasant life, enables the author to avoid the dangers with which the use of dialect is beset—dangers which threatened the success of *Bogland Studies,* as has been noted.

In most of Jane Barlow's work there is a suggestion of patronage, perhaps unavoidable in one who studies the peasant from outside, but the evident sympathy with which these idylls are written saves them from the reproach of offensiveness. Frequent passages testify to a complete comprehension of the precarious position of the dependent landholder, and the familiar figures of the countryside are sketched with considerable skill. There is, indeed, such intimacy with the life of the peasantry in its external aspects that one wonders how the necessary intercourse can have resulted in so scrupulous an absence of didacticism. Nobody would wish to see these pictures spoiled by the crude colours of the propagandist, but the unconscious propaganda of deep feeling might have stimulated the reader to supply the data excluded by the artist. It is precisely here that one feels that Jane Barlow lacks the requisite equipment for the study of rural Ireland. Everything she sees is softened in the glow of easy good humour or sentimental compassion, so that a rather superficial impression is all that remains when she has told her story. She almost never shows herself conscious of the spiritual entity concealed in these people whom she depicts in all manner of circumstances. Whether they are happy or sad, prosperous or ill-treated, they are portrayed solely as idyllic subjects whose problems are not stated in relation to any tangible reality. There is, in short, a decidedly unnatural detachment in Jane Barlow's conception of the Irish peasant. He is purely a creature of romance, whose existence is not to be measured by reference to unpleasant facts.

Two Northern storytellers are Shan F. Bullock and Seumas MacManus, each of whom published his first book in 1893. The latter is known also as a poet and dramatist, but his popularity derives from the numerous tales of Donegal life and fairy lore which began in 1896 with *The Leadin' Road to Donegal.* This work came after *Shuilers from Heathy Hills* (1893), a collection of prose and verse, but it may be said to mark the beginning of the author's career. In spite of its flagrantly "stage Irishman" humour and exaggerated dialect, Seumas MacManus was not destined to follow in the tracks of Lover and Lever. *'Twas in Dhroll Donegal* (1897) and *The Humours of Donegal* (1898) were still in the rollicking Lover manner, but *Through the Turf Smoke* (1899) showed more restraint and closer observation of actual peasant life. Three volumes of folk-tales, *The Bewitched Fiddle, In Chimney Cor-*

ners and *Donegal Fairy Tales,* followed in immediate succession, and afforded evidence of the author's increasing literary skill, which soon attained its fullest expression. *A Lad of the O'Friels,* which appeared in 1903, is superior to anything else Seumas MacManus has published, and may be counted as one of the best idealistic novels of the Irish peasantry we possess. Like most of its kind, the book inevitably tends to fall into a series of scenes, but the thread is sufficiently substantial to constitute a genuine story, instead of the more usual peg upon which to hang detached sketches. The community of Knocknagar is a living microcosm, studied with eyes which have seen from the inside the people and events described. Seumas MacManus succeeds in shaking off the obsession of broad comedy which has heretofore clung to him, and writes directly out of a life he knows so well, that one regrets his concessions to stereotype. The memorable picture of a Lough Derg pilgrimage is a perfect example of the fine material which lies at the disposal of the Irish novelist.

Shan F. Bullock is a writer of a very different calibre, and one who occupies an almost unique position in the literature produced under the influence of the Revival. He is that rare phenomenon amongst his contemporaries, a genuine novelist, who has eschewed both poetry and drama, and whose short stories are a very small part of his work. *Ring O'Rushes* (1896) and *Irish Pastorals* (1901) are the only volumes he has published in emulation of Seumas MacManus or Jane Barlow. But to these glimpses of rural manners in the County Fermanagh he has imparted a seriousness not characteristic of the more popular writers. *By Thrasna River,* his first important novel, appeared in 1895, and to this may be added *The Barrys* (1897), *The Squireen* (1903) and *Dan the Dollar* (1905). From a list of more than a dozen volumes these three will stand as representative of the author who has most consistently worked to obtain for Irish fiction something of the prestige reserved for poetry and drama. His novels deal almost exclusively with the people of Ulster, although in *The Barrys* half the action takes place in London, where the strange background throws into stronger relief the characteristics of the race from which the protagonists have sprung. Shan F. Bullock is not content to study Northern manners merely in their local manifestations. His two books of short sketches prove that he can write in the familiar, semi-idyllic manner as well as the chief exponents of the *genre,* but he is capable of more sustained effort. He alone has essayed to make the study of rural life simultaneously locally and universally human. He has analysed the Ulster temperament in conflict with fundamental problems, where deeper knowledge is demanded than is necessary to draw the picturesque outline of a peasant community. Consequently, one feels a gravity in his work utterly lacking in the romantic humour and pathos of Jane Barlow and Seumas MacManus. He does not see life as a sentimentalist, but as a realist, who cannot persuade himself that the smiles and tears of Hibernian romanticism are an adequate commentary upon the conditions he describes.

The three volumes of George Moore's *Hail and Farewell* might be included in the category of Irish fiction, were it not for their autobiographical form, coupled with the use of the names and attributes of living persons. Had the author chosen a more fictitious setting for this romance of literary Dublin, he would have spared us the pain of surrendering a remarkable work of imagination to the student of memoirs. Having previously drawn upon some of the people of his reminiscences for his novels, he might have continued the conventional disguise to the end. W. B. Yeats and A. E. were no less themselves when they figured successively as "Ulick Dean" in the early and later editions of *Evelyn Innes.* They would have lost nothing of their personality had they been similarly disguised in this narrative of a repatriated Irishman's adventures in the land of the Literary Revival. George Moore, however, crediting the subjects of his investigation, as well as the public, with his own capacity for artistic detachment, decided to elaborate the story of his return to Ireland, without troubling to conceal the identity of his material. With the perfect callousness of the realistic novelist, he took his "human documents" and arranged them with an eye only to their literary effectiveness. These were slices of life very much more personally alive than the anonymous *romans vécus* of his original French masters, but he exhibited them with the dispassionate enthusiasm of Zola reconstructing his picture of life during the Second Empire. *Ave, Salve* and *Vale,* in their strange juxtaposition of fact and fancy, form one of the most charming prose works associated with the Irish Literary Revival, of which they are the indispensable glossary and the sentimental history.

Fortunately, George Moore has left us a more enduring mark of his passage than his collaboration in the Irish Literary Theatre, and a less equivocal sign of his participation than *Hail and Farewell.* During his residence in Ireland he published one volume of short stories, *The Untilled Field* (1903), and one novel, *The Lake* (1905), which were, until recently, the only works of the first class in Irish fiction. In a preface to the Tauchnitz edition of the former book the author relates how, at the suggestion of John Eglinton, he began to write these stories, in order to preserve his impressions of Irish life, as it revealed itself to him after many years, absence. They were ostensibly published, however, for the purpose of supplying Irish prose writers with models, both Gaelic and English, and several appeared in *The New Ireland Review* in parallel versions, after the manner of Douglas Hyde's Connacht songs. Whether the translated volume, *An T-U'r-Ghort,* which was published the same year as the English edition, was an equally remarkable contribution to contemporary Gaelic literature, is doubtful. The author himself has recounted with much humour his failure to command the same attention from his Irish-speaking as from his English-speaking readers. It is not improbable that moral rather than literary considerations guided the Gaels in this, as in many other instances, with the result that Anglo-Ireland is the richer of the modern Gaelic disdain for æsthetic truth. *The Untilled Field* is the most perfect book of short stories in contemporary Irish literature and need not fear comparison with *A Sportsman Sketches,*—the model proposed by John Eglinton. In the Tauchnitz preface Moore denies the hope of fulfilling the demands of his friend, but only with Turgenev's analogous volume can his own be compared, for its exquisite sense of natural beauty.

Not content with his achievement in this characteristically Irish *genre,* he proceeded to meet our greatest need, by giving the literature of the Revival its first and only novel of distinction, *The Lake.* The personal and national metamorphosis which separated the author and his country from the distant period of *Parnell and his Island* was dramatically revealed in *The Untilled Field.* The former volume of impressions, dated 1887, showed the Ireland of Land League days in the distorted view of an absentee landowner, even more thoroughly denationalised than usual by his literary apprenticeship in Paris. Equally great is the distance separating *A Drama in Muslin* (1886) and *The Lake* (1905), both from a literary and chronological point of view, but the difference between the two novels is of another quality. Whatever objections may have been raised against *Muslin,*—to give the book its revised title of 1915,—it is unjust to assume, as has been the practise of Irish critics, that the author tried deliberately to calumny and misrepresent fashionable society in Dublin. Although contemporaneous with *Parnell and his Island,* the novel is a dispassionate study, in the realistic manner, of social conditions, not a personal criticism like the former work. After the magnificent portrayal of English manners in *A Mummer's Wife,* nothing could have been more legitimately interesting than a similar analysis of Irish society, and *Muslin* deserves no other criticism than that which has been applied to all the earlier works of George Moore prior to his return to Ireland. To make of it an occasion for patriotic indignation is merely to claim that preferential treatment which no writer of genius has ever conceded to his own people. The Irish setting is of no immediate significance, for at that time the novelist was innocent of any suspicion of national bias, unless towards France, his intellectual motherland.

It is precisely this fortuitous setting which constitutes the point of contrast between the earlier novel and *The Lake.* The latter is Irish, the former is about Ireland, and might, so far as its spirit is concerned, have been written by a foreigner. As befits Irish fiction, *The Lake* is composed of the simplest elements, and thereby stands in complete contrast to all the author's other novels. Here one does not find the amorous adventures, the rise and fall of fortunes, the amusing, discreditable and graphic incidents of modern life,—the vast fabric of a complicated social organism unrolled with the patient, unwearied gesture of the realistic novelist. On the contrary, the vital action takes place within the four walls of the parish-priest's house, in a remote Western village, where he receives the letters which are the occasion of an intensely interesting spiritual drama. Father Oliver Gogarty is the only one of the chief protagonists whom we meet face to face, after the first glimpse of Rose Leicester, as she flees from the parish under the shadow of sin. Her correspondence with her repentant accuser is all that we have, for it is his evolution, under the subtle influence of the woman he unconsciously loves, which is the interest of the story.

With delicate art Moore has outlined this drama of revolt against celibacy and belief, so that the banal theme is invested with a charm absent from the traditional rendering of the conflict. He avoids the querulous didacticism of the familiar novel of proselytism or agnosticism, just as he eliminates all suggestion of merely physical temptation. Oliver Gogarty's relation towards Rose is a profound piece of psychological analysis, in which the material factor is diminished to such a point that the woman becomes, as it were, a symbol. Having carefully summarised the circumstances of Gogarty's priesthood, having postulated his spiritual and temperamental disposition, he allows the interaction of ideas and emotions to divest the priest of the accidental and external accretions of his existence until, at last, the man emerges. The latter has stripped off the garments of convention, as well as the garb of his calling, before he plunges into the lake, on whose further shore the road to freedom lies open. The bundle he leaves on the bank behind him is the mere shell of a host of outworn ideals which have fallen away from him, and are abandoned on the threshold of his new life.

When one recalls the manner in which this subject has been treated by certain modern writers, and especially by George Moore's compatriots, it is not easy to be moderate in his praise. Add to this the tender beauty of the pictures forming the background of the story, the exquisite shading of light and colour, and the sensitive feeling for the landscape which seems, indeed, *un état d'âme,* so perfectly does it respond to the mood of the priest. Whether so intended, or not, like its companion volume of short stories, *The Lake* is a model for the prose-writers of the Revival. It was without an equal until the long-awaited Irish novelist appeared who has continued the work which George Moore so excellently began. Neither hypersensitive patriotism, nor a too strenuous desire for "literature at nurse," should obscure the fact that the author of that phrase has done most to restore the Anglo-Irish novel to literature. In the work of James Joyce we shall find that Moore's only successor has enriched Irish fiction with all that the older novelist might have given to it, had the portrayal of Irish life and character not been merely an incidental part of his great accomplishment.

There has been a vast crop of entertaining fiction which has come to be regarded, especially outside Ireland itself, as "very Irish," as the characteristic Irish contribution to the modern novel. The greatest of these disciples of Charles Lever were Œ. Somerville and Martin Ross, whose partnership was terminated by the death of Miss Martin in 1915. Their fox-hunting, rollicking tales of serio-comic peasants and devil-may-care Anglo-Irish gentry gave to *Some Experiences of an Irish R.M.* (1899), *Further Experiences of an Irish R.M.,* and *Dan Russell the Fox* the apparently irresistible charm of such literature for those who are satisfied with an effective convention. The popularity of the many volumes in this vein which these two collaborators published has somewhat overshadowed the real merit of the one novel of genuine power, originality and distinction which they wrote before they discovered the line of least resistance. *The Real Charlotte* (1894) is a Balzacian study of Irish provincial types, drawn with a seriousness and an impartial sense of reality, which serve to heighten regret for the subsequent squandering of the authors' great talent upon the trivialities of a superficial realism. The same attitude towards Irish life, but divorced from all semblance of reality, is found in the work of their successor, George Birmingham, whose *Seething Pot*

(1905) and *Hyacinth* (1906) were the first of a long line of stories designed rather as aids to digestion than to the immortality of the author.

Here and there an isolated volume of more literary quality appears, William Buckley's powerful and well written study of the Irish Rebellion of 1798, *Croppies Lie Down* (1903), St. John Ervine's *Mrs. Martin's Man* (1914). For a moment it seemed as if the latter might be regarded as something more than a fortunate accident, but the pseudo-Dickensian *Alice and A Family* revealed an imitator of Pett Ridge, and the author's next Irish novel, *Changing Winds* (1917) indicated the arrival of another circulationist. It is obviously written in the manner of the later discursive, "sociological" novels of H. G. Wells, and its many pages are largely made up of conversations in the now familiar manner of those youths from the English universities whose post-graduate philosophy has been recorded by a host of younger English novelists. Well known London personalities and almost every prominent figure in Dublin are freely used by St. John Ervine, and no less than three great catastrophes of recent history are worked into the story, which nevertheless remains lifeless. A curious economy is the introduction of the same people once under their real names and once in the feeblest of fictional disguise. The still life pictures of England at the outbreak of the war and Dublin during the insurrection in 1916 are the measure of the novelist's failure to infuse the quality of life into his book. His reflections on the Easter Rising in Ireland, with their fantastic anti-Catholic bias, and their complete blindness to the realities of that desperate adventure, are more suitable to the editorial columns of a Belfast newspaper than to the work of a writer whom Bernard Shaw has described as "an Irishman of real genius." Both in fiction and drama St. John Ervine seems unable to fulfil the promise of his first work, *Mrs. Martin's Man* and *Mixed Marriage.*

An Ulster novelist of a finer calibre is Forrest Reid, who was a contributor to *Uladh,* the organ of the Ulster Literary Theatre, in 1905, shortly after his 'prentice work, *The Kingdom of Twilight* was published. This was followed by another juvenile but more promising book, *The Garden God,* after which an interval of several years elapsed before the author offered the first of his mature novels, *The Bracknels* (1911). From the outset Forrest Reid showed his preoccupation with occult naturism, and his first books were rather naïve contributions to the cult of Pan, after the manner of Arthur Machen and Algernon Blackwood, but in *The Spring Song* (1916), this note of natural mystery is well sustained, and the vivid beauty of the author's visualisations of nature reveals a complete mastery over his style and his material. Out of the simplest elements an admirable work of art is contrived in this story of a group of children, whose adventures are described with so sure a sense of proportion that, while conscious of their intrinsic unimportance the reader is held by the intense interest which they assume in the sympathy and perspective of their creator.

A like simplicity of texture marks Forrest Reid's specifically Irish novels, *The Bracknels, Following Darkness* (1912), and *At the Door of the Gate* (1915). An ardent admirer of Henry James, he has been reproached for the ten-uousness of the fabric on which he embroiders his delicate and usually elusive themes. The first of these three is an amazing dissection of the mean souls of a family whose head is a self-made Belfast merchant. The second, and most remarkable of the three, is a slow moving but arresting study of spiritual loneliness, whose scene is set in the Mourne Mountains and then in the shabby streets of Belfast, where a sensitive young artist is crushed by the crude religion and harsh people about him. To the same subject in another form the novelist returned in *At the Door of the Gate,* which shows the development of a young man in the typical environment of lower middle-class Protestantism as practised in North-East Ulster. Except in the plays of Rutherford Mayne no more faithful studies of Northern Irish conditions have been drawn. At the same time Forrest Reid has a Celtic feeling for the spiritual beauty of nature which, allied with subtle craftmanship and a capacity for writing excellent English, makes this aloof and isolated writer a figure of the utmost distinction amongst his contemporaries.

About the time when St. John Ervine was turning from the theatre to the novel, and had published a little volume of sketches and stories under the title of *Eight O'Clock,* there also appeared a collection of stories by Dermot O'Byrne, *Children of the Hills* (1913), to which the author has since added *Wrack and Other Stories* (1918), both showing unusual qualities. O'Byrne is steeped in Gaelic lore and the old language and history are an essential part of his art. His realism is the realism of Synge, with whom his work has many points in common, as may be seen in *Hunger, The Call of the Road* and the title story of the second volume. The rhythmic, highly coloured speech of the Gaelic-speaking peasant has been rendered by an ear no less sensitive than Synge's, and the atmosphere of Celtic Ireland is skilfully evoked in the weird and grim historical tales which are included in *Wrack.* At the same time, there is in Dermot O'Byrne a quality of mystic imagination which is nowhere perceptible in Synge, and which redeems him from the charge of mere imitation.

Prior to his death in 1918 Seumas O'Kelly was known chiefly as a dramatist, although his first book was a volume of short stories, *By the Stream of Kilmeen* (1902), but his fame is now certain to rest upon his posthumous masterpiece, *The Golden Barque and The Weaver's Grave,* which was published in Dublin in 1919. *The Weaver's Grave* is composed of the simplest elements, the quest of three old men for the site of a friend's grave, and the grotesque humours and quarrels arising out of that situation. Mortimer Hehir, the weaver, had died, and by traditional right he was entitled to be buried in the old cemetery of Cloon na Morav. His young widow enlists the services of Meehaul Lynskey and Cahir Bowes, whose antiquity qualified them to decide where the weaver had staked out his last claim. The superb comedy of this search in the grave-yard, as full of memories for these old men as of graves, is the material out of which Seumas O'Kelly has made a story, vivid, humorous, haunting, bizarre. The setting is wonderful: the ancient country burial ground, still and forgotten beneath the tangle of shrubs and grasses, the mouldering tombstones, the relics of many centuries and

generations. Into this place come the two aged figures, bent double over their sticks, but filled with the exciting sense of their belated recall to useful activity, wandering about "with the labour of age and the hearts of children."

Above the dispute of doddering age, youth, in the person of the widow and one of the gravediggers, has its immemorial struggle, in which the woman is vanquished by the soft eyes and lips of the young man. The process whereby one of the hitherto indistinguishable twin gravediggers suddenly begins to differentiate himself in the eyes of the woman from "the one who did not count" is described with charming subtlety, and there is real poetry and dignity in the closing scene, when at last the grave has been dug, and the man climbs out from his labour. . . .

In the same volume *The Golden Barque* is made up of a series of sketches concerned with a river barge of that name. The adventures of its crew and the chronicle of its voyages are composed of such incidents as must come into the existences described, but, as they pass through the imagination of Seumas O'Kelly, they become invested with a mysterious element of beauty. *Michael and Mary* is typical in its picture of a girl who stands on the bank of a canal and watches a barge slowly passing. A bent figure leads the horse along the towing-path, and a young man stands at the tiller. One day she goes from one lock to the next at his side, in the rain. Another day she hears that he has gone voyaging to an unknown destination, "for he had the blood in him for the wide ocean, the wild blood of the rover." The story is nothing, but in its sheer simplicity it has become the purest poetry, and is the loveliest thing in the book after *The Weaver's Grave.* The supreme achievement of that longer story tends to dwarf the slighter, but remarkable accomplishment of the briefer sketches, as it surpasses the author's other stories in *Waysiders* (1917) and *Hillsiders* (1920), although these rarely lack distinction. Seumas O'Kelly died while he was still at work upon *The Weaver's Grave* which, even without his final revision, remains a perfect story, and emphasises his loss to Irish literature.

A fine gift for narrative prose was revealed by Padraic Colum in his volume of impressions, *My Irish Year* (1912), where he evokes with sympathetic charm a series of pictures of peasant life in the Irish Midlands. The author's power of creating atmosphere, that intangible something which differentiates his plays from those of his contemporaries, is nowhere more remarkable than in this work. Much of *My Irish Year* might be classified as fiction, so skilfully has Colum blended the material elements of his narrative with the imaginative qualities of intuition and instinct. No mere observer, on the outside of Irish life, could have reproduced so wonderfully the soul of rural Ireland. Similarly, in a later volume of prose, *A Boy in Eirinn* (1913), he contrives to invest a somewhat matter-of-fact presentation of Irish life and character with a delicate suggestion of the poetry and romance of childhood. Padraic Colum has since written several charming volumes of stories for children, such as *The King of Ireland's Son* (1916)—to mention the first, which is of specific Irish interest and confirms the hope that he may yet turn his genius for storytelling in the direction of the modern novel.

Daniel Corkery was known chiefly as a playwright and an occasional contributor to Irish periodicals until 1916, when he published his first book, *A Munster Twilight.* This little volume at once proved to be something more than the inevitable collection of short stories which, as we have seen, has always tended to usurp the place of the novel proper in Irish fiction. In an essay on *The Peasant in Literature* the author has defined the bulk of our popular Irish peasant literature as "real in the non-essentials and very untrue in the essentials," and his own stories seem to be designed to fulfil the conditions which that criticism implies. *A Munster Twilight* is a work belonging to the same class as Padraic Colum's *Wild Earth* and Synge's *Riders to the Sea,* both of which were excepted from the judgment passed by Daniel Corkery on his predecessors. He knows his Cork and Kerry as Synge knew Wicklow and the Aran Islands, and Colum the Midlands, and he describes the people with the same harsh humour that gives its savor to the writing of the dramatist. *The Lady of the Glassy Palace* and *Vanity,* for example, treat of death in the manner which was denounced as "brutality" in Synge, but which is in reality a manifestation against the lachrymose, conventional pathos of the "pleasant" playwrights and storytellers. *The Wake* also may be commended to those who desire realities rather than the jocosities of Samuel Lover and the Dickensian variations upon deathbed themes, which are commonly accepted as the only possible alternatives. Corkery can evoke the grim humour, as well as the pathos, of this hackneyed situation by the simple process of telling the truth.

His most conventional story (though admittedly in the "new" Irish convention) is the first in the book, *The Ploughing of Leaca-na-Naomh,* although the press as usual, singled it out for extravagant praise, doubtless because it is so "very Celtic." *The Return* is as grotesque and weird as anything in Poe but at the same time it is filled with a sense of Irish humanity. Not since *The Land* of Padraic Colum has the relation of the peasant to the soil been so finely expressed in prose as in that story of almost inarticulate emotion, *Joy,* which tells of the return to a rich farm of an old man who had been forced off the piece of poor land which he loved, and driven into the city. *The Spanceled* is another notable chapter, which reminds one of Synge in its challenging tragedy of a love which binds, or spancels, a man and a woman more irksomely because of the absence of legal bonds. In 1920 a second volume of short stories appeared under the title of *The Hounds of Banba,* vivid, imaginative studies of the Ireland of Sinn Féin, whose political interest naturally ensured their success. Political bias, though it may turn some readers away, is not by any means necessary to a proper appreciation of the artistic power of the book. Daniel Corkery has written the epic of resurgent and exalted nationalism, and his pictures of a whole people in revolt are admirable in the skill with which a single theme is developed without ever becoming forced or monotonous. The conditions portrayed are those which were outlined day by day in the newspaper reports of the Irish war, but here the outlines are filled in with the living matter of tradition, desperate devotion and heroic pride. Among a people aflame with the passion of nationality, harried yet undismayed, the author has found the stories of suffering and defeat, but never of despair. The rattle of machine guns and armoured cars, the tramp of men drilling in the darkness, the bitter memories of insurrection handed down from one generation to another, run through this book, giving it the value of an historical document which is, at the same time, literature. Here is the conflict of two races and two civilisations, not in terms of politics, but in terms of humanity.

The place of Daniel Corkery in Anglo-Irish literature is assured, however, not by his short stories, but by the novel which he published in 1917, *The Threshold of Quiet.* This work was written before *A Munster Twilight,* but the author was wise to offer the slighter book first, even at the risk of being expected to repeat himself in what was naturally regarded as his second book. There is not the slightest resemblance between them, for here he proceeds to unfold a leisured narrative in which the reader drifts along the quiet stream of provincial life. Connoisseurs of the picturesque phrase and those who cultivate literary plots will be rebuffed by Corkery's indifference to the dialectics of dialect and the requirements of "a good story." The substance of his novel is as tenuous as anything in the later works of Henry James; his manner is as garrulous and expansive as that of Dostoevsky. But his sentences have not the corresponding subtlety which makes or mars Henry James, according to one's fancy. "Swathed in relative clauses as an invalid in shawls," is not the description that can be aptly applied to them. Corkery writes a clear and forceful prose as devoid of mannerism as it is free from cliché; his style is as fresh and personal as his conception of character.

Reference has been made to the tendency of Irish fiction to resolve itself into a connected or unrelated series of episodes or incidents. The purveyors of humourous and sentimental novels for the libraries alone profess to tell a homogeneous story, and they are rewarded by a popularity denied either to the nouvelle, as such, or to the prose work of James Stephens. Although Corkery has shown in *A Munster Twilight* his ability to visualise the dramatic or humourous episode, his novel is innocent of all such effects. So completely has he emancipated himself from the common practice that one can easily imagine the impatient admirer of Katharine Tynan, Jane Barlow, George Birmingham, or Seumas MacManus turning aside from *The Threshold of Quiet,* with a complaint that it lacks incident, as it lacks a plot. It tells no story like *Spanish Gold;* it relates no scenes of country life, in the comic or sentimental manner of Jane Barlow and Seumas MacManus; it eschews the amiable idealisations of Katharine Tynan. If a parallel be sought it will be found, strange to say, in *A Portrait of the Artist as a Young Man.* Not that the morbid retrospection and analysis of James Joyce have their counterpart in the work of Daniel Corkery; but both writers have given their books the inchoate form to which the Russian novelists have reconciled us. The former has written a savage and, to some minds, a shocking indictment of Dublin; the latter has gently drawn aside the curtain, and softly illuminated the quiet and obscure corners of Cork.

One thinks of Chekhov and Dostoevsky while reading *The Threshold of Quiet,* for only in Russian literature does one find the portrayal of such secluded and uneventful lives as drift through these pages, as they drift through *The Cherry Orchard* or *Uncle Vanya.* The mysterious death of Frank Bresnan broods over the whole book; but it occurs at the beginning, and is the occasion of no greater suspense in the reader than was Raskolnikov's crime in Dostoevsky's masterpiece, for all Corkery's skill in allowing the truth of suicide to crystallise slowly and shyly in the minds of the circle whose existence is described. As in the case of *Crime and Punishment,* there is no attempt to exploit outward circumstance, and the story is almost purely cerebral, so carefully does the author restrict its movement to what is passing in the minds of his characters. When the book is closed all one has seen happening is the departure of Finnbarr Bresnan for America, after a hesitation as to whether he had not a vocation for the priesthood; the tragic ending to the story of Stevie Galvin and his brother; the crossing of the "threshold of quiet" by Lily Bresnan when she finally feels free to enter Kilvirra Convent, renouncing life and the love of Martin Cloyne. Even these few dramatic moments are not developed, but just cause a slight stir of the deep waters of consciousness in which these lives are submerged.

Yet only the most hasty reader will fail to succumb to the appeal of the book, which captures the mind by its simplicity and sincerity, its absence of factitious interest. Corkery plunges us at once into the slow current of these lonely lives, whose struggle for peace and happiness is no less intense and moving because it takes place on a plane only discernible to the intimate comprehension of a writer whose eyes are fixed on the truth nearest to his own heart. The high lights of grand tragedy and the crude glare of melodrama do not light up these pages, steeped in tender and alluring half tones. As a *genre* picture of provincial society in Ireland, *The Threshold of Quiet* is unique in its serious realism, from which the ugliness of naturalism has been eliminated without detriment to its fidelity. With a skill that amounts to genius Daniel Corkery avoids the falsity and mawkishness of the popular idealisations, while preserving the purity at which they aim. A great deal of careful pruning has gone to the creation of the mood in which it is possible by the merest hints and suggestions to obtain effects which his contemporaries have laboured and spoiled. The religious note is particularly delicate and beautiful, spontaneous and reserved, eloquent but never didactic. It is not only a remarkable first novel, but it is the one work of modern Irish fiction which can be compared with that of James Joyce, not because of any identity of mood and matter, but because of the psychological depth and the originality of these two writers. Dissimilar as they are in every respect Daniel Corkery and James Joyce have brought the Irish novel back into literature.

A serious effort towards the same end is discernible in the work of several young novelists who came forward about the same time as Corkery. Darrell Figgis with *Children of Earth* (1918), and *The House of Success* (1921), Eimar O'Duffy with *The Wasted Island* (1920), and Brinsley MacNamara, whose four novels, *The Valley of the Squinting Windows* (1918), *The Clanking of Chains* (1920), *In Clay and Bronze* (1921) and *The Mirror in the Dusk* (1921), deserve more than passing mention. The author is in evident revolt against the conventional Irish novel, and his work is a concerted attempt to break down the convention in fiction which the Abbey Theatre playwrights destroyed in Irish drama, to describe rural Ireland with realistic candour. Although the stories usually have their scene in the Midlands, Brinsley MacNamara closes his ears to the songs which the blackbird of Meath sang to Francis Ledwidge, nor does he bring the sympathy of Padraic Colum in describing the same countryside. Like the squinting windows of the valley of Tullanahogue as they peer malevolently at the doings of Garradrimna, the author's vision is not quite straight and clear. He is perhaps a little too complacently interested in the degrading existence of the "seven pubs" which absorb the time and money of the villagers, and his relish in the malicious gossip of the drunken men and back-biting women of the valley is not entirely unrelated to his own method of telling a story. He never loses an opportunity of emphasising the vileness of human nature in his portrayal of this agricultural slum. The theme is largely responsible for this one-sided characterisation. The story of the sin which wrecked the life of John Brennan's mother, defeated her ambitions for him, and brought him to the same ruin as his father, is developed through the gossip and feuds of Garradrimna, and the participants in these orgies of slander and hatred are the characters in Brinsley MacNamara's tragedy.

In *The Clanking of Chains* the subject is of more general significance, an exposure of the seamy side of Nationalist politics, as seen by an Irishman whose patriotism does not allow him to fall into the national habit of Narcissism. The malevolence of Tullanahogue was exercised under special conditions, and could have but a relative interest. The decadence of Ballycullen is the manifestation of a social disease which self-complacency has allowed the patrioteers to ignore. Michael Dempsey's struggle to stir his countrymen from their servile opportunism is, in a sense, the history of every Irish Nationalist leader. MacNamara allows no momentary gleam of hope or success to lighten these dark pages, and to that extent, it may be said, Michael Dempsey is not typical. He does not enjoy his hour of triumph even though it be merely the prelude to the ultimate disillusionment of rejected leaders, such as we have so often seen in this country. But the author has a vastly more important purpose than the creation of a tragic figure. Michael is never allowed to attain the dignity of tragedy—the brutal tragic-comedy of life is all powerful, and in the end he can do no more than retreat from the vindictive wrath of his inferiors. The Ballycullen community is composed of verbal patriots, who are content to belittle every heroic endeavour of Irish Nationalism until it succeeds. Then, when it is safe and profitable, they are the devoted admirers of each new political regime. In the course of the story these invertebrates evolve, with characteristic hesitations, from a soulless championship of constitutional Home Rule to an equally degrading conception of Sinn Féin. They touch nothing that they do not disfigure and destroy. The despairing idealist, Michael Dempsey, escapes, in order to avoid the fate of those tragic survivors of the Fenian and Agrarian movements, whom the author has described with the pitiless power of exasperated realism. Kevin Shanaghan and Connor Carberry, so different, yet alike in their misfortune of having outlived the day of their generation's glory, are remarkable studies.

The Clanking of Chains is an extremely effective study of the incurable loutishness of the undeveloped man. Brinsley MacNamara has chosen Ireland for the working out of his idea, but the *Leitmotiv* of the story is universal. Ibsen described it in *An Enemy of the People,* but, because we have not chosen to idealise the Scandinavians, nobody accuses Ibsen of having calumniated them. The romantic view of Nationalism will never lack exponents in Ireland and elsewhere. It is all the more necessary that a writer should come along who is not afraid to show us all the mean jealousies, the cowardice, and the corrupt servility, which shelter behind the deeds and words of great movements.

In his second novel the author shows a considerable advance upon his previous work. The characterisation is more distinct, and although the story in itself is not so "well-made," it is peopled by living types, Ambrose Donohoe, Gilbert McCormack, Marcus Flynn, and Mirandolina Conway. These are not just puppets serving the purpose of a thesis, but real men and women whose part in the shaping of Irish affairs is greater than that of the Michael Dempseys, because they are more numerous. It is they who have rivetted the chains whose heavy weight drags oppressively upon the community of which Ballycullen is a remarkable microcosm.

The autobiographical references of *In Clay and Bronze* date it as the second novel of Brinsley MacNamara, although circumstances deferred its publication, and eventually caused it to be published in London under the title of *The Irishman,* by "Oliver Blythe," although in New York the book appeared with its real title and over his own name. The story is that of Martin Duignan, a young farmer, who is drawn from the land to the city in pursuit of literary ambitions, has a disastrous spell of theatrical life in New York, and returns, disillusioned, to the clay from which he sprang. It is not until he has thus realised himself, and obeyed the traditional call of the soil to the peasant that is in him, that the artistically creative part of his being comes into play. At the close of the narrative his novel has been written and published, and he is back again in Dublin with high hopes in his breast. There the author leaves him with a slightly sardonic hint of the vanity of such hopes.

Brinsley MacNamara has an unrivalled faculty of seeing certain aspects of Irish life as they are. The peasantry, as he sees them, are neither the buffoons of Lover nor the visionaries of Yeats and Lady Gregory. They are the eternal peasant as Maupassant and others have described him, brutalised only too often by the intolerable conditions of existence in an agricultural slum. The types of Irish rural society which are elaborately and remorselessly exposed in *The Clanking of Chains* are sketched in here. MacNamara has a pitiless memory when he records the attitude of the mob mind towards Sinn Féin before it became patriotic to subscribe to that creed. In his pictures of Dublin he at once invites comparison with James Joyce's *A Portrait of the Artist as a Young Man* and *Ulysses.* Here, however, his effects are not so profound and his satire some-

what superficial. The "Tower Theatre" and its idiosyncrasies become the butt of many gibes, but they are neither good humoured enough to amuse nor serious enough to make a deep impression. But MacNamara has drawn an excellent picture of that curious pseudo-intellectual life of certain Dublin salons where an occasional fine talent may be found supporting a strange variety of parasites. Joyce has glanced at the fringe of that society, especially in *Ulysses,* but MacNamara's hero passes through it and returns to it.

It has been said of the Irish playwrights that they were too constantly preoccupied with the seamy side of Irish manners, with the ugly and sordid details of life. The riot over Synge's *Playboy* was a spectacular demonstration of the resentment felt by the romanticists. In his account of the "Tower Theatre" Mr. MacNamara hints satirically at the crude realism of peasant melodrama. His own novels, however, are the expression in fiction of precisely that mood of revolt and protest which enabled the dramatists of the Irish Theatre to drive out the old-fashioned stage Irishman of the Boucicault tradition. Brinsley MacNamara's work is a counterblast to the cheerful concoctions of George Birmingham, Dorothea Conyers, and even of Somerville and Ross, who never eliminated the Leveresque element from their novels. In the conventional form of the realistic school MacNamara's novels have widened the breach in the literary ramparts of romantic Ireland. But it is by the genius of James Joyce that the dilemma of the realists and the romanticists has been solved.

While the tranquil power and subtle qualities of *The Threshold of Quiet* have been recognised by discerning critics here and there, the book has had neither the popular suffrage of the general public nor the ardent championship of a coterie. The work of James Joyce, on the other hand, has enjoyed both in turn, and is now in danger of those antagonisms invariably aroused by extravagant enthusiasts and uncritical imitators. When he published his little booklet of Elizabethan songs, *Chamber Music,* in 1907, his name was unknown outside Ireland, and his first prose work, *Dubliners,* was actually accepted for publication about the same time by a Dublin publisher. Owing to a variety of peculiar circumstances, partly explained by the disadvantages under which the press always suffers when controlled by an alien administration, that first Irish edition of *Dubliners* was all destroyed except one copy delivered to the author, and the book did not appear until 1914, when it was published in London. Two years later a similar experience befell *A Portrait of the Artist as a Young Man,* which could not find a London publisher and was issued in New York. Finally neither London nor New York could meet the responsibility imposed by this daring and extraordinary genius, and his great experiment, *Ulysses* (1922), was issued in a limited edition for subscribers in Paris, but not until after *The Little Review* of New York had been rewarded with a fine for its praiseworthy attempt to publish portions of the work serially. With the exception of *Chamber Music* and his one play, *Exiles* (1918), the publication of Joyce's books has failed to answer to that definition of happiness which consists in having no history.

Charming as his little poems are they would no more have established James Joyce as one of the most original figures in the whole world of contemporary letters than would his remarkable psychological drama in three acts, which is undoubtedly the only Irish play to realise the first intentions of Edward Martyn in helping to launch the Dramatic Movement. In its morbid and profound dissection of the soul, *Exiles* suggests the social analysis of Ibsen combined with the acute sexual perceptions of Strindberg. The originality of Joyce and the justification of the high esteem in which he is held must be sought in those three volumes of fiction, *Dubliners, A Portrait of the Artist as a Young Man* and *Ulysses,* which have rightly aroused the attention of the intelligent public in Europe and America, even though a French critic has rashly declared that with them "Ireland makes a sensational re-entry into European literature." Apart from its affecting and ingenuous belief in the myth of a "European" literature, this statement of M. Valery Larbaud's has the obvious defect of resting upon two false assumptions. It is natural, perhaps, that he should know nothing whatever about Irish literature, and prove it by comparing the living Irish language to Old French. But a Continental writer might, at least, have remembered the vogue of Thomas Moore, who shared with Byron the curious distinction of a peculiarly "European" reputation due apparently to the enchantment which distance lends to the view of a foreign literature. In other words, to the Irish mind no lack of appreciation of James Joyce is involved by some slight consideration for the facts of Ireland's literary and intellectual evolution, and the effort now being made to cut him off from the stream of which he is a tributary is singularly futile. The logical outcome of this doctrinaire zeal of the coterie is to leave this profoundly Irish genius in the possession of a prematurely cosmopolitan reputation, the unkind fate which has always overtaken writers isolated from the conditions of which they are a part, and presented to the world without any perspective.

Fortunately, the work of James Joyce stands to refute most of the theories for which it has furnished a pretext, notably the theory that it is an unanswerable challenge to the separate existence of Anglo-Irish literature. The fact is, no Irish writer is more Irish than Joyce; none shows more unmistakably the imprint of his race and traditions. Those who have with some difficulty weaned themselves from the notion that the harum-scarum sportsmen and serio-comic peasants of the Lever school represent Ireland, only to adopt the more recent superstition of a land filled with leprechauns, heroes out of Gaelic legend, and Celtic twilight, naturally find James Joyce disconcerting. Accordingly, they either repudiate him altogether, or attempt to explain him at the expense of all his Irish contemporaries. The syllogism seems to be: J. M. Synge and James Stephens and W. B. Yeats are Irish, therefore James Joyce is not. Whereas the simple truth is that *A Portrait of the Artist as a Young Man* is to the Irish novel what *The Wanderings of Oisin* was to Irish poetry and *The Playboy of the Western World* to Irish drama, the unique and significant work which lifts the *genre* out of the commonplace into the national literature. Like most of his fellow-craftsmen in Ireland, as we have seen, Joyce began characteristically with a volume of short stories. *Dubliners* dif-

fered from the others, not in technique, but in quality, and above all, in its affinity with the best work of the French Naturalists, from whom Joyce learned his craft as George Moore did before him. It is not mere coincidence that the greatest novels of contemporary Irish life should come from the only two writers who submitted to that French influence, until they had mastered it and created out of it something of their own. The genesis of all that the author has since published is in that superb collection of studies of middle-class Dublin life.

Dublin is the frescoe upon which James Joyce has woven all the amazing patterns designed by an imagination which is at once romantic and realistic, brilliant and petty, full of powerful fantasy, yet preserving an almost incredible faculty of detailed material observation. He is governed by a horror and detestation of the circumstances which moulded the life of his Stephen Dedalus, in that city which he has carried away with him during the long years of his expatriation, and whose record he has consigned to the pages of *A Portrait of the Artist* and *Ulysses.* With a frankness and veracity as impressive as they are appaling Joyce sets forth the relentless chronicle of a soul stifled by material and intellectual squalor. Stephen Dedalus, the son of a well-to-do Catholic family, passes through the various educational and social experiences of his class in Ireland. He is sent from school and college to the university, and these institutions, their pupils and staff are described with a candour which might have been considered more sensational had the victims moved in a more prominent world. The autobiographical and realistic character of the history of Stephen Dedalus is dismissed by certain critics as of no importance, but except for some disguises of name, the two volumes of his adventures are as effectively indiscreet as *Hail and Farewell.*

The gradual downfall of the Dedalus family provides the framework of the first book. A deep undertone of filth and sordid shiftlessness is the fitting accompaniment to the disintegration of Stephen's life. The atmosphere in which he is expected to respond to the stimulus of higher education is sardonically suggested in the chapter where he is shown preparing to attend his lectures:

> He drained his third cup of watery tea to the dregs and set to chewing the crusts of fried bread that were scattered near him, staring into the dark pool of the jar. The yellow dripping had been scooped out like a boghole, and the pool under it brought back to his memory the dark turf-coloured water of the bath in Clongowes. The box of pawn tickets at his elbow had just been rifled and he took up idly one after another in his greasy fingers the blue and white dockets, scrawled and sanded and creased, and bearing the name of the pledger as Daly or MacEvoy. . . .

> Then he put them aside and gazed thoughtfully at the lid of the box, speckled with louse marks, and asked vaguely:

> "How much is the clock fast now?"

This hideous interior is typical of the material surroundings in which Stephen Dedalus lives. When he leaves the house we are told:

> The lane behind the terrace was waterlogged, and as he went down it slowly, choosing his steps amid heaps of wet rubbish, he heard a mad nun screeching in the nuns' madhouse beyond the wall:
>
> "Jesus! O Jesus! Jesus!"
>
> He shook the sound out of his ears by an angry toss of his head and hurried on, stumbling through the mouldering offal, his heart already bitten by an ache of loathing and bitterness. His father's whistle, his mother's mutterings, the screech of an unseen maniac were to him now so many voices offending and threatening to humble the pride of his youth.

It is not an escape, however, which the university provides, for he simply exchanges physical ugliness for intellectual ugliness, so far as Joyce reports his life there. The only ray of idealism which penetrates the gloom of his existence is the influence of religion, which comes upon him in college, when he recoils in terrified horror before the prospects of a hell, described with a wealth of dreadful detail which seems to be suggested by an elaboration of the filthiness of Stephen's moral and physical habits. It is apparently the author's purpose to empty Catholicism of all its spiritual content, in order to provide his hero with a congruous religious background. Similarly he is tempted to depart from the strictly horrible veracity of his pictures in order to romanticise the unclean initiation of Stephen into the adventure of love. It is, of course, possible, that the amorous and religious experiences of such a man should be on a level corresponding to the low quality of his own personality. But the redeeming feature of Stephen Dedalus is his sincerity, which enables him at all times to realise the significance of what he sees, and we find it hard to reconcile his realistic temperament with the preposterous idealisation of prostitution, in a city where it has not even a remote semblance of that disguise of joy, which is supposed to make it dangerous in more sophisticated places. So long as he describes the exterior of Dublin's underworld, Joyce is too good an observer to suggest anything more than its repulsiveness. It is the supreme irony of his portrait that the artist proceeds to Swinburnian romantics based upon material so unspeakably frowsy. The romance in Stephen's life is designedly of this degrading and degraded quality. For James Joyce shows himself throughout preoccupied with all that is mean and furtive in Dublin society, and so far as he permits his own views to emerge, he professes the greatest contempt for a social organisation which permits so much vileness to flourish squalidly, beneath a rigid formality of conduct. The pages of this book are redolent of the ooze of our shabby respectability, with its intolerable tolerance of most shameful social barbarism. Joyce shows how we breed and develop our Stephen Dedaluses, providing them with everything they crave, except the means of escape from the slime which envelops them. Culture for Dedalus is represented by the pedantries of medieval metaphysics, religion by the dread of hell. Left to drift abjectly between these extremes, the young artist disintegrates in a process whose analysis becomes a remarkable piece of personal and social dissection.

In *Ulysses* the analysis of Stephen Dedalus in particular, and of Dublin in general, is carried a step further, how much further may be imagined from the fact that this vast work, of more than seven hundred and twenty-five quarto pages, covers the events of less than twenty-four hours. It recounts a day in the life of Stephen Dedalus and Leopold Bloom, and shows in a marvellous microcosm the movement of the city's existence, in ever spreading circles and ripples of activity, correlated by a method which recalls that of Jules Romains and the *Unanimistes*. But its form is more akin to that of the German Expressionists. The technical innovations which began to show in *A Portrait of the Artist as a Young Man* are here advanced to the point of a deliberate stylistic method, whose cumulative effect is wonderful. The occasional use of monologue, the notation of random and unspoken thoughts as they pass through the mind of each character, the introduction without warning of snatches of conversation, of prolonged dialogues, now almost entirely takes the place of narrative. The final chapter, for instance, is a reverie of forty-two pages, without any kind of punctuation except the break of paragraphs, in which the whole sexual life of Leopold Bloom's wife rushes pell-mell into her consciousness. It is almost always in these passages of introspection that the author reveals the sex interests and experiences of his people, and in the emptying out of their minds naturally a great deal is uncovered to the discomfiture of convention. The charges of "immorality" which Joyce has had to face have been based as a rule upon such passages.

Yet, rarely in literature has eroticism appeared in such harsh and disillusioned guise as in the work of James Joyce, where it oscillates between contemptuous, Rabelaisian ribaldry, and the crude horror and fascination of the body as seen by the great Catholic ascetics. The glamour of love is absent, and there remains such an analysis of repressed and stunted instincts as only an Irishman could have made to explain the curious conditions of Irish puritanism. But the analysis is not put forward in any intention of criticism; didacticism is alien to all that Joyce has written. He has simply compiled the record, reconstructed a period in his life, and left us to draw conclusions. *Ulysses* is simultaneously a masterpiece of realism, of documentation, and a most original dissection of the Irish mind in certain of its phases usually hitherto ignored, except for the hints of George Moore. Dedalus and Bloom are two types of Dubliner such as were studied in Joyce's first book of stories, remarkable pieces of national and human portraiture. At the same time they serve as the medium between the reader and the *vie unanime* of a whole community, whose existence is unrolled before their eyes, through which we see, and reaches our consciousness as it filters into their souls. As an experiment in form *Ulysses* more effectively accomplishes its purpose than Jules Romains did in *La Mort de Quelqu'un,* for out of the innumerable fragments of which this mosaic is composed Joyce has created a living whole, the complete representation of life. The book might have been called *La Vie de Quelqu'un,* for it is not the personal existence of Dedalus and Bloom that matters so much as the social organism of which they are a part.

Hermann Bahr, in his *Expressionismus* (1916), describes the advent of Expressionism in terms which summarise appropriately the evolution of Joyce. "The eye of the body is passive to everything; it receives, and whatever is impressed upon it by outward charm is more powerful than the activity of the eye itself, more powerful than what it seizes of that outward charm. On the other hand, the eye of the mind is active and merely uses as the material of its own power the reflections of reality. . . . Now it seems that in the rising generation the mind is strongly asserting itself. It is turning away from exterior to interior life, and listening to the voices of its own secrets. . . . Such a generation will repudiate Impressionism and demand an art which sees with the eyes of the mind: Expressionism is the natural successor of Impressionism."

Much has been written about the symbolic intention of this work, of its relation to the Odyssey, to which the plan of the three first and last chapters, with the twelve cantos of the adventures of Ulysses in the middle, is supposed to correspond. Irish criticism can hardly be impressed by this aspect of a work which, in its meticulous detailed documentation of Dublin, rivals Zola in photographic realism. In its bewildering juxtaposition of the real and the imaginary, of the commonplace and the fantastic, Joyce's work obviously declares its kinship with the Expressionists, with Walter Hasenclever or Georg Kaiser.

With *Ulysses* James Joyce has made a daring and valuable experiment, breaking new ground in English for the future development of prose narrative. But the "European" interest of the work must of necessity be largely technical, for the matter is as local as the form is universal. In fact, so local is it that many pages remind the Irish reader of *Hail and Farewell,* except that the allusions are to matters and personalities more obscure. To claim for this book a European significance simultaneously denied to J. M. Synge and James Stephens is to confess complete ignorance of its genesis, and to invest its content with a mysterious import which the actuality of references would seem to deny. While James Joyce is endowed with the wonderful fantastic imagination which conceived the fantasmagoria of the fifteenth chapter of *Ulysses,* a vision of a Dublin Brocken, whose scene is the underworld, he also has the defects and qualities of Naturalism, which prompts him to catalogue the Dublin tramways, and to explain with the precision of a guide-book how the city obtains its water supply. In fine, Joyce is essentially a realist as Flaubert was, but, just as the author of *Madame Bovary* never was bound by the formula subsequently erected into the dogma of realism, the creator of Stephen Dedalus has escaped from the same bondage. Flaubert's escape was by way of the Romanticism from which he started, Joyce's is by way of Expressionism, to which he has advanced.

Until this revival of the art of fiction dealing with contemporary life, which has come about during the years of the war, the more original prose writers had shown no disposition to accept the novel proper as their medium. Prior to 1914 the two most important could not be classed as novelists except in the loosest sense of that term. Neither Lord Dunsany nor James Stephens had carried on the tradition of any previous writer of Irish fiction. They cannot be associated with the other storytellers. James Stephens began by making a slight concession to the accepted convention of the novel, but before *The Charwoman's Daughter* had reached many chapters that convention was abandoned. Lord Dunsany, on the other hand, has conceded only so much in his short stories as to suggest their ancestry in the fairy tale.

In 1905 *The Gods of Pegana* passed almost unperceived amidst the more avowedly Celtic literature of the moment. Indeed, it is unlikely that many readers who then saw the name of Lord Dunsany for the first time would have associated the book with the Irish movement in which its author was so generously interested. Coming forward as the creator of a new mythology, he could not readily be identified with a literary tradition whose strength was rooted in the soil of Gaelic legend and antiquity. Lord Dunsany invented his own antiquity, whose history was found in *The Gods of Pegana.* With a strange power of imagination he set forth the hierarchy of Pegana's gods, the greater and minor deities. Marvellous Beings, who play with worlds and suns, with life and death, their mere nomenclature is full of weird suggestion. There is not an event in the cosmic evolution known to us which Lord Dunsany has failed to elaborate into some beautiful legend. But, whereas the first volume was essentially the record of a new theogony, *Time and the Gods* (1908) is a collection of myths, which naturally attach themselves to the phenomena witnessed by the men whom the Pegana deities created for their amusement. In allowing his fancy to interpret the great elemental mysteries of nature, the rising of the winds or the coming of light, the author shows the same delicate poetic imagination as assisted him in the creation of the mighty figures who peopled his original cosmos. Yet, with a true sense of the mythus, Lord Dunsany controls fantasy, so that he is never betrayed into any conflict with the natural laws, as understood by contemporary science. His fable of the *South Wind,* for example, is as accurate in its representation of the facts as it is charming in its tender poetry.

The *Leitmotiv* of his work, whether the narrative be of gods or men, is the mysterious warfare between the phenomenal world and the forces of Time and Change. Even the "gods of Pegana" live beneath the shadow of this conflict which must one day result in their overthrow. Lord Dunsany's later work, *The Sword of Welleran* (1908), *A Dreamer's Tales* (1910) and *The Book of Wonder* (1912), is concerned more specifically with this aspect of existence. Here we learn of those wonderful cities, Perdondaris and Babbulkund, whose fabulous beauties are obliterated in a moment of Time, when something swift and terrible swallows them up, leaving only the whispering sands above them. The most beautiful prose the author has written is in these stories, beginning with *In the Land of Time* from *Time and the Gods,* which tell of the passing away of human achievement at the assault of nature aided by her relentless accomplices. Yet he has demonstrated his mastery of the grotesque and horrible in tales which recall those of Poe or Ambrose Bierce. His later work lacks glamour and spontaneity, and does not give the measure of his power, which is best seen in *The Sword of Welleran* and *A Dreamer's Tales*. There Lord Dunsany showed a wealth of bizarre and terrible fantasy of the same high quality as characterised his previous essays in mythological narrative. The latter, however, are his enduring share in the reawakening of the Celtic imagination of which the Literary Revival is the manifestation.

While Lord Dunsany was for many years the most neglected of our prose-writers, James Stephens has enjoyed a very different fate, being probably the best known of all the younger generation. It has rarely been given to an Irish genius so national to become famous in the short space of three years, which separated his first little book of verse, *Insurrections,* from *The Crock of Gold,* published in 1912. The same year saw the publication of his first prose work, *The Charwoman's Daughter,* and his second volume of poems, *The Hill of Vision,* but these were of necessity somewhat obscured by the remarkable success of *The Crock of Gold.* As was suggested in reference to his verse, the poet was the beneficiary of the prosaist. It may be said that everything he published at that time, or previously, came into consideration as a consequent and subsequent part of that success.

The immediate popularity of James Stephens must be attributed to the fact that he revealed at once his power to use prose as attractively as others used verse. The Celtic spirit which breathes through the poetry of the Revival is at last felt in a work of prose fiction, which, by contrast with the novels and stories of previous years, seemed a wonderful innovation. Yet *The Crock of Gold* could not have been a surprise to those who read *The Charwoman's Daughter* as it appeared in the first volume of *The Irish Review,* during the year 1911. The realism of the latter story of the Dublin streets could not repress the irresistible grotesquerie and good-humour, the fanciful charm so characteristic of the better-known book. Mrs. Makebelieve and her daughter personified a side of their creator's mentality. Like them he has the faculty of rising above reality and transporting himself into a world of pure fantasy. The co-existence of the ugly material facts of life with the beauty of an imaginary state, as shown in the lives of Mary Makebelieve and her mother, is a symbol of Stephen's work. He is eternally hovering on the line which divides the sublime from the ridiculous. He crosses it with an insouciance which comes, not from a lack of perception, but from an innate sense of the relativeness of all values.

The title of his first book was the forecast of an attitude towards life which subsequent works have confirmed. The "insurrection" of James Stephens is the revolt of an unsophisticated mind against unnatural decorum. When the Philosopher in *The Crock of Gold* goes to interview Angus Óg, his frame of mind is not, perhaps, as reverential as might be expected from a man who desired the presence of such a Being. His familiar *bonhomie* springs from a conviction of the necessary humanity of one's relations with all creatures, heavenly and terrestrial. Thus Stephens will contrive the conversation of a fly, a cow, a god or a spider, upon the assumption of a common relationship between all phenomena. This is not a mere literary artifice, "sophisticated infantilism," as severe critics pronounce it. It is the

reflection of the author's mind, which gambols in naïve irreverence about the gravest problems.

The Crock of Gold and *The Demi-Gods* (1914), his best works, are naturally most typical of his genius. At the same time, they are assertions of the claim of Irish prose to undertake some of the functions of poetry. Not that the author is prone to write "prose poems"; or to indulge in word-painting for its own sake. But his narratives are interwoven with the mysticism which we have heretofore found in A. E., and with the symbolism which has induced so many people to consider Yeats as a mystic. Irish mythology and fairy lore are skilfully blended, and the general impression left upon the reader is one entirely different from that of any other Irish story or fairy tale. The author's *gaminerie,* which enables him to contemplate the Cosmos with charming familiarity, has served him well, for he is not at all disconcerted when his fancy takes him from the domestic quarrels of the Philosopher and the farcical proceedings of the Policemen, to the realms of Pan and Angus Óg. The discourses of the gods are as much a part of his imaginative life as were of his actual life the charwomen, policemen and vagrants whose peculiarities he has not forgotten.

The dangers of this attitude were exemplified in *Here are Ladies* (1913) where the commonplace and the unusual jostle one another, this time to the discomfiture of the latter. In places one gets a glimpse of the author of *The Charwoman's Daughter* and *The Crock of Gold,* as in the grotesque fantasy of *The Threepenny Piece,* and in the delightful reverie of boyhood, *Three Happy Places,* where Stephens's peculiar power of visualising the outlook of a boy is exercised. Pessimists feared at one time that he was about to go the way of all Irish fiction writers, but *The Demi-Gods* has justified the optimists. Without breaking new ground the book marks an advance upon the earlier work to which it is closely akin. The author has firmer control of his material, and if there is a diminution of youthful exuberance, it is compensated by a note of deeper maturity. *The Demi-Gods* surpasses, where it does not equal, *The Crock of Gold,* which contains no character study to compare with Patsy MacCann.

When *The Demi-Gods* definitely placed James Stephens in the front rank of living prose-writers he was fortunately able to escape the compulsion to exploit the success which came to him so quickly after the appearance of *The Charwoman's Daughter.* He contented himself for six years by issuing an occasional little book of poems, none more beautiful than *Reincarnations,* a handful of exquisite variations upon themes from the later Gaelic poets. This slender work is a clue to the apparent inactivity of the author, who had plunged into the study of Irish, and was more absorbed in the Gaelic past than in the Irish present, although he had written that lively diary of an onlooker during the Rising of Easter 1916, *The Insurrection in Dublin.* He was at work upon a new version of the *Tain Bo-Cuailgne,* of which the two first volumes, as yet unpublished, promise his masterpiece. In prose, this time, he has achieved a "reincarnation" in which the great figures of legend, Deirdre and Naisi and Conchobar live and talk as they have never done since the days of the bards themselves. All the wit, the fantasy and the beauty which haunt the imagination and make the style of James Stephens have vivified those scenes and people, so often described since Standish O'Grady brought them back into literature, until they stand forth from his pages as the creations of the poet himself. Yet, with all this a scrupulous accuracy in details of chronology and local colour, carefully checked with reference to original documents and the findings of modern scholars and ancient bards.

Meanwhile a foretaste of this new quality in the work of Stephens, of this power of reincarnating from Gaelic material in a manner wholly original, may be found in the volume of *Irish Fairy Tales,* published in 1920, for which the author's major work was set aside temporarily. These are not the hackneyed fairy tales which usually serve, as this work has unfortunately done, as an excuse for a "gift-book" with illustrations by some artist in vogue. The author went to the fountain-head of Irish storytelling, the old legends and epics in which he was immersed, and the result is a volume as unmistakably of the soil of Ireland as it is the creation of the author's imagination. This fairyland is Irish, and were the characters of Grimm and Andersen to be substituted for Fionn, Tuan mac Cairill or Mongan, the tales would not lose their nationality in that universal land of fairy where no national frontiers hinder the wanderings of youthful adventurers. The descriptive passages are many and beautiful, but they are obviously meant for eyes and ears more sensitive than those of children. (pp. 374-419)

The author's power of grotesque fancy also adds to the effectiveness of his pictures of the strange and beautiful realm to which he acts as a guide. In *Mongan's Frenzy* the spectacle of the warriors of Ulster perched in the trees to escape from a flock of savage sheep is irresistible. "They roosted among the branches like great birds, while the venomous sheep ranged below, bleating terribly and tearing up the ground." The incongruity of this idea resides largely in an association of ideas to a sophisticated reader, but it will hardly come within the appreciation of children. Then there is the description of Mannanan's dog, which rescued the warriors from their plight:

> Now if the sheep were venomous, this dog was more venomous still, for it was fearful to look at. In body it was not large, but its head was of great size, and the mouth that was shaped in that head was able to open like the lid of a pot. It was not teeth which were in that head, but hooks and fangs and prongs. Dreadful was that mouth to look at, terrible to look into, woeful to think about, and from it, or from the broad, loose nose that waggled above it, there came a sound which no word of man could describe, for it was not a snarl, nor was it a howl, although it was both of these. It was neither a growl nor a grunt, although it was both of these; it was not a yowl nor a groan, although it was both of these: for it was one sound made up of these sounds, and there was in it, too, a whine and a yelp, and a long-drawn snoring noise, and a deep purring noise, and a noise that was like the squeal of a rusty hinge, and there were other noises in it also.

The rhythm of this prose, this delight in words, the gro-

tesque humour of each detail, are at once characteristic of the style of James Stephens and of the Gaelic storytellers. His study of Irish and prolonged absorption in the old literature have heightened the colour and strengthened the movement of his prose. His constructions have a delightful flavour of Gaelic; Irish forms are dexterously duplicated in English; cumulative epithets are effectively employed, yet the writing is as far removed from the manner of Synge as from the Kiltartan of Lady Gregory. The dignity and humour and easy, unaffected beauty of his style seem to find peculiarly happy expression in the re-clothing of these legendary tales, from which an episode, or even the hint of an episode, has enabled him to reconstruct a narrative of unsurpassed charm. These stories of the Fionn cycle are an indication of the direction in which James Stephens has been evolving, towards what already promises to be the greatest prose work in Anglo-Irish literature.

The retelling of the old stories of bardic literature has absorbed the energies of many Irish prose writers in recent years, apart from those who have been engaged in the work of translating and editing the classic texts of Gaelic literature. With the latter we are not concerned, except to note that this increasing knowledge of the Heroic Age has widened the field of tradition, and increased the resources of our poetry and drama. Those, however, who have contributed to the process of popularisation stand in a more direct relationship to Anglo-Irish literature. Their work has a literary rather than a scientific interest, although the intrinsic value of such work varies greatly, and interests the historian rather than the critic of literature.

Standish O'Grady had published his *History of Ireland: The Heroic Period* in 1878, but before the second volume was issued there appeared P. W. Joyce's *Old Celtic Romances* (1879), "the first collection of the old Gaelic prose romances that has ever been published in fair English translation," as the author described it in his preface. The book had none of the fire and poetic imagination of O'Grady's epic history; it did not, therefore, appeal in the same way to the young poets of the Eighties, but it was the forerunner of the popular literature of heroic Ireland. Its many editions prove that it can still survive the competition of numerous successors, some, fragmentary and fanciful, like Nora Hopper's *Ballads in Prose,* others, serious rivals, such as *The High Deeds of Finn* (1910) by T. W. Rolleston, where the value of a fine series of retellings is enhanced by the inclusion of material hitherto untranslated. Akin to O'Grady's *Finn and his Companions* is the recent volume, *Heroes of the Dawn* (1913), by Violet Russell, in which the wife of the poet essays, in turn, to bring the bardic heroes within the vision of boyhood. This work may be coupled with the *Celtic Wonder-Tales* (1910) of Ella Young as the two most charming collections of children's stories published in Ireland for many years.

Most of these versions have shown more regard for the literary and artistic quality of the stories than for the need of an ordered and accurate account of the bardic narratives. In this respect the best work is *The Cuchullin Saga in Irish Literature,* published by Eleanor Hull in 1898. A volume of fourteen stories embodying the history of Cuchulain, it was a valuable innovation in the manner of collating the Gaelic material. Its introduction and notes, and the careful selection of texts, made it at once a literary and scholarly contribution. But it was soon to make way for a similar volume outside the domain of scholarship, identical in content, but very different in form.

In 1902 Lady Gregory published her *Cuchulain of Muirthemne,* which was followed in 1904 by *Gods and Fighting Men.* The former is an ordered retelling of the Cuchulain legends, the latter treats of the gods and the Fianna, but, except in so far as it follows Eleanor Hull's choice of texts, Lady Gregory's work is very dissimilar. It is frankly a blend of scholarship and imaginative reconstruction. The author was no less desirous of clarifying the legendary material than was Eleanor Hull, but she did not allow considerations of fact to interfere with the success of her undertaking. Comparing all the translations of the scholars, she has co-ordinated and compressed them into a homogeneous narrative, by the simple expedient of making suppressions and additions of her own, whenever the textual versions threaten to disrupt her plan. Literary success came immediately to justify her experiments, but competent Gaelic criticism has severely condemned a procedure which has had the effect of conveying a very false idea of the classic age and literature of Ireland. Even so enthusiastic a commentator and apostle of Celticism as Fiona Mac-Leod felt constrained to admit the superiority of *The Cuchullin Saga in Irish Literature.*

Lady Gregory's "translations," however, are not to be judged for what that term implies. They are not so much translations as folk-versions of the old saga, adapted to literature. Their success has been mainly amongst readers already familiar with the correct text, or with those whose interest was of a less exacting nature. Both could submit to the undeniable charm of a style whose archaic flavour seemed peculiarly fitted to these evocations of ancient times. For Lady Gregory is the first and only writer of the Revival to employ the peasant idiom in narrative prose. That Kiltartan speech with which her comedies have made us familiar was consecrated to literary use by its effective elaboration in *Cuchulain of Muirthemne.* With the previous example of *The Love Songs of Connacht* before her, Lady Gregory was encouraged to extend the scope of Gaelicised English by adopting peasant speech in her most serious contribution to Anglo-Irish literature. It was a fine literary instinct that guided her in making this innovation, for, stripped of their language, her stories of Cuchulain and the Fianna would have been lost in the almost anonymous mass of similar popularisation. As it is, she has been saluted by many as an Irish Malory, and her work has shared in the general admiration for the beauties of an idiom illustrated shortly afterwards by the genius of J. M. Synge. The young writers of a generation unfamiliar with the emotion aroused by O'Grady, in the distant days when his rehandling of the bardic material was a revelation, may derive from Lady Gregory's pages that enthusiasm for heroic beauty which inspired the first movement of the Revival.

The literature of the Celtic Renaissance has been predominantly the creation of poets and dramatists, and in retrospect it presents a somewhat unequal appearance, owing to the absence of prose writers. The novel has fared badly, but criticism has fared worse, being unrepresented, except for the intermittent essays of John Eglinton, and that interesting, if isolated, work of collaboration, *Literary Ideals in Ireland,* of which some account has been given. The æsthetic reveries of W. B. Yeats, like the scattered articles of A. E. and others, do not bear witness to any deliberate critical effort on their part. Impartial criticism is a more than usually delicate task where a small country like Ireland is concerned. When the intellectual centre is confined within a restricted area, personal relations are unavoidable, and the critic finds discretion imperative, if he is to continue to dwell peaceably in the midst of his friends. Nevertheless, the Irish reviews have not shrunk from publishing the most candid criticism, and if little of this material has been collected, it is the fault of the critics. An interesting and hopeful innovation was the publication of Thomas MacDonagh's *Literature in Ireland.* This thoughtful volume of "studies in Irish and Anglo-Irish" was published shortly after the author's execution, and promised to be an introduction to further works of a similar character. MacDonagh was well equipped for the task he had set himself, and this book is an important contribution to the study of Anglo-Irish poetry.

The effect upon the literature of the smaller countries of this absence of critical judgment, publicly expressed, has been that honest criticism prefers to be silent where it cannot praise. Consequently, there is lack of intellectual discipline which allows the good and the mediocre to struggle on equal terms for recognition. In Ireland we have become accustomed to hearing Irish writers either enthusiastically advertised by the English press, or denounced as charlatans, usurping the fame reserved for the genuine heirs of England's literary glory. The phenomenon rarely calls for more than casual attention, so fortuitous does it seem. Yet, so far as it has any reasonable basis, it may be traced to our habit of allowing every writer who so desires to submit his work to outside criticism on the same terms as our most distinguished literary representatives. We cannot expect others to show more discrimination than ourselves, and when the storm of facile applause has broken over the head of the confiding poet or dramatist, we need not be surprised if some spirit more enquiring than the others leads an abusive reaction. So long as we continue to have our criticism written for us by journalists in England, these disconcerting alternations of idolatry and contempt will follow Irish literature abroad.

However flattering the cult of Celticism may seem to us, it is unwise to attach any significance to it. Anglo-Irish literature, as a whole, has not grown up to meet the desires of the devotees of this cult, but to meet the need of Ireland for self-expression. Should it incidentally produce a writer of such proportions as to entitle him to a place in comparative literary history, let us, by all means, encourage him to challenge the attention of the outside world. The main purpose, however, of the Literary Revival has not been to contribute to English literature, but to create a national literature for Ireland, in the language which has been imposed upon her—a circumstance which effectively disposes of the theory that Ireland is merely an intellectual province of England. The provincial Irishman is he who prefers to identify himself with the literary movement of another country but his own, and those writers who have addressed themselves to the English, rather than to the Irish, public are obviously in that category. They are always expatriates to their adopted countrymen.

The only question, therefore, which must be answered by such a survey as the present is: has the Literary Renaissance accomplished its purpose? Has it given us a body of work which may fairly be described as the nucleus of a national literature? In spite of various weaknesses, it seems as if Anglo-Irish literature had proved its title to be considered as an independent entity. It has not altogether escaped the literary traditions of the language in which it is written, but it has shown a more marked degree of originality, in respect of form and content, than Belgian or any other literature similarly dominated by a powerful neighbour. Possessing the advantage, denied to Switzerland and Belgium, of a great native literature, with all the traditions thereby implied, Ireland has been able to mould her second language according to the literary genius of the race.

It does not matter in the least whether the poetry of the Revival deserves, or does not deserve, the honours which enthusiasts have claimed for it. We must, first of all, determine whether the literature of the Revival is really national, and then attempt to estimate the relative importance of those who created it. If this history has helped in any way to attain that object, it will have corresponded to the intention with which it was conceived. Comparative criticism will in due course decide that question which obsesses certain minds, namely: is W. B. Yeats a greater poet than Shelley? France did not assign his status to her supreme poetic genius, Racine, by reference to Dante and Shakespeare. National (or local) values invariably take precedence of international, however disappointing that fact may seem to lovers of the absolute. (pp. 419-27)

> Ernest Boyd, "Fiction and Narrative Prose," in his Ireland's Literary Renaissance, revised edition, 1922. Reprint by Alfred A. Knopf, 1968, pp. 374-427.

Seamus Deane

[Deane is an Irish critic and educator who specializes in modern English and American literature. In the excerpt below, he examines predominant thematic and stylistic patterns in late nineteenth-century and early twentieth-century Irish fiction.]

In his last work, A Communication to my Friends (1933), George Moore gave his own peculiar account of his involvement with the Irish revival:

> After a year and a half's residence in Ireland I began to see Ireland as a portrait, and the form in which to choose to draw her portrait was the scene of a dozen short stories . . . if I succeeded in doing this, I would supply the Irish writers not yet in being with models on which they might make their stories more authentic than mine. The title of the book should have been A Portrait of Ireland, but that seemed too flagrant and I chose another title The Untilled Field,

which seemed to me sufficiently suggestive of the intention of the book, but I found no storyteller in Ireland who wished to take light from another; they all deemed that they possessed the light, and that when Ireland obtained her freedom she would rise higher than she had ever risen before; that the new Ireland would rival the Greece of Pericles.

The Untilled Field first appeared in Gaelic in 1902. The first English edition of the following year is substantially different and, characteristically, Moore included further revisions in the editions of 1914, 1926 and 1931. The half-dozen stories in Irish and the thirteen in English expressed a dualism in Moore and in the Irish revival, which was to endure for some decades afterwards. They are stories about the necessity for exile by an exile who found it necessary to return. They depict an Ireland which is spiritually stifling but in such a manner that the ideal of liberation gains strength only in virtue of the forces which would deny it. They identify the oppressive element in Irish society as Catholicism at the moment when Irish Catholicism was assuming to itself the role of liberator from the thrall of British rule and Protestant Ascendancy. In other words. Moore asserts the primacy of individual freedom and is sceptical, to say the least, about the capacity or willingness of the national cultural and political revival to allow for it. His Ireland is a vacuum in which the free soul withers and dies. It is difficult to avoid seeing here the first modern crystallization of the declarations of spiritual independence, which form such an important part of the tradition of Irish fiction in Joyce, Beckett and others throughout the century. Despite the soft malice of his words in A Communication to My Friends, others did take their light from him although, in them too, the light cast ambiguous shadows in their fictions. Moore amalgamated so much of Irish literary and social experience in his life and writings that he is a perfectly appropriate stepfather to the dishevelled and quarrelsome brood of novelists who were to succeed and, in some instances, outshine him.

He was a Catholic landlord from County Mayo, who witnessed the slow death of the semi-feudal relationship between landowners and tenantry from the Land League disturbances of the 1880s to the burning of the Big Houses in the 1920s. Moore Hall was burned down during the Irish Civil War in 1923. In 1880, George's sojourn in Paris had been ruined by a letter informing him that the tenants would pay no more rent until a reduction was granted. This presage of financial disaster impelled him to go to London to earn his living as a writer. His first aim, though, was to be a writer; as for earning a living, his tenants could do that for him, at a lower level and with more reluctance than he found agreeable. But to be a writer, Moore found he had to assemble a mass of new and sometimes ready-made materials provided by a number of miscellaneous sources—Zola, Flaubert, the Goncourt brothers, Turgenev, Tolstoy, Wagner, the French symbolists, led by Mallarmé, the French impressionists, led for him by Manet and Dégas, Walter Pater and, finally, W. B. Yeats and Edward Martyn. The various artistic movements represented by these names all gained his adherence for a time and all were repudiated in time. In the course of his various enthusiasms, Moore produced a series of books, which bore the imprint of his discipleship and, occasionally, demonstrated a temporary mastery over the competing influences which he courted so assiduously. He was a scholar of gossip, conversation and anecdote, not of books, so he wears his light learning lightly. But his ability to absorb French and English cultural models into his own Irish experience is almost as inexhaustible as that of Yeats. Like Yeats, he was thereby furnishing an example to the modern Irish tradition of writing by demonstrating the advantages to be gained from indulging an eclectic fury in the service of a single domineering ambition—to become an artist. In his search for an ultimate style—what he was later to call the 'melodic line'—he anticipates one of the anxieties of a literature which felt sharply the lack of a secure tradition and a consequent fascination with the twin problems of language and form.

Specifically, *The Untilled Field* is important because it demonstrated the art of composing a number of stories into a unified pattern, thereby making the total design of the collection more effective than the design of any individual story. This was a practice to be repeated, more famously, by Joyce in *Dubliners* and by Samuel Beckett in *More Pricks than Kicks*. The interwoven themes of exile and freedom, clerical despotism and the power of folk belief, repudiation of Ireland and attraction for it, sexual repression and sexual longing, were all to be taken up again and again in later years. But Moore's Ireland remains firmly lodged in the nineteenth century. It bears the marks of famine, emigration and dispossession. The people have almost melted into the lonely landscape:

> They were scanty fields, drifting from thin grass into bog into thin grass again, and in the distance there was a rim of melancholy mountains, and the peasants I saw along the road seemed a counterpart of the landscape. 'The land has made them', I said, 'according to its own image and likeness', and I tried to find words to define the yearning that I read in their eyes as we drove past. But I could find no words that satisfied me.

The limp syntax and the consequent limpidity of tone are characteristic features of Moore's style. The yearning in the peasants' eyes and the yearning of the artist to find the right words for it become as one, so that the reader is alerted to the intractability of the Irish experience for the Irish writer as much as for any agent of social improvement. (In fact the narrator in this instance is an agent for the Irish Industrial Society.) Socially, those who prohibit improvement are the priests. This is most painfully exposed in the volume's most famous story, 'Home Sickness', in which an exile, James Bryden, returns home to regain his health after thirteen years in the noisome atmosphere of a Bowery slum in New York. But, although he wants to marry a local girl, Margaret Dirken, and settle down in the beautiful landscape of his youth, the authoritarian interference of the local priest so discourages him that he finally returns to New York and abandons all that he loves. Yet, years later, the owner of the bar-room where he had served, married and with grown-up children, his memory lingers on Ireland and Margaret:

> There is an unchanging, silent life within every man that none knows but himself, and his un-

changing, silent life was his memory of Margaret Dirken. The bar-room was forgotten and all that concerned it and the things he saw most clearly were the green hill-side, and the bog lake and the rushes about it, and the greater lake in the distance, and behind it the blue line of wandering hills.

The tender note of regret had not always been prominent in Moore's reaction to his native land. In 1887, a book of essays, *Parnell and his Island*, appeared in London, having previously been published in a series in a French newspaper. It is difficult to describe the tone of this book. Regret lingers there, evoked for the most part by the spectacle of the decline of Irish landlordism. But there is also a note of hatred so savage that it borders on the pathological. This is evinced by the Irish peasantry and by the ruinous, squalid conditions of their life. Moore recognizes that the landlord system deserves to die, but he cannot bear the thought that the peasantry will, in turn, take over. His ambivalence on this point is matched by that of Standish O'Grady and Yeats. All the imagery of aristocratic elegance and civility, which survives to this day in Irish fiction and even in Irish poetry, is darkened by the recognition that it arose out of plunder and oppression. Violence is its natural companion:

> In Ireland every chicken eaten, every glass of champagne drunk, every silk dress trailed in the street, every rose worn at a ball, comes straight out of the peasant's cabin.

A writer who had trained himself in the French school of naturalism could hardly fail to emphasize the filth and degradation of the peasant's living conditions. He had already shown his gifts in that line with the account of the degradation of Kate Ede in *A Mummer's Wife* (1885), a study of the collapse of a personality under the stress of a total change in environment. In his 'Dublin novel', *A Drama in Muslin* (1886), the peremptory influence of environment is tempered by the force of the inner life of the heroine, Alice Barton. But the environment is, nevertheless, powerful; Dublin and Ireland in decay, presided over by the Dublin Castle, which has lost its political function and is reduced to a grim imitation of the London season to bolster its self-image as the nerve-centre of the nation:

> On the right murder has ended for the night; on the left, towards Merrion Square, the violins have ceased to sing in the ballrooms; and in their white beds the girls sleep their white sleep of celibacy. Passion and grief have ceased to trouble the aching heart, if not for ever, at least for a while; the murderer's and the virgin's reality are sunk beneath a swift-rolling tide of dreams—a tide deeper than the river that flows beneath the tears of the lonely lover. All but he are at rest; and now the city sleeps; wharves, walls, and bridges are veiled and have disappeared in the fog that has crept up from the sea; the shameless squalor of the outlying streets is enwrapped in the grey mist, but over them and dark against the sky the Castle still stretches out its arms as if for some monstrous embrace.

A Drama in Muslin (re-titled *Muslin* in the revised edition of 1915), tells the story of a group of Galway convent girls who enter into the marriage market of Anglo-Irish society on their presentation at the Viceregal Court in Dublin. Their different responses to the commercial-sexual world of the Castle and to the divided world of the rich and the poor provide us with a social commentary on the society of late Victorian Dublin. The central figure, Alice Barton, reacts against a system which produces such poverty for the mass of the people and such humiliation for women. In the end, she marries and leaves Ireland, having learned something of the shallowness and deception of the muslin world of the women who are entrapped within it. Most of all, perhaps, she has learned the futility of doing anything about the state of Ireland in 1882; evictions, political murder, Land League war and, in the midst of all, this pathetic muslin world of marriage and barter. She marries a dispensary doctor and they go off to a useful life in England. Moore was once more choosing exile as the only solution in a country where the problems, and the ambiguities, seemed insoluble.

Nothing could be more different than his greatest triumph in the naturalistic style, his answer to Hardy's *Tess of the D'Urbervilles* and perhaps also his answer to the futility and frustration that dominate *A Drama in Muslin.* The novel, *Esther Waters* (1894), is still the novel by which Moore is most remembered. It is subtitled 'An English Story' although many of its readers would regard it, along with Ford Madox Ford's *The Good Soldier,* as one of the best French novels in English. Moore always patronized the English novel as something attempted by 'only the inferior or—shall we say?—the subaltern mind'. No doubt he thought that a French infusion would reinvigorate it in the 1890s as an Irish one would at the turn of the century. The point is worth making only because it indicates how uneasy Moore was with the idea of any securely established tradition. Tradition was, like style, dependent on tone. The French and some of the Russians had it. In prose narrative the English did not. He would scarcely have acknowledged that the Irish had even prose narrative.

Yet, despite all these poses and snobberies, Moore produced in *Esther Waters* one of the most humane and sympathetic of all those stories of a blighted life, which are found so abundantly in late Victorian literature. Esther, an illiterate servant-girl, is seduced and deserted, then dismissed from her situation at Woodview by Mrs Barfield. She keeps her child against all odds, is partly won over to the religious views of the Plymouth Brethren, but meets up with her seducer William again and goes to live with him in his public house. His passion for gambling ruins the business and his health is broken. After his death, Esther goes back to her former position with Mrs Barfield at Woodview. The novel is naturalistic in the sense that Moore has done his homework and created the world of the bar and of the race-track with close attention to accurate detail. But it is also a psychological study of the instinctive will to survive in Esther, which overcomes the most crushing circumstances. Moore shows a sympathy with the lives of the poor, which he had kept carefully concealed up to this point. But he also displays, with that, an admiration for Esther's instincts, which is closely bound up with her illiteracy. This is no 'muslin martyr'; this is

a woman who has kept her primary instincts unviolated. It is possible to see here a reordering of his attitude towards the Irish peasantry and a certain, if incipient, benevolent feudalism towards these creatures of the soil and of instinct. Even at his most humane, Moore manages to be faintly maladroit and condescending.

Celibates, a volume of three novellas published in 1895, brings Moore closer to his preoccupation with the fate of a cloistered sexuality in a sensual world. The three figures, Mildred Lawson, John Norton and Agnes Lahens, deflect their natural desires into religious cravings. Moore is moving towards his analysis of his own country's condition in his various repetitions of the psychological intimacy between spirituality and sensuality. The most astonishing novel of his early career, *Evelyn Innes* (1898), explores this intimacy against a musical and mythological background not surpassed in its elaboration until Joyce's *Ulysses* appeared. The eponymous heroine, an opera singer, finds herself forced to choose between two lovers, Sir Owen Asher, the wealthy, sensual man, and Ulick Dean, the dedicated and spiritual Irish artist, modelled very obviously on W. B. Yeats, with whom Moore had begun to collaborate on the play *Diarmuid and Grania,* based on a legend in which the heroine is faced with a similar choice. The connection between this legend and that of Tristan and Isolde is also given due prominence in a work deeply impressed by the influence of Wagner. The French novelist Edouard Dujardin, the perfect Wagnerite, had already attempted to show how the Wagnerian motifs could be used in the structuring of a novel—his was called *Les Lauriers sont coupés,* frequently cited as the novel which introduced Joyce to the so-called 'stream-of-consciousness' method. This novel is Moore's most ambitious attempt to organize his material in such a way that his supple prose would achieve cumulative effects by the repetition of phrases and ideas operating like motifs. Moore's invertebrate syntax does not help him to avoid a lushness of effect, which is often overpowering. Nevertheless, *Evelyn Innes* is a remarkable novel, in which the search for a new language and a new form is decisively extended. Moore was now beginning to produce fiction which was neither 'French' nor 'English' in its provenance. His experimentalism had opened the way to the modern novel, which, in its endless interrogation of traditional forms, was to prove so attractive to Irish writers, for whom such interrogation was a necessity if they were to write at all.

Thus Moore moved to Dublin in 1901, seeking through Yeats and Martyn refreshment from a new centre of energy and abandoning England with the abruptness which marked all his temporary enthusiasms. After *The Untilled Field,* came *The Lake* (1905). As usual, it went through revisions—minor for the second impression of 1905, substantial for the edition of 1921. (Moore's constant revising and disowning of earlier works makes him a bibliographer's nightmare.) *The Lake,* which was originally to have been one of the stories in *The Untilled Field,* was warmly acclaimed as a masterpiece. Dedicated to Dujardin, it employs the interior monologue pioneered by the dedicatee but with greater subtlety. The story is simple, the treatment complex. An Irish Catholic priest, Fr. Oliver Gogarty, expels the local schoolmistress from the parish because she is pregnant. She goes to London and, through the intervention of another priest, who reproves Gogarty for his severity, they establish a correspondence, which becomes for him a process of education. He rediscovers the passional life he has buried and forsakes the priesthood by swimming across the lake on the first stage of his journey into exile and freedom in America. He leaves his clothes neatly folded to give the impression that he has drowned. It is the development of the priest's growing consciousness which stays in the memory of most readers. It is witnessed both from his own point of view and that of others, primarily from that of Rose Leicester (or Nora Glynn as she was renamed in the 1921 edition). She has learned to see the priest's plight as an example of the evolution of historical religious belief, although she also has her own personal involvement in the business. He sees it as a personal crisis, which can be overcome with the help of her sympathy and her more objective view of the situation. The discussions which dominate the letters are fused with descriptions of the lake in its various moods, the sky which it reflects, the landscape which it dominates. (pp. 168-75)

The sympathy which Moore brings to the examination of Fr. Gogarty's case is singularly absent when he treats the issues raised by religious belief in his great work of reminiscence *Hail and Farewell.* He was wise to leave Dublin before the first volume appeared, for it is a work of stylish malignance. Having used the name of Oliver St John Gogarty, the wit and friend of Joyce, in *The Lake,* he now went much further and paraded the literati of Dublin under their own names for the delectation of posterity. He wrote, as Susan Mitchell, his most acerbic critic, said, 'with a complete disregard for the feelings' of his friends, 'marvelling only that his friends should prefer immortality in any other form than that he had chosen for them'. Nevertheless, 'this new and daring form of the novel' was more than an epic work of gossip, although that aspect of it re-

mains one of its attractions, as it does of Joyce's *Ulysses.* Both writers convert Dublin from a capital city into the world's archetypal village. Edward Martyn, the type of the ascetic man, who transmutes his sensuality into the appreciation of art, and a devotion to religion, is the book's outstanding portrait. In him, Moore tries to tease out the complications of the Irish mind and the effect upon it of its contemporary social and cultural environment. Yeats too appears as a writer given to ritual and idealism of such an ethereal kind that he is unable to encompass within his work or within the movement that he led the simple, 'pagan' joys of sensual experience. Thus both men, and the country they represent, are portrayed as lacking in a deep inner vitality, which will finally have corrosive effects upon their creativity. Brooding over these is, of course, the humorous figure of George Moore himself, cast in the role of the messiah who has come to save Ireland from her spiritual and sensual disfranchisement. Like all messiahs, he is not honoured in his own country and must leave it so that it may learn more thoroughly just what it has missed. As always, Moore's fascination is with the figure of the artist and the difficulty of his role in trying to redeem society and life itself from the rigours of the self-imposed constraints with which it has been afflicted. In giving an account which will move easily from petty incident to philosophical disquisition, Moore developed further that flexible and insinuating style which can become saturated with sensations and impressions without ever quite losing its narrative, discursive drive. An intellectual crisis—his resolve to renounce Catholicism publicly and declare himself a Protestant, for instance—impels him to go on one of his walks in search of a friend to whom he can unbosom himself. The friend on this occasion is George Russell, better known as AE, the saint of the Literary revival:

> I wrote for an hour and then went out in search
> of AE: it is essential to consult AE on every mat-

The Abbey Theatre Company's dinner to honor Yeats on his reception of the Nobel Prize: 1) Sean O'Casey 2) Barry Fitzgerald 3) Arthur Shields 4) Lennox Robinson 5) Yeats 6) George Yeats.

ter of importance. . . . The night was Thursday, and every Thursday night, after finishing the last pages of *The Homestead,* he goes to the Hermetic Society to teach till eleven o'clock. But the rooms were not known to me, and I must have met a member of the Society who directed me to the house in Dawson Street, a great decaying building let out in rooms, traversed by dusty passages, intersected by innumerable staircases; and through this great ramshackle I wandered, losing myself again and again. The doors were numbered, but the number I sought seemed undiscoverable. At last, at the end of a short, dusty corridor, I found the number I was seeking, and on opening the door caught sight of AE among his disciples. He was sitting at a bare table, teaching, and his disciples sat on chairs, circlewise, listening. There was a lamp on the table and it lit up his ardent, earnest face, and some of the faces of the men and women, others were lost in shadows. He bade me welcome, and continued to teach as if I had not been there.

This is a memorable moment in this literary *flâneur's* sojourn through Dublin. It gives a brief snapshot of all that AE stood for—mysticism combined with the pragmatic wisdom which he provided in the columns of his newspaper *The Irish Homestead.* We recognize at once why AE is one of the heroes of this book. He concedes to both the sensual and the spiritual aspects of existence. His head is in the clouds but his feet are on the ground. No one quite captured, as Moore did, the secret of his enormous appeal and influence. Yet the reader who knows little or nothing of AE would recognize that, in the economy of this work, he is the inevitable father-confessor for someone like Moore, for Moore, in all the minuscule detail of his volumes, has steadily dwelt on the Irish as well as his own intellectual divisions. In this man, AE, they are harmoniously reconciled. The portraits of individuals are, therefore, memorably unique and yet they form part of a composite and interweaving pattern, which gives coherence to the medley of scenes and conversations. Again it is difficult to avoid thinking of Joyce in *Ulysses* and the manner in which he too composed a series of recurrent motifs within a thickly sown pattern of apparently random sensations and gossipy interludes.

Like his great contemporaries, Yeats and Joyce, Moore was prepared to rewrite history and myth in order to ratify his quest for a radical freedom which could be asserted in the face of all routinized attitudes and objections. *The Brook Kerith* (1916) is his most remarkable, *A Story-Teller's Holiday* (1918) is his most intractable effort to do so. In the first, he tells the story of a Jesus who did not die on the Cross, but was taken down and brought back to life and sent to become a shepherd among the Essenes. Twenty-five years later he meets St Paul, full of crusading zeal for the Christianity of Christ Crucified. In the final encounter between them, St Paul insists on continuing with his mission. He is willing to preach the spirit against the flesh, thereby re-enacting that schism in the religious mind which Moore found simultaneously fascinating and repellent. The same separation, more brutally imposed, characterizes the life of the famous lovers in his last large-scale work, *Heloise and Abelard* (1921). In *A Story-Teller's Hol-*

iday, he returns to the treatment of specifically Irish material, telling Irish legend through the medium of a highly improbable native story-teller, named Alec Trusselby. Old legend and contemporary story are linked by the recurrent theme of celibacy and the tragedies, minor or major, which flow from its enforcement. Part of the interest of the two volumes depends upon the exchange between the two narrators, Trusselby and Moore himself, described as 'a dialogue between the original and the acquired self'. The Dublin Moore describes at the outset had been shelled by the British in the 1916 Rebellion. Its famous buildings 'are but phantoms', it is 'a city that has passed away'. Babylon, Pompeii and Herculaneum are called upon to give the appropriate air of transience and desolation. Yeats has left, 'having become a myth from too long brooding on myths'. The world of *Hail and Farewell* has already begun to disappear, although the 'young doctor who supplies Dublin with jokes' and entertained Moore on the steps of the Shelbourne Hotel—almost certainly Oliver St John Gogarty—was not far from achieving his second immortalization in fiction of a kind which would reassemble the Dublin that was now disappearing, although under a different rubric. Having been the priest of *The Lake,* he was already transformed into the Buck Mulligan of *Ulysses.* Joyce, to his chagrin, did not merit an invitation to Moore's soirées in Dublin, although Gogarty did. Now it is sometimes difficult to remember that Moore and Gogarty had any other function than to have been associated with Joyce, whose experimentation with the novel and whose fascination with Ireland, the artist, sexual repression and the dedication of the work to the restoration of sundered flesh and spirit, past and present, had all been central preoccupations of Moore's career too. The Ireland he knew was, nevertheless, fading fast. He had a premonition of the end of Moore Hall, his ancestral house:

> Moore Hall will certainly fall into ruin. As soon as you have gone, the trees will be felled, and the lead taken from the roof; Moore Hall will be a ruin within a very few years; for not a great many years of life lie in front of you.

Moore Hall did become a ruin. The literature that had been produced by the people of the Irish Big House was disappearing with the conditions that had initially promoted it. Yeats in his tower will always be one of its symbols; Lady Gregory and Coole Park another; George Moore and Moore Hall the most ambiguous and yet, in many ways, the most characteristic of all. But another man in another kind of tower was to dominate the history of both Irish and modern fiction. This was James Joyce in his martello tower in Sandycove, County Dublin. Disguised as Stephen Dedalus, he was to find a new manner of walking and talking in Dublin and of making a narrative out of it.

So much has been written about James Joyce that there is no need to repeat much of it here, although it is remarkable that the commentary on his works should have turned into such an endless industry. That in itself says something about the later works in particular. *Ulysses* (1922) and *Finnegans Wake* (1939) present so many difficulties to the reader that they solicit guides and keys, dictionaries of allusion and reference, various sorts of exegetical compendia as well as interpretive essays, in which the shock of these new masterpieces is slowly absorbed and overcome. From the beginning he was opposed to the Literary Revival's cultural nationalism, believing that there had been quite enough of that already in the nineteenth century with disastrous results for the artists—like James Clarence Managan—who had been seduced by it. He looked instead to the world beyond, most especially to Europe and, among the Europeans, to Ibsen to whom he wrote on the occasion of the great dramatist's seventieth birthday, praising above all

> how in your absolute indifference to public canons of art, friends, and shibboleths you walked in the light of your inward heroism.

This is a suitable epigraph for Joyce's own career. Yet, for all his hostility to the reappearance of Ireland as a literary property in the years after Parnell's death, Joyce, more than anyone else, centred his work on the Ireland of that period. He shared with all his contemporaries, from Yeats and Synge to Moore and O'Casey, a preoccupation with the idea of a culture for which a wholly articulate and authentic literature had still to be found. Therefore, like them, he is deeply involved in the problems of language and of the various forms of censorship and disapproval that would deny its ultimate responsibility to truth. Like Moore, he made an artistic virtue out of his cosmopolitanism but he discovered a richer way of exploiting the analogies between his own, his country's past and the past of world history and world literature. His remembrance of things past is controlled by a variety of formal manoeuvres, which allow him to manifest them as being simultaneously present. His great synoptic narratives bring all history (everything that is crucial and much that is accidental) and all languages into the discipline of an art where everything exists in a felicitous present tense, where the most random detail can become meaningful and the most casual discovery is always *ben trovato*.

Joyce is the first and greatest of Irish urban writers. Dublin was the centre of his universe and the rapid transitions and dismembered sensations of modern urban life moulded his sensibility. Because of this, he is much more hospitable to the various kinds of popular entertainment and recreation which were a feature of the Catholic middle-class life into which he was born and from which he never entirely dissociated himself. In his writings, the Ireland of Daniel O'Connell, Thomas Moore, James Clarence Mangan and *The Spirit of the Nation* is given a new lease of life rather than the disdain which Yeats visited upon it. Yet, in his early fiction, this is a pharisaic world, coldly observed by an insider who had become estranged from it. In *Dubliners* (1914), we see another version of George Moore's Ireland, a place in which human desire and longing are frustrated by a deadening and powerful Catholicism and its social counterpart, a joyless and humiliating conformity. The opening story, *The Sisters*, first published in AE's journal, *The Irish Homestead* in 1904, introduces us in its first paragraph to the word 'paralysis'. This is a premonition of what is to come. The dead priest and the intricate bankrupt ritual of his wake are seen by a young boy who is becoming aware of the contrasting feelings within himself of attraction for this maleficent cul-

ture and rebellion against it. The desolation of the lives portrayed here rests on the abiding sense of something precious, even sacred, which has been violated—young love, the memory of Parnell, religious belief, a community's natural spirit of intimacy. The violation has produced a petrifaction of the spirit which has become institutionalized. Joyce wrote these stories in what he famously called a style of 'scrupulous meanness', making the gesture of his language the most prominent indication of his theme. Yeats's Ireland had discovered a new idealism. Joyce's Dublin has betrayed an old one—the idealism upon which the vision of a humane and living society rests. His people are driven inwards upon themselves by the pressure of their dilapidated surroundings, only to find no resource. The blankness of death covers all, as in the final vision of Gabriel Conroy in the last story, *The Dead*. The snow that falls on Dublin and extends westward to the Shannon and the grave of Michael Furey, his wife's former lover, brings the living and dead into a melancholy partnership. Just this once in *Dubliners*, we glimpse the mutual contracts that bind all together and on this sole occasion too we recognize that the wholeness of the Irish and of the human community has been perceived in the light of strong feeling. Joyce, we learn, is especially fond of such a final coda, suddenly suffusing his fiction with the retrospective power of the very energy which it had until then been denied. This closing vibrancy is, at times, sentimental. But so severe is the repudiation that precedes it that most readers find in it a solace from the unremitting bleakness that would otherwise dominate.

Joyce lived in the martello tower at Sandycove with Oliver St John Gogarty in 1904. He was by then a graduate of University College, Dublin, a student of languages and was locally known as an essayist, poet and writer of short stories. That year he also met Nora Barnacle, a chambermaid from Galway, and went away with her to Pola and then the following year to Trieste, where he began to teach English at the Berlitz school. This may have had an effect on the prose style of *Dubliners* and on that of his first novel, *Stephen Hero*, the twenty-six chapters of which he recast into the five chapters of *A Portrait of the Artist as a Young Man* in 1907-14. *Portrait* was first published in serial form in the English magazine *The Egoist* in 1915. The complete novel finally appeared in New York in 1916. Yeats and Pound were by then among his most fervent supporters and helped to get him grants from the British Royal Literary Fund and the British Treasury Fund to alleviate his appalling financial situation. Two years after moving to neutral Switzerland during the First World War, Joyce received the first of a series of munificent gifts from the wealthy and gifted Harriet Shaw Weaver, the first of many sponsors of his later career. He gradually became the centre of admiration of an inner clique of artists and avant-garde editors, especially after his move to Paris in 1920. At the same time, he began to achieve notoriety among the general public as a writer who managed to be obscene and opaque. Dublin frowned on the first two books. *The Irish Book Lover* claimed that Joyce was blind 'to the stirrings of literary and civic consciousness which give an interest and zest to social and political intercourse' in the capital. Joyce, however, did not waver in his resolve to 'write a chapter of the moral history of my country', seeing this as a liberating moment in the asphyxiating tradition of Irish writing. To the English publisher of *Dubliners* he wrote:

> in composing my chapter of moral history in exactly the way I have composed it I have taken the first step toward the spiritual liberation of my country. Reflect for a moment on the history of the literature of Ireland as it stands at present written in the English language before you condemn this genial illusion of mine.

In *Portrait,* the moral history of the development of Stephen Dedalus becomes an example of the liberation which Ireland sorely needed and implacably denied.

Portrait is not a thesis-novel. It is, in its latter part, either enriched or flawed by an ambiguity on the part of the author towards the protagonist, Stephen Dedalus, who had already figured in *Stephen Hero* as a young man entirely deserving of our sympathy and support in his struggle against the squalid morality of Irish life. It is possible to see Stephen as the greatest of all the artist heroes who had become so popular in the European novel since the 1880s. For once, we witness the growth of a consciousness which we can believe to be that of a young intellectual. Stephen begins by receiving the language of his world—nursery rhymes, Latin tags, political argument (over the fall of Parnell), hell-fire sermons, literary models. He ends by supplanting these forms of language with his own, so that the subject of the book becomes, in a formal sense, its author. In that light, the novel is a series of carefully orchestrated quotations, through which we see a young mind coming to grips with his world through an increasing mastery of language. Further, we recognize that this is a moral, not merely a formal, achievement. On the other hand, Stephen can be seen as a victim of Joyce's irony. He is the prototypical artist-aesthete, who is finally revealed to be a poseur, more gifted in theorizing about art and freedom than in producing either. It is not necessary to choose one emphasis at the expense of the other. The presence of both in the novel indicates Joyce's dissatisfaction with the limitations of the conventions of heroism, even if it be the heroism of the alienated artist in a mediocre society. This was already a worn theme by 1914. The weariness which beset it became visible in Richard Rowan, the hero of Joyce's one play, *Exiles,* written in 1915. An analyst of others, he cannot analyse his own perverse wish to have his wife betray him. Although he is an impoverished version of Stephen, Rowan does at least allow us to observe Joyce's almost neurotic fascination with treachery and betrayal, a symptom perhaps of the loneliness he felt in repudiating Ireland and in being repudiated by her.

In *Ulysses,* treachery and its accompanying loneliness is a pervasive preoccupation. Stephen Dedalus has betrayed his mother's dying request to kneel down and pray for her. His friend, Buck Mulligan, has betrayed him by refusing to acknowledge Stephen's importance. Leopold Bloom is betrayed by his wife, who commits adultery with Blazes Boylan. As a result, the intellectual Irishman, Stephen, and the commonplace Jew, Bloom, experience profound isolation in their wanderings through Dublin during 16 June 1904. Both men are members of broken families and citizens of a broken nation. Their interwoven sojourns, fit-

fully modelled on the wanderings of Homer's Ulysses in his journey towards wife, son and home in Ithaca, represent, among other things, an attempt on Joyce's part to reintegrate the project of the artist hero with the spirit of the community, specifically that of Dublin but generally that of mankind, from which he has been separated. For all its faults, Dublin is no longer the centre of paralysis. It is a city of talk and song, pub and restaurant, its physical and human detail registered with an almost preternatural freshness. Stephen, armed with an astonishing array of theories which assert the ultimate independence of the individual from all parentage, tradition and history, is a son in search of a father and agonized by his betrayal of his mother. Bloom, immersed in the world of physical sensation, is seeking companionship, a community—Irish, Jewish, familial—to which he might be permitted to belong, a father searching for a substitute for the child he lost. Both are involved in an intricate series of surrogate fantasies. Bloom philanders in his mild way among real and imagined women and attaches himself to the phalanx of Dublin males, led by Simon Dedalus, Stephen's father, without ever gaining acceptance among them. Stephen ranks himself in his mind with heretical heroes and betrayed writers—Arius, Photius, Valentine, Shakespeare— or with legendary son-victims like Icarus and Telemachus. The historical and mythical shadows that haunt their minds darken the naturalistic texture of the novel, allowing us—partly through the technique of the interior monologue—to observe the endless interchange between the inner and the outer worlds, one dominated by obsessions, the other characterized by randomness. In blending all these elements together, Joyce transformed the century's conception of the novel. He reconstructed the basic forms of fiction so that myth, history, intellectual theory and naturalistic detail could coexist within a narrative frame which was flexible enough to endure vertiginous variations of style. In *Ulysses,* the modern Irish experimentation with language and form reaches a culmination. After it, the tremendous prestige of the English novel was never again so oppressive for Irish writers.

Nevertheless, the rupture with traditional practice had its own dangers. The reader of *Ulysses* might well feel betrayed after the first ten episodes when a new kind of narrative takes over and the drama of Stephen and Bloom seems to give way to a virtuoso display of literary ventriloquism. The novel caricatures its own subject—the possibility of the restoration of a community between artist and public in modern conditions—by focusing our attention on the phenomenon of the production of language rather than on the more conventional consumption of a story or theme. Analogies proliferate as in the *Oxen of the Sun* episode, where the development of English prose style and the growth of the embryo in the womb are comically dovetailed in the account of Mrs Purefoy's labour in the Holles Street Lying-In Hospital. Even more enervating is the famous and very long-winded 'catechism' of the *Itchaca* episode, in which the act of communication between Bloom and Stephen is parodied to the point of absurdity and boredom. One has the impression of great language systems beginning to break away from the central mass of the novel and turning into offshore islands inhabited by Joycean specialists, while the general population looks on. The extension of *Ulysses* towards that mythic status at which it would be able to make any one thing representative of all things was not possible within the limits of that miraculous naturalism, which is its natural basis. In order to achieve that sense of unity in diversity, of all stories being one story, one man being all men, one country being all countries, Joyce had to break with this naturalism and found his new novel in the territory of dream. Thus, we enter the world of *Finnegans Wake.*

In this fluid world of the *Wake,* the distinction between chaos and order is cancelled. Chaos simply becomes the word we give to systems of order we do not at first perceive. Order is the word we give to chaotic materials over which we feel we have gained an ephemeral mastery. Every reader becomes his own novelist in a book that was more stringently organized by its author than any other novel. Since history is envisaged in this book as a cyclic pattern of recurrences, the blurred and gigantic figures which dominate it are archetypes of human experience. HCE, or Humphry Chimpden Earwicker, the publican in Chapelizod, who is dreaming the wake is also Here Comes Everybody and he Haveth Childers Everywhere, among them Shem and Shaun, the Cain and Abel brothers who represent the eternal principle of opposition. The microcosm of Irish history contains within itself the macrocosm of world history. The Fall of Man and the Fall of Parnell are the same event in different guises. Similarly, language, especially the English spoken by Irish people, becomes, through distortion, the idea to which all other languages are approximations. Every conceivable form of fusion, pun, malapropism and displacement is employed to set off an almost infinite train of associations, references and memories, which can easily become overburdened and go out of control. The medium of this book is its subject. Myth and story are secondary to it. In fact, the narrative line or lines, when they are perceived, are little more than organizing principles which help to provide some sense of sequence and symmetry for the protean vocabularies which shift and slide under their surfaces. Many of Joyce's greatest admirers were put off by the *Wake.* Yeats should have liked it more, for, as it moved through its complex development in serial form in the pages of the magazine *transition,* under the title *Work in Progress,* he might have glimpsed in it a comic version of his own theories of Eternal Recurrence which he had published in *A Vision.* Both of them shared a capacity to organize experience into strict patterns without conceding its diversity. Thus, in the *Wake,* for all the plainness of the informing idea of history, our sense of it is enriched by language which is comically and joyfully indulging in the extravagance of the actual. No matter how omnivorous the language is, we often have a sense that there is yet more which language, even when tortured to the point of collapse, cannot confess. In *Ulysses,* the shadow of an epic hero is cast over a text full of anti-heroic or mock-heroic references and we can infer from that how much Joyce wanted us to share the modernist view that we lived in a delinquent age. But in the *Wake,* the presence that moves behind the text is the presence of the ordinary workaday world and its workaday language. The dream slippages have transformed the quotidian into the mythic and, as we read this phantom script, we are drawn to reverse the process. It seems unlikely,

therefore, that Joyce was counterpointing the contemporary world against the world of myth in any disobliging manner. In fact, the curious effect of the *Wake* is to make us grateful for the particularized world we inhabit. Joyce, the master of ceremonies, transmogrifies everything for the sake of making it fresher and more endearing in its more conventional form. The introduction to the Mookse and the Gripes episode, for instance, is a perfect example of the text's yearning to be read straightforwardly, as a kind of nursery tale or music hall yarn, even though it is perversely deformed:

> Gentes and laitymen, fullstoppers and semicolonials, hybreds and lubberds!
>
> Eins within a space and a wearywide space it wast ere wohned a Mookse. The onesomeness wast alltolonely, archunsitslike, broady oval, and a Mookse he would a walking go (My hood! cries Antony Romeo), so one grandsumer evening, after a great morning and his good supper of gammon and spittish, having flabelled his eyes, pilleoled his nostrils, vacticanated his ears and palliumed his threats, he put on his impermeable, seized his impugnable, harped on his crown and steeped out of his immoble *De Rure Albo* (socolled becauld it was chalkfull of masterplasters and had borgeously letout gardens strown with cascadas pintacostecas, herthoducts and currycombs) and set off from Ludstown *a spasso* to see how badness was badness in the weirdest of all pensible ways.

One of the paradoxes of Joyce's achievement is that he did in the end give primacy to the idea of human solidarity and the ordinary secular life of the modern city in works which have gained, because of their extreme difficulty, a highly specialized audience. The liberal and democratic impulse in these books has been considerably deflected by the takeover of them by a class of experts. This indicates something ambiguous in Joyce as well as in the reception of his work. It was there in the double vision of Stephen as hero or as poseur in *Portrait.* It remains in *Ulysses* and in the *Wake* because the isolation of the artist and, by extension, of the individual seems to be too emphatic to be overcome by the emergent mass society which Joyce saw adumbrated in the Dublin of his youth. The *Wake* is a dream of community but it scarcely survives in the face of the 'nightmare of history' Stephen spoke of in *Ulysses.* It might be said that Joyce found Irish history and Irish tradition so fragmented that, in spite of his systematizing imagination, no hope for coherence could be entertained. Such a feeling would have been widespread in early twentieth-century Europe, when the premonitions of cultural disintegration had become universal. The battle between disorder and order, the individual consciousness and the communal mind, is waged by Joyce with such a dedication and energy that he changed the form of the traditional novel in his attempt to resolve it. He universalized the plight in which the nineteenth-century Irish novelists had been trapped. Caught between two cultures, two languages and two audiences, English and Irish, they had been mired by history. Joyce, inheriting these divisions, overcame them by bringing history into the ambit of fiction and revealing thereby the essentially linguistic and therefore ductile nature of both activities. In this respect, he emulated Yeats.

Joyce's *Ulysses* had been deemed pornographic after its publication in Paris in 1922. Eleven years passed before a New York judge cleared it of the charge and opened the way for its publication in a trade edition in the USA. By then Joyce was deeply engaged in *Work in Progress* and was gathering around him a group of disciples who would help him to complete it and help it to be received with some measure of comprehension. Samuel Beckett was one of the young recruits to the Joyce circle in 1928. His first publication was an essay on Joyce in 1929. In 1930 he helped translate the 'Anna Livia Plurabelle' section of the *Wake* into French. In 1937, the year in which his first novel, *Murphy,* was finally accepted for publication by the forty-third publisher to receive it, Beckett was involved as witness in a libel action in Dublin, taken out by a friend of his against the ineluctable Oliver St John Gogarty, who had so delighted Moore and displeased Joyce. Gogarty lost the case and left Ireland for the USA; Beckett lost face and left Ireland for France. Thereafter he visited Ireland only for family reasons. For him, as for Joyce and Moore, exile was a necessity. Like them too, language was for him a chosen rather than a naturally assumed action. After 1945, he began to write his works in French, later translating them into English himself. Thus, after his book of short stories, *More Pricks than Kicks* (1934), and his first two published novels, *Murphy* (1938) and *Watt* (1953, composed 1942-4), the works which made Beckett famous—the trilogy (*Molloy, Malone Meurt, L'Innommable,* composed 1947-9, published 1951-3), the *Nouvelles* ('La Fin', 'L'Expulsé', 'Le Calmant', 'Premier Amour', 1955)—were all written in his second language, as was the play, *En Attendant Godot,* which made him famous after its first production at the Théâtre de Babylone in Paris in 1953. Beckett has so many points of contact with Joyce that it is tempting to see him as a disciple or follower. Yet, although Joyce (along with Proust) remains for Beckett one of the greatest of writers, the differences between them are too marked to allow for any glib account of their relationship.

For one thing, Beckett grew up in the Protestant upper middle class of a Dublin that had become the capital of the Irish Free State the year before he began his career as an undergraduate at Trinity College. In the year his first essay was published, the Censorship of Publications Act was passed. Ireland entered on a long period of introversion and stabilization after the stormy years of the 1920s. The atmosphere was constricting. Cultural nationalism was degraded into a species of village bigotry. Writers, in particular, fought against the prevailing ideology, partly because they were among its most prominent victims in the matter of banning books and partly because the written word had such power in Ireland. Sean O'Faolain, Frank O'Connor and Liam O'Flaherty were among the most prominent spokesmen for the writers and for a general liberalization of the ethos of the new state. Beckett, however, played a little part in this dispute. He was certainly affected by the disenchantment and nullity of the Irish situation but, locked in his own personal depressions, was not disposed to do much about it other than escaping

from it. Going to Paris and becoming involved in the Joyce circle and in the Verticalist movement which was then associated with the journal *transition,* only confirmed his sense that he and his generation had nothing left but that 'integral pessimism' of which *transition* made such a fuss. Beckett had come after the Revival and after the great age of European modernism. The rich and multifarious world of Joyce's fiction had been replaced by the pure poverty of a world where only Habit ruled:

> Habit is a compromise effected between the individual and his environment, or between the individual and his own organic eccentricities, the guarantee of a dull inviolability, the lightning-conductor of his existence. Habit is the ballast that chains the dog to his vomit. Breathing is habit. Life is habit.

Ireland, we may say, functions in Beckett's work as a mode of absence. It is the anonymous landscape of the trilogy and of some of the later plays and fictions such as *All That Fall* and *First Love.* Within this vacuous space a series of meditations take place, the materials for which are sometimes stories, sometimes philosophical problems. But the stories lead nowhere and the problems are rendered ridiculous. Beckett's two languages of disquisition and of narrative are worked hard, to the point of exhaustion. When they resume, they carry with them an air of futility and resignation. Language aches to give up, to reach the silence which would signify death. But as long as consciousness remains, language proceeds. Two authors cast their shadows on all that he has written—Descartes and Dante. The Cartesian method of radical doubt is adapted, but the Cartesian premises are denied. *Cogito ergo sum* and *sum res cogitans* are declarations which, in Beckett's world, would appear ineffably smug. But the method by which everything inessential is pared away until the ultimate primary essence remains appeals to him, even though the paring away process will obviously be infinite for someone who does not or cannot believe in any primary essence. The effect of Cartesianism, its emotional consequence on Beckett's heroes, is deadening. They all suffer from an apathy of sublime proportions. They recognize the futility of existence and regard with venom anyone who dares to gloss it otherwise. So deep is their depression that it becomes the basis for a coherent and perfectly rational vision of the torment of everyday life. Here the Dante of the *Purgatorio* appears as the epic literary mentor and, particularly the figure of Belacqua from the ante-Purgatory, the epitome of Sloth, living or rather reliving the whole period of his life again under the shadow of a rock. Thus Beckett's novels and plays contain intellectually brilliant practitioners of the Cartesian method of radical doubt who are also stunned depressives, emotionally crippled by the vision of the meaninglessness of a life which must be lived and relived.

Belacqua Shuah is the odd name of the first Beckett hero, the ataraxic eccentric of *More Pricks than Kicks.* The ten stories in this volume are a record of his grotesque existence in Dublin, his marriages, his accidental death and his burial on the day his house is burned down. Except for the first of them, 'Dante and the Lobster', they are exercises in undergraduate affectation and humour. But the first novel, *Murphy,* is almost free of the excessive inkhorn extravagance of the short stories. Its hero has a 'Belacqua fantasy'—to escape from time. To that end, he practises various techniques of concentration, taking pleasure in the governance of his own mind just as he is goaded into displeasure by the requirements of the external world, represented by Celia, a prostitute who loves Murphy and wants him to find a job as a condition of her staying with him. Murphy does settle for a job in a lunatic asylum, where he feels more at home than elsewhere, especially with his chess-playing schizophrenic friend, Mr Endon. However, Murphy cannot gain full admission to the inner world of the insane and returns to his apartment to meet an untimely death in a gas explosion. Thus Beckett brings to a comic end the story of his gang of Irish misfits in London, dominated by the philosophic Murphy who had almost reached that state in which mind and body, self and world were happily and totally sundered from one another. This division, normally seen as tragic, is here viewed as desirable but tragic because not attainable. The novel rests firmly on this inconoclastic inversion.

In *Watt,* the power of the mind expresses itself in logic; the helplessness of the body is expressed in humiliation. Empirical data are frozen into analytic set-pieces which rob them of their natural interconnecting fluency. So Watt's manner of walking is described in such a manner that it becomes impossibly complicated; and yet he walks. Watt's stay in Mr Knott's house is dictated by a systematic arrangement which makes no sense; and yet it works. Beckett seems here to be stretching language to the point at which its connection with a meaningful world is broken, thereby indicating the possibility that the world is meaningless or that language is competent only to render meaningless what would otherwise be taken for granted. His favourite devices of the inventory and the series— exhaustive schema which include everything and mean nothing—are elaborated in this instance with a merciless rigour, which can sometimes be trying and sometimes comic. The story may be a parable or an allegory of Man confronting the Void, armed with his useless gift of ratiocination. But its irritable, obsessive turnings and twistings do not make it amenable to such translations. Mr Knott, for instance, appears to Watt differently each day. On each of eighty-one occasions he merits four descriptive epithets out of a total range of twelve possible. The listing takes two pages. There are numerous examples of the same manic cataloguing of the infinite choices which a novel, or language, or consciousness can make when faced with a presence which is an absence like Mr Knott. Occam's razor was never so badly needed nor so little used.

The difficulty of writing about people whose lives are completely internalized was solved when Beckett adopted the monologue as the dramatic form for the great trilogy he composed in the late forties. *Molloy, Malone Dies* and *The Unnamable* are narratives in which an orphic voice flows on relentlessly, unencumbered by the necessity to obey the usual conventions of fiction, which had so severely intruded upon Murphy's experimental journey into the fastness of his own mind. Physically bound or disabled, they become talking heads. Their inertia is deeper than anything imagined by Joyce or Moore. It is metaphysically, not so-

cially, dictated. Story is almost abandoned, but figures and names from earlier writings are introduced as though the character in the novel had been their creator. This is fiction vengefully representing as reality other fictions. Molloy and Moran, in the first of these novels, are writing reports about their pointless journeys into immobility. Molloy is the 'Irish', Moran the 'French' aspect of Beckett. One begins in despair, the other in confidence. Both end in ruin. Malone takes an unconscionably long time to die in his bedroom, tormented by memories, stories, the peremptory demands of his useless body. The Unnamable is limbless, trapped in an urn, condemned to talk until he goes almost berserk with grief and frustration at the endlessness of his plight. Language becomes more and more as reality becomes less and less. Everything is exact and measured and yet nothing has a boundary or limit. Journeys are undertaken by cripples. Escape is impossible so repetition is inescapable. The wish to be dead is countered by the wish that one had never been born. The desire for silence can only be expressed in words. With all these paradoxes and contradictions undermining the activity of language, it comes as no surprise to find that Beckett's prose, laden as always with pedantry and humour, is characterized by ramifying digressions, reservations, corrections and cancellations. Nothing can be said straightforwardly, including that last remark. The logic that had driven Murphy and Watt to the asylum now informs the structure of the sentences themselves. They dislocate sense by adhering rigidly to the strategies of formal analysis. The complications of these texts are intensified when their author translates them from their original French into English. One text becomes two, and although they are substantially the same, a host of minor differences seems to demand new emphases; altered cadences change the colour of feeling in particular passages. Language reproduces itself and finds that it has become different while remaining the same. The process of reading Beckett becomes labyrinthine.

Nouvelles et textes pour rien (1955, *Stories and Texts for Nothing* 1967) and *From An Abandoned Work* (1956) reveal even in their titles the extreme to which Beckett had brought the writing of fiction. *Waiting for Godot* and the radio play *All That Fall* (1957) remain within the tragic and neurotic zones explored in the fiction but the dramatic form liberates him in his treatment of it. As a dramatist, Beckett has more affinities with Yeats than with any other Irish writer. The stylized stage sets, the ritualized actions and speeches, the repudiation of the commercial theatre's idea of plot and its replacement by the monologues and dialogues of people who are 'mindtight' in a world which is 'bodytight'—these are all recognizable Yeatsian gestures. Wilde (with his Salomé, written in French), Synge, Moore, Joyce and Yeats had all paid their obeisance to France. Beckett made the interchange so intimate that he became a great Irish as well as a great French writer. In that sense, he broke the always dangerous connection between nationality and literature, although from another point of view it could be argued that he confirmed the ambition of the most important writers of the Revival to Europeanize Irish writing and thereby escape from insularity. The fondness of Irish dramatists in particular for vagrant or delinquent characters is a further symptom of their sceptical or disenchanted vision of established social forms, something common enough among oppressed peoples who feel that their communal experience is misrepresented by being regarded as peripheral. But Beckett excavates these rather inarticulate feelings with such vigour that they are re-presented in his writings as centrally human experiences. His drama has been particularly successful in this regard. Dramatic forms which had been associated with experimental theatre are refashioned by him into the norms of popular theatre.

The popularity of *Waiting for Godot* is partly explained by the fact that it combines the routines of slapstick comedy perfected in the music-hall and in the early cinema with the gestures of tragic theatre. The religious and philosophical references, the shadowy presence of the tragic (and therefore meaningful) death of the Crucifixion and the more substantial memories of attempted suicide by the clownish couple Vladimir and Estragon with their comic turns, their soliloquizing, their duets of despair and their anguished quartets with Pozzo and Lucky create a sense of the anomalous in the audience when the feeling deepens, as much as when it lightens. Categories like comedy and tragedy are as useless here as in O'Casey. The subtle mixture of tones can suddenly transform itself into sharp contrasts in the polarized light of a single speech, like Pozzo's outburst at the end. Then it resumes itself in the antiphonal response of Vladimir:

> Astride of a grave and a difficult birth. Down in the hole, lingeringly, the grave-digger puts on the forceps. We have time to grow old. The air is full of our cries. (*He listens*) But habit is a great deadener.

In *Endgame* and *Krapp's Last Tape* (both 1958) the waiting for someone or something to come is modified into a waiting for the past to return to give purpose or meaning to the desiccated present. The immobility of the personages in these plays is both the stillness of those who wait and the paralysis of those who have begun to die. Even in *All That Fall,* the first work originally written in English since 1945, Mrs Rooney staggering to the railway station near Dublin has difficulty in keeping the impression of death out of her vigorous words. Her husband remarks that 'one would think you were struggling with a dead language'. To this she gives the famous and hilarious—yet almost melancholy—response:

> Well, you know, it will be dead in time, just like our own poor dear Gaelic, there is that to be said.
>
> *Urgent baa.*

The lamb's bleat gives a delicious Special Effect to the remark.

The drama had its repercussion on Beckett's fiction. It helped him get rid of that neutered 'I' that had been the voice source in the trilogy. Instead, the later fictions or narratives, finally disembarrassed of plot, are voices in empty space, late night transmissions picked up through a cloud of static on some high-frequency wavelength. They come out of the silence abruptly and fade back just as suddenly. Yet for all the accidental and occasional aspect of pieces like *Ping* (1967) or *Lessness* (1970), *For To*

End Yet Again and Other Fizzles (1976), they retain, even intensify, the lucid, systematic rationale of inquiry, which the works of the 1930s and 1940s had more generously provided. As in Joyce, the random and the highly organized elements within a text are played against one another in a phantom chess-game. Sometimes, as in *Ping,* almost every organizing principle—punctuation, syntax, grammar, story—has vanished and we have only flickering images and the word 'Ping' itself to control the obsessive, wholly impersonal and yet totally confessional outpourings. Beckett seems to have gone as far as possible in abolishing from his writing the dimension of time. He wants neither sequence nor simultaneity but some intercalatory dimension in which the tension between the two is forgone entirely. These formal manoeuvres are the artifices for the control of those feelings which he blends in such estranging and disturbing ways. Feeling remains authentic as long as it remains intransitive. To find a language for it is to betray it. It is, therefore, appropriate that this inhabitant of Ireland, the 'Elysium of the roofless' should live in two languages, French and English, and still be able to say, 'Tears and laughter, they are so much Gaelic to me'.

Gaelic was no mystery to Flann O'Brien, who wrote one novel *An Béal Bocht* (*The Poor Mouth,* 1941, translated 1964) in that language. It is, characteristically, an outright attack on the various and misguided attempts to revive it. O'Brien, whose real name was Brian O'Nolan (or O Nualláin), is even better known as Myles, short for Myles na gCopaleen, the pen-name he used for the weekly column he wrote for *The Irish Times* between 1940 and 1966. Even Beckett's remorseless hilarity cannot quite match the humour of O'Brien's deadpan prose. But O'Brien achieved his best effects in only two novels—*An Béal Bocht* and *At-Swim-Two-Birds* (1939)—and in his newspaper column, now published in a useful selection, *The Best of Myles* (1968). Although his other novels have their attractions and brilliancies—especially *The Third Policeman* (completed 1940, published 1967)—they are flawed by the intermittent failure of that delicate balance between logic and fantasy which makes his early fiction so remarkable. *The Hard Life* (1961) and *The Dalkey Archive* (1964) are ingenious reworkings of the earlier novels, lacking the autonomy and finish of their predecessors. For this, James Joyce is to blame. O'Brien's reaction to Joyce's work and, later, to Joyce's fame is one of the most astonishing examples of the 'anxiety of influence' to be found, even in Ireland where the closeness of the small literary community stimulates fiction and friction of varied quality and unvaried regularity. At first, there was admiration and respect. Then, as the books on Joyce began to proliferate, especially in the USA, a certain modification occurred. In 1951, O'Brien declared that

> the true fascination of Joyce lies in his secretiveness, his ambiguity (his polyguity, perhaps?), his leg-pulling, his dishonesties, his technical skill, his attraction for Americans.

The publisher's refusal of *The Third Policeman* in 1940, the outbreak of war and the intense local Dublin-based cult of Myles na gCopaleen among the readers of *The Irish Times* served to enhance the contrast between O'Brien's fortunes and those of Joyce. O'Brien could see that he and

Beckett, along with Denis Devlin and Brian Coffey, were the only considerable writers of their generation to have escaped the wearisome enchantments of the Revival. He was not among the group Beckett christened 'the Antiquarians', who still lived parasitically off the cultural nationalism created by Ferguson, O'Grady and Yeats. O'Brien knew Old and Modern Irish. He admired the terseness and precision of the language and consequently found it distasteful to see these qualities transmogrified into Romantic vagueness and dishevelled dreaminess by people whose ignorance of the language was almost perfect. Yet there he was, in his 'homebased exile', shut off from the world by war, shut in with Ireland by his notoriety. The problem of provincialism and cosmopolitanism which he embodied (and which was to exercise so many of his contemporaries, like Patrick Kavanagh and Sean O'Faolain, who felt the burden of the 1940s, in Ireland in a similar way) was projected for him in the reception of Joyce, the most profoundly local of writers, who had now the most international of reputations. Thus the absorption of Joyce in the early novels, which led to their enrichment, declined into a running battle with his reputation in his later work, leading to its impoverishment. The culmination comes in *The Dalkey Archive,* where Joyce appears as a very religious curate serving in a pub twenty miles north of Dublin, anxious to become a Jesuit and horrified to hear that he is regarded as the author of *Ulysses,* 'that dirty book, that collection of smut'. As for *Finnegans Wake,* Joyce thinks it is still no more than a song.

The humour of this is darkened by the fact that this most unheroic Joyce has a counterpart in the idiot-genius de Selby, transposed now from *The Third Policeman* to the village of Dalkey, as far south of Dublin as Skerries, Joyce's refuge, is north. De Selby (whose name puns on the German *das Selbst,* the Self) has created a concoction which will destroy the world by relieving the atmosphere of its oxygen. Its intermediate use, so to speak, abolishes serial time and enables de Selby to converse with a number of figures from past history, all of them early fathers of the Church, including St Augustine. Their concerns, most of them heretical, are remarkably similar to those of James Augustine Joyce in *Ulysses.* (The comic and the more serious treatment of the anti-heroic theme, which depends on the fiction of a 'dead' here being alive in circumstances which make heroism suspect, had already been explored by Lennox Robinson's play *The Lost Leader* (1918), where Parnell is the victim, and in Moore's *The Book Kerith.*) The man whose (finally aborted) ambition is to bring de Selby and Joyce together is one Mick Shaughnessy, 'a lowly civil servant', who wants to stop the destruction of the world by the former and wonders if it could be done

> by bringing together de Selby and Joyce and inducing both to devote their considerable brains in consultation to some recondite, involuted and incomprehensible literary project, ending in publication of a book which would be commonly ignored and thus be no menace to universal sanity?

'Universal sanity' is, in fact, the ideal of O'Brien's writing. It is threatened by two forces. One is folly, the other self-involvement. Folly comes in every conceivable guise and

is hunted down in his newspaper column with such exquisite precision that the joy of the reader is provoked by the manner more than the object of the pursuit. The educational system, the language revival, government policies in general and a host of other samples of human folly are converted into mechanistic schemes for the suppression of the human element by a satirist who is himself a contriver of schemes and machines more elaborate than any ever devised. He defends ordinary common sense by using the weapons of its opponents. But in the case of Joyce (or Beckett), the inhuman element is created by the excessive concentration on the autonomous world of the work of art at the expense of common experience. Such a degree of self-involvement is the deepest form of exile. While O'Brien is more able than either to take pleasure in the self-enclosed world of art, he retains a suspicion that its relation to and effect on ordinary life is damaging. It is, therefore, appropriate to find that his fiction moves simultaneously in two directions—one towards a realism which is exaggeratedly squalid, the other towards a fantasy which is exaggeratedly pure. The transition from one to the other is always unforced and rapid because both are registered in a prose which is uniform in tone and economy. As in Swift, the plain style is ultimately more shocking in its effect than any virtuoso display could be.

The Third Policeman brings the worlds of realism and fantasy together in a particularly eerie manner. It begins with the murder of an old man called Mathers by the hero and his companion John Divney. It ends with the reappearance of the hero on Divney's threshold sixteen years later. This proves fatally upsetting for Divney, because he had murdered our hero sixteen years before so that he could keep Mathers' money and a farm and pub for himself. Now that both are dead, they can meet again in the de Selbian universe of lost souls, which our hero had just left after a series of strange adventures therein with the policemen Sergeant Pluck, Constable McCruiskeen and the third policeman himself, Fox. We can take it that the cycle (literally) of events will recur endlessly. These men are locked in a carefully arranged hell. Its 'reality' is confirmed by the theories of de Selby which proliferate in the footnotes and which open every chapter other than the first and last. Equally, its 'reality' is undermined by the disputes, recorded in the footnotes, which rage among the commentators on de Selby's works. (The application to Joyce needs no emphasizing.) Within the de Selbian world, there are various but cognate threats to be faced. The sergeant is obsessed with the fear that all the inhabitants of the parish are slowly turning into the bicycles which they ride, by a process of molecular interchange. The constable is obsessed with the theory of infinite recession, which he embodies in a series of boxes, which he makes with fanatical precision to fit one inside the other until they pass beyond the point of visibility—and beyond. Eternity is a machine run by the third policeman to keep the other two occupied. Even the landscape is a strictly composed illusion. Over all broods the de Selbian obsession with omnium—i.e. omniscience—and, typically, it is envisaged as something in a box which is also a bomb, which kills the hero and leads him into the phantom hell of the self. The moral parable is clear enough at one level. To seek omniscience is to concede to fantasy. We can also infer that the 'Joycean' world of aesthetic completeness is another version of such a search and has the same deplorable results, commentaries within commentaries *ad infinitum*. But the narrator, although his greed for money as well as his study of de Selby lead him through murder into these phantasmal punishments, belongs by nature in a very different world—that of sheer ordinariness. De Selby's world is the inverse of that. (The fact that the novel is a parody of the famous French novel, *A Rebours*, by J. K. Huysmans—one known to Moore, Wilde and Joyce— emphasizes the satiric parable on aesthetic self-containment and on the perversion associated with it.) The fact too that de Selby's world is controlled by policemen (prominent also in *The Dalkey Archive*) reminds us further of the connection between sinister fantasy and the world of officialdom—of government and its uniformed minions. Their wonderful malaprop jargon is redolent of the officialese, which O'Brien, as a civil servant, knew so well that he parodied it in his newspaper column into something which had its own unearthly beauty. However, any beauty that was unearthly was condemned on that account. O'Brien's protagonists are so deeply immersed in, so native to, the world of the slothful and ordinary that we finally give that world of the bed, the pub, the living-room, a moral priority over all the glittering alternatives of the mind's fictions. In *The Hard Life,* the young schoolboy hero Finbarr watches the obsessions of his older brother Manus and his half-uncle Mr Collopy grow into monstrous but comic fantasies while he remains rooted in the squalid quotidian world of the actual. However, their worlds become so grotesque that his final reaction to the latest development in his brother's mania is 'a tidal surge of vomit'. O'Brien's reaction to the monotony of human monomania became increasingly violent.

However, in his masterpiece, *At-Swim-Two-Birds,* delight is the dominant emotion. It is impossible to describe either the complications of its interwoven plots or the freshness of feeling, which remains intact through all the sophisticated parodies which are episodically developed with a casual aplomb. The book opens with four beginnings—the narrator, chewing bread and giving us examples of three separate openings for the novel he is about to write. He is an undergraduate at University College, Dublin. His life at home with his uncle and at college as an impecunious scholar-drunkard forms one narrative. Another is formed by his burlesque account of the legendary Gaelic heroes, Finn McCool and Mad Sweeney. The third consists of the story of Dermot Trellis, who is writing a novel, the characters of which lead an independent life while Trellis is asleep and revenge themselves upon him by writing a novel in which he is a character. All three narratives blend into one another until they fuse in the 'Conclusion of the book, ultimate'. The epigraph, from *Hercules furens,* is sweetly ironic; it means, 'For all proper things do stand out distinct from one another'. Yet the medley of styles and characters which we meet with here has not the imperious claim upon our admiration which we find in *Ulysses.* The narrator tells us that, 'The novel, in the hands of an unscrupulous writer, could be despotic'. He then goes on to propound his own theory of radical freedom in fiction. Author, reader and character are all free. The despotism of the monomaniac author (like Joyce) is disallowed. His

self-involvement is replaced by extroversion. The commonplace and the fantastic become two aspects of the one thing in a genial if closed universe of interchangeable parts:

> In reply to an inquiry, it was explained that a satisfactory novel should be a self-evident sham to which the reader could regulate at will the degree of his credulity. It was undemocratic to compel characters to be uniformly good or bad or poor or rich. Each should be allowed a private life, self-determination and a decent standard of living. This would make for self-respect, contentment and better service. It would be incorrect to say that it would lead to chaos. Characters should be interchangeable as between one book and another. The entire corpus of existing literature should be regarded as a limbo from which the discerning authors could draw their characters as required, creating only when they failed to find a suitable existing puppet. The modern novel should be largely a work of reference. Most authors spend their time saying what has been said before—usually said much better. A wealth of references to existing works would acquaint the reader instantaneously with the nature of each character, would obviate tiresome explanations and would effectively preclude mountebanks, upstarts, thimbleriggers and persons of inferior education from an understanding of contemporary literature.

This is a description of what *At-Swim-Two-Birds* is and what *Ulysses* and the *Wake,* the chief works of the Joycean egotistical sublime, are not. And yet the kinship between these novels is close and acknowledged to be so. O'Brien is making a gentle distinction, which allows him to absorb rather than be absorbed into Joyce's achievement. After this novel, that balance and irony were lost.

It would therefore be insulting to see O'Brien as nothing more than a Joycean disciple, even though he became as obsessed by Joyce as the most throughgoing de Selbian commentator ever did with de Selby. It is ironic that he never moved out of the shadow thrown by Joyce's reputation because he, along with Beckett, had found his way to the anti-novel as the ideal form in which the romantic conception of the artist-as-hero could finally be dismantled. He suspected the despotism of the Joycean artist but was vanquished by the despotism of the posthumous reputation he achieved. Although his failure can be attributed to the demands of his thrice-weekly column, to the misfortunes of the war, to the lack of a wider audience for his novels and to his excessive drinking, its roots were probably deeper. He gave way to the introversion which he had always countered by the precise evocation of the actualities of Dublin life. In *The Dalkey Archive,* the fantasy of Joyce and de Selby coming together is never seriously entertained because Mick, the pallid go-between, does not live in a sufficiently real world to give that fantasy a ground and a meaning. The fading of that genial realism made the fantasy thin and thereby revealed how paradoxically vital it was for O'Brien's (as it was for Beckett's) avant-garde fiction. Joyce, above all authors, could only be outfaced by a writer who, among all his other gifts, needed to register everything 'with perfection of detail and event'.

This is precisely what is lacking in other experimental fantasy-fictions of the period. The Revival had created a habit of mind which found the conjunction between myths of the past and the actualities of the present an appealing structural device both in poetry and in fiction. Few authors, however, found it possible to make the conjunction effective within a single work, with the result that their writing became polarized between the extremes of fantasy and the extremes of realism. Thus the same author produces fantasies of a peculiarly whimsical purity and realistic novels of a determined grimness. Among the outstanding examples of this schismatic division between two modes of writing are Eimar O'Duffy, Brinsley McNamara, Mervyn Wall and, above all, James Stephens. O'Duffy's first novel, *The Wasted Island,* is a bitter record of the ferment that preceded the 1916 rising and the disenchantment that came immediately after it. His best-known work, *King Goshawk and the Birds* (1926), the first in what is known as the Cuandine trilogy, is a strange mixture of satire and romance, relating the adventures of a mythic hero Cuandine in the degraded worlds of contemporary Ireland and England. Brinsley McNamara's first novel, *The Valley of the Squinting Windows* (1918), is one of the first and one of the most effective exposures of the narrow meanness of village life, sufficiently wounding to provoke the villagers concerned to burn the book publicly and hound his father from their midst. In contrast, *The Various Lives of Marcus Igoe* (1929) is a meditation on the autonomy of literature, elaborated in a fey and whimsical style. Mervyn Wall's two famous novels about a medieval Irish monk—*The Unfortunate Fursey* (1946) and *The Return of Fursey* (1948)—are among the subtlest and funniest of all modern Irish fantasies. But they too are countered by the unrelenting realism of *Leaves for the Burning* (1952), in which a journey undertaken by a group of friends to Sligo for the re-internment of the body of W. B. Yeats is offered as an image of the essential squalor of Irish society. The case of James Stephens is, perhaps, the most exemplary of all. At one time Joyce appointed him as the author who would finish the *Wake* in case Joyce should die before doing so. When we read Stephens's work we can see some method in this Joycean madness. The main novels—*The Charwoman's Daughter* (1912), *The Crock of Gold* (1912), *The Demi-Gods* (1914), *Irish Fairy Tales* (1920), *Deirdre* (1923) and *In The Land of Youth* (1924)—all achieve, though in different ratios, the intermingling of the fantastic or mythic and the realistic. But Stephens's realism is of a particularly powerful, because sober and understated, kind. (He also wrote one of the best eye-witness accounts of the Easter Rising, *The Insurrection in Dublin* 1916.) His world of gods and demi-gods, philosophers and leprechauns, is one of sunlit wisdom and instinctive happiness. The social world he depicts is dominated by the most unfeeling cruelties and selfishness, where the greatest crime is poverty. The opening of *The Charwoman's Daughter* is a well known instance of his plain exactitude:

> Mary Makebelieve lived with her mother in a small room at the very top of a big, dingy house in a Dublin back street. As long as she could re-

member she had lived in that top back room. She knew every crack in the ceiling, and they were numerous and of strange shapes. Every spot of mildew on the ancient wallpaper was familiar. She had, indeed, watched the growth of most from a greyish shade to a dark stain, from a spot to a great blob, and the holes in the skirting of the walls out of which at night time the cockroaches came rattling, she knew also. There was but one window in the room, and when she wished to look out of it she had to push the window up, because the grime of many years had so encrusted the glass that it was of no more than the demi-semi-transparency of thin horn. When she did look there was nothing to see but a bulky array of chimney-pots crowning a next-door house, and these continually hurled jays of soot against her window; therefore, she did not care to look out often, for each time that she did so she was forced to wash herself, and as water had to be carried from the very bottom of the five-storey house up hundreds and hundreds of stairs to her room, she disliked having to use too much water.

Comparing that with the opening of *The Crock of Gold* helps to give an impression of the distance between the two worlds in Stephens's fiction:

> In the centre of the pine wood called Coilla Doraca there lived not long ago two Philosophers. They were wiser than anything else in the world except the Salmon who lies in the pool of Glyn Cagny into which the nuts of knowledge fall from the hazel bush on its bank. He, of course, is the most profound of living creatures, but the two Philosophers are next to him in wisdom. Their faces looked as though they were made of parchment, there was ink under their nails, and every difficulty that was submitted to them, even by women, they were able instantly to resolve. The Grey Woman of Dun Gortin and the Thin Woman of Inis Magrath asked them the three questions which nobody had ever been able to answer, and they were able to answer them.

This is close to Flann O'Brien's parodies in *At-Swim-Two-Birds* but Stephens does not find that sustained ironic tone which subverts the O'Brien narrative and makes the activity of writing itself the subject of amused scrutiny. The repeated attempts on his part and on that of others to conjoin these worlds of Gaelic myth and Irish reality is, of course, a symptom of the increasing strain to which the heroicizing impulse of the Revival was subjected, especially in the aftermath of the political settlement of 1922. The society itself made the discrepancy between mythological grandeurs and quotidian pettiness so severe that it became impossible to incorporate them satisfactorily in fiction. Modern literature had exploited the discordant relationship between a vision of an integrated past and a disintegrated present to the point of exhaustion by the 1930s. The ambition to do so lingered in Ireland, partly because of the achievements of Yeats and Joyce and partly because the dream of a cultural revival was only reluctantly surrendered by a generation which was too vulnerable to accept its demise. However, when that acceptance was made, the savagery of the disillusion, the bitterness of the repudiation was, on occasion, quite awesome. Austin Clarke, for instance, became the scourge of the new Ireland of the 1950s and 1960s, even though no one had been more entranced by the possibility of calling in the old world of Gaelic civilization to balance and chasten the vulgarities of the oppressive present. His Celtic-Romanesque romances, *The Bright Temptation* (1932) and *The Singing Men at Cashel* (1936), or even the verse-drama *The Son of Learning* (1927), dedicated to George Moore and giving central prominence to the artist hero in a contest between Church and State, bespeak a faith in the idiom and the ideals of the Revival which he never entirely lost. The dangers of whimsy, undisciplined extravagance and folksy fake-wisdom were always in close attendance upon such writings. Perhaps Jack Yeats, the painter and brother of the poet, otherwise so 'rooted' a man, gave in to these dangers more helplessly than others when he turned to writing. *The Charmed Life* (1938), *Ah Well* (1942) and *And to You Also* (1944) are such flimsy affairs that they expose the vacuity that lay at the heart of the fantasy fictions of the long period from early to mid-century. The emptiness is in part social, but it is also the emptiness of a literary form which had outlived its usefulness. Moore, Joyce and O'Brien had exhausted the possibilities in prose, as had Yeats in poetry and Synge in drama, for the confrontation between mythological energy and contemporary penury of spirit. The theme was rewritten many times but it could not endure the disappearance of heroic ideals, which the new Catholic-bourgeois state so quickly and efficiently dispelled in the first three decades of its existence. Nationalism had certainly helped to create a new idea of Ireland, which had great and liberating consequences. But it also created a version of Irishness—compounded of whimsy, romantic populism, Celtic nativity heroisms, and a belief in the salience of the artist in political as well as cultural affairs—which was as restricting and as subject to caricature as the old colonialism had been. This was not surprising since the nationalism was a response to the colonialism and since it had been led by the Anglo-Irish section of the people, the colonials themselves. The long and lingering death of this nationalism became the aggrieved theme of much Irish writing of the middle decades of the century. It was a neo-colonial plight and it took the customary form of a battle between provincialism and cosmopolitanism, inwardness and outgoingness, native traditions and foreign importations. The Censorship was an expression of nationalism as much as was the literature it suppressed. Both were posited on an idea of Irishness, so much so that they sometimes forgot that literature could be quite distinct from it or any allegiance to it.

The more conventional fiction of the modern period, in Ireland as elsewhere, escaped most of the experimental novel's dizzy self-questionings and dislocations by assuming the existence of a scale of values which was expressed in a set of social attitudes or structures which could claim some degree of general assent. Among these, the most enduring social constellation in Irish fiction was represented by the Big House, the home of the landed gentry, which dominated the life of the Irish countryside from the eighteenth century. Its only serious competitor was the Roman Catholic Church but it did not, in modern times,

have the same appeal, partly because it was too powerful and pervasive a presence ever to play the role of representative image of a brilliant but threatened civilization, for which the Big House was so perfectly endowed. When Catholicism gained that sad eminence, it was usually in the form of the ideal construct it once had been in some distant past—generally the Celtic Church of the seventh to the ninth centuries or some other pre-Reformation image. Alternatively, Catholicism was often treated in a powerfully negative manner. It could be viewed as the organizing force which quelled the vibrant pagan personality of the race; or as the handmaiden of British imperial guile which helped to destroy late eighteenth-century and later forms of radicalism or liberalism; or it could be seen as the religion of the rabble, which established itself by keeping its congregation ignorant and civilization at bay. It is curious that so few Irish writers have shown any imaginative sympathy for Catholicism as such. This is, perhaps, a comment on the strong anti-intellectual features of a religion which was compelled by circumstances to minister to the oppressed and uneducated and was then unable to adapt in any effective way to the new forces released by the alleviation of these disadvantages. At any rate, it is clear that Irish literature has shown a marked predilection for idealized versions of civilization as they are represented in institutions which, like the Church or the Big House, arouse deeply felt ambivalences in the audience which reads about them. They are, of course, in a simple and direct sense, Catholic and Protestant images, but their sectarian distinctness does not preclude—indeed it demands—a recognition of the intimate animosities which they fostered in the enclosed conditions of rural life. By the close of the nineteenth century, it was clear that the Big House had no future in the new economic and political climate. It was at that point that it entered upon its long Indian summer as a cultural memory and myth, reproducing in a curious way the metamorphosis of the Irish language at the point of its disappearance some fifty years earlier. Irish literature sometimes reads like a series of studies in dying cultures; the moment of political death is the dawn of cultural life. Perhaps that is the ultimate reason for the anomalous position of Catholicism in Irish writing. When or if it ever reaches the moment of extinction, it will gain a literary respectability without which it is content to flourish in the meantime.

Edith Somerville and Violet Martin, known to literature as Somerville and Ross, anticipated the tragic cadence of the Big House novels (and, of course, of Yeats's poems on the Big Houses he immortalized) in a remarkable novel which is not about the Big House at all—*The Real Charlotte* (1894). It is a close and concentrated study of the destructive power of hatred within the confines of an Irish Protestant middle-class society which takes its tone from and looks up to the local Big House. The centre of attention is Charlotte Mullen and her victim, the young and beautiful Francie Fitzpatrick. But the Big House family of the Dysarts is stricken by all the ills that a too-refined aristocratic flesh is heir to—most especially the ill luck to have all the grace but none of the pressure of personality needed to give the society a moral as well as a social example. The financial frailty of this society, based on horses, land and an increasingly uncooperative tenantry, exacerbates the sensibilities of its inhabitants to the point of breakdown. The sinister element in their personalities is the incapacity to develop. They are all transfixed by circumstances. Like Charlotte, they have movements of feeling, but 'cannot be said to possess the power of development'. Such fixity of mind can be heroic, as in the case of Shibby Pindy in *The Big House of Inver* (1925), by Violet Martin (Martin Ross), whose Herculean efforts to save the Prendiville house and fortunes end in disaster with the burning of the Big House and the death in the fire of her helpless father. Since the nineteenth century, the decay of Anglo-Irish society had been expressed in novels of an increasingly sinister tone. Ruined houses consorted well with stories of hauntings, ghostly presences were readily available images of guilt and loneliness. Sheridan Le Fanu was the great Victorian master of this genre, although its most hysterical and popular development was achieved in Bram Stoker's *Dracula* (1897), which extends and vulgarizes the vampire motif Le Fanu had already introduced in his short story 'Carmilla' (1872). The living dead of the aristocratic vampire's tribe are victims of an historical crime from which the very bourgeois living—like Mina Harkness, the heroine—must be released by a joint Anglo-American assault, fortified by 'the wonderful power of money'. This is the power which Anglo-Irish landowners and middle classes sadly lacked. They were caught in an historical crisis from which there was no escape. In Elizabeth Bowen, the Le Fanu and the Somerville and Ross heritage is combined, especially in *The Last September* (1929), yet another tale of Big House life ending in the destruction both of the building and the way of life it represented. The central relationship between the daughter of the house, Lois Naylor, and the young English officer, Gerald Lesworth, is doomed by the stifling and disintegrating world of Ascendency snobbery, as much as by the War of Independence fought by the IRA against the British army. Gerald is killed in an ambush, and the three great houses of the district are burnt to the ground in a night.

> At Danielstown, half way up the avenue under the beeches, the thin iron gate twanged (missed its latch, remained swinging aghast) as the last unlit car slid out with the executioners bland from accomplished duty. The sound of the last car widened, gave itself to the open and empty country and was demolished. Then the first wave of a silence that was to be ultimate flowed back confidently to the steps. The door stood open hospitably upon a furnace.

Some of Bowen's best stories are set in London of the Second World War, a place similarly threatened by destruction and containing within itself the terrors which crisis precipitates. Her heroines are displaced people—orphans, divorcees—and her world is disoriented, a sequence of broken surfaces, perceptions, accidents. Sometimes there is a laboured attempt to confirm the possibility of a natural promise in the midst of threat. At the end of *The Heat of the Day* (1949), as the Second World War ends, a mother gathers up her child from the pram to let him see three swans flying west across a sky just traversed by homecoming bomber planes. But *The Death of the Heart* (1938) and *Eva Trout* (1969) both end with an abruptness which is

both shocking and familiar, for this is a world in which the likelihood of emotional and cultural amputation is bitterly strong. Elizabeth Bowen is the writer in whom the internal as well as the external collapse of an Irish and of an English civilization is finally registered. The strange death of liberal England included the stranger death of Ascendency Ireland. With her work, the last remnant of social faith disappeared from Irish fiction—that is, faith in the enduring power of contemporary society to confer meaning on the individual life. Although the Big House continued to reappear in novels from 1930 to the present day, its function was largely a nostalgic one; it was an image of memory, an indication of political conservatism, even an expression of cultural disdain for the contemporary moment. But, in all essentials, it had become one of the many Romantic ruins of the European mind.

As the Protestant and Anglo-Irish world lost its political and economic power in the new Free State (although not in the new Northern statelet), it also began to suffer cultural exclusions. In literature, the most fully developed statement came from Daniel Corkery, Professor of English at University College, Cork, in his book *Synge and Anglo-Irish Literature* (1931). This was a sequel to his earlier *The Hidden Ireland* (1925), in which he had tried to define the essence of the Gaelic literature of the eighteenth century and make that the basis for the quintessentially Irish spirit. Although he allows Synge into the Irish fold (just), he excludes almost everything and everyone else in the Revival and, beyond that, in the English language tradition in Ireland. In seeing the development of Irish society and literature in this way he was, at one level, expressing the triumphalism of the new-found state and its satisfaction at having finally destroyed the hegemony of the landowning class. He was also recognizing the harsh reality of the Protestant/Catholic distinction and attempting to find a literary gloss for it. The result is not bigotry, as many have said; for Yeats's defence of the Protestant tradition in his Senate speeches is of the same stripe. Both are acts of repossession which come too late. They are both assertions that Irish experience contains opposed elements, but their sponsorship of one over the other lacks charity, a fact dictated by the circumstances of the period rather than by a personal failure in generosity. There was and would continue to be a species of apartheid in Irish society. Elizabeth Bowen, remembering her young years in the Dublin of the 1890s, spoke of it in *Seven Winters: Memories of a Dublin Childhood* (1943):

> It was not until after the end of those seven winters that I understood that we Protestants were a minority, and that the unquestioned rules of our being came, in fact, from the closeness of a minority world. Roman Catholics were spoken of by my father and mother with a courteous detachment that gave them, even, no myth. I took the existence of Roman Catholics for granted but met few and was not interested in them. They were, simply 'the others', whose world lay alongside ours but never touched. As to the difference between the two religions, I was too discreet to ask questions—if I wanted to know. This appeared to share a delicate awkward aura with those two other differences—of sex, of

class. So quickly, in a child's mind, does prudery seed itself and make growth that I remember, even, an almost sexual shyness on the subject of Roman Catholics.

By the 1930s, the position had been transformed. The Protestant minority was now on the outside. The society remained divided. In Frank O'Connor's story 'My First Protestant' (1951), the narrator, Dan Hogan, says of a former girlfriend,

> She was my first Protestant. There were a number of them in our locality, but they kept to themselves.

That was published a quarter of a century after Lennox Robinson's play *The Big House* was staged at the Abbey, stimulating AE to speak of the 'liberating thrill' the final and defiant outburst of the Protestant heroine, Kate Alcock, gave him as she asserted her Anglo-Irish difference in the midst of yet another burned out mansion. (Between 1921 and 1923, 192 Big Houses were destroyed.) AE's aspiration towards 'the balancing of our diversities in a wide tolerance' in place of a stagnant uniformity remained no more than that, despite the heroic efforts of his journal *The Irish Statesman*. The Republican writers of the 1930s—O'Connor, Liam O'Flaherty, Peadar O'Donnell and Sean O'Faolain—were particularly disillusioned by the endurance of the old divisions. For, after all, the revolution had been fought. Yet everything seemed the same, the same utterly, only worse. The Revival and the Revolution had, between them, mobilized energies on behalf of a carefully selective image of Ireland's past. In doing so, they had concentrated so much attention on the phantom national spirit that they took little account of the actual dilapidation and provincialism which this, in the name of tradition, could encourage. Irish fiction transformed this situation into a scrutiny of the narrative convention of representation, for, where there was nothing to represent in fiction then fiction could be taught to represent nothingness. Equally, it could represent the long declension into nullity. After the revival and the Revolution, this declension remained, in the eyes of a new generation, a theme of unremitting fascination. For these new writers, the exit from the labyrinth of Irishness, the old essentialism, lay in modernization, the creation of a possible future rather than the recreation of an impossible past. (pp. 175-208)

> *Seamus Deane, "Irish Modernism: Fiction,"
> in his* Short History of Irish Literature,
> *Hutchinson, 1986, pp. 168-209.*

FURTHER READING

Anthologies

Canfield, Curtis, ed. *Plays of the Irish Renaissance: 1880-1930.* New York: Ives Washburn, 1929, 436 p.
    Includes thirteen plays by such notable figures as William Butler Yeats, Lady Gregory, and J. M. Synge.

Secondary Sources

Bramsbäck, Birgit, and Croghan, Martin, eds. *Anglo-Irish and Irish Literature: Aspects of Language and Culture—Proceedings of the Ninth International Congress of the International Association for the Study of Anglo-Irish Literature Held at Uppsala University, 4-7 August, 1986.* 2 vols. Stockholm: Almqvist & Wiksell International, 1988.
    Essay collection arranged according to subject matter and literary genre. Studies are included by such scholars as Croghan, James J. Blake, and Robert Welch.

Brown, Malcolm. *The Politics of Irish Literature: From Thomas Davis to W. B. Yeats.* Seattle: University of Washington Press, 1972, 431 p.
    Examines the Irish Literary Renaissance within a political and historical context. Brown includes sections on such topics as Fenianism and Irish Home Rule.

Colum, Mary. *Life and the Dream.* Garden City, N.Y.: Doubleday & Co., 1947, 466 p.
    Autobiography by notable Irish critic in which she reminisces about her professional and personal relationships with such figures as William Butler Yeats and Lady Gregory.

Donoghue, Denis. *We Irish.* New York: Alfred A. Knopf, 1986, 275 p.
    Includes chapters on the major figures of the Irish Literary Renaissance, including William Butler Yeats, James Joyce, and A. E., as well as commentary on political issues that influenced the development of Irish literature.

Fay, Gerard. *The Abbey Theatre: Cradle of Genius.* London: Hollis & Carter, 1958, 190 p.
    Traces the development of the Abbey Theatre, focusing specifically on the contributions of the Fay family.

Fay, W. G., and Carswell, Catherine. *The Fays of the Abbey Theatre: An Autobiographical Record.* New York: Harcourt, Brace and Co., 1935, 156 p.
    Autobiography of W. G. Fay, one of the founders of the Abbey Theatre.

Flannery, James W. *W. B. Yeats and the Idea of a Theatre: The Early Abbey Theatre in Theory and Practice.* New Haven, Conn.: Yale University Press, 1976, 404 p.
    Emphasizes the importance of Yeats's dramatic theories to the development of the Abbey Theatre. Flannery states: "[Throughout] his career as a dramatist and his involvement with the Irish dramatic movement, Yeats's basic struggle was to reconcile theory with practice."

Hogan, Robert, and Kilroy, James. *The Abbey Theatre: The Years of Synge—1905-1909.* Atlantic Highlands, N.J.: Humanities Press, 1978, 385 p.
    Examines J. M. Synge's contributions to the Irish National Theatre Society, the controversial nature of his work, and the impact of his death on the Irish Literary Renaissance.

Hogan, Robert, and O'Neill, Michael J., eds. *Joseph Holloway's Abbey Theatre: A Selection from His Unpublished Journal "Impressions of a Dublin Playgoer."* Carbondale and Edwardsville: Southern Illinois University Press, 1967, 296 p.
    Collection of journal entries in which Holloway recorded his reactions to the numerous productions he

saw at the Abbey Theatre and his impressions of the Irish Literary Renaissance's major figures.

Howarth, Herbert. *The Irish Writers, 1880-1940: Literature under Parnell's Star.* London: Rockliff, 1958, 318 p.

Examines the accomplishments of George Moore, Lady Gregory, William Butler Yeats, A. E., J. M. Synge, and James Joyce "in relation to the quick advance of Irish nationalism during their time."

Kain, Richard M. *Dublin: In the Age of William Butler Yeats and James Joyce.* Norman: University of Oklahoma Press, 1962, 216 p.

Describes Dublin in "its recent period of glory when it was the scene of a literary revival and the setting for a war of independence."

Kavanagh, Peter. *The Story of the Abbey Theatre: From Its Origins in 1889 to the Present.* New York: Devin-Adair Co., 1950, 243 p.

Traces the evolution of the Abbey Theatre and expounds upon the dramatic and critical ideals of its founders.

Komesu, Okifumi, and Sekine, Masaru, eds. *Irish Writers and Politics.* The Irish Literary Studies Series, Vol. 36. Gerrards Cross, England: Colin Smythe, 1990, 350 p.

Essay collection which focuses on the relationship between the Irish Nationalist movement and the Irish Literary Renaissance.

Malone, Andrew E. *The Irish Drama.* New York: Charles Scribner's Sons, 1929, 351 p.

Surveys twentieth-century Irish theater.

McCann, Sean, ed. *The Story of the Abbey Theatre.* London: New English Library, 1967, 157 p.

Discusses the Abbey Theatre's major productions and its distinct acting tradition.

Robinson, Lennox. *Ireland's Abbey Theatre: A History, 1899-1951.* London: Sidgwick and Jackson, 1951, 224 p.

Historical overview of the Abbey Theatre in which Robinson attempts to "build up a picture of our early Theatre and make it as authentic as possible."

Nuclear Literature:
Writings and Criticism in the Nuclear Age

INTRODUCTION

Nuclear, or A-bomb, literature explores the inevitability of nuclear warfare and the possibility of humanity's survival in a post-holocaust society. In such a world, individuals attempt to rebuild their lives and civilization while contending with such environmental disasters as nuclear winter, radiation fallout and disease, and famine, as well as battling hostile mutant beings and enemy human "tribes." Often considered a staple of the science fiction genre, these works may also be viewed as a modernist extension of apocalyptic theology and mythology, reflecting scientific discoveries, historical events, and the attitudes and concerns associated with life in the nuclear age.

The origin of nuclear literature is usually traced to three events: the Manhattan Project, which involved a group of scientists commissioned by the United States government to research and develop a nuclear reaction for military purposes and the resulting test explosion of an atomic device in July 1945 near Alamogordo, New Mexico; the August 1945 bombings of Hiroshima and Nagasaki; and the nuclear-weapons testings in the Marshall Islands in the 1950s. Literary scholars note, however, that as early as 1895, the year German physicist Wilhelm Conrad Röntgen began experimenting with x-rays and other radioactive materials, English novelist Robert Cromie began referring to these technological advances in his work, most notably in his novel *The Crack of Doom;* and, near the onset of World War I, H. G. Wells discussed the potential for global destruction in his *The World Set Free: A Study of Mankind.* In the United States, however, stories about nuclear wars, weapons, and post-holocaust societies were usually found only in such pulp magazines as *Astounding Science Fiction* and *Amazing Stories.* Many of these early narratives, which frequently describe what were perceived to be the medicinal properties of atomic fission, were wildly inaccurate, although critics note that most of these works did contain some element of truth. On one occasion, Joseph W. Campbell, Jr., editor of *Astounding Science Fiction,* was ordered by the United States War Department to withhold publishing stories that detailed, albeit unknowingly, classified information about nuclear weapons.

With the bombings of Hiroshima and Nagasaki and the advent of the Cold War, the threat of nuclear annihilation became more apparent, resulting in a proliferation of nuclear war fiction. While many works included space-age settings, atomic weapons, and alien beings, nuclear literature became a forum which allowed writers to speculate on social and political issues as well as the potential for an East-West confrontation. Such works as Aldous Huxley's *Ape and Essence,* Nevil Shute's *On the Beach,* and Pat Frank's *Alas, Babylon* additionally allowed nuclear fiction to be viewed as part of the mainstream Western literary tradition. Nuclear fiction was also popular in the Soviet Union, where many Russian authors who wrote about nuclear war and weaponry were closely monitored by government authorities. Unlike their American and English counterparts, Soviet works relied less on fantasy, reflecting instead the Kremlin's policy of either détente or nuclear supremacy. Japanese writers, however, approached nuclear literature from personal perspectives. As *hibakusha,* or survivors of Hiroshima and Nagasaki, Yoshi Hotta, Michihiko Hachiya, Yōko Ōta, and other writers provided readers with factual accounts of the bombings, employing the straightforward language of the "I-novel," to realistically convey the horrors they had encountered.

Because much apocalyptic literature, like most science fiction, can be interpreted as a warning about contemporary social and political problems, David Dowling has asserted that fictions "of nuclear disaster, as well as extending the horizons of fictional technique, call on the power of the word to defuse the power of the fused atom." While such scholars as Peter W. Schwenger, Mary Ann Caws, and philosopher and linguist Jacques Derrida have agreed with Dowling that there is a relationship between nuclear war and the written word, they have studied the nuclear referent in terms of literary criticism and philosophy. Using a deconstructionist approach and stressing that language is an imperfect medium, they question the validity of nuclear war fiction since nuclear war is a "hyperreality"—an experience humanity has yet to endure. They note that nuclear literature is closely related to Immanuel Kant's concept of the sublime, or the unknown, and is indicative of humanity's fear and fascination with death and destruction. Building upon the assumption that the nuclear referent has manifested itself throughout time, Schwenger has observed: "Situated in a future beyond the end, we are presented with a world whose objects and inhabitants function as metaphors, allowing the imagination to grasp through the tangible something that would otherwise be unthinkable. . . . pushing us toward a preliterate sensibility."

REPRESENTATIVE WORKS

Agawa Hiroyuki
    Hachigatsu muika (novel) 1947
    Devil's Hertage (novel) 1957

Ahern, Jerry
    Survivalist series (novels) 1981-

Aldiss, Brian

The Eighty-Minute Hour: A Space Opera (novel) 1974

Amis, Martin
Einstein's Monsters (short stories) 1987

Anderson, Poul
After Doomsday (novel) 1962
Thermonuclear Warfare (nonfiction) 1963
Orion Shall Rise (novel) 1983

Anthony, Piers
Sos the Rope (novel) 1968
Var the Stick (novel) 1972
Neq the Sword (novel) 1975

Auster, Paul
In the Country of Last Things (novel) 1987

Berriault, Gina
The Descent (novel) 1960

Blish, James
Black Easter; or, Faust Aleph-Nell (novel) 1968
The Day after Judgment (novel) 1971

Blumenfeld, Yorick
Jenny: My Diary (novel) 1982

Brackett, Leigh
The Long Tomorrow (novel) 1955

Bradbury, Ray
The Martian Chronicles (short stories) 1950

Buck, Pearl S.
Command the Morning (novel) 1959

Burdick, Eugene, and Wheeler, Harvey
Fail-Safe (novel) 1962

Caidin, Martin
The Long Night (novel) 1956

Charnas, Suzy McKee
Walk to the End of the World (novel) 1974
Motherlines (novel) 1978

Clarkson, Helen
The Last Day: A Novel of the Day after Tomorrow (novel) 1959

Cooper, Edmund
Seed of Light (novel) 1959
The Last Continent (novel) 1969
The Cloud Walker (novel) 1973
The Slaves of Heaven (novel) 1974

Coppel, Alfred
Dark December (novel) 1960

Cromie, Robert
The Crack of Doom (novel) 1895

Danin, Daniil Semenovich
Dobryǐ atom (nonfiction) 1957

Dement'ev, Alexander
Prekrasna zima v Sibiri (novel) 1960

Dick, Philip K.
The Penultimate Truth (novel) 1964

Frank, Pat [pseudonym of Harry Hart]
Dr. Bloodmoney; or, How We Got Along after the Bomb (novel) 1965

Efremov, Ivan
Tumannost' andromedy (novel) 1958
[*Andromeda: A Space Age Tale,* 1959]

Fenwick, Virginia
America R.I.P. (novel) 1965

Frank, Pat [pseudonym of Harry Hart]
Mr. Adam (novel) 1946
Alas, Babylon (novel) 1959

Freeling, Nicolas
Gadget (novel) 1977

Gee, Maggie
The Burning Book (novel) 1983

George, Peter
Red Alert (novel) 1958
Commander-1 (novel) 1965
Dr. Strangelove; or, How I Learned to Stop Worrying and Love the Bomb (novel) 1963

Gor, Gennadii
Universitetskaǐa naberezhnaǐa (novel) 1960

Hagedorn, Herman
The Bomb That Fell on America (poetry) 1946

Hersey, John
Hiroshima (nonfiction) 1946

Hoban, Russell
Riddley Walker (novel) 1980

Huxley, Aldous
Ape and Essence (novel) 1948

Ibuse Masuji
Kuroi ame (novel) 1966
[*Black Rain,* 1969]

Ineko Sata
Juei (novel) 1972

Johnson, Denis
Fiskadoro (novel) 1985

Jones, Mervyn
On the Last Day (novel) 1958

Kopit, Arthur
End of the World (drama) 1984

Kozhevnikov, Vadim
Znakom'tes, Baluev! (novel) 1961

Lanham, Edwin
The Clock at 8:16 (novel) 1970

Malamud, Bernard
God's Grace (novel) 1982

McIntyre, Vonda K.
The Exile Waiting (novel) 1975
Dreamsnake (novel) 1978

Merril, Judith
Shadow on the Hearth (novel) 1950

Michihiko Hachiya
Hiroshima nikki (diary) 1955

[*Hiroshima Diary: The Journal of a Japanese Physician, August 6–September 30, 1945,* 1955]

Miller, Walter M., Jr.
A Canticle for Leibowitz (novel) 1959

Minot, Stephen
Chill of Dusk (novel) 1964

Mitsuharu Inoue
Chi no mure (novel) 1970

Morris, Edita
The Flowers of Hiroshima (novel) 1959
The Seeds of Hiroshima (novel) 1965

Nichols, Robert, and Browne, Maurice
Wings over Europe: A Dramatic Extravaganza on a Pressing Theme (drama) 1928

Nikol'sky, Vadim
Cherez tysiachu let (novel) 1928

Norton, André [pseudonym of Alice Mary Norton]
Star Man's Son, 2250 A.D. (novel) 1952

O'Brien, Tim
Nuclear Age (novel) 1985

Orlovsky, Vladimir [pseudonym of Vladimir Grushvitsky]
Bunt atomov (novel) 1922

Padgett, Lewis [pseudonym of Henry Kuttner and C.L. Moore]
Mutant (novel) 1953

Pangborn, Edgar
Davy (novel) 1964
The Judgment of Eve (novel) 1966
The Company of Glory (novel) 1975

Prochnau, William
Trinity's Child (novel) 1983

Reed, Kit
Armed Camps (novel) 1969

Robinson, Kim Stanley
The Wild Shore (novel) 1984

Roshwald, Mordecai
Level 7 (novel) 1959

Rybak, Natan
Pora nadezhd i svershenii (novel) 1961

Sargent, Pamela
The Shore of Women (novel) 1986

Schell, Jonathan
The Fate of the Earth (nonfiction) 1982

See, Carolyn
Golden Days (novel) 1987

Shute, Nevil [pseudonym of Nevil Shute Norway]
On the Beach (novel) 1957

Sinclair, Upton

The Millenium: A Comedy of the Year 2000 (drama) 1924
A Giant's Strength: Drama in Three Acts (drama) 1948

Stacy, Ryder
Doomsday Warrior (novel) 1984
Doomsday Warrior, No. 2: Red America (novel) 1984

Strieber, Whitley, and Kunetka, James
Warday: And the Journey Onward (novel) 1984

Strugatskii, Arkadii and Boris
Obitaemyĭ ostrov (novel) 1971
[*Prisoners of Power,* 1977]

Tucker, Wilson
The Long Loud Silence (novel) 1952

Vonnegut, Kurt, Jr.
Galapagos (novel) 1985

Wells, H. G.
The World Set Free: A Story of Mankind (novel) 1914

Weston, Susan B.
Children of the Light (novel) 1984

Wilhelm, Kate [pseudonym of Katie Gertrude]
Where Late the Sweet Birds Sang (novel) 1976

Wolfe, Bernard
Limbo (novel) 1952

Wylie, Philip
Triumph (novel) 1963

Yōko Ōta
Shikabane no machi (memoirs) 1950

Yoshi Hotta
Shimpan (novel) 1963

OVERVIEWS

Jonathan Schell

[*An American nonfiction writer and historian, Schell has written full-length studies about the Vietnam war, Watergate, the nuclear threat, and the ways nuclear war can be averted. In the following excerpt, taken from his* The Fate of the Earth *(1982), Schell describes the immediate consequences and short-term effects of the atomic bombings of Hiroshima and Nagasaki.*]

On August 6, 1945, at 8:16 A.M., a fission bomb with a yield of twelve and a half kilotons was detonated about nineteen hundred feet above the central section of Hiroshima. By present-day standards, the bomb was a small one, and in today's arsenals it would be classed among the merely tactical weapons. Nevertheless, it was large enough to transform a city of some three hundred and forty thousand people into hell in the space of a few seconds. "It is no exaggeration," the authors of *Hiroshima and Nagasaki* tell us, "to say that the whole city was ruined instantaneously." In that instant, tens of thousands of people were burned, blasted, and crushed to death. Other tens of thousands suffered injuries of every description or were doomed to die of radiation sickness. The center of the city was flattened, and every part of the city was damaged. The trunks of bamboo trees as far away as five miles from ground zero—the point on the ground directly under the center of the explosion—were charred. Almost half the trees within a mile and a quarter were knocked down. Windows nearly seventeen miles away were broken. Half an hour after the blast, fires set by the thermal pulse and by the collapse of the buildings began to coalesce into a firestorm, which lasted for six hours. Starting about 9 A.M. and lasting until late afternoon, a "black rain" generated by the bomb (otherwise, the day was fair) fell on the western portions of the city, carrying radioactive fallout from the blast to the ground. For four hours at midday, a violent whirlwind, born of the strange meteorological conditions produced by the explosion, further devastated the city. The number of people who were killed outright or who died of their injuries over the next three months is estimated to be a hundred and thirty thousand. Sixty-eight per cent of the buildings in the city were either completely destroyed or damaged beyond repair, and the center of the city was turned into a flat, rubble-strewn plain dotted with the ruins of a few of the sturdier buildings.

In the minutes after the detonation, the day grew dark, as heavy clouds of dust and smoke filled the air. A whole city had fallen in a moment, and in and under its ruins were its people. Among those still living, most were injured, and of these most were burned or had in some way been battered or had suffered both kinds of injury. Those within a mile and a quarter of ground zero had also been subjected to intense nuclear radiation, often in lethal doses. When people revived enough from their unconsciousness or shock to see what was happening around them, they found that where a second before there had been a city getting ready to go about its daily business on a peaceful, warm August morning, now there was a heap of debris and corpses and a stunned mass of injured humanity. But at first, as they awakened and tried to find their bearings in the gathering darkness, many felt cut off and alone. In a recent volume of recollections by survivors called *Unforgettable Fire,* in which the effects of the bombing are rendered in drawings as well as in words, Mrs. Haruko Ogasawara, a young girl on that August morning, recalls that she was at first knocked unconscious. She goes on to write:

> How many seconds or minutes had passed I could not tell, but, regaining consciousness, I found myself lying on the ground covered with pieces of wood. When I stood up in a frantic effort to look around, there was darkness. Terribly frightened, I thought I was alone in a world of death, and groped for any light. My fear was so great I did not think anyone would truly understand. When I came to my senses, I found my clothes in shreds, and I was without my wooden sandals.

Soon cries of pain and cries for help from the wounded filled the air. Survivors heard the voices of their families and their friends calling out in the gloom. Mrs. Ogasawara writes:

> Suddenly, I wondered what had happened to my mother and sister. My mother was then forty-five, and my sister five years old. When the darkness began to fade, I found that there was nothing around me. My house, the next door neighbor's house, and the next had all vanished. I was standing amid the ruins of my house. No one was around. It was quiet, very quiet—an eerie moment. I discovered my mother in a water tank. She had fainted. Crying out, "Mama, Mama," I shook her to bring her back to her senses. After coming to, my mother began to shout madly for my sister: "Eiko! Eiko!"

> I wondered how much time had passed when there were cries of searchers. Children were calling their parents' names, and parents were calling the names of their children. We were calling desperately for my sister and listening for her voice and looking to see her. Suddenly, Mother cried "Oh Eiko!" Four or five meters away, my sister's head was sticking out and was calling my mother. . . . Mother and I worked desperately to remove the plaster and pillars and pulled her out with great effort. Her body had turned purple from the bruises, and her arm was so badly wounded that we could have placed two fingers in the wound.

Others were less fortunate in their searches and rescue attempts. In *Unforgettable Fire,* a housewife describes a scene she saw:

> A mother, driven half-mad while looking for her child, was calling his name. At last she found him. His head looked like a boiled octopus. His eyes were half-closed, and his mouth was white, pursed, and swollen.

Throughout the city, parents were discovering their wounded or dead children, and children were discovering their wounded or dead parents. Kikuno Segawa recalls seeing a little girl with her dead mother:

> A woman who looked like an expectant mother was dead. At her side, a girl of about three years of age brought some water in an empty can she had found. She was trying to let her mother drink from it.

The sight of people in extremities of suffering was ubiquitous. Kinzo Nishida recalls:

> While taking my severely wounded wife out to the riverbank by the side of the hill of Nakahiro-machi, I was horrified, indeed, at the sight of a stark naked man standing in the rain with his eyeball in his palm. He looked to be in great pain, but there was nothing that I could do for him.

Many people were astonished by the sheer sudden absence of the known world. The writer Yoko Ota later wrote:

> I just could not understand why our surroundings had changed so greatly in one instant. . . .

I thought it might have been something which had nothing to do with the war—the collapse of the earth, which it was said would take place at the end of the world, and which I had read about as a child.

And a history professor who looked back at the city after the explosion remarked later, "I saw that Hiroshima had disappeared."

As the fires sprang up in the ruins, many people, having found injured family members and friends, were now forced to abandon them to the flames or to lose their own lives in the firestorm. Those who left children, husbands, wives, friends, and strangers to burn often found these experiences the most awful of the entire ordeal. Mikio Inoue describes how one man, a professor, came to abandon his wife:

> It was when I crossed Miyuki Bridge that I saw Professor Takenaka, standing at the foot of the bridge. He was almost naked, wearing nothing but shorts, and he had a ball of rice in his right hand. Beyond the streetcar line, the northern area was covered by red fire burning against the sky. Far away from the line, Ote-machi was also a sea of fire.
>
> That day, Professor Takenaka had not gone to Hiroshima University, and the A-bomb exploded when he was at home. He tried to rescue his wife, who was trapped under a roofbeam, but all his efforts were in vain. The fire was threatening him also. His wife pleaded, "Run away, dear!" He was forced to desert his wife and escape from the fire. He was now at the foot of Miyuki Bridge.
>
> But I wonder how he came to hold that ball of rice in his hand. His naked figure, standing there before the flames with that ball of rice, looked to me as a symbol of the modest hopes of human beings.

In *Hiroshima,* John Hersey describes the flight of a group of German priests and their Japanese colleagues through a burning section of the city:

> The street was cluttered with parts of houses that had slid into it, and with fallen telephone poles and wires. From every second or third house came the voices of people buried and abandoned, who invariably screamed, with formal politeness, *"Tasukete kure!* Help, if you please!" The priests recognized several ruins from which these cries came as the homes of friends, but because of the fire it was too late to help.

And thus it happened that throughout Hiroshima all the ties of affection and respect that join human beings to one another were being pulled and rent by the spreading firestorm. Soon processions of the injured—processions of a kind that had never been seen before in history—began to file away from the center of the city toward its outskirts. Most of the people suffered from burns, which had often blackened their skin or caused it to sag off them. A grocer who joined one of these processions has described them in

an interview with Robert Jay Lifton which appears in his book *Death in Life:*

> They held their arms bent [forward] . . . and their skin—not only on their hands but on their faces and bodies, too—hung down. . . . If there had been only one or two such people . . . perhaps I would not have had such a strong impression. But wherever I walked, I met these people. . . . Many of them died along the road. I can still picture them in my mind—like walking ghosts. They didn't look like people of this world.

The grocer also recalls that because of people's injuries "you couldn't tell whether you were looking at them from in front or in back." People found it impossible to recognize one another. A woman who at the time was a girl of thirteen, and suffered disfiguring burns on her face, has recalled, "My face was so distorted and changed that people couldn't tell who I was. After a while I could call others' names but they couldn't recognize me." In addition to being injured, many people were vomiting—an early symptom of radiation sickness. For many, horrifying and unreal events occurred in a chaotic jumble. (pp. 36-42)

Physical collapse brought emotional and spiritual collapse

The mushroom cloud over Nagasaki, August, 1945.

with it. The survivors were, on the whole, listless and stupefied. After the escapes, and the failures to escape, from the firestorm, a silence fell over the city and its remaining population. People suffered and died without speaking or otherwise making a sound. The processions of the injured, too, were soundless. Dr. Michihiko Hachiya has written in his book *Hiroshima Diary:*

> Those who were able walked silently toward the suburbs in the distant hills, their spirits broken, their initiative gone. When asked whence they had come, they pointed to the city and said, "That way," and when asked where they were going, pointed away from the city and said, "This way." They were so broken and confused that they moved and behaved like automatons.

> Their reactions had astonished outsiders, who reported with amazement the spectacle of long files of people holding stolidly to a narrow, rough path when close by was a smooth, easy road going in the same direction. The outsiders could not grasp the fact that they were witnessing the exodus of a people who walked in the realm of dreams.

Those who were still capable of action often acted in an absurd or an insane way. Some of them energetically pursued tasks that had made sense in the intact Hiroshima of a few minutes before but were now utterly inappropriate. Hersey relates that the German priests were bent on bringing to safety a suitcase, containing diocesan accounts and a sum of money, that they had rescued from the fire and were carrying around with them through the burning city. And Dr. Lifton describes a young soldier's punctilious efforts to find and preserve the ashes of a burned military code book while people around him were screaming for help. Other people simply lost their minds. For example, when the German priests were escaping from the firestorm, one of them, Father Wilhelm Kleinsorge, carried on his back a Mr. Fukai, who kept saying that he wanted to remain where he was. When Father Kleinsorge finally put Mr. Fukai down, he started running. Hersey writes:

> Father Kleinsorge shouted to a dozen soldiers, who were standing by the bridge, to stop him. As Father Kleinsorge started back to get Mr. Fukai, Father LaSalle called out, "Hurry! Don't waste time!" So Father Kleinsorge just requested the soldiers to take care of Mr. Fukai. They said they would, but the little, broken man got away from them, and the last the priests could see of him, he was running back toward the fire.

In the weeks after the bombing, many survivors began to notice the appearance of petechiae—small spots caused by hemorrhages—on their skin. These usually signalled the onset of the critical stage of radiation sickness. In the first stage, the victims characteristically vomited repeatedly, ran a fever, and developed an abnormal thirst. (The cry "Water! Water!" was one of the few sounds often heard in Hiroshima on the day of the bombing.) Then, after a few hours or days, there was a deceptively hopeful period of remission of symptoms, called the latency period, which lasted from about a week to about four weeks. Radiation attacks the reproductive function of cells, and those that reproduce most frequently are therefore the most vulnera-

ble. Among these are the bone-marrow cells, which are responsible for the production of blood cells. During the latency period, the count of white blood cells, which are instrumental in fighting infections, and the count of platelets, which are instrumental in clotting, drop precipitously, so the body is poorly defended against infection and is liable to hemorrhaging. In the third, and final, stage, which may last for several weeks, the victim's hair may fall out and he may suffer from diarrhea and may bleed from the intestines, the mouth, or other parts of the body, and in the end he will either recover or die. Because the fireball of the Hiroshima bomb did not touch the ground, very little ground material was mixed with the fission products of the bomb, and therefore very little local fallout was generated. (What fallout there was descended in the black rain.) Therefore, the fatalities from radiation sickness were probably all caused by the initial nuclear radiation, and since this affected only people within a radius of a mile and a quarter of ground zero, most of the people who received lethal doses were killed more quickly by the thermal pulse and the blast wave. Thus, Hiroshima did not experience the mass radiation sickness that can be expected if a weapon is ground-burst. Since the Nagasaki bomb was also burst in the air, the effect of widespread lethal fallout on large areas, causing the death by radiation sickness of whole populations in the hours, days, and weeks after the blast, is a form of nuclear horror that the world has not experienced.

In the months and years following the bombing of Hiroshima, after radiation sickness had run its course and most of the injured had either died of their wounds or recovered from them, the inhabitants of the city began to learn that the exposure to radiation they had experienced would bring about a wide variety of illnesses, many of them lethal, throughout the lifetimes of those who had been exposed. An early sign that the harm from radiation was not restricted to radiation sickness came in the months immediately following the bombing, when people found that their reproductive organs had been temporarily harmed, with men experiencing sterility and women experiencing abnormalities in their menstrual cycles. Then, over the years, other illnesses, including cataracts of the eye and leukemia and other forms of cancer, began to appear in larger than normally expected numbers among the exposed population. In all these illnesses, correlations have been found between nearness to the explosion and incidence of the disease. Also, fetuses exposed to the bomb's radiation in utero exhibited abnormalities and developmental retardation. Those exposed within the mile-and-a-quarter radius were seven times as likely as unexposed fetuses to die in utero, and were also seven times as likely to die at birth or in infancy. Surviving children who were exposed in utero tended to be shorter and lighter than other children, and were more often mentally retarded. One of the most serious abnormalities caused by exposure to the bomb's radiation was microcephaly—abnormal smallness of the head, which is often accompanied by mental retardation. In one study, thirty-three cases of microcephaly were found among a hundred and sixty-nine children exposed in utero.

What happened at Hiroshima was less than a millionth

part of a holocaust at present levels of world nuclear armament. The more than millionfold difference amounts to
more than a difference in magnitude; it is also a difference
in kind. The authors of *Hiroshima and Nagasaki* observe
that "an atomic bomb's massive destruction and indiscriminate slaughter involves the sweeping breakdown of
all order and existence—in a word, the collapse of society
itself," and that therefore "the essence of atomic destruction lies in the totality of its impact on man and society."
This is true also of a holocaust, of course, except that the
totalities in question are now not single cities but nations,
ecosystems, and the earth's ecosphere. Yet with the exception of fallout, which was relatively light at Hiroshima and
Nagasaki (because both the bombs were air-burst), the immediate devastation caused by today's bombs would be of
a sort similar to the devastation in those cities. The immediate effects of a twenty-megaton bomb are not different
in kind from those of a twelve-and-a-half-kiloton bomb;
they are only more extensive. (The proportions of the effects do change greatly with yield, however. In small
bombs, the effects of the initial nuclear radiation are important, because it strikes areas in which people might
otherwise have remained alive, but in larger bombs—ones
in the megaton range—the consequences of the initial nuclear radiation, whose range does not increase very much
with yield, are negligible, because it strikes areas in which
everyone will have already been burned or blasted to
death.) In bursts of both weapons, for instance, there is a
radius within which the thermal pulse can ignite newspapers: for the twelve-and-a-half-kiloton weapon, it is a little
over two miles; for the twenty-megaton weapon, it is twenty-five miles. (Since there is no inherent limit on the size
of a nuclear weapon, these figures can be increased indefinitely, subject only to the limitations imposed by the technical capacities of the bomb builder—and of the earth's
capacity to absorb the blast. The Soviet Union, which has
shown a liking for sheer size in so many of its undertakings, once detonated a sixty-megaton bomb.) Therefore,
while the total effect of a holocaust is qualitatively different from the total effect of a single bomb, the experience
of individual people in a holocaust would be, in the short
term (and again excepting the presence of lethal fallout
wherever the bombs were ground-burst), very much like
the experience of individual people in Hiroshima. The Hiroshima people's experience, accordingly, is of much more
than historical interest. It is a picture of what our whole
world is always poised to become—a backdrop of scarcely
imaginable horror lying just behind the surface of our normal life, and capable of breaking through into that normal
life at any second. Whether we choose to think about it
or not, it is an omnipresent, inescapable truth about our
lives today that at every single moment each one of us may
suddenly become the deranged mother looking for her
burned child; the professor with the ball of rice in his hand
whose wife has just told him "Run away, dear!" and died
in the fires; Mr. Fukai running back into the firestorm; the
naked man standing on the blasted plain that was his city,
holding his eyeball in his hand; or, more likely, one of millions of corpses. For whatever our "modest hopes" as
human beings may be, every one of them can be nullified
by a nuclear holocaust. (pp. 42-7)

Jonathan Schell, "A Republic of Insects and
Grass," in his The Fate of the Earth, *Alfred A.*
Knopf, 1982, pp. 1-96.

Paul Boyer

[*An American editor, critic, and professor of history,*
Boyer is best known for his studies of the Salem witch
trials of 1692. In the following excerpt, he provides an
overview of American people's reaction to the August
1945 bombings of Hiroshima and Nagasaki.]

August 6, 1945. President Truman was aboard the U.S.S.
Augusta, steaming across the Atlantic on his way home
from the Postdam conference, when he received the word:
an American atomic bomb had been successfully detonated
over Hiroshima, Japan. Excitedly Truman rushed to the of-
ficers' wardroom and told them the news. The navy men
burst into cheers.

At the White House, it was a slow news day and only a few
reporters were on duty. In mid-morning, assistant press sec-
retary Eben Ayres strolled into the press room and told the
reporters something might be coming later. At 10:45 A.M.
Eastern War Time, Ayres released the story. At first the re-
porters seemed to hesitate, then they rushed for the tele-
phones. The first bulletin went out over the Associated Press
wire at 11:03.

John Haynes Holmes, minister of the Community Church
of New York City, was vacationing at his summer cottage
in Kennebunk, Maine, that day. Soon after, he described
his feelings on hearing the news: "Everything else seemed
suddenly to become insignificant. I seemed to grow cold, as
though I had been transported to the waste spaces of the
moon. The summer beauty seemed to vanish, and the waves
of the sea to be pounding upon the shores of an empty
world. . . . For I knew that the final crisis in human histo-
ry had come. What that atomic bomb had done to Japan,
it could do to us."

[*New York Times,* August 7, 1945]

How does a people react when the entire basis of its existence is fundamentally altered? Most such changes occur
gradually; they are more discernible to historians than to
the individuals living through them. The nuclear era was
different. It burst upon the world with terrifying sudden-
ness. From the earliest moments, the American people
recognized that things would never be the same again.

Perhaps the best way to convey a sense of the earliest days
of what almost immediately began to be called the "Atomic Age" is not to impose too much order or coherence on
them retrospectively. Out of the initial confusion of emotions and welter of voices, certain cultural themes would
quickly emerge. But first, the Event.

The first to hear the news that distant Monday were those
who happened to be near a radio at midday—housewives,
children, the elderly, war workers enjoying a vacation day
at home:

> This is Don Goddard with your news at noon.
> A little less than an hour ago, newsmen were
> called to the White House down in Washington,
> and there they were read a special announce-

ment written by President Truman. . . . This was the story of a new bomb, so powerful that only the imagination of a trained scientist could dream of its existence. Without qualification, the President said that Allied scientists have now harnessed the basic power of the universe. They have harnessed the atom.

As the sultry August afternoon wore on, the news spread by word of mouth. The evening papers reported it in screaming headlines:

> ATOMIC BOMB LOOSED ON JAPAN
> ONE EQUALS 20,000 TONS OF TNT
> FIRST TARGET IS ARMY BASE OF HIROSHIMA
> DUST AND SMOKE OBSCURE RESULT.

On his six o'clock newscast, Lowell Thomas of CBS radio, already assuming that everyone had heard the story, began in his folksy, avuncular voice:

> That news about the atomic bomb overshadows everything else today; and the story of the dropping of the first one on Japan. The way the Japanese describe last night's raid on Hiroshima indicates that this one bomb was so destructive that the Japs thought they had been blasted by squadrons of B-29s.

Meanwhile, over at NBC, the dean of radio news commentators, H. V. Kaltenborn, was preparing the script of his 7:45 P.M. broadcast. The first draft began by describing the atomic bomb as "one of the greatest scientific developments in the history of man." Hastily, Kaltenborn penciled in a punchier opening: "Anglo-Saxon science has developed a new explosive 2,000 times as destructive as any known before."

Continuing in his stern, professorial voice, Kaltenborn struck a somber note: "For all we know, we have created a Frankenstein! We must assume that with the passage of only a little time, an improved form of the new weapon we use today can be turned against us."

Kaltenborn was far from alone in perceiving the nightmarish possibilities. Science may have "signed the mammalian world's death warrant," warned the *St. Louis Post-Dispatch* on August 7, "and deeded an earth in ruins to the ants." A *Milwaukee Journal* editorial on the same day speculated about "a self-perpetuating chain of atomic destruction" that, like "a forest fire sweeping before high winds," could obliterate the entire planet.

In a broadcast that evening, Don Goddard added a chilling concreteness to these ominous forebodings:

> There is reason to believe tonight that our new atomic bomb destroyed the entire Japanese city of Hiroshima in a single blast. . . . It would be the same as Denver, Colorado, with a population of 350,000 persons being there one moment, and wiped out the next.

Thus in the earliest moments of the nuclear era, the fear that would be the constant companion of Americans for the rest of their lives, and of millions not yet born in 1945, had already found urgent expression.

The carefully orchestrated government press releases, il-

lustrated with a set of officially approved photographs, only partially allayed the gathering fear and uncertainty. Hiroshima itself was enveloped in an eerie silence that the outside world only gradually penetrated. "As for the actual havoc wrought by that first atomic bomb," said Lowell Thomas on August 7, "one earlier report was that the photographic observation planes on the job shortly after the cataclysmic blast at Hiroshima had been unable to penetrate the cloud of smoke and dust that hung over that devastated area." An air force spokesman on Okinawa said Hiroshima "seemed to have been ground into dust by a giant foot."

At a hectic news conference on Guam, Col. Paul Tibbets, Jr., pilot of the *Enola Gay,* the atomic-bomb plane, compared the cloud over the city to "boiling dust." Navy captain William S. Parsons, the scientist responsible for the final bomb assembly aboard the plane, extended an open palm to represent Hiroshima and said that only the fingers—the docks jutting into Hiroshima Bay—had been visible after the blast. The news conference was continually interrupted by a cigar-chomping Gen. Curtis LeMay with a terse, "No, you better not say that."

Speculation and "human interest" stories supplemented the tightly controlled official releases. Newsmen compared the atomic bomb to the 1917 explosion of a munitions ship in the harbor of Halifax, Nova Scotia, that had killed eighteen hundred people. They interviewed the wife of Gen. Leslie R. Groves, military chief of the Manhattan Project ("I didn't know anything about it until this morning, the same as everyone else"). They sought out Eleanor Roosevelt, who gave FDR's posthumous benediction to the atomic bomb: "The President would have been much relieved had he known we had it."

Journalists strove for a local angle: "DEADLIEST WEAPONS IN WORLD'S HISTORY MADE IN SANTA FE VICINITY" was the headline carried by the *Santa Fe New Mexican* over its story about tiny Los Alamos, nerve center of the Manhattan Project. Tennessee papers played up what the *New York Times* dramatically called the "secret empire" at Oak Ridge, where work on the atomic bomb had been conducted in a vast "labryinthine concrete fortress." In Hanford, Washington, reporters found the local residents surprised to learn that the vast secret facility nearby had been making plutonium; they had assumed poison gas. The Albany newspapers noted that General Groves was the son of a Presbyterian minister who had once had a church in that city.

The secret atomic-bomb test conducted at Alamogordo, New Mexico, on July 16, 1945, was now revealed. Lowell Thomas quoted a railway engineer who had been in the cab of the *Santa Fe* over 100 miles away at the moment of the predawn test: "All at once, it seemed as if the sun suddenly appeared out of the darkness. . . . The glare lasted about three minutes, then all was dark again." Newspaper stories told of Georgia Green, a blind girl in Albuquerque, 120 miles from Alamogordo, who at the moment of detonation had cried out, "What was that?"

On August 9, with Hiroshima still dominating the nation's consciousness, came a further shock: a second atomic bomb had been dropped on the Japanese city of Nagasaki. "It is an awful responsibility which has come to us," intoned President Truman on nationwide radio the next day. "We thank God that it has come to us instead of to our enemies; and we pray that He may guide us to use it in His ways and for His purposes."

Amid the stupefying rush of events, people could only assure each other that something momentous, almost unfathomable, had occurred. "[One] forgets the effect on Japan . . . ," said the *New York Herald Tribune,* "as one senses the foundations of one's own universe trembling." The papers were full of such observations. The bomb, commented *Christian Century* magazine, had "cast a spell of dark foreboding over the spirit of humanity." In the *New York Times*'s first letter-to-the-editor about the atomic bomb (forerunner of thousands that would appear in the years to follow), A. Garcia Diaz of New York City spoke of the "creeping feeling of apprehension" pervading the nation. (With characteristic understatement, the *Times* captioned this letter: "Atomic Bomb Poses Problem.") In the *New York Sun,* correspondent Phelps Adams described the mood in Washington: "For forty-eight hours now, the new bomb has been virtually the only topic of conversation and discussion. . . . For two days it has been an unusual thing to see a smile among the throngs that crowd the streets. The entire city is pervaded by a kind of sense of oppression." Political cartoonist D. R. Fitzpatrick of the *St. Louis Post-Dispatch* pictured a tiny human figure desperately clinging to a pair of reins attached to an awesome lightning bolt streaking across the skies. The caption was: "Little Man, Where To?"

On August 10, a day after the Nagasaki bombing, the Japanese offered to surrender if Emperor Hirohito could keep his throne. The Allies agreed, and on August 14, World War II ended. The nation's cities erupted in frenzied celebration, but the underlying mood remained sober and apprehensive. In Washington, the *New Republic* reported, the war's end did nothing to mitigate the post-Hiroshima gloom or the "curious new sense of insecurity, rather incongruous in the face of military victory." Thanks to the atomic bomb, wrote an official of the Rockefeller Foundation a few weeks later, the nation's mood at the moment of victory was bleaker than in December 1941 when much of the Pacific Fleet had lain in ruins at Pearl Harbor. "Seldom, if ever," agreed CBS radio commentator Edward R. Murrow on August 12, "has a war ended leaving the victors with such a sense of uncertainty and fear, with such a realization that the future is obscure and that survival is not assured."

On August 17, amid stories of the surrender ceremonies in Tokyo Bay, H. V. Kaltenborn reported a sobering assessment by air force general H. H. ("Hap") Arnold of what an atomic war would be like. "As we listen to the newscast tonight, as we read our newspapers tomorrow," said Kaltenborn, "let us think of the mass murder which will come with World War III." A few days later he added, "We are like children playing with a concentrated instrument of death whose destructive potential our little minds cannot grasp."

"The knowledge of victory was as charged with sorrow and doubt as with joy and gratitude," observed *Time* in its first postwar issue [August 20, 1945].

> In what they said and did, men are still, as in the aftershock of a great wound, bemused and only semi-articulate. . . . But in the dark depths of their minds and hearts, huge forms moved and silently arrayed themselves: Titans, arranging out of the chaos an age in which victory was already only the shout of a child in the street.

The war itself had shrunk to "minor significance," *Time* added, and its outcome seemed the "most grimly Pyrrhic of victories."

The best known of these early postwar editorials, Norman Cousins's "Modern Man Is Obsolete," which appeared in the [August 18th issue of the] *Saturday Review* four days after the Japanese surrender, exuded this spirit of apprehension. "Whatever elation there is in the world today," wrote Cousins,

> is severely tempered by . . . a primitive fear, the fear of the unknown, the fear of forces man can neither channel nor comprehend. This fear is not new; in its classical form it is the fear of irrational death. But overnight it has become intensified, magnified. It has burst out of the subconscious and into the conscious, filling the mind with primordial apprehensions.

Among book publishers, the post-Hiroshima race was won by Pocket Books, which on August 17 published *The Atomic Age Opens,* a 256-page paperback compendium of news stories, editorials, and pronouncements by world leaders intended to help those who were "grasping for solid ideas through the haze of the first excitement." The general tenor of these utterances is summed up in one chapter title: "The Whole World Gasped."

Perhaps the most important print medium through which the American people formed their initial impressions of the atomic bomb was Henry Luce's photo magazine *Life,* with its five million-plus circulation. *Life* devoted much of its August 20, 1945, issue to the bomb; here, in full-page photographs of Hiroshima and Nagasaki, many Americans encountered for the first time the towering mushroom-shaped cloud that would become the quintessential visual symbol of the new era. Hiroshima, said *Life,* had literally been "blown . . . off the face of the earth." Nagasaki, it added, choosing its words carefully, had been "disemboweled."

Underscoring a point made frequently in this early postwar period, *Life* noted that the atomic bombings were simply an extension of the massive B-29 "fire-bomb missions" under General LeMay that had already "ripped the guts out of Japan's great cities." These raids, *Life* explained, relied on

> the newly developed "jelly" bombs, which were aimed at different spots in a city and calculated to merge into one huge conflagration. Airmen called them "burn jobs" and a good-sized "burn job" did almost as much damage to property as the atomic bomb did and it also killed almost as many people.

In a lengthy background feature, *Life* insisted that the most important story concerning the debut of atomic energy was the scientific one: "Even the appalling fact that some 100,000 Japanese had died seemed incidental to the fact—which touched the destiny of everyone alive—that a way had been found to release the forces which killed these 100,000." Through several pages of simplified text and drawings, *Life* introduced its readers to the mysteries of the atom, uranium, and nuclear fission.

But what did it all mean? In an editorial titled "The Atomic Age" and in an essay, "The Atom Bomb and Future War," by *New York Times* military analyst Hanson W. Baldwin, *Life* tried to place the devastating events in context. Baldwin minced no words. As soon as the long-range rockets developed by the Germans were fitted with atomic warheads capable of "destroy[ing] cities at one breath," he wrote, echoing H. V. Kaltenborn, mankind would have "unleashed a Frankenstein monster." If conventional infantrymen had any future role at all, Baldwin continued, it would be as "an army of moles, specially trained in underground fighting."

In its editorial, by contrast, *Life* strove for a hopeful note: Atomic fission was a major breakthrough in humankind's long struggle to understand and subdue nature, and the world should be grateful that "Prometheus, the subtle artificer and friend of man, is still an American citizen." The future would be different, certainly, but it need not terrify. Even Hanson Baldwin's grim predictions could be viewed in an optimistic light. After all, "consider the ant, whose social problems much resemble man's":

> Ants have lived on this planet for 50 times as many millions of years as man. In all that time they have not committed race suicide and they have not abolished warfare either. Their nations rise and fall and never wholly merge. Constructing beautiful urban palaces and galleries, many ants have long lived underground in entire satisfaction.

But whatever the long-range reassurance offered by entomology or Greek mythology, the compelling immediate fact was that atomic fission had just been used to vaporize two cities. To its credit, *Life* confronted this fact squarely. The increasing ferocity of strategic bombing since the late 1930s, it said, "led straight to Hiroshima, and Hiroshima was, and was intended to be, almost pure *Schrecklichkeit* [terror]." All the belligerents, the United States no less than Nazi Germany, had emerged from World War II "with radically different practices and standards of permissible behavior toward others."

Despite these bleak reflections, the editorial concluded on a note of moral elevation. Above all else, the atomic bomb raised "the question of power. The atomic scientists had to learn new ways to control it; so now does political man":

> Power in society has never been controlled by anything but morality. . . . Our sole safeguard against the very real danger of a reversion to barbarism is the kind of morality which compels the individual conscience, be the group right or

wrong. The individual conscience against the atomic bomb? Yes, there is no other way.

> No limits are set to our Promethean ingenuity, provided we remember that we are not Jove.
>
> (pp. 3-10)

But what was *Life* actually saying? Evidently this: the same individuals who had acquiesced in the degradation of warfare into *Schrecklichkeit* were now being exhorted to confront the atomic bomb with consciences finely tuned to moral considerations. The American Prometheus who had assumed Jove's mantle and obliterated two cities with his newly discovered atomic thunderbolts was now being sternly told that he must resist the temptation ever again to play god.

After the initial shock, Americans seemingly rallied and took the atomic bomb in stride. Comedians (not all of them professionals) strained to find humor in the new weapon. A radio newscaster commented that Hiroshima "looked like Ebbetts Field after a game between the Giants and the Dodgers." Others joked that Japan was suffering from "atomic ache." Only one radio entertainer—Milton Berle—explicitly refused to make jokes about the atomic bomb.

Within hours of Eben Ayres's announcement, the bar at the Washington Press Club offered an "Atomic Cocktail"—a greenish blend of Pernod and gin. A letter in the *Philadelphia Inquirer* suggested that atomic vitamin pills be given to the slumping Athletics. *Time* said the Alamogordo test had "proved the bomb a smash-hit." Updating an old joke, *Life* reported that Oak Ridge workers, when asked what they were building, had replied: "We're making the fronts of horses, and shipping them to Washington for final assembly." One of the odder of the post-Hiroshima headlines appeared in the *Milwaukee Journal* on August 8: "The New Bomb Is So Staggering to the Mind, One Doesn't Dare Pun 'Up and Atom!' " *Stars and Stripes,* the military newspaper, reported one GI's comment: "Wait a minute, I got a gag for you. Just put in your paper: 'Now we're cooking—with atomic bombs!' and don't forget to credit me." On August 13, the *Chicago Tribune* ran an entire column of "Atomic Anecdotes." The *New Yorker,* while taking a dim view of all this "humor," dutifully recorded some of it "for the benefit of future social historians."

Nor could American business resist the bomb's commercial possibilities. Within days of the Hiroshima bombing, department stores were running "Atomic Sales" and advertisers offering "Atomic Results." Somewhat later, a jewelry company on New York's Fifth Avenue advertised:

> BURSTING FURY—Atomic Inspired Pin and Earring. New fields to conquer with Atomic jewelry. The pearled bomb bursts into a fury of dazzling colors in mock rhinestones, emeralds, rubies, and sapphires. . . . As daring to wear as it was to drop the first atom bomb. Complete set $24.75.

Other enterprising entrepreneurs gathered the greenish, glass-like fused sand at the Alamogordo test site and (oblivious to the danger of radioactivity) fashioned it into costume jewelry, which they advertised nationally. The Atomic Age Publishing Company of Denver announced a new magazine, *The Atom,* with a goal of one hundred thousand subscribers. By 1947, the Manhattan telephone directory listed forty-five businesses that had appropriated the magic word, including the Atomic Undergarment Company.

In 1946 the General Mills Corporation offered an "Atomic 'Bomb' Ring" for fifteen cents and a Kix cereal boxtop. Look into the "sealed atom chamber" in "the gleaming aluminum warhead," the advertisement said, and "see genuine atoms SPLIT to smithereens!" "Based on a scientific principle used in laboratories," the ring was "perfectly safe" and "guaranteed not to blow everything sky high." It was loaded with extras, including "bombardier's insignia embossed on cylindrical bomb grip." In fact, this little promotional premium managed to anticipate several cultural themes that would obsess America in the years ahead. Behind the bomb warhead was a space for secret messages: "You can outwit enemies by concealing a message of 100 words in this strategic compartment," the cereal-box copy promised; "It's so deceptive that anyone plotting to spy against you will be thrown off guard." Some 750,000 American children deluged General Mills with orders for their very own "Atomic 'Bomb' Ring."

In Hollywood, writers rushed to incorporate the atomic bomb into their movie scripts. The first film to accomplish this feat, *The House on 92nd Street,* was released in late September 1945. A spy thriller about Nazi agents operating in New York City early in World War II, it was revised at the last minute to make the object of the agents' quest be "Process 97, the secret ingredient of the atomic bomb."

The music industry was quick to cash in on the new national preoccupation as well. The Slim Gaillard Quartet recorded "Atomic Cocktail" in December 1945. The following year brought "Atom Buster" and "Atom Polka." In the interesting "Atom and Evil" by the San Francisco-based Golden Gate Quartet, a black gospel group, atomic energy is portrayed as an innocent, well-intentioned man seduced by a jaded "Miss Evil." A California company marketed a line of jazz recordings under the "Atomic" label complete with the picture of a mushroom-shaped cloud.

The complex psychological link between atomic destruction and Eros (a link that at the time of America's first postwar atomic test in 1946 led a French fashion designer to christen his new bathing suit the "Bikini") was established very early. Within days of Hiroshima, burlesque houses in Los Angeles were advertising "Atom Bomb Dancers." In early September, putting aside its pontifical robes for a moment, *Life* fulfilled a Hollywood press agent's dream with a full-page cheesecake photograph of a well-endowed MGM starlet who had been officially dubbed "The Anatomic Bomb." In "Atom Bomb Baby," a pop song of 1947, the bomb became a metaphor for sexual arousal.

Despite the outpouring of post-Hiroshima atomic ephemera, it would be wrong to conclude that Americans took the bomb casually or that its impact quickly faded. Just below the surface, powerful currents of anxiety and apprehension surged through the culture. As one cultural observer noted in January 1946, the attempts to make light of the atomic bomb were simply a by-product of the more profound underlying reaction: "paralyzing fear."

Some observers found this reaction rather contemptible. "Fantasy is running wild," complained Maj. Alexander de Seversky in the February 1946 *Reader's Digest.* "The hysteria with which Hiroshima was greeted . . . does not reflect credit on the United States," agreed a Yale University military strategist later that year. But whatever they thought of it, contemporary social observers agreed that the news of the atomic bomb had had a devastating effect, the impact made all the more traumatic by the unexpectedness of Truman's announcement. A flurry of journalistic stories in 1939 had publicized breakthroughs in the esoteric field of nuclear fission (arousing sufficient uneasiness that physicist Enrico Fermi went on CBS radio to assure the country there was "no cause for alarm"), but then a blanket of secrecy had descended and the atom largely disappeared from the public consciousness.

I am death, the destroyer of worlds.

—*J. Robert Oppenheimer, quoting from the* Bhagavadgītā, *1945.*

The spring and summer of 1945 had brought vague talk of new and terrible secret weapons, and the Postdam Declaration of July 26 had threatened the Japanese with "complete and utter destruction." Such isolated and generalized allusions, however, had prepared Americans no better than the Japanese for August 6. Except to a tiny circle of scientists and government officials, Truman's announcement came as a bolt from the blue.

To be sure, the immediate reaction was also influenced by the fact that for nearly four years Japan had been the hated, treacherous enemy. Vengeance was on many minds. "The Japanese began the war from the air at Pearl Harbor," said President Truman grimly; "They have been repaid manyfold." The moral symmetry of this equation appealed to many commentators and editorial writers. "No tears of sympathy will be shed in America for the Japanese people," said the *Omaha Morning World Herald* on August 8. "Had they possessed a comparable weapon at Pearl Harbor, would they have hesitated to use it?" The *New York Times*'s first editorial comment on the bomb, "Our Answer to Japan," was no less vindictive. The devastation of Hiroshima, it said [on August 7], was "but a sample" of what lay ahead. More atomic bombs were being built and could be "dropped on Japan at any time our military leaders choose."

"We are lucky to have found The Thing and are able to speed the war against the Japanese *before the enemy can devise countermeasures,*" observed the Communist Party's

New York Daily Worker. "Nip propagandists" protesting the atomic bomb should recall who started the war, said the *Los Angeles Times* on August 8. The "whining, whimpering, complaining" Japs, agreed the *Philadelphia Inquirer* three days later, were "good at dishing it out," but with the tables turned, "they now want to quit." "The Jap Must Choose," proclaimed *Newsweek* on August 13, "between surrender and annihilation." Outweighing the bomb's "wholesale slaughter," agreed the *Nation* on August 18, was its "spectacular success" in forcing the Japanese surrender. Two billion dollars, it added, "was never better spent." (pp. 10-13)

Many political cartoonists quickly assimilated this new motif into propagandistic anti-Japanese cartoons. A *Philadelphia Inquirer* cartoon of August 7 portrayed a grotesque, apelike brute staring up in dumb wonder as an atomic bomb exploded overhead. The cartoon in *PM,* the liberal New York City daily, was totally blank except for the words "So sorry" in a balloon at the top. The *Chicago Tribune* pictured the dove of peace flying over Japan, an atomic bomb in its beak. An *Atlanta Constitution* cartoon showing bodies flying into the air over Hiroshima was captioned: "Land of the Rising Sons."

But given the heavily racist wartime climate, post-Hiroshima vindictiveness proved surprisingly short-lived and was quickly overshadowed by a growing fear of what might lie ahead. The bomb might indeed force Japan to her knees, wrote Hanson W. Baldwin in the *New York Times* on August 7, but it would also bring incalculable new dangers. "We have," he concluded bleakly, "sowed the whirlwind."

Nor did the promise of a peactime atomic Utopia initially do much to diminish post-Hiroshima fear. Typically, the editor of a religious periodical noted in September 1945 that such speculations were being advanced, but confessed that "at the moment we can visualize only the unutterably shattering effect upon civilization and the wholesale destruction of millions of human beings."

The darkening national mood was intensified by the reaction from abroad. While the news of Hiroshima and Nagasaki did not have as sharp and immediate an impact in Europe (itself devastated and prostrate) as it did in the United States, awareness of the bomb's ominous implications came quickly. In a statement that somehow gained force from its stilted, Latinate English, the Vatican newspaper *Osservatore Romano* declared on August 7: "The last twilight of the war is colored by mortal flames never before seen on the horizons of the universe, from its heavenly dawn to this infernal era. This war gives us a catastrophic conclusion that seems not to put an end to its apocalyptic surprises." In contrast to President Truman's gloating, Winston Churchill struck a somber note: "This revelation of the secrets of nature, long mercifully withheld from man," he declared, "should arouse the most solemn reflections in the mind and conscience of every human being capable of comprehension."

Reinforced by such pronouncements from abroad, the "Great Fear" was open, palpable, and starkly literal in its expression. Newsman Don Goddard, as we have seen, quickly transmuted the devastation of Hiroshima into visions of American cities in smoldering ruins, and millions of Americans soon made the same imaginative leap. Physically untouched by the war, the United States at the moment of victory perceived itself as naked and vulnerable. Sole possessors and users of a devastating new instrument of mass destruction, Americans envisioned themselves not as a potential threat to other peoples, but as potential victims. "In that terrible flash 10,000 miles away, men here have seen not only the fate of Japan, but have glimpsed the future of America," wrote James Reston in the *New York Times.*

The *Milwaukee Journal* on August 8 published a large map of the city overlaid by concentric circles of destruction. And worse lay ahead. The primitive atomic bombs of 1945, observed the *New York Times* on August 12, were analogous to "the steam engine of James Watt, the telegraph of Morse, the flying machines of the Wrights." As soon as the atomic bomb was paired up with the guided missile, speculated the *Detroit News* on August 17, the threat to civilization would rise to "a new pitch of terror." In an interview with the *New Yorker,* John W. Campbell, Jr., the editor of *Astounding Science Fiction,* offered a similar vision of World War III: "Every major city will be wiped out in thirty minutes. . . . New York will be a slag heap. . . . Radioactive energy . . . will leave the land uninhabitable for periods ranging from ten months to five hundred years, depending on the size of the bomb." Speaking on a New York radio station days after Hiroshima, the sociologist Harvey W. Zorbaugh (a member of the wartime Committee for National Morale) predicted "an armament race such as the world has never seen." The life expectancy of the human species, said the *Washington Post* on August 26, had "dwindled immeasurably in the course of two brief weeks."

From our contemporary perspective, such fears seem so familiar as to be almost trite, but it is important to recognize how *quickly* Americans began to articulate them. Years before the world's nuclear arsenals made such a holocaust likely or even possible, the prospect of global annihilation already filled the national consciousness. This awareness and the bone-deep fear it engendered are the fundamental psychological realities underlying the broader intellectual and cultural responses of this period.

This primal fear of extinction cut across all political and ideological lines, from the staunchly conservative *Chicago Tribune,* which wrote bleakly of an atomic war that would leave Earth "a barren waste, in which the survivors of the race will hide in caves or live among ruins," to such liberal voices as the *New Republic,* which offered an almost identical vision of a conflict that would "obliterate all the great cities of the belligerents, [and] bring industry and technology to a grinding halt, . . . [leaving only] scattered remnants of humanity living on the periphery of civilization."

This fear pervaded all society, from nuclear physicists and government leaders to persons who barely grasped what had happened, but who sensed that it was deeply threatening. Indeed, the more knowledgeable and highly placed the individual, it seemed, the greater the unease. The "strange disquiet" and "very great apprehension" the atomic bomb had left in its wake, wrote theologian Reinhold Niebuhr, was particularly intense among "the more sober and thoughtful sections of our nation." Eugene Rabinowitch, a Manhattan Project chemist at the University of Chicago, later recalled walking the streets of Chicago in the summer of 1945 haunted by visions of "the sky suddenly lit by a giant fireball, the steel skeletons of skyscrapers bending into grotesque shapes and their masonry raining down into the streets below, until a great cloud of dust rose and settled over the crumbling city." As the members of the U.S. Strategic Bombing Survey probed the ruins of Hiroshima and Nagasaki in September 1945, an "insistent question" formed itself in their minds: "What if the target for the bomb had been an American city?"

So palpable was the depression in Washington, D.C., wrote newsman Phelps Adams, that many were admitting "they would be happier if this $2,000,000,000 gamble had failed," or if the new knowledge could be "bundled up in a sack and lost in the river like an unwanted kitten." The malaise gripping the capital, agreed the *New Republic,* was not rooted in dismay over what the atomic bomb had already done, but in "thoughts of its future use elsewhere and specifically against ourselves or our children." Even if the secret remained secure for fifteen years, said [ABC] radio commentator Elmer Davis on December 30, 1945, that was a short time "for people who are raising children."

Children were on many minds in these unsettled weeks. *Life* flippantly suggested that a generation weaned on Flash Gordon would be unfazed by the atomic bomb; but within days of Hiroshima, the *New Yorker* reported [in its August 18th issue] this moment observed among children at play in Manhattan:

> For years the playground in Washington Square has resounded to the high-strung anh-anh-anh of machine guns and the long-drawn-out whine of high-velocity shells. Last Saturday morning a great advance was made. We watched a military man of seven or eight climb onto a seesaw, gather a number of his staff officers around him, and explain the changed situation. "Look," he said, "I'm an atomic bomb. I just go 'boom.' Once. Like this." He raised his arms, puffed out his cheeks, jumped down from the seesaw, and went "Boom!" Then he led his army away, leaving Manhattan in ruins behind him.

Some time later, another observer of juvenile life in New York City noted a change in the Broadway penny arcades: "Where during the war for a nickel you could try your luck shooting at a helpless parachutist as he drifted toward the ground, you can now try your luck at wiping out a whole city, with an atomic bomb—all for five cents."

As the historian shifts focus to the level of individual experience, the evidence becomes tantalizingly fragmentary: the child who, in a prayer shortly after Hiroshima, asked God to let his family all die together; the little girl who, when asked what she wanted to be when she grew up, replied "alive"; the young mother in Pelham Manor, New York, who had just given birth to her second son when the Hiroshima news came and who three days later recorded her feelings in a letter to H. V. Kaltenborn:

Since then I have hardly been able to smile, the future seems so utterly grim for our two little boys. Most of the time I have been in tears or near-tears, and fleeting but torturing regrets that I have brought children into the world to face such a dreadful thing as this have shivered through me. It seems that it will be for them all their lives like living on a keg of dynamite which may go off at any moment, and which undoubtedly will go off before their lives have progressed very far.

Such scattered evidence gives us a glimpse into the consciousness and culture of childhood, as well as the concerns of adults trying to fathom the bomb's impact on the generation that would grow up in its shadow. It is perhaps noteworthy that John Hersey chose to conclude his influential 1946 work *Hiroshima* with the recollections of a ten-year-old survivor. The lad's account is terse and noncommittal, but Hersey does not assume that the emotional effects of the experience were therefore negligible. "It would be impossible to say," he observes, "what horrors were embedded in the minds of the children who lived through the day of the bombing in Hiroshima." Comparable fears about American children contributed to the larger uneasiness that seeped through the culture in the weeks after August 6, 1945.

Rather than diminishing, this mood deepened as weeks stretched into months. America was in the grip of a "fear psychosis," said anthropologist Robert Redfield in November 1945; atomic anxiety had become "a nightmare in the minds of men." *The First One Hundred Days of the Atomic Age,* a paperback published in late November, offered yet another potpourri of statements still "pouring forth from all sides" and reflecting "ever widening concern and alarm." Despite the passage of several months, wrote Hertha Pauli in the December *Commentary,* the bomb seemed to "weigh more and more heavily on the minds of more and more men." When *Time* named Harry Truman "Man of the Year" on December 21, 1945, the president's picture on the cover was dwarfed by a mushroom-shaped cloud and a hand gripping a lightning bolt. All the year's great events, said *Time,* including the deaths of FDR and Hitler and the surrender of Germany and Japan, paled before the awesome reality of the bomb:

> What the world would best remember of 1945 was the deadly mushroom clouds over Hiroshima and Nagasaki. Here were the force, the threat, the promise of the future. In their giant shadows . . . all men were pygmies. . . . Even Presidents, even Men of the Year, [were] mere foam flecks on the tide. . . . In such a world, who dared be optimistic?

Nor did the new year bring relief. In January, a State Department official commented on the undiminished "hysteria" and "poisonous fog" of suspicion and fear still prevading the country. Talk of the bomb was continuing to "boom on unceasingly from radio, press, and platforms," wrote another observer. A mental-health writer who made a national lecture tour that spring found "general fear and confusion." Bob Hope joked about this fear. "Have you noticed the modern trend in verses this year?" he said on his radio show on Valentine's Day 1946. "No more of this 'Roses are red, violets are blue.' I picked up one and it showed an atom bomb exploding, and under it a verse that read: 'Will you be my little geranium, until we are both blown up by uranium?'" The strain in such humor was apparent.

As late as 1948, a speaker before a New York City business and professional club began:

> The atomic age is here, and we're all scared to death; you, I, and everyone else. And no wonder. We woke up one morning, and either heard over the radio or read in big, black headlines, that an atomic bomb had been delivered, when we didn't even suspect the possibility of such a thing. Our very first contact was a shock, particularly since it told of the death of a great city.

But how accurate were all these comments? Were these cultural observers perhaps simply quoting each other, parroting what had quickly become conventional wisdom? Was the culture indeed in shock, or was this simply an instant media cliché? Some at the time wondered the same thing. "We know what the atomic bombs did to Hiroshima and Nagasaki," commented *Fortune* in December 1945. "What did they do to the U.S. mind?" (pp. 13-22)

[Clearly,] the weeks and months following August 6, 1945, were a time of cultural crisis when the American people confronted a new and threatening reality of almost unfathomable proportions. Equally clearly, the dominant immediate response was confusion and disorientation. But interwoven with all the talk of uncertainty and fear was another, more bracing theme: Americans must not surrender to fear or allow themselves to be paralyzed by anxiety; they must rally their political and cultural energies and rise to the challenge of the atomic bomb. (pp. 25-6)

Paul Boyer, "'The Whole World Gasped,'" in his By the Bomb's Early Light: American Thought and Culture at the Dawn of the Atomic Age, *Pantheon Books, 1985, pp. 3-26.*

FICTION

Paul Brians

[*An American educator and critic, Brians is the author of* Nuclear Holocausts: Atomic War in Fiction, 1895-1984 *(1984), which has been called by the editors of the science fiction magazine* FUTURES *"the authoritative account and complete bibliography of the atomic war in fiction." In the following excerpt from* Nuclear Holocausts, *Brians provides a historical and thematic overview of nuclear holocaust fiction written between 1895 and 1984.*]

Many authors have pondered the significance of the bomb in the years since 1945. World War III—the nuclear holocaust—has been fought over and over in the pages of books and magazines. In a way, these are war stories; but nuclear war is different from earlier wars in ways that affect its depiction in fiction. First, it is short. Although some of our fiction depicts lengthy atomic warfare, most of it assumes the war will be over in minutes, or hours at most. Concepts familiar from other wars become irrelevant: conscription, the noble sacrifice of soldiers to defend loved ones at home, the civilian support of the war effort. Indeed, the distinction between civilian and military is largely erased except that the military personnel most directly engaged in conducting the war are the most sheltered, and innocent civilians the most likely casualties. In Helen Clarkson's *The Last Day: A Novel of the Day After Tomorrow* (1958), one character comments: "In the old days, men at arms were always sustained through the immoral act of killing by the thought that they were not fighting for themselves, but for their children. Today men ask their children to die for them."

Because nuclear war leaves no time for the traditional distinctions, many of the qualities central to other modes of war fiction are irrelevant. Courage is of little use, even for the preservation of one's own life. No amount of loyalty, determination, self-sacrifice or heroism will deflect an incoming intercontinental ballistic missile one jot from its programmed course. The hope of victory, which is all that makes war worthwhile for most, is absent. Mere retaliation can produce at best a pyrrhic victory, at worst, the end of life on Earth. And where traditional war fiction appeals to the notion that in combat human character is tested and the inner self revealed, nuclear war stories are dominated by machinery, not human beings. The rockets and bombs dwarf the officials who launch them, and the logic of battle is dictated by technological considerations as much as it is by the strategic decisions of such officials.

The paradox that the entire point of nuclear war is its own

prevention—deterrence—leads to yet other paradoxes. A commander in chief must convince the enemy that he is determined to fight, if necessary, a war which can only be a catastrophe for his own nation. The details of strategy must be carefully laid out so that they may never be used. The more unthinkable the war becomes, the more we must think about it. Unlike in other wars, the enemy must be well informed of our plans and resources, for a secret deterrent is no deterrent at all.

A peculiar feature of the age of nuclear combat is the possibility of accidental war. Wars have in the past been begun on the basis of trivial incidents, misunderstandings, and errors in judgment; but the notion that civilization might be ended or life on Earth be destroyed through a technical malfunction or an error in judgment presents an absurdity of such enormous dimensions that it can scarcely be grasped. The resultant air of futility about much nuclear war fiction is convincing in ways that similar views of conventional wars could not be. Even those few writers who try to establish that atomic war might be purposeful or beneficent seem led by its internal logic to depict it as absurd.

The author of a nuclear war story, then, lacks many of the resources of traditional war narratives. The genre it has most in common with is not in fact the war story at all, but the narrative of a great catastrophe: fire, flood, plague. Nuclear war fiction has necessarily evolved its own conventions, the specifics of which will be explored in the following pages. It is disheartening to see how soon the conventions that emerged from this new type of fiction became clichés, how quickly it became possible to write utterly unoriginal works on the subject. To see the potentially most awesome of subjects trivialized enlarges one's sense of the capacity of the human mind for irrelevance. Yet the genre has also produced thoughtful, powerful works, even a few works of high literary merit.

Hiroshima has had nothing like the literary impact of other great military events. Even though this study surveys well over eight hundred items—even allowing for a generous number overlooked—the number of novels, short stories, and plays depicting nuclear war and its aftermath published in English in any given year since 1945 has seldom exceeded two dozen. Stories of the atomic holocaust have never rivalled in number stories of other conflicts such as the American Civil War or World War II. Even in those years when a good many nuclear war stories were published, they were rarely widely read: most of them are science fiction, and until recently science fiction has had a very restricted audience.

There is another, more important reason for the relative unpopularity of nuclear war fiction: it can be disturbing. Even at its most escapist, it deals with a war many readers feel to be as inevitable and as final as death itself. Unlike historical wars, World War III will not stay safely in the past to allow itself to be enjoyed. The armchair general of World War II is reassured by the knowledge that he or she has survived; the armchair victim of World War III has no such assurance.

Nuclear war must be the most carefully avoided topic of

general significance in the contemporary world. People are not curious about the details. Once in a decade a book will receive a broad audience: John Hersey's *Hiroshima* (1946), Nevil Shute's *On the Beach* (1957), Jonathan Schell's *The Fate of the Earth* (1982). But whereas Civil War buffs who will consume volume after volume about Bull Run and Vicksburg are commonplace, there are few World War III buffs: almost everyone seems to feel adequately informed by reading one book about nuclear war. So thoroughly neglected is the genre that there are many notable novels which have been almost entirely overlooked or forgotten. This study aims to bring them to the attention of a wider public. (pp. 2-4)

Novelists did not wait until August 6, 1945 to begin writing accounts of atomic warfare. The public imagination had been inflamed with all manner of wild fancies in reaction to the discoveries of X-rays by Roentgen in 1895, of radioactivity in uranium by Becquerel in 1896, of radium and polonium by the Curies in 1898, and of the possibility of converting matter into energy according to Einstein's relativity theory of 1905. Popular fiction was not slow to adapt the new knowledge to military uses.

The atom was viewed as harboring world-shattering power as early as 1895: in Robert Cromie's *The Crack of Doom,* a group of madmen are barely thwarted in their plot to use an atomic device to undo creation. Novelists were particularly prodigal in the invention of all manner of miraculous rays. In George Griffith's *The Lord of Labour* (written in 1906, published in 1911) the Germans invent a ray which can "demagnetize" metal in such a manner that it crumbles into dust on impact. The British fleet is manipulated into destroying itself when it fires its guns at the ray-wielding enemy fleet of wooden ships. But Anglo-Saxon ingenuity and civilization triumph as the English retaliate with helium-radium bullets of stupendous explosive power. The supposed healing powers of radioactivity were touted as early as 1907 in a story titled "Itself" by Edgar Mayhew Bacon. Also in 1907 Upton Sinclair wrote a play concerning atomic weapons which remained unpublished and unproduced until he revised it as a novel in 1924: *The Millenium: A Comedy of the Year 2000.* In it tiny radium weapons are carried by guards. The new element radiumite, which produces atomic energy, kills all life on Earth when a mad professor smashes a jar full of it. Only eleven humans who happen to be flying in an airplane survive. (p. 4)

Popular articles and books on the mysterious new sort of energy proliferated during the early years of the twentieth century, among them Frederick Soddy's *Interpretation of Radium* (1908). Soddy's lucid explanation of the new science was cited by H. G. Wells in 1913 when he wrote what is usually cited as the first novel depicting a war involving atomic weapons, *The World Set Free* (published in 1914, on the eve of World War I). As Ritchie Calder points out in his introduction to the Collins edition, Wells made plenty of errors. He imagined bombs behaving rather like reactors, sustaining continuous seventeen-day-long volcano-like explosions. He confused chemical and atomic reactions and erroneously supposed that the end product of radioactivity would be gold (fortuitously destroying the precious-metal monetary standard). Yet, considering that most popular writers saw in radioactivity a form of magic capable of all manner of miracles (for instance, Philip Francis Nowlan's *Armageddon 2419,* first published 1928-29), and that early science fiction was distracted by variegated rays which could cause invisibility or shrink a man to the size of an atom, it is remarkable that Wells was able to make as much sense out of the knowledge of his day as he did. He understood Einstein's theory well enough to grasp that atomic energy would be derived from the annihilation of matter; the "Carolinium" used in his bombs bears some resemblance to plutonium; and his atomic bombs are delivered from the air.

The novel, which appeared in 1914, belongs to Wells's pontificating middle period and is relatively plotless, consisting in the main of lectures on history and an account of a utopian but authoritarian world government with a monopoly on atomic weapons. Wells's vision of a united world did not, of course, need the new scientific discoveries to prompt it; but he was not to be alone in imagining that the overwhelming power of the atom would force humanity to set aside its petty nationalistic disputes. Indeed this sanguine view was a mere repetition of the hopes expressed upon the invention of weapons such as TNT, which were also supposed to make war inconceivable. Wells's novel, like Hollis Godfrey's *The Man Who Ended War* (1908), and other, similar tales discussed in Merritt Abrash's "Through Logic to Apocalypse: Science-Fiction Scenarios of Nuclear Deterrence Breakdown" (*Science-Fiction Studies* 13 [1986]) anticipated post-1945 works in which atomic blackmail per se forces peace on the world—stories that might best be called "muscular disarmament" fiction.

Growing interest in the theme is illustrated by *Wings Over Europe: A Dramatic Extravaganza On a Pressing Theme,* a play by Robert Nichols and Maurice Browne (1929). The British cabinet is confronted by a young man, the son of the prime minister, who has penetrated the secrets of the atom sufficiently to create world-wrecking bombs and the transmutation of matter. He envisions a utopia administered by benevolent England, but the greed and militarism of the cabinet members frustrate his endeavor. In despair, he determines to destroy the world, but is killed by a truck just before setting off the explosion. Just as the world seems safe for capitalism and warfare once more, word arrives that the Guild of United Brain Workers has independently discovered the secret and has placed atomic bombs in airplanes circling above all the major capitals of the world, aiming at global rule, underlining the theme that scientific discoveries cannot be kept secret indefinitely. The secretary of state for foreign affairs gains possession of the first discoverer's triggering mechanism and plans to confront the Guild with it. The ending is left in suspense. (pp. 4-6)

In 1932 Harold Nicolson, diplomat and biographer (also the husband of Vita Sackville-West), published another early muscular disarmament novel, *Public Faces;* in it the British impose universal disarmament through their monopoly of atomic bombs delivered by rockets strongly resembling cruise missiles. Nicolson's weapons are far more powerful than those of Wells: one dropped off the coast of Florida creates a tidal wave which kills eighty thousand people, shifts the course of the Gulf Stream, and permanently alters the climate. Nicolson was less interested in technical matters than in the political maneuvering of the great powers in which peace and British supremacy are ensured by the boldly illegal stroke of an imaginative, headstrong minister.

J. B. Priestley escalated the potential carnage in his 1938 novel, *The Doomsday Men,* in which a group of religious fanatics come close to succeeding in their plot to destroy the world by bombarding a lump of a newly discovered radioactive element with a cyclotron, creating a reaction which would have completely disrupted the Earth's crust, peeling it like an orange. But throughout the twenties and thirties most popular articles and books on atomic energy focused on its peaceful uses. The utopia of tomorrow would be created through cheap and abundant atomic power, not through atomic blackmail. (p. 6)

The U.S.-supported research which led to the Manhattan Project began in 1939 amid the greatest secrecy, and the following year the publication of further articles on atomic theory was prohibited in Britain and America. But just before wartime censorship was imposed, the announcement of the successful splitting of uranium 235 and the possibility of power derived from a chain reaction led to a spate of newspaper and magazine articles hailing the atomic utopia of the future and darkly hinting at the possibility of weapons being designed by Nazi scientists. . . . In a sense, the Manhattan Project shut the door after the horse had been stolen, as was acknowledged in a September 8, 1945, editorial in *The Saturday Evening Post* revealing that the War Department tried to prevent the distribution and reading of the *Post*'s 1940 issue even in public libraries across the country. The basic principles of atomic fission and the possibility of a uranium bomb were common knowledge, and wartime censorship hid little that spies did not already know; but popular articles on the subject ceased to appear and the public seemed to forget about the whole issue during much of World War II.

Only in science fiction did speculation continue, principally in the pages of *Astounding Science Fiction.* Editor John W. Campbell, Jr., was by far the most influential editor in science fiction during the thirties and forties, fostering new approaches to science fiction, introducing new writers, and assigning story topics to his authors. He was fascinated by things atomic, and continually urged others to create stories on the theme. Throughout the 1930s he had written stories depicting the atomic weapons of the future. While often upstaged by various rays and beams, atomic blast weapons and bombs appear again and again in stories written both under his own name and under his pseudonym, "Don A. Stuart." Sometimes the atomic weapons are capable of ending civilization, or even obliterating the human race, but ultimately they prove in almost every case to be a means of liberation.

Evidently unaware of the wartime ban, Campbell published in May 1941 a story with a more alarmist view, Robert A. Heinlein's "Solution Unsatisfactory," which came very close to describing the Manhattan Project itself:

"Someone in the United States government had realized the terrific potentialities of uranium 235 quite early, and, as far back as the summer of 1940, had rounded up every atomic research man in the country and sworn them to silence." Heinlein overestimated the difficulty of controlling an atomic explosion, so that what his scientists develop by 1945 is not an atomic bomb, but radioactive dust, which they drop with devastating consequences on Berlin.

Heinlein's technical errors are unimportant. More significantly, he understood that atomic weapons research could not be kept a secret, and that America's nuclear monopoly would be unlikely to create international stability unless it imposed a new world order. Accordingly, the President issues a peace proclamation, that, "divested of its diplomatic surplusage," says, "The United States is prepared to defeat any power, or combination of powers, in jig time. Accordingly, we are outlawing war and are calling on every nation to disarm completely at once. In other words, 'Throw down your guns, boys; we've got the drop on you!' "

Unfortunately, the scientists of the USSR—in the story dubbed the "Eurasian Union"—have also discovered the uses of atomic dust, and the result is the devastating Four-Days War. (If Heinlein's understanding had been more widely shared by his countrymen, the U.S. might have been spared the atom spy hysteria of the postwar era in which politicians seemed to think that the secrets of fission could be patented and kept secret.) In the war the enemy is destroyed, but power is seized by the colonel who conceived of using the radioactive dust in the first place. The world is now at peace, but it has become a vast dictatorship; hence the story's title. (pp. 6-8)

So long as the Manhattan Project security remained in force, stories of atomic doom remained rare. Another notable exception is Lester del Rey's *Nerves* (originally in *Astounding,* September 1942; expanded [into book form in] 1956), which describes a near-disaster in a malfunctioning atomic power plant which threatens to destroy several states. The scientists who keep the true extent of the danger secret from the public are depicted as heroes whose titanic efforts preserve the future of atomic energy by preventing the unscientific hysteria which would inevitably result were the nature of the threat to become generally known.

Another and much more fantastic atomic plant disaster story was Malcolm Jameson's "The Giant Atom," in which a device resembling a cyclotron creates an ever-growing atom which threatens to consume the entire planet. Published in *Startling Stories* in 1943, it was reprinted posthumously after Hiroshima and Nagasaki under the opportunistic title *Atomic Bomb,* although Jameson's variation on the Frankenstein's monster theme bears little relationship to the new weapon. Heinlein's "Solution Unsatisfactory" demonstrates clearly that during the early 1940s anyone possessing a more than casual familiarity with the material published on atomic science before the imposition of censorship could extrapolate the possibilities more accurately than Jameson had.

A crisis of sorts was reached in the publication of pre-Hiroshima atomic war fiction with the appearance in *Astounding,* March 1944, of Cleve Cartmill's "Deadline," containing a description of an atomic bomb accurate enough to cause FBI agents to call on both Cartmill and editor Campbell. . . . Campbell argued, apparently successfully, that his readers were so used to reading stories involving atomic science that if he were to ban such tales from *Astounding* in the future they would become conspicuous by their absence. In February of 1945, the magazine published "The Piper's Son"—the first of Henry Kuttner's "Baldy" tales, later collected as *Mutant*—depicting telepathic mutants whose powers are the result of radiation from an atomic war. One can hardly avoid the conclusion that Campbell was preparing himself a reputation as a prophet as he continued to publish Kuttner's sequels in June and July. The fourth tale, "Beggars in Velvet," undoubtedly also written before Hiroshima, was published in December in the same issue with an editorial by Campbell hailing the advent of the atomic age.

Kuttner's stories hardly posed a threat to national security: the war was placed in the distant past, and its effects, though they were later to become commonplace in fiction, were thoroughly fantastic. Campbell was treading on thinner ice in publishing Robert Abernathy's "When the Rockets Come" in March 1945. It depicts the atomic bomb as a horrifying weapon whose effects expose its users as morally bankrupt. Abernathy's story anticipated the liberal reaction to the bomb which would be fully developed in fiction only years later.

In Fritz Leiber's "Destiny Times Three" (*Astounding,* March, April 1945), Heinlein's fears that the new technology may be incompatible with democratic government are reflected as "subtronic" weapons are developed on three alternate versions of Earth. On one world the knowledge is public property; on another an attempt is made to suppress it; and on a third it is monopolized by a dictatorship. The dictatorship invades the other two. Just as America was reaching the pinnacle of its power in the world, these science fiction writers were warning that the new atomic age was as likely to prove a disaster as a triumph. Their warnings went unnoticed by the general public, of course, and were probably unheeded even by most seasoned science fiction fans, jaded by decades of stories of planet-busting beams and rays depicted with casual bravado.

Author Philip Wylie, not fortunate enough to be working for the privileged Campbell, found that when he wrote a story depicting a Nazi conspiracy to rule the world through atomic bombs he could not get it published. According to records in agent Harold Ober's files, Wylie submitted "The Paradise Crater" to him on January 13, 1944; *Blue Book,* a popular men's fiction magazine, bought the story, then cancelled its publication. A note dated July 3, 1945 explains the cancellation as prompted by security considerations: "War Dept. objects to the use of this. President Conant of Harvard is working on something similar. He promised not to offer to any magazine. Cancel sale." (James Conant was chairman of the National Defense Research Committee and very much a part of the Manhattan Project. . . .) According to H. Bruce Franklin, Wylie was placed under house arrest and even threatened with death for his indiscretion. A month later, the magazine repurchased the story, and a note was added to the file reading, "Atomic bomb released on Japan Aug. 6, 1945." So *Blue Book* accomplished the coup of publishing the first atomic bomb story after Hiroshima even though it had been written over a year and a half before. Thus inadvertantly began Wylie's long collaboration with the government's nuclear weapons planners which was to result in four short stories and three novels relating to nuclear war.

"The Paradise Crater" is an unexceptional counterespionage story in which the hero sabotages the Nazi villains' store of atomic bombs. An enormous explosion results: flames shoot forty thousand feet into the air; an earthquake wreaks havoc throughout much of the western United States and Canada; a tidal wave roars west from the shores of California and inundates thousands of "Japanese savages on distant Nippon" (the defeated Asian enemy having evidently reverted to barbarism). The mountain within which the bombs were built becomes a crater two miles deep and thirty across. Ever since writers began to grasp the significance of Einstein's $E=mc^2$, they had been enthusiastically predicting that a cupful of coal could power an entire city. It is not surprising that Wylie supposed that the detonation of a large number of nuclear weapons would create a cataclysm.

As we have seen, the tendency to think of atomic weapons in apocalyptic terms existed even well before the first one was detonated; it has persisted ever since, although this is not a universal pattern, nor even the dominant one. The earliest reactions to use of the bomb on Japan were fraught with ambivalence. For example, Wylie's first postbomb article, published in *Collier's,* September 29, 1945, was entitled "Deliverance or Doom?" The first published fictional response to Hiroshima was a brief sketch written by Theodore Sturgeon and entitled "August Sixth 1945," which appeared in the letters column of the December issue of *Astounding.* According to a personal conversation with the author, it had been intended as a regular submission, and Sturgeon remained to the end of his life disgruntled that Campbell avoided paying him for the piece by treating it as mere correspondence. It encapsulates and gives classic expression to the science fiction community's ambivalent reaction to the bomb: self-congratulation on having predicted the astonishing new technology, mixed with apprehension about the threat it posed to civilization. Man, wrote Sturgeon, "knows—he learned on August 6, 1945, that he alone is big enough to kill himself, or to live forever." Atomic science threatens universal extinction, but it also holds out the promise of immortality.

Albert I. Berger has shown how widespread was the self-congratulatory mood among science fiction writers at that time in an important article, "The Triumph of Prophecy: Science Fiction and Nuclear Power in the Post-Hiroshima Period." (*Science-Fiction Studies* 3 [1976]). The jubilation with which so many writers greeted the new era matched the general American euphoria over the defeat of Japan. Brian Aldiss, who was to write one of the most moving accounts of the aftermath of a nuclear holocaust in his 1964 nuclear accident novel *Greybeard,* recalls with what relief he and his fellow soldiers poised to invade the islands

greeted the news of the bombing of Hiroshima and Nagasaki (personal conversation with author). The generally optimistic mood of the popular press is reflected in an anthology hastily assembled by Pocket Books in August of 1945, *The Atomic Age Opens.* The cover blurb conveys the same message as Sturgeon's little sketch: "THE END—THE BEGINNING? When the United States Army Air Forces dropped the first atomic bomb on Hiroshima, it meant the end of Japan as a war-making power—and the beginning of a new age. For, with this newly-released force, man can destroy himself or create a world rich and prosperous beyond all previous dreams."

Campbell immediately began to publish editorials about the wonders of the atomic age. The following year Pat Frank—later more well known for his sobering account of atomic war, *Alas, Babylon*—reduced the threat of universal sterilization through radiation to a joke in his best-selling *Mr. Adam.* In this work, a nuclear accident leaves only one man fertile, and he is pursued by millions of desperate, would-be mothers. At about the same time, Captain Walter Karig of the U.S. Naval Reserves produced a little pamphlet partly aimed at arguing for the continuing importance of the navy in the atomic era, but which provided his sailors with all manner of Buck Rogers gimmickry suddenly made plausible by the new technology. A. E. Van Vogt, like Kuttner before him, seized on the notion of war-induced radiation creating superhuman traits in his series of stories begun in 1946 and later collected as *Empire of the Atom.* Arthur C. Clarke treated the invention of the bomb whimsically, as an example of human feistiness and gumption, in "Loophole" (*Astounding,* April 1946). Henry Kuttner's "Rain Check" (*Astounding,* July 1946) was hardly more serious. (pp. 8-11)

During 1947 *Astounding* overwhelmingly dominated the publishing of nuclear war fiction with over a dozen stories, many of them awful warnings sharply in contrast with Campbell's generally optimistic editorial stance. Poul Anderson's first published story, "Tomorrow's Children," written jointly with F. N. Waldrop, took a less sanguine view of radiation-induced birth defects than preceding stories like those of Kuttner. The best known story published that year was Theodore Sturgeon's "Thunder and Roses," which—despite the fact that most of its literary merit resides in its title—remains a striking argument against the theory of nuclear deterrence.

But Campbell's taste reasserted itself forcefully in the following year, in which the number of atomic war stories in *Astounding* dropped by three quarters and only one (Judith Merril's memorable "That Only a Mother") could be considered an awful warning. Despite this fact, a correspondent complained in the September 1948 issue of the excessive number of nuclear war stories appearing in the magazine. Campbell reassured him and other concerned readers: "We have specified to our authors that the 'atomic doom' stories are not wanted. . . ."

Despite this announced change in policy, Campbell published some "atomic doom" stories in 1949 (Alfred Coppel, "Secret Weapon"; Kris Neville, "Cold War") and succeeding years, but most of the atomic war tales in *Astounding* were either frivolous (like Van Vogt's continuing

"Empire of the Atom" series) or absurdly upbeat. An atomic war story perfectly reflecting Campbellian optimism—though it departs from the realistic style which Campbell preferred—is A. E. Van Vogt's "Resurrection" (published as "The Monster" in August 1948). When creatures from another world investigating the cause of Earth's destruction resurrect a man in order to question him, he uses a nuclear device to battle them in an atomic duel from which he emerges triumphant. The resuscitated hero will use the technology of the defeated aliens to revive and grant immortality to the entire human race. Lest the preceding holocaust raise any doubts about the goodness of human nature, it is strongly hinted that Earth had been devastated not by people but by the ancestors of these very aliens.

Fredric Brown's 1949 story "Letter to a Phoenix" also matched Campbell's philosophy, mixing positivism with the power of positive thinking. Brown's protagonist is made nigh-immortal by exposure to bomb radiation and thus can report that the holocausts which periodically almost annihilate the human race are actually necessary to perpetuate the species, which—without this invigorating tonic—would die out like every other race in the universe.

Henry Kuttner's 1947 *Astounding* story, "Tomorrow and Tomorrow," similarly argued that atomic war might prove a fine method of birth control and stimulate scientific research, creating a utopia. Irrelevance could go no further, and the magazine soon almost ceased publishing atomic war stories altogether, with occasional exceptions reminiscent of the immediate postwar period (Walter M. Miller, "Dumb Waiter" [1952]; Morton Klass, "In the Beginning" [1954]). The 1951 Twentieth-Century Fox muscular disarmament fable, *The Day the Earth Stood Still,* was based on a pre-atomic age *Astounding* story ("Farewell to the Master" by Harry Bates, October 1940), but the original tale entirely lacked the antiwar message of the film. The filmmakers would have been hard pressed to find a real anti-nuclear war story in the fifties version of the magazine. The days when *Astounding* had dominated nuclear war fiction were over. (pp. 12-13)

Outside of science fiction, novelists and short story writers were slow to respond to Hiroshima. Aside from Wylie, who maintained a connection for many years with science fiction, the only generally well known author to write an atomic war novel by 1948 was Aldous Huxley, whose *Ape and Essence* was more of a restatement of the antiutopian themes of *Brave New World* than a serious meditation on the probable consequences of a future holocaust. He did grasp the genetic danger, and remains one of the few writers to treat seriously the problems of radioactive soil for agriculture. In fact, few novels depicting nuclear war either outside or inside of science fiction were published before 1950. Those that were were not well known or not widely reviewed or sold. Some of the reluctance of authors to explore the new theme may be attributed to war-weariness. In the five years after Hiroshima, not much conventional war fiction was published either. Of course, George Orwell's *1984* (1949) uses atomic war as part of its background, but nuclear weapons play such a minor role in the novel that most readers have probably forgotten that he touched on the subject at all.

However, during this same period Ray Bradbury was writing a series of stories which would appear knitted together in book form in 1950 and become for many years (until Shute's *On the Beach* [1957]) the best known fictional work dealing with nuclear war: *The Martian Chronicles.* Indeed, it was for over a decade the best-known piece of modern science fiction writing. Although the immense success of Bradbury's book can be attributed mostly to the sensuous exoticism of his Martian setting and characters, the book is significant for the political development it marked. *The Martian Chronicles* turns its back on the postwar vision of the American Century. It deplores our crass commercialism, reminds readers of the nation's crimes against the Indians and blacks, and battles against the forces of censorship, albeit in a distinctly bizarre fashion, in the tale entitled "Usher II." No modern writer is more typically American in his themes and attitudes than Bradbury; yet repeatedly his fiction hints at or clearly depicts the monstrous crimes that lurk beneath the Norman Rockwell exteriors of his protagonists.

The Martian Chronicles is the story of humanity which is punished for its genocidal deeds by committing genocide on itself. Having killed off most of the Indians, having driven desperate blacks to flee the lynch-law South for Mars, and having contemptuously—almost without noticing—annihilated the wise, gentle Martians, humanity destroys itself in an atomic holocaust which is one last act of typical, unexplained stupidity. It is not necessary to explain why nuclear war consumes the Earth: it is the logical consequence of the parochialism, bigotry, and greed which are displayed in the earlier chapters.

The book concludes on a muted note of hope as the human race survives in two families who have fled to Mars. In Bradbury, any hope for the future lies not in society at large, but in the decency of individuals. This story, "The Million-Year Picnic," had been his first published response to Hiroshima, and it comes close to condemning humanity in toto. So anxious is the protagonist to eradicate the past that he resorts to censorship, burning various papers and volumes in a way that clashes curiously with the theme of "Usher II," and even more with Bradbury's passionate denunciation of book-burning, *Fahrenheit 451* (earliest version, 1951). Ironically, book-burning is the solution to the failure of civilization caused by nuclear war in *The Martian Chronicles* whereas a nuclear war ends the tyranny which instituted book-burning in *Fahrenheit 451.*

It is inconceivable that John Campbell could have published "The Million-Year Picnic," even if Bradbury had offered it to him. In fact it is surprising to find such a work widely read and appreciated by a nation which we have been told was undergoing The Great Celebration. But even in the early fifties, there were plenty of Americans who abstained from the nation's love affair with itself, and a disproportionate number of them were science fiction fans. (pp. 14-15)

The traditional formula for science fiction had been to pose a problem and find a technical development which would solve it. In the early 1950s, the formula for many *Galaxy* and *Fantasy and Science Fiction* stories was to posit a technical development and discover what could go wrong with it. Atomic war stories with a distinctly jaundiced cast to them poured forth: Fritz Leiber's "Coming Attraction" and "A Bad Day for Sales," Damon Knight's "World Without Children," Cyril M. Kornbluth's "With These Hands," Ward Moore's "Flying Dutchman" and "Lot," Wilson Tucker's *The Long Loud Silence,* Ray Bradbury's "The Garbage Collector," Philip K. Dick's "The Defenders" and "Second Variety," and James Gunn's "The Boy with Five Fingers." So powerful was the trend that editor H. L. Gold complained in the January 1952 issue of *Galaxy,* "Over 90% of stories submitted still nag away at atomic, hydrogen and bacteriological war, the post-atomic world, reversion to barbarism, mutant children killed because they have only ten toes and fingers instead of twelve. . . . Look, fellers, the end isn't here yet."

Meanwhile most American writers were ignoring the entire subject. There were two principal reasons for this fact. One was that the ghettoization of science fiction in the United States tended to prevent mainstream authors from writing stories set in the future. The other was that most Americans feared communism far more than the bomb, and were not prone to criticize the maintenance of a nuclear balance of terror which seemed to favor the West. Some even urged a preventative war, a first strike in which America's God-given might would crush the evil Soviet empire, as in the hypocritically titled October 27, 1951 issue of *Collier's* magazine, "Preview of the War We Do Not Want." (p. 16)

It was the explosion of the first American thermonuclear device in November of 1952 and of the first Russian hydrogen bomb a year later, obviously the product of independent research not inferior to our own, which reawakened public concern. Whereas some public officials like Bernard Baruch had spoken of the atomic bomb in apocalyptic terms immediately after Hiroshima, the general public seemed to be unable to comprehend the magnitude of the destructive potential it represented. . . . If the average reader happened upon one of the narratives depicting a cataclysmic atomic war, he or she probably dismissed it as wildly hyperbolic. This judgment might not have been too far wrong, considering that a writer as sober as Philip Wylie was depicting a chain reaction capable of consuming in a flash both Earth and Moon (in "Blunder" [1946]). But the H-bomb had a somewhat different effect on the public than had the A-bomb. Whereas the threat posed by the latter had been somewhat obscured by its role in ending World War II, the new weapon was developed by both East and West during a period of extreme tension highlighted by the ongoing Korean War and by the appointment of John Foster Dulles to the post of U.S. secretary of state. Dulles developed the doctrine of "massive retaliation" and harbored fantasies of "rolling back" the Russians from Eastern Europe. Despite the fact that fans and editors alike had complained that nuclear war was an exhausted theme, 1953 proved a record year for science fiction dealing with the subject. In Britain, John Wyndham reflected the tensions of the time in *The Kraken Wakes,* in which the Americans and Russians almost fail

to defeat invading tentacled sea monsters because each is convinced their predations are the work of the other side.

The next year another event marked the decisive point in turning public attention to the danger of atomic war. On March 1, 1954, the Bravo H-bomb test near the Marshall Islands fatally contaminated sailors aboard a Japanese fishing vessel known as the *Lucky Dragon.* That their citizens—now our allies—should once more be victims of American radioactive fallout created an uproar which destroyed forever the conspiracy of silence which had made the topic taboo in postwar Japan. In the West, people finally realized that even when one was not exposed to the direct effects of the bomb, its fallout could be deadly.

The year 1954 had provided an abundance of other news stories calculated to attract the attention of the public to atomic warfare. After long delays, negotiations about the uses of atomic power began seriously, although no agreement was to be reached for four more years. A new version of the Atomic Energy Act was passed. On March 31 Atomic Energy Commission Chair Lewis Strauss aroused a furor by commenting to the press that a single bomb could destroy any city on Earth. Robert Oppenheimer's security clearance was removed in April, and interest in the atomic spy theme was revived. On September 24, Aikichi Kuboyama, fisherman, died of the radiation disease to which he had fallen victim on the *Lucky Dragon* during the Bravo H-Bomb test.

Interest was sustained by related events the next year. On January 31, 1955, the Russians modified their long-held position disparaging the effectiveness of atomic bombs when they pointed out that only a few weapons would be needed to destroy crucial Western centers of power. The United States continued to test bombs in Nevada that spring. In March, Dulles and Eisenhower threatened the Communist Chinese with tactical nuclear weapons if they should attempt to seize the islands of Quemoy and Matsu, although Leo Szilard had warned the previous month that such an act would likely precipitate a devastating holocaust in which both sides would be destroyed. And Federal Civil Defense Administrator Val Peterson speculated about the possibility of creating a cobalt doomsday bomb, a device which was to find a prominent place in much later fiction (probably as much because of its repeated discussion by Herman Kahn as for any other reason). In Great Britain the Campaign for Nuclear Disarmament, spearheaded by philosopher Bertrand Russell, was claiming headlines. Russell wrote a number of fictional sketches on the theme of atomic war about this time, although some of them remained unpublished until after his death. At no time until the Cuban missile crisis did the world seem poised so close to the brink of nuclear war.

The result of all this activity and concern was the publication in 1955 of a large number of novels depicting atomic war or its aftermath, including such notable works as Leigh Brackett's *The Long Tomorrow,* C. M. Kornbluth's *Not This August,* John Wyndham's *The Chrysalids,* and the first part of Walter M. Miller, Jr.'s *A Canticle for Leibowitz.* The nuclear war novel had come of age. Magazine editors may have wearied of the subject, but book publishers were becoming interested and would dominate the genre henceforth. In no year before had so many novels been published depicting nuclear war.

During the next year's presidential campaign, Democratic candidate Adlai Stevenson called for an atomic test ban, with considerable initial support from the public. The long debate which followed kept public attention focused on the bomb, but to some extent the test-ban debate was a distraction which directed attention away from any attempt to deal with the greater danger of nuclear war itself. Even in the midst of this debate, authors were not able to sustain readers' interest in nuclear war: 1956 marked a low point in the publication of such fiction, although two mainstream works attacted some attention—Martin Caidin's *The Long Night* and Herman Wouk's *The Lomokome Papers.*

Though Eisenhower had abandoned the notion of beginning negotiations for a test ban treaty when the Russians publicly supported Stevenson's proposals—thus laying the administration open to the possibility of charges that it was not being sufficiently anti-Communist—the debate continued, as did the testing. America exploded no fewer than twenty-four bombs in Nevada in 1957. In April, Khruschev boasted that the Russians possessed a super-bomb capable of melting the polar icecap. But the impact of all of this was slight compared to the shock created by the Russian launching of the world's first satellite, *Sputnik 1,* on October 4. Clearly, if the USSR had rockets good enough to place a satellite in orbit, they were a serious threat to our security. When they followed up their feat by launching even heavier satellites, the effect was shattering.

For the first time Americans felt themselves to be in an inferior position, although in fact their atomic arsenal still enormously outweighed that of the Soviet Union. Russian proposals for some kind of a treaty began to look more attractive. Not much nuclear war fiction of significance was published in English that year (although Agawa Hiroyuki's important *Devil's Heritage* was published in Japan). In fact there was just one novel which was widely read, and it was to prove the most influential work of its kind for the next quarter of a century and the only one most people ever read: Nevil Shute's *On the Beach.*

Shute used an Australian perspective ideally situated to address the fears about fallout which had been mounting since 1954. As his novel begins, the atomic war is already over. The powerful effect which this slickly written tale had on its readers can be attributed to its insistence on the relentless, inescapable advance of the zone of radioactivity, removing all trace of human life from latitude after latitude on its way south. Inferior to the 1959 film based on it, the novel is unconvincing in its plot, its characters are stereotypes (too many of them deny the inevitable in the same way), and the love story is mawkish. But what makes *On the Beach* nevertheless one of the most compelling accounts of nuclear war ever written is its almost unique insistence that everyone—without exception—is going to die. Shute directly addresses the most primal fears of the human race, which has spent most of its history denying or compensating for the fact of personal death, and does so with a relentlessness which the complex technique of

a more sophisticated writer might have muted. For once, there are no distractions: no invading aliens, no super-fallout shelters to protect the protagonists, no struggle back from a dreadful but exciting postwar barbarism. There are simply a man and a woman reaching the agonizing decision to kill their only child in its crib and commit suicide as the rest of the human race expires around them. (pp. 17-20)

What gives [*On the Beach*] its significance is the fact that it forced the general public to focus on atomic war as a threat to personal existence at a time when there was widespread concern about fallout from testing. The experience was a harrowing one for many readers, and most of them seem to have considered it sufficient. Although many nuclear war novels superior to Shute's were to be published in succeeding years, none of them would be nearly as widely read. Its closest competitor was Pat Frank's *Alas, Babylon* in 1959, which was considered shocking in its day but which is remarkable mainly for the good fortune of its principal characters who survive nicely with only a minimum of preparation on the bare fringes of a distantly depicted holocaust.

The worldwide success of *On the Beach* finally caught the attention of mainstream writers who began to turn out holocaust novels, innocent of the fact that the theme was considered exhausted by many in the science fiction community. The year 1958 saw the publication of such works as Peter Bryant's *Two Hours to Doom* (later to be transformed into *Dr. Strangelove*), Helen Clarkson's *The Last Day,* and Mervyn Jones's *On the Last Day.* Although interest in the topic began to revive in the science fiction magazines as well, it was no longer the property of the science fiction community. In 1959 mainstream realistic works written in a serious vein dominated the field. John Brunner, who wrote mostly science fiction and who was then involved in British bomb protest activities, suggested in his political novel, *The Brink,* that Western paranoia about the Russians was more hazardous to world peace than the Russians themselves. In Britain, where left-wing politics were not absolutely beyond the pale, the novel could be marketed; but it is unique among his many books in never having been published in the United States.

During 1959 the history of the bomb was explored in Pearl S. Buck's fictional account of the Manhattan Project, *Command the Morning.* Edita Morris, like Brunner an antibomb activist, movingly depicted the impact of the bomb from the Japanese point of view in *The Flowers of Hiroshima.* Hans Hellmut Kirst's best-selling *The Seventh Day* made the escalation of a war over Germany all too credible. And in England, Mordecai Roshwald's *Level 7* made the death of the human race even more compelling than had Shute; the novel does not strive for scientific credibility but succeeds as a parable.

This was also the year in which the most nuclear war fiction of high quality appeared until 1984. It also marked the definitive end of the illusion fostered for so long in the science fiction community that the theme had been exhausted. The nuclear war science fiction of the early 1960s rose to new heights as writers took up the challenge signified by the achievements of authors in 1959, and as the field as a whole matured with the advent of a new generation of writers bent on wrenching science fiction out of the pulp ghetto. Along with a large number of inconsequential works, some important ones appeared, including Edgar Pangborn's *Davy* (1962) and Philip K. Dick's *Dr. Bloodmoney; or, How We Got Along After the Bomb* (1956). Science fiction writers may have temporarily lost their ascendancy in the nuclear war novel in the late 1950s, but they reclaimed it in the sixties and have retained it ever since.

The year 1960, marked by the U-2 incident and the Sino-Soviet split, produced few notable works other than Alfred Coppel's *Dark December* (one of the best nuclear war novels ever published) and H. A. Van Mierlo's *By Then Mankind Ceased to Exist* (probably the worst). The next year was dominated by discussion of fallout shelters in the public press, as the Russians built the Berlin Wall and resumed testing in the atmosphere, and the United States undertook its first major shelter program. Shelters both natural and artificial are prominent in the fiction published in 1961 and 1962, in works like Gina Berriault's *The Descent,* a marvelous satire on the entire civil defense craze; Daniel F. Galouye's moving *Dark Universe,* in which refugees have lived in the dark underground for so many generations that they have forgotten what light is; James White's *Second Ending,* with its fantastic automated hospital which preserves the single specimen from which the human race will be recreated; Robert Moore Williams's absurd *The Day They H-Bombed Los Angeles,* in which ordinary folks mingle with movie stars in Los Angeles fallout shelters; and George H. Smith's *The Coming of the Rats.* Novels set in various sorts of shelters had been published at intervals before this, but not in such numbers.

The Cuban missile crisis of October 1962 did not find much resonance in nuclear war fiction. After reaching the brink of a real nuclear war, most people seemed to want to forget the subject as quickly as possible; and a year later Kennedy's assassination rendered fiction which might imply criticism of his nuclear diplomacy in bad taste. Pierre Salinger did not publish his novel loosely based on the missile crisis until nearly a decade later (*On Instructions of My Government* [1971]). Out of the considerable amount of nuclear war fiction published in 1962, the most notable literary achievement was the beginning of Edgar Pangborn's *Davy* in which he created the postholocaust world in which he was to work for the rest of his life. The dangers of brinksmanship were illustrated in 1962's best-selling *Fail-Safe* by Eugene Burdick and Harvey Wheeler.

The United States, Great Britain, and the USSR finally signed a treaty banning testing in the atmosphere in 1963, and there was for a time a general easing of tensions with the Soviet Union. But all during the early sixties there arose in the West an extreme paranoia about the Chinese, no longer on the leash of the Russians, who were perceived as being far more reasonable. This paranoia finds its quintessential expression in Bernard Newman's absurd classic of Sinophobia, *The Blue Ants* (1962).

Now permanently established as a subgenre of science fiction, nuclear war stories and novels of merit continued to appear throughout the sixties from such authors as Ray

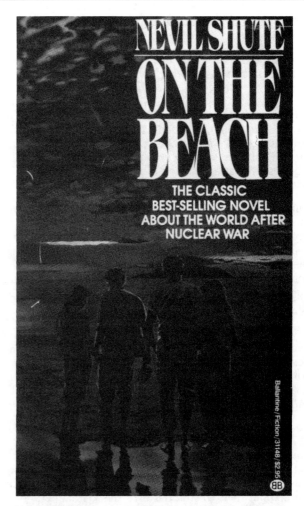

1984 book cover of Nevil Shute's On the Beach *(1947).*

Bradbury ("To the Chicago Abyss" [1963]), Philip K. Dick (*The Penultimate Truth* [1964] and *Dr. Bloodmoney*), Edgar Pangborn (besides *Davy,* mentioned above, *The Judgment of Eve* [1966]), Thomas M. Disch ("Casablanca" [1967]), and Harlan Ellison ("I Have No Mouth, and I Must Scream" [1967]), among many others. But the nuclear war science fiction of the sixties had no focus. There was no equivalent of the old *Astounding* (now retitled *Analog* and still rejecting atomic doom stories) to develop a tradition. In any case, the magazines were ceasing to play an important role in developing new themes as paperback books began to dominate the market.

The nuclear war theme flourished in the sixties at least partly because of the "New Wave" phenomenon in science fiction which involved many younger writers who were drawn to apocalyptic and anti-technological themes. They found in nuclear war the perfect expression of what disgusted them in much traditional science fiction. In the 1940s science fiction had promoted itself as prophetic and inspirational. In the 1950s it had been diagnostic and critical, but typically provided some sort of happy ending. But in the 1960s the dominant mood of much of the best writing could only be described as nihilistic. At last science fiction found a fictional voice appropriate to the nightmare of nuclear war.

As had been true since 1945, isolated individuals outside of this tradition or any other tradition passionately turned out deeply felt warnings against atomic Armageddon which went almost entirely unread. Among the better idiosyncratic sixties novels are Derek Ingrey's absurdist *Pig on a Lead* (1963), Stephen Minot's sternly intellectual anti-intellectual *Chill of Dusk* (1964), Virginia Fenwick's uneven but interesting *America R.I.P.* (1965), and John R. Vorhies's remarkable study of nuclear strategy and politics, *Pre-Empt* (1967).

Public attention was briefly captured by the antiballistic missile debate of 1969, a year which witnessed the publication of more nuclear war fiction than any other between 1965 and 1974. But throughout most of the latter sixties, the U.S. was preoccupied with Black Power, psychedelia, student protest, and—above all—Vietnam. Traditional nuclear war fiction seemed incongruent in this setting. Nuclear blackmail and sabotage novels proliferated, especially in Britain, for an audience that yearned for simpler days; but the younger generation which dominated the readership of science fiction and therefore of nuclear war fiction was absorbed in other pursuits. Few of the young American antiwar protesters knew of or cared about the earlier generation of ban-the-bomb protesters in the U.S. and Britain.

The protesters' concerns were reflected in nuclear war fiction through heavy irony in 1969 in Harlan Ellison's *A Boy and His Dog* and Norman Spinrad's "The Big Flash," but these stories were not expressions of the youth movement, merely observations on it. Authors on the Right worked out their frustrations over the Vietnam era after the youth revolt was stifled, in works such as Clive Egleton's *A Piece of Resistance* (1970) and its sequels, *Last Post for a Partisan* (1971), and *the Judas Mandate* (1972), Oliver Lange's *Vandenberg* (1971), Mario Pei's "1976" (1971), Christopher Priest's *Fugue for a Darkening Island* (1972), W. D. Pereira's *Aftermath 15* (1973), and General Sir John Hackett's *The Third World War: A Future History* (1978).

The most dyspeptic—nay, apoplectic—of these nuclear war novels which used the holocaust to berate duped, treasonous, destructive youth is Allen Drury's culmination of the series he began with *Advise and Consent,* titled *The Promise of Joy* (1975). In this delirious attack on the late antiwar movement, a courageous president battles almost alone against a spineless Congress, gruesomely violent pacifists, and a wildly leftist partisan press to defeat the Reds and avert the holocaust by negotiating from strength. If in the early sixties the rage of the young in revolt found its expression in nuclear war themes, the same themes were used in the seventies to express the rage they had aroused in their elders.

The outstanding achievements in science fiction during the seventies were James Blish's *The Day After Judgment* (1971), James Tiptree, Jr.'s "The Man Who Walked Home" (1972), Edgar Pangborn's *The Company of Glory* (1975) and *Still I Persist in Wondering* (1978), Brian Al-

diss's *The Eighty-Minute Hour* (1974), Suzy McKee Charnas's *Motherlines* (1978), and Vonda McIntyre's *Dreamsnake* (1978). It is no coincidence that half of these authors (including Tiptree, whose real name is Alice Sheldon) are women; during the seventies the women's movement profoundly influenced science fiction. Stars like Ursula Le Guin and Joanna Russ attracted unprecedented numbers of young female readers, and many outstanding women writers began using science fiction to address the concerns of a new audience profoundly influenced by feminism. Writers like Charnas and McIntyre are part of a revisionist movement within the field which has been reshaping the postholocaust landscape along with every other element in science fiction in recent years. They have concentrated in particular on rejecting the traditional misogynistic neobarbarian fantasy, an endeavor in which they have been joined by male feminist writers like Paul O. Williams (The Pelbar Cycle [1981-85]).

Aside from right-wing thrillers and science fictional treatments of the post-holocaust world, however, the last half of the seventies marked a low point in the creation of nuclear war fiction. In absolute numbers, never had so little been published since 1945. By way of an exception, one of the finest of all postholocaust novels, Russell Hoban's *Riddley Walker,* appeared in 1980 and sold well.

Not until protests in Europe and America over the deployment of new missiles and agitation for a weapons freeze reawakened public concern with the issue did nuclear war fiction began to revive, with works like Yorick Blumenfeld's *Jenny* (1981), Raymond Briggs's *When the Wind Blows* (1982), and Whitley Strieber and James Kunetka's *Warday* (1984), its title suggestive of the controversial 1983 made-for-television movie *The Day After.* The most recent development is the proliferation of right-wing adventure novels with postholocaust settings. . . . Whether the current flurry of interest in the subject can be sustained remains to be seen. The year 1984 marked the all-time high point of nuclear war fiction publishing in terms of numbers of works. The past pattern has been a sharp peak of activity followed by a decline, and 1985 saw the appearance of a somewhat smaller, though still substantial, number.

This survey would be incomplete without reference to what I consider the finest novel ever published in English depicting the consequences of nuclear war, Ibuse Masuji's *Black Rain.* Written in 1965 and translated from the Japanese in 1967, the historical event to which this work responds is the bombing of Hiroshima. Ibuse is a journalist who drew on the diary of an acquaintance and the memories of other survivors to recreate the experience of the *hibakusha,* the victims of the Hiroshima bombing. Written in an understated tone, and with a thread of subtle irony running through it, this novel is nevertheless by far the most devastating account of the effects of nuclear war ever written. The destruction, the wounds, and the effects of radiation disease are depicted in minute detail. A host of powerful images is presented: telephone poles burn like candles, lead from melted power lines has left a trail of silver droplets, a baby girl plays with her dead mother's breasts. The main psychological reaction of the victims is shock. Some try to go on about their business as usual, absurdly attempting, for instance, to report to offices which have been vaporized. The traditional modesty of Japanese women prevents many of them from seeking medical attention, as this example highlights:

> At one sundry goods store this side of Mitaki Station on the Kobe line, they had found a woman who had got in unnoticed and died in one of their closets. When the owner of the store dragged the body out, he found that the garment it was wearing was his daughter's best summer kimono. Scandalized, he had torn the best kimono off the body, only to find that it had no underwear on underneath. She must have been burned out of her home and fled all the way there naked, yet still—being a young woman—sought something to hide her nakedness even before she sought water or food.

The vast bulk of accounts of imaginary nuclear wars pales in contrast to such touching, vivid reports of human suffering. There are a number of works containing such stories: Agawa's *Devil's Heritage;* Joy Kogawa's *Obasan* (1982); Morris's *Flowers of Hiroshima* and *The Seeds of Hiroshima* (1965); Edwin Lanham's *The Clock at 8:16* (1970); and the stories collected in Oe Kenzaburo's *The Crazy Iris and Other Stories of the Atomic Aftermath* (1985). All of them are affecting, but none possesses the powerfully simple artistry of *Black Rain*. Nuclear war fiction has been written from the perspective of politicians who started it, of our descendants who may undergo it, and of investigating aliens from the distant stars; but the perspective which makes the experience a vivid reality is that adopted by Ibuse, of the real-life victims. Most other authors have written about nuclear war without really confronting it. They show how it can be prevented or survived, use it as a club to thrash a political foe, fantasize about it as a source of magic, revel in the disorder which follows in its wake, wield it to clear the way for a future utopia, or create through it a kind of nostalgic—albeit radioactive—pastoral. (pp. 20-5)

During the years of research on this book I have often been asked which works I recommend most highly. . . . Here it is appropriate to list those works with the greatest potential for political impact on readers still uninformed about or unmoved at the threat posed by the world's nuclear arsenals. Avoiding a holocaust in this sense is, after all, the most serious purpose such fiction can perform. For its persuasiveness and contemporaneity, Prochnau's book certainly ranks high on the list. No other novel is as effective in depicting the probable course of a nuclear war. In portraying the effects of fallout, no one has done a better job than Helen Clarkson in *The Last Day*. And the work which best conveys the tragedy of the destruction of civilization is Russell Hoban's *Riddley Walker*.

But if I were to single out one work which should be read with attention by persons concerned with nuclear war, it would be Masuji Ibuse's *Black Rain*. No writer has more affectingly depicted the human tragedy that is nuclear warfare. Nuclear deterrence remains an acceptable policy of national defense largely because of the failure of imagination which our leaders willfully impose on themselves.

The cloud of "nukespeak" which surrounds the atomic arms debate obscures the reality of the danger confronting us. Creative writers like Ibuse make the abstractions of the scenario writers concrete and remind us that nuclear war cannot be other than a crime against humanity and against the Earth itself. Blunted by decades of professional jargon and simple avoidance of the topic, the best of the fiction writers can reawaken our sensitivity to the holocaust that has loomed over the horizon for the past four decades and which threatens to shadow the future of our children unless we are stirred, at last, to do something to prevent it. (pp. 93-4)

> *Paul Brians, "The History of the Holocaust," and "Avoiding the Holocaust," in his* Nuclear Holocausts: Atomic War in Fiction, 1895-1984, *The Kent State University Press, 1987, pp. 1-26, 83-94.*

David Dowling on the value of nuclear war literature:

If the creation of fictions about nuclear disaster is so difficult, one may ask, why bother? Such fictions are not to be valued for their predictive value, to be put away safely like Orwell's *1984* once the dread year is past. Nor are they essentially polemical, dire warnings for moral rearmament; fictions which do attempt these ends risk trivialising the very calamity they wish to warn against. No, their value lies in the notion of maturity. . . . They are the means whereby an adolescent humanity—that is to say, unperfected, unfulfilled—can wisely consider the essential qualities of humanness, under the most challenging conditions of personal and public crisis, in the grandest spiritual (good and evil) and secular (time past and time future) terms.

Although they are about endings and change, nuclear fictions have that sense of an ending, as Frank Kermode argues, which is of crucial relevance to us, people living in the 'middest.'

> *David Dowling, in his* Fictions of Nuclear Disaster, *Macmillan, 1987.*

Peter Schwenger

[In the following excerpt, Schwenger examines nuclear fiction's ability to address the phenomenon of "psychic numbing"—a reaction to a severe threat that results in decreased sensitivity—by anticipating the reader's response and utilizing a variety of narrative techniques.]

It was a novel, among other things, which originated the atomic bomb. H. G. Wells dedicated *the World Set Free*, published in 1913, to Frederick Soddy, a pioneer in the exploration of radioactivity. Using Soddy's research as a base, Wells predicted the advent of artificial radioactivity in 1933, the year in which it actually took place; and he foresaw its use for what he named the "atomic bomb." In Wells' novel these bombs are used in a world war that erupts in mid-century and is so catastrophic that a world government is formed, initiating a new age powered by the peaceful use of the atom. The physicist Leo Szilard, a long-time admirer of Wells, read this novel in 1932, the year before he first intuited the possibility of a nuclear chain reaction. The novel seems to have become part of his own mental chain reaction, one that took place at an almost unconscious level during the spring that Szilard spent at the Strand Palace Hotel in London, by his own admission doing nothing. He would only monopolize the bath from around nine to twelve in the morning, since "there is no place as good to think as a bathtub." The theories that resulted from this prolonged immersion were introduced by references to Wells; and Szilard, having realized the atomic bomb, spent the rest of his life trying to realize the world government which, in the Wells novel, was its consequence.

Literature, which was part of the genesis of nuclear weaponry, continues to be an inextricable aspect of its nature. For [Jacques] Derrida, in fact, we are facing

> a phenomenon whose essential feature is that of being *fabulously textual,* through and through. Nuclear weaponry depends, more than any weaponry in the past, it seems, upon structures of information and communication, structures of language, including nonvocalizable language, structures of codes and graphic decoding. But the phenomenon is fabulously textual also to the extent that, for the moment, a nuclear war has not taken place: one can only talk and write about it.

The linguistic nature of the arms race, of peace talks and negotiations, has been thoroughly analyzed. Likewise there is a growing number of books on the nature of nuclear war. But there is also a growing body of novels, poems, and plays making up a literature of nuclear holocaust. As the example of Wells' novel shows, this is not altogether unprecedented; nuclear literature predates Hiroshima. But the subject of nuclear war has, up till now, mainly served the purposes of science fiction; only rarely—as in the cases of *A Canticle for Leibowitz* and *On the Beach*—have science fiction authors risen above the lowest common denominator of that genre. In the 1980s, every year sees the publication of works which demand serious attention both as literature and as fictive strategies for comprehending a subject that is commonly called "unthinkable." Russell Hoban's *Riddley Walker,* Bernard Malamud's *God's Grace,* Maggie Gee's *The Burning Book,* Tim O'Brien's *Nuclear Age*—these works explicitly preoccupied with nuclear holocaust may be supplemented by other works of the eighties with a persistent apocalyptic undertone, works such as Doris Lessing's *Canopus in Argos* series, Umberto Eco's *Name of the Rose,* and Mario Vargas Llosa's *War of the End of the World.* And these are only the literary manifestations of a widespread movement in all the arts aimed at expressing the dominant condition of our time.

What we are seeing is a break in the state of suspended emotion that has endured for forty years, a state which Robert Jay Lifton has called "numbing." This lack of an adequate response to the possibility of nuclear warfare is perfectly explicable. To begin with,

> we would rather avoid looking at events that, by

their very nature, must change us and our relation to the world. We prefer to hold on to our presuppositions and habits of personal and professional function. And we may well sense that seriously studying such an event means being haunted by it from then on, taking on a lifelong burden of responsibility to it.

If we can overcome this reluctance to think about the subject, being willing does not mean that we are able: nuclear war is unthinkable in one sense because none of the images that characterize our previous experiences is adequate to this one. What images we can come up with are so painful, so unacceptable, that they, or the emotions associated with them, are blocked; and this, properly speaking, is the numbing phenomenon. . . . [Lifton notes that one] pays a high psychic price for this emotional defense system:

> When numbing occurs, the symbolizing process—the flow and recreation of images and forms—is interrupted. And in its extreme varieties, numbing itself becomes a symbolic death: One freezes in the manner of certain animals facing danger, becomes as if dead in order to prevent actual physical or psychic death.

What, then, accounts for the current release from the numbing that has lasted so long? It would be easy to argue that it arises from the sense of urgency provoked by recent escalations in the arms race; literature responds with, in Wallace Stevens' words, "a violence from within that protects us from a violence without." But given the fact that numbing arises precisely because of the magnitude of the felt threat, an increase in magnitude should only reinforce the numbing. George Steiner suggests another reason, finding the very time period to be significant: "Psychologists tell us that there is a critical period before which you simply cannot endure or recollect what you have experienced. After thirty or forty years, not only can you begin to, but perhaps you have to, in order to come to some kind of peace with yourself." Steiner is here speaking not of nuclear holocaust but of the Jewish Holocaust; and indeed the Jewish Holocaust provides the only body of literature—and, increasingly, of literary theory—which is at all comparable to the evolving body of nuclear holocaust literature. "Fictions are for finding things out," Frank Kermode has said, "and they change as the needs of sensemaking change." In somewhat the same way as an "aesthetics of atrocity" has evolved, is evolving, to meet the terrible need of the Holocaust, so a new aesthetic is evolving now. Experimental, pluralistic, it must resort to more strategies than one to accommodate its complex subject.

Of these strategies, it might be claimed that the documentary form is most true to the subject; one Holocaust critic maintains that it "preserves a kind of sacred attitude toward broad historical processes that precludes . . . artistic 'interference.' " But this is not, cannot be, the case: there is no such thing as a purely factual narrative, viewed through an innocent eye. The traditional problem of "point of view," indeed, assumes boggling proportions when the subject is nuclear holocaust. "The right vantage point from which to view a holocaust is that of a corpse," says Jonathan Schell, "but from that vantage point, of course, there is nothing to report." Nor would any individual report be adequate: a holocaust is characterized by what Yeats called "the emotion of multitude." Two documentary treatments, John Hersey's *Hiroshima* and James Kunetka and Whitley Streiber's *Warday,* try to resolve this problem by an *accumulation* of individual points of view. Of the two, Hersey's is the more honest about the inadequacies of its form, as can be seen in a comparison of endings. *Warday* cannot resist a final interpretation of its imagined documents in a moralizing, classical act of closure: "If only we have gained wisdom from the fire. If only we can accept how alike we all are, one and another." Hersey's book ends not with his own words but with the words of a document, a schoolboy essay on the events of 6 August 1945 as a child remembers them. To this child the pleasurable spectacle of a burning gas tank across the river is as memorable as the news of a neighbor's death; and he commemorates each with a sentence, only adding a conventional "Alas" to the latter. The inadequacy of the boy's words reflects on the inadequacy of *any* words to evoke a full emotional comprehension of this subject. When my students read Hersey's book they emerge from the experience with a kind of survivor's guilt: it makes them uneasy that they do not feel more, that they are not changed. They feel better when it is pointed out to them that even those who lived through the bombing of Hiroshima returned as soon as possible to the old pattern of their lives, summing up the experience with the Japanese equivalent of "it can't be helped." At the moment of the catastrophe itself, the citizens of Hiroshima were no more enlightened. There are many descriptions of the numbed state of the survivors, Dr. Michihiko Hachiya's [*Hiroshima Diary,* 1955], for instance:

> Outsiders . . . reported with amazement the spectacle of long files of people holding stolidly to a narrow, rough path when close by was a smooth, easy road going in the same direction. The outsiders could not grasp the fact that they were witnessing the exodus of a people who walked in the realm of dreams.

Perhaps one's numbness to catastrophe while it is happening and the numbness with which one sees catastrophe approach are not utterly different things. In our inability to comprehend nuclear disaster we are united with the people who lived it.

Grasping at documentary for the sense of something solid, we are only returned to ourselves and to the central problem of nuclear holocaust literature, that of reader response. The problem has been central to visions of the end from the beginning, but is peculiarly intensified in this version of apocalypse; for the defining feature of a nuclear holocaust, the one that sets it apart from its apocalyptic predecessors, is that this apocalypse is man-made. It is not part of a divine plan, nor of any order of things larger than the human. The individual, then, is not free from the suspicion of complicity, responsibility, and guilt. Even hope becomes a burden when it must evoke action. The pain of complicity added to the pain of fear and loss gives new intensity to a classical aporia of apocalyptic texts: the paradoxical relationship between the pleasure and the pain which the reader feels. As a text, an apocalypse must give some version of the pleasure of the text; yet how can a

reader respond with pleasure to such a painful subject? If the text does succeed in giving pleasure, it is surely perverting, distorting the painful reality of its subject. If it does not succeed, the reader recoils from that painful reality in the rejection strategies of numbing.

The aesthetic which addresses itself precisely to this paradox is that of the sublime.

> The sublime, as observers like Burke and Kant and Schopenhauer insist, arises from terror, terror beheld and resisted, the terror of revolution for Wordsworth, of the abyss for Whitman, of nuclear annihilation for any poet today who would make a language to match our extremity.

Terrence des Pres' version here can be countered by Frances Ferguson's "nuclear sublime," which is less a matter of resistance than of recognition—and what is recognized is our own attraction to nuclear annihilation. "To think the sublime would be to think the unthinkable and to exist in one's own nonexistence," claims Ferguson. "Thus when Schiller describes suicide . . . as the inevitable outcome of the logic of the sublime, he is of course right." Moreover, in pursuing this logic to its end, one rids oneself not only of the burden of one's own existence but of the claustrophobic burden of the existence of others; for "the existence of other people seems like an accident that has befallen us." This is a justification of nuclearism in terms of an "egotistical sublime": sublimity is translated to a self-destroying egotism, and then the claims of the ego, even against the "unborn," are argued. This explains the pleasure we take in contemplating apocalypse, though it does so unpleasantly.

The merit of such a theory is that it does not allow us to deny the element of attraction in nuclear holocaust, an element which has also been expressed in an evil little poem by Alia Johnson:

Why We Should Drop the Bombs

it would be so exciting
it would be so powerful
it would punish us for our sins
things wouldn't be so boring anymore
we could get back to basics
we would remember who we love
it would be so loud
it would be so hot
the mushroom clouds would rise up
we could start over
we wouldn't have to be afraid of it anymore
we wouldn't have to be afraid anymore
we would finally have done it
    better than Raskolnikov
it would release our anger
    in the ultimate tantrum
then we could rest

Each of the items on this list of "reasons" is capable of extensive exegesis: the "hard survivalism," with its promise of purification and return to fundamentals; a different kind of fundamentalism which views nuclear holocaust in religious terms; and [as the editor of *Diacritics* writes] the potent force of boredom, "the deep-seated boredom of an alienated public that dreams of debris, of swallowing the world with a yawn." Such a public is attracted to the subject of nuclear holocaust because of its "thrill"—a twitch that momentarily galvanizes deadened sensibilities. Eventually this strategy too lapses into another form of numbness: "The stereotypes of nuclear destruction, like the proliferative figure of the mushroom cloud, aim to make us forget by their mechanical repetition the reality they are supposed to designate. . . ." Emerging from Johnson's list is above all the tyranny of the unconscious, of that part of the unconscious which has been created by the nuclear peril. Anger finds expression in the very act whose suspended and prolonged threat created that anger in the first place. In a typical movement of reader response to this subject, the process is circular and paradoxical. Equally paradoxical is the fact that attraction to the pleasures of nuclear holocaust and revulsion from its pains both find their resolution in a form of numbness. A literature of nuclear holocaust must encompass the full circle of these responses without lapsing into this perverse still point. Literature must not be anodyne; its true function, as Kafka knew, is to awaken.

Arthur Kopit's *End of the World* not only anticipates the full range of reader responses; those responses are its subject. The play is about a playwright, Michael Trent, who is approached by a wealthy patron to write a play about the nuclear arms race—as Kopit himself was approached in the spring of 1981. We watch Trent's attempts to find out the "truth" about nuclear weaponry; we watch his confusion, dismay, and resistance to the process. The play is then about the difficulties of writing about this subject or, indeed, of formulating any response to it. Trent becomes the audience's stand-in. His assignment, and ours, is given by the patron, Philip Stone: "What I have come to know, on my own, you must somehow come to know on your own, as well. . . ." This difficult task is made easier for us by Kopit's dramatic strategies. Tongue in cheek, he presents his playwright in the mode of a private detective, more Philip Marlowe than Christopher. This conventional mode is reassuring to the audience, as the play's subject, and title, are not. At the same time the detective story is, according to Umberto Eco, the most metaphysical and philosophical of the model plots, with scope for investigation in its fullest sense. Trent's private-eye posture has a comic effect which is only one of many in the play. The absurd paradoxes of nuclear "deterrence" become occasions for hilarity rather than existential despair. Leaking laughter all the way, the play proceeds to its end. There, after numerous instances of comic catharsis, enough of the audience's tensions have been dissipated so that they can hear two long monologues in succession, by Stone and Trent. Stone's description of his reactions to witnessing an atomic bomb test is paralleled by Trent's memory of an impulse to drop his infant son from a highrise apartment window. Both recognize in themselves the capacity for evil (to use an old-fashioned word); both understand that the nature of their *response* to that recognition is what can make a difference. The play thus fulfills its stated purpose, of enabling the audience to "believe what they know."

A basic strategy for overcoming the problems of reader response to the subject of nuclear holocaust is to situate readers in a position of Olympian detachment. Here, rather than being overwhelmed by the subject matter, they can take comfort in knowing more than the characters they observe; and in this way, too, they are enabled to "believe what they know." This is the strategy of Raymond Briggs' highly effective *When the Wind Blows*. Nuclear holocaust is presented in the least threatening of conventions, that of the comic strip. The unusually small frames both distance us from the characters and emphasize the ludicrous littleness of their preoccupations and of their idea of what is happening to them. What is happening to them is represented by double-page spreads depicting nuclear weaponry—looming, in this context, on a gigantic scale—and finally a nuclear explosion, which literally shatters all frames. It does not, however, shatter the characters' faith that the system will make it all come out right if they only do the Correct Thing. And so, all unknowing, they settle into the long business of dying. The inadequate understanding of these people is savagely satirized as unwittingly complicit in the death of the world; at the same time, it is tenderly cherished as an affirmation of life on the purely human scale. Readers witness a kind of massacre of the innocents; and distance allows them to feel pity and rage on behalf of these little people where they are unable to feel these emotions on their own behalf.

This basic strategy, with some complex variations, is that of Maggie Gee's *The Burning Book*. The novel is a family chronicle, whose generations are "small" people, innocents. As a chronicle it is a study of time, and of the looming threat of the end of time—or at least of chronicles. The threat invades even the temporal form of the novel, as voices from the future and elsewhere in the present interrupt the narrative line.

> *with such a hubbub outside, great cracks appear in my novel* other novels do better, build us a paper home

Yet these cracks, these intrusions into the conventional narrative of people's lives, are the real subject of the novel. They foreshadow nuclear war's ultimate and final intrusion into the world. For the "book" of the title is a microcosm, a fictive model of the world. Gee's book, as a physical object, is its own most powerful metaphor: the effect of nuclear holocaust is as unthinkable as the coming of real fire to the pages of a fictive world consumed by it.

One's response to the characters of any narrative is also a response to the nature of narrative itself, which shapes character in time: "We spend our years as a tale that is told," says the psalmist. The verse would make an apt motto for *God's Grace*. "This is that story," Malamud begins, admitting the familiarity of apocalypse in general and our prolonged anticipation of nuclear apocalypse in particular. Actually the book is a number of stories, each shaping the life of the central character. Primarily it is the narrative of Calvin Cohn, lone survivor of the apocalyptic story. Attempting to begin anew on an island with a remnant of simian survivors, he finds his plan undermined and destroyed as the monkeys replay the patterns of human evil. But besides being the story of Calvin Cohn, *God's Grace* is also, plainly, a Robinsonade; it is also the story of Romeo and Juliet, transposed to Cohn and a female chimpanzee named Mary Madelyn; above all it is the story of Abraham and Isaac, which Kierkegaard used to call in question comfortable Christian notions of the relationship between man and God. God here is Author, the maker of all stories, enamored of beginnings and endings; he is "made of words." So language is, in Lacanian terms, the "Name of the Father." And yet another story that recurs throughout the book is the primordial story of the father, that of Oedipal rivalry: it is sexual jealousy which initiates the downfall of Cohn's ordered island. Castration is replaced here by another symbolic wound. Cohn as vengeful father punishes his rebellious adopted son, the monkey Buz, by snipping the wires in the monkey's throat which give him the power of speech. Those wires have been implanted before the apocalypse in an operation performed by the scientist Walther Bünder, another father figure to Buz. And in the last scene of the book, the Abraham-Isaac story is perversely replayed: Buz cuts the throat of Cohn, now a white-bearded patriarch looking much like conventional portrayals of God. The wound in the throat is a central image in this story about the power of speech, the power to make stories. For Malamud, nuclear holocaust raises problems that are as much literary as theological; indeed, one becomes the other.

Both Gee and Malamud, then, construct their works to call into question the notion of "story"—or that notion is called into question from the beginning by the subject matter, which baffles conventional narrative structures. All such structures depend on an ultimate revelation; what motivates the reader of what Barthes calls classical "readerly texts" is the expectation of the end, with its final revelation of meaning. When we recall that apocalypse *means* "revelation," we see that all such readerly texts are in this sense apocalyptic. Moreover, the plenitude of that revelation is inevitably connected with death, for only with death is the meaning of a life summed up. Thus for Walter Benjamin the reader's desire for meaning is a desire for the central character's death or, at least, that figurative death which is the novel's end.

In the light of these apocalyptic overtones in the conventional narrative, it is ironic that a narrative of nuclear holocaust can provide no apocalypse at all, no revelation. When the people of Hiroshima were discussing plans for a memorial at the site of ground zero, one survivor suggested leaving a large empty space around the place where the bomb struck, a representation of nothingness—"because that is what there was." Nuclear holocaust is what Derrida calls the "wholly unimaginable other"; it is for this reason that he recognizes in it the underlying paradigm of deconstruction, trace without truth: "it is thus the only ineffaceable truth, it is so as the trace of what is entirely other. . . ." In this view Barthes' distinctions collapse and *all* literature becomes not apocalyptic but nuclear narrative. "Literature belongs to this nuclear epoch," Derrida asserts. "Literature has always belonged to the nuclear epoch." It is useful, however, to maintain Barthes' distinctions, to maintain any distinctions from this final and empty common denominator, even if this is and always will be the referent. Derrida again: "Literature and literary criticism cannot speak of anything else, they can have no other ultimate referent, they can only multiply their strategic maneuvers in order to assimilate that unassimilable wholly other." But it is precisely those strategies which are ultimately more interesting than the ultimate, because they tell us something about our own human nature. If these strategies are far from full apocalyptic revelation, they are nevertheless revealing.

Underlying all strategies is the desire for *postponement.* "Words beat on against death," writes Maggie Gee, as she resolutely refuses to end her *Burning Book.* Arms talks have helped us to feel that words are there to stave off an ultimate action. Like Scheherazade, the writer is continually postponing an anticipated end—has always done so, even before the nuclear age. The whole classic array of plot devices—obstacles, withheld knowledge, reversals of fortune, and so on—can be seen as a series of delaying tactics to hold in suspense an ending which the reader anticipates almost from the beginning. The connection of that ending to apocalypse has already been mentioned. Frank Kermode goes further to see parallels between the delays and diversions of plot and the tendency in folk apocalypse for the end of the world to be announced and then postponed. An example is the use of peripeteia ("a falsification of expectation so that the end comes as expected, but not in the manner expected"):

> Peripeteia depends on our confidence of the end; it is a disconfirmation followed by a consonance; the interest of having our expectations falsified is obviously related to our wish to reach the discovery or recognition by an unexpected and instructive route. . . . In assimilating the peripeteia we are enacting that readjustment of expectations in regard to an end which is so notable a feature of naïve apocalyptic.

At the same time, the plot's flexibility in relation to its anticipated ending may serve another purpose: "We concern ourselves with the conflict between the deterministic pattern any plot suggests, and the freedom of persons within that plot to choose and so to alter the structure, the relations of beginning, middle, and end." Again, it is conventional narrative which is being spoken of here. When the narrative being analyzed in these terms is a nuclear one, the theory is curiously transformed.

Nevil Shute's *On the Beach* shows such a transformation in the writing of a conventional novelist. Devices like peripeteia or the withholding of knowledge which Barthes calls "reticence" become ironic in this context. The peripeteia here is the round-trip voyage by a submarine to check on an erratic radio transmission from a North America which has been devastated by nuclear war. When it is found that the transmission key is being pressed by a Coke bottle tangled in a window cord, it is less a reversal of expectations than a confirmation of them. As for reticences, those of the opening ("What war? What has happened?") are quickly replaced by the reticences of the characters themselves. In the epigraph, taken from T. S. Eliot's *The Hollow Men,* "we grope together and avoid speech." The fundamental tension of the novel is that between the novel's words—which implicitly offer the hope of postponement, a space of time during which a meaning can be found—and the characters' agreement (unspoken, of course) that words are to be avoided. A spare style, similar to Hemingway's, reinforces a code like his, in which talking, with its danger of emotional release, is always to be guarded against. Moira Davidson, the most vital character in the novel, breaks down at the end of the first chapter; in the following chapters she learns to suppress such behavior. She learns this above all from her platonic love affair with Dwight Towers, an American submarine captain whose leading characteristic is his lack of imagination, even when confronted with the end of the world. He is oriented only toward his duty and his death; and death he sees in terms of going "home," by which he means his now destroyed home in Mystic, Connecticut. His goal, like that of all the inhabitants of radiation-threatened Australia, is death with dignity—but also with passivity. If the characters succeed in controlling their passions it is, as Blake would point out, because those passions are weak enough to be controlled. This is doubtless another blessing of a lack of imagination. Alternative attitudes or strategies do not suggest themselves. The one scientist whose theories hold out hope is not merely disproved; he is disapproved of from the start. The characters within the novel are wary of any suggestion of flexibility in the deterministic plot; the lesson they are bent on teaching themselves is that no freedom is possible in the face of their nuclear fate.

On the Beach is plainly a study of the numbing phenomenon; it is a projection past a future holocaust of the kind of attitude that precedes one. Endings are of course often projections of middles, of the *medias res* that is our life now. And this may be another reason why a novel such as this can provide no final revelation, nor even a new one. The entire novel is a postponement followed by a confirmation, confirming a complex of psychological factors which are only those already possessed by the readers. The condition of postponement which underlies the whole novel is utilized by the characters not to achieve a new sense of meaning, but to canonize the old patterns. Death becomes a duty to be performed by the characters with no more and no less of a sense of ritual than has attended all the duties of their lives.

Postponement, then, is used very differently in Shute's novel and in Gee's. *On the Beach* uses postponement only to give the characters time to acquiesce. In *The Burning Book* the characters have no time to acquiesce, even if they had the inclination; all the postponement is on the readers' behalf, so that they, not the characters, can evolve a meaning *before* the anticipated holocaust. Yet the sense of meaning finally inheres in the characters, and in the small-scale dramas of their ordinary lives. These dramas have a narrative element, one which is finally nullified by the blast: people are not allowed to finish their stories. Narrative time is played against nuclear holocaust, which is the abolition of time. This sense of interruption renders Gee's novel again different from Shute's, where people numb themselves into a continuity with their past lives which is at the same time a continuity with the slow approach of their death-laden future. Narrative time in Shute has become pure interim, defined and measured by the rate of radioactive drift.

The narrative time of both Shute's and Gee's books is un-

usual for nuclear novels, most of which are set well after a nuclear holocaust. To deal with such a holocaust in the present poses all the difficulties that have already been indicated; and to deal with the past which precedes that terrible present is merely to find ourselves in our own present, with all its imaginative difficulties in comprehending our nuclear condition. Situated in a future beyond the end, we are presented with a world whose objects and inhabitants function as metaphors, allowing the imagination to grasp through the tangible something that would otherwise be unthinkable. Moreover, the express activity of the inhabitants of a postnuclear world is often to decipher the nature of the catastrophe—which is our activity too. Such, to various degrees, are *Warday, Fiskadoro, A Canticle for Leibowitz*, and *Riddley Walker*. The last two are examples of another temporal structure which even more explicitly connects this projected future to our present condition: circularity. What E. M. Forster called the "unlovely worm of time" puts its tail in its mouth to yield not so much a world without end as a world that is always ending.

Circularity provides both structure and theme in *Riddley Walker*. Through the eyes of its twelve-year-old narrator, the novel depicts England a thousand years after what is simply referred to as "Bad Time." This world is most like a Neolithic one, or the darkest of the Dark Ages. In the course of the novel gunpowder is rediscovered—the "One Little One" as opposed to the "One Big One" which resulted in Bad Time. That too, it is implied, will come again, further along the temporal circle. The spatial circle here is the ring of eight settlements surrounding Canterbury—or Cambry, as it is now called. "Fools Circel 9wys," a children's rhyme and game of the time, sums up the journey which Riddley actually takes. Fugitive and outcast, he must traverse the circle and its center—Cambry, which so long ago was ground zero. In Riddley's day, as in ours, that dead center represents everything that is unknowable. Yet Riddley, "Fool" that he is, attempts to know it. He attempts to unravel the riddle of the central myth of his culture, the so-called Eusa story, in which the reader recognizes—though with some confusion—events from the time of a nuclear holocaust.

Riddley's activity, and that of the reader, is hermeneutic. Indeed, for the reader the difficulty of deciphering meaning begins with the very language of the book, which is a curious combination of slang, street argot, and debased terminology from a dead computer culture. Moreover, all this is written in a phoneticized spelling, so that the reader is slowed down and often forced to speak aloud what is on the page in order to make sense of it. The novel thus illustrates Derrick de Kerckhove's provocative theory that the bomb, by fragmenting established patterns of meaning, is pushing us toward a preliterate sensibility. What words there are, in Riddley Walker's world, are not trusted to convey meaning even by those who use them: "Some times theres mor in the emty paper nor there is when you get the writing down on it." So silence involuntarily replaces words in Riddley's first "tell," as he steps into his dead father's role of "connexion man" for his settlement—the official interpreter of the connections between things. As Riddley later launches into his new life as an outcast, he is still trying to make connections, but the only truth he finds is that expressed by the old Eusa story: "Lukin for the 1 yu wil aul ways fyn thay 2." So throughout the book the old mythic symbols are continually dividing into new meanings as they emerge in new contexts. And from this fission of meanings results a hermeneutic fool's circle with, at its center, something unspeakable, unknowable: "the idear of us." There is no way to intuit that idea except by traveling the circle—or, in the terms of the Eusa story, by going through all one's changes.

> Eusa sed . . . Woan yu pleas tel me how menne Chaynjis thayr ar? The Littl Man sed, As menne as reqwyrd. Eusa sed, Reqwyrd by wut? The Littl Man sed, Reqwyrd by the idear uv yu. Eusa sed, Wut is the idear uv me? The Littl Man sed, That we doan no til yuv gon thru aul yur Chaynjis.

Riddley Walker is thus a novel whose ultimate revelation is about nonrevelation. It admits that the question of the bomb is bound up with the whole question of man's nature, and it gives us the courage to endure the process of questioning. The "chaynjis" that we go through in coming to terms with the bomb and with ourselves will be many; all are inadequate for understanding the ground zero of our existence. Yet, as with all the fictive strategies considered here, the points on this Fool's Circle may imply its center.

What I am saying is perhaps only the obvious: that any art of nuclear holocaust must proceed by implication—must "by indirections find directions out." The true subject of such an art is not the bomb itself but its psychological penumbra. Within this we live, neither free of the shadow of the bomb nor finally confronted with it. Uneasy, uncomprehending, we find its diffuse horror seeping into our unconscious and even into the texture of our daily life. De Kerckhove refers to

> the psychological fallout of the nuclear technology: shock, numbing, denial, fear, helplessness, aggression, narcissism, fetishism, assimilation, transformation. . . . It is precisely because the bomb has been imagined for so long as a mere object, that so few people have perceived it as an information environment. And yet, as it penetrated to ever deeper recesses of our unconscious, it was informing deep-seated feelings and attitudes.

We sense what is happening to us only at moments, moments whose evanescent content has traditionally been caught by the lyric. And so we have a proliferation of lyric poems about this subject, which often capture the subtle tremor of catastrophe at the edge of our ordinary vision. William Stafford and Leonard Nathan, for instance, repeatedly write on the subject. Their approach is summed up by Nathan:

> What we cannot imagine but know somehow to be true—like death or the possibility of nuclear war—affects us in ways that are hard to define because the effects are often indirect, as when otherwise harmless objects terrorize us in dreams and leave behind echoes of the same terror when we awaken. Indirection seems to be the

only unhysterical way we can deal with the terrible but true. That is why perhaps the best modern poetry about death and cataclysm is indirect.

These indirections are necessary in part because of the privileged position of the subject in the innermost recesses of our minds. The "sacred attitude" held toward the Jewish Holocaust is prematurely and inappropriately applied to nuclear holocaust as well. [Lifton writes:]

> Our sense is that a force capable of *destroying* human history must not be of it but beyond it. Similarly, weapons that can obliterate virtually all of human mind . . . seem to us to be, in Otto Rank's term, "beyond psychology." The weapons so encompass us and diminish us as to seem not of us but to have entered our realm mysteriously from somewhere "outside" and "beyond."

So, only a few decades after its birth, the bomb has become mythologized. In novels such as *A Canticle for Leibowitz* and *Riddley Walker* such mythologizing is carried out literally, as complex myths are constructed around an historical nuclear war. Whenever this is done in a nuclear narrative, it serves a number of purposes. First, it creates a specific form for our vague sense of sacred terror, providing a vehicle adequate to its expression and, perhaps, its catharsis. Second, it allows us to see the mythologizing process at work, usually in retrospect, which is a process that most of us have assented to without choice or even awareness. Finally, and as a consequence, it demystifies the process, both the one within the novel and by extension the one which has already taken place in our minds. That process is somewhat like mummifying and produces as awesome an aspect. If we unwind the wrappings one by one, we eventually see a human face, perhaps only our own.

Most of the works I have discussed here do not dictate a response to the nuclear threat so much as they make response possible. Imagining, as best we can, what might lie in the future has left us with little more than numbness. But the literature of nuclear holocaust shows that the same imagination which presents to us unendurable possibilities may also help us to endure—not to endure a holocaust but our anticipations of one, our fears and even our hopes. Diffuse as these may be, inchoate denizens of our unconscious, they are nevertheless real. They are among the realities of our existence quite as much as, or more than, the warheads we have never seen. Our task now is, in Martin Buber's phrase, "to imagine the real." And this must mean not only to comprehend a world poised for nuclear annihilation but also to comprehend our responses to this fact. Among Blake's *Proverbs of Hell* is this one: "What is now proved was once only imagin'd." We have seen this in the case of Wells and Szilard and the first atom bomb; we might see it in the case of a nuclear war, if there are any of us left to do the seeing. But we might also see another kind of reality, the kind that is beginning to unfold itself from our imaginations at this time. De Kerckhove, for one, sees the continual pressure of the bomb's presence in our lives as a force for change. If the imagination is pushed into going through all of its changes, in Riddley Walker's terms, the whole idea of us might change as well. For de Kerckhove, "The psychic end of the bomb will be reached when the whole culture is so completely transformed that it is structured for integration rather than for its present trend of disintegration." As much as anything else, it will be the literary imagination that determines whether this "psychic end" is reached, or the other one. (pp. 33-48)

Peter Schwenger, "Writing the Unthinkable," in Critical Inquiry, Vol. 13, No. 1, Autumn, 1986, pp. 33-48.

Michael Dorris and Louise Erdrich

[*An American educator, novelist, poet, and critic, Dorris is also an anthropologist who specializes in Native-American culture. Erdrich is an American novelist, poet, and short story writer best known for her novels* Love Medicine *(1984),* The Beet Queen *(1986), and* Tracks *(1988), in which she explored her Chippewa heritage. In the following essay, which was originally published as "Bangs and Whimpers: Novelists at Armageddon" in the* New York Times Book Review *in 1988, they examine the different ways authors have depicted post-nuclear society.*]

Faced with extinction, we imagine reprieve. The 19th-century Paiute prophet Wovoka postulated that through the revitalization of ancient beliefs and through the newly begun practice of the Ghost Dance, military defeat, slaughtered buffalo herds and cultural genocide could be exchanged for a utopia guided by traditional values of co-operation and moderation. The devastating history of European invasion and dominance were, these Indians desperately theorized, but a test of their faith, a punishment for assimilation, a catalyst through which the past might become the future. For both the individual and the tribe, hope of continuity was an antidote to annihilation, and there was a dream life accessible beyond the apparent destruction of the familiar world.

Living with the menace of instant, global, nuclear war, many people today feel vulnerable to an analogous threat of extinction. But ours is still an abstract apprehension; we do not rely upon exhaustion-induced trances to see past the immediacy of our fragile mortality and connect with prospective alter egos and descendants. In the years since Aug. 6, 1945, writers of fiction have repeatedly and variously attempted to conceive a future beyond an Armageddon which, if and when it comes, is guaranteed to exact casualties on a scale beyond precedent, beyond comprehension. In a range that parallels the theoretical grapplings of scientists and the machinations of politicians, these novels as a group are a curious mixture of facile hopefulness and utter nihilism of myopia and experimentation.

Some of the earliest work displays a curious fascination of the inconvenience that middle-class Caucasians may suffer in the war's aftermath. There is a touch of *The Swiss Family Robinson* in the resourceful, determined postattack inhabitants of Pat Frank's *Alas, Babylon!* (1959). As short supplies and broken communications are countered with backwoods folklore, a little girl must wait to flush her toilet after every use until the pump of the artesian well is hooked up to an improvised generator. A Westchester maid is forced to stand in food lines at a suburban supermarket in Judith Merril's *Shadow on the Hearth* (1950). War seems awful not so much because of massive anonymous death tolls heard on emergency frequency broadcasts, but, because the tidy structure of a "Leave It to Beaver" world is disrupted, women may take charge of governments or repair a gas leak, while men find it impossible to contact their brokers.

Adversity, however, sometimes cleanses. Since the breach between yesterday and tomorrow in these books is only a millisecond of fission and fusion, materialistic preoccupations seem to melt in the firestorm's blast, and a core of red-white-and-blue basics solidifies. Characters experience loss, but after the smoke clears, husbands return or widows are provided with new mates. Only unadaptive, greedy people or faceless urban masses actually perish.

The Last Day (1959) by Helen Clarkson and *On the Beach* (1957) by Nevil Shute are distinctive in their rejection of cozy survivalist endings. Their scale is personal, their gaze unblinking. Protagonists mourn the death of their own children, and thus the symbolic extinction of humanity. They have the vision of no vision, imagine a world empty of human consciousness. Slow, inexorable radiation sickness, like the invisible societal psychosis that led to war in the first place, terminates all plucky short-term solutions, and the world ends in a sea of old newspapers blowing down deserted streets.

In 1987, Carolyn See's *Golden Days* continued this before-and-after convention, but with greater optimism. In a New Age view of female toughness and regeneration, Ms. See creates a heroine, Edith Langley, who has battled sexism to achieve financial security and identity, and damn well isn't going to roll over and die just because of atomic holocaust. She hunkers down, literally embodies her past by encrusting herself with her own jewels, and changes everything except her own resolve. Her recollections become protectively selective and she endures. "What if," she offers, "we tried to remember John Donne and the Rolling Stones and driving the car with the radio on, and lying on clean sheets with perfect bodies looking out at palm fronds, and the clean blue of the biggest ocean, what if we only remember *California?*"

In *Warday* (1984), Whitley Strieber and James Kunetka's mock-documentary novel, two friends travel the country, bearing witness to the social and environmental fallout of a small-scale war. The authors meticulously detail a United States in which law exists only in isolated pockets and where the fabric uniting the disparate factions of the country has eroded beyond recognition. The narrators encounter feudalism, anarchy and decline in most sectors, a landscape predicted by a 1987 M.I.T. computer simulation in which the loss of fossil fuel following a limited nuclear exchange soon results in worldwide famine and a Middle-Ages level of subsistence.

Other controversial but chilling warnings are even more drastic. Studies have recently forecast that in an atomic attack, a nuclear electromagnetic pulse might well render useless all electric-powered technology, and the atmospheric dust of destroyed cities might create a nuclear winter severe enough to eliminate agriculture for centuries to come.

Yet in spite of all this, a majority of postnuclear war novels of the last 25 years are irrationally optimistic, if only in their lack of true realism. Often degraded, mutated and dazed, human beings—or some facsimile of them—*do* survive to tell the tale.

Why now, when the lethal consequences of ultimate weapons are understood and when the means of their efficient delivery exist in greater numbers, are there fewer writers with the bleak vision of a Nevil Shute or a Helen Clarkson? Perhaps the very naivete of the 1950s made the concept of annihilation tolerable. Perhaps some of today's younger authors, born and raised in the context of nuclear threat, fallout shelters and evacuation plans, have become anesthetized by the crossed fingered wishfulness of Deterrence.

Perhaps the postnuclear landscape has simply become a part of contemporary consciousness. Our children learn what to expect by perusing the J.C. Penney Christmas catalogue, which features in its toy section pages of Transformer robots, hybridized machines and medieval-futuristic figures called Visionaries, set in rocky ruins meant to resemble our increasingly familiar dystopia. In popular films, white knights and punk outlaws cavort, not in the burned and bloodied everyday clothing of Hiroshima's witnesses, but in chic leather duds and studs. Mad Max retains his spiked hair, his white teeth, and has the strength to tote heavy souped-up machinery as he quests for fuel and adventure in a rough-and-tumble Australian outback, the opposite of its lifeless, untitillating counterpart in *On the Beach.*

As we acquire a sense of living in the Before, and take for granted fantasies of how the new A.D. (after detonation) will look and feel, the blighted future becomes for some writers almost an actual place, a shadowland that exists an instant away, a wretched but intriguing playground for the literary and semantic imagination. Though characters survive, the novels are deeply anguished and sardonic in their views of a devolved and ailing humanity.

The narrowed perimeters of this imaginary terrain, simultaneously ordinary and alien, are used as a philosophical and linguistic proving ground retaining elements of language and custom, but with a shuffled detritus. Commencing with Walter Miller Jr.'s *Canticle for Leibowitz* (1959), and continuing through Angela Carter's *Heroes and Villains* (1969), Russell Hoban's *Riddley Walker* (1981), Bernard Malamud's *God's Grace* (1982), Denis Johnson's *Fiskadoro* (1985) and Paul Auster's *In the Country of Last Things* (1987), we hear the voices of victims—paranoid, comic, agonized, suspicious, adrift in dangerous neocivilizations. These are cultural orphans, uncertain even of the rules of languages altered as drastically and carelessly as the rearranged topography.

"Entire categories of objects disappear," says Paul Auster's Anna, "flowerpots for example, or cigarette filters, or rubber bands—and for a time you will be able to recognize those words, even if you cannot recall what they mean. But then, little by little the words become only sounds, a random collection of glottals and fricatives, a storm of whirling phonemes, and finally the whole thing just collapses . . . Your mind will hear it, but it will register as something incomprehensive, a word from a language you cannot speak."

The monks of the Albertian Order of Leibowitz dedicate their lives to copying and preserving pre-conflagration fragments in *A Canticle for Leibowitz,* though all referential meaning is lost. These texts, so meticulously saved on bits of paper, have no bearing on the capacity to understand blueprints, circuit designs, memos and racing forms.

Angela Carter's dysphoric young protagonist, Marianne, studies dictionaries, which contain "innumerable incomprehensible words she could only define through their use in other books, for these words had ceased to describe facts and now stood only for ideas or memories." In Ms. Carter's vision, humans are no longer capable or deserving of Adam's task; and when her characters can no longer identify the ceaseless variety of natural forms, they lose their primal link with nature, that of words. With the loss of civilization, they are not returned to a pastoral state of union with the cosmos; rather, they are unmoored, shaken to the core. "Losing their names . . . things underwent a process of uncreation and reverted to chaos, existing only to themselves in an unstructured world where they were not formally acknowledged, becoming an ever-widening margin of undifferentiated and nameless matter." Bereft of the ability to name, to control, to describe human vocabulary becomes a pattern of arcana referring to an antique lexicon.

In *God's Grace,* the last human survivor in the world, Calvin Cohn, teaches chimpanzees to speak. "God was Torah. He was made of words," Cohn remembers. In attempting to preserve language, he seeks to endow his primates with idealized reason, but his failure, or theirs, is grim and farcical. His half-human offspring is cannibalized by renegade members of the group, and Cohen's agonized protest—"We have a functioning community and are on the verge of an evolutionary advance, if not breakthrough" is to no avail. Cohen joins the rest of his species, a burnt offering.

The actual texts of *Riddley Walker* and *Fiskadoro* mirror a universe whose structure is barely recognizable. Both books feature invented pidgins that reflect a collapsed social order degenerated because of disease yet energized by exotic orthographies and folklores. Riddley Walker's dialect is the most extreme, a richly decomposed English, mixing elision and whimsey. He speaks of "fizzics" and the Puter and Power Leat, the Eusa folk and those "who ben bernt out after Bad Time all the clevver is bernt out with all the clevverness." The protagonists of both novels are adolescent boys who embark on coming-of-age quests after the deaths of their fathers. In *Fiskadoro,* utterance is a mixture of Spanish, English, and static. The war is still going on, somewhere; its artifacts and idioms are curiosities in the isolated, superstitious, cancer-ridden fishing village where the narrator lives.

Erstwhile brand names and the flotsam of a former world

linger like fallout, ludicrous, out of context—Jimi Hendrix sings on "Cubaradio," the god Bob Marley is revered, and the solemn gift of a half-pint bottle of Kikkomon soy sauce, "never opened," is a treasure. In *Canticle for Leibowitz*, a sacred relic is solemnly preserved, a hand-scribbled note: *"Pound pastrami, can kraut, six bagels—bring home for Emma."* A Punch-and-Judy show in *Riddley Walker* becomes quasi-religious, sinister. What trash survives by luck, becomes endowed with mana.

Riddley Walker's quest, pursued through a maze of tortuous clues, ends in an acting out of Nietzsche's idea of eternal recurrence. Gunpowder is rediscovered, and the first explosion since "Bad Time" is ugly and sensational. "I minim they were men and the nex they wer peaces of meat nor it wernt done by knife nor spear nor arrer nor sling stoan it were clevverness done it and the 1 Big 1. That old chard coal berners head took off strait up like a sky lark only parbly not singing. Up it gone and down it came thwock on a poal and ripe for telling. Goodparley sitting there dead with a stoan pounder in his skul. You myt say after all them years of looking for that 1 Big 1 it finely come in to his mynd."

Two of the most provocative recent novels offer a more drastic and a more benign forecast for future humanity. Extrapolating less from immediate cultural fact than from fantasy or theory, they suggest that true change can only come about through a drastic reorganization of our species, or the radical shift of our deepest values.

Galapagos (1985), Kurt Vonnegut's satire about "The Nature Cruise of the Century" on the "new Noah's ark," projects a million years hence the results of today's international strife. Though in fictional Guyaquil the incendiaries are "dagonite," "the latest advance in the evolution of high explosives" rather than thermonuclear, the calamitous results are the same: the population of the world is wiped out except for a few expatriate castaways, and no precedent of recuperation is applicable. "What humanity was about to lose . . . was the ability to heal itself. As far as humanity was concerned, all wounds were about to become very permanent, and high explosives weren't going to be a branch of show business any more."

Devolution, as opposed to learning from mistakes, insures that, with the shrinkage of "big brains," there is no second opportunity at global suicide. "As for human beings making a comeback, of starting to use tools and build houses and play musical instruments and so on again: They would have to do it with their beaks this time. Their arms have become flippers in which the hand bones are almost entirely imprisoned and immobilized."

Reading Ursula K. LeGuin's *Always Coming Home* (1985), a less bizarre but equally original version of a projected postcatastrophe world, one encounters an eventual emanation that rectifies elements of the present. Though there are mentions of chemical contamination zones and "a congenital degenerative condition affecting the motor nerves . . . evidently related to residual ancient industrial toxins in soil and water," the book is mute on the particular causes—be they nuclear war or another disaster—of the previous society's collapse.

The Kesh, members of the novel's central community, are described, through a myriad of perspectives, internal and external to society, as relentlessly and stubbornly gentle, connected by webs of kinship and respect for nature. The entrapments of technological violence and sexual inequality have been revealed, the lessons have been internalized, and unlike the neighboring aggressive, patriarchal Condor people, the Kesh have achieved enduring balance.

Always Coming Home more than even the most sanguine books discussed in this essay, finds the seeds of a superior, less dangerous revitalization in the treasury of culture's traditional values. Its perspective is as nostalgic as a memory of childhood—filled with straightforward simplicity and clarity of choice. The insights gained *in extremis* or after the fact in other fictional creations have reached fruition here, and even *with* "big brains," there is no chance that this branch of humankind will elect to reinvent weapons capable of its own destruction. This is Wovoka's ghost dance, culturally generalized and come true in the most enriching sense: a return of abiding peace, of sanity, a movement from the brink, a test passed, a logical conclusion averted forever. (pp. 52-7)

> *Michael Dorris and Louise Erdrich, "The Days After Tomorrow: Novelists at Armageddon," in* The Nightmare Considered: Critical Essays on Nuclear War Literature, *edited by Nancy Anisfield, Bowling Green State University Popular Press, 1991, pp. 52-7.*

David Leon Higdon

[*An American educator, editor, and critic, Higdon is known for his studies on Joseph Conrad. In the following essay, Higdon examines how British nuclear holocaust literature can be placed into three categories that depict a nuclear Dark Age, the end of all life, or the end of civilization.*]

Early in Nevil Shute's best-selling novel, *On the Beach* (1957), two characters, John Obsorne and Peter Holmes, calmly weigh the gradual spread of radioactive fallout throughout the world as it slowly but inexorably annihilates all forms of animal life. Since he has seen no physical damage of the kind usually associated with war on his reconnaissance trips, Peter confesses he "can't really believe it's going to happen." When chided for his lack of imagination, he responds, "I suppose I haven't got any imagination. . . . It's—it's the end of the world. I've never had to imagine anything like that before," to which John laughingly responds, "It's not the end of the world at all. . . . It's only the end of us."

Imagining the unimaginable and framing a terminal vision of "the end of us" has long been and continues to be a peculiar province of several disciplines—myth, theology, literature, and science, to name but the most obvious. Whether telling of the wrath of Jehovah or Zeus, myth has presented numerous cautionary tales concerning the destruction of mankind, and theologians have made eschatology, or the study of last things, a key part of religious training and inquiry whether the religion is Hindu, Buddhist, or Christian. Science has given us periodic glimpses

The Stars Fall, *one of sixteen woodcuts in a series on the apocalypse by Albrecht Dürer.*

of terminality on massive time scales ranging from the life cycle of stars to the greenhouse effect to the so-called death comet which periodically visits extinction on Earth's life forms. Nowhere, though, has imagining terminality found more fruitful ground than in literature, and nothing has focused attention more firmly on the necessity of envisioning the end than the detonation of a twelve-and-a-half kiloton fission bomb at 8:16 a.m. on 6 August 1945, the day "World War III began on the installment plan," as J. G. Ballard tartly put it in a recent issue of *Newsweek*.

Brian Aldiss spoke for an entire generation of writers when he commented in *Hell's Cartographers* that

> the new-born nuclear power was something greater than social life, greater than almost all the people (not greater than *all* people: not greater than Truman: for it was he who decided that the Bomb remained in the hands of politicians instead of being passed to the generals; that decision forms one of the nodal points of modern history). The Bomb dramatized starkly the overwhelming workings of science and technology, applied science, in our lives.

In confronting this nodal point of history and the potential for future catastrophe such as the *Thing,* the *Flame Deluge,* the *Accident,* and the *Bad Time,* literature developed nuclear fiction, a branch of traditional catastrophe fiction, which, in the view of Ballard, "represents a constructive and positive act by the imagination rather than a negative one, an attempt to confront the terrifying void of a patently meaningless universe by challenging it at its own game, to remake zero by provoking it in every conceivable way." Indeed, this paradigm is exactly the one addressed by nuclear ordeal fiction and non-fiction from H. G. Wells' prophetic the *World Set Free* (1914) to Jonathan Schell's *The Fate of the Earth* (1982), which argues "yet it may be only by descending into this hell in imagination now that we can hope to escape descending into it in reality at some later time. . . . A society which systematically shuts its eyes to an urgent peril to its physical survival and fails to take any steps to save itself cannot be called psychologically well."

As catastrophe fiction increasingly moved questions of responsibility from the gods and nature to man himself and as futuristic potentialities became present possibilities, several directions became evident. In the forty years of nuclear fiction, we can see a gradual darkening in tone, an emerging confrontation between national tempers, and ever-increasing doubts over the ability of civilization to use and to control its own technologies. Douglas Adams's *The Hitchhiker's Guide to the Galaxy* (1979) reminds its readers that "the History of every major Galactic Civilization tends to pass through three distinct and recognizable phases, those of Survival, Inquiry and Sophistication, otherwise known as the How, Why and Where phases." After hearing this, its characters adjourn to the Restaurant at the End of the World. I propose, instead, to trace three phases by contrasting British visions of post-holocaust worlds with American responses to these works and by demarcating what events have contributed to changing directions in the fiction.

One of the first British authors to respond to the new nuclear age was Aldous Huxley in *Ape and Essence* (1948). Early in 1948, Huxley wrote Fairfield Osborn, author of *Our Plundered Planet,* that: "The great question now is: will the public and those in authority pay any attention to what you say, or will the politicians go on with their lunatic games . . . ignoring the fact that the world they are squabbling over will shortly cease to exist in its old familiar form, but will be transformed, unless they mobilize all available intelligence and . . . good will, into one huge dust bowl." He did not add that he was only weeks away from completing his own sardonic and savage vision of this dust bowl of the year 2108 in which clothing is secured by exhuming corpses, where human bones are transformed into tools, and where 80 percent of all live births result in deformed infants. It is a world bereft of human affection, human joy, and human companionship, for these have been replaced by hunger, fear, and cruelty. Civilization has been replaced by a puritanical blood worship of Belial. A new Dark Age has descended upon mankind. Though it is first an attack on the technology Huxley had made his target since *Brave New World* (1932), the narrator of *Ape and Essence* generalizes the attack further:

> Progress is the midwife of Force. Doubly the midwife, for the fact of technological progress provides people with the instruments of ever more indiscriminate destruction, while the myth of political and moral progress serves as the excuse for using these means to the very limit.

In the novel and its reviews, we glimpse a confrontation between British pessimism, reserved distrust of technology as solution, and seasoned, tested assumptions concerning human nature and American optimism, faith in technology, and naïveté concerning human nature typical of this period. One reviewer oddly claimed that "perhaps the Huxley name will carry this to a certain market but for the average normal reader, this form of satire at its most extreme may well prove disastrous," or as Paul Brians succinctly characterized the difference: "Let the effete English weep over the impending doom of humanity . . . American grit and know how will cope with even the worst disaster." *Catholic World* accused Huxley of letting "his imagination run in a riotous extreme, giving us pictures grotesque and horrible, and not always decent," adding as a further warning to its readers that "the motif of sex is repeatedly and obscenely stressed." Most reviewers simply dismissed Huxley as a soured man who had fallen out of love with humanity. *Time* stated that "he simply can't stand the world any more, not even enough to pillory it," and the *New York Tribune Weekly Book Review,* calling *Ape and Essence* a "rather sterile fantasy," marvelled at Huxley's "grand disgust with all of us alive today." As we have recently seen, at times people prefer to hear good news even when there is little or none. No wonder then that American reviewers failed to see that Huxley held out a slight hope in allowing his main characters to escape this world, that the United States government would soon give us "Duck and Cover" programs, and that John Campbell, the influential editor of *Astounding,* would shortly inform contributors that "we have specified to our authors that the 'atomic doom' stories are not wanted."

At one point, the Arch-Vicar in *Ape and Essence* tells its protagonist, the New Zealander Doctor Poole, that "[Belial] created an entirely new race of men, with deformity in their blood, with squalor all around them and ahead, in the future, no prospects but of more squalor, worse deformity, and, finally, complete extinction." It was left to Nevil Shute to realize this vision of "complete extinction" in *On the Beach* (1957), a novel whose impact was seen not only in the sale of three million copies but also in the popularity of the 1959 motion picture adaptation. This novel also brought yelps of tortured logic from some reviewers. One argued that "*On the Beach* must set a record for suicides. I know of no other novel in which all the major characters, all, commit suicide. For this reason . . . *On the Beach* definitely cannot be recommended to any reader." This remark well illustrates the intellectual paucity, indeed the bankruptcy, of many responses which, when confronted with the absolute annihilation of the species, desperately clung to the idea that individual existence is of such value that it must be preserved until the last moment because perhaps. . . .

By 1957, however, the climate had begun to shift, as signalled by reviewers praising the novel for its "powerful theme," its "crusading earnestness," its "cautionary tale," and its "obsessive nightmarish" qualities. George Harrison of the *New York Tribune* exclaimed: "I believe *On the Beach* should be read by every thinking person." Why the shift in only a decade? Paul Brians notes that "1955 saw the publication of more nuclear war fiction than any year since 1946" and suggests that authors and public alike had become sensitized to the dangers of fallout as a result of the "Lucky Dragon" incident in which a Japanese fishing vessel was contaminated during the Bravo tests in the Marshall Islands, tests which alerted the world "to the real magnitude . . . of the peril from nuclear fallout." Since 1945, testing had proliferated as nations rushed to possess nuclear technological capabilities. The United States had tested two devices in 1946, three in 1948, seventeen in 1951, and the hydrogen bomb in 1952. Russia joined testing in 1949, 1952, and 1953; the British in 1952 and 1957. Not until 1958 was testing suspended, and in February of that year the Campaign for Nuclear Disarmament was launched in the United Kingdom with the twin aims of mobilizing mass opinion against that nation's nuclear weapons program and of favoring unilateral nuclear disarmament.

In the midst of such public concerns, Shute's *On the Beach* stands as a remarkably quiet, understated work, with no particularly memorable characters, no spectacular events, and no shrill rhetoric. In counter-pointing the mundane ordinariness of everyday life against the impending extinction of the species, Shute's novel acquires a powerful resonance and a sharply-honed shock value remarkably similar to that exploited in Shirley Jackson's "The Lottery." When Shute's key thematic statement comes, its hopes are all the more wistful and all the more compelling in enunciating our central duty to our race:

> I mean, if a couple of hundred million people all decide that their national honour requires them to drop cobalt bombs upon their neighbors, well, there's not much that you or I can do about it.

The only possible hope would have been to educate them out of their silliness.

Before making this comment, however, the novel occupies us with the daily realities of Lieutenant Commander Peter Holmes, his wife, and his infant daughter, with the detached love affair of Moira Davidson and Dwight Towers, and with assorted minor characters denying the inevitable through their very ordinariness which gives them the dignity and strength not to let the remnants of their civilization collapse into chaos. Futile, perhaps; silly, probably—but very, very Commonwealth. Dwight Towers accepts that "the human race was to be wiped out" but consoles himself with the thought that "the world [was to be] made clean again for wiser occupants without undue delay. Well, that probably makes sense." Notice that Shute holds out no hopes whatever of a remnant surviving to begin anew. No falsities are allowed; in their place stands absolute confrontation with the end, envisioned as a group of decent people who love one another enough and who love existence enough that they are willing to kill themselves to assert the dignity of existence. Peter Holmes' last words, spoken to his wife, are "I've had a grand time, too . . . Let's end on that."

The decade following publication of Shute's novel brought Mordecai Roshwald's *Level 7* (1959), Walter Miller's *A Canticle for Leibowitz* (1960), and Philip Wylie's *Triumph* (1963), which called attention to an increasingly darker vision of future horrors, preparing the ground for yet a third direction in nuclear fiction. W. Warren Wagar states that "after 1965 . . . a significant shift in scenarios took place, with just over half still forecasting terminal wars, and the rest evenly divided between the accidents and miscalculations of scientists and catastrophic events in the environment." Gone largely are faith in technology and belief that a remnant will survive; gone, too, is the optimistic faith in human nature and civilization. In their place one finds the nuclear winter scenario, the transmuted gene scenario, and the ever more troubling questions about the nature of civilization itself.

This is anticipated in the angry voice of Brian Aldiss, who fuses Huxley's distrust of technology with Shute's bleakness. In his autobiographical essay for *Hell's Cartographers,* Aldiss dismisses the smug and naive political and philosophical assumptions of much science fiction, concluding that "we are at the end of the Renaissance period. New and darker ages are coming. We have used up most of our resources and most of our time. Now nemesis must overtake hubris, for this is the last act of our particular play." He calls for a fiction treating this "landscape of destruction" which will "be shot through with a sense that our existences have been overpowered . . . by gigantic forces borne of the Renaissance and achieving ferocious adolescence with the Industrial Revolution." Throughout his novels, Mary Shelley's *Frankenstein* (1818) remains an available touchstone because to Aldiss it embodies "the archetype of the scientist whose research, pursued in the sacred name of increasing knowledge, takes on a life of its own and causes untold misery before being brought under control."

In *Greybeard* (1964), Aldiss marks the new scenarios by

exploring the future from the time of the 1981 Accident, a disruption of the Van Allen radiation belts as a result of "a series of 'controlled' nuclear detonations in space," until the year 2030. As Alby Timberlane, Aldiss's protagonist, journeys backwards in memory and forwards down the Thames, recording for DOUCH(E)—the Documentation of Universal Contemporary History (Europe)— Aldiss foresees a savage future world peopled not by us but whose inhabitants nevertheless will find the "records . . . a link for them between their past and their future."

Greybeard gives us a near future world of anarchy where the average age "already stood high in the seventies." The Accident has rendered the animal world largely sterile. Aldiss's novel arrives at a somewhat unearned optimistic conclusion only after having Algy proclaim the "values of the twentieth century . . . invalid" and argue that "otherwise they wouldn't have wrecked the world. Don't you think," he asks his wife, "that the Accident has made us more appreciative of the vital things, like life itself, and like each other?"; to this, she responds, "No, I don't." Aldiss's novel less questions science and human nature than it questions the very directions of civilization and the validity of civilization. It regrets less that man may die than that "there was no longer a place on earth for mind." Again, though, American reviewers simply failed to address the "vast unknown" imaginatively embodied in the novel. *Best Seller* turned to a distinction between fact and fiction as old as the Greeks, commenting that if it "had a real scientific basis, it would be the finest bit of propaganda against atom bomb testing instead of the figment of the author's imagination" and concluding that "most readers would expect more of a human race that managed to survive the effects of 'fall-out' even on a world-wide scale," thereby totally missing the point of Aldiss's theme.

The Day of the Bomb has thus secularized and demythified the *Dies Irae*, but we should take little comfort or assurance in Gary Wolfe's claim that "with the exception of a few works . . . most nuclear holocaust stories assure us that humanity can rebuild against the most staggering odds," and heed the admonitions and cautions of the works themselves. As Wagar has argued,

> Terminal visions are not just stories about the end of the world, or the end of the self. They are also stories about the nature and meaning of reality as interpreted by world views. They are propaganda for a certain understanding of life in which the imaginary end serves to sharpen the focus and heighten the importance of certain structure of value. They are games of chance, so to speak, in which the players risk all their chips on a single hand.

Lest we ever forget what the game involves, consider in closing a few lines from Ted Sturgeon's 1947 story, "Thunder and Roses," one of the very first stories to address the nuclear war threat:

> He looked down through the darkness at his hands. No planet, no universe, is greater to a man than his own ego, his own observing self. These hands were the hands of all history, and like the hands of all men, they could by their

small acts make human history or end it. . . . "You'll have your chance," he said into the future. "And by Heaven, you'd better make good."

Nuclear fiction is, without doubt, the most serious game we have ever played, for it makes immediately accessible the ends that threaten us presently and may await us in the none-too-distant future. That we have made it this far is exceedingly scant proof that we will endure further, so "by Heaven [we'd] better make good." (pp. 117-23)

> *David Leon Higdon, " 'Into the Vast Unknown': Directions in the Post-Holocaust Novel," in* War and Peace: Perspectives in the Nuclear Age, *edited by Ulrich Goebel and Otto Nelson, Texas Tech University Press, 1988, pp. 117-24.*

Martha A. Bartter

[*In the following essay, Bartter asserts that nuclear literature that focuses on the destruction of human civilization advocates urban renewal, a return to nature, and a simpler way of life.*]

Mrs O'Leary's cow did Chicago a big favor. The earthquake of 1906 did the same for San Francisco. Once such a disaster is distanced by time, we can see how these major cities benefited by having to rebuild. Similarly, we may marvel at the modernity, functionality, and beauty of some European cities—those most devastated by World War II. Cities get old, worn-out, dirty, dysfunctional. No technological "fix" seems to satisfy us as we struggle with deteriorating neighborhoods, narrow streets, and ineffective sewers. We long for the opportunity to clean house from top to bottom, to "make it new." Typically, we alternate between the kind of urban renewal that blasts all old structures to make room for high-rise low-income housing and the kind that salvages the shell of old buildings while "modernizing" the interior. While we would deny actually *wanting* our major cities destroyed, and with them our landmarks and our history, we note the popularity of movies like *Godzilla,* which show the fragility of our urban culture.

Since Sodom and Gomorrah, cities have been identified with sin. Now we spend much of our time and energy trying to make our cities "habitable," while seeing them as a prime target for atomic bombs; they sin by their very existence. For us, the underground "shelters" that simultaneously protect and confine the fictional survivors of nuclear "war" metaphorically represent the most-feared features of the city: crowded, dark, technologically dependent, complicated prisons, they are necessary only because the city itself exists. The city is both womb and tomb.

[Bartter adds in a footnote: "We continue to use outdated linguistic tags to discuss the Nuclear Era: e.g., 'war,' which has connotations of 'battle' for territory between opposing armies ending in 'victory' for one side and 'defeat' for the other, probably accompanied by invasion and occupation of 'defeated' territory. While a number of political, economic, and psychological goals are served by such 'conquest,' we should note that none of these can be satisfied by an exchange of nuclear devices; radioactive territory cannot be "occupied" nor can disintegrated populations be 'defeated,' even supposing there might be survivors on the "winning" side. The aim of nuclear 'war' is annihilation rather than conquest. As our fiction shows, the best we can hope for is to derive some benefit from the next 'war,' assuming that we survive it.]

Our attitude towards nuclear holocaust appears similarly ambivalent. Early, serious fictional descriptions of atomic weapons used in war predicted their horrifying destructive properties, mostly aimed at civilian populations in urban centers; yet these fictions usually found ways to explain the survival of a select group. This group, purified through the sacrifice of a large percentage of its members (and perhaps by a return to primitive conditions), might eventually be able to build a new, infinitely better world. Thus, atomic war has traditionally been presented both as obvious disaster and as secret salvation. This covert message is usually overlooked in fiction, even by authors, but it powerfully influences our cultural subconscious.

In fiction we explore who we "are" (or "were"). Through the medium of a story, we expose our assumptions about ourselves and our world, although very often *we* don't see what we have said. [Edward T. Hall writes:] "Culture hides much more than it reveals, and strangely enough what it hides, it hides most effectively from its own participants. . . . [T]he real job is not to understand foreign culture but to understand our own." Comparing our culture to another is invaluable; we can "see" ourselves, perhaps for the first time. We obtain much the same result by observing our fiction, which is produced from our own cultural matrix, responds to it, and subtly but definitively influences it, while being "made new" by passing through the eye of an artist. Looking back at our fictions, we can see some of our own cultural "blind spots," some of which seem not to have changed very much over the years, even though [according to James Gunn] SF is a "literature of change." In fiction, we still expect to "renew" society by surviving the "inevitable" atomic war, rather than by changing the conditions that lead to it. While we give lip service to the concept of "renewal," what we truly believe, as Mircea Eliade notes, is that any remnant of the old structure will get in the way of the new: "life cannot be *repaired,* it can only be *re-created* by a return to sources."

For Americans, a "return to sources" implies a return to the wilderness. (Evoking the past subtly assures us that we will survive again, as we demonstrably did before.) In our cultural mythology, we canonize the frontiersman, who, untrammeled by law and undisturbed by neighbors, carves a living from the virgin land. Like the typical Heinlein hero, he *has* to be competent or die; he has no one to depend on but himself. Unlike the pioneer, who sets out to create a community in the wilderness, the frontiersman sees the city as pure evil: it represents physical pollution of the landscape and moral pollution of its inhabitants through overcrowding, exposure to the peculiarities of other kinds of people, and forced interdependence. Yet the city also embodies our highest educational, technological, and aesthetic achievements, the market for the frontiersman's furs and the source of his weapons. Our spiritual

kinship with the frontiersman leads us to adopt his values, at least in part; like him, we treat the city with respectful dislike.

Thus, urban renewal through nuclear "war" may seem relatively attractive, as Bernard Wolfe shows in *Limbo* (1952). Years after World War III, Martine, Wolfe's protagonist (who has spent the interval on a tropical island), finds a rebuilt city unexpectedly beautiful. With "most basic industry . . . underground," Los Alamos presents "the sheer geometric beauty" of a "glass-and-concrete diorama." Martine muses: "Apparently the H-bomb had in one great continental sizzle accomplished what the reformers and uplifters had never been able to: with a spurt of social-engineering efficiency it had cleared the slums from America overnight."

Wolfe describes a society that has apparently undergone radical change following nuclear holocaust: literal "disarmament," rather than "defense," is now the dominant political slogan, and there is much talk about "the moral equivalent of war." But some things remain the same. Like ours, Wolfe's world labels large parts of human experience as "bad" and rejects them. Emotions are considered overwhelmingly dangerous. Since mere humans cannot control their "evil" emotions under stress, men replace their arms and legs with artificial ("controllable") prostheses to feel safe from their own feelings. (Women are not permitted self-amputation, although some of them protest this discrimination.) But by attempting to amputate anger, men succeed in eliminating love.

Martine soon recognizes how clearly the city represents the culture that built it. On the surface it looks open, efficient, highly attractive; but a "Slot" runs down the center, deep underground. Here all the necessary machinery of living, the reproductive and alimentary/excretory systems, and most particularly the emotions (symbolized by Blacks and women) are buried and "forgotten." But these should not be hidden, and cannot be eliminated. Like the new city, the society is inherently unstable; repressed antagonisms lead again to war, one that stuffs the antiseptic buildings of Los Alamos and their self-rejecting, half-mechanical inhabitants into its visceral "Slot."

We must uneasily agree with Wolfe, that human beings "cause" war. Hobbes, whom we officially refute and tacitly follow, argues that man's "nature" is selfish, lustful, greedy, and bellicose, and that man's life, if not constrained by "civilizing" institutions, is "solitary, poor, nasty, brutish, and short." Rousseau, whose philosophy formally underlies both the "American dream" and the myth of the American frontier, but whose optimism we refute in practice, holds that "human nature" is intrinsically noble, but corrupted morally and physically by civilization. Both philosophers tacitly reject the city: Rousseau, as the source of contamination; Hobbes, as the means of concentrating large numbers of unpleasant, dangerous, half-civilized humans where they can influence each other. No wonder that the hero of American fiction is so often the "lone gunman," the "competent man" who can survive without the debilitating luxuries of the city.

We may eulogize the frontiersman in fiction, but for our

own living, we prefer to emulate the pioneer. Our fiction shows that an ideal world would consist of small, self-supporting communities, full of people "just like us": decent, hard-working, respectable people who get along with their neighbors. These people would have the resources and the freedom to engage in science, technology, and the arts, while living simply but comfortably, in groups small enough for everyone to know everyone else, and no one could get away with evil-doing. We cling to this myth of the small town, no matter how often it is debunked. Ideal communities, we somehow believe, *could* exist if only our world were renewed as a better (less urban, mechanized, depersonalized) place.

We demonstrate the power of this dream by continually destroying cities in our fiction without destroying the society that built them. H. G. Wells, in *The World Set Free* (1914), raised the issue of warfare aimed at cities full of civilians, even before World War I changed our consciousness of war. As World War II became a visible possibility, a number of writers described the result of atomic warfare: mutual, mass destruction of civilian society. Wells destroyed Paris (along with the rest of Europe) to "set the world free" from nationalism. In 1932, *Wonder Stories* printed Carl Spohr's "The Final War." Less a novel than a long, vivid explication of war, possibly from personal experience, "The Final War" describes an "inevitable" progression from the alignment of nations into blocs to the onset of hostilities. War is vicious and wholesale. Any new weapon is instantly duplicated by the other side. An officer explains:

> We had underestimated the tenacity of life. We meant to wipe each other from the face of the earth. There were several million people killed in a few hours, immense property damage was done, but no decision was forced. Retaliation, that was all.

Cities are dispersed. There are no civilians: women run underground factories; even young children fight. When a scientist invents a way of releasing atomic power, he does so in the hope that it will enforce peace. He is, of course, wrong. Like Nobel's dynamite, the new weapon is employed not only on the "fronts" but carried by air to every part of the world.

> These plans were carried out, after the ground commanders, that had sent the ships, were dead. They were completed, after the men, in whose power-mad brains the plans had originated, were crushed in their deep concrete dugouts. There were no staffs, no governments, only these orders, that had to be carried out.

A few surviving soldiers band together, determined never to fight another war (though they will fight anyone who tries to make them fight), and ready to create a society based on the dictates of individual conscience. The nation-state, as exemplified by the urban center, is dead; now, Spohr hopes, human beings can live together in peace—as long as the group stays small. When a plane bearing the representative of the "World Government" arrives, the protagonist's first suspicious question is

> 'What countries?'

> 'There are no countries anymore, there is only the earth and the Freedom of Conscience.'

> Young stepped forward, his hand extended. 'Welcome, friend.'

Reassured that no large, unified government is about to take over, the little band of ex-soldiers continue to build their community in the wilderness.

Except that it lacks details of battle, Pat Frank's *Alas, Babylon* (1959) is startlingly similar to "The Final War." Warned of imminent hostilities, the protagonist finds refuge from atomic attack in a small Florida town. Most of the story depicts the efforts of survivors to create a self-sufficient community in the wake of a very limited nuclear war. Frank's little town is incredibly lucky. It escapes not only bombs but fallout, so uncontaminated food and water remain available; it attracts people with essential skills, including a doctor; the protagonist is an efficient organizer who can defend the town against marauders. But the people who truly hold the key to the group's survival are black ex-sharecroppers, who understand the farming techniques and resources of the area.

When a "rescue" helicopter arrives, the group rejects relocation to a "camp," electing to remain together in their hard-won community. They have a few needs that only an urban center can supply, like prescription glasses for their doctor, but only one question: "Who won the war?"

The soldier's answer is bitter: "We won it. We really clobbered 'em. . . . Not that it matters." The cities are gone. Some nations that avoided the war are sending aid to the suffering ex-combatants, but nationalism is dead so far as the survivors are concerned. Their job, as the novel ends, is to "face the thousand-year night."

Having assigned the "blame" for war to the nation-state, Wells, Spohr, and Frank set out to show its destruction, embodied in the death of cities, as the salvation of humanity. Each ends his grim warning with reassurance: the survival of a simpler culture with a purer ethic (signified in Spohr and Frank by the ability of their group to repel raiders operating on evil, urban standards) proves the pragmatic virtue of the return to origins, no matter how horrifying the circumstances may seem.

The Kuttners show this particularly clearly. Their "Baldies," for example, are clearly a beneficial post-holocaust mutation, whose telepathic ability makes them different from the "normal" population; they must endure discrimination, while protecting themselves from "psychotic" Baldies who wear wigs and hide their telepathic abilities. These radicals endanger the "normal" Baldies as they seek to rule the world.

In these stories, all cities have already been destroyed. Everyone, Baldy and normal alike, lives in small, self-sufficient communities. Any town that threatens to accumulate too large a population risks being "dusted off" by its neighbors as a potent danger to others; a concentration of power could be the target of the next attack. Yet no one seems to heed the danger. Towns that get "dusted off" have grown not from intrinsic conditions, to support an industrial, educational, or trading center, for instance, but simply from a desire to rule, a desire the Kuttners seem to feel is basic to "human nature." Cities are thus equated with the power-mad "psychotic" Baldies, who have little to gain from alienating themselves from their fellow mutants except the chance to wield power. And since every town has its generous supply of radioactives, just as every "normal" Baldy has defenses against "psychotic" ones, the recurring attempt to gain political power seems pathetically futile.

That the "Baldies" represent an advanced state of humanity is amply demonstrated in the book: eventually, they develop a method of sharing their mental technology with "normal" humans. No longer discriminated against, they can help to organize a world in which everyone lives at peace with his or her neighbors (so long as not too many of them are nearby).

In "Tomorrow and Tomorrow" (*Astounding Science Fiction,* Jan.-Feb. 1947), the Kuttners set out to show that a "small atomic war" can be preferable to peace.

> Civilization and technology had, in the middle of the twentieth century, approached the critical mass. Only the creation of a unified world government with its practically unlimited powers, could have kept the global pile from beginning a chain reaction.

The only alternative to a chain reaction is absolute stasis. As in the "Baldy" stories, everyone in the world of "Tomorrow and Tomorrow" possesses atomic weapons; fear of global atomic war has caused the world government to bring *all* change, even medical research, to a complete stop. A small group of revolutionaries fears the result of such rigidity, particularly the stopping of research. Led by radiation-induced mutants, they contact an alternate Earth, whose representative, Omega, convinces them that atomic war is the only alternative to elimination of humanity from present cancer and a coming plague. Omega, on whose planet World War III was fought with devastating atomic and biological weapons, assures the rebels: "Don't worry about the earth exploding. It won't. And as long as the planet itself survives, mankind and civilization will survive." The war killed all but a few humans on Omega's world, but it broke the power of the government—with beneficial results for research. Those who survive live well. The revolutionaries expect to create a similar situation, in which a small, select, nonurban population will inherit a renewed and purified Earth.

Many authors see atomic war not only as destroying cities but also as leaving the survivors with a widespread fear of them. In Robert Abernathy's "Heirs Apparent" (*Fantasy & Science Fiction,* June 1954), the only culture that survives World War III is that of the nomadic Mongols, who sweep out of the Russian steppes to scatter the small community laboriously reconstructed by the two surviving men of education and spirit—one Russian, one stranded American. Like the Baldies, the nomads believe that any town, no matter how small, may attract more bombs. In vain, the leaders argue that no war-making state still exists. Fear is stronger than reason, and civilization dies. The aftermath of such population dispersal is shown in stories like Nelson Bond's series about Meg the Priestess:

"Pilgrimage" (*Amazing,* Oct. 1939), "The Judging of the Priestess" (*Fantastic Adventures,* Apr. 1940), and "Magic City" (*Astounding Science Fiction,* Feb. 1941); and Andre Norton's *Star Man's Son* (1952). In these tales, noble but primitive tribes fear the ruined cities, usually for good reason: they may still be polluted with radioactive residue, or inhabited only by mutants, deformed in mind and body.

Cities represent the aspects of "ourselves" that we dislike: emotionally unstable, subject to the influence of others, and forced to rely on a network of interdependent forces we can neither fully understand nor control. We find special reassurance when the post-nuclear community is shown not as a small, self-sufficient town, but as an institution like a monastery or college. An ordered community exists to fulfill an explicit purpose, as a town does not. College and monastery are similar in this regard; education and prayer both imply conservation of knowledge, culture, and belief. A. E. van Vogt's *Empire of the Atom* (1956) no less than Walter M. Miller, Jr's *A Canticle for Leibowitz* (*Fantasy & Science Fiction,* Apr. 1955; book form, 1959) and James Gunn's *This Fortress World* (1955) rely on this perception. Indeed, the most successful small communities in post-holocaust fiction are those which demonstrate: explicit, clearly perceived leadership, especially if chosen for excellence rather than by inheritance; an explicit code of ethical behavior; and explicit rewards for "good behavior." These criteria are most readily observed in coherent communities. On the other hand, monasteries frequently lack opportunities for free choice: movement, occupation, and association are determined, as they are not in a town. But if what we seek is stability and safety, then a high level of control, even when it limits our "freedom," may seem welcome. In an unstable world, we dream of a contained, controlled environment that will neither surprise nor bore us. As part of our cultural heritage, these unrealistic dreams remain invisible but potent influences on our attitudes and behavior.

This can most clearly be seen by contrast. Instead of rediscovering the village, the "atomic scenario" fiction of Robert A. Heinlein "returns to sources" by recreating the frontiersman. Heinlein rejects the city by effectively removing his protagonists from its polluting presence early in the action. These pure-hearted heroes, men of outstanding capability and resourcefulness, rise to danger like striking muskies, and usually run away with the fisherman's line. Though they may *save* society, his protagonists never use their extraordinary capability to *renovate* it. Elected to some heroic task by their special competence, they have no fondness for the common man. Like the "lone gunman," Heinlein heroes tend to ride off into the sunset when their task is done. Neither the city nor the town is for them.

In *Sixth Column* (*Astounding Science Fiction,* Jan.-Mar. 1941), a small group of research scientists led by a public-relations man defeat an entire army of highly trained, sophisticated, intelligent Pan-Asians. From a cave in the wilderness, they meet urban technology with ingenuity, craftiness, and American know-how disguised as religion, blasting large sections of the Pan-Asian capital city with their magic weapons.

In *The Puppet Masters* (1951) and *Starship Troopers* (1959), cities exist so that they can be destroyed by alien invasion, disease, and nuclear bombs, while alien cities exist so that "we" can invade and destroy them. The protagonists, meanwhile, are removed from urban contamination into small, elite groups with special knowledge, responsibilities, and power. This is particularly evident in *Starship Troopers,* where much attention is paid to the hero's boot-camp training and his separation from "ordinary" people. One cannot, however, say that he is separated from "ordinary citizens," for no one in this society becomes a genuine citizen, with the right to vote, unless he or she participates in the "Federal Service." Heinlein proposes that no one who has not voluntarily left soft urban culture for the rigors of military training is capable of exercising the responsibilities and privileges of government (something we never see in the book). But only an elite few are strong enough to follow this route to the wilderness.

Whether the city is rejected for its technology, sophistication, and degeneracy, or for its sheeplike stupidity that demands to be "saved" by a frontier hero, our fiction suggests that civilization can be cleansed by ritual sacrifice and a return to its roots. Yet even an ideal small town must be shown as inhabited by human beings, "naturally" imperfect, belligerent, and untrustworthy. Most writers would agree with the Kuttners:

> The moment a man is born—in fact, the moment he is conceived—he is at war. Metabolism fights catabolism; his mind is a battlefield; there is a perpetual struggle with orientation and adjustment to the arbitrary norm. Some men adjust fairly well to their environment, but no man is ever entirely at peace. Death brings the only armistice.
>
> ["Tomorrow and Tomorrow"]

If that is how man "is," then there is no hope for anything better than survivable war. Cities are pits of corruption because they concentrate people, who can't even get along with themselves, much less with others. No wonder they are "naturally" warlike. The larger the concentration of humanity, the more likely war becomes.

Some authors propose that, although such character traits are inherited, not all humans are evil. Robert Spencer Carr's "Mutation" (*Beyond Infinity*, 1951) and Sherwood Springer's "No Land of Nod" (*Thrilling Wonder Stories,* Dec. 1952) demonstrate that atomic war can purify small communities by conveniently killing off all the bad guys, so that the meek and loving can inherit the Earth, which they were too "weak" to take by force. Unless *all* the bad seeds are uprooted, however, they will sprout again with the recovery of the technological potential of the city, and recurring "war," as shown in *A Canticle for Leibowitz,* seems inevitable. Despite the innocence and beauty of Rachel's awakening on the shoulder of Mrs Grales, despite the loving hope represented by monks and children boarding the spaceship that flees Armageddon on Earth, Miller gives us no real assurance that "human nature" will not take war with it into the heavens.

The cycle of the city represents the rise and fall of the nation-state: a flowering of technology with a concentration of wealth and power, followed inexorably by luxury, degeneracy, and destruction. Some authors have explicitly and terrifyingly envisioned not only the death of cities, but the death of all humanity, as do Helen Clarkson in *The Last Day* and Mordecai Roshwald in *Level 7* (both 1959); but even their visions do not lack hope: after all, the very presence of the storyteller who describes the end belies its finality. While we may willingly suspend our disbelief long enough to feel the impact of the tale, we do not *believe* it. Others may die; we shall not. We shall find or create our ideal small community even in a world where urban renewal has been accomplished by nuclear holocaust. Although we realize that to "renew" society in "one great continental sizzle" risks absolute disaster, the concept still seems reassuringly familiar. We have, after all, a long history of "successful" war; Carthage was simply a mistake, the result of an excess of Roman zeal.

Analyzing the assumptions we have recorded in literature is valuable, for we tend to act on our assumptions, especially those we are most successful at hiding from ourselves. But literature also serves another function: to create new visions, new assumptions for us to act upon. This does not mean that we can, or should, take fiction literally; *Limbo* stands as a fictional warning against such folly. Bernard Wolfe's "dis-armament" is, on the face of it, absurd; yet is it more absurd than a world kept "peaceful" by the threat of Mutual Assured Destruction? Absurdity has its place. We cannot even *think* about trying solutions we cannot *imagine*.

It is useful, therefore, to see what alternatives have been suggested to the cycle of city, holocaust, wilderness, city (as portrayed so vividly in *A Canticle for Leibowitz*). The few writers like Theodore Sturgeon and Bernard Wolfe who have sought to transcend the cycle of the city usually do so by looking for ways to re-create "human nature." As long as we believe that each man "is a battlefield," engaged in "a perpetual struggle" with himself and his environment, we cannot create peace. Wolfe's hero achieves "renewal," not by his return to his island village, but by rigorously (and painfully) learning to accept himself.

Theodore Sturgeon often writes of societies made genuinely habitable because the people in them, like the inhabitants of Xanadu ("The Skills of Xanadu," in *Galaxy,* July 1956) and the Ledom in *Venus Plus X* (1960), learn genuinely to *like* themselves and each other. This is rarely easy, as we see in "The [Widget], the [Wadget], and Boff " (*Fantasy & Science Fiction,* Nov.-Dec. 1955). Although he explores the concept of nuclear holocaust as thoroughly as anyone (in "Memorial," *Astounding Science Fiction,* Apr. 1946, and "Thunder and Roses," *Astounding Science Fiction,* May 1947), Sturgeon rejects nuclear triage as a "solution" to the problems caused by "human nature." If it should become "possible for mankind to live with itself in health," as Sturgeon shows in *The Cosmic Rape,* people could live in small rural villages or create beautiful, functional cities with equal success. Urban renewal by nuclear holocaust would no longer be necessary, nor would it be apt to occur.

Few authors see such radical change in human behavior as likely, however, so nuclear war remains a probability in their fiction. Indeed, many show that any change that affects how "human nature" works is even more frightening than a cycle of recurring war, which we accept as "realistic," no matter how dreadful. Most tend to forget that "renewal" is only a *process,* and make it an end in itself. This destroys its value; unless we have a positive goal to achieve by renewal, our efforts will fail as miserably as the high-rise low-income apartment complexes that stand as mute evidence of our failure to remake people by changing the conditions they live in.

The lack of new vision in our fiction shows that we have no genuine goal to work towards; we do not know what peace is like, nor can we define it except as a negative condition. Even the *American Heritage Dictionary* agrees: peace is (1) "The absence of war or other hostilities. . . . (3) Freedom from quarrels and disagreement; harmonious relations." War may be hell, but it is at least interesting. In the "battle of life," peace is an epitaph. Nowhere do we see it portrayed as vital, interesting, fun, or creative. By finding a new vision of peace in our fiction, we may create new assumptions to live by; we may even become willing to give up our fearful ambivalence, our cycles of urban "renewal," for something like the functional community of human beings that Bernard Wolfe and Sturgeon point to. (pp. 148-56)

> *Martha A. Bartter, "Nuclear Holocaust as Urban Renewal," in* Science-Fiction Studies, *Vol. 13, No. 2, July, 1986, pp. 148-58.*

William J. Scheick

[*Scheick is an American educator, author, and editor of* Texas Studies in Language and Literature *whose critical works include* The Will and the Word: The Poetry of Edward Taylor *(1974) and* The Slender Human Word: Emerson's Artistry in Prose *(1978). In the following excerpt, he contends that the purpose of post-holocaust fiction is to "deconstruct" the reader's belief in the possibility for atomic war.*]

The serious novelist who describes the post-nuclear holocaust world faces a curious situation. If his or her work proves untrue, it "dies" in the future, where it might be dismissed as mere fantasy; if it forecasts correctly, it also "dies" in the future, where its potential readers have expired. What use can such a book have in either world? Perhaps such fiction might be constructed only as a timeless aesthetic artifact, a work of serious art designed by its author to endure forever; but its subject matter, so urgent and apocalyptic, presses hard against this objective of aloofness. Its subject matter would perhaps expose any purely aesthetic objective in this instance as callous, as if the artist were merely remotely musing upon his species' proclivity for self-destruction; and its subject matter would certainly expose this aesthetic objective as patently irrelevant in a predicted future without the capacity for the passive enjoyment of such rarefied expressions of art.

As a result, fiction treating the post-nuclear holocaust world might be better constructed as self-consuming artifacts. Self-consuming artifacts transfer the reader's attention away from the aesthetic nature of the work itself and

toward its effects in that reader's mind, which ideally is challenged to confront and change its sense of what is normal. If it succeeds, this kind of post-nuclear holocaust novel would technically no longer be needed and so might also "die," just as if it were a mere document that proved correct or incorrect; but at least the novel which is a self-consuming artifact would have played a role in "making the world safe" for a future aesthetics of life and of art.

Such self-consuming artifacts have a deconstructive feature. They are (to apply Roland Barthes' terms) narratives of bliss (*jouissance*) rather than texts of pleasure. That is, apropos language, they unsettle the reader's values and memories, and they challenge the reader's historical, cultural, and psychological assumptions. These post-nuclear holocaust novels are like the shattered world they describe, for their portrayal of a profound unmitigated loss fractures any conventional expectations of comfort the reader might seek in the structure of reading. Their thought-defying picture of the total or near-total loss of human life occasions a disorientation of the reader's familiar sense of the known, particularly in such axiological matters as values. The ideal reader (in Iser's sense) experiences a crisis at some level of his or her mind, which cannot fathom such worldwide destruction and which registers a sense of complicity in this devastation. This deconstructive experience of crisis is necessary before reconstructive thought can begin. In the best nuclear holocaust fiction of the 1980s, this aimed-for sense of crisis, suggesting the need to replace one set of social values with a new perspective, is generated not only through a horrifying depiction of the end of the world, but also through a specific disorientation of the implied reader's normal sense and valuation of language, time, and reality.

Several of these contemporary novels suggest that the average reader unconsciously believes in a firm relation between language (the experience of shared denotative meanings) and reality (the experience of shared temporal eventuation). Sometimes, moreover, recent authors of post-nuclear holocaust fiction indicate that language, as the fundamental expression of the human mind, lies at the heart of the nuclear threat in the reader's world. Their fiction suggests that language not only cloaks ideological and other biased agendas, but also conceals its own arbitrariness in fashioning our unsafe world. To most people, at least in their day-to-day lives, language seems readily to signify the signified. However, like Barthes, some contemporary authors of nuclear holocaust fiction sense how conventional language can authoritatively repress all alternative discourse.

This point is made in David Graham's *Down to a Sunless Sea* (1981), which specifically notes how the language of all political ideologies is pernicious to human survival, and in Denis Johnson's *Fiskadoro* (1985), which argues for the transformation of the language of both political and religious ideologies into a mythic discourse capable of furthering a better dream of life. Similarly, Michael Swanwick's *In the Drift* (1985) is especially grounded in the problem of ideology.

Set in the east coast of America, where a nuclear accident has created a radioactive no-man's-land called the Drift inhabited by mutants, Swanwick's novel demonstrates how language serves as a tool of repressive governmental forces. The word *drift,* designating the zone of genetically mutated outcasts, functions to sharpen ideological boundaries and to justify a lack of compassion toward others in general, most particularly toward deformed humans in the Drift, who are treated like slaves and even killed at random. Moreover, the governmental application of the word *drift* keeps from common knowledge the fact that during the last century the zone has slowly spread across previously uninfected areas. Even more subtly, the distinction implied by the word *drift* conceals from the average citizen in the novel the fact that all life has become hellish: in the Drift, where life-expectancy is a mere twenty-two years, and outside the Drift, where a harsh militaristic organization called the Mummers patrol the borders of the badlands and try to keep Philadelphia a "safe haven from all that lay behind." Such a slogan reverberates with echoes of a similar use of language in the reader's world of the 1980s.

In Swanwick's novel this alleged safe haven is dominated by males, whereas in the Drift a female vampire, a Joan-of-Arc figure, emerges as a sacrificial leader. Similar to such other novels of this decade as David Graham's *Down to a Sunless Sea,* Poul Anderson's *Orion Shall Rise* (1983), David Brin's *The Postman* (1986), Whitley Strieber's *Wolf of Shadows* (1986), and Paul Theroux's *O-Zone* (1987), Swanwick's story urges as part of its agenda the idea that women must have a more central place in any effort to reform human sensibility in a post-nuclear holocaust world. Like Hélène Cixous, some of these novelists of post-nuclear holocaust fiction suggest that it is essentially *male* authoritarian discourse that asserts its dominance over another, possibly transformative language.

Two contemporary post-nuclear holocaust novels written by women indicate that women will have a more central role in the future, but caution about the limits of suggesting that women might readily derive a viable alternative discourse. In *The Shore of Women* (1986) Pamela Sargent describes a post-nuclear holocaust world in which women live separately from men, who are kept in a state of barbarity by the fear-inducing "wicked spell" of delusive female discourse. In this novel, as in Brin's *The Postman,* women wage war against men, and even if their cause is to end the era of male aggression, they are nonetheless engaged in the same activity. Brin seems unaware of this problem in his book, but Sargent sees it clearly. She makes the point that an ideal rapprochement between the sexes can only occur when each recognizes that though their natures indeed differ, yet "there is something of us in them and something of them in us." If Sargent emphasizes the need to expand the discourse of love to include genuine friendship and to transcend all gender discourse by means of a "worship . . . [of] life itself," Sheri Tepper wonders in *The Gate to Women's Country* (1988) whether the articulation of love will be possible at all in the post-nuclear world, a "Hades" where "there's no love" because love leads to betrayal between the sexes. Although the women in Tepper's novel are slowly breeding gentle males, a practice unknown to the men who live separate warrior lives outside women's country, her protagonist ends in silence,

her final discourse not a specifically female alternative to male language, but only silent tears of grief over the sorry state of affairs.

That language, whether assessed from gender or ideology, is indeed an agent in the prevalence of the nuclear threat informs James Morrow's *This Is the Way the World Ends* (1986). In Morrow's novel an American assistant secretary of defense, on trial by the post-apocalyptic unborn, protests hotly: "Can't you use a goddamn metaphor any more without being dragged into court?" But, as the novel shows, metaphors have been at the bottom of the disaster. The assistant secretary asserts that "your missiles must send the right message," but as a Pentagon arms controller, also on trial, unwittingly complains, "It's a real pain arriving at certain definitions." Missiles convey a message, for they are powered by the language of the human mind. However, the real message they convey points not to endurance (the strength to deter nuclear destruction) but to the essential instability of the meaning of our life and of our interpretations (language) of life. That the final authority for meaning, in life and in language, resides in us is the main message of serious nuclear holocaust fiction. This fiction is (to apply Jacques Derrida's comments on the metaphor of nuclear holocaust) a missile-like missive (language) returned for deconstruction to the sender, who is humanity, its only authorizing author.

This missile of the post-nuclear holocaust text sends its message through the deconstruction of the reader's normal sense not only of language (as we have seen) but also of time. The post-nuclear holocaust novel records the characters' past, which paradoxically remains the reader's future. This paradox amounts to a disorienting coalescence of the reader's sense of the past and the future. Such an erasure of distinctness of time periods corresponds to the assault in these novels on a distinctness of concrete denotative meaning in language.

Collapsing past and future, several of these works represent a disorienting linguistic timefold similar to the holocaustal rip in time literally described in the plot of some of these novels. Tears in time occur, for example, in John Varley's *Millennium* (1983), in which a small group of contaminated individuals in the dying Last Age try to start civilization over again by going back in time to rescue select people from airplanes which are known to have crashed in the past. In Morrow's *This Is the Way the World Ends,* too, George Paxton learns that "time is ruined," that "one of the many effects of nuclear war that nobody quite anticipated" was the annihilation of fundamental particles so that "time gets twisted and folded."

In post-nuclear holocaust fiction, this literal and linguistic timefold suggests that time, like the nature of all language (metaphor), is not fixed, but is always an arbitrary present moment rife with unseen alternative possibilities. As the metaphoric timewarp in these books describe and represent, there is an instability in the fabric of the seemingly fixed material world and its language. These works, as self-consuming artifacts, emphasize this instability in order to challenge the average reader's comfortable sense of material reality. However, this destabilization intimates more than a threat of dissolution. The destabilization of time, like the decentering of the fixed meaning of language, also suggests the openness of human experience to potential change for the better.

To elicit a sense of this possibility, these novelists focus on memory, the faculty which uses seemingly fixed language to record seemingly fixed time. If, as we have noted, language is the subtle tool of political, religious, gender and cultural ideologies, so too is the sense of time as documented by human memory. This relationship between memory and political control is evident in the process of selection, for memory (as unstable as are the language and time comprising it) is always selective. It privileges this; it brackets that. Just as language is an instrument of the authoritative domination of people (by whatever forces), so too is memory. As Michel Foucault has observed, "Memory is actually a very important factor in struggle. . . . If one controls people's memory, one controls their dynamism. . . . It is vital to have possession of this memory, to control it, administer it, tell it what is must contain."

So, finally, serious authors of contemporary post-nuclear holocaust fiction emphasize their characters' past (memory) as the reader's future to conflate time palindromically to give the reader a sense of *déjà vu,* which possibly makes this reader reassess his or her own memory. These writers, to apply Foucault's point, struggle for control over their reader's memory, the reader's sense of the past that will shape the direction of the human future (the authors' characters' past). In Whitley Strieber and James Kunetka's *WarDay* (1984) we are told that "words like *history* have lost their weight. They seem as indefinite as memories and as unimportant." But this is only a minority report in post-nuclear holocaust fiction during the 1980s.

Johnson's *Fiskadoro* at first seems similarly to suggest that since "memories . . . make you crazy," the remnants of humanity might try to avoid "waking up and remembering the past and thinking it's real"; perhaps such an erasure of the past, as if merely forgetting a bad dream, might allow a new possible mode of human existence. So Fiskadoro suffers a severe memory loss, from which he never recovers. The narrator of Johnson's novel, however, clings to bits and pieces of past lore, as typically do the narrator of Russell Hoban's *Riddley Walker* (1980), who writes "in memberment" and the narrator of Kim Stanley Robinson's *The Wild Shore* (1984), who writes, in imitation of an old story-teller, "to hold on to the part of the past that's of value." Finally, as these three characters indicate, memory is critical to human mental evolution, whether distorted, collaged memory, or new post-destruction current memory (like Fiskadoro's). As the palindrome of reader future and character past in these timefold novels suggest, memory is for their authors as important a means of access to their readers as Foucault notes it is a crucial means of political control over people.

Hoban's and Robinson's protagonists are pessimistic about the ability of their narratives to achieve anything. But behind the pessimism of each of these narrators hides their respective novelist's hope in the possibility that his characters' memory might serve as a reminder of the reader's choices for the future. Just as Robinson's protagonist, despite his despair, continues to contemplate the duplicitous selfishness of humanity even in the post-nuclear holocaust world and just as Hoban's Riddley accepts how his ongoing pursuit of the meaning of human existence, which he "parbly . . . won't never know," is "jus on me to think on it," the ideal reader of these two books, and many others in their genre, is left *in medias res,* in the midst of contemplating human nature.

Put another way, there is a profound subtextual question lurking in the presentation of the reader's future as a narrative past: can humanity finally develop a "deep *memory,*" value "painful memories" "with a bite," recover "those things not so much lost as unremembered," and learn from the past, even a fictional past in a fantasy about the future? Is humanity, so "capable of anything," able to learn to value an evolution of mind, not merely to crave the survival of body even in a hellish world? Can such a reminding (a character's memory) provide an opportunity for a re-minding (a reader's future), a revision/re-vision in human consciousness? When reminding/re-minding is experienced by the ideal reader, through the destabilization of that reader's perspective of time and language, the post-nuclear holocaust novel manifests its potential as a writerly (*scriptible*) text, defined by Barthes in *S/Z* as a work which displaces the mere consumer of fixed meaning with the reader who produces meanings; or, in a related sense, it manifests its potential as a self-consuming artifact, defined by Fish as a work which transfers the reader's attention from the aesthetic nature of the work itself to the challenge in the reader's mind to conventional notions of what is normal. Then it urges the reader not to be a mere consumer of fixed meaning (prevalent values) but to be a producer of new meanings (alternative values) in his or her sense of both the temporal world and the language which gives that world actuality.

This destabilization of reader perspective through a revision of comfortable notions of language and time includes for many contemporary post-nuclear holocaust novelists a break from mimetic representation of the sort typical of realistic fiction. These authors use the vehicle of fantasy, if not entirely then at least to a degree, as an assault on their reader's complacent sense of the concreteness of their experience of reality, especially as expressed in the conventions of realistic fiction. Fantasy provides these writers with a freedom to use language, unmoored from the demands of mimesis, to communicate an urgent message about alternative possibilities. Like a missive missile (in Derrida's sense), this message must break through the reader's defense systems, the defense systems of fixed (culturally or politically determined) signified meaning; for a re-minding requires an explosion of the conventional—not only in presentations of language and time, but also in presentations of characterization and setting.

It is true that a character presented mimetically can be a companion in consciousness for the reader. Mimetic characterization serves as a mirrorlike reflection of the reader, or at least of some features of the reader. The reader, consequently, might find a character's voice comfortably recognizable, and might find him- or herself readily seduced to companionship by this sense of familiarity. Identifying oneself with post-nuclear holocaust characters might generate sympathy, ultimately self-sympathy, but can it communicate the need for a radical re-vision as forcefully as sensing mere fragments of recognizable human sensibility in bizarre characters? Mimetic characters, I think, tend to support the status quo because they keep the reader interiorized, locked within the self and the given values of that self's sense of reality, whereas bizarre characters with only the rudiments of human sensibilities potentially force the reader to confront an *Other* outside the reader's valorized self. Such characters contribute to the work of fantasy, which as a polysemous genre departs from consensus reality, suggests the mutability of the present, and provokes intensity of engagement by circumventing verbal defenses. Such fantastical characterization forces a dual perspective upon the ideal reader, who looks within him- or herself sympathetically and at the same time looks outward at him- or herself as a monster.

If, as Hélène Cixous notes (1976), mimetic characters convey a sense of the present as everlasting, then fantastic alternatives to such characters might more successfully defy the reader's impression of the firmness of his or her sense of the present. When George Paxton discovers, in *This Is the Way the World Ends,* that his daughter is really an android, a rupture occurs for him and the reader between signifier and signified—such an explosion of expectations that the very nature of reality (in our world, in our memory [mind], and in our language) is called into question.

Consider, as well, Martin Amis' *Einstein's Monsters* (1987), the five stories of which evince a progression from mimetic to fantastical characters. In this book, accounts of how average lives reflect the threat and violence endemic to a world defined by a nuclear referent steadily give way to a post-nuclear holocaust reality in which a sacrificial puppy (with more consciousness than many people) transforms into a human form; and an eight-feet-long, four-feet-wide, five-legged, crimson-eyed mutated dog is fed Queers (human defectives); and an allegedly single immortal man, clearly insane, laments the fact (to an audience dying before his eyes) that humanity "will all be gone and I will be alone forever." This shift from mimesis is informed by Amis' conviction that a post-nuclear holocaust world would be as fantastical a version of hell as ever conceived of by humanity, that such a world would in its nonhuman nature be almost beyond imagining. This shift from mimesis to the fantastical also, and more importantly, conveys Amis' recognition that if there is to be a reminding, his readers must see themselves outwardly as Other, as "terrible mutations," as well as inwardly as Self, as "human beings." As the title of his book indicates, we are "energetic actors, vivid representations of the twentieth century—Einstein's monsters." Similar to Tepper's intimation in her abiding metaphor of role playing in *The Gate to Women's Country,* Amis reveals that we are not *only* what we appear to be on the surface. We could be more or we could be less, as both Tepper and Amis suggest. In Amis' book we, whatever our outward features, are like actors with a hidden conflicted nature below the surface. We are, on the one hand, potentially the very human descendents of Einstein, that symbol of our capacity for transformative thought; we are, on the other hand,

potentially degenerate monsters subhumanly perverting our Einstein-like capacity for thought (re-minding).

If fantastical characters like the alleged Immortal in *Einstein's Monsters,* the Joan-of-Arc vampire of *In the Drift,* the ghosts of the unborn in *This Is the Way the World Ends,* the apparently psychic dogs in *Riddley Walker,* the clairvoyant servitors in *The Gate to Women's Country,* and the cosmic overseer in *Millennium* typically represent assaults on the reader's comfort in mimetic characterization, the descriptions of reality itself in post-nuclear holocaust fiction can equally thwart the reader's desire for mimetic representation and thereby potentially provoke a revision of reality. A thoroughly mimetic presentation, *War Day* depicts in unforgettable detail what nuclear devastation might be like, but it also is enmeshed in the status quo insofar as it emphasizes human limitations and evades the question of how or what changes in human sensibility might occur.

In contrast, Denis Johnson's *Fiskadoro* supplants mimesis with dream reality (the fantastical). Johnson's narrative technique suggests that life at any moment exists as if in a dream. Just as a person tends to forget his dreams upon awakening, so too can the race forget its past as humanity evolves out of the holocaust and forms new memories. In this way the human race might yet redeem itself from the hell it tends to make out of life; this process is the Romantic hope implied in the closing words of Johnson's novel: "And in her state of waking, she jerked awake. And from that waking, she woke up." The *ands,* and the successive wakings from a preceding dream state these *ands* connect, imply a potentially regenerative process which goes on and on.

But Johnson is no starry-eyed optimist. In *Fiskadoro* he implies that in the long run the post-holocaust new life-dream-story might not be any different than the pre-holocaust one. Johnson has Mr. Cheung say, "Some of us are aligned with a slight force, a frail resistance that shapes things for the better.' Fiskadoro is slight and frail, and he does indeed bring change. But the words "slight" and "frail" hint at the precariousness of the possibility for an improvement in the human condition. And this suggestion is supported later in the novel when a minor character ponders how "everything came to an end before. Now it will happen again. Many times. Again and again." Maybe post-holocaust humanity will merely recapitulate the pattern of pre-holocaust humanity; maybe the human mind is so insistent in its hell-making self-destructive force that the slight, frail resistance in that same mind will be overpowered. Still Johnson (like Robinson and Hoban) posits the reality of this resistant force, and he hopes for the small chance, which seems to exist, for its emergence from the myth-engendering human mind and for the possibility for a better dream (life) to which this emergence could give rise.

In post-nuclear holocaust fiction similarly characterized by the nature of dreams, the reader cannot tell what is dream and what is actual in the narrative. This confusion makes the point—a point H. G. Wells insisted upon throughout most of his career—that life is like a dream, that life is not a fixed immutable reality but an open-ended series of alternative possibilities. . . . [Morrow writes that humanity] is "living in a dream world" replete with nebulous "frail memor[ies]"; human life, as aptly imaged by Amis, is "a gorgeous and dreadful dream, the two states—panic and rapture—welded as close as the two faces of a knife." And, as we have noted, the characters in this *mise en scene,* replete with fantastic possibilities, may be outlandish caricatures, insane immortals, psychic dogs, mutant vampires, clairvoyant servitors, bizarre aliens, or unborn ghosts. Such characters are appropriate to a dreamlike setting. If revision/re-vision in the reader's future, if an emphasis on possibility, rather than an emphasis on limitation, is the goal of the post-nuclear holocaust novel, then the fantastical past of the fictional character's memory should ideally distort or breach usual mimetic representations of the commonplace. Such disorientation in the reader might lead to revisionary thought.

The assault on mimetic representations of language, time, and reality for the purpose of provoking thought in the disoriented reader is essentially a deconstructive feature of the post-nuclear holocaust novel of the 1980s. As the narrator of Sargent's *The Shore of Women* learns, "Doubt can show us how we might make things better." But in these works deconstruction is not merely a measure of reality, but also a means of encouraging reconstructive mental patterns. In contrast to the sense of *aporia*—the sense of an infinite regress of meaning that denies any possible "outside" perspective of an ultimate truth, the authors of serious post-nuclear holocaust fiction suggest that there is one external ultimate fact we all indeed know to be true: death.

With death there is no problem of *difference,* the deferment of presence with a sign which is not the thing itself. Death is non-being, the nothing at the end of life. Death is, to adapt Wallace Stevens' line, the "Nothing that is not there and the nothing that is." Reminding the reader of the "outside," fixed, and real referential fact of death requires not only the re-minding that is a devastating missile-like message destroying the ideal reader's conventional sense of things (the deconstruction of conventional sense of language, time, and reality), but also the re-minding that is a possible re-creation (reconstruction of new world possibilities). Grounded in the singular reality of death (non-being or nothing), this fictional re-minding becomes a potentialist discourse, as J. Fisher Solomon cogently suggests in *Discourse and Reference in the Nuclear Age.*

Post-nuclear holocaust fiction uses the fantastical in a way that conforms with a post-structural reading of humanity's subjectivization and relativization of reality; but even while conceding that reality, in an ontological sense, is not ultimately knowable, it insists upon a single empirical potentiality, the potential external reality of death. The death of the post-nuclear holocaust text itself (as we have seen) is at issue, but essentially the possible extinction of the reader's life, perhaps of all life on Earth, by nuclear destruction serves as a limiting "objective" referential ground (*épistémè*) for subjective belief (*doxa*) and action because it can be projected or calculated through our experience of probability, propensity, or regularity. Indeed,

for these novelists, as for J. Fisher Solomon, the most urgent instance of the propriety for such a potentialist metaphysics is the nuclear threat of our time.

This threat can be defined as an empirical potentiality: a predictability of human extinction which has objective reality because the possibility of nuclear holocaust bears within itself real propensities for probable development. So, for Solomon and these novelists, as for writers in the field of nuclear criticism, the nuclear referent is not merely the fantastical product of our imaginations that requires a suspension of belief (as Derrida seems to contend), but it is also something extrinsic to us, something with *real* extra-conjectural, extra-interrelational, extra-linguistic dispositional potentialities. In a world which is like an open-ended dream for authors of post-nuclear holocaust fiction, the nuclear referent is a subjective dream and *at the same time* something extrinsic to us, something utterly *real* in its dispositional potentiality to kill the dreamer. The only chance the dreamer (humanity) has for survival in the nuclear age lies (according to serious nuclear holocaust novelists) in his or her ability to dream into "external" existence a "fantastical reality" of alternative potentialities.

In this sense, appearances at once fictionally deceive and factually tell the truth, for everything is the product of the

Book jacket for A Canticle for Leibowitz *by Walter M. Miller, Jr.*

333

dream-capacity of the human mind. This faith in the protean ability of the human mind counters, anxiously to be sure, the pessimism of such post-nuclear holocaust visions as Robinson's *The Wild Shore* and Varley's *Millennium*. In Neal Barrett, Jr.'s *Through Darkest America* (1986), the father of sixteen-year-old Howie Ryder says, "What you see on the outside's not near as important as the part you can't see"; "it's not what you call something that makes it what it is." Howie learns this lesson about the deceptiveness of appearances and language in painful ways, and the force of his discoveries suggests a rather pessimistic conclusion and outlook. Nevertheless, at the periphery of Howie's main experiences are several little disclosures which abrade a solely pessimistic reading of his encounters. These marginal revelations include the fact that, contrary to popular opinion, some members of the black race have survived the holocaust, some species of animals are reappearing, and (most important of all) "once and a while a ship comes in to port" on the coast of California even though "there weren't supposed to be any" other "places in the world" after the War.

These intimations of possibilities for regeneration are reinforced by Howie's response (his last words in the novel) to the remark that "there ain't nothin' up that way you can do." Howie replies, "I got to go see if that's so." Informing Howie's uncertain comment—he is not even sure he says it aloud—is a deep sense of the lesson he has learned (as stated by his father) about the deceptiveness of appearances. If, as his encounters indicate, appearances in the world deceive, then even the pessimistic impression they suggest collectively might itself also deceive. Before he accepts the conclusion that he can do nothing at all, he wants to *see* for himself.

Howie's final words in the book, however uncertain, amount to a commitment to search (as he does in the sequel *Dawn's Uncertain Light* [1989]) below the composite appearance of things to discover whether there is in fact nothing he can do to change his world. Implied readers of such post-nuclear holocaust fiction presumably should be left with the same thought: that we should resist a pessimistic capitulation to forces seemingly out of our control and should press on with a commitment to life, even if only tentatively against the seemingly great odds suggested by the appearance that nothing can be done about the threat of the nuclear destruction of our world.

Resisting the pessimism of several post-nuclear holocaust works is a tentative hope in alternative appearances, dreams, fictions that might become fact. If one subjective dream (the nuclear referent of the 1980s) could become an objective reality, then possibly alternative dreams could become a new human reality. As is suggested in the assault on language and memory, fact is fiction, and fiction is fact in the repository of the human mind, not only in art but also in the dream that is life. This belief informs the subjective visions of the stories serious post-nuclear holocaust novelists tell. In these timefold works, the fictional memories of future humanity coalesce with the seemingly factual memories of present readers in the 1980s because reality is always the objectification of dream possibilities emanating from the human mind. Post-nuclear novelists deconstruct the language, time, and reality of our present version of the world, a dream reality *really* characterized by the nuclear referent, in the hope that an alternative reconstructive story might somehow emerge. They believe in the fantastical power of stories, of art, to make a difference because all reality, including memory, is only an artistic dream. In this sense, the nuclear reality we now know, albeit real in its propensity for extinguishing all life, is only the product of a mind-invented story.

In Robinson's *The Wild Shore* Old Tom tells stories "to hold on to the part of our past that's of value," and the narrator Henry resolves to continue to contemplate the meaning of life through his writing. In Brin's *The Postman* Gordon Krantz exchanges stories and songs for food, and his fictional works salvage something factual from the past. Laissa in Sargent's *The Shore of Women* records from the outside previously outlawed stories, legendary amalgamations of fact and fiction. These narratives infect the barbarous men, seemingly so immune to thought. As Sargent's narrator says, "I had triggered a flood of words and an orgy of self-examination among the men. They told their stories, listened to others, and reflected on their lives; this was something new for most of them." In her hope that these "stories can be powerful in time," that they might also cause the civilized women to think and thereby change too, Laissa expresses the aim of Sargent's use of fiction to urge upon her readers to reflect upon some deep truths about the nuclear age of the 1980s.

The protagonist of Hoban's *Riddley Walker* similarly ponders "what the idear of us myt be" by recording stories with a mythic and allegorical undercurrent. When Lorna says to Riddley, "there ain't never ben no strait story I ever heard," Hoban means that human accounts are as "crookit" (fallen, devious, distorted) as is every postlapsarian post-nuclear holocaust person; that these accounts are, like Riddley's and like human history, nonlinear, or disorderly, in their eventuation; that these accounts are allegorical rather than straightforward; and that these accounts are fiction. Indeed, Robinson, Brin, Sargent, and Hoban make the point that whereas in the pre-holocaust world alleged factual accounts presented fictions as truth, in the post-holocaust world fiction preserves some truths, although these truths might well remain elusive to even such sensitive survivors as Henry, Krantz, Laissa, and Riddley. By presenting in their own "crookit" fictions, allegories of truths, about the perilous direction of twentieth-century crooked humanity, Robinson, Sargent, Brin, and Hoban use fiction, not a *straight*forward mode, to reach a not-straight humanity, and in doing so align themselves with the superior role and value of post-holocaust storytelling.

Like Robinson's, Sargent's, Brin's and Hoban's novels, Johnson's *Fiskadoro* posits the immense value of the embodiment of deep truth in fiction, particularly in the post-nuclear holocaust world of his book. The stories told in Robinson's book are heightened embellishments; those told in Sargent's and Brin's books are legendary; those told in Tepper's book are ritualistic; those told in Hoban's book are allegorical; those told in Johnson's book are anthropologically mythic, especially the central story of the book itself that is rendered by a first-person narrator (never identified) who "like[s] to tell stories." If these authors share the view that fiction is a useful vehicle for truth, the difference among them is not only the degree of increasing value attributed to story-telling from Robinson's embellishments, to Sargent's and Brin's legends, to Tepper's rituals, to Hoban's allegories, to Johnson's mythic patterns. Beyond this difference of degree, and perhaps explaining it, is Johnson's implication that fiction, like dreamwork (art, memory, and life), has the capacity to heal, renew, and redirect human endeavors, if not in the twentieth century, then perhaps in a post-nuclear holocaust age when everything is so levelled that healthy mythic patterns might once again be evoked from the human mind.

Johnson and other authors of post-nuclear holocaust fiction portray a future for the reader that is simultaneously the past of the narrator in the hope that this fictional projected memory might result in a different projected future than the one predictable in the present world, a dream reality, defined by the fantastic yet utterly real nuclear referent. In deconstructing our comfortable reliance on the nature of language (denotation), time (memory), and reality (mimesis), they create fantastical fiction as self-consuming artifacts designed to disorient and then to provoke reconstructive thought in their readers. As spent, self-consuming textual missiles, post-nuclear holocaust fiction indicates that humanity will either die through a failed re-minding or live through a successful re-minding. (pp. 71-82)

> *William J. Scheick, "Post-Nuclear Holocaust Re-Minding," in* The Nightmare Considered: Critical Essays on Nuclear War Literature, *edited by Nancy Anisfield, Bowling Green State University Popular Press, 1991, pp. 71-83.*

POETRY

Jan Barry

[In the following essay, Barry, an American poet, journalist, and editor asserts that nuclear war poetry, like nuclear war fiction, may depict the immediate effects of war, but it exists, first and foremost, as a form of protest literature.]

[Where] are the poems of the nuclear age?

Poets have addressed the subject. But poetry in America has had dwindling cultural impact since 1945. Besides the massive shadow cast on most other arts by movies, television and rock music (the electronic triangle which defines American culture in the nuclear age), another possible factor in the loss of cultural impact for modern poetry has been national attitudes toward nuclear war—that the "unthinkable" is a topic in which speculation is best left to ex-

perts or Hollywood's cinema chamber of horrors, that the underlying temper of the times is too terror-filled to be "poetic," that the end of our era could well be disaster beyond words.

What could poets, whose baliwick in the popular perception has been to compose light verse or sentimental ballads, what could these moody dreamers add to the heart-churning reality of space age inventions spinning out of the trillion-dollar technology of the nuclear arms race, technology with the power of God to create a world-destroying Doomsday of nuclear holocaust? This is visual, eye-popping stuff—flame-spewing missiles, cities turned into hell in an instant—made for the giant silver screen and eagle's eye-view of television.

The nature of nuclear war may have brought great pause to poets, as well. Perhaps poets sensed better than others knew that nuclear Armageddon would mean the death of art, that nuclear war contained the power to destroy art's illusion of immortality.

Imagining Doomsday, Hollywood mythmakers assumed that after the dust settles something like the Death Valley desert and feuding Wild West (or *Star Wars*) characters would still survive, providing comforting continuity to audiences raised on gunfighter westerns. Novelists and journalists and television writers' scenarios also assumed a fierce struggle among survivors after nuclear apocalypse, not much different from the heroic stories of survivors of civilizations devastated in World War II.

Perhaps poets weighed the literal weight of the words in the Cold War patter about nuclear war: "the end of the world." What if there *were* no one left to admire the breathtaking warnings of the world's end? What could a poet, whose canvas is the human soul, whose passion is casting lines of words to hook immortality—what could the poetic mind facing total extinction—do with such a hopeless vision?

In any case, when I edited a collection of poets' responses to the Vietnam War and the nuclear age, [*Peace Is Our Profession: Poems and Passages of War Protest,*] published in 1981, I found it difficult to find many memorable poems imagining nuclear war.

What I did discover was a fierce, nearly underground wave of poetry on waging peace to prevent nuclear war. And I found some bleak, Beckettian images of nuclear holocaust—in poetry that had seldom reached American audiences—conveying a Biblical, stark, lyrical power.

> There was a sadness in the land
> And silence.
> The northern birds had ceased to sing
> And blue fire had grown in the east.
>
> From the depths of hell blood welled
> And spewed across the valleys and the plains.
> Vipers came when the blood had dried
> And slithered through the dead, gray grass.
>
> Hearts were sick with longing for the color
>   green,
> but it was gone, covered in rust red and gray.
> They cried out in their grief . . .

Lord, have mercy on us! We have seen the pit!

LORD, WE DID NOT UNDERSTAND.
LORD, IF WE HAD ONLY KNOWN.
Lord, let the birds sing. We will listen.
Lord, let the grass grow. We will see.
      [Joseph M. Shea, "After the Bomb"]

Several other poets included in the anthology recovered startling images from accounts of the atomic bombing of Hiroshima to warn of humanity's likely outcome.

a flat black shadow
etched into the solid
stone had arms outflung
and feet running forward,
as welcome to our future.
      [R. B. Weber, "On a Bridge at Hiroshima"]

And exactly now, across the world,
behind a plane, the *Enola Gay,*
there falls a thin tube
with a small fuse at one end
that will fire one of two parts
into the larger part at the other end
and explode this filament
with a light brighter than the sun. Below,
in the wooden city Hiroshima
can it not be that a man
has just rolled back
one of his living-room shutters
and is looking out on his garden, thinking,
The morning glories on their bamboo sticks,
the blue sky,
how beautiful everything is! Let me enjoy it . . .
      (from "August 6, 1945" by Millen Brand)

Can we speak of the flesh falling from bones
the roaring of matter torn
as loud as the horror screams
deep into the ears
of a hundred thousand burning souls?
The flash, the river, the blast, the storm,
and the sickness
the long slow radiating pain
that will stalk a thousand hallways
into now
and lie in the cribs of the future.
The horror of 8:15
will tear at a billion dreams
      (from "Enola Gay" by Don Ogden)

Other poets wrote biting, icily ironic, appalled responses to the proliferating nuclear arsenals and global battle plans during the depths of the Cold War.

Mrs. Smith, old widow
with her television loaded
with big colored pictures
of grandchildren—
burn her up.
This is the national defense.

It is necessary. History
forced our hand. Our honor
is at stake, our national place.

Michael Grady Maxwell,
fourth grade shortstop
with knee patches and
a d-plus in math,

cremate him alive,
an acceptable loss.

Diplomacy and wealth,
the day-to-day feeling
that we are unsafe,
seeing our beliefs pushed
too long and too far
into the mud.

The Umanoff family,
the father a leather worker
wife a brick mason,
six children in steps
with wide trusting smiles,
reduce them to ash
. . .

Dmitri in his crib,
eight weeks old,
learns to use his eyes
and gurgles.
Bring his internal organs
to a rapid boil.
Simmer them midair
out of his skin.

All the earth contaminant,
Christ and Marx done proud.

Big brave athletically accomplished men
with clear minds and in a time of peace
figured this out and decided it was best.
      (from "Pax" by Tom Hawkins)

Neither you nor I nor children
nor the unborn nor the aged nor
the ill nor the lilies of the field
nor the fish of the sea nor
harvest nor planting nor skies
nor seasons nor
the works of Shakespeare
or Dante or Picasso nor the
blood of martyrs
nor the tears of exiles . . .
  . . .None of these
not one is safe nothing is safe if
their plans are consummated if their
weapons are lit if mischance
occurs they would declare god a
nonentity . . .
      (from untitled poem by Daniel Berrigan)

As I gathered these and other poems together, the aftermath of nuclear war acquired tragic shapes unimagined in the Pentagon or the Kremlin or Hollywood. Some prescient poems foreshadowed subsequent warnings by scientists in the mid-1980s that dense smoke from global firestorms from nuclear war could create "nuclear winter," blocking sunlight possibly long enough to extinguish life on earth.

It is night; the bomb
has fallen.
Here was our mistake:
we marched, but not
to the arsenals.

We never went in, tools in hand,
to dismantle what should never
have been built.

In Russia, it will always
be night.
Tomorrow, our own lights
go out . . .
        (from "Dead Wrong" by Shel Horowitz)

Night drifts coldly into dawn
  . . .

Terror and alarm, confusion,
fire, death, apocalyptic change—
all these we imagined.
In the darkest alleys of our minds
we covered every possibility.

No one thought of this.

The sun climbs in the east;
still the streets and roads
are empty. No one moves;
each is locked forever

in a dream.
        [from "The Last Day" by W. D. Ehrhart]

The images of nuclear war in American poetry composed during the Cold War are chilling. The chill is deepened when one realizes that most of these poems appeared only in an American form of *samizdat,* the underground Soviet literature. Most of the works cited in this essay were circulated only in manuscript, or had appeared in obscure publications, when I sought poetry for the anthology which I published in a small press venture in partnership with W. D. Ehrhart.

Perhaps these images of nuclear war were too naked, too much like seeing our own bones exposed by a nuclear flash, to appeal to many Americans. It was a terrible subject for poets to grapple with, as well. Once the horror of nuclear holocaust had been held up—like a handmade sign warning that the road ahead is washed out—what more was there to say to a society which kept speeding past all warning signs?

Most of my own poetry has been inspired, and I've been spiritually sustained, by the work of other poets. But poetry on nuclear warfare inspired in me only despair. I found dreaming my own death too difficult to deal with, let alone imagining the death of the world. Editing this anthology, I gained a great admiration for those poets who could convey their horror of nuclear war in poetry.

But the apocalyptic vision was just a part of what I discovered about poetry on the nuclear age. Beyond some memorable poems in a retrospective of Vietnam War protests, the works in *Peace Is Our Profession* that appealed to the widest audience were impassioned, yet practical calls to not just abhor nuclear war, but work to prevent it.

Beneath the dangling sword
the nations rage and snarl and starve
while inept men debate the means of peace.
  . . .

That mounting fire,
the coming stench,
like vapors from the deep
assail the nations,
transcend their borders
and rise to debase the nostrils of our God.

He abhors our wars,
our hate,
our violence.
It's not just hating war,
despising war,
sitting back and waiting for war to end.
It's not just loving peace,
wanting peace,
sitting back and waiting for peace to come.
Peace, like war, is waged.
        (from "The Peacemaker" by Walker Knight)

This poem, which first appeared in *Home Missions,* a publication of the Southern Baptist Convention, was quoted by President Carter at the signing of the Israeli-Egyptian peace treaty in Washington in 1979, and was prominently cited in a news account of the historic event in *Time* magazine. As I sought to put together a new literary vision of war and peace in the nuclear age, "The Peacemaker" provided the central motif of the anthology—greatly helping to change the thrust of the book from war protest to war prevention.

In a subsequent review of *Peace Is Our Profession,* [R. Z. Sheppard] called attention to the theme of waging peace thread through the anthology, quoting a Muriel Rukeyser poem [entitled "Peace the great meaning"]:

Peace the great meaning has not been defined.
When we say peace as a word, war
As a flare of fire leaps across our eyes.
We went to this school. Think war;
Cancel war, we were taught.
What is left is peace.
No, peace is not left, it is no canceling;
The fierce and human peace is our deep power
Born to us of wish and responsibility.

I had included a trio of Rukeyser poems in the anthology in a section designed to show the context of protests of the Vietnam War, waged in the midst of the continuing nuclear arms race. But these and other protest poems by well-known and unknown poets were scarcely part of the popular culture; indeed, they were difficult to discover. Poetry reflected the passion of the '60s and '70s peace movement. But (with the singular exception of Allen Ginsberg's coining of "flower power"), it did not provide the rebellious slogans and fiery phrases that helped to fuel the protest.

The Vietnam War was followed by a much different era of peace activism: working to prevent future wars. As I began seeking poetry on war and peace in the post-Vietnam era, Walker Knight and other poets were offering a new vision of peacemaking. Allen Ginsberg made a spectacular effort to change national consciousness about the nuclear age with "Plutonian Ode," a Whitmanesque sweeping song of the times which he chanted like a New Age mantra at nuclear weapons protests and college poetry readings in the late '70s.

Poems on waging peace created by a number of poets inspired many Americans who worked to help prevent nuclear disaster, in a groundswell of public reaction to belligerent calls by the Reagan administration to prepare to wage and win nuclear war, in the 1980s.

One of the most effective poems was Wendell Berry's "To

a Siberian Woodsman"—a lifeline of poetry shooting out across the Cold War to the Russians, the people of Pushkin, which the Fellowship of Reconciliation printed on posters with photos of Soviet people, that were hung on walls in churches and schools across America in the desperate years of prodding the Reagan administration to respond to Gorbachev's peace initiatives.

Lines from Berry's poem hanging on church walls were cited by a Soviet editor of a Moscow-based news magazine as one of the most impressive things he discovered in a visit to small-town America.

Grappling for solutions beyond protest, seeking a path to prevent war, other poets hit upon the same theme of reaching out to enemies and estranged strangers to wage peace. Some American poets and peace activists were profoundly influenced by the unexpected, hardy humanism of Vietnamese writers, who reached out to us despite the destruction of their nation by our military machine.

> We will invite the youth
> Who bear on their bodies
> And in their minds and hearts
>   the sounds of war
> The brothers from the Chinese border
>   to the Gulf of Thailand.
>
> We will invite our friends
>   from the West
>   Those whose fathers went
>   and never returned
>   Those whom the war has taken
>   their loved ones.
>
> We will invite our friends
>   from north and south Korea
>   From east and west Germany . . .
>
> From behind the mushroom
>   columns of smoke
> of Hiroshima and Nagasaki . . .
>
> We will say new words
>
> Our hearts filled with human love
> And a new language
> For those who were the enemy.
>   (from "Invitations" by Hai Ha)

The most profound poet on waging peace in the nuclear age I encountered in compiling *Peace Is Our Profession* was Millen Brand, who died shortly before the anthology was published. In 1977, at age 71, he traveled to Japan and joined a marathon peace march from Nagasaki to Hiroshima; and in the fashion of ancient Japanese poets, he recorded the journey in a volume of poems, titled *Peace March,* acutely attuned to the country and culture he was passing through.

Each day of the journal of his journey he entered an insightful poem on the interaction of Japanese and Americans, the shattering wounds of our wartime enmity still raw, working together to prevent nuclear war. [The following is entitled "July 23. Moji Station."]

> At noon and still in Kitakyushu,
> half a hundred new marchers
> meet us at Moji Station.

> Among them is a man
> with white hair, thin and fine,
> down the back of his neck. Yet
> he looks young. He takes my hand.
> His name is Yojiro Taya.
> I tell him I am seventy-one.
> He says he is seventy-six
> and again takes my hand.
> "Haiku," he says. He explains
> through our interpreter,
> "For fifty-five years
> I have been walking around Japan
> writing haiku."
>   "What kind?" I ask him.
>   "All kinds. Country scenes,
> nature, the seasons, but mainly
> in the last twenty years
> haiku against war."
>   "And now you're marching with us."
>   "Every year I've marched
> in demonstrations against war.
> I march and write.
> I've written thousands of haiku."
>   Seventeen syllables
> each a breath
> against death.

There is much more to be discovered in surveying poetry on nuclear war and waging peace in the nuclear age. At the beginning of the '80s, these poems were like Biblical cries in the wilderness. By the end of the decade, they had deftly foreshadowed the dramatic power of an international movement for waging peace that, unexpectedly, crumbled the military barriers of the Cold War.

Refusing to be silenced by the roaring, sleepless shadow show cast by the movies, TV and rock music, or to remain silent as hermits in the face of impending oblivion, these poets proclaimed that the end of poetry has not yet arrived. They reclaimed the cultural tradition that the power of poetry—the very best "end of art"—is to sustain and recharge the human spirit, when the future looks most bleak. (pp. 85-94)

> *Jan Barry, "The End of Art: Poetry and Nuclear War," in* The Nightmare Considered: Critical Essays on Nuclear War Literature, *edited by Nancy Anisfield, Bowling Green State University Popular Press, 1991, pp. 85-94.*

NUCLEAR WAR IN RUSSO-JAPANESE LITERATURE

Robert Jay Lifton

[*Lifton is an American psychiatrist, writer, and editor who was the first to study the effects of "psychic numbing." A prominent figure in the field of psychohistory, a discipline Christopher Lehmann-Haupt has termed an "endeavor to define how individual human behavior interacts with the historical currents of a given age," Lif-*

ton has written about the events surrounding Hiroshima, the Nazi concentration camps of World War II, and the Vietnam war. In the following excerpt taken from his book Death in Life: Survivors of Hiroshima *(1967), Lifton briefly addresses the belief, held by many Japanese, that atomic-bomb literature is an invalid form of writing and has been exhausted.*]

[When looking at Japanese A-bomb literature,] the dilemma which immediately presents itself is whether or not there is such a thing as "A-bomb literature"—a term that has been used to include just about everything written which mentions the atomic bomb. Like "A-bomb disease," it illuminates important problems by its very ambiguity, as well as by the contention it inspires. (p. 399)

Yōko Ōta's *Town of Corpses* and Dr. Michihiko Hachiya's *Hiroshima Diary* [are examples of one Kind of A-bomb literature, the personal diary or memoir]. Memoirs, of course, never merely record events, but re-create them through the author's personal formulation of them, however hidden this formulation may be. In Miss Ōta's case, we have observed the blending of exquisite psychological sensibilities with an angry anti-militarism; and in Dr. Hachiya's, a combination of medical commitment and non-judgmental detachment (not to mention the further distillation of his *Hiroshima Diary,* and in a sense reformulation of it, by Warner Wells, the articulate and morally responsive American physician who rendered the book into English).

Such memoirs derive, at least in part, from two longstanding Japanese literary conventions: the use of the personal diary; and the related "I-novel," a form of first-person narrative which all but obliterates the boundaries between autobiography and fiction. We are therefore hardly surprised that many A-bomb memoirs, including Miss Ōta's, have been labeled novels.

But the distinction between memoir and fictional transformation is of considerable importance. Indeed, the difficulty in taking the imaginative leap from the one to the other was a preoccupation of just about every writer I spoke to who was concerned with A-bomb literature. A Hiroshima literary critic conversant with these matters told me that there have been three sequential stages of writing about the A-bomb: first, that of "reportage" (or what we have called the "personal memoir"), beginning at the time of the bomb and extending until about the mid-1950s; then, that of a "novel" so autobiographical that it differs only slightly from reportage (and perhaps is best termed the "memoir-novel"), lasting roughly until 1955; and a subsequent "stage of confusion" in which writers have attempted, with relatively little success, to convert the A-bomb experience into a genuinely fictional idiom. The critic's conviction was that writers "have already exhausted the resources of the immediate experience," and that they must now deal with it as "something of a more symbolic nature" by portraying "ordinary people and ordinary circumstances while having the A-bomb unmistakably present in the background." He went on to describe a pattern of moral and literary compulsion among Hiroshima writers which we can immediately recognize to be a product of the A-bomb's circle of guilt:

The fact that they are in Hiroshima . . . makes many feel that they must write about this special experience of the A-bomb . . . and those who don't want to write about the A-bomb . . . feel that they have to try to work out reasons for not writing about it. . . .

He stressed the literary problem presented by the A-bomb as "an alien object removed from human beings"—that is, by its technologically induced distance. And like many other Hiroshima writers I spoke to, he insisted that "past literary methods . . . are inadequate for dealing with the A-bomb," but could say little about what new approaches might suffice. He thought too superficial the "shifting of literary focus from the A-bomb itself to more political elements . . . and peace movements," and also raised the dilemma of how to evoke the bomb's unprecedented dimensions:

> . . . If you describe the A-bomb in an ordinary way, from a standpoint of personal relationships, your description differs very little from that of other disasters—such as ordinary bombings or earthquakes. But writers feel that the A-bomb has special significance . . . and is different from these other disasters. Yet they are unable to find a way to bring out this special significance. . . .

Finally, he raised the issue of the *hibakusha*-writer's [or the "explosion-affected person's"] particular inclination toward silence:

> Those who have been through the experience are hesitant about writing about it—and therefore seem, at least outwardly, to be more passive in their attitudes.

But this silence is acceptable neither to *hibakusha*-writers themselves . . . , nor to their critics—notably those from the highly centralized Tokyo "literary establishment," perceived by Hiroshima writers as a kind of Big Brother, now chastising provincial colleagues for failing to speak up about the A-bomb in their work, now ridiculing the entire genre of "A-bomb literature" with the disdainful challenge, "What is A-bomb literature anyway?" And of course there is the very real question of how many gifted writers could be expected to appear in a particular provincial area, whatever its special historical experience.

No wonder, then, that some wished to abandon the whole concept of A-bomb literature, and indeed the A-bomb itself as a literary subject—as did one provocative woman writer [Miyoko Shijō] in a somewhat sensational proposal put forth in an article in a Hiroshima newspaper in early 1953:

> The A-bomb is not a special genre of literature. So-called A-bomb literature was written mostly from immediate feelings of indignation, anger, hatred, and repentance. But now that seven years have passed, isn't it about time to stop writing in this fashion and instead to deal with the more essential things of life? . . . What is important to us is not death but love, romance, peace, happiness. . . . It is important for writers to think seriously about love and romance . . . in order to try to understand the

essential meaning of life. Literature should not be used for special purposes, whether political or scientific, and A-bomb literature has been used for such purposes. . . .

This plea for a "cheerful" literature of individual sensual experience was partly a reaction to the self-consciously "purposeful," even manipulative, tendency of much that had previously been written. The trouble, of course, was that her proposal came close to advocating that Hiroshima's unique history be totally ignored. In the lively debate that followed, some writers angrily denounced her "escapist attitude," while others, in more measured tones, granted the weaknesses of existing A-bomb literature but insisted upon its general significance. One observer wryly summed up the debate: "Just about everything that could be said about A-bomb literature was said . . . but this did not necessarily produce any A-bomb literature."

As a way out of this literary and psychological bind, some, like the literary critic, suggested that Hiroshima writers turn away from preoccupation with victims alone and "write about the A-bomb from the other side"—that is, from the standpoint of those who dropped the bomb and possibly deal with "the story of the pilot who went insane," keeping in mind that "it is quite possible that if the Japanese had the A-bomb, they would have used it." (pp. 399-401)

> *Robert Jay Lifton, "Creative Response: 1) 'A-Bomb Literature',"in his* Death in Life: Survivors of Hiroshima, *Simon and Schuster, 1967, pp. 399-450.*

Kenzaburō Ōe

[*Kenzaburō Ōe is a major Japanese novelist, critic, and educator. In the following excerpt, taken from his introduction to* The Crazy Iris and Other Stories of the Atomic Aftermath *(1985), Ōe surveys the works of Japanese writers who emphasize the effects of the atomic bombings of Hiroshima and Nagasaki in their fiction, asserting that their work is an attempt to make the "unknowable future" of the nuclear age readily comprehensible to all people.*]

The massive wreckage of life, limb, and livelihood caused by the atomic bombings of Hiroshima and Nagasaki was, for single-bomb attacks, unprecedented in human history. In trying to comprehend this extensive damage in the aftermath of the Pacific War, the Japanese faced many uncertainties and ambiguities. Efforts to reach an accurate understanding of this problem, which concerns all humanity in the latter half of the twentieth century, have been made by a wide range of citizens' organizations in which A-bomb survivors themselves have taken a central role. Literary works dealing with the atomic bombings have also wrestled with this crucial problem.

Literary treatments of A-bomb damage and suffering have not all focused solely on the "victim" approach to interpreting the bombings. The "second-generation survivors" (children of those directly affected) were the first to acknowledge clearly that Japan and the Japanese were aggressors in the Pacific War that brought on the atomic

bombings and, before that, in Japan's war on China. Thus, they sought to comprehend the atomic bombings in relation to what the Japanese call the "Fifteen-years War" (1931-45). The second generation's views found common ground in the A-bomb survivors' organizations to which their fathers and mothers belonged. From this common ground emerged the core ideas and values by which they not only question both the American and Japanese governments' responsibilities for the atomic bombings but also have repeatedly urged the Japanese government to take international initiatives to abolish all nuclear arms.

With this broad perspective, the movement has embraced the concerns of various non-Japanese persons, particularly the large numbers of Koreans who were in Hiroshima and Nagasaki in August 1945 and also suffered atomic death, injury, and damage—thus challenging the widespread trend of referring to Japan as "the only country to suffer atomic bombings." The movement has since expanded to join Pacific-area peoples in protests against nuclear contamination of the Pacific Ocean by aggressor nations, including Japan (for nuclear waste dumping). This understanding, rooted in the Japanese experiences of Hiroshima and Nagasaki, is the cornerstone of the growing global antinuclear movement that seeks the eradication of all nuclear arms.

Most literature that has taken A-bomb experiences as its basic subject matter has attempted to see the experiences of Hiroshima and Nagasaki A-bomb survivors as a vital factor in the lives and livelihood of all the Japanese people. The English translation of this anthology of A-bomb short stories is an effort to make the original A-bomb experiences a part of the shared experience of peoples throughout the world.

Among intellectuals who experienced the atomic bombing of Hiroshima and subsequently wrestled with the questions of how to live and how to express themselves as writers, the most outstanding is Tamiki Hara (1905-51). A master of poetic prose suffused with gentleness, Hara experienced the Hiroshima bombing because he had returned there, his hometown, to place in his family's ancestral tomb the ashes of his recently deceased wife. He resolved to give expression, as an eyewitness, to the wretchedness of A-bomb suffering and damage, which he himself had experienced. Beginning with "Natsu no Hana" ("Summer Flower"), he persistently resisted censorship restrictions of the Allied Occupation and published many works. Five years later, however, during the Korean War, when it was rumored that atomic bombs might again be used, he committed suicide. The work he left behind at that time, *Shingan no Kuni* (*The Land of Heart's Desire*), is filled with profound insights for us who must continue living in the nuclear age. Machine-centered civilization, having introduced nuclear devastation, then pushed forward madly along a course of development fueled by nuclear energy. Toward this vigorous pursuit—that could lead to global annihilation and, in any case, faces an "unknowable future"—Hara harbored profound misgivings.

Writer Yōko Ōta (1906-63) had already produced a number of literary works before experiencing the Hiroshima bombing; but she subsequently concentrated all of her en-

Yasuko Yamagata's version of the immediate consequences of the atomic bomb in Hiroshima.

ergies on writing about A-bomb experiences. While, unlike Hara, she did not succumb to suicide, her untimely death is doubtless evidence that the intense physical and mental anguish she suffered over survivors' A-bomb injuries and illnesses exhausted her strength prematurely. She riveted her sight on human beings at the time of the bombing; her works *Ningen Ranru* (*Human Shabbiness*) and *Han-ningen* (*Half-human*) are fruits of her perceptive powers. Viewing the survivors' pains and problems in terms of relations between self and others, she penned a stinging indictment of discrimination against A-bomb survivors. She was particularly gifted at depicting life in Hiroshima in the immediate post-bombing days—the Nagasaki situation was essentially the same—as the survivors struggled amidst a multitude of hardships to rebuild their lives.

Masuji Ibuse (1898-), a major representative of modern Japanese literature, did not personally experience the atomic bombings. But, in addition to his award-winning *Kuroi Ame* (*Black Rain*), he wrote a number of superb short stories about Hiroshima survivors in the context of the local culture and customs he knew so well (he grew up in a town near Hiroshima). In "Kakitsubata" ("The Crazy Iris"), Ibuse portrays the misery caused by the atomic bombing; but he does so from the vantage point of daily life in the provincial setting of wartime Japan. The result is a penetratingly accurate portrayal of A-bomb survivors. By focusing on the abnormality of an iris blooming unseasonally, out of step with nature's cycles, and then on the abnormality of "man's inhumanity to man" in the use of atomic weapons and the consequent misery, Ibuse pinpoints at one stroke the views of nature and of life and death involved. Ibuse is surely the best example of literary excellence achieved by writers who throughout a lifetime have dared to face squarely the extraordinary agonies of atomic warfare.

Another outstanding representative of modern Japanese literature and one who, like Ibuse, did not personally experience the atomic bombing of her city, is Ineko Sata (1904-). A native of Nagasaki, she has over the years cultivated close relationships with Nagasaki survivors, and she drew on her cumulative insights to produce the full-length novel *Juei* (*Shadow of a Tree*), which treats the long-term hardships of A-bomb survivors. In the short story "Iro no Nai E" ("The Colorless Paintings") she depicts the inner processes—reflected in the colorless paintings—of an A-bomb survivor-painter who, as time passes, sinks into deep depression. Another impressive human dimension of this story is the inclusion of the painter's refusal, as an A-bomb survivor, to participate in a highly politicized world rally against atomic and hydrogen bombs, along with the painter's warm feelings toward the writer herself. World rallies against atomic and hydrogen bombs, held alternatively each year in Hiroshima and Nagasaki on their respective memorial bombing days, with many foreign participants, constitute an important political movement to abolish nuclear arms. Further social significance is added by wide citizen participation in these rallies. Writer Sata, an active leader in progressive women's movements, has played a key role in these world rallies. That she manifests concern for, but without criticizing, A-bomb survivors who turn their backs on overly politicized rallies, reveals Sata's distinctive character.

Hiroko Takenishi (1929-), Sata's junior by a quarter of a century, is a writer best known for her studies of classical Japanese literature. She personally experienced the Hiroshima bombing, but she has not resorted to strident expressions to voice her political opinions relative to that experience. Her short story "Gishiki" ("The Rite") depicts the inner thought processes of a woman who, having experienced the Hiroshima bombing as a young girl, becomes a mature and independent intellectual; a love affair, however, arouses in her anxiety about possible abnormal genetic effects induced by A-bomb illness, and this leads to various misgivings about marriage and childbirth. This depiction of A-bomb experiences as seen by a woman of intellectual bent who pursues a career in business may well convey to the larger world a new image of women in Japan. Also of special interest is the depiction in bold relief—through the main character's observations as a young girl—of the circumstances of a family of Korean residents in Japan who experienced the atomic bombing.

Another writer who experienced the atomic bombing as a young girl—in her case, in Nagasaki—and has since written various works about that experience is Kyōko Hayashi (1930-). She possesses unusual powers of imagination for recalling past experiences with great fidelity and for reconstructing them in detail. And for her, the most significant of all past experiences is that of suffering the atomic bombing as a young girl. Central in her memory are her classmates, both those who were killed instantly by the bombing and those who later died, one after another, from A-bomb injuries and illnesses. The grown, middle-aged woman realizes that, though still living, neither she nor the rest of her classmates are physically or mentally free from the dark shadow cast by the first atomic bombs. "Akikan" ("The Empty Can") is one of her many short stories that weave current thoughts and feelings into a portrayal of the cruel events of August 1945. A young girl named Kinuko, not knowing what to do with the remains of her parents who died in the atomic bombing, places their ashes in an empty can, which she then carries with her to school. This past happening is depicted in the manner of a mythical episode. Then, under Hayashi's deft pen, this young girl becomes a grown woman who has all along lived with glass fragments, sprayed widely by the atomic blast, still imbedded in her back; tomorrow, it seems, she will enter a hospital for treatment after thirty long years. Hayashi skillfully connects past and present in this story about a young woman who survives an atomic bombing and goes on living.

Though not himself an A-bomb victim, Mitsuharu Inoue (1926-) has also written extensively about Nagasaki A-bomb survivors, focusing especially on the discrimination they suffer in provincial communities. His piercing social sensitivity, first manifested in his full-length novel *Chi no Mure* (*People of the Land*), comes through also in his short story "Te no Ie" ("The House of Hands"). This tale involves A-bomb orphans of Nagasaki who are raised in an institution that teaches them manual skills. When they reach marriageable age, one of them, a girl, develops symptoms of A-bomb disease and has a difficult childbirth. By treating fears of radiation aftereffects, a new dimension of social discrimination against survivors is exposed in this story's depiction of a dark crisis. In a postscript to this short story, Inoue presents thought-provoking correlations between discrimination against A-bomb survivors and the historically older, though still active, discrimination against members of outcast communities (*buraku*) in Japan.

The authors thus far introduced, both the A-bomb survivors and those who are not, are all professional writers whose works represent the high quality of Japanese literature. There are, however, many A-bomb survivors of both the Hiroshima and the Nagasaki bombings who have thought through their experiences and, while not professional writers, have expressed themselves in novels and short stories. Choosing to make their primary contributions to society through other occupational channels, they have nonetheless produced many literary works. As a whole, their stories based on A-bomb experiences possess two distinctive characteristics. One is that their way of portraying A-bomb experiences relies on a method of stark realism. Their sometimes artless realism is extremely powerful; and, indeed, their works force one to reconsider the very nature and purpose of a novel. The other point is that almost all of these nonprofessional writers experienced the atomic bombings in their late childhood or early adolescence. They retained vivid memories of their experiences until they reached mature adulthood, when they then performed the valuable service to society of writing stories based on their experiences. "Ningen no Hai" ("Human Ashes") by Katsuzō Oda (1931-) is included in this volume as representative of works by these writers. (pp. 9-15)

In compiling this anthology I have come to realize anew that the short stories included herein are not merely literary expressions, composed by looking back at the past, of what happened at Hiroshima and Nagasaki in the summer of 1945. They are also highly significant vehicles for thinking about the contemporary world over which hangs the awesome threat of vastly expanded nuclear arsenals. They are, that is, a means for stirring our imaginative powers to consider the fundamental conditions of human existence; they are relevant to the present and to our movement toward all tomorrows. As I noted at the outset, in the work he left behind before committing suicide, Hara Tamiki warned that, because civilization is headed either toward extinction or toward salvation from that fate, we inescapably face an "unknowable future." The fundamental condition of life, then, is that we are assailed by overwhelming fear yet, at the same time, beckoned by the necessity to rebuild hope, however difficult, in defiance of that fear. (pp. 15-16)

> *Kenzaburō Ōe, in an introduction, translated by David L. Swain, to* The Crazy Iris and Other Stories of the Atomic Aftermath, *edited by Kenzaburō Ōe, Grove Press, Inc., 1985, pp. 9-16.*

Nobuko Tsukui

[*A professor of American and Japanese literature, Tsukui is also the translator of Yoshi Hotta's novel* Shimpan *(1963; The Judgment). In the following excerpt, she examines the intentions of major Japanese writers who specialize in* genbaku bungaku, *or atomic-bomb literature.*]

Most literary forms have doubtful origins: Arthurian literature, the American Western, the Gothic novel, the pastoral. One literary form, however, can be dated to the day and hour: *genbaku bungaku,* the atomic-bomb literature of Japan. It begins in August 1945 at the moment when a writer (or potential writer) recovers sufficient awareness to tell herself or himself, I am alive. I must write. What gave birth to this new category of literature is one of the most unfortunate events in the history of humanity.

Immediately after the bombing of Hiroshima and Nagasaki, the surviving victims (*hibakusha*)—both professional writers and ordinary citizens of all ages from all walks of life—began to write about their experience, the utterly incomprehensible catastrophe which fell upon them without any warning. Virtually all *hibakusha* realized that they had survived an unprecedented event, and many of them felt a duty to write about their direct personal experience, to record what they witnessed. In its four decades of history, atomic-bomb literature has produced a large number of works in every form and genre: poetry (traditional Japanese haiku and tanka as well as free verse); fiction; drama; various forms of prose such as personal memoirs, diaries, and testimonies; children's literature; film scripts; and comic books, as well as books of pictures or photographs. Quite naturally, the predominant subject matter of early *genbaku bungaku,* written primarily by the *hibakusha,* was their direct experience of atomic bombing in the two cities in August 1945, but subsequent atomic-bomb literature, written by both *hibakusha* and non-*hibakusha* writers, deals with a wider range of subjects, indicating a certain direction in which this body of literature is moving: from a recording of direct, personal experience of atomic-bomb victims to an expression, in artistic creation, of greater concerns for the present condition and for the future, if any, of humankind in the nuclear age. Among the *hibakusha* writers stirred by a sense of mission in the immediate aftermath of the bombing, Yoko Ota writes: "I am watching with two eyes, one a human being's and one a writer's . . . I must write about [this experience] some day as a duty of a writer who witnessed it"; and Tamiki Hara: "The realization that I was alive and the significance [of this fact] suddenly struck me. I whispered to my heart that I must live to write about this experience." Clearly here we find a fundamental answer to the question, Why do these writers write?

Faced with the utterly incomprehensible catastrophe, they made conscious efforts to record accurately the nature of the devastation and destruction, seeking additional information from other victims, from newspapers, and from other sources. But providing accurate information on the physical facts of destruction is by no means the only purpose of atomic-bomb literature. More importantly, the authors have written about the effects of atomic bombing on their entire existence, on their souls as well as their bodies, on their spiritual lives, and ultimately on the destiny of humankind. Again, to quote Hara:

> I survived the tragedy of the atomic bombing, and at that moment myself and my literature were violently driven forward by some force. I wanted to write down the raw scenes I had witnessed even at the risk of death. I recorded that unprecedented experience in a series of writings including *Summer Flowers* and *From the Ruins.*
>
> In the midst of the cries of death and confusion, I was burning with a fervent prayer for a new human race. . . .

And yet, despite their strong sense of mission, these authors, like most *hibakusha,* would rather forget their experiences, if they could. For through no fault of theirs, atomic bombing caused a deep sense of alienation in the *hibakusha,* as Hara writes:

> One morning, he was subjected to a black attack above his head, then watched the collapse of his house, and ran away from there. It may be that from that time on, he had been deprived of the right to exist on earth. . . .

In short, these *hibakusha* writers had to overcome injury, illness, grief: physical and emotional suffering, often intensified by poverty and the dread of latent illnesses and future wars. To add to these obstacles came censorship, imposed by people determined to minimize and obscure the horror of what had taken place. From September 1945 to September 1951, while the occupation authorities enforced the Press Code, which imposed *prior censorship* on everything written for publication or broadcasting, these authors were forbidden to express their thoughts and fears. The censorship meant not only an infringement of their basic rights but a harassment or even a threat for some. For example, Yoko Ota was interrogated by an American official about her novel, *The Town of Corpses;* and Shinoe Shoda defied censorship. She writes:

> In those days the GHQ censorship was strict; and I was told that if my secret publication of the tanka collections was found out, I would certainly be sentenced to die. I made up my mind that I would face the death penalty if I must; and despite my family's objections, I published the book secretly because I felt compelled to do so.

Furthermore, the Press Code often resulted in self-restraint or self-censorship by editors and publishers, as in the case of Tamiki Hara's *Summer Flowers,* the publication of which was delayed by two years.

Nevertheless, despite their physical, mental, and spiritual suffering, the surviving *hibakusha* writers felt that writing was the only way to console those killed instantly in the blast. But their writing was not solely for the dead. They wrote so that non-*hibakusha* citizens of the world might read to know, to understand, and ultimately to work toward peace on earth. Herein lies a most fundamental value of these works. Let us listen to some of these authors. Yoko Ota:

> . . . I have tried to write novels unrelated to the atomic bombing, but the vision of my home town, Hiroshima, branded in my brain would push aside those images which were to be my other novels. . . . the reality of the annihilation of the city and the people which I have witnessed . . . becomes the closest and most concrete image of a work to be written and destroys my desire for other works. . . .

Tamiki Hara: "Do not live for yourself. Live only for the sorrow of the dead people." Shinoe Shoda:

> I composed my tanka collection . . . with an intention to mourn those victims who were killed instantly and those who died later and to comfort those survivors who are grieved and suffering. . . .
>
> I dedicate the diary of sorrow
> To the souls of my fellow countrymen
> Who were forced to die before their time.

Sankichi Toge:

> This book is dedicated to those who lost their lives by the atomic bombs dropped in Hiroshima . . . and in Nagasaki . . . ; to those who, even to this day, have been tormented by the fear of death and pain; to those who cannot erase their anguish and sorrow as long as they live; and to all the people of the world who abhor the atomic bomb.

and Kyoko Hayashi:

> The flash of August 9 is rekindled in my brain at every opportunity. The flash momentarily burns out my thought and senses and scalds my brain blank.
>
> The woman wishes to be the reciter of August 9. She is a *hibakusha,* and she wishes to pass on the story of August 9 from generation to generation as faithfully as possible.

So overwelming are their memories and visions that most *hibakusha* writers try to find a new language or a new form to describe the unprecedented experience. Within the confines of the thirty-one syllables of tanka poetry, Shinoe Shoda used unconventional form and vocabulary for her poetic expression. Yoko Ota's unnovelistic novel may be considered as a new novel, with its autobiographical elements, its unflinching objectivity in recording the "reality of Hiroshima," and, most importantly, her self-conscious striving for inclusiveness, to lend her pen to the entire city and beyond, to warn against the impending tragedy of humankind. Tamiki Hara's blend of fiction and poetry in his highly personal writing is a new form fused into shape by the blast of atomic destruction, as Yoshie Hotta recognizes. Kyoko Hayashi consciously chooses to be the reciter of August 9, the experience of Nagasaki. Her role as the uniter of the past and the present and her conviction that Hiroshima and Nagasaki ought to be remembered and passed on to the generations to come give her work its essential feature: a strong sense of continuity. She pursues relentlessly, yet with the understanding and compassion of a fellow *hibakusha,* those survivors who grow older, carrying intangible yet never-fading memories of the bombing in their minds as well as visible reminders on their bodies, as in the case of a woman, Oki, in "An Empty Can," who has a piece of glass removed from her back almost a quarter of a century after the blast and discovers that the glass has been wrapped in a silky, flosslike fat in her flesh as a pearl would be inside its shell.

Clearly, then, the *hibakusha* authors write from a sense of mission: their responsibility to the dead, for whose silence they must speak, and to the living, whom they must dissuade from self-destruction. Equally dedicated and involved are non-*hibakusha* writers of atomic-bomb literature, who also perform, in their own way, what they see as a duty. For instance, Masuji Ibuse, who is known for his reticence and detachment, nonetheless allows us in an interview a rare glimpse of his motives in his novel *Black Rain,* in which he makes the blending of truth and fiction his own "new" approach to novel writing. There is a memorable scene in which a woman screams, her arms outstretched toward the mushroom cloud, "Hey, you, horrible monster of a cloud, go away! We are noncombatants! Go away!" "It is I," says Ibuse at an interview, "who made that person scream. In actuality, probably no one shouted like that. But that [scream] is what I wanted to express. . . . " Another non-*hibakusha* writer, Yoshie Hotta, presents his involvement and commitment in yet another way.

Among works of atomic-bomb literature, Hotta's novel, *Judgment,* distinguishes itself in several ways. First, the novel places the atomic bombing in a wider geographical and historical context, much beyond the purely personal experience of Japanese A-bomb victims. The novel connects East and West through the events of World War II and illustrates the author's global perspective and his concern for the human condition on this planet. This inclusiveness is clearly his way of dealing with the subject. Second, though itself appropriately defined as atomic-bomb literature, *Judgment* can be read as questioning the premises on which such works are based. Was the bombing of Hiroshima and Nagasaki indeed an unprecedented action, or was it rather the latest and most extreme instance of terrorism against civilians? Looting and burning to break the will of noncombatants, thus depriving the military of support, dates far back in the dishonorable annals of warfare. By linking the atrocity of the bombing to the atrocities of conventional war, Hotta makes the essential connection. Thirdly, insofar as one of the characteristics of atomic-bomb literature is to seek a new language and new literary modes, *Judgment* again diverges from the type. It is pretty much a traditional novel. Here is nothing of the informal, fragmentary, lyrical, autobiographical quality of some *genbaku bungaku.* A novel of thought and action, *Judg-*

ment employs an onmiscient author and a variety of point-of-view characters, revealed through both narration and interior monologue, with sudden shifts of place and person. In reading it, Americans discover what a Japanese author thinks an American would have felt after helping to bomb Hiroshima. Japanese readers presumably explore the psychology of a repentant enemy. All readers encounter characters who search, with varying degrees of success, for an understanding of life, or at least for a mode of living. (pp. 197-202)

The writers of atomic-bomb literature . . . seek to unfold in fiction and poetry the form and essence of experience, the reality of nuclear war enacted in Hiroshima and Nagasaki. Moreover, in their writings, we find not an encapsulated, self-reflected misery, but a grief and compassion that looks outward, claiming kinship with all human misery, past and present. Instead of sameness, we find variety. Instead of hopeless acquiescence, we find a striving to communicate. By its very determination to be heard, this message from the dead and those about to die affirms some kind of hope, however frail, however contingent, for a new spirit of understanding, and even for the continuing existence of humankind on this planet.

In short, these writers provide not only historical insight but a source of that sensuous and emotional involvement which, according to the traditional faith of poets, can transform hearts, minds, and purposes. What atomic-bomb literature can tell human beings is not, after all, the catalog of horrors but the ways individual human beings have met these horrors. Only by learning to see life through the eyes of people other than ourselves can we escape the cumulative poison of our own selfishness. Herein lies the fourfold value of atomic-bomb literature: as history, as art, as an admonition against self-destruction, and as an inspiration to work for peace. (p. 212)

John Hersey on the events at Hiroshima:

Mr. Tanimoto found about twenty men and women on the sandspit. He drove the boat onto the bank and urged them to get aboard. They did not move and he realized that they were too weak to lift themselves. He reached down and took a woman by the hands, but her skin slipped off in huge, glovelike pieces. He was so sickened by this that he had to sit down for a moment. Then he got out into the water and, though a small man, lifted several of the men and women, who were naked, into his boat. Their backs and breasts were clammy, and he remembered uneasily what the great burns he had seen during the day had been like: yellow at first, then red and swollen, with the skin sloughed off, and finally, in the evening, suppurated and smelly. With the tide risen, his bamboo pole was now too short and he had to paddle most of the way across with it. On the other side, at a higher spit, he lifted the slimy living bodies out and carried them up the slope away from the tide. He had to keep consciously repeating to himself, "These are human beings."

John Hersey, in his Hiroshima, *originally published by Knopf in 1946, reprinted by Vintage Books, 1985.*

Nobuko Tsukui, "Yoshie Hotta's Judgment: An Approach To the Atomic-Bomb Literature of Japan," in Arizona Quarterly, *Vol. 42, No. 3, Autumn, 1986, pp. 197-212.*

Rosalind J. Marsh

[*Marsh, an English educator and critic, specializes in Eastern European studies. In the following excerpt, she examines how recent Soviet A-bomb literature reflects public opinion as well as government programs and policies of the post-Stalin era.*]

Since nuclear physics is a particularly vital area of Soviet scientific research which closely impinges upon defence and foreign policy, the treatment of this theme in post-Stalin literature provides an illuminating case study of the Soviet writer's approach to politically sensitive subjects. The following essay seeks, firstly, to investigate how much real information about the Soviet nuclear programme can be extrapolated from Soviet fiction; secondly, to explore the degree to which fiction on this theme corresponds to the fluctuating propaganda needs of the party; and thirdly, to discuss the contrasting viewpoints adopted by Soviet writers to the moral and philosophical problems raised by the development of nuclear weapons.

Very little information about the Soviet nuclear research programme was revealed in the USSR during the period between Stalin's death and the fall of Khrushchev; the first, cautious Soviet account was not published until 1966. Although the history of the Soviet nuclear programme still remains veiled in obscurity, émigré and Western sources provide additional information. Soviet atomic research began in the 1920s in Moscow, Leningrad and Kharkov. George Gamow, an eminent Russian physicist who escaped from the USSR in 1933, gave a lecture in 1927 at the Soviet Academy of Sciences on the atomic fusion which creates the energy of the stars, after which he was approached by Bukharin who asked him if it would be possible to produce such energy on earth. The Soviet A-bomb project, however, was not started until 1943 when scientists were taken off other war work to join an institute under Igor Kurchatov. A stimulus to the Soviet programme was provided by a young engineer, N. I. Flerov, who in 1942 wrote to Stalin pointing out that American research into nuclear fission had suddenly become classified, suggesting that military research was being carried out in this area; intelligence reports that a German bomb project was under way also had a significant effect. In the spring of 1944 the physicists Karl Szilard, Yuri Rumer and Yuri Krutkov were transferred from the aviation *sharashka* (special prison) to an atomic *sharashka* near Sukhumi to join a crash research and development project under Beria's direction. In 1945, when the Americans tested their first atomic bomb, the CIA claimed that the USSR would be unable to build an atomic bomb until well into the 1950s. However, the Soviet Union conducted its first nuclear explosion in September 1949 and in 1950 produced a workable A-bomb, to the astonishment of the world. It is difficult to determine exactly how far the Soviet success was dependent on espionage, but undoubtedly the information acquired from such scientific spies as Klaus Fuchs and defectors like Bruno Pontecorvo, as well as from 'open' American sources relating to the technology of nuclear weapons, contributed to the speed of the Soviet achievement.

In 1949 Andrei Sakharov and Igor Tamm were assigned to top-secret work on the development of the principles of the H-bomb, which they perfected by 1950. On 8 August 1953, nine months after the first American H-bomb test, Malenkov, the Chairman of the Council of Ministers, casually announced that the USSR now possessed the H-bomb too; and four days later the Russians tested their first thermonuclear bomb in Siberia. It is still a matter of dispute as to whether the USSR did in fact have priority over the USA for some months in 1953.

In order to equal the Americans in quantity of nuclear weapons the Soviet Union initiated a long-range missile and rocket programme which eventually produced the inter-continental ballistic missile and Sputnik. For 18 years after 1950 Sakharov was caught up in 'a special world of military designers and inventors, special institutes, committees and learned councils, pilot plants and proving grounds' operating in conditions of extreme secrecy. He felt the tremendous impact of the sight of the huge material, intellectual and nervous resources of thousands of people being poured daily into the creation of a means of total destruction, potentially capable of annihilating all human civilisation. He realised that the project was controlled by people who, though talented, were cynical: until the summer of 1953 the chief of the nuclear project was Beria, 'who ruled over millions of slave-prisoners'. However, it was not until the late 1950s that Sakharov got a clear picture of 'the collective might of the military-industrial complex and of its vigorous, unprincipled leaders, blind to everything except their "job"'.

Because a special atomic censorship vets all literary references to nuclear research, very little information about the development of the Soviet atomic and hydrogen bombs has been revealed in fiction published in the Soviet Union. A significant exception is Granin's novel [*Ida na grozu* (*Into the Storm*)] (1962) which demonstrates that in Stalin's time atomic physicists enjoyed a relative immunity from arrest because of the immense military importance of their work. The physicist Anikeev, engaged in work on 'the problem' (a term used to refer to the atomic bomb), comes into conflict with Beria, the director of the project. Anikeev is angry at Beria's 'ignorant, sometimes disastrous interference' with his research, and writes to the Central Committee asking them 'to protect "the problem" from the ignorant management of Beria'. Although such a challenge was 'positively suicidal' at that time, Anikeev's reputation and the importance of his work save him from 'swift reprisals'. When Beria orders him to leave his work on the bomb and go into exile to a northern pedagogical institute, Anikeev risks his life by staying on the project illegally for a while to finish testing the bombs. This portrait of Anikeev is probably modelled on the famous physicist Kapitsa who refused to collaborate on the atomic project and was kept under house arrest for eight years. It is a matter of some controversy whether Kapitsa's decision was prompted by moral opposition to nuclear weapons or

a specialist's dislike of mismanagement and interference with his research, as evinced by Granin's Anikeev.

Gennadii Gor's novel [*Universitets Kaya naberezhnaya* (*The University Embankment*)] (1959) gives a less frank account of the conditions in which Soviet atomic physicists worked during and after the war. The physicist Chukhlyaev, who is described as studying the motion of atomic particles in a cyclotron, continues his research during the war after his laboratory has been evacuated to the Urals—a possible reference to the special industrial complex in the South Urals area under Beria's control where free scientists worked with their imprisoned colleagues. Since Chukhlyaev's topic is vital for the future of the Soviet Union, he is given good facilities and frequently summoned by party officials who give him plenty of time to complete his work; the nature of his potential achievement is elucidated when Hiroshima provides a spur to his research. While disclosing some truth about the Soviet atomic project by admitting that Chukhlyaev is interested in the work of the German nuclear physicists Hahn and Strassman (who in 1939 discovered the fission of uranium nuclei), Gor's statement that the German intelligence services are curious about Chukhlyaev's research is an intriguing misrepresentation of the true situation, for in actual fact the Soviet atomic programme benefited from the knowledge of German nuclear specialists who were brought to Russia after the capture of Berlin. This fact has not, of course, been revealed in histories of atomic research published in the Soviet Union.

Literature of the Brezhnev era is not as revealing about the history of atomic research as fiction published during the more liberal periods of Khrushchev's rule, but during the 1960s writers still occasionally afford fascinating glimpses into the realities of the Soviet nuclear programme. A novel by the young writer V. Makanin, [*Pryamaya liniya* (*Straight Line*)] (1967), for example, even treats such a seemingly taboo subject as the death of two people on a missile testing site because of a mathematical miscalculation caused by the need to rush the work.

It is only dissident writers who discuss the Soviet nuclear programme with any degree of frankness and, occasionally, provide genuinely new information. Stalin's personal encouragement of nuclear physicists is depicted in Vasilii Grossman's novel [*Zhizn' i sud'ba* (*Life and Fate*)] which was completed in 1960, confiscated by the KGB in 1961 and given up for lost, but eventually published posthumously in the West after the émigré writer Vladimir Voinovich had smuggled out a copy on microfilm. Grossman portrays the Jewish nuclear physicist Shtrum, who is afraid of arrest because of his disparaging references to Stalin, but during the war receives a telephone call from Stalin telling him he is working in 'a very important area' and wishing him success in his work. Solzhenitsyn, in the new version of [*V Kruge pervom* which was translated as *The First Circle* in 1978 and] restores much of his original uncut manuscript, depicts a real incident based on his own personal experience. He portrays the diplomat Innokentii Volodin who telephones the American embassy in Moscow with a warning that Koval', a Soviet agent, is about to obtain information about the atomic bomb in New

York. This episode is based on the case of a real Soviet diplomat, Ivanov, who rang the American and Canadian embassies about Koval' in December 1949 and whose voice Lev Kopelev and Solzhenitsyn were required to identify in the special prison. Solzhenitsyn does, however, alter historical reality for his own didactic purposes: the act of Innokentii's prototype Ivanov was, most probably, motivated by considerations of personal gain rather than idealism; and although Solzhenitsyn eventually came to regard the betrayal of a Soviet agent to a foreign power as preferable to the Soviet state's acquisition of more powerful weapons, he did not adopt this position in 1949, but cursed the caller and willingly cooperated with Kopelev.

In the post-Stalin era the party has considered it very important for Soviet writers to discuss the problems of nuclear war and disarmament, thus contributing to the Soviet propaganda effort at home and abroad. The significance which the authorities attach to writers' grasp of correct party policy on foreign and defence matters is illustrated by the periodic meetings held in the Union of Writers at which prominent military men outline current party thinking, and by frequent speeches by the party leaders and articles by literary functionaries exhorting writers to treat this subject.

From 1954 to 1964 a number of Soviet writers laboured hard to present the contradictions of Khrushchev's policy of 'peaceful coexistence' in a plausible manner, combining propaganda for world peace with a justification of the arms race and a desire for the overthrow of capitalism. Granin introduces this theme into [*Iskatel: (The Seekers)*] (1954), although it is only tenuously related to the rest of the novel. Granin's hero, the engineer Lobanov, looks through American journals concerned with the development of the H-bomb, and reflects: 'Those people would have dropped their bombs if we hadn't got similar bombs. And so we will have exactly what they have, and even more'. In a provocative passage omitted from the foreign-language edition of the novel Lobanov berates the American firm Bell for having distorted the original worthy aim of its founder, Alexander Bell—the creation of hearing aids—in order to become involved instead in the mass-production of nuclear weapons. The Americans' aim of profiting from the destructive side of science is contrasted with Russian scientists' concern about the terrible power of the thermonuclear bomb.

An injunction by the Central Committee of the party to the Third Congress of Soviet Writers in 1959 to treat such questions as the threat of nuclear war and the maintenance of world peace was followed by Ivan Ryadchenko in his poem ["Na ulitse Zhanny—vesna" ("On Jeanae's Street It is Spring)] (1959) which uses the technological achievement of the Soviet Sputnik as propaganda in favour of a 'communist' peace. In the early 1960s, however, Soviet writers faced the difficult task of adapting to Khrushchev's professed and probably real desire to achieve relaxation with the USA to ensure Soviet internal development, while at the same time taking account of Khrushchev's actions which periodically placed a strain on Soviet-US relations. Dogmatist writers, encouraged by the U-2 incident of 1960 and the continuing Berlin crisis,

began to express virulent anti-American feeling in their literary work. In V. Kochetov's novel [*Sekretar' obkoma (The Secretary of the District Party Committee)*] (1961) two children discuss whether the USSR should send missiles to defeat America or continue the policy of peaceful coexistence. In V. Kozhevnikov's [*Znakom'tes, Baluev! (Introduce Yourself, Baluev!)*] (1960), which was hailed as a new model work to be added to the socialist realist canon, a character asks: 'Why are they flaunting their bombs under our nose, why? We know war. . . . ' He regrets that 'our noble science' has been used to create such a terrible weapon, but comments favourably on a speech by Khrushchev warning capitalists not to play with the bomb, which will produce not a conventional war, but an elemental disaster. Kozhevnikov launches a violent diatribe against 'numerous meetings of NATO, SEATO and other military organisations on the lowest human level which are conspiring against peace' and preventing the peace-loving Soviet marshals from organising 'grandiose, planetary, international cooperative defence installations'.

Other writers, however, continued to hold more moderate views. Alexander Dement'ev, in [*Prekrasna Zima v Sibiri (Glorious is the Winter in Siberia)*] (1960), expresses fear of nuclear war, but is convinced that the Soviet nuclear deterrent will save the world from disaster. Perhaps the best known work written in the period of 'peaceful coexistence' was Evtushenko's poem ["Khotyat li russkie voiny?" ("Do the Russians Want War?")] (1961), which was made into a popular song. Although this poem became a useful tool of party propaganda and is much quoted to foreigners, it also undoubtedly corresponds to the deepest feelings of the Soviet population, who are fully conscious of the devastation which war can cause.

Soviet writers were also exhorted to emphasise the peaceful uses of atomic energy, a field in which the USSR was a genuine pioneer. Sakharov and Tamm had started work in 1950 on the problem of a controlled nuclear reaction for the purpose of industrial power; and in 1954 the world's first atomic power station at Obninsk started to produce electricity. In 1954 the press was full of reports about the 'great success of the peaceful use of atomic energy'; but much Soviet nuclear research remained classified until 1955, when Kurchatov persuaded Khrushchev to declassify many works in order to impress foreign countries by the Soviet contribution to the First United Nations Conference on the Peaceful Uses of Atomic Energy.

Fiction was enlisted as another means of publicising Soviet achievements in this field. In Kozhevnikov's *Introduce Yourself, Baluev!* two radiographers discuss a recent article by Academician Nesmeyanov about the use of nuclear power in Soviet power stations and the icebreaker *Lenin,* welcoming his claim that, when scientists have learnt to control thermonuclear reactions and concern about sources of energy has disappeared, the USSR will enter the era of full communism. D. Danin's popular science documentary [*Dobryi atom (The Good Atom)*] (1956) describes the author's visit to the first (still unnamed) Soviet experimental nuclear power station, and provides a persuasive defence of the official Soviet view of the alleged contrast between the peaceful Soviet use of atomic energy and the destructive capitalist exploitation of the atomic bomb. Soviet writers, naturally, fail to mention that the Obninsk power station was not economically viable (the first commercial station was built at Calder Hall in Cumberland) and that the icebreaker *Lenin* lay in dry dock for a year and a half until all the faults in its atomic motors had been eliminated.

Both Danin's work and the lengthy didactic novel by the neo-Stalinist Ukrainian writer, Natan Rybak, [*Pora nadezha i svershenii (The Time of Hopes and Achievements)*] (1961) appear to have been influenced by Robert Jungk's history of the atomic scientists, *Brighter than a Thousand Suns* (translated into Russian in a heavily censored edition in 1961), since both contain views and imagery identical to those encountered in Jungk's book, notably the description of Hiroshima as a 'black day for Albert Einstein'. Rybak's novel is an isolated work which became notorious among the progressive intelligentsia for its crude, chauvinistic propaganda and total ignorance of science, but received praise in the official press. Rybak's subject is the development of atomic energy in the USSR and the West in the period from the Potsdam Conference of 1945 to the Paris Peace Conference of 1955. His novel, with its bitter satire of President Truman, reflects Soviet anti-American propaganda which was becoming particularly intense by the early 1960s; and his sympathetic portrayal of Stalin suggests that Soviet dogmatists were eager for a partial rehabilitation of Stalin. Rybak emphasises that at the Potsdam Conference, when Truman announced the testing of the first American atomic bomb at Alamogordo, Stalin expressed no surprise at the news, but retained his dignified composure and refused to make concessions. Stalin is also depicted as the initiator of the peaceful atomic research programme in the USSR.

Rybak gives a less than detached history of Western atomic research, incorporating several commonplaces of Soviet propaganda—the role of the CIA and great American corporations in promoting the development of nuclear weapons, the employment of former Nazis on the Manhattan Project and the moral scruples of émigré scientists after the dropping of the bombs on Japan. Expressing a view now shared by some Western 'revisionist' historians, he suggests that Hiroshima was a threat aimed against the Soviet Union in order to prevent her from helping Korea, China and the countries of Eastern Europe. Without providing any new information, Rybak also outlines a highly nationalistic history of Soviet atomic research, claiming that Ya. Frenkel, independently of Niels Bohr in Princeton, evolved a new theory of the structure of the nucleus; and that the idea of the synchrocyclotron was suggested by V. Veksler independently of the American scientist E. McMillan. Rybak's novel makes a striking contribution to the 'Khrushchev cult' of the early 1960s, depicting Soviet nuclear physicists working for international peace under Khrushchev's direction. The work ends with an impassioned plea for disarmament and the peaceful channelling of atomic energy—an appeal which was also relevant to the situation in 1961, although the violent anti-American feeling expressed in this novel somewhat undermines the sincerity of the Soviet demands for 'peaceful coexistence' at that time.

Vladimir Orlov's documentary work [*Bogatyrskii atom (The Mighty Atom)*] (1962) expresses many of the same views as Danin and Rybak, but lays greater emphasis on Khrushchev's disarmament campaign. Orlov claims that, although Soviet scientists were the first to make the thermonuclear bomb, this achievement was forced upon them. However, while arguing that the USSR would be glad of a disarmament treaty, he also justifies Khrushchev's policy of continuing nuclear tests on the grounds that they are essential for defence purposes, and that successful tests inspire the Soviet people with pride in their country.

Although fiction of the post-Stalin period generally adhered to the party line in its attitude to nuclear weapons, by the late 1950s some liberal writers began to express a growing concern about the social and moral consequences of atomic research, reflecting the views of the scientific intelligentsia rather than those of the party leaders. A horrified reaction to nuclear weapons had been common in both the Soviet Union and the Western world since the Second World War, but at no time had protest in the USSR approached the proportions of the CND marches in Britain. Between the years 1945 and 1953, as the USSR was racing to produce the atomic, and later the hydrogen bomb, discussion of this subject was kept to a minimum, while the Soviet authorities encouraged propaganda for peace. It seems that both Sakharov and Tamm believed at the time that they were 'working for peace'; they felt, as did many of the physicists who worked on the American A-bomb, such as Oppenheimer, Bethe and Leo Szilard, that if both the USSR and the USA possessed an equal nuclear deterrent then the balance of power would be maintained, and the two countries would be forced to negotiate their differences rather than destroy themselves and the world. The dangers of nuclear radiation were not publicly admitted until 1954, when the adverse consequences of the American nuclear test on Bikini Atoll were publicised in connection with the Soviet government's decision to reopen disarmament negotiations. With some reservations, Khrushchev approved Soviet participation in the Pugwash international conferences, at which prominent scientists discussed world political problems and the social implications of different scientific projects. The main points on the agenda of the first Pugwash Conference held in 1957 were disarmament, arms control and international co-operation. Although these conferences did not exert much influence on the activities of politicians, they raised the consciousness of Soviet scientists about their role in Soviet society and the world in general.

The anxiety felt by some Soviet scientists about the Soviet government's continuation of nuclear tests was also confirmed by the nuclear disaster which occurred in the South Urals area at the end of 1957 or the beginning of 1958: nuclear waste, stored in underground shelters close to the first Soviet military reactors, exploded, distributing radioactive products over a large area, perhaps more than a thousand square miles, and subsequently causing the death of several hundred people from radiation sickness.

By 1960 Sakharov became convinced that further testing of nuclear bombs was no longer necessary on scientific grounds, but was being undertaken for purely political reasons. He attempted to halt the series of nuclear tests planned for 1961-62, but although he convinced the head of the project, Igor Kurchatov, his challenge to Khrushchev proved unsuccessful. Subsequently liberal scientific opinion must have been at least partially satisfied by the 1963 Soviet-American agreement to halt tests in the atmosphere, in space and under water. According to Nadezhda Mandelshtam, however, it would seem that a fear of nuclear war, a sense of approaching doom was spreading among the Soviet people, all the more so because it had originally been artificially suppressed by the Soviet authorities.

The new concern felt by scientists and Soviet intellectuals in general about the social consequences of atomic research is reflected, if only obliquely, in Soviet literature of the late 1950s and early 1960s, in which, as we have seen, an attack on nuclear weapons usually still had to be connected with anti-capitalist propaganda. This is the approach adopted by Soloukhin in his poem ["Zhitelyam zemli" ("To the Inhabitants of the Earth")] (1958) which, while emphasising the guilt of the Americans who were responsible for dropping the first nuclear bombs on Japan, nevertheless generalises from this episode and implies that science is not always constructive and beneficial to mankind if it is placed in the wrong hands. Soloukhin reminds his readers that although the great geniuses of the past, such as Pavlov, have widened man's horizons, 'the black concentrate of death has already been developed and is kept in storage'.

Gor's *University Embankment* provides an interesting example of a device used by Soviet writers to raise the subject of nuclear weapons: discussion of the present in the guise of depicting the past. Through his portrait of the atomic physicist Chukhlyaev Gor anachronistically projects back to the war and immediate post-war periods the anxiety about the effects of atomic radiation expressed by Soviet scientists after 1954, when information about the destructive power of nuclear weapons, withheld for eight years, was disclosed in a flood of publicity. This was probably not a consideration which had weighed heavily with the prisoners who raced to produce the first Soviet A-bomb; Chukhlyaev's attitude more closely resembles the concern of scientists in the 1950s about the significant increase in radiation sickness among people employed in the nuclear and radiochemical industries, and about the nuclear catastrophe in the Urals.

Another 'Aesopian device' is employed by Granin, in a didactic passage about nuclear weapons inserted, somewhat incongruously, at the end of his novel *Into the Storm* (1962). Granin's hero, the physicist Krylov, argues with a pessimistic French scientist who believes that the nuclear bomb will destroy human civilisation. In Krylov's view it is tragic that science created the bomb before the world had been freed from capitalism; the history of science has therefore overtaken the history of man. Yet although he realises that science is not always channelled towards the good of mankind, Krylov expresses faith in man's future and a desire to fight for world peace. In this way Granin bows to the official view that Soviet scientists have a more positive approach to atomic research and the state of the world than foreigners, while managing to voice fears prev-

alent among the Soviet intelligentsia through the mouth of his 'negative character'.

V. Tendryakov's story ["chrezvychairoe proisshestvie" ("An Exceptional Event")] (1961) concentrates on general moral questions, omitting any explicit anti-capitalist bias. When a school debate is held on the topical issue of the relative importance of art and science in the modern world two teachers write rival 'declarations' in favour of the 'physicist' and 'lyricist' positions. The manifesto of the 'lyricists', who win a resounding victory, asserts that science has produced atomic bombs as well as peaceful Sputniks, and that scientists have a moral responsibility to ensure that their discoveries are not misused.

The possible harmful consequences of nuclear research was not a theme favoured by the Soviet authorities. However, in his poem ["Produkty raspada urana" ("Products of the Disintegration of Uranium")] (1960) the Kazan poet Rafgat Dovletshin, writing under the pseudonym M. L'vov, expresses concern that nuclear waste may endanger mankind, and that 'it is not too soon' to think about its safe disposal. L'vov's anxiety may have been aroused, not by the 'monstrous dreams' mentioned in the poem, but by a real event—the Urals nuclear disaster of 1958.

The subject of the harmful impact of Soviet nuclear tests was forbidden by the censorship. Nevertheless, Andrei Voznesensky, in some poems inspired by his journey to the USA in 1961, uses the Aesopian technique of referring to America in order to highlight the horror of nuclear war. His ["Monolog bitnika" ("Beatnik's Monologue")] (1962) evokes the terrifying effect of nuclear fall-out:

> Women will give birth to Rolls-Royces through-
> out the nation—Radiation.

In ["N'ya-Yorkskaya Ptitsa" ("New York Bird")] (1962) the mechanical bird symbolising the soul of America refuses to predict the future, and the threat of war remains:

> The atomic age groans in this hotel room.

Voznesensky's long poem "Oza" (1964), which is set in the nuclear research station at Dubna, won great popularity among Soviet scientists for its exploration of many of the moral and philosophical implications of scientific development. The poet expresses an ambivalent attitude towards scientific progress: on the one hand he praises Dubna, where his 'wonderful, independent' scientist friends, the 'flower of the nation', are engaged in research designed to protect him; but on the other hand, he condemns the depersonalisation of man through modern technology. The heroine of the poem, a physicist, is called Oza, or sometimes by the more common Russian name Zoya, derived from the Greek word for life, *zoē*, suggesting that she is a symbol of life or the human soul. The changes in her name as she stands by the cyclotron beyond the reach of the poet who loves her imply that human individuality is constantly in danger of being distorted or transformed by the power of modern technology, and that the values of love and poetry may be irrevocably lost. Various figures in the poem represent different attitudes towards scientific development. The Scientist, who embodies the amoral worship of scientific progress for its own sake, has invented a 'nuclear aggregate' and proposes an experiment to cut the earth into two and place one hemisphere inside the other, stating: 'True, half of mankind would perish, but the other half will get a kick out of the experiment'. The benevolent Historian in the poem argues that progress is necessary and valuable, but the poet's 'friend from abroad' asserts that science and technology are powerful weapons which can be misused if evil, inhuman men control them. Although Voznesensky insures against criticism by putting this sentiment into the mouth of a foreigner, he is also issuing a scarcely veiled warning to the current Soviet leaders about the dangers of research into weapons of destruction. The clearest expression of the poet's own position is in the words:

> All progress is retrogression
> If the process breaks man down.

Voznesenky expresses values similar to those of Pasternak, defending love, nature, poetry and the free human spirit against the worship of technological 'pseudo-progress' for its own sake; science is meaningless unless it is used to serve man. Technology and politics are transient, whereas the human soul, expressed in love or poetry, is eternal.

In the early 1960s the ideas of Sakharov were reflected in the growth of a certain internationalist, pacifist sentiment among young people which was fed by the party's own peace propaganda. Evtushenko's remarks on the eve of his departure from Germany in 1963 demonstrate his clear support for world unity and apolitical humanism: 'The basis of all fruitful discussion is trust. When is a new Messiah going to appear on earth who simply tells men to 'trust one another', and we not crucify him? How can we facilitate such trust? I can criticise the West in many things and with justice. And the West can, with equal justice, criticise the East'. The obloquy to which Evtushenko was subjected, however, suggests that the party's peace propaganda was not intended to be taken too literally by Soviet people, but was primarily aimed at foreign countries. Similarly, Okudzhava's [*Bud'zdorov, shkolyar! Good Luck Schoolboy!*)] (1961), which presents war in a starkly realistic way, was accused of 'Remarquism'—a reference to Erich Maria Remarque, the author of *All Quiet on the Western Front*—that is of painting war in such dark colours that the work implied that war itself was wrong. In 1964 the Ministry of Defence called a special conference for writers, artists and film makers at which Marshal Malinovsky upbraided authors for composing unheroic works containing pacifist sentiments. Their failure to respond adequately was, however, demonstrated by the further accusations of 'Remarquism' directed against Grigorii Baklanov for his novel *July 1941* (1965) and against the Byelorussian writer Vasil Bykau for *The Dead Feel No Pain* (1966).

In the post-Khrushchev period the strengthening of the censorship and renewed repression against Soviet writers have meant that the issue of the harmful effects of Soviet nuclear research cannot be directly confronted in literature. Works dealing with Soviet physicists, such as D. Konstantinovsky's [*Sledovatel'no, sushchestvuyu (. . . Ergo Sum)*] (1974) and Boris Bondarenko's [*Piramida*

(*Pyramid*)] (1978), have concentrated on peaceful aspects of atomic research. The subject of nuclear weapons has, however, been obliquely treated in science fiction. Several works by Arkadii and Boris Strugatsky, including *Roadside Picnic* (1972), raise the question of the desirability of scientific and technological development, and whether it should be limited. The Strugatskys depict a scientific institute in Canada which is studying the Zone, an area which, according to one interpretation, was a place visited by extra-terrestrial beings who had a picnic on their way, leaving behind some of the technological litter of their existence. These discarded objects, products of a totally alien civilisation, defy most earthly logic and scientific analysis, but men called Stalkers, like the protagonist Redrick Schuhart, venture into the Zone to fulfil orders for objects which people require for various reasons: the quest for pure knowledge for its own sake (as in the case of the Russian scientist Kirill); the search for new devices and techniques to improve human well-being; and the thirst to make profit out of the creation of new and more terrible weapons, using the mysterious 'itchers', 'so-sos' and 'witches' jelly'. Perhaps in order to 'cover' themselves if called to account, the Strugatskys set their Zone in a capitalist country and explicitly deny any direct allusions to nuclear waste, as 'there is no radiation in the Zone'; nuclear contamination is, nevertheless, suggested by the fact that the Zone is a dangerous place which can cause death, madness and genetic mutations in the children of Stalkers. Schuhart, the epitome of 'natural man', eventually discovers the symbolic golden ball in the heart of the Zone which promises the fulfilment of all man's desires. At the moment of discovery, however, he realises that he has no ideals of his own, and repeats the words of his Russian friend Kirill who asked for happiness, freedom and the satisfaction of everyone's needs. Although the conclusion is somewhat simplistic, the main theme of the story is a sceptical attitude towards scientific research into the unknown, which, it is implied, has become such a dangerous, yet attractive pursuit that humanitarian ideals have been lost in the process. The Strugatskys' story formed the basis of Tarkovsky's film *Stalker*, although the authors are alleged to have dissociated themselves from the film.

Since the fall of Khrushchev until the present day a vast amount of material has continued to appear in the press and literature about the USSR's victory over fascism. 'War prose', which has always accounted for a significant proportion of the programmes of Soviet publishing houses, is relevant to the issue of Soviet nuclear policy, since the very prevalence of the theme in Soviet fiction, like the well-kept cemeteries, is a reflection of the terrible trauma war caused in the USSR and the desire that it should never be repeated. The works of Bondarev and Bykaŭ, for example, do not refer directly to nuclear weapons, but implicit in their writing is a warning against future wars and a concern with the moral questions of peace. War literature is an enormous subject which cannot be treated in detail here; our discussion will concentrate on works which directly refer to nuclear weapons and the international situation, or historical works which are used to reflect more recent political and social developments.

Soviet sources date the beginning of the Brezhnev regime's

policy of detente to the Declaration on Strengthening Peace and Security in Europe issued by the Political Consultative Committee of the Warsaw Pact powers in Bucharest in July 1966; but there seems to be no noticeable change of attitude towards the West in literature of the late 1960s and early 1970s. Indeed, there was a resurgence of neo-Stalinist intransigence in Kochetov's notorious [*Chego zhe ty Khochesh'? (What Do You Really Want?*)] (1969) which depicts foreigners as agents of an international anti-Soviet conspiracy attempting to undermine the USSR ideologically by the export of suspect films, novels, pop singers and dancers. The anti-Soviet organiser of a UNESCO expedition ostensibly designed to collect material on medieval Russian art speaks of the impossibility of winning a nuclear war against the USSR: 'The possibility of atomic and nuclear strikes against communism, which the generals are always making a song and dance about, is becoming more problematical year by year. We would suffer an attack similar to any we could deliver, possibly more powerful, and in a nuclear war there won't be any winners, only bodies. Or, more precisely, their ashes'. Kochetov implies that although the enemies of the USSR realise the futility of a nuclear strike, their new tactic is to 'undermine the Soviet system beforehand', and, particularly, to erode 'their strict communist aesthetics' with the help of liberals and de-Stalinisers within the USSR.

There is no doubt that Kochetov's neo-Stalinism reflected a certain current of opinion among the Central Committee Secretariat and the higher echelons of the bureaucracy which was coming to the fore again in 1969 in connection with the projected celebration of the ninetieth anniversary of Stalin's birth. Kochetov's appeals for political vigilance and the strengthening of the Soviet economy, and his emphasis on the need for very high military expenditure to prevent another war, which might overturn the Soviet regime and lead either to a fascist order or to domination by the NATO powers, played on deep Soviet fears and insecurities. However, after the neo-Stalinists had failed to secure the complete rehabilitation of Stalin in December 1969, Kochetov was attacked for his overt chauvinism, even though such views continued to be held by certain elements in the party, the managerial class and the army.

The real beginning of detente can be dated to the XXIV Congress of April 1971 when Brezhnev outlined his Peace Programme, further elaborated at the XXV Congress of 1976, which laid down the basic principles of Soviet detente policy in the 1970s. It is a matter of some controversy whether detente sprang from a position of Soviet weakness or strength, although the argument that Brezhnev's policy resulted directly from the USSR's achievement of strategic parity with the USA appears highly plausible. In any case, detente certainly possessed a different meaning for the USSR and the West. The USA regarded detente as a means of changing Soviet behaviour, restraining Soviet expansionism by offering the USSR cooperation in areas of mutual trust. The USSR, however, saw detente as a relationship of both cooperation and conflict; while agreeing that cooperation in such areas as arms control and trade is mutually beneficial, the Soviet leaders never contemplated changing their political system or modifying their foreign policy. During the 1970s the Brezhnev regime

built up its stockpile of armaments, including the medium-range SS-20s aimed at Western Europe. The Soviet view of detente was clearly stated by Brezhnev at the XXV Congress: 'Detente does not in the slightest abolish and cannot abolish or alter the laws of the class struggle'.

Soviet fiction did not immediately respond to Brezhnev's peace initiative. M. Kolesnikov's novel [*Pravo vybora (The Right of Choice)*] (1971), for example, differs little from the propaganda of the 1950s and 1960s. The working-class hero praises peaceful Soviet atomic research and contrasts it with the imperialists' preparation for atomic, chemical and biological warfare against the USSR. He declares vehemently: 'I believe in peaceful coexistence. But I don't believe an imperialist can become tame, harmless in class terms, just as if he's not the kind of exploiter a capitalist is bound to be'. In the same breath he cites the death of his father in Berlin, the killing in Vietnam and Africa and the existence of West Germany, thus implicitly linking German Nazism with the contemporary menace of the USA and Western Europe. Kolesnikov's espousal of the view that it is necessary at the same time to fight for peace and to prepare for war, militarily and psychologically, can be regarded as either a pre-detente party position or a realistic interpretation of detente by a conformist Soviet writer.

By 1972, with Nixon's visit to Moscow in May, the impact of Brezhnev's Peace Programme was beginning to be felt. The edition of *Literaturnaya gazeta* celebrating the 27th anniversary of the victory over fascism published Pavlenko's ["Mariya" ("Maria)], a work written in the early post-war years, which presents a relatively balanced view of the Germans. Pavlenko points out the common cultural heritage—a Russian officer appreciates Goethe, Schiller and Bach—and not only refers to Nazi atrocities, but also depicts German opponents of fascism. Although in works of the 1970s references to the destructive power of the American bomb and the pangs of conscience suffered by Oppenheimer and Szilard and the bomber pilot at Hiroshima were still common in literature and criticism, the general decrease in anti-American rhetoric reflects Soviet writers' response to the new detente policy. (pp. 248-60)

From 1976 international relations deteriorated considerably, leading to what can now be seen as a new 'Cold War'. At the XXVI Congress in 1981 Brezhnev did not exactly renounce the detente policy announced ten years earlier; indeed, he still tried to portray the USSR as the champion of world peace, while at the same time expressing his dislike of the worsening political climate. Soviet writers had to adapt to the new situation, expressing more hostility to the West than before, while continuing to stress the Soviet desire for peace. Patriotic themes were popularised again in 1978 by Brezhnev's war memoir *Little Earth*, the first part of an autobiographical trilogy (probably created by a team of ghost writers, as the émigré writers Topol and Neznansky suggest in their thriller *Red Square*) for which he was awarded the Lenin Prize for Literature in 1979. In the 1980s critics demanded works displaying *global' nost'* (global scope) and *masshtabnost'* (an impressive scale), and writers responded with works concerned with international affairs. Anti-German and anti-American sentiments began to surface again in such historical works as A. Chivilikhin's *Memory* (1980) and V. Semin's *The Dam* (1981). Yet although condemnation of the moral bankruptcy and militarism of the West was generally expected from Soviet writers, an analysis of literature of the 1980s demonstrates that within certain limits writers were able to treat this theme in very different ways.

Chingiz Aitmatov's interesting novel [*Novyimir* (*The Day Lasts More Than a Hundred Years*)] (1980) juxtaposes a story about the humane Kirghiz workman Burannyi Edigei with a science fiction tale which emphasises the need to preserve world peace. Aitmatov depicts a Soviet and an American cosmonaut co-operating on the space station *Parity* which has been established to work on an energy programme designed to help the whole of mankind. With a glance back at the Apollo-Soyuz space mission of 1975, Aitmatov postulates a future of even greater international scientific and political co-operation, but the name of the space station suggests that this can only occur when the USA and the USSR maintain strategic parity. The cosmonauts unexpectedly receive a communication from extra-terrestrial beings and journey to the planet Lesnaya Grud' (Forest Breast) where they meet an advanced civilisation which wishes to make contact with Earth. The people are friendly, do not believe in war or weapons, and want to help solve the earth's problems. They believe, for example, that: 'The present energy crisis, which has led people to rage, to despair, to the desire to take up the atomic bomb, is really just a very big technical problem which all countries could solve if they chose to discuss it'. However, when the cosmonauts wire back to base asking if Lesnaya Grud' can make contact with Earth, both the Soviet and American authorities refuse and the earth is ringed with lethal weapons. Earth is so unprepared for a meeting with a harmonious extraterrestrial civilisation that it avoids the challenge.

At the VII Congress of Soviet Writers in 1981 the Chairman of the Writers' Union, Georgii Markov, declared that 'the "cosmic" line of the novel has been deemed by majority opinion to be questionable in many of its aspects', and that it is not successfully integrated with the rest of Aitmatov's novel, which he praised for its 'humanist values'. Soviet critics clearly objected to the science fiction tale not merely on aesthetic grounds, but also because it suggested that distrust and war are still endemic on the earth, and that the USSR and the USA are equally responsible for poor international relations. Aitmatov had evidently failed to disarm criticism by a preface in which he asserted that his aim in inventing the science fiction tale was 'to draw attention in a paradoxical hyperbolic fashion to a situation full of potential danger for people on earth'. Aitmatov not only made the general statement that 'pointless conflicts between peoples and the waste of material resources and mental energy on the arms race are the most monstrous crimes against mankind', but also bowed to party policy, making ritual references both to imperialism and the Chinese cultural revolution, and condemning the Olympic boycott of 1980 as 'an excuse for Cold War' (a complaint which now sounds ironic in view of the 1984 Olympic boycott by the Eastern bloc).

As Katerina Clark has shown [in her essay 'The Mutability of the Canon: Socialist Realism and Chingiz Aitmatov's "I dol'she veka dlitsia den" ', *Slavic Review,* 1984], Aitmatov's novel is so ambiguous that it admits of diametrically opposed interpretations by Soviet critics who wish to minimise its problematic aspects. Evgenii Sidorov conceded that the world is far from universal harmony, but took Aitmatov to task for depicting the parity of the two sides and failing to emphasise the irreconcilable differences between capitalism and communism. He regarded the establishment of the cordon of rockets round the earth as regrettable, but necessary because: 'We must endure and build our earthly fate ourselves, without the magical participation of reason from another planet'. Another critic, Yurii Mel'vil', speculated that the ban was imposed by the Americans, who could not allow a visit from emissaries of a higher civilisation that knew neither wars nor violence because this would undermine the very foundation of the capitalist world; the Soviet side was forced to agree in order to avoid war. Moreover, he claimed, if contact had been made, the reactionary forces would only have misused the advanced technology of the extra-terrestrial beings for their own militaristic purposes, and hence intensified the threat of world war.

Notwithstanding the ingenious interpretations advanced by Soviet critics in order to admit Aitmatov's novel to the pantheon of socialist realism, it is worth noting that the refusal of bureaucrats to meet a highly intelligent extraterrestrial civilisation on the grounds that the earth is not yet ready was one of the themes of the Strugatsky brothers' controversial [*Ulitka na sklone* (*Tale of a Triumvirate*)], published in the provincial journal *Angara* in 1968. The Strugatskys' depiction of the triumvirate which rejects the alien's request for a meeting in incomprehensible ideological jargon was reminiscent of the kangaroo courts of three judges in the Stalin period. Shortly after publication this issue of the journal was taken out of circulation, the editorial board was dismissed for 'political blindness', and the work has never appeared in book form in the USSR. Both the Strugatskys and Aitmatov, perhaps, were guilty of suggesting that Soviet society (as well as the modern Western world) could by no means be considered an advanced, harmonious civilisation.

Aitmatov's novel, which has been disparaged by Sinyavsky as 'a bad book', nevertheless struck a chord among the Soviet population. The émigré Victor Nekrasov reported in 1981 that a friend of his, a psychiatrist living in exile after seven years of imprisonment, had written that he was 'amazed by this book' and asked him to send three copies of it to Siberia. Aitmatov's genuine commitment to peace and international cooperation was demonstrated again in his speech at the VII Writers' Congress of 1981 which made no ideological points, but argued only that 'the end of the world . . . the suicide of the human race' was unthinkable, and expressed the hope that man would 'avoid technological barbarism and not dare to press that nuclear button in which all lives are connected'. Aitmatov's emphasis on the total catastrophe of nuclear war has been official party policy since Brezhnev's speech at Tula in January 1977. At the XXVI Congress in 1981 Brezhnev made it clear that the USSR did not want nuclear war or military superiority: 'To try to outstrip each other in the arms race or to expect to win a nuclear war is dangerous madness'. (pp. 261-63)

After Brezhnev's death both Andropov's peace initiatives and the original intransigence of the party leadership under Chernenko signalled changes of style in the Kremlin but no basic change of policy. The continuing 'Cold War' atmosphere was demonstrated by a novel directly concerned with the possibility of nuclear war, Victor Stepanov's [*Gromoverzhtsy, Nash sovremennik* (*The Thunderers*)] (1983), published during Andropov's short term of office. The novel follows Gromyko's policy of concentrating exclusively on relations between the USSR and the USA: a parallel is drawn between the breakdown of the friendship between a Soviet and an American nuclear submarine commander and the deterioration in Soviet-US relations. Stepanov includes certain new themes which reflect current Soviet concerns. Firstly, the USA is perceived as wishing to recover the nuclear superiority it possessed in the 1940s by testing new weapons in space. Secondly, although the novel is extremely anti-American in tone, a distinction is drawn between militaristic circles in the USA and an American scientist who becomes involved in the US peace movement. She is sympathetic to Soviet views, and eventually abandons her work on the training of dolphins for anti-submarine warfare. The USSR is presented as the wise protector not only of the human race, but also of 'the whole world . . . the whole planet'. (p. 266)

Post-Stalin fiction treating the themes of atomic energy and nuclear policy provides a good illustration of the Soviet writer's function as populariser of party policy. Because of the particularly stringent censorship which applied to such a politically sensitive subject, literature on this theme has tended to conform very closely to the party line. However, the prevalence of the themes of war, peace and nuclear weapons in Soviet literature is not merely, or even primarily, a response to party directives to write on these subjects; it also undoubtedly reflects the deepest preoccupations of individual writers, which may well correspond to widespread attitudes in Soviet society.

The study of Soviet fiction has certain implications for the Soviet interpretation of detente. A notable feature of post-Stalin literature is that, despite occasional changes of rhetoric, it has continued to express a remarkably consistent view on nuclear policy. In the successive eras of Khrushchev's 'peaceful coexistence', the reaction caused by the Vietnam War and the invasion of Czechoslovakia, Brezhnev's period of detente and the tension of the 1980s, fiction has faithfully reflected the ambiguous Soviet position which can be defined as the combination of an avowedly defensive policy with an offensive posture. Such consistency would seem to suggest that Soviet military policy has not changed much over the years: the differences between the periods of 'detente' and 'Cold War' reflect changes in the presentation rather than the substance of Soviet policy. Within this broad framework of conformity, however, different views held by 'liberals' and 'dogmatist' writers can be distinguished: such liberal writers as Evtushenko, Bondarev and Aitmatov lay more emphasis on peace; dogmatists, such as Kochetov and Chakovsky, on confronta-

tion. This difference of emphasis perhaps reflects the continuing debate in the USSR between adherents of a 'scientific' view that nuclear war would mean total catastrophe, and the 'dogmatists' who believe that victory is possible.

While the majority of writers used the margin of freedom permitted to them after 1953 to demonstrate their obedience to the dictates of the party, others exploited it effectively to express their own ideas, often through Aesopian devices. Post-Stalin fiction affords some real information about the history of the A-bomb programme, and offers, if only indirectly, some insight into the feelings of individual writers about such subjects as the disarmament campaign and the disposal of nuclear waste. It is, however, only dissident writers who directly challenge the party's military and foreign policy. In the new edition of *The First Circle* Solzhenitsyn claims that Stalin unwisely rejected the 1946 Baruch Plan to ban further research on nuclear weapons and place the American bomb under the control of an independent United Nations Atomic Energy Committee. He implies that the Soviet bomb is not merely a deterrent to capitalist aggression, but also a powerful means of internal control in the hands of the Soviet regime. Innokentii's Uncle Avenir states that if Stalin has the bomb, 'we shall never see freedom'. Solzhenitsyn also takes a sceptical view of peace propaganda by both the USSR and the USA: in his play *Candle in the Wind* (written in 1960, but not published abroad until 1969), which is set in an imaginary country containing elements of both capitalism and socialism, a journalist preparing for a congress admits: 'The idea is that every country should have the right to have nuclear weapons, but we have to serve it up as part of the struggle for peace. It's a very subtle business'. A similar attack on both sides can be discerned in Solzhenitsyn's protest against expulsion from the Writers' Union in 1969, when he spoke of the need for a sense of man's common humanity, since the Marxist concept of the class struggle would be irrelevant after the nuclear holocaust, 'when the few surviving bipeds will be wandering over the radioactive earth, dying'.

Alexander Zinov'ev, in *The Yawning Heights,* takes an ironic view of detente, which he dubs 'the Great Global Kissing', suggesting that it makes very little difference to Soviet policy. Leadiban (Brezhnev) announces the end of detente, declaring: 'There is no one left to kiss, and no one left to do the kissing. So we shall increase our military might not by a 100%, as had been planned, but by 200%'.

Although the USSR genuinely desires arms limitation as a means of freeing scarce resources for economic development, the study of Soviet fiction tends to corroborate Zinov'ev's view that Soviet peace propaganda is largely for foreign consumption only. During periods of international relaxation liberal writers, with their modified anti-capitalist rhetoric, are encouraged, because they project a more sophisticated image of the USSR abroad; but even in periods of detente writers are subjected to criticism if they venture beyond the party line, stressing the similarities between the West and the East, implying that both sides are equally to blame for the arms race, or expressing a desire for peace at any price. Pure pacifism is frowned upon, as has been shown by the harassment of such writers as Evtushenko and Okudzhava in the 1960s and Bykaŭ in the 1980s. Further evidence of the Soviet dislike of pure pacifism was provided by the arrest of members of the fledgeling independent dissident 'peace group' as early as June 1982. This does not, however, mean that the USSR does not desire peace; the central message of Soviet fiction, whether conformist, liberal or dissident, is that peace is essential—opinions are, however divided in the USSR, as in the West, about how this can best be achieved. (pp. 266-68)

Rosalind J. Marsh, "Soviet Fiction and the Nuclear Debate," in Soviet Studies, Vol. XXXVIII, No. 2, April, 1986, pp. 248-69.

Vladimir Gakov and Paul Brians

[*In the following excerpt, Gakov and Brians provide a brief overview of what they consider the most influential works of nuclear war fiction published in the Soviet Union.*]

It is sometimes claimed that writers in the USSR have not been allowed to create works corresponding to the vast body of nuclear-war fiction published in the West. It is not surprising that scholars looking for such material have been unable to locate it, since the theme has hardly been a popular one in the Soviet Union. However, Soviet SF authors, who have often dealt with the dangers posed by nuclear weapons, have in fact also depicted nuclear wars as having taken place. A survey of how Soviet authors have imagined a nuclear holocaust may be of special interest now that the dangers posed by the nuclear arms race are being brought forcefully to the world's attention by the successful negotiation of an agreement reducing the number of intermediate-range nuclear missiles in Europe.

Whether the extrapolation of nuclear holocaust will be as "successful" as other SF prophecies is, of course, not our main concern. If a holocaust comes, very likely no one will survive to assess the accuracy of our imaginings; or if some do survive, they will have more urgent concerns than debating literary matters. For the most part, these are not major contributions to fiction, and their style and technique are seldom worthy of much attention (although there are exceptions). It is precisely in what they reveal about Soviet attitudes that their principal interest lies. (p. 67)

It is true that for many years frank explorations of nuclear-war themes were discouraged by Soviet publishers. Not that there was any officially articulated policy on the subject; there was instead an unspoken taboo on depicting a future nuclear holocaust as occurring on Earth. True, holocaust fictions such as Bradbury's *Martian Chronicles* and *Fahrenheit 451* were translated and published, and films such as *On the Beach* were viewed by Soviet audiences; but it was felt by many authorities that the "social optimism" traditionally associated with Soviet writers should make them shun such nightmare visions of the future. Depicting a nuclear war as possible or probable was viewed as a sort of defeatism. The theme was labelled as "Western"—and dangerous for Soviet readers.

This taboo was not absolute, however. It was possible to depict nuclear-war themes in certain limited ways. For instance, such a war could be the result of a conspiracy by evil imperialists, or Western intelligence agencies might scheme to steal Soviet nuclear secrets. Such propagandistic works strikingly resembled their anti-Soviet counterparts in the West. Writers who preferred a more serious approach often depicted a nuclear war on another planet or even in the distant past (for instance, in ancient Atlantis or even before the Deluge). Nuclear wars could also be depicted in dreams or fantasies, so long as it was made clear that the wars had not really occurred.

A few SF authors went beyond these constraints and succeeded in publishing more or less realistic accounts of nuclear wars set on Earth. Some of these works escaped censorship on account of the very fact that they *were* SF and were therefore considered trivial and unworthy of serious attention.

The treatment of nuclear-war themes in Soviet literature developed long before Hiroshima, just as it did in the West. In 1922 there appeared Vladimir Orlovsky's [*Bunt atomov (Revolt of the Atoms)*], and in 1928. Vadim Nikol'sky's [*Cherez tysiachu let (A Thousand Years Hence)*]. These novels, rediscovered in the 1970s by Soviet scholars and bibliographers, have created something of a sensation. Both authors foresaw atomic wars, radiation disease, and even a powerful worldwide anti-nuclear movement. Nikol'sky's novel, remarkably enough, depicts a "terrible explosion in the year 1945 which blasted half of Europe." After the '20s, the subject seems to have been neglected until the late '50s.

1957 was a watershed year for Soviet SF. It was the first year after Stalin's crimes were exposed at the 20th Party Congress, and—of course—the year Sputnik was launched. The year was marked in SF by the publication of Ivan Efremov's [*Tumannost' Andromedy (The Andromeda Nebula)*], the first full-scale Communist utopia in Soviet literature, a landmark of the period and a launching pad for contemporary Soviet SF. In the prologue to his novel, Efremov mentions a nuclear holocaust, set on another planet, in more realistic terms than had been common before, blazing the way for many others, including the most famous of the new generation of courageous, socially responsible SF writers: [Arkady and Boris Strugatsky].

Their 1971 novel, [*Obitaemyi ostrov (Prisoners of Power)*], marked another important turning point in the development of Soviet nuclear-war fiction. Though set on an alien planet, its civilization is so similar to our own as to render unmistakable their warnings against the nuclear peril facing Earth. The world of this story has actually undergone a limited nuclear war and is still suffering from the aftermath when the Earthman-protagonist appears. The authors provide details clearly connected with nuclear war and familiar from their appearance in Western SF: weapons "gone mad" without human action, for instance. One of the more remarkable scenes is a tank attack which takes place in the epicenter of a nuclear blast. But more significant than these details is the almost pacifist atmosphere of the novel, rejecting war in general and nuclear war spe-

"Baby Play with Nice Ball?"

LIFE OR DEATH

THE ATOM

HUMANITY

Editorial cartoon recognizing humanity's newfound capability for destruction.

cifically, which is reminiscent of *All Quiet on the Western Front* or *A Farewell to Arms.*

For the generation coming of age in the early 1970s, this novel had a powerful impact, creating a conceptual breakthrough which helped to make possible the changes now described as the "new political thinking." During the early years of the current decade, which marked the final phase of the "years of stagnation," SF led the way in courageously depicting the subject of nuclear war in hitherto taboo ways. This breakthrough was assisted by the development of the "nuclear winter" theory, worked on simultaneously by both Western and Soviet scientists. As the probable consequences of a full-scale nuclear conflict became apparent, attitudes began to shift, both in the minds of politicians and among writers of SF. The topic took on a new urgency. Both established mainstream and SF authors and newer, younger authors contributed to the development of this new body of nuclear-war SF, which in some ways anticipated, and even paved the way for, the drastic changes in Soviet society now defined by the two magic words, "perestroika" (restructuring) and "glasnost" (openness).

A group of young, highly-talented SF writers emerged during this decade who, if they did not form a self-conscious movement like the British New Wave or today's cyberpunks, experienced similar problems with their own old guard. They faced adverse criticism and often found it difficult to get their works published. But they persevered. Perhaps the greatest success of this group was the making of *Letters from a Dead Man,* the [1986 film directed by Konstantin Lopushansky]. . . . Paradoxically, just as this group is finding its voice and boldly exploring new themes, it is having difficulty getting published for another reason: at present Soviet readers are fascinated more by old works than by new. The formerly suppressed classics are being published: *Doctor Zhivago, We, Brave New World, Animal Farm, 1984,* and even *Darkness at Noon.* Everyone is especially fascinated with accounts of Soviet

history uncovering the secrets of the Stalin years, trying to recover the legacy of the past. Such material naturally crowds out much of the more speculative writing done by younger writers who, if they no longer risk suppression, do not appeal as directly to the popular taste. Soviet SF fans are as dedicated and enthusiastic as those in the West, but they do not make up a large proportion of the readership; and their desires are seldom taken into account in selecting which fiction should be published. Nevertheless, depictions of nuclear war continue to appear in the Soviet press. The theme is now clearly recognized as not only legitimate but important.

In all this varied body of work one characteristic stands out: Soviet fiction does not treat the theme of nuclear war frivolously, as have so many Western SF novels, thrillers, and survivalist adventure stories. In all recent Soviet nuclear-war fiction, the authors are deadly serious about the subject and view themselves as participants in the worldwide movement towards peace in a world in which nuclear weapons have been eliminated. (pp. 68-70)

Vladimir Gakov and Paul Brians, "Nuclear-War Themes in Soviet Science Fiction: An Annotated Bibliography," in Science-Fiction Studies, *Vol. 16, No. 1, March, 1989, pp. 67-84.*

NUCLEAR WAR AND WOMEN WRITERS

Martha A. Bartter

[*In the following essay, Bartter surveys works of nuclear fiction, determining whether women writers portray nuclear war differently than their male counterparts.*]

Stories seriously exploring the kind of world that might follow an atomic war appeared in American science fiction as early as 1927. Most are very pessimistic. Those that reflect the World War I experience of prolonged stalemates and escalation of deadly inventions expect atomic weapons to be used by both sides, with horrible consequences. Many predict a forced return to primitive or medieval conditions, often with complications from residual radiation. A few writers posit advantageous radiation-induced mutations, including the ability to read minds, longevity, and the like, in a kind of desperate denial. But for most, atomic war stands as the ultimate representation of human self-hatred and self-destruction, calling racial survival into serious question.

During its "Golden Age," science fiction wasn't supposed to be a woman's genre, and war was never supposed to be a woman's issue. Survival of the human race, however, has always been women's responsibility. Do women science fiction writers treat this topic in some special way? (p. 254)

In contrast to the familiar science fiction pattern that removes action to a safe distance in time or space, nuclear war stories immediately responding to the bombing of Hiroshima and Nagasaki are usually set on earth in the near future. The first were written by men; they usually consider the outcome for humanity in broad metaphorical terms. Women writers brought the fallout home. Judith Merril's "That Only a Mother" (1948) takes place during a prolonged atomic war, and deals with teratogenic mutations: the hopeful young mother who tells the story delivers a phocomelic infant whose deformity she refuses to recognize. The child is abnormally bright and precocious. A gender-based conflict then arises, since the father sees only his daughter's physical abnormalities while the mother is aware only of her abilities. The story ends with the unresolved question: Will the father kill his child?

Just a month later, Margaret St. Clair published "Quis Custodiet . . . ?" in which a "final solution" seems possible to the continuing, apparently inevitable conflict between the few humans remaining after an atomic war and a race of mechanically practical mutants whose hatred of all living things depicts postwar sterility even more clearly than does the nearly desertified planet. The humans decide not to wipe out the mutants, even at their own peril; they failed as custodians of life once, and the resulting mutants are their constant reminder of their responsibility to life now.

"The Hole in the Moon" (1952) by the same author is set in a junkyard representing the postatomic world. Some of the women have been infected with a disease that makes them physically coarse and avid for sex, but does not kill them. It is, however, deadly to males. The male protagonist simultaneously desires and fears sexual contact. After he repulses an apparently healthy "dream woman," he invites an obviously infected woman into his shack, assuring her, in drunken despair, that *he* won't hurt *her.*

Alice Eleanor Jones's "Created He Them" (1955) is narrated by Ann, mother of seven children, who must submit to her arrogant, hated husband because he can breed and she can bear normal children. Other women, sterile or the mothers of defective children destroyed by the "Center," bribe her with scarce food for the opportunity to lavish attention on two children still at home; they will be taken to the Center at the age of three, presumably to be trained for war or for further breeding. Fritz Leiber explores the same theme in "The Moon Is Green" (1952), which ends with the woman's madness and death. Jones more realistically if less artistically shows her protagonist's grim resignation to intolerable life: "In this desolate, dying, bombed-out world," Ann muses, "we have to live, and we have to live together. Because . . . we are among the tiny percentage of the people in this world who can have normal children. We hate each other, but we breed true."

In each of these early stories, women took a jaundiced view of the post-atomic future. They are less interested in winning than in reproduction—life itself—which men, with their mutilated intra- and interpersonal skills, fail to cope with. Maggie may be mad in "That Only a Mother," but she nurtures the mutant girl-child who may represent the human race's only future; her husband, whose war-work has exposed them both to psychological and genetic hazard, probably will kill it. In a world where even the moon is damaged, Margaret St. Clair denies that the sex

act has a future. A woman reminds the men of their failed custodianship in "Quis Custodiet . . . ?" but women have become sexual victims in the equally sterile world of "Created He Them." Carol Emshwiller's "Day at the Beach" (1959) seems more cheerful; it shows the day-to-day struggle for normality by the mother of an unpleasant "throwback" son, who may represent the best the postwar human race can breed. A story that particularly contrasts with Emshwiller's is Robert Spencer Carr's "Mutation" (1951), where the savage throwback Kane, representing humanity, is naturally supplanted by his equally mutant but angelically beautiful brother. Unlike Carr, Emshwiller does not opt for miracles, only for the ability to live each day in the most humane fashion possible even though the race may have lost the ability to reproduce itself.

Before and immediately after World War II, science fiction was largely a pulp literature. In the 1950s science fiction novels began to show up in bookstores, largely due to the popularity of Heinlein's young adult novels. While science fiction magazines encouraged grim stories of atomic war, regular publishers usually rejected them. An exception is Helen Clarkson's *The Last Day* (1959), which offers no hope of survival whatever. While Clarkson does not provide the evidence of worldwide death from nuclear fallout that Nevil Shute does in *On the Beach* (1957), her intimate, homely details certainly imply it.

In the 1950s, women followed established, androgynous patterns in their postnuclear war novels: Andre Norton's *Star Man's Son* (1952) and Leigh Brackett's *The Long Tomorrow* (1955) each shows regression to a "primitive" society, Norton to Amerindian tribalism, and Brackett to an anti-technological New Mennonite agrarianism. Each uses the "Grail quest" form of coming-of-age story, with a male protagonist. In each book the quest is for knowledge. Like the first story in Miller's *A Canticle for Leibowitz* (1955-59), the novels by Norton and Brackett assume that the post-holocaust world will reject science. Norton's Fors, who would have been trained as an acknowledged seeker, or Star Man, had he not been declared mutant and thrown out of the tribe, has to make his quest without the aid of his society. Brackett's young men are beaten when they seek to extend their schooling beyond the prescribed age of fifteen, and must leave their society completely to acquire the new knowledge they so desperately want.

Each story assumes that a patriarchal system relying strongly on tradition will naturally dominate the postholocaust society. Brackett's New Mennonites are perhaps more rigid about their social organization than are Norton's Star Men, but each society is unforgiving of differences within the group and murderous of differences without. Whole populations are declared "the enemy" and warred upon. At the end of *Star Man's Son,* the various tribes unite—but only to fight the mutated Beast Men more effectively. While the patriarchal tradition is challenged by the young men's quest in each book, and some (slow, gradual) changes toward recreating a modern world will probably occur, Brackett faces, far more consciously than Norton, the realization that knowledge can be dangerous in and of itself.

By 1960, the public had apparently tired of postnuclear war stories. They became less popular with science fiction writers, particularly with women. In fact, none were published by American women between 1959 and 1973, when Vonda K. McIntyre's "Of Mist, and Grass, and Sand" described a desertified, possibly postnuclear world developed more explicitly in her later books. This fifteen-year hiatus is significant: it spans the inception of the women's liberation movement. It also marks the end of stories set in unselfconsciously patriarchal societies, and the beginning of postnuclear societies based on overt domination of one sex by the other. If we have found few radical differences in the way men and women treat the topic of racial survival before the 1970s, we may now expect radical differences to appear. They do.

Suzy McKee Charnas' *Walk to the End of the World* (1974) is an angry book. Human culture seems limited to the Holdfast, a small relatively fertile coastal area. Women (called "fems") are blamed by the men for the destruction of prewar society, and are treated like animals; they would have to rise several degrees to approach slavery. One man plans to breed fems as food. The men treat each other badly, too; they lie, cheat, use, and kill each other to obtain severely limited resources. The fems believe that somewhere outside the Holdfast women may live free of men, and they help Alldera, a fem trained to carry messages, to escape her master in order to bring help for her fellows, even as the men's feuds continue the destruction of Holdfast.

In the sequel, *Motherlines* (1978), Alldera is found by the "Riding Women" of the plains, who live entirely without men. Pregnant and starving when found, Alldera learns to live with the Riding Women, descendents of a prewar genetic experiment who can give birth parthenogenetically when stimulated by mating with a young stallion. Unlike most escaped fems, Alldera is accepted for the sake of her daughter, who the Riding Women hope may give a new Motherline to their race, and stays with them. Alldera also finds the Free Fems she has been seeking; organized under a matriarch, they hope to liberate the fems of the Holdfast, but have been prevented by the Riding Women who fear retaliation by the men. Now the Holdfast seems too weak to fear, and the Riding Women see that, under Alldera's leadership, such a foray might indeed be useful. But unlike the Riding Women, who cannot initiate new lines but can reproduce, fem society has little hope of survival; they cannot breed without men nor will they live with men of Holdfast, if any remain.

Vonda K. McIntyre's *The Exile Waiting* (1975) takes place in a bomb shelter big enough to hold a small city, built in natural caves. Long after the war that devastated Earth, it remains a closed society, clutching the remains of technology that permit life to continue underground. But people are not very healthy, nor is the society: run by a capricious oligarchy, it oppresses most for the pleasure of a very few. Many children are defective, and mutants are banished to the lower caverns, where they lead a difficult but less brutal life than people do in Center. The heroine, a young thief, manages to escape but we see no sign that the society itself will change.

Kate Wilhelm's *Where Late the Sweet Birds Sang* (1976) has a somewhat different premise: worldwide ecological disaster sets off a nuclear war. The combination destroys human fertility, even among a small group of well-prepared and sheltered people; anticipating this possibility, they clone themselves. A few generations later, their society consists of groups of clones who are empathic almost to the point of telepathy, but who must venture in small bands into the world beyond their valley to salvage necessary equipment from the ruins. (Their inability to reproduce old equipment and their inability to reproduce biologically new individuals forms a metaphoric counterpoint.) Leaving the valley disrupts the clone group and causes some to go mad, although one woman learns to enjoy solitude. Her naturally conceived child is the only one able to think independently, and the only one with any imagination or creativity. He learns woodscraft and survival skills, eventually kidnaps some of the fertile women, who are kept by the clones as brainwashed, isolated prisoners, and starts his own colony. Some years later he returns to find the valley deserted; his now-healthy group may literally be all that is left of humanity.

Pamela Sargent's *The Shore of Women* (1986) deliberately reverses the situation in Charnas's *Walk to the End of the World*. Sargent's women live in technologically comfortable walled cities scattered broadly across the face of North America, while locking all men out in the wilderness. The men live in primitive fashion; if they begin to band together, the women attack and kill them. At intervals, men are attracted to "shrines" where they are deliberately given erotic dreams, both to collect their semen and to ensure their allegiance to the woman-centered religion. Inside the city, women who form attachments to their male infants are punished, since all boys are brainwashed and put outside the wall at an early age. The protagonist is a girl thrown out of the city for not condemning her mother's behavior. She survives, mates with, and comes to love a man (in the city women enjoy physical love only with each other), bears a daughter, and returns to the city to begin the subversion of the status quo.

In these later books, we do find more feminine protagonists, and more competent ones, than we did before the raising of women's consciousness. Vonda K. McIntyre's *Dreamsnake* and Joan Vinge's "Phoenix in the Ashes" (both 1978) each depict an attractive and vital woman coping with a difficult world. Carol Amen's film *Testament* (1983) reflects Clarkson's *The Last Day;* both protagonists remain loving, competent and sane to the end, no easy feat. In Susan B. Weston's *Children of the Light* (1984) the protagonist is male, but the most effective characters are female. M. J. Engh's *Arslan* (1976) consciously and deliberately denies value or voice to the women who are Arslan's chief victims. Only James Tiptree, Jr.'s, "The Man Who Walked Home" (1979) assumes a male-dominated social structure and a male narrative voice. Of the nineteen works considered here, nine and one-third (considering the three sections of Wilhelm's *Where Late the Sweet Birds Sang* separately) employ a female protagonist: Merril, Jones, Clarkson, Emshwiller, Charnas, McIntyre, Wilhelm [in the first section of *Where Late the Sweet Birds Sang*], and Amen; the first four were written before 1959. Seven and two-thirds employ a male protagonist: St. Clair, Norton, Brackett, Engh, Tiptree, Weston, and Wilhelm [in the second section of *Where Late the Sweet Birds Sang*]; again, the first four precede the women's movement. Vinge and Sargent divide their stories fairly evenly between male and female protagonists, though Sargent gives almost all the important action to the females.

Once a writer has posited life after nuclear death, she has the opportunity to describe the society that gets established. How much it resembles prewar society is the author's option, since one of the reasons to posit atomic destruction is to clear the decks for the next stage of human development. In each of these works, we see a society organized along hierarchical lines, generally resisting change. Whether the society is dominated by men (as it is in all but two of the books) or by women, it is run by the few for the few, and the maintenance of control seems a paramount concern. This is not surprising in *The Long Tomorrow* and *Star Man's Son,* in which tradition and fear of change run the society as much as do the leaders. They were written when the natural assumption of male domination went more or less unquestioned. But it does seem surprising that this tacit assumption has remained unchallenged in the postholocaust stories by Wilhelm and Tiptree.

Very few works that posit any postnuclear future for the human race anticipate a more egalitarian society. Most writers assume that a highly authoritarian social structure will naturally follow nuclear war. Nine describe male-dominated hierarchies: Merril, Norton, Jones, Brackett, Clarkson, [Charnas in *Walk to the End of the World,* McIntyre in *The Exile Waiting*], Engh, Vinge, and Wilhelm; only Charnas [in *Motherlines*] and Sargent describe female-dominated systems, and these do so only by eliminating male competition. St. Clair [in "Quis Custodiet . . .?"] and Charnas [in *Motherlines*] show a higher level of caring and sharing than do the unambiguously male-dominated works, while McIntyre [in *Dreamsnakes*] and Weston present systems with some genuine freedom of choice and humanitarian goals. It should be noted that these less authoritarian systems function in a world as ecologically damaged as that of the hierarchically ordered works, if not more so; we cannot ascribe the sometimes savage dominance systems solely to the need for physical survival.

Political dominance is frequently evidenced by sexual dominance, often including sexual bondage or separation of the sexes. True to the science fiction tradition of questioning accepted patterns, males do not automatically dominate females in these works: Charnas [in *Walk to the End of the World*] and [in *The Exile Waiting*] show a high level of male-dominated sexual repression, while Sargent describes an equally high level of female-dominated repression. Charnas [in *Walk to the End of the World*], Jones, McIntyre [in *The Exile Waiting*], Wilhelm, and Engh all show enslavement of women to some degree, including rape, forced breeding, and prostitution; Sargent applies the same enslavement to men. Vinge shows a religious society that rigidly prescribes "correct," submissive behavior for women, including arranged marriage. Wilhelm's clones employ a group-dominated repression of women, in which infertile females cooperate in the reproductive slavery of fertile ones. Charnas [in *Motherlines*] and Sargent present female single-sex communities. Normal sexual relations occur only in five stories: Merril, Norton, Brackett, McIntyre [in *Dreamsnake*], and Weston. This ratio differs significantly from the postholocaust stories written by men during this period, most of which take marriage and reproduction for granted. I have found only one book by a male author which suggests that coercion might be necessary to maintain postwar reproduction—J. Neil Schulman's *The Rainbow Cadenza* (1983). Stories by male writers usually focus on technology, especially on methods of recovering or retaining a technological society, while assuming either a "primitive" (male-dominated) social structure or a familiar one in which men naturally make the important decisions, but graciously allow women their proper sphere (production and reproduction) and some autonomy.

Technology can look quite unmechanical when a woman writes about it. McIntyre's *Dreamsnake* is set in the same world as *The Exile Waiting,* but has little to do with the underground Center. Instead, the ecologically devastated Earth itself becomes a character in the story, which follows Snake, a healer in a world without drugs, research, or hospitals. The healers have developed a medical technology which treats disease with mutated snakes, including the rare, alien Dreamsnake. The scarcity of Dreamsnakes limits the effectiveness of the healers, so learning to breed them becomes a metaphor for the potential health of the planet itself. McIntyre explores societies varying from extended families run by a dominant person (male or female) with democratic input, to a full dictatorship run by a sadistic man, to a kind of creative anarchy among the healers.

Eventually Snake learns that by overprotecting the Dreamsnakes they have prevented them from reaching maturity. This metaphor also applies to the underground Center: as we saw in *The Exile Waiting,* living shut away from the dangers of the natural environment has produced a hot-house culture where the few completely dominate the many, where mutations abound and are discarded, and where everything outside their own shelter is made to seem so dangerous that those who leave cannot distinguish these paranoid warnings from true ones. True knowledge leads to true understanding; as the Dreamsnake will breed when allowed to mature, so may the world someday come to healthy maturity. McIntyre's Healers stand in opposition to Engh's Arslan, a gnostic idealist who conquers the world with nuclear blackmail so he can sterilize all females, thus neatly eliminating the human race. Each employs biotechnology; Arslan's sterilizing virus becomes a metaphoric complement to McIntyre's healing serpent.

In Weston's *Children of the Light,* a concerned and informed young man of today is thrown forward into a small community, a lifetime after holocaust. He brings knowledge that he cannot communicate to share with the people he finds there; they don't even know what the atomic war was, much less what caused it. He also brings undamaged sperm that they not only can use but cannot survive without. But in their struggle to survive and reproduce in their tainted environment, they have formed a caring society based on ability and cooperation. Given a choice, a woman from a rigid, hierarchical society joins their group and becomes warmly human.

We can now address the question initially posed in this paper: Do women science fiction writers treat postnuclear survival in some special way? Long-term survival of the human race essentially depends upon two factors: peace and procreation. Women writers are not optimistic about either one. Merril and Jones depict a technologically competent world engaging in permanent war, with resultant social and genetic damage. Nine works that describe the world as reverting to a less technological condition assume "naturally" recurring intergroup conflict: [St. Clair in "Quis Custodiet . . . ?"], Norton, Bracket, Charnas [in *Walk to the End of the World*] (in [her *Motherlines*] there is conflict but no killing), [McIntyre in *The Exile Waiting*] Vinge, Weston and Sargent. Only St. Clair [in "Quis Custodiet . . .?"] and Weston include a concerted attempt to substitute a cooperative society for the combative one.

Given a high level of radiation and a damaged ecology, procreation is problematic. In such a world, Jones says, the race will continue only if those who can breed will—or must—do so. Merril, Emshwiller, and Weston suggest that males may be more susceptible to genetic damage than females. Clarkson, Engh, and more recently, Carol Amen's movie *Testament* (1983) go further, assuming that future war will leave no survivors. . . . Only Norton, Brackett, Vinge, and Tiptree take the human race's ability to replenish the postnuclear earth for granted.

This evidence that women write more pessimistically than men about postnuclear reproduction raises another question: Why do women so often represent feminist concerns not by portraying strong, independent female protagonists, but by combining images of nuclear war with sexual slavery? (We should note that women are inevitably constrained either to overtly reject or to tacitly accept patriarchy in their work. Even those who most detest the conditions that inform their stories, including the threat of nuclear war, cannot assume that feminist issues will simply go away, as many male writers seem to do.)

Patriarchy depends upon what we may call the *genetic fantasy* in which masculinity is proven by fertility. This fantasy has various corollaries, including the castration complex (a woman "castrates" a man by refusing to bear his child) and the inheritance complex (the belief that "blood will tell" and its corollary, that a man can't ensure his bloodline unless he owns "his woman"). Note that the patronymic—a mark of ownership—still dies out in our culture if no male children survive, no matter how many girls do.

Postholocaust stories by men usually assume the genetic fantasy as a given, while simultaneously employing the *technology fantasy:* humans can fix anything if they apply enough intelligence and effort. The corollaries to this fantasy include the belief that machines are necessary to survival, and that intelligence and effort are by themselves

good and deserve to be rewarded. Even a reduced biosphere and genetic damage can be overcome by proper machinery and hard work. Wilhelm and Vinge raise this fantasy only to refute it. Although Sargent most clearly assumes it, the technology fantasy seems to be mainly a masculine preoccupation.

The genetic fantasy and the technology fantasy are both corollaries of the *control fantasy;* both depend upon the same basic assumption: The world is dangerous; control makes it safe(r). To be "out of control" is to be unmanly (hysterical, womb-sick). Being "masculine" means domination (by hierarchy, religion, bureaucracy, etc.) of people, and technological control (by agriculture, cities, power sources, machines, science, etc.) of everything else. Oppression and ownership of women stems from male fear of losing control over reproduction. In their science fiction stories, few women reject technology entirely, but they do demonstrate how many things can't be controlled. Either overtly or tacitly, they recognize that domination opposes and denies fecundity—the spontaneous possibilities of reproduction.

Few women opt to play the genetic fantasy game, though they frequently show themselves as the victims of it. They recognize the inter- and intrapersonal damage these fantasies inflict upon those who live by them, and present this damage in fiction by metaphors of domination and sterility. This may be interpreted as radical feminism, but it has much wider implications. Women who use nuclear war to highlight the lethal self-hatred that permits anyone to reject those aspects of self that represent "the other"—sexually or psychologically—naturally must show the postwar society as continuing this rejection of self. Most writers recognize that the resulting rigid, domineering society is implicitly unstable, but manage only to anticipate and deplore its self-destruction. Unlike many male novelists, women do not anticipate a postholocaust utopia. If the present society is so anti-life that it has destroyed our culture and our world in nuclear war, they show that the result will represent our worst fears, not our secret hopes.

The message of these works is clear: survival of the race depends on humans living cooperatively with their world and themselves. The relationship between nations, like that between man and his environment, can most powerfully be represented in fiction by the relationship between men and women. If the male-female relationship is destroyed—by infertility, by sexual domination, or by separation of the sexes, each a malignant aspect of control—then the human race is finished, no matter how well stabilized the technological, political, and social situation may seem. Given our contemporary situation, it is no accident that only Charnas's Riding Women, McIntyre's Healers, and Weston's Idamore settlers actively explore the possibility of a cooperative society. "The hand that rocks the cradle rules the world" takes on new meaning in the context of postatomic holocaust. (pp. 254-63)

Martha A. Bartter, "The Hand That Rocks the Cradle," in Extrapolation, *Vol. 30, No. 3, Fall, 1989, pp. 254-66.*

Louise Kawada

[In the following essay, Kawada examines how American women poets have responded to the threat of nuclear war. Noting that nuclear war poetry is popular with women writers, she attempts to discover why this genre appeals to them and whether their work is "gender-marked."]

The topics of nuclear destruction and the Promethean gamble with leak-prone power plants have attracted the attention of several women poets: Amy Clampitt, June Jordan, Sharon Olds, Carole Oles, Marge Piercy, Maxine Kumin, and most notably Denise Levertov, who has continued to be one of the most prominent voices in the antinuclear movement. The number of poets surprises, for war and the machinery of war have traditionally been the domain of male poets. Among even these poets, however, the attitude toward conventional warfare has undergone a metamorphosis, and the mark of modern poetry appears to be a very unsentimental and antiheroic response toward war. Whitman, for example, while in the process of writing *Drum-Taps* and nursing the wounded, recanted his early hawkish enthusiasm for war. In like manner Siegfried Sassoon and Wilfrid Owen (in contrast to their fellow Englishman Rupert Brooke) described the horror of war, refusing to see its carnage as a sign of patriotic benevolence. The axiom to be derived from the history of poetry is that those poets who knew war firsthand (as did Whitman, Sassoon, and Owen) hated war; and a second principle follows that the more massive and faceless war has grown in its destructive force, the less likely it is to excite celebratory fervor.

A kind of military millennialism is abroad that suffers the success of its own enterprise and knows now (or should know) that there cannot be, in any effective sense, a war to end all wars. How then to rise out of this situation when the fathers have taken provisions to their care-taking limits? Nuclear war is yet another matter—the massive and faceless taken to unimaginable extremes. The situation is not accommodating to the writer, for as Terrence Des Pres observes, "Nuclear threat engenders cynicism, despair, allegiance to a mystique of physical force, and to say No to such destructive powers requires an enormously vehement Yes to life and human values." This yes-saying, in fact, seems to be the logical and necessary next stage to the earlier denial by the poets of war's uplifting grandeur. Arguably, moreover, women poets have expanded their range of themes and subjects and found a voice and vision that affirm life, even in their awareness of efforts to suppress or efface that life. The issue of nuclear threat for women writers on its most fundamental level is the issue of the use and abuse of power, which often manifests itself as racism, sexism, or environmental pollution. For a woman poet, the act of confronting nuclear threat and the social ills that accompany that threat somehow reminds her of the extraordinary richness and beauty of what must be protected and saved. That vehement yes-saying to life is the most distinguishing and striking characteristic of women's writing on nuclear themes, and it stands as a reminder of poetry's own power to offer salvation and renew a sense of value.

The emergence of several American women poets who write so compellingly on nuclear issues is the subject of this paper, which tries to understand this phenomenon by asking three different questions:

1. What is it about the prospect of nuclear war more so than conventional war that compels this level of feminine response?

2. Is this response, aside from the fact of its female authorship, in any sense gender-marked? Do women poets contemplate and write about nuclear war in ways that are different from a male poet's response to nuclear threat?

3. And finally, is the poetic response, its techniques, form and tropes in the writing by women poets itself gender-marked?

Have women poets in their confrontation with nuclear issues modified or challenged principles of poetic decorum? Have they in their political vision begun to radicalize an esthetic?

To ask the questions is to begin to move toward comprehending the uniqueness of these poets' contributions. Women are likely to speak out against nuclear power and nuclear arms buildup because they feel they possess certain habits of mind, that, if shared and transferred, might effect a change of consciousness. In recent years much has been written about women's developmental patterns and their concepts of order and value. A new theory states that what were once deficits in the pattern of women's maturation—their failure to achieve a strongly demarcated identity, their tendency to merge and empathize with others often at the expense of self, and their need to be loved as well as to love—can from another point of view be perceived as strengths. Jean Baker Miller has written that women are "more thoroughly prepared to move toward more advanced, more affiliative ways of living—and less wedded to the dangerous ways of the present." Writing on the ways women acquire an ethical sense, Carol Gilligan has observed that women define the issues in a moral problem as "a problem of care and responsibility in relationships rather than as one of rights and rules. . . . The inflicting of hurt is considered selfish and immoral in its unconcern, while the expression of care is seen as the fulfillment of moral responsibility."

The research of Miller and Gilligan reinforce on many levels women's preference for connectedness over separation. Clearly, a stance that values connection and relatedness and that denies a hierarchical mode of thinking intrinsic to separation is one that can be effectively applied to a world that needs to renew its sense of connection. Perhaps women poets are now speaking out against nuclear issues and political injustice because women as a group have learned to value their habits of mind that favor cooperation and recognize interdependence.

This ethos is reflected thematically in several of the poems examined here. In a manner that sets these poems apart form a masculine treatment of the same material, women poets tend to contextualize nuclear threat and see it in relation to other social ills and problems. If the bomb has been a means of stabilizing a nation's supremacy, then women poets from their marginalized position as women within society are likely to examine the concept of supremacy along with the problems of hunger, poverty, suppression, and resentment that ensue in maintaining supremacy. Moreover, the act of speaking out is in itself a positive act; and by some turning—the driving force of the survivor perhaps—the poems themselves tend to sound a positive note, suggesting, if not optimism, then a willed refusal to despair.

In anticipation of a more elaborate answer to the question of poetic style, it would appear that women poets are strongly conscious of a need to speak out clearly and openly on the threats posed by nuclear power. The depersonalization of the nuclear age calls for a corresponding change in esthetic principles, one that values directness over indirectness, specificity over suggestion. The poets presented here are, in effect, revising the ideas of poetic decorum in order to fashion a new poetry for a new age.

Alternative visions often take root in the unpromising soil of anger and outrage. One of the sources of women's anger mentioned in their poetry is the favoring by the dominant, decision-making culture of abstract "higher" principles and the consequent devaluing of everyday realities and needs. This split that promotes absence of feeling and hierarchizes the intellect over the senses—doing what it must "to make the world safe for Democracy"—is explored by several women poets, in particular Denise Levertov. "Reason has brought us / more dread than ignorance did," Levertov tells us in one poem, while in another, significantly titled, "A Split Mind," she describes a governor who offers to his granddaughter as a plaything an architect's model of a nuclear power plant he is trying to get approval for, despite warnings about the health hazards the plant would pose:

> "Goddamn commies," he mutters, crushing
> the report on nuclear hazards into a ball and
> tossing it across the room, ignoring
> the wastebasket and plutonium and the idea
> that he could be wrong, one gesture
> sufficing for all.

The poem concludes with a question, directed back upon the governor but also outward to readers:

> How deep, how deep
> does the split go, the fault line
> under the planned facility,
> into his mind?

Levertov suggests that there well may be more than a natural split in the earth that would make the facility unsafe, but there is also a sad irony in the use of "split mind" to describe the governor. His mind is split, not in the sense that he deliberates between two choices ("to be of a split mind"), but rather that his beliefs are already so entrenched that he refuses to examine new data and hear different opinions.

"The Split Mind" with its word plays and implicit ironies is more literarily self-conscious than other poems Levertov has written when she confronts her own disgust and outrage. Her most recent volume, *Oblique Prayers* (1984), is more outspoken. "Rocky Flats" talks about the hubris

of scientists who have not "tamed" (itself a word suggesting dominance) the wild mushroom but propose out of their pride to domesticate the nuclear mushroom cloud and its spores of death. As they work in the lab, they "shield their minds from horror, shield their hands / with rubber." The first "covering up" can prove fatal in its consequences, while the second seems laughably futile.

Scientists, here specifically those hired to do research for the Pentagon, are again the object of Levertov's ire in "Watching *Dark Circle.*" She recalls a sequence in the film *Dark Circle* in which laboratory pigs are burned to simulate the responses of human beings to nuclear fire. This act is not a scientific experiment, Levertov tells her readers, but an obscenity:

> Men are willing
> to call the roasting of live pigs
> a simulation of certain conditions. It is
> not a simulation. The pigs (with their high-rated
>   intelligence,
> their uncanny precognition of disaster) are real,
> their agony real agony, the smell
> is not archetypal breakfast nor ancient feasting
> but a foul miasma irremovable from the nostrils,
> and the simulation of hell these men
> have carefully set up
> is hell itself,
>   and they in it, dead in their lives,
> and what can redeem them? What can redeem
>   them?

Levertov's directness here, her denial of the aptness of "simulation," is an important poetic act to perform in an age that shields the mind from awareness through a smoke screen of language. Language, that element of civilized life that should be on the side of preserving its content, often is used to distort truth. Celia Gilbert, for example, in her long poem "Lot's Wife" quotes directly from Frank W. Chinnock's *Nagasaki: The Forgotten Bomb* to illustrate how language can suppress the truth and deny connection between the doer and the deed. Chinnock describes the bomber pilot, Sweeney:

> Sweeney was like most bomber pilots who have
> formed a defensive armor about their particular
> role in war. Their function is to drop bombs on
> targets not on people. Were they to think otherwise, to be ordered to drop a bomb on say, 2,567
> men, women, and children, they would probably
> go mad. A target was a different matter.

What is important to perceive in the poems referred to so far is that persons in authority—governors, scientists, soldiers—have pursued what they define as a higher law, a nobler set of principles, at the expense of human lives and the human spirit. The only way to live with that compromise is to deny that a compromise has ever been made.

A poem by Amy Clampitt, "A New Life," describes a young woman, allegorically named Autonomy, who has traded any real human qualities for an image-setting style and life in the fast track. The problem of compromise and any reflection on moral decisions never trouble Autonomy, who could not fit these thoughts into her busy schedule of job, Econ class, husband, and toddler (Autonomy, Jr.). Autonomy's life resembles the hurtled rush along a freeway; and, appropriately, Clampitt speculates on endings, whether by some new "mother-lode of still smarter bombs, the germ / of an ever cleverer provocation to instability / within the neutron" or by the muddled, madding rush of her life as "artifice of the pursuit of happiness." The only question that remains is whether the end will be "as the green-haired prophets of punk would have it, / a total, or only a partial / apocalyptic freakout." Clampitt's bitingly acerbic language of wit mocks its own fall. To call either a mental breakdown or a nuclear holocaust an "apocalyptic freakout" is a decadent yet somehow familiar gesture. The vernacular has co-opted the mysterious and the dreaded, literally melting down the aspect of terror in its own cool idiom.

Canadian poet and novelist Margaret Atwood presents cryptic Blakean proverbs and questions that stand as a gloss on the poems just discussed and offer a bridge to other themes. She addresses a spectral "you who started the countdown," and asks:

> When will you learn
> the flame and the wood/flesh
> it burns are whole and the same?
>
> You attempt merely power
> you accomplish merely suffering
> How long do you expect me to wait
> while you cauterize your
> senses, one
> after another
> turning yourself to an
> impervious glass tower?
> How long will you demand I love you?
> I'm through, I won't make
> any more flowers for you
> I judge you as the trees do
> by dying.

The split in sensibility that favors reason and denies the sense can lead to other kinds of deterioration and loss, as Atwood implies in the concluding couplets. The Earth, its beauty and its bounty, is doomed if mankind persists in its careless pollution and wanton destruction. As Atwood observes in another poem:

> In view of the fading animals
> the proliferation of sewers and fears
> the sea clogging, the air
> nearing extinction
> we should be kind, we should
> take warning, we should forgive each
>   other. . . .

While both men and women poets have linked nuclear power issues to a concern for ecology and a sense of the earth's precious fragility, women poets are more likely to ask why the ecosystem has been thrown into imbalance and what mind-set has caused the decline. For women writers, no one social problem exists in isolation from another; connections must be made to find a common etiology among a set of problems—pollution, poverty, racism, misogyny—before a new web of connections can be woven to reflect the sacredness and unity of life.

In an "Address to the Commission on the Environment and Energy" at the World Peace Parliament in 1980,

Levertov named anthropocentrism, the view that man is "the natural ruler of the world, whose 'manifest destiny' is to 'conquer Nature,' " as the mindset that is leading the earth towards destruction. She appealed in the Address "to think deeply about what it means to be a human being, and realize that we cannot attain our beautiful common goals, our vision of justice and compassion for all, by arrogantly violating our Mother, the Earth." [In *Candles in Babylon*] Levertov reiterates this appeal in her poetry by asking for "A culture of gardens, of horticulture not agribusiness." In another poem, "Beginners," dedicated to the memory of Karen Silkwood and Eliot Gralla, she asks her readers to envision "how it might be to live as siblings with beast and flower, / not as oppressors."

In one of her most recent poems, "Gathered at the River," Levertov describes how she gathered with others in late summer along the banks of the Charles River in Cambridge, Massachusetts, to launch candle boats in commemoration of the bombings of Hiroshima and Nagasaki. As the small gathering intones "Never again," Levertov senses the animate presence of the trees as watchful—and utterly dependent—witnesses. The trees listen, she claims,

> because the war
> we speak of, the human war with ourselves,
> the war against earth,
> against nature,
> is a war against them.

Levertov's poem neither resolves itself in any facile affirmation nor concludes with despair. The tension between the will and hope of the participants and their awareness of both history and current capability resonates throughout the poem, while the trees, which might have been mere landscape, are foregrounded as in themselves intelligent witnesses.

Other poets besides Levertov try to reawaken a sense of the holiness and the redemptive wholeness of nature in their readers. In "You Are In Bear Country," which serves as prologue to *The Long Approach,* Maxine Kumin asks the question, "*Is death / by bear to be preferred / to death by bomb?*" She answers "yes" and then invites the reader to "Come on in, Cherish / Your wilderness." "Wilderness," as the rest of the volume will explain, is the untamed beauty and mystery in organic life as well as a reorganized sense of order that would dislocate patterns of dominance.

Probably one of the most remarkable expressions of the connection between a devaluing of the earth and the looming potential for nuclear holocaust occurs in the prose poem "No Rock Ever Scorned Me As A Whore" by native American writer Chrystos. The concluding passage reads:

> I realized one day after another nuclear protest,
> another proposed bill to make a nuclear waste
> disposal here, that I had no power with
> those   My power rests with a greater being,
> a silence which goes on behind the uproar. . . .
> My distant ancestors knew some things that are
> lost to me & I would not have the insidious luxu-
> ry of this electric heat, this journal & pen with-
> out the concurrent problems of nuclear waste
> storage   When we are gone, someone else

will come   Dinosaur eggs might hatch in the
intense heat of nuclear explosions   I will be
sad to see the trees & birds on fire   Surely
they are innocent as none of us has been

With their songs, they know the sacred   I am
in a circle with that soft, enduring word   In
it is the wisdom of all peoples   Without a
deep, deep understanding of the sacredness of
life, the fragility of each breath, we are
lost   The holocaust has already occurred   What follows is only the burning
brush   How my heart aches & cries to write
these words   I am not as calmly indifferent as
I sound   I will be screaming no no no more
destruction in that last blinding light

Disregard for "the Earth, our Mother" is only one of
many issues, however, that women poets in particular perceive as related to a proliferation of nuclear weapons and
power plants. These poets also address racial and sexual
domination and violence, issues they feel are symptomatic
or parallel reflectors of this same drive for power. In
"Lot's Wife," for example, Celia Gilbert draws comparisons between the Avenging Angels in Genesis and the
bomber pilots in World War II, between a patriarchal au-
thorization of violence to compel morality and the destruction of Hiroshima and Nagasaki as a means of preserving "the American way." Principles may be at stake
here, but women in either half of the metaphoric equation
are not privileged. As Gilbert comments on the biblical
narrative:

And there were violent gangs of men
who raped men, and that seemed to many
especially horrible. When women were raped
that was wrong, they said
but there was no special horror to it.

Likewise, in Minnie Bruce Pratt's "Strange Flesh," it is female flesh in particular that is made to feel strange. The
poem begins with the speaker, Beatrice, entering a building where a nuclear die-in is about to take place. She passes by young men working in cubicles who have been
taught by older men how "to abstract from the particular
instant, how their minds / set them apart from gross matter." Beatrice reflects that since she was twelve she had
known that "breasts were the opposite of thinking / could
have murdered hers for pulling her down." Her body is
"strange flesh" in the sense of its being made alien to her,
but that is only the first example of strangeness and alienation the poem offers.

Beatrice watches as photographs of Hiroshima and Nagasaki are projected on the wall, one of which shows the butterfly print of a kimono impressed on a woman's skin by
the intensity of the nuclear fire. The other participants of
the die-in seem unmoved, "watching yellow people die,
people of a different color dying in another country." Sickened with a sense of shame, Beatrice then recalls her father's voice, clearly racist in his comparison of insects to
"little black wizened men" and narrowly self-righteous in
his theology.

"Strange Flesh" becomes defined in the father's "moral
voice of Apocalypse, Sunday morning" as he explains to
her

how those who know
as beasts naturally, the followers after strange
     flesh,
the filthy dreamers who despise dominion,
     would burn,
ashes of Sodom and Gomorrah, wells without
     water, trees of
withered fruit, twice dead.

What her father would not tell Beatrice are stories of
women—Navajo women, Black women by the Savannah
River, her own mother—who went blind from the dust of
uranium waste or who sickened and died from plutonium
or radiation contamination in the strange flesh of their
cancerous bodies. In a second-sight vision, Beatrice also
realizes that her father would not tell her (if he ever could)
that "she was both / us and them, that opposites did not
have to kill / each other off."

Pratt helps her reader to understand the deep-seated sense
of division and hierarchy that opposes men and women,
mind and body, white and black (or yellow), scientific arrangements and natural design. In a desire to gain and
maintain control, these oppositions go deliberately unnoticed and unhealed. Pratt's poem, however, brings to the
fore this suppressed subtext of violence, and as it does so,
it opens the way for the poem's conclusion with its decisive rejection of despair:

In the hall a door shut
behind the scientist. People dropped silent to the
     floor,
a die-in, crumpled like a heap of defeated bodies.
Beatrice looked at the predictable despair, and
     left.
She wouldn't just lie down and die: she would
     act contrary
somehow, like hair, or an angry wasp.

For this twentieth-century Beatrice, this moment of rejection is her epiphany, her vision of a world that transcends
passive acquiescence and imagines instead the possibilities
for action.

Living in a world marked by a power-hungry quest for
domination over others or over the earth itself leads to
feelings of despair, particularly if one is part of the group
that others wish to control. Yet despite their vulnerability
as outsiders, women almost self-consciously resist despair
in their poems, and this resistance in itself constitutes another theme that informs their poems. The turning point
from despair usually occurs only after a long look at its
causes; and thus the hope that emerges seems both merited
and substantiated. In "How to Survive Nuclear War," for
example, Maxine Kumin begins by describing a state of
mind that is anything but hopeful. Sick with fever in a
hotel room in Kyoto, she dwells on images that fill her
with a sense of her own powerlessness. She imagines herself "pursued by Nazis, kidnapped, stranded / when the
dam bursts, my life / always in someone else's hands." In
her feverish state, she contemplates the Japanese who just
the week before had celebrated the Holy Radish Festival
and had honored even the insects trampled beneath the
farmers' feet. Distressed, she admits she has nothing to re-
pent: "I kill to keep whatever / pleases me."

The images of personal terror and the religious elements then combine in her semiconscious with recollections of the novel she has been reading, Masuje Ibuse's *Black Rain*. The novel presents the attack on Hiroshima, with a docudrama starkness and intensity, and Kumin's mind dwells on some of the images:

> Everywhere the black rain fell
> it stains the flesh like a tatoo
> but weeks later, when
> survivors must expel
> day by day in little pisses
> the membrane lining the bladder
> pain becomes an extreme grammar.

At the poet's lowest ebb, she acknowledges to herself a historic culpability:

> I understand we did this.
> I understand
> we may do this again
> before it is done to us.

With that realization her consciousness subsides into sleep and a dream state. The dream is restorative and affirming, for she dreams of ginkgos, ritually maimed each year in Japan to produce their polypoid stumps, and she is filled with a sense of hope for humanity. "The severed shoot," she tells us,

> comes back, takes on a
> human form, fan-shaped,
> ancient, all-knowing,
> tattered like us.
> This means
> *we are all to be rescued.*

A little later when she awakes from her dream, she looks out her window and sees an actual line of old ginkgos and observes:

> The new sprouts that break from
> their armless shoulders are
> the enemies of despair.

The unconscious has worked on its own deep level to heal the psychic tearing of the poet, who felt unable to join in any ritual atonement and therefore unable to be absolved from guilt.

In the inner logic of the poem, the drama projected is that of a Jewish-American woman visiting Japan during a season when the Japanese are paying homage to even the lowliest forms of life. As a Jew she has been victimized; as an American she acknowledges the bombings; as a woman she admits in the poem that when it serves her even she kills beetles, or eats meat, or condones the wearing of skins of animals. The dream image that comes to her of the "tattered" gingko reaffirms because it is tattered, a reminder of the human form that fails or suffers loss but finds strength to continue. Despite the "how-to" title of the poem suggesting the operations of a step-by-step rationality, the poet realizes that she can find release from her psychic dilemma only through submission to the deeper and more intricate workings of the unconscious. Nevertheless, she retains the insight of that dream wisdom and brings it to bear on her waking life.

June Jordan, like Kumin, opens herself to a different kind of order, one that will lead her beyond despair. The issue of reordering priorities forms the subject of one of Jordan's best-known poems, "From Sea to Shining Sea." The poem opens with the proclamation (promise or warning?) that "Natural order is being restored." One of the "signs" of this order, as Jordan meticulously informs her readers, is a pyramid of 104 pomegranates priced at eighty-nine cents each. She later elaborates on some of the far-reaching extensions of this order:

> Designer jeans will be replaced by the designer
> of the jeans.
> Music will be replaced by reproduction
> of the music.
> Food will be replaced by information.
> Above all the flag is being replaced by the flag.

Implicitly she warns that symbol is replacing substance, that the ad man appeal to surface and style is driving out the real essence of the commodity. Old cultural connections with the sacred—costume, music, food, national symbols—have been distorted and emptied of meaning by the technicians and image makers. As a result, both the real value and the symbolic meaning of these items are severely diminished.

"Natural order" comes to mean in this poem anything that is contrived and set up to serve some purpose beyond its own essence. It is "not a good time" to be against the natural order, Jordan tells us. In fact, it is a "bad time" to be black, to be gay, to be a child, to be old, to be a woman—or even to live in Arkansas where

> Occasional explosions caused by mystery
> nuclear missiles have been cited
> as cause for local alarm, among
> other things.

Jordan continues to catalog in her poem the injustices and disparities as well as the economic and racial provocations to social equality and equanimity. In a manner reminiscent of Whitman, she almost derails her poem in despair. She pulls herself up, though, with the same abrupt decisiveness as the earlier New York poet and says, simply, "Wait a minute." The turning point comes when Jordan summons up the lusciousness of the pomegranate, its succulence exploding in her mouth with "voluptuous disintegration." In that recollection, she announces:

> This is a good time
> This is the best time
> This is the only time to come together
> > Fractious
> > Kicking
> > Spilling
> > Burly
> > Whirling
> > Raucous
> > Messy
>
> > Free
> Exploding like the seeds of a natural disorder.

Whether it is the associative logic of a dream or the sweet bursting succulence of a pomegranate, Kumin and Jordan are able to draw from their worlds an idea of order that is not hierarchical, but cooperative and affirming. Pratt,

Kumin, and Jordan all acknowledge the horrors of contemporary history and the social problems that affect daily life, but they are able to use their awareness of these problems to push forward to new energy and hope. The use of associative logic, dream imagery, and specific detail drawn from everyday life suggests, moreover, a particularly feminine way of finding a way to deeper comprehension of truth. Dream, intuition, and the imagination are important operations whereby one counteracts the despair along with the desire for supremacy that might drag the world toward its end. As these poets show us, the vitality of the imagination, combined with a physical vitality expressed in action, can effectively confront the threat of nuclear annihilation.

Given the fact that women poets often refuse to despair and almost always present nuclear issues contextually with other social problems, might they not also have evolved a means of expressing their ideas in a style with identifiable characteristics? Have they begun to forge a poetics that enables them to say what they wish to say?

An early feminist poem on nuclear "preparedness" recalls an older, more traditional style that women writers have since found to be unaccommodating. In 1964 Marge Piercy published "Homo faber: the shell game," a poem which suggests the allure of power that modern weapons possess. Whether it is a weapon or a building, man constructs visible edifices to prove his power, as Piercy enumerates:

> The ziggurat, the acropolis, the palace of our
> 　　dream
> whose shape rings in the blood's cave like bella-
> 　　donna,
> all scream in the eagle's prey-seeing swoop of the
> 　　bomber,
> those planes expensive as cities,
> the sharklean submarine of death,
> the taut kinetic tower of the missile,
> the dark fiery omphalos of the bomb.

In many ways this lyric with its alliteration and other carefully crafted sound patterns figures too attractively the force of the weapons. As a highly crafted work, it allies itself with older canons of poetic decorum. This lyric might serve as an example of poetry that John Stuart Mill described as "overheard," rather than "eloquence" which is written to be heard and to move others to action. In Mill's words, "Poetry, accordingly, is the natural fruit of solitude and meditation; eloquence, of intercourse with the world."

The proposed intention of writing poetic eloquence has not been an aesthetically popular platform, even in recent years. In a note that accompanied a submission to *Writers in the Nuclear Age,* [William Carpenter] voiced his hesitation:

> It's pretty difficult for most poets to participate
> in the nuclear protest with their work—it's not
> a good time for propaganda in poetry—but I do
> think that most good writing at this time must
> show at some level the urgency of this historic
> context.

Terrence Des Pres, a contributor to the same volume, was far more caustic in his appraisal of the contemporary poetry scene. He observed:

> In a time of nuclear threat, with absolutely ev-
> erything at stake, our poetry grows increasingly
> claustrophobic and small-themed, it contracts
> its domain, it retires still further into the narrow
> chamber of the self; and we see in this not only
> the exhaustion of a mode and a tradition, but
> also the spectacle of a spirit cowed and retreat-
> ing.

Arguably, if this survey of poems is any indication, women poets do not retreat into a narrow world of self, ignoring political and social issues. Their responses are sometimes filled with anger, often with a special intensity, as Alicia Ostriker demonstrates in her poem, "An Army of Lovers." She describes how she confronts the routinized and apparently sanctioned violence in everyday life—including a man shouting "Nuke 'em" at an airport—and then claims, "I am writing this letter with my blood, and estrogen, true ink." Almost twenty years earlier Levertov observed that "The interaction of life on art and of art on life is continuous. Poetry is necessary to the whole man, and that poetry be not divided from the rest of life is necessary to *it*. Both life and poetry fade, wilt, shrink, when they are divorced." Body/word, life/art, politics/poetics: for the health of either side of the dialectic, there must be flow and continuity.

If anything, contemporary women poets seem deliberately to strive in their poetry for the immediacy and directness of "eloquence." The sense of an audience pervades the poems, sometimes in the form of address, such as "we" or "you," or sometimes in the setting up of literal speech-giving situations, such as Levertov's poem entitled, "A Speech: For Antidraft Rally, D.C., 22 March 1980." Even the specificity of the title of this poem insists on the poem itself as a real event. Whether the events in the poems, moreover, are public, such as a protest or a die-in, or more private and contained, such as the remembered fragments of conversation in Pratt's "Strange Flesh," the feeling is that of a community in the world of the poem—people acting and reacting to each other with immediacy and energy. The image of the poet removed from society, reflecting and meditating in tranquility and solitude, is not the image projected by contemporary women poets who write with an urgency of the blood (and estrogen) of their age, its oppressions, terrors, and needs.

Out of a need to create a new code of poetic decorum, women poets have substituted a poetry of symbol making and indirection with a poetry of plain speech and directness. In the draft rally poem, for example, Levertov refuses to stylize the diction or the flow of her lines to serve some outworn poetic ideal. She writes:

> Let us unite to tell
> all we have learned about old-fashioned war's
> vomit and shit, about new-fashioned war's
> abrupt end to all hope.

Other poets point to instances where language is used to conceal truth. June Jordan, in particular, inveighs against the lies of manipulative politicians and policy makers. Unlike Levertov, who counters the bureaucrats or the scientists with her own spirited declamation of the truth, Jordan's tactic is to reproduce those voices on the page and let the reader judge. In "From Sea to Shining Sea," for example, she deadpans the "official" report, or press release. The poem announces, *"This was not a good time to live in Grand Forks North Dakota,"* and then proceeds to explain:

> Given the presence of a United States nuclear
> missile base in Grand Forks North Dakota
> the non-military residents of the area feel
> that they are living only a day by day distance
> from certain
> annihilation, etcetera.

The bald presentation of official-sounding, sense-defying language (what could the "etcetera" after annihilation be, anyway?) operates to make the reader aware of other examples of empty Muzak-verbiage that plays itself out in the world. Jordan's act of framing this language within a poem makes its insidious emptiness even more apparent. In other poems, however, Jordan uses the length and directness of the prose line, not to speak ironically, but in the clearest way possible. Other poets (Kumin, Chrystos, Pratt) also employ the prose idiom in their writing, an impulse which surely must have something to do with a desire to be heard and understood. This writing often reflects speech patterns and so, in some sense, confers value upon the human voice by placing it within the esthetic structure of a poem. (pp. 112-30)

Despite, or perhaps because of, the anger with which women writers view the prospect of nuclear annihilation, they bring enormous energy and positive force to an examination of the causes behind this crisis. One writer, June Jordan, even manages to treat the topic with dark, often parodic humor, which functions as a strategy to make readers confront the potential for global devastation. Besides the humor inherent in the mangled language in "From Sea to Shining Sea," Jordan exhibits humor in another poem, "War Verse," parodying Frost's "Mending Wall" ("Something there is that sure must love a plane"). On one level Jordan criticizes the antiseptic depersonalized killings of the bomber plane:

> No matter how many you kill with what kind of
> bombs or how much blood you manage to spill
> you never will hear the cries of pain. . . .

On another level the poem may be a criticism of the Establishment esthetic of Frost, who insisted that the narrative materials in a poem always conformed to the regularity of meter.

Jordan uses in "Song of the Law-Abiding Citizen" pop-tune rhythms and lyrics that help to both engage and insure the reader's attention and comprehension. She describes a good citizen, on welfare, who prides himself on his upright character and returns some ten thousand food stamps received through an administrative error "to the President (and his beautiful wife)." "Song" juxtaposes a humorous instance of governmental inefficiency with a serious, harmful assault on the safety and welfare of citizens, as trucks are permitted to cruise through Manhattan

> carrying nuclear garbage right next to you

> and it's legal
> it's radioaction ridin' like a regal
> load of jewels. . . .

The talking blues rhythms (reminiscent of 1960s protest songs) serve to ridicule what the government names as legal and as illegal; on the other hand, virtually the same idiom reveals all too glaringly the unquestioning obedience of the law-abiding citizen. A dull-witted ethos, Jordan implies, can be as harmful to the citizenry as an obsession with power that sees itself positioned outside any law. Humor here metes out a fuller dimension of criticism than the more one-sided stance of moral outrage.

All of these poets, particularly Jordan and Levertov, have experimented with ways of concluding their poems to suggest hope for the future and a continuing flow of energy. Jordan's conclusion to "From Sea to Shining Sea" with its adjectives describing the energy of a natural disorder 'Fractious' 'Kicking' 'Spilling' 'Burly' is one such example; another, Levertov's "The Cry," dedicated to nuclear activist and writer Jonathan Schell, recalls the anguished and reverberating image of Edward Munch's "The Shriek." It opens with the admission that

> No pulsations
>   of passionate rhetoric
>   suffice
>
> In this time
>   in this time
>   this time

The only response that can be summoned to this horror is the inarticulate cry of "mouths gaping to 'Aayy!'" As the poem progresses, it searches out some relief from anguish and postulates the hope of avoiding nuclear war "by luck / by chance / grace perhaps." With this hope, Levertov commutes inarticulate anguish and the longing, half-despairing cry of "O" into a vision of wholeness and spiritual affirmation:

>   only O
>   maybe
> some wholly
>   holy
>   holy
> unmerited call:
>   bellbird
>   in branch of
> snowrose
>   blossoming
>   newborn cry
> demanding
>   with cherubim
>   and seraphim
> eternity:
>   being:
>   milk:

The colons after the final three words signify an open-ended sense of possibility, of being and action that will continue for an eternity. The ordering of the last three words—'eternity', 'being', 'milk'—literally restores heaven to earth, with a privileging of the flow and essence of maternal nurturance. Through my vision, my body— Levertov seems to be saying along with several other women poets—we will survive and endure, for we know ourselves to be enemies of despair. (pp. 130-33)

> Louise Kawada, *"Enemies of Despair: American Women Poets Confront the Threat of Nuclear Destruction," in* Papers on Language and Literature, *Vol. 26, No. 1, Winter, 1990, pp. 112-33.*

THE NUCLEAR REFERENT AND LITERARY CRITICISM

Diacritics

[*In the following essay, originally published as a preface to the Summer 1984 issue of* Diacritics *devoted to nuclear criticism, the author justifies the need to study contemporary literature in the context of nuclear war.*]

By Nuclear Criticism is meant something positive and something unavowed, a new topic and an explicitation of what is already everywhere being done. This proposal arises, on the one hand, out of reading a certain amount of recent criticism and critical theory and feeling that without exception it recounts an allegory of nuclear survival; and, on the other, out of the sense that critical theory ought to be making a more important contribution to the public discussion of nuclear issues. The field would invite both kinds of criticism, the sort that reads other critical or canonical texts for the purpose of uncovering the unknown shapes of our unconscious nuclear fears, and that which aims to show how the terms of the current nuclear discussion are being shaped by literary or critical assumptions whose implications are often, perhaps systematically ignored.

In the second category, taking our hints from work which is already underway, in disparate forms and fields, one might investigate subjects such as these:

—The conjunction of the second millenium with the literally apocalyptic power of the nuclear arsenal has excited virulent forms of eschatological thinking like that which has periodically raged through our culture. Eschatology, as a concept and a discursive practice, has a textual tradition, a social history, and a logic which deserve to be recalled. The use value, as well as the profit, that can be derived from predicting the end of things ought to be examined critically.

—The current arms race has arisen under the conditions of a bilateral conflict between the two superpowers. The tendency therefore of both sides to enact the dialectic of mimetic rivalry is powerful and increasingly visible, confirming the necessity to explore further the nature of its compulsion, the consequences of its application to the mutual representations and policy decisions of the antagonists.

—The power of horror, which the nuclear horizon proposes, has its own abject influence on the quality of our lives and on the cultural climate we engender, and may determine in ways we do not yet understand our capacity to act, even to will. That power itself has begun to be analyzed.

—Critical theory for some time has been given over to analyzing the interpretations of origin in our culture. The danger of nuclear destruction arises out of a technological program aimed at discovering the atomic origin of things. The nature of the desires, the concepts of use and aim, the value of the values which have motivated the theory and practice of *technè* in our culture require urgent philosophical repetition.

—The psychology of arms racers must be analyzed. What do scientists want? Why do they go on building what many of them wish to disarm? What do soldiers dream? Why do they so love peace, above all when they retire? The role of gender in motivating the choice of goals ought to be determined. On one side are mostly men who make policy decisions and invent the vocabulary of arms talk. On the other are frequently women leading men against installations, with figures and scenarios for anti-nuclear struggle taken from the vocabulary of their own.

—It is not just "nukespeak," but all the forms of nuclear discourse which obey rhetorical constraints, which submit to forms of censorship, exploit narrative figures and tropological devices, in order to persuade. Rhetorical analysis of the forms, the themes, the performance of nuclear political argument as it is presently enacted must begin.

—The calculus of negotiations depends on epistemological assumptions and theories of strategy which may well be illuminated by the insights of critical theory into the structure of discourse, the functions of signs, and the conditions of sending messages.

—The representation of nuclear war in the media as well as in the literary canon demands to be analyzed ideologically, that is, in terms of the interests it seeks to promote and to conceal, in terms of the whole critique of representation which for some time has been engaged. To what extent do all the current versions of apocalypse now merely feed the vice of the hypocritical reader, the deep-seated boredom of an alienated public that dreams of debris, of swallowing the world with a yawn? To what degree do the stereotypes of nuclear destruction, like the proliferative figure of the mushroom cloud, aim to make us forget by their mechanical repetition the reality they are supposed to designate?

—Crises usually have their origin in the interpretation of unexpected, frequently aleatory events. The attribution of motives, the misreading of intentions, the sometimes cynical fabrications elaborated around an occurrence serve to invest it with meaning, to constitute it historiographically, not only as an object of understanding but as a significant fact which has the power to change the course of events. Critical theory must play a role in analyzing the mechanisms by which nuclear narratives are construed and enacted. (pp. 2-3)

"Nuclear Criticism," in Diacritics, *Vol. 14, No. 2, Summer, 1984, pp. 2-3.*

De Kerckhove on the role of the bomb in Western civilization:

The bomb is not an accidental by-product of our industrial-military complex, it is a bio-cultural artifact which is grounded in the history of Western civilization. Its production was inevitable. However, beside threatening global destruction, it can also serve the purpose of educating us to a new level of global maturity.

The image of the nuclear explosion, with its sequence of fission, reaction, mushrooming, fall-out, and radioactivity, is an accelerated analogue of the history of the West. Our first major cultural mutation dates back to the invention of the phonetic alphabet. Western history began with the atomization of human speech. An increasingly rapid growth of technical progress followed soon after along the patterns of a dialectical chain reaction. At the top of this vertical drive of accelerated and mechanized invention, we are witnessing a reversal: with electricity, we are girding the earth with a crown of heat and light as the planet is being electronically wired for energy and instant communication. We are now experiencing the psychoactive fall-out and we have no choice but to undergo another global mutation within the next few decades.

As a ground for the policies of deterrence, the nuclear bomb has become, quite unexpectedly, the greatest communication medium mankind has ever invented, not for information but for transformation. Its impact is pure energy and its effect could be to precipitate either the elimination or the crystallization of a planetary consciousness.

> *Derrick de Kerckhove, in his "On Nuclear Communication," in* Diacritics, *Summer 1984.*

Jacques Derrida

[*Derrida is an Algerian-born French philosopher, critic, translator, and author of* L'ecriture et la différence *(1967;* Writing and Difference*) and* De la grammatologie *(1967;* Of Grammatology*). Often studied in the social sciences and the liberal arts, Derrida is an influential proponent of the deconstructionist approach to literature, which posits that words have no inherent meaning and are therefore unable to relay completely and unambiguously the speaker's intentions. In the following excerpt, Derrida states that language and nuclear war literature are closely related and even interdependent because both attempt to describe reality which can never be known in its entirety and, in the case of nuclear war, an event that humanity has yet to experience.*]

Let me say a word first about speed.

At the beginning there will have been speed.

We are speaking of stakes that are apparently limitless for what is still now and then called humanity. People find it easy to say that in nuclear war "humanity" runs the risk of its self-destruction, with nothing left over, no remainder. There is a lot that could be said about that rumor. But whatever credence we give it, we have to recognize that these stakes appear in the experience of a race, or more precisely of a *competition,* a rivalry between two rates of speed. It's what we call in French a *course de vitesse,* a *speed race.* Whether it is the arms race or orders given to start a war that is itself dominated by that economy of speed throughout all the zones of its technology, a gap of a few seconds may decide, irreversibly, the fate of what is still now and then called humanity—plus the fate of a few other species. As no doubt we all know, no single instant, no atom of our life (of our relation to the world and to being) is not marked today, directly or indirectly, by that speed race. And by the whole strategic debate about "no use," "no first use," or "first use" of nuclear weaponry. Is this new? Is it the first time "in history"? Is it an invention, and can we still say "in history" in order to speak about it? The most classical wars were also speed races, in their preparation and in the actual pursuit of the hostilities. Are we having, today, *another,* a different experience of speed? Is our relation to time and to motion qualitatively different? Or must we speak prudently of an extraordinary—although qualitatively homogeneous—acceleration of the same experience? And what temporality do we have in mind when we put the question that way? Can we take the question seriously without re-elaborating all the problematics of time and motion, from Aristotle to Heidegger by way of Augustine, Kant, Husserl, Einstein, Bergson, and so on? So my first formulation of the question of speed was simplistic. It opposed quantity and quality as *if* a quantitative transformation—the crossing of certain thresholds of acceleration within the general machinery of a culture, with all its techniques for handling, recording, and storing information—could not induce qualitative mutations, as *if* every invention were not the invention of a process of acceleration or, at the very least, a new experience of speed. Or as *if* the concept of speed, linked to some quantification of objective velocity, remained within a homogeneous relation to every experience of time—for the human subject or for a mode of temporalization that the human subject—as such—would have himself covered up.

Why have I slowed down my introduction this way by dragging in such a naive question? No doubt for several reasons. . . .

Reason number one. Let us consider the form of the question itself: is the war of (over, for) speed (with all that it entails) an irreducibly new phenomenon, an invention linked to a set of inventions of the so-called nuclear age, or is it rather the brutal acceleration of a movement that has always already been at work? This form of the question perhaps constitutes the most indispensable formal matrix, the keystone or, if you will, the *nuclear* question, for *any* problematics of the "nuclear criticism" type, in *all* its aspects.

Naturally, I don't have time to demonstrate this. I am offering it, therefore, as a hasty conclusion, a precipitous assertion, a *belief,* an opinion-based argument, a doctrine or a dogmatic weapon. But I was determined to begin with it. I wanted to begin as quickly as possible with a warning in the form of a dissuasion: watch out, don't go too fast. There is perhaps no invention, no radically new predicate in the situation known as "the nuclear age." Of all the dimensions of such an "age" we may always say one thing: it is neither the first time nor the last. The historian's critical vigilance can always help us verify that repetitiveness; and that historian's patience, that lucidity of memory must always shed their light on "nuclear criticism," must oblige it to decelerate, dissuade it from rushing to a conclusion on the subject of speed itself. But this dissuasion and deceleration I am urging carry their own risks: the critical zeal that leads us to recognize precedents, continuities, and repetitions at every turn can make us look like suicidal sleepwalkers, blind and deaf *alongside the unheard-of;* it could make us stand blind and deaf alongside that which cuts through the assimilating resemblance of discourses (for example of the apocalyptic or bimillenarist type), through the analogy of techno-military situations, strategic arrangements, with all their wagers, their last-resort calculations, on the "brink," their use of chance and risk factors, their mimetic resource to upping the ante, and so on—blind and deaf, then, alongside what would be absolutely unique; and it, this critical zeal, would seek in the stockpile of history (in short, in history itself, which in this case would have this blinding search as its function) the wherewithal to neutralize invention, to translate the unknown into a known, to metaphorize, allegorize, domesticate the terror, to circumvent (with the help of circumlocutions: turns of phrase, tropes and strophes) the inescapable catastrophe, the undeviating precipitation toward a remainderless cataclysm. The critical slowdown may thus be as critical as the critical acceleration. One may still die after having spent one's life recognizing, as a lucid historian, to what extent all that was not new, telling oneself that the inventors of the nuclear age or of nuclear criticism did not invent the wheel, or, as we say in French, "invent gunpowder." That's the way one always dies, moreover, and the death of what is still now and then called humanity might well not escape the rule.

Reason number two. What is the *right* speed, then? Given our inability to provide a good answer for that question, we at least have to recognize gratefully that the nuclear age allows us to think through this aporia of speed (i.e., the need to move both slowly and quickly); it allows us to confront our predicament starting from the limit constituted by the absolute acceleration in which the uniqueness of an ultimate event, of a final collision or collusion, the temporalities called subjective and objective, phenomenological and intra-worldly, authentic and inauthentic, etc., would end up being merged into one another. But, wishing to address these questions to the participants of a colloquium on "nuclear criticism," I am also wondering at what speed we have to deal with these aporias: with what rhetoric, what strategy of implicit connection, what ruses of potentialization and of ellipsis, what weapons of irony? The "nuclear age" makes for a certain type of colloquium, with its particular technology of information, diffusion and storage, its rhythm of speech, its demonstration procedures, and thus its arguments and its armaments, its modes of persuasion or intimidation.

Reason number three. Having raised, very rapidly, my question on the subject of speed, I am unilaterally disarming, I am putting my cards on the table. I am announcing that, for want of time—time for preparation and time for the speech act—I shall not make a real "speech." By which means, you will say, I shall have taken more time than all my partners. I am thus choosing, as you have already observed, the genre or rhetorical form of tiny atomic nuclei (in the process of fission or division in an uninterruptable chain) which I shall arrange or rather which I shall project toward you, like tiny inoffensive missiles: in a discontinuous, more or less haphazard fashion. This will be my little strategic and capitalistic calculation, in order to say, potentially, without being too tedious and as quickly as possible, as many things as possible. Capitalization—or capitalism—always has the structure of a certain potentialization of speed. This has been, in three points, my *first missile,* or my *first missive,* or my first nuclear aphorism: *in the beginning there will have been speed,* which is always *taking on speed,* in other words, overtaking or—as we say in French, *prendre de vitesse, doubler,* doubling, passing—both the act and the speech. At the beginning was the word; at the beginning was the act. No! At the beginning—faster than the word or the act—there will have been *speed,* and a speed race between them. But of course, speed was only a beginning for *my* speech, for my speech act, today.

For such a feat, we may consider ourselves competent.

And for the reason I have just stated very quickly: because of speed.

Indeed: nowhere has the dissociation between the place where competence is exercised and the place where the stakes are located ever *seemed* more rigorous, more dangerous, more catastrophic. *Seemed,* I said. Is it not *apparently the first time* that that dissociation, more unbridgeable than ever for *ordinary mortals,* has put in the balance the fate of what is still now and then called humanity *as a whole,* or even of the earth as a whole, at the very moment when your president is even thinking about waging war beyond the earth? Doesn't that dissociation (which is dissociation itself, the division and the dislocation of the *socius,* of sociality itself) allow us to think the essence of knowledge and *technè* itself, as socialization *and* desocialization, as the constitution and the deconstruction of the *socius?*

Must we then take that dissociation seriously? And what is seriousness, in this instance? That is the first question, and thus *the first reason* why it is not totally irrelevant, inconsistent, to hold a colloquium on the nuclear in a space, our own, which is essentially occupied by non-experts, by questioners who doubtless don't know very well who they are, who don't very well know what justifies them or what legitimates their community but who know at least that they are not military professionals, are not professionals of strategy, diplomacy, or nuclear techno-science.

Second reason. So we are not experts in strategy, in diplomacy, or in the techno-science known as nuclear science, we are oriented rather toward what is called not humanity but the humanities, history, literature, languages, philology, the social sciences, in short all that which in the Kant-

The Trumpets Distributed, *a woodcut in Albrecht Dürer's* Apocalypse *series.*

ian university was situated in the inferior class of the philosophy school, foreign to any exercise of power. We are specialists in discourse and in texts, all sorts of texts.

Now I shall venture to say that in spite of all appearances this specialty is what entitles us, and doubly so, to concern ourselves seriously with the nuclear issue. And by the same token, if we have not done so before, this entitlement, this responsibility that we would thus have been neglecting until now, directs us to concern ourselves with the nuclear issue—*first,* inasmuch as we are representatives of humanity and of the incompetent humanities which have to think through as rigorously as possible the problem of competence, given that the stakes of the nuclear question are those of humanity, of the humanities. How, in the face of the nuclear issue, are we to get speech to circulate not only among the self-styled competent parties and those who are alleged to be incompetent, but among the competent parties themselves. For we are more than just suspicious; we are certain that, in this area in particular, there is a multiplicity of dissociated, heterogeneous competencies. Such knowledge is neither coherent nor totalizable. Moreover, between those whose competence is techno-scientific (those who invent in the sense of unveiling or of "constative" discovery as well as in the sense of production of new technical or "performing" mechanisms) and those whose competence is politico-military, those who are empowered to make decisions, the deputies of performance or of the performative, the frontier is more undecidable than ever, as it is between the good and evil of all nuclear technology. If on the one hand it is apparently the first time that these competencies are so dangerously and effectively dissociated, on the other hand and from another point of view, they have never been so terribly accumulated, concentrated, entrusted as in a dice game to so few hands: the military men are also scientists, and they find themselves inevitably in the position of participating in the final decision, whatever precautions may be taken in this area. All of them, that is, very few, are in the position of inventing, inaugurating, improvising procedures and giving orders where no model—we shall talk about this later on—can help them at all. Among the acts of observing, revealing, knowing, promising, acting, simulating, giving orders, and so on, the limits have never been so precarious, so undecidable. Today it is on the basis of that situation—the limit case in which the limit itself is suspended, in which therefore the *krinein, crisis,* decision itself, and choice are being subtracted from us, are abandoning us like the remainder of that subtraction—it is on the basis of that situation that we have to re-think the relations between knowing and acting, between constative speech acts and performative speech acts, between the invention that finds what was already there and the one that produces new mechanisms or new spaces. In the undecidable and at the moment of a decision that has no common ground with any other, we have to reinvent invention or conceive of another "pragmatics."

Third reason. In our techno-scientifico-militaro-diplomatic incompetence, we may consider ourselves, however, as competent as others to deal with a phenomenon whose essential feature is that of being *fabulously textual,* through and through. Nuclear weaponry depends, more than any weaponry in the past, it seems, upon structures of information and communication, structures of language, including non-vocalizable language, structures of codes and graphic decoding. But the phenomenon is fabulously textual also to the extent that, for the moment, a nuclear war has not taken place: one can only talk and write about it. You will say, perhaps: but it is not the first time; the other wars, too, so long as they hadn't taken place, were only talked about and written about. And as to the fright of imaginary anticipation, what might prove that a European in the period following the war of 1870 might not have been more terrified by the "technological" image of the bombings and exterminations of the Second World War (even supposing he had been able to form such an image) than we are by the image we can construct for ourselves of a nuclear war? The logic of this argument is not devoid of value, especially if one is thinking about a limited and "clean" nuclear war. But it loses its value in the face of the hypothesis of a total nuclear war, which, as a hypothesis, or, if you prefer, as a fantasy, or phantasm, conditions every discourse and all strategies. Unlike the other wars, which have all been preceded by wars of more or less the same type in human memory (and gunpowder did not mark a radical break in this respect), nuclear war has no precedent. It has never occurred, itself; it is a non-event. The explosion of American bombs in 1945 ended a "classical," conventional war; it did not set off a nuclear war. The terrifying reality of the nuclear conflict can only be the signified referent, never the real referent (present or past) of a discourse or a text. At least today apparently. And that sets us to thinking about to*day,* our day, the presence of this present in and through that fabulous textuality. Better than ever and more than ever. The growing multiplication of the discourse—indeed, of the literature—on this subject may constitute a process of fearful domestication, the anticipatory assimilation of that unanticipatable entirely-other. For the moment, today, one may say that a non-localizable nuclear war has not occurred; it has existence only through what is said of it, only where it is talked about. Some might call it a fable, then, a pure invention: in the sense in which it is said that a myth, an image, a fiction, a utopia, a rhetorical figure, a fantasy, a phantasm, are inventions. It may also be called a speculation, even a fabulous specularization. The breaking of the mirror would be, finally, through an act of language, the very occurrence of nuclear war. Who can swear that our unconscious is not expecting this? dreaming of it, desiring it? You will perhaps find it shocking to find the nuclear issue reduced to a fable. But then I haven't said simply that. I have recalled that a nuclear war is for the time being a fable, that is, something one can only talk about. But who can fail to recognize the massive "reality" of nuclear weaponry and of the terrifying forces of destruction that are being stockpiled and capitalized everywhere, that are coming to constitute the very movement of capitalization. One has to distinguish between this "reality" of the nuclear age and the fiction of war. But, and this would perhaps be the imperative of a nuclear criticism, one must also be careful to interpret critically this critical or diacritical distinction. For the "reality" of the nuclear age and the fable of nuclear war are perhaps distinct, but they are not two separate things. It is the war (in other words the fable) that triggers this fabulous war effort, this senseless capitalization of sophisticated weaponry, this speed race in search of speed, this crazy precipitation which, through techno-science, through all the techno-scientific inventiveness that it motivates, structures not only the army, diplomacy, politics, but the whole of the human *socius* today, everything that is named by the old words culture, civilization, *Bildung, scholè, paideia.* "Reality," let's say the encompassing institution of the nuclear age, is constructed by the fable, on the basis of an event that has never happened (except in fantasy, and that is not nothing at all), an event of which one can only speak, an event whose advent remains an invention by men (in all the senses of the word "invention") or which, rather, remains to be invented. An invention because it depends upon new technical mechanisms, to be sure, but an invention also because it does not exist and especially because, at whatever point it should come into existence, it would be a grand premiere appearance.

Fourth reason. Since we are speaking of fables, of language, of fiction and fantasy, writing and rhetoric, let us go even further. Nuclear war does not depend on language just because we can do nothing but speak of it—and then as something that has never occurred. It does not depend on language just because the "incompetents" on all sides can speak of it only in the mode of gossip or of *doxa* (opinion)—and the dividing line between *doxa* and *épistémè* starts to blur as soon as there is no longer any such thing as an absolutely legitimizable competence for a phenomenon which is no longer strictly techno-scientific but techno-militaro-politico-diplomatic through and through, and which brings into play the *doxa* or incompetence even in its calculations. There is nothing but *doxa,* opinion, "belief." One can no longer oppose belief and science, *doxa* and *épistémè,* once one has reached the decisive place of the nuclear age, in other words, once one has arrived at the critical place of the nuclear age. In this critical place, there is no more room for a distinction between belief and science, thus no more space for a "nuclear criticism" strictly speaking. Nor even for a truth in that sense. No truth, no apocalypse. (As you know. Apocalypse means Revelation, of Truth, *Un-veiling.*) No, nuclear war is not *only* fabulous because one can *only* talk about it, but because the extraordinary *sophistication* of its technologies—which are also the technologies of delivery, sending, dispatching, of the missile in general, of mission, missive, emission, and transmission, like all *technè*—the extraordinary sophistication of these technologies coexists, cooperates in an essential way with sophistry, psycho-rhetoric, and the most cursory, the most archaic, the most crudely opinionated psychagogy, the most vulgar psychology. (pp. 20-4)

As for the aporias of the nuclear referent, we don't believe in them.

Under the heading of *nuclear criticism,* in a colloquium organized by *Diacritics,* we have to talk about literature, about the literature that I shall distinguish here from poetry, from the epic, from *belles-lettres* in general. Now it seems that the constitution of literature has not been possible without (1) a project of stockpiling, of building up an

> **Nuclear weaponry depends, more than any weaponry in the past . . . , upon structures of information and communication, structures of language, including non-vocalizable language, structures of codes and graphic decoding. But the phenomenon is fabulously textual also to the extent that, for the moment, a nuclear war has not taken place: one can only talk and write about it.**
>
> —*Jacques Derrida*

objective archive over and above any traditional oral base; (2) without the development of a positive law implying authors' rights, the identification of the signatory, of the corpus, names, titles, the distinction between the original and the copy, the original and the plagiarized version, and so forth. Literature is not reduced to this form of archiving and this form of law, but it could not outlive them and still be called literature. Now what allows us perhaps to think the uniqueness of nuclear war, its being-for-the-first-time-and-perhaps-for-the-last-time, its absolute inventiveness, what it prompts us to think even if it remains a decoy, a belief, a phantasmatic projection, is obviously the possibility of an irreversible destruction, leaving no traces, of the juridico-literary archive—that is, total destruction of the basis of literature and criticism. Not necessarily the destruction of humanity, of the human habitat, nor even of other discourses (arts or sciences), nor even indeed of poetry or the epic; these latter might reconstitute their living process and their archive, at least to the extent that the structure of that archive (that of a nonliterary memory) implies, structurally, reference to a real referent external to the archive itself. I am taking care to say: to that extent, and on that hypothesis. It is not certain at all that all the other archives, whatever their material basis may be, have such a referent absolutely outside themselves, outside their own possibility. If they do have one, then they can rightfully reconstitute themselves and thus, in some other fashion, survive. But if they do not have one, or to the extent that they do not have one outside themselves, they find themselves in the situation of literature. One might say that they participate in literature in that literature produces its referent as a fictive or fabulous referent, which in itself is dependent on the possibility of archiving, indeed constituted in itself by the archivizing act. That would lead to a considerable extension—some would say an abusive one—of the field of literature. But who has proven that literature is a field with indivisible and simply assignable limits? The events known by the name of literature are definable; and there is in principle a possible history of this name and of the conventions attached to the naming. But the same cannot be said of the structural possibilities of what goes by the name literature, which is not limited to the events already known under this name.

Here we are dealing hypothetically with a total and remainderless destruction of the archive. This destruction would take place for the first time and it would lack any common proportion with, for example, the burning of a library, even that of Alexandria, which occasioned so many written accounts and nourished so many literatures. The hypothesis of this total destruction watches over deconstruction, it guides its footsteps; it becomes possible to recognize, in the light, so to speak, of that hypothesis, of that fantasy, or phantasm, the characteristic structures and historicity of the discourses, strategies, texts, or institutions to be deconstructed. That is why deconstruction, at least what is being advanced today in its name, belongs to the nuclear age. And to the age of literature. If "literature" is the name we give to the body of texts whose existence, possibility, and significance are the most radically threatened, for the first and last time, by the nuclear catastrophe, that definition allows our thought to grasp the essence of literature, its radical precariousness and the radical form of its historicity; but at the same time, literature gives us to think *the totality* of that which, like literature and henceforth in it, is exposed to the same threat, constituted by the same structure of historical fictionality, producing and then harboring its own referent. We may henceforth assert that the historicity of literature is contemporaneous through and through, or rather structurally indissociable, from something like a nuclear *epoch* (by nuclear "epoch," I also mean the *épochè* suspending judgment before the absolute decision). The nuclear age is not an epoch, it is the absolute *épochè;* it is not absolute knowledge and the end of history, it is the *épochè* of absolute knowledge. Literature belongs to this nuclear epoch, that of the crisis and of nuclear criticism, at least if we mean by this the historical and ahistorical horizon of an absolute self-destructibility without apocalypse, without revelation of its own truth, without absolute knowledge.

This statement is not abstract, it does not concern general and formal structures, some equation between a literarity extended to any possible archive and a self-destructibility in general. No, according to my hypothesis it would rather be a question of the sudden "synchronous" appearance, of a cohabitation of two formations: on the one hand, we have the principle of reason (interpreted since the seventeenth century according to the order of representation, the domination of the subject/object structure, the metaphysics of will, modern techno-science, and so on [I refer here in passing to Heidegger, who moreover is less interested in nuclear *war* than in the atomic age as an age of in-formation which forms and in-forms a new figure of man]) and on the other hand we have the project of literature in the strict sense, the project which cannot be shown to antedate the seventeenth and eighteenth centuries. To advance the hypothesis of their conjugation, it is not necessary to follow Heidegger in his interpretation of the principle of reason and in his evaluation of literature (as distinguished from poetry), as it appears for example in *Was heisst Denken.* But I have discussed this elsewhere and I cannot pursue this direction further here. In what I am here calling in another sense an absolute epoch, literature comes to life and can only experience its own precariousness, its death menace and its essential finitude. The movement of its inscription is the very possibility of its effacement. Thus one cannot be satisfied with saying that,

in order to become serious and interesting today, a literature and a literary criticism must refer to the nuclear issue, must even be obsessed by it. This has to be said, and it is true. But I believe also that, at least indirectly, they have always done this. Literature has always belonged to the nuclear epoch, even if it does not talk "seriously" about it. And in truth I believe that the nuclear epoch is dealt with more "seriously" in texts by Mallarmé, of Kafka, or Joyce, for example, than in present-day novels that would offer direct and realistic descriptions of a "real" nuclear catastrophe.

Such would be the *first* version of a *paradox of the referent.* In two points. 1. Literature belongs to the nuclear age by virtue of the performative character of its relation to the referent, and the structure of its written archive. 2. Nuclear war has not taken place, it is a speculation, an invention in the sense of a fable or an invention to be invented in order to make a place for it or to prevent it from taking place (as much invention is needed for the one as for the other), and for the moment all this is only literature. Some might conclude that therefore it is not real, as it remains entirely suspended in its fabulous and literary *épochè.*

But we do not believe, such is the other version or the other side of the same paradox, in any thing except the nuclear referent.

If we are bound and determined to speak in terms of reference, nuclear war is the only possible referent of any discourse and any experience that would share their condition with that of literature. If, according to a structuring hypothesis, a fantasy or phantasm, nuclear war is equivalent to the total destruction of the archive, if not of the human habitat, it becomes the absolute referent, the horizon and the condition of all the others. An individual death, a destruction affecting only a part of society, of tradition, of culture may always give rise to a symbolic work of mourning, with memory, compensation, internalization, idealization, displacement, and so on. In that case there is monumentalization, archivization and *work on the remainder, work of the remainder.* Similarly, my own death as an individual, so to speak, can always be anticipated phantasmatically, symbolically too, as a negativity at work—a dialectic of the work, of signature, name, heritage, image, grief: all the resources of memory and tradition can mute the reality of that death, whose anticipation then is still woven out of fictionality, symbolicity, or, if you prefer, literature; and this is so even if I live this anticipation in anguish, terror, despair, as a catastrophe that I have no reason not to equate with the annihilation of humanity as a whole: this catastrophe occurs with every individual death; there is no common measure adequate to persuade me that a personal mourning is less serious than a nuclear war. But the burden of every death can be assumed symbolically by a culture and a social memory (that is even their essential function and their justification, their *raison d'être*). Culture and memory limit the "reality" of individual death to this extent, they soften or deaden it in the realm of the "symbolic." The only referent that is absolutely real is thus of the scope or dimension of an absolute nuclear catastrophe that would irreversibly destroy the entire archive and all symbolic capacity, would destroy the "movement of survival," what I call *"surviv-ance,"* at the very heart of life. This absolute referent of all possible literature is on a par with the absolute efface-ment of any possible trace; it is thus the only ineffaceable trace, it is so as the trace of what is entirely other, *"trace du tout autre."* This is the only absolute trace—effaceable, ineffaceable. The only "subject" of all possible literature, of all possible criticism, its only ultimate and a-symbolic referent, unsymbolizable, even unsignifiable; this is, if not the nuclear age, if not the nuclear catastrophe, at least that toward which nuclear discourse and the nuclear symbolic *are still beckoning:* the remainderless and a-symbolic de-struction of literature. Literature and literary criticism cannot speak of anything else, they can have no other ulti-mate referent, they can only multiply their strategic ma-neuvers in order to assimilate that unassimilable wholly other. They are nothing but those maneuvers and that dip-lomatic strategy, with the "double talk" that can never be reduced to them. For simultaneously, that "subject" can-not be a nameable "subject," nor that "referent" a name-able referent. Then the perspective of nuclear war allows us to re-elaborate the question of the referent. What is a referent? In another way, to elaborate the question of the transcendental ego, the transcendental subject, Husserl's phenomenology needed, at some point, the fiction of total chaos. Capable of speaking only of that, literature cannot help but speak of other things as well, and invent strategies for speaking of other things, for putting off the encounter with the wholly other, an encounter with which, however, this relationless relation, this relation of incommensura-bility cannot be wholly suspended, even though it is pre-cisely its epochal suspension. This is the only invention possible.

What I am saying can be transposed into a discourse of contemporary diplomatico-military strategy. Consider for example what Theodore Draper says in an article entitled "How Not to Think about Nuclear War" [*New York Re-view of Books,* July 15, 1982]. In the early going Draper has criticized the whole strategy of "no first use" of nucle-ar weapons, which would amount to "no use," and direct-ed his irony at the "realm of utopian obscurantism" of Jonathan Schell who, in *The Fate of the Earth,* spoke about "reinventing politics" and "reinventing the world" ("a global disarmament, both nuclear and conventional, and the invention of political means by which the world can peacefully settle the issues that throughout history it has settled by war"). Now Draper falls back upon what may appear to be wisdom or an economy of deferral (*dif-férance*): gain as much time as possible while taking into account the unmovable constraints; return, if possible (as if it were possible) to the original meaning of deterrence or dissuasion, which would seem by and large to have been lost or perverted in recent times. To quote Draper: "De-terrence is all we have. Like many such terms that are abused and misused, it is best to get back to its original meaning." I cannot deal with this discourse in detail; it would warrant a meticulous and vigilant analysis, espe-cially at that point where, referring to Solly Zuckerman's *Nuclear Illusion and Reality,* Draper imputes to scientists a greater responsibility than that of the military and politi-cal authorities. Draper reminds us that in a chapter about "the advice of scientists," Zuckerman "shows how they

have been pushing the politicians and the military around; the arms race, he warns, can be brought to an end only if the politicians 'take charge of the technical men.' This re-versal of the commonly understood roles may come as a surprise to most readers."

An absolute missile does not abolish chance.

There is nothing serious to be said against that "rational" and "realistic" wisdom of dissuasion, against that econo-my of deferral or deterrence. The only possible reserva-tion, beyond objection, is that if there are wars and a nu-clear threat, it is because "deterrence" has neither "origi-nal meaning" nor measure. Its "logic" is the logic of devia-tion and transgression, it is rhetorical-strategic escalation or it is nothing at all. It gives itself over, by calculation, to the incalculable, to chance and luck. Let us start again from that conception of sending or "missivity" on the basis of which Heidegger finally relaunches the thought of being as the thought of a gift, and of what gives impetus to thought—gives to be thought, gives forth into thought, *"ce qui donne à penser"*—of the *"es gibt Sein,"* of the dis-pensation or the emission (*envoi:* sending) of being (*Gesch-ick des Seins*). This emission or sending of Being is not the firing of a missile or the posting of a missive, but I do not believe it is possible, in the last analysis, to *think* the one without the other. Here I can do no more than designate titles of possible discourses. I have often tried, elsewhere, to stress the divisibility and the irreducible dissemination of the *envois* (sendings, dispatches), of the acts of sending. Even what I have called "destinerrance" [—a wandering that is its own end, etc. . . .] no longer gives us the as-surance of a sending of being, of a recovery of the sending of being. If the ontico-ontological difference ensures the gathering-up of that sending (*le rassemblement de cet envoi*), the dissemination and the destinerrance I am talk-ing about go so far as to suspend that ontico-ontological difference itself. The dissemination epochalizes the differ-ence in its turn. Of this movement I can only indicate the path. The destinerrance of the *envois,* (sendings, missives, so to speak), is connected with a structure in which ran-domness and incalculability are essential. I am not speak-ing here of factors of undecidability or incalculability that function as reservations in a calculable decision. I am not speaking of the margin of indeterminacy that is still homo-geneous to the order of the decidable and the calculable. As it was in my lecture on "Psychè, Inventions of the Other," it is a question here of an aleatory element that appears in a heterogeneous relation to every possible cal-culation and every possible decision. That unthinkable ele-ment offers itself to (be) thought in the age when a nuclear war is possible: one, or rather, from the outset, *some* send-ings, many sendings, missiles whose destinerrance and randomness may, in the very process of calculation and the games that simulate the process, escape all control, all reassimilation or self-regulation of a system that they will have *precipitously* (too rapidly, in order to avert the worst) but irreversibly destroyed.

Just as all language, all writing, every poetico-performative or theoretico-informative text dispatches, sends itself, allows itself to be sent, so today's missiles, whatever their underpinnings may be, allow themselves to be described more readily than ever as dispatches in writing (code, inscription, trace, and so on). That does not reduce them to the dull inoffensiveness that some would naively attribute to books. It recalls (exposes, explodes) that which, in writing, always includes the power of a death machine.

The aleatory destinerrance of the *envoi* allows us to think, if we may say so, the age of nuclear war. But this thought has been able to become a radical one, as a thought left over from the "remainderless," only in the nuclear age. This contemporaneity is not historical in the trivial sense of the term. It had to have given signs of itself *even before* nuclear techno-science reached the point where it is now with its inventions: in Democritean physics as well as in Nietzsche or Mallarmé, among many others. But let us not eradicate the broad scansion of this history which has constructed a concept of history lacking any proportion with it: the moment when Leibnitz's formation of the Principle of Reason (and all that Reason prescribes for modern techno-science) comes to resonate with the nuclear question of metaphysics, the question that Leibnitz himself formulates and around which Heidegger organizes the very repetition of the essence of metaphysics in 1929 (between the first and the last "world war") in *What is Metaphysics?* The question is, "Why *is* there something rather than nothing?"

Hence we meet once again the necessity and the impossibility of thinking the event, the coming or venue of a first time which would also be a last time. But the destinerrance of the sendings is precisely what both divides and repeats the first time and the last time alike.

The name of nuclear war is the name of the first war which can be fought in the name of the name alone, that is, of everything and of nothing.

Let us start again, for this the last dispatch, from the homonymy between Kantian criticism and "nuclear criticism." First, on the topic of this name, "nuclear criticism," I foresee that soon, after this colloquium, programs and departments in universities may be created under this title, as programs or departments of "women's studies" or "black studies" and more recently of "peace studies" have been created—things which, no matter how quickly they are reappropriated by the university institution, are nonetheless, in principle and conceptually, irreducible to the model of the *universitas* (but it would take too long to demonstrate this here). "Nuclear criticism," like Kantian criticism, is thought about the limits of experience as a thought of finitude. The *intuitus derivativus* of the receptive (that is, perceiving) being, of which the human subject is only one example, cuts its figure on the (back)ground of the possibility of an *intuitus originarius,* of an infinite intellect which creates its own objects rather than inventing them. As for the history of humanity, that example of finite rationality, it presupposes the possibility of an infinite progress governed according to an Idea of Reason, in Kant's sense, and through a treatise on Perpetual Peace.

Such a criticism forecloses a finitude so radical that it would annul the basis of the opposition and would make it possible to think the very limit of criticism. This limit comes into view in the groundlessness of a remainderless self-destruction of the self, auto-destruction of the *autos* itself. Whereupon the kernel, the nucleus of criticism, itself bursts apart.

Now when Hegel *on the one hand* sets forth the implicit consequence of Kantian criticism and recalls or postulates that one must begin *explicitly* with a thought about the infinite of which Kantian criticism has indeed had to begin implicitly, and *on the other hand* defines access to the life of the mind and to consciousness by the passage through death or the risk of biological (let us say natural) death, through war and the struggle for recognition, he still has to hold on to that remainder of natural life which, in symbolization, makes it possible to capitalize (on) what is gained from the risk, from war and from death itself. As individual or community, the master has to survive in order to enjoy the symbolic profit (in mind and consciousness) from death risked or endured. He takes risks and he dies *in the name* of something which is worth more than life, but something which will still be able to *bear his name* in life, in a residue of living support. That is what made Bataille laugh: the master has to live on in order to cash in on and enjoy the benefits of the death risk he has risked.

Today, in the perspective of a remainderless destruction, without mourning and without symbolicity, those who contemplate launching such a catastrophe do so no doubt in the name of what is worth more in their eyes than life ("better dead than red"). On the other hand, those who want nothing to do with that catastrophe are ready to prefer any sort of life at all, life above all, as the only value worthy to be affirmed. But nuclear war—as a hypothesis, a phantasm, of total self-destruction—can only come about in the name of that which is worth more than life, that which, giving its value to life, has greater value than life. Thus it is indeed waged *in the name of.* . . . That, in any case, is the story that the war-makers always tell. But as it is in the name of something whose name, in this logic of total destruction, can no longer be borne, transmitted, inherited by anything living, that name in the name of which war would take place would be the name of nothing, it would be pure name, the "naked name." That war would be the first and the last war in the name of the name, with only the non-name of "name." It would be a war without a name, a nameless war, for it would no longer share even the name of war with other events of the same type, of the same family. Beyond all genealogy, a nameless war in the name of the name. That would be the End and the Revelation of the name itself, the Apocalypse of the Name.

You will say: but all wars are waged in the name of the name, beginning with the war between God and the sons of Shem who wanted to "make a name for themselves" and transmit it by constructing the tower of Babel. This is so, but "deterrence" had come into play among God and the Shem, the warring adversaries, and the conflict was temporarily interrupted: tradition, translation, transference have had a long respite. Absolute knowledge too. Neither God nor the sons of Shem (you know that Shem means "name" and that they bore the name "name") knew absolutely that they were confronting each other in the name of the name, and of nothing else, thus of nothing. That is why they stopped and moved on to a long compromise. We have absolute knowledge and we run the risk, precisely because of that, of not stopping. Unless it is the other way around: God and the sons of Shem having understood that a name wasn't worth it—and this would be absolute knowledge—they preferred to spend a little more time together, the time of a long colloquy with warriors in love with life, busy writing in all languages in order to make the conversation last, even if they didn't understand each other too well. One day, a man came, he sent messages to the seven churches and they called that the Apocalypse. The man had received the order, "What you see, write in a book and send to the seven churches." When the man turned around to see what voice was giving him this order, he saw in the middle of seven golden candlesticks, with seven stars in his hand, someone from whose mouth "a sharp double-bladed sword" was emerging, and who told him, among other things: "I am the first and the last." The name of the man to whom he was speaking, the one who was appointed to send messages, to deliver the seven messages, was John. (pp. 26-31)

> *Jacques Derrida, "No Apocalypse, Not Now (Full Speed Ahead, Seven Missiles, Seven Missives)," translated by Catherine Porter and Philip Lewis, in* Diacritics, *Vol. 14, No. 2, Summer, 1984, pp. 20-31.*

William J. Scheick

[*In the following excerpt, Scheick notes that there are numerous definitions of "nuclear criticism" and that all of them ultimately attempt to define the essence of humanity by its potential for self-destruction.*]

Insofar as I can determine, the expression "nuclear criticism" was first used as a classification in an issue of *Diacritics* (1984), which contained a number of essays addressing literature, culture, and thought in terms of a possible nuclear holocaust. If only a few sentences toward a working definition of nuclear criticism appeared in that issue, an uncertain explanation and an incomplete self-consciousness still remain as problems for its practitioners today. Nuclear criticism includes writers who vary from those with a fervent social commitment to denuclearize the world to those who engage in its practice somewhat more abstractly as an interesting philosophical or critical concern. Moreover, nuclear criticism encompasses a wide variety of discourse, ranging, for example, from decoding various kinds of nukespeak (Hilgartner), to advancing programs for classroom instruction to encourage awareness of the nuclear threat, to enumerating themes and plot patterns in fiction on the subject of nuclear destruction, to analyzing and relating patterns of thought, apropos a nuclear world, to popular culture, politics, or literary and social traditions, to relating writings with a nuclear referent to other modes of cultural and critical expression, to forging a vocabulary and methodology whereby texts throughout the ages can be read in terms of the nuclear referent, to making critical assessments of nuclear criticism itself.

As this inventory suggests, nuclear criticism is not one

thing. It is a polymorphous ethical mode of critical enquiry encompassing, at least at this incipient stage of its practice, an open-ended opportunity to explore epistemologically, in every manner of way, the applicability of the human potentiality for nuclear self-destruction to the study of human cultural myths, structures, and artifacts.

That nuclear criticism should include so much is perhaps appropriate given the meaning of the word *nuclear*. This word obviously derives from the word *nucleus,* and *nucleus* has an interesting and instructive history. The earliest use of the word, if the *OED* is accurate in this instance, occurred in two highly technical contexts during the opening decade of the eighteenth century, when it referred (botanically) to the center of a nut and (astronomically) to the condensed portion of the head of a comet. The technical nature of the word kept it comet-like, far away from everyday human life; things nuclear were technically extraordinary, remote. By the second decade of the eighteenth century this word was also used technically to describe the interior crust of the earth. Things nuclear were now remotely overhead (in comets), remotely hidden in our midst (in nuts), and also remotely underfoot (in the earth)—still safely far away on the frontier of communal human concerns insofar as the word remained technical and the reality it described continued to refer to matters extra-human. By 1760, however, *nucleus* came to mean, in nontechnical usage, a central part around which other parts were grouped in the material world, which was a definition on the verge of impinging on human affairs. By the end of the eighteenth century this pattern specifically included communal human structures, and by the second decade of the nineteenth century the word no longer was restricted to the external world or to material human affairs; it now included the human mind and referred to such immaterial concerns as the kernel of fine thinking or the core of a cultural manifestation of the human mind.

The very history of the word *nucleus,* mutating from something seemingly extrinsic and remote to humanity, to something internal within the human mind, parallels the degree to which the development of nuclear technology has, from 1945 to 1990, increasingly invaded human consciousness. The pervasiveness of the capacity of nuclear technology to threaten us personally has moved from the relative safety of "out there" (in a seemingly remote Nevada Test Site, or Hiroshima, or Bikini) to "right here" (in our backyards and in our heads).

Moreover, the history of the word *nucleus* adumbrates what has become the informing motive of the mode of discourse called nuclear criticism. Whether written with social/political fervor or intellectual abstraction, nuclear criticism aims for a redirection of critiques of cultural artifacts from the remote spatial void of poststructuralism to the apposite inner-spatial realm of human ethos. Just as the meaning of the word "nucleus" altered from something faraway to something nearby, nuclear criticism aims to transform the poststructuralist distant and abstract emphasis on the indeterminacy of the meaning of any thought or word to an immediate and relevant emphasis on the determinacy of at least one meaning: the utter reality of predictable death, of the total extinction of all life, in terms of the nuclear referent.

In this sense, nuclear criticism endeavors to penetrate to the core of human mental constructions, including literary or cultural criticism itself, in order to expose the one ultimate concern that has always mattered to humanity throughout history: the preservation of life. Nuclear criticism seeks (sometimes directly, sometimes indirectly) to become the nucleus of renewed ethical critical discourse, and in this sense it finds itself borne on the same tide of ethical concern evident in feminist, ethnic, third world, and (to a degree) new historicist critical practice. Making ethical judgments of texts is an inevitable and natural human act, as Wayne Booth has recently and forcefully reminded us, and nuclear criticism demonstrates one way how, in Booth's sense, we make spiritual or emotional use of cultural artifacts. Nuclear criticism intrinsically seeks to discover by the beginning of the twenty-first century the *nucleus* of a renewed or new ethical sensibility in the human mind, which is precisely where the meaning of the word "nucleus" instructively came to reside by the beginning of the nineteenth century.

Does my analogical maneuvering here seem too fantastic or farfetched? Perhaps I am desperate. I must accept the risk of censure that my similitude might provoke: the nuclear risk against which my observation is (in some sense) deterrently lodged is exceedingly critical in its demand for a response from me. In taking the risk of seeming to be farfetched, I disclose the kernel, or nucleus, of my hope pressing against this menacing nuclear referent. And might not my musing over the implications of the history of the word *nucleus* as a paradigm for the direction of nuclear criticism finally demonstrate one way how nuclear criticism proceeds?

In other words, in response to the nuclear referent, nuclear criticism often tries to combine matter-of-fact reason and imaginative intuition, reflection and speculation. If the juxtaposition of reason and intuition seems to be an oxymoron, might not an incongruity be pragmatically useful—and, as a result, a kind of truth-telling—in the cause of urging a communal reminding that might also become a re-minding? If nuclear criticism expresses anything, it affirms the tentative possibility of a re-minding, a hoped-for reinterpretation of communal memory (e.g., the history of a word) that would contribute to a revision of human consciousness. Practitioners of nuclear criticism, even in its more abstract modes, evidence anxious hope in the capacity of the human mind to redirect itself. But this reminding requires more than a mere leap of faith; it requires a deliberate leap of the human mind into the seemingly farfetched. The revision of human consciousness requires a fetching from afar (as if the human spirit were a cometary head or a planetary core), an imaginative intuitive revision, a seeing anew, within the matter-of-fact rational boundaries of the ordinary, where (like the interior of a nut) lay the hidden nuclei of human ideological patterns.

At its best, then, nuclear criticism requires a neo-Romantic intuitive vaulting of mind: speculative archeological decodings of cultural artifacts of every kind (the past); inventive coalescences of imagery and coinages of affective vocabulary (the present); and fanciful conjectures of what might for better or for worse eventuate in human experience (the future). In making seemingly, farfetched, imaginative leaps, nuclear criticism implicitly seeks to discover and uncover, by whatever act of "intuitive rationality" necessary, some "nuclear" features hidden within the human unconscious. It might, for instance, suggest how an apparently minor and innocuous exchange with a colleague evinces a semiotic code replicating the underlying pattern of governmental rhetoric and practice pertaining to nuclear deterrence. Nuclear criticism undertakes to dig in excavated sites (e.g., to unearth the buried treasure of a pertinent word) to the heart of the human psyche, as if it were a cometary head or a planetary core. By combining reason and intuition, reflection and speculation, nuclear criticism not only discovers and uncovers, it potentially urges through its disclosures a similar revisionary reminding; it urges humanity to reinterpret its communal memory in the context of "living" with the threat of the nuclear referent.

This goal of nuclear criticism has been faulted, most notably by Tobin Siebers, who remarks that in this mode of discourse "the image of nuclear war provides only a new metaphor for the old practice of marking literature with the frustration felt by those who desire to act morally within society"; "the metaphor of nuclear war becomes a convenient image with which to express one's critical inadequacies, hesitations, and guilty conscience about the problems of ethical criticism." That nuclear criticism has antecedents in its intellectual impulse is no troublesome charge, for as Siebers notes in another context, nuclear criticism at heart affirms community. The remainder of Siebers's rebuke amounts to unearned assertions, and his reduction of nuclear war to a metaphor amounts to a misperception. However, underlying his dismissal is an assessment of what he discerns as a fundamental contradiction at the center of nuclear criticism: that its practitioners wish to give up war in order to find literature, but also *hopelessly* find literature to be allied with war; nuclear criticism "enters the public discussion of nuclear war on the side of peace and proposes aesthetic values as an antidote to those of violence. But it insists on bringing literature into the war zone to make its point. Literary theory begins to resemble nuclear war in its assault on literature." Even my own preceding discourse can in part be construed in these terms, for in speaking of excavated sites to discover and uncover unconscious ideological patterns in human cultural myths, structures, and artifacts I imply the trope of penetration and rupture as well as suggest the deleterious nature of what is unearthed.

But does nuclear criticism only manifest a negative capability? If the unfavorable findings, the revelation of subtle "nuclear" expressions of human suicidal impulses, characterize most of nuclear criticism at this time, the practice of this discourse does so because it is immediately situated at a precarious, desperate moment of human history and finds it necessary to explore the darkness of the human unconscious. That resistant darkness (like the mystical dark night of the soul) must be known first before the positive enlightenment of re-minding and re-vision is possible. The stress of nuclear criticism on the negative, on the alignment of human cultural expressions with the nuclear threat itself, is the necessary prelude to an awakening of humanity to its potentiality for re-minding and re-vision.

Furthermore, the tendency of nuclear criticism at present to disclose so much incriminating evidence in its excavated sites at the core of the human mind only indicates, finally, something to which the nuclear referent already attests: humanity's penchant for self-destruction. This negative finding, however, is not the only feature of human potentiality, nor does it impugn all human cultural artifacts as expressions only of humanity's negative capability. Many of the very works which reveal the bleak dimensions of human thought also reveal the positive traits of the human mind. But in a time of acute nuclear threat, nuclear criticism can hardly blithely dwell on old values or try to discover new ones, for the nuclear age calls for radical rethinking. This revision or reformation cannot occur unless humanity is first convinced of the prevalence of its negative, self-destructive impulses written large everywhere, especially in expressions of the nuclear referent in cultural myths, structures, and artifacts.

Moreover, as an antidote to its negative findings in aligning art and war, nuclear criticism implicitly offers its method of combining matter-of-fact reason and imaginative intuition, reflection and speculation, as one heuristic feature of its program of reminding/re-minding. Rationally and intuitively fetching from afar, nuclear criticism not only makes imaginative leaps toward insights into human negative capability, but also *always already* suggestively exhibits one method of re-minding for a future revision, if humanity is to have a future. That nuclear criticism heuristically invites humanity likewise to combine reason and intuition, as a *positive* mode of possible human re-minding, is what Siebers fails to observe.

More threatening to the agenda of nuclear criticism than Siebers's focus on its temporary and necessary preoccupation with the alignment of cultural expressions with war is, as I mentioned in passing earlier, the poststructuralist mood in which it finds itself. Poststructuralist attitudes have saturated contemporary thought to such an extent that many critics have come to treat such questions as what is real, what is true, or what is good as useless issues. Given the nature of this sense of permanent indeterminacy and tentative situationality, Barbara Herrnstein Smith typically concludes that in criticism the language of value should be assiduously avoided.

In response to the emphasis of poststructuralism on the historization, subjectivization, and relativization of reality, nuclear criticism not only implies a potentialist human capacity for revision but also struggles toward a potentialist metaphysics. This feature of nuclear criticism can be appreciated if we apply to it J. Fisher Solomon's remarkable discussion of reference in a nuclear age. Conceding that (as the poststructuralists have indicated) reality is not ultimately knowable, Solomon insists upon an empirical potentiality, a potential external reality, which can serve as a limiting "objective" referential ground (*episteme*) for subjective belief (*doxa*) and action because it can be pro-

jected or calculated through our experience of probability, propensity, or regularity.

For Solomon, the most urgent instance of the need for such a potentialist metaphysics is the nuclear threat of our time. This threat can be defined as an empirical potentiality: a predictability which has objective reality because the possibility of nuclear holocaust bears within itself real propensities for probable development. So, for Solomon as for the practitioners of nuclear criticism, the nuclear referent is not only the mere product of our imaginations that requires a suspension of belief (as Derrida seems to contend), but it is also something extrinsic to us, something with *real* extraconjectural, extra-interrelational, extra-linguistic dispositional potentialities.

In this light, the nuclear referent is the "most real" of empirical potentialities; situationally verifiable, it "really" threatens the extinction of life. Death is the ultimate enactment of devaluation, paradoxically the "most real" experience to the living, whose common sense value throughout time has always been the continuation of life. In a world of occluded perception and of a relativity and situationality of values, there is one fact, one possibility that is not humanly experienced as equal in value to other empirical encounters: death.

Precisely this shared human commonsensical valuation of life, countering the ever-potential devaluing alternative "reality" of the complete extinction of all life, is a collective memory of which nuclear criticism positively reminds us when focusing on the negative capability of the "situational" and "real" nuclear referent. To reveal this valuation of life (contesting with alternative suicidal proclivities) at the nucleus of the conflicted human mind and at the hidden core of its cultural expressions comprises the implicit agenda of nuclear criticism when it heuristically combines matter-of-fact reason and imaginative intuition, reflection and speculation, as an example of a kind of reminding (reinterpretation of communal memory) and revision (seeing anew). Just as the nuclear referent is an afflictive real potentiality derived from the divided human mind, other occasions might well evince equally beneficial "real" potentialities derived from that same mind. Hope in this reformational alternative potentiality, especially in the human capacity to sustain life in spite of its current penchant to destroy life, defines the vital communal heart, the core, the nucleus of nuclear criticism.

Here we stand. How can we do otherwise? (pp. 3-10)

William J. Scheick, "Nuclear Criticism: An Introduction," in Papers on Language and Literature, *Vol. 26, No. 1, Winter, 1990, pp. 3-12.*

Klaus R. Scherpe

[*In the following excerpt, Scherpe examines the influence nuclear war has had on modernist and postmodernist thought.*]

In the age of *posthistorie,* the end of the world [*Weltuntergang*] can no longer be a topic, at least not a dramatic one. The historical, philosophical, and theological power of the apocalypse to conjure up images of the end, in order to make life more meaningful, seems to be exhausted. As Hans Magnus Enzensberger remarks in his "Two Notes on the End of the World": "Finality, which was formerly one of the major attributes of the apocalypse, and one of the reasons for its power of attractions, is no longer vouchsafed us." The nuclear catastrophe, viewed as "pure" terror, as the fatal consolidation and refinement of all the vital power of labor and knowledge, excludes every metaphysical reflection and paralyzes our fantasy and imagination. The transformation of the catastrophe into a multimedia show with its proliferation of images, stories, and commentaries from the treasure trove of Biblical, literary and psychoanalytic exegesis can only confirm the loss. The novel feature of the impending end of the world is its producibility. Not only has it become producible but, perhaps, even interchangeable: an ecological disaster and the catastrophic developments now underway in genetic engineering are both just as suitable for snuffing out human existence or making it unrecognizable. The producibility of the catastrophe *is* the catastrophe. If this formulation is valid pretext for the postmodern condition, beyond the historical trends and exhausted "grand narratives," as [Jean-François] Lyotard puts it, then there really is no more space for a narrative dramatization of the end of the world. "The actual nuclear event will not occur, because it already has occurred," says [Jean] Baudrillard. If this explosive force has already penetrated things, if the "fission" implicit in the decentering and deterritorialization of every substantive assumption about collective rationality and about the role of subjective agency in the historical process is already complete, then the theory has itself taken on catastrophic dimensions.

For Jean Baudrillard the "nuclear is the apotheosis of simulation." The nuclear bomb is nothing more than the final sign in the game of simulation. But it is not so much "reality" as our understanding of reality that collapses. In Baudrillard's reflection on the "agony of reality," the capitalist system of exchange is, in a sense, expanded to subsume every phenomena and every discourse, which are themselves interchangeable—including all the categorical assumptions of traditional Marxism. In the complete dominance of dead labor over living labor embodied in the "bomb" every dialectic of production crumbles, which excludes both the revolutionary event and the nuclear explosion. And it is apparently only in this impossibility, in the total absence of "eventfulness" [*Ereignishaftigkeit*] from reality, that the theory can retain for itself some of the fascination that has always been a component part of the apocalyptic idea. Baudrillard claims for his theory, and for himself as a theoretician, an awareness of "objective irony" and "radical indifference." This awareness is achieved when reality is displaced into the time frame of the future perfect tense: "it will have been . . . it will have happened." What he predicts is, perhaps, no more and no less than a shift in the grammar of the end of the world.

It is difficult to escape the suggestive force of a social theory like the one proposed by the latest popular philosophers of French poststructuralism, Baudrillard and Lyotard, especially given the aggressive fashion with which they address their German audience. Its power might be a result

of the "subversive ecstacy" unleashed by a theory that is able to totalize various individual phenomena, as well as complete discourses, by sucking (almost like a vampire) every differentiation, argumentation, and every scrap of evidence from them. The "emotional antipathy to universals" (when made accessible with the help of a set of dialectical tools) and the final renunciation of historical referents, which have become unrecognizable under the flood of information produced by society, herald a new form of Nietzsche's "joyful wisdom"—also, and especially in conjunction with, "final matters."

This is not the place to wage a final battle with the "structural" theory of exchange, which is the radical product of the theory of simulation, nor is it the place for political dissent, which is necessary when Baudrillard, like [André] Glucksmann, advocates a high level of nuclear armaments as a consequence of his theory. Criticism and dissent have already been registered by competent people. What is at issue here, with reference to the threatened impoverishment of modernity's critical potential, is the unique phenomenon represented by the transformation of social theory and socio-critical discussion into a new aesthetic consciousness, or at least into aesthetic values, most notably in the fascinating power of "indifference." The statement that finality has lost its power of attraction, that the "big bang" no longer has its theatrical fascination, can only be justified as an aesthetic expression. It is precisely the abstract reality of the destructive potential of nuclear weapons that creates a thoroughly concrete reality, namely that of the threat, which apparently continues to fascinate the aesthetic consciousness.

When railing against the dominance of instrumental reason, the aesthetic consciousness of modernity always admitted its allegiance to "another state of being," i.e., to the explosive break or rupture with the continual inertia of linear social development. In the literature written at the turn of the century this was symbolized in the "life of danger" that contrasted with the normality of ordinary bourgeois life. The images and conundrums that were intended to challenge the Weimar Republic's secure, fact-oriented consciousness exhibit an aesthetic fascination with representations of the "state of emergency [*Ausnahmezustand*]." Postmodern consciousness seems to have lost the ability to imagine "another state of being" with its explosive force. How and why, we might ask, do terrorism, threats, and, more comprehensively, nuclear deterrence still retain a specifically aesthetic fascination in our era?

Postmodern thought thrives on the destabilization of signifiers, on the destruction of the symbolic order. In a certain sense postmodern thought is predicted on the finality of "reality," which it only perceives voyeuristically. When viewing the "modernist project" retrospectively, one does not even remember the concepts that were proclaimed dead, one after another: God, metaphysics, history, ideology, revolution, and finally death itself; not even "sacrifical death" is accorded an "independent existence." Structuralist thought already seals the fate of the subjective and the humane, freezing them out to the extent that they are based on substantialist assumptions. Poststructuralist thought adopts the only conceivable perspective left, a sense of déjà vu for everything that was proclaimed dead; all that can be done is to add more items to the list. Baudrillard's theory of simulation seems to have been constructed for the sole purpose of eradicating the last remnants of substantialist assumptions and rational calculations. If death had been accepted as the last possible bastion of revolutionary consciousness, it too would be eliminated as a referent in the next publication, left to drown in the infinite sea of indifference. The accelerating effect of the theory, through which the historical temporality of observed phenomena is made to disappear, can be imagined metaphorically as a vampire or a rapacious Moloch. Finally, the theory even incorporates the eschatological consciousness of the apocalypse. Baudrillard calls the catastrophic effect of the threat emanating from simulation an "implosion," not an "explosion"; it results from the fact that under pressure from a merely simulated reality every social energy is expended internally in the "play of signifiers," evaporating and disappearing in some "catastrophic process."

Of note is not only the curious manner in which this form of theorizing constantly creates new objects in order to make them disappear, but also the complaint that is always inscribed in this signifying game; in spite of all the indifference there is a noticeable defense against the loss of "eventfulness." One has to surface for a moment from the stream of verbal indifference, with which Baudrillard floods every indication of possible differentiations, to remember the thoroughly original potential of the protest that poststructuralist thought since Foucault has mounted against ideological consciousness. The break with a history that was firmly identified with the discourse of power was not a spontaneous act but rather one carried out under protest against rationality's functional system, against the prison-house of language, against the terroristic sense of security contained in the grammatical rules of social consciousness and institutions. It is probably not accidental that Baudrillard, who has perhaps taken the destabilization of signifiers further than anyone else, is the most energetic, even polemical proponent of the loss of "eventfulness."

On the one hand, Baudrillard proclaims a condition of the absolute absence of events; only "pseudo-events" occur: "The whole scenario of public information and all the media have no other function than maintaining the illusion of eventfulness or the illusion of real actions and objective facts." Everything that happens is conditioned by the illusion that something "really" does take place. And yet, Baudrillard continues to regard "the event" as the actual danger and threat in the "system" and to the system. The strategy of nuclear deterrence only appears to be directed towards preventing an "emergency"; in reality [?!] its purpose is to ensure the strengthening of the system of protection, obstruction, and control of the "event." "The deterring effect is in no way related to the nuclear inferno . . . but to the much larger probability of a real event, that is, to anything in the system that could produce an event and throw everything else out of balance." Why, one could ask, does the "system" direct all its energy towards something (the incalculable event, the intrusion of the uncontrollable, the revolutionary shock) that is not

only not real, but that cannot even claim the illusion of reality? Even Baudrillard's theory of simulation, in which the crisis of overproduction in capitalism is to be understood as the "total" shift of production into reproduction, can only ground the *abstraction of an absence of events* by referring to the *dynamic of events* whose presence is at least latent. His position has consequences for the idea of the "catastrophic" nature of the present social situation and for the aesthetic means with which it can finally be thought.

One consequence is the assertion of an "objective irony," an attitude of indifference characterized by the statement: "Everything has already happened," and Baudrillard willingly concedes that this attitude possesses a certain "seductiveness" or "passionate" quality. The aesthetic fascination is apparently contained in the subject's almost ecstatic surrender and submission to the indifference emanating from the object and to the incomprehensible "objectivity" of the system, whose purely abstract existence constitutes the catastrophe. Yet another consequence is the recourse to eventfulness, whose non-existence is apparently not so complete, since it is not only destroyed by the system but also produced anew. Eventfulness itself produces a threatening dynamic, which can be noted, if nowhere else, as an acceleration towards the end. To be sure, this acceleration can be, indeed has to be, described as the system's own continued functioning, but in this motion energies are set free that require or even demand an event "here and now" (death, revolution, catastrophe). "The revolution will never rediscover death if it doesn't demand it immediately." Although Baudrillard has disavowed this pathos in the course of articulating his theory (perhaps one should speak of "pseudo-progress"), the de-dramatization carries with itself a notion that requires the validity of one particular illusion within the state of disillusion [*Illusionslosigkeit*], namely, the "intensification" of the catastrophic condition. The "pseudo-revolution" of May 1968 is accorded a certain "eventful tone": "All in all, it was an intensive event, timely and with a special tone." The formulation alone shows that Baudrillard at this point is still betting on the aesthetic fascination with the intensity that can emanate from such an event. In the relatively uneventful 1980s Baudrillard announces his affinity to the "fatal strategy of the era," which wants to counter the absence of hope for the future by calling for an anticipation of the end, wishing for the sudden event of total destruction in place of the deadly "waiting." "Apocalypse now" is the last possible event that can be pitted against the abstraction of eventlessness. The aesthetic consciousness of post-modernity insists on "objective irony" when confronted with the social situation of "pure" reproduction. Yet, the aesthetic fascination with events does not seem to have disappeared completely in the process.

If my observations are correct, then "playing with the apocalypse" is an integral part of postmodern social philosophy. One consequence of the "postmodern condition" is that the de-dramatization of the end has become a dominant image—in spite of the fact that among Baudrillard's followers, especially among his German followers, a re-dramatization of the end is at hand. Baudrillard's theory represents itself as a particular constellation of *aesthetic consciousness,* which is supposed to embody postmodernist thought. This consciousness has been fatally enriched with reflections on the "end of finality" and is therefore identifiable as a theory of catastrophe, or as a theoretical catastrophe when compared with the consciousness and theory of crisis contained in modernism. The specifically aesthetic dimension of the consciousness of catastrophe refers to a particular constellation in the theory and literature of modernism visible in Germany since the end of WWI. If postmodern knowledge insists, as Lyotard writes, on treating its own development as discontinuous, catastrophic, and irrevocably flawed, the aesthetic consequences of such a position can already be seen in the aesthetic representations of this epistemological paradox produced at a point in history when the social process of modernization and rationalization was so obvious that it became necessary to posit "different conditions" for art and for aesthetic reflection ("freedom from rules," the "state of emergency," productive destruction). When Baudrillard reflects on the permanent "recycling" of all social phenomena and discourses and speaks of a "world irradiated with norms," in which every instance of heterogeneity and contradiction is made to disappear, he is radicalizing ideas whose roots lie in the theoretical and literary critique of civilization put forth by writers like Ernst Jünger, Carl Schmitt, Walter Benjamin, Franz Kafka, or Thomas Mann—however different the proportion of destructive to liberating criticism in their ideologies. If, in view of his post-historical theory, Baudrillard fancies himself to be theorizing under conditions of seductive or impassioned aesthetic "indifference," from which he is nevertheless able to remind us of the aesthetic intensity of events, he merely accentuates aesthetic phenomena that have been constantly reflected in the development of modernism. The historical difference is, however, not to be denied: where Baudrillard includes a remnant of eventfulness in his theory retrospectively, modernism in German literature and in German literary theory since Weimar had banked on the power of the revolutionary event.

The more it comes to be accepted, the more the postmodern phenomenology of society and art will have to accept its own historicity, not its dialectical sublation but rather its historical significance. Post-modern theory prefers to think of itself in terms of the "death of modernity," as the liquidation of modernity's enlightening potential and as the praxis of contradicting and deconstructing its utopian hopes. On the other hand, criticism of postmodernity, as formulated by [Jürgen] Habermas and [Peter] Bürger, consists of the "completion of the project of modernity" without it ever becoming clear how the arguments implicit in the call for a renewal of the Enlightenment discourse through communicative acts could defend themselves against the destructive forces, which are every bit as much a part of the "project of modernity" as its Enlightenment impulses. One needs to differentiate among the various positions at stake in the current dispute between the "modern" self-defense of reason and its "postmodern" self-destruction. To begin with, there is the double character of the "project of modernity," the recognition of its enlightening *and* its destructive energies. This would allow for a more precise understanding of the success of post-

The mushroom cloud over Hiroshima, August 6, 1945 around 8:20 A.M., *as remembered by Hidehiko Okazaki.*

modernity's radicalization of modernity's destructive energies, which is itself the result of a failure to make use of the Enlightenment's potential for protest. (pp. 95-103)

. . . . .

The constellation implicit in the dramatization or de-dramatization of the end dominates current thinking about apocalyptic consciousness. In the theory of modernity, particularly in Benjamin's version, the drama of the catastrophe is retained or reconstituted historically and philosophically in the notions of "shock" and "state of emergency." But at the same time, the theory includes the opposite position, most prominently presented by Ernst Jünger, of the non-dramatic observation of a permanent catastrophe without resorting to what Jünger viewed as the sentimental memory of the power of humanity. Jünger's potential de-dramatization is most apparent in his pose of *désinvolture,* an indifference that is as painful as it is appealing. The *aesthetic* consciousness of modernity contains both positions without differentiating them clearly; perhaps, they are often related to each other. Postmodern consciousness, born in an age of "agony at reality," insists on separating the reflective connection that one can locate in the history of the debates that raged within modernity, with authors like Jünger and Thomas Mann ranged on various sides of the front. By dismissing apocalyptic metaphysics and insisting instead on a pure and self-sufficient logic of catastrophe, postmodern thought frees itself from the necessity of expecting an event that will alter or end history.

A number of German essayist-philosophers are presently engaged in eradicating enlightenment-oriented modernity, in which the complacency brought on by the irony or indifference that can be observed in French philosophers of *posthistoire* is missing completely. What the Germans apparently overlook is something they could learn from French poststructuralists, namely the ability to think in terms of *differences* rather than in (fanaticized) oppositions. The "critique of reason" that Ulrich Horstmann develops in his *Philosophie der Menschenflucht* (Philosophy of Human Escape) or that is advocated by Gerd Bergfleth, a profound prophet of Jean Baudrillard, in spite of the fact that the latter's thought is more abstinent than ecstatic, has tended to become a new form of metaphysics and a re-dramatization of the end. What they are doing here is transforming the postmodern "heaven" (*Jenseits*) into something mythical and primitive—in a way that is so fanatically true to the original that they are probably creating a typically German version of the postmodern condition. One should perhaps concede them the last possible variation on the theme of self-realization, the apocalypse they can only carry out on themselves, as self-destruction.

In his "meditation on the bomb" Peter Sloterdijk proposes a version of this form of thinking that has been therapeutically tempered. He presupposes a postmodern accounting of modernism after the "termination" of the belief in progress, after the elimination of the free space for subjective actions, and after the de-dramatization of potentially explosive heterogeneity in a society that has become homogenous: "The overkill atmosphere is constantly becoming more pervasive. . . . The structure of overkill has become the real subject of current developments." The difference between the life-styles of the punkers and the members of the establishment is only one of appearance. The "subjective excesses" disappear in the face of "objective" ones: "Cynical eruptions burst forth from the catastrophic mass of civilization." Seen in this light, the atomic bomb is just the "most extreme form of objectification" in the process of civilization, "the purest reality and the purest potentiality" of the catastrophic social principle in capitalism. This is precisely the point that Sloterdijk finds so fascinating. The bomb is "a damnably ironical machine; it is 'good' for nothing, and yet it can produce the most powerful effects." Sloterdijk uses this constellation to imagine a new, fantastic sort of "break through," which would simultaneously reverse and surpass the fantasies of escape and breakthrough contained in the theory of modernity: "For a long time the bomb has not been a means to an end, because it is such an immeasurable means; it overshadows every possible end. Since it can no longer be a means to an end, it has become a medium for self-discovery. It is an anthropological development. . . ." The methodology employed by Sloterdijk uses an infinite chain of analogies and short-circuits to eliminate every antagonism and contradiction, and therefore presupposes the "most extreme

form of objectification"; it arrives—"objectively," having been moved rather than moving itself—at a point of indifference that becomes the point of departure for a new, hyper-realistic identification: "The bomb demands of us neither resistance nor resignation, but rather an experience of self-discovery. We are it. There the western 'subject' is brought to fruition." The compulsive drive and longing for a new eventfulness and ability to experience— Thomas Mann spoke of the "desire for the breakthrough" in this connection—leads to an extreme form of identification in the face of the nuclear catastrophe. Sloterdijk's "mediation on the bomb," enriched as it is with a dose of oriental wisdom—"All secrets are contained in the art of giving in, of not resisting."—stages the encounter with the bomb as a final act of love, an infinitely seductive coupling that can only be interrupted by one thing: "If you look very closely, it seems now and again, that the bombs are grinning mockingly to themselves."

For Kafka and Thomas Mann the "shameless" and mocking smile of the artist who is branded by the deconstructive principle of modernism serves as a warning against its horror and its terror. The smile and the image of the smile are filled with irony or cynicism, but also with pain. Sloterdijk would like to discover nothing less than a grand and fascinating "detente" in the bomb's "mocking smile." All of the pangs of anxiety and hope mobilized by the threat of the bomb would dissipate there. Yet, if the apocalyptic attraction of the bomb is reinterpreted therapeutically so that it becomes an "anthropological event" of self-discovery, the danger is just what Ernst Jünger feared the most: the subject's becoming unable to feel pain, a state characterized by the absence of pain, in which the individual's capacity to resist gives up its last line of defense. In the name of the bomb the "shameless smile" that repelled Kafka is surpassed by the insolent smile of cynical reason. Compared to the demonic laughter that Thomas Mass attempted to ward off by conjuring it up, the insolent smile of the bomb means certain death through radiation. Sloterdijk's buddhist inspired suggestion that we become at one with the bomb by embracing it can really only serve the interests of certain adherents and confessors, in the form of their "own" collective death.

It is no accident that recent German intellectual life finds the shift produced by the transition to the "postmodern condition," namely from a mentality of indifference to one that can be characterized as a striving for a new myth of primary experiences, particularly attractive. While Sloterdijk immerses himself in the wisdom of the orient in order to make nuclear self-discovery conceivable, Ulrich Horstmann invokes the whole tradition of western intellectual history to support his "anthropofugal perspective." He fantasizes about the redemption of humanity through a form of collective suicide that is as necessary as it is desirable. Whereas Sloterdijk is only engaged, as it seems to me, in an apparent de-dramatization of the end, Horstmann carries the redramatization of the apocalypse to its logical conclusion, namely to the "Archimedian point of humanism," which served modernism, historically in the sense of the Enlightenment, as both the center and fulcrum for the consciousness of impending catastrophe. Horstmann interprets the producibility of a nuclear catastrophe, which Günter Anders had called the point of absolute danger as early as 1956 (we have become the "masters of the apocalypse"), as the starting point for an act of apocalyptic self-discovery, which should be transformed into an event here and now. Horstmann relates the release from the painful syndrome of Hegel's "unhappy consciousness" to what Foucault has termed an epistemological "fold." In so doing he limits Foucault's archaeology of the human sciences to the teleological perspective of an indifferent realm of "things" and "the void left by man's disappearance," which is a dreadful misunderstanding of Foucault's argument. The notion that a nuclear strike would constitute an instance of absolute indifference, one in which the "monster" called humanity would realize itself in a completely negative and destructive event, is nothing more than a radical, yet banal reversal of the Enlightenment impulse implicit in the "project of modernity." What is fascinating is not the momentary interruption that allows us to remember the "humane" history we never experienced, nor is it the "breakthrough" to the new reality of revolutionary experience; the fascination lies in self-discovery in the moment of annihilation. The crux of Horstmann's philosophy is its fixation on the individual's own death, another attempt to "concretize" the incomprehensible abstraction of the destruction of society. Thus the apocalypse reclaims a certain drama as "self-discovery," a kind of spiritual drama, which French postmodernism can, perhaps, only ridicule as a typically German desire for authenticity and immediacy.

If the "death of modernity" has already been decided upon, the only option left in the "postmodern" condition is self-sacrifice. Using this fatal strategy for a "break through" all by oneself, Gert Bergfleth shortcircuits what Baudrillard calls death's revolt, where death becomes the last possible means of escaping the "system's ability to integrate everything." Having retreated from the attractions of simulation theory and the "territory" he had staked out there, Baudrillard claims in his most recent publications "to have completely crossed over to the other side of objective irony." His German prophet, on the other hand, is now proclaiming death's ecstasy, and he claims, in an obvious perversion of Baudrillard's position, that the individuals who are ready to sacrifice themselves can be redeemed:

> Isn't a sacrificial death so other-worldly and remote that anything said from the perspective of survival has to be false; and isn't our task first [!] principally [!] actually [!] and only [!] to contemplate that remoteness and to organize our lives in a way that is consistent with what is being sanctified there. . . . What is being advocated here is a refusal to accede to the moralistic obligations that the system demands, and this does not include a warning against suicide. Neither is any encouragement being offered. There is a third option that consists of the affirmation of this sacred but fatal passion.

Bergfleth's intense desire for some sort of deadly seriousness can scarcely be comprehended within any theoretical explanatory framework. The reader has to decide whether to add the irony that seems to be missing from such intellectual, yet anti-rational outpourings or to resort once

more to analytic reason. A longing for death and "intensity" seems to constitute the turning point for a frustrated form of postmodern thought; the most immediate consequence would be the re-emergence of barbarism and other archaisms. Like Horstmann, Bergfleth allows his argument to sink to the level of enthusiastic and passionate destructiveness that Thomas Mann identifies so terrifyingly in his portrait of pre-fascist thought in *Doktor Faustus*. The "critique of reason" carried out by these German essay-philosophers has, for all practical purposes, become identical with that form of eschatological thought that contains all the well-known components of the ancient apocalyptic drama. The ability to exercise critical judgement disappears in the apparently novel "experience of one's own groundlessness," in the feat of "making oneself absolutely invulnerable." The result is to free up enormous energies for the purpose of committing suicide: "Every energy should be concentrated on bringing about the end!" The "system" itself is to suffer the death without the qualities that it deserves: elimination, cessation, neutralization. But the individual who works actively and passionately for the end is rewarded with the apocalyptic promise of rebirth in the catastrophe: "I would call this other end the beginning of a new world."

. . . . .

It appears that the German adherents and proponents of French *posthistoire* want to transform the perversion of Enlightenment thought into a new morality of death. The sing-song tones of recent German thought about the end are nothing more than the "vile ditty" of destructive reason, which complements the songs of those friends of peace whose anxiety about their own death leads them to oppose dying in general. If French philosophers are making different music, it is perhaps because under the sign of the "end of finality" the moral and aesthetic posturing that turns the drama of the apocalypse into the last possible event no longer seems sensible. They favor its transformation into a different kind of non-dramatic, aesthetic consciousness.

When Baudrillard, the theoretician of capitalism's "hypertely," lays claim to the theoretical gesture of "indifference" and "objective irony," when Lyotard actualizes the aesthetic category of the sublime as a feeling that "nothing further might happen," and when Glucksmann uses the threat of nuclear deterrence to agitate for an aesthetically productive state of "vertigo," which he sees as our "sporadic perception of the void that shows we are capable of digging our own graves," the de-dramatization of the apocalypse in the nuclear "event" is always present in their minds. The point of proclaiming the illusion of "eventfulness" in the salvation of an "otherworldly" catastrophe is to contemplate the present system's "catastrophic logic." Like Glucksmann in his *La Force du Vertige*, Baudrillard is hoping for *aesthetic* consequences from his *political* advocacy of nuclear armaments:

> Fortunately they have produced a hundred times more of them than they need! If they should ever succeed in finding a small but appropriate place to wage a war, the break through [!] could finally be at hand. We are protected by this

luxuriant growth, by the ecstacy of destruction. We remain in a state of nuclear phantasmagoria, which will never become reality.

The transformation of postmodern knowledge about the nuclear society into aesthetic consciousness, which is free from moralizing aesthetization, is no longer linked in the way that the theory of modernity was to the chimera of the "breakthrough" or the "interruption" as historical events—even though it is clear that Baudrillard has not completely relinquished the "catastrophic" event as a reference. The fascination with fright [*Schrecken*], which served "destructive" modernity as a point for the crystallization of aesthetic perception, is overtaken to a degree by fascination with deterrence [*Abschreckung*, literally being frightened away]. The threat that something might happen or could happen is dissolved and disappears under the permanent threat that nothing will. As Glucksmann writes: "The war's results precede it." The notion of "It will have happened," with which one imagines a retrospective look at a future that will never occur and that cannot be achieved, certainly not as a utopia, produces the aesthetic consciousness of "distance" and "indifference" that sounds the death knell for critical thinking in terms of negation, anticipation, and causal connections. Such distance is the result of deterrence rather than fear. Suspending the expectation of death and one's anxiety about it are supposed to effect new "intensity" for an existence that is always already marked by death. While Glucksmann seems to be interested in some kind of aesthetic catharsis that would purify the motives behind our beliefs and our fear of the "balance of terror," Lyotard reactivates the concept of the sublime to describe the imagination's impotence when faced with the same always already existent set of problems with which the avant-garde had to deal. Lyotard sees the "avant-garde search for the event-producing work," which is reflected in a postmodern context by the desire for "apocalypse now," being contradicted by the "sublime element" in the capitalist economy. The capitalist system's abstract functional mechanism is just as impenetrable to our imaginative capacities and to aesthetic experience as the nuclear catastrophe, which is the final and highest stage of accumulation achieved by the system. And so it is only logical to redirect the artistic energies, which were apparently wasted in attempts at representing something that is ultimately impossible to represent, back to theorizing itself. In fact, to the extent that it duplicates the "catastrophic" structures in society, the theory is to be understood as a kind of aesthetic consciousness. Yet, if reflecting about the lack of eventfulness were the final event, the "project of postmodernity" would be over before it ever started.

Apocalypse forever? (pp. 122-29)

Klaus R. Scherpe, "Dramatization and Dedramatization of 'the End' The Apocalyptic Consciousness of Modernity and Post-Modernity," translated by Brent O. Peterson, in Cultural Critique, *No. 5, Winter, 1986-87, pp. 95-129.*

> **Our tragedy today is a general and universal physical fear so long sustained by now that we can even bear it. There are no longer problems of the spirit. There is only the question: When will I be blown up?**
>
> **—William Faulkner, in his Nobel Prize for Literature acceptance speech, 1950.**

Thomas M. F. Gerry

[*In the following essay, Gerry maintains that the threat of nuclear war requires that the tenets of literary criticism be reevaluated if they are to accurately represent the "nuclear age."*]

The most significant events of our time are the invention, use and proliferation of nuclear weapons. Literary criticism regularly has ignored the nuclear fact. In her recent article, "Lifton's Law and the Teaching of Literature," Gillian Thomas suggests that "we must begin by examining the ways in which our own modes of thinking and expression have been deformed and brutalized by living in the nuclear age." . . . I agree with Thomas that by acknowledging the interactions between the nuclear peril and our activities as critics and teachers of literature we can begin to loosen ourselves from the paralysis deterring us from being fully alive in this profession.

The development of the atomic bomb, its use on Japan and the physical and psychic aftermath of those events, coincided with the intensification of critics' attention to the text exclusively. This coincidence is not fortuitous: they were swept up in the sudden society-wide awakening and the subsequent society-wide inattention which occurred. As Paul Boyer documents in his book *By the Bomb's Early Light: American Thought and Culture at the Dawn of the Atomic Age*, within two months after the bombing of Hiroshima and Nagasaki in August 1945, writers, broadcasters, politicians, scientists and the public had articulated every aspect of the nuclear consciousness with which we are today familiar, except the concept of Nuclear Winter. Shortly after this extraordinarily quick and pervasively felt illumination (an exhaustive study in 1946 by the Social Science Research Council found that fully ninety-eight per cent of American adults knew about the bomb) the fearful consciousness diminished. It resurfaced in the mid-1950s, faded in 1963, and emerged again in the late 1970s. Writers and critics in common with everyone, then, experience these swings of awakening and sleeping.

The most widely accepted explanation for the diminution of awareness is that it is a form of denial called psychic numbing. Robert Jay Lifton depicts psychic numbing in *Indefensible Weapons: The Political and Psychological Case Against Nuclearism* as a combination of the blocking of images which create too much stress, with the absence of images because of a lack of prior experience. Ultimately the effect of psychic numbing, both individually and culturally, is to exclude feeling from life.

It is important to understand that the public's receding consciousness of the nuclear peril is not simply a spontaneous response to the fearful reality; the State actively fosters what Jonathan Schell in *The Fate of the Earth* calls "the strange double life of the world." The nuclear states' strategies to suppress consciousness include emphasising civilian uses of atomic energy, and trying to convince people that the policy of Mutually Assured Destruction, the deterrence theory, will work to protect them. In addition, governments admonish citizens to act reasonably within the overall insanity and to let the government handle these (unpatriotic) fears at the bargaining table. With these strategies the state deliberately obfuscates the underlying insane reality with jargon and other forms of "misinformation," leading people to believe that because of the complexities, the whole matter had best be left to the experts. Should one decide that government is wrong in its reliance on nuclear weapons, and decide to express such dissent, the state is fully prepared to back up its position with policies, delays, palliatives, even confessions on the part of its officials that they are powerless to change the situation. In common with everyone, literary critics are the victims of such state-induced confusion and apathy.

But in his collection of essays, *The World, the Text, and the Critic,* Edward W. Said adds an even more chilling dimension to the role of literary critics in the nuclear madness:

> . . . it is our technical skill as critics and intellectuals that the culture has wanted to neutralize, and if we have cooperated in this project, perhaps unconsciously, it is because that is where the money has been.

Publishing and teaching ingenious refinements of texts in a literary universe with little critical reference to the outside world have been the activities central to many English departments. Said maintains that between critics, who engage only in "formal, restricted analysis," and the State, extends a chain of validation which is also the conduit through which funding is distributed, but in reverse, of course, from the State to the textually-absorbed critics.

According to a number of influential books that have recently been published, the chief problem for literary critics and theorists now is whether and how to incorporate history in the study of texts. Frank Lentricchia describes this ongoing crisis in his book of 1980, *After the New Criticism:*

> The crisis is generated . . . by, on the one hand, a continuing urge to essentialize literary discourse by making it a unique kind of language—a vast, enclosed, textual and semantic preserve—and, on the other hand, by an urge to make literary language 'relevant' by locating it in larger contexts of discourse and history. . . . The traces of the New Criticism are found . . . in the repeated and often extremely subtle denial of history by a variety of contemporary theorists.

To demonstrate this denial is the fundamental concern of *After the New Criticism.* For example, Lentricchia begins

his analysis of the most important theoretical documents which purport to reject the New Criticism with Northrop Frye's *Anatomy of Criticism* (1957), the basic tenet of which is that literature is made out of literature. According to Lentricchia,

> For Frye actual history can be nothing but a theatre of dehumanization, a place of bondage and torture . . . [W]hat is celebrated . . . is a fantastical utopian alternative to the perception of a degraded social existence: a human discoursing free of all contingency, independent of all external forces, a discoursing empowered by unconditional human desire.

Noting Frank Kermode's argument in *Romantic Image,* that by the writings of Kant and Coleridge "we were sunk in aesthetic isolationism," Lentricchia shows that while the New Criticism overtly intensified the isolation, most subsequent theorists continue to turn away from historical contexts:

> Whether New Critical or poststructuralist, the formalist critic is concerned to demonstrate the history-transcending qualities of the text, and whether he wields the textual cleaver of difference or that of irony, he portrays the writer as a type of Houdini, a great escape artist whose deepest theme is freedom, whose great and repetitious feat is the defeat of history's manacles.

Said agrees with Lentricchia's insights about contemporary literary theory, similarly depicting it as a closed system. Said channels this awareness towards the world outside the text:

> For the most part our critical ethos is formed by a pernicious analytic of blind demarcation by which, for example, imagination is separated from thought, culture from power, history from form, texts from everything that is *hors texte,* and so forth. In addition, we misuse the idea of what method is, and we have fallen into the trap of believing that method is sovereign and can be systematic without also acknowledging that method is always part of some larger ensemble of relationships headed and moved by authority and power.

Lifton describes three major "Nuclear Illusions" in the opening section of *Indefensible Weapons.* In addition to the illusion of limit and control and the illusion of foreknowledge, he discusses the illusion of rationality of which the self-referentiality of literary studies is a particular instance. Within the "basic structural absurdity" that in the process of destroying their enemies, various nuclear-armed states are prepared at a moment's notice to destroy virtually all of humankind (including, as they seem to need reminding, themselves), people are urged to behave rationally, to keep on with business as usual.

> The illusion is of a 'systems rationality'—of a whole structure of elements, each in logical relation to the other components and to the whole. We are dealing here with nothing less than the logic of madness.

Analogous to the nuclear "systems rationality" illusion is formalist literary theorists' insistence on isolating the text from outside factors, particularly . . . the nuclear factor, which undermines the traditional assumptions of literary studies and obliges these studies to focus exclusively on the literary universe. Another example of this illusion's influence is the way the English departments of universities have conformed to the model of the Sciences—rationalized themselves, as it were. Most obvious, perhaps, is the emphasis on research and publication as the primary measures of their members' performance; but also, in their mimicking of the supposedly value-free "scientific" attitude, English departments follow the model of the nuclear "systems rationality" Lifton characterizes as the "logic of madness."

With "post-structuralism" the madness spreads, according to Terry Eagleton. He argues that post-structuralists' tendency to regard the world as itself textual and therefore as problematically indeterminable is an extension of the contemporary isolation of texts from the world. Post-structuralism, Eagleton writes:

> reaches out and colonizes [material] history, re-writing it in its own image, viewing famines, revolutions, soccer matches and sherry trifle as yet more undecidable 'text.' Since prudent men and women are not prone to take action in situations whose significance is not reasonably clear, this viewpoint is not without its implications for one's social and political life.

In his analysis of the condition of literary studies, Said locates the relevant "authority and power," which literary methodology serves, in Western nuclear-armed states, much as Lifton does, substituting for "systems rationality" the phrase "a liberal consensus":

> the formal, restricted analysis of literary-aesthetic works validates the culture, the culture validates the humanist, the humanist the critic, and the whole enterprise the State. Thus authority is maintained by virtue of the cultural process, and anything more than refining power is denied the refining critic. By the same token, it has been true that 'literature' as a cultural agency has become more and more blind to its actual complicities with power. That is the situation we need to comprehend.

A necessary step towards such comprehension is to acknowledge our governments' most meaningful activity: the development and employment of the nuclear arsenal.

A number of factors in addition to their consciously isolating themselves from "the world" contribute to literary critics' apparent helpless passivity in the presence of the nuclear dilemma. Inherent in the commonly used label for the present period, "Postmodern," is its fundamental orientation to the past, to the Modern period. This characteristic of the term is emblematic of the practice of teachers and critics of literature, as well as of many writers today. One devastating effect of nuclearism is its drastically undermining our sense of the future. To hold in one's mind the reality that at any moment our whole world could end—meaning not merely our individual deaths, but our entire species' extinction by a nuclear cataclysm—is to displace the sense, available to all human beings prior to 1945, that our world will continue even if we personally are dead. Schell elaborates on the significance of this condition:

> Since the future generations are specifically what is at stake, all human activities that assume the future are undermined directly. To begin with, desire, love, childbirth, and everything else that has to do with the biological renewal of the species have been administered a powerful shock by the nuclear peril.

Not only has this radical impoverishment occurred physically and emotionally, but concomitantly in the realm of symbolism. One aspect of the way traditional symbolic relationships have become problematic may be suggested by the following examples. Under the burden of the nuclear threat, marriage, the central action of comic literature, cannot stand up as the symbolic promise of society's continuance. Regarded in the context of the total extinction that nuclear weapons threaten, even death, which in the past could give increased significance to the hero's life, loses meaning. Apocalyptic imagery, so effectively exploited by writers in the past, becomes in the Nuclear Age almost a mockery of our real prospects. Schell sums up the dilemma for traditional artistic aims in these words:

> if it wishes to truthfully reflect the reality of its period, whose leading feature is the jeopardy of the human future, art will have to go out of existence, while if it insists on trying to be timeless it has to ignore this reality—which is nothing other than the jeopardy of human time—and so, in a sense, tell a lie.

The dilemma is similar for criticism. Either we read literature's symbols with their pre-nuclear significations—another motive for sealing literary discourse into a history-denying discipline—or we acknowledge the nuclear threat and face the emptiness of traditional symbolism: face, in fact, the impossibility of any lasting meaning which involves futurity. Besides avoidance or an Existentialist despair, what sort of artistic or critical resolution is possible in these circumstances? Schell maintains, citing the visual art criticism of Harold Rosenberg, that the blurring of the distinctions between art and artist and between art and other activities is one reaction to the dilemma. Peter Schwenger's work on literature which involves nuclear weapons is a rare exception to the response of critics who are busily avoiding the issue of meaning by concentrating exclusively on form. Obviously this avoidance is understandable, considering the ominousness of our circumstances. As the poet Carolyn Forché put it: "There is no metaphor for the end of the world and it is horrible to search for one."

Besides in the area of symbols, literature has been robbed by nuclearism of its traditional structures, causing another radical dilemma for the critic. Similar to the comic ending involving a marriage, the pastoral pattern—in C. L. Barber's phrase, the path "through release to clarification"—does not function fully in the presence of the nuclear threat. I have mentioned the loss of significance for individual death in the context of humanity's extinction: the loss is comparable for the genre of tragedy. As Lifton remarks, "We have no experience with a narrative of potential extinction"; again the choice is to bury oneself in the past or to face the absurdity.

Particular words too have become problematic. The word "war" in the nuclear context is a misnomer. The philosopher John Somerville states why and proposes a replacement:

> What we are dealing with is, first of all, a massive case of linguistic self-deception which arises out of the fact that we have gone on using an old and familiar word—war—to denote a new thing that has a superficial resemblance to the old thing called war, but which in reality has been transformed into something quaiitatively different. . . .
>
> That is, whenever we spoke of war prior to World War II we were referring to an activity that presupposed the possibility of a human future. . . . Since we already have a series of nouns which denote successively wider ranges of killing—suicide for killing oneself, infanticide for killing infants, genocide for killing national or ethnic groups—and since nuclear weapons can now kill all human beings and obliterate all human creations in one relatively brief conflict, it seems appropriate to call such a conflict *omnicide*.

The word "peace," much-touted by believers in nuclear deterrence, is also an erroneous usage. From stories my grandfather told me about his experiences in World War I, I learned of the severe tension the soldiers had to endure because of the knowledge that at any instant a shell might land and explode in their trench. The precarious vulnerability of which we all are victims right now is surely more like an experience of war than peace. One could advance a similar objection to contemporary uses of "security" and "defence."

In addition to the uncritical application of archaic terms, language is perverted by the unconscious acceptance and use of euphemisms deliberately proliferated by the nuclear powers. One of the most striking early examples is the terminology for the first bombs: the result of the Alamogordo test explosion of July 16, 1945 was encoded as "The baby is born"; the Hiroshima bomb was called "Little Boy," and the Nagasaki bomb "Fat Man." Later euphemisms lack the gruesome irony and therefore more easily become habits of thought and understanding. The manufacturing and deploying of nuclear armaments by various countries is sportily called the nuclear arms "race." By shifting metaphors, supposedly these weapons become a protective umbrella. The appellation "Star Wars" glamorizes a sinister escalation of the nuclear peril. Lifton says that by such linguistic abuse "we *domesticate* these weapons in our language and attitudes. Rather than feel their malignant actuality, we render them benign."

Schell describes another pervasive corruption of language, observing we have all come to live a lie: "the pretense that life lived on top of a nuclear stockpile can last" He goes on:

> Meanwhile, we are encouraged not to tackle our predicament but to inure ourselves to it: to de-

velop a special, enfeebled vision, which is capable of overlooking the hugely obvious, a special, sluggish nervous system, which is conditioned not to react even to the most extreme and urgent peril. . . . In this timid, crippled thinking, 'realism' is the title given to beliefs whose most notable characteristic is their failure to recognize the chief reality of the age, the pit into which our species threatens to jump; 'utopian' is the term of scorn for any plan that shows serious promise of enabling the species to keep from killing itself (if it is 'utopian' to want to survive, then it must be 'realistic' to be dead); and the political arrangements that keep us on the edge of annihilation are deemed 'moderate,' and are found to be 'respectable,' whereas new arrangements, which might enable us to draw a few steps back from the brink, are called 'extreme' or 'radical.'

Finally, the term "Postmodernism," commonly used to denote the literary period from about 1950 to the present, betrays even through its compounded blandness some salient features of the criticism that makes do with it. As I mentioned, the term is fundamentally oriented to the past. While I recognize that period labels are never entirely accurate, to me the most objectionable quality of this term, "Postmodern," is that it says nothing directly about the actualities it purports to label. Instead, "Postmodern" clouds with pseudo-technical jargon the most characteristic actuality of our time: the invention, use and proliferation of nuclear weaponry. By contrast, then, I suggest we use the term "The Nuclear Age" for this period as a precise indicator which places literature in its appropriate historical and cultural context.

The political analysis by Richard Falk in his section of *Indefensible Weapons,* contains the following sentence:

> The challenges posed by nuclearism are overwhelmingly questions of values, belief systems, and underlying imagery of human destiny; specialized rational discourse contributes little to the resolution of such questions.

As I have suggested, literary discourse contributes little because often it is almost entirely self-absorbed. But the questions Falk raises, it seems to me, are highly appropriate as subjects for students of literature. Are these not the sorts of issues that we are trained to address, albeit normally within the confines of purely literary study? This confinement is not only unnecessary, but to acquiesce in it is basically immoral. As Falk writes:

> to write about nuclear weapons is inevitably to adopt a cause. . . . It is also a matter of integrity. To pretend dispassion is to mask a commitment at some level of consciousness to a continued reliance on these infernal weapons of mass destruction.

The cause which the writer about nuclear weapons adopts is the cause of the future of human life: a cause about which nobody can be complacent. However, the literary critic's isolation in textual studies not only parallels the nuclear "logic of madness," but reaffirms it. Utterly paradoxically, the literary critic and teacher subscribes to and actively, because of her or his educative role, perpetuates the nonchalant—uncritical—attitude which is the lock confining us to the state of nuclear insanity.

The key to freeing ourselves—as critics, as teachers, as human beings—is to expose and to challenge the absurdity wherever we find its influence; and as I have tried to show, nuclear absurdity is evident in many ways in our professional as well as in our personal lives.

Language and literature are not abstract phenomena with no bearing on the material world; they are the basic tools and components of consciousness. As anyone who has visited a place where many people are illiterate may be impressed, reading and writing—at all levels of sophistication—are powerful instruments of liberation. Literary critics and teachers have vital roles to play in exposing the nuclear "logic of madness." To recognize, to accept, and to act on this responsibility are of the utmost urgency. (pp. 297-305)

> *Thomas M. F. Gerry, "The Literary Crisis: The Nuclear Crisis," in* The Dalhousie Review, *Vol. 67, Nos. 2 & 3, Summer-Fall, 1987, pp. 297-305.*

FURTHER READING

Anthologies

Barry, Jan, ed. *Peace Is Our Profession: Poems and Passages of War Protest.* Montclair, N.J.: East River Anthology, 1981, 312 p.

Collection of poetry, short fiction, and essays about war. Barry writes: "The focus of this collective challenge to the power of war is two-fold: one aim is to illuminate the force of language, the often overlooked sparks of words that unite explosions of human action, inflame passions for war or peace. The other aim is frankly to startle or enchant or draw the reader stone sober into listening to how humans struggle for survival, yet often fail to communicate, shouting past each others' speech, blundering into war, blundering out again, blaming others but seldom reexamining our own responsibility."

Kenzaburō Ōe. *The Crazy Iris and Other Stories of the Atomic Aftermath.* New York: Grove Press, 1985, 204 p.

Anthology of short stories by Japanese writers, including Masuji Ibuse and Hiroko Takenishi, depicting life after the bombings of Hiroshima and Nagasaki.

Schley, Jim, ed. *Writings in a Nuclear Age.* Hanover, N.H.: University Press of New England, 1984, 234 p.

Reprint of a special issue of *New England Review and Bread Loaf Quarterly* (Summer 1983) featuring an anthology of poems, short stories, and essays about nuclear war and weaponry.

Secondary Sources

Anisfield, Nancy, ed. *The Nightmare Continued: Critical Essays on Nuclear War Literature.* Bowling Green, Ohio: Bowling Green State University Popular Press, 1991, 201 p.

Collection of essays by various authors, including Jim Schley, Paul Brians, and Hara Tamiki. The book is divided into two parts: the first provides an overview of issues and trends explored in nuclear war movies and fiction, while the second part examines specific cinematic and literary texts.

Berger, Albert I. "Nuclear Energy: Science Fiction's Metaphor of Power." *Science-Fiction Studies* 6, No. 2 (July 1979): 121-28.

Contends that science fiction writers' use of technology as a metaphor for power allowed many authors to "predict" the bomb's ability to alter human existence even before the effects of nuclear explosive devices were made known to the general public.

——. "Love, Death and the Atomic Bomb: Sexuality and Community in Science Fiction, 1935-55." *Science-Fiction Studies* 8, No. 3 (November 1981): 280-96.

Argues that the lack of realistic characterization and depictions of interpersonal and sexual relationships in nuclear holocaust fiction, as well as the emphasis on the social and political contexts in which nuclear technology develops, have contributed to the genre's assumptions that social collapse is inevitable and often an unconscious desire of modern society.

Berger, Harold L. "Catastrophe." In his *Science Fiction and the New Dark Age,* pp. 147-55. Bowling Green, Ohio: Bowling Green University Popular Press, 1976.

Analyzes the portrayal of nuclear war and its consequences in Nevil Shute's *On the Beach,* Philip Wylie's *Triumph,* Mordecai Roshwald's *Level 7,* and Walter M. Miller, Jr.'s *A Canticle for Leibowitz.*

Brians, Paul. "Nuclear War in Science Fiction, 1945-59." *Science-Fiction Studies* 11, No. 3 (November 1984): 253-63.

Contends that American science fiction writers who published between 1945 and 1959 portrayed nuclear energy and war with scientific inaccuracy, exaggerated optimistism, and "not [as] an apocalyptic horror, but as a problem with a solution." Brians also notes that the most realistic works of this period were written by authors considered part of the literary mainstream.

——. "And That Was the Future . . . The World Will End Tomorrow." *FUTURES* 20, No. 4 (August 1988): 424-33.

Attributes the popularity and abundance of modern post-holocaust fiction to historical events and trends.

——. "Nuclear Family/Nuclear War." *Papers on Language & Literature* 26, No. 1 (Winter 1990): 134-42.

Refers to works by Judith Merril, Helen Clarkson, Carol Amen, and Lynne Littman to demonstrate that women depict nuclear holocausts and their effects on individuals and families more intelligently and sensitively than male writers.

Diacritics: A Review of Contemporary Criticism 14, No. 2 (Summer 1984): 2-82.

Special issue devoted to the impact nuclear war has had on literary theory and contemporary society. Essays by Jacques Derrida, Zoë Sofia, and Mary Ann Caws are included.

Ketterer, David. *New Worlds for Old: The Apocalyptic Imagi-*

nation, Science Fiction, and American Literature. Blooming-ton: Indiana University Press, 1974, 347 p.

> Examines how the use of apocalyptic imagery in the fiction of such nineteenth-century writers as Edgar Allan Poe and Herman Melville as well as in the works of modern science fiction authors secures this genre, and thus nuclear fiction, a place in the traditional American literary canon.

Lifton, Robert Jay, and Falk, Richard. *Indefensible Weapons: The Political and Psychological Case against Nuclearism.* New York: Basic Books, 1982, 301 p.

> Discusses humanity's "psychological, political, and military dependence on nuclear weapons, the embrace of the weapons as a solution to a variety of human dilemmas," and the "fundamental deformation of *attitude* toward the weapons, as well as their immediate dangers."

Matsuoka, Naomi. "The Wrong Stuff: The Hiroshima Pilot in Japanese Fiction." *Comparative Literature Studies* 24, No. 3 (1987): 264-76.

> Explores Japanese versions of and reactions to the story of Claude Eatherly, whom many American and European writers mistakenly described as the pilot of the *Enola Gay,* the aircraft that dropped the bomb on Hiroshima, as found in Iida Momo's novel *Amerika no eiyû* (*The American Hero*) and Hotta Yoshie's *Shimpan* (*The Judgment*).

Messmer, Michael W. "Nuclear Culture, Nuclear Criticism." *The Minnesota Review,* Nos. 30-31 (Spring-Fall 1988): 161-80.

> Proposes that literary critics and other members of "the human sciences can make a contribution to the current nuclear debate different from and supplementary to those made by policy makers, strategic theorists, military figures, scientists and engineers, peace activists, and politicians" by recognizing the extent to which the threat of nuclear annihilation has pervaded humanity's collective unconscious.

————. " 'Thinking It Through Completely': The Interpretation of Nuclear Culture." *Centennial Review* XXXII, No. 4 (Fall 1988): 397-413.

> Attributes contemporary concepts about nuclear war, which he describes as a "hyperreality," to the works of Jacques Baudrillard, Umberto Eco, and such philosophers as Immanuel Kant and Edmund Burke.

Morrisey, Thomas J. "Armageddon from Huxley to Hoban." *Extrapolation* 25, No. 3 (Fall 1984): 197-213.

> Asserts that Aldous Huxley's *Ape and Essence,* Walter M. Miller, Jr.'s *A Canticle for Leibowitz,* and Russell Hoban's *Riddley Walker* share similar themes— "whether or not human love, divine love, or art have any future at all after a thermonuclear war"—and are "the most significant works of . . . [this] genre."

Papers on Language & Literature 26, No. 1 (Winter 1990): 3-186.

> Special issue devoted to the depiction of nuclear holocausts in contemporary fiction and the relationship between the nuclear referent, the humanities, and modern culture.

Parnov, Yeremei. "Science Fiction against Nuclear Madness." *Soviet Literature,* No. 6 (1985): 180-84.

> Defends science fiction as a genre that foresees potential social problems rather than one which merely exaggerates modern times.

Rabkin, Eric S.; Greenberg, Martin H.; and Olander, Joseph D., eds. *The End of the World.* Carbondale: Southern Illinois University Press, 1983, 204 p.

> Examines how "stories of the end of the world display the consequences of our social values . . . [and] the meanings of our wishes" as a form of rebirth and renewal. The collection includes essays on the role of the survivor, nature, and technological catastrophes in apocalyptic literature.

Reid, J. H. "Homburg-Machine—Heiner Müller in the Shadow of Nuclear War." In *A Radical Stage: Theatre in Germany in the 1970s and 1980s,* edited by W. G. Sebald, pp. 145-60. Oxford: Berg Publishers, 1988.

> Explores German dramatist Heiner Müller's plays in connection with his belief that "[nuclear] war will be the alternative to communism."

Science-Fiction Studies 13, No. 2 (July 1986): 115-233.

> Special issue devoted to the manner in which nuclear war is depicted in science fiction. Essays on the role of the military, deterrence policies, and the scientific community in nuclear fiction as well as papers on Walter M. Miller, Jr. and Theodore Sturgeon are included.

Smith, Jeff. *Unthinking the Unthinkable: Nuclear Weapons and Western Culture.* Bloomington: Indiana University Press, 1989, 190 p.

> Analyzes various literary and non-literary texts and their relationship to the public's attitudes and opinions about the nuclear debate.

Solomon, J. Fisher. *Discourse and Reference in the Nuclear Age.* Norman: University of Oklahoma, 1988, 298 p.

> Examines the cultural connections between discourse theory, literary criticism, philosophy, and the potential for nuclear war. Solomon devotes a chapter to Jacques Derrida's "No Apocalypse, Not Now," in which he summarizes and responds to Derrida's arguments.

Strada, Michael J. "Kaleidoscopic Nuclear Images of the Fifties." *Journal of Popular Culture* 20, No. 3 (Winter 1986): 179-98.

> Examines how nuclear weapons and their presence were delineated by American politicians, fiction and nonfiction writers, and in the science fiction films during the 1950s. Strada demonstrates that although each interpretation of nuclear war is unique, all are thematically interdependent.

Thomas, Gillian. "Lifton's Law and the Teaching of Literature." *Dalhousie Review* 66, Nos. 1-2 (Spring-Summer 1986): 14-21.

> Contends that universities avoid incorporating nuclear war literature into their curricula because nuclear war and the threat of global destruction is "beyond words," and, as Robert Jay Lifton notes, a "violation . . . of traditional patterns of teaching and learning. We generally understand our teaching function as one of transmitting and recasting knowledge, in the process of which we explore a variety of narratives. We have no experience with a narrative of potential extinction."

Treat, John Whittier. "Atomic Bomb Literature and the

Documentary Fallacy." *The Journal of Japanese Studies* 14, No. 1 (Winter 1988): 27-57.

Surveys the life of Hara Tamiki, a Japanese writer who gained prominence as a writer of A-bomb literature and analyzes the documentary nature of his Hiroshima memoir, "Natsu no hana."

Wagar, W. Warren. *Terminal Visions: The Literature of Last Things.* Bloomington: Indiana University Press, 1982, 241 p.

Draws upon various literary texts which incorporate apocalyptic myth and imagery to examine how "a dying culture—in this case, the national-bourgeois culture of the post-Christian West—has chosen to express the loss or decline of its faith in itself."

Wilson, Robert. "Fleeing the Ashes: Catastrophe Situations in Canadian Literature." *North Dakota Quarterly* 52, No. 3 (Summer 1984): 8-23.

Examines thematic concerns of recent Canadian fiction dealing with nuclear holocausts and their effects in an attempt to explain why post-catastrophic stories, a staple of American science fiction writers, are rare in Canadian literature.

The Vampire in Literature

INTRODUCTION

While the vampire can be traced throughout literary history and world folklore to antiquity, vampirism as the focus of narrative and theme in works of literature first became prominent in the early nineteenth century. John William Polidori's novella *The Vampyre*, published in 1819, is generally considered to be the first work of vampire fiction and introduced several traits of the literary vampire, including a deathlike countenance and hypnotic powers. This work sparked popular interest, and a deluge of vampire stories followed, most prominently Thomas Preskett Prest's *Varney the Vampyre; or, The Feast of Blood*. Another influential work of vampire literature was Joseph Sheridan LeFanu's "Carmilla," which depicted a lesbian relationship between vampire and victim, further expanding the conventions of vampirism to include an ambiguous sexual attraction between predator and prey, the vampire's aversion to religious symbols, and aspects of sadism. With the publication of Bram Stoker's *Dracula* in 1897, the popular conception of vampires and their portrayal in literature became codified, resulting in the familiar stereotype of an aristocratic bloodsucker who preys upon beautiful young women. Stoker's novel has been the focus of diverse social, psychological, and historical interpretations. Many critics, for example, have asserted that the work is an admonition against deviant sexual behavior, emphasizing the association between vampires and the subversion of Christian and Victorian morality. Although much twentieth-century vampire fiction continues to incorporate characteristics of the nineteenth-century vampire, commentators have noted a trend toward depictions of vampires as sympathetic and morally ambiguous characters, which contrasts with the traditional image of the vampire as threatening and thoroughly evil. Both as character and as symbol, critics find that the vampire in literature serves to reflect society's views on sexuality, death, religion, and the role of women, and functions as a psychological metaphor for humanity's most profound fears and desires.

REPRESENTATIVE WORKS

Aickman, Robert
"Pages from a Young Girl's Journal"   (short story) 1976; published in *Cold Hand in Mine*

Blackwood, Algernon
"The Transfer"   (short story)   1912; published in *Pan's Garden*

Charnas, Suzy McKee

The Vampire Tapestry   (novel)   1980

Christie, Agatha
"The Last Seance"   (short story)   1926; published in *Double Sin, and Other Stories*

Crawford, F. Marion
"For the Blood Is the Life"   (short story)   1905; published in *Uncanny Tales*

Daniels, Les
The Black Castle   (novel)   1978
The Silver Skull   (novel)   1979
Citizen Vampire   (novel)   1981
Yellow Fog   (novel)   1988

De la Mare, Walter
The Return   (novel)   1910
"Seaton's Aunt"   (short story)   1923; published in *The Riddle, and Other Stories*

Ewers, Hanns Heinz
Vampir   (novel)   1921
[*Vampire*, 1934; also published as *Vampire's Prey*]

Gautier, Théophile
"La morte amoureuse"   (short story)   1836
["The Dead Beloved" published in *The Works of Théophile Gautier*, 1900-03]

James, M. R.
"Wailing Well"   (short story)   1931; published in *The Collected Ghost Stories of M. R. James*

King, Stephen
Salem's Lot   (novel)   1975

LeFanu, Joseph Sheridan
"Carmilla"   (short story)   1872; published in *In a Glass Darkly*

Ligotti, Thomas
"The Lost Art of Twilight"   (short story)   1989; published in *Songs of a Dead Dreamer*

Martin, George R. R.
Fevre Dream   (novel)   1982

Matheson, Richard
I Am Legend   (novel)   1954

McCammon, Robert R.
They Thirst   (novel)   1981

McGrath, Patrick
"Blood Disease"   (short story)   1988; published in *Blood and Water, and Other Tales*

Monette, Paul
Nosferatu   (novel)   1979

Nodier, Charles
Le Vampire (drama) [first publication] 1820

Polidori, John William
The Vampyre (novella) 1819

Powers, Tim
Dinner at Deviant's Palace (novel) 1985

Prest, Thomas Preskett
Varney the Vampyre; or, The Feast of Blood
(novella) 1840

Ptacek, Kathryn
Blood Autumn (novel) 1985

Raven, Simon
Doctors Wear Scarlet (novel) 1960

Rice, Anne
Interview with the Vampire (novel) 1976
The Vampire Lestat (novel) 1985
The Queen of the Damned (novel) 1988

Roman, Victor
Four Wooden Stakes (novel) 1925

Romero, George A.
Martin (novel) 1977

Rudorff, Raymond
The Dracula Archives (novel) 1972

Russell, Ray
"Sanguinarius" (novella) 1967; published in
Unholy Trinity

Saberhagen, Fred
The Dracula Tape (novel) 1975

Scott, Jody
I, Vampire (novel) 1984

Simmons, Dan
Carrion Comfort (novel) 1990

Somtow, S. P.
Vampire Junction (novel) 1984

Southey, Robert
Thalaba the Destroyer (poetry) 1801

Stableford, Brian
The Empire of Fear (novel) 1988

Stenbock, Count Eric Stanislaus
"The True Story of a Vampire" (short story)
1894; published in *Studies of Death*

Stoker, Bram
Dracula (novel) 1897
"Dracula's Guest" (short story) 1914; published in
Dracula's Guest, and Other Weird Stories

Strieber, Whitley
The Hunger (novel) 1981

Sturgeon, Theodore
Some of Your Blood (novel) 1961

Tolstoy, Alexey
Vampires: Stories of the Supernatural (short stories)
1969

Tonkin, Peter
The Journal of Edwin Underhill (novel) 1981

Viereck, George Sylvester
The House of the Vampire (novel) 1907

Wakefield, H. R.
"The Seventeenth Hole at Duncaster" (short story)
1928; published in *They Return at Evening*

Wilson, Colin
The Mind Parasites (novel) 1967
The Space Vampires (novel) 1976

Wilson, F. Paul
The Keep (novel) 1981

Yarbro, Chelsea Quinn
Hotel Transylvania (novel) 1978
The Saint-Germain Chronicles (short stories) 1983

ORIGINS AND EVOLUTION

M. M. Carlson

[*In the following essay, Carlson discusses several influential works of vampire fiction and distinguishes between the literary vampire and its folkloric prototype.*]

When Bram Stoker's *Dracula* first came out in 1897, it was an immediate success, a horror writer's "stroke of genius." But Stoker's novel was not a work based on Stoker's imagination alone. Two elements contributed to the success of his novel: a great deal of historical and ethnographic research, and an extensive, already existing body of vampire fiction.

It is to this existing body of vampire literature that the modern reader owes his notion of what a vampire is. We tend to think of vampires as figures from folklore, but the image we have of them has been largely predetermined by the literary, not the folkloric, vampire. The origin of the literary vampire lies in folklore, but literature has greatly reworked and remolded the vampire into a recognizable literary type to suit its own needs and purposes.

Though vampires and lamias appear in classical tales and literature (Ovid, Apuleius, Petronius' *Satyricon,* Flavius Philostratos, and others), references to these supernatural creatures are not sufficiently numerous or consistent to be considered a coherent and developed body of vampire literature. This literature, though of interest, will not be considered here.

The modern literary vampire first made its appearance in a period of reaction against the domination of rationalism. Vampire literature *per se* is a post-Enlightenment phenomenon, a result of Romanticism and of the interest in folklore encouraged by Herder's romantic nationalism. Through German Romanticism, the vampire made his way from folklore into the realm of literature, where he soon became comfortable in certain character types already existing in the literature of the day.

Among the first works of modern vampire literature was Goethe's "Die Braut von Korinth" (1797), an extremely popular and influential ballad about a young woman who returns from the tomb to suck the heart's blood of her former betrothed. Influenced by this ballad, Robert Southey introduced the female vampire into English poetry in 1801 with "Thalaba the Destroyer." Even though the exotic nature of the vampire was calculated to appeal to the Gothic and Romantic writers, the vampire did not become a stock character in the Gothic tradition until the short novel *The Vampyre, A Tale* by Dr. John Polidori (1819).

The Vampyre was originally attributed to Byron, whose prose fragment of a vampire story, written during the same session that produced Mary Shelley's *Frankenstein,* formed the basis of Polidori's novel. The artistically undistinguished but interesting *Vampyre* introduces the detestable Lord Ruthven. This typical misanthropic Byronic hero, however, wears a new and exotic costume: he is a vampire.

The importance of this short novel cannot be overestimated, since Lord Ruthven became the prototype of male vampires in European fiction. He possesses all the characteristics we continue to meet in vampire literature: the personification of evil, great physical strength, pale, drinks blood, sexually hypnotic. The story is fast-paced and full of terrifying action. It ends with general tragedy as Lord Ruthven makes his escape, leaving only death and destruction behind him.

Though Polidori's introduction claims his dependence on scholarly ethnographic sources, it is clear that his vampire is really the disguised gothic villain (Manfred in Walpole's *Castle of Otranto* (1764), Clara Reeve's *The Old English Baron* (1777), Montoni in Mrs. Radcliffe's *Mysteries of Udolpho* (1794), the dark romantic heroes of Byron, and so on).

Lord Ruthven's ruthlessness, his vengefulness, his evil desire to corrupt the innocent and destroy the beautiful, his frequenting of exotic places and castle ruins, his immorality, his world-weariness—all these are characteristics of the gothic villain. To this character type Polidori added some of the more spectacular elements of vampire lore to emphasize his villain's demonic nature and to thrill the reader.

Lord Ruthven is not the standard vampire described in the scientific and psuedo-scientific literature on vampires that appeared on the continent (and particularly in Germany) in the 18th century. In fact, Polidori plays fast and loose with actual vampire lore for the sake of both his plot and his characterization. Ruthven leaves his native soil to seek victims in London (a motif that will reappear in Stoker's novel). All of his victims are young women; in fact, the sexual element is very strong. (The two major climactic points of the story center on a "love crime"). One of the characters relates that the vampire drinks the blood of one woman each year (are there no female vampires?), yet Ruthven helps himself to several. Though Ruthven is abroad both day and night, we learn that vampires have

only nocturnal powers. Ruthven's victims do not become vampires in turn; they die, while he remains the only vampire. Nor does Polidori discuss methods for the destruction of vampires. He was not concerned with these particular problems because he was not really dealing with a vampire; he was still writing about the gothic villain. But the possibilities suggested by Polidori's tale did not escape the more creative artists who followed him.

Polidori's *Vampyre* was immensely popular and was soon transformed into dozens of plays, numerous comic operettas, vaudevilles, and even two operas (Marschner, 1828, and Lindpainter, 1829). In the 19th century, just as in our own day, the vampire was most appreciated through the dramatic medium. Needless to say, many plays, novels, and stories tried to exploit the vampire craze of the 19th century. Most were of low quality, and many had nothing to do with vampires beyond the use of that intriguing word in their titles.

Polidori's novel started a deluge of translations and imitations. In England, the best-known was Thomas Preskett Prest's sensationalistic thriller *Varney the Vampire,* or *The Feast of Blood* (1847). France was a particularly ripe territory. In 1820 Charles Nodier wrote a stage play, *Le Vampire,* and vampire plays continued to be popular in France until after the turn of the 20th century. Even Dumas (*père*) wrote a play paraphrasing Polidori's tale (*Le Vampire,* 1851). The vampire captured Dumas' imagination. Dennis Wheatley recently discovered a long-lost Dumas novel, *The Horror at Fontenay,* an interesting little volume which adds two motifs to the tradition of the literary vampire: the vampire casts no shadow and has no reflection. This corresponds to the popular belief that the soul can be manifested in a shadow or reflection, and since the vampire is an animated corpse, he would not have a soul.

One of the best vampire stories in French (or in any language) is Theophile Gautier's "La Morte Amoreuse" (1836). This fascinating little story followed Goethe's lead, not Polidori's, for Gautier's vampire is a lovely courtesan whose influence involves a young priest in a double life. To the biblically-prohibited act of drinking human blood, Gautier adds the sacrilegious act of carnally seducing a man of God. Clarimonde, the vampire, is destroyed by holy water at the end of the story.

In Russia, Count Aleksei K. Toistoi wrote two vampire novellas, *La Famille du Vourdalak* and *Oupyr* (1841). The latter is a society tale with gothic coloring, but *La Famille du Vourdalak* discusses the customs of the Southern Slavs relating to vampires. The story even refers to Dom Calmet's "curious book" and briefly discusses the Slavic vampire in an effort to stress "exotic authenticity." However, Tolstoi wrote the tales in French; only later were they translated into his native Russian. This fact indicates that A. K. Tolstoi's inspiration for the stories came not so much from Slavic folklore as from the established Western European literary tradition of supernatural fiction.

German literature also produced a number of vampire novels under Polidori's influence. Generally speaking, they belong to the realm of sensationalistic literature and include such works as H. Zschokke's *Der tote Gast* and

Spindler's *Der Vampir und seine Braut* (1826). A little more sophisticated is Theodor Hildebrand's *Der Vampyr oder die Totenbraut: ein Roman nach neugriechischen Volkssagen* (1828). Few are of any real merit; several of the later German vampire novels were crudely pornographic (Dr. Seltzam's *Die Vampyre der Rezidenz,* (1900).

Literary interest in vampires did not wane in the second half of the 19th century. On the contrary, a new type of vampire joined Lord Ruthven: the Fatal Woman, "La Belle Dame sans merci." Following the tradition of Goethe, Gautier, and Keats ("Lamia"), this new female vampire was more the product of literary tradition than of folklore. She was the sensual, dark heroine of romantic fiction—erotic, cruel, sadistic, demonic. She was Lilith returned, the Lamia. She was Edgar Allan Poe's embodiment of vampire love (Ligea, Berenice, Elleonora). She appeared in Baudelaire's *Les Fleurs du Mal* (1857) and (under the influence of de Sade) in A. C. Swinburne's *Chastelard* (1865) and "Satie Te Sanguine." We find her at her most spiritual in Ivan Turgenev's "Prizraki-Fantaziia" (1863). She became the ultimate blend of pain, death, and love. In most cases, she was only vaguely related to the folkloric vampire, for her function in decadent literature lay elsewhere. Decadent literature spiritualized and psychologized the vampire.

But the Fatal Woman vampire did not completely dominate the vampire literature of the second half of the 19th century. In 1872 a very important English short story appeared. This was Joseph Sheridan LeFanu's "Carmilla." It particularly influenced Bram Stoker and is a fine piece of literature in its own right. It is the story of Mircalla, a Styrian countess of the 17th century, who preys on young noblewomen. The relationship between the vampire and her victims is psychological as well as physical: there is a lesbian quality about Carmilla. Before Carmilla is discovered and staked, she draws not only Laura's blood, but her personality and being as well. This is a new, sophisticated twist in the vampire story and one of LeFanu's greatest contributions to vampire literature. The vampire is no longer simply a disguised gothic villain or a supernatural monster, but is a motivated character with his own complex psychology.

LeFanu took his material from a variety of sources. He certainly knew Dom Calmot's work and Delrio's *Disquisitionum magicarum libri sex* (1755), for he took an episode directly from the latter (on trapping a vampire by stealing its graveclothes). Many vampire features later appropriated by Stoker appear in "Carmilla": metamorphosis of the vampire, the ability to enter through locked doors and small apertures, inactivity during the day and the need to repose in the coffin, aversion to Christian relics, hypnotic ability, and superhuman strength. LeFanu tries not to stray too far from the documented folklore vampire in "Carmilla": still, he cannot help adding interesting literary features. For example, LeFanu's vampire must call herself by an anagram of her name: Mircalla, Millarca, Carmilla.

The turn of the century saw a renascence of vampire literature, a tendency possibly generated by the morbidity of the Victorian period. New, unusual kinds of vampires began to appear in literature: the botanical vampires of H. G. Wells ("The Flowering of the Strange Orchid," 1895) and F. M. White ("The Horla," 1887), Conan Doyle ("The Parasite," 1891), and Algernon Blackwood ("The Transfer," 1912). There was a rash of sensationalistic stories and novels following the publication of *Dracula,* their titles designed to attract attention: Marion Crawford's "For the Blood is the Life" (1911), Victor Roman's *Four Wooden Stakes* (1925), H. R. Wakefield's *They Return at Evening* (1928). Enthusiasm for *Dracula* continues even today (Raymond Rudorff's *The Dracula Archives,* 1972).

In our own century, the cinema has been the major medium for transmitting the vampire image. Some of the best include Murnau's *Nosferatu* (1922), Browning's *Dracula* (1931), Hammer's *Horror of Dracula* (1958), and Warhol's *Dracula* (1974). This is a well-documented tradition and deserves no further elaboration here.

The best-known vampire novel continues to be Bram Stoker's *Dracula* (1897). Stoker did a great deal of research in the British Museum Library in preparation for writing his novel. There is no doubt that he did considerable work on vampirism in Eastern Europe, and probably started with Emily Gerard's travel book on Romania, *The Land Beyond the Forest* (Edinburgh, 1888). Gerard's book provided much of the material Stoker used about the "undead." Stoker may have been led to actually use Dracula as his main character by a suggestion from Professor Ármin Vámbery, a famous Hungarian orientalist then travelling in England. Stoker was much taken by the exoticism of the name "Dracula" and did some historical research on the figure.

The historical Dracula was Vlad V, Voivode of Wallachia (1431-76), called Vlad Țepeș (The Impaler). The origin of the name "Dracula" has caused a fair amount of discussion. Grigore Nandris, who has written an article about its etymology, concludes that the word derives from "dracul" (dragon), an epithet for Vlad III, the Impaler's father, who belonged to the Order of the Dragon; the -a is a genetive suffix added to Vlad V's name by Orthodox scribes writing in Cyrillic. Some scholars have assumed that "Dracula" comes from the Romanian word for devil (also "dracul"), and in this way they connect Vlad the Impaler with the literary vampire. In Romanian folklore, however, the material for devils and vampires is mutually exclusive. Nor is it likely that this taboo word would be used to describe a line of Christian princes who built many churches and were considered heroic in their own land.

Vlad Țepeș was a Wallachian prince brought to power by János Hunyadi of Hungary in 1456. Together with Hunyadi, he managed to repel the Ottoman Turks for a brief time. He earned himself the reputation of a cruel tyrant, but historically he was no more cruel than his contemporaries—Richard III, Mahomet II, Ivan IV (the Terrible). Vlad liked to impale people on large stakes. His excesses achieved a degree of popularity, for the European reading public was mad to read about him in the broadsheets that circulated his story from about 1485 on. (Over one dozen incunabula dealing with Vlad Țepeș exist from this period). Handwritten copies of his story circulated everywhere; wandering minstrels sang of his excesses. Vlad was *very* popular.

In Russia, Vlad also achieved a degree of notoriety, but not for the same reasons as in Europe. In the *Povest' o Mutianskom Voivode Drakule* (m.s. 1490), he was a hero in the struggle against the Turks (who were a threat to Orthodox, not Roman, Christianity). Then in the 1530s and 1540s, the many episodes of the *Povest'* were used to justify the autocracy of Ivan IV (the Terrible), and many of the incidents in the *Povest'* were in time transferred from Vlad V to Ivan IV.

Though there are many real horror stories about Vlad Ţepeş, there is nothing in his historical character to connect him to vampire mythology. Nor did local folk legend make him a hero. The folklore of Hungary and Romania, however, is very rich in vampire beliefs. There is one story in particular which may have facilitated Stoker's connection between Dracula and the idea of vampirism. This is the story of Elizabeth Báthory, an early 17th century countess from the Carpathians who was called the Vampire Lady. She drank and bathed in the blood of an estimated 650 virgins before she was walled up in her room in 1611. In his research, Stoker may have read about the notorious Countess who came from the same general geographical area as Dracula, and considered merging the two stories. This is speculation, of course, but the folklore and the history of the area certainly could suggest many things to an enterprising writer of horror fiction.

Be that as it may, there is little doubt that Stoker purposely chose Vlad Ţepeş for his Dracula because of Vlad's notoriety and his connection with an exotic area already strongly associated with vampire beliefs in reality and in the minds of his readers. Even the description of Dracula in the novel corresponds to the popularly circulated woodcut of Vlad V (though the description also owes a debt to Polidori).

Once he had his Count, Bram Stoker proceeded to write his thriller in the tradition of Victorian supernatural fiction, a genre that obviously owes much to the Gothic novel. Stoker did incorporate some new features from Romanian folklore into his novel: the connection of the vampire and the wolf, the appearance of vampires as points of light, the introduction of St. George's Eve as the time when evil spirits freely roam the earth, the the use of garlic to repel vampires. In the novel Stoker also used the traditional motif that the devil can make contracts only with willing victims. Harker enters Dracula's castle to the words: "Enter freely and of your own free will!" Stoker also preserves the motif that the dead cannot cross water. Dracula is most helpless when on the water and must arrange to be transported by others across rivers and oceans.

Stoker deviates from traditional fictional vampire dogma in that his Dracula can be abroad during the day, though in a weakened state. Otherwise, Dracula is a traditional literary vampire in all other major respects, and owes his existence as much to Lord Ruthven, Varney, and Carmilla, as to folklore. The novel contains many allusions to previous horror fiction.

A catalog of general features will help us distinguish the literary vampire from his folkloric prototype:

1. The literary vampire is almost exclusively of aristocratic usually titled, background. This is a feature of the Gothic and Byronic heroes, and justifies the literary vampire's entrance into an elite and interesting society. In folklore, the vampire can be of any class, though most of them are from among the peasantry.

2. Although he comes from a remote and exotic area (usually in Romania or Hungary), the literary vampire travels to cities to "hunt", since urban life provides anonymity. Cities like London or Paris also provide a familiar locale for both author and reader, and heighten the necessary contrast between the known and the unknown, the commonplace and the exotic. The uninvited intrusion of the supernatural into everyday life provides the tension necessary to horror fiction. The folkloric vampire, on the other hand, remains in the vicinity of his native village.

3. The literary vampire does not "hunt" his own family. His victims are usually outside his own ethnic group and of the opposite sex. The folkloric vampire, however, does not distinguish his victims by sex. He also begins by appearing to his own family first, then to other relatives and friends in the village.

4. While the folkloric vampire is usually a recently-made vampire, the literary vampire is inevitably centuries old. Nor is he sullen or stupid, as the folkloric vampire often is; instead, he is devilishly clever, worldly-wise, and even well-read and intellectual. He is a worthy antagonist.

5. The sexual element in the relationship between the literary vampire and his victim is strong (love-death). In folklore, the vampire can return to his wife or pursue young girls, but in literature this motif is carried much further. The pursuit of the victim (the innocent female pursued by the male vampire, the helpless, weak, and often willing male pursued by the voracious female vampire) and the subsequent bite have strong overtones of eroticism and perversion. The "love crime" is the central episode in much vampire fiction.

6. The presence and function of Christianity and of the clergy assume a very important role in vampire literature, greater by far than their role in later folklore of the vampire. This is a reflection of contemporary European religious values, and not a motif taken from folklore. Folkloric vampires are usually contained by extra-Christian methods (staking, powerful plants, burning, and so on).

7. The folkloric vampire is a supernatural monster. The literary vampire began by imitating this, and early fictional vampires are personifications of pure evil (Lord Ruthven). By the end of the 19th century, the literary vampire had developed beyond the level of a supernatural demon; he had become a sufferer. As Dracula is struck by Harker's and Morris' knives, Mina Harker observes Dracula's face: "In that moment of final dissolution, there was in the face a look of peace, such as I never could have imagined might have rested there." Anyone familiar with literary tradition will recognize in the literary vampire the traditional Gothic and Byronic heroes. The vampire is

often an individual who has challenged God and lost, but who continues willfully, stubbornly, on his way. At times he tires of what he is, but his own pride and divine retribution negate his penitence. The literary vampire belongs to the tradition of Prometheus, Milton's Satan, Faust, and Ahasuerus, the Wandering Jew. To this basic figure were added the colorful and decorative superstitions of Eastern Europe. The accommodation of this literary type, however, accounts for most of the major differences between the literary and the folkloric vampire.

8. In folklore, one can become a vampire in a variety of ways: by being the victim of a vampire, by dying as a sorcerer or witch, by being a particularly evil or cursed person, by permitting an animal to jump over the corpse, and in scores of other ways. The origin of the literary vampire is most often very mysterious, but an ancient pact with the devil is often indicated.

9. Vampires in literature have remarkable staying power. Unlike the folkloric vampire, who is discovered through a ritual and then burned or staked, the literary vampire has remarkable regenerative powers. Lord Ruthven, for instance, is wounded and appears to die. He is revived when the full moon's rays strike his body as it lies in his coffin on a mountain top. The folkloric vampire lacks this ability. The actual killing of the vampire in literature usually conforms to the sensationalistic methods suggested by folklore (such as staking). It is hard even for a talented horror writer to improve on a good thing.

The vampire became a stock literary character only when the scientific, rationalistic 19th century forced him out of his folkloric environment and into the new image-carrying element in our culture: literature. His appearance in literature was facilitated by Herder's romantic nationalism and a renewed interest in the folklore heritage of the various European nations. In literature, the vampire found his own level, combining his historical and folkloric features with the character of the Gothic villain. In this new environment the character of the vampire gradually underwent a psychological probing—impossible in his folklore environment—which elucidated the meaning of his character in a new and exciting way. Literature examined, more explicitly and from a wide variety of view points the nature of evil locked within the figure of the vampire, and adapted that figure to suit the needs and understandings of the authors who generated it and the reading public it served. So we see that the images and figures of folklore do not die and disappear. Being fluid, the vampire metamorphoses and disguises himself, appearing again in new ways as times and conditions change. (pp. 26-31)

M. M. Carlson, "What Stoker Saw: An Introduction to the History of the Literary Vampire," in Folklore Forum, *Vol. X, No. 2, Fall, 1977, pp. 26-32.*

Clive Leatherdale

[*In the following excerpt from his critical study* Dracula: The Novel and the Legend, *Leatherdale provides an overview of nineteenth-century vampire tales.*]

The vampire epidemic and its reverberations which swept across much of the Continent in the second quarter of the eighteenth century was ready-made to excite German academia rather than her writers and artists. The haughty intellectual atmosphere of the Enlightenment viewed vampirism as a phenomenon to be analysed, not romanticized. The plethora of explanatory dissertations streaming from German universities were, in time, translated and worked their way across the English Channel, so that as early as the 1730s the term 'vampire' had made its debut in English writing. For the moment, these startling revelations of walking corpses would find little enthusiastic reception in the higher literary circles of either Britain or Germany while the Age of Reason flourished; but then, as Gothic, followed by the broader Romantic sentiments became fashionable amongst educated society in the later decades of the century, and natural human fascination with the mysteries of love, life, death and the supernatural re-emerged, the vampire became something of a vogue. It would take a century for the transformation to be complete, but the folkloric vampire of central and eastern Europe would eventually metamorphose into the British-built vampire of Romantic literature. Purported fact would live on and derive nourishment as fiction, as a post-Enlightenment literary phenomenon.

Abetted by the earlier labours of their academic countrymen, it was the poets of Germany who first realized the potential of the vampire, and who transported the undead from the Church-dominated plagues of superstition into the respectable channels of verse. Ossenfelder's *The Vampire* (1748), Bürger's *Lenore* (1773) and Goethe's *The*

The Vampire of Kisilova:

In the village of Kisilova, three leagues from Gradisch, an old man of sixty-two died in September; three days after the funeral he appeared before his son in the night and asked for food. His son gave him some and he disappeared. The next day the son told his neighbors what had happened. That night the old man did not appear; but the following night he appeared and demanded food; no one knows whether his son gave it to him or not, but in the morning the son was found dead in his bed, and on that same day five or six others in the village suddenly fell ill, and they died one after the other a few days later. The governor of the district forwarded a report to the Tribunal in Belgrade, and they sent two officials and an executioner to deal with the matter. The governor who first reported it traveled from Gradisch to see with his own eyes what had happened. All the bodies that had been buried for the last six weeks were disinterred; when they reached the body of the old man, they found his eyes were open and of a red color, and his respiration was normal, though he was quite still and dead. From this they concluded that he undoubtedly was a vampire. The hangman drove a stake through his heart. A great fire was made, and the corpse was reduced to ashes. It is said that "none of the marks of vampirism was found on the body of the son, nor on any of the others."

Augustin Calmet, in his Traité sur les apparitions des esprits, et sur les vampires, ou Les revenans de Hongrie, de Moravie, *1751.*

The Bride of Corinth (1797) announced the new medium for the vampire tale. *Lenore* was clearly known to Bram Stoker, who would include in *Dracula* its vivid phrase *'Denn die Todten reiten schnell'* (For the dead travel fast). Goethe, in *The Bride of Corinth,* demonstrates his awareness of Greek vampire lore when he fuses the quest for love and blood. A young woman returns from the grave to seek her lover:

> From my grave to wander I am forced,
>   Still to seek the God's long sever'd link,
> Still to love the bridegroom I have lost,
>   And the lifeblood of his heart to drink.

In Britain, Samuel Taylor Coleridge's "The Rime of the Ancient Mariner" (1797) comes close to the vampire essence with these lines:

> Her lips were red, her looks were free,
> Her locks were yellow as gold:
> Her skin was white as leprosy,
> The Nightmare Life-in-Death was she,
> Who thicks man's blood with cold.

(Part III, lines 190-4)

But credit for the dramatically unambiguous arrival of the vampire into English verse goes to Robert Southey's high Gothic epic *Thalaba the Destroyer* (1797), which was published complete with explanatory notes for bewildered readers:

> 'Yea, strike her!' cried a voice, whose tones
>   Flow'd with such a sudden healing through
>   his soul,
>   As when the desert shower
>   From death deliver'd him;
> But obedient to that well-known voice,
>   His eye was seeking it,
>   When Moath, firm of heart,
> Perform'd the bidding: through the vampire
>   corpse
>   He thrust his lance; it fell,
>   And howling with the wound,
>   Its fiendish tenant fled.
> A sapphire light fell on them,
> And garmented with glory, in their sight
>   Oneiza's spirit blood.

(Book 8, Stanza II)

The following year Southey's "The Old Woman of Berkeley" ranged widely over lamias, ghosts, and witches, providing a sound base for the explosion of the literary vampire that would arrive in the second decade of the new century. John Stagg's grisly *The Vampyre* (1810) emphasized the blood and gore aspect of the undead:

> The choir then burst the funeral dome
>   Where Sigismund was lately laid,
> And found him, tho' within the tomb,
>   Still warm as life, and undecay'd.
> With blood his visage was distain'd,
>   Ensanguin'd were his frightful eyes,
> Each sign of former life remain'd,
>   Save that all motionless he lies.

By this time, the great Romantic poets could discern the potential of the vampire for their own creative purposes. By 1820 many of them had experimented in detail with the vampire motif—some making use of the male vampire as an instrument of domination; others working with the she-vampire/lamia tradition to project female seduction. Among the latter category is to be found Sir Walter Scott's *Rokeby:*

> For like the bat of Indian brakes,
> Her pinions from the womb she makes,
> And soothing thus the dreamer's pains,
> She drinks the life-blood from his veins.

Coleridge told of the she-vampire *Christabel;* Shelley preferred to explore the male version in *The Cenci;* while Keats' prolific output of vampirish poems—"The Eve of St Agnes," "Lamia," and above all "La Belle Dame sans Merci"—alternated the sex of the undead. In "This Living Hand" Keats uses vampiric language to illustrate the power of love:

> This living hand, now warm and capable
> Of earnest grasping, would, if it were cold
> And in the icy silence of the tomb,
> So haunt thy days and chill thy dreaming nights
> That thou wouldst wish thine own heart dry of
>   blood
> So in my veins red life might stream again,
> And thou be conscience-calm'd—see here it is.
> I hold it towards you.

Most prominent of all was the influence exerted by Byron, steeped in vampire folklore, whose curse of *The Giaour* spells out all the terror of the vampire—prince of phantoms.

> But first on earth, as Vampyre sent,
> Thy corpse shall from its tomb be rent;
> Then ghastly haunt thy native place,
> And suck the blood of all thy race;
> There from thy daughter, sister, wife,
> At midnight drain the stream of life;
> Yet loathe the banquet, which perforce
> Must feed thy livid living corse,
> Thy victims, ere they yet expire,
> Shall know the demon for their sire . . .
>
> . . . Yet with thine own best blood shall drip
> Thy gnashing tooth, and haggard lip;
> Then stalking to thy sullen grave
> Go—and with Ghouls and Afrits rave,
> Till these in horror shrink away
> From spectre more accursed than they.

What will already be clear from these assembled extracts is that the vampire has radically changed its image—from the pestilential outgrowth of superstition to a vehicle for artistic expression. If the vampire of folklore is notoriously difficult to define—because of its cultural diversity, lack of undisputed corroboration, and the embellishments of Church, rumour, and panic—such an amorphous concept in the hands of poets and writers could only dilute the substance of vampirism still further, as they freely adapted folklore for their own ends. Romantics were not interested in the undead as such. In their hands, vampires ceased to be the 'end', and became the 'means', the catalyst, the medium. The creatures now depicted frequently bore little resemblance to the hideous foamy-mouthed, walking corpses of Slavonic legend. In Romantic literature, generally, vampire imagery is employed not to threaten or frighten, but to illuminate and enlighten.

The Gothic and Romantic, as literary epochs, were well-served by several durable and adaptable myths—among them the Wandering Jew, Don Juan, and the Seeker After Forbidden Knowledge—but the vampire myth could be uniquely harnessed to illustrate one particular aspect of human emotional entanglement: that one partner could mysteriously gain vitality by draining that of the other. Literary vampirism is frequently an expression of energy transfer, psychological as much as intravenous. The central theme became love, not blood, and the nocturnal visits prompted by earthly rather than spiritual intent. Any vestigial supernatural element may be reduced to no more than a lover returning from death to pursue the source of his unrequited affections. As for the flexibility with which the myth became endowed, this has been well essayed by Twitchell:

> In the works of such artists as Coleridge, Byron, Shelley, Keats, Emily and Charlotte Brontë, Stoker, Wilde, Poe and Lawrence the vampire was variously used to personify the force of maternal attraction/repulsion (Coleridge's Christabel), incest (Byron's Manfred), oppressive paternalism (Shelley's Cenci), adolescent love (Keats' Porphyro), avaricious love (Poe's Morella and Berenice), the struggle for power (E. Brontë's Heathcliff), sexual suppression (C. Brontë's Bertha Rochester), homosexual attraction (Le Fanu's Carmilla), repressed sexuality (Stoker's Dracula), female domination (D. H. Lawrence's Brangwen women), and, most Romantic of all, the artist himself exchanging energy with aspects of his art (Coleridge's Ancient Mariner, Poe's artist in 'The Oval Portrait', Wordsworth's Leech Gatherer, Wilde's Dorian Gray, and the narrator of James's *The Sacred Fount*).

This metaphorical utilization of vampirism to serve social, emotional and erotic purposes meant that the central character would not necessarily be explicitly labelled as a vampire. Further, it would not always be clear whether the person performing the energy transfer *is* actually a vampire, though it is important to appreciate that s/he *acts* as if s/he is. In some cases it was superfluous for the writer to announce the presence of overt vampirism, though the association may be obvious. In other instances greater room for manoeuvre was maintained by the artist distancing himself as far as possible from recognizable features of vampirism—to the point of being unconscious of their very presence.

With the greatest poets of a generation turning their talents to the vampire motif it was only a matter of time before it appeared in English prose. Whereas it is not possible to cite with any precision the date of its entry into poetry (strains of vampire-like activity being depicted long before Southey's explicit reference to 'the vampire'), there is no comparable difficulty in dating its advent into prose. Before the nineteenth century there had been no discernible vampire motif in an English short story or novel, though Matthew Lewis' notorious *The Monk* (1796) does include an episode in which a legendary Bleeding Nun appears in bloodstained habit to drain the blood from the

hero with a long, cold kiss. On the Continent, an early obsession with spilled blood was evidenced by the Marquis de Sade's *Justine* (1796), a morbid excursion through blood, sex and excessive violence. *Justine* was, however, devoid of any supernatural presence, unlike Johann Ludwig Tieck's *Wake Not the Dead* (c. 1800).

As it turned out, both *Dracula* and that other horror classic, *Frankenstein,* emerged from the same seed. In 1816 Lord Byron was at the peak of his fame and, on account of his personal indiscretions, of his notoriety. Making news for the wrong reasons he left London for Geneva in the company of a young physician and travelling companion, John Polidori, there to meet up with fellow poet Percy Shelley and his young wife-to-be, Mary. A horror-writing contest was decided upon, but it was neither Byron nor Shelley who provided a new direction for English literature. It was Mary who came up with *Frankenstein,* while Polidori developed on a rough outline scribbled by Byron to complete a short twenty-page tale of his own. It was published in 1819 under the title *The Vampyre* and became with hindsight one of the most influential works of the century—albeit unconsciously.

The Vampyre's initial impact was almost entirely due to the association with Byron—a coincidence happily encouraged by the publishers—and his lordship was long credited with authorship, despite repeated disavowals. Goethe added to the interest, describing it as Byron's best work, so that it won for itself a readership that spanned western Europe and left Polidori to be pilloried, unjustly, for plagiarism.

Its later impact derived from its seminal position in the development of vampire literature. Not only was *The Vampyre* the first work of its kind in English prose, but its leading character, Lord Ruthven, encapsulated many of the basic ingredients of the literary vampire that would shape the genre to the present day. Ruthven is an aristocrat, world weary, coldly evil, aloof, cunning, and irresistible to innocent women, whom he willingly corrupts. In short, he is the stereotypical, misanthropic, moody, nocturnal libertine—a classic Byronic hero (with whom Polidori had occasion to be personally acquainted) endowed with supernatural trappings. By casting Ruthven as a nobleman, Polidori invests him with greater literary potential: the vampire thereby becomes more mobile, his erotic qualities are enhanced, and he is able to exercise sexual *droit de seigneur* over his victims. Parts of the tale are also situated in Greece (authentic vampire country) to provide added local colour. The 'blood' aspect of vampirism is played down—Ruthven acting more as a psychological sponge—but the overall impression and originality of the story were sufficient for it to be translated and adapted for the Paris stage within a year of publication. In time, it would appear in comic operas and vaudeville, and invite a host of imitations.

Polidori probably did not think of his tale in vampire terms—to him it was a further variation on the theme of the Gothic villain—but it initiated new possibilities for the fictional vampire. Bram Stoker's *Dracula* would, in time, eventually stand as the apotheosis of the tradition inaugurated by Lord Ruthven, but for the moment the vampire motif would explore new avenues. The lamia-esque appeal of the vampire *femme fatale,* as revealed in the style of 'Christabel' and 'La Belle Dame sans Merci,' began to break out of its poetic confines on both sides of the Atlantic. Theophile Gautier's little French tale 'La Morte Amoreuse' (1836) tells of a priest carnally seduced by a she-vampire, who is ultimately destroyed by holy water. From the United States in the 1830s Edgar Allan Poe wove vampire elements into many of his short stories, without identifying the vampire for what it was. He preferred to explore the ways and means through which lovers—one of whom is usually dead—can suffocate one another outside prescribed conventions concerning vampire behaviour. Poe's stories are full of women dead but alive: Berenice, Morella, Ligeia, Madeleine Usher; and in an innovative twist in 'The Oval Portrait' the artist paints a portrait of his wife, but as the colours are added to the picture they are drained from her. When the portrait is complete and totally lifelike, his wife is dead. The energy exchange has not taken place between people, but between a person and her image.

Several other isolated vampire tales appeared during the mid-nineteenth century which deserve mention: Alexander Dumas' (père) *The Pale Faced Lady,* with its setting in the Carpathian mountains; the anonymously written *The Vampire of Kring;* and contributions by Hoffman, Baudelaire, and Alexis Tolstoy. The year 1847 would turn out to be an eventful one in the history of the literary vampire. The adaptation of Continental superstition was now infiltrating literature of all kinds. Both Charlotte and Emily Brontë took advantage of it. In *Jane Eyre,* Bertha Rochester's promiscuity is presented as so abhorrent that she is described by Charlotte Brontë as reminiscent 'of that foul German spectre—the Vampyre'. As for Heathcliff in Emily's *Wuthering Heights,* his nocturnal wanderings, bloodless hue, refusal to eat, and his ability to drain the vitality of others are suggestive in themselves. But then in the concluding chapter the question is explicitly asked: 'Is he a ghoul or a vampire?' and Brontë includes the following passage: 'I tried to close his eyes: to extinguish, if possible, that frightful, life-like gaze of exultation before any one else beheld it. They would not shut: they seemed to sneer at my attempts: and his parted lips and sharp white teeth sneered too!' Brontë does not *say* that Heathcliff is a vampire, but her readers in the 1840s, more so than today, knew enough of the legend to draw their own conclusions.

Mention of *Jane Eyre* and *Wuthering Heights* demonstrates how rarefied and pervasive the original vampire motif had become. Neither sister was writing about, or was especially interested in, vampires *per se,* yet they both reveal themselves to be familiar with its use as a social metaphor. The real significance of 1847, however, lies not with the Brontës but with a contribution from the lower end of the literary spectrum. By this time literacy was increasing and newly-installed steam presses and assembly-line publishing techniques were churning out a succession of 'penny dreadfuls'—blood-thirsty, proletarian pot-boilers, comprising tales of murder, lurid romance, and any other sensationalist happenings that could be laced with sexual innuendo. It was out of these developments

that *Varney the Vampire; or, the Feast of Blood* first appeared.

Polidori had told his tale in some twenty pages: the author of *Varney*—James Malcolm Rymer or Thomas Pecket Prest (the authorship is disputed)—needed 868 double-columned pages divided into 220 chapters. Not surprisingly it was reissued in 1853 in penny parts. With *Varney* there is no pretence at literary art; just a rattling story-line told over and over again to be taken on its own terms. Set in the 1730s, the exploits of Sir Francis Varney mark him as the principal literary precursor of Count Dracula. Those ingredients in *Varney* later employed by Bram Stoker include: the maidens' sexual initiation and their mixed reactions of desire and fear; the vampire's roots in central Europe; the quasi-medical-scientific methods of vampire disposal; and the Keystone-Cops-style hunt for the vampire—plus innocent, sleep-walking victims, and the villain dressed in a black cloak, able to climb down castle walls, who arrives in Britain aboard a shipwrecked vessel during a tempest.

After *Varney* there seemed no other avenues for the fictional vampire to explore; the genre seemed exhausted, both as a literary metaphor and as a scaremonger in its

Title page from Thomas Preskett Prest's Varney the Vampyre.

own right. But there remains to be considered one further mainstream vampire work pre-dating *Dracula,* whose author, like Stoker, was an Irishman. Among the five tales comprising *In a Glass Darkly* (1872), by Joseph Sheridan Le Fanu, appeared the novelette 'Carmilla'—credited by many aficionados as the finest vampire tale ever written. Despite its advanced date, 'Carmilla' is soundly Gothic, down to evening mists, full moons, black stagecoaches and central European locations.

Unlike *Varney,* 'Carmilla' is a tasteful, sensuous work; yet what gives it its distinctive flavour is not so much the fact of Carmilla being a she-vampire, but that she is a lesbian. The monopoly of the feminine perspective for both vampire and victim serves to heighten the sexual quality of the vampire act, which is described in greater erotic detail than in any previous example of the genre. Moreover, the vampire is here no longer a supernatural fiend or disguised Gothic villain, but a complex, self-motivated personality. The female vampire would become a popular acquisition for film makers, who would link Carmilla with the real-life Hungarian mass-murderess Elizabeth Bathory to create a further sub-cult of the vampire species.

The dying years of the nineteenth century witnessed a curious Indian summer for the Gothic novel. Stevenson's *Dr Jekyll and Mr Hyde* (1886) and Oscar Wilde's *Picture of Dorian Gray* (1891) are—along with *Dracula*—perhaps the most memorable examples of this unexpected burst of symbolic energy; but the vampire motif once again began to sprout and bloom in unexplored directions. H. G. Wells' 'The Flowering of the Strange Orchid' dealt with vampire plants; Conan Doyle's 'The Parasite' delved into psychic sponges; and Jules Verne's *Carpathian Castle* presented evil scientists posing as vampires. Guy de Maupassant's little cameo, 'The Horla', vividly tells of the anguish and symptoms of a vampire assault from the perspective of the victim and the madness it induces.

Dracula would be the next, and last, great vampire work, so it will be useful to enumerate the various changes that had taken place over the course of a century from the vampire of folklore to the totally different creature presented by the vampire of literature. The one is something to be believed in and feared: the other an artificial construct to illuminate and to entertain. In literature, the social background of the undead is commonly transformed from the peasantry to the nobility, and they are able to travel beyond their native community to plague great cities where they can hide in total anonymity. Whereas the folkloric vampire tends to restrict its activities, at least initially, within its immediate family and friends, and is not strictly bound to visit the opposite sex, the literary vampire frequently has no family and can attack whom it pleases where it pleases. Victims would often be from outside the vampire's own ethnic group, and (with the notable exception of Carmilla) will usually be drawn from the opposite sex.

With regard to its age, the vampire of superstition will not have been long dead, yet will be zombie-like, thick-headed and stupid—the opposite of his fictional counterpart, who, though he may have been dead for centuries, will have used his time profitably to become learned, intelligent, and

adroit. The sexual element is latent in folklore; exaggerated in fiction, and embellished by perversions and the corruption of innocents. The religious ingredient is usually indispensable in literature, the arrival of the priest/hero being integral to the plot. In addition there may be a sense of pity for the vampire—not encountered in folklore—a feeling that he is as much a victim as victimizer, in keeping with the tradition of Faust and the Wandering Jew. The vampire of folklore, as earlier outlined, may have acquired its condition for any one of countless reasons. The origins of its literary cousins will either be left undisclosed, or else will result from some form of pact with the devil. Finally, the vampire of literature possesses remarkable staying powers and regenerative abilities (like the villain in modern crime thrillers, the vampire must not be caught and destroyed too easily), and the means for his/her destruction will normally comply with the more sensational methods prescribed by folklore—the gorier the better from the reader's point of view.

The wealth of folklore and literary antecedents was thoroughly assimilated by Bram Stoker. *Dracula* fuses the tradition of the Byronic hero/Gothic villain with that of the *femme fatale,* and overlays the whole with a rich veneer of folklore. Stoker ignores the popular device of siting his tale in a remote land in a bygone age, and brings his all-powerful Count to contemporary England—to the crowded streets of London in the 1890s. The late Victorian upsurge in tales of the supernatural assisted him to construct a character far more evil than Carmilla and far more substantial than Varney, for as Wolf has said: 'There is nothing in Varney, nothing at all, that is capable of sounding

---

Characteristics to be Determined on Disinterment of a Suspected Vampire:

1. Are there a number of holes (about the breadth of a man's finger) in the soil above the grave?

2. Does the revealed corpse have any of the following:
   A. wide-open eyes
   B. a ruddy complexion
   C. no signs of corruption

3. Have the nails and hair grown as in life?

4. Are there two small livid marks on the neck?

5. Is the shroud partially devoured?

6. Is there blood in the veins of the corpse?

7. Is the coffin full of blood?

8. Does the body look well-fed?

9. Are the limbs fully flexible?

If the answer to these questions is 'yes' refer to your neighbourhood Dhampir, priest or witch to provide exorcism recipe.

Anthony Masters, in his The Natural History of the Vampire, *G. P. Putnam's Sons, 1972.*

anything like the chords of dark understanding that reverberate in page after page of Stoker's *Dracula*'. (pp. 46-55)

> *Clive Leatherdale, "The Vampire in Literature," in his* Dracula: The Novel & The Legend, A Study of Bram Stoker's Gothic Masterpiece, *The Aquarian Press, 1985, pp. 46-55.*

Devendra P. Varma

[Varma is a Canadian critic and educator specializing in the Gothic novel. In the following essay, he examines the origins and meaning of the vampire as a figure in myth and literature.]

The vampire motif is an anthropomorphic theme, a human-animal, life-death configuration. The vampire kills and re-creates. He is the Destroyer and the Preserver, for the passive vampires of life turn into active ones after death. Westerners have viewed the vampire lore as a fascinating but unsolved enigma, but the origins of this myth lie in the mystery cults of oriental civilizations.

The carved vampire fangs and canine teeth of the oriental images of gods shed a strange light on the clues of the origin of vampire lore. The Nepalese Lord of Death, the Tibetan Devil and Mongolian God of Time, whose specific vampire-fanged images adorn many monasteries take us to the very source of this curious legend. Stories of these weird gods who subsisted by drinking the blood of sleeping persons originated with the Hindus of ancient India. And Tibetan manuscripts concerning vampires were held in such high regard that they were embalmed in images to increase their sanctity.

On the antique oriental frescoes the vampire-god is painted with a face in ghastly green, his lustreless body bathed in diffused grey-blue shadows. Represented as a dead soul with an expression of anguish and perversity, his portrait exerts a petrifying effect with the grisly power of a Medusa. He seems to survey the scene with an insolent indifference, while a grotesque female figure, like some fierce Maenad, huddled in agony, her face covered in a tangle of dishevelled locks, gazes in fixed adoration at the vampire-god she holds in icy embrace. It is difficult to communicate the impelling nature of its symbolism, but it is sublime in its belligerent power. The dead soul emerges as a living psyche; the beholders are horror-struck, hide their faces and fly!

The vampire-mural, rich in its mystic symbolism, first emerged in the Indus valley civilization of the Third Millenium B.C. Worshipped as a fierce deity he was portrayed in blue skin set in appropriate scenes of a deep seated demonism that later influenced the aboriginal faiths of Himalayan kingdoms. Its terrifying figure characterized the night-side of its aspect of fertility and salvation. The horrifying deities of Mongolia, Tibet and Nepal, supposedly nourished on flesh, bones and blood, reveal those cross currents of history and styles of worship, the uncurbed primordial urges of primitive peoples forced to explore the hell of the soul.

The antique Buddhist murals and paintings expound terrifying figures of a grotesque world. These were meant to strike terror—an emotion which, for a brief spell, thrusts an individual beyond the self. In Tibet, the grinning *Yama,* the sombre Lord of Death, holds in his claws the Wheel of Life. The Indian *Kali* is a hideous black monster clad in the skins of the dead, eating brains from a human skull, the goddess of disease, battle and death, her black colour symbolic of black magic, like the dark Egyptian Isis and the Black Virgin of the Europe of Middle Ages. These terrifying Gods and awesome figures of Tantric Buddhism were manifestations of a great faith. Their timelessly transcending images and paintings in remote mountain shrines, looming terrifyingly in their demonic forms, stimulated the mystics to comprehend that a man can arrive in heaven only if he has the daring and perseverance to wade right through hell.

In Nepal, the blood-drinking God of Death has three blood-shot eyes; yellow-red flames issue from his eyebrows; from his two nostrils burst forth rain-clouds, raging thunder and lightning. With his right hand he brandishes a flaming sword defiantly against Heaven; in his left hand he holds a skull-cup brimming with warm blood. His head is festooned with a crown of five bleached skulls, and he wears a garland of freshly severed, blood-dripping human heads. The Nepalese cartographers of Hell, thus describe this God, this devilish cannibal with vampire fangs, standing on a mount of skeletons in the ocean of billowing blood.

In outer Mongolia the Vampire God is pictured in a setting of horrible, fierce fires where stormy winds sweep up tremendous waves of a wild sea of blood. In the centre filled with decapitated beings stands a mound of skeletons while poisonous vapours flash terrible streaks of lightning. Ravens, owls, bats, vultures and other demoniacal birds circle round the sky. Waves of blood billow tremendously as human corpses—mummified and decomposed—are scattered around. In the interior of this gruesome and frightening supernatural abode, the Mongolian God of Time bares his canine teeth, sharp like the ice of a glacier.

Between India and Mongolia, ringed by sacred mountains lie the dark and desolate plateaus of Tibet, a country of fierce winds, of sudden calm, and snowy wasteland stretching for thousands of miles. Through the passage of centuries, protected by forbidding barriers of ice and snow, beneath skies of purest turquoise blue, the Tibetans have fostered superstitious dreams and nourished a primitive religion. Extremely isolated, in the highest country on earth with a unique culture, Tibetans are deeply convinced of the reality of mountain spirits and the importance of blood offerings. A country of grotesque cults, fascinating folklore, rituals of exorcising ceremonies and sacred dances, its gods are mountains whose sharp-edged peaks shine like vampire fangs glistening in moonlight.

Their remote temples and monasteries nestled in the fastnesses of snowy ranges or perched on jagged crests silhouetted darkly against the sky, have nourished some fantastic legends and lore. Their isolation has fostered belief in a culture which is forebodingly mysterious. These mountain shrines are embellished with incredible frescoes and sculptures that make the visitors gasp in awe. The Monastery of Muru at the north-east corner of Lhasa, famed for its teaching of the occult, black art and gross forms of heathen sorcery; and the monastery of Gyantsé, a place celebrated for Devil-dances, both maintain Devil's Chambers of Horror, Satanic caves in the dark, designed to awe and impress the superstitious pilgrim.

Sacred to the denizens of the supernatural world, the frescoes and painted scrolls with their elaborate ornamentation and rich texture portray demoniac forces of life. Here stand the hideously colossal infernal images which infest the world. These have human forms but wear heads of ogres and monstrous beasts. One particular statue of a glaring demon is called *Bhayankara* or the Awful, a hideous nightmare creation worshipped with offerings of blood. The eerie gloom of the chamber is adorned with huge skins, teeth and claws of ferocious animals and the remains of sacrificial victims, while the walls are decorated with paintings of evil spirits, sorcerers, witches, bats and vultures. This bizarre spectacle of barbaric idolatry is perceived in the lurid light and suffocating atmosphere of smoky rancid-butter lamps where no daylight can ever penetrate its muffled secrets. Its pitch-dark and eternal night is intensified by coleopterous lights of butter candles and burning incense, as the figures of priests loom out of darkness through the thin clouds of incense fumes, twirling their prayer-wheels, like shadows vivid yet veiled, droning their mystic spells to exorcise devils in intervals between their dreamy meditations.

In Tibet it is a happy omen to see a corpse, and belief exists that devils bring salvation. "Gods too are demons" quotes the epic of *Gesar.* Their deity is an embodiment of positive and negative qualities, bestowing both good and evil, and life itself bears the double face of death and life, of devil and god.

Spirit-evocation is still practised in Tibet by their funerary priests who through their trances and ecstasies attempt to render the dead innocuous and to get rid of him. The Tibetans still believe that the spirits of the dead pursue the living; and the lamas offer fox-liver and hot blood in sacrifice to appease the vampire gods. The Tibetans object to earth-burial for belief is prevalent that when a corpse is interred, the spirit of the deceased, upon seeing it, attempts to re-enter it, and that if the attempt be successful, a vampire results, whereas cremation or other methods of quickly dissipating the elements of the dead body prevent vampirism.

Under the sway of the first King of Tibet Srong-Tsan-Gampo, during the middle of the seventh century, Buddhism had entered Tibet from two sources: the queen was the daughter of a royal family of Nepal, and his second wife was a princess of the Chinese Imperial family. The two ladies converted their young husband to Lamaism or Tantric Buddhism which ultimately became a disastrous parasitical disease—a cloak to the worst forms of devil worship. And the savage Tibetans were placed in constant dread of malignant devils in this life and in the world to come.

Story goes that Padmasambhava, the far-famed professor of occult sciences at the great Buddhist University of Na-

landa, was summoned to Lhasa in 747 A.D. by the Emperor of Tibet Thi-Srong-Detsan, to exorcise a demoniacal and malignant spirit, and to rid the natives of "a dangerous affliction." A demon was supposedly creating havoc, hunting men and beasts, devastating villages, "sucking the blood" of cattle and men in the stillness of night. Padmasambhava was originally a native of Udyana or Swat, from North-West India, and it was reported that he could raise spirits of the dead and conjure up to his assistance the demons of darkness.

Crossing the glacier-clad heights of Himalayan ranges, and trekking over high snowy passes glittering in cold and relentless sunshine, Padmasambhava arrived in the most savage and least known part of the Trans-Himalayas. He discovered that wreathed in the romance of centuries Lhasa stood shrouded in impenetrable mystery, and the savage natives believed in demons, sorcery, vampirism, and the pervasive presence of malevolent spirits.

It is not known what cures Padmasambhava effected but he stayed on in Tibet to expound the mystical elements of Tantric philosophy and iconography, and to establish the first community of Tibetan Buddhist lamas in 749 and rose to be a Great Master of Tibetan Wisdom. He translated several Sanskrit texts on the Supernatural into the Tibetan language, some of which have been preserved in the monasteries of Tibet and concealed in secret with appropriate mystic ceremonies in monastic vaults.

The Vampire is a fascinating poetic manifestation of the occult, inextricably woven in strands of mystery, terror and fantasy. Chronicling the history of vampires may be a dubious enterprise, but this legend surely appears to have originated in the East. Sir Richard Burton seems to acknowledge the provenance when he calls the legends translated from the Sanskrit in his *Baital-Pachisi* or *Twenty-five Tales of a Vampire* "an old and thoroughly Hindu repertory."

But vampires and vampire-gods can be traced in many parts of Asia and eastern Europe, and in many ages. The ancient Egyptians and the Chinese, like the Tibetans had their own vampire beliefs. In Assyrian demonology the Ekimmu was a vampire demon. According to the Hindu mythology, Ralarati was supposedly a combination of a witch and a vampire. Katakhanes is a Cingalese variant, while the Burmese worshipped the Swawmx. The ancient Greeks knew the bisexual demon called Lamia that stole children and sucked their blood. In Solomonic legend, Ornias was a handsome vampire. A Slavic expression for vampire is Vikodlak, while in Poland these are called Upirs. Even in remote valleys and clustering villages of Greece the vampire stalks, unquestioned and accepted as Brucolacas.

Trade caravans and pilgrims traversing the deep river valleys and tortuous passes fanned the culture of India into the Trans-Himalayas, disseminating the philosophy and religion of the great monastic centres of the Ganges basin. And as Tantric Buddhism got its firm grip upon Tibet, its vampire motifs funnelled through age-old routes from India to central Asia, and then travelled on the first transcontinental and diplomatic highway, called the Great Silk

Route, that ran from China to the Mediterranean across Parthean and Kushan dominions. The important land route over the steppes apparently branched from central Asia to eastern Europe and to those ancient cities nestling on the northern Black Sea coast.

Passed on to the Arabs, the vampire legend arrived in Greece shortly after Christ had delivered the Sermon on the Mount, and then in the West it spread all over Transylvania, Hungary, Poland, Silesia, Moravia, Bohemia, Austria and Lorraine.

Meanwhile, the Magyars, a race of ferocious horsemen of Asiatic origin, had come sweeping from the Mongolian steppes and crossed the passes of the eastern Carpathians during the ninth century to occupy the basin of Hungary and the Transylvanian Alps. Their Finno-Ugric language was akin to the Ostyak and Vogul tongues spoken on the eastern slopes of the Ural mountains. They brought their old beliefs from their Asiatic home-land, and what seems most likely is that the Transylvanian vampire beliefs, Burton's bat-winged spirit, and the Tibetan and Nepalese vampire gods, all go back to some extremely ancient common source. The Magyars' pagan background must have been Shamanistic and thus possibly linked with Tibet, where animistic religion embraced a belief in powerful spirits.

The superstition prevalent in eastern Europe, in Greece and the Balkan countries—current in Hungary about 1730, provides evidence that the Transylvanian vampire-beliefs precede the Romantic Revival. One supposes from its wide-spread nature, that in Europe it goes back to misty Middle Ages, and may have been first a peasant belief and not a literary mode.

Dracula's name is Hungarian, and the Hungarians are not really a western race. They are Asiatic in origin, and their language does not belong to the Indo-European group. It was only after they had settled in Europe and become Christianised that they began to consider themselves European.

Indian and Tibetan vampire stories were as fashionable as oriental spices and silk in the markets of Greece and Rome. Ships that sailed regularly over the Indian Ocean and the Red Sea, between Egypt, conquered by Rome, and the ports of western India, carried those oriental myths and legends to the centres of the Western civilized world. Sir Richard Burton in his 1870 edition of *Vikram and the Vampire* noted that Miletus, the great maritime city of Asiatic Ionia, was of old the meeting place of the East and the West. Here the Phoenician trader bargained with the Hindu merchant from the Gangetic valley, and the Hyperborean rubbed shoulders with the Nubian and the Arab. And here was produced and publicised the genuine Oriental apologue, those fabulous narratives and romantic adventures, the blend of all myths and legends. Burton notes that the ancestral tale-teller never collected a larger purse of coppers than when he related the worst of his "aurei."

Like all true myths the vampire legend has been subjected to manifold interpretations, but surely it is logical within the realms of fantasy. This fabulous legend of horror got nourished and richly ornamented, in the passage of centuries, through attendant hints of Satanism, necrophilia, sado-masochism and the myth of the lycanthrope. Some scholars have equated the vampire with plague and pestilence and sickness of the soul, and under the light of the latest advances in psychological research some have discovered sexual undertones in the vampire myth. The young and handsome vampire slobbering blood over the exposed throats of his beautiful victims—the demon lover who dies and yet loves—the stake driven through the naked body of a beauteous vampire, and the nocturnal scenes drenched in a wealth of gory detail, are all surely susceptible of being given a Freudian or Jungian twist. But they all miss the covert symbolism of the vampire concept.

Many explanations have been offered for vampirism: it was the delusions of superstitious and primitive countries, or it was cases of premature burial. To the German romantics it was the practice of black magicians who conjured up the Devil to invoke spirits of the dead to work evil among the world of the living. The promulgation of the vampire myth has also been attributed to a group of Christians who professed to have solved the mysteries of Christ's resurrection, and who, consequently exiled from Palestine, had to emigrate to central Europe where they became despotic rulers.

In Greece it was considered as a punishment for some heinous crime committed during life that the deceased was doomed to vampirise and compelled to confine his infernal visitations only to those whom he loved most while upon earth. It was further emphasized by the recurrent embodiment of the secular myth where the golden-haired virgin was offered to the barbarous demigod, a unicorn or an anthropoid as a suitable prize. Most of it was archetypical, and the vampire stories contain scenes in which fiends hover over white-clad reclining heroines. By ancient sanction of the romantic mode, this erotic content became an intrinsic manifestation in European tradition.

The concept of the dead arising from their graves to feed upon the blood of the innocent and the beautiful is not a macabre but a voluptuous idea. The vampire works out his spell in the dark, in Gothic landscapes of gloomy mansions, wind washed valleys or the crumbling ruins of some great château nestling on a wooded hillside. He rises from the moist and damp earth in a glowing mist or black fog through the vaults that rest under cobwebs faintly lighted by the dim radiance of the rising moon. The moon-drenched clouds etched across by a pattern of naked branches establish a psychological mood of anguish and foreboding.

The vampire is not a ghastly figure appearing like a demon from hell with fangs bared or eyes bloodied. He is tall and handsome, his hair dark and well-groomed; despite the waxen pallor of his face and hands, he has flashing dark eyes and a vivid redness in his lips curled in a smile. As the Undead he casts no shadow and has no reflection, but what is prominent are his canine teeth. The hollow beneath his eyes adds to his romantic expression of undefinable melancholy diffusing a lonesome sadness. His black cloak flutters in the breeze as he silently glides along empty corridors while the wind rustles through shroudlike ghostly curtains.

There is a sort of yearning, hunger and thirst, an aching longing in his heart which takes the intensity of sheer torment. An awakened nostalgia, a rueful agony draws him out of the shadows with a magnetic attraction transcending time and space. And then there comes a whiff from the langorous Gothic: his victim has been lying awake in her bed awaiting his coming as the night wind rustles the decayed autumnal leaves on her balcony. Her young body is taut, reclining and drinking the moonlight until the aura of silver mist clings about her. The slim silhouette of her white body caresses every line and curve of her tender figure as her golden tresses cloak her beauty in a luxuriant voluptuousness. She lies in an occult swoon for her midnight visitor, and awakens in langorous stillness at the break of dawn, like a sensuous maid after a night of love.

It is, indeed, a sensuous, romantic situation—the victim falling into a soothing unconsciousness, drifting into the realm of sleep, falling like a child into a territory of the unknown, in an uncharted blackness! And what an experience it is to be embraced by a female vampire!—by a lady of utterly bewitching beauty—a lady of lovely countenance, full cheeks, straight nose, lush Italianate lips, and teeth of such sparkling whiteness and perfection as to make her seem as unreal as a portrait in an artist's gallery—, to look at her large, luminous eyes shadowed with pensive sadness, to listen to the sudden rustle of silk and a tiny jingle of bracelets or pendant ear-rings, before swooning into oblivion!

Sin must follow temptation. Evil may be terrible, but it is also irresistible. Even a loathsome embrace marks the naked cruelty of passion. The vampire's embrace may plumb the bottomless pit of damnation; nonetheless, it ravages the heights of heaven with rage and rapture.

In the European concept the vampire may be odious yet still attractive. Creation of a delirious imagination possessing ingredients of a gossamer fantasy, he is a symbol of love transcending time and space. The idea of the physical body being a vessel of some inscrutable force is as antique as the stars. However, the vampire does not destroy but dehumanises, creating a state where emotional life gets suspended, where the victim is deprived of individual emotions, freedom of will or moral judgment. He gives a new dimension to concepts of love, tenderness and autumnal light. It is easy, therefore, to see why Surrealists, in their quest for the absolute in love and freedom, were attracted to Gothic romance.

But the concept of the vampire is not only firmly rooted in legends and folk-myths of antiquity but also established by facts of history and eye-witness accounts. There exist many curious and interesting notices of this beautiful and horrid superstition. In the public record for the years 1693 and 1694 there are accounts of vampires and their visitations in Poland and Russia. There are stories current in the mountains of Silesia and Moravia and on the Hungarian frontiers in the village of Kisilova, three leagues from Gradisch, about authentic vampire visitations. Arnold Paul, a Hungarian soldier, related how he had been tormented by a Turkish vampire near Cassova on the frontiers of Turkish Serbia. The veracious Tournefort gives a long account in his travels of several astonishing cases of vampirism to which he had been an eye witness.

While Calmet narrating a variety of anecdotes and traditional folklore about these visitations, dismisses them all as samples of superstitious barbarism, Montague Summers had examined many factual cases very scrupulously. Commenting upon vampirism he said, "Not that they do not occur but that they are carefully hushed and stifled. More than one such instance has come to my notice. . . . Such cases, in truth, are happening every day, and I have met with not a few instances in my own experience."

Pozdnejev tells of the mystics of Mongolia who worshipped the Vampire-God. Alexandra David-Neel while practising rituals in funerary fields, saw every night a skinny, sickly-looking young man with glittering eye, dressed in ragged ascetic garb, climb to a cave high up in the mountains and disappear in moonlit mists. F. Maraini in *Geheim Tibet* recalls the belief that dead lamas often "return" as terrifying vampires. In the 1920's a lama who was robbed and killed in South Tibet revenged himself as a terrible vampire whose devastations ravaged a whole village. Another wise and sagacious *fakir* who had been condemned to death by the monastic authorities of Lhasa, turned into a terrible revengeful vampire until he was tamed and made into a protector of the faith.

In the backdrop of the eternal snows of Kanchenjunga nestles the ancient monastery of Sinon displaying some of the loveliest frescoes of Sikkim. A beautiful painting is that of Princess Pedi Wangmo, born in 1686, the half-sister of the monarch Chador Namgyal. In a weird conspiracy, very much reminiscent of medieval Europe, she plotted with a Tibetan doctor to assassinate the ruler by opening his vein. The monarch bled to death and the princess drank his blood in a skull-bowl and then escaped. However, she was pursued and captured in Namchi where the doctor was brutally murdered and the princess was "strangled to death with a silken scarf." It is said that she turned into a vampire.

The vampire of myth and legend stemming from grotesque cults and aboriginal faiths, gradually stalked into the dim corridors of literature. The steadily intensifying interest in mysteries of life, death and immortality, gave the vampire motif a felicitous welcome into the orbits of the *Schauerroman*.

And who else could have written the first vampire tale [*The Vampyre*] but Dr. John William Polidori (1795-1821), the young and handsome "gentleman who travelled with Lord Byron, as physician," whose well-groomed hair, dark flashing eyes and continental unctuous complexion, added a strange fascination to the Mediterranean charm of his personality? This youngest medical graduate of the University of Edinburgh, who flirted alternately with medicine and literature, who in the ghostly soirées in Geneva during 1816 would cast a hypnotic and penetrating gaze on Claire Clairmont, Mary Shelley's half-sister and Byron's mistress, would also seek the society of the fabulous Russian Countess of Breuss crossing the lake alone at midnight in a solitary boat as clouds lowered and thunders rumbled on the mountain peaks while jagged lightnings forked across the sombre sky.

By training and temperament Dr. Polidori was well-equipped to inaugurate the new species of *Schauerroman.* The vituperating critics babbled out damaging imputations and defamatory obloquies that Polidori had plagiarised his plot from Byron's feverish and unfinished *Fragment,* but there were quite a few interesting precursors of Byron's own abortive attempt.

Earlier, John Stagg had penned a ballad called *The Vampyre* (1810), a story wondrously grisly, prefaced by a learned disquisition on vampires. In this ballad, Gertrude wonders at the "deadly pale" face of her Lord Herman and is curious about "the fading crimson from his cheek." She finds him lingering in a state of "pensive gloom" while his eyes are getting "lustreless" and "dim." At midnight hour he "pants" and "tugs for breath" and "starts with convulsive horrors."

Herman relates the horrid cause of his "uncommon anguish"; his dear young friend Sigismund, recently buried, visits him every night from the "dreary mansions of the tomb" and "the low regions of the dead" to suck from his veins "the stream of life," and to drain "the fountain of his heart." Herman predicts his own death during the next night but threatens to return again to seek Gertrude's life.

The live-long night Gertrude keeps vigil on her sleeping, dying Lord, and just as the convent bell tolls vesper time, Herman dies. She beholds, in the dim light of the lantern, the ghastly shade of Sigismund:

> His jaws cadaverous were besmear'd
>> With clotted carnage o'er and o'er,
> And all his horrid whole appear'd
>> Distent, and fill'd with human gore!

With hideous scowl the spectre flies, Gertrude shrieks and then swoons away. Next morning Sigismund's sepulchre is opened, and he is discovered "still warm as life, and undecay'd" within his tomb:

> With blood his visage was distain'd,
>> Ensanguin'd were his frightful eyes.

The story ends with a stake being driven into his heart.

And then there had been Monk Lewis's first noteworthy Gothic ballad in English, *Alonzo the Brave, and the Fair Imogene,* behind which lurks the shadow of Bürger's *Lenore* (1773).

This German ballad narrates the tale of a maiden longing for her lover's return from battle. Endlessly waiting in tears, she listens to the gallop of a horse one night. The demon lover has come to carry her off to their bridal. She mounts behind him and they ride furiously through moonlit woods. He speaks of the dead, and they pass a host of spectres before arriving in a churchyard when the dawn breaks. There the lover, a skeleton, crumbles piece by piece, the great black horse is engulfed in the earth, and screams resound in the air.

> **In the European concept the vampire may be odious yet still attractive. Creation of a delirious imagination possessing ingredients of a gossamer fantasy, he is a symbol of love transcending time and space.**
>
> **—*Devendra P. Varma***

The vampirish elements of this story are widely diffused in folk tales. As to Bürger's immediate source one cannot doubt the veracity of his own confession that he was drawing from an ancient ballad of which he could discover no text. Maury has argued, "Il nous parait incontestable que Bürger s'est inspiré d'une série de ballades écossaises, qui roulent sur l'idée fondamentale du retour du fiancé tant pleuré sous forme de revenant," and he quotes two verbal parallels from *Fair Margaret and Sweet William* and *Sweet William's Ghost,* both in Percy's *Reliques,* and both known to Bürger. While Percy, like Herder, may have been as inspiration behind Bürger's experiment, one fails to establish whether the Percy ballads furnished more

Dr. John William Polidori, author of The Vampyre.

than incidental hints. *Lenore* appears to be entirely out of the English tradition. And Lewis was well acquainted with German literature at first hand having studied in Germany during 1792-3.

Lewis's *Alonzo the Brave* absorbs the shades of Bürger's *Lenore:* a knight goes to the wars and fails to return to his lady love. Meanwhile, the fair maiden gets married to a rich baron, and at the nuptial banquet, precisely as the clock is striking one, a stranger appears:

> His vizor was closed, and gigantic his height;
>   His armour was sable to view;
> All pleasure and laughter was hushed at his
>   sight;
> The dogs as they eyed him drew back in affright;
>   The lights of the chamber burnt blue.

Lights burning blue at the appearance of a spectre is an old Radcliffean device.

So the lover has returned to reproach the maid for her infidelity. He grapples with her and wheels her down to death with him. Her spectre still haunts the castle, where the abduction scene is re-enacted each year by spectres who "drink out of skulls" a health "in blood" to Alonzo and his reluctant sweetheart.

Polidori's *The Vampyre* (1819) is an artistically executed tale, rising like a crescendo to a climax, very compelling from a stylistic point of view. It gave reality to a folk-myth, and pointed out the future techniques of romantic supernatural fiction with an increased stress upon local colour and folklore, and with a heavier shade of the supernatural no longer rationalised and explained away. It abandoned the "disinheritance plot" of the conventional Gothic romance, and pointed out a shift in focus from the earlier "hero" as a passive noble soul to a more dynamic and consummate "villain." But this change, too, is another spot-light on an aspect of "Byronism."

Returning to England in 1817, Polidori had planned to migrate to South America but eventually settled to practice medicine in Norwich, the city of Francis Lathom, the Gothic novelist and author of *The Midnight Bell*. Having failed professionally, Polidori made a futile attempt at a literary career, but worried by gambling debts and desperate finances, in August 1821 he drugged himself to death. This was the end of his short and tumultuous career.

In the cascade of a whole torrent of vampire tales and plays which gushed after the pioneering effort of Polidori, perhaps none had been so grisly and hair-raising as Thomas Preskett Prest's *Varney the Vampyre, or Feast of Blood*. Published in 1847, this novel was widely plagiarised, and having enjoyed "unprecedented success" it was reprinted in 1853 in penny parts. Its ghastly vampire hero and his gruesome deeds gave the novel such notorious popularity that it was soon out of print. Varney went to sleep again in the repository and treasure chests of book-collectors. In 1927, Montague Summers, an avid searcher of rare Gothic items, tried to raise Varney's ghost by offering fabulous sums to procure a copy but without success.

This particular vampire-romance had excited the impossible quest of book-lovers perhaps because of its authenticity. Prest had followed his researches with an indefatigable zeal. He was a prolific author of blood and thunder melodramas and stocked his narratives with tangible Gothic horrors. *Varney* was the climax of his achievement, and despite its length it contains a meticulously drawn, suspenseful plot. Vivid incidents come crowding thick upon us and the story offers a masterly integration of atmosphere and description capable of raising grisly shudders. The quality of the visual narrative is superb. It can be called the true *roman-noir* where black, ornate settings and incidents float in a sequent motion, like a bat or a hearse, traversing a spectral landscape.

Prest has been called the "Prince of Lurid Shockers." His complete works, scarce but full of vitality, should engage the attention of some enthusiastic Gothic researcher. His genius reveals a significant chapter in the history of the Gothic movement, for he stands as a link between John Polidori and the later Bram Stoker, celebrated author of *Dracula* (1897).

Doubtlessly, Bram Stoker had read the novel by Prest with delight and profit, for he bequeathed upon the tale of his vampire count and his evil castle, a far superior shade of beauty. By transferring his setting from Transylvania to Victorian England, he brought a greater sense of actuality to this most eminent Gothic vampire saga.

Stoker is a past master of creating a mood and providing a stage-setting. Even before we penetrate deep into the Carpathian mountains, a kind of stillness slides into our soul. The last light of day is gone and the sunlight dips beyond the Transylvanian Alps. Darkness seems like the end of the world. Time once again appears to stand still. The picturesque taverns and inns are left far behind. The pastel shades of greens, browns and pale yellows that suffuse the landscape, give way to unreality of time and place as darkness and silence brood over trees and foliage.

The roadway lies precipitous, snaked and twisted through dim, craggy hills, as gathering twilight settles upon the gorges, ravines, cascades and torrents. The jagged horizon of mountainous ridges lifts starkly against the night sky, and the surrounding countryside is lost in a sea of darkness. In the portentous gloom of the night, ominous rumblings are heard in the distance. Soon a jagged streak of lightning illumines the sky, and the boom of thunder reverberates across the darkened hills. A raw, biting wind sweeps up from the pass.

And there stands the sinister castle of Count Dracula, gray and ghostly by pale moonshine, so vague, so steeped in age-old terrors and superstitions, guarded by slavering wolves and inhabited by a sinister fiend who feasts on human blood. Engulfed in great dark shadows, it evokes an atmosphere of the unknown, and a state of dread and uneasy heart. Wrapped in multiple mysteries, its high turreted outline stands silent and foreboding, climbing to a smoke-hazed sky. Its lichen-covered walls, its stony floor, glisten with dampness, and wear the damaging marks of centuries of rain, wind and storm.

The gloom is unfathomable and eerie with the tapers burning low. The candlelight flickers, casting wavering shadows across the walls as we listen to the moan of the wind whistling through the ivy creeping on its ancient walls of stone. We enter a wide baronial hall; thick cobwebs and ancient dust lie over everything; the texture and colour of red velvet cushions have crumpled and faded. At the yawning entrance of a chamber, we see the shadowy silhouette of a tall, cloaked, and incredibly handsome figure; his dark sheen of hair rustling faintly in the breeze; a candlestick poised in his right hand, impressing us as the magnificent Prince of Darkness.

This is Dracula—the aristocratic Count who lived at the beginning of the sixteenth century, and who fought glorious battles against the Turks. A born leader, a distinguished aristocrat, a man of vision and implacable ferocity,—it was believed that he had like Faustus made pacts with the Devil for "power and omnipotence." We make the acquaintance with this Undead monster who has ravaged humanity for centuries.

But Count Dracula is essentially a human being. Although a monster of ferocity, he is still very real. He has dignity and stillness about him until he explodes into ravenous action. A man of immense physical appeal, he exercises a hypnotic effect upon the desires of women! His movements are deft and amazingly graceful. Even within the folds of his dark, flowing cape, every gesture is rich with command. His broad shoulders are framed in the glare of the candles, his pointed cane whose ferrule is of hammered silver, reflects flashes of lightning in the night sky or sparkles like a star. The flowing cape, the cane—all seem integral parts of his personality as if he had been born with them! And what a faded splendour his clothes have: the swallow-tail coat of dark serge worn out and shiny; the edges of his cuffs and shirt collar wilted; the purple cravat at his throat bravely affecting a swirl no longer natural to fine silk. But what impresses us is the vast sadness of his face and a voice filled with hypnotic power. The majestic glint of his enigmatic eyes, dark and sensuous and still holding sorrow, are like burning embers fighting for survival in a dying fire.

Dracula is an idea, a concept full of fantasies and wonders, beyond the reaches of darkness and imagination. Dracula symbolizes "the loneliness of evil." Despite his ravenous activities, there lingers an eternal sadness about his personality, a brooding, withdrawn unhappiness. He lingers in this world, but he is not of this world. He is a demon, but above all he is a man. We may question his authenticity but there exists a living Dracula within us all,—something ravenous, blood-sucking and intense, something ferocious with the powers of greed, lust and violence. Dracula is essentially human and pathetic, not totally evil, and his message is transcendence over the transitory. (pp. xiv-xxviii)

> *Devendra P. Varma, "The Vampire in Legend, Lore, and Literature," in* Varney the Vampire; or, The Feast of Blood: A Series of Gothic Novels *by Thomas Preskett Prest, edited by Sir Devendra P. Varma, Arno Press, 1970, pp. xiii-xxx.*

Summers on the vampire:

In all the darkest pages of the malign supernatural there is no more terrible tradition than that of the vampire, a pariah even among demons. Foul are his ravages; gruesome and seemingly barbaric are the ancient and approved methods by which folk must rid themselves of this hideous pest. Even to-day in certain quarters of the world, in remoter districts of Europe itself, Transylvania, Slavonia, the isles and mountains of Greece, the peasant will take the law into his own hands and utterly destroy the carrion who—as it is yet firmly believed—at night will issue from his unhallowed grave to spread the infection of vampirism throughout the countryside. Assyria knew the vampire long ago, and he lurked amid the primaeval forests of Mexico before Cortes came. He is feared by the Chinese, by the Indian, and the Malay alike; whilst Arabian story tells us again and again of the ghouls who haunt ill-omened sepulchres and lonely crossways to attack and devour the unhappy traveller.

> *Montague Summers, in his* The Vampire: His Kith and Kin, *Hegan Paul, Trench, Trubner & Co., 1928.*

Margaret L. Carter

[*Carter is an American novelist, screenwriter, critic, and editor who specializes in horror fiction and has edited several works concerning the vampire in literature. In the following essay, she discusses the development of conventional vampire characteristics in several works of nineteenth-century literature and classifies the types of vampires depicted in numerous twentieth-century works, emphasizing the tendency of twentieth-century writers to portray vampires as sympathetic characters.*]

The "dead gray eye" of the vampire, as everyone knows, first glares from the pages of English prose fiction in *The Vampyre,* by John Polidori. How Byron, the Shelleys, and Polidori, at the Villa Diodati in 1816, participated in a ghost story contest that resulted in Mary Shelley's *Frankenstein* and a "Fragment" by Byron from which Polidori extracted the seed of *The Vampyre,* how the tale was at first attributed to Byron and became so popular that numerous dramatic adaptations were based upon it, have been retold by various commentators and need not be repeated here. The literary vampire as we know him—or her—is a product of the Romantic movement, either a Gothic-Byronic villain or a fatal seductress. Polidori's seminal tale established the deathlike countenance and mesmeric power of the vampire, as well as the device, later abandoned, of the undead monster's revival by the rays of the moon. In other respects, aside from his appetite for blood, Polidori's Lord Ruthven, probably a distorted picture of Byron himself, appears outwardly human.

The title character of *Varney the Vampyre; or, The Feast of Blood,* attributed to either Thomas Preskett Prest or James Malcolm Rymer, also lacks the plethora of supernatural powers and limitations we associate with vampires. Although strong, hypnotically compelling, and almost impossible to kill, Varney cannot change into a bat, wolf, or mist, nor does he have to rest by day in a coffin lined with earth. This mid-century "penny dreadful" establishes the conventional means of destroying the undead: the stake and the fire. Without such extreme measures, a vampire can always be restored to life by the full moon. In *Varney* we find a miscellaneous array of motifs—a mysterious stranger who neither eats nor drinks, a somnambulistic female victim, inexplicable illness, a methodical team of vampire hunters, and a descent into a vault where an empty coffin lies—later used more skillfully by Stoker and his successors. *Varney* combines fast-moving, melodramatic action and provocative hints of terror and passion with sloppy construction and outright inconsistencies. (For instance, Varney offers three irreconcilable stories of his past.) Unlike Ruthven, Varney grows to evoke the reader's sympathy. As the concluding chapters narrow to the vampire's point of view, we see him as a creature driven by forces beyond his control, so that we view his suicide in the crater of Vesuvius with pity.

The other classic pre-Stoker vampire tale, J. Sheridan Le Fanu's "Carmilla," presents a vampire who, if not a sympthetic figure, is an alluring one. Carmilla shares the bloodlust, preternatural strength, mesmeric personality, and near-indestructibility of Ruthven and Varney, though she seems to have lost the affinity for moonlight. She adds fear of religious objects, a propensity for resting in a tomb, and, perhaps, shape-shifting ability (the heroine, Laura, sees her as a large, black animal). Stoker's vampire-hunting polymath, Dr. Van Helsing, probably descends from both the Baron, a student of occult arts, who helps to expose Carmilla, and Dr. Hesselius, Le Fanu's frame narrator. Moreover, "Carmilla" breathes an atmosphere of sexuality unmatched until certain passages in *Dracula.*

By the third quarter of the nineteenth century, then, all the elements of the conventional literary vampire had been introduced. While certain variants to be exploited in later fiction—such as vampirism as a hoax or misunderstanding in [Mary] Braddon's "Good Lady Ducayne," psychic predation in [A. Conan] Doyle's *The Parasite,* and the vampire as a nonhuman but natural creature in [Phil] Robinson's "Last of the Vampires"—had appeared by the 1890s, they were not amplified upon at the time. It was the supernatural vampire derived from folklore and modified by Romanticism that provided the focus for Bram Stoker's masterpiece.

In no other fictional category, perhaps, is one work accepted as definitive in quite the same way as *Dracula* is for the literary vampire. All tales of vampirism, whether they explicitly mention Stoker's novel or not, implicitly assume the reader's acquaintance with it. As [James B.] Twitchell points out in *Dreadful Pleasures,* even those who have not read *Dracula* know the essentials of the story; the figure of the Transylvanian Count has assumed archetypal status. Few people in the English-speaking world can be unfamiliar with the components of the vampire legend as assembled by Stoker from folklore and earlier works such as "Carmilla": The vampire feeds on blood, lives for centuries unless killed, can be destroyed only in certain prescribed ways, can assume various animal shapes, can take the form of mist to pass through near-solid barriers, hypnotizes his prey, casts no reflection, sleeps in a coffin on

a bed of his native soil, controls animals and the weather, has visibly pointed fangs and hairy palms, avoids sunlight, cannot cross running water except at limited times, cannot enter a dwelling without an invitation, and transforms victims who die of his bite into creatures like himself. Vampire fiction after Stoker has either followed his pattern, self-consciously departed from it, or used pieces of it in weaving new patterns. Hence this bibliography is a guide, not to the literary vampire in the strictest sense, but to tales of vampirism in all its fragmented forms. One or more motifs extracted from the total complex frequently appear in a story whose author would not call it a vampire tale.

Before laying out categories of vampirism according to content I shall briefly explore some tentative divisions according to the stories' formal characteristics. In view of the documentary format and multiple narrators of *Dracula,* it is natural to glance at the implications of narrative structure in later vampire fiction. An outstanding pastiche of Stoker, [Fred] Saberhagen's *The Dracula Tape* provides an appropriate starting point since it retells the incidents of Stoker's novel from the viewpoint of Count Dracula himself. Speaking in the first person, the Count narrates the notorious events of 1890 as he recalls them, recording his apologia on the tape deck of a car belonging to a descendant of Jonathan and Mina Harker. The Count's narrative is conditioned by his audience, for he attempts to vindicate himself in the eyes of the family of the woman he loves (Mina). Saberhagen's tour de force preserves the "facts" of the case as reported by Stoker's various narrators (with the single exception of the date of Mina's pregnancy), while transforming the events' meaning. Since Dracula's own narrative is, of course, as self-serving as Jonathan's or Dr. Seward's, the reader confronting *The Dracula Tape* in isolation may well wonder how truthful the Count's report is. Saberhagen's four sequels, however, make it clear that he intends to present his own Dracula as a reliable witness.

In the first of these sequels, *The Holmes-Dracula File,* Saberhagen presents a counterpoint of two narrators, Dracula himself and Dr. Watson. In quest of the solution to the novel's mystery, Dracula and Holmes travel separate but sometimes intersecting paths toward a common goal. Comparing this tale to [Loren D.] Estleman's *Sherlock Holmes vs. Dracula,* I find Saberhagen's treatment superior. As a Sherlock Holmes pastiche, Estleman's novel is competent enough. Watson tells the events of Dracula's attempted invasion of England (also following Stoker's "facts") in the cryptic fragments of the truth available to him; while in Doyle's original series, the reader shares Watson's ignorance, in Estleman's story the reader, like Holmes, knows what Dracula is from the beginning, a factor that robs the narrative of mystery. As a vampire tale, *Sherlock Homes vs. Dracula* adds nothing to the form. Estleman's Count makes even fewer appearances "onstage" than Stoker's does and, when he appears, proves to be a rather flat, conventional villain—a reflection, perhaps, of Watson's uncompromising revulsion, rendering him incapable of seeing whatever personality the Count might possess.

Greater complexity in the presentation of a vampire appears in Stoker's predecessor and model, Le Fanu's "Carmilla". The first-person narrator, Laura, though victimized by the vampire, describes Carmilla in ambiguous terms of mingled fascination and fear. Even at a distance of many years, she remains unsure of how to evaluate her experience with Carmilla, since she did not witness the most terrible events, but learned of them through secondhand reports. Two factors, the distortion of memory and Laura's affection for Carmilla, allow the reader to question this narrator's reliability. Hence the vampire, even after her destruction, remains a figure of beauty as well as horror.

Twentieth-century authors of vampire fiction manipulate point of view in a variety of ways to communicate nontraditional images of the vampire. At the opposite pole from the impressionistic, highly personal memoir that constitutes "Carmilla," [Bob] Leman's "The Pilgrimage of Clifford M" presents itself as a scientific paper informing the public about a newly discovered species. The fictitious author begins his report with an account of the vampire's life cycle, which he then applies to the case of one atypical vampire, the unfortunate Clifford. A less objective narrative style enters only at the climax, with a farewell message penned by Clifford himself before his suicide. The scientific reporter of this tale presents himself as an authoritative, informed observer and invites the reader to share this privileged position. The narrator of [Peter] Tonkin's *The Journal of Edwin Underhill,* on the other hand, gropes in ignorance for the first half of the novel. Enjoying no retrospective knowledge of the significance of his ordeal, he reports its phases day by day, as they unfold. The reader stands in a superior position, well aware that Underhill is turning into a vampire. Underhill's confusion and skepticism contrast with the reader's certainty that the supernatural is at work. Moreover, after the transformation Underhill's possession by the demonic intelligence of "the Dead"—the dominant vampire who transformed him—introduces a second point of view, for he sometimes speaks of his former, human self as a separate person. Shifting points of view are masterfully employed by [Suzy McKee] Charnas in *The Vampire Tapestry,* which leads the reader from an external, distant contemplation of the vampire to an intimate sharing of his thought processes. In the novel's first section, the viewpoint character is his enemy, a woman who knows nothing of the enigmatic Dr. Weyland beyond what he, perhaps misleadingly, chooses to reveal; in the second, we see through the eyes of a teenage boy who sympathizes with the vampire and becomes his ally. Next we progress to the viewpoint of Weyland's therapist; here, for the first time, he speaks for himself at length. The fourth section alternates between Weyland's perspective and that of various minor characters, while the final episode places us entirely within Weyland's consciousness. By this point, our understanding of Weyland's unique nature and problems produces sympathy as well; he now functions, not as villain, but as hero.

Manipulation of point of view frequently involves issues of sympathy as well as belief. In the earliest English prose vampire tale, Polidori's *The Vampyre,* Ruthven, viewed through the eyes of the bewildered young Aubrey, appears

An illustration from Polidori's The Vampyre *depicting the discovery of a victim.*

not only distant and enigmatic but threatening. Though we read of Ruthven's fatal fascination, we get no emotional sense of it. Another nineteenth-century tale, [Eric] Stenbock's "True Story of a Vampire," told, like "Carmilla," in the first person by an emotionally involved observer, expresses compassion for the vampire's reluctant destruction of the boy he loves. Here the monster appears a pathetic rather than frightfully alluring figure. [William] Tenn's "She Only Goes Out at Night" portrays the vampire through the eyes of a first-person narrator who initially views the vampire as the bloodthirsty monster of legend but comes to sympathize with her when he sees the love she shares with his employer's son. Numerous twentieth-century stories present vampirism from the vampire's own viewpoint. Curiously, however, these do not necessarily show the vampire in a favorable light. [James] Hart's "The Traitor," for instance, stays entirely within the consciousness of a vampire who views his condition as a curse he strives to overcome. The narrator of [Robert] Bloch's "The Bat Is My Brother" is driven by a need for vengeance on the vampire who condemned him to undeath. [Anne] Rice's vampiric narrators in *Interview with the Vampire* and *The Vampire Lestat* appear to regard vampirism amorally, as a change of state to which they must adjust as well as they can. Whatever scruples each feels about his predatory nature gradually vanish as he becomes more inhuman. A rare glimpse of positive values inherent in vampirism appears in [Lee] Killough's *Blood Hunt,* whose viewpoint character becomes a vampire while retaining his human personality and motivations. He solves the problems of living as a vampire in twentieth-century America in ingenious and morally acceptable ways, while attempting to use his new powers for good.

Moral orientation in vampire fiction since *Dracula* cannot be taken for granted. Stoker and his predecessors assumed vampirism, if not the vampire himself or herself, to be unequivocally evil; the vampire must be either hated or pitied. While the majority of later vampire stories maintain that conventional attitude, conspicuous exceptions exist. In [Marion Zimmer] Bradley's "Treason of the Blood" and [Richard] Purtill's "Something in the Blood," a vampiric nature is a neutral phenomenon easily vulnerable to abuse, but capable of being turned to good ends. Purtill's vampires actually become public benefactors by opening a blood bank and using their peculiar senses to weed out tainted blood. The aliens of [Colin] Wilson's *The Space Vampires* function structurally as villains, yet authoritative characters within the story suggest that psychic vampirism can be directed into harmless or even beneficial channels. [Chelsea Quinn] Yarbro's aristocratic vampire, Saint-Germain, functions as hero, more noble than most of the human characters surrounding him, yet the series featuring him includes at least one vampire who conforms to the stereotype of conscienceless predator. As one might expect, unambiguously good fictional vampires are seldom found. One example of such is [Susan] Petrey's Varkela race, a subspecies of humankind famed for their expertise as horse trainers and healers, priding themselves on never taking blood except when their services have earned it. [Spider] Robinson's Pyotr, in a story from the "Callahan's Bar" series, uses his vampiric appetite to save his heavy-drinking friends from hangovers and, in one more serious case, death from alcohol poisoning.

Though nontraditional vampires such as the Varkela and Pyotr abound in contemporary fantasy and science fiction, stories on the conventional *Dracula* pattern continue to be written. Numerous authors, moreover, create supernatural (rather than scientifically rationalized) vampires who alter the traditional pattern ingeniously while retaining a strong flavor of its influence. Other authors besides Saberhagen attempt to rewrite Stoker or use Dracula as a character in adventures of their own devising. In [Raymond] Rudorff's *The Dracula Archives,* purporting to occur shortly before Stoker's narrative, the vampire lord does not appear in his own person until the concluding pages. Throughout the story his spirit reaches out, over thousands of miles, to manipulate lives by a kind of demonic possession in an attempt to effectuate his bodily resurrection. In his trilogy, [Peter] Tremayne rewrites Dracula's story partly from the viewpoint of Vlad the Impaler's son, Mircea. Drawing upon Stoker's hints that Dracula practiced Satanism in life, Tremayne presents vampirism as a flawed byproduct of an occult search for immortality. Unlike these two authors, [Robert] Lory deals with Dracula's fate after his destruction by the heroes of Stoker's tale; Lory's series has the vampire revived by a retired, wheelchair-bound criminologist, who uses Dracula as a tool for dealing with crimes of a particularly gruesome or mysterious nature. Occultism plays a role here also, for Dracula has as ally an immortal sorceress from ancient Atlantis. Lory's version adds little to the character of the vampire Count, who functions mostly as an animated information bank and killing machine.

Perhaps overshadowed by Stoker's influence, few authors manage to produce outstanding fiction with Dracula as central character. More successful are novelists who adapt the literary vampire, as shaped by that overwhelming influence, into creations of their own. [Stephen] King's Barlow in *Salem's Lot,* for instance, physically resembles Dracula and projects a similar aura of mingled fascination and repulsiveness. Yarbro's Saint-Germain might be characterized as Dracula with a difference. Saint-Germain, too, is a Transylvanian count who bewitches young women into his unnatural afterlife. His debut in *Hotel Transylvania,* however, as we have noted, casts him as hero rather than villain. Unlike Dracula, Yarbro's vampire has no aversion to holy symbols; a stunning reversal of conventional roles has Saint-Germain holding a coven of Satanists at bay with a consecrated Host. In most other respects Saint-Germain conforms to the *Dracula* pattern: he casts no reflection, requires a bed of his native soil, and avoids sunlight (like Dracula—contrary to the impression given by innumerable film versions—he is not helpless by day). He differs from Stoker's Count in being unable to change shape. If Saint-Germain possesses any supernatural mesmeric power, he de-emphasizes it, though he often uses his superhuman strength to deadly effect. Deriving her character from the enigmatic historical figure of that name, Yarbro makes her vampire an alchemist. She attributes his undead condition to his initiation, in boyhood, into a vampiric priesthood, but she wisely leaves veiled the ultimate origin of vampirism itself. Yarbro's novels blend omniscient narrative with the epistolary method, interspersing characters' letters among blocks of action to present a variety of viewpoints regarding Saint-Germain. In *Hotel Transylvania,* particularly, this technique gradually unfolds the secret of Saint-Germain's nature by alternately increasing and decreasing the reader's distance from him, while in the later books of the series the implied reader is assumed to start from a prior acquaintance with the vampiric hero.

Another adaptation of the supernatural vampire, Rice's *Interview with the Vampire,* retains different aspects of Stoker's prototype from those chosen by Yarbro. Inert by day, Rice's vampires keep to the shadows even at night, since their physical appearance changes, after transformation, to render them more obviously inhuman than either Dracula or Saint-Germain. Thus they conform more closely to the monstrous vampire of folklore than to the Byronic villain-hero epitomized by the typical literary vampire. Still, they are capable of passing as ordinary human beings, despite the blood-thirst that, unlike Saint-Germain's, usually destroys the victim in a single attack. Whereas Stoker asserts that all victims of vampirism share that fate after death, both Rice and Yarbro postulate that vampirism can be passed on only by a mutual exchange of blood (or, according to Yarbro, by a prolonged liaison). Hence the vampire must deliberately choose to effect the transformation. The second novel in Rice's series, *The Vampire Lestat,* attempts to explain the origin of vampirism in terms of the Isis-Osiris myth, tracing the contagion back to a single incident of demonic possession in ancient Egypt. This total unveiling of the mystery proves incompletely satisfying, for no explicit account could live up to the expectation sustained through the narrator's long, convoluted quest for his ultimate origins. The image of the archetypal vampiric pair, however, a male and female so ancient that they have virtually become animate stone, seldom moving or feeding, sustaining all other vampires' lives by their continued existence, remains compelling. Both vampire narrators, Louis and Lestat, seem driven to unveil and justify themselves—Louis to a single sympathetic listener, and Lestat, in defiance of vampiric ethics, to the entire human world. Lestat apparently views his act of self-revelation—symbolically, through the rock band he leads to fame, and literally, through the book-within-a-book of the same title—as a means of transmuting both vampire and human society.

Rice's vampires exemplify a kind of rationalized supernaturalism, for aside from their undead status, virtual indestructibility, and superior strength and speed, they share few of the traditional supernatural stigmata. They do not sleep on beds of earth, lack reflections, assume animal shape, or shun garlic and holy objects. Still more fully rationalized, of course, are the vampires of science fiction. Science-fiction attempts to fit the vampire into the taxonomy of life as we know it generally fall into two categories: (1) vampirism as disease; (2) vampires as members of a separate species.

In the subcategory of communicable disease [Richard] Matheson's *I Am Legend* stands out, even after several decades, as the most detailed and coherent treatment, leaving few details of the legend unrationalized. The vampire bacillus is spread by biting, by insects, and (in spore form) by dust storms. Sunlight destroys the organism, and garlic acts as a violent antigen to the reanimated dead infected by it. When a deep wound, as from the traditional wooden stake, pierces the flesh, the bacillus consumes its host, causing the body to disintegrate. Matheson explains the power of holy symbols, the bat transformation, the lack of a reflection, and the difficulty of crossing water as superstitions, often believed by the brain-damaged undead and producing psychosomatic effects on them. The protagonist, the last uninfected human being, combats the plague-animated vampires with *Dracula* as his flawed guidebook, until the vampires establish their own society, whose lore reduces him to a feared and loathed minority of one. "Normal" humanity, paradoxically, becomes the "legend." [Bill] Johnson's "Business as Usual," a humorous treatment of a vampiric political action group, attributes the condition to a virus producing symptoms similar to those of porphyria. Numerous tales, such as Purtill's "Something in the Blood" and Killough's *Blood Hunt,* while not developing an elaborate theory, hint that vampirism may be an infectious disease rather than a supernatural curse. Such stories, however, do not always maintain consistency; Killough's vampire, for instance, has no trouble with mirrors or crosses but cannot enter a dwelling without an invitation. Vampirism as a mental illness, communicable through hypnotic suggestion and a kind of psychological addiction, characterizes [Simon] Raven's *Doctors Wear Scarlet,* which maintains just enough ambiguity to preclude discounting the supernatural altogether.

The second subcategory under "disease" presents vampirism as a metabolic disorder, usually hereditary. The lovely young Tatiana in Tenn's "She Only Goes Out at Night" begins to suffer from her vampiric taint in early adulthood. Along with the blood-craving, she acquires an allergy to sunlight and the power of becoming invisible. Her fiancé's physician-father treats her with dark glasses, hormone injections, and nightly doses of reconstituted blood. [George] Romero's *Martin* (a novelization of the film of the same title) involves a congenital taint conferring longevity and unnatural youth on the title character. Although a savage predator who frequently kills to satisfy his blood-need, Martin still longs to be understood and spends hours telephoning a radio call-in program in search of sympathy. His elderly uncle, considering Martin a vampire in the traditional sense, destroys him in the traditional manner.

A slight shift in emphasis divides vampirism as hereditary disease from vampirism as membership in another species. Such a race may originate either on Earth or on another planet. Probably the best-known of novels in this category, [Colin] Wilson's *The Space Vampires,* postulates entities who move from body to body in a manner analogous to demon possession. They feed on, not blood, but life-force, a concept Wilson scientifically rationalizes with accounts of measurement of this hypothetical energy and its fluctuation during predator-prey encounters. [A. E.] Van Vogt's "Asylum" and "The Proxy Intelligence" introduce aliens practicing similar psychic vampirism. More traditionally humanoid and blood-drinking, Sabella in [Tanith] Lee's novel of that name is actually an alien who has taken over a human girl's identity and memories at the moment of the child's death. True to the legend, Sabella avoids sunlight, though in other respects she appears human. [Niel] Straum's "Vanishing Breed" explains the vampires who have haunted Earth's history as a race of long-lived, blood-drinking aliens who travel from world to world as their predatory nature becomes known, forcing them to flee. Having fostered the legend of the reanimated dead as a cover, they find that their scheme backfires when their own young people come to believe the legend, too.

One of the largest and most fruitful groups of science-fiction vampire tales comprises stories in which vampires are another species evolving on Earth concurrently with *Homo sapiens.* Such stories range from light, undeveloped treatments, such as [Fredric] Brown's "Blood" and Robinson's "Pyotr's Story," to the elaborate constructs unfolded in, for example, [George R. R.] Martin's *Fevre Dream* and Petrey's Varkela series. The Varkela, a nocturnal tribe inhabiting the Russian steppes, eat ordinary food but also require about a pint of blood per month to sustain life. They have an affinity for horses and are famed as shamanistic healers, trading their medical skill for "blood payment." Among their peculiarities are retractable fangs, a long, doglike tongue, fur on the chest, and two kinds of salivary glands, one containing an anticoagulant, the other a rapid clotting agent. The Varkela can interbreed with human beings, unlike the more bizarre vampires of Leman's "The Pilgrimage of Clifford M." Differing so radically from *Homo sapiens* that even copulation is impossible, these vampires live for centuries, gradually metamorphosing from mindless, furry carnivores to outwardly human creatures living only on blood and spending the daylight hours in a deathlike coma. Like the more conventional literary vampire, they can take bat form, an ability, seemingly inconsistent with a "scientific" theory, which is presented without explanation. Clifford, an anomaly among his race, brought up by human foster-parents, discovers that adult vampires, over centuries of life, degenerate into unthinking beasts despite their human appearance. Hence this tale ends pessimistically, with the assumption that Clifford's civilized conditioning has no chance against the pull of his bestial nature. More optimistic is Martin's *Fevre Dream*, set in the heyday of the Mississippi steamboats. Martin's viewpoint character is a riverboat captain who befriends and learns to trust a vampire, Joshua, striving to become the savior of his race by breaking their bondage to the "red thirst." Unlike most fictional vampires, Joshua's people suffer bloodlust only once a month, when they are compelled to kill, however rational and civilized they may be at other periods. Long-lived and extremely hard to destroy, they even regenerate lost limbs. As befits a long-lived species, they breed very seldom, females being subject to estrus and males being sexually inert except in the presence of a fertile female.

In contrast to Martin's vampire subculture, [Suzy McKee] Charnas' Dr. Weyland epitomizes the solitary predator. He himself does not know whether he is a member of a separate species, a visitor from another plant, or a human mutation; so far as he knows, he is unique. He recalls no parents or childhood. Living for millennia, he falls into an extended period of suspended animation whenever the present becomes too hazardous. He wakes with the skills and general knowledge of previous lifetimes but no specific memories. He hunts by night out of necessity but is not seriously hampered by sunlight. Instead of fangs, a retractable dart beneath his tongue serves for drawing blood. Though possessing none of the traditional vampire's occult powers, Weyland has inhuman speed, strength, hearing, and eyesight, qualities Charnas justifies by citing similar abilities in the animal kingdom. Indeed, animal metaphors dominate the book—Weyland is a tiger, a lynx, a bird of prey, in deceptively human form. His ability but disinclination to copulate with his victims—his "livestock"—encapsulates his attitude toward humanity. Using his superior intelligence to study the people around him, he remains aloof, treasuring his detachment as necessary to survival. *The Vampire Tapestry* traces his unwilling growth toward a more human point of view, a transmutation he finally rejects, choosing to withdraw into another deathlike sleep.

From the anomalous Weyland, we move on to stories of vampirism by entities not strictly vampires, in many cases not humanoid, some entirely sui generis. . . . Lovecraft and authors influenced by him—for instance, Bloch in "Shambler from the Stars" and [Frank Belknap] Long in "Horror from the Hills"—portray amorphous entities from other dimensions, feeding on either blood or life-force. Such an entity takes possession of a human body in [Tim] Powers' *Dinner at Deviant's Palace;* however, that novel also features spectral, bloodthirsty doppelgangers split off from living people, as well as an addictive drug synthesized from human blood. Nonhuman blood-drinkers, of course, invade Earth in [H. G.] Wells' *War of the Worlds*, while his "The Flowering of the Strange Orchid" is one among many stories of blood-sucking plants. A rabbit plays the role of a vegetarian vampire—sucking juices from vegetables by night—in [James] Howe's juvenile novel *Bunnicula*. A part of a human body returns from death to attack the living in [F. Marion] Crawford's

"The Screaming Skull" and Bloch's "Skull of the Marquis de Sade." A patch of ground leeches life from victims in [Algernon] Blackwood's "The Transfer," a grove of trees in [E. F.] Benson's "And No Bird Sings." Inanimate objects sometimes prey on people—a building in Poe's "The Fall of the House of Usher," a car in King's *Christine* (for Christine appears to become stronger and "younger" with every kill). The latter book also features possession by the dead, as the car's deceased former owner devours the personality of young Arnie—a form of vampirism seen also in Poe's "Morella" and "Ligeia."

Psychic predation, whether by the living or the dead, encompasses a large category of fiction, sometimes shading into the mainstream. . . . More problematic are *Jane Eyre* and *Wuthering Heights*, particularly the latter, for references to Heathcliff as a vampire sometimes appear to be more than metaphor. I have reluctantly concluded, however, that neither Brontë seriously intends the supernatural as an interpretative option. [Edgar Allan] Poe's "Oval Portrait" does suggest that the artist's obsession literally drains the model's life-force into the work. An unrationalized psychic vampire appears in [Fritz] Leiber's "Girl with the Hungry Eyes," while a similar emotion-feeder in [C. M.] Kornbluth's "Mindworm" is the product of radiation-induced mutation. [Peter] Saxon's more specialized predator in *The Torturer* feeds only on pain; like the classic vampire, he has risen from death and ages instantaneously when destroyed. The predator in [Charles] DeLint's *Yarrow*, thousands of years old, apparently learned through occult means to prolong his life by consuming his peculiar food—the essence of others' dreams.

Some fictional vampires defy classification—for instance, the child vampire of [S. P.] Somtow's *Vampire Junction*, who, though supernatural, does not appear to be a revenant created by another vampire's attack. Rather, he explains himself as a spontaneous birth from the collective unconscious; the novel has a strong Jungian flavor, and one of the central characters is the boy vampire's Jungian analyst. The child's victims become vampires; however, the exact nature of their vampirism depends on which mass-media images of the legend they are most familiar with. . . . Not all legendary vampires drink blood; some consume other human products, while some spread death by their mere proximity. Literary vampirism, likewise, may involve consuming substances such as marrow, bone, or neural fluid. Moreover, an undead revenant may conform to vampiric guidelines in other respects while not preying on people at all, as in [Ray] Bradbury's "Pillar of Fire." Yarbro's rapacious "ghoul" in "Disturb Not My Slumbering Fair" is essentially an "undead" except that she devours flesh as well as blood and prefers her food well aged. . . . [In *The Screwtape Letters* C. S.] Lewis' devils drink the fear and anguish of human souls, even while the victims still live. Where to draw the boundary line depends ultimately on personal judgment. (pp. 31-44)

Margaret L. Carter, "An Anatomy of Vampirism," in The Vampire in Literature: A Critical Bibliography, *edited by Margaret L. Carter, UMI Research Press, 1989, pp. 31-44.*

SOCIAL AND PSYCHOLOGICAL PERSPECTIVES

Peter Penzoldt

[*In the following excerpt from his critical study* The Supernatural in Fiction, *Penzoldt presents a psychological analysis of vampire fiction.*]

The psychological problem of the vampire motif is a complex one. Literary criticism has never to my knowledge taken pains to analyse it completely, probably because the discoveries to which such an investigation would lead are anything but pleasant. Yet since modern psychology has taught us to speak more freely of the subconscious, I see no reason why psychoanalysis should not contribute to the investigation of a problem which certainly concerns literature. This problem is further complicated by the fact that there are two distinct types of vampire in fiction. The vampire sometimes appears as a mere physical being, as the 'un-dead' corpse of a deceased person who comes back to feed upon the blood of the living, sometimes as a 'psychic vampire' drawing the vital power from his victims. I believe that these ideas are closely related, and that, in fact, the second is merely an evolved form of the first. The 'physical vampire' is not simply an allegory as many authors believed, but the outbreak of deeply rooted subconscious fears. These fears may be neurotic, but they are to a certain extent found even in normal beings. If this were not the case, the motif would raise much less interest among the public.

Modern psychology shows us that whenever we deal with the fear of imaginary beings we must look for its cause in one of the stages of infantile development. The vampire is a sucking monster. In order to find the key to the mystery, we must therefore examine the oral stage of development. The small child is usually asleep. It awakens only when hunger compels it to cry for nourishment. Thus the act of being fed is at first its only contact with reality. This contact is a pleasurable one, so pleasurable indeed that occasions for sucking are soon sought independently of nourishment. The child begins to suck its thumb, although it yields no milk, and later it puts all sorts of objects into its mouth: the pleasure has become 'erotic'. In the language of psychology this means that feelings of love or affection manifest themselves by the desire to devour the beloved object. Such a form of 'love' is based on identification, on the desire to become one with the beloved object by incorporating it. Of course the child soon realises that eating something means destroying it. If the desire is applied to persons, a guilt-feeling develops, which later normally causes the oral tendencies to be replaced by other modes of affection. Now for every primitive mind, a crime has to be punished in the same fashion as it has been perpetrated. Thus the child that dreams of eating a person or a pet dog is liable to develop fancies about horrible monsters by which it might be devoured itself. The fear children have of wolves and other big animals, and the subjects of many fairy-tales, are good proof of that. The vampire is nothing but one of those horrors that an imagination tormented by retaliation fears might invent. Thanks to certain unconscious memories of our childhood terrors it impresses even the adult. Its erotic character is still evident later: The

women vampires always prey on young men, the men on women. Goethe's 'Braut von Korinth', for example, is a vampire brought back to life by sheer sex desire.

The vampire motif is crude and primitive. It seems natural that modern authors have preferred either to use it as an allegory or to transfer the problem into the psychic domain, describing a supernatural agency that is able to steal people's vitality or will-power. A short historical survey of the vampire theme in both its primitive and its more evolved form will make this development clear.

Since Hollywood has taken over Bram Stoker's novel *Dracula* (1897) and made about a dozen more or less convincing pictures out of it, the blood-sucking 'un-dead' has become quite a popular figure in America and wherever American films are shown. From what I remember of my own schooldays in the United States, any American child can tell you that a vampire is able to transform itself into a bat, that it must spend the day in a wooden coffin filled with earth from its native country, that all its victims become vampires also, that it can only be killed by driving a stake of holly through its heart, and so on. Yet it was not Bram Stoker who invented these traditional details, nor was it he who introduced the vampire in English literature. The motif is much older. It is already referred to on Assyrian and Chaldean tablets. In the twelfth century William Newbury relates several vampire stories. A vampire was buried in Melrose Abbey and the grave of another is still shown to tourists in Ireland. The vampire superstition was general in the East. In Europe it probably appeared first in Greece with the myth of the 'lamias', the beautiful girls who lured young men to death. After 1800 it begins to be common in English fiction. Southey wrote his 'Thalaba' in 1801, Byron his 'Giaour' in 1813, Keats his 'Lamia' in 1819. Besides the poems there are plays on the vampire theme. First an anonymous romantic play of two acts, *The Vampire,* then a play with the same title, and then *The Vampire Bride,* by John Dorset (1821). As far as the short story is concerned the vampire probably made its first appearance in Polidori's novelette *The Vampyre* (1819).

In the short story we usually find the more evolved form, the psychic vampire. Of course, the blood-sucking monster appears in a number of stories, although usually in a slightly modified form. Sheridan Le Fanu's 'Carmilla,' E. F. Benson's 'Mrs. Anworth' and Marion Crawford's 'The Blood is the Life' are orthodox vampire stories. Benson's 'Negotium Perambulans' deals with a slimy blood-sucking fiend, its stench and stickiness creating additional horror. Last but not least 'The Flowering of the Strange Orchid', by H. G. Wells, and Oscar Cook's 'Si Urag of the Tail' describe man-eating, blood-sucking orchids, thus preserving the Greek tradition of the beautiful vampire.

In fiction, descriptions of such physical attacks from the other world appear both clumsy and contradictory when we compare them with the tragedy of the vampirised soul. We may really speak of a progress when we consider the transition from the crude physical horrors of the earlier writers to the refinement of a symbolised inner conflict. Our reasonable age has taught us not to fear imaginary physical dangers. Yet the terrors of the soul seem to have increased rather than diminished. Mental disease and neurosis have become everyday themes of conversation, and the black menace of insanity seems to threaten more humans now than ever before. Is it therefore so astonishing that poetic imagination should conceive evil beings that are capable of sucking away man's mental strength and life-power, and that the medieval idea of possession and dispossession finds new life in fiction? Authors simply give the above-mentioned infantile fears the form that they wear in adult society. . . . The main difference between the forms seems to lie in the degree of objectivity of the apparition. The more the vampire becomes merely a symbol or allegory of inner conflicts, e.g. the personification of neurosis or a beginning of insanity, the closer we move to the domain of fictional psychiatry. In most vampire stories the degree of objectivity remains rather high.

The more developed form of the vampire motif first appears in Poe's 'Morella' and 'Ligeia'. Although these might be considered as stories on metempsychosis, the fact remains that in both tales the spirit of a dead person takes possession of a living body. In 'Ligeia' the spirit of the dead wife actually kills her rival and then enters and transforms the corpse. We find the same theme later in such stories as 'God Grante that She Lye Stille', by Cynthia Asquith, 'The Story of the Late Mr. Elvesham', by H. G. Wells, 'Dispossession', by C. H. B. Kitchin, 'The Return', by Walter de la Mare, 'Lazarus Returns', by Guy Endore, 'Miss Avenal', by W. F. Harvey, some of Mr. Blackwood's stories and others less well conceived. In contrast with the earlier writers, who preferred an Eastern or Continental setting for a theme which is essentially foreign, the modern authors choose English scenes for their stories. Each of the authors mentioned above freely modified the traditional vampire theme. Mrs. Asquith describes a beautiful, strangely impersonal young lady, whose body is more and more usurped by the spirit of an evil ancestress, until she dies in a final, but victorious, struggle with the invader. Kitchin uses exactly the same theme, only here the victim is a young man, and the story does not end with a tragedy. Walter de la Mare and Guy Endore make the usurper change the victim's body as well as the soul. In de la Mare's story, this change is entirely confined to the physical being. Wells describes a forced exchange of bodies. Considered as allegories, some of these stories have a strange power of fascination. Modern times have shown us how the evil spirit of one being, dead or alive, can possess millions of men, and how his influence can become so strong that his spiritual slaves will even try to resemble him physically. Harvey's 'Miss Avenal' is the kind of vampire that by some mysterious process is enabled to steal other people's vitality without even touching them. First an ailing patient, she grows more and more vigorous while her nurse's health declines. We can hardly refrain from drawing a parallel between such a vampire and a kind of person every one of us meets now and then, a short conversation with whom leaves us feeling unpleasantly empty and exhausted. Whoever has had occasion to converse with a typical neurotic will appreciate Harvey's story to the full.

Thus the vampire theme has undergone an interesting development since it first appeared in the English short story. The original superstition, that English authors received as a heritage from the Middle East and later the Continent, appears in its traditional form at first, but is soon considered too primitive and is developed into symbols and allegories. Yet even there, it is always used to represent conflicts of the soul, and its subconscious origin is thus tacitly admitted, or openly displayed. (pp. 37-40)

Peter Penzoldt, "The Main Motif," in his The Supernatural in Fiction, *P. Nevill, 1952, pp. 29-66.*

Rosemary Jackson

[*In the following excerpt from her critical study* Fantasy: The Literature of Subversion, *Jackson discusses the concept of the vampire as a dark reflection of the self, a subversion of Christian and Victorian morality, and a symbol of a primal father who claims all women for himself.*]

[Bram Stoker's *Dracula* (1897) provides] a culmination of nineteenth-century English Gothic. It engages with a similar desire for and dismissal of transgressive energies. The consequences of a longing for immortality from a merely human context are horrifically realized by Dracula, who is not content with a promise of eternal life elsewhere. He dissolves the life/death boundary, returning from an otherworld to prey upon the living. He occupies a paraxial realm, neither wholly dead nor wholly alive. He is a present absence, an unreal substance. Dr Van Helsing points out that Dracula produces no mirror image. 'He throws no shadow; he makes in the mirror no reflect.' He is beyond organic life. 'This Thing is not human—not even beast', writes Jonathan Harker. 'I was beginning to shudder at the presence of this being, this Un-dead . . . and to loathe it.' Dracula comes from an inorganic realm, before cultural formation. 'The very place', says Helsing, 'where he have been alive [sic], Undead for all these centuries, is full of strangeness of the geologic and chemical world. There are deep caverns and fissures that reach none know whither.'

Dracula's victims share his un-dead quality. They become parasites, feeding off the real and living, condemned to an eternal interstitial existence, *in between* things: 'We all looked on in horrified amazement as we saw the woman, with a corporeal body as real at that moment as our own, pass in through the interstice where scarce a knife-blade could have gone!' Like the elusive demon of Hogg's *Confessions,* Dracula has no fixed form. He metamorphoses as bat, rat, rodent, man. He is without scruple, without form. His appearance means that chaos is come again, for he is *before* good or evil, outside human categorization. The text is never completely 'naturalized' as a moral allegory. Van Helsing realizes that Dracula is the inverse side of his legality, that only a thin line separates them. Adapted from Herzog's film version of the tale, Paul Monette's *Nosferatu* emphasizes this symbiotic link, for Harker *becomes* Dracula. The 'other', the vampire, is a reflection of the self. Harker's name suggests it is his *listening* which calls up the vampire as his echo. He admits a vague familiarity with the female vampire who visits him. 'I seemed somehow to know her face, and to know it in connection with some dreamy fear . . . a longing and at the same time some deadly fear.' *Dracula* remains one of the most extreme inversions of Christian myth and subversions of Victorian morality. It blasphemes against Christian sacraments—Renfield, the count's disciple, chants 'The blood is the life! The blood is the life!' It offends sexual taboos. Not only the count, but also his female converts, return like repressed memories to suck away life: the sexual undertones are barely concealed.

Dracula—and any vampire myth—is also a re-enactment of that killing of the primal father who has kept all the women to himself—a pattern which is found in ancient mythology, as Freud elaborated in *Totem and Taboo*. Fraternal groups, he wrote, at some stage banded together to murder and devour the father who had retained the right to keep various women to himself. 'The violent primal father had doubtless been the feared and envied model of each one of the company of brothers: and in the act of devouring him they accomplished their identification with him, and each one of them acquired a portion of his strength.' The close link between Van Helsing and Count Dracula in Stoker's version points to this identification—indeed, the fantasizing activities of the whole novel point to a barely concealed *envy* for the count's erotic and sadistic and appropriating pleasures. By defeating these desires, the narrative reasserts a prohibition on exogamy. An excellent article by Richard Astle [in *Sub-Stance*, 1980] has explored in greater detail the ways in which *Dracula* enacts a killing of the father and re-enacts the process of the subject's insertion into human culture, borrowing from Freud and Lacan to deepen the argument.

The vampire myth is perhaps the highest symbolic representation of eroticism. Its return in Victorian England (drawing upon legendary material, Polidori's *Vampyr,* the popular *Varney the Vampire* and implicit vampiric elements of *Frankenstein*) points to it as a myth born out of extreme repression. It is during his period of engagement to Lucy that Harker enters the world of Dracula and vampirism: a bourgeois family structure, to which his engagement is the key, gives rise to its own undead, suggesting that the law contains, through repression, its 'other.' The fantasy of vampirism is generated at the moment of maximum social repression: on the eve of marriage (a similar balance is established in *Frankenstein,* when the monster murders Elizabeth on the wedding night). It introduces all that is 'kept in the dark': the vampires are active *at night,* when light/vision/the power of the *look* are suspended.

What is represented in the vampiric myth in *Dracula* is a symbolic *reversal* of the Oedipal stage and of the subject's cultural formation in that stage. In relation to the theories of Lacan . . . it could be claimed that the act of vampirism is the most violent and extreme attempt to negate, or reverse, the subject's insertion into the symbolic. The vampiric act is divided into two: firstly, a penetration of the victim with canine (phallic) teeth; secondly, a sucking of the victim's (life-supporting) blood. The first re-enacts the subject's insertion into the order of the phallus (father), through reversal; the second implies that through such negation, a return has been established to the pre-Oedipal

stage, replacing the subject in a symbiotic relation to the mother (the blood sucking repeats sucking at the breast as well as the condition of being provided with life-as-blood inside the womb). With each penetration and 'return' to the unity of the imaginary, a new vampire is produced: further objects of desire are endlessly generated, creating an 'other' order of beings, for whom desire never dies and whose desire prevents them from dying—hence the subversive power of the vampire myth and a consequent recourse to magic and mechanical religious rites (the stake through the heart, the crucifix) to fix and defeat desire. The sadistic piercing of the vampire with the stake reasserts the rule of the father, re-enacting the original act of symbolic castration visited upon the subject for desiring union with the mother. Stoker's version of the myth repeats this castration, and rids the world at the same time of all non-bourgeois elements. (pp. 118-21)

> *Rosemary Jackson, "Gothic Tales and Novels," in her* Fantasy: The Literature of Subversion, *Methuen, 1981, pp. 95-122.*

James B. Twitchell

[*Twitchell is an American critic and educator who has written extensively on vampirism in literature. In the following excerpt from his critical study* Dreadful Pleasures: An Anatomy of Modern Horror, *he discusses the vampire as a central image in popular culture, surveys the development of vampire literature in the nineteenth century, and offers a psychoanalytic reading of Bram Stoker's* Dracula *(1897).*]

We are currently plagued by two vampires. The emaciated snaggle-toothed fiend, who is straight from folklore, is feral, mindless, and barbaric; the foppish gentleman, who is from the arts, is articulate, sensitive, and cultured. They both dedicate their waking hours to the same activity—draining blood and hence the life energy of innocent women. If ever Sir Philip Sidney wanted an example of the sugar-coating powers of art, this is it, for the suave gentleman is ever so much more palatable (if that is the right word) than the scruffy menace, the nosferatu. But like a china doll the nosferatu, literally the "not dead," is just under the skin of the gentlemanly Dracula, and what they both promise to do still lifts the hairs on the nape of our necks and sends ripples down our spines.

These monsters are vampires and the verb "plague" is not inappropriate, for they are members of a genus of monsters that, like the werewolf, reproduce themselves through their victims. In a most unsophisticated doppelgänger transformation, the vampire's victim becomes a second-generation vampire who, in turn, inducts a third, fourth, and so on. So it is no wonder that, although the vampire is one of mankind's oldest horror images, he really entered Western popular culture in the seventeenth century as a logical way to account for the geometric progression of deaths caused by the fast-acting plague bacteria. We now know that the toxic strain was carried to man from mice via fleas, but it was ever so much more logical, ever so much more plausible, to think that the vampire did it. Plague victims were burned for more than sanitary reasons: they were burned because incineration was one of the most effective methods of vampire disposal.

But the only way for Occam's razor to cut so sharply through the medical confusion of the plague was for the vampire already to be considered alive and well. And indeed he was. Long before Christ, the vampire had roamed Middle European mythologies, migrating from the high steppes of India eastward into China and westward into Greece. The rise of Christianity, ironically, did as much to nurture the vampire as the plague would later do, for the Catholic Church found in the story of this fiend a most propitious analogy to describe the intricate workings of evil.

Aside from the devil, the vampire is the most popular malefactor in Christianity. In fact, the competition is unfair, not just because the vampire is now probably more popular, but because the vampire really *is* the devil. The vampire is simply the husk of a human that has been commandeered by the spirit of Satan. The force of evil has gained control of the sinner's body and has trapped the psyche, or the soul, depending on the culture, and is sealing it off from eternal rest. In Christian worlds the devil has done this because the human sinner died unbaptized, was excommunicated, was buried in unhallowed ground, committed suicide, or—most commonly used today, but relatively unheard of before the seventeenth century—was the victim of a vampire's attack. The human form is simply the soma, the undead hulk, carrying around the demon and letting it pass through society undetected.

Or almost undetected, because this avatar still carries vestiges of satanic possession; for instance, the nosferatu/vampire stinks of putrefaction, has tufts of hair in the palm (a reminder of the lycanthropic transformation), has bloodshot, incandescent eyes, often a cleft palate, fingernail claws and, of course, those extended teeth. It has been appropriately pointed out that many of these traits were Victorian symptoms of sexual excess, particularly self-abuse. Little wonder the vampire should only feel safe alone at night. Incidentally, the vampire's fear of daylight seems an example of reasoning *post hoc, ergo propter hoc,* for he was a nocturnal molester in folklore first, a daylight despiser second. In pre-cinematic folklore the vampire was superpowerful in moonlight and only ordinary during the day. Hence Bram Stoker's Dracula walked undetected around London at noontime in a business suit and straw hat. We have, however, made the vampire so photophobic that for a while during the 1960s and 1970s it was a sure sign that the vampire's demise was near at hand when the string section of the studio orchestra was cued-up and the camera panned over to the rising crest of light on the horizon.

The other method of vampire destruction in both contemporary and ancient folklore was the stake. Here one sees the wonderfully concentrated logic of the folk imagination, for while the audience was unperturbed that, with the vampire's geometric population burst the poor fiends would soon run out of virgin blood to drink, they always demanded that the logic of vampire destruction be maintained. Since the vampire is the devil inside an already dead human carcass, he must be destroyed, not killed.

There is simply nothing alive left to kill. That is why he cannot be shot or knifed or bludgeoned to death. The husk is then either burned or staked to the ground, and often the head is cut off and stuffed with garlic for good measure. Once again the stake is not to kill, it simply holds the carrion in place. To a purist, this stake should be of the same wood from which Christ's cross was fashioned—aspen, buckthorn, or oak, depending on the culture—and the vampire should be placed chest down, so if the leech somehow revives, he will dig down to the center of the earth, not up to the crust.

For all the vampire's quaint habits, for all his serendipitous encounters with Satan and the plague, he might never have survived in Western horror art had he not been adopted by the Holy Roman Church. The results of this sponsorship are still visible in the myth as the principal symbols used in destroying the vampire: holy water, the sign of the cross, church icons of all sorts and, of course, the vampire's most common enemy, the parish priest. But the Church could have fostered other monsters—why not the zombie or the ghoul or some other already extant ogre? Why the vampire? What the medieval church found in the vampire legend was not just an apt mythologem for evil, but an elaborate allegory for the transubstantiation of evil. The reason this was so important was that the vampire myth explained the most difficult concept in the last of the sacraments to be introduced—the Eucharist. It explained the doctrine of transubstantiation in reverse. In the Middle Ages the Church fathers found their congregation understandably hesitant about accepting that the wafer and the wine were the actual, let alone the metaphoric, body and blood of Christ. How better could the transubstantiation be explained than on the more primitive level, the level the folk already knew and believed in—namely, the vampire transformation. For just as the devil-vampire drank the blood and then captured the spirit of a sinner, so too could the penitent drink the blood, eat the body, and possess the divinity of Christ.

There is every indication that, without this syncretic layering with Christian dogma, the vampire might have shriveled up to become a lesser monster as he did in most non-Christian cultures. But thanks to the Church, the vampire found a niche in the occidental chamber of horrors and has yet to be dislodged. By the Renaissance the folk myth had been almost completely expropriated by the Church. The vampire destroyer in folklore, usually the fiend's son, called a "dhampire," who intuitively knew how best to destroy the father, became the priest. Garlic and certain berries, which had been the bane of the vampire, evolved into holy water and icons. Decapitation and burning became staking, complete with all the rigamarole about the choice of proper wood. The folklore beast even made it into the register of the Inquisition, the *Malleus Maleficarum,* or *Witch Hammer.* This *vade mecum* of Church prosecutors did not name the vampire as such but acknowledged the existence of the blood-sucking undead and prescribed the requisite legal tests. Thus did the folk vampire, the nosferatu, slowly but surely become the Christian vampire, the dracula.

The vampire has now become such a part of the whole

Christian ethos that in the 1960s Hammer Studios even attempted to make this the theme of one of its then-endless celluloid resuscitations. In *Dracula Has Risen from the Grave* (1968) we find that a village church in Middle Europe has fallen on hard times. The local priest has given himself over to liquor and gambling and neglected his flock. Atheists have flourished and so too has the neighborhood Dracula. When the monsignor comes to inspect the parish he is outraged and collars the backsliding priest, promising to straighten matters out. Together they climb up to Castle Dracula, which overlooks the town (Hammer seemed to use the same matte work for Castle Dracula or Castle Frankenstein or Castle Fu Manchu, and it always looked like cardboard), in order to "sanitize the devil's lair." The modern priest is clearly bored by all this superstitious fiddle-de-dee such as putting crosses all over—especially a big golden one in the door latch—spraying holy water and mumbling prayers. He is so blasé that en route home he wanders off the steep path and stumbles over a cliff. Meanwhile, the monsignor is so rapt in his prayers that he does not notice that his young charge has been cut on a jagged rock and that his blood is dripping onto the frozen body of . . . Dracula. The king vampire has lain there in an ice chunk since he was trapped in an ice flow at the end of *Dracula, Prince of Darkness* (1965). Dracula, now revived and furious, makes the priest erase all unsightly graffiti from his castle as well as remove the big golden cross from the door. The priest heaves it over the cliff. Dracula will have his revenge for this defacement of his castle and the now-powerless priest will be his instrument.

Dracula avenges himself in typical Hammer style: he "attacks" (seduces) the monsignor's full-breasted niece who is, of course, "almost a daughter" to the churchman. To make matters worse, just as the young priest should have protected his flock, so the requisite boyfriend, Paul, should be protecting his comely girlfriend. But Paul is an atheist! The monsignor clearly has his hands full, having a careless surrogate son in the church and a faithless surrogate son-in-law-to-be at home. Typically, the monsignor now dies of a broken heart and a punch or two from Dracula, but not before he has deputized Paul to collar the wayward priest and promise to destroy the evil patriarch. The girl must be saved before it is too late. The boys catch Dracula, but when they try to stake him it won't take—Paul is an atheist and can't pray; the priest is a coward and won't. So the vampire is on the loose once again.

Only luck saves them now. Dracula returns to make the girl his "bride," but Paul surprises him and is badly beaten for his troubles. The vampire is now able to take her to his castle to make a queen of her (she's not so unwilling), but who should appear at the gate but a revived Paul. Another fight, and this time it's Dracula who trips over the cliff, to be impaled on that big golden cross that the priest had earlier heaved over the cliff. Just happening to be passing by is that wayward priest. He sees Dracula fall, is reconciled with his God, can now say the proper prayers, and Dracula is once again fried. Unbeknownst to us in the audience, a merchant is standing close by to collect that dust so that lusty Lord Courtly can mix with a little blood to get *Taste the Blood of Dracula* (1970) started. In *Dracula Has Risen from the Grave* the boys finally learned the value of Christianity; popular culture got one of its most alluring theater posters—a sexually sated young beauty with two puncture marks just over her cleavage: "Dracula Has Risen from the Grave . . . obviously"; and Hammer Studios got the Queen's Award for Industry.

Clearly, the vampire, even the Hammer Dracula, has more going for him than just being the resident demon in Christian folklore. For the last few generations he has also served to explain the dynamics of human social and sexual behavior. And it is here, especially as a paradigm of suppressed interfamilial struggles, that the vampire has become a central figure in popular culture. He is no longer a figure of demonic terror; he has become an eidolon of sexual horror. How this transformation occurred is illustrative not only of the romantic imagination, but of the mythopoetic process in general, for it shows how certain myths continually re-magnetize themselves around the audience's changing lodestones.

The vampire was not a subject of artistic concern prior to the turn of the nineteenth century. Although mentioned in a few ballads like "Sweet William's Ghost," in travelogues (usually ones that detailed English adventures in Central Europe) or in histories, especially those of an ecclesiastical bent where the pre-Reformation church fathers carried the day against the "Sanguisugae" or bloodsuckers, such references were always made in passing. I suppose a case could be made (and it has been) that the Beowulf monster, Grendel, is vampiric, or that Caliban is also, but such an interpretation usually mixes the vampire with his stronger mythic cousin, the incubus. Most pre-romantic blood-thirsty monsters are more informed by the incubus myth than by the vampire.

The fact is that the vampire was too raw, too uncouth, too predictable to be of much interest to any but the most gothic of imaginations. This may partially explain why he left the fireside of the folk and the parchment of church scholars to enter the slightly soiled world of late-eighteenth-century poetry and prose fiction. He started his migration in German gothicism, in Ossenfelder's "The Vampire" (1748) and Bürger's *Lenore* (1773), in which he played the part of a revenant come back from the dead to collect his living bride. By the time Goethe wrote his more allusive *The Bride of Corinth* (1797) it is clear that "collect the bride" was a code for "sexually molest." And what better image of gothic terror, of the master of the castle and the farmer's daughter, than this new vampire as lover, coming up out of the grave (later up from the cellar) to collect his tabooed bride, princess, queen.

The most important English translator of German shivers into English was Robert Southey. Southey was a poet more eager than most to be current, and he was more able than most to be inappropriate. In book eight of *Thalaba the Destroyer* (1797) Southey takes his chivalric hero, Thalaba, into a buried vault where he pays his respects to his one-time bride, Oneiza. She was taken from him on their wedding day by a demon. Now, rising from the mist like her Teutonic male counterpart, Oneiza beckons Thalaba to follow her beyond the grave. But Thalaba has a wise friend who has read all those German poems and warns the ephebic hero; the fiend is "lanced" and we're off to another adventure.

Southey realized his readers might have some problem here (it all happens in two stanzas) so he appended a prose commentary, which is really the first extended psychological explanation of the vampire in English. In retrospect Southey summed up what the French Benedictine scholar Dom Augustin Calmet had expounded in his most important *Traité sur les apparitions des espirits, et sur les vampires . . .* (Paris, 1746). Southey's well-researched, five-page gloss introduced the vampire to the best of people, especially the Lake Poets, Wordsworth and Coleridge, and this is just the kind of entrée into literary society that no monster should be without.

Although the vampire's debut did not go unnoticed, it had stiff competition. There were many other new archetypes after the turn of the century who were also appealing: the reclusive poet, the melancholy man of feeling, the emotive child, the Promethean overreacher, to say nothing of Don Juan or the Wandering Jew. But the vampire was not neglected for long. His image can be seen lurking in the shadow of Schedoni in *The Italian,* or beside Ambrosio in *The Monk,* or stepping out in such characters as Geraldine in "Christabel," the Ancient Mariner in "The Rime of the Ancient Mariner," the leech gatherer in *Resolution and Independence,* Lamia and La Belle Dame Sans Merci in Keats' poems of the same names, or in the menacing protagonists of Byron's *Manfred* and Shelley's *The Cenci.*

The poets especially understood that here in the vampire archetype was an apt mythologem that could be used to express some psychological truth. And the "truth" they were most fascinated by had to do with the interaction between artist and family, and art and audience. This fascination was carried from the romantic poets into such works as Poe's "The Oval Portrait," where the artist "vamps" the sitter of a painting so that the subject on the canvas can "come alive," Wilde's *The Picture of Dorian Gray,* where this theme is reversed, and even into Henry James' experiments in *The Sacred Fount,* where the narrator enervates his characters in order to create both a work of art and a "theory of reality."

The vampire who skulks about in romantic polite literature is certainly a far distant cousin of the vampire who was to strut around the backlot at Universal Studios and who now seems omnipresent on late night airwaves. The modern vampire, however, is related to the romantic-art vampire in one important way: the modern vampire is not only interested in blood, he is interested in the process of seduction and forbidden possession, in the transfer of energy, of life, from someone to himself. He is a psychosexual leech. Thanks in large part to his transformations in romantic art, he is no longer a facinorous beast snarling at all who come between him and his victim; instead, he has become almost an aesthete who seeks and "loves" particular victims. And what "evil" he does is strangely attractive to his victim. His actions are surely sexual, but without the confusions of the body. The vampire has become part of an elaborate cultural fantasy: he finds young females, he does something to them, and he leaves them. Now the problem is to determine what, exactly, he does and, more important, to whom.

To understand the complexity of the modern vampire and his victim, we need to trace his progress not through poetry, but through prose and drama. If the modern vampire is both a literal and a figurative lady-killer, then how appropriate that the first extended vampire story should have indirectly come from the pen of that arch-adolescent himself, George Gordon, Lord Byron. *The Vampyre,* the first English story, came to us by a most circuitous route, and although it has been retraced often enough before, let me briefly travel the route again if only because it leads to the Frankenstein myth as well.

In the early summer of 1816 a most unusual colony of English poets and poetasters convened around the Villa Diodati on the shores of Lake Geneva. It was an unusual enough assemblage so that even the professionally blasé Swiss took to their telescopes to spy on the proceedings. The local people were excitedly outraged by stories of drugs, free sex, and general debauchery characterized by Robert Southey as a "league of incest." The central characters were already well known: Percy Shelley, recently separated from his wife and now squiring Mary Godwin, the seventeen-year-old daughter of William Godwin and Mary Wollstonecraft; and Lord Byron, at once the most famous and infamous person in Europe, and his young retinue which included (along with a veritable menagerie) a young Scotsman and Byron's traveling physician, Dr. John Polidori. The Shelley and Byron parties had not previously known each other, but they had much in common: both were organized around prestigious and aristocratic poets, both poets were in self-imposed exile (Byron for his supposed incest with his half-sister, Shelley for his adultery), and both poets were involved in varying sexual degrees with Mary Godwin's stepsister Claire Clairmont. Young Polidori was also attracted to Miss Clairmont and this inappropriate attraction—he was an irritable and melancholy young man as well as an employee—may well have had considerable bearing on how the first vampire story ever made it into print.

On a rainy night sometime between June 15 and 17, both groups made a friendly wager that was to influence the shape of modern horror profoundly. As they had all been reading gothic tales from German, it was only natural that they should try their hands at composing one. So they made a pact—each member of both groups should write a scary tale and they would then see whose was best. Percy Shelley wrote a scary tale which, if his early attempts at the genre are any indication, happily he destroyed; Claire Clairmont contributed something but probably not much, since she had more pressing interests elsewhere (she was at this time carrying Byron's child); Polidori wrote something which Mary Shelley reports as being "about a skull-headed lady" who saw something through a keyhole that drove her insane; and so only two contestants were left— the seventeen-year-old Mary Godwin and Lord Byron. Mary Godwin wrote the first draft of what . . . was to be not just the most famous and popular early-nineteenth-century gothic novel, but the copy-text of one of the most stable archetypes of twentieth-century horror, *Franken-*

stein. Lord Byron, meanwhile, wrote a series of notes in the back of his wife's account book about a mysterious man who, according to Polidori in his introduction to *Ernestus Brechtold* (1819), was traveling east with a young friend, died of some strange disease after extracting an oath from the friend to keep mum, then reappeared a year later in London to "make love to his former friend's sister."

Certainly, this is not much of a horror story, but Polidori, ever mindful of his patron's eminence, re-formed the tale; and after he was discharged from Byron's service for a cause Polidori did not consider just (Polidori was not just a whiner, he was paying too much attention to Claire), he wrote up the story himself and sold it to Henry Colburn, then the most notorious publisher and literary entrepreneur in London. In the April 1819 issue of Colburn's *New Monthly Magazine* a tale entitled *The Vampyre* appeared, written by a "Lord B." From the editorial introduction there was no doubt who this "Lord B." really was—he was a friend of "P.S." living at the Villa Diodati. When John Murray, Byron's London publisher, saw the story, he described to Byron

> a copy of a thing called *The Vampire,* which Mr. Colburn had had the temerity to publish with your name as its author. It was first printed in the New Monthly Magazine, from which I have taken the copy which I now enclose. The Editor of that Journal has quarrelled with the publisher, and has called this morning to exculpate himself from the baseness of the transaction. He says that he received it from Dr. Polidori for a small sum, Polidori saying that the whole plan of it was yours, and that it was merely written out by him. The Editor inserted it with a short statement to this effect, but to his astonishment Colburn cancelled the leaf on the day previous to its publication, and contrary to, and in direct hostility to his positive order, fearing that this statement would prevent the sale of this work in a separate form, which was subsequently done. He informs me that Polidori, finding that the sale exceeded his expectation, and that he sold it too cheap, went to the Editor, and declared he would deny it. . . .
>
> (John Murray to Lord Byron, April 27, 1819)

To substantiate his non-authorship, Byron found his fragment and sent it off to Murray who was to attach it to the end of *Mazeppa* and later include it in Byron's *Complete Works.* It is a poorly crafted tale, not just incoherent but often nonsensical, and it is a testament to how much Byron disliked Polidori that he was willing to have it published at all. Colburn, who may have used the young doctor to capitalize on Byron's name, finally admitted the authorship; Polidori conceded the truth in public—the idea was Byron's but the actual prose was his. Polidori was so disgraced that a year later he committed suicide.

Polidori's story is not bad at all—in any case, certainly better than the one projected by Byron. It tells of Lord Ruthven, a heartless lady-killer in London society, who goes to the continent with a young neophyte named Aubrey. They have a series of adventures, the most important of which involves a young girl, Ianthe, who is cruelly mur-

dered by a vampire. This vampire obligingly leaves his knife beside her body. Why the vampire should need a knife is unclear, but to quibble is quite beside the point: it is a *clue.* For when Ruthven dies, he leaves a bejeweled sheath that just fits the knife. But before Ruthven dies, he extracts a pledge from Aubrey not to mention a word of his eccentric behavior for a year and, when Aubrey foolishly consents, he asks for just one more thing: Would Aubrey be kind enough to bury him on top of a nearby hill open to the rays of the moon? After all, Ruthven has been kind enough to show Aubrey European nightlife.

We all know the rest from here on—we've heard it often enough. Ruthven revives in moonlight, returns to England, enraptures Aubrey's sister (exactly as in the Byron outline reported by Polidori, but not in Byron's written fragment), and Aubrey can't say a thing because of the oath. Finally, a year and a day after the oath, and one day after Ruthven has married Miss Aubrey, he blurts out the truth. The authorities pursue the fiend and his bride, "but when they arrived, it was too late. Lord Ruthven had disappeared and Aubrey's sister had glutted the thirst of a VAMPYRE."

Goethe, at least, claimed this was the best thing Byron ever wrote, and had Byron really written it, it probably would have been his most influential piece of prose. In the history of popular culture it often makes no difference who actually does what; if a media hero is perceived to be connected with some new development in taste, let no reality intrude. And Byron was the first great character in popular culture; his name alone was sufficient to introduce this new image to the consumers of pulp.

The vampire didn't need much introduction, for in just a few years he was already on stage. The first adaptation of Polidori's work was J. R. Planche's *The Vampire: Or the Bride of the Isles,* which was first performed August 9, 1820 complete with this explanatory playbill:

> This piece is founded on the various traditions concerning THE VAMPIRES, which assert that they are Spirits, deprived of all Hope of Futurity, by the Crimes committed in their Mortal State—but, that they are permitted to roam the Earth, in whatever Forms they please, *With Supernatural Powers of Fascination*—and, that they cannot be destroyed, so long as they sustain their dreadful Existence by imbibing the BLOOD OF FEMALE VICTIMS, whom they are first compelled to Marry.

Planche's vampire must have cut quite a figure, dressed in plaid kilt and sporran, and was such a success that some twenty other vampire plays, including an opera, "Der Vampyr," followed his lead. Two facts about the vampire melodrama for students of the arcane: (1) the trapdoor, complete with smoke screen, was first used in these plays and still continues to be called by its original name, "the vampire trap," even in the most recent Broadway revival (1979) and (2) one of the first twin bills in the English theater was Planche's *The Vampyre* and R. B. Peake's *Presumption: Or the Fate of Frankenstein.* This is probably the longest playing double feature in Western theatre—the vampire and the manmade monster are still very much together.

In one important way, however, Byron's presence in the introduction of the vampire into popular culture should not go unnoticed. Byron, no doubt inadvertently, first coupled the folklore nosferatu with his own magnificent creation—himself. The character of the Byronic hero, that lusty libertine in the open shirt that Byron made such a part of his verse dramas and life dramas, is simply the vampire with a pedigree. This figure is the eternal searcher for sexual happiness, even if he has to destroy women in the process. Before Bram Stoker finally transformed the barbaric nosferatu into the suave Dracula, Byron had already started the metamorphosis. Polidori may even have realized this, for he consciously patterned Ruthven (a name already coined by Lady Caroline Lamb to satirize Byron in her novel *Glenarvon*) on Byron in order to take a poke at his erstwhile employer. On one level *The Vampyre* is clearly a roman à clef with the innocent Aubrey being Polidori himself.

More important, for our purposes, is that later in the summer of 1816 Byron wrote *Manfred,* in which he created his most thoughtful and thought-provoking Byronic hero around the skeleton of the vampire. Manfred is a superhuman seeker of pleasure who now wants only death, but is condemned, fated, to live. Here is a man with extraordinary magical powers, yet who cannot extricate himself from the chains of memory. Here is a moody lover who has so transgressed the bounds of eroticism that he has destroyed those whom he loves in the process. Here is a man who, unlike the Hollywood Dracula, cannot even drink red wine for it reminds him of the blood he has already swallowed. And whose blood is that? It is the blood of a woman he should not have loved; it is blood of his blood, the blood of his sister Astarte (Byron's half-sister, Augusta Leigh).

I would not emphasize the connection between the implied vampirism and incest had Byron not already done so. Byron knew only too well what everyone else knew—he was himself now a pariah for breaching the most hallowed sexual taboo. Here in *Manfred* Byron begs the reader to commit the biographical fallacy, and he doesn't have to beg much. What is interesting is that in portraying his incestuous hero, Byron uses the same archetype he had been discussing at the beginning of the summer, the same demon he had decided to write his scary story about, the vampire. And still more interesting is that Byron seemed to understand, albeit unconsciously, that the connection between incest and vampirism would become the mainstay of the myth, the prime generator of the horror.

It is not surprising, considering the events of the summer of 1816, that Shelley too should have been drawn to this new bogey, for he was more than passingly interested in the dynamics of forbidden love. But while vampirism is implied and tangential in Byron, it is quite actual and straightforward in Shelley. This is a little unexpected, for Shelley wrote his most gothic and macabre work, *The Cenci,* at the same time he was composing his most ethereal and glorious hosannahs in *Prometheus Unbound.* In fact, it seems at the end of Act III Shelley was so entangled

in wisps and sprites and nixies and pixies that he almost had to reassert the world of blood and gore.

I suppose there is some preparation for this change of tenor, for at the end of Act III in *Prometheus Unbound* we are told that as the millenium approaches, "The wretch [who] crept a vampire among men, / Infecting all with his own hideous ill" (scene iv) has been cast out. Perhaps this reference reminded Shelley of his earlier gothic endeavors, such as his boyhood novels; perhaps it reminded him of his pact to write a scary story; or perhaps he was just tired of "pinnacl[ing man] dim in the intense inane." Before he finally etherealized what was left of mankind in the last act of *Prometheus Unbound,* the work he chose to write was as gruesome a bit of the gothic as was ever produced in the nineteenth century.

Shelley's story is of the Cenci family, a family devoured from within by the fiendish appetites of a cruel father and then left to moulder by a paternalistic church and oppressive state. The family's story was already famous by the time Shelley retold it, except that the story was usually told as a piece of tabloid journalism—"Mad father tortures family, rapes daughter, destroys sons, and escapes on a legal technicality; daughter then takes law into her own hands, kills father, is caught and legally killed." Shelley, however, tells the story as an allegory of contagious evil, just as he was telling *Prometheus Unbound* as an allegory of contagious good. If the means for apocalyptic release is forgiveness, then the means for evil entrapment is incest. Evil for Shelley is a plague, a contagious virus that spreads outward from a specific violation of just order. It is a disease inseminated by a demonic parasite into an innocent and ignorant host.

No one who has ever read Shelley's *Cenci* has ever doubted that incest was the dominant motif; in fact, that is essentially why the play went unproduced until the 1920s. To make Count Cenci a credible carrier of the plague of evil, Shelley had to first make a credible virus, and this he found in the actual and metaphorical spermlike germ: blood. Blood is a botular poison in the play, and much of the initial action centers around how Cenci delivers his rot into others. As with Byron, it was almost inevitable that Shelley would use the emerging image of vampire-virgin, except that in Shelley's case the victim was not his protagonist's sister, but his daughter. *Manfred* was unactable, in part because of the supernatural machinery, but *The Cenci* was unproduceable because of the unsupportable and continual violation of mores.

Here, for instance, is Count Cenci, a half-century before Count Dracula, preparing for his Eucharist of evil:

> (*Filling a bowl of wine, and lifting it up*)
> Oh, thou
> bright wine whose purple splendour leaps
> And bubbles gaily in this golden bowl
> Under the lamplight, as my spirits do,
> To hear the death of my accursed sons!
> Could I believe thou wert their mingled blood,
> Then would I taste thee like a sacrament,
> And pledge with thee the mighty Devil in Hell,
> Who, if a father's curses, as men say,

Climb with swift wings after their children's
  souls,
And drag them from the very throne of Heaven,
Now triumphs in my triumph—But thou art
Superfluous; I have drunken deep of joy,
And I will taste no other wine to-night.

(Act I, scene iii)

Although Cenci claims he will drink no more—that he is sated with evil for a while—this is not to be. Later that evening, after Beatrice has initiated a confrontation, he again returns to the communion wine:

(Exeunt all but Cenci and Beatrice)

My brain is swimming round;
Give me a bowl of wine!

(To Beatrice.)

Thou painted viper!
Beast that thou art! Fair and yet terrible!
I know a charm shall make thee meek and tame,
Now get thee from my sight!

(Exit Beatrice.)

Here, Andrea,
Fill up this goblet with Greek wine. I said
I would not drink this evening, but I must;
For, strange to say, I feel my spirits fail
With thinking what I have decreed to do.

(Drinking the wine)

Be thou the resolution of quick youth
Within my veins, and manhood's purpose stern,
And age's firm, cold, subtle villainy;
As if thou wert indeed my children's blood
Which I did thirst to drink! The charm works
  well;
It must be done; it shall be done, I swear!

(Act I, scene iii)

Cenci spills more than wine that night: Beatrice, his daughter, is commanded to come to him "at midnight and alone," and she is inducted into the nightmare world of his evil. She wakes the next morning profoundly distressed:

My God!
The beautiful blue heaven is flecked with blood!
The sunshine on the floor is black! The air
Is changed to vapours such as the dead breathe
In charnel pits! Pah! I am choked! There creeps
A clinging, black, contaminating mist
About me. . . .

(Act III, scene i)

It is here in Beatrice's transformation from innocence to experience, from virgin to vamp, from passive goodness to active evil, that Shelley attempts to picture the growth of embryonic evil. Her "pernicious mistake," as he called it, is that, in order to redress a wrong she now must act, must seek vengeance, and this willy-nilly leads to the casuistry that, for Shelley (at least in 1819), allows evil to breed elsewhere. Meeting evil with evil actions is evil, and to make sure he gets his heroine properly evil, Shelley depends on our knowing the doppelgänger transformation inherent in the vampire myth. Beatrice is virtuous only to the point at which she decides to destroy malignity with malevolence.

I mention Byron's Count Manfred and Shelley's Count Cenci not to comment on the artistic appropriateness of romantic vampirism, but to point out that here in these closet melodramas of the early 1800s the old menacer of young women—that staple first of Elizabethan drama and then of the gothic novel—is getting a bit long in the tooth. He is still a figure of some sympathy, but he is turning into a horror monster. Cenci is not happy—he is possessed. Manfred is not pleased—he is driven. They thirst for what is forbidden; they hunger for sexual knowledge that is tabooed. Incest has always been embedded in the vampire folklore; after all, the vampire (like the werewolf) is supposed to return to attack first those whom he most loved in life, but what the romantic poets did was to so exaggerate the family context that the vampire *only* attacks his female kin.

The vampire stays at home for the rest of the century unhappily feeding off family, lustily violating sexual taboos. When you look at later art treatments of this horror myth, say in Poe, you find the family relationship always implied, if not stated. With the famous triplets—*Berenice, Morella,* and *Ligeia*—Poe has a narrator attempt to explain away some strange sexual behavior with a "cousin" (whom he has "married") by encouraging us to believe that he was crazy or on drugs. But if you look carefully at these stories you will find the narrator is a psychological rapist; he is, in fact, a vampire. Finding this stated or implied vampirism in Poe is, as D. H. Lawrence first explained, an occupational hazard for the reader. Here in Lawrence's own coruscating prose:

> [The] secondary law of all organic life is that each organism only lives through contact with other matter, assimilation, and contact with other life, which means assimilation of new vibrations, non-material. Each individual organism is vivified by intimate contact with fellow organisms. . . . In spiritual love, the contact is purely nervous. The nerves in the lovers are set vibrating in unison like two instruments. The pitch can rise higher and higher. But carry this too far, and the nerves begin to break, to bleed, as it were, and a form of death sets in. . . . It is easy to see why each man kills the things he loves. To *know* a living thing is to kill it. You have to kill a thing to know it satisfactorily. For this reason, the desirous consciousness, the SPIRIT, is a vampire.
>
> ("Edgar Allan Poe," Studies in Classic American Literature)

For Poe, the family is always a hothouse of energy. Each human plant struggles for the life-energy of others. Family life is a battle for nourishment, and Poe shows us the extreme consequences of this struggle. So in *The Fall of the House of Usher*, the house actually tumbles down as the last of the survivors, Madeline and Roderick, finally collapse in each other's arms. We will never know who was host and who was violator—all we know is that the "vibrations" between brother and sister have reached too high a pitch and now both partners are "bled" to death.

By no means do I mean to imply that the vampire was progressively more sophisticated in the nineteenth century, but only that certain aspects of the myth were being refined in art. In popular culture the vampire was still the night molester, the bedroom intruder, the fiend who kept coming in from the cold with hot-blooded rape on his mind. He is still a beast and his bestiality is still obvious in his animal transformations: he is lupine or batlike. And one can see his feral qualities whenever he is visually reproduced. Regardless of how the artist may want him to appear, the folk want him monstrous—a fiend first, a family man second.

The greatest work in popular culture on the vampire theme before Bram Stoker's *Dracula* (1898) was a bloody pulp, *Varney the Vampyre, or the Feast of Blood. Varney* first came out as a penny throwaway in the late 1840s and was read until it was almost in shreds; then it was collected into book form and again was read almost into tatters. *Varney* guaranteed that no popular artist would ever allegorize this demon into respectability, for he kept returning month after month, always doing the same thing—only the necks changed. Published during the height of the sensational pulps, Varney was king of vampires. In 868 pages of double-columned, miniscule print, he wandered around London and England and the Continent doing what vampires always do best and doing it with admirable panache. It was Varney first, then Dracula, who was the people's vampire. He is as responsible for all the vampire costumes, fangs, capes, blood, and coffins in moonlight as is the Count. But as E. E. Bleiler has contended in his introduction to the Dover edition, *Varney the Vampire* "may well qualify as the most famous book that almost no one has read."

No wonder! Here is the plot: in the first hundred or so thousand words Varney attacks Miss Flora Bannerworth again and again and again, each time in different disguise, but with the same results—at the moment of success he is thwarted and must redouble his efforts. In Volume II he tries his hands, or rather his teeth, on other victims with varying success (he even travels to Italy where he attacks the daughter of Count Polidori), until finally exhausted, bored, and a little conscience-stricken, he jumps into Mount Vesuvius and is incinerated. The only other such self-effacing vampire who committed suicide was the cinematic Blacula, who in the early 1970s voluntarily submitted himself to the California sun rather than continue to live off the public blood.

Varney was written by many hands, including two of the most famous shiver-masters, James Malcolm Rymer and Thomas Pecket Prest, was spewed from the maw of the first steam presses in the House of Edward Lloyd, and might have been forgotten—like *Wagner the Wehr-Wolf; The Coral Island, or The Hereditary Curse; The Bronze Statue, or The Virgin's Curse; Pope Joan, or the Female Pontiff; The Greek Maiden, or The Banquet of Blood; Ada the Betrayed, or The Murder at the Old Smithy; The Child of Mystery, or The Cottager's Daughter; The Maniac Father, or The Victim of Seduction; Ernestine de Lacy, or The Robber's Foundling; Almira's Curse, or The Black Tower of Bransdorf; The Skeleton Clutch, or The Goblet of Gore; The Death Ship, or The Pirate's Bride and the Maniac of the Deep; Sawney Bean, The Man Eater of Bidlothian*— had not *Dracula* come along thirty years later to pick up the gauntlet. Bram Stoker had read *Varney,* as well as ev-

erything else about vampires in the British Museum. Thanks to *Varney,* most of the myth's major données—the moonlight revival motif, the Middle European ancestry, the courtly manner, the hunt by the mob, the quasi-medical explanation, and, most important, the theme of forbidden heroine initiated through contact with the vampire—were already in place for Stoker to assimilate.

And assimilate them he did, as well as so much else. With the exception of the Transylvanian accent, everything now included in the vampire myth was either stated or implied in *Dracula.* Stoker maintained both the tradition of the vampire as sexual oppressor (an interpretation that had grown still stronger as the century progressed, thanks to J. Sheridan Le Fanu's gem of a horror story "Carmilla," 1871) as well as the episodic attack that had been the staple of the sensation novel. What is more, he introduced a historical basis for Dracula. There really had been a Middle European Dracula. His name was Vlad Tepes and he was an obscure Wallachian prince caught between opposing Christian and Moslem cultures, who happened to have a fondness for staking his victims—staking them in the stomach, in the heart, and in the groin. He even impaled the whole population of a town in concentric circles leading up a hill with the mayor, like a cherry, stuck at the top. For this, and many like exploits, he earned the nickname "tepes" or "the impaler," but this was not the name that stuck. His father had been a "Dracul," a member of a paramilitary sect, and since "a" is a Rumanian suffix meaning "son of," Vlad junior would be forever known as "Dracula."

Because *Dracula* has become the copy-text for the most pervasive horror myth, I will discuss the novel in some detail, emphasizing what I take to be its main contribution— namely, the projection of interfamilial sexual fantasies. This is not to imply that *Dracula* does not have many other important facets—for it does, as recent books like Leonard Wolf, *A Dream of Dracula: In Search of the Living Dead* (1972); Anthony Masters, *The Natural History of the Vampire* (1972); Raymond T. McNally and Radu Florescu, *In Search of Dracula* (1973); and Gabriel Ronay, *The Truth about Dracula* (1974) clearly attest. But there must be something special in this coding of the vampire story that is so potent that "Dracula" has become an eponym for "vampire."

Like *Frankenstein* and *Dr. Jekyll and Mr. Hyde, Dracula* was produced as one of the aftershocks of a nightmare. In contrast to the dreams of Mary Shelley and Robert Louis Stevenson, however, we know very little of Bram Stoker's nightmare other than that it came, so he said, as the result of eating too much dressed crab meat at London's famous Beefsteak Room. In the dream he reported seeing a huge crab king rising up from the plate and slowly approaching him with open pincers. This image is certainly not much to go on, even though a critic writing in *The American Imago* some years ago claimed that a crab, "viewed horoscopically," is the astrological sign of Bram's younger brother George, and so "eating the dressed crab meat meant unconsciously eating up and killing baby George."

There is a more tantalizing relationship between *Dracula* and what was actually going on in Bram Stoker's life at the time, of which this dream is only a symptom. During the 1880s and 1890s Stoker was the factotum of Henry Irving, an actor and impressario of great renown and a demanding employer. The suggestion has been occasionally made that Dracula is a caricature of Irving, and indeed the physical similarities are striking. Was Irving the crablike figure rising up to torment his aide? Equally tantalizing is the fact that Stoker in 1890 had met Arminius Vamberuy, a professor from the University of Budapest, who told him wondrous tales of the Transylvanian undead and encouraged the young man to look into the esoteric holdings at the British Museum. Stoker had already read *The Vampyre,* "Carmilla," *Varney,* the pioneering *The Land Beyond the Forest* (i.e., Trans-sylvania) by Emily Gerard, and Sabine Baring-Gould's *The Book of Werewolves,* so when he found a cache of documents on the Viovode Drakula he must have realized that life was intruding into art. All three forces, the unconscious recreation of the dream, the biographical portrayal of "Father" Irving, and the conscious fictionalization of a historical character seem to be interwoven in the novel. Behind this fabric is yet another design that makes all the parts fit: the unfolding of the vampire myth as a fable of sexual initiation.

What sets *Dracula* apart from other gothic romances is that here somehow is a web of modern horror. Other works still are caught up in its patterns: this is the text that the others continually re-create; the anxiety of its influence is still felt. Yet, when you read it, it seems an unsubstantial and even feeble piece of prose. It is striking in its absolute lack not just of causality, but of probability. Nothing important is ever really completely explained, yet the text is full of explanations. Who is this King of the Vampires? Where is he from? How did he get so rich? Why haven't we heard of him before? Most important, why is he coming to England and why is he choosing these women, our women? This novel has the internal organization of a dream or a fairy tale. All we ever know for sure is that Dracula is a bloodsucker who comes out of the East to attack specific women. He is the uncanny personified. Even the Frankenstein monster and Mr. Hyde provide some sense of predictability in their choice of prey, but not Stoker's Dracula. He just *is,* that's all. The movies, of course, can't stand this indeterminacy and so have filled in all the blanks. "Is this your wife?" the cinematic Dracula now says to the requisite young man who has entered Transylvania. "My, what a lovely neck she has." But Stoker did no such thing. He packed his monster in special dirt, moved him to England, and then let him hunt a woman he supposedly never even heard of—Miss Lucy Westenra. (Stoker's names are well chosen, in this case the name meaning "Light in the West," and it is unfortunate that invariably retellers of Stoker's tale have first changed the names or coupled various names in order to not just get extraneous characters out, but to "make sense" of Dracula's appetites.)

The dreamlike pattern of the novel's causality has caused critics, as well as screen adapters, some consternation. *Dracula* really is, as one contemporary critic has put it, a "spoiled masterpiece," especially if you judge it by the standards of the conventional novel. Of course it's not a traditional novel; like *Dr. Jekyll* and *Frankenstein* it is a mess. In the first place, the story is told from a series of narrative points of view, which is fine, but then these points of view are delivered to us in the form of diaries, letters, stenographic transcriptions (one of the first instances of the dictaphonic mode in literature), all of which sound exactly alike. Bram Stoker is not Wilkie Collins; he has only one voice and whenever he tries to alter even the tone, as he does with van Helsing or Quincey Morris, it too often sounds silly. Second, the middle of the book—especially the Mina-Lucy correspondence—is tedious, even distracting. Third (maybe this is an asset), Stoker simply cannot delineate young male characters. Jonathan Harker, Arthur Holmwood, and John Seward all sound exactly alike. The fourth "boy," Quincey Morris, the Winchester-packing American, sounds as if his speeches were written by John Wayne.

If *Dracula's* claim on our attention is not artistic, it must be psychological. Here is a gothic novel that has rarely appeared in classrooms, yet makes money for any publisher. Here is a book that has been condensed, mutilated, rewritten, revamped as a classic comic-book, yet, like the vampire itself, does not die. There is only one vampire text—nothing has displaced it. Here is a work, like *Dr. Jekyll and Mr. Hyde* and *Frankenstein,* that has simply left the literary world to be absorbed by popular culture. These works have left the medium of print, but have never gone out of print. The sense of uncomfortable admiration that we associate with liking what we are not supposed to like can be seen in the announcement by Oxford University Press that *Dracula* was to be the one-hundredth title in its acclaimed World Classic Series. The Press admitted that many of the authors in this series, which includes Thoreau, Dickens, Trollope, Henry James, and Tolstoy, would "no doubt turn over in their graves" if they knew what was going to be the one-hundredth World Classic.

Bram Stoker, author of Dracula.

Why did *Varney* perish and *Dracula* survive? What gives *Dracula* its endurance? Why has it become a classic, albeit a slightly embarrassing one? It must be that there is some other story enfolded within Stoker's endpapers—some story that we want to hear badly enough to put up with all the cardboard characters, dull asides, and desultory plotting—a story we *wish* to be horrified by; a story we want made classic.

There is, I think, this other story, and it is buried just below the surface of the printed text. This story is of incest, of the primal horde, and of the establishment of social and sexual taboos. Essentially, the story between the covers of *Dracula* describes the struggle of a band of boys (Jonathan Harker, Quincey Morris, Arthur Holmwood, John Seward) against a foe of great strength and cunning. The foe is, of course, Dracula—a man of eternal retirement age, subtle intelligence, and social position, a man who already has his own castle, already has his own wealth and serfs, already has his own women. Dracula's women are, by the way, not old hags, but the stuff adolescent boys can only dream of, and so why Dracula should want to leave these women is of more than passing interest. Here are Dracula's women as perceived by a recumbent Jonathan Harker:

> In the moonlight opposite me were three young women, ladies by their dress and manner. I thought all the time that I must be dreaming when I saw them, for, though the moonlight was behind them, they threw no shadow on the floor. They came close to me, and looked at me for some time, and then whispered together. Two were dark and had high aquiline noses, like the Count, and great dark piercing eyes, that seemed to be almost red when contrasted with the pale yellow moon. The other was fair, as fair as can be, with great wavy masses of golden hair and eyes like pale sapphires. I seemed somehow to know her face, and to know it in connection with some dreamy fear, but I could not recollect at the moment how or where. All three had brilliant white teeth that shone like pearls against the ruby of their voluptuous lips. There was something about them that made me uneasy, some longing and at the same time some deadly fear. I felt in my heart a wicked, burning desire that they would kiss me with those red lips. It is not good to note this down, lest some day it should meet Mina's eyes and cause her pain; but it is the truth.

> . . . . .

> The fair girl advanced and bent over me till I could feel the movement of her breath upon me. Sweet it was in one sense, honey-sweet, and sent the same tingling through the nerves as her voice, but with a bitter underlying the sweet, a bitter offensiveness, as one smells in blood.

> I was afraid to raise my eyelids, but looked out and saw perfectly under the lashes. The girl went on her knees, and bent over me, simply gloating. There was a deliberate voluptuousness which was both thrilling and repulsive, and as she arched her neck she actually licked her lips like an animal, till I could see in the moonlight the moisture shining on the scarlet lips and on the red tongue as it lapped the white sharp teeth. Lower and lower went her head as the lips went below the range of my mouth and chin and seemed to fasten on my throat. Then she paused, and I could hear the churning sound of her tongue as it licked her teeth and lips, and I could feel the hot breath on my neck. Then the skin of my throat began to tingle as one's flesh does when the hand that is to tickle it approaches nearer—nearer. I could feel the soft, shivering touch of the lips on the super-sensitive skin of my throat, and the hard dents of two sharp teeth, just touching and pausing there. I closed my eyes in languorous ecstasy and waited—waited with beating heart.

Perhaps Dracula wants to leave these voluptuaries because he has already "loved" them; or maybe he is such a dog in the manger that he wants only the women the "boys" want. His first Western victim is exactly that; she is almost a mirage, and her name, "Lucy Westenra" (light in the West), tells it all. She has been courted by all the boys except Jonathan, who is already engaged, yes, but secretly lusting after those vampire princesses in Dracula's cellar. Lucy has entertained marriage proposals from Messrs. Seward, Holmwood, and Morris, and she has, as the action begins, just chosen Arthur Holmwood. Arthur's wealthy father now conveniently dies, thereby passing his title, Lord Godalming, on to his son. So whatever doubt we may have had about Arthur's appropriateness is over: he is quite simply the best of English, nay Western, manhood—noble, honest, robust, stalwart, just a little dim, and very rich.

Dracula would have the woman of the boys' dreams to add to his collection were it not for the intercession of wily Herr Professor, Doctor, Lawyer Abraham Van Helsing, "M.D., D.Ph., D.Lit., etc., etc." (How Van Helsing, whose English teacher seems to have been a New York cabbie, ever won a D.Lit., an Oxford-only degree for advanced studies, is anyone's guess.) Van Helsing is of Dracula's apparent age, position, and reputation, except that he has no women in his basement, only a wife who has recently been committed to an asylum. Yet, clearly, he would not be averse to joining the boys in their pursuit of Lucy if he thought he could get away with it. But he can't and so he represses his barely sublimated sexual drives to struggle instead for propriety and social justice. Into this struggle he brings all that Western culture has to offer: logic, science, reason, and an abiding faith in God and superstition.

The central action of this book, which really has little action, entails the boys joining forces with the wise father, Van Helsing, in order to pursue and destroy the evil patriarch, Count Dracula. They must get him before he gets their women. The metaphor to describe this "getting" process is the transfusion: who is going to get into whose blood. At the center of the vampire myth transfusion is always implied—the vampire sucks blood from the victim and somehow leaves some strain of himself, some evil germ that will transform the host. But in *Dracula* there is another series of transfusions that is far more revealing of the embedded psychosexuality of the myth.

After Lucy has been twice bled by Dracula, Van Helsing realizes she desperately needs replenishment. He realizes that she languishes by day because she is being "loved" by Dracula at night. Usual defensive measures are taken (garlic, cross, and so on) but to no avail, so Van Helsing takes John Seward aside and from his instrument bag (a motif that is almost always in the myth) removes "the ghastly paraphernalia of our beneficial trade"—not hammer and stake, but the needles and tubing necessary to connect John with his erstwhile inamorata, Lucy. He is going to let the life fluid pass from John to Lucy. Neither doctor worries about matching blood types, nor does Van Helsing do anything in the way of "prepping" donor or host; he simply plugs them together and shunts John's life elixir into Lucy's emaciated body. After all, she must be saved. Who should now appear but Arthur, Lord Godalming, the Jack who has won this Jill fair and square, and he is understandably bewildered at the sight of this hose connecting his boyfriend to his own fiancée. At once Van Helsing understands and explains:

> "Young miss is bad, very bad. She wants blood, and blood she must have or die. My friend John and I have consulted; and we are about to perform what we call transfusion of blood—to transfer from full veins of one to the empty veins which pine for him. John was to give his blood, as he is the more young and strong than me"— here Arthur took my hand and wrung it hard in silence—"but, now you are here, you are more good than us, old or young, who toil much in the world of thought. Our nerves are not so calm and our blood not so bright as yours!"

Setting aside the "empty vein" and "bright blood" references, Van Helsing realizes Arthur is the only proper one for Lucy to draw from and so he pulls the tubes, reconnects them properly, and "performs the operation" once again. It is a direct body-to-body transfusion and, as C. F. Bentley first pointed out a decade ago, is clearly suggestive of coitus.

Arthur, alas, is soon called away on business, so Dracula returns to his and two days later Lucy is again in need of blood. This time Doctor Seward must finally perform the deed himself. Lucy is hazy and Van Helsing, afraid that she might wake and "that would make danger," gives her a dose of morphine. All hooked up to Lucy now, young John realizes he too can perform the task: "It was a feeling of personal pride that I could see a faint tinge of colour steal back into the pallid cheeks and lips. No man knows, till he experiences it, what it is to feel his own life-blood drawn away into the veins of the woman he loves." Van Helsing warns his young colleague to stay quiet: "Mind, nothing must be said of this. If our young lover should turn up unexpected, as before, no word to him. It would at once frighten him and enjealous him, too." Lucy wakes, sees her pale donor, and remarks rather too perceptively:

> "We owe you so much, Dr. Seward, for all you have done, but you really must take care not to overwork yourself. You are looking pale yourself. You want a wife to nurse and look after you a bit; that you do!" As she spoke, Lucy turned crimson, though it was only momentarily, for her poor wasted veins could not stand for such

an unwonted drain to the head. The reaction came in excessive pallor as she turned imploring eyes on me. I smiled and nodded, and laid my finger on my lips; with a sigh, she sank back amid her pillows.

This is Lucy's second transfusion, this one from her cast-off suitor, but she has other young gentleman friends, especially the straight-talking, straight-shooting Texan, Quincey Morris. A few days later Dracula makes yet another visit and Quincey is looked for, but can't be found. Van Helsing himself is pressed into service. It's over in a nonce—just a sentence: "As he [Van Helsing] spoke he took off his coat and rolled up his shirt sleeve. After the operation. . . ." Then Lucy is attacked for the third time and no new donor can be found, even though there is a houseful of devoted and healthy female servants. Women, it seems, cannot perform this life-giving task. The donor must be a man, a young, well-born man—if not an Englishman, then maybe a virile American. Van Helsing explains: "A brave man's blood is the best thing on this earth when a woman is in trouble. You're a man and no mistake. Well, the devil may work against us for all he's worth, but God sends us men when we want them." Quincey has his turn.

During all this hubbub the young people's parents are removed from the text by death: Arthur loses his father, Lucy her mother, Jonathan his mentor, Mr. Hawkins; they are now all orphaned adolescents in the care of fatherly Van Helsing. And soon they are even to lose the one character around whom the family has now re-formed: Dracula is about to get "sister" Lucy and make her his Queen. "Check to the King," Van Helsing unironically says, but still, one might add, not yet a "mate." They can never allow Him to get Her.

Just how important these transfusions were finally becomes apparent on the day of Lucy's burial. The disappointed young men are all gathered around when Arthur provides exactly the information Van Helsing wants kept secret. "Arthur was saying [reports Seward] that he felt then as if the two of them had really been married and that she was his wife in the sight of God." The boys all blanch, knowing that if Arthur thinks the transfusion has married him to Lucy, then he has been cuckolded a number of times by his best friends. It is Van Helsing, however, who is most embarrassed, and he erupts into his confusing "King Laugh" hysterics. When the paroxysm is over he finally explains to his protégé, John Seward, why he was so upset. Van Helsing claims that at moments of intense anxiety one can either dissipate pressure through laughter or tears. He favors laughter. Seward sees nothing laughable:

> "Well, for the life of me, Professor," I said, "I can't see anything to laugh at in all that. Why, your explanation makes it a harder puzzle than before. But even if the burial service was comic, what about poor Art and his trouble? Why, his heart was simply breaking."
>
> "Just so. Said he not that the transfusion of his blood to her veins had made her truly his bride?"
>
> "Yes, and it was a sweet and comforting idea for him."

"Quite so. But there was a difficulty, friend John. If so that, then what about the others? Ho, ho! Then this so sweet maid is a polyandrist, and me, with my poor wife dead to me, but alive by Church's law, though no wits, all gone—even I, who am faithful husband to this now-no-wife, am bigamist."

"I don't see where the joke comes in there either!" I said; and I did not feel particularly pleased with him for saying such things. He laid his hand on my arm, and said:—

"Friend John, forgive me if I pain. I showed not my feeling to others when it would wound, but only to you, my old friend, whom I can trust. If you could have looked into my very heart then when I want to laugh; if you could have done so when the laugh arrived; if you could do so now when King Laugh have pack up his crown, and all that is to him—for he go far, far away from me, and for a long, long time—maybe you would perhaps pity me the most of all."

I was touched by the tenderness of his tone, and asked why.

"Because I know!"

Seward still sees nothing laughable, for if the transfusions were sexually conjunctive, coital, then Van Helsing, the superego himself, has transgressed one of the great sexual taboos. Van Helsing has been a bigamist, to be sure, but worse yet, he has been incestuous. For if the boys are his surrogate sons then, indeed, as he himself says, Lucy has been "almost a daughter" to him.

Certainly in the text of *Dracula* blood and semen are closely linked, even psychologically interchangeable. But is this relationship true outside the text? Yes, or at least so says Ernest Jones, the Freudian analyst. Here is Jones explaining this particular aspect of the vampire myth as it relates specifically to adolescent masturbatory fantasies:

> The explanation of these phantasies is surely not hard. A nightly visit from a beautiful or frightful being, who first exhausts the sleeper with passionate embraces and then withdraws from him a vital fluid; all this can point only to a natural and common process, namely to nocturnal emissions accompanied with dreams of a more or less erotic nature. In the unconscious mind blood is commonly an equivalent for semen.
>
> (*On the Nightmare,* 1931)

Jones is not alone in believing this; other analysts have concurred, if only because blood and semen are such observable plasmas of life that mixing them up or displacing them in dream life seems inevitable.

Although blood and semen are elixirs, they are most definitely not to be drunk. The vampire drinks blood and so signals his demonism; the sexual degenerate indulges in acts of fellatio and in so doing signals his perversion—at least to high Victorians. In this context we might recheck the other important scene of transfusion that occurs, not between the boys and their "sister" Lucy, but between Dracula and their "mother," Mina. Here is the scene set down by John Seward in his diary. He recalls how he burst into Mina's room to see exactly how Dracula was attacking his second victim:

> The moonlight was so bright that through the thick yellow blind the room was light enough to see. On the bed beside the window lay Jonathan Harker, his face flushed and breathing heavily as though in a stupor. Kneeling on the near edge of the bed facing outwards was the white-clad figure of his wife. By her side stood a tall, thin man, clad in black. His face was turned from us, but the instant we saw all recognized the Count—in every way, even to the scar on his forehead. With his left hand he held both Mrs. Harker's hands, keeping them away with her arms at full tension; his right hand gripped her by the back of the neck, forcing her face down on his bosom. Her white nightdress was smeared with blood, and a thin stream trickled down the man's bare breast which was shown by his torn-open dress. The attitude of the two had a terrible resemblance to a child forcing a kitten's nose into a saucer of milk to compel it to drink.

Seward's physiological response tells all: "What I saw appalled me. I felt my hair rise like bristles on the back of my neck and my heart seemed to stand still." He is literally horrified.

I do not want to go too far with the implied fellatio because it is an aspect of the vampire myth that has not really been assimilated into popular renditions. But things are fast changing in the myth. To the best of my recollection, it first appeared in a number of Hammer versions of the late 1960s, starting with *Dracula, Prince of Darkness,* in which Christopher Lee first slowly draws his razor-sharp finger talon across his breast, leaving a footlong serration, and grabs his victim by the hair, forcing her to his chest in an unsubtle-enough way to titillate the audience and also get past the censor. I suppose this scene was implied in the 1931 *Dracula* when Helen Chandler says, "He opened a vein in his arm and made me drink," but somehow it is not the same. The chest incision scene is so much a part of the myth now that when it appeared in the 1978 *Count Dracula* (with Louis Jourdan), the video-effects man went crazy with dissolves, fades, and all manner of computer-assisted design. And in the more recent Frank Langella versions on both Broadway and in film, the scene played as *the* central image of forbidden romance. In fact, in the movie the camera shoots through gauze and chest hair to make sure we understand the nether counterparts.

While it would be a mistake to force the blood/semen analogy, it may account for the myth's almost uncanny ability to reflect the audience's sexual excitements as well as sexual anxieties. In this context one should look at Mina's response to Dracula's advances, for it prefigures the "modern" view of the female victim of such assaults. Lucy, we recall, was a giddy child-woman whose naiveté and zest for sexual excitement made her easy prey for Dracula's appetites. She even thrives on the encounter, becoming far more ravishing in deathlessness than she ever was in life. She was raped by Dracula but, in street talk, she "was asking for it." In terms of the novel, as a result of "it" she becomes by turns "langorous," "voluptuous," "sensuous," and "wanton." Lucy becomes La Belle Dame

Sans Merci. On the other hand, Mina is no "la belle dame" either before or after Dracula's attack. And what separates her from fluffy Lucy? Only this: she is respectable; she is married; she is within a family. Mina is the Victorian woman's idea of the "new" woman: helpmate, stenographer, all-night typist, bookkeeper, but most of all, wife. She has a woman's heart and a man's brain. So she should not, if literary history can be taken as prescriptive, have to deal with the advances of a Schedoni, Melmoth, Antonio, let alone a Dracula.

But she does; Dracula almost makes her his wife. "When I call, you will come," he says to Mina. "Together we will make a new world," he says to Lucy. From the perspective of the late twentieth century we might expect her response to him to be one of revulsion and, of course, to a considerable extent it is, but if you look again at this scene and its aftermath you will see a little of Lucy lingering in Mina. As Dracula bends to Mina's body, he whispers, "You may as well be quiet; it is not the first time, or the second, that your veins have appeased my thirst"; and she later numbly explains, "I was bewildered, and, strangely enough, I did not want to hinder him." She colludes, just a bit. Why?

Is it part of the vampire curse that she should be so willingly unwilling on this his third invasion of her body, or is there something in the evil father's phallic bite that she secretly desires? Is there a craving under her revulsion, just as there was in her husband's terror at Castle Dracula, when he secretly sought the bite of, which was it, Dracula's daughters or wives? Lest we conclude that Mina's "desire with loathing strangely mix'd" is just a momentary feeling of guilt and should thus be treated as the confused rape victim's occasional confession that somehow she has encouraged the attack when indeed she hasn't, we should remember that Mina's self-acknowledged complicity lasts until the end. Months later, on the night before the intrepid band of vampire hunters has at last cornered the fiend in his native Transylvania, Mina has this strange confession:

> Oh, what will tomorrow bring to us? We go to seek the place where my poor darling suffered so much. God grant that we may be guided aright, and that He will deign to watch over my husband and those dear to us both, and who are in such deadly peril. As for me, I am not worthy in His sight. Alas! I am unclean to His eyes, and shall be until He may deign to let me stand forth in His sight as one of those who have not incurred His wrath.

Why does she, a good Christian woman, not consider herself redeemable unless she realizes that to some degree she has been a conscious participant in desired but forbidden acts?

The vampire "attack" on first Lucy and then on Mina constitutes the first half of the myth and is noticeable for its conspicuous lack of violence. I cannot think of another night molester who does such ghastly and horrible things in such a gentlemanly manner. Certainly, this is not the behavior of Dracula's forebearers—certainly not the nosferatu who ripped his victims apart in order to get at the blood. But as we have seen, Dracula is after more than

blood; he is after a certain kind of sex. The sexual act he performs is, ostensibly at least, sucking. Could it be that on one level the most immature audience, say the prelatency audience, interprets the "horror" as simply the result of violating what for them has been recently tabooed, namely nursing. To this still androgynous audience Dracula himself is orally cannibalistic and this, they know, simply will not do. This audience knows Dracula is a big bad boy and so must be punished and suffer. If you continue to look at the psychosexual dynamics of the myth, you realize that the victim, the woman, also enjoys it; as a matter of fact it gives them both sensual pleasure—but it is still wrong. And if she continues to receive his advances, she will have to suffer as well.

To the slightly older audience, however, the scenario becomes sexually more complex because, as the vampire takes blood, he inseminates his victim with the germ of his forbidden obsessions. He makes her, by turns, "langorous . . . sensual . . . wanton." The attack is an impure carnal defilement of family. Again, no mention of this in the text of *Dracula* is explicit, but both in the characters' responses and in the constellating mythography that has radiated from this novel we find evidence of the perverse effect of violation. The female victim now almost invariably wants what is forbidden, even after she knows what it will cost, and so she encourages her own defloration before it begins (as she had done in the pre-Dracula folklore) as well as after. Victim and violator both desire each other, and both know that this desire is horribly wrong.

Perhaps we can best understand this ambivalence by seeing the assault not only from the viewpoints of the participants, but from the vantage point of that adolescent audience. In this context the vampire story seems a playback of an already recorded program—the primal young male audience witnesses the older man defile the virgin (for indeed to this audience the mother is eternally virginal), while at the same time imagining himself to be that powerful man. Hence the audience response to the vampire is oxymoronic: on one hand, the vampire is bad, evil, sucking what he should not be sucking, being sexual where he should not be; yet it's all somehow very alluring. The vampire himself is powerful; he has all the night to himself, all the women he wants, especially this one. This ambivalence is played out in the affective response in which the audience seems to say: "The vampire, if he would play by the rules and not attack (my) woman/mother/sister, is wonderful, but if he mistakes and overreaches his limits, I'll have to fight with him." Hence the young male must abandon the old patriarch and join the youthful throng that seeks his overthrow.

From the young woman's point of view, feelings are also ambivalent. She may well sympathize with the victim for she too is virginal, she too hungers to satisfy those strange new appetites, and she too is anxious to cross that threshold into the presumed wonderland of adulthood—namely, genital sexuality. So what stops her? What stops her is what stops all of us—fear. Fear not just of the unknown, or of performance, but fear that an improper partner can make her pregnant and that pregnancy caused by the wrong man can result in her being cast out of the tribe. And so what does the vampire do but remove all fear. He comes in the dead of night; he knows exactly what to do; he will not make her pregnant (for vampires breed sideways from victim to victim); all she has to do is be a bit interested and he'll do the rest.

But who is he to her? If (1) the vampire is a projection of self for the male and the victim is a projection of self for the female, and (2) if the victim for the male is maternal, then shouldn't the vampire for the female be paternal? Is he not, on one level, a surrogate father? For he is lord of the manor exercising the *droit du seigneur* and he is also the elder priest, the holy man who baptizes the unenlightened into the ways of his sensualism. Along with the word "marriage" and all its attendant terms like "bride" and "wife," and along with the perversion of transubstantiation, the other Christian ceremony subverted in *Dracula* is "baptism." So Van Helsing, the wise but initially impotent father-priest, refers to Mina as "tainted . . . with that Vampire baptism," while she herself earlier has recognized, wiping her face clean of blood, that some perfidious sacrament has been performed.

Essentially, the horror that resides in the modern myth of the vampire, as translated through the text of *Dracula,* is not generated by the sexual act per se, but by the psychological and social undesirability of these particular participants. To both sexes in the adolescent audience, the myth articulates and upholds the taboo of incest. Break the code and invite a punishment worse than death. "There are," the cinematic Dracula keeps reminding us, "things far worse than death . . . to die, to be really dead—that would be wonderful." Still the young male audience is ambiguous: they want to do what the vampire does, but they now know the consequences. And the young female audience is also nonplussed: they want the "love" of the vampire, but they too now know the eventualities. The myth makes these ever so clear—female victims are condemned to become "bloofer" ladies, lamias, vamps, unable to be sexually reproductive or satisfied, while the vampire himself remains a prisoner of his unsatisfied desires, unable to know the relief of death.

Understanding the dynamics of vampire attack leads us into the second half of the myth, namely the destruction, or, in Van Helsing's more appropriate trope, "the sanitizing" of such a stain. Again, it is to the text of *Dracula* that we must turn, for Stoker unconsciously assimilated the folklore and then rearranged it into the pattern we now so easily recognize. The first victim/sinner is Lucy. Lucy is twice a victim of displaced incest: first, when she is attacked by Dracula, which causes her to start her metamorphosis, and second, when she is metaphorically "victimized" by Van Helsing (via the transfusions), which slows the doppelgänger process but is still a violation of sorts. The "evil" father, however, finally has his way and she is transformed, made vampiric. She must then be "destroyed" for her sins by Van Helsing and the young men. Van Helsing leads the prospective bridegroom, Lord Godalming, up to her charnel bed and places the phallic stake in his hands:

> Arthur took the stake and the hammer, and

when once his mind was set on action his hands never trembled nor even quivered. Van Helsing opened the missal and began to read, and Quincey and I followed as well as we could. Arthur placed the point over the heart, and as I looked I could see its dint in the white flesh. Then he struck with all his might.

> The Thing in the coffin writhed; and a hideous, blood-curdling screech came from the opened red lips. The body shook and quivered and twisted in wild contortions; the sharp white teeth champed together till the lips were cut, and the mouth was smeared with a crimson foam. But Arthur never faltered. He looked like a figure of Thor as his untrembling arm rose and fell, driving deeper and deeper the mercy-bearing stake, whilst the blood from the pierced heart welled and spurted up around it. His face was set, and high duty seemed to shine through it; the sight of it gave us courage so that our voices seemed to ring through the little vault.

Lucy is culpable because she has been sexually careless. It is in the destruction of the male vampire that we are vouchsafed insight into what really generates the horror. In the young boy's pursuit of the old vampire we see what the English anthropologist Maurice Richardson first pointed out in "The Psychoanalysis of Ghost Stories" (1959)—an almost exact retelling of Freud's primal horde theory. Dracula, the fallen father, has attempted to withdraw two of the most important women from the breeding pool: Lucy, the about-to-wed, and Mina, the mother-to be. He will not let the boys, in a sense his sons, near them. Lucy is clearly the more sexually exciting, but Mina is more important to the tribe, and the fact that she is able not just to survive, but to reproduce, is as damaging to the foul patriarch as any stake through his heart. It is not co-incidental, I think, that the novel ends not with Dracula's death, but with the birth of Mina's boy child—a lad appropriately named John Quincey Arthur (the order is not clear) Harker. For the boys have all participated in his creation, and his presence proves that they are able to reproduce now without fear. The adolescents are adults now; they have had to sacrifice Lucy and Quincey, but at last they are potent and free.

The retelling of the vampire myth buttresses the more modern explanation of the Oedipal desire in the male: namely, there is no specific desire to possess the mother (or sister), but rather such incest is tied to more fundamental social drives. The boys need women; they don't necessarily want them. To be sure, Mina does mother the boys; in fact, she speaks consolingly of Arthur after he has "staked" Lucy:

> We women have something of the mother in us that makes us rise above smaller matters when the mother-spirit is invoked; I felt this big, sorrowing man's head resting on me, as though it were that of the baby that some day may lie on my bosom, and I stroked his hair as though he were my own child. I never thought at the time how strange it all was.

It would be a mistake to see Mina as the primary love object of the boys, for they clearly most want what Dracula most wants—the virgin, Miss Lucy.

It is in this context that Van Helsing's role is so enlightening. The boys can undergo supervised transfusions with Lucy, but the older men must not approach so close. Van Helsing and Dracula do, and their reactions show exactly what the deed entails. Dracula has an easy victim; Van Helsing a nervous breakdown. Note that Van Helsing never suggests transfusing the boys' blood into Mina, even though with Lucy this was prescribed. Van Helsing has sexually desired Lucy, repressed the urge, then found an opportunity to express it. And what does "it" do to him? It summons up "King Laugh," an irrational return of the repressed desires, signaling a momentary lapse of superego control. Dracula, on the other hand, follows the same desire seemingly without deflection and thereby commits a horror so potent that it calls forth the combined wrath of the civilized world. He must now contend with the wrath of Harker a lawyer, Seward a doctor, Lord Godalming an aristocrat, and Morris a New World colonist. And who is the leader of this British Empire? None other than the new Urizen from the Old World, Van Helsing. In spite of his momentary transgression, Van Helsing has, in Blakean terms, learned to "suppress desire"; in Freudian terms, to sublimate libido; and so it is he who leads the posse of the primal horde to destroy his tyrannical double, Dracula.

The vampire myth, like all horror stories, is conservative. The superego finally contains the id. This mythic parable continually articulates the need for repression, a lesson we will see again in the adventures of Frankenstein, of the werewolf, and of Dr. Jekyll/Mr. Hyde. They are the morality plays of our time. Their moral is biological efficiency, repression in the service of protecting established reproductive patterns. Such sagas articulate the best way to ensure the generative safety, not so much of the individual but of society. From such stories adolescents learn what is sexually permissible and what is sexually damaging, again not damaging to the specific person, but to the species. The horror of Dracula is not that he sleeps in the dirt, or doesn't brush after meals, or can grimace and growl, or can be lupine or batlike, or even that he preys on young virgins. The horror of Dracula is that within his infantile desires, within his misdirected libido, is the promise of profound interfamilial strife, and hence nonproductive sexual behavior. And this is the fear that has generated the taboos that have produced the institution of the family and, as Lévi-Strauss argued, culture as well. In our early teenage years we learn that Dracula must be driven out, even though what he promises is so attractive. We know he is so rich, so much a man of the evening, so sexually knowledgeable, so suave; and yet we must learn that he is so awful. (pp. 105-40)

> *James B. Twitchell, "The Rise and Fall and Rise of Dracula," in his* Dreadful Pleasures: An Anatomy of Modern Horror, *Oxford University Press, 1985, pp. 105-59.*

Carol A. Senf

[In the following excerpt from her critical study The Vampire in Nineteenth-Century English Literature, *Senf asserts that the depiction of the vampire in literature has reflected periods of social change.]*

[My] interest in vampires began in the late 1960s, when a student recommended that I read *Dracula.* At the same time, I was becoming interested in the women's liberation movement, and I initially became interested in women vampires in nineteenth-century literature because of what I perceived as hostility to women in that literature. A greater awareness of historical conditions has made me change my mind—partially—and has enabled me to see that writers like Stoker, Dickens, and Eliot are not necessarily antifeminists or anti-women even though their ideal women are very different from twentieth-century ideals. Understanding the social conditions that influenced such writers has not caused me to wish to adopt a nineteenth-century standard of values—or behavior—however. (pp. 140-41)

Although the vampire certainly has no "cookie-cutter" uniformity, nineteenth-century vampires appear in roughly three kinds of literary works: those in which living-dead characters suck the blood of victims and in which characters identify "real" vampires within their fictional world; those in which one of the characters suspects another character of being a vampire, and the author neither confirms nor denies this possibility; and those in which one of the characters deliberately uses the term "vampire" as a significant metaphor to focus the attention of another character or the reader on the destructive human being's resemblance to the supernatural figure. (p. 141)

[Why] did a primitive superstition suddenly become a popular literary figure at the beginning of the nineteenth century? After all, as most commentators on the subject have observed, the belief in vampires is indigenous to almost all cultures and all periods. Moreover, why has the vampire evolved so significantly over the past (roughly) two centuries and why has it seemed to change at specific historical times? Finally, why is the vampire in the twentieth century primarily a character in *popular* literature (and in its cinematic equivalents) while its nineteenth-century predecessor attracted the attention of some of that century's most original thinkers—economists and historians as well as imaginative writers—and therefore became an important part of the literary mainstream?

Although there have been numerous variations on the subject of vampires, including vampire plants and people who simply pretend to be vampires, this study does not attempt to come to terms with these one-of-a-kind variations. In fact, all the vampires in this study fit the following definition: . . .

> The vampire is a reanimated corpse that perpetuates its unnatural existence by feeding on blood, an act of parasitism that drains the victim's life force and can transform the victim into a vampire; it is also an ordinary human being who is characterized as a vampire and who is clearly modeled on vampires with whom writer and reader are familiar.

Despite the apparent uniformity, however, there is a huge difference in the typical twentieth-century vampire and its predecessors. Although identified by three characteristics that were also common to vampires both in folklore and in nineteenth-century literature (bloodsucking, rebellious behavior and eroticism), these characteristics are generally much more positive in the twentieth century. For example, although still requiring blood to survive, the vampire in the twentieth century no longer destroys human beings by sucking their blood. Thus the vampire becomes a more sympathetic figure, a misunderstood outsider rather than a bestial destroyer of human life. Moreover, both the rebelliousness and the erotic behavior tend to be presented in a more favorable light.

The difference can be seen most clearly by contrasting these twentieth-century variations with the vampire from folklore. That the vampire in folklore destroys human beings (often the most innocent or helpless, such as newborn infants or women in labor) by sucking their blood is its main—sometimes its only—characteristic. In fact, most versions tend to emphasize the bestial or inhuman by ignoring any human motivation and by stressing the differences, not the similarities, in vampires and human beings. One of the most extreme examples is the Malaysian Penanggalan, which is little more than a mouth with attached entrails (an image that emphasizes both its oral fixation and habit of destroying its victims by sucking their blood). However extreme the Penanggalan may appear, the majority of folklore examples tend to undermine any possible resemblance between vampire and human.

Furthermore, the vampire in folklore has none of the attractive rebelliousness of the twentieth-century vampire. In fact, the emphasis on rebellion—especially the romantic conflict with a cruel and oppressive world—seems to be a literary invention. There is, however, a latent rebelliousness that writers may have seen and modified. For example, the mere fact that the vampire is a dead body that refuses to stay dead constitutes a subtle form of rebellion even though it was necessary for nineteenth-century writers to add the Faustian elements of grandeur and heroism. Moreover, the connection to certain religious beliefs tends to suggest a kind of latent rebelliousness as well. For example, people might become vrykolakas (a type of Greek vampire) by not being buried according to the rites of the Greek Church, by living an immoral life, or by practicing witchcraft. Similarly, many Roman Catholics believed that the excommunicated became vampires. Thus there was a tendency to believe that those who rebelled against the tenets of the established church—whatever that church might be—were likely to become vampires after death.

If a latent rebelliousness exists in many folklore versions, a subtle eroticism may also exist there as well. Certainly many of the psychological explanations of vampirism focus on the similarities between the vampire's bloodsucking, the "love bite," and infantile incestuous desires. At least there was material for later writers to explore and develop though I am convinced that much of the significance of these characteristics (the rebelliousness and the eroticism though possibly not the fear of violent death, a reality much more common during earlier historical periods) has been attached by twentieth-century commentators.

A nineteenth-century engraving of a female vampire.

For example, Montague Summers, the rather unorthodox Anglican clergyman tends to see moral—even religious—significance in many forms of vampire belief. Jones, on the other hand, sees many of the pressures that are characteristic of a nuclear family. However, the kind of love-hate relationship between parents and children that Jones argues is responsible for the belief in vampires is not likely to occur in families before the eighteenth century or in families in most primitive cultures. In fact, Lawrence Stone's description of families in the Early Modern period suggests that the intense emotions so often associated with the modern family could not have existed in families during earlier historical periods (certainly not during the middle ages, where Jones locates the superstitious belief in vampires) or in many of the primitive cultures described by Summers and Masters:

> . . . this combination of delayed marriage, low life expectation and early fostering out of the surviving children resulted in a conjugal family which was very short-lived and unstable in its composition. Few mutual demands were made on its members, so that it was a low-keyed and undemanding institution which could therefore weather this instability with relative ease.

These casual family relationships were unlikely to produce the kinds of intensely emotional responses that Jones associates with the family. That Jones is wrong about family relationships in the middle ages does not keep his analysis from helping us analyze the vampire in the nineteenth and twentieth centuries, a period characterized by a totally different kind of family. Here again, Stone is helpful in providing an overview of the modern nuclear family, one that contrasts with the family in the Early Modern Period:

> The four key features of the modern family—intensified affective bonding of the nuclear core

at the expense of neighbours and kin; a strong sense of individual autonomy . . . ; a weakening of the association of sexual pleasure with sin and guilt; and a growing desire for physical privacy—were all well established by 1750. . . . Further stages in the diffusion of this new family type did not take place until the late nineteenth century during which many of the developments that have been described had gone into reverse.

Thus Stone reinforces the strong emotional bonds between family members that constitute such a strong core for psychoanalysis. Furthermore he observes that evolving notions of both individualism and sexuality may have contributed to the nineteenth-century response to both eroticism and rebellion. That these same traits are seen as positive attributes in twentieth-century literature may stem directly from a changing notion of the self (especially a growing sense of the rights of the individual) and its relationship to other human beings.

Knowing a little about changing patterns of family relationships and notions of the individual may help us to understand one major difference in the typical vampire in folklore and his literary offspring. For example, the literary vampire originated during a period when Romantic literature emphasized the power of the individual. The vampire in folklore, on the other hand, is little more than an animal with a thoughtless appetite for human blood, a creature moreover who happened to attack family members simply because of physical conditions, including the fact that primitive people are likely to live on farms or in villages, where they are also likely to be related to their near neighbors.

Although the vampire as we know it is primarily a creation of nineteenth-century literature, the initial changes in the folklore vampire came during the Enlightenment, when many thinkers became aware of the primitive belief in vampirism; and many of them attempted to explain the phenomenon rationally by speculating about its relationship to disease—especially epidemic disease—and premature burial. Others—including Voltaire—capitalized on the metaphoric possibilities associated with a creature that destroyed others by sucking their blood. These rational explanations continued throughout the nineteenth and twentieth centuries and undoubtedly had much more resonance during the Victorian Era, a period that was literally preoccupied with the idea of death.

Despite these rational explanations, which admittedly helped to keep the vampire before the public eye, the vampire seems to have entered popular consciousness primarily through Romantic literature. Indeed, as many writers have commented, the vampire with which we in the twentieth century are most familiar is a literary creature, not a direct product of folklore. Thus most people would have associated it with awe and mystery rather than with disease or other rational causes (though even a few twentieth-century writers, including Matheson in *I Am Legend,* attribute vampirism to epidemic disease), for the earliest literary versions certainly make little attempt to explain the vampire. Instead, early works of literature—including *Lenore,* "Wake Not the Dead," "The Vampyre" and even the relatively late *Varney the Vampire*—simply accept the fact that such supernatural creatures exist and that they exist primarily to prey on ordinary human beings.

Later, as the nineteenth century progresses, these supernatural beings become incorporated into realistic literature, with writers like the Brontës, George Eliot, and Charles Dickens using the motif more or less metaphorically to emphasize certain characteristics in their ordinary human characters. For example, Charlotte Brontë, who was apparently influenced by German literature, combines the bestial behavior of Tieck's Brunhilda with a violent and irrational eroticism and adds to it the kind of economic dependence that was expected of married women in the nineteenth century. Dickens and Eliot, on the other hand, continue to emphasize economic predation—although not simply the kind mandated for married women—and also suggest that vampiric behavior is connected with aggressive masculinity.

Although the movement in mainstream nineteenth-century literature is from Romanticism to realism, the evolution in the vampire motif is not quite so simple, however, for two of the most Gothic treatments of the vampire—"Carmilla" and *Dracula*—occur late in the century. Even more confusing is the fact that the vampire in the twentieth century has been associated with fantasy rather than with realistic works.

> **It is likely that all these factors—fashion, religious views, and the very presence of death as well as the Romantic fascination with what was mysterious and awe inspiring—contributed to the nineteenth-century celebration of death and that interest in the vampire, in that century a bringer of death to the young and beautiful rather than to the old and diseased, was part and parcel of that fascination.**
>
> **—Carol A. Senf**

However, if the formal changes in the works that feature the vampire have not been consistent, the thematic changes as the vampire evolves from folklore through mainstream literature to popular culture have been more so. Granted that there are numerous individual exceptions—certainly not surprising for a figure that has been so popular—the vampire has evolved from a merely bestial creature in folklore to an appealing figure in twentieth-century popular culture, becoming literally heroic in Badham's [1979 film] version of *Dracula* and in Martin's *Fevre Dream* (*Live Girls* even suggests this evolution by having the ancient vampire much more cruel than her young "recruits"); and the nineteenth-century literary character occupies a kind of mid-range between the beast and the hero.

This change is perhaps most dramatic when one looks at the vampire as a bloodsucker, the one characteristic that is common to all vampiric figures. While many twentieth-century vampires attempt to alter their unsavory reputations by drinking the blood of animals or minute amounts of human blood and many vampires in folklore drink blood but do not kill their victims, vampires in nineteenth-century literature are almost always responsible for the deaths of those they touch. The exceptions are Varney, who may not be a vampire, and Bertha Mason, who is revealed to be a suffering human being rather than a supernatural figure. In fact, even George Eliot, whose vampiric characters are ordinary human beings rather than supernatural creatures, underlines the utter destructiveness of her vampiric characters by showing that their behavior destroys their victims.

Changing attitudes toward death and dying may be partially responsible for different perceptions of that bringer of death, the vampire. Vampire epidemics and the folklore that accumulated around them were often associated with periods of epidemic disease, including smallpox. Such epidemics continued to plague the Victorians while death continued to strike all ages rather than primarily the old and diseased. Nonetheless the Victorian attitude toward death seems to be more than just a response to these facts. For example, both James Stevens Curl, who wrote the appropriately titled *The Victorian Celebration of Death,* and John Morley, who wrote *Death, Heaven, and the Victorians,* provide the twentieth-century reader with curious illustrations of the Victorian attitude to death, including the fact that Victorian crematoria, which "allowed the mourners to see the coffin disappear into the fire," made the reality of death much more immediate and the fact that even children were surrounded by reminders of ever-present death in the form of memorial cards and "samplers stitched intricately . . . with epitaphs for parents and grandparents."

Furthermore Curl contrasts twentieth-century burial customs with nineteenth and thus suggests a significant difference in attitude:

> The romantic nineteenth-century tradition that created Pere-la-Chaise, Kensal Green, Highgate, Mount Auburn, Green-wood, and, to a lesser extent, Arlington National Cemetery, has given way to a new concept. The term 'cemetery' is now in some danger of extinction . . . for the euphemism 'Memorial-Park' is in vogue. These 'Memorial-Parks' . . . appear to be superseding the nineteenth-century model cemeteries. . . . Gentility, euphemism, comfortable suburban death, and banality are replacing the splendours of nineteenth-century cemetery design.

Thus Curl reveals an important fact: the Victorians glorified death while people in the twentieth century attempt to deny its power. Curl attributes this fascination merely to fashion and explains that the modern attitude toward death is simply the result of a changed fashion:

> The post-war generation, and indeed the post-first war generation rejected the dark romantic gloom of Victoriana, and demanded an unmysterious church, a neatly clipped garden of rest, a bright and shining world. . . . Indeed,

the contemporary trend is to look on the Victorian Celebration of Death as something of a joke.

However, such significant cultural changes are rarely the result of fashion. Nancy Hill, who places the Victorian fascination with death within a much larger social and cultural framework—one that differs markedly from its twentieth-century counterpart—offers a more convincing argument:

> Paradoxically we seem to tolerate nearly perpetual warfare, the expectation of atomic annihilation . . . yet death as an actual occurrence affecting our personal lives has virtually no reality for us. We have to be taught . . . to deal with death, or else turn the whole unpleasant business over to an antiseptic institution.
>
> In Dickens' age death was still a religious event, . . . Dickens' contemporaries were still capable of being moved by the medieval Dance of Death . . . because their religious beliefs still accepted many of the same premises. In Dickens' still Christian era Death serves a summons to appear before the Creator and to answer for one's activities. Death as a conductor between the earthly and the eternal is a far more terrifying figure than Death as a signalman announcing journey's end.

It is likely that all these factors—fashion, religious views, and the very presence of death as well as the Romantic fascination with what was mysterious and awe inspiring—contributed to the nineteenth-century celebration of death and that interest in the vampire, in that century a bringer of death to the young and beautiful rather than to the old and diseased, was part and parcel of that fascination.

Moreover, when we look at the vampire as a destructive creature, a bringer of death, we see one more significant difference between the nineteenth-century vampire and its twentieth-century offspring: Vampires in nineteenth-century literature are generally revealed as being more destructive than their human opponents although—with the exception of Dracula, Bulstrode and Vincy, and the vampires mentioned by social writers—vampires threaten individuals rather than groups of human beings. In fact, it is only in *Dracula,* a kind of turning point for the literary vampire at any rate, that the reader gets a sense of a war between monsters and humans, a war that is explored further in twentieth-century works although often with a surprising difference. In the following passage, Dracula—proud of his warrior heritage—attempts to explain to Jonathan Harker the connection between bloodshed and heroism:

> Is it a wonder that we were a conquering race; that we were proud . . . when, after the battle of Mohacs, we threw off the Hungarian yoke, we of the Dracula blood were amongst their leaders, for our spirit would not brook that we were not free. Ah, young sir, the Szekeleys—and the Dracula as their heart's blood, their brains, and their swords—can boast a record that mushroom growths like the Hapsburgs and the Romanoffs can never reach. The warlike days are over. Blood is too precious a thing in these days

of dishonourable peace; and the glories of the great races are as a tale that is told.

Momentarily impressed by the heroic Dracula, Harker is later terrified when he realizes that the vampire plans to attack everything that Harker holds dear. In addition, although Harker eventually attacks the somnolent Dracula with a sword and Van Helsing and his small band of followers ultimately "declare war" on Dracula, there seems to be no doubt in Stoker's mind that Dracula is the aggressor, his attacks on individuals only an indication of his plan to subdue the entire human species. In fact, Harker sees Dracula's plan to settle in England as nothing less than a declaration of guerrilla warfare:

> This was the being I was helping to transfer to London, where, perhaps, for centuries to come he might, amongst its teeming millions, satiate his lust for blood, and create a new and ever-widening circle of semi-demons to batten on the helpless.

While Stoker is the only nineteenth-century writer to link the vampire with the mass annihilation of warfare, this connection is made more frequently in twentieth-century works. For example, Sergeant Stanslas in Wellman's "The Horror Undying" and Private Lunkowski in Drake's "Something Had To Be Done" use the horrors of warfare as a cover for their bloodthirsty exploits. However, both Wellman and Drake suggest that their vampires are no more violent than the human beings on whom they prey. Furthermore, Yarbro, in *Hotel Transylvania,* and Chetwynd-Hayes, in *The Monster Club,* indicate that vampires and other supernatural monsters are actually less aggressive and destructive than human beings. Chetwynd-Hayes has one of his monsters, a ghoul, draw the human character's attention to recent history to focus the attention of both fictional character and reader on the horror of *human* aggression:

> In the past sixty years the humes [or humans] have exterminated one hundred and fifty million of their own kind. . . . The humes began with many serious disadvantages, but these they overcame with wonderful ingenuity . . . they invented guns, tanks, aeroplanes, bombs, poisonous gas, extermination camps, swords, daggers, bayonets, booby-traps, atomic bombs, flying missiles, submarines, warships, aircraft carriers, and motor-cars. . . . During their short history they have subjected other humes to death by burning, hanging, decapitation, electrocution, strangulation, shooting, drowning, racking, crushing, disembowelling and other methods too revolting for the delicate stomachs of this assembly.

Certainly far from subtle, this long catalogue is a poignant reminder of why the vampire, a threat only to individuals, is no longer terribly frightening to people in the Post-Hiroshima Age.

As a member of one of the generations born after World War II, I am well aware that warfare today can result in global destruction. However, the social historian Asa Briggs observes that this fear is nothing new, that the horrors of warfare on a global scale and the threat of mass an-

nihilation have been a major part of human consciousness during the entire twentieth century:

> The great European wars of the twentieth century . . . were very different in scale and character from the 'little wars' of the nineteenth. . . . The latter had been fought along the lines of many of the wars of the Roman Empire, by small numbers of regular soldiers against hostile forces on distant frontiers . . . sometimes they were punitive expeditions to enforce law and order, sometimes they were more ambitious campaigns to annexe territory.

Briggs suggests that changes in military strategy as well as technological developments—I hesitate to label these developments advancements—have also altered human attitudes to death and dying. As a result, human beings in the twentieth century have come to fear, not vampires and other threats to the individual self, but vast impersonal forces over which they as individuals have no control.

Moreover, during the twentieth century, the horrors of warfare have become a part of everyone's life, not just part of the lives of professional military men. That warfare has entered the living rooms of ordinary human beings is partially—in recent decades—because modern telecommunications have enabled people continents away to experience the horrors of war and partially because the possibility of being personally affected seems so immediate.

On the other hand, Brigg's discussion of World War I provides a sense that mass awareness of the horrors of war was a reality long before the days of television and nuclear weapons:

> Slaughter was, in fact, appalling. . . . Death, which was a matter of luck, was not the only human sacrifice to a new Moloch. Injured, gassed, shell-shocked, blinded men staggered back from the wars to a life that would never be the same again.

Compared to the real horrors that people in the twentieth century see around them—either on the battlefield or back at home—dying from a vampire attack appears innocuous—even attractive. Here, at least is an adversary against which one might battle honorably and openly. The vampire is typically a personal threat, not an invisible whiff of poisonous gas, a bomb dropped on an unsuspecting populace, or—most unspeakable of all—what came to be known during the Vietnam War as "friendly fire."

If changing notions of warfare and the possibility of mass annihilation in the twentieth century have been responsible for writers and readers taking a more sympathetic view of the vampire, changing attitudes toward authority and toward rebellion against that authority have also led to a more sympathetic treatment of the vampire, especially when the vampire is shown rejecting a corrupt or vicious society or choosing to live in seclusion. Significant examples of the vampire as an attractive rebel are Badham's Dracula, Yarbro's St. Germain, Saberhagen's Dracula, to name only a few. There are several important exceptions, however, that possibly—it is too soon to tell—signify a changing attitude toward rebellion: *Fright Night* (Columbia Pictures, 1985) and *Last Rites* (1985). *Fright Night,* which was written and directed by Tom Holland, features a truly despicable vampire who feeds on the blood of prostitutes and who turns the young hero's best friend into a vampire also. Dolores, the ancient vampire in *Last Rites* is even more hideous. Wearing the gem-studded cross that had once belonged to the archbishop, one of her former lovers, is an obvious reminder of her contempt for religious authority. It is tempting to draw an analogy between the present social and political climate (especially the renewed strength of fundamentalist religious groups and the fact that once again authority of whatever kind seems to signify right) and the fact that the vampire—always a rebel against authority—is perceived as a threat. However, one movie does not necessarily indicate a trend. (*Fright Night* is complicated by being an artistic attempt to do something new with an old genre. Thus it combines a parody of horror movies with genuinely frightening material.) Furthermore, as Briggs cautions, it is especially difficult for writers to come to terms with their own present:

> The closer the social historian gets to his own times, the more difficult it is for him to be sure that he has grasped what is essential about his period. This is largely a matter of vantage point. Some features of the pattern may not yet even be clearly visible.

Holding Briggs's caution in mind, I will conclude—albeit cautiously—that vampires in the twentieth century have been perceived as more or less attractive rebel figures, ones who *choose* to live outside the society that they, their creators, and their readers (or viewers) regard as problematic—even corrupt. To put it succinctly, vampires have become heroes and heroines in the twentieth century.

Unlike their twentieth-century offspring, writers in the nineteenth century do not choose to make heroes/heroines of their vampires; and the reasons for the change in attitude is partially caused by a changed attitude toward authority. During the nineteenth century the middle classes (which formed the bulk of the reading public) in Great Britain, the United States, and Germany, as Peter Gay observes, were overwhelmingly religious and therefore receptive to both religious authority and to other kinds of authority. Their counterparts one hundred years later, as Briggs observes, are strikingly different:

> Even at the beginning of the 1950s . . . only 10% of the population were regular church goers. Now, in the late 1950s and early 1960s there was a sharp decline, particularly among the Nonconformist sects. The power of the chapel . . . sharply declined, and many of the great Victorian chapels were pulled down or used for other purposes, even as bingo halls.

Without question, the decline in church attendance suggests that religious authority has diminished significantly since the beginning of the nineteenth century. However, Briggs observes that other factors accompanied the decrease in religious power during the 1950s and further undermined traditional authority: "The real break had come . . . when, with increased prosperity, educational opportunity and social and physical mobility, society seemed to be more fluid and less willing to accept old ways."

Briggs does not mention the effect that various scandals involving cabinet officials might have had on British respect for political authority although the Hammer films featuring arrogant and sensual vampires had their heyday in the 1960s. Furthermore, vampire films in this country have been most popular during periods of political unrest (for example, during both the Depression and the 1970s, when the lack of faith in political institutions that resulted from both the bungled Vietnam War and Watergate was at an all-time high.) Moreover, greater social and physical mobility had already begun to undermine traditional sources of authority even in the nineteenth century as people immigrated from rural areas to large metropolitan centers and from Europe to the Untied States and other countries. (Gay estimates that 62 million people left Europe between the early 1820s and the early 1920s.) However, in spite of immigration, established institutions, including the church, the government, and even the public house, managed to retain their authority over the individual until mid-twentieth century. At that point, greater suspicion—even contempt—of established authority created more interest in and respect for individuals who rebelled against established authority.

Even though they are not presented as attractive figures who offer positive alternatives to the status quo, many vampires in the nineteenth century are presented as rebels, the most prominent being Lucy Westenra, Dracula, Catherine Earnshaw, Heathcliff, and Bertha Mason. Lucy, who is modeled on the New Woman of the 1890s, rebels subconsciously against the constraints (especially the sexual constraints) placed on women even before she meets Dracula; and she becomes openly rebellious after her "initiation." Dracula himself also rejects English authority though he is usually careful to be circumspect about that rejection. In fact, he invites Jonathan Harker to Transylvania to learn more about English law and customs. Furthermore, Dracula is especially frightening to Stoker's middle class narrators (and probably to his middle class readers as well) because he flaunts his freedom from everything that restricts them. Catherine, Heathcliff, and Bertha Mason simply long for the evasive freedom that Dracula possesses. Unable to find the freedom that they seek within their society—freedom to marry whomever they choose, for example, or to adopt a more congenial social role—Catherine and Heathcliff rebel against that society; and Emily Brontë, who lived during a time when both women and propertyless orphans like Heathcliff had very few social options, suggests that they can find the freedom they seek only in death. Her sister Charlotte also uses the vampire to reveal the circumstances that were likely to cause women to rebel; and her vampire, Bertha Mason, is literally imprisoned (appropriately in the attic of her husband's ancestral home) by a society that regards openly sexual behavior—indeed any kind of assertive behavior—in women as inappropriate. Brontë shows that Jane is also tempted to rebel against the society that attempts to imprison her, but she also provides acceptable ways for Jane to rebel against the constraints of her society even if that rebellion ultimately falls short of the mark for most twentieth-century feminists.

Lucy Westenra, Dracula, Catherine Earnshaw, Heathcliff, and Bertha Mason are perhaps the most rebellious vampires in nineteenth-century literature. Nonetheless, a kind of latent rebellion exists in *all* vampires—even in those like Lord Ruthven, Carmilla, Vholes, Bulstrode, and Vincy whose exploitative behavior is used by their creators to mirror the corruption that exists in an exploitative society. That rebellion consists of a refusal to live by the rules of their society and even—in the case of the supernatural vampires—the natural laws that govern the human species.

Though bloodsucking and rebellion are common traits of the literary vampire in the nineteenth century, the single most prominent trait is their eroticism. In fact . . . , the exceptions prove the rule. Vholes and Tulkinghorn, Bulstrode and Vincy are the *only* nineteenth-century vampires who are not defined by their erotic behavior; and Eliot even hints at a degree of sensuality in Bulstrode's past character when she refers to his power over his wives.

There is, however, one critical difference in the ways this eroticism is depicted. While twentieth-century writers treat the eroticism of their vampires as a positive trait, their nineteenth-century counterparts definitely do not. To see the difference clearly, one need only contrast Mr. Varri's gentle seduction of Anna in "Softly While You're Sleeping" with Varney's brutal attack on the sleeping Flora Bannerworth or with Lord Ruthven's even more bestial attack on Ianthe. Furthermore, one might also contrast Yarbro's scholarly St. Germain, Daniel's Don Sebastian, Herzog's Nosferatu and the interpretations of Dracula by Frank Langella [in the 1979 film *Dracula*] or George Hamilton [in the 1979 film *Love at First Bite*] with Lord Ruthven, Vholes, or Dracula. The comparison reveals that men vampires in the twentieth century—except when they merely imitate Stoker's character—are courtly and gentle, often as vulnerable as their human victims. Men vampires in the nineteenth century, on the other hand, use great physical and political power to attack sleeping or otherwise defenseless victims, giving them no opportunity to protect themselves or even to understand what is happening to them. In this sense, even Lydgate reveals his origins in the eighteenth-century rake and Gothic villain, for he uses his aristocratic family and cosmopolitan background to overwhelm—albeit unconsciously in his case—the provincial Rosamond. Eliot's use of literary source material is much more subtle than Polidori's, however, so Lydgate is a realistic character in his own right as well as an inheritor of a popular eighteenth-century literary tradition that emphasized diabolical masculine power.

An even more striking change takes place in women vampires, who are more interesting because they are somewhat less dependent on a popular literary tradition and are, therefore, the products of their creator's individual imaginations. Understanding the social conditions that influenced their creators enables us to see that the vampire motif enabled writers to explore changes in women's lives and especially to focus on questions of power and powerlessness. In the twentieth century, women vampires—including Miriam, Sterling, Valan, Madelaine, and Vampirella—are both overwhelmingly sensual and appealing, but their nineteenth-century counterparts are considerably less attractive. Like Varney and Lord Ruthven, Carmilla and Bertha Mason are characterized by their brutal attacks on sleeping victims; Lucy Westenra and the women in Dracula's castle are murderers of children as well as violently sexual beings, who both seduce and terrify their male victims; and even Catherine Earnshaw—perhaps the most sympathetic vampire in nineteenth-century literature—is terrifying when she first appears outside Lockwood's window.

Thus, one can begin to see a trend. Not only are vampires in twentieth-century popular culture more attractive than their forerunners in nineteenth-century literature, but they seem to be more appealing *and* less destructive precisely because of the same characteristics.

Before going on to discuss the reasons for these changes in the vampire motif, however, one more related trend should be noted—the fact that women vampires . . . tend to replace men vampires in the middle of the nineteenth century. Frayling explains:

> In general, the Satanic Lord was fashionable . . . up to 1847, when he gorged himself to death in *Varney the Vampire*. The Fatal Woman made tentative appearances in Germany and France during the early period of Romanticism, but came into her own during 1840-80.

Part of the reason is undoubtedly literary influence just as the numerous versions of Dracula in the twentieth century are a tribute to the immense popularity of Stoker's novel. However, both Frayling and Mario Praz (who erroneously attributes the interest in vampires entirely to the fascination with Lord Byron) seem to oversimplify the paradigm while Judith Newton, who analyses both fiction written by women and household manuals addressed to middle class women, suggests that the growing nineteenth-century interest in powerful women characters may have stemmed from its concern—even obsession—with women's actual power, an obsession that increased as the century progressed:

> This same tension and counterinsistence in relation to women's power leave traces on periodical literature addressed to the "woman question." In 1810, for example, an author for the *Edinburgh Review* makes only one reference to women's influence, giving far more emphasis to the dignity, the delightfulness, and the ornamental quality of women's character and to the importance of their personal happiness. But by 1831, in literature of the same kind, power and influence are frequent subjects of concern and references to both are accompanied by a sharpening distinction between what is appropriate to women and what to men.

This particular passage concerns non-fiction prose rather than fiction, but it reveals the same trend that we have observed in popular fiction. In fact, the growing awareness of women's power and influence may explain the increasing popularity of fatal women (of which the woman vampire is merely one important sub-type) during the second half of the nineteenth century when women gained power and influence and feminists began to petition for additional rights for women. Concerned with women's power and influence, writers in the nineteenth century often responded by creating powerful women characters, the vampire being one of the most powerful negative images.

Though the observations of Praz, Carter, and Frayling focus on literary influence, Newton and Gay, who look at the relationship between literature and the society that influences its creators, offer a more complete analysis of a complex phenomenon. Gay, who observes that "no century depicted woman as vampire, as castrater, as killer so consistently . . . as the nineteenth," connects "the vengeful female, the murderous courtesan, the immortal vampire . . . the castrating sisterhood: Salome beheading John the Baptist, Judith punishing Holofernes" with social concerns, especially with the increase in feminist activity. Looking back over this study reveals that the bulk of the vampires in the nineteenth century were women—Catherine Earnshaw, Bertha Mason, Carmilla, Rosamond Vincy, Lucy Westenra and the three vampires in Dracula's castle—and that even Dracula and Heathcliff share characteristics with their women companions. (Varney and Ruthven are more specifically Byronic in origin.) Furthermore, as Gay correctly observes, this dialectical relationship between the evolving position of women (and feminists' demands for increased social, economic, and political power) and negative responses to powerful women or even to potentially powerful women seems to have originated during a period when many people were exploring the position of women within their society. For a variety of reasons, the hostile responses to powerful women diminish greatly during the twentieth century. . . . The result is a vastly different response to women in general and an increasingly attractive portrayal of women vampires in twentieth-century popular culture.

Nonetheless, despite the fact that hostility toward powerful women continues throughout the nineteenth century, it would be a mistake to assume that the actual condition of women did not evolve during that period or that the focus for hostility and fear did not change accordingly. Sheila Rothman, in fact, cautions against looking for "a unitary, static, and invariably subservient role for women." Nonetheless, both Rothman, who studies the changing roles for American women in *Woman's Proper Place: A History of Changing Ideals and Practices, 1870 to the Present,* and Jane Lewis, who evaluates English women during roughly the same period in *Women in England 1870-1950: Sexual Divisions and Social Change,* discover that women's roles have changed according to certain stages though both recognize "links before and survivals afterward." Rothman, Lewis and other students of women's history identify roughly five major stages for middle-class women since the 1870s and acknowledge that working class women typically had lives outside their homes that made their existence less restricted though undoubtedly more physically arduous:

1. During the first three-quarters of the nineteenth century, the virtuous woman as wife and mother was expected to isolate herself within the home. As a result, women had a certain degree of influence within their "proper sphere."

However, single women during the period, even those who were forced to support themselves financially, had few economic opportunities.

2. During the latter decades of the nineteenth century and the beginning decades of the twentieth, feminists attempted to introduce the virtues of women's sphere into the wider public arena. Single women gained economic and educational opportunities, but married women (especially those with children) were still expected to devote themselves to their families. In fact, the cult of educated motherhood made that particular part of woman's role more important (and possibly more restrictive) than ever before.

3. World War I temporarily changed the lives of women as more of them were given the opportunities to work outside the home. However, after the war, women were expected to return to the home. The biggest change was that wives were now encouraged to be sexual companions to their husbands, in fact to be more interested in their husbands than in their children.

4. World War II gave women even more opportunities for advancement. However, the biggest change came in the post-war years when many women chose not to return to their homes. Furthermore, those who did return home grew increasingly disenchanted with the restricted roles permitted to them.

5. The end result of women's disenchantment with their roles as housewives and mothers came during the 1960s, when the women's liberation movement began to demand equality (both professional and sexual) with men. At the same time advances in birth control technology made sexual equality possible for the first time in human history.

As we can readily infer, these stages have had a profound impact on the lives of women during the past hundred years. Moreover, the increasing acceptability of women's sexuality (first within monogamous marriage and gradually outside marriage as well) and the rising sense that men and women are more equal than different (at least in terms of their educational and economic needs) has had a profound effect on men as well, not to mention [on] the vampire. (pp. 141-56)

While there seems to be some question about the degree and kind of sexuality recommended for married men and women, the sexuality so often associated with the vampire—the crude excesses of Bertha Mason, the lesbianism of Carmilla, the violent and exploitative behavior of Ruthven and Varney, and the promiscuity of Lucy Westenra and Dracula's three companions—fall outside what was recommended behavior. Besides being violent and excessive it also fell outside monogamous marriage. Thus this behavior was regarded as threatening both to individual health and to the social order.

Aside from reasons of health, however, one of the reasons that physicians and other thinkers encouraged the sexuality of married couples was the immense value placed on motherhood; and Gay argues that "the bourgeois conscience, whether religious or secular," during most of the nineteenth century assumed that motherhood was a woman's highest duty. Moreover, Lewis suggests yet another reason that the wife and mother at home became an important moral force especially after mid-century—the fact that "evolutionary ideas had shaken the religious faith of so many. The hearth itself became sacred, and the chief prop of a moral order no longer buttressed by belief."

During the last few decades of the nineteenth century and the first few decades of the twentieth, motherhood became even more important, partially because the new schools for women emphasized women's responsibility to bring up healthy, well-adjusted children. Lewis adds yet one more reason for the increasingly positive view of motherhood, "eugenic concern about the quality of the race." Certainly this emphasis on maternal virtues suggests one reason that the woman vampire changes from the sexual temptresses presented by Gautier at the beginning of the century and even by Emily Bronte at mid-century to the bad mothers created by LeFanu, Eliot, and Stoker later in the century. While the ideal woman at the end of the century was characterized by her desire to nurture and protect children, Carmilla, Lucy, and Dracula's three companions are characterized by their predatory relationships to children. Carmilla, for example, though revealed primarily as a threat to young women, first appears to Laura when Laura is a child of six. Stoker's women vampires, although they are also threats to other adults, seem to practice their vampire skills on children; and Harker is horrified when Dracula presents his hungry companions with a bag containing a "half-smothered child." Lucy tempts young children as the "bloofer lady" before she drinks their blood. Even Rosamond, who miscarries when she defies her husband's warning against horseback riding, can be viewed as a bad mother, certainly in this case as the destroyer of her unborn child. Thus, women vampires in the second half of the nineteenth century, though still presented as erotic threats to the men around them, are also shown to be bad mothers who, instead of nurturing and protecting children, destroy them. Despite the change in the woman vampire, however, the continuing interest in powerful women characters suggests that people continued to be concerned with the evolving role of women within their society. (pp. 158-59)

The past centuries have involved great social flux; and it is during the periods of greatest social flux that the vampire—especially the woman vampire—seems to thrive. Our study suggests that men vampires seem to be products of literary influence—including such popular types as the rake, the Gothic villain, and the Byronic hero—although they too are likely to appear during periods when human beings feel most threatened by the forces that surround them. However, women vampires have appeared during periods of intense interest in individual identity, periods during the past two centuries that have focused directly on the changing social condition of women and indirectly on the social condition of men.

Because of these changing attitudes to individual identity and because of the changing attitudes toward rebellion, death, and warfare, the man vampire has also evolved to become more attractive and less threatening in the twentieth century. One need only compare the Count on Sesame Street or more serious literary versions—Anne Rice's

Lestat, Saberhagen's Dracula, or Martin's Joshua York—to their nineteenth-century counterparts—especially Ruthven and Dracula—to see that the vampire is no longer a serious threat to the human race.

However, the evolving nature of the woman vampire is much more significant and interesting because it is directly linked to changing social and personal ideals for women, ideals that have contributed to the popularity of the woman vampire during the past two hundred years.

As a direct response to the sexually indulgent eighteenth century, both men and women vampires in the early years of the nineteenth century are characterized as sexually voracious creatures. In fact, Varney is often described as an eighteenth-century gentleman though the distinction is sometimes blurred by the writer's frequent anachronisms. However, during a period that demanded female purity, the sexually aggressive woman vampire is doubly condemned in French, German, and English literature. Gautier's beautiful courtesan, Hoffman's returning wife, Le-Fanu's Carmilla, and Bronte's Bertha Mason all reveal their authors' loathing of overt expressions of women's sexuality; and even the character of Catherine Earnshaw, who seems to prefer freedom to her wifely responsibilities and motherhood, is influenced by this attitude.

Although Catherine Earnshaw dies in childbirth and never gets an opportunity to prove herself a bad mother, women vampires after the mid-nineteenth century often directly contradict the view—held even by feminists—that women's chief responsibility was to be good mothers. In fact, Carmilla, who is perceived as a sexual threat, is also a bad mother who seeks out motherless adolescent girls to seduce. Rosamond Vincy is directly responsible for the miscarriage of her first child, but she presumably settles down to provide for the training of her four daughters, daughters who one imagines will be carbon copies of her. Presented even less ambivalently are Lucy Westenra and the three women in Dracula's castle, who openly prey on children, and Catherine, the formerly doting mother in Bierce's "The Death of Halpin Frasier," who turns on her son and destroys him.

Sexually aggressive, rebellious, or bad mothers, women vampires in nineteenth-century literature invariably destroy the human beings around them. Thus, they become a negative version of what nineteenth-century women were expected to do and be; and the major emphasis changes as the corresponding ideals for women change.

Although vampires of both sexes figure prominently in literature and drama during the last decades of the nineteenth century, the first half of the twentieth century represents a relative low point for the vampire. In fact, many vampires—including Tod Browning's *Dracula* and Murneau's *Nosferatu* (Germany, 1922)—merely rehash earlier versions of the vampire myth. (Murneau's version was, in fact, so close to Stoker's *Dracula* that Stoker's widow filed suit.) Notable exceptions are Stoker's *The Lady of the Shroud,* in which the belief in vampires is used to provide a cover for a political refugee and *Dracula's Daughter* (Lambert Hillyer, USA, 1936), in which Gloria Holden plays a reluctant vampire, almost in the spirit of

An illustration from LeFanu's "Carmilla."

vampires in the 1960s, 70s, and 80s. However, unlike these later vampires, the Countess Marya Zaleska is unable to control her blood lust despite her attraction to a young human physician.

The genre remained viable during the 1940s and 50s, mostly through a variety of parody versions, including *Abbott and Costello Meet Frankenstein* (Charles T. Baron, USA, 1948). However, as many commentators, including Stephen King and Raymond T. McNally note, few "serious" vampire films were released between 1940 and 1965. McNally observes:

> Pearl Harbor on December 7, 1941, delivered the *coup de grace* to the horror movies and to horror fiction. When faced with *real* horrors, the straightforward horror movie found no audience.

Thus McNally concurs with the idea that changing attitudes to warfare and death are responsible for the evolution of the vampire motif.

Genuine fears about mass annihilation, however, do not explain the increasing interest in the vampire—especially in the woman vampire—during the 1960s, 70s, and 80s; and it was my questions about what caused this change that led me to explore the vampire motif to begin with. Indeed the change in the vampire motif seems more directly linked to changing attitudes toward sexuality than to increased fears about death. Certainly the numerous Ham-

mer films, beginning with *Horror of Dracula* (England, 1958), feature Christopher Lee as a vampire whose sensuality delights his equally sensual women victims. Michael Carreras, of Hammer Films, agrees:

> The greatest difference between our Dracula and anybody else's was the sexual connotations. There was no real horror in it, the women were eager to be nipped by Dracula and I think that gave it a fresh look.

More significant changes occur later, however, with appealing women vampires, such as Miriam, Sterling, Valan, and Madelaine, and with human women who openly choose to seduce their vampire lovers rather than wait to be seduced. In fact, both Lucy (played by Kate Nelligan in John Badham's 1979 version of *Dracula*) and the neurotic model (played by Susan St. James in Stan Dragoti's 1979 *Love at First Bite*) are appealing precisely because they recognize their full human potential as individuals, a potential that includes the right to choose a fulfilling sexual relationship. Like the buxom cartoon character Vampirella, these new women vampires openly acknowledge that sexuality is a healthy and normal response, not a threat to the individual or the society. In fact, in most recent versions, the vampire often appears as more positive than his or her human counterparts.

During the past three decades, writers who have featured the vampire have focused on the individual's right to choose a different kind of existence, especially when that alternative does not cause harm to other individuals. Thus there has been increasing emphasis on the positive aspects of the vampire's eroticism and on his or her right to rebel against the stultifying constraints of society and a decreasing emphasis on the vampire's quarrel with traditional religious beliefs. In fact, recent writers have emphasized their vampires' desires for peaceful coexistence with human beings.

As a result of this more positive attitude, most twentieth-century interpretations of the vampire have been more light and playful than either their counterparts in nineteenth-century literature or even earlier folklore. This greater tolerance is undoubtedly the result of our growing acceptance of variations—even extreme variations—in individual behavior, an acceptance revealed partially by the number of films featuring lesbian vampires during the 1970s. In fact, Margaret L. Carter comments specifically on this growing toleration when she observes that the vampire is no longer "the universally feared and hated villain of nightmare tradition":

> Increase in knowledge of psychology and sociology no doubt contributes to the change in attitude. Today we no longer feel qualified to judge any man . . . as a monster. Current emphasis on minority problems may even cause a monster to be an appealing character, because he suffers for being "different." Furthermore, moral ambiguity is more acceptable in this century than the last; we are less apt than Stoker to consign any creature to irrevocable damnation. There is also the simple artistic problem of an overworked plot motif. Too many imitations of the "Dracula" pattern must inevitably pall on the reader.

Although Carter persists in referring to the vampire as a male figure, she is undoubtedly correct about the reasons for this increasing toleration, not to mention simple boredom with a literary motif that has become a cliche. Formerly monsters to be feared, both because of their sexual preferences and their bloodthirsty habits, vampires in twentieth-century popular culture are often presented as appealing figures rather than as threats; and the rare exceptions to this trend—*Fright Night* and *Last Rites*—suggest that the pendulum may be swinging away from this acceptance of human differences. However, it is simply too soon to make that judgment.

The character of the vampire continues to evolve, but one thing remains certain: The vampire in the twentieth-century has returned to being a kind of folk figure, a character in paperback novels—especially in science fiction, fantasy, and children's literature—in popular films and television, even in advertising. Originating in that most popular of literary forms—folklore—the vampire in the eighteenth- and nineteenth-centuries entered the cultural mainstream, when it attracted the attention of serious artists, writers, and thinkers. Today, despite the tremendous evolution in the vampiric character, the vampire itself seems to have returned to its rightful place as a subject of folk interest. Laughing uneasily about the obvious Freudian references or even aroused by the openly sensual na-

ture of the twentieth-century vampire, the modern reader or viewer grasps intuitively a fact that his more avant garde eighteenth and nineteenth century counterparts often attempted to present through various artistic media: The haunting face of the vampire is simply a darker version of our own. (pp. 160-64)

> *Carol A. Senf, "Making Sense of the Changes," in her* The Vampire in Nineteenth-Century English Literature, *Bowling Green State University Popular Press, 1988, pp. 140-64.*

Ronald Foust

[*In the following essay, Foust discusses psychological symbolism in vampire fiction.*]

Since its inception in the late eighteenth century, Gothic fiction has been such a popular and influential literary form that "an understanding of the literature of the last two hundred years requires a knowledge of the nature of Gothic" [Andrew Wright in an introduction to *The Castle of Otranto,* by Horace Walpole]. Despite its popularity, however, the "Gothic novel has not fared well among literary critics" who typically "treat the subject with chilly indifference or condescension" [Robert D. Hume, "Gothic versus Romantic," *PMLA* (1969)].

Of course, this general critical indifference has extended to the vampire tale. For example, Devendra Varma [in his *The Gothic Flame*] has called *Dracula* "probably the greatest horror tale of modern times," and yet criticism has not treated it seriously and, more surprisingly, has made no effort to connect it to the Gothic tradition. This aversion to the vampire motif includes even aficionados of "weird" fiction. Thus, although Peter Penzoldt [in his *The Supernatural in Fiction*], admits that "the psychological problem at the root of the Vampire archetype is a complex one," he nonetheless concludes that "the vampire motif is crude and primitive" because he can see in it merely a projection of Freudian somatic wish-fulfillment. Such critical aversion ignores the fact that the vampire motif has been employed in many of our greatest literary works, beginning with Book XI of *The Odyssey.*

As Varma has pointed out, the tale of terror appeals "to some deeply rooted instinct; an irresistible, inexplicable impulse drives us toward the macabre." Thus, despite critical neglect, Gothicism continues to thrive among a mass audience because it satisfies a hunger for an experience that is otherwise proscribed by social conventions. This experience constitutes for the reader-protagonist a psychological "rite of passage" based upon an imaginative encounter with the chthonic doppelgänger that Jung called the Shadow. Since this encounter is ultimately purgative—defamiliarizing and thus enriching the reader's diurnal experience—it is desired; however, since it initially awakens a dim species memory of man's original separation from and conquest of natural chaos, it involves him in peril (the "madness" that is a favored metaphor of the form) and is therefore feared. Finally, the uncanny effect that characterizes the vampire tale is attributable to the fact that the demonic adversary is a projection of the "buried Self," a dark double of both the reader and the fictive protagonist.

The earliest prose narrative of this kind is John Polidori's *The Vampyre* (1819), which is based on a five-page fragment by Lord Byron. In it we meet Lord Ruthven (Byron), the original Undead, a nobleman pallid and burdened with ennui whose "dead grey eye . . . pierce[s] through to the inward workings of the heart," causing awe in all who meet him. He takes an orphaned "young gentleman of the name of Aubrey" as his traveling companion, and together they set off on a Grand Tour.

Ruthven proceeds to debauch everyone he meets as the pair travel across Europe. Finally, in Athens, Aubrey falls in love with a Greek girl, Ianthe, who tells him "the tale of the living vampyre." Aubrey laughs at the superstition but is rebuked by the peasants who "shudder at his daring thus to mock a superior, infernal power." Later, while examining some ruins, he becomes so engrossed in his research that night falls and a storm breaks before he remembers to return to the village. Suddenly he hears a woman's cries coming from nearby. He rushes into a dark hovel and is "gripped by one whose strength seemed superhuman." As his attacker flees, the storm abruptly ceases and he discovers Ianthe dead: "upon her neck and breast was blood, and upon her throat were the marks of teeth having opened the vein." Still later Ruthven is shot during a struggle with bandits; on his deathbed he extracts an oath of silence from Aubrey concerning his habits and his fate. He dies and his body is placed on a rock so that it is "exposed to the first cold ray of the moon that rose after his death." Aubrey then returns to England to live with his sister, whom he takes to a ball where he sees "Lord Ruthven again before him, . . . the dead rise again!" Shock at seeing this revenant brings on a depression that deepens into temporary insanity as Aubrey broods over the mystery and power that Ruthven represents. Even when he learns that his sister has become engaged to marry "the monster," he cannot expose him, for each time he tries, a voice telepathically bids him "remember his oath." Although he feels powerless before Ruthven's supernatural reality, he finally rouses himself to action on the day of his sister's wedding and writes a note to her guardians exposing Ruthven. They rush to protect her but arrive to find that Lord Ruthven has disappeared and that Aubrey's sister has "glutted the thirst of a VAMPYRE!"

Polidori's novel both initiates the modern vampire story and adumbrates the major elements that will become the archetypal staples of the form. These include the vampire's "evil eye" or hypnotic power, its tremendous strength, its pallor and association with the moon, its immortality, its identity as a self-absorbed egotist who brings ruin on individuals and societies, its thirst for blood (an ancient attribute of the dead), and its associations with the grave (the hovel), with Satan, and with the love-crime that Mario Praz feels is at the heart of the vampire story. Thus, Polidori's narrative initiates the prose tradition of the vampire as waste-maker and introduces the master-slave relation that obtains between the demonic monster and the representatives of ordinary decency and innocence. In addition, we note that Aubrey is both drawn to and repelled by Ruthven and that both he and the guardians are ineffectual in protecting the treasure (the virginal sister). I shall return to the meaning of the relation between the vampire and a treasure; here I will merely point out that the vampire constitutes a threat to the integrity of a beloved object in Polidori's flawed original version of the theme.

The first full treatment of the motif occurs in Sheridan Le Fanu's beautiful but neglected "Carmilla," a minor masterpiece that greatly influenced Bram Stoker. It is the story of an eighteen-year-old English girl, Laura, who lives in Styria with her father, a retired English soldier, some miles from a ruined village, the former domain "of the proud family of Karnstein, now extinct." Early in the narrative, Laura recounts a dream she had as a child in which "I saw a solemn, but very pretty face. . . . It was that of a young lady who was kneeling, with her hands under the coverlet. . . . She caressed me with her hands, and lay down beside me on the bed, and drew me towards her, smiling. . . . I was awakened by a sensation as if two needles ran into my breast."

As this image implies, "Carmilla" is a story of lesbianism, which is the love-crime that is so necessary to the vampire motif. As the story begins, clouds of mist gather on Laura's estate as a servant discusses the moon's magnetic influence. Suddenly a runaway carriage approaches, "thundering along the road . . . with the speed of a hurricane." Since it is a lunary avatar, the vampire enters at night in moonlight and in mist. Furthermore, the images of thunder and of hurricane are appropriate to the vampire motif for reasons that will become apparent. The carriage overturns and its passenger, Carmilla Karnstein (stone-flesh), is invited to remain as Laura's guest. The two are mysteriously drawn to each other, and Laura recalls that Carmilla "used to place her pretty arms about my neck, draw me to her, and . . . murmur with her lips near my ear. . . . 'In the rapture of my enormous humiliation I live in your warm life, and you shall die—die, sweetly die—into mine. . . . [You will] learn the rapture of that cruelty, which is yet love.' " Carmilla's algolagnic passion is "like the ardour of a lover" and creates in Laura "a strange tumultuous excitement" that is compounded of both pleasure and "a vague sense of fear and disgust." In keeping with the vampire's role as lunar deity, Carmilla is pale and languid, eats nothing and appears only late in the afternoon. Her chthonic nature is implied when she is likened to a fish and to a cat. In addition, she has the gleaming eyes and the passionate gaze that are attributes of the vampire. As the two girls grow increasingly close, Carmilla makes her climactic demand of Laura: "You must come with me, loving me, to death. . . . Love will have its sacrifices. No sacrifice without blood." Love, blood, and death: it is this insistence upon *Liebestod* that most clearly reveals the vampire motif to be the epitome of Gothic *Schauer-Romantik* and that relates both to the Romantic tradition.

The vampire tale is a projection of the ancient theme of demonic possession. As Laura is being possessed, a friend, General Spielsdorf, arrives. His adopted daughter has died

> [The] uncanny effect that characterizes the vampire tale is attributable to the fact that the demonic adversary is a projection of the "buried Self," a dark double of both the reader and the fictive protagonist.
>
> —*Ronald Foust*

under odd circumstances, and he is convinced that she was the victim of their beautiful guest, Millarca (like Carmilla, an anagram of Mircalla, the vampire's true name), who sometimes takes "the shape of a beast" and who Spielsdorf is convinced is a revenant or vampire. His sole mission in life is now to find and destroy the monster in "the usual way, by decapitation, by the stake, and by burning." Together they travel to the ruined Karnstein village where they meet the original vampire-killer, Baron Vordenburg, a "fantastic old gentleman," who helps them find the monster's lair in a deserted churchyard. There they corner Carmilla, whose features undergo "an instantaneous and horrible transformation"; they grapple with her and are overwhelmed by her prodigious strength; and she then returns to her "amphibious existence" in the tomb. They eventually discover her coffin and, "in accordance with the ancient practice," drive a stake through her heart. Carmilla shrieks, writhes, and dies, whereupon the hunters decapitate her.

It is primarily in the manner of the vampire's destruction that one most clearly recognizes the myth of the dragon-battle that underlies the modern vampire tale. In its tremendous strength, destructiveness, and manner of dying, the vampire is a displaced version of the ancient image of the dragon that menaces a social unit, the members of which are individually powerless, until its threat is collectively overcome. Thus the conquest of the vampire represents at one level the victory of conventional society over a powerful, ancient, attractive but lethal prehistoric foe representing natural chaos.

Le Fanu elaborates all of Polidori's materials, including the vampire's association with mist, moonlight, and storms; the ambivalently attractive and repulsive effect it has upon its victim; its identity as a destroyer (the "deserted village" theme); its algolagnia (the love-crime), and its shape-shifting. In addition, Le Fanu adds the important elements of the picturesque castle, the vampire's chthonic anti-Christian connotations, and the mythopoeic importance of the dragon-battle culminating in staking and beheading as the effective means of liberating society from its ambiguously hated and loved Enemy.

Bram Stoker's *Dracula* (1897) is the masterpiece of *Schauer-Romantik* and the culmination of Gothic as a genre. It is Stoker's work which has been drawn upon by filmmakers and imitated by epigones such as Stephen King in *Salem's Lot*. Since *Dracula* is the most complete embodiment of the displaced myth of the dragon-battle that generates all vampire fiction, I shall discuss it at some length.

It opens as Jonathan Harker, an "orphan" who is engaged to be married, travels by carriage on May 4, "the eve of St. George's Day," from the village of Bistritz in Transylvania through the Borgos Pass toward the mountain that the native population calls "Isten szed!—God's seat!" Dracula's forbidding and ancient castle adorns the peak of the "cosmic mountain"; that is, castle and mountain together constitute a sacred center, a threshold that opens onto the three levels of heaven, earth, and the underworld. During the trip the coach rocks and sways through the darkness like a ship in a storm, and the vampire's association with the chaos of storms is again established. As the journey continues, Harker feels that he is "simply going over and over the same ground again." Thus the journey is the fictive equivalent of the mythic night-sea crossing in which the young initiate leaves the security of his home, is disoriented by experience, and enters a labyrinth. The mazelike quality of the temporal journey will be duplicated spatially in the form of the interior of the castle itself. This induction of the initiate into experience is a central feature of all Gothic fiction and is the narrative equivalent of the myth of engorgement, of being swallowed into a monster's belly.

When he arrives at the castle, Harker enters a courtyard which is constructed as a labyrinthine maze. He then meets Count Dracula, who introduces himself as a hunter—and indeed he is. The novel divides evenly into two parts based upon the metaphor of the hunt. During the first half, the vampire hunts his human prey; the narrative movement is from Transylvania to England as Dracula's power waxes to fullness. During the second half, his menace wanes as the human society wrests power from him and becomes the hunter, tracking him from civilization back to Transylvania, where his power disappears as they stake and behead him on the mountaintop at the foot of the castle. The story's form, then, is that of a circle divided, Yin-Yang-like, into sigmoid halves. This structure, suggestive of the waxing and waning of the moon, is apropos of the narrative's latent meaning, since the vampire tale is a modern displacement of an ancient myth in which a demonic lunar avatar is combated and finally overcome by a solar hero.

Harker's induction into supernatural reality soon deepens into horror as he realizes that he is Dracula's captive. Imprisoned at the top of the castle, he is visited by three of Dracula's sister-brides; they are succubi, "phantom shapes," who simply materialize from the moonlight. He pretends to sleep as one of them bends over him and prepares to kiss his throat. He feels "longing and at the same time deadly fear," a "voluptuousness which was both thrilling and repulsive"; Dracula arrives "in a storm of fury" and saves Harker for his own purposes. At his arrival the succubi suddenly "fade into the rays of the moonlight."

In desperation he decides to explore Dracula's room, which he enters perilously by scaling a portion of the castle wall. It is empty, and all that he discovers is a large pile of gold in one corner, all of it at least three hundred years old. He passes through an open door, a threshold, which leads "through a stone passage to a circular stairway." It is yet another maze, and he descends to the bottom where, in the bowels of the earth, he enters "a dark, tunnel-like passage, through which [comes] a deathly, sickly odor." There, in the interior of an ancient, dilapidated chapel, he finds the count lying in a coffin in the moribund state that is the nocturnal vampire's lot during the half of each day that is dominated by the influence of the sun. Later, when Van Helsing and the others corner Dracula in England, Harker slashes at him with his knife, tearing Dracula's clothing, from which falls a stream of gold. Thus Harker's discovery of Dracula's treasury is a crucial scene establishing the vampire as the guardian of a treasure hoard. I shall return to the meaning of this important motif. Harker finally escapes by scaling the castle ramparts and drops out of the narrative; we later learn that he has lain in delirium in a hospital in Budapest for weeks. In the meantime, Dracula has chartered a ship, the *Demeter,* which arrives covered with mist on the English coast during a storm. The ship's crew is missing, and only a corpse is found lashed to the helm. However, the ship's log is discovered, and it recounts the events aboard the *Demeter* for the month of July, during which time Dracula systematically has destroyed the ship's entire "society." It is important to note that the height of the vampire's power occurs in midsummer at sea where, taking the shape of mist, he creates yet another ruin, just as he has depopulated the area surrounding his castle. It is in its role as destroyer of social organizations that the modern vampire most clearly reveals its kinship with the mythic dragon which is its prototype.

In England, Dracula preys on Lucy Westenra, Arthur Holmwood's fiancée. Throughout this section Dracula's chthonic attributes are insisted upon: he is associated with mist, moonlight, and bats and seems "more like a wild beast than a man." As Lucy declines, the orthodox physician, John Seward, calls for assistance from his former teacher, Abraham Van Helsing. A more complex version of Le Fanu's Baron Vordenburg, Van Helsing, the vampire-killer, is a shaman: he is a physician, a teacher, a jurist, and a priest whose most effective medicines are the Christian armaments of crucifix, holy water, and the sanctified Host. Two things of importance now occur: Van Helsing adopts the members of the beleaguered society—Seward, Quincy Morris, Harker, Arthur, Mina, and Lucy each becomes "my child"—and he begins to use vegetation metaphors as analogies for human action. "My friend John, when the corn is grown . . . while the milk of its mother-earth is in him . . . the husbandman will pull the ear . . . I have sown my corn [i.e., made his plan of action], and Nature has her work to do in making it sprout"; Dracula has come to England where humanity grows "like the multitude of standing corn."

Lucy progressively weakens as Van Helsing struggles to save her life. Finally he is forced to give her blood transfusions from each of the four men to sustain her life. Nevertheless, she dies and becomes another of Dracula's brides. After her death, Arthur is in such shock that "his stalwart manhood seemed to have shrunk." Thus, possession by the Undead has a clear psychosexual dimension which gives a special urgency to the hunt for Dracula conducted throughout the remaining portion of the text. Lucy is now a lamia preying upon the children of London. When Van Helsing discovers this, she is tracked to her lair, where the men look upon her with loathing, and her transformed flesh is likened to that of Medusa. Van Helsing warns Arthur that "you are now in the bitter waters, my child" and must master this terror in order to drink "of the sweet waters"; that is, he must undergo this initiatory experience to achieve his manhood and Lucy's freedom. Thus, Arthur, looking "like a figure of Thor," hammers the stake into Lucy's heart. At this the "thing in the coffin writhed; and a hideous blood-curdling screech came from the opened lips. The body shook and quivered and twisted in wild contortions." The small band of humans, a microcosmic social order, by now associate Dracula with Satan and pledge to destroy the vampire, emblem of Night and chthonic chaos, in order to set "the earth free from a monster of the nether world."

The possession of Lucy, a love-crime occurring about midway in the story, represents the climactic point of the vampire's power. The division of the plot into halves is a structural device reifying Stoker's treatment of the motif since, among other things, the vampire is a lunar deity (hence its paleness, its languor, and its association with moonlight), whose progress is associated with the four cycles of the moon. The first half of the narrative is equivalent to the waxing of the moon and its fullness of influence; the second half recapitulates in dramatic form its waning and disappearance. This lunar association explains several important aspects of the vampire tale. As J. E. Cirlot points out [in *A Dictionary of Symbols*] "Man, from the earliest times, has been aware of the relationship between the moon and the tides, and of the more mysterious connexion between the lunar cycle and the physiological cycle of women." Thus the vampire is a personification of the moon, "the Master of Women." In addition, the moon's phases are "the source of inspiration for the Dismemberment myth" since the moon "is the being which does not keep its identity but suffers 'painful' modifications to its shape." The moon is the primordial and original shape-shifter, and this is a partial explanation of the vampire's ability to alter its form, as well as its association with that other archetypal shape-changer, the *loup-garou* or werewolf. However, there is another explanation of the vampire's ability to alter its form to which I shall return.

After his encounter with Dracula, Harker suffers so severely from the malady that had afflicted Arthur that Mina begs Van Helsing to restore her husband. Harker's journal entry explains the malady: "I felt impotent," he writes, and Van Helsing "made a new man of me" by his vigorous resistance to the vampire. Indeed, the making of an adolescent into a man is the novel's buried theme. The essential point is that the vampire does not produce the future—children through sexual union—but only a static, changeless present. He is an egotist who possesses others for the purpose of reproducing images of himself through an asexual "vamping" of the innocent. This is the psychological import behind the multitude of ruins the vampire creates and rules, as well as its association with the moon.

It is now October as the small band of humans turn hunter and stalk their enemy, whose power, though waning, remains great. The vampire is able still to attack and wound Mina in a hideous parody of the Christian sacrament of marriage. As she sleeps, Dracula comes to her as a red-capped column of mist during the full moon and performs a mock marriage ritual by chanting: "And you . . . are now to me, flesh of my flesh; blood of my blood; kin of my kin . . . my companion and my helper." The men rush to her bedroom only to see the vampire holding her in a "terrible and horrid position, with her mouth to the open wound in his breast." Upon their arrival Dracula becomes savage, and they banish him with the sacred wafer and crucifix. Mina honestly admits that her unnatural mating with the vampire was horrible but that, "strangely enough, I did not want to hinder him." The remainder of the story constitutes an act of ritual atonement, the result of which is the union of a cleansed Harker and Mina, the divine pair, in a marriage resulting in the restoration of sexual vitality and in childbearing.

We are now in a position to see a pattern emerging: the vampire threatens the cosmic *hieros gamos,* the "sacred marriage," that is the primordial model of human social organization. Lord Ruthven destroys Aubrey's Ianthe (and Aubrey's self-confidence, his "manhood") and then, on her wedding night, his sister; Carmilla seduces Laura and offers a lesbian substitute for marriage and reproduction; Dracula blasts Arthur's and Lucy's fruitfulness and then turns his ruinous passion upon Mina. Having rendered Harker impotent, he begins his seduction of Harker's bride, and he taunts his human enemies thus: "Your girls that you all love are mine already . . . my creatures, to do my bidding and to be my jackals when I want to feed."

However, his boast is forced; from this point on, the vampire's power is clearly on the wane as the human band organize against him, find and sterilize all but one of his coffin-homes, and force him to take flight. A white-haired but rejuvenated Harker takes command of the hunters, who track the vampire back to Transylvania. The experience of the ancient Enemy has been so estranging that the hunters begin to lose track of modern "objective" time and instead become "accustomed to watch for sunrise and sunset"; that is, they are perilously close to falling back into the rhythms of nature.

It is now November and snow is falling around Castle Dracula as the little band overtake the gypsy wagoneers who are conveying the vampire's coffin to the castle. A struggle ensues at the peak of "God's seat," the gypsies are overcome, and in the *sparagmos* or ritualistic tearing to pieces, Harker is able to slash Dracula's throat with his Kukri knife as Quincy Morris, fatally wounded, plunges his bowie knife into the vampire's heart at the exact moment that the sun falls behind the horizon. With this ritual act of staking and dismemberment, the curse passes away, and Mina stands cleansed and bathed in rosy light.

A "Note" is appended in which Harker relates that "Seven years ago we all went through the flames"; in the meantime, Mina has given birth to a boy who is given a "bundle of names" that link "all our little band of men together." Harker and Mina also return to Castle Dracula—which stands "as before, reared high above a waste of desolation"—but now the labyrinth, divested of the Minotaur at its center, is harmless and merely picturesque.

We now are prepared to understand both the myth of which the vampire tale is a displaced version and the crypto-religious nature of the reader's encounter with this epitome of Gothicism. It is no accident that Harker's initiation into supernatural reality begins on the eve of St. George's Day. The vampire tale is the most powerful modern reenactment of the ancient myth of the dragon-slaying, of which the contest between St. George and the dragon is the premier English version. In the myth society is threatened by a waste-making dragon, chthonic emblem of the forces of Night and Chaos; a solar hero reestablishes social order (i.e., rescues a treasure, often in the form of a virginal maiden, or alternatively, the reawakening of the fertility of the land) by pursuing, destroying, and dismembering the *feond mancynnes,* mankind's ancient Enemy. Typically, the *sparagmos* or dismemberment ushers in new life and returned social vigor.

The reader's encounter with the vampire reenacts perhaps our most ancient ritual experience and "one of the oldest battles in literature," which is "the fight between the sun-god and a monster deity," [according to Paul Newman in his *The Hill of the Dragon*]. The best-known version in Anglo-American mythology is the legend of St. George, although its origins are much more ancient and extend backward in time through the Norse legend of Thor and the Midgard Serpent, to Greek tales of Zeus and Typhon, Apollo and the Python, and Cadmus and the founding of Thebes from the dragon's sown teeth. However, the original version is contained in our oldest written document, the *Enuma Elish* (Babylonian Genesis, circa 1500 B.C.). There the solar god, Marduk, "combats the evil she-dragon, Tiamat," his mother. She is also the spirit of salt water who symbolizes [according to Peter Hogarth and Cal Clery in their *Dragons*] "evil or primeval chaos," which explains the dragon's frequent association with storms and the ocean. The serpentine Tiamat "was the first dragon, and her awesome ever-changing image has haunted mankind ever since."

This is the myth that informs such later mythico-religious documents as *Beowulf,* where, we recall, the solar hero encounters "the serpent, the dread malicious spirit," the "people's foe, the dread fiery dragon," and strikes it in the head with his sword. The dragon then takes Beowulf's "whole neck between his sharp teeth" and inflicts a mortal wound, as Wiglaf strikes "the vengeful stranger a little lower," killing it. The wounded Beowulf cuts the dragon in half and bids Wiglaf enter "the lair of the serpent, the ancient creature who flew by twilight" and bring out the treasure the dragon had guarded. There Wiglaf finds "glittering gold lying on the ground." (As in Stoker's tale the gold in *Beowulf* has lain in the ground for three hundred years.) Beowulf dies, and his men push "the dragon, the serpent, over the cliff—let the waves take the guardian of the treasure, the flood enfold him." The dragon is buried in the sea because that is the chaotic natural element it emblemizes. Thus, the modern vampire's attributes—its power, its chthonic characteristics, its ritualized manner of dying—are the necessary results of the requirements of the archetypal story, that of the dragon-battle, that lies at the heart of all Gothic fiction.

"The Dragon is the greatest of all serpentes and bestes," says a Medieval document. It "dwelleth in depe caves of the ground"; it also "fleeth in to the ayre & bethet in the ayre in such wyse that it semeth to be a gret tempest in the ayre & his wynges . . . be facyoned lyke the wynges of a battle that flyeth in the twy lyght & where the dragon abideth there is the ayre dark and full of venymous corruption." Mythographically considered, the vampire is a displaced form of the dragon. When discovered and staked, it writhes and agonizes because that is the ritualized behavior of the dragon symbol of chaos and is thus associated with the moon, storms, fogs and mist, and the night. It is also a chthonic divinity and thus a shape-shifter, appearing now as a bat, now as a wolf, now as an elemental mist or dust motes, and is likened to cats, fish, serpents, and lizards. It is, in effect, the personified spirit of the multitudinous power of the various elements of primordial Nature wreaking vengeance on social organizations *because* they are organized and, thus, "unnatural." Its prime targets, then, are marriage and the family since these constitute the cornerstones of civilization. Hence the vampire's typical victim is a young, marriageable innocent tremulously poised at the vulnerable turning point between childhood freedom and adult responsibility.

The popularity of all Gothic fiction, especially the vampire tale, is understandable in terms of the reader's repressed desire to experience vicariously this myth in which the villain, always some displacement of the dragon, threatens the reader's psychological integrity with "possession." The resultant effect is what Freud called "the uncanny," the ambivalent desire and dream which are the result of experiencing the alien Other as a projection of our own buried impulse toward disorder and, perhaps, death. It is projected repeatedly in these fictions as a wish-fulfillment in which the threatened innocent—Aubrey, Laura, Mina, or Harker—is momentarily overcome by the loved and hated Other, only to be rescued by the archetype that Jung called "the wise old man." The villain is the Shadow, the "negative side of the personality" of which the reader must become aware by "recognizing the dark aspects of the personality as present and real." The villain, then, is a psychopomp, "a mediator between the conscious and the unconscious and a personification of the latter," [according to R. F. C. Hull in his *The Portable Jung.*]

Psychologically considered, the fictive dragon-battle "has three main components: the hero, the dragon, and the treasure" [Erich Newmann, *The Origins and History of Consciousness*]. Dracula sleeps at the foot of a passageway linked to a treasure hoard because he is a modern manifestation of the dragon. The treasure represents the hero's Self, his maturity which must be won from a serpentine adversary who represents a fear of "relapse into the body-bound chthonic world of animality." Thus, the vampire tale constitutes an initiation ritual, a "rite of passage," for the reader-protagonist. As Mircea Eliade has pointed out [in his *The Sacred and the Profane: The Nature of Religion*], the initiate must pass "beyond the profane, unsanctified condition" and discover "the true dimensions of existence" before he can "assume the responsibility that goes with being a man . . . [since] access to spirituality is expressed "in a symbolism of death and rebirth." Only when Harker has slain the chthonic dragon of his own primordial animality can he "cleanse" Mina and redeem the sexual function necessary for the regeneration of society.

Dracula begins in May and ends in November, spanning the six-month vegetation cycle; the vampire charters a ship, the *Demeter,* in July and while at sea (where, being an avatar of Tiamat, he has his greatest strength) he destroys an entire microcosmic society as he had done before. He then threatens a new society, characterized by preparations for multiple weddings, with similar ruin. His destructive efforts partially succeed until he is overthrown by a "solar youth" and a "wise old man." Together they dismember him in ancient fashion, and from this act new life arises.

Overcoming the dragon constitutes an imaginative cosmogony; that is, it recapitulates the myth of an originative creative act of consciousness by which primordial man imperfectly separated himself from the preconsciousness of Nature. The vampire, therefore, is not merely a "crude motif"; rather, it is a hierophany, an "*act of manifestation* of the sacred" in which the reader shares. The reader experiences what may be called crypto-religious emotions in his purely imaginative encounter with the numinosity—the power, the mystery, the awesomeness—of the vampire. As Glen St. John Barclay notes [in his *Anatomy of Horror: The Masters of Occult Fiction*], "The inherent appeal of the story of the occult lies in its capacity not to exorcise faith in the unknown, but to reinforce it," since any fiction that "refers to the intervention of the supernatural in human affairs necessarily affirms that the supernatural exists."

The vampire tale can be thought of as the climactic development of the Gothic novel, the appeal of which lies in its ability to satisfy an ancient hunger for numinous experiences repressed by the reader's conscious understanding of the limits of reality. Behind the lurid image of the vampire lurks the shadowy dragon, our repressed double, psychopomp of the Id, our barely buried "secret sharer." Thus, the vampire tale is the epitome of Gothic fiction, an understanding of which is essential to a complete literary history, since "the study of dragons is the study of the human mind." (pp. 73-83)

Ronald Foust, "Rite of Passage: The Vampire Tale as Cosmogonic Myth," in Aspects of Fantasy: Selected Essays from the Second International Conference on the Fantastic in Literature and Film, *edited by William Coyle, Greenwood Press, 1986, pp. 73-84.*

VAMPIRE FICTION AND SCIENCE FICTION

Joan Gordon

[*In the following essay, Gordon distinguishes between "the evil vampire of horror fiction" and "the good vampire of speculative fiction," asserting that since 1980 writers have increasingly depicted vampires as characters with moral sensitivity.*]

Vampires in fiction presently enjoy a rebirth of popularity. Certainly the recent craze for horror fiction offers some explanation, but because many vampires of the eighties invite our sympathy, their horrific nature sometimes pales next to other, more intriguing concerns. I would like, then, to examine a number of sympathetic vampires, all in fiction published since 1980.

I do not mean to suggest that all modern vampire novels sympathize with the vampire. Skipp and Spector's *The Light at the End* (1986) features utterly unredeemable vampires, utterly inexplicable in their motives and utterly loathsome in their feeding habits. In the fine old tradition of horror fiction, this novel seeks only to scare the bejesus out of its readers. David Bischoff's vampires, android creatures, are unsympathetic, parasitic, and destructive, if not absolutely repellent or even particularly scary (*Vampires of Nightworld:* 1981). I am more interested, however, in the vampires with whom we sympathize, because such an allegiance is surprising. Although one can find pleasant vampires in earlier science fiction, they are rare. There are Theodore Sturgeon's *Some of Your Blood* (1961) and Hal Clement's two stories, "Assumption Unjustified" (1946) and "A Question of Guilt" (1976). Chelsea Quinn Yarbro's *Saint-Germain* series of vampire novels begins in 1978 with the publication of *Hotel Transylvania* but continues well into the 1980s. Anne Rice's *Interview With the Vampire* was published in 1976 but its much richer companion volume, *The Vampire Lestat,* appeared in 1985.

Since 1980, in contrast, there have been a great many novels with sympathetic vampires. In *Crimson Kisses* by Asa Drake (pseud. Nina and Dean Andersson, 1981), the vampire is satanic, guilty of the most despicable carnage, yet shown as an admirable creature. Timmy Valentine of S. P. Somtow's *Vampire Junction* (pseud. Somtow Sucharitkul, 1984) accepts the nauseating crimes of his fellow vampires and for a while, so do we. George R. R. Martin's *Fevre Dream* (1982) shows a vampire trying to mend his bloodthirsty ways. The vampires of Whitley Strieber's *The Hunger* (1981), Anne Rice's *The Vampire Lestat* (1985), and Suzy McKee Charnas's *Vampire Tapestry* (1980) all kill discreetly, making it yet easier for us to accept their predatory natures. The eponymous heroes of Tanith Lee's *Sabella* (1980) and Chelsea Quinn Yarbro's *The Saint-Germain Chronicles* (1983), the narrator of *I, Vampire* (1984) by Jody Scott, and the vampires of Michael Talbot's *The Delicate Dependency* (1982) find it unnecessary to kill. Regardless of the mayhem level, we are meant to sympathize with these vampires in every case, they are, almost always, the protagonists of the stories, and we see the world from their vantage point. In a single

exception, *The Delicate Dependency,* we learn along with the narrator to understand the vampire.

Imagine two poles: at one lies the vampire as utterly despicable and at the other the vampire as perfectly admirable. Somewhere along the path between these two poles lie all these sympathetic vampires. At the despicable pole, we find the evil vampire of horror fiction; at the other, the good vampire of speculative fiction. Toward the evil pole the vampire is a supernatural being, his behavior is violent and disgusting, the "ick factor" is high in numerous, lovingly described scenes of gore, and our sympathies put us in a morally untenable position. The vampires of *Crimson Kisses, Vampire Junction, Fevre Dream,* and *The Hunger* lie at varying degrees between this pole and some neutral equator.

For example, Asa Drake's Vlad, the dashing and romantic impaler of *Crimson Kisses,* is an agent of the devil; his sadistic and ruthless treatment of everyone he meets is described in graphic and vile detail, and we are horrified to find ourselves anxiously hoping for his success in these grisly endeavors. At this dismal pole, our unlikely sympathy is evoked through a third person viewpoint limited to Vlad and his satanic girlfriend. It is only because we see through Vlad's eyes and hear his thoughts—never seeing through the eyes of his victims or hearing their anguish—that we come to side with Vlad. There is no attempt to justify Vlad's behavior; rather, the glamor is meant to lie with his sadistic evil—he is an instrument of Satan.

Somtow Sucharitkul comes close to this nadir in *Vampire Junction.* His vampire is sympathetic all the while he, and especially his cohorts, behave reprehensibly. We find him sympathetic not only because of the viewpoint, but also because Timmy Valentine has the form and seemingly helpless charm of a child, and because he is not an agent of evil but the embodiment of a universal archetype. Although we are never meant to approve of his mass-murdering companions, we tend to duplicate Timmy's mere sadness with their indiscretion, rather than having a more appropriate moral response to the carnage. We are distanced morally also because the vampires' existence hinges somehow upon our own Jungian race consciousness—it's our fault.

Most of the vampires of George R. R. Martin's steamboat gothic *Fevre Dream* are not only evil, disgusting, and supernatural, but also unsympathetic; only one, Joshua, is sympathetic. He recognizes the immoral nature of his kind's predation and rejects it, struggling to become something harmless; he even attempts to reform his colleagues. There is no attempt to glamorize the evil or shift blame; thus, Martin manages to give us a sympathetic vampire without forcing us into a dubious moral position.

And just a bit farther from that evil pole is the elegant vampire of Whitley Strieber's *The Hunger.* Miriam Blaylock is the last of an ancient species; she is a super-predator, not supernatural, and she kills discreetly for her survival. Of course, she has an undead friend who is far less discreet and far more morally problematic, who also provides the reader with the requisite gore of a horror story. As in *Crimson Kisses* and *Vampire Junction,* we find ourselves expected to accept morally reprehensible behavior—indiscriminate killing—because Blaylock accepts it among her companions.

As I look toward this evil pole in my paradigm of sympathetic vampires, I notice first that all the novels which allow the vampires an elemental evil are written as horror novels. That makes obvious sense—the horror genre requires evil as well as ick to make our skin crawl. In most cases (Strieber's is the exception) the vampire is supernatural: an agent of the devil, an embodiment of an archetype, or just an inexplicable monster. Supernatural beings are unknowable and uncontrollable, hence scarier.

More intriguingly, all are written by men, suggesting perhaps that the vampire is more compellingly creepy for male writers than for female ones or that women writers tend to avoid the horror genre even when they use its typical characters. Why might the vampire be a more terrifying character for male writers? The answer may lie in traditional male views of power and predation. The vampire is a predator who exerts power over his prey; every successful predator does. If one is acculturated to viewing relationships in terms of competitive power—the punishment of the weak by the strong, the subjugation of the inferior by the superior, the determinism of evolution or the chain of being—then a vampire or any other superior predator will necessarily seem threatening (and most threatening through its evocation in the reader of self-doubt). Supporting this view of power are such traditional notions as the male head of the household and the male being physically stronger than the female, especially when these roles are combined with the equations of "fittest" with the winner in combat and of might with right.

When we think of power as the ability to overpower, the predator overpowers his prey; the emphasis is upon an unequal relationship and inevitably upon cruelty—thus, the evil vampire whose power over his prey is both extraordinary and cruel. His prey is clearly a victim, forced into subjugation, cruelly treated, suffering pain. If this is indeed the culturally male view of power, then a super-predator whose ability to subjugate goes beyond that of a human male is particularly threatening to a man: ideal subject matter for a scary story.

But I also made another suggestion: that women writers tend to avoid the genre even when using its typical characters. If female notions of power and strength differ from male ones, it would not be surprising if the creatures who represent power were different as well. In feminist rethinking of the traditional power structure, the male head of household has been replaced not by a female boss but by equal partners. Female physical strength has lain not in the ability to overpower but in stamina and flexibility. Thus, power does not involve a rigid chain of command or competition; instead, it focuses on cooperation and endurance. Such creatures as vampires, associated with power, no longer hold threatening positions. Rather, predators or not, they become super-survivors instead of super-killers. To survive, they must live in harmony with their world, be flexible, adaptable, and possess stamina. These are hardly threatening or fearsome traits; the vampire retains its strength but loses its terror.

And it is true that in the recent vampire novels by women, the vampires are not, in themselves, terrifying. I might add that some of the least blood-thirsty vampires in recent fiction reside in Michael Talbot's *The Delicate Dependency,* illustrating that, while the domain of the vicious vampire may be exclusively male territory these days, the domain of the gentle vampire is not exclusively female territory.

So we come to the other pole in my paradigm where stands the perfectly admirable vampire. I have said that toward this pole the novels are not horror fiction but speculative fiction. Their marketing would seem to belie that: Yarbro's series is described as "historical horror"; the others are often shelved with horror fiction simply because that's where vampires belong. I would argue, however, that horror is the least of the concerns in these novels. When I asked Chelsea Quinn Yarbro (at the 1986 WisCon) why she wrote about vampires, she said that her real interest was in writing historical fiction but that since horror fiction is so much more marketable, she chose to elide the two genres. Each volume of the *Saint-Germain* series offers at least one passage of entertainingly graphic carnage that is historically accurate, plot-forwarding, and completely unprovoked by the gentlemanly vampire. But the carnage is not the central point in any of these novels: Historical ambiance and the development of Saint-Germain's character are much more important. Although they may please the horror fiction reader, these novels are not really part of the genre. As for the other novels I shall be discussing, the presence of such well-disciplined and urbane vampires and the absence of any evil night-stalkers puts them outside the compass of horror fiction.

So what characteristics do these novels share which reside nearer the good pole in my paradigm? I place above the equator and heading toward the benign zenith: Charnas's *Vampire Tapestry,* Rice's *The Vampire Lestat,* Lee's *Sabella,* Scott's *I, Vampire,* Yarbro's *Saint-Germain* series, and Talbot's *The Delicate Dependency.* It is easier to find sympathetic vampire novels in which the author finds something good to say about vampirism than it is to find novels where the vampires do evil while we may sympathize with them. All but one are by women, suggesting some feminist connection. The vampire is always sophisticated, urbane, knowledgeable in the ways of the world—he or she has usually been around for a long time. In four of these six novels, the vampire does not need to kill; in the other two (*Tapestry* and *Lestat*) the vampire kills discreetly and in modest quantity. In all six cases, the vampire examines the morality of its behavior.

In none of these novels is the vampire supernatural. Rather he, or in two cases (*Sabella* and *I, Vampire*) she, is transformed perhaps by a virus (*Lestat* and *Dependency*) or by a defective gene (*I, Vampire*). Or it may be a member of a different species, as was the case in *The Hunger,* and is so more sympathetically in *Vampire Tapestry* and *Sabella.* Saint-Germain may be an exception since his vampirism is connected with some proto-Etruscan priesthood, but his origins are only discussed vaguely, religion holds no power over him, and his strengths and limitations are so carefully delineated that there is no sense of the supernatural about him. In fact, though all of these vampires are more powerful than human beings, they are, being natural, controllable and understandable, less than fearsome. We do not sympathize with them in spite of their evil ways, but because they aren't really evil.

Why might the vampire be a more terrifying character for male writers? The answer may lie in traditional male views of power and predation.

—Joan Gordon

Connected with these characteristics—the vampires' natural existence, their knowledgeability, their self-examination, and their feminist tendencies—and as a result of them, we can find several thematic concerns which all six novels share. These themes include the nature of power, the nature of love, and the connection between the two; male and female approaches to the archetype of the vampire; and cross-species responsibility with its implications about ecology and human relations. I have previously written of the first two sets of issues so I shall discuss only the last set.

Cross-species responsibility is, of course, more than a purely speculative concern—how to behave when confronted by our first alien being. It has to do, in our mundane world, with ecology—the relationships among all the creatures on this planet—and by analogy, with human dynamics—the relationships between the sexes, among individuals, and among the many ethnic, racial, religious, and political groups of human beings. One way to explore all these relationships is to look at the relationship between predator and prey. As we have already seen, novels with evil vampires portray an unequal relationship between predator and prey. In the natural world, such an unfair relationship would result in an imbalance between predators and prey; first the prey would be decimated and the world overrun by predators, and next the predators would die of starvation. So we might argue that benign vampires are more realistic.

Edward Weyland, the vampire in Suzy McKee Charnas's *Tapestry,* and Anne Rice's vampire Lestat lie closest to the equator because they do indeed kill human beings. They are natural predators and their prey is human. Wolves don't feel guilty about eating deer: they must to survive, and besides, they aren't self-aware. Weyland and Lestat must kill humans to survive, and they only kill to survive; so why should they feel guilty? We may feel uncomfortable and find vampires evil because we are their prey, but surely we are not evil just because beef cattle, for instance, might find us so. Of course, beef cattle aren't thinking beings so they cannot judge us—or at least they can't know what we're up to. But we are thinking beings and we can judge our predators. Does the fact of our understanding devalue their need to survive? If all our food sources knew what we were up to, would we be morally obligated to

starve? No. Each species has the obligation to survive, though not at the expense of destroying another species. Fictional vampires, then, are evil when they destroy wantonly—they'll destroy our species (and then their own). But killing to survive is morally acceptable—we accept it in ourselves, we accept it in these novels.

Here is one side of the issue of cross-species responsibility: each species' obligation to allow the existence of the others has nothing to do with relative superiority or inferiority. Self-awareness makes no difference. By extrapolation, then, these novels imply that cultures, races, and clusters of believers must allow diversity as well, even if they find other groups of people inferior.

But there is another side to this issue of cross-cultural responsibility. It has everything to do with sentience and it is morally more ambiguous. The wolf doesn't feel guilty—it isn't a thinking being—but we, like the vampire, are self-aware, and we may feel guilty. In both *Tapestry* and *Lestat,* the vampire's sentience makes him aware of the suffering of his prey, and of its existence not just as a species but as an individual. Such awareness is a kind of love and it makes predation and survival a moral conundrum. When Weyland sees his prey as individuals, cares for and loves a few of those individuals, he can no longer function as a predator, and so he sleeps until he can "rise restored, eyes once more bright and unreflective as a hawk's and heart as ruthless as a leopard's." The thinking predator cannot resolve his survival with the killing it necessitates; so he must sacrifice his awareness. The novel ends.

Similarly, Lestat is warned early in his career of the dangers of seeing his prey as individuals: "He grows irresistibly to love mortals. He comes to understand all things in love. . . . There finally comes a moment when he cannot bear to take life, or bear to make suffering, and nothing but madness or his own death will ease his pain." Lestat does not resolve this anguish with madness, death, or sleep, but struggles to resolve self-awareness with survival. The closest he comes to resolution is a world view in which vampires exist not as a part of a divine plan but as part of a Savage Garden, the world of nature without gods or spiritual meaning. Here Lestat finds meaning as an existentialist does, by making it through the exercise of moral choice. Lestat's pain is not greatly eased by this philosophy but Anne Rice promises a third book in *The Chronicles of the Vampires* where he might have better luck.

Other vampires resolve the moral puzzle by surviving without killing. Sabella and *I, Vampire*'s Sterling O'Blivion come of age as vampires, mature morally, when they learn how to survive without killing. Under the auspices of an alien lover, Sterling learns to grow a more suitable morality through "advanced physics," to "project whatever reality you want." This option is not available to the rest of us, however, so we look to Sabella. She learns that the relationship between predator and prey does not require the death of one. Her lover shows her that she can control her appetite. If she takes only what she needs to survive, her prey will survive as well, and furthermore, the relationship can be one of sharing rather than victimizing. The prey offers nourishment, the predator takes only what is needed. The relationship works because each partner understands and trusts the other; the individual can be acknowledged. The vampires of *The Delicate Dependency* make similar acknowledgement. Their relationship to their food supply is not so intimate as Sabella's is to her lover, but it is compassionate. The prey do not suffer; rather, they are employees with job security and beneficent employers.

In the *Saint-Germain* books, Yarbro's kindly and urbane vampire offers even more: a symbiotic arrangement. Saint-Germain survives on the nourishment he takes from human blood; but instead of just taking, he exchanges. The human being takes erotic and emotional pleasure, feels emotional well-being. For Saint-Germain as well, the point is in the touch, the love exchanged in the process. Predation would diminish the nourishment.

In all three works, nourishment is freely given and gratefully received. Power resides not only with the taker but with the nurturer as well, though less so in Michael Talbot's novel than in the other two. I suspect that it is a feminist vision to see power in the giver of nourishment as well as in the taker, to see that giving and taking can be an equal exchange rather than a one-way movement.

Perhaps the final question to be asked is: why is the vampire a hero for the 'eighties? Well, there is a cynical answer: a greedy and rapacious age requires a greedy and rapacious hero. *Crimson Kisses, Vampire Junction,* and *The Hunger* supply that kind of hero. But all the other sympathetic vampire novels I have discussed suggest less cynical answers. Perhaps we are beginning to rethink survival in a culturally diverse world. Perhaps exchange rather than hierarchy is the way to a global village. (pp. 227-34)

> *Joan Gordon, "Rehabilitating Revenants, or Sympathetic Vampires in Recent Fiction," in* Extrapolation, *Vol. 29, No. 3, Fall, 1988, pp. 227-34.*

Veronica Hollinger

[In the following essay, Hollinger compares the theme of vampirism in science fiction to the traditional treatment of the vampire in Dracula.*]*

That SF is capable of evoking in its readers "a sense of wonder" has become something of a critical cliché. Another and equally characteristic side of the SF coin, however, is its role in what we might term "the domestication of the fantastic." H. G. Wells introduces this issue, for example, in his "Preface to the *Scientific Romances*" (1933). "Nothing," he writes, "remains interesting where anything may happen." For this reason, the SF writer should provide the reader with orderly ground-rules for his or her fictional universes. Wells concludes that "[the writer] must help [the reader] in every possible unobtrusive way to *domesticate* the impossible hypothesis" (Wells's emphasis). This is reiterated, in different terms, by Eric S. Rabkin, who argues that

> what is important in the definition of science fiction is . . . the idea that paradigms do control our view of all phenomena, that within these paradigms all normal problems can be solved,

and that abnormal occurrences must either be explained or initiate the search for a better (usually more inclusive) paradigm.

For this reason, while the SF genre expands the scope and the variety of the physical universe, it often does so—ironically perhaps—at the expense of what cannot be explained in terms of natural law and scientific possibility—i.e., at the expense of the super-natural or the un-natural, the ontologically indeterminate area of the fantastic.

From the generic perspective of SF, the territory of the fantastic lies just across the border, and SF has always been effective at expanding its own territories through the scientific rationalization of elements originally located in the narrative worlds of fantasy. In Colin Manlove's words, "the science fiction writer throws a rope of the conceivable (how remotely so does not matter) from our world to his [or hers] . . . ." Manlove points out that "as soon as the 'supernatural' has become possible we are no longer dealing with fantasy but with science fiction."

A classic example of this domestication of the fantastic occurs in Arthur C. Clarke's *Childhood's End* (1953), a novel which draws the conventional figure of the devil—bat-wings, barbed tail, and all—across the border of the supernatural into SF territory. *Childhood's End* not only provides a "plausible" narrative framework for its demystification of the devil-figure; it also aims to explain the powerful ongoing presence of this figure in our collective race-memory. Clarke thus manages to transform mythic fantasy into alien reality while maintaining the "sense of wonder" inscribed in the original figure.

The vampire, a less grandiose but equally horrific archetype, is one satanic figure which is currently enjoying a resurgence of literary and critical popularity. "Immortalized" by Bram Stoker in his classic Gothic novel, *Dracula* (1897), and still most typically associated with the horror genre, the vampire too has occasionally crossed the border from fantasy to SF, undergoing varieties of domestication in works such as Richard Matheson's *I Am Legend* (1954), Tanith Lee's *Sabella, or the Blood Stone* (1980), and David Bischoff's *Vampires of Nightworld* (1981).

I want to concentrate in this essay on two other texts which introduce the figure of the vampire into the narrative worlds of SF in very different ways: Colin Wilson's *The Space Vampires* (1976) and Jody Scott's *I, Vampire* (1984). Although each may be said to parody—in the broadest sense of the term—both traditional vampire narratives and traditional SF treatments of the alien invasion story, it is interesting to examine the extent to which Wilson's compliance with previously established conventions serves to consolidate a conservative ideology, while Scott's more playful rejection of the absolutes of generic boundaries both derives from and results in a more radical ideological coloration. As Linda Hutcheon notes in her study of the forms and functions of parody, "the presupposition of both a law and its transgression bifurcates the impulse of parody: it can be normative and conservative, or it can be provocative and revolutionary."

The Space Vampires is strongly influenced by A. E. van Vogt's novella, "Asylum" (1942), as Wilson acknowledges in an introductory note to his text. The makers of *Life-force,* the film version of *The Space Vampires,* took their title from van Vogt's story of evil aliens whose "unnatural lusts" include a passion for human energy. Wilson's vampiric aliens share this appetite for the "life force" and are thus not particularly remote displacements of Stoker's quintessential blood-drinkers.

Wilson's text is directly concerned with the expansion of scientific paradigms to include the "abnormal occurrence" of the vampire in ways which will rationally account for its existence. His narrative is based upon the theory that a kind of metaphorical vampirism is natural to human beings and that it may be either malevolent (as when one deliberately drains another's psychic energy) or benevolent (as when one shares one's own energy). This theory is developed after the discovery of "the space vampires," ruthless aliens who suck the life-energy from their victims and leave them either dead or helplessly enslaved.

The story follows the efforts of Wilson's human characters, led by the heroic Commander Carlsen, to find and then expel three of these vampire-like aliens, who have inadvertently been brought back to Earth by a team of human explorers under the mistaken assumption that they are dead. Wilson rather neatly plays by the rules of popular vampire lore here, since, as the text later reminds us, "it is a characteristic of vampires that they *must* be invited. They cannot take the initiative" (Wilson's emphasis).

While Scott's novel was published by Ace Books under the SF rubric, it is rather more careless of generic boundaries than is Wilson's. It, too, peoples its narrative world with aliens from outer space, but, apart from a casual reference to the defective gene inherited by its vampire protagonist, it makes very little effort to explain the "abnormal occurrence" of this figure within its fictional world. Among the ironically surreal events which take place in *I, Vampire,* there are no fewer than two alien invasions: the background conflict of the novel is between the benevolent race of Rysemians, who are determined to drag humanity up the evolutionary ladder in spite of itself, and the sinister Sajorians, for whom humanity provides a booming market in intergalactic slaves. Scott's vampire, however, is neither human nor alien: a kind of link between the two, Sterling O'Blivion remains an inexplicable phenomenon inhabiting a narrative world which can accommodate both "semi-mythological creature[s]" like herself and genuine SF aliens.

While *I, Vampire* can be read as a self-contained narrative, it is also the sequel to Scott's SF novel, *Passing for Human* (1977). The protagonist of this earlier work is Benaroya, the repulsively fish-like Rysemian "anthropologist" who reappears in *I, Vampire* disguised as Virginia Woolf. It is interesting to note here that, in *Passing for Human,* Scott, like Clarke in *Childhood's End,* makes use of a "domesticated" version of the devil. In her satiric fiction, however, this devil-as-alien is no benevolent savior but the quintessentially evil leader of the Sajorian invasion. Scaulzo, "the Prince of Darkness," is able to mesmerize his human victims because of their inherent gullibility: "primitives always go for that type of schmaltz. . . ."

Passing for Human was recently reprinted by The Women's Press as part of its series of feminist SF, and *I, Vampire* continues Scott's critique of contemporary social and sexual politics. Specific to the latter novel, however, is her satiric attack on the repressive nature of social and discursive representations of the Other, accomplished through the delineation of Sterling O'Blivion's struggles against "readings" which attempt to appropriate her both as a woman and as a vampire. Benaroya/Woolf addresses this problem directly at the end of the narrative: "What is a vampire? Who projected that image onto you? My guess is, the people of Transylvania *created* you out of boredom and frustration" (Scott's emphasis). Even before this realization, however, Sterling refuses to rationalize or to justify her existence: "if my actual history sounds like outtakes from a tacky B movie, or worse, well, that's not my problem. I am what I am, as God and Popeye both say when you wake them out of a sound sleep."

After centuries of keeping a low profile, Scott's vampire finds herself enlisted by the Rysemians in their battle against the Sajorians. And thanks to a time-travel machine which she has invented in her spare time, she also finds herself jumping five years into the future to market the Famous Men's Sperm Kit as part of the Rysemian effort to hasten the evolution of the human race. Most importantly, perhaps, courtesy of Rysemian lessons in "psychic evolution," Sterling overcomes her craving for blood, repudiating, within the terms of Scott's fictional world, the limitations projected onto her by the representations of others.

From the perspective of the "tradition" of vampire literature, what Wilson and Scott have produced are intertexts. *The Space Vampires* and *I, Vampire* inevitably invoke the entire "history" of the vampire in literature and film at the same time as they make use of previously established narrative codes and conventions for their own purposes. Within the terms of Hutcheon's analysis of parody, this history is "grafted onto the text[s]" and becomes available as a significant contextual element to readers who, as "decoders of encoded intent" have the role of activating it. While Wilson's and Scott's texts are also traversed by typical SF conventions in general and, in the case of *Space Vampires,* by details of previous SF stories in particular, I want to focus my attention here upon the way in which the figure of the vampire is positioned within each narrative structure and the ideological implications of its positioning. In order to accomplish this, I will, for the most part, confine my own "activation" of backgrounded material to certain aspects of Stoker's classic treatment of the vampire in *Dracula.*

In Stoker's text, the sinister Count is the enemy in one version of the eternal battle between Good and Evil. This opposition, which is central to romance narratives, is always constructed upon specific ideological foundations. In his discussion of "magical [i.e., romance] narratives" in *The Political Unconscious,* Fredric Jameson explains the foundation of this opposition as follows:

> The concept of good and evil is a positional one that coincides with categories of Otherness. . . . The essential point to be made here [about the Other] is not so much that he is feared

because he is evil; rather he is evil *because* he is Other, alien, different, unclean, and unfamiliar.

And in a fascinating consideration of "fantasy antagonists, R. E. Foust reminds us of Freud's theory of the *doppelgänger* and his postulation of the "phenomenon of the 'double' "; from this perspective, the Other is a projection of certain undesirable aspects of the self, a "monstrous adversary" constructed out of repressed psychological material. As such, it is a source of fear and loathing whose return threatens to overcome the forces of Consciousness and Culture (the forces in whose interests it has been repressed in the first place). "The fantasy conflict," Foust concludes, "is structured upon an implicit assumption of the binary, rather than the unilateral, relationship between nature and culture." As I shall presently argue, it is this kind of binary thinking, endemic to the enterprises of logocentrism and patriarchy, which is sustained (even as it is parodied) in Wilson's text and deconstructed in Scott's.

One of the ways in which Stoker's text maintains the position of the vampire as evil Other is through its epistolary narrative technique. The entire novel is a compendium of diaries, journals, letters, newspaper articles, and other forms of I/eye-witness reports. The ideological outcome of this narrative method, of course, is the exclusion of the voice of the monstrous Other from the novel; that is, it keeps the outsider on the outside. As has been frequently noted, Stoker's narrative voices are exclusively human. Indeed, Dracula himself appears on only 62 pages of the original 390-page edition of the novel. In *Dracula,* the Other has no voice, no point of view; he merely *is.* While this, of course, ensures that he is all the more terrifying because almost completely unknown, it also effectively silences him.

As we might expect from its narrative strategies, *Dracula* is an extremely conservative text, one that valorizes human reason and privileges human over "alien" life. The inhabitants of its narrative world are neatly divided into "us" and "them."

The narrative perspective of *Space Vampires* achieves very much the same kind of result. Although Wilson replaces Stoker's eye-witnesses with an omniscient narrator, the point of view is again that of the human characters, and in particular of the Commander of the *Hermes,* Olaf Carlsen, leader of the expedition which brings the three aliens to Earth and the central character in the subsequent battle to overcome them. There is no real attempt in *Space Vampires* to explore the point of view of the aliens. Like Stoker's Count, they are more often off stage than on, objects of human fear and loathing, variously described as "deadly unknown germs" and "galactic criminals." During the course of the narrative, their vampirism is equated with sexual perversion, criminality, and outright evil.

Unlike Stoker, however, Wilson does provide his alien vampires with one opportunity to speak for themselves: when the human heroes trap one of the three "Nioth-Korghai" in the body of a human victim, they wrest a confession from him of his people's fall into vampirism and their subsequent history. He admits to these crimes but makes it clear that the alternative to their vampirism is

death: "After all, this seems to be a law of nature; all living creatures eat other living creatures."

Any sympathy aroused in the reader through this exposition is quickly smothered when Carlsen refuses to believe the alien's peaceful overtures: "I've got an instinct about it. Nothing in their behaviour leads me to trust them." As it turns out, Carlsen is right. The space vampires cannot be trusted; by its very nature, the other is always evil.

There are several interesting similarities between *Space Vampires* and Wilson's 1967 novel *The Mind Parasites,* which postulates a similar kind of alien possession and makes use of the metaphor of vampirism: "for more than two centuries now, the human mind has been constantly a prey to these energy vampires." What is most disturbing about *Mind Parasites* is Wilson's speculation that the cause of human *malaise* lies outside human agency. This is both a negation of human responsibility and another instance of the (paranoid) projection of undesirable elements of the human psyche onto conveniently non-human scapegoats.

For the most part, the reader of *Space Vampires* has no access to the perspective of Wilson's aliens. Such a perspective is unnecessary, since there is no doubt in the minds of the human characters, and consequently in the minds of Wilson's readers, that these aliens must be destroyed if possible, or at least expelled from Earth. Under the circumstances, it is both appropriate and ironic that the human characters refer to the alien spaceship as "the Stranger" (if they are not conversant with Camus' existentialist classic, we can be sure that Wilson is). *Space Vampires* fits rather neatly into that longstanding SF tradition of representing the alien as the threat from the outside, the other who must be driven from human territory if humankind is to rest secure.

Space Vampires is exemplary of Wilson's ongoing flirtation with various forms of popular literature, especially SF. His latest effort, a three-part epic whose collective title is *Spider World,* promises to continue his appropriation of traditional SF formulas in ways which sustain, even as they exploit, the potential conservatism of these formulas.

Given the ideological parallels between *Dracula* and *Space Vampires* in regard to the figure of the "alien," it is also appropriate that Wilson's text contains some intriguing allusions to Stoker's. While the concept of energy-sucking aliens is borrowed from van Vogt, *Dracula* is perhaps a more interesting background text against which to read *Space Vampires.* It is not accidental that the opening pages of Wilson's story owe so much of their atmosphere to details which are overtly Gothic. The alien craft is compared to "some damn great castle floating in the sky" and to "Frankenstein's castle"; and it exudes "the quality of a nightmare."

Wilson's allusions to *Dracula* are even more pronounced in the area of narrative event. Carlsen's companion in his quest to find and expel the aliens is Dr Hans Fallada, a British criminologist whose research into the phenomena of human vampirism emphasizes his role as the SF analogue of Professor Abraham Van Helsing, the evil Count's original nemesis. Wilson's vampire hunters are able to pinpoint the whereabouts of at least one of the aliens through her mind-link with Olaf Carlsen, who must be hypnotized before he can disclose the information. This incident directly recalls that in which Mina Harker, also partially possessed, also hypnotized, reveals Dracula's hiding place to the heroic band of men who will rescue her at last from his spell.

The fact that Wilson's allusions to *Dracula* are not always straight-forward gives an interesting complexity to the narrative structure of *Space Vampires*. One of his most intriguing revisions of Stoker appears in the character of the mysterious Count von Geijerstam, who lives in seclusion in northern Sweden in a castle which was once the home of "our famous vampire, Count Magnus de la Gardie." It cannot be coincidence that von Geijerstam is living with three beautiful young women who are practicing a form of "benevolent vampirism" under his tutelage. The reader is inevitably reminded of the three female vampires, the "brides of Dracula," who come so close to destroying Jonathan Harker at the beginning of Stoker's text. *Space Vampires* also recounts a scene in which Carlsen—at this point clearly an avatar of Jonathan Harker—is approached by one of these young women. In a further revisionary movement, however, the text demonstrates that it is Carlsen rather than the woman who plays the role of vampire, as he drains her of life-energy until she is all but unconscious.

Returning to *I, Vampire* at this point—and recalling Hutcheon's identification of the dual potential of parody ("it can be normative and conservative, or it can be provocative and revolutionary")—we can now see that Jody Scott's reworking of *Dracula* is far more unorthodox in its manipulation of the traditions and conventions of the classic vampire story than is *Space Vampires*.

One of Scott's most obvious revisions is highlighted in her title. Just as *Space Vampires* describes obviously oppositional figures who arrive from "out there," so Scott's title indicates the shift in perspective from the human to the Other. The first 13 chapters of *I, Vampire* are narrated by the vampire herself, displacing the human voice from its privileged position at the center of the text. Suddenly the outsider is on the inside and the voice of the Other, glittering with angry wit and the cynicism born of sharing the world with human beings for 700 years, is heard in no uncertain terms. Sterling O'Blivion is the subject of her own story rather than the object of another's, the interpreter of events rather than the event interpreted. She is only too aware that "when you are a . . . semi-mythological creature like myself, you are expected to act out a script written by others; one that ignores your true nature." While this particular narrative strategy serves to demystify the Other even more definitively than does Wilson's text, it also shifts the perspective in ways which break down the oppositional barriers between human and other which *Space Vampires* leaves standing.

Sterling O'Blivion, the centuries-old and ravishingly beautiful manager of the Max Arkoff dance studio in Chicago, is a victim of the kind of binary thinking which defines the Other as evil. She sets out to explode "a few pernicious myths" about vampires, pointing out that all she takes

from her own victims is "six skimpy ounces [of blood]. Less than they take at the blood bank. Cheap, selfish bastards! . . . and for this I suffered the curse of excommunication and was enrolled among the damned." She also warns that "[o]nly a fool sets out to kill any living creature. You don't know what forces you are releasing."

The target of Scott's sometimes vicious satire is that very humanity which has forced the vampire to live in the shadows for 700 years. The Rysemians bluntly inform Sterling that the human race is psychotic, that it will have to be quarantined or destroyed if it cannot evolve into a fit inhabitant of the universe beyond its own borders. *I, Vampire,* as it casts humanity as dangerous life-form, thus effects a satiric inversion of the conventional alien-invasion plot.

Scott's feminist parody of *Dracula* is particularly effective in its subversion of the sexual politics of the earlier story. An examination of the roles played by the female characters in *Dracula* soon reveals that they are as dependent upon their relationship with Stoker's sinister Count as they are upon the ordinary men by whom they are befriended or to whom they are betrothed. Lucy Westenra and Mina Harker are cast as prizes in the contest between the Vampire and his human opponents, while the three vampire brides have already been won. In their passive receptivity, women are at once the susceptible mediators through which the Other may penetrate into human territory and the spoils of war which fall to the victor in this battle between Good and Evil. If Mina Harker enjoys peace and prosperity at the end of her adventures, it is because she submits herself to the values of Stoker's Victorian reality and returns to the patriarchal fold cleansed of any contact with the Other who both attracts and threatens from the outside.

This implicit identification of woman and vampire, which operates as a powerful subtextual element in Stoker's original story—a kind of hidden agenda—is both acknowledged and satirized in Scott's. Indeed, her work goes several steps further in its deconstruction of the human/other opposition. O'Blivion becomes involved in a passionate love affair with Benaroya, who has temporarily abandoned her own alien body in order to infiltrate the human community disguised as Virginia Woolf. On the one hand, Sterling is not only a female vampire, but a lesbian vampire, and one who has made love "out of [her] species." On the other hand, as Benaroya assures her, there are no limits to what the mind can create out of the physical universe, "or P.U., as we call it." She also makes it clear that, from the perspective of the Rysemians, "there are no aliens," or, as she revises Terence, "nothing alien is alien to me." *I, Vampire* ultimately acknowledges the nature of reality as social and linguistic construction. Any logocentric dependence upon "the thing in itself" is thoroughly undermined in this postmodern universe of continuously shifting bodies and perspectives.

Given the structural parallels in the position of the vampire in *Dracula* and *Space Vampires,* it is perhaps not surprising to find in Wilson's text an uncomfortably ambivalent attitude towards women—the same discomfort that we can read in *Dracula* itself. *Space Vampires* weaves a complex interconnection between the ideas of vampirism and masculinist versions of sexuality, which becomes apparent, for example, in Carlsen's realization that "the vampire responded to desire like a shark to blood" and that "the energy-loss [resulting from psychic vampirism] produced much the same effect as masculine domination." Wilson's human females are invariably ready to yield, both mentally and physically, to Carlsen as his own powers as a psychic vampire develop, but it is made clear that "his gentlemanly self-control" will prevent him from taking advantage of their weakness.

Wilson implies, however, that female vampires will not act so benignly. Just as the women in *Dracula* are either pure Victorian maidens or ravening (i.e., sexual) monsters, so Wilson's text represents the sexually active woman as somehow linked to the alien forces which threaten from "out there." The scene in which Carlsen defeats one of the aliens who temporarily inhabits a female body, for example, bears a disturbing resemblance to a sexual encounter in which male physical desire is equated with strength of will: "Without moving his body he was holding her as a bird might hold a worm." The alien, of course, was about to destroy him completely. Wilson's women-as-alien-vampires are incapable of restraining their appetites, and for this reason, are tremendously threatening figures.

Carlsen's wife, Jelka, on the other hand, is a modern version of the Victorian angel in the house. The text's references to Goethe's principle of the *ewig weibliche,* the eternal feminine which "draws us upwards and on" draws the reader downwards, back into the sexual politics of *Dracula,* which also separates the good woman from the sexual woman. When Carlsen's "basic masculine tenderness" is aroused by one of von Geijerstam's young pupils, the sexual-political ideology of *Space Vampires* becomes even clearer: "It struck him that her body *was* Jelka's. Both were embodiments of a female principle that lay beyond them, looking out of the body of every woman in the world as if out of so many windows."

At this point we might recall Sterling O'Blivion's complaint that a "semi-mythological creature . . . [is] expected to act out a script written by others; one that ignores your true nature." In its essentialist representations, *Space Vampires* not only reduces its female characters to the status of "semi-mythological" beings, but undertakes to supply the script for their subsequent behavior. If there is parody here waiting to be activated, the reader might well be forgiven for missing the point entirely.

I would like to return now to Foust's contention that the Other is created through the projection of undesirable psychic material. The result in Wilson's text is the *expression* of this undesirable material embodied in the form of vampire-aliens; his narrative can be read as a metaphorical dramatization of the return of the repressed, an *expression* of the anxiety of the divided self which has constructed a reality defined through binary oppositions such as inside vs. outside, human vs. alien, masculine vs. feminine. As is inevitably the case, such binary thinking is also rigidly hierarchical. In each instance, one of the terms is privileged over the other: inside over outside, human over alien, masculine over feminine.

The deconstruction of such antitheses is an important activity in Scott's text and a driving force in her parody of the conventional treatment of the vampire. Whereas Wilson's narrative casts the vampire-alien in opposition to the human, Scott's replaces the two-term system (with its underlying hierarchical privilege) with a three-term one: vampire, alien, human.

Any attempt to return her narrative to the dramatization of binary thinking breaks down in view of the shifting relationships among the terms of this system, relationships which emphasize complicity rather than opposition. The human cannot remain antithetical to the vampire in the presence of the alien; nor can the human/alien opposition hold up in a narrative which interposes the figure of the vampire between these two conventionally opposed terms.

While Wilson's text is an intriguing revision of the traditional vampire tale—a successful crossing of the border from fantasy into SF—it maintains rather than revises the ideological paranoia towards the figure of the alien Other which pervades Stoker's *Dracula.* In its echoes of the latter's sexual politics, it seems also to support conventional patriarchal attitudes about women, casting its female characters as pawns in the contest of human heroes and alien vampires in a way which underscores the human/alien opposition around which the narrative is structured.

Scott's *I, Vampire,* though lacking the coherence and the direction of *Space Vampires* and suffering periodically from a kind of New Age valorization of psychic over physical reality, is more skeptical about the usefulness of borders and boundaries than Wilson's fiction is. Its fusion of fantasy and SF parallels on the generic level its deconstruction of the human/other opposition on the narrative level. Sterling O'Blivion is the vampire as intertext, a figure combining the characteristics of both human and alien, mediating between the two in a way which demonstrates the artificiality of an opposition which is, after all, only a difference.

The vampire, like that other 19th-century avatar of horror, Frankenstein's monster, always functions within a context which resonates with implications beyond the mere telling of an exciting tale. Stoker's original literary vampire, for example, has been usefully examined from a variety of critical perspectives, ranging from the sexual-political to the socio-political to the psychoanalytic. While the intrusion of the vampire into SF heralds a relatively untraditional treatment of this typically Gothic archetype, Wilson's conflation of vampire with alien maintains the role of the former as the threat-from-outside, the quintessential Other. Scott's revision, by contrast, is one of a small but growing number of works, most of them by women, which are interested in creating new scripts for this particular "semi-mythological creature"—scripts which are applicable to the "real" world as well.

Roger C. Schlobin has suggested that many contemporary treatments of the vampire have "emasculated" this traditionally potent figure, and he cites works by Chelsea Quinn Yarbro (the six-volume *Saint-Germain Chronicles* [1978-83]) and Suzie McKee Charnas (*The Vampire Tap-*

estry [1980]), among others, to support his contention. To this particular list should be added the works of Anne Rice, Angela Carter, Tanith Lee, and Jody Scott. What these writers have effected is a rejection of the vampire as what we might term a "metaphorical rapist." Schlobin makes it clear that the vampire, as it functions within the framework of the conventional horror story or film, threatens its victims, whether male or female, with a kind of violation that has its clearest analogue in the act of physical rape. It is not therefore surprising that even when the vampire is male (as in Charnas's *Vampire Tapestry* or Rice's "Chronicles"), he is developed from outside the conventional male perspective (i.e., he is *e*masculated). When the vampire is female, as in Scott's text, the rejection of this perspective is even more obvious. I would suggest, therefore, that the "emasculation" of the "fantasy antagonist" in all these instances is also—and results in—a "feminization." There can be little incentive for women writers to contribute to the literary tradition of the "monstrous adversary" as rapist. Instead, these works might be said to constitute a new literary canon developed around the figure of the Outsider. This is no longer, of course, the modernist Outsider identified by Wilson in his 1950s' book on the subject, but a new representation created by a politicized contemporary literature in its protests against the coercive nature of patriarchal marginalization.

Given the rapidly increasing popularity of horror literature and film over the last few years, it is not surprising that the vampire archetype has been resurrected, nor that it has occasionally been appropriated by SF writers. What is especially interesting about this "return," however, is the significant ideological differences apparent in the works of writers like Scott who have taken over the figure of the vampire in order to develop explorations and deconstructions of conventionalized oppressor/victim relationships.

Wilson's domestication of the fantastic is more successful than Scott's insofar as *The Space Vampires* offers its readers a rational paradigm from within which it can explore the "abnormal occurrence" of the figure of the vampire. What Scott's text succeeds in preserving, however, is that sense of wonder about our own human nature—actual and potential—which becomes suffocated in *The Space Vampires,* buried under an earlier and far less desirable view of reality. (pp. 145-56)

> *Veronica Hollinger, "The Vampire and the Alien: Variations on the Outsider,"* in Science-Fiction Studies, *Vol. 16, No. 2, July, 1989, pp. 145-60.*

FURTHER READING

Anthologies

Datlow, Ellen. *Blood Is Not Enough.* New York: William Morrow, 1989, 308 p.

Collection of new and reprinted stories focusing on non-bloodsucking vampires.

McNally, Raymond T. *A Clutch of Vampires.* New York: Warner Books, 1975, 239 p.

Collection of vampire fiction and folklore reflecting the history of vampirism in literature and culture.

Shephard, Leslie. *The Dracula Book of Great Vampire Stories.* Secaucus, N.J.: Citadel, 1975, 621 p.

Collection of nineteenth-century vampire stories, including Count Stenbock's "The True Story of a Vampire," and Joseph Sheridan LeFanu's "Carmilla."

Secondary Sources

Baran, Henryk. "Some Reminiscences in Blok: Vampirism and Its Antecedents." In *Aleksandr Blok Centennial Conference,* edited by Walter N. Vickery, pp. 43-60. Columbus, Ohio: Slavica Publishers, 1984.

Discusses the theme of vampirism in the works of Aleksandr Blok and asserts that he "responded significantly to three separate sources of vampiric thematics: Russian folklore, Stoker's *Dracula,* and Romantic literature."

Clapp, Edwin R. "La Belle Dame as Vampire." *Philological Quarterly* XXVII, No. 1 (January 1948): 89-92.

Discusses the theme of vampirism in John Keats's *La Belle Dame sans Merci.*

Copper, Basil. *The Vampire in Legend, Fact and Art.* London: Robert Hale & Co., 1973, 208 p.

Discusses vampirism in legend, literature, film, theater, and fact.

Cranny-Francis, Anne. "Sexual Politics and Political Repression in Bram Stoker's *Dracula*." In *Nineteenth-Century Suspense: From Poe to Conan Doyle,* edited by Clive Bloom, Brian Docherty, Jane Gibb, and Keith Shand, pp. 65-92. New York: St. Martin's Press, 1988.

Discusses the theme of sexuality associated with vampirism in *Dracula* and asserts that the characters and situations depicted in the novel provide insight into the social, political, and psychological crises experienced by the middle classes in late nineteenth-century England, concentrating on Stoker's portrayal of female characters and the theme of male power and dominance.

Day, William Patrick. *In the Circles of Fear and Desire: A Study of Gothic Fantasy.* Chicago and London: The University of Chicago Press, 1985, 208 p.

Explores Gothic fantasy from its origins in the late eighteenth century through the end of the nineteenth century, emphasizing the theme of descent to the underworld in search of lost identity and asserting that the vampire is "the most striking image of a human being fully transformed by the descent."

Douglas, Drake. "The Vampire." In his *Horror!,* pp. 15-50. Toronto: The Macmillan Co., 1966.

Discussion of the characteristics of the vampire in legend followed by an overview of several major works of vampire literature.

Dresser, Norine. *American Vampires: Fans, Victims & Practitioners.* New York: W. W. Norton & Co., 1989, 255 p.

Explores the American fascination with vampires.

Frayling, Christopher. "Vampyres." *London Magazine* 14, No. 2 (June-July 1974): 94-104.

> Review of several critical studies on vampires. Frayling asserts that there is still research to be done on vampirism and that no writers have surpassed the achievements of Bram Stoker and Joseph Sheridan LeFanu.

Griffin, Gail B. "The Girls That You All Love Are Mine." *International Journal of Women's Studies* 3, No. 5 (September-October 1980): 454-65.

> Discusses female vampirism in *Dracula* as a reflection of male attitudes, asserting that Stoker's female vampires exhibit traits of the "Victorian Bad Woman: sexual aggressiveness, anger, and perverted maternal instincts."

Masters, Anthony. *The Natural History of the Vampire.* New York: G. P. Putnam's Sons, 1972, 259 p.

> Debates "the causes of the fear that created mythical vampirism and the climate for real-life vampirism," and analyzes "the sexual, religious and psychiatric motivation behind the creation of the vampire cult." Masters also discusses the vampire in the contexts of literature, Christianity, and contemporary culture.

McFarland, Ronald E. "The Vampire on Stage: A Study in Adaptations." *Comparative Drama* 21, No. 1 (Spring 1987): 19-33.

> Credits Polidori's *The Vampyre* with establishing several standard characteristics of literary vampires and discusses adaptations of the work for the stage, emphasizing the prominence of the vampire theme in nineteenth-century melodrama.

Murgoci, Agnes. "The Vampire in Roumania." *Folklore* XXXVII, No. 4 (31 December 1926): 320-49.

> Discusses the folk beliefs about vampires that originated in Russia, Rumania, and the Balkan states.

Nandris, Grigore. "The Historical Dracula." *Comparative Literature Studies* III, No. 3 (1966): 367-96.

> Examines the influence of Rumanian vampire legends on *Dracula* and analyzes the psychological significance and historical background of the novel.

Oinas, Felix. "East European Vampires & Dracula." *Journal of Popular Culture* 16, No. 1 (Summer 1982): 108-16.

> Examines the origins and characteristics of vampires in Eastern European folklore and legend and asserts that *Dracula* established the convention of vampirism in literature and film.

Riccardo, Martin V. *Vampires Unearthed: The Complete Multi-Media Vampire and Dracula Bibliography.* New York and London: Garland Publishing, 1983, 135 p.

> Bibliography of vampire literature encompassing works of fiction, drama, nonfiction, and children's literature, as well as listings of vampire journals and clubs.

Senf, Carol A. "The Vampire in *Middlemarch* and George Eliot's Quest for Historical Reality." *New Orleans Review* 14, No. 1 (Spring 1987): 87-97.

> Examines Eliot's use of the vampire motif in *Middlemarch,* asserting that she focuses on the vampire's predatory nature as a distinctly human possibility and realistically portrays horror and cruelty as a part of daily existence.

Stevenson, John A. "A Vampire in the Mirror: The Sexuality of Dracula." *PMLA* 103, No. 2 (March 1988): 139-49.

> Reconsiders *Dracula* as a story of "interracial" sexual competition rather than as one of intrafamilial strife or incest, asserting that the threat of the vampire is associated with his status as a foreign outsider.

Summers, Montague. *The Vampire: His Kith and Kin.* London: Kegan Paul, Trench, Trubner & Co., 1928, 356 p.

> Critical study of vampires by one of the earliest and foremost authorities on witchcraft and the supernatural, including a chapter devoted to the origins and development of the vampire in literature.

Twitchell, James B. *The Living Dead: A Study of the Vampire in Romantic Literature.* Durham: Duke University Press, 1981, 188 p.

> Organized into chapters on the vampire in pre-Romantic English literature, the female vampire, the male vampire in poetry, the vampire in prose, the artist as vampire, and D. H. Lawrence and the modern vampire.

Veeder, William. "Carmilla: The Arts of Repression." *Texas Studies in Language and Literature* 22, No. 2 (Summer 1980): 197-223.

> Discusses the portrayal of vampirism in LeFanu's "Carmilla" as it relates to the theme of women's sexuality and the duality of human nature.

Waller, Gregory A. *The Living and the Undead: From Stoker's "Dracula" to Romero's "Dawn of the Dead."* Urbana: University of Illinois Press, 1986, 228 p.

> Discusses the genre of horror stories concerning the "undead," the twentieth-century portrayal of vampires in literature and popular culture, and various literary and theatrical versions of *Dracula.*

Weissman, Judith. "Woman as Vampires: *Dracula* as a Victorian Novel." *The Midwest Quarterly* XVII, No. 4 (Summer 1977): 392-405.

> Explores the literary theme of vampirism as a representation of sexual terror and focuses on *Dracula* as "an extreme version of the stereotypically Victorian attitudes toward sexual roles."

Twentieth-Century
Literary Criticism

Cumulative Indexes
Volumes 1-46

This Index Includes References to Entries in These Gale Series

Black Literature Criticism provides excerpts from criticism of the most significant works of black authors of all nationalities over the past 200 years. Complete in three volumes.

Children's Literature Review includes excerpts from reviews, criticism, and commentary on works of authors and illustrators who create books for children.

Classical and Medieval Literature Criticism offers excerpts of criticism on the works of world authors from classical antiquity through the fourteenth century.

Contemporary Authors series encompasses five related series. **Contemporary Authors** provides biographical and bibliographical information on more than 100,000 writers of fiction, nonfiction, poetry, journalism, drama, and film. **Contemporary Authors New Revision Series** provides completely updated information on active authors covered in previously published volumes of *CA*. **Contemporary Authors Permanent Series** consists of updated listings for deceased and inactive authors removed from the original volumes 9-36 when those volumes were revised. **Contemporary Authors Autobiography Series** presents specially commissioned autobiographies by leading contemporary writers. **Contemporary Authors Bibliographical Series** contains primary and secondary bibliographies as well as analytical bibliographical essays by authorities on major modern authors.

Contemporary Literary Criticism presents excerpts of criticism on the works of novelists, poets, dramatists, short story writers, scriptwriters, and other creative writers who are now living or who have died since 1960.

Dictionary of Literary Biography comprises four related series. **Dictionary of Literary Biography** furnishes illustrated overviews of authors' lives and works and places them in the larger perspective of literary history. **Dictionary of Literary Biography Documentary Series** illuminates the careers of major figures through a selection of literary documents, including letters, interviews, and photographs. **Dictionary of Literary Biography Yearbook** summarizes the past year's literary activity and includes updated and new entries on individual authors. A cumulative index to authors and articles is included in each new volume. **Concise Dictionary of**

American Literary Biography, a six-volume series, collects revised and updated sketches on major American authors that were originally presented in *Dictionary of Literary Biography.*

Drama Criticism provides excerpts of criticism on the works of playwrights of all nationalities and periods of literary history.

Literature Criticism from 1400 to 1800 compiles significant passages from the most noteworthy criticism on authors of the fifteenth through the eighteenth centuries.

Nineteenth-Century Literature Criticism offers significant passages from criticism on authors who died between 1800 and 1899.

Poetry Criticism presents excerpts of criticism on the works of poets from all eras, movements, and nationalities.

Short Story Criticism combines excerpts of criticism on short fiction by writers of all eras and nationalities.

Something about the Author series encompasses three related series. **Something about the Author** contains well-illustrated biographical sketches on authors and illustrators of juvenile and young adult literature from all eras. **Something about the Author Autobiography Series** presents specially commissioned autobiographies by prominent authors and illustrators of books for children and young adults. **Authors & Artists for Young Adults** provides high school and junior high school students with profiles of their favorite creative artists.

Twentieth-Century Literary Criticism contains critical excerpts by the most significant commentators on poets, novelists, short story writers, dramatists, and philosophers who died between 1900 and 1960.

World Literature Criticism, 1500 to the Present provides excerpts from criticism on 225 authors from the Renaissance to the present. Complete in six volumes.

Yesterday's Authors of Books for Children contains heavily illustrated entries on children's writers who died before 1961. Complete in two volumes.

Literary Criticism Series
Cumulative Author Index

This index lists all author entries in the Gale Literary Criticism Series and includes cross-references to other Gale sources. References in the index are identified as follows:

AAYA: *Authors & Artists for Young Adults,* Volumes 1-7
BLC: *Black Literature Criticism,* Volumes 1-3
CA: *Contemporary Authors* (original series), Volumes 1-136
CAAS: *Contemporary Authors Autobiography Series,* Volumes 1-15
CABS: *Contemporary Authors Bibliographical Series,* Volumes 1-3
CANR: *Contemporary Authors New Revision Series,* Volumes 1-35
CAP: *Contemporary Authors Permanent Series,* Volumes 1-2
CA-R: *Contemporary Authors* (first revision), Volumes 1-44
CDALB: *Concise Dictionary of American Literary Biography,* Volumes 1-6
CLC: *Contemporary Literary Criticism,* Volumes 1-72
CLR: *Children's Literature Review,* Volumes 1-25
CMLC: *Classical and Medieval Literature Criticism,* Volumes 1-9
DC: *Drama Criticism,* Volumes 1-2
DLB: *Dictionary of Literary Biography,* Volumes 1-114
DLB-DS: *Dictionary of Literary Biography Documentary Series,* Volumes 1-9
DLB-Y: *Dictionary of Literary Biography Yearbook,* Volumes 1980-1990
LC: *Literature Criticism from 1400 to 1800,* Volumes 1-19
NCLC: *Nineteenth-Century Literature Criticism,* Volumes 1-36
PC: *Poetry Criticism,* Volumes 1-5
SAAS: *Something about the Author Autobiography Series,* Volumes 1-14
SATA: *Something about the Author,* Volumes 1-68
SSC: *Short Story Criticism,* Volumes 1-10
TCLC: *Twentieth-Century Literary Criticism,* Volumes 1-46
WLC: *World Literature Criticism, 1500 to the Present,* Volumes 1-6
YABC: *Yesterday's Authors of Books for Children,* Volumes 1-2

Afton, Effie 1825-1911
See Harper, Francis Ellen Watkins

Agee, James 1909-1955 . . . . **TCLC 1, 19**
See also CA 108; DLB 2, 26;
CDALB 1941-1968

Agnon, S(hmuel) Y(osef Halevi)
1888-1970 . . . . **CLC 4, 8, 14**
See also CAP 2; CA 17-18;
obituary CA 25-28R

Ai 1947- . . . . **CLC 4, 14, 69**
See also CAAS 13; CA 85-88

Aickman, Robert (Fordyce)
1914-1981 . . . . **CLC 57**
See also CANR 3; CA 7-8R

Aiken, Conrad (Potter)
1889-1973 . . . **CLC 1, 3, 5, 10, 52; SSC 9**
See also CANR 4; CA 5-8R;
obituary CA 45-48; SATA 3, 30; DLB 9,
45, 102; CDALB 1929-1941

Aiken, Joan (Delano) 1924- . . . . **CLC 35**
See also CLR 1, 19; CANR 4; CA 9-12R;
SAAS 1; SATA 2, 30

Ainsworth, William Harrison
1805-1882 . . . . **NCLC 13**
See also SATA 24; DLB 21

Aitmatov, Chingiz 1928- . . . . **CLC 71**
See also CA 103; SATA 56

Ajar, Emile 1914-1980
See Gary, Romain

Akhmadulina, Bella (Akhatovna)
1937- . . . . **CLC 53**
See also CA 65-68

Akhmatova, Anna
1888-1966 . . . . **CLC 11, 25, 64; PC 2**
See also CAP 1; CA 19-20;
obituary CA 25-28R

Aksakov, Sergei Timofeyvich
1791-1859 . . . . **NCLC 2**

Aksenov, Vassily (Pavlovich) 1932-
See Aksyonov, Vasily (Pavlovich)

Aksyonov, Vasily (Pavlovich)
1932- . . . . **CLC 22, 37**
See also CANR 12; CA 53-56

Akutagawa Ryunosuke
1892-1927 . . . . **TCLC 16**
See also CA 117

Alain 1868-1951 . . . . **TCLC 41**
See also Chartier, Emile-Auguste

Alain-Fournier 1886-1914 . . . . **TCLC 6**
See also Fournier, Henri Alban
See also DLB 65

Al-Amin, Jamil Abdullah 1943-
See also BLC 1; CA 112, 125

Alarcon, Pedro Antonio de
1833-1891 . . . . **NCLC 1**

Alas (y Urena), Leopoldo (Enrique Garcia)
1852-1901 . . . . **TCLC 29**
See also CA 113

Albee, Edward (Franklin III)
1928- . . . **CLC 1, 2, 3, 5, 9, 11, 13, 25, 53**
See also WLC 1; CANR 8; CA 5-8R;
DLB 7; CDALB 1941-1968

Alberti, Rafael 1902- . . . . **CLC 7**
See also CA 85-88

Alcott, Amos Bronson 1799-1888 . . **NCLC 1**
See also DLB 1

Alcott, Louisa May 1832-1888 . . . . **NCLC 6**
See also CLR 1; WLC 1; YABC 1; DLB 1,
42, 79; CDALB 1865-1917

Aldanov, Mark 1887-1957 . . . . **TCLC 23**
See also CA 118

Aldington, Richard 1892-1962 . . . . . . **CLC 49**
See also CA 85-88; DLB 20, 36

Aldiss, Brian W(ilson)
1925- . . . . **CLC 5, 14, 40**
See also CAAS 2; CANR 5; CA 5-8R;
SATA 34; DLB 14

Alegria, Fernando 1918- . . . . **CLC 57**
See also CANR 5; CA 11-12R

Aleixandre, Vicente 1898-1984 . . . **CLC 9, 36**
See also CANR 26; CA 85-88;
obituary CA 114

Alepoudelis, Odysseus 1911-
See Elytis, Odysseus

Aleshkovsky, Yuz 1929- . . . . **CLC 44**
See also CA 121, 128

Alexander, Lloyd (Chudley) 1924- . . **CLC 35**
See also CLR 1, 5; CANR 1; CA 1-4R;
SATA 3, 49; DLB 52

Alexander, Margaret Abigail Walker 1915-
See Walker, Margaret

Alfau, Felipe 1902- . . . . **CLC 66**

Alger, Horatio, Jr. 1832-1899 . . . . . **NCLC 8**
See also SATA 16; DLB 42

Algren, Nelson 1909-1981 . . . . **CLC 4, 10, 33**
See also CANR 20; CA 13-16R;
obituary CA 103; DLB 9; DLB-Y 81, 82;
CDALB 1941-1968

Ali, Ahmed 1910- . . . . **CLC 69**
See also CANR 15, 34; CA 25-28R

Alighieri, Dante 1265-1321 . . . . **CMLC 3**

Allard, Janet 1975- . . . . **CLC 59**

Allen, Edward 1948- . . . . **CLC 59**

Allen, Roland 1939-
See Ayckbourn, Alan

Allen, Sarah A. 1859-1930
See Hopkins, Pauline Elizabeth

Allen, Woody 1935- . . . . **CLC 16, 52**
See also CANR 27; CA 33-36R; DLB 44

Allende, Isabel 1942- . . . . **CLC 39, 57**
See also CA 125

Alleyne, Carla D. 1975?- . . . . **CLC 65**

Allingham, Margery (Louise)
1904-1966 . . . . **CLC 19**
See also CANR 4; CA 5-8R;
obituary CA 25-28R; DLB 77

Allingham, William 1824-1889 . . . **NCLC 25**
See also DLB 35

Allston, Washington 1779-1843 . . . . **NCLC 2**
See also DLB 1

Almedingen, E. M. 1898-1971 . . . . . . **CLC 12**
See also Almedingen, Martha Edith von
See also SATA 3

Almedingen, Martha Edith von 1898-1971
See Almedingen, E. M.
See also CANR 1; CA 1-4R

Alonso, Damaso 1898- . . . . **CLC 14**
See also CA 110; obituary CA 130

Alta 1942- . . . . **CLC 19**
See also CA 57-60

Alter, Robert B(ernard) 1935- . . . . . **CLC 34**
See also CANR 1; CA 49-52

Alther, Lisa 1944- . . . . **CLC 7, 41**
See also CANR 12; CA 65-68

Altman, Robert 1925- . . . . **CLC 16**
See also CA 73-76

Alvarez, A(lfred) 1929- . . . . **CLC 5, 13**
See also CANR 3; CA 1-4R; DLB 14, 40

Alvarez, Alejandro Rodriguez 1903-1965
See Casona, Alejandro
See also obituary CA 93-96

Amado, Jorge 1912- . . . . **CLC 13, 40**
See also CA 77-80

Ambler, Eric 1909- . . . . **CLC 4, 6, 9**
See also CANR 7; CA 9-12R; DLB 77

Amichai, Yehuda 1924- . . . . . . **CLC 9, 22, 57**
See also CA 85-88

Amiel, Henri Frederic 1821-1881 . . **NCLC 4**

Amis, Kingsley (William)
1922- . . . . . . **CLC 1, 2, 3, 5, 8, 13, 40, 44**
See also CANR 8; CA 9-12R; DLB 15, 27

Amis, Martin 1949- . . . . **CLC 4, 9, 38, 62**
See also CANR 8, 27; CA 65-68; DLB 14

Ammons, A(rchie) R(andolph)
1926- . . . . **CLC 2, 3, 5, 8, 9, 25, 57**
See also CANR 6; CA 9-12R; DLB 5

Anand, Mulk Raj 1905- . . . . **CLC 23**
See also CA 65-68

Anaya, Rudolfo A(lfonso) 1937- . . . . **CLC 23**
See also CAAS 4; CANR 1; CA 45-48;
DLB 82

Andersen, Hans Christian
1805-1875 . . . . **NCLC 7; SSC 6**
See also CLR 6; WLC 1; YABC 1

Anderson, Jessica (Margaret Queale)
19??- . . . . **CLC 37**
See also CANR 4; CA 9-12R

Anderson, Jon (Victor) 1940- . . . . **CLC 9**
See also CANR 20; CA 25-28R

Anderson, Lindsay 1923- . . . . **CLC 20**
See also CA 125

Anderson, Maxwell 1888-1959 . . . . . **TCLC 2**
See also CA 105; DLB 7

Anderson, Poul (William) 1926- . . . . **CLC 15**
See also CAAS 2; CANR 2, 15; CA 1-4R;
SATA 39; DLB 8

Anderson, Robert (Woodruff)
1917- . . . . **CLC 23**
See also CA 21-24R; DLB 7

Anderson, Roberta Joan 1943-
See Mitchell, Joni

Anderson, Sherwood
1876-1941 . . . . . . **TCLC 1, 10, 24; SSC 1**
See also WLC 1; CAAS 3; CA 104, 121;
DLB 4, 9; DLB-DS 1

Andrade, Carlos Drummond de
1902-1987 . . . . **CLC 18**
See also CA 123

Andrade, Mario de 1892-1945 . . . . . **TCLC 43**

Andrewes, Lancelot 1555-1626 ...... **LC 5**

Andrews, Cicily Fairfield 1892-1983
See West, Rebecca

Andreyev, Leonid (Nikolaevich)
1871-1919 .... **TCLC 3**
See also CA 104

Andrezel, Pierre 1885-1962
See Dinesen, Isak; Blixen, Karen
(Christentze Dinesen)

Andric, Ivo 1892-1975 .... **CLC 8**
See also CA 81-84; obituary CA 57-60

Angelique, Pierre 1897-1962
See Bataille, Georges

Angell, Roger 1920- .... **CLC 26**
See also CANR 13; CA 57-60

Angelou, Maya 1928-....... **CLC 12, 35, 64**
See also BLC 1; CANR 19; CA 65-68;
SATA 49; DLB 38

Annensky, Innokenty 1856-1909... **TCLC 14**
See also CA 110

Anouilh, Jean (Marie Lucien Pierre)
1910-1987 ...... **CLC 1, 3, 8, 13, 40, 50**
See also CA 17-20R; obituary CA 123

Anthony, Florence 1947-
See Ai

Anthony (Jacob), Piers 1934- ...... **CLC 35**
See also Jacob, Piers A(nthony)
D(illingham)
See also DLB 8

Antoninus, Brother 1912-
See Everson, William (Oliver)

Antonioni, Michelangelo 1912-..... **CLC 20**
See also CA 73-76

Antschel, Paul 1920-1970....... **CLC 10, 19**
See also Celan, Paul
See also CA 85-88

Anwar, Chairil 1922-1949 .... **TCLC 22**
See also CA 121

Apollinaire, Guillaume
1880-1918 .... **TCLC 3, 8**
See also Kostrowitzki, Wilhelm Apollinaris
de

Appelfeld, Aharon 1932- .... **CLC 23, 47**
See also CA 112

Apple, Max (Isaac) 1941-........ **CLC 9, 33**
See also CANR 19; CA 81-84

Appleman, Philip (Dean) 1926-..... **CLC 51**
See also CANR 6; CA 13-16R

Apuleius, (Lucius) (Madaurensis)
125?-175?................... **CMLC 1**

Aquin, Hubert 1929-1977.......... **CLC 15**
See also CA 105; DLB 53

Aragon, Louis 1897-1982........ **CLC 3, 22**
See also CA 69-72; obituary CA 108;
DLB 72

Arany, Janos 1817-1882........ **NCLC 34**

Arbuthnot, John 1667-1735.......... **LC 1**

Archer, Jeffrey (Howard) 1940- .... **CLC 28**
See also CANR 22; CA 77-80

Archer, Jules 1915- .... **CLC 12**
See also CANR 6; CA 9-12R; SAAS 5;
SATA 4

Arden, John 1930- .... **CLC 6, 13, 15**
See also CAAS 4; CA 13-16R; DLB 13

Arenas, Reinaldo 1943- .... **CLC 41**
See also CA 124, 128

Arendt, Hannah 1906-1975 .... **CLC 66**
See also CA 19-20R; obituary CA 61-64

Aretino, Pietro 1492-1556.......... **LC 12**

Arguedas, Jose Maria
1911-1969 .... **CLC 10, 18**
See also CA 89-92

Argueta, Manlio 1936-............ **CLC 31**

Ariosto, Ludovico 1474-1533........ **LC 6**

Aristophanes
c. 450 B. C.-c. 385 B. C. ..... **CMLC 4;
DC 2**

Arlt, Roberto 1900-1942 .... **TCLC 29**
See also CA 123

Armah, Ayi Kwei 1939-......... **CLC 5, 33**
See also BLC 1; CANR 21; CA 61-64

Armatrading, Joan 1950-.......... **CLC 17**
See also CA 114

Arnim, Achim von (Ludwig Joachim von
Arnim) 1781-1831 .... **NCLC 5**
See also DLB 90

Arnold, Matthew
1822-1888 .... **NCLC 6, 29; PC 5**
See also WLC 1; DLB 32, 57;
CDALB 1832-1890

Arnold, Thomas 1795-1842 ..... **NCLC 18**
See also DLB 55

Arnow, Harriette (Louisa Simpson)
1908-1986 .... **CLC 2, 7, 18**
See also CANR 14; CA 9-12R;
obituary CA 118; SATA 42, 47; DLB 6

Arp, Jean 1887-1966............. **CLC 5**
See also CA 81-84; obituary CA 25-28R

Arquette, Lois S(teinmetz) 1934-
See Duncan (Steinmetz Arquette), Lois
See also SATA 1

Arrabal, Fernando 1932- ... **CLC 2, 9, 18, 58**
See also CANR 15; CA 9-12R

Arrick, Fran 19??- .... **CLC 30**

Artaud, Antonin 1896-1948 ..... **TCLC 3, 36**
See also CA 104

Arthur, Ruth M(abel) 1905-1979.... **CLC 12**
See also CANR 4; CA 9-12R;
obituary CA 85-88; SATA 7;
obituary SATA 26

Artsybashev, Mikhail Petrarch
1878-1927 .... **TCLC 31**

Arundel, Honor (Morfydd)
1919-1973 .... **CLC 17**
See also CAP 2; CA 21-22;
obituary CA 41-44R; SATA 4;
obituary SATA 24

Asch, Sholem 1880-1957 .... **TCLC 3**
See also CA 105

Ashbery, John (Lawrence)
1927- ... **CLC 2, 3, 4, 6, 9, 13, 15, 25, 41**
See also CANR 9; CA 5-8R; DLB 5;
DLB-Y 81

Ashton-Warner, Sylvia (Constance)
1908-1984 .... **CLC 19**
See also CA 69-72; obituary CA 112

Asimov, Isaac 1920-.... **CLC 1, 3, 9, 19, 26**
See also CLR 12; CANR 2, 19; CA 1-4R;
SATA 1, 26; DLB 8

Astley, Thea (Beatrice May)
1925- .... **CLC 41**
See also CANR 11; CA 65-68

Astley, William 1855-1911
See Warung, Price

Aston, James 1906-1964
See White, T(erence) H(anbury)

Asturias, Miguel Angel
1899-1974 .... **CLC 3, 8, 13**
See also CAP 2; CA 25-28;
obituary CA 49-52

Atheling, William, Jr. 1921-1975
See Blish, James (Benjamin)

Atherton, Gertrude (Franklin Horn)
1857-1948 .... **TCLC 2**
See also CA 104; DLB 9, 78

Attaway, William 1911?-1986
See also BLC 1; DLB 76

Atwood, Margaret (Eleanor)
1939- .... **CLC 2, 3, 4, 8, 13, 15, 25, 44;
SSC 2**
See also WLC 1; CANR 3, 24; CA 49-52;
SATA 50; DLB 53

Aubin, Penelope 1685-1731? .... **LC 9**
See also DLB 39

Auchincloss, Louis (Stanton)
1917-.............. **CLC 4, 6, 9, 18, 45**
See also CANR 6; CA 1-4R; DLB 2;
DLB-Y 80

Auden, W(ystan) H(ugh)
1907-1973 ..... **CLC 1, 2, 3, 4, 6, 9, 11,
14, 43; PC 1**
See also WLC 1; CANR 5; CA 9-12R;
obituary CA 45-48; DLB 10, 20

Audiberti, Jacques 1899-1965 ...... **CLC 38**
See also obituary CA 25-28R

Auel, Jean M(arie) 1936-.......... **CLC 31**
See also CANR 21; CA 103

Auerbach, Erich 1892-1957 .... **TCLC 43**
See also CA 118

Augier, Emile 1820-1889 .... **NCLC 31**

Augustine, St. 354-430.......... **CMLC 6**

Austen, Jane
1775-1817 .... **NCLC 1, 13, 19, 33**
See also WLC 1

Auster, Paul 1947-............... **CLC 47**
See also CANR 23; CA 69-72

Austin, Mary (Hunter)
1868-1934 .... **TCLC 25**
See also CA 109; DLB 9

Averroes 1126-1198 .... **CMLC 7**

Avison, Margaret 1918-.......... **CLC 2, 4**
See also CA 17-20R; DLB 53

Ayckbourn, Alan 1939- .... **CLC 5, 8, 18, 33**
See also CA 21-24R; DLB 13

Aydy, Catherine 1937-
See Tennant, Emma

Ayme, Marcel (Andre) 1902-1967... **CLC 11**
See also CA 89-92; DLB 72

Ayrton, Michael 1921-1975 . . . . CLC 7
See also CANR 9, 21; CA 5-8R;
   obituary CA 61-64

Azorin 1874-1967 . . . . CLC 11
See also Martinez Ruiz, Jose

Azuela, Mariano 1873-1952 . . . . TCLC 3
See also CA 104

"Bab" 1836-1911
See Gilbert, (Sir) W(illiam) S(chwenck)

Babel, Isaak (Emmanuilovich)
   1894-1941 . . . . TCLC 2, 13
See also CA 104

Babits, Mihaly 1883-1941 . . . . TCLC 14
See also CA 114

Babur 1483-1530 . . . . LC 18

Bacchelli, Riccardo 1891-1985 . . . . . CLC 19
See also CA 29-32R; obituary CA 117

Bach, Richard (David) 1936- . . . . CLC 14
See also CANR 18; CA 9-12R; SATA 13

Bachman, Richard 1947-
See King, Stephen (Edwin)

Bachmann, Ingeborg 1926-1973 . . . . . CLC 69
See also CA 93-96; obituary CA 45-48

Bacon, Sir Francis 1561-1626 . . . . LC 18

Bacovia, George 1881-1957 . . . . TCLC 24

Bagehot, Walter 1826-1877 . . . . . . NCLC 10
See also DLB 55

Bagnold, Enid 1889-1981 . . . . CLC 25
See also CANR 5; CA 5-8R;
   obituary CA 103; SATA 1, 25; DLB 13

Bagryana, Elisaveta 1893- . . . . CLC 10

Bailey, Paul 1937- . . . . CLC 45
See also CANR 16; CA 21-24R; DLB 14

Baillie, Joanna 1762-1851 . . . . NCLC 2

Bainbridge, Beryl
   1933- . . . . CLC 4, 5, 8, 10, 14, 18, 22, 62
See also CANR 24; CA 21-24R; DLB 14

Baker, Elliott 1922- . . . . CLC 8, 61
See also CANR 2; CA 45-48

Baker, Nicholson 1957- . . . . CLC 61

Baker, Russell (Wayne) 1925- . . . . . . CLC 31
See also CANR 11; CA 57-60

Bakshi, Ralph 1938- . . . . CLC 26
See also CA 112

Bakunin, Mikhail (Alexandrovich)
   1814-1876 . . . . NCLC 25

Baldwin, James (Arthur)
   1924-1987 . . . . . CLC 1, 2, 3, 4, 5, 8, 13,
         15, 17, 42, 50, 67; DC 1; SSC 10
See also BLC 1; WLC 1; CANR 3,24;
   CA 1-4R; obituary CA 124; CABS 1;
   SATA 9, 54; DLB 2, 7, 33; DLB-Y 87;
   CDALB 1941-1968; AAYA 4

Ballard, J(ames) G(raham)
   1930- . . . . CLC 3, 6, 14, 36; SSC 1
See also CANR 15; CA 5-8R; DLB 14

Balmont, Konstantin Dmitriyevich
   1867-1943 . . . . TCLC 11
See also CA 109

Balzac, Honore de
   1799-1850 . . . . NCLC 5, 35; SSC 5
See also WLC 1

Bambara, Toni Cade 1939- . . . . CLC 19
See also BLC 1; CANR 24; CA 29-32R;
   DLB 38; AAYA 5

Bandanes, Jerome 1937- . . . . CLC 59

Banim, John 1798-1842 . . . . NCLC 13

Banim, Michael 1796-1874 . . . . . . NCLC 13

Banks, Iain 1954- . . . . CLC 34
See also CA 123

Banks, Lynne Reid 1929- . . . . CLC 23
See also Reid Banks, Lynne

Banks, Russell 1940- . . . . CLC 37, 72
See also CANR 19; CA 65-68

Banville, John 1945- . . . . CLC 46
See also CA 117, 128; DLB 14

Banville, Theodore (Faullain) de
   1832-1891 . . . . NCLC 9

Baraka, Imamu Amiri
   1934- . . . CLC 1, 2, 3, 5, 10, 14, 33; PC 4
See also Jones, (Everett) LeRoi
See also BLC 1; CANR 27; CA 21-24R;
   CABS 3; DLB 5, 7, 16, 38; DLB-DS 8;
   CDALB 1941-1968

Barbellion, W. N. P. 1889-1919 . . . TCLC 24

Barbera, Jack 1945- . . . . CLC 44
See also CA 110

Barbey d'Aurevilly, Jules Amedee
   1808-1889 . . . . NCLC 1

Barbusse, Henri 1873-1935 . . . . TCLC 5
See also CA 105; DLB 65

Barea, Arturo 1897-1957 . . . . TCLC 14
See also CA 111

Barfoot, Joan 1946- . . . . CLC 18
See also CA 105

Baring, Maurice 1874-1945 . . . . TCLC 8
See also CA 105; DLB 34

Barker, Clive 1952- . . . . CLC 52
See also CA 121

Barker, George (Granville)
   1913- . . . . CLC 8, 48
See also CANR 7; CA 9-12R; DLB 20

Barker, Howard 1946- . . . . CLC 37
See also CA 102; DLB 13

Barker, Pat 1943- . . . . CLC 32
See also CA 117, 122

Barlow, Joel 1754-1812 . . . . NCLC 23
See also DLB 37

Barnard, Mary (Ethel) 1909- . . . . CLC 48
See also CAP 2; CA 21-22

Barnes, Djuna (Chappell)
   1892-1982 . . . CLC 3, 4, 8, 11, 29; SSC 3
See also CANR 16; CA 9-12R;
   obituary CA 107; DLB 4, 9, 45

Barnes, Julian 1946- . . . . CLC 42
See also CANR 19; CA 102

Barnes, Peter 1931- . . . . CLC 5, 56
See also CA 65-68; DLB 13

Baroja (y Nessi), Pio 1872-1956 . . . . TCLC 8
See also CA 104

Barondess, Sue K(aufman) 1926-1977
See Kaufman, Sue
See also CANR 1; CA 1-4R;
   obituary CA 69-72

Barrett, (Roger) Syd 1946-
See Pink Floyd

Barrett, William (Christopher)
   1913- . . . . CLC 27
See also CANR 11; CA 13-16R

Barrie, (Sir) J(ames) M(atthew)
   1860-1937 . . . . TCLC 2
See also CLR 16; YABC 1; CA 104;
   DLB 10

Barrol, Grady 1953-
See Bograd, Larry

Barry, Philip (James Quinn)
   1896-1949 . . . . TCLC 11
See also CA 109; DLB 7

Barth, John (Simmons)
   1930- . . . . . . CLC 1, 2, 3, 5, 7, 9, 10, 14,
                        27, 51; SSC 10
See also CANR 5, 23; CA 1-4R; CABS 1;
   DLB 2

Barthelme, Donald
   1931-1989 . . . . . CLC 1, 2, 3, 5, 6, 8, 13,
                        23, 46, 59; SSC 2
See also CANR 20; CA 21-24R, 129;
   SATA 7; DLB 2; DLB-Y 80

Barthelme, Frederick 1943- . . . . CLC 36
See also CA 114, 122; DLB-Y 85

Barthes, Roland 1915-1980 . . . . CLC 24
See also obituary CA 97-100

Barzun, Jacques (Martin) 1907- . . . . CLC 51
See also CANR 22; CA 61-64

Bashevis, Isaac 1904-1991
See Singer, Isaac Bashevis

Bashkirtseff, Marie 1859-1884 . . . NCLC 27

Basho, Matsuo 1644-1694 . . . . PC 3

Bass, Kingsley B. 1935-

Bassani, Giorgio 1916- . . . . CLC 9
See also CA 65-68

Bataille, Georges 1897-1962 . . . . CLC 29
See also CA 101; obituary CA 89-92

Bates, H(erbert) E(rnest)
   1905-1974 . . . . CLC 46; SSC 10
See also CANR 34; CA 93-96;
   obituary CA 45-48

Baudelaire, Charles
   1821-1867 . . . . NCLC 6, 29; PC 1
See also WLC 1

Baudrillard, Jean 1929- . . . . CLC 60

Baum, L(yman) Frank 1856-1919 . . . TCLC 7
See also CLR 15; CA 108; SATA 18;
   DLB 22

Baumbach, Jonathan 1933- . . . . . . CLC 6, 23
See also CAAS 5; CANR 12; CA 13-16R;
   DLB-Y 80

Bausch, Richard (Carl) 1945- . . . . . . CLC 51
See also CA 101

Baxter, Charles 1947- . . . . CLC 45
See also CA 57-60

Baxter, James K(eir) 1926-1972 . . . . CLC 14
See also CA 77-80

Bayer, Sylvia 1909-1981
See Glassco, John

Beagle, Peter S(oyer) 1939- . . . . CLC 7
See also CANR 4; CA 9-12R; DLB-Y 80

Burroughs, William S(eward)
1914- .... **CLC 1, 2, 5, 15, 22, 42**
See also WLC 1; CANR 20; CA 9-12R;
DLB 2, 8, 16; DLB-Y 81

Busch, Frederick 1941- ... **CLC 7, 10, 18, 47**
See also CAAS 1; CA 33-36R; DLB 6

Bush, Ronald 19??- .... **CLC 34**

Butler, Octavia E(stelle) 1947- ..... **CLC 38**
See also CANR 12, 24; CA 73-76; DLB 33

Butler, Samuel 1612-1680 .... **LC 16**
See also DLB 101

Butler, Samuel 1835-1902 ...... **TCLC 1, 33**
See also WLC 1; CA 104; DLB 18, 57

Butor, Michel (Marie Francois)
1926- .... **CLC 1, 3, 8, 11, 15**
See also CA 9-12R

Buzo, Alexander 1944- .... **CLC 61**
See also CANR 17; CA 97-100

Buzzati, Dino 1906-1972 .... **CLC 36**
See also obituary CA 33-36R

Byars, Betsy 1928- .... **CLC 35**
See also CLR 1, 16; CANR 18; CA 33-36R;
SAAS 1; SATA 4, 46; DLB 52

Byatt, A(ntonia) S(usan Drabble)
1936- .... **CLC 19, 65**
See also CANR 13, 33; CA 13-16R;
DLB 14

Byrne, David 1953?- .... **CLC 26**

Byrne, John Keyes 1926-
See Leonard, Hugh
See also CA 102

Byron, George Gordon (Noel), Lord Byron
1788-1824 .... **NCLC 2, 12**
See also WLC 1

Caballero, Fernan 1796-1877..... **NCLC 10**

Cabell, James Branch 1879-1958 ... **TCLC 6**
See also CA 105; DLB 9, 78

Cable, George Washington
1844-1925 .... **TCLC 4; SSC 4**
See also CA 104; DLB 12, 74

Cabrera Infante, G(uillermo)
1929- .... **CLC 5, 25, 45**
See also CANR 29; CA 85-88

Cade, Toni 1939-
See Bambara, Toni Cade

CAEdmon fl. 658-680 .... **CMLC 7**

Cage, John (Milton, Jr.) 1912- ..... **CLC 41**
See also CANR 9; CA 13-16R

Cain, G. 1929-
See Cabrera Infante, G(uillermo)

Cain, James M(allahan)
1892-1977 .... **CLC 3, 11, 28**
See also CANR 8; CA 17-20R;
obituary CA 73-76

Caldwell, Erskine (Preston)
1903-1987 .... **CLC 1, 8, 14, 50, 60**
See also CAAS 1; CANR 2; CA 1-4R;
obituary CA 121; DLB 9, 86

Caldwell, (Janet Miriam) Taylor (Holland)
1900-1985 .... **CLC 2, 28, 39**
See also CANR 5; CA 5-8R;
obituary CA 116

Calhoun, John Caldwell
1782-1850 .... **NCLC 15**
See also DLB 3

Calisher, Hortense 1911-.... **CLC 2, 4, 8, 38**
See also CANR 1, 22; CA 1-4R; DLB 2

Callaghan, Morley (Edward)
1903-1990 .... **CLC 3, 14, 41, 65**
See also CANR 33; CA 9-12R;
obituary CA 132; DLB 68

Calvino, Italo
1923-1985 .... **CLC 5, 8, 11, 22, 33, 39;**
SSC 3
See also CANR 23; CA 85-88;
obituary CA 116

Cameron, Carey 1952- .... **CLC 59**

Cameron, Peter 1959-.............. **CLC 44**
See also CA 125

Campana, Dino 1885-1932....... **TCLC 20**
See also CA 117

Campbell, John W(ood), Jr.
1910-1971 .... **CLC 32**
See also CAP 2; CA 21-22;
obituary CA 29-32R; DLB 8

Campbell, Joseph 1904-1987 .... **CLC 69**
See also CANR 3, 28; CA 4R;
obituary CA 124; AAYA 3

Campbell, (John) Ramsey 1946- .... **CLC 42**
See also CANR 7; CA 57-60

Campbell, (Ignatius) Roy (Dunnachie)
1901-1957 .... **TCLC 5**
See also CA 104; DLB 20

Campbell, Thomas 1777-1844 .... **NCLC 19**

Campbell, (William) Wilfred
1861-1918 .... **TCLC 9**
See also CA 106

Camus, Albert
1913-1960 ... **CLC 1, 2, 4, 9, 11, 14, 32,**
63, 69; DC 2; SSC 9
See also WLC 1; CA 89-92; DLB 72

Canby, Vincent 1924-............. **CLC 13**
See also CA 81-84

Canetti, Elias 1905- .... **CLC 3, 14, 25**
See also CANR 23; CA 21-24R; DLB 85

Canin, Ethan 1960-............... **CLC 55**

Cape, Judith 1916-
See Page, P(atricia) K(athleen)

Capek, Karel
1890-1938 .... **TCLC 6, 37; DC 1**
See also WLC 1; CA 104

Capote, Truman
1924-1984 ..... **CLC 1, 3, 8, 13, 19, 34,**
38, 58; SSC 2
See also WLC 1; CANR 18; CA 5-8R;
obituary CA 113; DLB 2; DLB-Y 80, 84;
CDALB 1941-1968

Capra, Frank 1897-............... **CLC 16**
See also CA 61-64

Caputo, Philip 1941-.............. **CLC 32**
See also CA 73-76

Card, Orson Scott 1951- .... **CLC 44, 47, 50**
See also CA 102

Cardenal, Ernesto 1925-........... **CLC 31**
See also CANR 2; CA 49-52

Carducci, Giosue 1835-1907....... **TCLC 32**

Carew, Thomas 1595?-1640 .... **LC 13**

Carey, Ernestine Gilbreth 1908-.... **CLC 17**
See also CA 5-8R; SATA 2

Carey, Peter 1943-........... **CLC 40, 55**
See also CA 123, 127

Carleton, William 1794-1869...... **NCLC 3**

Carlisle, Henry (Coffin) 1926-...... **CLC 33**
See also CANR 15; CA 13-16R

Carlson, Ron(ald F.) 1947-........ **CLC 54**
See also CA 105

Carlyle, Thomas 1795-1881 ...... **NCLC 22**
See also DLB 55

Carman, (William) Bliss
1861-1929 .... **TCLC 7**
See also CA 104

Carpenter, Don(ald Richard)
1931- .... **CLC 41**
See also CANR 1; CA 45-48

Carpentier (y Valmont), Alejo
1904-1980 .... **CLC 8, 11, 38**
See also CANR 11; CA 65-68;
obituary CA 97-100

Carr, Emily 1871-1945.......... **TCLC 32**
See also DLB 68

Carr, John Dickson 1906-1977 ...... **CLC 3**
See also CANR 3; CA 49-52;
obituary CA 69-72

Carr, Virginia Spencer 1929-....... **CLC 34**
See also CA 61-64

Carrier, Roch 1937-.............. **CLC 13**
See also DLB 53

Carroll, James (P.) 1943-.......... **CLC 38**
See also CA 81-84

Carroll, Jim 1951- .... **CLC 35**
See also CA 45-48

Carroll, Lewis 1832-1898........ **NCLC 2**
See also Dodgson, Charles Lutwidge
See also CLR 2; WLC 1; DLB 18

Carroll, Paul Vincent 1900-1968.... **CLC 10**
See also CA 9-12R; obituary CA 25-28R;
DLB 10

Carruth, Hayden 1921- .... **CLC 4, 7, 10, 18**
See also CANR 4; CA 9-12R; SATA 47;
DLB 5

Carson, Rachel 1907-1964 .... **CLC 71**
See also CANR 35; CA 77-80; SATA 23

Carter, Angela (Olive) 1940-..... **CLC 5, 41**
See also CANR 12; CA 53-56; DLB 14

Carver, Raymond
1938-1988 ... **CLC 22, 36, 53, 55; SSC 8**
See also CANR 17; CA 33-36R;
obituary CA 126; DLB-Y 84, 88

Cary, (Arthur) Joyce (Lunel)
1888-1957 .... **TCLC 1, 29**
See also CA 104; DLB 15

Casanova de Seingalt, Giovanni Jacopo
1725-1798 .... **LC 13**

Casares, Adolfo Bioy 1914-
See Bioy Casares, Adolfo

Casely-Hayford, J(oseph) E(phraim)
1866-1930 .... **TCLC 24**
See also BLC 1; CA 123

Casey, John 1880-1964
See O'Casey, Sean

Conrad, Robert Arnold 1904-1961
See Hart, Moss

Conroy, Pat 1945-............... CLC 30
See also CANR 24; CA 85-88; DLB 6

Constant (de Rebecque), (Henri) Benjamin
1767-1830 .... NCLC 6

Cook, Michael 1933- .... CLC 58
See also CA 93-96; DLB 53

Cook, Robin 1940- .... CLC 14
See also CA 108, 111

Cooke, Elizabeth 1948- .... CLC 55

Cooke, John Esten 1830-1886..... NCLC 5
See also DLB 3

Cooney, Ray 19??- .... CLC 62

Cooper, Edith Emma 1862-1913
See Field, Michael

Cooper, J. California 19??- .... CLC 56
See also CA 125

Cooper, James Fenimore
1789-1851 .... NCLC 1, 27
See also SATA 19; DLB 3;
CDALB 1640-1865

Coover, Robert (Lowell)
1932- .... CLC 3, 7, 15, 32, 46
See also CANR 3; CA 45-48; DLB 2;
DLB-Y 81

Copeland, Stewart (Armstrong)
1952- .... CLC 26
See also The Police

Coppard, A(lfred) E(dgar)
1878-1957 .... TCLC 5
See also YABC 1; CA 114

Coppee, Francois 1842-1908 ...... TCLC 25

Coppola, Francis Ford 1939-....... CLC 16
See also CA 77-80; DLB 44

Corcoran, Barbara 1911-.......... CLC 17
See also CAAS 2; CANR 11; CA 21-24R;
SATA 3; DLB 52

Corman, Cid 1924- .... CLC 9
See also Corman, Sidney
See also CAAS 2; DLB 5

Corman, Sidney 1924-
See Corman, Cid
See also CA 85-88

Cormier, Robert (Edmund)
1925-.................... CLC 12, 30
See also CLR 12; CANR 5, 23; CA 1-4R;
SATA 10, 45; DLB 52

Corn, Alfred (Dewitt III) 1943-..... CLC 33
See also CA 104; DLB-Y 80

Cornwell, David (John Moore)
1931-.................... CLC 9, 15
See also le Carre, John
See also CANR 13; CA 5-8R

Corso, (Nunzio) Gregory 1930-... CLC 1, 11
See also CA 5-8R; DLB 5, 16

Cortazar, Julio
1914-1984 ..... CLC 2, 3, 5, 10, 13, 15,
33, 34; SSC 7
See also CANR 12; CA 21-24R

Corvo, Baron 1860-1913
See Rolfe, Frederick (William Serafino
Austin Lewis Mary)

Cosic, Dobrica 1921- .... CLC 14
See also CA 122

Costain, Thomas B(ertram)
1885-1965 .... CLC 30
See also CA 5-8R; obituary CA 25-28R;
DLB 9

Costantini, Humberto 1924?-1987... CLC 49
See also obituary CA 122

Costello, Elvis 1955-............. CLC 21

Cotter, Joseph Seamon, Sr.
1861-1949 .... TCLC 28
See also BLC 1; CA 124; DLB 50

Couperus, Louis (Marie Anne)
1863-1923 .... TCLC 15
See also CA 115

Courtenay, Bryce 1933-........... CLC 59

Cousteau, Jacques-Yves 1910-...... CLC 30
See also CANR 15; CA 65-68; SATA 38

Coward, (Sir) Noel (Pierce)
1899-1973 .... CLC 1, 9, 29, 51
See also CAP 2; CA 17-18;
obituary CA 41-44R; DLB 10

Cowley, Malcolm 1898-1989 .... CLC 39
See also CANR 3; CA 5-6R;
obituary CA 128; DLB 4, 48; DLB-Y 81

Cowper, William 1731-1800...... NCLC 8

Cox, William Trevor 1928- ... CLC 9, 14, 71
See also Trevor, William
See also CANR 4; CA 9-12R; DLB 14

Cozzens, James Gould
1903-1978 .... CLC 1, 4, 11
See also CANR 19; CA 9-12R;
obituary CA 81-84; DLB 9; DLB-Y 84;
DLB-DS 2; CDALB 1941-1968

Crabbe, George 1754-1832....... NCLC 26

Crace, Douglas 1944-............. CLC 58

Cram, Ralph Adams 1863-1942.... TCLC 45

Crane, (Harold) Hart
1899-1932 .... TCLC 2, 5; PC 3
See also WLC 2; CA 127;
brief entry CA 104; DLB 4, 48;
CDALB 1917-1929

Crane, R(onald) S(almon)
1886-1967 .... CLC 27
See also CA 85-88; DLB 63

Crane, Stephen
1871-1900 ..... TCLC 11, 17, 32; SSC 7
See also WLC 2; YABC 2; CA 109;
DLB 12, 54, 78; CDALB 1865-1917

Craven, Margaret 1901-1980....... CLC 17
See also CA 103

Crawford, F(rancis) Marion
1854-1909 .... TCLC 10
See also CA 107; DLB 71

Crawford, Isabella Valancy
1850-1887 .... NCLC 12
See also DLB 92

Crayencour, Marguerite de 1903-1987
See Yourcenar, Marguerite

Creasey, John 1908-1973.......... CLC 11
See also CANR 8; CA 5-8R;
obituary CA 41-44R; DLB 77

Crebillon, Claude Prosper Jolyot de (fils)
1707-1777 .... LC 1

Creeley, Robert (White)
1926-........ CLC 1, 2, 4, 8, 11, 15, 36
See also CANR 23; CA 1-4R; DLB 5, 16

Crews, Harry (Eugene)
1935-.................CLC 6, 23, 49
See also CANR 20; CA 25-28R; DLB 6

Crichton, (John) Michael
1942-.................... CLC 2, 6, 54
See also CANR 13; CA 25-28R; SATA 9;
DLB-Y 81

Crispin, Edmund 1921-1978........ CLC 22
See also Montgomery, Robert Bruce
See also DLB 87

Cristofer, Michael 1946-.......... CLC 28
See also CA 110; DLB 7

Croce, Benedetto 1866-1952 ...... TCLC 37
See also CA 120

Crockett, David (Davy)
1786-1836 .... NCLC 8
See also DLB 3, 11

Croker, John Wilson 1780-1857 .. NCLC 10

Cronin, A(rchibald) J(oseph)
1896-1981 .... CLC 32
See also CANR 5; CA 1-4R;
obituary CA 102; obituary SATA 25, 47

Cross, Amanda 1926-
See Heilbrun, Carolyn G(old)

Crothers, Rachel 1878-1953....... TCLC 19
See also CA 113; DLB 7

Crowley, Aleister 1875-1947 .... TCLC 7
See also CA 104

Crowley, John 1942-
See also CA 61-64; DLB-Y 82

Crumb, Robert 1943-............. CLC 17
See also CA 106

Cryer, Gretchen 1936?- .... CLC 21
See also CA 114, 123

Csath, Geza 1887-1919........... TCLC 13
See also CA 111

Cudlip, David 1933-............. CLC 34

Cullen, Countee 1903-1946 ..... TCLC 4, 37
See also BLC 1; CA 108, 124; SATA 18;
DLB 4, 48, 51; CDALB 1917-1929

Cummings, E(dward) E(stlin)
1894-1962 ..... CLC 1, 3, 8, 12, 15, 68;
PC 5
See also WLC 2; CANR 31; CA 73-76;
DLB 4, 48; CDALB 1929-1941

Cunha, Euclides (Rodrigues) da
1866-1909 .... TCLC 24
See also CA 123

Cunningham, J(ames) V(incent)
1911-1985 .... CLC 3, 31
See also CANR 1; CA 1-4R;
obituary CA 115; DLB 5

Cunningham, Julia (Woolfolk)
1916-.................... CLC 12
See also CANR 4, 19; CA 9-12R; SAAS 2;
SATA 1, 26

Cunningham, Michael 1952- .... CLC 34

Currie, Ellen 19??-............... CLC 44

Dabrowska, Maria (Szumska)
1889-1965 .... CLC 15
See also CA 106

Dabydeen, David 1956?-.......... **CLC 34**
See also CA 106

Dacey, Philip 1939- .... **CLC 51**
See also CANR 14; CA 37-40R

Dagerman, Stig (Halvard)
1923-1954 .... **TCLC 17**
See also CA 117

Dahl, Roald 1916-........... **CLC 1, 6, 18**
See also CLR 1, 7; CANR 6; CA 1-4R;
SATA 1, 26

Dahlberg, Edward 1900-1977... **CLC 1, 7, 14**
See also CA 9-12R; obituary CA 69-72;
DLB 48

Daly, Elizabeth 1878-1967........ **CLC 52**
See also CAP 2; CA 23-24;
obituary CA 25-28R

Daly, Maureen 1921- .... **CLC 17**
See also McGivern, Maureen Daly
See also SAAS 1; SATA 2

Daniken, Erich von 1935-
See Von Daniken, Erich

Dannay, Frederic 1905-1982
See Queen, Ellery
See also CANR 1; CA 1-4R;
obituary CA 107

D'Annunzio, Gabriele
1863-1938 .... **TCLC 6, 40**
See also CA 104

Dante (Alighieri)
See Alighieri, Dante

Danvers, Dennis 1947-........... **CLC 70**

Danziger, Paula 1944- .... **CLC 21**
See also CLR 20; CA 112, 115; SATA 30,
36

Dario, Ruben 1867-1916 .... **TCLC 4**
See also Sarmiento, Felix Ruben Garcia
See also CA 104

Darley, George 1795-1846 .... **NCLC 2**

Daryush, Elizabeth 1887-1977.... **CLC 6, 19**
See also CANR 3; CA 49-52; DLB 20

Daudet, (Louis Marie) Alphonse
1840-1897 .... **NCLC 1**

Daumal, Rene 1908-1944........ **TCLC 14**
See also CA 114

Davenport, Guy (Mattison, Jr.)
1927- .... **CLC 6, 14, 38**
See also CANR 23; CA 33-36R

Davidson, Donald (Grady)
1893-1968 .... **CLC 2, 13, 19**
See also CANR 4; CA 5-8R;
obituary CA 25-28R; DLB 45

Davidson, John 1857-1909........ **TCLC 24**
See also CA 118; DLB 19

Davidson, Sara 1943- .... **CLC 9**
See also CA 81-84

Davie, Donald (Alfred)
1922- .... **CLC 5, 8, 10, 31**
See also CAAS 3; CANR 1; CA 1-4R;
DLB 27

Davies, Ray(mond Douglas) 1944- .. **CLC 21**
See also CA 116

Davies, Rhys 1903-1978........... **CLC 23**
See also CANR 4; CA 9-12R;
obituary CA 81-84

Davies, (William) Robertson
1913- .... **CLC 2, 7, 13, 25, 42**
See also WLC 2; CANR 17; CA 33-36R;
DLB 68

Davies, W(illiam) H(enry)
1871-1940 .... **TCLC 5**
See also CA 104; DLB 19

Davis, Frank Marshall 1905-1987
See also BLC 1; CA 123, 125; DLB 51

Davis, H(arold) L(enoir)
1896-1960 .... **CLC 49**
See also obituary CA 89-92; DLB 9

Davis, Rebecca (Blaine) Harding
1831-1910 .... **TCLC 6**
See also CA 104; DLB 74

Davis, Richard Harding
1864-1916 .... **TCLC 24**
See also CA 114; DLB 12, 23, 78, 79

Davison, Frank Dalby 1893-1970 ... **CLC 15**
See also obituary CA 116

Davison, Peter 1928- .... **CLC 28**
See also CAAS 4; CANR 3; CA 9-12R;
DLB 5

Davys, Mary 1674-1732............. **LC 1**
See also DLB 39

Dawson, Fielding 1930- .... **CLC 6**
See also CA 85-88

Day, Clarence (Shepard, Jr.)
1874-1935 .... **TCLC 25**
See also CA 108; DLB 11

Day, Thomas 1748-1789............. **LC 1**
See also YABC 1; DLB 39

Day Lewis, C(ecil)
1904-1972 .... **CLC 1, 6, 10**
See also CAP 1; CA 15-16;
obituary CA 33-36R; DLB 15, 20

Dazai Osamu 1909-1948 .... **TCLC 11**
See also Tsushima Shuji

De Crayencour, Marguerite 1903-1987
See Yourcenar, Marguerite

Deer, Sandra 1940-............... **CLC 45**

De Ferrari, Gabriella 19??- .... **CLC 65**

Defoe, Daniel 1660?-1731 .... **LC 1**
See also WLC 2; SATA 22; DLB 39

De Hartog, Jan 1914-............. **CLC 19**
See also CANR 1; CA 1-4R

Deighton, Len 1929-....... **CLC 4, 7, 22, 46**
See also Deighton, Leonard Cyril
See also DLB 87

Deighton, Leonard Cyril 1929-
See Deighton, Len
See also CANR 19; CA 9-12R

De la Mare, Walter (John)
1873-1956 .... **TCLC 4**
See also CLR 23; WLC 2; CA 110;
SATA 16; DLB 19

Delaney, Shelagh 1939-........... **CLC 29**
See also CA 17-20R; DLB 13

Delany, Mary (Granville Pendarves)
1700-1788 .... **LC 12**

Delany, Samuel R(ay, Jr.)
1942- .... **CLC 8, 14, 38**
See also BLC 1; CANR 27; CA 81-84;
DLB 8, 33

de la Ramee, Marie Louise 1839-1908
See Ouida
See also SATA 20

De la Roche, Mazo 1885-1961 ..... **CLC 14**
See also CA 85-88; DLB 68

Delbanco, Nicholas (Franklin)
1942-..................... **CLC 6, 13**
See also CAAS 2; CA 17-20R; DLB 6

del Castillo, Michel 1933-......... **CLC 38**
See also CA 109

Deledda, Grazia 1871-1936 .... **TCLC 23**
See also CA 123

Delibes (Setien), Miguel 1920- ... **CLC 8, 18**
See also CANR 1; CA 45-48

DeLillo, Don
1936-........ **CLC 8, 10, 13, 27, 39, 54**
See also CANR 21; CA 81-84; DLB 6

De Lisser, H(erbert) G(eorge)
1878-1944 .... **TCLC 12**
See also CA 109

Deloria, Vine (Victor), Jr. 1933-.... **CLC 21**
See also CANR 5, 20; CA 53-56; SATA 21

Del Vecchio, John M(ichael)
1947-...................... **CLC 29**
See also CA 110

de Man, Paul 1919-1983 .... **CLC 55**
See also obituary CA 111; DLB 67

De Marinis, Rick 1934-........... **CLC 54**
See also CANR 9, 25; CA 57-60

Demby, William 1922-............. **CLC 53**
See also BLC 1; CA 81-84; DLB 33

Denby, Edwin (Orr) 1903-1983 ..... **CLC 48**
See also obituary CA 110

Dennis, John 1657-1734........... **LC 11**

Dennis, Nigel (Forbes) 1912-........ **CLC 8**
See also CA 25-28R; obituary CA 129;
DLB 13, 15

De Palma, Brian 1940-........... **CLC 20**
See also CA 109

De Quincey, Thomas 1785-1859 ... **NCLC 4**

Deren, Eleanora 1908-1961
See Deren, Maya
See also obituary CA 111

Deren, Maya 1908-1961........... **CLC 16**
See also Deren, Eleanora

Derleth, August (William)
1909-1971 .... **CLC 31**
See also CANR 4; CA 1-4R;
obituary CA 29-32R; SATA 5; DLB 9

Derrida, Jacques 1930-........... **CLC 24**
See also CA 124, 127

Desai, Anita 1937-............ **CLC 19, 37**
See also CA 81-84

De Saint-Luc, Jean 1909-1981
See Glassco, John

De Sica, Vittorio 1902-1974 .... **CLC 20**
See also obituary CA 117

Desnos, Robert 1900-1945........ **TCLC 22**
See also CA 121

Destouches, Louis-Ferdinand-Auguste
1894-1961
See Celine, Louis-Ferdinand
See also CA 85-88

Duerrenmatt, Friedrich
1921- .... **CLC 1, 4, 8, 11, 15, 43**
See also CA 17-20R; DLB 69

Duffy, Bruce 19??- .... **CLC 50**

Duffy, Maureen 1933- .... **CLC 37**
See also CA 25-28R; DLB 14

Dugan, Alan 1923- .... **CLC 2, 6**
See also CA 81-84; DLB 5

Duhamel, Georges 1884-1966 .... **CLC 8**
See also CA 81-84; obituary CA 25-28R;
DLB 65

Dujardin, Edouard (Emile Louis)
1861-1949 .... **TCLC 13**
See also CA 109

Duke, Raoul 1939-
See Thompson, Hunter S(tockton)

Dumas, Alexandre (Davy de la Pailleterie)
(pere) 1802-1870.......... **NCLC 11**
See also WLC 2; SATA 18

Dumas, Alexandre (fils)
1824-1895 .... **NCLC 9; DC 1**

Dumas, Henry 1918-1968 .... **CLC 62**

Dumas, Henry (L.) 1934-1968....... **CLC 6**
See also CA 85-88; DLB 41

Du Maurier, Daphne 1907- ... **CLC 6, 11, 59**
See also CANR 6; CA 5-8R;
obituary CA 128; SATA 27

Dunbar, Paul Laurence
1872-1906 .... **TCLC 2, 12; PC 5; SSC 8**
See also BLC 1; WLC 2; CA 124;
brief entry CA 104; SATA 34; DLB 50,
54, 78; CDALB 1865-1917

Duncan (Steinmetz Arquette), Lois
1934- .... **CLC 26**
See also Arquette, Lois S(teinmetz)
See also CANR 2; CA 1-4R; SAAS 2;
SATA 1, 36

Duncan, Robert (Edward)
1919-1988 ... **CLC 1, 2, 4, 7, 15, 41, 55;**
PC 2
See also CANR 28; CA 9-12R;
obituary CA 124; DLB 5, 16

Dunlap, William 1766-1839 ...... **NCLC 2**
See also DLB 30, 37, 59

Dunn, Douglas (Eaglesham)
1942- .... **CLC 6, 40**
See also CANR 2; CA 45-48; DLB 40

Dunn, Elsie 1893-1963
See Scott, Evelyn

Dunn, Katherine 1945- .... **CLC 71**
See also CA 33-36R

Dunn, Stephen 1939- .... **CLC 36**
See also CANR 12; CA 33-36R

Dunne, Finley Peter 1867-1936.... **TCLC 28**
See also CA 108; DLB 11, 23

Dunne, John Gregory 1932-........ **CLC 28**
See also CANR 14; CA 25-28R; DLB-Y 80

Dunsany, Lord (Edward John Moreton Drax
Plunkett) 1878-1957......... **TCLC 2**
See also CA 104; DLB 10

Durang, Christopher (Ferdinand)
1949- .... **CLC 27, 38**
See also CA 105

Duras, Marguerite
1914- ...... **CLC 3, 6, 11, 20, 34, 40, 68**
See also CA 25-28R; DLB 83

Durban, Pam 1947-................ **CLC 39**
See also CA 123

Durcan, Paul 1944-............ **CLC 43, 70**
See also CA 134

Durrell, Lawrence (George)
1912-1990 .... **CLC 1, 4, 6, 8, 13, 27, 41**
See also CA 9-12R; DLB 15, 27

Durrenmatt, Friedrich
1921- .... **CLC 1, 4, 8, 11, 15, 43**
See also Duerrenmatt, Friedrich
See also DLB 69

Dutt, Toru 1856-1877.......... **NCLC 29**

Dwight, Timothy 1752-1817...... **NCLC 13**
See also DLB 37

Dworkin, Andrea 1946- .... **CLC 43**
See also CANR 16; CA 77-80

Dylan, Bob 1941-........ **CLC 3, 4, 6, 12**
See also CA 41-44R; DLB 16

Eagleton, Terry 1943-............ **CLC 63**

East, Michael 1916-
See West, Morris L.

Eastlake, William (Derry) 1917-..... **CLC 8**
See also CAAS 1; CANR 5; CA 5-8R;
DLB 6

Eberhart, Richard 1904-... **CLC 3, 11, 19, 56**
See also CANR 2; CA 1-4R; DLB 48;
CDALB 1941-1968

Eberstadt, Fernanda 1960-........ **CLC 39**

Echegaray (y Eizaguirre), Jose (Maria Waldo)
1832-1916 .... **TCLC 4**
See also CA 104

Echeverria, (Jose) Esteban (Antonino)
1805-1851 .... **NCLC 18**

Eckert, Allan W. 1931- .... **CLC 17**
See also CANR 14; CA 13-16R; SATA 27,
29

Eckhart, Meister c. 1260-c. 1327 .. **CMLC 9**

Eco, Umberto 1932-.......... **CLC 28, 60**
See also CANR 12; CA 77-80

Eddison, E(ric) R(ucker)
1882-1945 .... **TCLC 15**
See also CA 109

Edel, Leon (Joseph) 1907-...... **CLC 29, 34**
See also CANR 1, 22; CA 1-4R

Eden, Emily 1797-1869 .... **NCLC 10**

Edgar, David 1948-.............. **CLC 42**
See also CANR 12; CA 57-60; DLB 13

Edgerton, Clyde 1944-............ **CLC 39**
See also CA 118

Edgeworth, Maria 1767-1849...... **NCLC 1**
See also SATA 21

Edmonds, Helen (Woods) 1904-1968
See Kavan, Anna
See also CA 5-8R; obituary CA 25-28R

Edmonds, Walter D(umaux) 1903- .. **CLC 35**
See also CANR 2; CA 5-8R; SAAS 4;
SATA 1, 27; DLB 9

Edson, Russell 1905- .... **CLC 13**
See also CA 33-36R

Edwards, Eli 1889-1948
See McKay, Claude

Edwards, G(erald) B(asil)
1899-1976 .... **CLC 25**
See also obituary CA 110

Edwards, Gus 1939- .... **CLC 43**
See also CA 108

Edwards, Jonathan 1703-1758....... **LC 7**
See also DLB 24

Ehle, John (Marsden, Jr.) 1925-.... **CLC 27**
See also CA 9-12R

Ehrenburg, Ilya (Grigoryevich)
1891-1967 .... **CLC 18, 34, 62**
See also CA 102; obituary CA 25-28R

Eich, Guenter 1907-1971
See also CA 111; obituary CA 93-96

Eich, Gunter 1907-1971.......... **CLC 15**
See also Eich, Guenter
See also DLB 69

Eichendorff, Joseph Freiherr von
1788-1857 .... **NCLC 8**
See also DLB 90

Eigner, Larry 1927- .... **CLC 9**
See also Eigner, Laurence (Joel)
See also DLB 5

Eigner, Laurence (Joel) 1927-
See Eigner, Larry
See also CANR 6; CA 9-12R

Eiseley, Loren (Corey) 1907-1977.... **CLC 7**
See also CANR 6; CA 1-4R;
obituary CA 73-76

Eisenstadt, Jill 1963- .... **CLC 50**

Ekeloef, Gunnar (Bengt) 1907-1968
See Ekelof, Gunnar (Bengt)
See also obituary CA 25-28R

Ekelof, Gunnar (Bengt) 1907-1968 .. **CLC 27**
See also Ekeloef, Gunnar (Bengt)

Ekwensi, Cyprian (Odiatu Duaka)
1921- .... **CLC 4**
See also BLC 1; CANR 18; CA 29-32R

Elder, Lonne, III 1931-
See also BLC 1; CANR 25; CA 81-84;
DLB 7, 38, 44

Eliade, Mircea 1907-1986 .... **CLC 19**
See also CA 65-68; obituary CA 119

Eliot, George 1819-1880.... **NCLC 4, 13, 23**
See also WLC 2; DLB 21, 35, 55

Eliot, John 1604-1690 .... **LC 5**
See also DLB 24

Eliot, T(homas) S(tearns)
1888-1965 .... **CLC 1, 2, 3, 6, 9, 10, 13,**
15, 24, 34, 41, 55, 57; PC 5
See also WLC 2; CA 5-8R;
obituary CA 25-28R; DLB 7, 10, 45, 63;
DLB-Y 88; CDALB 1929-1941

Elizabeth 1866-1941............. **TCLC 41**
See also Russell, Mary Annette Beauchamp

Elkin, Stanley (Lawrence)
1930- ...... **CLC 4, 6, 9, 14, 27, 51**
See also CANR 8; CA 9-12R; DLB 2, 28;
DLB-Y 80

Elledge, Scott 19??- .... **CLC 34**

Elliott, George P(aul) 1918-1980..... CLC 2
  See also CANR 2; CA 1-4R;
  obituary CA 97-100

Elliott, Janice 1931-.............. CLC 47
  See also CANR 8; CA 13-16R; DLB 14

Elliott, Sumner Locke 1917-....... CLC 38
  See also CANR 2, 21; CA 5-8R

Ellis, A. E. 19??-.................. CLC 7

Ellis, Alice Thomas 19??-......... CLC 40

Ellis, Bret Easton 1964-........ CLC 39, 71
  See also CA 118, 123; AAYA 2

Ellis, (Henry) Havelock
  1859-1939 .... TCLC 14
  See also CA 109

Ellis, Trey 1964-................. CLC 55

Ellison, Harlan (Jay) 1934-... CLC 1, 13, 42
  See also CANR 5; CA 5-8R; DLB 8

Ellison, Ralph (Waldo)
  1914-............CLC 1, 3, 11, 54
  See also BLC 1; WLC 2; CANR 24;
  CA 9-12R; DLB 2, 76;
  CDALB 1941-1968

Ellmann, Lucy 1956- .... CLC 61
  See also CA 128

Ellmann, Richard (David)
  1918-1987 .... CLC 50
  See also CANR 2; CA 1-4R;
  obituary CA 122; DLB-Y 87

Elman, Richard 1934-............. CLC 19
  See also CAAS 3; CA 17-20R

El-Shabazz, El-Hajj Malik 1925-1965
  See Malcolm X

Eluard, Paul 1895-1952 .... TCLC 7, 41
  See also Grindel, Eugene

Elyot, Sir Thomas 1490?-1546...... LC 11

Elytis, Odysseus 1911-........ CLC 15, 49
  See also CA 102

Emecheta, (Florence Onye) Buchi
  1944- .... CLC 14, 48
  See also BLC 2; CANR 27; CA 81-84

Emerson, Ralph Waldo
  1803-1882 .... NCLC 1
  See also WLC 2; DLB 1, 59, 73;
  CDALB 1640-1865

Eminescu, Mihail 1850-1889 ..... NCLC 33

Empson, William
  1906-1984 .... CLC 3, 8, 19, 33, 34
  See also CA 17-20R; obituary CA 112;
  DLB 20

Enchi, Fumiko (Veda) 1905-1986 ... CLC 31
  See also obituary CA 121

Ende, Michael 1930-............. CLC 31
  See also CLR 14; CA 118, 124; SATA 42;
  DLB 75

Endo, Shusaku 1923-..... CLC 7, 14, 19, 54
  See also CANR 21; CA 29-32R

Engel, Marian 1933-1985......... CLC 36
  See also CANR 12; CA 25-28R; DLB 53

Engelhardt, Frederick 1911-1986
  See Hubbard, L(afayette) Ron(ald)

Enright, D(ennis) J(oseph)
  1920- .... CLC 4, 8, 31
  See also CANR 1; CA 1-4R; SATA 25;
  DLB 27

Enzensberger, Hans Magnus
  1929- .... CLC 43
  See also CA 116, 119

Ephron, Nora 1941- .... CLC 17, 31
  See also CANR 12; CA 65-68

Epstein, Daniel Mark 1948- .... CLC 7
  See also CANR 2; CA 49-52

Epstein, Jacob 1956- .... CLC 19
  See also CA 114

Epstein, Joseph 1937-.......... CLC 39
  See also CA 112, 119

Epstein, Leslie 1938-.......... CLC 27
  See also CANR 23; CA 73-76

Equiano, Olaudah 1745?-1797...... LC 16
  See also BLC 2; DLB 37, 50

Erasmus, Desiderius 1469?-1536..... LC 16

Erdman, Paul E(mil) 1932- .... CLC 25
  See also CANR 13; CA 61-64

Erdrich, Louise 1954-......... CLC 39, 54
  See also CA 114

Erenburg, Ilya (Grigoryevich) 1891-1967
  See Ehrenburg, Ilya (Grigoryevich)

Erickson, Steve 1950-............ CLC 64
  See also CA 129

Eseki, Bruno 1919-
  See Mphahlele, Ezekiel

Esenin, Sergei (Aleksandrovich)
  1895-1925 .... TCLC 4
  See also CA 104

Eshleman, Clayton 1935-.......... CLC 7
  See also CAAS 6; CA 33-36R; DLB 5

Espriu, Salvador 1913-1985......... CLC 9
  See also obituary CA 115

Estleman, Loren D. 1952- .... CLC 48
  See also CA 85-88

Evans, Marian 1819-1880
  See Eliot, George

Evans, Mary Ann 1819-1880
  See Eliot, George

Evarts, Esther 1900-1972
  See Benson, Sally

Everett, Percival L. 1957?- .... CLC 57
  See also CA 129

Everson, Ronald G(ilmour) 1903- ... CLC 27
  See also CA 17-20R; DLB 88

Everson, William (Oliver)
  1912- .... CLC 1, 5, 14
  See also CANR 20; CA 9-12R; DLB 5, 16

Everyman 1495- .... DC 2

Evtushenko, Evgenii (Aleksandrovich) 1933-
  See Yevtushenko, Yevgeny

Ewart, Gavin (Buchanan)
  1916- .... CLC 13, 46
  See also CANR 17; CA 89-92; DLB 40

Ewers, Hanns Heinz 1871-1943 ... TCLC 12
  See also CA 109

Ewing, Frederick R. 1918-
  See Sturgeon, Theodore (Hamilton)

Exley, Frederick (Earl) 1929- .... CLC 6, 11
  See also CA 81-84; DLB-Y 81

Ezekiel, Nissim 1924-............ CLC 61
  See also CA 61-64

Ezekiel, Tish O'Dowd 1943-....... CLC 34

Fagen, Donald 1948-............. CLC 26

Fair, Ronald L. 1932-............. CLC 18
  See also CANR 25; CA 69-72; DLB 33

Fairbairns, Zoe (Ann) 1948- .... CLC 32
  See also CANR 21; CA 103

Fairfield, Cicily Isabel 1892-1983
  See West, Rebecca

Fallaci, Oriana 1930-............. CLC 11
  See also CANR 15; CA 77-80

Faludy, George 1913-............. CLC 42
  See also CA 21-24R

Fanon, Frantz 1925-1961
  See also BLC 2; CA 116; obituary CA 89-92

Fante, John 1909-1983............ CLC 60
  See also CANR 23; CA 69-72;
  obituary CA 109; DLB-Y 83

Farah, Nuruddin 1945-............ CLC 53
  See also BLC 2; CA 106

Fargue, Leon-Paul 1876-1947 ..... TCLC 11
  See also CA 109

Farigoule, Louis 1885-1972
  See Romains, Jules

Farina, Richard 1937?-1966......... CLC 9
  See also CA 81-84; obituary CA 25-28R

Farley, Walter 1920- .... CLC 17
  See also CANR 8; CA 17-20R; SATA 2, 43;
  DLB 22

Farmer, Philip Jose 1918-....... CLC 1, 19
  See also CANR 4; CA 1-4R; DLB 8

Farrell, J(ames) G(ordon)
  1935-1979 .... CLC 6
  See also CA 73-76; obituary CA 89-92;
  DLB 14

Farrell, James T(homas)
  1904-1979 .... CLC 1, 4, 8, 11, 66
  See also CANR 9; CA 5-8R;
  obituary CA 89-92; DLB 4, 9, 86;
  DLB-DS 2

Farrell, M. J. 1904-
  See Keane, Molly

Fassbinder, Rainer Werner
  1946-1982 .... CLC 20
  See also CA 93-96; obituary CA 106

Fast, Howard (Melvin) 1914- ...... CLC 23
  See also CANR 1; CA 1-4R; SATA 7;
  DLB 9

Faulkner, William (Cuthbert)
  1897-1962 .... CLC 1, 3, 6, 8, 9, 11, 14,
  18, 28, 52, 68; SSC 1
  See also WLC 2; CANR 33; CA 81-84;
  DLB 9, 11, 44, 102; DLB-Y 86;
  DLB-DS 2; CDALB 1929-1941

Fauset, Jessie Redmon
  1882-1961 .... CLC 19, 54
  See also BLC 2; CA 109; DLB 51

Faust, Irvin 1924-................. CLC 8
  See also CA 33-36R; DLB 2, 28; DLB-Y 80

Fearing, Kenneth (Flexner)
  1902-1961 .... CLC 51
  See also CA 93-96; DLB 9

Federman, Raymond 1928- ...... CLC 6, 47
  See also CANR 10; CA 17-20R; DLB-Y 80

Federspiel, J(urg) F. 1931-........ CLC 42

Francis, Robert (Churchill)
     1901-1987 . . . . CLC 15
     See also CANR 1; CA 1-4R;
       obituary CA 123

Frank, Anne 1929-1945 . . . . TCLC 17
     See also WLC 2; CA 113; SATA 42

Frank, Elizabeth 1945- . . . . CLC 39
     See also CA 121, 126

Franklin, (Stella Maria Sarah) Miles
     1879-1954 . . . . TCLC 7
     See also CA 104

Fraser, Antonia (Pakenham)
     1932- . . . . CLC 32
     See also CA 85-88; SATA 32

Fraser, George MacDonald 1925- . . . . CLC 7
     See also CANR 2; CA 45-48

Fraser, Sylvia 1935- . . . . CLC 64
     See also CANR 1, 16; CA 45-48

Frayn, Michael 1933- . . . . . . CLC 3, 7, 31, 47
     See also CA 5-8R; DLB 13, 14

Fraze, Candida 19??- . . . . CLC 50
     See also CA 125

Frazer, Sir James George
     1854-1941 . . . . TCLC 32
     See also CA 118

Frazier, Ian 1951- . . . . CLC 46
     See also CA 130

Frederic, Harold 1856-1898 . . . . . . NCLC 10
     See also DLB 12, 23

Frederick the Great 1712-1786 . . . . . . LC 14

Fredman, Russell (Bruce) 1929-
     See also CLR 20

Fredro, Aleksander 1793-1876 . . . . . NCLC 8

Freeling, Nicolas 1927- . . . . CLC 38
     See also CANR 1, 17; CA 49-52; DLB 87

Freeman, Douglas Southall
     1886-1953 . . . . TCLC 11
     See also CA 109; DLB 17

Freeman, Judith 1946- . . . . CLC 55

Freeman, Mary (Eleanor) Wilkins
     1852-1930 . . . . TCLC 9; SSC 1
     See also CA 106; DLB 12, 78

Freeman, R(ichard) Austin
     1862-1943 . . . . TCLC 21
     See also CA 113; DLB 70

French, Marilyn 1929- . . . . . . CLC 10, 18, 60
     See also CANR 3; CA 69-72

Freneau, Philip Morin 1752-1832 . . NCLC 1
     See also DLB 37, 43

Friedman, B(ernard) H(arper)
     1926- . . . . CLC 7
     See also CANR 3; CA 1-4R

Friedman, Bruce Jay 1930- . . . . CLC 3, 5, 56
     See also CANR 25; CA 9-12R; DLB 2, 28

Friel, Brian 1929- . . . . CLC 5, 42, 59
     See also CA 21-24R; DLB 13

Friis-Baastad, Babbis (Ellinor)
     1921-1970 . . . . CLC 12
     See also CA 17-20R; SATA 7

Frisch, Max (Rudolf)
     1911- . . . . CLC 3, 9, 14, 18, 32, 44
     See also CA 85-88; DLB 69

Fromentin, Eugene (Samuel Auguste)
     1820-1876 . . . . NCLC 10

Frost, Robert (Lee)
     1874-1963 . . . CLC 1, 3, 4, 9, 10, 13, 15,
                              26, 34, 44; PC 1
     See also WLC 2; CA 89-92; SATA 14;
       DLB 54; DLB-DS 7; CDALB 1917-1929

Fry, Christopher 1907- . . . . CLC 2, 10, 14
     See also CANR 9; CA 17-20R; DLB 13

Frye, (Herman) Northrop
     1912-1991 . . . . CLC 24, 70
     See also CANR 8; CA 5-8R;
       obituary CA 133; DLB 67, 68

Fuchs, Daniel 1909- . . . . CLC 8, 22
     See also CAAS 5; CA 81-84; DLB 9, 26, 28

Fuchs, Daniel 1934- . . . . CLC 34
     See also CANR 14; CA 37-40R

Fuentes, Carlos
     1928- . . . . . CLC 3, 8, 10, 13, 22, 41, 60
     See also WLC 2; CANR 10; CA 69-72

Fugard, Athol 1932- . . . CLC 5, 9, 14, 25, 40
     See also CA 85-88

Fugard, Sheila 1932- . . . . CLC 48
     See also CA 125

Fuller, Charles (H., Jr.)
     1939- . . . . CLC 25; DC 1
     See also BLC 2; CA 108, 112; DLB 38

Fuller, John (Leopold) 1937- . . . . CLC 62
     See also CANR 9; CA 21-22R; DLB 40

Fuller, (Sarah) Margaret
     1810-1850 . . . . NCLC 5
     See also Ossoli, Sarah Margaret (Fuller
       marchesa d')
     See also DLB 1, 59, 73; CDALB 1640-1865

Fuller, Roy (Broadbent) 1912- . . . . CLC 4, 28
     See also CA 5-8R; DLB 15, 20

Fulton, Alice 1952- . . . . CLC 52
     See also CA 116

Furabo 1644-1694
     See Basho, Matsuo

Furphy, Joseph 1843-1912 . . . . TCLC 25

Futabatei Shimei 1864-1909 . . . . . . TCLC 44

Futrelle, Jacques 1875-1912 . . . . . . TCLC 19
     See also CA 113

Gaboriau, Emile 1835-1873 . . . . . . NCLC 14

Gadda, Carlo Emilio 1893-1973 . . . . CLC 11
     See also CA 89-92

Gaddis, William
     1922- . . . . CLC 1, 3, 6, 8, 10, 19, 43
     See also CAAS 4; CANR 21; CA 17-20R;
       DLB 2

Gaines, Ernest J. 1933- . . . . . . CLC 3, 11, 18
     See also BLC 2; CANR 6, 24; CA 9-12R;
       DLB 2, 33; DLB-Y 80;
       CDALB 1968-1988

Gaitskill, Mary 1954- . . . . CLC 69
     See also CA 128

Gale, Zona 1874-1938 . . . . TCLC 7
     See also CA 105; DLB 9, 78

Galeano, Eduardo 1940- . . . . CLC 72
     See also CANR 13-32; CA 29-35R

Gallagher, Tess 1943- . . . . CLC 18, 63
     See also CA 106

Gallant, Mavis
     1922- . . . . CLC 7, 18, 38; SSC 5
     See also CA 69-72; DLB 53

Gallant, Roy A(rthur) 1924- . . . . CLC 17
     See also CANR 4; CA 5-8R; SATA 4

Gallico, Paul (William) 1897-1976 . . . CLC 2
     See also CA 5-8R; obituary CA 69-72;
       SATA 13; DLB 9

Galsworthy, John 1867-1933 . . . . TCLC 1, 45
     See also WLC 2; brief entry CA 104;
       DLB 10, 34, 98

Galt, John 1779-1839 . . . . NCLC 1

Galvin, James 1951- . . . . CLC 38
     See also CANR 26; CA 108

Gamboa, Frederico 1864-1939 . . . . . TCLC 36

Gann, Ernest K(ellogg) 1910- . . . . . . CLC 23
     See also CANR 1; CA 1-4R

Garcia Lorca, Federico
     1898-1936 . . . . . TCLC 1, 7; DC 2; PC 3
     See also WLC 2; CA 131;
       brief entry CA 104; DLB 108

Garcia Marquez, Gabriel (Jose)
     1928- . . . CLC 2, 3, 8, 10, 15, 27, 47, 55,
                                       68; SSC 8
     See also WLC 3; CANR 10, 28;
       CA 33-36R; AAYA 3

Gardam, Jane 1928- . . . . CLC 43
     See also CLR 12; CANR 2, 18; CA 49-52;
       SATA 28, 39; DLB 14

Gardner, Herb 1934- . . . . CLC 44

Gardner, John (Champlin, Jr.)
     1933-1982 . . . . CLC 2, 3, 5, 7, 8, 10, 18,
                                  28, 34; SSC 7
     See also CA 65-68; obituary CA 107;
       obituary SATA 31, 40; DLB 2; DLB-Y 82

Gardner, John (Edmund) 1926- . . . . . CLC 30
     See also CANR 15; CA 103

Gardons, S. S. 1926-
     See Snodgrass, W(illiam) D(e Witt)

Garfield, Leon 1921- . . . . CLC 12
     See also CA 17-20R; SATA 1, 32

Garland, (Hannibal) Hamlin
     1860-1940 . . . . TCLC 3
     See also CA 104; DLB 12, 71, 78

Garneau, Hector (de) Saint Denys
     1912-1943 . . . . TCLC 13
     See also CA 111; DLB 88

Garner, Alan 1935- . . . . CLC 17
     See also CLR 20; CANR 15; CA 73-76;
       SATA 18

Garner, Hugh 1913-1979 . . . . CLC 13
     See also CA 69-72; DLB 68

Garnett, David 1892-1981 . . . . CLC 3
     See also CANR 17; CA 5-8R;
       obituary CA 103; DLB 34

Garrett, George (Palmer, Jr.)
     1929- . . . . CLC 3, 11, 51
     See also CAAS 5; CANR 1; CA 1-4R;
       DLB 2, 5; DLB-Y 83

Garrick, David 1717-1779 . . . . LC 15
     See also DLB 84

Garrigue, Jean 1914-1972 . . . . CLC 2, 8
     See also CANR 20; CA 5-8R;
       obituary CA 37-40R

Goldman, Emma 1869-1940 . . . . . . TCLC 13
  See also CA 110

Goldman, William (W.) 1931- . . . . CLC 1, 48
  See also CA 9-12R; DLB 44

Goldmann, Lucien 1913-1970 . . . . . CLC 24
  See also CAP 2; CA 25-28

Goldoni, Carlo 1707-1793 . . . . LC 4

Goldsberry, Steven 1949- . . . . CLC 34

Goldsmith, Oliver 1728?-1774 . . . . LC 2
  See also WLC 3; SATA 26; DLB 39, 89,
  104, 109

Gombrowicz, Witold
  1904-1969 . . . . CLC 4, 7, 11, 49
  See also CAP 2; CA 19-20;
  obituary CA 25-28R

Gomez de la Serna, Ramon
  1888-1963 . . . . CLC 9
  See also obituary CA 116

Goncharov, Ivan Alexandrovich
  1812-1891 . . . . NCLC 1

Goncourt, Edmond (Louis Antoine Huot) de
  1822-1896 . . . . NCLC 7

Goncourt, Jules (Alfred Huot) de
  1830-1870 . . . . NCLC 7

Gontier, Fernande 19??- . . . . CLC 50

Goodman, Paul 1911-1972 . . . . CLC 1, 2, 4, 7
  See also CAP 2; CA 19-20;
  obituary CA 37-40R

Gordimer, Nadine
  1923- . . . . CLC 3, 5, 7, 10, 18, 33, 51, 70
  See also CANR 3, 28; CA 5-8R

Gordon, Adam Lindsay
  1833-1870 . . . . NCLC 21

Gordon, Caroline
  1895-1981 . . . . CLC 6, 13, 29
  See also CAP 1; CA 11-12;
  obituary CA 103; DLB 4, 9; DLB-Y 81

Gordon, Charles William 1860-1937
  See Conner, Ralph
  See also CA 109

Gordon, Mary (Catherine)
  1949- . . . . CLC 13, 22
  See also CA 102; DLB 6; DLB-Y 81

Gordon, Sol 1923- . . . . CLC 26
  See also CANR 4; CA 53-56; SATA 11

Gordone, Charles 1925- . . . . CLC 1, 4
  See also CA 93-96; DLB 7

Gorenko, Anna Andreyevna 1889?-1966
  See Akhmatova, Anna

Gorky, Maxim 1868-1936 . . . . TCLC 8
  See also Peshkov, Alexei Maximovich
  See also WLC 3

Goryan, Sirak 1908-1981
  See Saroyan, William

Gosse, Edmund (William)
  1849-1928 . . . . TCLC 28
  See also CA 117; DLB 57

Gotlieb, Phyllis (Fay Bloom)
  1926- . . . . CLC 18
  See also CANR 7; CA 13-16R; DLB 88

Gould, Lois 1938?- . . . . CLC 4, 10
  See also CA 77-80

Gourmont, Remy de 1858-1915 . . . . TCLC 17
  See also CA 109

Govier, Katherine 1948- . . . . CLC 51
  See also CANR 18; CA 101

Goyen, (Charles) William
  1915-1983 . . . . CLC 5, 8, 14, 40
  See also CANR 6; CA 5-8R;
  obituary CA 110; DLB 2; DLB-Y 83

Goytisolo, Juan 1931- . . . . CLC 5, 10, 23
  See also CA 85-88

Gozzi, (Conte) Carlo 1720-1806 . . NCLC 23

Grabbe, Christian Dietrich
  1801-1836 . . . . NCLC 2

Grace, Patricia 1937- . . . . CLC 56

Gracian y Morales, Baltasar
  1601-1658 . . . . LC 15

Gracq, Julien 1910- . . . . CLC 11, 48
  See also Poirier, Louis
  See also DLB 83

Grade, Chaim 1910-1982 . . . . CLC 10
  See also CA 93-96; obituary CA 107

Graham, Jorie 1951- . . . . CLC 48
  See also CA 111

Graham, R(obert) B(ontine) Cunninghame
  1852-1936 . . . . TCLC 19

Graham, W(illiam) S(ydney)
  1918-1986 . . . . CLC 29
  See also CA 73-76; obituary CA 118;
  DLB 20

Graham, Winston (Mawdsley)
  1910- . . . . CLC 23
  See also CANR 2, 22; CA 49-52;
  obituary CA 118

Granville-Barker, Harley
  1877-1946 . . . . TCLC 2
  See also CA 104

Grass, Gunter (Wilhelm)
  1927- . . CLC 1, 2, 4, 6, 11, 15, 22, 32, 49
  See also WLC 3; CANR 20; CA 13-16R;
  DLB 75

Grau, Shirley Ann 1929- . . . . CLC 4, 9
  See also CANR 22; CA 89-92; DLB 2

Graver, Elizabeth 1965- . . . . CLC 70

Graves, Richard Perceval 1945- . . . . CLC 44
  See also CANR 9, 26; CA 65-68

Graves, Robert (von Ranke)
  1895-1985 . . . CLC 1, 2, 6, 11, 39, 44, 45
  See also CANR 5; CA 5-8R;
  obituary CA 117; SATA 45; DLB 20;
  DLB-Y 85

Gray, Alasdair 1934- . . . . CLC 41
  See also CA 123

Gray, Amlin 1946- . . . . CLC 29

Gray, Francine du Plessix 1930- . . . . CLC 22
  See also CAAS 2; CANR 11; CA 61-64

Gray, John (Henry) 1866-1934 . . . . TCLC 19
  See also CA 119

Gray, Simon (James Holliday)
  1936- . . . . CLC 9, 14, 36
  See also CAAS 3; CA 21-24R; DLB 13

Gray, Spalding 1941- . . . . CLC 49

Gray, Thomas 1716-1771 . . . . . . LC 4; PC 2
  See also WLC 3

Grayson, Richard (A.) 1951- . . . . CLC 38
  See also CANR 14; CA 85-88

Greeley, Andrew M(oran) 1928- . . . . CLC 28
  See also CAAS 7; CANR 7; CA 5-8R

Green, Hannah 1932- . . . . CLC 3, 7, 30
  See also Greenberg, Joanne
  See also CA 73-76

Green, Henry 1905-1974 . . . . CLC 2, 13
  See also Yorke, Henry Vincent
  See also DLB 15

Green, Julien (Hartridge) 1900- . . CLC 3, 11
  See also CA 21-24R; DLB 4, 72

Green, Paul (Eliot) 1894-1981 . . . . . . CLC 25
  See also CANR 3; CA 5-8R;
  obituary CA 103; DLB 7, 9; DLB-Y 81

Greenberg, Ivan 1908-1973
  See Rahv, Philip
  See also CA 85-88

Greenberg, Joanne (Goldenberg)
  1932- . . . . CLC 3, 7, 30
  See also Green, Hannah
  See also CANR 14; CA 5-8R; SATA 25

Greenberg, Richard 1959?- . . . . CLC 57

Greene, Bette 1934- . . . . CLC 30
  See also CLR 2; CANR 4; CA 53-56;
  SATA 8

Greene, Gael 19??- . . . . CLC 8
  See also CANR 10; CA 13-16R

Greene, Graham (Henry)
  1904-1991 . . . CLC 1, 3, 6, 9, 14, 18, 27,
  37, 70, 72
  See also CANR 35; CA 13-16R;
  obituary CA 133; SATA 20; DLB 13, 15,
  77, 100; DLB-Y 85

Gregor, Arthur 1923- . . . . CLC 9
  See also CANR 11; CA 25-28R; SATA 36

Gregory, J. Dennis 1925-
  See Williams, John A.

Gregory, Lady (Isabella Augusta Persse)
  1852-1932 . . . . TCLC 1
  See also CA 104; DLB 10

Grendon, Stephen 1909-1971
  See Derleth, August (William)

Grenville, Kate 1950- . . . . CLC 61
  See also CA 118

Greve, Felix Paul Berthold Friedrich
  1879-1948
  See Grove, Frederick Philip
  See also CA 104

Grey, (Pearl) Zane 1872?-1939 . . . . . TCLC 6
  See also CA 104; DLB 9

Grieg, (Johan) Nordahl (Brun)
  1902-1943 . . . . TCLC 10
  See also CA 107

Grieve, C(hristopher) M(urray) 1892-1978
  See MacDiarmid, Hugh
  See also CA 5-8R; obituary CA 85-88

Griffin, Gerald 1803-1840 . . . . NCLC 7

Griffin, John Howard 1920-1980 . . . . CLC 68
  See also CANR 2; CA 2R; obituary CA 101

Griffin, Peter 1942- . . . . CLC 39

Griffiths, Trevor 1935- . . . . CLC 13, 52
  See also CA 97-100; DLB 13

Grigson, Geoffrey (Edward Harvey)
   1905-1985 .... CLC **7, 39**
   See also CANR 20; CA 25-28R;
   obituary CA 118; DLB 27

Grillparzer, Franz 1791-1872 ...... NCLC **1**

Grimke, Charlotte L(ottie) Forten 1837?-1914
   See Forten (Grimke), Charlotte L(ottie)
   See also CA 117, 124

Grimm, Jakob Ludwig Karl
   1785-1863 .... NCLC **3**
   See also SATA 22; DLB 90

Grimm, Wilhelm Karl 1786-1859 .. NCLC **3**
   See also SATA 22; DLB 90

Grimmelshausen, Johann Jakob Christoffel
   von 1621-1676 .... LC **6**

Grindel, Eugene 1895-1952
   See also brief entry CA 104

Grossman, David 1954- .... CLC **67**

Grossman, Vasily (Semenovich)
   1905-1964 .... CLC **41**
   See also CA 124, 130

Grove, Frederick Philip
   1879-1948 .... TCLC **4**
   See also Greve, Felix Paul Berthold
   Friedrich

Grumbach, Doris (Isaac)
   1918- .... CLC **13, 22, 64**
   See also CAAS 2; CANR 9; CA 5-8R

Grundtvig, Nicolai Frederik Severin
   1783-1872 .... NCLC **1**

Grunwald, Lisa 1959-............. CLC **44**
   See also CA 120

Guare, John 1938- .... CLC **8, 14, 29, 67**
   See also CANR 21; CA 73-76; DLB 7

Gudjonsson, Halldor Kiljan 1902-
   See Laxness, Halldor (Kiljan)
   See also CA 103

Guest, Barbara 1920-............. CLC **34**
   See also CANR 11; CA 25-28R; DLB 5

Guest, Judith (Ann) 1936-....... CLC **8, 30**
   See also CANR 15; CA 77-80

Guild, Nicholas M. 1944-.......... CLC **33**
   See also CA 93-96

Guillen, Jorge 1893-1984.......... CLC **11**
   See also CA 89-92; obituary CA 112

Guillen, Nicolas 1902-1989 .... CLC **48**
   See also BLC 2; CA 116, 125;
   obituary CA 129

Guillen y Batista, Nicolas Cristobal
   1902-1989
   See Guillen, Nicolas

Guillevic, (Eugene) 1907-.......... CLC **33**
   See also CA 93-96

Guiney, Louise Imogen
   1861-1920 .... TCLC **41**
   See also DLB 54

Guiraldes, Ricardo 1886-1927 ..... TCLC **39**

Gunn, Bill 1934-1989 .... CLC **5**
   See also Gunn, William Harrison
   See also DLB 38

Gunn, Thom(son William)
   1929-.................CLC **3, 6, 18, 32**
   See also CANR 9; CA 17-20R; DLB 27

Gunn, William Harrison 1934-1989
   See Gunn, Bill
   See also CANR 12, 25; CA 13-16R;
   obituary CA 128

Gunnars, Kristjana 1948-......... CLC **69**
   See also CA 113; DLB 60

Gurganus, Allan 1947- .... CLC **70**

Gurney, A(lbert) R(amsdell), Jr.
   1930-................. CLC **32, 50, 54**
   See also CA 77-80

Gurney, Ivor (Bertie) 1890-1937... TCLC **33**

Gustafson, Ralph (Barker) 1909-.... CLC **36**
   See also CANR 8; CA 21-24R; DLB 88

Guthrie, A(lfred) B(ertram), Jr.
   1901-................. CLC **23**
   See also CA 57-60; DLB 6

Guthrie, Woodrow Wilson 1912-1967
   See Guthrie, Woody
   See also CA 113; obituary CA 93-96

Guthrie, Woody 1912-1967 .... CLC **35**
   See also Guthrie, Woodrow Wilson

Guy, Rosa (Cuthbert) 1928-........ CLC **26**
   See also CLR 13; CANR 14; CA 17-20R;
   SATA 14; DLB 33

Haavikko, Paavo (Juhani)
   1931-................. CLC **18, 34**
   See also CA 106

Hacker, Marilyn 1942- .... CLC **5, 9, 23, 72**
   See also CA 77-80

Haggard, (Sir) H(enry) Rider
   1856-1925 .... TCLC **11**
   See also CA 108; SATA 16; DLB 70

Haig-Brown, Roderick L(angmere)
   1908-1976 .... CLC **21**
   See also CANR 4; CA 5-8R;
   obituary CA 69-72; SATA 12; DLB 88

Hailey, Arthur 1920-............. CLC **5**
   See also CANR 2; CA 1-4R; DLB-Y 82

Hailey, Elizabeth Forsythe 1938-... CLC **40**
   See also CAAS 1; CANR 15; CA 93-96

Haines, John 1924-............... CLC **58**
   See also CANR 13; CA 19-20R; DLB 5

Haldeman, Joe 1943- .... CLC **61**
   See also CA 53-56; DLB 8

Haley, Alex (Palmer) 1921-...... CLC **8, 12**
   See also BLC 2; CA 77-80; DLB 38

Haliburton, Thomas Chandler
   1796-1865 .... NCLC **15**
   See also DLB 11

Hall, Donald (Andrew, Jr.)
   1928-..............CLC **1, 13, 37, 59**
   See also CAAS 7; CANR 2; CA 5-8R;
   SATA 23; DLB 5

Hall, James Norman 1887-1951 ... TCLC **23**
   See also CA 123; SATA 21

Hall, (Marguerite) Radclyffe
   1886-1943 .... TCLC **12**
   See also CA 110

Hall, Rodney 1935- .... CLC **51**
   See also CA 109

Halpern, Daniel 1945- .... CLC **14**
   See also CA 33-36R

Hamburger, Michael (Peter Leopold)
   1924-...................... CLC **5, 14**
   See also CAAS 4; CANR 2; CA 5-8R;
   DLB 27

Hamill, Pete 1935-............... CLC **10**
   See also CANR 18; CA 25-28R

Hamilton, Edmond 1904-1977....... CLC **1**
   See also CANR 3; CA 1-4R; DLB 8

Hamilton, Gail 1911-
   See Corcoran, Barbara

Hamilton, Ian 1938-.............. CLC **55**
   See also CA 106; DLB 40

Hamilton, Mollie 1909?-
   See Kaye, M(ary) M(argaret)

Hamilton, (Anthony Walter) Patrick
   1904-1962 .... CLC **51**
   See also obituary CA 113; DLB 10

Hamilton, Virginia (Esther) 1936-... CLC **26**
   See also CLR 1, 11; CANR 20; CA 25-28R;
   SATA 4; DLB 33, 52

Hammett, (Samuel) Dashiell
   1894-1961 .... CLC **3, 5, 10, 19, 47**
   See also CA 81-84; DLB-DS 6

Hammon, Jupiter 1711?-1800? .... NCLC **5**
   See also BLC 2; DLB 31, 50, 31, 50

Hamner, Earl (Henry), Jr. 1923- ... CLC **12**
   See also CA 73-76; DLB 6

Hampton, Christopher (James)
   1946-...................... CLC **4**
   See also CA 25-28R; DLB 13

Hamsun, Knut 1859-1952....... TCLC **2, 14**
   See also Pedersen, Knut

Handke, Peter 1942- .. CLC **5, 8, 10, 15, 38**
   See also CA 77-80; DLB 85

Hanley, James 1901-1985 ...CLC **3, 5, 8, 13**
   See also CA 73-76; obituary CA 117

Hannah, Barry 1942-.......... CLC **23, 38**
   See also CA 108, 110; DLB 6

Hansberry, Lorraine (Vivian)
   1930-1965 .... CLC **17, 62; DC 2**
   See also BLC 2; CA 109;
   obituary CA 25-28R; CABS 3; DLB 7, 38;
   CDALB 1941-1968

Hansen, Joseph 1923-............. CLC **38**
   See also CANR 16; CA 29-32R

Hansen, Martin 1909-1955 .... TCLC **32**

Hanson, Kenneth O(stlin) 1922-.... CLC **13**
   See also CANR 7; CA 53-56

Hardenberg, Friedrich (Leopold Freiherr) von
   1772-1801
   See Novalis

Hardwick, Elizabeth 1916- .... CLC **13**
   See also CANR 3; CA 5-8R; DLB 6

Hardy, Thomas
   1840-1928 ... TCLC **4, 10, 18, 32; SSC 2**
   See also CA 104, 123; SATA 25; DLB 18,
   19

Hare, David 1947- .... CLC **29, 58**
   See also CA 97-100; DLB 13

Harlan, Louis R(udolph) 1922-..... CLC **34**
   See also CANR 25; CA 21-24R

Harling, Robert 1951?-............ CLC **53**

Harmon, William (Ruth) 1938-..... CLC **38**
   See also CANR 14; CA 33-36R

Henry, O. 1862-1910 . . . **TCLC 1, 19; SSC 5**
See also Porter, William Sydney
See also YABC 2; CA 104; DLB 12, 78, 79;
CDALB 1865-1917

Henry VIII 1491-1547 . . . . **LC 10**

Henschke, Alfred 1890-1928
See Klabund

Hentoff, Nat(han Irving) 1925- . . . . . **CLC 26**
See also CLR 1; CAAS 6; CANR 5, 25;
CA 1-4R; SATA 27, 42; AAYA 4

Heppenstall, (John) Rayner
1911-1981 . . . . **CLC 10**
See also CANR 29; CA 1-4R;
obituary CA 103

Herbert, Frank (Patrick)
1920-1986 . . . . **CLC 12, 23, 35, 44**
See also CANR 5; CA 53-56;
obituary CA 118; SATA 9, 37, 47; DLB 8

Herbert, George 1593-1633 . . . . **PC 4**

Herbert, Zbigniew 1924- . . . . **CLC 9, 43**
See also CA 89-92

Herbst, Josephine 1897-1969 . . . . . . **CLC 34**
See also CA 5-8R; obituary CA 25-28R;
DLB 9

Herder, Johann Gottfried von
1744-1803 . . . . **NCLC 8**

Hergesheimer, Joseph
1880-1954 . . . . **TCLC 11**
See also CA 109; DLB 9

Herlagnez, Pablo de 1844-1896
See Verlaine, Paul (Marie)

Herlihy, James Leo 1927- . . . . **CLC 6**
See also CANR 2; CA 1-4R

Hermogenes fl. c. 175- . . . . **CMLC 6**

Hernandez, Jose 1834-1886 . . . . . . **NCLC 17**

Herrick, Robert 1591-1674 . . . . **LC 13**

Herriot, James 1916- . . . . **CLC 12**
See also Wight, James Alfred
See also AAYA 1

Herrmann, Dorothy 1941- . . . . **CLC 44**
See also CA 107

Hersey, John (Richard)
1914- . . . . **CLC 1, 2, 7, 9, 40**
See also CA 17-20R; SATA 25; DLB 6

Herzen, Aleksandr Ivanovich
1812-1870 . . . . **NCLC 10**

Herzl, Theodor 1860-1904 . . . . **TCLC 36**

Herzog, Werner 1942- . . . . **CLC 16**
See also CA 89-92

Hesiod c. 8th Century B.C.- . . . . . . **CMLC 5**

Hesse, Hermann
1877-1962 . . . **CLC 1, 2, 3, 6, 11, 17, 25,**
69; SSC 9
See also CAP 2; CA 17-18; SATA 50;
DLB 66

Heyen, William 1940- . . . . **CLC 13, 18**
See also CAAS 9; CA 33-36R; DLB 5

Heyerdahl, Thor 1914- . . . . **CLC 26**
See also CANR 5, 22; CA 5-8R; SATA 2,
52

Heym, Georg (Theodor Franz Arthur)
1887-1912 . . . . **TCLC 9**
See also CA 106

Heym, Stefan 1913- . . . . **CLC 41**
See also CANR 4; CA 9-12R; DLB 69

Heyse, Paul (Johann Ludwig von)
1830-1914 . . . . **TCLC 8**
See also CA 104

Hibbert, Eleanor (Burford) 1906- . . . . **CLC 7**
See also CANR 9, 28; CA 17-20R; SATA 2

Higgins, George V(incent)
1939- . . . . **CLC 4, 7, 10, 18**
See also CAAS 5; CANR 17; CA 77-80;
DLB 2; DLB-Y 81

Higginson, Thomas Wentworth
1823-1911 . . . . **TCLC 36**
See also DLB 1, 64

Highsmith, (Mary) Patricia
1921- . . . . **CLC 2, 4, 14, 42**
See also CANR 1, 20; CA 1-4R

Highwater, Jamake 1942- . . . . **CLC 12**
See also CLR 17; CAAS 7; CANR 10;
CA 65-68; SATA 30, 32; DLB 52;
DLB-Y 85

Hijuelos, Oscar 1951- . . . . **CLC 65**
See also CA 123

Hikmet (Ran), Nazim 1902-1963 . . . . **CLC 40**
See also obituary CA 93-96

Hildesheimer, Wolfgang 1916- . . . . . **CLC 49**
See also CA 101; DLB 69

Hill, Geoffrey (William)
1932- . . . . **CLC 5, 8, 18, 45**
See also CANR 21; CA 81-84; DLB 40

Hill, George Roy 1922- . . . . **CLC 26**
See also CA 110, 122

Hill, Susan B. 1942- . . . . **CLC 4**
See also CANR 29; CA 33-36R; DLB 14

Hillerman, Tony 1925- . . . . **CLC 62**
See also CANR 21; CA 29-32R; SATA 6

Hilliard, Noel (Harvey) 1929- . . . . . . **CLC 15**
See also CANR 7; CA 9-12R

Hillis, Richard Lyle 1956-
See Hillis, Rick

Hillis, Rick 1956- . . . . **CLC 66**
See also Hillis, Richard Lyle

Hilton, James 1900-1954 . . . . **TCLC 21**
See also CA 108; SATA 34; DLB 34, 77

Himes, Chester (Bomar)
1909-1984 . . . . **CLC 2, 4, 7, 18, 58**
See also BLC 2; CANR 22; CA 25-28R;
obituary CA 114; DLB 2, 76

Hinde, Thomas 1926- . . . . **CLC 6, 11**
See also Chitty, (Sir) Thomas Willes

Hine, (William) Daryl 1936- . . . . **CLC 15**
See also CANR 1, 20; CA 1-4R; DLB 60

Hinton, S(usan) E(loise) 1950- . . . . . **CLC 30**
See also CLR 3, 23; CA 81-84; SATA 19,
58; AAYA 2

Hippius (Merezhkovsky), Zinaida
(Nikolayevna) 1869-1945 . . . . . . **TCLC 9**
See also Gippius, Zinaida (Nikolayevna)

Hiraoka, Kimitake 1925-1970
See Mishima, Yukio
See also CA 97-100; obituary CA 29-32R

Hirsch, Edward (Mark) 1950- . . . **CLC 31, 50**
See also CANR 20; CA 104

Hitchcock, (Sir) Alfred (Joseph)
1899-1980 . . . . **CLC 16**
See also obituary CA 97-100; SATA 27;
obituary SATA 24

Hoagland, Edward 1932- . . . . **CLC 28**
See also CANR 2; CA 1-4R; SATA 51;
DLB 6

Hoban, Russell C(onwell) 1925- . . **CLC 7, 25**
See also CLR 3; CANR 23; CA 5-8R;
SATA 1, 40; DLB 52

Hobson, Laura Z(ametkin)
1900-1986 . . . . **CLC 7, 25**
See also CA 17-20R; obituary CA 118;
SATA 52; DLB 28

Hochhuth, Rolf 1931- . . . . **CLC 4, 11, 18**
See also CA 5-8R

Hochman, Sandra 1936- . . . . **CLC 3, 8**
See also CA 5-8R; DLB 5

Hochwalder, Fritz 1911-1986 . . . . . . **CLC 36**
See also CA 29-32R; obituary CA 120

Hocking, Mary (Eunice) 1921- . . . . . **CLC 13**
See also CANR 18; CA 101

Hodgins, Jack 1938- . . . . **CLC 23**
See also CA 93-96; DLB 60

Hodgson, William Hope
1877-1918 . . . . **TCLC 13**
See also CA 111; DLB 70

Hoffman, Alice 1952- . . . . **CLC 51**
See also CA 77-80

Hoffman, Daniel (Gerard)
1923- . . . . **CLC 6, 13, 23**
See also CANR 4; CA 1-4R; DLB 5

Hoffman, Stanley 1944- . . . . **CLC 5**
See also CA 77-80

Hoffman, William M(oses) 1939- . . . **CLC 40**
See also CANR 11; CA 57-60

Hoffmann, E(rnst) T(heodor) A(madeus)
1776-1822 . . . . **NCLC 2**
See also SATA 27; DLB 90

Hoffmann, Gert 1932- . . . . **CLC 54**

Hofmannsthal, Hugo (Laurenz August
Hofmann Edler) von
1874-1929 . . . . **TCLC 11**
See also CA 106; DLB 81

Hogg, James 1770-1835 . . . . **NCLC 4**

Holbach, Paul Henri Thiry, Baron d'
1723-1789 . . . . **LC 14**

Holberg, Ludvig 1684-1754 . . . . **LC 6**

Holden, Ursula 1921- . . . . **CLC 18**
See also CAAS 8; CANR 22; CA 101

Holderlin, (Johann Christian) Friedrich
1770-1843 . . . . **NCLC 16; PC 4**

Holdstock, Robert (P.) 1948- . . . . **CLC 39**

Holland, Isabelle 1920- . . . . **CLC 21**
See also CANR 10, 25; CA 21-24R;
SATA 8

Holland, Marcus 1900-1985
See Caldwell, (Janet Miriam) Taylor
(Holland)

Hollander, John 1929- . . . . . . **CLC 2, 5, 8, 14**
See also CANR 1; CA 1-4R; SATA 13;
DLB 5

Holleran, Andrew 1943?- . . . . **CLC 38**

Ibsen, Henrik (Johan)
1828-1906 . . . . . TCLC **2, 8, 16, 37**; DC **2**
See also CA 104

Ibuse, Masuji 1898- . . . . CLC **22**
See also CA 127

Ichikawa, Kon 1915- . . . . CLC **20**
See also CA 121

Idle, Eric 1943- . . . . CLC **21**
See also Monty Python
See also CA 116

Ignatow, David 1914- . . . . . . CLC **4, 7, 14, 40**
See also CAAS 3; CA 9-12R; DLB 5

Ihimaera, Witi (Tame) 1944- . . . . CLC **46**
See also CA 77-80

Ilf, Ilya 1897-1937 . . . . TCLC **21**

Immermann, Karl (Lebrecht)
1796-1840 . . . . NCLC **4**

Ingalls, Rachel 19??- . . . . CLC **42**
See also CA 123, 127

Ingamells, Rex 1913-1955 . . . . TCLC **35**

Inge, William (Motter)
1913-1973 . . . . CLC **1, 8, 19**
See also CA 9-12R; DLB 7;
CDALB 1941-1968

Innaurato, Albert 1948- . . . . CLC **21, 60**
See also CA 115, 122

Innes, Michael 1906-
See Stewart, J(ohn) I(nnes) M(ackintosh)

Ionesco, Eugene
1912- . . . . CLC **1, 4, 6, 9, 11, 15, 41**
See also CA 9-12R; SATA 7

Iqbal, Muhammad 1877-1938 . . . . . TCLC **28**

Irving, John (Winslow)
1942- . . . . CLC **13, 23, 38**
See also CANR 28; CA 25-28R; DLB 6;
DLB-Y 82

Irving, Washington
1783-1859 . . . . NCLC **2, 19**; SSC **2**
See also YABC 2; DLB 3, 11, 30, 59, 73,
74; CDALB 1640-1865

Isaacs, Susan 1943- . . . . CLC **32**
See also CANR 20; CA 89-92

Isherwood, Christopher (William Bradshaw)
1904-1986 . . . . CLC **1, 9, 11, 14, 44**
See also CA 13-16R; obituary CA 117;
DLB 15; DLB-Y 86

Ishiguro, Kazuo 1954- . . . . . . CLC **27, 56, 59**
See also CA 120

Ishikawa Takuboku 1885-1912 . . . . TCLC **15**
See also CA 113

Iskander, Fazil (Abdulovich)
1929- . . . . CLC **47**
See also CA 102

Ivan IV 1530-1584 . . . . LC **17**

Ivanov, Vyacheslav (Ivanovich)
1866-1949 . . . . TCLC **33**
See also CA 122

Ivask, Ivar (Vidrik) 1927- . . . . CLC **14**
See also CANR 24; CA 37-40R

Jackson, Jesse 1908-1983 . . . . CLC **12**
See also CANR 27; CA 25-28R;
obituary CA 109; SATA 2, 29, 48

Jackson, Laura (Riding) 1901- . . . . . . CLC **7**
See also Riding, Laura
See also CANR 28; CA 65-68; DLB 48

Jackson, Shirley
1919-1965 . . . . CLC **11, 60**; SSC **9**
See also CANR 4; CA 1-4R;
obituary CA 25-28R; SATA 2; DLB 6;
CDALB 1941-1968

Jacob, (Cyprien) Max 1876-1944 . . . TCLC **6**
See also CA 104

Jacob, Piers A(nthony) D(illingham) 1934-
See Anthony (Jacob), Piers
See also CA 21-24R

Jacobs, Jim 1942- and **Casey, Warren**
1942- . . . . CLC **12**
See also CA 97-100

Jacobs, Jim 1942-
See Jacobs, Jim and Casey, Warren
See also CA 97-100

Jacobs, W(illiam) W(ymark)
1863-1943 . . . . TCLC **22**
See also CA 121

Jacobsen, Jens Peter 1847-1885 . . NCLC **34**

Jacobsen, Josephine 1908- . . . . CLC **48**
See also CANR 23; CA 33-36R

Jacobson, Dan 1929- . . . . CLC **4, 14**
See also CANR 2, 25; CA 1-4R; DLB 14

Jagger, Mick 1944- . . . . CLC **17**

Jakes, John (William) 1932- . . . . CLC **29**
See also CANR 10; CA 57-60; DLB-Y 83

James, C(yril) L(ionel) R(obert)
1901-1989 . . . . CLC **33**
See also CA 117, 125; obituary CA 128

James, Daniel 1911-1988
See Santiago, Danny
See also obituary CA 125

James, Henry (Jr.)
1843-1916 . . . TCLC **2, 11, 24, 40**; SSC **8**
See also CA 132; brief entry CA 104;
DLB 12, 71, 74; CDALB 1865-1917

James, M(ontague) R(hodes)
1862-1936 . . . . TCLC **6**
See also CA 104

James, P(hyllis) D(orothy)
1920- . . . . CLC **18, 46**
See also CANR 17; CA 21-24R

James, William 1842-1910 . . . . . TCLC **15, 32**
See also CA 109

Jami, Nur al-Din 'Abd al-Rahman
1414-1492 . . . . LC **9**

Jandl, Ernst 1925- . . . . CLC **34**

Janowitz, Tama 1957- . . . . CLC **43**
See also CA 106

Jarrell, Randall
1914-1965 . . . . . . CLC **1, 2, 6, 9, 13, 49**
See also CLR 6; CANR 6; CA 5-8R;
obituary CA 25-28R; CABS 2; SATA 7;
DLB 48, 52; CDALB 1941-1968

Jarry, Alfred 1873-1907 . . . . TCLC **2, 14**
See also CA 104

Jeake, Samuel, Jr. 1889-1973
See Aiken, Conrad

Jean Paul 1763-1825 . . . . NCLC **7**

Jeffers, (John) Robinson
1887-1962 . . . . CLC **2, 3, 11, 15, 54**
See also CA 85-88; DLB 45;
CDALB 1917-1929

Jefferson, Thomas 1743-1826 . . . . NCLC **11**
See also DLB 31; CDALB 1640-1865

Jeffrey, Francis 1773-1850 . . . . . . NCLC **33**

Jellicoe, (Patricia) Ann 1927- . . . . . . CLC **27**
See also CA 85-88; DLB 13

Jen, Gish 1955- . . . . CLC **70**

Jenkins, (John) Robin 1912- . . . . CLC **52**
See also CANR 1; CA 4R; DLB 14

Jennings, Elizabeth (Joan)
1926- . . . . CLC **5, 14**
See also CAAS 5; CANR 8; CA 61-64;
DLB 27

Jennings, Waylon 1937- . . . . CLC **21**

Jensen, Johannes V. 1873-1950 . . . . TCLC **41**

Jensen, Laura (Linnea) 1948- . . . . . . CLC **37**
See also CA 103

Jerome, Jerome K. 1859-1927 . . . . . TCLC **23**
See also CA 119; DLB 10, 34

Jerrold, Douglas William
1803-1857 . . . . NCLC **2**

Jewett, (Theodora) Sarah Orne
1849-1909 . . . . TCLC **1, 22**; SSC **6**
See also CA 108, 127; SATA 15; DLB 12,
74

Jewsbury, Geraldine (Endsor)
1812-1880 . . . . NCLC **22**
See also DLB 21

Jhabvala, Ruth Prawer
1927- . . . . CLC **4, 8, 29**
See also CANR 2, 29; CA 1-4R

Jiles, Paulette 1943- . . . . CLC **13, 58**
See also CA 101

Jimenez (Mantecon), Juan Ramon
1881-1958 . . . . TCLC **4**
See also CA 104

Joel, Billy 1949- . . . . CLC **26**
See also Joel, William Martin

Joel, William Martin 1949-
See Joel, Billy
See also CA 108

John of the Cross, St. 1542-1591 . . . . LC **18**

Johnson, B(ryan) S(tanley William)
1933-1973 . . . . CLC **6, 9**
See also CANR 9; CA 9-12R;
obituary CA 53-56; DLB 14, 40

Johnson, Charles (Richard)
1948- . . . . CLC **7, 51, 65**
See also BLC 2; CA 116; DLB 33

Johnson, Denis 1949- . . . . CLC **52**
See also CA 117, 121

Johnson, Diane 1934- . . . . CLC **5, 13, 48**
See also CANR 17; CA 41-44R; DLB-Y 80

Johnson, Eyvind (Olof Verner)
1900-1976 . . . . CLC **14**
See also CA 73-76; obituary CA 69-72

Johnson, Fenton 1888-1958
See also BLC 2; CA 124;
brief entry CA 118; DLB 45, 50

Keane, Mary Nesta (Skrine)   1904-
See Keane, Molly
See also CA 108, 114

Keane, Molly   1904- . . . .   **CLC 31**
See also Keane, Mary Nesta (Skrine)

Keates, Jonathan   19??- . . . .   **CLC 34**

Keaton, Buster   1895-1966 . . . .   **CLC 20**

Keaton, Joseph Francis   1895-1966
See Keaton, Buster

Keats, John   1795-1821 . . . . . .   **NCLC 8; PC 1**

Keene, Donald   1922- . . . .   **CLC 34**
See also CANR 5; CA 1-4R

Keillor, Garrison   1942- . . . .   **CLC 40**
See also Keillor, Gary (Edward)
See also CA 111; SATA 58; DLB-Y 87;
AAYA 2

Keillor, Gary (Edward)
See Keillor, Garrison
See also CA 111, 117

Kell, Joseph   1917-
See Burgess (Wilson, John) Anthony

Keller, Gottfried   1819-1890 . . . .   **NCLC 2**

Kellerman, Jonathan (S.)   1949- . . . . .   **CLC 44**
See also CANR 29; CA 106

Kelley, William Melvin   1937- . . . . . .   **CLC 22**
See also CANR 27; CA 77-80; DLB 33

Kellogg, Marjorie   1922- . . . .   **CLC 2**
See also CA 81-84

Kelly, M. T.   1947- . . . .   **CLC 55**
See also CANR 19; CA 97-100

Kelman, James   1946- . . . .   **CLC 58**

Kemal, Yashar   1922- . . . .   **CLC 14, 29**
See also CA 89-92

Kemble, Fanny   1809-1893 . . . .   **NCLC 18**
See also DLB 32

Kemelman, Harry   1908- . . . .   **CLC 2**
See also CANR 6; CA 9-12R; DLB 28

Kempe, Margery   1373?-1440? . . . .   **LC 6**

Kempis, Thomas á   1380-1471 . . . .   **LC 11**

Kendall, Henry   1839-1882 . . . . . .   **NCLC 12**

Keneally, Thomas (Michael)
1935- . . . . . .   **CLC 5, 8, 10, 14, 19, 27, 43**
See also CANR 10; CA 85-88

Kennedy, Adrienne   1931-
See also BLC 2; CANR 26; CA 103;
CABS 3; DLB 38

Kennedy, Adrienne (Lita)   1931- . . . .   **CLC 66**
See also CANR 26; CA 103; CABS 3;
DLB 38

Kennedy, John Pendleton
1795-1870 . . . .   **NCLC 2**
See also DLB 3

Kennedy, Joseph Charles   1929- . . . . . .   **CLC 8**
See also Kennedy, X. J.
See also CANR 4, 30; CA 1-4R; SATA 14

Kennedy, William (Joseph)
1928- . . . .   **CLC 6, 28, 34, 53**
See also CANR 14; CA 85-88; SATA 57;
DLB-Y 85; AAYA 1

Kennedy, X. J.   1929- . . . .   **CLC 8, 42**
See also Kennedy, Joseph Charles
See also CAAS 9; DLB 5

Kerouac, Jack
1922-1969 . . . .   **CLC 1, 2, 3, 5, 14, 29, 61**
See also Kerouac, Jean-Louis Lebris de
See also DLB 2, 16; DLB-DS 3;
CDALB 1941-1968

Kerouac, Jean-Louis Lebris de   1922-1969
See Kerouac, Jack
See also CANR 26; CA 5-8R;
obituary CA 25-28R; CDALB 1941-1968

Kerr, Jean   1923- . . . .   **CLC 22**
See also CANR 7; CA 5-8R

Kerr, M. E.   1927- . . . .   **CLC 12, 35**
See also Meaker, Marijane
See also SAAS 1; AAYA 2

Kerr, Robert   1970?- . . . .   **CLC 55, 59**

Kerrigan, (Thomas) Anthony
1918- . . . .   **CLC 4, 6**
See also CAAS 11; CANR 4; CA 49-52

Kesey, Ken (Elton)
1935- . . . . . .   **CLC 1, 3, 6, 11, 46, 64**
See also CANR 22; CA 1-4R; DLB 2, 16;
CDALB 1968-1987

Kesselring, Joseph (Otto)
1902-1967 . . . .   **CLC 45**

Kessler, Jascha (Frederick)   1929- . . . .   **CLC 4**
See also CANR 8; CA 17-20R

Kettelkamp, Larry   1933- . . . .   **CLC 12**
See also CANR 16; CA 29-32R; SAAS 3;
SATA 2

Kherdian, David   1931- . . . .   **CLC 6, 9**
See also CLR 24; CAAS 2; CA 21-24R;
SATA 16

Khlebnikov, Velimir (Vladimirovich)
1885-1922 . . . .   **TCLC 20**
See also CA 117

Khodasevich, Vladislav (Felitsianovich)
1886-1939 . . . .   **TCLC 15**
See also CA 115

Kielland, Alexander (Lange)
1849-1906 . . . .   **TCLC 5**
See also CA 104

Kiely, Benedict   1919- . . . .   **CLC 23, 43**
See also CANR 2; CA 1-4R; DLB 15

Kienzle, William X(avier)   1928- . . . .   **CLC 25**
See also CAAS 1; CANR 9; CA 93-96

Kierkegaard, SOren   1813-1855 . . .   **NCLC 34**

Killens, John Oliver   1916- . . . .   **CLC 10**
See also CAAS 2; CANR 26; CA 77-80,
123; DLB 33

Killigrew, Anne   1660-1685 . . . .   **LC 4**

Kincaid, Jamaica   1949- . . . .   **CLC 43, 68**
See also BLC 2; CA 125

King, Francis (Henry)   1923- . . . . .   **CLC 8, 53**
See also CANR 1; CA 1-4R; DLB 15

King, Martin Luther, Jr.   1929-1968
See also BLC 2; CANR 27; CAP 2;
CA 25-28; SATA 14

King, Stephen (Edwin)
1947- . . . .   **CLC 12, 26, 37, 61**
See also CANR 1, 30; CA 61-64; SATA 9,
55; DLB-Y 80; AAYA 1

Kingman, (Mary) Lee   1919- . . . .   **CLC 17**
See also Natti, (Mary) Lee
See also CA 5-8R; SAAS 3; SATA 1

Kingsley, Charles   1819-1875 . . . . .   **NCLC 35**
See also YABC 2; DLB 21, 32

Kingsley, Sidney   1906- . . . .   **CLC 44**
See also CA 85-88; DLB 7

Kingsolver, Barbara   1955- . . . .   **CLC 55**
See also CA 129

Kingston, Maxine Hong
1940- . . . .   **CLC 12, 19, 58**
See also CANR 13; CA 69-72; SATA 53;
DLB-Y 80

Kinnell, Galway
1927- . . . .   **CLC 1, 2, 3, 5, 13, 29**
See also CANR 10; CA 9-12R; DLB 5;
DLB-Y 87

Kinsella, Thomas   1928- . . . . . .   **CLC 4, 19, 43**
See also CANR 15; CA 17-20R; DLB 27

Kinsella, W(illiam) P(atrick)
1935- . . . .   **CLC 27, 43**
See also CAAS 7; CANR 21; CA 97-100

Kipling, (Joseph) Rudyard
1865-1936 . . . .   **TCLC 8, 17; PC 3; SSC 5**
See also YABC 2; CANR 33; CA 120;
brief entry CA 105; DLB 19, 34

Kirkup, James   1918- . . . .   **CLC 1**
See also CAAS 4; CANR 2; CA 1-4R;
SATA 12; DLB 27

Kirkwood, James   1930-1989 . . . .   **CLC 9**
See also CANR 6; CA 1-4R;
obituary CA 128

Kis, Danilo   1935-1989 . . . .   **CLC 57**
See also CA 118, 129; brief entry CA 109

Kivi, Aleksis   1834-1872 . . . .   **NCLC 30**

Kizer, Carolyn (Ashley)   1925- . . .   **CLC 15, 39**
See also CAAS 5; CANR 24; CA 65-68;
DLB 5

Klabund   1890-1928 . . . .   **TCLC 44**
See also DLB 66

Klappert, Peter   1942- . . . .   **CLC 57**
See also CA 33-36R; DLB 5

Klausner, Amos   1939-
See Oz, Amos

Klein, A(braham) M(oses)
1909-1972 . . . .   **CLC 19**
See also CA 101; obituary CA 37-40R;
DLB 68

Klein, Norma   1938-1989 . . . .   **CLC 30**
See also CLR 2, 19; CANR 15; CA 41-44R;
obituary CA 128; SAAS 1; SATA 7, 57;
AAYA 2

Klein, T.E.D.   19??- . . . .   **CLC 34**
See also CA 119

Kleist, Heinrich von   1777-1811 . . . .   **NCLC 2**
See also DLB 90

Klima, Ivan   1931- . . . .   **CLC 56**
See also CANR 17; CA 25-28R

Klimentev, Andrei Platonovich   1899-1951
See Platonov, Andrei (Platonovich)
See also CA 108

Klinger, Friedrich Maximilian von
1752-1831 . . . .   **NCLC 1**

Klopstock, Friedrich Gottlieb
1724-1803 . . . .   **NCLC 11**

Knebel, Fletcher 1911- .... CLC 14
See also CAAS 3; CANR 1; CA 1-4R;
SATA 36

Knight, Etheridge 1931-1991 ...... CLC 40
See also BLC 2; CANR 23; CA 21-24R;
DLB 41

Knight, Sarah Kemble 1666-1727 ..... LC 7
See also DLB 24

Knowles, John 1926- ...... CLC 1, 4, 10, 26
See also CA 17-20R; SATA 8; DLB 6;
CDALB 1968-1987

Koch, C(hristopher) J(ohn) 1932- ... CLC 42
See also CA 127

Koch, Kenneth 1925- .... CLC 5, 8, 44
See also CANR 6; CA 1-4R; DLB 5

Kochanowski, Jan 1530-1584 .... LC 10

Kock, Charles Paul de
1794-1871 .... NCLC 16

Koestler, Arthur
1905-1983 .... CLC 1, 3, 6, 8, 15, 33
See also CANR 1; CA 1-4R;
obituary CA 109; DLB-Y 83

Kohout, Pavel 1928- .... CLC 13
See also CANR 3; CA 45-48

Kolmar, Gertrud 1894-1943 ...... TCLC 40

Konigsberg, Allen Stewart 1935-
See Allen, Woody

Konrad, Gyorgy 1933- .... CLC 4, 10
See also CA 85-88

Konwicki, Tadeusz 1926- ..... CLC 8, 28, 54
See also CAAS 9; CA 101

Kopit, Arthur (Lee) 1937- .... CLC 1, 18, 33
See also CA 81-84; CABS 3; DLB 7

Kops, Bernard 1926- .... CLC 4
See also CA 5-8R; DLB 13

Kornbluth, C(yril) M. 1923-1958.... TCLC 8
See also CA 105; DLB 8

Korolenko, Vladimir (Galaktionovich)
1853-1921 .... TCLC 22
See also CA 121

Kosinski, Jerzy (Nikodem)
1933-1991 ... CLC 1, 2, 3, 6, 10, 15, 53,
70
See also CANR 9; CA 17-20R;
obituary CA 134; DLB 2; DLB-Y 82

Kostelanetz, Richard (Cory) 1940- .. CLC 28
See also CAAS 8; CA 13-16R

Kostrowitzki, Wilhelm Apollinaris de
1880-1918
See Apollinaire, Guillaume
See also CA 104

Kotlowitz, Robert 1924- .... CLC 4
See also CA 33-36R

Kotzebue, August (Friedrich Ferdinand) von
1761-1819 .... NCLC 25

Kotzwinkle, William 1938- ... CLC 5, 14, 35
See also CLR 6; CANR 3; CA 45-48;
SATA 24

Kozol, Jonathan 1936- .... CLC 17
See also CANR 16; CA 61-64

Kozoll, Michael 1940?- .... CLC 35

Kramer, Kathryn 19??- .... CLC 34

Kramer, Larry 1935- .... CLC 42
See also CA 124, 126

Krasicki, Ignacy 1735-1801 ...... NCLC 8

Krasinski, Zygmunt 1812-1859 .... NCLC 4

Kraus, Karl 1874-1936 .... TCLC 5
See also CA 104

Kreve, Vincas 1882-1954 .... TCLC 27

Kristofferson, Kris 1936- .... CLC 26
See also CA 104

Krizanc, John 1956- .... CLC 57

Krleza, Miroslav 1893-1981 .... CLC 8
See also CA 97-100; obituary CA 105

Kroetsch, Robert (Paul)
1927- .... CLC 5, 23, 57
See also CANR 8; CA 17-20R; DLB 53

Kroetz, Franz Xaver 1946- .... CLC 41
See also CA 130

Kropotkin, Peter 1842-1921 ...... TCLC 36
See also CA 119

Krotkov, Yuri 1917- .... CLC 19
See also CA 102

Krumgold, Joseph (Quincy)
1908-1980 .... CLC 12
See also CANR 7; CA 9-12R;
obituary CA 101; SATA 1, 48;
obituary SATA 23

Krutch, Joseph Wood 1893-1970.... CLC 24
See also CANR 4; CA 1-4R;
obituary CA 25-28R; DLB 63

Krylov, Ivan Andreevich
1768?-1844................. NCLC 1

Kubin, Alfred 1877-1959 .... TCLC 23
See also CA 112; DLB 81

Kubrick, Stanley 1928- .... CLC 16
See also CA 81-84; DLB 26

Kumin, Maxine (Winokur)
1925- .... CLC 5, 13, 28
See also CAAS 8; CANR 1, 21; CA 1-4R;
SATA 12; DLB 5

Kundera, Milan
1929- .... CLC 4, 9, 19, 32, 68
See also CANR 19; CA 85-88; AAYA 2

Kunitz, Stanley J(asspon)
1905- .... CLC 6, 11, 14
See also CANR 26; CA 41-44R; DLB 48

Kunze, Reiner 1933- .... CLC 10
See also CA 93-96; DLB 75

Kuprin, Aleksandr (Ivanovich)
1870-1938 .... TCLC 5
See also CA 104

Kureishi, Hanif 1954- .... CLC 64

Kurosawa, Akira 1910- .... CLC 16
See also CA 101

Kuttner, Henry 1915-1958 .... TCLC 10
See also CA 107; DLB 8

Kuzma, Greg 1944- .... CLC 7
See also CA 33-36R

Kuzmin, Mikhail 1872?-1936...... TCLC 40

Labrunie, Gerard 1808-1855
See Nerval, Gerard de

La Bruyere, Jean de 1645-1696...... LC 17

Laclos, Pierre Ambroise Francois Choderlos
de 1741-1803 .... NCLC 4

La Fayette, Marie (Madelaine Pioche de la
Vergne, Comtesse) de
1634-1693 .... LC 2

Lafayette, Rene
See Hubbard, L(afayette) Ron(ald)

Laforgue, Jules 1860-1887 .... NCLC 5

Lagerkvist, Par (Fabian)
1891-1974 .... CLC 7, 10, 13, 54
See also CA 85-88; obituary CA 49-52

Lagerlof, Selma (Ottiliana Lovisa)
1858-1940 ....TCLC 4, 36
See also CLR 7; CA 108; SATA 15

La Guma, (Justin) Alex(ander)
1925-1985 .... CLC 19
See also CANR 25; CA 49-52;
obituary CA 118

Lamartine, Alphonse (Marie Louis Prat) de
1790-1869 .... NCLC 11

Lamb, Charles 1775-1834 .... NCLC 10
See also SATA 17

Lamming, George (William)
1927- .... CLC 2, 4, 66
See also BLC 2; CANR 26; CA 85-88

LaMoore, Louis Dearborn 1908?-
See L'Amour, Louis (Dearborn)

L'Amour, Louis (Dearborn)
1908-1988 .... CLC 25, 55
See also CANR 3, 25; CA 1-4R;
obituary CA 125; DLB-Y 80

Lampedusa, (Prince) Giuseppe (Maria
Fabrizio) Tomasi di
1896-1957 .... TCLC 13
See also CA 111

Lampman, Archibald 1861-1899 .. NCLC 25
See also DLB 92

Lancaster, Bruce 1896-1963 .... CLC 36
See also CAP 1; CA 9-12; SATA 9

Landis, John (David) 1950- .... CLC 26
See also CA 112, 122

Landolfi, Tommaso 1908-1979... CLC 11, 49
See also CA 127; obituary CA 117

Landon, Letitia Elizabeth
1802-1838 .... NCLC 15

Landor, Walter Savage
1775-1864 .... NCLC 14

Landwirth, Heinz 1927-
See Lind, Jakov
See also CANR 7; CA 11-12R

Lane, Patrick 1939- .... CLC 25
See also CA 97-100; DLB 53

Lang, Andrew 1844-1912 .... TCLC 16
See also CA 114; SATA 16

Lang, Fritz 1890-1976 .... CLC 20
See also CANR 30; CA 77-80;
obituary CA 69-72

Langer, Elinor 1939- .... CLC 34
See also CA 121

Langland, William 1330?-1400?...... LC 19

Lanier, Sidney 1842-1881 .... NCLC 6
See also SATA 18; DLB 64

Lanyer, Aemilia 1569-1645 .... LC 10

Lao Tzu c. 6th-3rd century B.C.... CMLC 7

Loti, Pierre 1850-1923 . . . . TCLC 11
See also Viaud, (Louis Marie) Julien

Louie, David Wong 1954- . . . . CLC 70

Lovecraft, H(oward) P(hillips)
    1890-1937 . . . . TCLC 4, 22; SSC 3
See also CA 104

Lovelace, Earl 1935- . . . . CLC 51
See also CA 77-80

Lowell, Amy 1874-1925 . . . . TCLC 1, 8
See also CA 104; DLB 54

Lowell, James Russell 1819-1891 . . NCLC 2
See also DLB 1, 11, 64, 79;
    CDALB 1640-1865

Lowell, Robert (Traill Spence, Jr.)
    1917-1977 . . . CLC 1, 2, 3, 4, 5, 8, 9, 11,
                              15, 37; PC 3
See also CANR 26; CA 9-10R;
    obituary CA 73-76; CABS 2; DLB 5

Lowndes, Marie (Adelaide) Belloc
    1868-1947 . . . . TCLC 12
See also CA 107; DLB 70

Lowry, (Clarence) Malcolm
    1909-1957 . . . . TCLC 6, 40
See also CA 105, 131; DLB 15

Loy, Mina 1882-1966 . . . . CLC 28
See also CA 113; DLB 4, 54

Lucas, Craig . . . . CLC 64

Lucas, George 1944- . . . . CLC 16
See also CANR 30; CA 77-80; SATA 56;
    AAYA 1

Lucas, Victoria 1932-1963
See Plath, Sylvia

Ludlam, Charles 1943-1987 . . . . . CLC 46, 50
See also CA 85-88; obituary CA 122

Ludlum, Robert 1927- . . . . CLC 22, 43
See also CANR 25; CA 33-36R; DLB-Y 82

Ludwig, Ken 19??- . . . . CLC 60

Ludwig, Otto 1813-1865 . . . . NCLC 4

Lugones, Leopoldo 1874-1938 . . . . . TCLC 15
See also CA 116

Lu Hsun 1881-1936 . . . . TCLC 3

Lukacs, Georg 1885-1971 . . . . CLC 24
See also Lukacs, Gyorgy

Lukacs, Gyorgy 1885-1971
See Lukacs, Georg
See also CA 101; obituary CA 29-32R

Luke, Peter (Ambrose Cyprian)
    1919- . . . . CLC 38
See also CA 81-84; DLB 13

Lurie (Bishop), Alison
    1926- . . . . CLC 4, 5, 18, 39
See also CANR 2, 17; CA 1-4R; SATA 46;
    DLB 2

Lustig, Arnost 1926- . . . . CLC 56
See also CA 69-72; SATA 56; AAYA 3

Luther, Martin 1483-1546 . . . . LC 9

Luzi, Mario 1914- . . . . CLC 13
See also CANR 9; CA 61-64

Lynch, David 1946- . . . . CLC 66
See also CA 129; brief entry CA 124

Lynn, Kenneth S(chuyler) 1923- . . . . CLC 50
See also CANR 3, 27; CA 1-4R

Lytle, Andrew (Nelson) 1902- . . . . . . CLC 22
See also CA 9-12R; DLB 6

Lyttelton, George 1709-1773 . . . . LC 10

Lytton, Edward Bulwer 1803-1873
See Bulwer-Lytton, (Lord) Edward (George
    Earle Lytton)
See also SATA 23

Maas, Peter 1929- . . . . CLC 29
See also CA 93-96

Macaulay, (Dame Emilie) Rose
    1881-1958 . . . . TCLC 7, 44
See also CA 104; DLB 36

MacBeth, George (Mann)
    1932- . . . . CLC 2, 5, 9
See also CA 25-28R; SATA 4; DLB 40

MacCaig, Norman (Alexander)
    1910- . . . . CLC 36
See also CANR 3; CA 9-12R; DLB 27

MacCarthy, Desmond 1877-1952 . . TCLC 36

MacDermot, Thomas H. 1870-1933
See Redcam, Tom

MacDiarmid, Hugh
    1892-1978 . . . . . . CLC 2, 4, 11, 19, 63
See also Grieve, C(hristopher) M(urray)
See also DLB 20

Macdonald, Cynthia 1928- . . . . . . CLC 13, 19
See also CANR 4; CA 49-52

MacDonald, George 1824-1905 . . . . . TCLC 9
See also CA 106; SATA 33; DLB 18

MacDonald, John D(ann)
    1916-1986 . . . . CLC 3, 27, 44
See also CANR 1, 19; CA 1-4R;
    obituary CA 121; DLB 8; DLB-Y 86

Macdonald, (John) Ross
    1915-1983 . . . . CLC 1, 2, 3, 14, 34, 41
See also Millar, Kenneth
See also DLB-DS 6

MacEwen, Gwendolyn (Margaret)
    1941-1987 . . . . CLC 13, 55
See also CANR 7, 22; CA 9-12R;
    obituary CA 124; SATA 50, 55; DLB 53

Machado (y Ruiz), Antonio
    1875-1939 . . . . TCLC 3
See also CA 104

Machado de Assis, (Joaquim Maria)
    1839-1908 . . . . TCLC 10
See also BLC 2; brief entry CA 107

Machen, Arthur (Llewellyn Jones)
    1863-1947 . . . . TCLC 4
See also CA 104; DLB 36

Machiavelli, Niccolo 1469-1527 . . . . . . LC 8

MacInnes, Colin 1914-1976 . . . . . . CLC 4, 23
See also CANR 21; CA 69-72;
    obituary CA 65-68; DLB 14

MacInnes, Helen (Clark)
    1907-1985 . . . . CLC 27, 39
See also CANR 1, 28; CA 1-4R;
    obituary CA 65-68, 117; SATA 22, 44;
    DLB 87

Macintosh, Elizabeth 1897-1952
See Tey, Josephine
See also CA 110

Mackenzie, (Edward Montague) Compton
    1883-1972 . . . . CLC 18
See also CAP 2; CA 21-22;
    obituary CA 37-40R; DLB 34

Mac Laverty, Bernard 1942- . . . . . . CLC 31
See also CA 116, 118

MacLean, Alistair (Stuart)
    1922-1987 . . . . CLC 3, 13, 50, 63
See also CANR 28; CA 57-60;
    obituary CA 121; SATA 23, 50

MacLeish, Archibald
    1892-1982 . . . . CLC 3, 8, 14, 68
See also CANR 33; CA 9-12R;
    obituary CA 106; DLB 4, 7, 45;
    DLB-Y 82

MacLennan, (John) Hugh
    1907- . . . . CLC 2, 14
See also CA 5-8R; DLB 68

MacLeod, Alistair 1936- . . . . CLC 56
See also CA 123; DLB 60

Macleod, Fiona 1855-1905
See Sharp, William

MacNeice, (Frederick) Louis
    1907-1963 . . . . CLC 1, 4, 10, 53
See also CA 85-88; DLB 10, 20

Macpherson, (Jean) Jay 1931- . . . . . . CLC 14
See also CA 5-8R; DLB 53

MacShane, Frank 1927- . . . . CLC 39
See also CANR 3; CA 11-12R

Macumber, Mari 1896-1966
See Sandoz, Mari (Susette)

Madach, Imre 1823-1864 . . . . NCLC 19

Madden, (Jerry) David 1933- . . . . CLC 5, 15
See also CAAS 3; CANR 4; CA 1-4R;
    DLB 6

Madhubuti, Haki R. 1942- . . . . CLC 6; PC 5
See also Lee, Don L.
See also BLC 2; CANR 24; CA 73-76;
    DLB 5, 41; DLB-DS 8

Maeterlinck, Maurice 1862-1949 . . . TCLC 3
See also CA 104

Mafouz, Naguib 1912-
See Mahfuz, Najib

Maginn, William 1794-1842 . . . . . . NCLC 8

Mahapatra, Jayanta 1928- . . . . CLC 33
See also CAAS 9; CANR 15; CA 73-76

Mahfuz Najib 1912- . . . . CLC 52, 55
See also DLB-Y 88

Mahon, Derek 1941- . . . . CLC 27
See also CA 113, 128; DLB 40

Mailer, Norman
    1923- . . . . . . CLC 1, 2, 3, 4, 5, 8, 11, 14,
                              28, 39
See also CANR 28; CA 9-12R; CABS 1;
    DLB 2, 16, 28; DLB-Y 80, 83;
    DLB-DS 3; CDALB 1968-1987

Maillet, Antonine 1929- . . . . CLC 54
See also CA 115, 120; DLB 60

Mais, Roger 1905-1955 . . . . TCLC 8
See also CA 105, 124

Maitland, Sara (Louise) 1950- . . . . . . CLC 49
See also CANR 13; CA 69-72

Major, Clarence 1936- .... **CLC 3, 19, 48**
See also BLC 2; CAAS 6; CANR 13, 25;
CA 21-24R; DLB 33

Major, Kevin 1949- .... **CLC 26**
See also CLR 11; CANR 21; CA 97-100;
SATA 32; DLB 60

Malamud, Bernard
1914-1986 ..... **CLC 1, 2, 3, 5, 8, 9, 11,**
18, 27, 44
See also CANR 28; CA 5-8R;
obituary CA 118; CABS 1; DLB 2, 28;
DLB-Y 80, 86; CDALB 1941-1968

Malcolm X 1925-1965
See Little, Malcolm
See also BLC 2

Malherbe, Francois de 1555-1628..... **LC 5**

Mallarme Stephane
1842-1898 .... **NCLC 4; PC 4**

Mallet-Joris, Francoise 1930- ...... **CLC 11**
See also CANR 17; CA 65-68; DLB 83

Maloff, Saul 1922- .... **CLC 5**
See also CA 33-36R

Malone, Louis 1907-1963
See MacNeice, (Frederick) Louis

Malone, Michael (Christopher)
1942- .... **CLC 43**
See also CANR 14; CA 77-80

Malory, (Sir) Thomas ?-1471....... **LC 11**
See also SATA 33, 59

Malouf, David 1934- .... **CLC 28**

Malraux, (Georges-) Andre
1901-1976 ...... **CLC 1, 4, 9, 13, 15, 57**
See also CAP 2; CA 21-24;
obituary CA 69-72; DLB 72

Malzberg, Barry N. 1939- .... **CLC 7**
See also CAAS 4; CANR 16; CA 61-64;
DLB 8

Mamet, David (Alan)
1947- .... **CLC 9, 15, 34, 46**
See also CANR 15; CA 81-84, 124;
CABS 3; DLB 7; AAYA 3

Mamoulian, Rouben 1898-......... **CLC 16**
See also CA 25-28R; obituary CA 124

Mandelstam, Osip (Emilievich)
1891?-1938?................TCLC 2, 6
See also CA 104

Mander, Jane 1877-1949 .... **TCLC 31**

Mandiargues, Andre Pieyre de
1909- .... **CLC 41**
See also CA 103; DLB 83

Mandrake, Ethel Belle 1902-1934
See Thurman, Wallace

Mangan, James Clarence
1803-1849 .... **NCLC 27**

Manley, (Mary) Delariviere
1672?-1724................... **LC 1**
See also DLB 39, 80

Mann, (Luiz) Heinrich 1871-1950... **TCLC 9**
See also CA 106; DLB 66

Mann, Thomas
1875-1955 ... **TCLC 2, 8, 14, 21, 35, 44;**
SSC 5
See also CA 104, 128; DLB 66

Manning, Frederic 1882-1935 ..... **TCLC 25**
See also CA 124

Manning, Olivia 1915-1980 ...... **CLC 5, 19**
See also CANR 29; CA 5-8R;
obituary CA 101

Mano, D. Keith 1942- .... **CLC 2, 10**
See also CAAS 6; CANR 26; CA 25-28R;
DLB 6

Mansfield, Katherine
1888-1923 .... **TCLC 2, 8, 39; SSC 9**
See also CA 104

Manso, Peter 1940- .... **CLC 39**
See also CA 29-32R

Manzoni, Alessandro 1785-1873 .. **NCLC 29**

Mapu, Abraham (ben Jekutiel)
1808-1867 .... **NCLC 18**

Marat, Jean Paul 1743-1793....... **LC 10**

Marcel, Gabriel (Honore)
1889-1973 .... **CLC 15**
See also CA 102; obituary CA 45-48

Marchbanks, Samuel 1913-
See Davies, (William) Robertson

Marie de France
c. 12th Century- .... **CMLC 8**

Marie de l'Incarnation 1599-1672.... **LC 10**

Marinetti, F(ilippo) T(ommaso)
1876-1944 .... **TCLC 10**
See also CA 107

Marivaux, Pierre Carlet de Chamblain de
(1688-1763).................... **LC 4**

Markandaya, Kamala 1924-...... **CLC 8, 38**
See also Taylor, Kamala (Purnaiya)

Markfield, Wallace (Arthur) 1926-... **CLC 8**
See also CAAS 3; CA 69-72; DLB 2, 28

Markham, Robert 1922-
See Amis, Kingsley (William)

Marks, J. 1942-
See Highwater, Jamake

Markson, David 1927-............ **CLC 67**
See also CANR 1; CA 49-52

Marley, Bob 1945-1981 .... **CLC 17**
See also Marley, Robert Nesta

Marley, Robert Nesta 1945-1981
See Marley, Bob
See also CA 107; obituary CA 103

Marlowe, Christopher 1564-1593 ..... **DC 1**
See also DLB 62

Marmontel, Jean-Francois
1723-1799 .... **LC 2**

Marquand, John P(hillips)
1893-1960 .... **CLC 2, 10**
See also CA 85-88; DLB 9

Marquez, Gabriel Garcia 1928-
See Garcia Marquez, Gabriel

Marquis, Don(ald Robert Perry)
1878-1937 .... **TCLC 7**
See also CA 104; DLB 11, 25

Marryat, Frederick 1792-1848 .... **NCLC 3**
See also DLB 21

Marsh, (Dame Edith) Ngaio
1899-1982 .... **CLC 7, 53**
See also CANR 6; CA 9-12R; DLB 77

Marshall, Garry 1935?- .... **CLC 17**
See also CA 111; AAYA 3

Marshall, Paule 1929- .. **CLC 27, 72; SSC 3**
See also BLC 3; CANR 25; CA 77-80;
DLB 33

Marsten, Richard 1926-
See Hunter, Evan

Martin, Steve 1945?- .... **CLC 30**
See also CANR 30; CA 97-100

Martin du Gard, Roger
1881-1958 .... **TCLC 24**
See also CA 118; DLB 65

Martineau, Harriet 1802-1876.... **NCLC 26**
See also YABC 2; DLB 21, 55

Martinez Ruiz, Jose 1874-1967
See Azorin
See also CA 93-96

Martinez Sierra, Gregorio
1881-1947 .... **TCLC 6**
See also CA 104, 115

Martinez Sierra, Maria (de la O'LeJarraga)
1880?-1974................... **TCLC 6**
See also obituary CA 115

Martinson, Harry (Edmund)
1904-1978 .... **CLC 14**
See also CA 77-80

Marvell, Andrew 1621-1678......... **LC 4**

Marx, Karl (Heinrich)
1818-1883 .... **NCLC 17**

Masaoka Shiki 1867-1902 .... **TCLC 18**

Masefield, John (Edward)
1878-1967 .... **CLC 11, 47**
See also CAP 2; CA 19-20;
obituary CA 25-28R; SATA 19; DLB 10,
19

Maso, Carole 19??-................ **CLC 44**

Mason, Bobbie Ann
1940- .... **CLC 28, 43; SSC 4**
See also CANR 11; CA 53-56; SAAS 1;
DLB-Y 87

Mason, Nick 1945-................ **CLC 35**
See also Pink Floyd

Mason, Tally 1909-1971
See Derleth, August (William)

Masters, Edgar Lee
1868?-1950.......... **TCLC 2, 25; PC 1**
See also CA 104; DLB 54;
CDALB 1865-1917

Masters, Hilary 1928- .... **CLC 48**
See also CANR 13; CA 25-28R

Mastrosimone, William 19??- ...... **CLC 36**

Matheson, Richard (Burton)
1926- .... **CLC 37**
See also CA 97-100; DLB 8, 44

Mathews, Harry 1930-.......... **CLC 6, 52**
See also CAAS 6; CANR 18; CA 21-24R

Mathias, Roland (Glyn) 1915-...... **CLC 45**
See also CANR 19; CA 97-100; DLB 27

Matthews, Greg 1949- .... **CLC 45**

Matthews, William 1942-.......... **CLC 40**
See also CANR 12; CA 29-32R; DLB 5

Matthias, John (Edward) 1941-...... **CLC 9**
See also CA 33-36R

Matthiessen, Peter
1927- . . . . **CLC 5, 7, 11, 32, 64**
See also CANR 21; CA 9-12R; SATA 27;
DLB 6

Maturin, Charles Robert
1780?-1824. . . . . **NCLC 6**

Matute, Ana Maria 1925- . . . . **CLC 11**
See also CA 89-92

Maugham, W(illiam) Somerset
1874-1965 . . . . **CLC 1, 11, 15, 67; SSC 8**
See also CA 5-8R; obituary CA 25-28R;
SATA 54; DLB 10, 36, 77, 100

Maupassant, (Henri Rene Albert) Guy de
1850-1893 . . . . **NCLC 1; SSC 1**

Mauriac, Claude 1914- . . . . **CLC 9**
See also CA 89-92; DLB 83

Mauriac, Francois (Charles)
1885-1970 . . . . **CLC 4, 9, 56**
See also CAP 2; CA 25-28; DLB 65

Mavor, Osborne Henry 1888-1951
See Bridie, James
See also CA 104

Maxwell, William (Keepers, Jr.)
1908- . . . . **CLC 19**
See also CA 93-96; DLB-Y 80

May, Elaine 1932- . . . . **CLC 16**
See also CA 124; DLB 44

Mayakovsky, Vladimir (Vladimirovich)
1893-1930 . . . . **TCLC 4, 18**
See also CA 104

Mayhew, Henry 1812-1887 . . . . . . **NCLC 31**
See also DLB 18, 55

Maynard, Joyce 1953- . . . . **CLC 23**
See also CA 111, 129

Mayne, William (James Carter)
1928- . . . . **CLC 12**
See also CA 9-12R; SATA 6

Mayo, Jim 1908?-
See L'Amour, Louis (Dearborn)

Maysles, Albert 1926- and **Maysles, David**
1926- . . . . **CLC 16**
See also CA 29-32R

Maysles, Albert 1926- . . . . **CLC 16**
See also Maysles, Albert and Maysles,
David
See also CA 29-32R

Maysles, David 1932- . . . . **CLC 16**
See also Maysles, Albert and Maysles,
David

Mazer, Norma Fox 1931- . . . . **CLC 26**
See also CLR 23; CANR 12; CA 69-72;
SAAS 1; SATA 24

Mazzini, Guiseppe 1805-1872 . . . . **NCLC 34**

McAuley, James (Phillip)
1917-1976 . . . . **CLC 45**
See also CA 97-100

McBain, Ed 1926-
See Hunter, Evan

McBrien, William 1930- . . . . **CLC 44**
See also CA 107

McCaffrey, Anne 1926- . . . . **CLC 17**
See also CANR 15; CA 25-28R; SATA 8;
DLB 8

McCarthy, Cormac 1933- . . . . **CLC 4, 57**
See also CANR 10; CA 13-16R; DLB 6

McCarthy, Mary (Therese)
1912-1989- . . . **CLC 1, 3, 5, 14, 24, 39, 59**
See also CANR 16; CA 5-8R;
obituary CA 129; DLB 2; DLB-Y 81

McCartney, (James) Paul
1942- . . . . **CLC 12, 35**

McCauley, Stephen 19??- . . . . **CLC 50**

McClure, Michael 1932- . . . . **CLC 6, 10**
See also CANR 17; CA 21-24R; DLB 16

McCorkle, Jill (Collins) 1958- . . . . . . **CLC 51**
See also CA 121; DLB-Y 87

McCourt, James 1941- . . . . **CLC 5**
See also CA 57-60

McCoy, Horace 1897-1955 . . . . **TCLC 28**
See also CA 108; DLB 9

McCrae, John 1872-1918 . . . . **TCLC 12**
See also CA 109; DLB 92

McCullers, (Lula) Carson (Smith)
1917-1967 . . **CLC 1, 4, 10, 12, 48; SSC 9**
See also CANR 18; CA 5-8R;
obituary CA 25-28R; CABS 1; SATA 27;
DLB 2, 7; CDALB 1941-1968

McCullough, Colleen 1938?- . . . . **CLC 27**
See also CANR 17; CA 81-84

McElroy, Joseph (Prince)
1930- . . . . **CLC 5, 47**
See also CA 17-20R

McEwan, Ian (Russell) 1948- . . . **CLC 13, 66**
See also CANR 14; CA 61-64; DLB 14

McFadden, David 1940- . . . . **CLC 48**
See also CA 104; DLB 60

McFarland, Dennis 1956- . . . . **CLC 65**

McGahern, John 1934- . . . . **CLC 5, 9, 48**
See also CANR 29; CA 17-20R; DLB 14

McGinley, Patrick 1937- . . . . **CLC 41**
See also CA 120, 127

McGinley, Phyllis 1905-1978 . . . . . . **CLC 14**
See also CANR 19; CA 9-12R;
obituary CA 77-80; SATA 2, 44;
obituary SATA 24; DLB 11, 48

McGinniss, Joe 1942- . . . . **CLC 32**
See also CANR 26; CA 25-28R

McGivern, Maureen Daly 1921-
See Daly, Maureen
See also CA 9-12R

McGrath, Patrick 1950- . . . . **CLC 55**

McGrath, Thomas 1916- . . . . **CLC 28, 59**
See also CANR 6; CA 9-12R, 130;
SATA 41

McGuane, Thomas (Francis III)
1939- . . . . **CLC 3, 7, 18, 45**
See also CANR 5, 24; CA 49-52; DLB 2;
DLB-Y 80

McGuckian, Medbh 1950- . . . . **CLC 48**
See also DLB 40

McHale, Tom 1941-1982 . . . . **CLC 3, 5**
See also CA 77-80; obituary CA 106

McIlvanney, William 1936- . . . . **CLC 42**
See also CA 25-28R; DLB 14

McIlwraith, Maureen Mollie Hunter 1922-
See Hunter, Mollie
See also CA 29-32R; SATA 2

McInerney, Jay 1955- . . . . **CLC 34**
See also CA 116, 123

McIntyre, Vonda N(eel) 1948- . . . . . **CLC 18**
See also CANR 17; CA 81-84

McKay, Claude
1889-1948 . . . . **TCLC 7, 41; PC 2**
See also BLC 3; CA 104, 124; DLB 4, 45,
51

McKay, Claude 1889-1948
See McKay, Festus Claudius

McKay, Festus Claudius 1889-1948
See also BLC 2; CA 124; brief entry CA 104

McKuen, Rod 1933?- . . . . **CLC 1, 3**
See also CA 41-44R

McLuhan, (Herbert) Marshall
1911-1980 . . . . **CLC 37**
See also CANR 12; CA 9-12R;
obituary CA 102; DLB 88

McManus, Declan Patrick 1955-
See Costello, Elvis

McMillan, Terry 1951- . . . . **CLC 50, 61**

McMurtry, Larry (Jeff)
1936- . . . . **CLC 2, 3, 7, 11, 27, 44**
See also CANR 19; CA 5-8R; DLB 2;
DLB-Y 80, 87; CDALB 1968-1987

McNally, Terrence 1939- . . . . . . **CLC 4, 7, 41**
See also CANR 2; CA 45-48; DLB 7

McNamer, Deirdre 1950- . . . . **CLC 70**

McNeile, Herman Cyril 1888-1937
See Sapper
See also DLB 77

McPhee, John 1931- . . . . **CLC 36**
See also CANR 20; CA 65-68

McPherson, James Alan 1943- . . . . . **CLC 19**
See also CANR 24; CA 25-28R; DLB 38

McPherson, William 1939- . . . . **CLC 34**
See also CA 57-60

McSweeney, Kerry 19??- . . . . **CLC 34**

Mead, Margaret 1901-1978 . . . . **CLC 37**
See also CANR 4; CA 1-4R;
obituary CA 81-84; SATA 20

Meaker, M. J. 1927-
See Kerr, M. E.; Meaker, Marijane

Meaker, Marijane 1927-
See Kerr, M. E.
See also CA 107; SATA 20

Medoff, Mark (Howard) 1940- . . . **CLC 6, 23**
See also CANR 5; CA 53-56; DLB 7

Megged, Aharon 1920- . . . . **CLC 9**
See also CANR 1; CA 49-52

Mehta, Ved (Parkash) 1934- . . . . **CLC 37**
See also CANR 2, 23; CA 1-4R

Mellor, John 1953?-
See The Clash

Meltzer, Milton 1915- . . . . **CLC 26**
See also CLR 13; CA 13-16R; SAAS 1;
SATA 1, 50; DLB 61

Melville, Herman
1819-1891 . . . . . . **NCLC 3, 12, 29; SSC 1**
See also SATA 59; DLB 3, 74;
CDALB 1640-1865

Membreno, Alejandro 1972- . . . . **CLC 59**

Menander
  c. 342 B.C.-c. 292 B.C......... **CMLC 9**

Mencken, H(enry) L(ouis)
  1880-1956 .... **TCLC 13**
  See also CA 105, 125; DLB 11, 29, 63;
  CDALB 1917-1929

Mercer, David   1928-1980........... **CLC 5**
  See also CANR 23; CA 9-12R;
  obituary CA 102; DLB 13

Meredith, George   1828-1909...... **TCLC 17**
  See also CA 117; DLB 18, 35, 57

Meredith, George   1858-1924...... **TCLC 43**

Meredith, William (Morris)
  1919- .... **CLC 4, 13, 22, 55**
  See also CANR 6; CA 9-12R; DLB 5

Merezhkovsky, Dmitri
  1865-1941 .... **TCLC 29**

Merimee, Prosper
  1803-1870 .... **NCLC 6; SSC 7**

Merkin, Daphne   1954-............ **CLC 44**
  See also CANR 123

Merrill, James (Ingram)
  1926- .... **CLC 2, 3, 6, 8, 13, 18, 34**
  See also CANR 10; CA 13-16R; DLB 5;
  DLB-Y 85

Merton, Thomas (James)
  1915-1968 .... **CLC 1, 3, 11, 34**
  See also CANR 22; CA 5-8R;
  obituary CA 25-28R; DLB 48; DLB-Y 81

Merwin, W(illiam) S(tanley)
  1927- ...... **CLC 1, 2, 3, 5, 8, 13, 18, 45**
  See also CANR 15; CA 13-16R; DLB 5

Metcalf, John   1938-.............. **CLC 37**
  See also CA 113; DLB 60

Mew, Charlotte (Mary)
  1870-1928 .... **TCLC 8**
  See also CA 105; DLB 19

Mewshaw, Michael   1943-........... **CLC 9**
  See also CANR 7; CA 53-56; DLB-Y 80

Meyer-Meyrink, Gustav   1868-1932
  See Meyrink, Gustav
  See also CA 117

Meyers, Jeffrey   1939- .... **CLC 39**
  See also CA 73-76

Meynell, Alice (Christiana Gertrude
    Thompson)   1847-1922 .... **TCLC 6**
  See also CA 104; DLB 19

Meyrink, Gustav   1868-1932....... **TCLC 21**
  See also Meyer-Meyrink, Gustav

Michaels, Leonard   1933-........ **CLC 6, 25**
  See also CANR 21; CA 61-64

Michaux, Henri   1899-1984 ...... **CLC 8, 19**
  See also CA 85-88; obituary CA 114

Michelangelo   1475-1564........... **LC 12**

Michelet, Jules   1798-1874....... **NCLC 31**

Michener, James A(lbert)
  1907- .... **CLC 1, 5, 11, 29, 60**
  See also CANR 21; CA 5-8R; DLB 6

Mickiewicz, Adam   1798-1855 ..... **NCLC 3**

Middleton, Christopher   1926-...... **CLC 13**
  See also CANR 29; CA 13-16R; DLB 40

Middleton, Stanley   1919-........ **CLC 7, 38**
  See also CANR 21; CA 25-28R; DLB 14

Migueis, Jose Rodrigues   1901-..... **CLC 10**

Mikszath, Kalman   1847-1910 ..... **TCLC 31**

Miles, Josephine (Louise)
  1911-1985 .... **CLC 1, 2, 14, 34, 39**
  See also CANR 2; CA 1-4R;
  obituary CA 116; DLB 48

Mill, John Stuart   1806-1873..... **NCLC 11**
  See also DLB 55

Millar, Kenneth   1915-1983 .... **CLC 14**
  See also Macdonald, Ross
  See also CANR 16; CA 9-12R;
  obituary CA 110; DLB 2; DLB-Y 83;
  DLB-DS 6

Millay, Edna St. Vincent
  1892-1950 .... **TCLC 4**
  See also CA 103; DLB 45;
  CDALB 1917-1929

Miller, Arthur
  1915- ...... **CLC 1, 2, 6, 10, 15, 26, 47;
                                          DC 1**
  See also CANR 2, 30; CA 1-4R; CABS 3;
  DLB 7; CDALB 1941-1968

Miller, Henry (Valentine)
  1891-1980 .... **CLC 1, 2, 4, 9, 14, 43**
  See also CA 9-12R; obituary CA 97-100;
  DLB 4, 9; DLB-Y 80; CDALB 1929-1941

Miller, Jason   1939?-............... **CLC 2**
  See also CA 73-76; DLB 7

Miller, Sue   19??-................. **CLC 44**

Miller, Walter M(ichael), Jr.
  1923- .... **CLC 4, 30**
  See also CA 85-88; DLB 8

Millett, Kate   1934-.............. **CLC 67**
  See also CANR 32; CA 73-76

Millhauser, Steven   1943-....... **CLC 21, 54**
  See also CA 108, 110, 111; DLB 2

Millin, Sarah Gertrude   1889-1968 .. **CLC 49**
  See also CA 102; obituary CA 93-96

Milne, A(lan) A(lexander)
  1882-1956 .... **TCLC 6**
  See also CLR 1, 26; YABC 1; CA 104, 133;
  DLB 10, 77, 100

Milner, Ron(ald)   1938-............ **CLC 56**
  See also BLC 3; CANR 24; CA 73-76;
  DLB 38

Milosz Czeslaw
  1911- .... **CLC 5, 11, 22, 31, 56**
  See also CANR 23; CA 81-84

Milton, John   1608-1674............. **LC 9**

Miner, Valerie (Jane)   1947-........ **CLC 40**
  See also CA 97-100

Minot, Susan   1956- .... **CLC 44**

Minus, Ed   1938-................. **CLC 39**

Miro (Ferrer), Gabriel (Francisco Victor)
  1879-1930 .... **TCLC 5**
  See also CA 104

Mishima, Yukio
  1925-1970 .... **CLC 2, 4, 6, 9, 27; DC 1;
                                          SSC 4**
  See also Hiraoka, Kimitake

Mistral, Gabriela   1889-1957 .... **TCLC 2**
  See also CA 104

Mistry, Rohinton   1952-........... **CLC 71**

Mitchell, James Leslie   1901-1935
  See Gibbon, Lewis Grassic
  See also CA 104; DLB 15

Mitchell, Joni   1943-.............. **CLC 12**
  See also CA 112

Mitchell (Marsh), Margaret (Munnerlyn)
  1900-1949 .... **TCLC 11**
  See also CA 109, 125; DLB 9

Mitchell, S. Weir   1829-1914...... **TCLC 36**

Mitchell, W(illiam) O(rmond)
  1914- .... **CLC 25**
  See also CANR 15; CA 77-80; DLB 88

Mitford, Mary Russell   1787-1855.. **NCLC 4**

Mitford, Nancy   1904-1973........ **CLC 44**
  See also CA 9-12R

Miyamoto Yuriko   1899-1951...... **TCLC 37**

Mo, Timothy   1950-............... **CLC 46**
  See also CA 117

Modarressi, Taghi   1931- .... **CLC 44**
  See also CA 121

Modiano, Patrick (Jean)   1945-..... **CLC 18**
  See also CANR 17; CA 85-88; DLB 83

Mofolo, Thomas (Mokopu)
  1876-1948 .... **TCLC 22**
  See also BLC 3; brief entry CA 121

Mohr, Nicholasa   1935-............ **CLC 12**
  See also CLR 22; CANR 1; CA 49-52;
  SAAS 8; SATA 8

Mojtabai, A(nn) G(race)
  1938- .... **CLC 5, 9, 15, 29**
  See also CA 85-88

Moliere   1622-1673 .... **LC 10**

Molnar, Ferenc   1878-1952........ **TCLC 20**
  See also CA 109

Momaday, N(avarre) Scott
  1934- .... **CLC 2, 19**
  See also CANR 14; CA 25-28R; SATA 30,
  48

Monroe, Harriet   1860-1936....... **TCLC 12**
  See also CA 109; DLB 54, 91

Montagu, Elizabeth   1720-1800 .... **NCLC 7**

Montagu, Lady Mary (Pierrepont) Wortley
  1689-1762 .... **LC 9**

Montague, John (Patrick)
  1929- .... **CLC 13, 46**
  See also CANR 9; CA 9-12R; DLB 40

Montaigne, Michel (Eyquem) de
  1533-1592 .... **LC 8**

Montale, Eugenio   1896-1981... **CLC 7, 9, 18**
  See also CANR 30; CA 17-20R;
  obituary CA 104

Montesquieu, Charles-Louis de Secondat
  1689-1755 .... **LC 7**

Montgomery, Marion (H., Jr.)
  1925- .... **CLC 7**
  See also CANR 3; CA 1-4R; DLB 6

Montgomery, Robert Bruce   1921-1978
  See Crispin, Edmund
  See also CA 104

Montherlant, Henri (Milon) de
  1896-1972 .... **CLC 8, 19**
  See also CA 85-88; obituary CA 37-40R;
  DLB 72

Monty Python . . . . CLC 21

Moodie, Susanna (Strickland)
 1803-1885 . . . . NCLC 14

Mooney, Ted 1951- . . . . CLC 25

Moorcock, Michael (John)
 1939- . . . . CLC 5, 27, 58
 See also CAAS 5; CANR 2, 17; CA 45-48;
 DLB 14

Moore, Brian
 1921- . . . . CLC 1, 3, 5, 7, 8, 19, 32
 See also CANR 1, 25; CA 1-4R

Moore, George (Augustus)
 1852-1933 . . . . TCLC 7
 See also CA 104; DLB 10, 18, 57

Moore, Lorrie 1957- . . . . CLC 39, 45, 68
 See also Moore, Marie Lorena

Moore, Marianne (Craig)
 1887-1972 . . . CLC 1, 2, 4, 8, 10, 13, 19,
 47; PC 4
 See also CANR 3; CA 1-4R;
 obituary CA 33-36R; SATA 20; DLB 45;
 DLB-DS 7; CDALB 1929-1941

Moore, Marie Lorena 1957-
 See Moore, Lorrie
 See also CA 116

Moore, Thomas 1779-1852 . . . . NCLC 6

Morand, Paul 1888-1976 . . . . CLC 41
 See also obituary CA 69-72; DLB 65

Morante, Elsa 1918-1985 . . . . CLC 8, 47
 See also CA 85-88; obituary CA 117

Moravia, Alberto
 1907- . . . . CLC 2, 7, 11, 18, 27, 46
 See also Pincherle, Alberto

More, Hannah 1745-1833 . . . . NCLC 27

More, Henry 1614-1687 . . . . LC 9

More, Sir Thomas 1478-1535 . . . . LC 10

Moreas, Jean 1856-1910 . . . . TCLC 18

Morgan, Berry 1919- . . . . CLC 6
 See also CA 49-52; DLB 6

Morgan, Edwin (George) 1920- . . . . . CLC 31
 See also CANR 3; CA 7-8R; DLB 27

Morgan, (George) Frederick
 1922- . . . . CLC 23
 See also CANR 21; CA 17-20R

Morgan, Janet 1945- . . . . CLC 39
 See also CA 65-68

Morgan, Lady 1776?-1859 . . . . NCLC 29

Morgan, Robin 1941- . . . . CLC 2
 See also CA 69-72

Morgan, Seth 1949-1990 . . . . CLC 65
 See also CA 132

Morgenstern, Christian (Otto Josef Wolfgang)
 1871-1914 . . . . TCLC 8
 See also CA 105

Moricz, Zsigmond 1879-1942 . . . . . TCLC 33

Morike, Eduard (Friedrich)
 1804-1875 . . . . NCLC 10

Mori Ogai 1862-1922 . . . . TCLC 14
 See also Mori Rintaro

Mori Rintaro 1862-1922
 See Mori Ogai
 See also CA 110

Moritz, Karl Philipp 1756-1793 . . . . . . LC 2

Morris, Julian 1916-
 See West, Morris L.

Morris, Steveland Judkins 1950-
 See Wonder, Stevie
 See also CA 111

Morris, William 1834-1896 . . . . NCLC 4
 See also DLB 18, 35, 57

Morris, Wright (Marion)
 1910- . . . . CLC 1, 3, 7, 18, 37
 See also CANR 21; CA 9-12R; DLB 2;
 DLB-Y 81

Morrison, James Douglas 1943-1971
 See Morrison, Jim
 See also CA 73-76

Morrison, Jim 1943-1971 . . . . CLC 17
 See also Morrison, James Douglas

Morrison, Toni 1931- . . . . . CLC 4, 10, 22, 55
 See also BLC 3; CANR 27; CA 29-32R;
 SATA 57; DLB 6, 33; DLB-Y 81;
 CDALB 1968-1987; AAYA 1

Morrison, Van 1945- . . . . CLC 21
 See also CA 116

Mortimer, John (Clifford)
 1923- . . . . CLC 28, 43
 See also CANR 21; CA 13-16R; DLB 13

Mortimer, Penelope (Ruth) 1918- . . . . CLC 5
 See also CA 57-60

Mosher, Howard Frank 19??- . . . . . . CLC 62

Mosley, Nicholas 1923- . . . . CLC 43, 70
 See also CA 69-72; DLB 14

Moss, Howard
 1922-1987 . . . . CLC 7, 14, 45, 50
 See also CANR 1; CA 1-4R;
 obituary CA 123; DLB 5

Motion, Andrew (Peter) 1952- . . . . . . CLC 47
 See also DLB 40

Motley, Willard (Francis)
 1912-1965 . . . . CLC 18
 See also CA 117; obituary CA 106; DLB 76

Mott, Michael (Charles Alston)
 1930- . . . . CLC 15, 34
 See also CAAS 7; CANR 7, 29; CA 5-8R

Mowat, Farley (McGill) 1921- . . . . . CLC 26
 See also CLR 20; CANR 4, 24; CA 1-4R;
 SATA 3, 55; DLB 68; AAYA 1

Mphahlele, Es'kia 1919-
 See Mphahlele, Ezekiel

Mphahlele, Ezekiel 1919- . . . . CLC 25
 See also BLC 3; CANR 26; CA 81-84

Mqhayi, S(amuel) E(dward) K(rune Loliwe)
 1875-1945 . . . . TCLC 25
 See also BLC 3

Mrozek, Slawomir 1930- . . . . CLC 3, 13
 See also CAAS 10; CANR 29; CA 13-16R

Mtwa, Percy 19??- . . . . CLC 47

Mueller, Lisel 1924- . . . . CLC 13, 51
 See also CA 93-96

Muir, Edwin 1887-1959 . . . . TCLC 2
 See also CA 104; DLB 20

Muir, John 1838-1914 . . . . TCLC 28

Mujica Lainez, Manuel
 1910-1984 . . . . CLC 31
 See also CA 81-84; obituary CA 112

Mukherjee, Bharati 1940- . . . . CLC 53
 See also CA 107; DLB 60

Muldoon, Paul 1951- . . . . CLC 32, 72
 See also CA 113, 129; DLB 40

Mulisch, Harry (Kurt Victor)
 1927- . . . . CLC 42
 See also CANR 6, 26; CA 9-12R

Mull, Martin 1943- . . . . CLC 17
 See also CA 105

Munford, Robert 1737?-1783 . . . . LC 5
 See also DLB 31

Mungo, Raymond 1946- . . . . CLC 72
 See also CANR 2; CA 49-52

Munro, Alice (Laidlaw)
 1931- . . . . CLC 6, 10, 19, 50; SSC 3
 See also CA 33-36R; SATA 29; DLB 53

Munro, H(ector) H(ugh) 1870-1916
 See Saki
 See also CA 104; DLB 34

Murasaki, Lady c. 11th century- . . . CMLC 1

Murdoch, (Jean) Iris
 1919- . . . . . . CLC 1, 2, 3, 4, 6, 8, 11, 15,
 22, 31, 51
 See also CANR 8; CA 13-16R; DLB 14

Murphy, Richard 1927- . . . . CLC 41
 See also CA 29-32R; DLB 40

Murphy, Sylvia 19??- . . . . CLC 34

Murphy, Thomas (Bernard) 1935- . . . CLC 51
 See also CA 101

Murray, Les(lie) A(llan) 1938- . . . . . CLC 40
 See also CANR 11, 27; CA 21-24R

Murry, John Middleton
 1889-1957 . . . . TCLC 16
 See also CA 118

Musgrave, Susan 1951- . . . . CLC 13, 54
 See also CA 69-72

Musil, Robert (Edler von)
 1880-1942 . . . . TCLC 12
 See also CA 109; DLB 81

Musset, (Louis Charles) Alfred de
 1810-1857 . . . . NCLC 7

Myers, Walter Dean 1937- . . . . CLC 35
 See also BLC 3; CLR 4, 16; CANR 20;
 CA 33-36R; SAAS 2; SATA 27, 41;
 DLB 33; AAYA 4

Myers, Walter M. 1937-
 See Myers, Walter Dean

Nabokov, Vladimir (Vladimirovich)
 1899-1977 . . . . CLC 1, 2, 3, 6, 8, 11, 15,
 23, 44, 46, 64
 See also CANR 20; CA 5-8R;
 obituary CA 69-72; DLB 2; DLB-Y 80;
 DLB-DS 3; CDALB 1941-1968

Nagy, Laszlo 1925-1978 . . . . CLC 7
 See also CA 129; obituary CA 112

Naipaul, Shiva(dhar Srinivasa)
 1945-1985 . . . . CLC 32, 39
 See also CA 110, 112; obituary CA 116;
 DLB-Y 85

Naipaul, V(idiadhar) S(urajprasad)
 1932- . . . . CLC 4, 7, 9, 13, 18, 37
 See also CANR 1; CA 1-4R; DLB-Y 85

Nakos, Ioulia 1899?-
 See Nakos, Lilika

Pink Floyd . . . . CLC 35

Pinkney, Edward 1802-1828 . . . . . NCLC 31

Pinkwater, D(aniel) M(anus)
1941- . . . . CLC 35
See also Pinkwater, Manus
See also CLR 4; CANR 12; CA 29-32R;
SAAS 3; SATA 46; AAYA 1

Pinkwater, Manus 1941-
See Pinkwater, D(aniel) M(anus)
See also SATA 8

Pinsky, Robert 1940- . . . . CLC 9, 19, 38
See also CAAS 4; CA 29-32R; DLB-Y 82

Pinter, Harold
1930- . . . . . CLC 1, 3, 6, 9, 11, 15, 27, 58
See also CA 5-8R; DLB 13

Pirandello, Luigi 1867-1936 . . . . . TCLC 4, 29
See also CA 104

Pirsig, Robert M(aynard) 1928- . . . CLC 4, 6
See also CA 53-56; SATA 39

Pisarev, Dmitry Ivanovich
1840-1868 . . . . NCLC 25

Pix, Mary (Griffith) 1666-1709 . . . . LC 8
See also DLB 80

Plaidy, Jean 1906-
See Hibbert, Eleanor (Burford)

Plant, Robert 1948- . . . . CLC 12

Plante, David (Robert)
1940- . . . . CLC 7, 23, 38
See also CANR 12; CA 37-40R; DLB-Y 83

Plath, Sylvia
1932-1963 . . . . CLC 1, 2, 3, 5, 9, 11, 14,
17, 50, 51, 62; PC 1
See also CAP 2; CA 19-20; DLB 5, 6;
CDALB 1941-1968

Plato 428? B.C.-348? B.C. . . . . CMLC 8

Platonov, Andrei (Platonovich)
1899-1951 . . . . TCLC 14
See also Klimentov, Andrei Platonovich
See also CA 108

Platt, Kin 1911- . . . . CLC 26
See also CANR 11; CA 17-20R; SATA 21

Plimpton, George (Ames) 1927- . . . . . CLC 36
See also CA 21-24R; SATA 10

Plomer, William (Charles Franklin)
1903-1973 . . . . CLC 4, 8
See also CAP 2; CA 21-22; SATA 24;
DLB 20

Plumly, Stanley (Ross) 1939- . . . . . . CLC 33
See also CA 108, 110; DLB 5

Poe, Edgar Allan
1809-1849 . . . NCLC 1, 16; PC 1; SSC 1
See also SATA 23; DLB 3, 59, 73, 74;
CDALB 1640-1865

Pohl, Frederik 1919- . . . . CLC 18
See also CAAS 1; CANR 11; CA 61-64;
SATA 24; DLB 8

Poirier, Louis 1910-
See Gracq, Julien
See also CA 122, 126

Poitier, Sidney 1924?- . . . . CLC 26
See also CA 117

Polanski, Roman 1933- . . . . CLC 16
See also CA 77-80

Poliakoff, Stephen 1952- . . . . CLC 38
See also CA 106; DLB 13

Police, The . . . . CLC 26

Pollitt, Katha 1949- . . . . CLC 28
See also CA 120, 122

Pollock, Sharon 19??- . . . . CLC 50
See also DLB 60

Pomerance, Bernard 1940- . . . . CLC 13
See also CA 101

Ponge, Francis (Jean Gaston Alfred)
1899- . . . . CLC 6, 18
See also CA 85-88; obituary CA 126

Pontoppidan, Henrik 1857-1943 . . . TCLC 29
See also obituary CA 126

Poole, Josephine 1933- . . . . CLC 17
See also CANR 10; CA 21-24R; SAAS 2;
SATA 5

Popa, Vasko 1922- . . . . CLC 19
See also CA 112

Pope, Alexander 1688-1744 . . . . LC 3

Porter, Connie 1960- . . . . CLC 70

Porter, Gene Stratton 1863-1924 . . TCLC 21
See also CA 112

Porter, Katherine Anne
1890-1980 . . . . . CLC 1, 3, 7, 10, 13, 15,
27; SSC 4
See also CANR 1; CA 1-4R;
obituary CA 101; obituary SATA 23, 39;
DLB 4, 9; DLB-Y 80

Porter, Peter (Neville Frederick)
1929- . . . . CLC 5, 13, 33
See also CA 85-88; DLB 40

Porter, William Sydney 1862-1910
See Henry, O.
See also YABC 2; CA 104; DLB 12, 78, 79;
CDALB 1865-1917

Post, Melville D. 1871-1930 . . . . . . TCLC 39
See also brief entry CA 110

Potok, Chaim 1929- . . . . CLC 2, 7, 14, 26
See also CANR 19; CA 17-20R; SATA 33;
DLB 28

Potter, Dennis (Christopher George)
1935- . . . . CLC 58
See also CA 107

Pound, Ezra (Loomis)
1885-1972 . . . . . CLC 1, 2, 3, 4, 5, 7, 10,
13, 18, 34, 48, 50; PC 4
See also CA 5-8R; obituary CA 37-40R;
DLB 4, 45, 63; CDALB 1917-1929

Povod, Reinaldo 1959- . . . . CLC 44

Powell, Adam Clayton, Jr. 1908-1972
See also BLC 3; CA 102;
obituary CA 33-36R

Powell, Anthony (Dymoke)
1905- . . . . CLC 1, 3, 7, 9, 10, 31
See also CANR 1; CA 1-4R; DLB 15

Powell, Dawn 1897-1965 . . . . CLC 66
See also CA 5-8R

Powell, Padgett 1952- . . . . CLC 34
See also CA 126

Powers, J(ames) F(arl)
1917- . . . . CLC 1, 4, 8, 57; SSC 4
See also CANR 2; CA 1-4R

Powers, John J(ames) 1945-
See Powers, John R.

Powers, John R. 1945- . . . . CLC 66
See also Powers, John J(ames)
See also CA 69-72

Pownall, David 1938- . . . . CLC 10
See also CA 89-92; DLB 14

Powys, John Cowper
1872-1963 . . . . CLC 7, 9, 15, 46
See also CA 85-88; DLB 15

Powys, T(heodore) F(rancis)
1875-1953 . . . . TCLC 9
See also CA 106; DLB 36

Prager, Emily 1952- . . . . CLC 56

Pratt, E(dwin) J(ohn) 1883-1964 . . . . CLC 19
See also obituary CA 93-96; DLB 92

Premchand 1880-1936 . . . . TCLC 21

Preussler, Otfried 1923- . . . . CLC 17
See also CA 77-80; SATA 24

Prevert, Jacques (Henri Marie)
1900-1977 . . . . CLC 15
See also CANR 29; CA 77-80;
obituary CA 69-72; obituary SATA 30

Prevost, Abbe (Antoine Francois)
1697-1763 . . . . LC 1

Price, (Edward) Reynolds
1933- . . . . CLC 3, 6, 13, 43, 50, 63
See also CANR 1; CA 1-4R; DLB 2

Price, Richard 1949- . . . . CLC 6, 12
See also CANR 3; CA 49-52; DLB-Y 81

Prichard, Katharine Susannah
1883-1969 . . . . CLC 46
See also CAP 1; CA 11-12

Priestley, J(ohn) B(oynton)
1894-1984 . . . . CLC 2, 5, 9, 34
See also CA 9-12R; obituary CA 113;
DLB 10, 34, 77; DLB-Y 84

Prince (Rogers Nelson) 1958?- . . . . . CLC 35

Prince, F(rank) T(empleton) 1912- . . CLC 22
See also CA 101; DLB 20

Prior, Matthew 1664-1721 . . . . LC 4

Pritchard, William H(arrison)
1932- . . . . CLC 34
See also CANR 23; CA 65-68

Pritchett, V(ictor) S(awdon)
1900- . . . . CLC 5, 13, 15, 41
See also CA 61-64; DLB 15

Probst, Mark 1925- . . . . CLC 59
See also CA 130

Procaccino, Michael 1946-
See Cristofer, Michael

Prokosch, Frederic 1908-1989 . . . . CLC 4, 48
See also CA 73-76; obituary CA 128;
DLB 48

Prose, Francine 1947- . . . . CLC 45
See also CA 109, 112

Proust, Marcel 1871-1922 . . TCLC 7, 13, 33
See also CA 104, 120; DLB 65

Pryor, Richard 1940- . . . . CLC 26
See also CA 122

Przybyszewski, Stanislaw
1868-1927 . . . . TCLC 36
See also DLB 66

Author Index

Rolvaag, O(le) E(dvart)
1876-1931 . . . . TCLC 17
See also CA 117; DLB 9

Romains, Jules 1885-1972 . . . . CLC 7
See also CA 85-88

Romero, Jose Ruben 1890-1952 . . . TCLC 14
See also CA 114

Ronsard, Pierre de 1524-1585 . . . . LC 6

Rooke, Leon 1934- . . . . CLC 25, 34
See also CANR 23; CA 25-28R

Roper, William 1498-1578 . . . . LC 10

Rosa, Joao Guimaraes 1908-1967 . . . CLC 23
See also obituary CA 89-92

Rosen, Richard (Dean) 1949- . . . . . . CLC 39
See also CA 77-80

Rosenberg, Isaac 1890-1918 . . . . . . TCLC 12
See also CA 107; DLB 20

Rosenblatt, Joe 1933- . . . . CLC 15
See also Rosenblatt, Joseph

Rosenblatt, Joseph 1933-
See Rosenblatt, Joe
See also CA 89-92

Rosenfeld, Samuel 1896-1963
See Tzara, Tristan
See also obituary CA 89-92

Rosenthal, M(acha) L(ouis) 1917- . . . CLC 28
See also CAAS 6; CANR 4; CA 1-4R;
SATA 59; DLB 5

Ross, (James) Sinclair 1908- . . . . CLC 13
See also CA 73-76; DLB 88

Rossetti, Christina Georgina
1830-1894 . . . . NCLC 2
See also SATA 20; DLB 35

Rossetti, Dante Gabriel
1828-1882 . . . . NCLC 4
See also DLB 35

Rossetti, Gabriel Charles Dante 1828-1882
See Rossetti, Dante Gabriel

Rossner, Judith (Perelman)
1935- . . . . CLC 6, 9, 29
See also CANR 18; CA 17-20R; DLB 6

Rostand, Edmond (Eugene Alexis)
1868-1918 . . . . TCLC 6, 37
See also CA 104, 126

Roth, Henry 1906- . . . . CLC 2, 6, 11
See also CAP 1; CA 11-12; DLB 28

Roth, Joseph 1894-1939 . . . . TCLC 33
See also DLB 85

Roth, Philip (Milton)
1933- . . . . . . CLC 1, 2, 3, 4, 6, 9, 15, 22,
31, 47, 66
See also CANR 1, 22; CA 1-4R; DLB 2, 28;
DLB-Y 82; CDALB 1968-1988

Rothenberg, James 1931- . . . . CLC 57

Rothenberg, Jerome 1931- . . . . CLC 6, 57
See also CANR 1; CA 45-48; DLB 5

Roumain, Jacques 1907-1944 . . . . . . TCLC 19
See also BLC 3; CA 117, 125

Rourke, Constance (Mayfield)
1885-1941 . . . . TCLC 12
See also YABC 1; CA 107

Rousseau, Jean-Baptiste 1671-1741 . . . LC 9

Rousseau, Jean-Jacques 1712-1778 . . . LC 14

Roussel, Raymond 1877-1933 . . . . . TCLC 20
See also CA 117

Rovit, Earl (Herbert) 1927- . . . . CLC 7
See also CANR 12; CA 5-8R

Rowe, Nicholas 1674-1718 . . . . LC 8

Rowson, Susanna Haswell
1762-1824 . . . . NCLC 5
See also DLB 37

Roy, Gabrielle 1909-1983 . . . . . . CLC 10, 14
See also CANR 5; CA 53-56;
obituary CA 110; DLB 68

Rozewicz, Tadeusz 1921- . . . . CLC 9, 23
See also CA 108

Ruark, Gibbons 1941- . . . . CLC 3
See also CANR 14; CA 33-36R

Rubens, Bernice 192?- . . . . CLC 19, 31
See also CA 25-28R; DLB 14

Rubenstein, Gladys 1934-
See Swan, Gladys

Rudkin, (James) David 1936- . . . . . . CLC 14
See also CA 89-92; DLB 13

Rudnik, Raphael 1933- . . . . CLC 7
See also CA 29-32R

Ruiz, Jose Martinez 1874-1967
See Azorin

Rukeyser, Muriel
1913-1980 . . . . CLC 6, 10, 15, 27
See also CANR 26; CA 5-8R;
obituary CA 93-96; obituary SATA 22;
DLB 48

Rule, Jane (Vance) 1931- . . . . CLC 27
See also CANR 12; CA 25-28R; DLB 60

Rulfo, Juan 1918-1986 . . . . CLC 8
See also CANR 26; CA 85-88;
obituary CA 118

Runyon, (Alfred) Damon
1880-1946 . . . . TCLC 10
See also CA 107; DLB 11

Rush, Norman 1933- . . . . CLC 44
See also CA 121, 126

Rushdie, (Ahmed) Salman
1947- . . . . CLC 23, 31, 55, 59
See also CA 108, 111

Rushforth, Peter (Scott) 1945- . . . . . CLC 19
See also CA 101

Ruskin, John 1819-1900 . . . . TCLC 20
See also CA 114; SATA 24; DLB 55

Russ, Joanna 1937- . . . . CLC 15
See also CANR 11; CA 25-28R; DLB 8

Russell, George William 1867-1935
See A. E.
See also CA 104

Russell, (Henry) Ken(neth Alfred)
1927- . . . . CLC 16
See also CA 105

Russell, Mary Annette Beauchamp 1866-1941
See Elizabeth

Russell, Willy 1947- . . . . CLC 60

Rutherford, Mark 1831-1913 . . . . . . TCLC 25
See also CA 121; DLB 18

Ruyslinck, Ward 1929- . . . . CLC 14

Ryan, Cornelius (John) 1920-1974 . . . CLC 7
See also CA 69-72; obituary CA 53-56

Ryan, Michael 1946- . . . . CLC 65
See also CA 49-52; DLB-Y 82

Rybakov, Anatoli 1911?- . . . . . . CLC 23, 53
See also CA 126

Ryder, Jonathan 1927-
See Ludlum, Robert

Ryga, George 1932- . . . . CLC 14
See also CA 101; obituary CA 124; DLB 60

Séviné, Marquise de Marie de
Rabutin-Chantal 1626-1696 . . . . . LC 11

Saba, Umberto 1883-1957 . . . . TCLC 33

Sabato, Ernesto 1911- . . . . CLC 10, 23
See also CA 97-100

Sacher-Masoch, Leopold von
1836?-1895 . . . . NCLC 31

Sachs, Marilyn (Stickle) 1927- . . . . . CLC 35
See also CLR 2; CANR 13; CA 17-20R;
SAAS 2; SATA 3, 52

Sachs, Nelly 1891-1970 . . . . CLC 14
See also CAP 2; CA 17-18;
obituary CA 25-28R

Sackler, Howard (Oliver)
1929-1982 . . . . CLC 14
See also CA 61-64; obituary CA 108; DLB 7

Sacks, Oliver 1933- . . . . CLC 67
See also CANR 28; CA 53-56

Sade, Donatien Alphonse Francois, Comte de
1740-1814 . . . . NCLC 3

Sadoff, Ira 1945- . . . . CLC 9
See also CANR 5, 21; CA 53-56

Safire, William 1929- . . . . CLC 10
See also CA 17-20R

Sagan, Carl (Edward) 1934- . . . . CLC 30
See also CANR 11; CA 25-28R; SATA 58

Sagan, Francoise
1935- . . . . CLC 3, 6, 9, 17, 36
See also Quoirez, Francoise
See also CANR 6; DLB 83

Sahgal, Nayantara (Pandit) 1927- . . . CLC 41
See also CANR 11; CA 9-12R

Saint, H(arry) F. 1941- . . . . CLC 50

Sainte-Beuve, Charles Augustin
1804-1869 . . . . NCLC 5

Sainte-Marie, Beverly 1941-1972?
See Sainte-Marie, Buffy
See also CA 107

Sainte-Marie, Buffy 1941- . . . . CLC 17
See also Sainte-Marie, Beverly

Saint-Exupery, Antoine (Jean Baptiste Marie
Roger) de 1900-1944 . . . . TCLC 2
See also CLR 10; CA 108; SATA 20;
DLB 72

Saintsbury, George 1845-1933 . . . . . TCLC 31
See also DLB 57

Sait Faik (Abasiyanik)
1906-1954 . . . . TCLC 23

Saki 1870-1916 . . . . TCLC 3
See also Munro, H(ector) H(ugh)
See also CA 104

Salama, Hannu 1936- . . . . CLC 18

Salamanca, J(ack) R(ichard)
1922- . . . . CLC 4, 15
See also CA 25-28R

Sale, Kirkpatrick 1937- .... **CLC 68**
See also CANR 10; CA 13-14R

Salinas, Pedro 1891-1951........ **TCLC 17**
See also CA 117

Salinger, J(erome) D(avid)
1919- .... **CLC 1, 3, 8, 12, 56; SSC 2**
See also CA 5-8R; DLB 2;
CDALB 1941-1968

Salter, James 1925- .... **CLC 7, 52, 59**
See also CA 73-76

Saltus, Edgar (Evertson)
1855-1921 .... **TCLC 8**
See also CA 105

Saltykov, Mikhail Evgrafovich
1826-1889 .... **NCLC 16**

Samarakis, Antonis 1919- .... **CLC 5**
See also CA 25-28R

Sanchez, Florencio 1875-1910..... **TCLC 37**

Sanchez, Luis Rafael 1936-........ **CLC 23**

Sanchez, Sonia 1934-.............. **CLC 5**
See also BLC 3; CLR 18; CANR 24;
CA 33-36R; SATA 22; DLB 41;
DLB-DS 8

Sand, George 1804-1876......... **NCLC 2**

Sandburg, Carl (August)
1878-1967 ... **CLC 1, 4, 10, 15, 35; PC 2**
See also CA 5-8R; obituary CA 25-28R;
SATA 8; DLB 17, 54; CDALB 1865-1917

Sandburg, Charles August 1878-1967
See Sandburg, Carl (August)

Sanders, (James) Ed(ward) 1939- ... **CLC 53**
See also CANR 13; CA 15-16R, 103;
DLB 16

Sanders, Lawrence 1920-......... **CLC 41**
See also CA 81-84

Sandoz, Mari (Susette) 1896-1966 .. **CLC 28**
See also CANR 17; CA 1-4R;
obituary CA 25-28R; SATA 5; DLB 9

Saner, Reg(inald Anthony) 1931- .... **CLC 9**
See also CA 65-68

Sannazaro, Jacopo 1456?-1530 .... **LC 8**

Sansom, William 1912-1976....... **CLC 2, 6**
See also CA 5-8R; obituary CA 65-68

Santayana, George 1863-1952..... **TCLC 40**
See also CA 115; DLB 54, 71

Santiago, Danny 1911-............ **CLC 33**
See also CA 125

Santmyer, Helen Hooven
1895-1986 .... **CLC 33**
See also CANR 15; CA 1-4R;
obituary CA 118; DLB-Y 84

Santos, Bienvenido N(uqui) 1911-... **CLC 22**
See also CANR 19; CA 101

Sapper 1888-1937 .... **TCLC 44**

Sappho
c. 6th-century B.C.- ..... **CMLC 3; PC 5**

Sarduy, Severo 1937-............. **CLC 6**
See also CA 89-92

Sargeson, Frank 1903-1982 .... **CLC 31**
See also CA 106, 25-28R; obituary CA 106

Sarmiento, Felix Ruben Garcia 1867-1916
See Dario, Ruben
See also CA 104

Saroyan, William
1908-1981 ..... **CLC 1, 8, 10, 29, 34, 56**
See also CA 5-8R; obituary CA 103;
SATA 23; obituary SATA 24; DLB 7, 9;
DLB-Y 81

Sarraute, Nathalie
1902- .... **CLC 1, 2, 4, 8, 10, 31**
See also CANR 23; CA 9-12R; DLB 83

Sarton, Eleanore Marie 1912-
See Sarton, (Eleanor) May

Sarton, (Eleanor) May
1912- .... **CLC 4, 14, 49**
See also CANR 1; CA 1-4R; SATA 36;
DLB 48; DLB-Y 81

Sartre, Jean-Paul (Charles Aymard)
1905-1980 ... **CLC 1, 4, 7, 9, 13, 18, 24,
44, 50, 52**
See also CANR 21; CA 9-12R;
obituary CA 97-100; DLB 72

Sassoon, Siegfried (Lorraine)
1886-1967 .... **CLC 36**
See also CA 104; obituary CA 25-28R;
DLB 20

Saul, John (W. III) 1942- .... **CLC 46**
See also CANR 16; CA 81-84

Saura, Carlos 1932- .... **CLC 20**
See also CA 114

Sauser-Hall, Frederic-Louis
1887-1961 .... **CLC 18**
See also Cendrars, Blaise
See also CA 102; obituary CA 93-96

Savage, Thomas 1915- .... **CLC 40**
See also CA 126

Savan, Glenn 19??-............... **CLC 50**

Sayers, Dorothy L(eigh)
1893-1957 .... **TCLC 2, 15**
See also CA 104, 119; DLB 10, 36, 77

Sayers, Valerie 19??-............. **CLC 50**

Sayles, John (Thomas)
1950- .... **CLC 7, 10, 14**
See also CA 57-60; DLB 44

Scammell, Michael 19??-.......... **CLC 34**

Scannell, Vernon 1922- .... **CLC 49**
See also CANR 8; CA 5-8R; DLB 27

Schaeffer, Susan Fromberg
1941- .... **CLC 6, 11, 22**
See also CANR 18; CA 49-52; SATA 22;
DLB 28

Schell, Jonathan 1943-............ **CLC 35**
See also CANR 12; CA 73-76

Schelling, Friedrich Wilhelm Joseph von
1775-1854 .... **NCLC 30**
See also DLB 90

Scherer, Jean-Marie Maurice 1920-
See Rohmer, Eric
See also CA 110

Schevill, James (Erwin) 1920-....... **CLC 7**
See also CA 5-8R

Schisgal, Murray (Joseph) 1926-..... **CLC 6**
See also CA 21-24R

Schlee, Ann 1934-................ **CLC 35**
See also CA 101; SATA 36, 44

Schlegel, August Wilhelm von
1767-1845 .... **NCLC 15**

Schlegel, Johann Elias (von)
1719?-1749..................... **LC 5**

Schmidt, Arno 1914-1979......... **CLC 56**
See also obituary CA 109; DLB 69

Schmitz, Ettore 1861-1928
See Svevo, Italo
See also CA 104, 122

Schnackenberg, Gjertrud 1953-..... **CLC 40**
See also CA 116

Schneider, Leonard Alfred 1925-1966
See Bruce, Lenny
See also CA 89-92

Schnitzler, Arthur 1862-1931 ...... **TCLC 4**
See also CA 104; DLB 81

Schor, Sandra 1932?-1990 .... **CLC 65**
See also CA 132

Schorer, Mark 1908-1977 .... **CLC 9**
See also CANR 7; CA 5-8R;
obituary CA 73-76

Schrader, Paul (Joseph) 1946-...... **CLC 26**
See also CA 37-40R; DLB 44

Schreiner (Cronwright), Olive (Emilie
Albertina) 1855-1920........ **TCLC 9**
See also CA 105; DLB 18

Schulberg, Budd (Wilson)
1914- .... **CLC 7, 48**
See also CANR 19; CA 25-28R; DLB 6, 26,
28; DLB-Y 81

Schulz, Bruno 1892-1942......... **TCLC 5**
See also CA 115, 123

Schulz, Charles M(onroe) 1922- .... **CLC 12**
See also CANR 6; CA 9-12R; SATA 10

Schuyler, James (Marcus)
1923- .... **CLC 5, 23**
See also CA 101; DLB 5

Schwartz, Delmore
1913-1966 .... **CLC 2, 4, 10, 45**
See also CAP 2; CA 17-18;
obituary CA 25-28R; DLB 28, 48

Schwartz, John Burnham 1925- .... **CLC 59**

Schwartz, Lynne Sharon 1939-..... **CLC 31**
See also CA 103

Schwarz-Bart, Andre 1928-....... **CLC 2, 4**
See also CA 89-92

Schwarz-Bart, Simone 1938-........ **CLC 7**
See also CA 97-100

Schwob, (Mayer Andre) Marcel
1867-1905 .... **TCLC 20**
See also CA 117

Sciascia, Leonardo
1921-1989 .... **CLC 8, 9, 41**
See also CA 85-88

Scoppettone, Sandra 1936-........ **CLC 26**
See also CA 5-8R; SATA 9

Scorsese, Martin 1942- .... **CLC 20**
See also CA 110, 114

Scotland, Jay 1932-
See Jakes, John (William)

Scott, Duncan Campbell
1862-1947 .... **TCLC 6**
See also CA 104; DLB 92

Scott, Evelyn 1893-1963.......... **CLC 43**
See also CA 104; obituary CA 112; DLB 9,
48

Williamson, David   1932- .... **CLC 56**

Williamson, Jack   1908- .... **CLC 29**
See also Williamson, John Stewart
See also DLB 8

Williamson, John Stewart   1908-
See Williamson, Jack
See also CANR 123; CA 17-20R

Willingham, Calder (Baynard, Jr.)
1922- .... **CLC 5, 51**
See also CANR 3; CA 5-8R; DLB 2, 44

Wilson, A(ndrew) N(orman)   1950- .. **CLC 33**
See also CA 112, 122; DLB 14

Wilson, Andrew   1948-
See Wilson, Snoo

Wilson, Angus (Frank Johnstone)
1913- .... **CLC 2, 3, 5, 25, 34**
See also CANR 21; CA 5-8R; DLB 15

Wilson, August
1945- .... **CLC 39, 50, 63; DC 2**
See also BLC 3; CA 115, 122

Wilson, Brian   1942- .... **CLC 12**

Wilson, Colin   1931- .... **CLC 3, 14**
See also CAAS 5; CANR 1, 122; CA 1-4R;
DLB 14

Wilson, Edmund
1895-1972 .... **CLC 1, 2, 3, 8, 24**
See also CANR 1; CA 1-4R;
obituary CA 37-40R; DLB 63

Wilson, Ethel Davis (Bryant)
1888-1980 .... **CLC 13**
See also CA 102; DLB 68

Wilson, Harriet   1827?-?
See also BLC 3; DLB 50

Wilson, John   1785-1854 .... **NCLC 5**

Wilson, John (Anthony) Burgess   1917-
See Burgess, Anthony
See also CANR 2; CA 1-4R

Wilson, Lanford   1937- .... **CLC 7, 14, 36**
See also CA 17-20R; DLB 7

Wilson, Robert (M.)   1944- .... **CLC 7, 9**
See also CANR 2; CA 49-52

Wilson, Sloan   1920- .... **CLC 32**
See also CANR 1; CA 1-4R

Wilson, Snoo   1948- .... **CLC 33**
See also CA 69-72

Wilson, William S(mith)   1932- ..... **CLC 49**
See also CA 81-84

Winchilsea, Anne (Kingsmill) Finch, Countess
of   1661-1720 .... **LC 3**

Wingrove, David   1954- .... **CLC 68**
See also CA 133

Winters, Janet Lewis   1899-
See Lewis (Winters), Janet
See also CAP 1; CA 9-10

Winters, (Arthur) Yvor
1900-1968 .... **CLC 4, 8, 32**
See also CAP 1; CA 11-12;
obituary CA 25-28R; DLB 48

Winterson, Jeanette   1959- .... **CLC 64**

Wiseman, Frederick   1930- .... **CLC 20**

Wister, Owen   1860-1938 .... **TCLC 21**
See also CA 108; DLB 9, 78

Witkiewicz, Stanislaw Ignacy
1885-1939 .... **TCLC 8**
See also CA 105; DLB 83

Wittig, Monique   1935?- .... **CLC 22**
See also CA 116; DLB 83

Wittlin, Joseph   1896-1976 .... **CLC 25**
See also Wittlin, Jozef

Wittlin, Jozef   1896-1976
See Wittlin, Joseph
See also CANR 3; CA 49-52;
obituary CA 65-68

Wodehouse, (Sir) P(elham) G(renville)
1881-1975 ... **CLC 1, 2, 5, 10, 22; SSC 2**
See also CANR 3; CA 45-48;
obituary CA 57-60; SATA 22; DLB 34

Woiwode, Larry (Alfred)   1941-... **CLC 6, 10**
See also CANR 16; CA 73-76; DLB 6

Wojciechowska, Maia (Teresa)
1927- .... **CLC 26**
See also CLR 1; CANR 4; CA 9-12R;
SAAS 1; SATA 1, 28

Wolf, Christa   1929- .... **CLC 14, 29, 58**
See also CA 85-88; DLB 75

Wolfe, Gene (Rodman)   1931-....... **CLC 25**
See also CAAS 9; CANR 6; CA 57-60;
DLB 8

Wolfe, George C.   1954- .... **CLC 49**

Wolfe, Thomas (Clayton)
1900-1938 .... **TCLC 4, 13, 29**
See also CA 104; DLB 9; DLB-Y 85;
DLB-DS 2

Wolfe, Thomas Kennerly, Jr.   1931-
See Wolfe, Tom
See also CANR 9; CA 13-16R

Wolfe, Tom   1931-... **CLC 1, 2, 9, 15, 35, 51**
See also Wolfe, Thomas Kennerly, Jr.

Wolff, Geoffrey (Ansell)   1937- ..... **CLC 41**
See also CA 29-32R

Wolff, Tobias (Jonathan Ansell)
1945- .... **CLC 39, 64**
See also CA 114, 117

Wolfram von Eschenbach
c. 1170-c. 1220 .... **CMLC 5**

Wolitzer, Hilma   1930- .... **CLC 17**
See also CANR 18; CA 65-68; SATA 31

Wollstonecraft Godwin, Mary
1759-1797 .... **LC 5**
See also DLB 39

Wonder, Stevie   1950- .... **CLC 12**
See also Morris, Steveland Judkins

Wong, Jade Snow   1922- .... **CLC 17**
See also CA 109

Woodcott, Keith   1934-
See Brunner, John (Kilian Houston)

Woolf, (Adeline) Virginia
1882-1941 .... **TCLC 1, 5, 20, 43; SSC 7**
See also CA 130; brief entry CA 104;
DLB 36, 100

Woollcott, Alexander (Humphreys)
1887-1943 .... **TCLC 5**
See also CA 105; DLB 29

Wordsworth, Dorothy
1771-1855 .... **NCLC 25**

Wordsworth, William
1770-1850 .... **NCLC 12; PC 4**
See also DLB 93, 107

Wouk, Herman   1915-......... **CLC 1, 9, 38**
See also CANR 6; CA 5-8R; DLB-Y 82

Wright, Charles   1935- .... **CLC 6, 13, 28**
See also BLC 3; CAAS 7; CANR 26;
CA 29-32R; DLB-Y 82

Wright, Charles (Stevenson)   1932- .. **CLC 49**
See also CA 9-12R; DLB 33

Wright, James (Arlington)
1927-1980 .... **CLC 3, 5, 10, 28**
See also CANR 4; CA 49-52;
obituary CA 97-100; DLB 5

Wright, Judith   1915- .... **CLC 11, 53**
See also CA 13-16R; SATA 14

Wright, L(aurali) R.   1939-........ **CLC 44**

Wright, Richard (Nathaniel)
1908-1960 ... **CLC 1, 3, 4, 9, 14, 21, 48;
SSC 2**
See also BLC 3; CA 108; DLB 76;
DLB-DS 2; CDALB 1929-1941; AAYA 5

Wright, Richard B(ruce)   1937- ...... **CLC 6**
See also CA 85-88; DLB 53

Wright, Rick   1945-
See Pink Floyd

Wright, Stephen   1946- .... **CLC 33**

Wright, Willard Huntington   1888-1939
See Van Dine, S. S.
See also CA 115

Wright, William   1930- .... **CLC 44**
See also CANR 7, 23; CA 53-56

Wu Ch'eng-en   1500?-1582? .... **LC 7**

Wu Ching-tzu   1701-1754 .... **LC 2**

Wurlitzer, Rudolph   1938?-..... **CLC 2, 4, 15**
See also CA 85-88

Wycherley, William   1640?-1716 ...... **LC 8**
See also DLB 80

Wylie (Benet), Elinor (Morton Hoyt)
1885-1928 .... **TCLC 8**
See also CA 105; DLB 9, 45

Wylie, Philip (Gordon)   1902-1971... **CLC 43**
See also CAP 2; CA 21-22;
obituary CA 33-36R; DLB 9

Wyndham, John   1903-1969 .... **CLC 19**
See also Harris, John (Wyndham Parkes
Lucas) Beynon

Wyss, Johann David   1743-1818 .. **NCLC 10**
See also SATA 27, 29

X, Malcolm   1925-1965
See Little, Malcolm

Yanovsky, Vassily S(emenovich)
1906-1989 .... **CLC 2, 18**
See also CA 97-100; obituary CA 129

Yates, Richard   1926- .... **CLC 7, 8, 23**
See also CANR 10; CA 5-8R; DLB 2;
DLB-Y 81

Yeats, William Butler
1865-1939 .... **TCLC 1, 11, 18, 31**
See also CANR 10; CA 104; DLB 10, 19

Yehoshua, A(braham) B.
1936- .... **CLC 13, 31**
See also CA 33-36R

Literary Criticism Series
Cumulative Topic Index

This index lists all topic entries in the Gale Literary Criticism Series *Contemporary Literary Criticism, Literature Criticism from 1400 to 1800, Nineteenth-Century Literature Criticism,* and *Twentieth-Century Literary Criticism.*

Topic Index

Yellow Journalism   NCLC 36: 383-456
   overviews, 384-96
   major figures, 396-413
   the role of reporters, 413-28
   the Spanish-American War, 428-48
   Yellow Journalism and society, 448-
     54

Young Playwrights Festival
   1988—CLC 55: 376-81
   1989—CLC 59: 398-403
   1990—CLC 65: 444-48

Topic Index

TCLC Cumulative Nationality Index

AMERICAN

Adams, Henry **4**
Agee, James **1, 19**
Anderson, Maxwell **2**
Anderson, Sherwood **1, 10, 24**
Atherton, Gertrude **2**
Austin, Mary **25**
Barry, Philip **11**
Baum, L. Frank **7**
Beard, Charles A. **15**
Belasco, David **3**
Bell, James Madison **43**
Benchley, Robert **1**
Benét, Stephen Vincent **7**
Benét, William Rose **28**
Bierce, Ambrose **1, 7, 44**
Black Elk **33**
Bodenheim, Maxwell **44**
Bourne, Randolph S. **16**
Bradford, Gamaliel **36**
Bromfield, Louis **11**
Burroughs, Edgar Rice **2, 32**
Cabell, James Branch **6**
Cable, George Washington **4**
Cather, Willa **1, 11, 31**
Chambers, Robert W. **41**
Chandler, Raymond **1, 7**
Chapman, John Jay **7**
Chesnutt, Charles Waddell **5, 39**
Chopin, Kate **5, 14**
Comstock, Anthony **13**
Cotter, Joseph Seamon, Sr. **28**
Cram, Ralph Adams **45**
Crane, Hart **2, 5**
Crane, Stephen **11, 17, 32**
Crawford, F. Marion **10**
Crothers, Rachel **19**
Cullen, Countee **4, 37**
Davis, Rebecca Harding **6**

Davis, Richard Harding **24**
Day, Clarence **25**
DeVoto, Bernard **29**
Dreiser, Theodore **10, 18, 35**
Dunbar, Paul Laurence **2, 12**
Dunne, Finley Peter **28**
Fisher, Rudolph **11**
Fitzgerald, F. Scott **1, 6, 14, 28**
Flecker, James Elroy **43**
Fletcher, John Gould **35**
Forten, Charlotte L. **16**
Freeman, Douglas Southall **11**
Freeman, Mary Wilkins **9**
Futrelle, Jacques **19**
Gale, Zona **7**
Garland, Hamlin **3**
Gilman, Charlotte Perkins **9, 37**
Glasgow, Ellen **2, 7**
Goldman, Emma **13**
Grey, Zane **6**
Guiney, Louise Imogen **41**
Hall, James Norman **23**
Harper, Frances Ellen Watkins **14**
Harris, Joel Chandler **2**
Harte, Bret **1, 25**
Hawthorne, Julian **25**
Hearn, Lafcadio **9**
Henry, O. **1, 19**
Hergesheimer, Joseph **11**
Higginson, Thomas Wentworth **36**
Hopkins, Pauline Elizabeth **28**
Howard, Robert E. **8**
Howe, Julia Ward **21**
Howells, William Dean **7, 17, 41**
James, Henry **2, 11, 24, 40**
James, William **15, 32**
Jewett, Sarah Orne **1, 22**
Johnson, James Weldon **3, 19**
Kornbluth, C. M. **8**

Kuttner, Henry **10**
Lardner, Ring **2, 14**
Lewis, Sinclair **4, 13, 23, 39**
Lewisohn, Ludwig **19**
Lindsay, Vachel **17**
Locke, Alain **43**
London, Jack **9, 15, 39**
Lovecraft, H. P. **4, 22**
Lowell, Amy **1, 8**
Marquis, Don **7**
Masters, Edgar Lee **2, 25**
McCoy, Horace **28**
McKay, Claude **7, 41**
Mencken, H. L. **13**
Millay, Edna St. Vincent **4**
Mitchell, Margaret **11**
Mitchell, S. Weir **36**
Monroe, Harriet **12**
Muir, John **28**
Nathan, George Jean **18**
Nordhoff, Charles **23**
Norris, Frank **24**
O'Neill, Eugene **1, 6, 27**
Oskison, John M. **35**
Phillips, David Graham **44**
Porter, Gene Stratton **21**
Post, Melville **39**
Rawlings, Marjorie Kinnan **4**
Reed, John **9**
Roberts, Kenneth **23**
Robinson, Edwin Arlington **5**
Rogers, Will **8**
Rölvaag, O. E. **17**
Rourke, Constance **12**
Runyon, Damon **10**
Saltus, Edgar **8**
Santayana, George **40**
Sherwood, Robert E. **3**
Slesinger, Tess **10**

517

Nationality Index

ISBN 0-8103-2428-8